TCP/IP

Protocol Suite

McGraw-Hill Forouzan Networking Series

Titles by Behrouz A. Forouzan:

Data Communications and Networking
TCP/IP Protocol Suite
Local Area Networks
Business Data Communications

EBCDIC extended binary coded decimal interchange code
EIA Electronics Industries Association
email electronic mail
EMI electromagnetic interference
ESP Encapsulating Security Payload
ESP Encrypted Security Payload
ESS Extended Service Set

FCC Federal Communications Commission
FCS frame check sequence
FHSS frequency hopping spread spectrum
FQDN fully qualified domain name
FTAM file transfer, access, and management
FTP File Transfer Protocol

HDSL high bit rate digital subscriber line
HTML hypertext markup language
HTTP hypertext transfer protocol

IAB Internet Architecture Board
IANA Internet Assigned Numbers Authority
ICANN Internet Corporation for Assigned Names and Numbers
ICMP Internet Control Message Protocol
ICMPv6 Internet Control Message Protocol, version 6
IEEE Institute of Electrical and Electronics Engineers
IESG Internet Engineering Steering Group
IETF Internet Engineering Task Force
IGMP Internet Group Management Protocol
IMAP4 Internet Mail Access Protocol, version 4
INTERNIC Internet Network Information Center
IP Internetworking Protocol
IPng Internetworking Protocol, next generation
IPSec IP Security
IPv6 Internetworking Protocol, version 6
IR infrared
IRTF Internet Research Task Force
ISO International Organization of Standardization
ISOC Internet Society
ISP Internet service provider
ITU-T International Telecommunications Union–Telecommunication Standardization Sector

KDC key distribution center

LAN local area network
LANE LAN emulation
LCP Link Control Protocol
LEC LAN emulation client
LECS LAN emulation configuration server
LES LAN emulation server
LIS logical IP subnet
LRC longitudinal redundancy check
LSA link state advertisement
LSP link state packet

MAN metropolitan area network
MAU multistation access unit

TCP/IP

Protocol Suite

Second Edition

Behrouz A. Forouzan

with

Sophia Chung Fegan

Boston Burr Ridge, IL Dubuque, IA Madison, WI New York San Francisco St. Louis
Bangkok Bogotá Caracas Kuala Lumpur Lisbon London Madrid Mexico City
Milan Montreal New Delhi Santiago Seoul Singapore Sydney Taipei Toronto

McGraw-Hill Higher Education
A Division of The McGraw-Hill Companies

TCP/IP PROTOCOL SUITE, SECOND EDITION

Published by McGraw-Hill, a business unit of The McGraw-Hill Companies, Inc., 1221 Avenue of the Americas, New York, NY 10020.

Some ancillaries, including electronic and print components, may not be available to customers outside the United States.

This book is printed on acid-free paper.

International 2 3 4 5 6 7 8 9 0 DOC/DOC 0 9 8 7 6 5 4 3
Domestic 3 4 5 6 7 8 9 0 DOC/DOC 0 9 8 7 6 5 4 3

ISBN 0–07–246060–1
ISBN 0–07–119962–4 (ISE)

Publisher: *Elizabeth A. Jones*
Senior developmental editor: *Emily J. Lupash*
Executive marketing manager: *John Wannemacher*
Project manager: *Sheila M. Frank*
Production supervisor: *Sherry L. Kane*
Media project manager: *Jodi K. Banowetz*
Senior media technology producer: *Phillip Meek*
Coordinator of freelance design: *Rick D. Noel*
Cover designer: *Joanne Schopler/Graphic Visions*
Cover image: *©Index Stock, Image number 362261, Head of the Charles Regatta, Cambridge MA by James Lemoss*
Compositor: *Interactive Composition Corporation*
Typeface: *10/12 Times Roman*
Printer: *R. R. Donnelley & Sons Company/Crawfordsville, IN*

Library of Congress Cataloging-in-Publication Data

Forouzan, Behrouz A.
TCP/IP protocol suite / Behrouz A. Forouzan. — 2nd ed.
p. cm. — (McGraw-Hill Forouzan networking series)
Includes bibliographical references and index.
ISBN 0–07–246060–1 — ISBN 0–07–119962–4 (ISE)
1. TCP/IP (Computer network protocol). I. Title. II. Series.
TK5105.585 .F67 2003
004.6'2—dc21 2002024414
CIP

INTERNATIONAL EDITION ISBN 0–07–119962–4

www.mhhe.com

To the memory of my father,
the source of my inspiration

—Behrouz Forouzan

BRIEF TABLE OF CONTENTS

TABLE OF CONTENTS

Chapter 5 Subnetting/Supernetting and Classless Addressing 119

Chapter 6 Delivery and Routing of IP Packets 147

Chapter 14 Multicasting and Multicast Routing Protocols 405

Chapter 15 Application Layer and Client-Server Model 429

Chapter 20 File Transfer Protocol (FTP) 555

Chapter 21 Trivial File Transfer Protocol (TFTP) 575

Chapter 23 Simple Network Management Protocol (SNMP) 623

Chapter 24 Hypertext Transfer Protocol (HTTP) 649

Chapter 27 Mobile IP 717

Chapter 28 Real-Time Traffic over the Internet 733

Preface

Technologies related to networks and internetworking may be the fastest growing in our culture today. One of the ramifications of that growth is a dramatic increase in the number of professions where an understanding of these technologies is essential for success—and a proportionate increase in the number and types of students taking courses to learn about them.

This is a book about TCP/IP. It provides the information necessary for students who seek a degree in data communications and networking. It is also a reference for professionals who are supporting or preparing to work with networks based on TCP/IP. In short, this book is for anyone who needs to understand the TCP/IP protocols.

The book assumes the reader has no prior knowledge of the TCP/IP protocols, although a previous course in data communications is desirable.

Organization

This book is divided into five parts. The first part, comprising Chapters 1 to 3, reviews the basic concepts and underlying technologies that, although independent from the TCP/IP protocols, are needed to support them.

The second part of the text discusses the protocols in the network and transport layer. Chapters 4 to 10 emphasize the network layer protocols. Transport layer protocols are fully described in Chapters 11 and 12. Chapters 13 and 14 are devoted to a detailed description of routing protocols.

The third part discusses the application programs that use the network and transport layer protocols. Chapter 15 and 16 give a brief review of the client–server paradigm and socket programming and lay the foundation for Chapters 17 to 25, which discuss the application protocols.

The fourth part (Chapters 26 to 30) covers issues and topics relatively new to the Internet. We discuss IP over ATM, Mobile IP, Real-Time Communication, Internet Security, and Private Networks (including real and virtual private networks).

The fifth part of the book (Chapter 31) is devoted to the next generation of TCP/IP. We describe IPv6, ICMPv6, and the transition strategies from version 4 to version 6.

Features

Several features of this text are designed to make it particularly easy for students to understand TCP/IP.

Visual Approach

The book presents highly technical subject matter without complex formulas by using a balance of text and figures. The approximately 590 figures accompanying the text provide a visual and intuitive opportunity for understanding the material. Figures are particularly important in explaining networking concepts, which are based on connections and transmission. These are both often more easily grasped visually than verbally.

Highlighted Points

We have repeated important concepts in boxes for quick reference and immediate attention.

Examples and Applications

Whenever appropriate, we have included examples that illustrate the concept introduced in the text. Also, we have added real-life applications throughout each chapter to motivate students.

Protocol Packages

Although we have not tried to give the detailed code for implementing each protocol, many chapters contain a section that discusses the general idea behind the implementation of each protocol. These sections provide an understanding of the ideas and issues involved in each protocol. They are optional.

Key Terms

The new terms used in each chapter are listed at the end of the chapter with definitions included in the glossary.

Summary

Each chapter ends with a summary of the material covered by that chapter. The summary is a bulleted overview of all the key points in the chapter.

Practice Set

Each chapter includes a practice set designed to reinforce salient concepts and encourage students to apply them. It consists of three parts: multiple-choice questions, exercises, and programming exercises. Multiple-choice questions test students' grasp of basic concepts and terminology. Exercises require deeper understanding of the material. The programming exercises are for those students or readers who have taken one or two programming courses in C or a similar language. These exercises prepare students for client–server programming courses.

Appendixes

The appendixes are intended to provide quick reference material or a review of materials needed to understand the concepts discussed in the book.

Glossary and Acronyms

The book contains an extensive glossary and a list of acronyms.

New to the Second Edition

There are six totally new chapters in the second edition:

- Chapter 14, Multicast Routing Protocols
- Chapter 26, IP over ATM
- Chapter 27, Mobile IP
- Chapter 28, Real-Time Traffic over the Internet
- Chapter 29, Internet Security
- Chapter 30, Private Networks

Several chapters have been revised. Classless addressing was added to Chapter 5. Chapter 10 was revised to reflect the new version of IGMP. Chapter 23 was revised to make the concepts easier to understand. Several examples were added to each chapter to provide real applications of theoretical issues. Key terms were added at the end of each chapter.

How to Use the Book

This book is written for both academic and professional audiences. The book can be used as a self-study guide for interested professionals. As a textbook, it can be used for a one-semester or one-quarter course. The chapters are organized to provide a great deal of flexibility. The following are some suggestions:

- Chapters 1 to 3 can be skipped if students have already taken a course in data communications and networking.
- Chapters 4 through 14 are essential for understanding TCP/IP.
- Chapters 15 and 16 can be covered briefly to open the way for a network programming course.
- Chapters 17 to 25 can be covered in detail in a semester system and briefly in a quarter system.
- Chapters 26 to 30 can be skipped if there are time constraints.
- Chapter 31 can be used as a self-paced chapter.

Acknowledgments for the Second Edition

It is obvious that the development of a book of this scope needs the support of many people. We acknowledged the contribution of many people in the preface of the first edition. For the second edition, we would like to acknowledge contributions to the development of a book from peer reviews. We would especially like to acknowledge the contributions of the following reviewers:

- Walter Read, California State University, Fresno
- Wayne D. Smith, Mississippi State University
- Ronald R. Srodawa, Oakland University
- Rod Fatoohi, San Jose State University
- Abdullah Abonamah, University of Akron
- Douglas Jacobson, Iowa State University
- Sam C. Hsu, Florida Atlantic University
- Dale Liu, Indiana University-Purdue University-Indianapolis
- Dennis Karvelas, New Jersey Institute of Technology

Special thanks go to the staff of McGraw-Hill. Betsy Jones, our publisher, proved how a proficient publisher can make the impossible, possible. Emily Lupash, the developmental editor, gave us help whenever we needed it. Sheila Frank, our project manager, guided us through the production process with enormous enthusiasm. We also thank Sherry Kane in production, Rick Noel in design, and Barbara Somogyi, the copy editor.

Special thanks also go to Andy Yu who read the book for technical content.

Trademark Notices

Throughout the text we have used several trademarks. Rather than insert a trademark symbol with each mention of the trademarked name, we acknowledge the trademarks here and state that they are used with no intention of infringing upon them. Other product names, trademarks, and registered trademarks are the property of their respective owners.

- Apple, AppleTalk, EtherTalk, LocalTalk, TokenTalk, and Macintosh are registered trademarks of Apple Computer, Inc.
- Bell and StarLan are registered trademarks of AT&T.
- DEC, DECnet, VAX, and DNA are trademarks of Digital Equipment Corp.
- IBM, SDLC, SNA, and IBM PC are registered trademarks of International Business Machines Corp.
- Novell, Netware, IPX, and SPX are registered trademarks of Novell, Inc.
- Network File System and NFS are registered trademarks of Sun Microsystems, Inc.
- PostScript is a registered trademark of Adobe Systems, Inc.
- UNIX is a registered trademark of UNIX System Laboratories, Inc., a wholly owned subsidiary of Novell, Inc.
- Xerox is a trademark, and Ethernet is a registered trademark of Xerox Corp.

CHAPTER 1

Introduction

The Internet has revolutionized many aspects of our daily lives. It has affected the way we do business as well as the way we spend our leisure time. Count the ways you've used the Internet recently. Perhaps you've sent electronic mail (email) to a business associate, paid a utility bill, read a newspaper from a distant city, or looked up a local movie schedule—all by using the Internet. Or, maybe you researched a medical topic, booked a hotel reservation, chatted with a fellow Trekkie, or comparison-shopped for a car. The Internet is a communication system that has brought a wealth of information to our fingertips and organized it for our use.

The Internet is a structured, organized system. Before we discuss how it works and its relationship to TCP/IP, we first give a brief history of the Internet. We then define the concepts of protocols and standards and their relationships to each other. We discuss the various organizations that are involved in the development of Internet standards. These standards are not developed by any specific organization, but rather through a consensus of users. We discuss the mechanism through which these standards originated and matured. Also included in this introductory chapter is a section on Internet administrative groups.

1.1 A BRIEF HISTORY

A **network** is a group of connected, communicating devices such as computers and printers. An internet (note the lowercase *i*) is two or more networks that can communicate with each other. The most notable internet is called the **Internet** (uppercase *I*), a collaboration of more than hundreds of thousands interconnected networks. Private individuals as well as various organizations such as government agencies, schools, research facilities, corporations, and libraries in more than 100 countries use the Internet. Millions of people are users. Yet this extraordinary communication system only came into being in 1969.

ARPANET

In the mid-1960s, mainframe computers in research organizations were stand-alone devices. Computers from different manufacturers were unable to communicate with one another. The **Advanced Research Projects Agency (ARPA)** in the Department of Defense (DOD) was interested in finding a way to connect computers together so that the researchers they funded could share their findings, thereby reducing costs and eliminating duplication of effort.

In 1967, at an Association for Computing Machinery (ACM) meeting, ARPA presented its ideas for **ARPANET,** a small network of connected computers. The idea was that each host computer (not necessarily from the same manufacturer) would be attached to a specialized computer, called an *interface message processor* (IMP). The IMPs, in turn, would be connected to each other. Each IMP had to be able to communicate with other IMPs as well as with its own attached host.

By 1969, ARPANET was a reality. Four nodes, at the University of California at Los Angeles (UCLA), the University of California at Santa Barbara (UCSB), Stanford Research Institute (SRI), and the University of Utah were connected via the IMPs to form a network. Software called the *Network Control Protocol* (NCP) provided communication between the hosts.

Birth of the Internet

In 1972, Vint Cerf and Bob Kahn, both of whom were part of the core ARPANET group, collaborated on what they called the *Internetting Project.* They wanted to link different networks together so that a host on one network could communicate with a host on a second, different network. There were many problems to overcome: diverse packet sizes, diverse interfaces, and diverse transmission rates, as well as differing reliability requirements. Cerf and Kahn devised the idea of a device called a *gateway* to serve as the intermediary hardware to transfer packets from one network to another.

Transmission Control Protocol/Internetworking Protocol (TCP/IP)

Cerf and Kahn's landmark 1973 paper outlined the protocols to achieve end-to-end delivery of packets. This was a new version of NCP. This paper on transmission control protocol (TCP) included concepts such as encapsulation, the datagram, and the functions of a gateway. A radical idea was the transfer of responsibility for error correction from the IMP to the host machine. This ARPA Internet now became the focus of the communication effort. Around this time responsibility for the ARPANET was handed over to the Defense Communication Agency (DCA).

In October 1977, an internet consisting of three different networks (ARPANET, packet radio, and packet satellite) was successfully demonstrated. Communication between networks was now possible.

Shortly thereafter, authorities made a decision to split TCP into two protocols: **Transmission Control Protocol (TCP)** and **Internetworking Protocol (IP).** IP would handle datagram routing while TCP would be responsible for higher level functions such as segmentation, reassembly, and error detection. The internetworking protocol became known as TCP/IP.

In 1981, under a DARPA contract, UC Berkeley modified the UNIX operating system to include TCP/IP. This inclusion of network software along with a popular operating system did much to further the popularity of networking. The open (non-manufacturer-specific) implementation on Berkeley UNIX gave every manufacturer a working code base on which they could build their products.

In 1983, authorities abolished the original ARPANET protocols, and TCP/IP became the official protocol for the ARPANET. Those who wanted to use the Internet to access a computer on a different network had to be running TCP/IP.

MILNET

In 1983, ARPANET split into two networks: **MILNET** for military users and ARPANET for nonmilitary users.

CSNET

Another milestone in Internet history was the creation of CSNET in 1981. **CSNET** was a network sponsored by the National Science Foundation (NSF). The network was conceived by universities that were ineligible to join ARPANET due to an absence of defense ties to DARPA. CSNET was a less expensive network; there were no redundant links and the transmission rate was slower. It featured connections to ARPANET and Telenet, the first commercial packet data service.

By the middle 1980s, most U.S. universities with computer science departments were part of CSNET. Other institutions and companies were also forming their own networks and using TCP/IP to interconnect. The term *Internet,* originally associated with government-funded connected networks, now referred to the connected networks using TCP/IP protocols.

NSFNET

With the success of CSNET, the NSF, in 1986, sponsored **NSFNET,** a backbone that connected five supercomputer centers located throughout the United States. Community networks were allowed access to this backbone, a T1 line with a 1.544 Mbps data rate, thus providing connectivity throughout the United States.

In 1990, ARPANET was officially retired and replaced by NSFNET. In 1995, NSFNET reverted back to its original concept of a research network.

ANSNET

In 1991, the U.S. government decided that NSFNET was not capable of supporting the rapidly increasing Internet traffic. Three companies, IBM, Merit, and MCI, filled the void by forming a nonprofit organization called Advanced Network and Services (ANS) to build a new, high-speed Internet backbone called **ANSNET.**

The Internet Today

The Internet today is not a simple hierarchical structure. It is made up of many wide and local area networks joined by connecting devices and switching stations. It is difficult to give an accurate representation of the Internet because it is continuously changing—new networks are being added, existing networks need more addresses, and networks of defunct companies need to be removed. Today most end users who want Internet connection use the services of Internet service providers (ISPs). There are international service providers, national service providers, regional service providers, and local service providers. The Internet today is run by private companies, not the government. Figure 1.1 shows a conceptual (not geographical) view of the Internet.

International Service Providers

At the top of the hierarchy are the international service providers that connect nations together.

National Service Providers (NSPs)

National service providers (NSPs) are backbone networks created and maintained by specialized companies. There are many NSPs operating in North America; some of the most well-known are SprintLink, PSINet, UUNet Technology, AGIS, and internet MCI. To provide connectivity between the end users, these backbone networks are connected by complex switching stations (normally run by a third party) called **network access points (NAPs).** Some NSP networks are also connected to each other by private switching stations called peering points. NSPs normally operate at a high data rate (up to 600 Mbps).

Regional Internet Service Providers

Regional internet service providers or **regional ISPs** are small ISPs that are connected to one or more NSPs. They are at the third level of hierarchy with a lesser data rate.

Local Internet Service Providers

Local Internet service providers provide direct service to the end users. The local ISPs can be connected to regional ISPs or directly to NSPs. Most end users are connected to the local ISPs. Note that in this sense, a local ISP can be a company that just provides Internet services, a corporation with a network to supply services to its own employees, or a nonprofit organization, such as a college or a university, that runs its own network. Each of these can be connected to a regional or national service provider.

Time Line

The following is a list of important Internet events in chronological order:

- **1969.** Four-node ARPANET established.
- **1970.** ARPA hosts implement NCP.
- **1973.** Development of TCP/IP suite begins.
- **1977.** An internet tested using TCP/IP.

Figure 1.1 *Internet today*

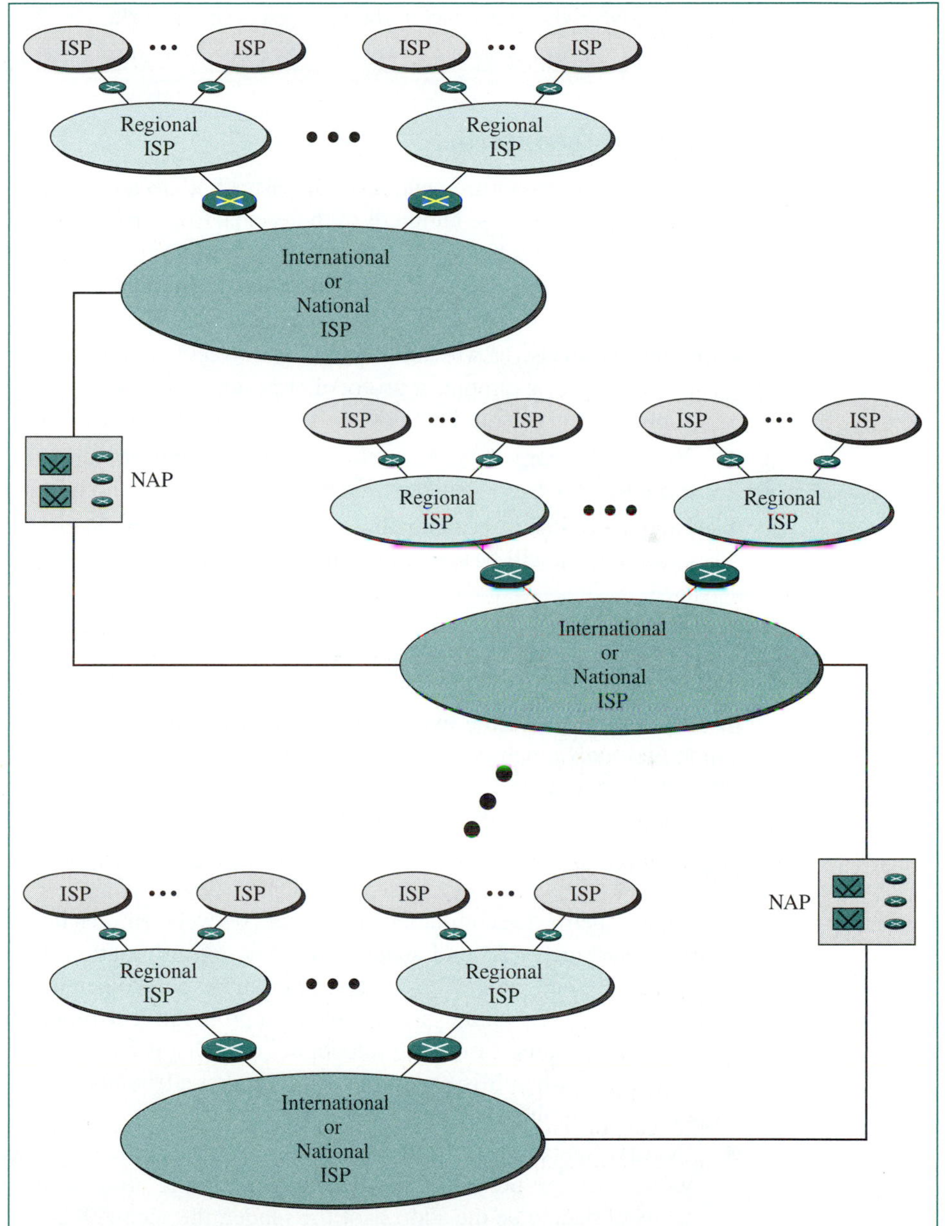

- **1978.** UNIX distributed to academic/research sites.
- **1981.** CSNET established.
- **1983.** TCP/IP becomes the official protocol for ARPANET.
- **1983.** MILNET was born.
- **1986.** NSFNET established.

- **1990.** ARPANET decommissioned and replaced by NSFNET.
- **1995.** NSFNET goes back to being a research network.
- **1995.** Companies known as **Internet Service Providers (ISPs)** started.

Growth of the Internet

The Internet has grown tremendously. In just a few decades, the number of networks has increased from tens to hundreds of thousands. Concurrently, the number of computers connected to the networks has grown from hundreds to hundreds of millions. The Internet is still growing. Factors that have an impact on this growth include the following:

- **New Protocols.** New protocols need to be added and obsolete ones need to be removed. For example, a protocol superior in many respects to IPv4 has been approved as a standard but not yet fully implemented (see IPv6, Chapter 31).
- **New Technology.** New technologies are under development that will increase the capacity of networks and provide more bandwidth to the Internet's users.
- **Increasing Use of Multimedia.** It is predicted that the Internet, once just a vehicle to share data, will be used more and more for multimedia (audio and video).

1.2 PROTOCOLS AND STANDARDS

In this section, we define two widely used terms: protocols and standards. First, we define *protocol,* which is synonymous with "rule." Then we discuss *standards,* which are agreed-upon rules.

Protocols

In computer networks, communication occurs between entities in different systems. An **entity** is anything capable of sending or receiving information. However, two entities cannot simply send bit streams to each other and expect to be understood. For communication to occur, the entities must agree on a protocol. A **protocol** is a set of rules that governs data communication. A protocol defines what is communicated, how it is communicated, and when it is communicated. The key elements of a protocol are syntax, semantics, and timing.

- **Syntax.** Syntax refers to the structure or format of the data, meaning the order in which they are presented. For example, a simple protocol might expect the first 8 bits of data to be the address of the sender, the second 8 bits to be the address of the receiver, and the rest of the stream to be the message itself.
- **Semantics.** Semantics refers to the meaning of each section of bits. How is a particular pattern to be interpreted, and what action is to be taken based on that interpretation? For example, does an address identify the route to be taken or the final destination of the message?

- **Timing.** Timing refers to two characteristics: when data should be sent and how fast it can be sent. For example, if a sender produces data at 100 Megabits per second (Mbps) but the receiver can process data at only 1 Mbps, the transmission will overload the receiver and data will be largely lost.

Standards

Standards are essential in creating and maintaining an open and competitive market for equipment manufacturers and also in guaranteeing national and international interoperability of data and telecommunications technology and processes. They provide guidelines to manufacturers, vendors, government agencies, and other service providers to ensure the kind of interconnectivity necessary in today's marketplace and in international communications.

Data communication standards fall into two categories: *de facto (*meaning "by fact" or "by convention") and *de jure (*meaning "by law" or "by regulation").

- **De facto.** Standards that have not been approved by an organized body but have been adopted as standards through widespread use are **de facto standards.** De facto standards are often established originally by manufacturers that seek to define the functionality of a new product or technology.
- **De jure. De jure standards** are those that have been legislated by an officially recognized body.

1.3 STANDARDS ORGANIZATIONS

Standards are developed through cooperation of standards creation committees, forums, and government regulatory agencies.

Standards Creation Committees

While many organizations are dedicated to the establishment of standards, data telecommunications in North America rely primarily on those published by the following:

- **International Standards Organization (ISO).** The International Standards Organization (ISO; also referred to as the International Organization for Standardization) is a multinational body whose membership is drawn mainly from the standards creation committees of various governments throughout the world. Created in 1947, the ISO is an entirely voluntary organization dedicated to worldwide agreement on international standards. With a membership that currently includes representative bodies from 82 industrialized nations, it aims to facilitate the international exchange of goods and services by providing models for compatibility, improved quality, increased productivity, and decreased prices. The ISO is active in developing cooperation in the realms of scientific, technological, and economic activity. Of primary concern to this book are the ISO's efforts in the field of information technology, which have resulted in the creation of the Open Systems Interconnection (OSI) model for network communications. The United States is represented in the ISO by ANSI.

- **International Telecommunications Union–Telecommunication Standards Sector (ITU-T).** By the early 1970s, a number of countries were defining national standards for telecommunications, but there was still little international compatibility. The United Nations responded by forming, as part of its International Telecommunications Union (ITU), a committee, the **Consultative Committee for International Telegraphy and Telephony (CCITT).** This committee was devoted to the research and establishment of standards for telecommunications in general and phone and data systems in particular. On March 1, 1993, the name of this committee was changed to the International Telecommunications Union–Telecommunication Standards Sector (ITU-T).
- **American National Standards Institute (ANSI).** Despite its name, the American National Standards Institute (ANSI) is a completely private, nonprofit corporation not affiliated with the U.S. federal government. However, all ANSI activities are undertaken with the welfare of the United States and its citizens occupying primary importance. ANSI's expressed aims include serving as the national coordinating institution for voluntary standardization in the United States, furthering the adoption of standards as a way of advancing the U.S. economy, and ensuring the participation and protection of the public interests. ANSI members include professional societies, industry associations, governmental and regulatory bodies, and consumer groups.
- **Institute of Electrical and Electronics Engineers (IEEE).** The Institute of Electrical and Electronics Engineers (IEEE) is the largest professional engineering society in the world. International in scope, it aims to advance theory, creativity, and product quality in the fields of electrical engineering, electronics, and radio as well as in all related branches of engineering. As one of its goals, the IEEE oversees the development and adoption of international standards for computing and communication.
- **Electronic Industries Association (EIA).** Aligned with ANSI, the Electronic Industries Association (EIA) is a nonprofit organization devoted to the promotion of electronics manufacturing concerns. Its activities include public awareness education and lobbying efforts in addition to standards development. In the field of information technology, the EIA has made significant contributions by defining physical connection interfaces and electronic signaling specifications for data communication.

Forums

Telecommunications technology development is moving faster than the ability of standards committees to ratify standards. Standards committees are procedural bodies and by nature slow moving. To accommodate the need for working models and agreements and to facilitate the standardization process, many special-interest groups have developed *forums* made up of representatives from interested corporations. The forums work with universities and users to test, evaluate, and standardize new technologies. By concentrating their efforts on a particular technology, the forums are able to speed acceptance and use of those technologies in the telecommunications community. The forums present their conclusions to the standards bodies. Some important forums for the telecommunications industry include the following:

- **Frame Relay Forum.** The Frame Relay Forum was formed by Digital Equipment Corporation, Northern Telecom, Cisco, and StrataCom to promote the acceptance and implementation of frame relay. Today, it has around 40 members representing North America, Europe, and the Pacific Rim. Issues under review include flow control, encapsulation, translation, and multicasting. The forum's results are submitted to the ISO.
- **ATM Forum.** The ATM Forum promotes the acceptance and use of Asynchronous Transfer Mode (ATM) technology. The ATM Forum is made up of Customer Premises Equipment (e.g., PBX systems) vendors and Central Office (e.g., telephone exchange) providers. It is concerned with the standardization of services to ensure interoperability.

Regulatory Agencies

All communications technology is subject to regulation by government agencies such as the Federal Communications Commission in the United States. The purpose of these agencies is to protect the public interest by regulating radio, television, and wire/cable communications.

- **Federal Communications Commission (FCC).** The Federal Communications Commission (FCC) has authority over interstate and international commerce as it relates to communications.

The websites for the above organizations are given in Appendix G.

1.4 INTERNET STANDARDS

An **Internet standard** is a thoroughly tested specification that is useful to and adhered to by those who work with the Internet. It is a formalized regulation that must be followed. There is a strict procedure by which a specification attains Internet standard status. A specification begins as an Internet draft. An **Internet draft** is a working document (a work in progress) with no official status and a six-month lifetime. Upon recommendation from the Internet authorities, a draft may be published as a **Request for Comment (RFC).** Each RFC is edited, assigned a number, and made available to all interested parties.

RFCs go through maturity levels and are categorized according to their requirement level.

Maturity Levels

An RFC, during its lifetime, falls into one of six **maturity levels:** proposed standard, draft standard, Internet standard, historic, experimental, and informational (see Figure 1.2).

Figure 1.2 *Maturity levels of an RFC*

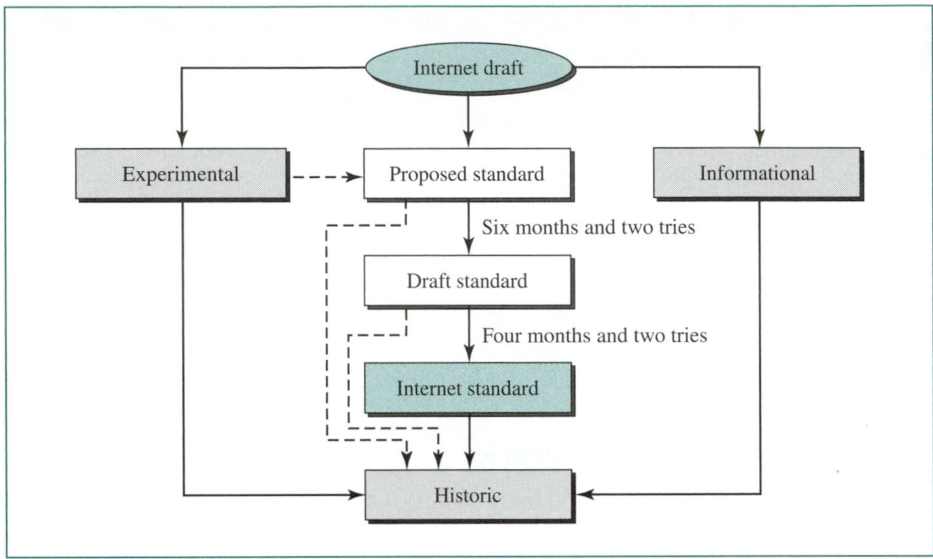

Proposed Standard

A proposed standard is a specification that is stable, well understood, and of sufficient interest to the Internet community. At this level, the specification is usually tested and implemented by several different groups.

Draft Standard

A proposed standard is elevated to draft standard status after at least two successful independent and interoperable implementations. Barring difficulties, a draft standard, with modifications if specific problems are encountered, normally becomes an Internet standard.

Internet Standard

A draft standard reaches Internet standard status after demonstrations of successful implementation.

Historic

The historic RFCs are significant from a historical perspective. They either have been superseded by later specifications or have never passed the necessary maturity levels to become an Internet standard.

Experimental

An RFC classified as experimental describes work related to an experimental situation that does not affect the operation of the Internet. Such an RFC should not be implemented in any functional Internet service.

Informational

An RFC classified as informational contains general, historical, or tutorial information related to the Internet. It is usually written by someone in a non-Internet organization, such as a vendor.

Requirement Levels

RFCs are classified into five **requirement levels:** required, recommended, elective, limited use, and not recommended (see Figure 1.3).

Figure 1.3 *Requirement levels of an RFC*

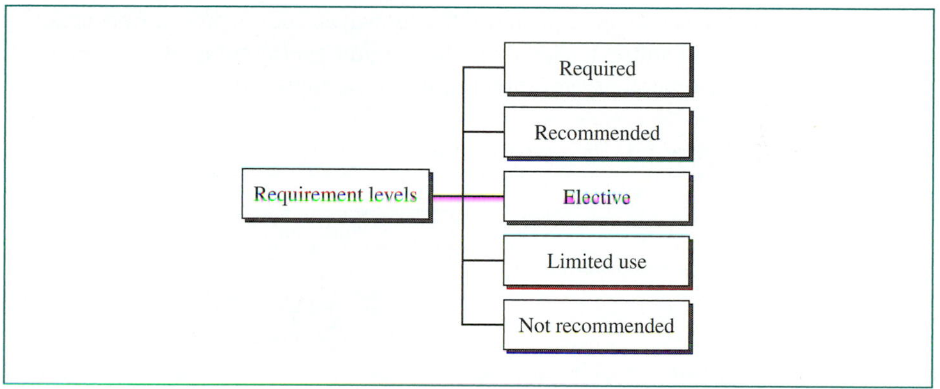

Required

An RFC is labeled *required* if it must be implemented by all Internet systems to achieve minimum conformance. For example, IP (Chapter 8) and ICMP (Chapter 9) are required protocols.

Recommended

An RFC labeled *recommended* is not required for minimum conformance; it is recommended because of its usefulness. For example, FTP (Chapter 20) and TELNET (Chapter 19) are recommended protocols.

Elective

An RFC labeled *elective* is not required and not recommended. However, a system can use it for its own benefit.

Limited Use

An RFC labeled *limited use* should be used only in limited situations. Most of the experimental RFCs fall under this category.

Not Recommended

An RFC labeled *not recommended* is inappropriate for general use. Normally a historic (obsolete) RFC may fall under this category.

RFCs can be found at **http://www.faqs.org/rfcs**

1.5 INTERNET ADMINISTRATION

The Internet, with its roots primarily in the research domain, has evolved and gained a broader user base with significant commercial activity. Various groups that coordinate Internet issues have guided this growth and development. Appendix G gives the addresses, email addresses, and telephone numbers for some of these groups. Figure 1.4 shows the general organization of Internet administration.

Figure 1.4 *Internet administration*

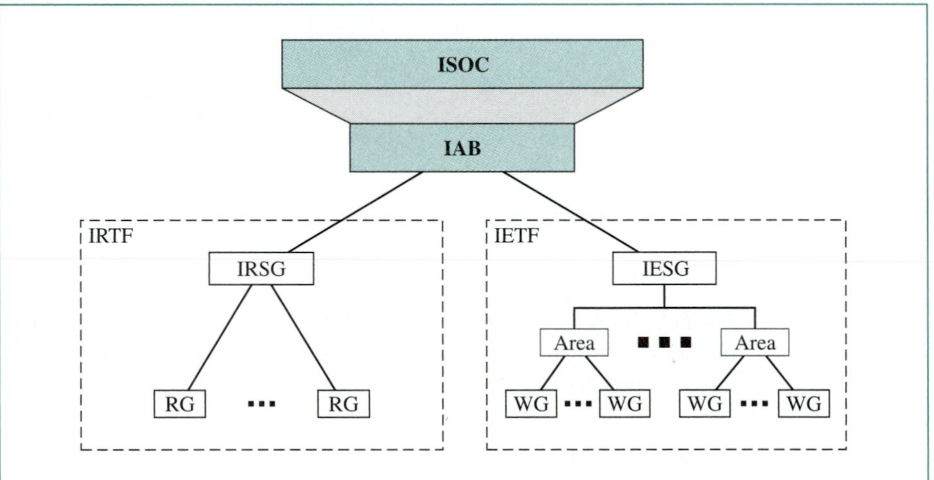

Internet Society (ISOC)

The **Internet Society (ISOC)** is an international, nonprofit organization formed in 1992 to provide support for the Internet standards process. ISOC accomplishes this through maintaining and supporting other Internet administrative bodies such as IAB, IETF, IRTF, and IANA (see the following sections). ISOC also promotes research and other scholarly activities relating to the Internet.

Internet Architecture Board (IAB)

The **Internet Architecture Board (IAB)** is the technical advisor to the ISOC. The main purposes of the IAB are to oversee the continuing development of the TCP/IP Protocol Suite and to serve in a technical advisory capacity to research members of the Internet community. IAB accomplishes this through its two primary components, the

Internet Engineering Task Force (IETF) and the Internet Research Task Force (IRTF). Another responsibility of the IAB is the editorial management of the RFCs, described earlier in this chapter. IAB is also the external liaison between the Internet and other standards organizations and forums.

Internet Engineering Task Force (IETF)

The **Internet Engineering Task Force (IETF)** is a forum of working groups managed by the Internet Engineering Steering Group (IESG). IETF is responsible for identifying operational problems and proposing solutions to these problems. IETF also develops and reviews specifications intended as Internet standards. The working groups are collected into areas, and each area concentrates on a specific topic. Currently nine areas have been defined, although this is by no means a hard and fast number. The areas are:

- Applications
- Internet protocols
- Routing
- Operations
- User services
- Network management
- Transport
- Internet protocol next generation (IPng)
- Security

Internet Research Task Force (IRTF)

The **Internet Research Task Force (IRTF)** is a forum of working groups managed by the Internet Research Steering Group (IRSG). IRTF focuses on long-term research topics related to Internet protocols, applications, architecture, and technology.

Internet Assigned Numbers Authority (IANA) and Internet Corporation for Assigned Names and Numbers (ICANN)

The **Internet Assigned Numbers Authority (IANA),** supported by the U.S. government, was responsible for the management of Internet domain names and addresses until October 1998. At that time the **Internet Corporation for Assigned Names and Numbers (ICANN),** a private nonprofit corporation managed by an international board, assumed IANA operations.

Network Information Center (NIC)

The **Network Information Center (NIC)** is responsible for collecting and distributing information about TCP/IP protocols.

The websites for Internet organizations can be found in Appendix G.

1.6 KEY TERMS

American National Standards Institute (ANSI)

ANSNET

Advanced Research Projects Agency (ARPA)

ARPANET

ATM Forum

Consultative Committee for International Telegraphy and Telephony (CCITT)

CSNET

de facto standards

de jure standards

Electronic Industries Association (EIA)

entity

Federal Communications Commission (FCC)

Frame Relay Forum

Institute of Electrical and Electronics Engineers (IEEE)

International Standards Organization (ISO)

International Telecommunications Union–Telecommunication Standards Sector (ITU-T)

Internet

Internet Architecture Board (IAB)

Internet Assigned Numbers Authority (IANA)

Internet Corporation for Assigned Names and Numbers (ICANN)

Internet draft

Internet Engineering Task Force (IETF)

Internet Research Task Force (IRTF)

Internet Service Providers (ISPs)

Internet Society (ISOC)

Internet standard

local Internet service providers

maturity levels

MILNET

national service providers (NSPs)

network

Network Information Center (NIC)

network access points (NAPs)

NSFNET

protocol

regional ISPs

Request for Comment (RFC)

requirement levels

semantics

syntax

timing

Transmission Control Protocol/ Internetworking Protocol (TCP/IP)

1.7 SUMMARY

- The Internet is a collection of more than 100,000 separate networks.
- ARPANET began as a network with four nodes.
- TCP/IP is the protocol suite for the Internet.
- CSNET provided communication between networks ineligible to join ARPANET.
- NSFNET provided communication between networks throughout the United States.
- Local Internet service providers (ISPs) connect individual users to the Internet.
- Regional Internet service providers connect local Internet service providers.
- National service providers (NSPs) are backbone networks created and maintained by specialized companies
- A protocol is a set of rules that governs data communication; the key elements of a protocol are syntax, semantics, and timing.
- Standards are necessary to ensure that products from different manufacturers can work together as expected.
- The ISO, ITU-T, ANSI, IEEE, and EIA are some of the organizations involved in standards creation.
- Forums are special-interest groups that quickly evaluate and standardize new technologies.
- Two important forums are the Frame Relay Forum and the ATM Forum.
- The FCC is a regulatory agency that regulates radio, television, and wire/cable communications.
- A Request for Comment (RFC) is an idea or concept that is a precursor to an Internet Standard.
- An RFC goes through the proposed standard level, then the draft standard level before it becomes an Internet standard.
- An RFC is categorized as required, recommended, elective, limited use, or not recommended.
- The Internet Society (ISOC) promotes research and other scholarly activities relating to the Internet.
- The Internet Architecture Board (IAB) is the technical advisor to the ISOC.
- The Internet Engineering Task Force (IETF) is a forum of working groups responsible for identifying operational problems and proposing solutions to these problems.
- The Internet Research Task Force (IRTF) is a forum of working groups focusing on long-term research topics related to Internet protocols, applications, architecture, and technology.
- The Internet Corporation for Assigned Names and Numbers (ICANN), formerly known as IANA, is responsible for the management of Internet domain names and addresses.
- The Network Information Center (NIC) is responsible for collecting and distributing information about TCP/IP protocols.

1.8 PROBLEM SET

Multiple-Choice Questions

1. In the original ARPANET, _______ were directly connected together.
   a. IMPs
   b. host computers
   c. networks
   d. routers
2. _______ was formed to connect universities with no defense ties.
   a. ARPANET
   b. CSNET
   c. NSFNET
   d. ANSNET
3. This was the first network.
   a. CSNET
   b. NSFNET
   c. ANSNET
   d. ARPANET
4. Which agency is the U.S. voting member to the ISO?
   a. USO
   b. IEEE
   c. NATO
   d. ANSI
5. Which organization has authority over interstate and international commerce in the communications field?
   a. ITU-T
   b. IEEE
   c. FCC
   d. ISOC
6. _______ are special-interest groups that quickly test, evaluate, and standardize new technologies.
   a. Forums
   b. Regulatory agencies
   c. Standards organizations
   d. All of the above

7. Which agency developed standards for physical connection interfaces and electronic signaling specifications?
   a. EIA
   b. ITU-T
   c. ANSI
   d. ISO
8. _______ is the protocol suite for the current Internet.
   a. TCP/IP
   b. NCP
   c. UNIX
   d. ACM
9. A version of the _______ operating system included TCP/IP.
   a. DARPA
   b. NCP
   c. UNIX
   d. ACM
10. The _______ oversees the IETF and the IRTF.
    a. ISOC
    b. IAB
    c. IANA
    d. NIC
11. The _______ maintains and supports IAB.
    a. ISOC
    b. IETF
    c. IANA
    d. ICANN
12. _______ is the precursor to ICANN.
    a. ISOC
    b. IETF
    c. IANA
    d. NIC

Exercises

13. Do some research and find some standards developed by ITU-T.
14. Do some research and find some standards developed by ANSI.
15. One of the standards developed by IEEE is project 802. Do some research and find some information about this project. What is 802.1? What is 802.2? What is 802.3? What is 802.5?

16. EIA has developed some standards for interfaces. Do some research and find some of these standards. What is EIA 232?
17. Do some research and find some regulations devised by FCC concerning AM and FM transmission.
18. Use the Internet to find the number of RFCs.
19. Use the Internet to find the subject matter of RFCs 2418 and 1603.
20. Use the Internet to find the RFC that discusses the IRTF working group guidelines and procedures.
21. Use the Internet to find two examples of an historic RFC.
22. Use the Internet to find two examples of an experimental RFC.
23. Use the Internet to find two examples of an informational RFC.
24. Use the Internet to find the RFC that discusses the FTP application.
25. Use the Internet to find the RFC for the Internet Protocol (IP).
26. Use the Internet to find the RFC for the Transmission Control Protocol (TCP).
27. Use the Internet to find the RFC that details the Internet standards process.

CHAPTER 2

The OSI Model and the TCP/IP Protocol Suite

The layered model that dominated data communication and networking literature before 1990 was the **Open Systems Interconnection (OSI) model.** Everyone believed that the OSI model would become the ultimate standard for data communication—but this did not happen. The TCP/IP protocol suite became the dominant commercial architecture because it was used and tested extensively in the Internet; the OSI model was never fully implemented.

In this chapter, we first briefly discuss the OSI as a model and then we concentrate on TCP/IP as a protocol suite.

2.1 THE OSI MODEL

Established in 1947, the **International Standards Organization (ISO)** is a multinational body dedicated to worldwide agreement on international standards. An ISO standard that covers all aspects of network communications is the Open Systems Interconnection (OSI) model. It was first introduced in the late 1970s. An **open system** is a set of protocols that allows any two different systems to communicate regardless of their underlying architecture. The purpose of the OSI model is to show how to facilitate communication between different systems without requiring changes to the logic of the underlying hardware and software. The OSI model is not a protocol; it is a model for understanding and designing a network architecture that is flexible, robust, and interoperable.

> ISO is the organization. OSI is the model.

The OSI model is a layered framework for the design of network systems that allows communication between all types of computer systems. It consists of seven separate but related layers, each of which defines a part of the process of moving information across a network (see Figure 2.1). Understanding the fundamentals of the OSI model provides a solid basis for exploring data communication.

Figure 2.1 *The OSI model*

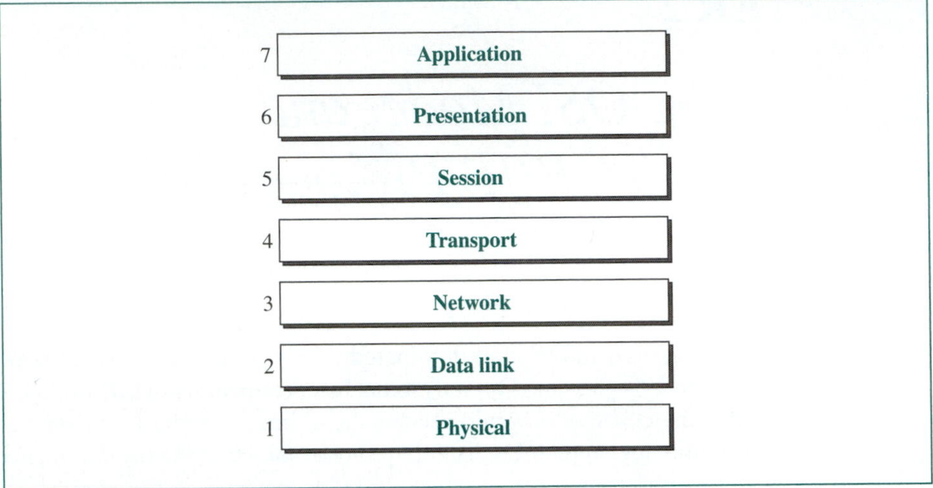

Layered Architecture

The OSI model is composed of seven ordered layers: physical (layer 1), data link (layer 2), network (layer 3), transport (layer 4), session (layer 5), presentation (layer 6), and application (layer 7). Figure 2.2 shows the layers involved when a message is sent from device A to device B. As the message travels from A to B, it may pass through many intermediate nodes. These intermediate nodes usually involve only the first three layers of the OSI model.

In developing the model, the designers distilled the process of transmitting data to its most fundamental elements. They identified which networking functions had related uses and collected those functions into discrete groups that became the layers. Each layer defines a family of functions distinct from those of the other layers. By defining and localizing functionality in this fashion, the designers created an architecture that is both comprehensive and flexible. Most important, the OSI model allows complete interoperability between otherwise incompatible systems.

Within a single machine, each layer calls upon the services of the layer just below it. Layer 3, for example, uses the services provided by layer 2 and provides services for layer 4. Between machines, layer *x* on one machine communicates with layer *x* on another machine. This communication is governed by an agreed-upon series of rules and conventions called protocols. The processes on each machine that communicate at a given layer are called **peer-to-peer processes.** Communication between machines is therefore a peer-to-peer process using the protocols appropriate to a given layer.

Peer-to-Peer Processes

At the physical layer, communication is direct: In Figure 2.2, device A sends a stream of bits to device B (through intermediate nodes). At the higher layers, however, communication must move down through the layers on device A, over to device B, and then

Figure 2.2 *OSI layers*

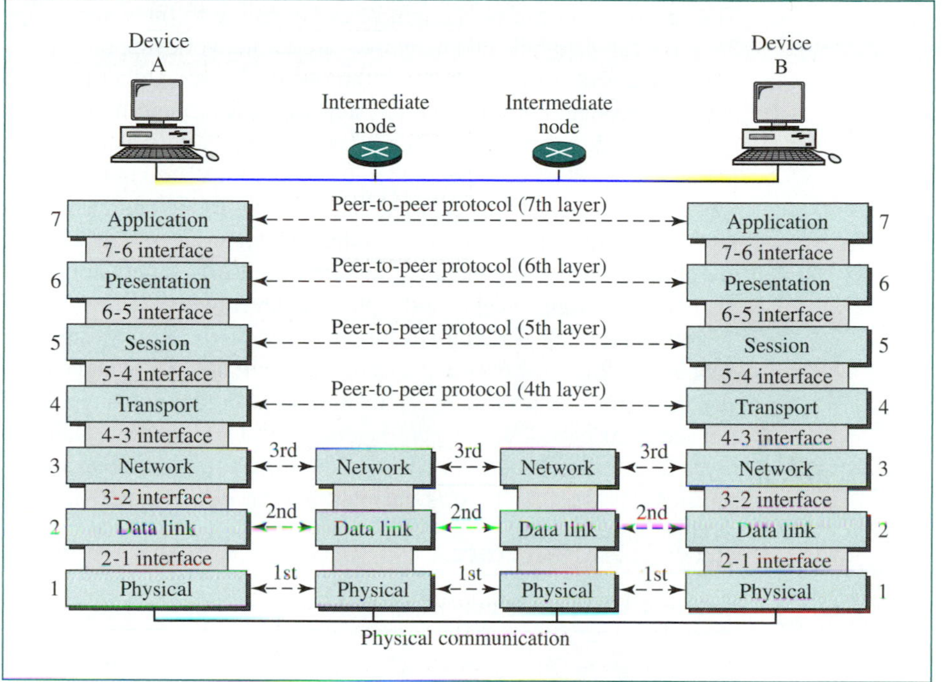

back up through the layers. Each layer in the sending device adds its own information to the message it receives from the layer just above it and passes the whole package to the layer just below it.

> Headers are added to the data at layers 6, 5, 4, 3, and 2. Trailers are usually added only at layer 2.

At layer 1 the entire package is converted to a form that can be transferred to the receiving device. At the receiving machine, the message is unwrapped layer by layer, with each process receiving and removing the data meant for it. For example, layer 2 removes the data meant for it, then passes the rest to layer 3. Layer 3 then removes the data meant for it and passes the rest to layer 4, and so on.

Interfaces between Layers

The passing of the data and network information down through the layers of the sending device and back up through the layers of the receiving device is made possible by an **interface** between each pair of adjacent layers. Each interface defines what information and services a layer must provide for the layer above it. Well-defined interfaces and layer functions provide modularity to a network. As long as a layer provides the expected services to the layer above it, the specific implementation of its functions can be modified or replaced without requiring changes to the surrounding layers.

Organization of the Layers

The seven layers can be thought of as belonging to three subgroups. Layers 1, 2, and 3—physical, data link, and network—are the network support layers; they deal with the physical aspects of moving data from one device to another (such as electrical specifications, physical connections, physical addressing, and transport timing and reliability). Layers 5, 6, and 7—session, presentation, and application—can be thought of as the user support layers; they allow interoperability among unrelated software systems. Layer 4, the transport layer, links the two subgroups and ensures that what the lower layers have transmitted is in a form that the upper layers can use. The upper OSI layers are almost always implemented in software; lower layers are a combination of hardware and software, except for the physical layer, which is mostly hardware.

In Figure 2.3, which gives an overall view of the OSI layers, L7 data means the data unit at layer 7, L6 data means the data unit at layer 6, and so on. The process starts at layer 7 (the application layer), then moves from layer to layer in descending, sequential order. At each layer (except layers 7 and 1), a header is added to the data unit. At layer 2, a trailer is added as well. When the formatted data unit passes through the physical layer (layer 1), it is changed into an electromagnetic signal and transported along a physical link.

Figure 2.3 *An exchange using the OSI model*

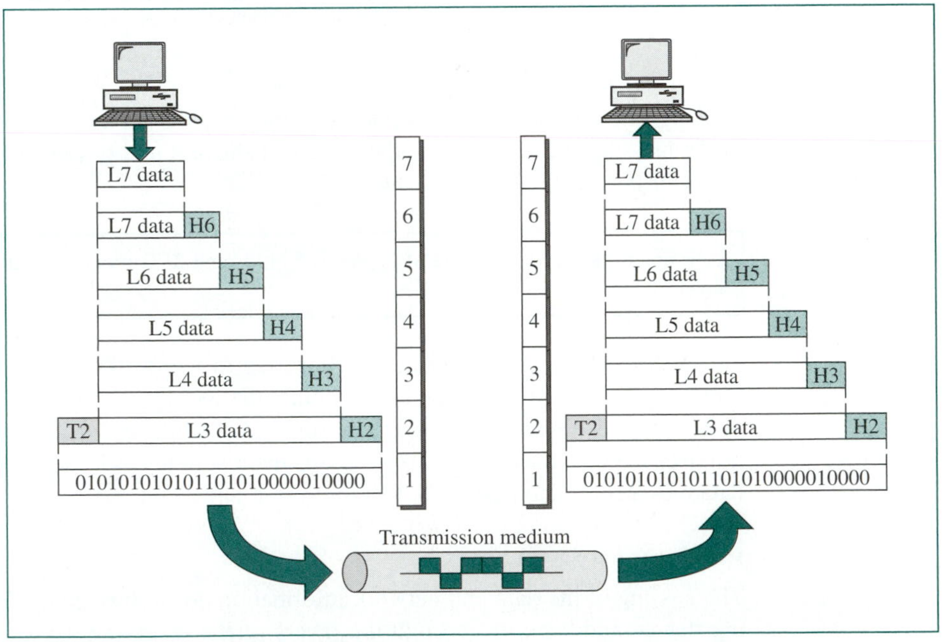

Upon reaching its destination, the signal passes into layer 1 and is transformed back into digital form. The data units then move back up through the OSI layers. As each block of data reaches the next higher layer, the headers and trailers attached to it at the corresponding sending layer are removed, and actions appropriate to that layer are taken. By the time it reaches layer 7, the message is again in a form appropriate to the application and is made available to the recipient.

2.2 LAYERS IN THE OSI MODEL

In this section we briefly describe the functions of each layer in the OSI model.

Physical Layer

The **physical layer** coordinates the functions required to transmit a bit stream over a physical medium. It deals with the mechanical and electrical specifications of the interface and transmission media. It also defines the procedures and functions that physical devices and interfaces have to perform for transmission to occur. Figure 2.4 shows the position of the physical layer with respect to the transmission media and the data link layer.

Figure 2.4 *Physical layer*

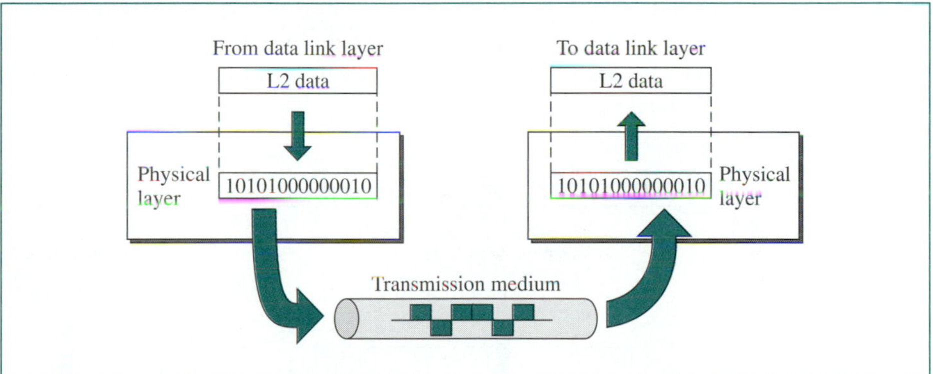

The physical layer is concerned with the following:

- **Physical characteristics of interfaces and media.** The physical layer defines the characteristics of the interface between the devices and the transmission media. It also defines the type of transmission media (see Chapter 3).
- **Representation of bits.** The physical layer data consists of a stream of **bits** (sequence of 0s or 1s) without any interpretation. To be transmitted, bits must be encoded into signals—electrical or optical. The physical layer defines the type of **encoding** (how 0s and 1s are changed to signals).
- **Data rate.** The **transmission rate**—the number of bits sent each second—is also defined by the physical layer. In other words, the physical layer defines the duration of a bit, which is how long it lasts.
- **Synchronization of bits.** The sender and receiver must not only use the same bit rate but must also be synchronized at the bit level. In other words, the sender and the receiver clocks must be synchronized.

- **Line configuration.** The physical layer is concerned with the connection of devices to the media. In a **point-to-point configuration,** two devices are connected together through a dedicated link. In a **multipoint configuration,** a link is shared between several devices.
- **Physical topology.** The physical topology defines how devices are connected to make a network. Devices can be connected using a **mesh topology** (every device connected to every other device), a **star topology** (devices are connected through a central device), a **ring topology** (each device is connected to the next, forming a ring), or a **bus topology** (every device on a common link).
- **Transmission mode.** The physical layer also defines the direction of transmission between two devices: simplex, half-duplex, or full-duplex. In the **simplex mode,** only one device can send; the other can only receive. The simplex mode is a one-way communication. In the **half-duplex mode,** two devices can send and receive, but not at the same time. In a **full-duplex** (or simply duplex) **mode,** two devices can send and receive at the same time.

Data Link Layer

The **data link layer** transforms the physical layer, a raw transmission facility, to a reliable link. It makes the physical layer appear error free to the upper layer (network layer). Figure 2.5 shows the relationship of the data link layer to the network and physical layers.

Figure 2.5 *Data link layer*

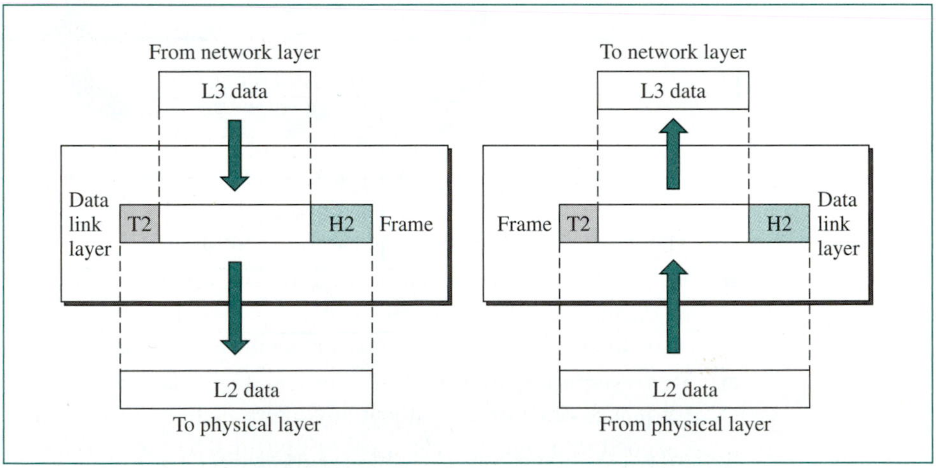

Specific responsibilities of the data link layer include the following:

- **Framing.** The data link layer divides the stream of bits received from the network layer into manageable data units called **frames.**
- **Physical addressing.** If frames are to be distributed to different systems on the network, the data link layer adds a header to the frame to define the sender and/or

receiver of the frame. If the frame is intended for a system outside the sender's network, the receiver address is the address of the connecting device that connects the network to the next one.

- **Flow control.** If the rate in which the data is absorbed by the receiver is less than the rate produced in the sender, the data link layer imposes a flow control mechanism to prevent overwhelming the receiver.
- **Error control.** The data link layer adds reliability to the physical layer by adding mechanisms to detect and retransmit damaged or lost frames. It also uses a mechanism to prevent duplication of frames. Error control is normally achieved through a trailer added to the end of the frame.
- **Access control.** When two or more devices are connected to the same link, data link layer protocols are necessary to determine which device has control over the link at any given time.

Figure 2.6 illustrates hop-to-hop (node-to-node) delivery by the data link layer.

Figure 2.6 *Node-to-node delivery*

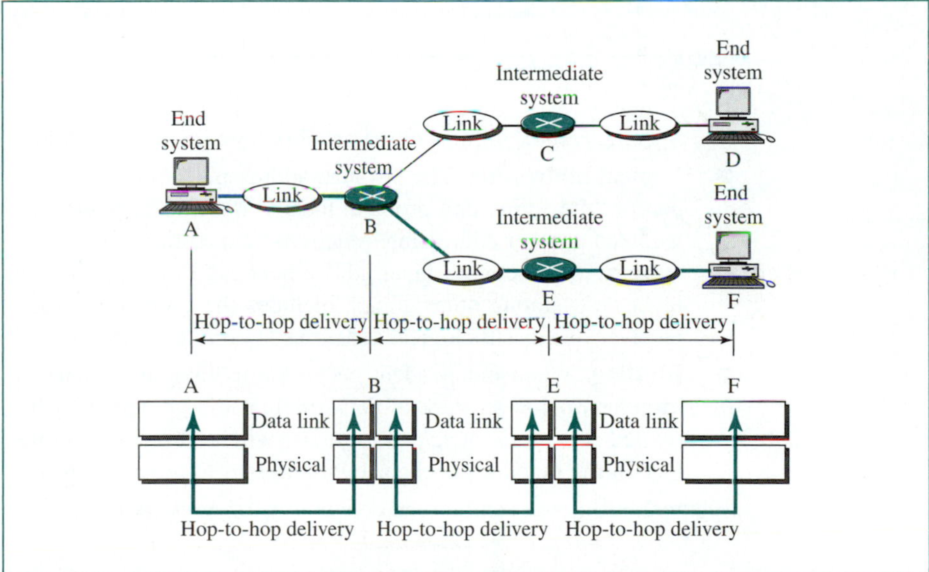

Network Layer

The **network layer** is responsible for the source-to-destination delivery of a packet possibly across multiple networks (links). Whereas the data link layer oversees the delivery of the packet between two systems on the same network (links), the network layer ensures that each packet gets from its point of origin to its final destination.

If two systems are connected to the same link, there is usually no need for a network layer. However, if the two systems are attached to different networks (links) with connecting devices between the networks (links), there is often a need for the network layer to accomplish source-to-destination delivery. Figure 2.7 shows the relationship of the network layer to the data link transport layers.

Figure 2.7 *Network layer*

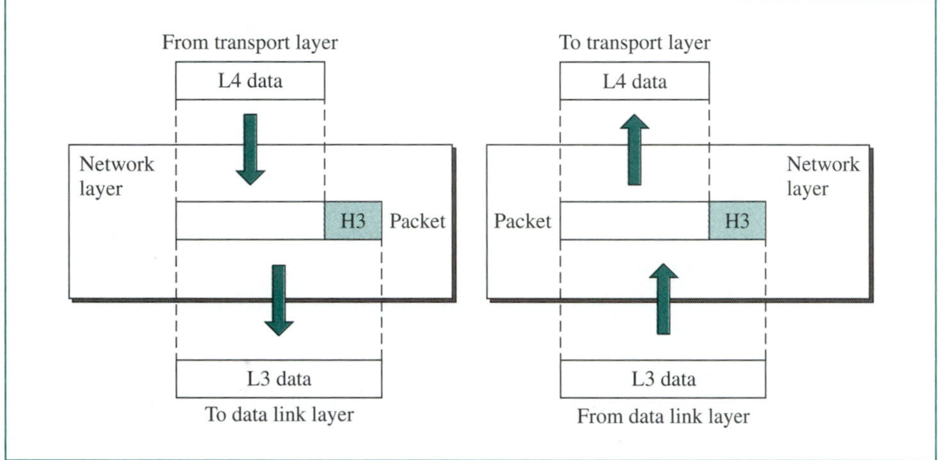

Specific responsibilities of the network layer include the following:

- **Logical addressing.** The physical addressing implemented by the data link layer handles the addressing problem locally. If a packet passes the network boundary, we need another addressing system to help distinguish the source and destination systems. The network layer adds a header to the packet coming from the upper layer that, among other things, includes the logical addresses of the sender and receiver. We discuss logical addresses later in this chapter.
- **Routing.** When independent networks or links are connected together to create **internetworks** (network of networks) or a large network, the connecting devices (called *routers* or *switches*) route or switch the packets to their final destination. One of the functions of the network layer is to provide this mechanism.

Figure 2.8 illustrates end-to-end delivery by the network layer.

Transport Layer

The **transport layer** is responsible for **source-to-destination** (end-to-end) **delivery** of the entire message. Whereas the network layer oversees end-to-end delivery of individual packets, it does not recognize any relationship between those packets. It treats each one independently, as though each piece belonged to a separate message, whether or not it does. The transport layer, on the other hand, ensures that the whole message arrives intact and in order, overseeing both error control and flow control at the source-to-destination level. Figure 2.9 shows the relationship of the transport layer to the network and session layers.

Figure 2.8 *End-to-end delivery*

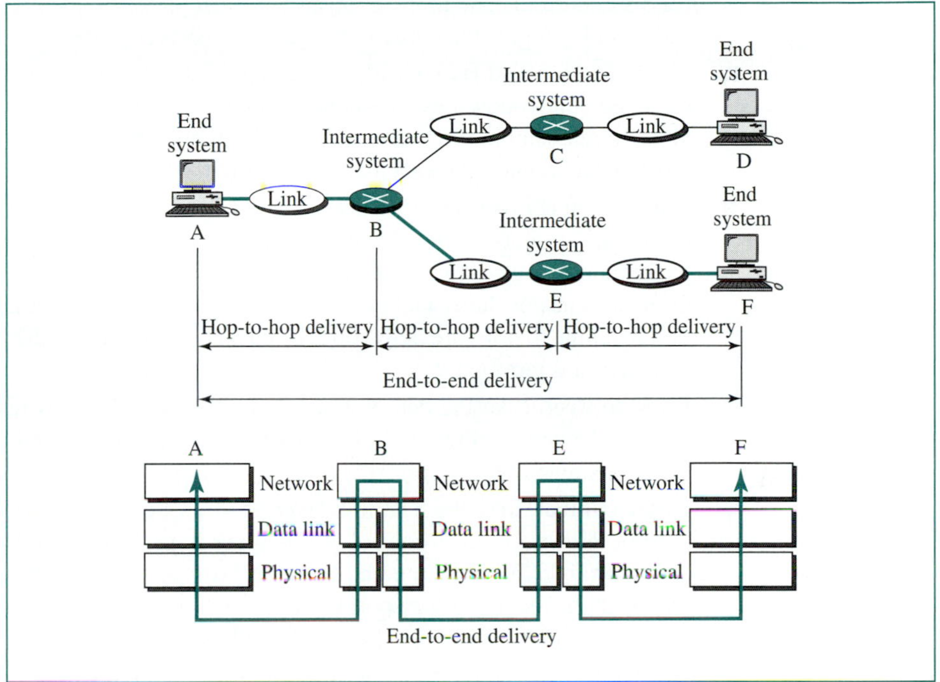

Figure 2.9 *Transport layer*

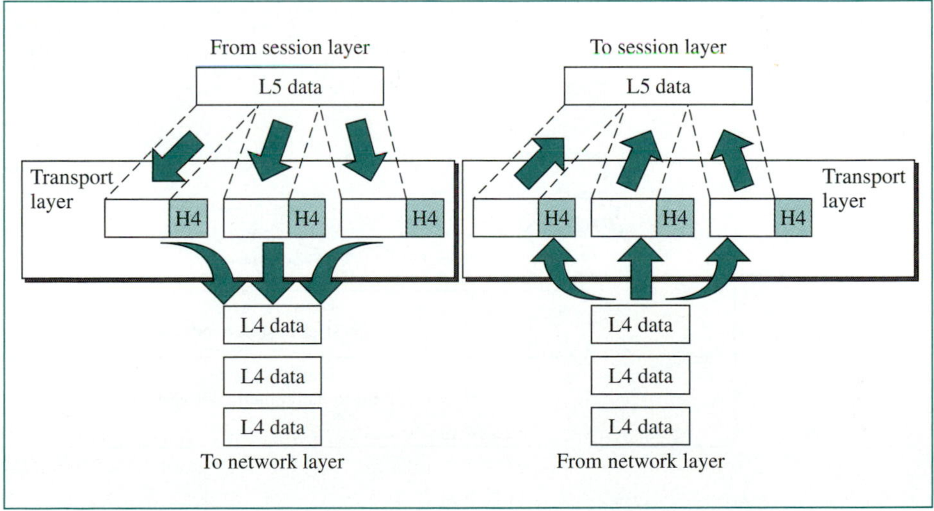

Specific responsibilities of the transport layer include the following:

- **Service-point addressing.** Computers often run several programs at the same time. For this reason, source-to-destination delivery means delivery not only from one computer to the next but also from a specific process (running program) on one computer to a specific process (running program) on the other. The transport layer header must therefore include a type of address called a *service-point address* (or port address). The network layer gets each packet to the correct computer; the transport layer gets the entire message to the correct process on that computer.

- **Segmentation and reassembly.** A message is divided into transmittable segments, each segment containing a sequence number. These numbers enable the transport layer to reassemble the message correctly upon arriving at the destination and to identify and replace packets that were lost in the transmission.
- **Connection control.** The transport layer can be either connectionless or connection-oriented. A connectionless transport layer treats each segment as an independent packet and delivers it to the transport layer at the destination machine. A connection-oriented transport layer makes a connection with the transport layer at the destination machine first before delivering the packets. After all the data is transferred, the connection is terminated.
- **Flow control.** Like the data link layer, the transport layer is responsible for flow control. However, flow control at this layer is performed end to end rather than across a single link.
- **Error control.** Like the data link layer, the transport layer is responsible for error control. However, error control at this layer is performed end to end rather than across a single link. The sending transport layer makes sure that the entire message arrives at the receiving transport layer without *error* (damage, loss, or duplication). Error correction is usually achieved through retransmission.

Figure 2.10 illustrates end-to-end delivery by the transport layer.

Figure 2.10 *Reliable end-to-end delivery of a message*

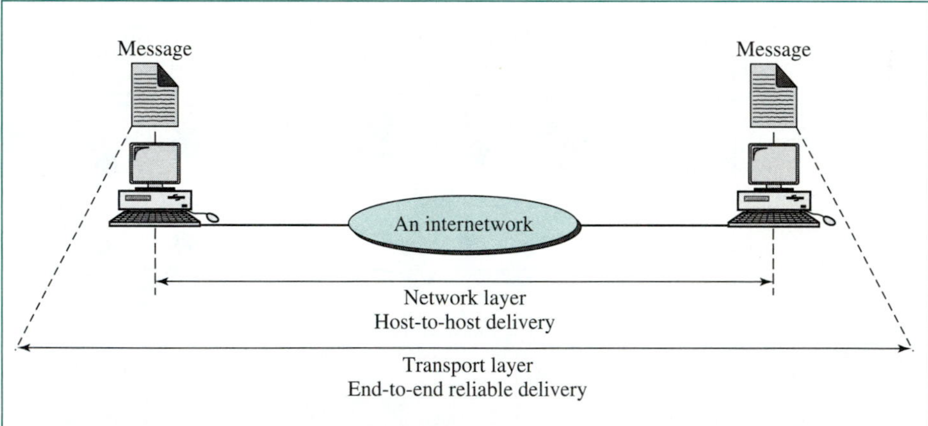

Session Layer

The services provided by the first three layers (physical, data link, and network) are not sufficient for some processes. The **session layer** is the network *dialog controller*. It establishes, maintains, and synchronizes the interaction between communicating systems.

Figure 2.11 *Session layer*

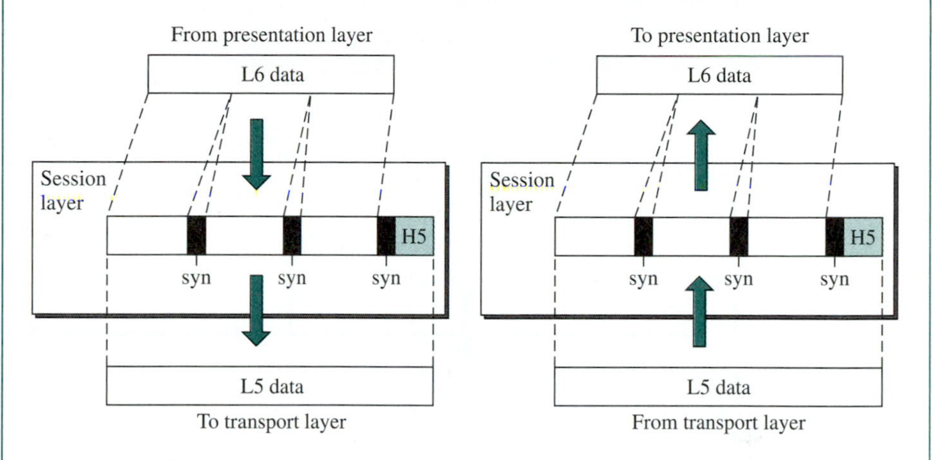

Specific responsibilities of the session layer include the following:

- **Dialog control.** The session layer allows two systems to enter into a dialog. It allows the communication between two processes to take place either in half-duplex (one way at a time) or full-duplex (two ways at a time) mode. For example, the dialog between a terminal connected to a mainframe can be half-duplex.
- **Synchronization.** The session layer allows a process to add checkpoints (**synchronization points**) into a stream of data. For example, if a system is sending a file of 2,000 pages, it is advisable to insert checkpoints after every 100 pages to ensure that each 100-page unit is received and acknowledged independently. In this case, if a crash happens during the transmission of page 523, the only pages that need to be resent after system recovery are pages 501 to 523. Pages previous to 501 need not be resent. Figure 2.11 illustrates the relationship of the session layer to the transport and presentation layers.

Presentation Layer

The **presentation layer** is concerned with the syntax and semantics of the information exchanged between two systems. Figure 2.12 shows the relationship between the presentation layer and the application and session layers.

Specific responsibilities of the presentation layer include the following:

- **Translation.** The processes (running programs) in two systems are usually exchanging information in the form of character strings, numbers, and so on. The information should be changed to bit streams before being transmitted. Because different computers use different encoding systems, the presentation layer is responsible for interoperability between these different encoding methods. The presentation layer at the sender changes the information from its sender-dependent format into a common format. The presentation layer at the receiving machine changes the common format into its receiver-dependent format.

Figure 2.12 *Presentation layer*

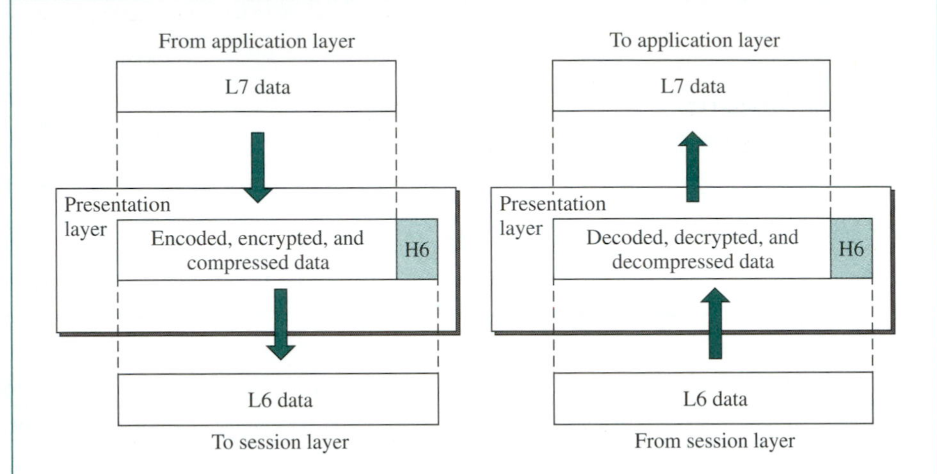

- **Encryption.** To carry sensitive information a system must be able to assure privacy. Encryption means that the sender transforms the original information to another form and sends the resulting message out over the network. Decryption reverses the original process to transform the message back to its original form.
- **Compression.** Data compression reduces the number of bits contained in the information. Data compression becomes particularly important in the transmission of multimedia such as text, audio, and video.

Application Layer

The **application layer** enables the user, whether human or software, to access the network. It provides user interfaces and support for services such as electronic mail, remote file access and transfer, shared database management, and other types of distributed information services.

Figure 2.13 shows the relationship of the application layer to the user and the presentation layer. Of the many application services available, the figure shows only three: X.400 (message-handling services), X.500 (directory services), and file transfer, access, and management (FTAM). The user in this example uses X.400 to send an email message. Note that no headers or trailers are added at this layer.

Specific services provided by the application layer include the following:

- **Network virtual terminal.** A network virtual terminal is a software version of a physical terminal and allows a user to log on to a remote host. To do so, the application creates a software emulation of a terminal at the remote host. The user's computer talks to the software terminal, which, in turn, talks to the host, and vice versa. The remote host believes it is communicating with one of its own terminals and allows you to log on.

Figure 2.13 *Application layer*

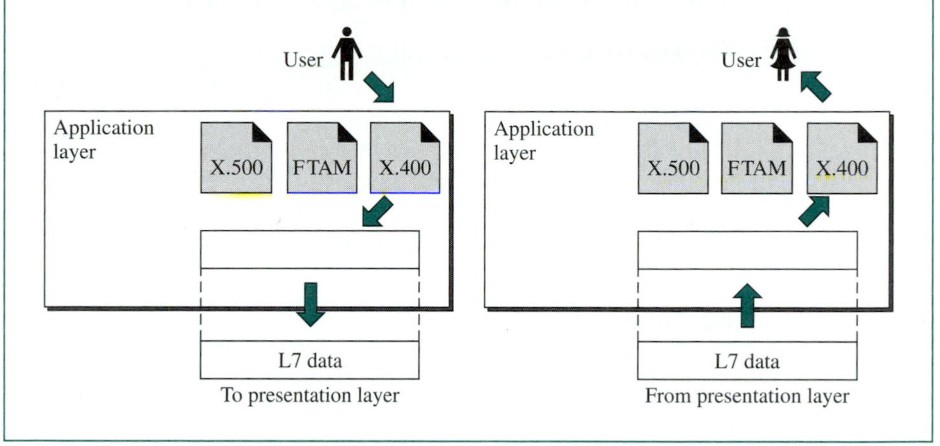

- **File transfer, access, and management (FTAM).** This application allows a user to access files in a remote host (to make changes or read data), to retrieve files from a remote computer for use in the local computer, and to manage or control files in a remote computer locally.
- **Mail services.** This application provides the basis for email forwarding and storage.
- **Directory services.** This application provides distributed database sources and access for global information about various objects and services.

Summary of Layers

Figure 2.14 shows a summary of duties for each layer.

Figure 2.14 *Summary of layers*

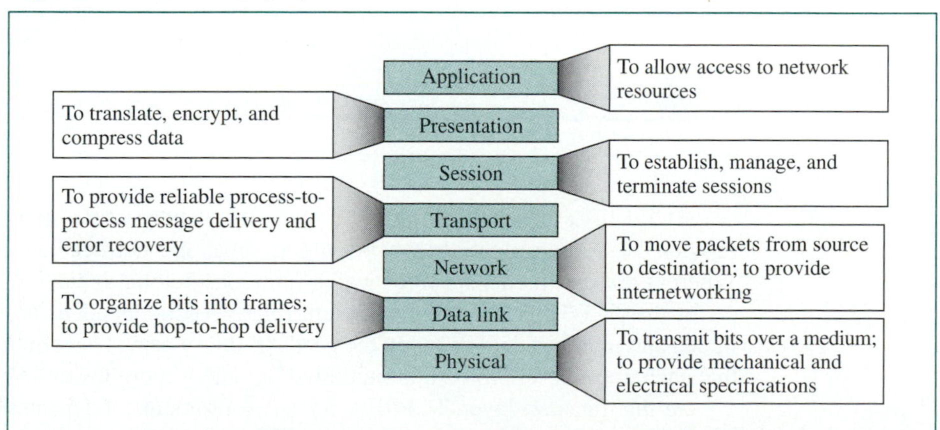

2.3 TCP/IP PROTOCOL SUITE

The **TCP/IP protocol suite** was developed prior to the OSI model. Therefore, the layers in the TCP/IP protocol suite do not match exactly with those in the OSI model. The TCP/IP protocol suite is made of five layers: physical, data link, network, transport, and application. The first four layers provide physical standards, network interface, internetworking, and transport functions that correspond to the first four layers of the OSI model. The three topmost layers in the OSI model, however, are represented in TCP/IP by a single layer called the *application layer* (see Figure 2.15).

Figure 2.15 *TCP/IP and OSI model*

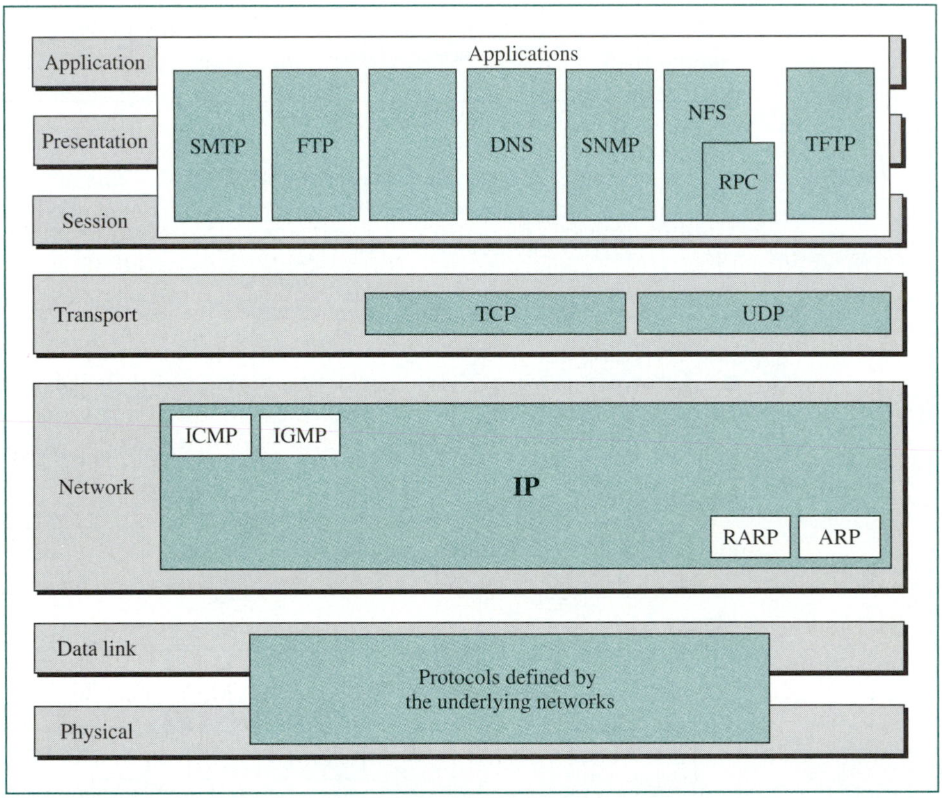

TCP/IP is a hierarchical protocol made up of interactive modules each of which provides a specific functionality, but the modules are not necessarily interdependent. Whereas the OSI model specifies which functions belong to each of its layers, the layers of the TCP/IP protocol suite contain relatively independent protocols that can be mixed and matched depending on the needs of the system. The term *hierarchical* means that each upper level protocol is supported by one or more lower level protocols.

At the transport layer, TCP/IP defines two protocols: Transmission Control Protocol (TCP) and User Datagram Protocol (UDP). At the network layer, the main protocol defined by TCP/IP is the Internetworking Protocol (IP), although there are some other protocols that support data movement in this layer.

Physical and Data Link Layers

At the physical and data link layers, TCP/IP does not define any specific protocol. It supports all of the standard and proprietary protocols. A network in a TCP/IP internetwork can be a local area network (LAN), a metropolitan area network (MAN), or a wide area network (WAN).

Network Layer

At the network layer (or, more accurately, the internetwork layer), TCP/IP supports the Internetworking Protocol (IP). IP, in turn, contains four supporting protocols: ARP, RARP, ICMP, and IGMP. Each of these protocols is described in more detail in later chapters.

Internetworking Protocol (IP)

The **Internetworking Protocol (IP)** is the transmission mechanism used by the TCP/IP protocols. It is an unreliable and connectionless datagram protocol—a **best-effort delivery** service. The term *best-effort* means that IP provides no error checking or tracking. IP assumes the unreliability of the underlying layers and does its best to get a transmission through to its destination, but with no guarantees.

IP transports data in packets called *datagrams,* each of which is transported separately. Datagrams can travel along different routes and can arrive out of sequence or be duplicated. IP does not keep track of the routes and has no facility for reordering datagrams once they arrive at their destination.

The limited functionality of IP should not be considered a weakness, however. IP provides bare-bones transmission functions that free the user to add only those facilities necessary for a given application and thereby allows for maximum efficiency.

Address Resolution Protocol (ARP)

The **Address Resolution Protocol (ARP)** is used to associate an IP address with the physical address. On a typical physical network, such as a LAN, each device on a link is identified by a physical or station address usually imprinted on the network interface card (NIC). ARP is used to find the physical address of the node when its Internet address is known. ARP will be discussed in Chapter 7.

Reverse Address Resolution Protocol (RARP)

The **Reverse Address Resolution Protocol (RARP)** allows a host to discover its Internet address when it knows only its physical address. It is used when a computer is connected to the network for the first time or when a diskless computer is booted. We will discuss RARP in Chapter 7.

Internet Control Message Protocol (ICMP)

The **Internet Control Message Protocol (ICMP)** is a mechanism used by hosts and gateways to send notification of datagram problems back to the sender. ICMP sends query and error reporting messages. We will thoroughly discuss ICMP in Chapter 9.

Internet Group Message Protocol (IGMP)

The **Internet Group Message Protocol (IGMP)** is used to facilitate the simultaneous transmission of a message to a group of recipients. We will thoroughly discuss IGMP in Chapter 10.

Transport Layer

The transport layer is represented in TCP/IP by two protocols: TCP and UDP. The IP is a **host-to-host protocol,** meaning that it can deliver a packet from one physical device to another. UDP and TCP are **transport level protocols** responsible for delivery of a message from a process (running program) to another process.

User Datagram Protocol (UDP)

The **User Datagram Protocol (UDP)** is the simpler of the two standard TCP/IP transport protocols. It is a process-to-process protocol that adds only port addresses, checksum error control, and length information to the data from the upper layer.

Transmission Control Protocol (TCP)

The **Transmission Control Protocol (TCP)** provides full transport layer services to applications. TCP is a reliable stream transport protocol. The term *stream,* in this context, means connection-oriented: a connection must be established between both ends of a transmission before either can transmit data.

At the sending end of each transmission, TCP divides a stream of data into smaller units called *segments.* Each segment includes a sequence number for reordering after receipt, together with an acknowledgment number for the segments received. Segments are carried across the internet inside of IP datagrams. At the receiving end, TCP collects each datagram as it comes in and reorders the transmission based on sequence numbers.

Application Layer

The *application layer* in TCP/IP is equivalent to the combined session, presentation, and application layers in the OSI model. Many protocols are defined at this layer. We cover many of the standard protocols in later chapters.

2.4 ADDRESSING

Three different levels of addresses are used in an internet using the TCP/IP protocols: **physical** (link) **address, internet** (IP) **address,** and **port address** (see Figure 2.16).

Figure 2.16 *Addresses in TCP/IP*

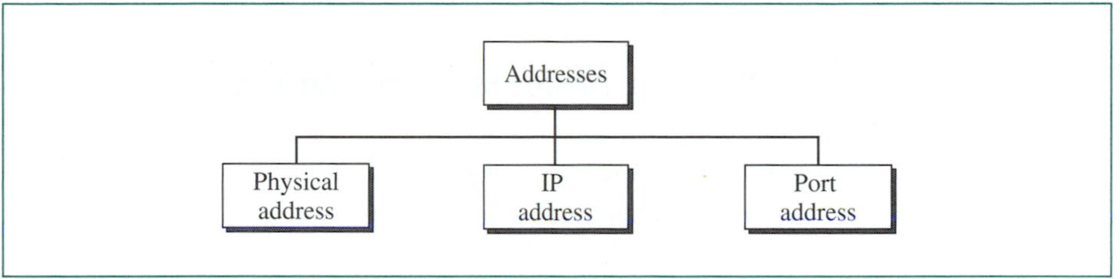

Each address belongs to a specific layer of TCP/IP architecture, as shown in Figure 2.17.

Figure 2.17 *Relationship of layers and addresses in TCP/IP*

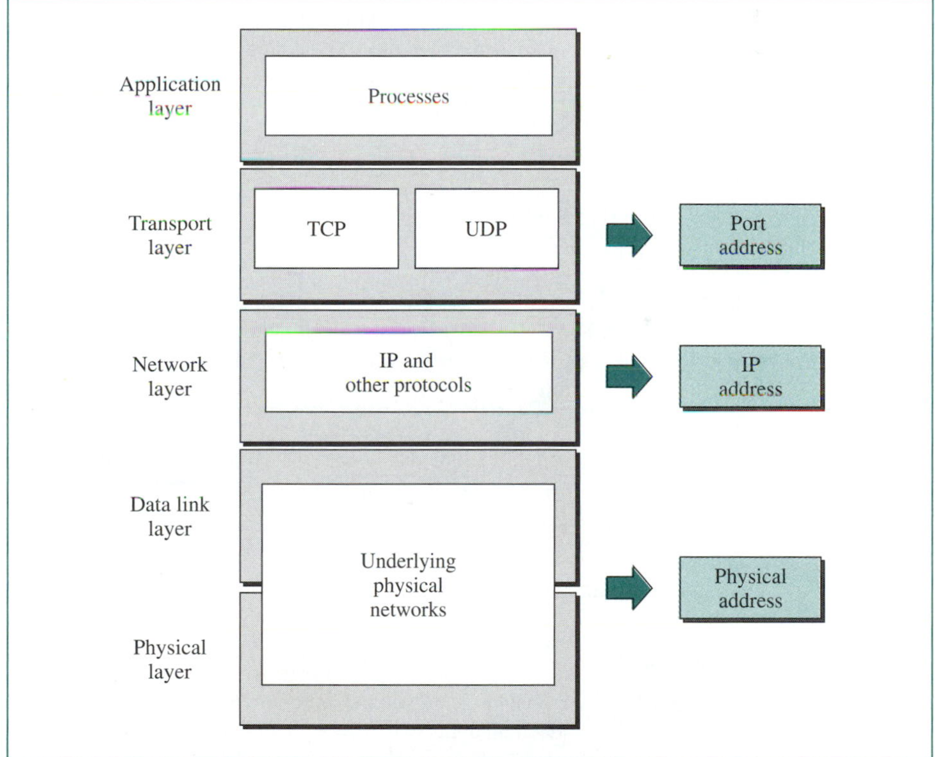

Physical Address

The **physical address,** also known as the link address, is the address of a node as defined by its LAN or WAN. It is included in the frame used by the data link layer. It is the lowest level address.

The physical addresses have authority over the network (LAN or WAN). The size and format of these addresses vary depending on the network. For example, Ethernet uses a 6-byte (48-bit) physical address that is imprinted on the network interface card

(NIC). LocalTalk, however, has a 1-byte dynamic address that changes each time the station comes up.

Unicast, Multicast, and Broadcast Physical Addresses

Physical addresses can be either **unicast** (one single recipient), **multicast** (a group of recipients), or **broadcast** (to be received by all systems in the network). Some networks support all three addresses. For example, Ethernet (see Chapter 3) supports the unicast physical addresses (6 bytes), the multicast addresses, and the broadcast addresses. Some networks do not support the multicast or broadcast physical addresses. If a frame must be sent to a group of recipients or to all systems, the multicast or broadcast address must be simulated using unicast addresses. This means that multiple packets are sent out using unicast addresses.

Example 1

In Figure 2.18 a node with physical address 10 sends a frame to a node with physical address 87. The two nodes are connected by a link. At the data link level this frame contains physical (link) addresses in the header. These are the only addresses needed. The rest of the header contains other information needed at this level. The trailer usually contains extra bits needed for error detection.

Figure 2.18 *Physical addresses*

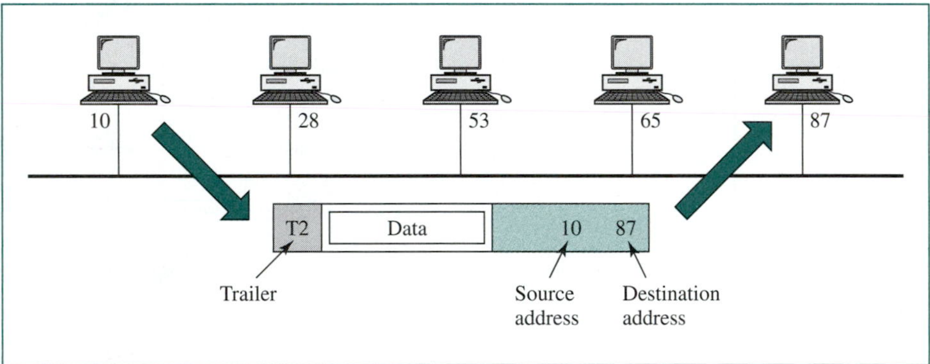

Example 2

As we will see in Chapter 3, most local area networks use a 48-bit (6 bytes) physical address written as 12 hexadecimal digits, with every 2 bytes separated by a hyphen as shown below:

07-01-02-01-2C-4B	A 6-byte (12 hexadecimal digits) physical address

Internet Address

Internet addresses are necessary for universal communication services that are independent of underlying physical networks. Physical addresses are not adequate in an internetwork environment where different networks can have different address formats. A universal addressing system in which each host can be identified uniquely, regardless of the underlying physical network, is needed.

The Internet addresses are designed for this purpose. An Internet address is currently a 32-bit address that can uniquely define a host connected to the Internet. No two hosts on the Internet can have the same IP address.

Unicast, Multicast, and Broadcast Addresses

The Internet addresses can be either unicast (one single recipient), multicast (a group of recipients), or broadcast (all systems in the network). There are limitations on broadcast addresses. We will discuss the three types of addresses in Chapter 4.

Example 3

In Figure 2.19 we want to send data from a node with network address A and physical address 10, located on one LAN, to a node with a network address P and physical address 95, located on another LAN. Because the two devices are located on different networks, we cannot use link addresses only; the link addresses have only local jurisdiction. What we need here are universal addresses that can pass through the LAN boundaries. The network (logical) addresses have this characteristic. The packet at the network layer contains the logical addresses, which remain the same from the original source to the final destination (A and P, respectively, in the figure). They will not change when we go from network to network. However, the physical addresses will

Figure 2.19 *IP addresses*

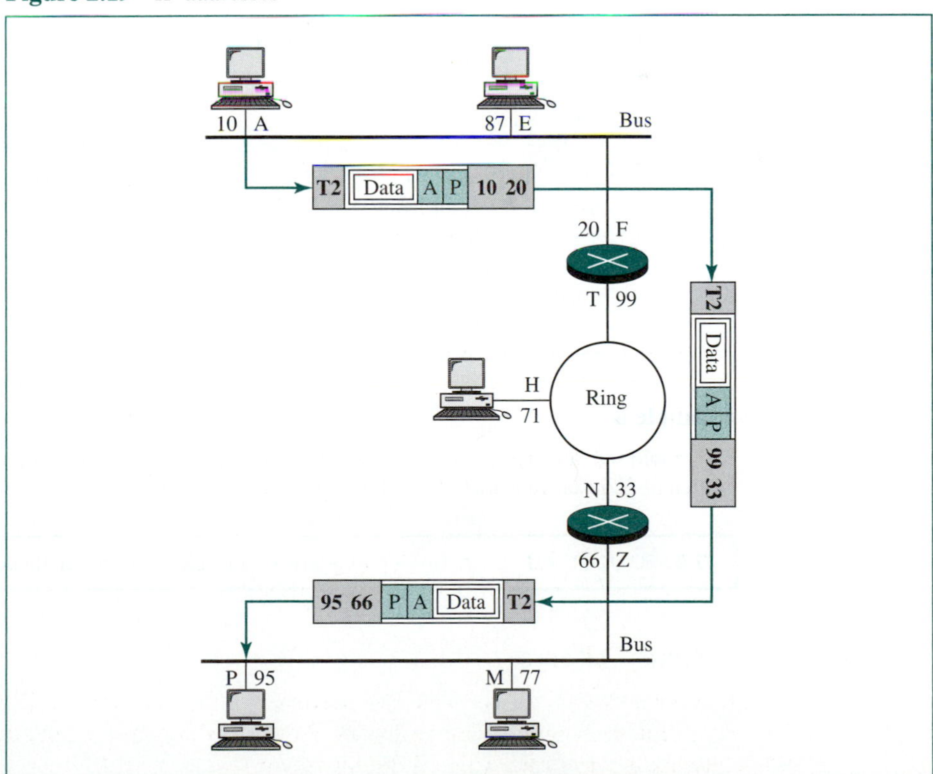

change as the packet moves from one network to another. The box with the R is a router (internetwork device), which we will discuss in Chapter 3.

Example 4

As we will see in Chapter 4, an Internet address (in IPv4) is 32 bits in length, normally written as four decimal numbers, with each number representing 1 byte. The numbers are separated by a dot. Below is an example of such an address.

132.24.75.9	An internet address in IPv4 in decimal numbers

Port Address

The IP address and the physical address are necessary for a quantity of data to travel from a source to the destination host. However, arrival at the destination host is not the final objective of data communication on the Internet. A system that sends nothing but data from one computer to another is not complete. Today, computers are devices that can run multiple processes at the same time. The end objective of internet communication is a process communicating with another process. For example, computer A can communicate with computer C using TELNET. At the same time, computer A communicates with computer B using File Transfer Protocol (FTP). For these processes to occur simultaneously, we need a method to label different processes. In other words, they need addresses. In TCP/IP architecture, the label assigned to a process is called a port address. A port address in TCP/IP is 16 bits long.

Example 5

Figure 2.20 shows an example of transport layer communication. Data coming from the upper layers have port addresses *j* and *k* (*j* is the address of the sending process, and *k* is the address of the receiving process). Since the data size is larger than the network layer can handle, the data are split into two packets, each packet retaining the service-point addresses (*j* and *k*). Then in the network layer, network addresses (A and P) are added to each packet. The packets can travel on different paths and arrive at the destination either in order or out of order. The two packets are delivered to the destination transport layer, which is responsible for removing the network layer headers and combining the two pieces of data for delivery to the upper layers.

Example 6

As we will see in Chapters 11 and 12, a port address is a 16-bit address represented by one decimal number as shown below.

753	A 16-bit port address represented as one single number

Figure 2.20 *Port addresses*

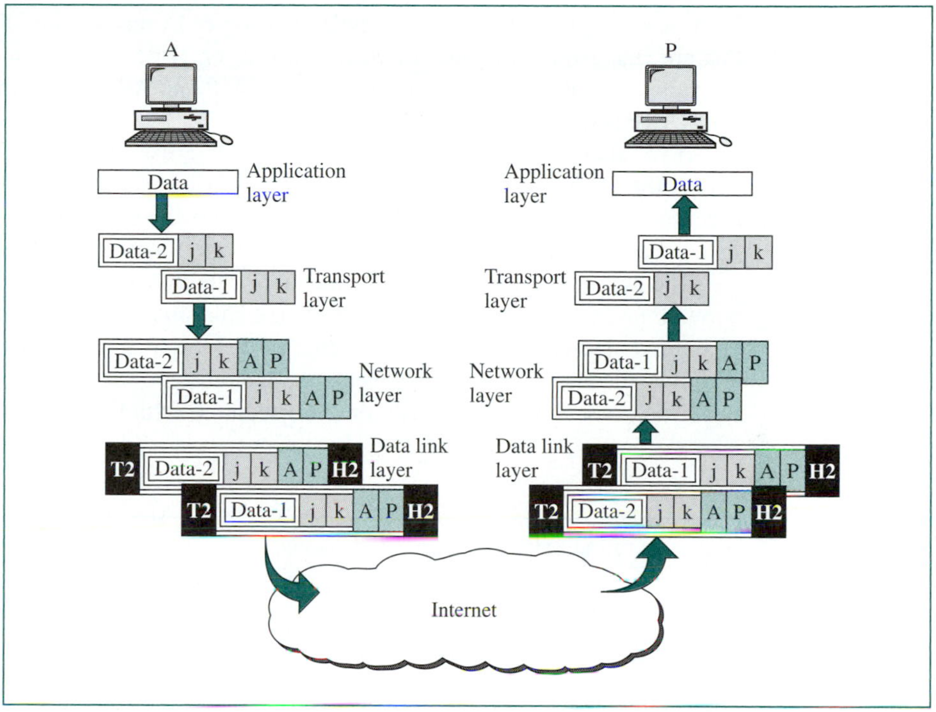

2.5 TCP/IP VERSIONS

TCP/IP became the official protocol for the Internet (then known as ARPANET; see Chapter 1) in 1983. As the Internet has evolved, so has TCP/IP. There have been six versions since its inception. We look at the latter three versions here.

Version 4

Most networks on the Internet are currently using version 4. However, this version has significant shortcomings. The primary problem is that the Internet address is only 32 bits in length with the address space divided into different classes. With the rapid growth of the Internet, 32 bits is not sufficient to handle the projected number of users. Also, the division of the space into different classes further limits the available addresses.

Version 5

Version 5 was a proposal based on the OSI model. This version never went beyond the proposal stage due to extensive layer changes and the projected expense.

Version 6

IETF has designed a new version called version 6. In this version, the only protocols that are changed are the ones in the network layer. **IPv4** (IP version 4) becomes **IPv6** (IP version 6), ICMPv4 becomes ICMPv6, IGMP and ARP are merged into ICMPv6, and RARP is deleted.

IPv6, also known as IPng (IP *next generation*), uses 128-bit (16-byte) addresses, versus the 32-bit (4-byte) addresses currently used in version 4. IPv6 can thereby accommodate a larger number of users. In version 6, the packet format has been simplified, yet at the same time it is more flexible to allow for the future addition of features.

The new version supports authentication, data integrity, and confidentiality at the network layer. It is designed to handle the transmission of real-time data such as audio and video, and can carry data from other protocols. IPng can also handle congestion and route discovery better than the current version.

This book is based primarily on the version 4, with Chapter 31 concentrating on IPng.

2.6 KEY TERMS

access control

Address Resolution Protocol (ARP)

application layer

best-effort delivery

bits

broadcast physical address

bus topology

compression

connection control

data link layer

dialog control

directory services

encoding

encryption

error control

file transfer, access, and management (FTAM)

flow control

frames

full-duplex mode

half-duplex mode

host-to-host protocol

interface

International Standards Organization (ISO)

Internet address

Internet Control Message Protocol (ICMP)

Internet Group Message Protocol (IGMP)

internetworks

Internetworking Protocol (IP)

IPv4

IPv6

line configuration

logical addressing

mail services

mesh topology

multicast physical address

multipoint configuration

network layer

network virtual terminal

open system

Open Systems Interconnection (OSI) model

peer-to-peer processes

physical address

physical layer

physical topology

point-to-point configuration

port address

presentation layer

Reverse Address Resolution Protocol (RARP)

ring topology

routing

segmentation

service-point addressing

session layer

source-to-destination delivery

star topology

synchronization points

TCP/IP protocol suite

translation

transmission mode

transmission rate

transport layer

transport level protocol

unicast physical address

User Datagram Protocol (UDP)

2.7 SUMMARY

- The International Standards Organization (ISO) created a model called the Open Systems Interconnection (OSI), which allows diverse systems to communicate.
- The seven-layer OSI model provides guidelines for the development of universally compatible networking protocols.
- The physical, data link, and network layers are the network support layers.
- The session, presentation, and application layers are the user support layers.
- The transport layer links the network support layers and the user support layers.
- The physical layer coordinates the functions required to transmit a bit stream over a physical medium.
- The data link layer is responsible for delivering data units from one station to the next without errors.
- The network layer is responsible for the source-to-destination delivery of a packet across multiple network links.
- The transport layer is responsible for the source-to-destination delivery of the entire message.

- The session layer establishes, maintains, and synchronizes the interactions between communicating devices.
- The presentation layer ensures interoperability between communicating devices through transformation of data into a mutually agreed-upon format.
- The application layer enables the users to access the network.
- TCP/IP is a five-layer hierarchical protocol suite developed before the OSI model.
- The TCP/IP application layer is equivalent to the combined session, presentation, and application layers of the OSI model.
- Three types of addresses are used by systems using the TCP/IP protocol: the physical address, the internetwork address (IP address), and the port address.
- The physical address, also known as the link address, is the address of a node as defined by its LAN or WAN.
- The IP address uniquely defines a host on the Internet.
- The port address identifies a process on a host.
- Most networks use IPv4.
- IPv6 is supposed to replace IPv4 in the near future.

2.8 PRACTICE SET

Multiple-Choice Questions

1. Why was the OSI model developed?
   a. manufacturers disliked the TCP/IP protocol suite
   b. the rate of data transfer was increasing exponentially
   c. standards were needed to allow any two systems to communicate
   d. none of the above
2. The _______ model shows how the network functions of a computer ought to be organized.
   a. CCITT
   b. OSI
   c. ISO
   d. ANSI
3. The physical layer is concerned with the transmission of _______ over the physical medium.
   a. programs
   b. dialogs
   c. protocols
   d. bits

4. The OSI model consists of _______ layers.
   a. three
   b. five
   c. seven
   d. eight
5. As a data packet moves from the lower to the upper layers, headers are _______.
   a. added
   b. subtracted
   c. rearranged
   d. modified
6. When data is transmitted from device A to device B, the header from A's layer 5 is read by B's _______ layer.
   a. physical
   b. transport
   c. session
   d. presentation
7. Which layer functions as a liaison between user support layers and network support layers?
   a. network layer
   b. physical layer
   c. transport layer
   d. session layer
8. What is the main function of the transport layer?
   a. node-to-node delivery
   b. process-to-process message delivery
   c. synchronization
   d. updating and maintenance of routing tables
9. Session layer checkpoints _______.
   a. allow just a portion of a file to be resent
   b. detect and recover errors
   c. control the addition of headers
   d. are involved in dialog control
10. Encryption and decryption are functions of the _____________ layer.
    a. transport
    b. session
    c. presentation
    d. application

11. Which of the following is an application layer service?
    a. network virtual terminal
    b. file transfer, access, and management
    c. mail service
    d. all of the above
12. When a host on network A sends a message to a host on network B, which address does the router look at?
    a. port
    b. IP
    c. physical
    d. none of the above
13. To deliver a message to the correct application program running on a host, the _______ address must be consulted.
    a. port
    b. IP
    c. physical
    d. none of the above
14. IPv6 has _______ -bit addresses.
    a. 32
    b. 64
    c. 128
    d. variable
15. ICMPv6 includes _______.
    a. IGMP
    b. ARP
    c. RARP
    d. a and b

Exercises

16. How are OSI and ISO related to each other?
17. Match the following to one of the seven OSI layers:
    a. route determination
    b. flow control
    c. interface to outside world
    d. provides access to the network for the end user
    e. changes ASCII to EBCDIC
    f. packet switching

18. Match the following to one of the seven OSI layers:
    a. reliable process-to-process message delivery
    b. network selection
    c. defines frames
    d. provides user services such as email and file transfer
    e. transmission of bit stream across physical medium
19. Match the following to one of the seven OSI layers:
    a. communicates directly with user's application program
    b. error correction and retransmission
    c. mechanical, electrical, and functional interface
    d. responsibility for information between adjacent nodes
    e. reassembly of data packets
20. Match the following to one of the seven OSI layers:
    a. format and code conversion services
    b. establishes, manages, and terminates sessions
    c. ensures reliable transmission of data
    d. log-in and log-out procedures
    e. provides independence from differences in data representation
    f. synchronization of users
21. Domain Name System or DNS (see Chapter 18) is an application program in the TCP/IP protocol suite. Do some research and find the equivalent of this protocol (if any) in the OSI model. Compare and contrast the two.
22. File Transfer Protocol or FTP (see Chapter 20) is an application program in the TCP/IP protocol suite. Do some research and find the equivalent of this protocol (if any) in the OSI model. Compare and contrast the two.
23. Trivial File Transfer Protocol or TFTP (see Chapter 21) is an application program in the TCP/IP protocol suite. Do some research and find the equivalent of this protocol (if any) in the OSI model. Compare and contrast the two.
24. There are several transport layer models proposed in the OSI model. Do some research and find all of them. Explain the differences between them.
25. There are several network layer models proposed in the OSI model. Do some research and find all of them. Explain the differences between them.

CHAPTER 3

Underlying Technologies

We can think of the Internet as a series of backbone networks that are run by international, national, and regional ISPs. The backbones are joined together by connecting devices such as routers or by switching stations. The end users are either part of the local ISP LAN or connected via point-to-point networks to the LANs. Conceptually, the Internet is a set of switched WANs (backbones), LANs, point-to-point WANs, and connecting or switching devices as shown in Figure 3.1.

Figure 3.1 *Internet model*

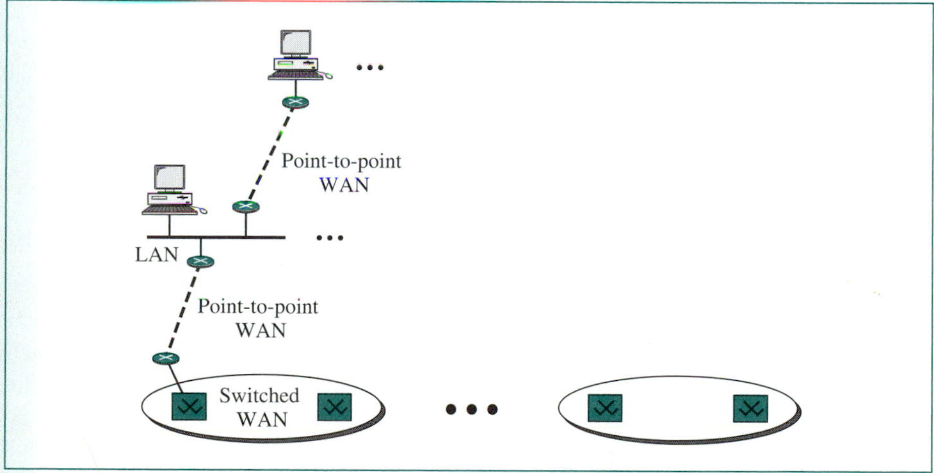

Although the TCP/IP protocol suite is normally shown as a five-layer stack, it only defines protocols for the upper three layers; TCP/IP is only concerned about the network, transport, and application layers. This means that TCP/IP assumes the existence of these WANs, LANs, and the connecting devices that join them.

We do the same. We assume that the reader is already familiar with the underlying technology of data communications, telecommunications, LANs, WANs, and connecting devices.

However, as a brief review, we touch upon these underlying technologies in this chapter. Note that we cannot cover any of these topics in detail; this would require a book or two. For more in-depth coverage, see Forouzan, *Introduction to Data Communications and Networking,* 2 ed., McGraw-Hill, 2001, and Forouzan, *Local Area Networks,* McGraw-Hill, 2003.

3.1 LOCAL AREA NETWORKS (LANs)

A **local area network (LAN)** is a data communication system that allows a number of independent devices to communicate directly with each other in a limited geographic area such as a single department, a single building, or a campus. A large organization may need several connected LANs.

The most popular LANs are Ethernet LANs, Token Ring LANs, wireless LANs, and ATM LANs. We briefly review the first three technologies in this section; we discuss ATM LANs after we have discussed ATM technology.

For further discussion of LANs, see Forouzan, *Local Area Networks,* McGraw-Hill, 2003.

Ethernet

Ethernet is the most widely used local area network protocol. The protocol was designed in 1973 by Xerox with a data rate of 10 Mbps and a bus topology. Today it has a data rate of 100 Mbps and 1000 Mbps (1 gigabit per second). Ethernet is formally defined by the IEEE 802.3 standard (see Appendix F).

Traditional Ethernet (10 Mbps)

The original Ethernet, usually referred to as traditional Ethernet, had a 10-Mbps data rate. We discuss this Ethernet version first.

Access Method: CSMA/CD The IEEE 802.3 standard defines **carrier sense multiple access with collision detection (CSMA/CD)** as the access method for traditional Ethernet. Stations on a traditional Ethernet can be connected together using a physical bus or star topology, but the logical topology is always a bus. By this, we mean that the medium (channel) is shared between stations and only one station at a time can use it. It also implies that all stations receive a frame sent by a station (broadcasting). The real destination keeps the frame while the rest drop it. In this situation, how can we be sure that two stations are not using the medium at the same time? If they do, their frames will collide with each other. CSMA/CD is designed to solve the problem according to the following principles:

1. Every station has an equal right to the medium (multiple access).
2. Every station with a frame to send first listens to (senses) the medium. If there is no data on the medium, the station can start sending (carrier sense).
3. It may happen that two stations both sense the medium, find it idle, and start sending. In this case, a collision occurs. The protocol forces the station to continue to listen to the line after sending has begun. If there is a collision, all stations sense

the collision; each sending station sends a jam signal to destroy the data on the line and, after each waits a different random time, try again. The random times prevent the simultaneous re-sending of data.

Figure 3.2 shows CSMA/CD.

Figure 3.2 *CSMA/CD*

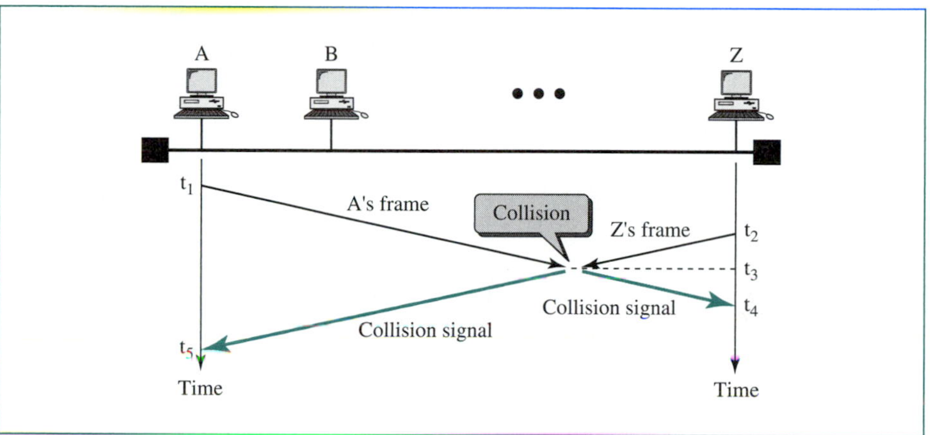

Three factors are related in the CSMA/CD standard: the minimum frame length, the data transmission rate, and the collision domain. The time the station needs to wait to be sure that there is no data on the line is the minimum frame length divided by the transmission rate (the time required to send out the minimum frame length). This time is proportional to the time needed for the first bit to travel the maximum network distance (collision domain). In other words, we have

> Minimum frame length / Transmission rate
> is proportional to
> Collision domain / Propagation speed

In traditional Ethernet, the minimum frame length is 520 bits, the transmission rate is 10 Mbps, the propagation speed is almost the speed of light, and the collision domain is almost 2500 meters.

Layers Figure 3.3 shows the 10-Mbps Ethernet layers. The data link layer has two sublayers: the logical link control (LLC) sublayer and the media access control (MAC) sublayer. The LLC layer is responsible for flow and error control at the data link layer. The MAC sublayer is responsible for the operation of the CSMA/CD access method. The MAC sublayer also frames data received from the LLC layer and passes the frames to the physical layer for encoding. The physical layer transfers data into electrical signals and sends them to the next station via the transmission medium. This bottom layer also detects and reports collisions to the data link layer.

Frame IEEE 802.3 specifies one frame type containing seven fields: preamble, SFD, DA, SA, length/type of PDU, 802.2 frame, and the CRC. Ethernet does not provide any

Figure 3.3 *Ethernet layers*

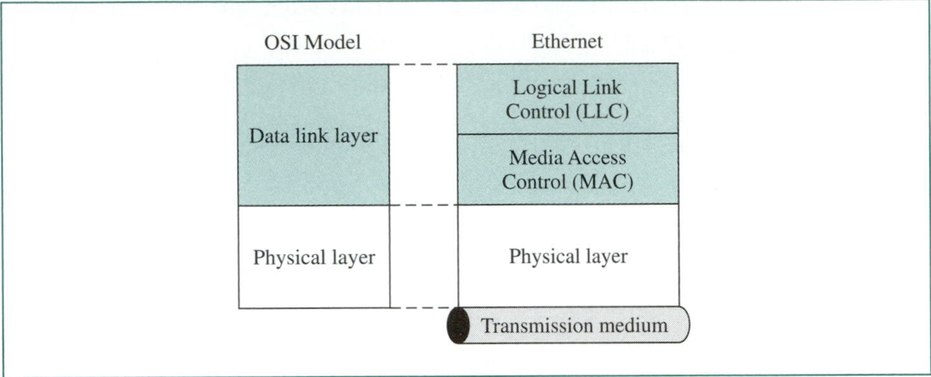

mechanism for acknowledging received frames, making it what is known as an unreliable medium. Acknowledgments must be implemented at the higher layers. The format of the CSMA/CD MAC frame is shown in Figure 3.4.

Figure 3.4 *Ethernet frame*

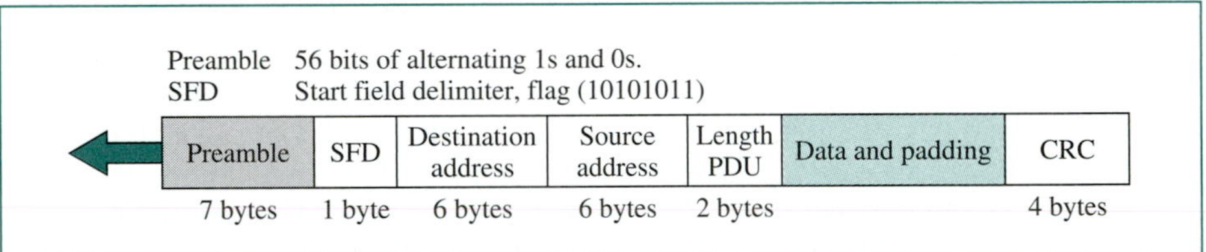

- **Preamble.** The preamble of the 802.3 frame contains 7 bytes (56 bits) of alternating 0s and 1s that alert the receiving system to the coming frame and enable it to synchronize its input timing. The preamble is actually added at the physical layer and is not (formally) part of the frame.
- **Start frame delimiter (SFD).** The SFD field (1 byte: 10101011) of the 802.3 frame signals the beginning of the frame. The SFD gives the station a last chance for synchronization. The last two bits are 11 and are a signal that the next field is the destination address.
- **Destination address (DA).** The DA field is 6 bytes and contains the physical address of the intermediate or destination station.
- **Source address (SA).** The SA field is also 6 bytes and contains the physical address of the sending or intermediate station.
- **Length/type.** The length type field has one of two meanings. If the value of the field is less than 1518, it is a length field and defines the length of the data field that follows. If the value of this field is greater than 1536, it defines the upper layer protocol that uses the service of the Internet.
- **Data.** The data field carries data encapsulated from the upper layer protocols. It is a minimum of 46 and a maximum 1500 bytes.

- **CRC.** The last field in the 802.3 frame contains the error detection information, in this case a CRC-32 (see Appendix D).

Addressing Each station such as a PC, workstation, or printer on an Ethernet network has its own **network interface card (NIC).** The NIC fits inside the station and provides the station with a 6-byte physical address. The Ethernet address is 6 bytes (48 bits) that is normally written in hexadecimal notation with a hyphen to separate bytes as shown below:

07-01-02-01-2C-4B

The addresses in Ethernet are sent byte by byte, left to right; however, for each byte, the least significant bit is sent first and the most significant bit is sent last.

There are three types of addresses in Ethernet: unicast, multicast, and broadcast. In a **unicast address,** the least significant bit of the first byte is 0; in the **multicast address,** the least significant bit is 1. A **broadcast address** is 48 1s. A source address is always unicast. The destination address can be unicast (one single recipient), multicast (a group of recipients), or broadcast (all stations connected to the LAN).

Implementations The IEEE standard defines several implementations for traditional Internet. The following four are common:

- **10BASE5** (thick Ethernet) uses a bus topology with a thick coaxial cable as the transmission medium.
- **10BASE2** (thin Ethernet or Cheapernet) uses a bus topology with a thin coaxial cable as the transmission medium.
- **10BASE-T** (twisted-pair Ethernet) uses a physical star topology (the logical topology is still a bus) with stations connected by two pairs of twisted-pair cable to the hub.
- **10BASE-FL** (fiber link Ethernet) uses a star topology (the logical topology is still a bus) with stations connected by a pair of fiber-optic cables to the hub.

A simple representation of these four implementations is shown in Figure 3.5. The transceiver, which can be external or internal, is responsible for encoding, collision detection, and transmitting/receiving signals.

Fast Ethernet

The need for a higher data rate resulted in the **Fast Ethernet** protocol (100 Mbps). In the MAC layer, Fast Ethernet uses the same principles as traditional Ethernet (CSMA/CD) except that the transmission rate has been increased from 10 Mbps to 100 Mbps. For CSMA/CD to work, we have two choices: either increase the minimum frame length or decrease the collision domain (the speed of light cannot be changed). Increasing the minimum length of the frame involves additional overhead. If the data to be sent is not long enough, we must add extra bytes, which means more overhead and loss of efficiency. Fast Ethernet has chosen the other option; the collision domain has been decreased by a factor of 10 (from 2500 meters to 250 meters). With a star topology, 250 meters is acceptable in many cases. In the physical layer, Fast Ethernet uses different signaling methods and different media to achieve a data rate of 100 Mbps.

Figure 3.5 *Ethernet implementations*

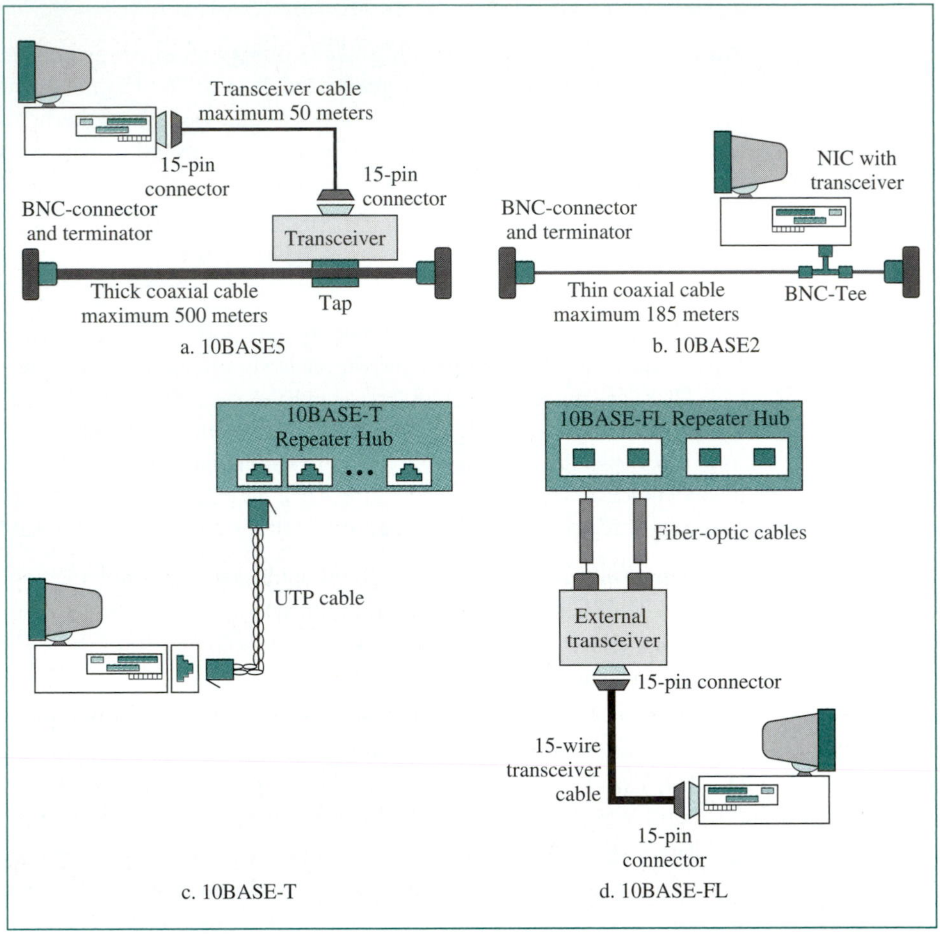

Fast Ethernet Implementation Fast Ethernet can be categorized as either a two-wire or four-wire implementation. The two-wire implementation is called 100BASE-X, with either twisted-pair cable (100BASE-TX) or fiber-optic cable (100BASE-FX). The four-wire implementation is designed only for twisted-pair cable (100BASE-T4). In other words, we have three implementations: 100BASE-TX, 100BASE-FX, and 100BASE-T4 (see Figure 3.6).

Gigabit Ethernet

The need for a data rate higher than 100 Mbps resulted in the **Gigabit Ethernet** protocol (1000 Mbps). To achieve this data rate the MAC layer has two options: keeping CSMA/CD or dropping it. For the former, the two choices are, once again, to decrease the collision domain or increase the minimum frame length. Since a collision domain of 25 meters is unacceptable, the minimum length of the frame is increased in a very elegant way.

Figure 3.6 *Fast Ethernet implementations*

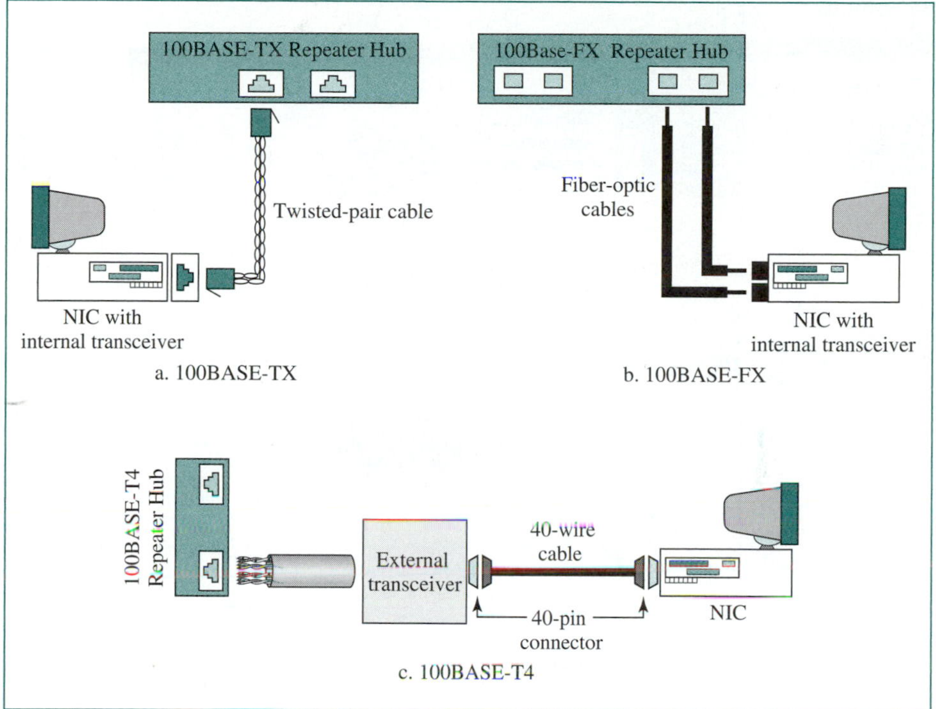

In the second option, dropping CSMA/CD, every station is connected by two separate paths to the central hub. This is called full-duplex Ethernet with no collision and no need for CSMA/CD.

At the physical level, many changes have been made to allow the transmission of data at this rate.

Gigabit Ethernet Implementation Gigabit Ethernet can be classified as either a two-wire or four-wire implementation. The two-wire implementation is called 1000BASE-X, with optical fibers transmitting short-wave laser signals (1000BASE-SX), optical fibers transmitting long-wave laser signals (1000BASE-LX), and shielded twisted pair transmitting electrical signals (1000BASE-CX). The four-wire version uses twisted-pair cables (1000BASE-T). In other words, we have four implementations, three of which are shown in Figure 3.7.

Token Ring

Token Ring is a protocol defined in IEEE Project 802.5. It uses a token passing access method. Token passing is illustrated in Figure 3.8. Whenever the network is unoccupied, a simple 3-byte token circulates. This token is passed from station to station until it encounters a station with data to send. The station keeps the token and sends a data frame. This data frame proceeds around the ring, being regenerated by each station. Each intermediate station examines the destination address, finds that the frame is

Figure 3.7 *Gigabit Ethernet implementations*

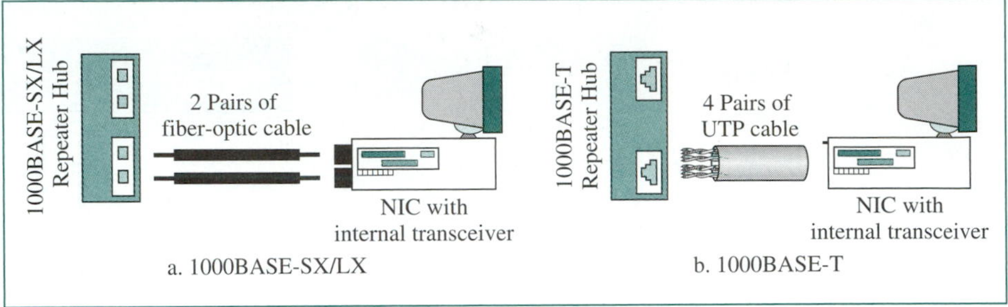

Figure 3.8 *Token passing*

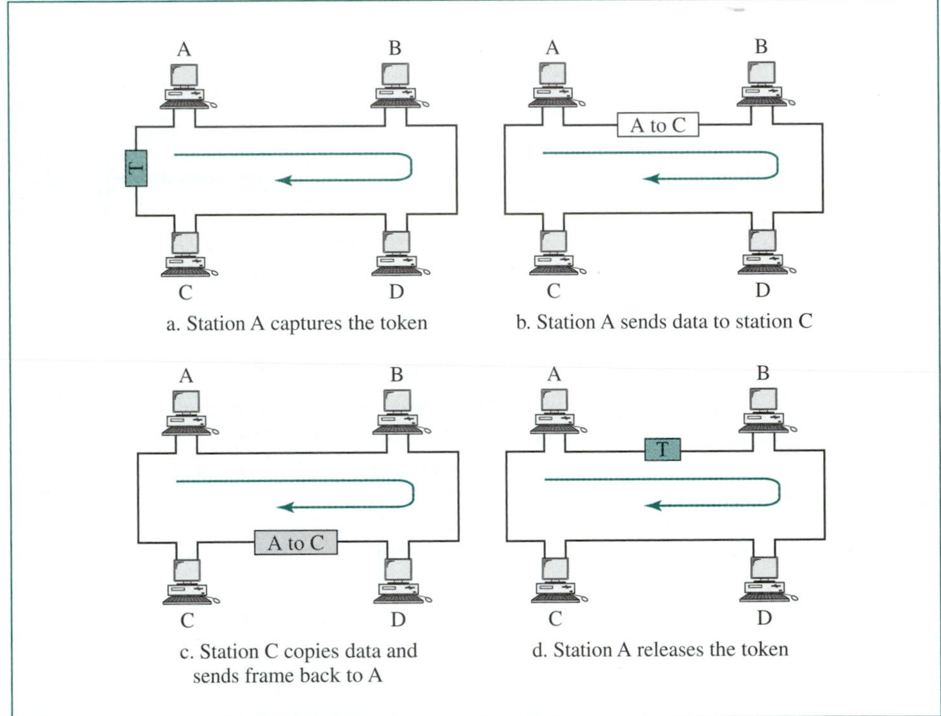

addressed to another station, and relays it to its neighbor. The intended recipient recognizes its own address, copies the message, checks for errors, and changes 4 bits in the last byte of the frame to indicate address recognized and frame copied. The full packet then continues around the ring until it returns to the station that sent it.

Layers

Token Ring uses the same two layers as Ethernet. The data link layer is divided into two sublayers: LLC and MAC. The LLC plays the same role as in Ethernet. The MAC sublayer is responsible for the token passing and reservation operations. It is also responsible for frame creation and frame delivery to the physical layer.

Frame

Token Ring defines three types of frames: data, token, and abort.

Data Frame In Token Ring, the data frame is the only one of the three types of frames that can carry a protocol data unit (PDU) and the only one addressed to a specific destination rather than being available to the ring at large. Figure 3.9 shows the format of the data frame.

Figure 3.9 *Data frame*

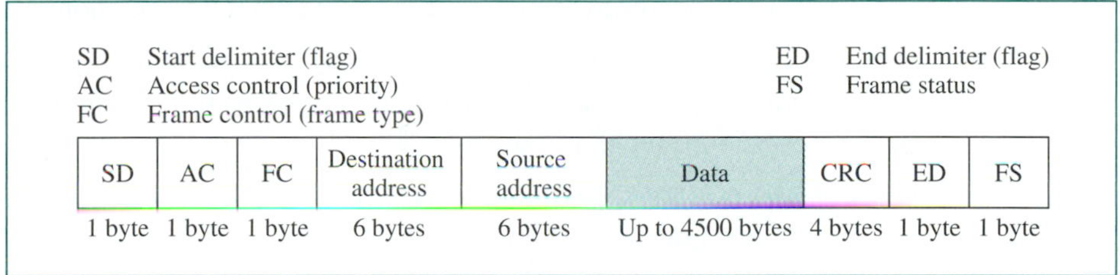

The following describes each field in the frame:

- **Start delimiter (SD).** The first field of the data frame, SD, is 1 byte long and is used to alert the receiving station to the arrival of a frame as well as to allow it to synchronize its retrieval timing.
- **Access control (AC).** The AC field is 1 byte long and includes four subfields. The first 3 bits are the priority field. The fourth bit is called the token bit and is set to indicate that the frame is a data frame rather than a token or an abort frame. The token bit is followed by a monitor bit. The last 3 bits are a reservation field that can be set by stations wishing to reserve access to the ring.
- **Frame control (FC).** The FC field is 1 byte long and contains two fields. The first is a 1-bit field used to indicate the type of information contained in the PDU (whether it is control information or data). The second uses the remaining 7 bits of the byte and contains information used by Token Ring (e.g., how to use the information in the AC field).
- **Destination address (DA).** The 6-byte DA field contains the physical address of the frame's next destination.
- **Source address (SA).** The SA field is also 6 bytes long and contains the physical address of the sending station.
- **Data.** The sixth field, data, is allotted 4500 bytes and contains the PDU. A Token Ring frame does not include a PDU length or type field.
- **CRC.** The CRC field is 4 bytes long and contains a CRC-32 error detection sequence.
- **End delimiter (ED).** The ED is a second flag field of 1 byte and indicates the end of the sender's data and control information.

- **Frame status (FS).** The last byte of the frame is the FS field. It can be set by the receiver to indicate that the frame has been read, or by the monitor to indicate that the frame has already been around the ring. This field is not an acknowledgment, but it does tell the sender that the receiving station has copied the frame, which can now be discarded.

Token Frame Because a token is really a placeholder and reservation frame, it has only three fields: SD, AC, and ED. The SD indicates that a frame is coming. The AC indicates that the frame is a token and includes the priority and reservation fields. The ED indicates the end of the frame.

Abort Frame An abort frame carries no information at all—just starting and ending delimiters. It can be generated either by the sender to stop its own transmission (for whatever reason), or by the monitor to purge an old transmission from the line.

Addressing Like Ethernet, most Token Ring implementations use a 6-byte address. The addressing mechanism is the same as the Ethernet, except that Token Ring sends the most significant bit of each byte first.

Implementation The ring in a Token Ring consists of a series of shielded twisted-pair sections linking each station to its immediate neighbors. Configuring the network as a ring introduces a potential problem: One disabled or disconnected node could stop the flow of traffic around the entire network. To solve this problem, each station is connected to an automatic switch. This switch can bypass an inactive station. While a station is disabled, the switch closes the ring without it. When the station comes on, a signal sent by the NIC moves the switch and brings the station into the ring. For practical purposes, individual automatic switches are combined into a hub called a multistation access unit (MAU); see Figure 3.10. One MAU can support up to eight stations. Looked at from the outside, this system looks like a star with the MAU at the middle. But, it is in fact a ring. MAUs can be combined to create a larger ring.

Figure 3.10 *MAU*

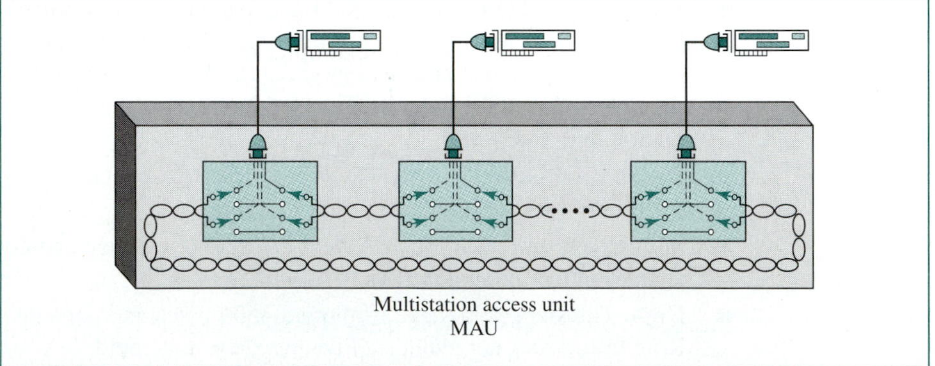

Wireless LANs

Wireless communication is one of the fastest growing technologies. The demand for mobile devices has led to a need for wireless wide and local area networks. In this section, we first discuss the general concept of wireless transmission techniques before we discuss wireless LAN technology.

Spread Spectrum

Wireless devices can transmit signals using several techniques including radio frequency spread spectrum and radio frequency narrow band and infrared waves. We discuss here only the spread spectrum technique because of its applications in the Internet.

The spread spectrum technique requires a bandwidth that is several times the original bandwidth. There are two spread spectrum techniques: frequency hopping and direct sequence as shown in Figure 3.11.

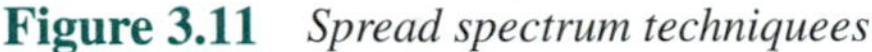

Figure 3.11 *Spread spectrum techniquees*

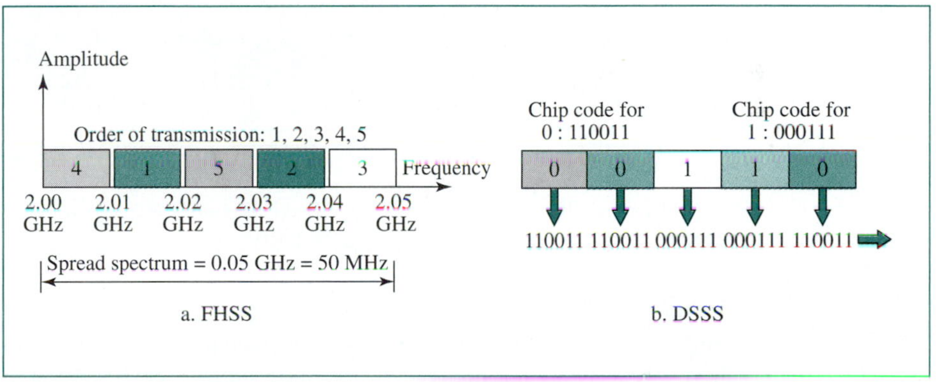

Frequency Hopping Spread Spectrum (FHSS) In this scheme, the sender transmits at one carrier frequency for a short period of time, then hops to another carrier frequency for the same amount of time, hops again for the same amount of time, and so on. After N hops, the cycle is repeated. If the spectrum (bandwidth) of the original signal is B, the spread spectrum (bandwidth) that is allocated for transmission is $N \times B$, where N is the number of hops in each cycle. For example, Figure 3.11 shows FHSS for $B = 10$ Mbps and $N = 5$. In our example, transmission requires only 0.01 GHz or 10 MHz, but the system needs 0.05 GHz to spread the spectrum.

Spreading prevents an intruder from obtaining confidential information. The sender and receiver agree on the sequence of the allocated bands. In the figure, the first bit (or group of bits) is sent in band 1 (between 2.01 and 2.02 GHz), the second bit (or group of bits) is sent in band 2 (2.03 to 2.04 GHz), and so on. An intruder who tunes his receiver to frequencies between 2.01 and 2.02 may receive the first bit, but receives nothing in this band during the next 4 bit intervals.

Direct Sequence Spread Spectrum (DSSS) In this scheme, each bit to be sent by the sender is replaced by a sequence of bits called a chip code. To avoid buffering, however, the time needed to send one original bit is the same as the time needed to send one chip code. This means that the data rate for sending chip codes is N (N is the number of bits in each chip code) times the data rate of the original bit stream. For example, if the sender generates the original bit stream at 1 Mbps, and the chip code is 6 bits long, the data rate for transmitting chip codes is $1 \times 6 = 6$ Mbps.

It is obvious that the bandwidth required to send the chip codes is N times greater than the bandwidth for sending the original bit stream. If the original bit stream needs B Hz, the chip codes need $N \times B$ Hz, the same as in FHSS.

ISM Frequency Band In 1985, the Federal Communications Commission (FCC) modified the radio spectrum regulations for unlicensed devices. The modification authorizes wireless LANs to operate in Industrial, Scientific, and Medical (ISM) bands. The use of these bands does not require a license from the FCC if the equipment operates under 1 W of power. Figure 3.12 shows the ISM bands.

Figure 3.12 *ISM bands*

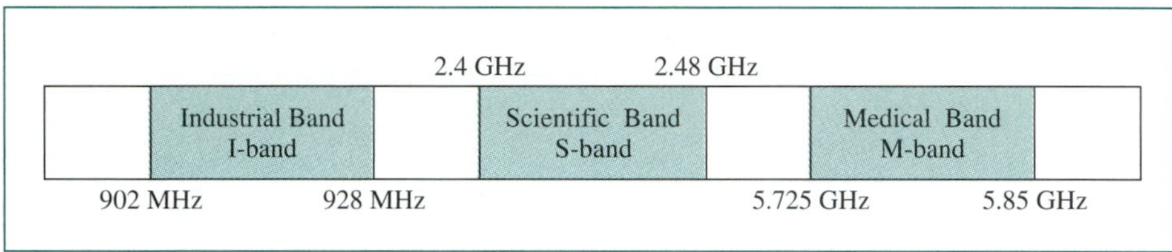

The 902 MHz band and the 5.725 GHz band are available only in the United States; the 2.4 GHz band is available globally.

Architecture

Our discussion of wireless LANs here is limited to the IEEE 802.11 standard. The standard defines two kinds of services: the basic service set (BSS) and the extended service set (ESS).

Basic Service Set The IEEE 802.11 defines the **basic service set (BSS)** as the building block of a wireless LAN. A basic service set is made of stationary or mobile wireless stations and an optional central base station, known as the access point (AP). Figure 3.13 shows two sets in this standard.

Figure 3.13 *BSSs*

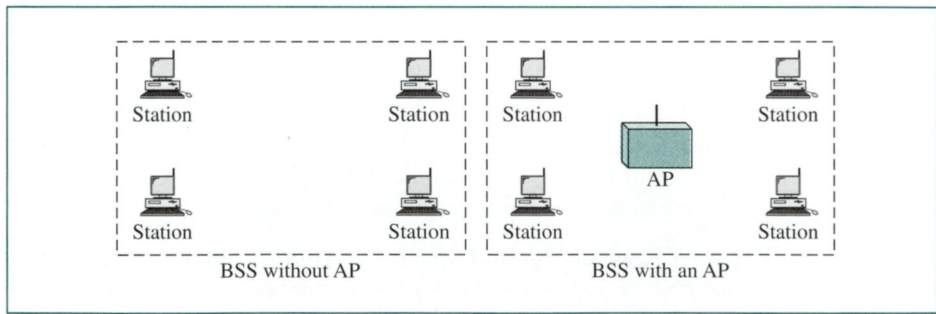

The BSS without an AP is a stand-alone network and cannot send data to other BSSs. It is an *ad hoc architecture.*

Extended Service Set An **extended service set (ESS)** is made of two or more BSSs with APs. In this case, the BSSs are connected through a *distribution system,* which is usually a wired LAN. The distribution system connects the APs in the BSSs. The IEEE 802.11 does not restrict the distribution system; it can be any IEEE LAN such as an Ethernet or Token Ring. Note that the ESS uses two types of stations: mobile and stationary. The mobile stations are normal stations inside a BSS. The stationary stations are AP stations that are part of a wired LAN. Figure 3.14 shows an ESS.

Figure 3.14 *ESS*

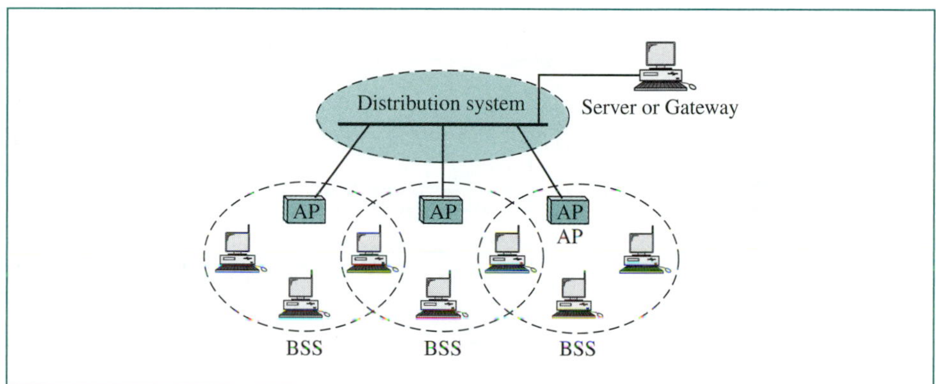

When BSSs are connected together, we have an *infrastructure network.* In this network, the stations within reach of each other can communicate without the use of an AP. However, two stations in two different BSSs usually communicate via two APs. The idea is similar to communication in a cellular network if we consider each BSS to be a cell and each AP to be a base station. Note that a mobile station can belong to more than one BSS at the same time.

Access Method Wireless LANs use an access method called carrier sense multiple access with collision avoidance (CSMA/CA). The first two principles of CSMA/CD also apply to CSMA/CA; each station has equal access to the medium (multiple access) and each station senses the medium before sending. However, collision detection is not applicable for several reasons, the dominant one being the **hidden terminal problem.**

To understand the hidden terminal problem, imagine we have three stations (1, 2, and 3). Station 1 sends a frame to station 2 at the same time that station 3 sends a frame to station 2. It may happen that stations 1 and 3 cannot hear each other (perhaps because of some obstruction like a mountain or a wall). In this case, collision may occur, with stations 1 and 3 unable to detect it: they think their packets have arrived safely.

To prevent this situation, collision must be avoided. Each station defines how long it needs the medium and tells other stations to refrain from sending data during this period. The procedure is as follows:

1. The sending station, after sensing that the medium is idle, sends a special small frame called request to send (RTS). In this message, the sender defines the total time it needs the medium.

2. The receiver acknowledges the request (broadcast to all stations) by sending a small packet called clear to send (CTS).
3. The sender sends the data frame.
4. The receiver acknowledges the receipt of data.

Figure 3.15 shows the procedure.

Figure 3.15 *CSMA/CA*

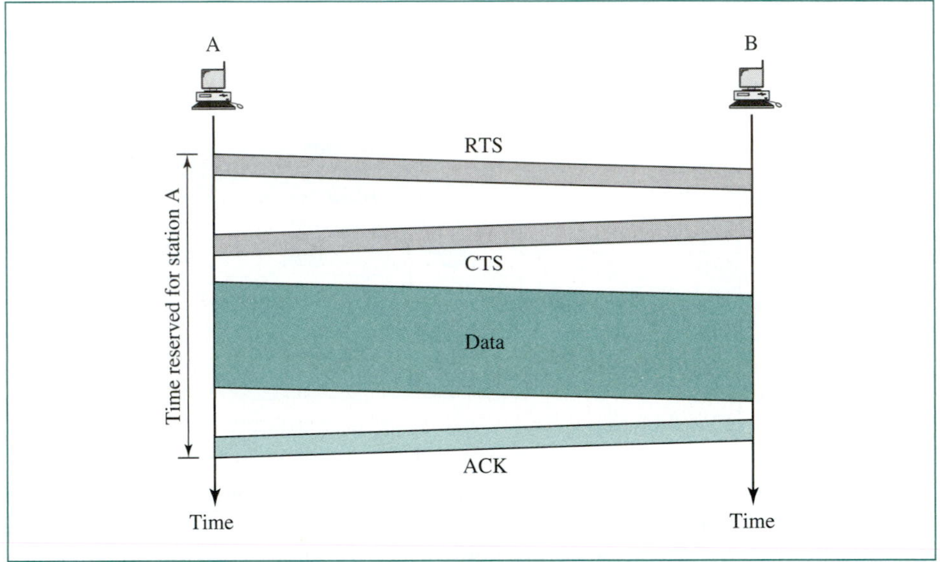

3.2 POINT-TO-POINT WANs

The second type of network we encounter in the Internet is the point-to-point wide area network. A point-to-point WAN connects two remote devices using a line available from a public network such as a telephone network. These public companies normally provide the service at the physical layer; the user is responsible for the protocol at the data link layer.

Physical Layer

At the physical layer, the point-to-point connection between two devices can be accomplished using one of the services available today such as traditional modem technology with the regular telephone line, a DSL line, cable modem, a T-line, or SONET.

V.90 (56K) Modem

Many end users of the Internet are connected from home or small businesses to an ISP through a traditional modem. One current development is the V.90 (56K) modem which uses the existing telephone line. The subscriber is connected to the switching station of the telephone company and uses the connection from the switching station to the ISP computer (server). The connection is asymmetric; the user can download data at 56 kbps, but uploading is only at 33.6 kbps.

Digital Subscriber Line (DSL)

The **digital subscriber line (DSL)** is a newer technology that uses the existing telecommunication networks such as the local loop telephone line (a connection between subscriber resident and the telephone company) to accomplish high-speed delivery of data, voice, video, and multimedia.

DSL is a family of technologies. Five of them will be discussed here: ADSL, RADSL, HDSL, VDSL, and SDSL.

ADSL Telephone companies have installed high-speed digital wide area networks to handle communication between their central offices. The link between the user (subscriber) and the network, however, is still an analog line (at least part of it). The challenge is to make these links digital—a digital subscriber line—without changing the existing local loops. The local loop uses twisted-pair cable with a potential bandwidth of at least 1 MHz.

Asymmetric digital subscriber line (ADSL) is asymmetrical, which means it provides higher bit rates in the downstream direction (from the telephone central office to the subscriber's site) than the upstream direction (from the subscriber site to the telephone central office). This is what subscribers usually want. They want to receive high-volume files quickly from the Internet, but they usually have small files, such as a short email message, to send.

ADSL divides the bandwidth of a twisted-pair cable (1 MHz) into three bands, as shown in Figure 3.16. The first band, normally between 0 and 25 kHz, is used for regular telephone service (known as plain old telephone service or POTS). This service uses only 4 kHz of this band; the rest is used as a guard band to separate the voice channel from the data channels. The second band, usually between 25 and 200 kHz, is used for upstream communication. The third band, usually 250 kHz to 1 MHz, is used for downstream communication. Some implementations overlap the downstream and upstream band to provide more bandwidth in the downstream direction.

Figure 3.16 *Bands for ADSL*

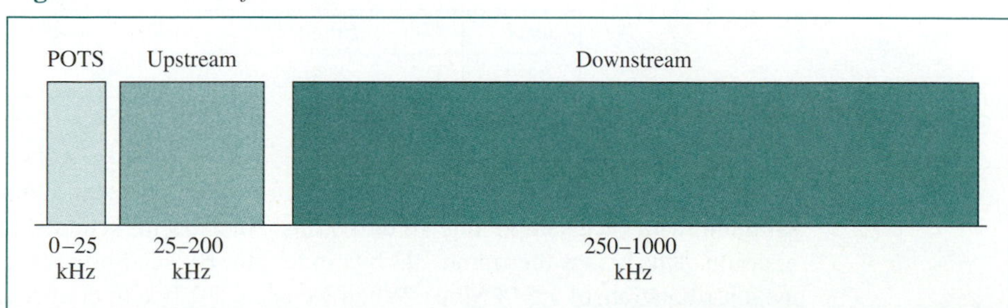

RADSL The **rate adaptive asymmetrical digital subscriber line (RADSL)** is a technology based on ADSL. It allows different data rates depending on the type of communication: voice, data, multimedia, and so on. Differing rates may also be assigned to subscribers based on their demand of the bandwidth. RADSL is beneficial to the customer because the cost is based on the data rate needed.

HDSL The **high bit rate digital subscriber line (HDSL)** was designed by Bellcore (now Telcordia) as an alternative to the T-1 line (1.544 Mbps) which has a 1 km length restriction. HDSL can operate at lengths up to 3.6 km.

SDSL The **symmetric** (or single-line) **digital subscriber line (SDSL)** is the same as HDSL but uses one single twisted-pair cable, available to most residential subscribers, to achieve the same data rate as HDSL. A technique called *echo cancellation* is employed to create a full-duplex transmission.

VDSL The **very high bit rate digital subscriber line (VDSL),** an alternative approach that is similar to ADSL, uses coaxial, fiber-optic, or twisted-pair cable for short distances (300 to 1800 meters). A bit rate of 50 to 55 Mbps downstream and 1.5 to 2.5 Mbps upstream can be achieved with VDSL.

Cable Modem

Another technology used for remote connection is the cable modem. This technology uses the cable TV services available in most areas. The technology uses a 500 MHz coaxial cable to deliver TV channels to residential areas. Because each TV channel needs only 6 MHz, more than 75 channels can be simultaneously broadcast through the cable. Some of these channels can be used to transmit data through the cable TV provider to the Ethernet.

T Lines

T lines are standard digital telephone carriers designed originally to multiplex voice channels (after being digitized). Today, however, T lines can be used to carry data from a residence or an organization to the Internet. They can also be used to provide a physical link between nodes in a switched wide area network. T lines are commercially available in two data rates: T-1 and T-3 (see Table 3.1).

Table 3.1 *DS and T line rates*

Service	*Line*	*Rate (Mbps)*	*Voice Channels*
DS-1	T-1	1.544	24
DS-3	T-3	44.736	672

T-1 Line The data rate of a T-1 line is 1.544 Mbps. Twenty-four voice channels are sampled, with each sample digitized to 8 bits. An extra bit is added to provide synchronization. This makes the frame 193 bits in length. By sending 8000 frames per second, we get a data rate of 1.544 Mbps. When we use a T-1 line to connect to the Internet, we can use the whole or part of the capacity of the line to send digital data.

T-3 Line A T-3 line has a data rate of 44.736 Mbps. It is equivalent to 28 T-1 lines.

Many subscribers may not need the entire capacity of a T line. To accommodate these customers, the telephone companies have developed fractional T line services, which allow several subscribers to share one line by multiplexing their transmissions.

SONET

The high bandwidths of fiber-optic cable are suitable for today's highest data rate technologies (such as video conferencing) and for carrying large numbers of lower-rate technologies at the same time. ANSI created a set of standards called **Synchronous Optical Network (SONET)** to handle the use of fiber-optic cables. It defines a high-speed data carrier.

SONET first defines a set of electrical signals called **synchronous transport signals (STSs).** It then converts these signals to optical signals called **optical carriers (OCs).** The optical signals are transmitted at 8000 frames per second.

Table 3.2 shows the data rates for STSs and OCs. Note that the lowest level in this hierarchy has a data rate of 51.840 Mbps, which is greater than that of a T-3 line (44.736 Mbps).

Table 3.2 *SONET rates*

STS	*OC*	*Rate (Mbps)*
STS-1	OC-1	51.840
STS-3	OC-3	155.520
STS-9	OC-9	466.560
STS-12	OC-12	622.080
STS-18	OC-18	933.120
STS-24	OC-24	1244.160
STS-36	OC-36	1866.230
STS-48	OC-48	2488.320
STS-96	OC-96	4976.640
STS-192	OC-192	9953.280

Data Link Layer

To have a reliable point-to-point connection, a user needs a protocol at the data link layer. The most common protocol for this purpose is **Point-to-Point Protocol (PPP).**

PPP

The telephone line or cable companies provide a physical link, but to control and manage the transfer of data, there is a need for a special protocol. The Point-to-Point Protocol (PPP) was designed to respond to this need.

PPP Layers PPP has only physical and data link layers. No specific protocol is defined for the physical layer by PPP. Instead, it is left to the implementer to use whatever is available. PPP supports any of the protocols recognized by ANSI. At the data link layer, PPP defines the format of a frame and the protocol that are used for controlling the link and transporting user data. The format of a PPP frame is shown in Figure 3.17.

Figure 3.17 *PPP frame*

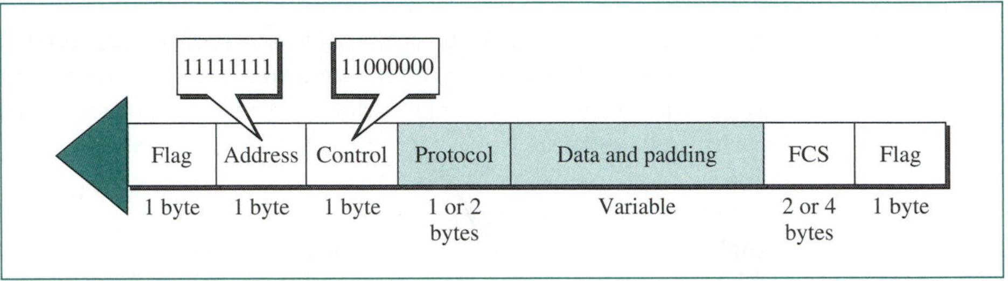

The descriptions of the fields are as follows:

1. **Flag field.** The flag field identifies the boundaries of a PPP frame. Its value is 01111110.
2. **Address field.** Because PPP is used for a point-to-point connection, it uses the broadcast address used in most LANs, 11111111, to avoid a data link address in the protocol.
3. **Control field.** The control field is assigned the value 11000000 to show that, as in most LANs, the frame has no sequence number; each frame is independent.
4. **Protocol field.** The protocol field defines the type of data being carried in the data field: user data or other information.
5. **Data field.** This field carries either user data or other information.
6. **FCS.** The frame check sequence field is simply a 2-byte or 4-byte CRC used for error detection.

Link Control Protocol (LCP)

The **Link Control Protocol (LCP)** is responsible for establishment, maintenance, and termination of the link. When the data field of a frame is carrying data related to this protocol, it means that PPP is handling the link; it does not carry data.

Network Control Protocol (NCP)

The **Network Control Protocol (NCP)** has been defined to give flexibility to PPP. PPP can carry data from different network protocols, including IP. After establishment of the link, PPP can carry IP packets in its data field.

3.3 SWITCHED WANs

The backbone networks in the Internet are usually a switched WAN. A switched WAN is a wide area network that covers a large area (a state or a country) and provides access at several points to the user. Inside the network, there is a mesh of point-to-point networks that connects switches. The switches, multiple port connectors, allow the connection of several inputs and outputs.

Switched WAN technology differs from LAN technology in many ways. First, instead of a bus or star topology, switches are used to create multiple paths. LAN technology is consider a connectionless technology; there is no connection between packets sent by a sender to a receiver. Switched WAN technology, on the other hand, is a connection-oriented technology. Before a sender can send a packet, a connection must be established between the sender and the receiver. After the connection is established, it is assigned an identifier, which is used during the transmission. The connection is formally terminated when the transmission is over. The connection identifier is used instead of the source and destination addresses in LAN technology.

We discuss three common switched WANs in this section. The first, X.25, is almost obsolete. The second, Frame Relay, will still be in use for a few more years to come. The third, ATM, is the prevalent technology. Our discussion for the first two will be short; we devote more time to the third.

X.25

X.25, introduced in the 1970s, was the first switched WAN to become popular both in Europe and United States. Although still used in Europe, it is disappearing from the United States. It was mostly used as a public network to connect individual computers or LANs. It provides an end-to-end service.

Although X.25 was (and still is, to some extent) used as the WAN to carry IP packets from one part of the world to another, there was always a conflict between IP and X.25. IP is a third- (network) layer protocol. An IP packet is supposed to be carried by a frame at the second (data link) layer. X.25, which was designed before the Internet, is a three-layer protocol; it has its own network layer. IP packets had to be encapsulated in the X.25 network-layer packet to be carried from one side of the network to another. This is analogous to a person who has a car but has to load it in a truck to go from one point to another.

Another problem with X.25 is that it was designed at a time when transmission media were not very reliable (no use of optical fibers). For this reason, X.25 performs flow and error control at both the data link layer and the network layer. This makes transmission very slow and is not popular given the ever increasing demand for speed.

For the above reasons, X.25 will most likely soon disappear from the Internet.

Frame Relay

Frame Relay, a switched technology that provides low-level (physical and data link layers) service, was designed to replace X.25. Frame Relay has some advantages over X.25:

1. **High Data Rate.** Although Frame Relay originally was designed to provide a 1.544-Mbps data rate (equivalent to a T-1 line), today most implementations can handle up to 44.736 Mbps (equivalent to a T-3 line).
2. **Bursty Data.** Some services offered by wide area network providers assume that the user has a fixed-rate need. For example, a T-1 line is designed for a user who

wants to use the line at a consistent 1.544 Mbps. This type of service is not suitable for the many users today that need to send **bursty data** (nonfixed-rate data). For example, a user may want to send data at 6 Mbps for 2 seconds, 0 Mbps (nothing) for 7 seconds, and 3.44 Mbps for 1 second for a total of 15.44 Mb during a period of 10 seconds. Although the average data rate is still 1.544 Mbps, the T-1 line cannot fulfill this type of demand because it is designed for fixed-rate data, not bursty data. Bursty data requires what is called **bandwidth on demand.** The user needs different bandwidth allocations at different times. Frame Relay accepts bursty data. A user is granted an average data rate that can be exceeded when needed.

3. **Less Overhead Due to Improved Transmission Media.** The quality of transmission media has improved tremendously since the last decade. They are more reliable and less error prone. There is no need to have a WAN that spends time and resources checking and double-checking potential errors. X.25 provides extensive error checking and flow control. Frame Relay does not provide error checking or require acknowledgment in the data link layer. Instead, all error checking is left to the protocols at the network and transport layers that use the services of Frame Relay.

Frame Relay Architecture

The devices that connect users to the network are DTEs. The switches that route the frames through the network are DCEs (see Figure 3.18). Frame Relay is normally used as a WAN to connect LANs or mainframe computers. In the first case, a router or a bridge can serve as the DTE and connects, through a leased line, the LAN to the Frame Relay switch, which is considered a DCE. In the second case, the mainframe itself can be used as a DTE with the installation of appropriate software.

Figure 3.18 *Frame Relay network*

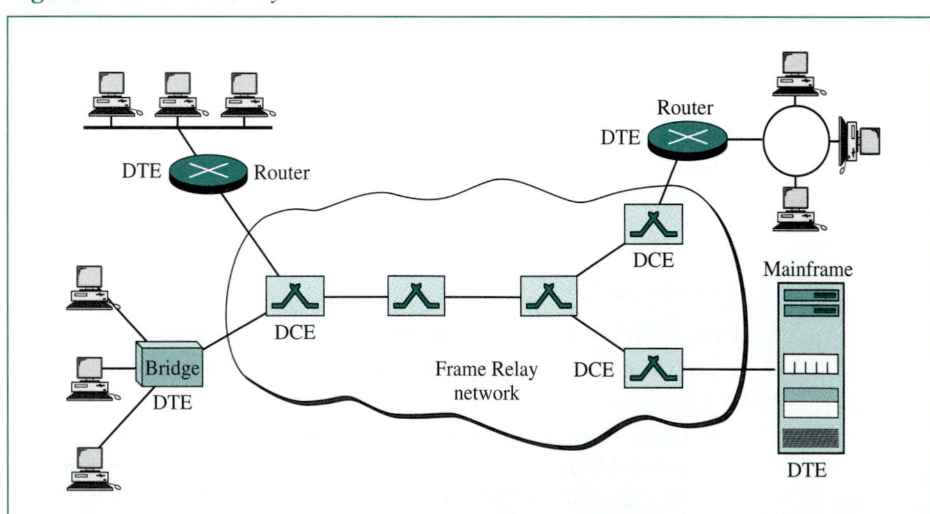

Virtual Circuits

Frame Relay like other switched LANs uses a virtual circuit and virtual circuit identifiers called DLCIs.

Frame Relay Layers

Frame Relay has only physical and data link layers. No specific protocol is defined for the physical layer in Frame Relay. Instead, it is left to the implementer to use whatever is available. Frame Relay supports any of the protocols recognized by ANSI.

At the data link layer, Frame Relay employs a simple protocol responsible for delivering data from one DTE to another.

ATM

Asynchronous Transfer Mode (ATM) is the *cell relay* protocol designed by the ATM Forum and adopted by the ITU-T.

Design Goals

Among the challenges faced by the designers of ATM, six stand out. First and foremost is the need for a transmission system to optimize the use of high-data-rate transmission media, in particular optical fiber. Second is the need for a system that can interface with existing systems, such as the various packet networks, and to provide wide area interconnectivity between them without lowering their effectiveness or requiring their replacement. Third is the need for a design that can be implemented inexpensively so that cost would not be a barrier to adoption. If ATM is to become the backbone of international communications, as intended, it must be available at low cost to every user who wants it. Fourth, the new system must be able to work with and support the existing telecommunications hierarchies (local loops, local providers, long-distance carriers, and so on). Fifth, the new system must be connection-oriented to ensure accurate and predictable delivery. And last but not least, one objective is to move as many of the functions to hardware as possible (for speed) and eliminate as many software functions as possible (again for speed).

Cell Networks

ATM is a *cell network.* A **cell** is a small data unit of fixed size that is the basic unit of data exchange in a cell network. In this type of network, all data are loaded into identical cells that can be transmitted with complete predictability and uniformity. Cells are multiplexed with other cells and routed through a cell network. Because each cell is the same size and all are small, any problems associated with multiplexing different-sized packets are avoided.

> A cell network uses the cell as the basic unit of data exchange. A cell is defined as a small, fixed-sized block of information.

Asynchronous TDM

ATM uses **asynchronous time-division multiplexing**—that is why it is called Asynchronous Transfer Mode—to multiplex cells coming from different channels. It uses fixed-size slots the size of a cell. ATM multiplexers fill a slot with a cell from any input channel that has a cell; the slot is empty if none of the channels has a cell to send.

Figure 3.19 shows how cells from three inputs are multiplexed. At the first tick of the clock, channel 2 has no cell (empty input slot), so the multiplexer fills the slot with a cell from the third channel. When all the cells from all the channels are multiplexed, the output slots are empty.

Figure 3.19 *ATM multiplexing*

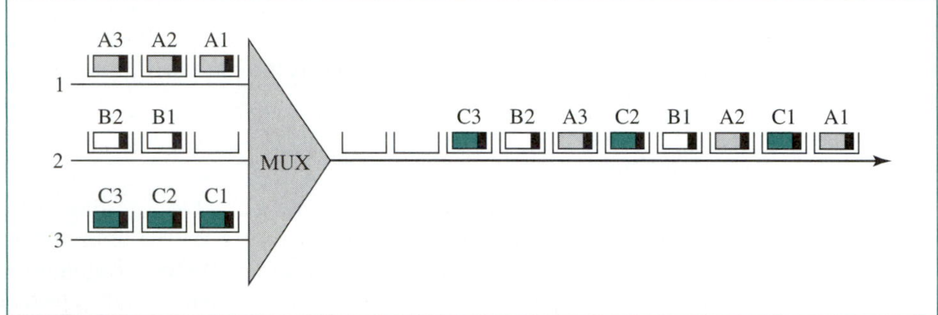

ATM Architecture

ATM is a cell-switched network. The user access devices, called the end points, are connected through a **user-to-network interface (UNI)** to the switches inside the network. The switches are connected through **network-to-network interfaces (NNIs).** Figure 3.20 shows an example of an ATM network.

Figure 3.20 *Architecture of an ATM network*

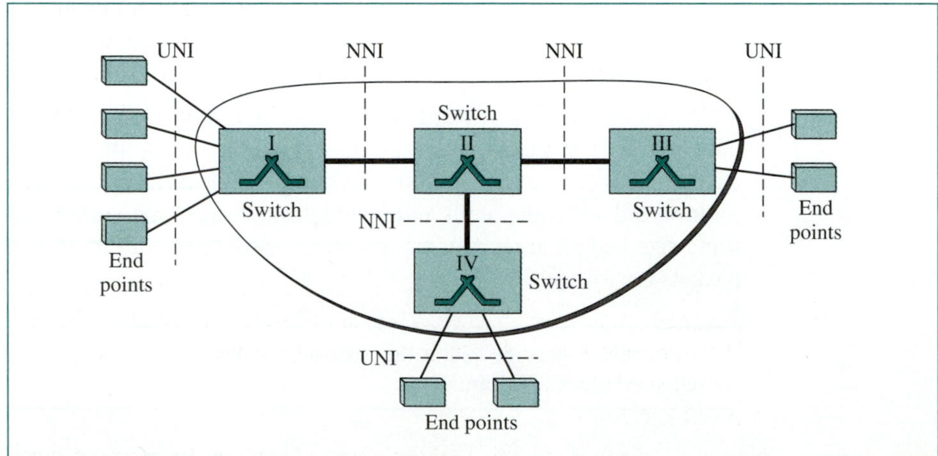

Virtual Connection Connection between two end points is accomplished through transmission paths (TPs), virtual paths (VPs), and virtual circuits (VCs). A **transmission path (TP)** is the physical connection (wire, cable, satellite, and so on) between an end point and a switch or between two switches. Think of two switches as two cities. A transmission path is the set of all highways that directly connects the two cities.

A transmission path is divided into several virtual paths. A **virtual path (VP)** provides a connection or a set of connections between two switches. Think of a virtual path as a highway that connects two cities. Each highway is a virtual path; the set of all highways is the transmission path.

Cell networks are based on **virtual circuits (VCs).** All cells belonging to a single message follow the same virtual circuit and remain in their original order until they reach their destination. Think of a virtual circuit as the lanes of a highway (virtual path) as shown in Figure 3.21.

Figure 3.21 *Virtual circuits*

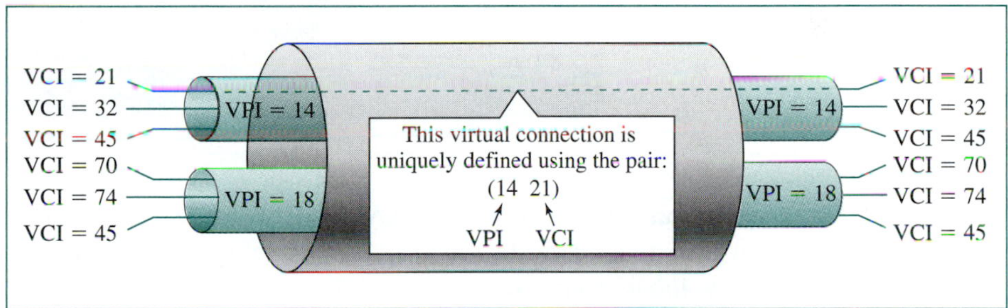

The figure also shows the relationship between a transmission path (a physical connection), virtual paths (a combination of virtual circuits that are bundled together because parts of their paths are the same), and virtual circuits that logically connect two points together.

In a virtual circuit network, to route data from one end point to another, the virtual connections need to be identified. For this purpose, the designers of ATM created a hierarchical identifier with two levels: a **virtual path identifier (VPI)** and a **virtual circuit identifier (VCI).** The VPI defines the specific VP and the VCI defines a particular VC inside the VP. The VPI is the same for all virtual connections that are bundled (logically) into one VP.

> Note that a virtual connection is defined by a pair of numbers: the VPI and the VCI.

Cells A cell is 53 bytes in length with 5 bytes allocated to header and 48 bytes carrying payload (user data may be less than 48 bytes). Most of the header is occupied by the VPI and VCI. Figure 3.22 shows the cell structure.

ATM Layers

The ATM standard defines three layers. They are, from top to bottom, the application adaptation layer, the ATM layer, and the physical layer as shown in Figure 3.23.

Figure 3.22 *An ATM cell*

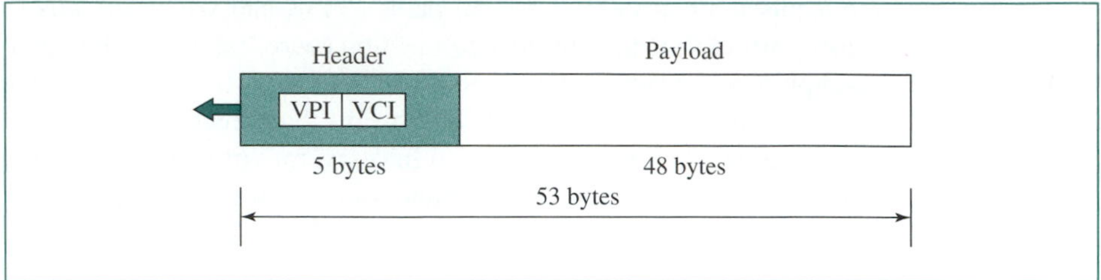

Figure 3.23 *ATM layers*

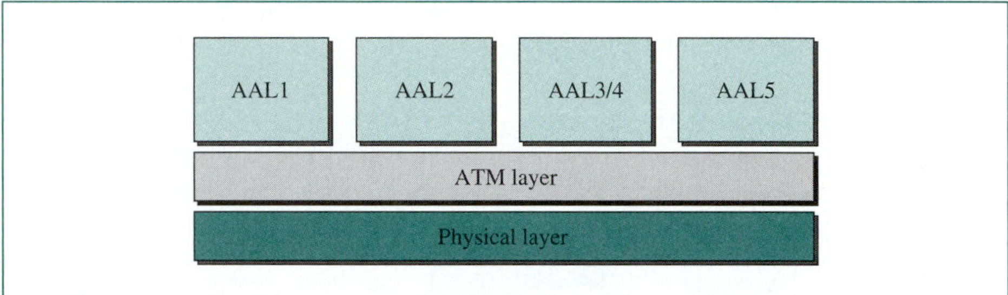

Application Adaptation Layer (AAL) The **application adaptation layer (AAL)** allows existing networks (such as packet networks) to connect to ATM facilities. AAL protocols accept transmissions from upper-layer services (e.g., packet data) and map them into fixed-sized ATM cells. These transmissions can be of any type (voice, data, audio, video) and can be of variable or fixed rates. At the receiver, this process is reversed—segments are reassembled into their original formats and passed to the receiving service.

- **AAL1.** AAL1 is designed for **constant-bit-rate (CBR)** data coming from applications that generate and consume bits at a constant rate. In this type of application, transmission delays must be minimal and transmission must simulate real time. Examples of constant-bit-rate applications include real-time voice (telephone calls) and real-time video (television).
- **AAL2.** AAL2 is designed for **variable-bit-rate (VBR)** data coming from applications that generate and consume bits at variable rates. In this type of application, the bit rate varies from section to section of the transmission, but within established parameters. Examples of variable-bit-rate applications include compressed voice, data, and video.
- **AAL3/4.** AAL3/4 is designed for connection-oriented packet protocols (such as X.25) that use virtual circuits.
- **AAL5.** AAL5 is designed for connectionless packet protocols that use a datagram approach to routing (such as the IP protocol in TCP/IP).

The IP protocol uses the AAL5 sublayer.

ATM Layer The ATM layer provides routing, traffic management, switching, and multiplexing services. It processes outgoing traffic by accepting 48-byte segments from the AAL sublayers and transforming them into 53-byte cells by the addition of a 5-byte header.

Physical Layer The physical layer defines the transmission medium, bit transmission, encoding, and electrical to optical transformation. It provides convergence with physical transport protocols, such as SONET and T-3, as well as the mechanisms for transforming the flow of cells into a flow of bits.

We will discuss IP over ATM in Chapter 26.

ATM LANs

ATM is mainly a wide area network (ATM WAN); however, the technology can be adopted to local area networks (ATM LAN). In this section we discuss the technology as applied to LANs.

The high data rate of the technology (155 and 622 Mbps) has attracted the attention of designers who are looking for increased data rates in LANs.

ATM LAN Architecture

Today, we have three ways to incorporate ATM technology in a LAN architecture: creating a pure ATM LAN, making a legacy ATM LAN, or a mixture of both as shown in Figure 3.24.

Pure ATM Architecture In a pure ATM LAN, an ATM switch is used to connect the stations in a LAN, in the same way stations are connected to an Ethernet switch. In this way, stations can exchange data at one of two standard rates of ATM technology (155 and 652 Mbps). However, the station uses a virtual path identifier (VPI) and a virtual connection identifier (VCI) instead of a source and destination address. This approach has a major drawback. The system needs to be built from the ground up; existing LANs cannot be upgraded into pure ATM LANs.

Legacy LAN Architecture A second approach is to use ATM technology as a backbone to connect traditional LANs.

In this way, stations on the same LAN can exchange data at the rate and format of traditional LANs (Ethernet, Token Ring, etc.). But when two stations on two different LANs need to exchange data, they can go through a converting device that changes the frame format. The advantage here is that output from several LANs can be multiplexed together to create a high data rate input to the ATM switch. We will see that there are several issues that should be resolved first.

Mixed Architecture Probably the best solution is to mix the two previous architectures. This means keeping the existing LANs and, at the same time, allowing new stations to be directly connected to an ATM switch. This approach allows the gradual migration of legacy LANs into ATM LANs by adding more and more directly connected stations to the switch. Again, the stations in one specific LAN can exchange data

Figure 3.24 *ATM LAN architectures*

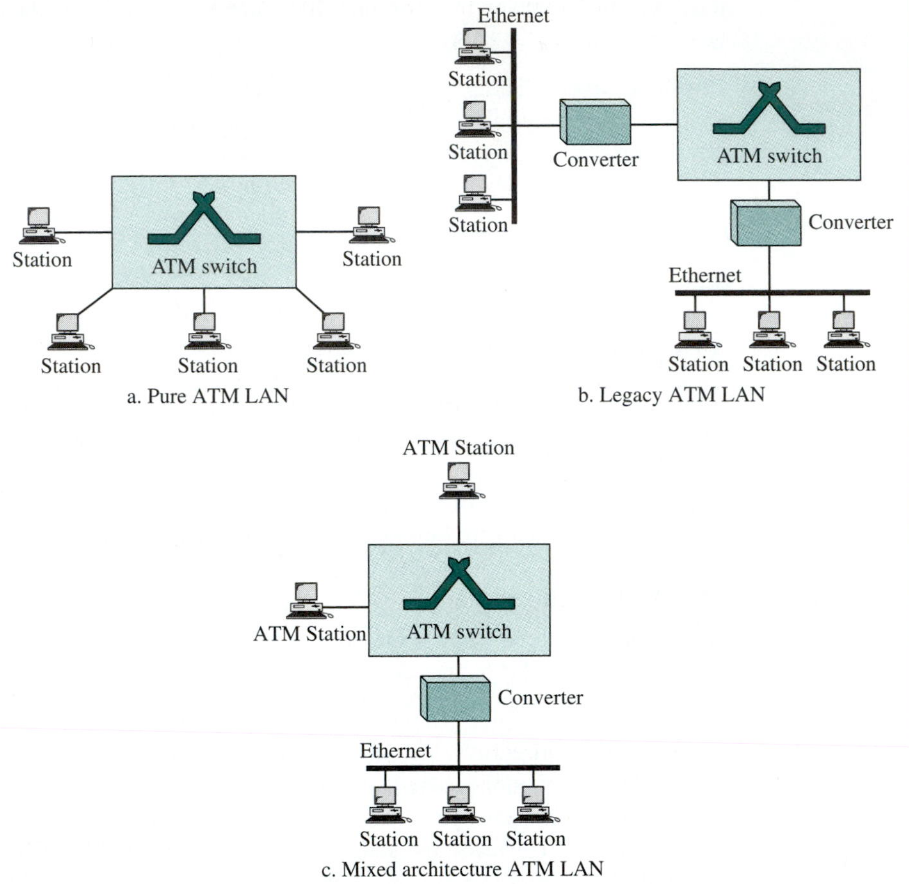

a. Pure ATM LAN

b. Legacy ATM LAN

c. Mixed architecture ATM LAN

using the format and data rate of that particular LAN. The stations directly connected to the ATM switch can use an ATM frame to exchange data. However, the problem is how a station in a traditional LAN can communicate with a station directly connected to the ATM switch or vice versa.

LAN Emulation (LANE)

At the surface level, the use of ATM technology in LANs seems very natural. However, the similarity is only at the surface level; many issues need to be resolved, as summarized below:

- **Connectionless vs. Connection-oriented.** Traditional LANs, such as Ethernet, are connectionless protocols. On the other hand, ATM is a connection-oriented protocol; a station that wishes to send cells to another station first establishes a connection and, after all of the cells are sent, terminates the connection.
- **Physical Addresses vs. Virtual Connection Identifiers.** Closely related to the first issue is the difference in addressing. A connectionless protocol, such as Ethernet,

defines the route of a packet through source and destination addresses. However, a connection-oriented protocol, such as ATM, defines the route of a cell through virtual connection identifiers (VPIs and VCIs).

- **Multicasting and Broadcasting Delivery.** Traditional LANs, such as Ethernet, can both multicast and broadcast packets; a station can send packets to a group of stations or to all stations. There is no easy way to multicast or broadcast on an ATM network although point-to-multipoint connections are available.
- **Interoperability.** In a mixed architecture, a station connected to a legacy LAN must be able to communicate with a station directly connected to an ATM switch.

An approach called **Local Area Network Emulation (LANE)** solves the above-mentioned problems and allows stations in a mixed architecture to communicate with each other. The approach uses emulation. Stations can use a connectionless service that emulates a connection-oriented service. Stations use the source and destination addresses for initial connection and then use VPI and VCI addressing. The approach allows stations to use unicast, multicast, and broadcast addresses. Finally, the approach converts frames using a legacy format to ATM cells before being sent through the switch.

Client/Server Model

LANE is designed as a client/server model to handle the four previously discussed problems. The protocol uses one type of client and three types of servers.

LAN Emulation Client (LEC) All stations have LANE client software installed on top of the three ATM protocols. The upper-layer protocols are unaware of the existence of the ATM technology. These protocols send their requests to LEC for a LAN service such as connectionless delivery using MAC unicast, multicast, or broadcast addresses. The LEC, however, just interprets the request, and passes the result on to the servers.

LAN Emulation Configuration Server (LECS) The LANE configuration server is used for initial connection between the client and LANE. This server is always waiting to receive the initial contact. It has an address that is known to every client in the system.

LAN Emulation Server (LES) LANE server software is installed on the LES server. When a station receives a frame to be sent to another station using a physical address, LEC sends a special frame to the LES server. The server creates a virtual circuit between the source and the destination station. The source station can now use this virtual circuit (and the corresponding identifier) to send the frame or frames to the destination.

Broadcast/Unknown Server (BUS) Multicasting and broadcasting require the use of another server called the Broadcast/Unknown Server or BUS. If a station needs to send a frame to a group of stations or to every station, the frame first goes to the BUS server; this server has permanent virtual connections to every station. The server creates copies of the received frame and sends a copy to a group of stations or to all stations, simulating a multicasting or broadcasting process. The server can also deliver a unicast frame by sending the frame to every station. In this case the destination address is unknown. This is sometimes more efficient than getting the connection identifier from the LES server.

Figure 3.25 shows clients and servers in a mixed architecture ATM LAN.

Figure 3.25 *A mixed architecture ATM LAN using LANE*

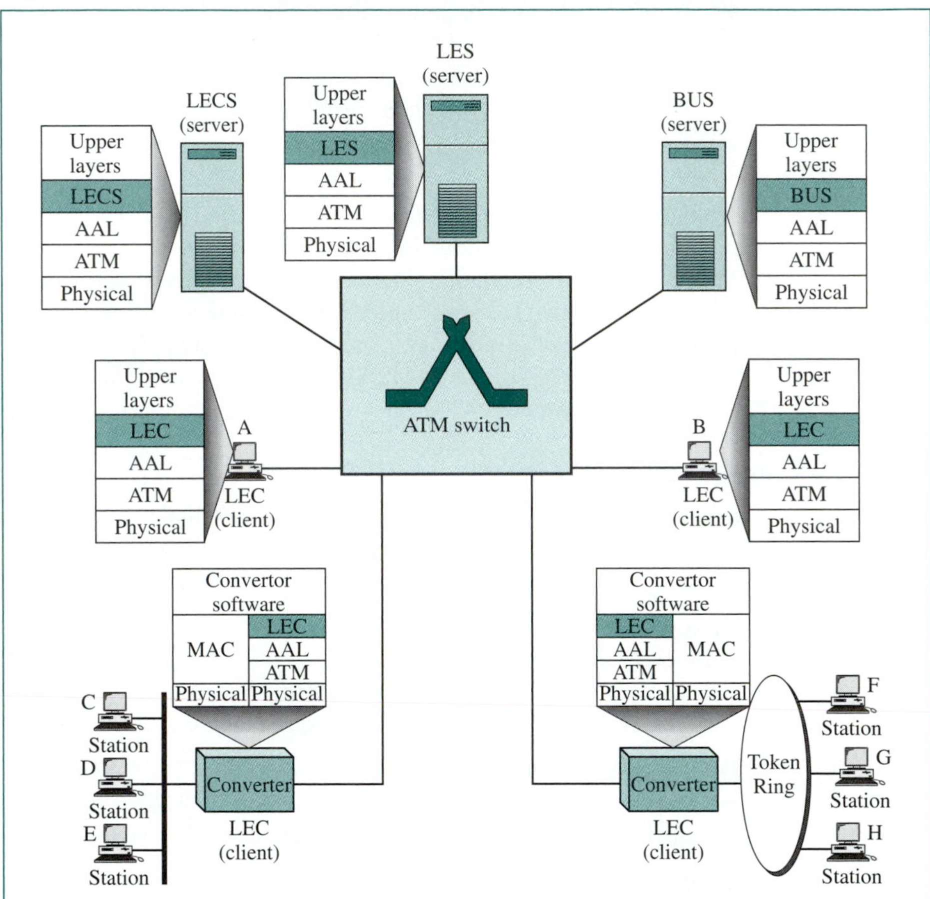

In the figure, three types of servers are connected to the ATM switch (they can actually be part of the switch). Also we show two types of clients. Stations A and B, LANE stations designed to send and receive LANE communication, are directly connected to the ATM switch. Stations C, D, E, F, G, and H, in traditional legacy LANs are connected to the switch via a converter. These converters act as LEC clients and communicate on behalf of their connected stations.

3.4 CONNECTING DEVICES

In this chapter, we discussed LANs and WANs as the underlying technologies for the Internet and the TCP/IP protocol. However, the Internet today is not made of a single LAN or a single WAN. The Internet is a combination of LANs and WANs. There must be a way to join these LANs and WANs together. We call these joining tools *connecting devices.*

We discuss five kinds of devices in this section: repeaters, hubs, bridges, routers, and switches. Repeaters and hubs operate in the first layer of the TCP/IP protocol suite. (This is comparable to the physical layer of the OSI model.) Bridges operate in the first two layers. Routers operate in the first three layers. We have two types of switches; the first type is a sophisticated bridge and the second is a sophisticated router. Figure 3.26 shows the layers in which each device operates.

Figure 3.26 *Connecting devices*

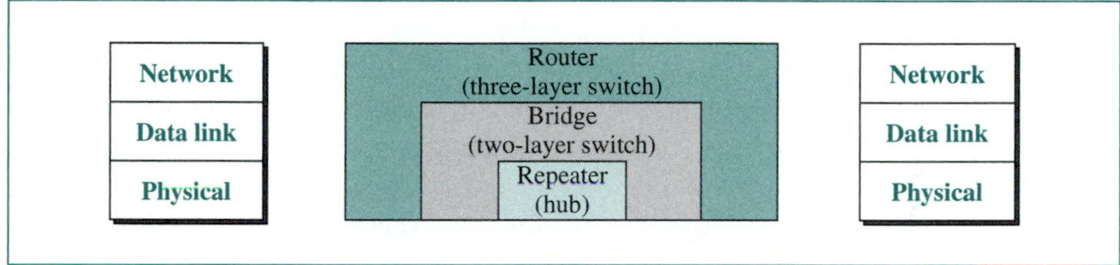

Repeaters

A repeater is a device that operates only in the physical layer. Signals that carry information within a network can travel a fixed distance before attenuation endangers the integrity of the data. A repeater receives a signal, and before it becomes too weak or corrupted, regenerates the original bit pattern. It then sends the refreshed signal. A repeater can extend the physical length of a network as shown in Figure 3.27.

Figure 3.27 *Repeater*

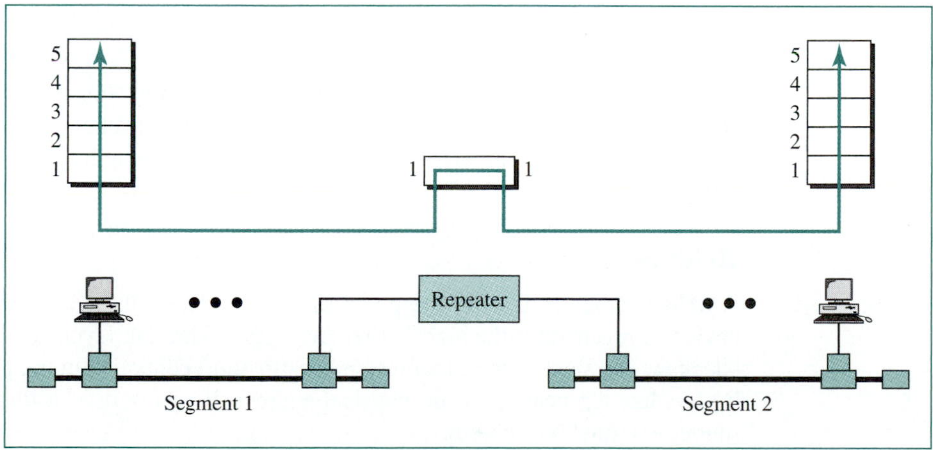

A repeater connects segments of a LAN together.

A repeater can overcome the length restriction on a 10BASE5 Ethernet. In this standard, the length of the cable is limited to 500 meters. To extend this length, we divide the cable into segments and install repeaters between segments. Note that the whole network is still considered one LAN, but the portion of the networks separated by repeaters are called *segments*. The repeater acts as a two-interface node, but operates only in the physical layer. When it receives a packet from any of the interfaces, it regenerates and forwards it to the other interface.

> A repeater forwards every packet; it has no filtering capability.

Hubs

Although, in a general sense, the word hub can refer to any connecting device, it does have a specific meaning. A hub is actually a multiport repeater. It is normally used to create connections between stations in a physical star topology. We have seen examples of hubs in some Ethernet implementations (10BASE-T, for example). However, hubs can also be used to create multiple levels of hierarchy as shown in Figure 3.28.

Figure 3.28 *Hubs*

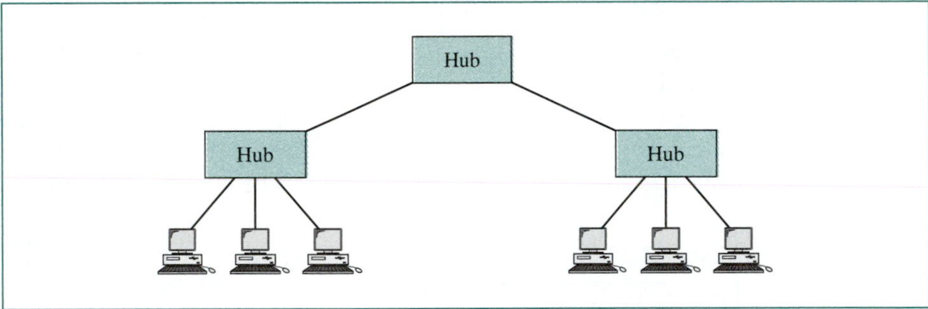

Note that the whole network is still one single LAN. Note also that the network is considered a logical bus topology (if a station sends a packet, it is received by every other station. The hierarchical use of hubs removes the length limitation of 10BASE-T (100 meters).

Bridges

A **bridge** operates in both the physical and the data link layers. As a physical layer device, it regenerates the signal it receives. As a data link layer device, the bridge can check the physical address (source and destination) contained in the packet. Note that a bridge, like a repeater, has no physical address. It acts only as a filter, not an original sender to a final destination.

Filtering

One may ask what is the difference, in functionality, between a bridge and a repeater? A bridge has filtering capability. It can check the destination address of a packet and decide if the packet should be forwarded or dropped. If the packet is to be forwarded, the decision must specify the interface. A bridge has a table that maps addresses to interfaces.

> A bridge has a table used in filtering decisions.

Let us give an example. In Figure 3.29, a LAN is divided into two segments separated by a bridge. If a packet destined for station 712B13456141 (or 712B13456142) arrives at interface 1, the bridge consults its table to find the departing interface. According to its table, packets for 712B13456141 leave through interface 1. Therefore, there is no need for forwarding; the packet is dropped. On the other hand, if a packet for 712B13456141 arrives at interface 2, the departing interface, again, is interface 1, and the packet is forwarded. In the first case, segment 2 remains free of traffic; in the second case, both segments have traffic. In our example, we show a two-interface bridge; in reality a bridge can have several interfaces. Note that all the segments connected to a bridge are still part of one LAN.

Figure 3.29 *Bridge*

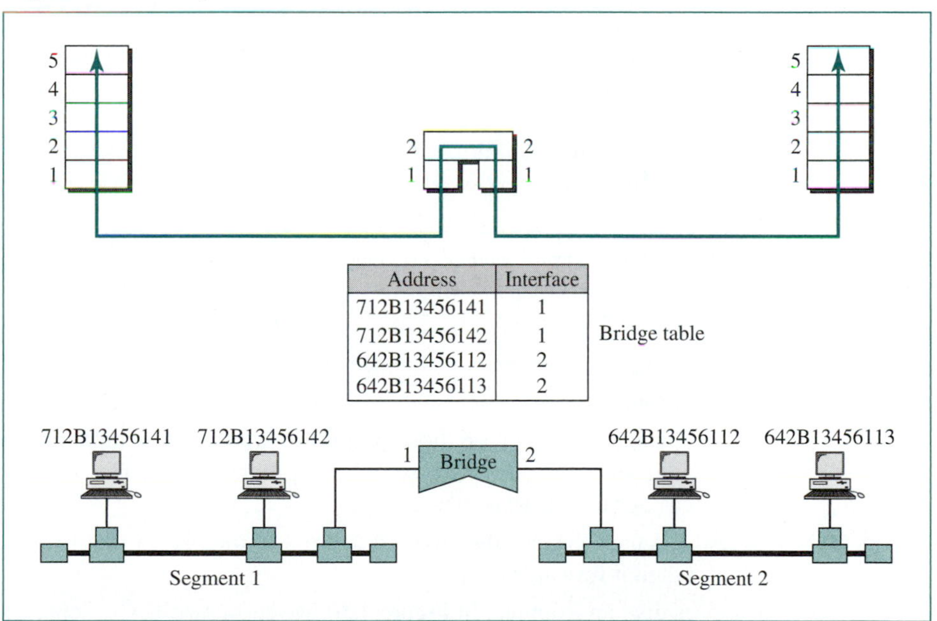

Address	Interface
712B13456141	1
712B13456142	1
642B13456112	2
642B13456113	2

> A bridge connects segments of a LAN together.

Note also that a bridge does not change the physical addresses contained in the packet.

Transparent Bridges

Today's bridges are transparent (or learning) bridges; they can be easily installed between two segments of a LAN (plug and play). The bridge's table is originally empty, but as soon as a bridge receives and forwards a packet, it creates an entry in its table with the source address and the arriving interface. From then on, the bridge knows that every packet to that destination departs from that interface. The bridge also records information about the destination using the information contained in the packet. We do something similar when we reply to mail (or email).

Routers

A **router** is a three-layer device; it operates in the physical, data link, and network layers. As a physical layer device, it regenerates the signal it receives. As a data link layer device, the router checks the physical addresses (source and destination) contained in the packet. As a network layer device, a router checks the network layer addresses (addresses in the IP layer).

> A router is a three-layer (physical, data link, and network) device.

A router can connect LANs together; a router can connect WANs together; and a router can connect LANs and WANs together. In other words, a router is an internetworking device; it connects independent networks together to form an internetwork. According to this definition, two networks (LANs or WANs) connected by a router become an internetwork or an internet.

> A repeater or a bridge connects segments of a LAN.
> A router connects independent LANs or WANs to create an internetwork (internet).

There are three major differences between a router and a repeater or a bridge.

1. A router has a physical and logical (IP) address for each of its interfaces.
2. A router acts only on those packets in which the destination address matches the address of the interface at which the packet arrives. This is true for unicast, multicast, or broadcast addresses.
3. A router changes the physical address of the packet (both source and destination) when it forwards the packet.

Let us give an example. In Figure 3.30, we show two LANs separated by a router. The left LAN has two segments separated by a bridge. The router changes the source and destination addresses of the packet. When the packet travels in the left LAN, its source address is the address of the sending station; its destination address is the address of the router. When the same packet travels in the second LAN, its source address is the address of the router and its destination address is the address of the final destination.

Routers route packets among multiple interconnected networks. They route packets from one network to any of a number of potential destination networks on an internet.

Figure 3.30 *Routing example*

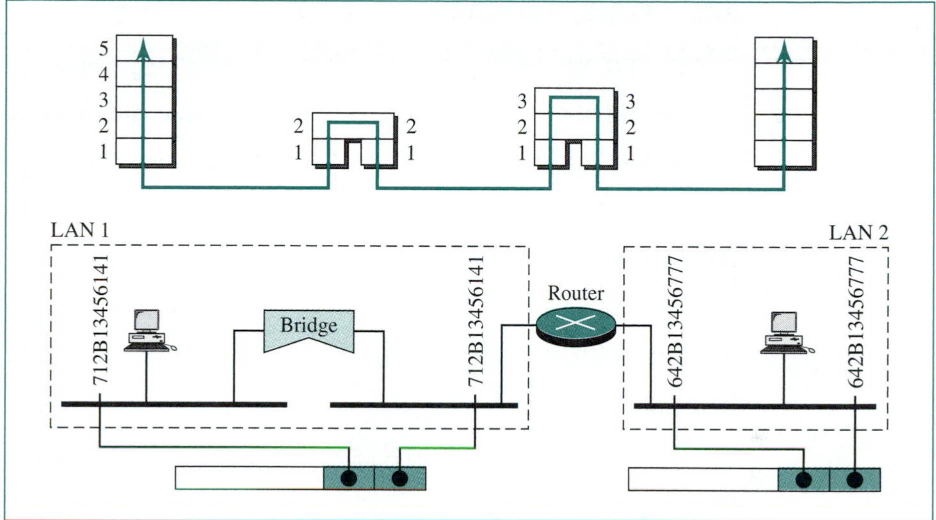

Routers act like stations on a network. But unlike most stations, which are members of only one network, routers have addresses on, and links to, two or more networks.

> A router changes the physical addresses in a packet.

We will learn more about routers and routing in future chapters after we have discussed IP addressing.

Switches

When we use the term switch, we should be careful because a switch can mean two different things. We must clarify the term by adding the level at which the device operates. We can have a two-layer switch or a three-layer switch. Let us briefly discuss each.

Two-Layer Switch

A two-layer switch is a bridge with many interfaces and a design that allows better (faster) performance. A bridge with a few interfaces can connect a few segments of a LAN together. A bridge with many interfaces may be able to allocate a unique interface to each station, with each station on its own independent segment. This means no competing traffic (no collision as we saw in Ethernet). In this book, to avoid confusion, we use the term bridge for a two-layer switch.

Three-Layer Switch

A three-layer switch is a router with an improved design to allow better performance. A three-layer switch can receive, process, and dispatch a packet much faster than a traditional router even though the functionality is the same. In this book, to avoid confusion, we use the term router for a three-layer switch.

3.5 KEY TERMS

1000BASE-CX
1000BASE-LX
1000BASE-SX
1000BASE-T
100BASE-FX
100BASE-T4
100BASE-TX
100BASE-X
10BASE2
10BASE5
10BASE-FL
10BASE-T
abort frame
application adaptation layer (AAL)
asymmetric digital subscriber line (ADSL)
asynchronous time-division multiplexing
Asynchronous Transfer Mode (ATM)
ATM switch
bandwidth on demand
basic service set (BSS)
bridge
broadcast/unknown server (BUS)
broadcast address
carrier sense multiple access with collision detection (CSMA/CD)
cell
channel
collision
connecting device
connectionless protocol
connection-oriented protocol
destination address (DA)
digital subscriber line (DSL)
direct sequence spread spectrum (DSSS)
ESS-transition mobility
Ethernet
extended service set (ESS)
Fast Ethernet
fractional T line
frame
frame check sequence (FCS)
Frame Relay
frequency hopping spread spectrum (FHSS)
full-duplex Ethernet
Gigabit Ethernet
high bit rate digital subscriber line (HDSL)
infrared (IR)
LAN emulation (LANE)
LAN emulation client (LEC)
LAN emulation configuration server (LECS)
LAN emulation server (LES)
legacy LAN
Link Control Protocol (LCP)
local area network (LAN)
local loop

mixed architecture LAN

multicast address

multistation access unit (MAU)

Network Control Protocol (NCP)

network interface card (NIC)

network-to-network interfaces (NNIs)

optical carrier (OC)

packet

physical address

Point-to-Point Protocol (PPP)

preamble

pure ATM LAN

radio frequency wave

rate adaptive asymmetrical digital subscriber line (RADSL)

repeater

router

source address (SA)

spread spectrum

start frame delimiter (SFD)

switch

switched Ethernet

symmetric digital subscriber line (SDSL)

Synchronous Digital Hierarchy (SDH)

Synchronous Optical Network (SONET)

synchronous transport module (STM)

synchronous transport signal (STS)

T lines

T-1 line

T-3 line

token

token frame

token passing

Token Ring

transceiver

unicast address

user-to-network interface (UNI)

very high bit rate digital subscriber line (VDSL)

virtual circuit identifier (VCI)

virtual connection identifier (VCI)

virtual path identifier (VPI)

wide area network (WAN)

wireless transmission

X.25

3.6 SUMMARY

- Ethernet is the most widely used local area network protocol.
- Traditional Ethernet uses CSMA/CD with a data rate of 10 Mbps and a collision domain of 2500 meters.
- The data link layer of Ethernet consists of the LLC sublayer and the MAC sublayer.
- The MAC sublayer is responsible for the operation of the CSMA/CD access method.

- Each station on an Ethernet network has a unique 48-bit address imprinted on its network interface card (NIC).
- The common implementations of 10-Mbps Ethernet are 10BASE5, 10BASE2, 10BASE-T, and 10BASE-FL.
- Fast Ethernet uses CSMA/CD with a data rate of 100 Mbps and a collision domain of 250 meters.
- The common Fast Ethernet implementations are 100BASE-TX, 100BASE-FX, and 100BASE-T4.
- Gigabit Ethernet has a data rate of 1000 Mbps. Common implementations are 1000BASE-SX, 1000BASE-LX, and 1000BASE-T.
- A point-to-point connection to the Internet is possible using regular telephone lines and traditional modems, DSL lines, cable modems, T-lines, or SONET networks.
- The Point-to-Point Protocol (PPP) was designed for users who need a reliable point-to-point connection to the Internet.
- PPP operates at the physical and data link layers of the OSI model.
- The Link Control Protocol (LCP) is responsible for establishing, maintaining, configuring, and terminating links.
- X.25 is a switched WAN that is being replaced by other technologies.
- Frame Relay eliminates the extensive error checking necessary in X.25 protocol. Frame Relay operates in the physical and data link layers of the OSI model.
- Asynchronous Transfer Mode (ATM) is the cell relay protocol designed to support the transmission of data, voice, and video through high data rate transmission media such as fiber-optic cable.
- The ATM data packet is called a cell and is composed of 53 bytes (5 bytes of header and 48 bytes of payload).
- A cell network is based on permanent virtual circuit routing.
- The ATM standard defines three layers: the application adaptation layer (AAL), the ATM layer, and the physical layer.
- There are four different AALs, each specific for a data type. TCP/IP uses AAL5, which converts data coming from a connectionless packet switching network.
- ATM technology can be adopted for use in a LAN (ATM LAN).
- In a pure ATM LAN, an ATM switch connects stations. In a legacy ATM LAN, the backbone that connects traditional LANs uses ATM technology. A mixed architecture ATM LAN combines features of a pure ATM LAN and a legacy ATM LAN.
- Local Area Network Emulation (LANE) is a client/server model that allows the use of ATM technology in LANs.
- LANE software includes LAN emulation client (LEC), LAN emulation configuration server (LECS), LAN emulation server (LES), and broadcast/unknown server (BUS) modules.
- Connecting devices can connect segments of a network together; they can also connect networks together to create an internet.
- There are five types of connecting devices: repeaters, hubs, bridges, routers, and switches.

- Repeaters regenerate a signal at the physical layer.
- A hub is a multiport repeater.
- Bridges have access to station addresses and can forward or filter a packet in a network. They operate at the physical and data link layers.
- Routers determine the path a packet should take. They operate at the physical, data link, and network layers.
- A two-layer switch is a sophisticated bridge; a three-layer switch is a sophisticated router.

3.7 PRACTICE SET

Multiple-Choice Questions

1. 10BASE2 uses _______ cable while 10BASE5 uses _______.
   a. thick coaxial, thin coaxial
   b. twisted-pair, thick coaxial
   c. thin coaxial, thick coaxial
   d. fiber-optic, thin coaxial
2. _______ specifies a star topology featuring a central hub and unshielded twisted-pair wire as the medium.
   a. 10BASE5
   b. 10BASE2
   c. 10BASE-T
   d. none of the above
3. Frame Relay operates in the _______.
   a. physical layer
   b. data link layer
   c. physical and data link layers
   d. physical, data link, and network layers
4. Which ATM layer specifies how user data should be packaged into cells?
   a. physical
   b. ATM
   c. application adaptation
   d. data adaptation
5. Which ATM layer has a 53-byte cell as an end product?
   a. physical
   b. ATM
   c. application adaptation
   d. cell transformation

6. Which application adaptation layer type can process a data stream having a non-constant bit rate?
   a. AAL1
   b. AAL2
   c. AAL3/4
   d. AAL5
7. Which AAL type is designed to support a data stream that has a constant bit rate?
   a. AAL1
   b. AAL2
   c. AAL3/4
   d. AAL5
8. Which of the following is not a connecting device?
   a. bridge
   b. transceiver
   c. router
   d. repeater
9. Repeaters function in the _______ layer.
   a. physical
   b. data link
   c. network
   d. a and b
10. Bridges function in the _______ layer.
   a. physical
   b. data link
   c. network
   d. a and b
11. A bridge has access to the _______ address of a station on the same network.
   a. physical
   b. network
   c. service access point
   d. all of the above
12. Routers function in the _______ layers.
   a. physical and data link
   b. physical, data link, and network
   c. data link and network
   d. network and transport

13. In a _______ ATM LAN, all stations are connected to the ATM switch.
    a. pure
    b. legacy
    c. mixed architecture
    d. any of the above
14. A ______ ATM LAN could have Ethernet LANs and Token Ring LANs connected to an ATM switch.
    a. pure
    b. legacy
    c. mixed architecture
    d. b and c
15. In an ATM LAN, a station on an Ethernet LAN needs _______ to exchange data with a Token Ring LAN.
    a. repeaters
    b. hubs
    c. timers
    d. converters
16. _______ software is installed on the client machine.
    a. LEC
    b. LECS
    c. LES
    d. BUS
17. The ______ server is used for the initial connection between the client and LANE.
    a. LEC
    b. LECS
    c. BUS
    d. none of the above
18. In an ESS the _______ station is mobile.
    a. AP
    b. server
    c. BSS
    d. all of the above
19. In an ESS the _______ stations are part of a wired LAN.
    a. AP
    b. server
    c. BSS
    d. all of the above

20. SONET is a standard for _______ networks.
    a. twisted-pair cable
    b. coaxial cable
    c. Ethernet
    d. fiber-optic cable
21. SONET is an acronym for _______ Network.
    a. Synchronous Optical
    b. Standard Optical
    c. Symmetrical Open
    d. Standard Open
22. PPP is a _______ layer protocol.
    a. physical
    b. data link
    c. physical and data link
    d. seven
23. What is the purpose of LCP?
    a. establishment of a link
    b. maintenance of a link
    c. termination of a link
    d. all of the above

Exercises

24. What is a collision?
25. Suppose there is heavy traffic on both a CSMA/CD LAN and a Token Ring LAN. A station on which system is more likely to wait longer to send a frame? Why?
26. Why do you think that an Ethernet frame should have a minimum data size?
27. Imagine the length of a 10BASE5 cable is 2500 meters. If the speed of propagation in a thick coaxial cable is 200,000,000 meters/second, how long does it take for a bit to travel from the beginning to the end of the network? Ignore any propagation delay in the equipment.
28. Using the data in Exercise 27, find the maximum time it takes to sense a collision. The worst case occurs when data are sent from one end of the cable and the collision happens at the other end. Remember that the signal needs to make a round-trip.
29. The data rate of 10BASE5 is 10 Mbps. How long does it take to create the smallest frame? Show your calculation.
30. Using the data in Exercises 28 and 29, find the minimum size of an Ethernet frame for collision detection to work properly.
31. An Ethernet MAC sublayer receives 42 bytes of data from the LLC sublayer. How many bytes of padding must be added to the data?

32. An Ethernet MAC sublayer receives 1510 bytes of data from the LLC layer. Can the data be encapsulated in one frame? If not, how many frames need to be sent? What is the size of the data in each frame?

Programming Exercises

33. Complete the following **struct** declaration for the Ethernet packet.

```
struct   Ethernet
{
..............................................................;
unsigned long  int            CRC ;
} ;
```

34. Complete the following **struct** declaration for the Token Ring packet.

```
struct   Token_Ring
{
.............................................................. ;
unsigned long int             CRC ;
} ;
```

35. Complete the following **struct** declaration for an FDDI packet.

```
struct     FDDI
{
.............................................................. ;
unsigned long int             CRC ;
..............................................................;
} ;
```

CHAPTER 4

IP Addresses: Classful Addressing

At the network (or IP) layer, we need to uniquely identify each device on the Internet to allow global communication between all devices. This is analogous to the telephone system, where each telephone subscriber has a unique telephone number if we consider the country code and the area code as part of the identifying scheme.

In this chapter, we discuss classful addressing, one of the addressing mechanisms of the current version (IPv4) of the TCP/IP protocol suite. In Chapter 5, we introduce classless addressing, another addressing mechanism in the current protocol. In Chapter 31 we discuss the addressing mechanism of the next-generation TCP/IP protocol suite (IPv6).

4.1 INTRODUCTION

The identifier used in the IP layer of the TCP/IP protocol suite to identify each device connected to the Internet is called the Internet address or IP address. An IP address is a 32-bit binary address that *uniquely* and *universally* defines the connection of a host or a router to the Internet.

> An IP address is a 32-bit address.

IP addresses are unique. They are unique in the sense that each address defines one, and only one, connection to the Internet. Two devices on the Internet can never have the same address. However, if a device has two connections to the Internet, via two networks, it has two IP addresses.

> The IP addresses are unique.

The IP addresses are universal in the sense that the addressing system must be accepted by any host that wants to be connected to the Internet.

Address Space

A protocol like IP that defines addresses has an address space. An address space is the total number of addresses used by the protocol. If a protocol uses N bits to define an address, the address space is 2^N because each bit can have two different values (0 and 1) and N bits can have 2^N values.

IPv4 uses 32-bit addresses, which means that the address space is 2^{32} or 4,294,967,296 (more than four billion). This means that, theoretically, if there were no restrictions, more than 4 billion devices could be connected to the Internet. We will see shortly that the actual number is much less.

> The address space of IPv4 is 2^{32} or 4,294,967,296.

Notation

There are three common notations to show an IP address: binary notation, dotted-decimal notation, and hexadecimal notation.

Binary Notation

In binary notation, the IP address is displayed as 32 bits. To make the address more readable, one or more spaces is usually inserted between each octet (8 bits). Each octet is often referred to as a byte. So it is common to hear an IP address referred to as a 32-bit address, a 4-octet address, or a 4-byte address. The following is an example of an IP address in binary notation:

01110101 10010101 00011101 11101010

Dotted-Decimal Notation

To make the IP address more compact and easier to read, Internet addresses are usually written in decimal form with a decimal point (dot) separating the bytes. Figure 4.1 shows an IP address in dotted-decimal notation. Note that because each byte (octet) is only 8 bits, each number in the dotted-decimal notation is between 0 and 255.

Figure 4.1 *Dotted-decimal notation*

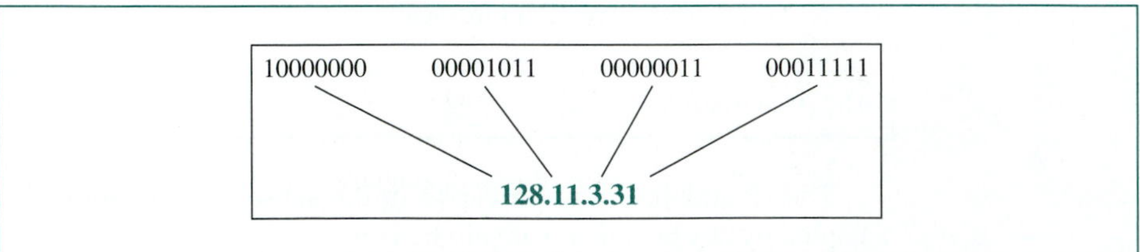

> The binary, decimal, and hexadecimal number systems are reviewed in Appendix B.

Example 1

Change the following IP addresses from binary notation to dotted-decimal notation.

a. 10000001 00001011 00001011 11101111
b. 11000001 10000011 00011011 11111111
c. 11100111 11011011 10001011 01101111
d. 11111001 10011011 11111011 00001111

Solution

We replace each group of 8 bits with its equivalent decimal number (see Appendix B) and add dots for separation:

a. 129.11.11.239
b. 193.131.27.255
c. 231.219.139.111
d. 249.155.251.15

Example 2

Change the following IP addresses from dotted-decimal notation to binary notation.

a. 111.56.45.78
b. 221.34.7.82
c. 241.8.56.12
d. 75.45.34.78

Solution

We replace each decimal number with its binary equivalent (see Appendix B):

a. 01101111 00111000 00101101 01001110
b. 11011101 00100010 00000111 01010010
c. 11110001 00001000 00111000 00001100
d. 01001011 00101101 00100010 01001110

Example 3

Find the error, if any, in the following IP addresses:

a. 111.56.045.78
b. 221.34.7.8.20
c. 75.45.301.14
d. 11100010.23.14.67

Solution

a. There are no leading zeroes in dotted-decimal notation (045).
b. We may not have more than four numbers in an IP address.
c. In dotted-decimal notation, each number is less than or equal to 255; 301 is outside this range.
d. A mixture of binary notation and dotted-decimal notation is not allowed.

Hexadecimal Notation

We sometimes see an IP address in hexadecimal notation. Each hexadecimal digit is equivalent to four bits. This means that a 32-bit address has 8 hexadecimal digits. This notation is often used in network programming.

Example 4

Change the following IP addresses from binary notation to hexadecimal notation.

a. 10000001 00001011 00001011 11101111

b. 11000001 10000011 00011011 11111111

Solution

We replace each group 4 bits with its hexadecimal equivalent (see Appendix B). Note that hexadecimal notation normally has no added spaces or dots; however, 0X (or 0x) is added at the beginning or the subscript 16 at the end to show that the number is in hexadecimal.

a. 0X810B0BEF or $410B0BEF_{16}$

b. 0XC1831CFF or $C1831CFF_{16}$

4.2 CLASSFUL ADDRESSING

IP addresses, when started a few decades ago, used the concept of classes. This architecture is called **classful addressing.** In the mid-1990s, a new architecture, called **classless addressing,** was introduced that will eventually supersede the original architecture. However, most of the Internet is still using classful addressing and the migration is slow. In this chapter, we introduce the concept of classful addressing; in the next chapter, we discuss classless addressing. The concept of "classful" is needed to understand the concept of "classless."

In classful addressing, the IP address space is divided into five classes: A, B, C, D, and E. Each class occupies some part of the whole address space. Figure 4.2 shows the class occupation of the address space (approximation).

Figure 4.2 *Occupation of the address space*

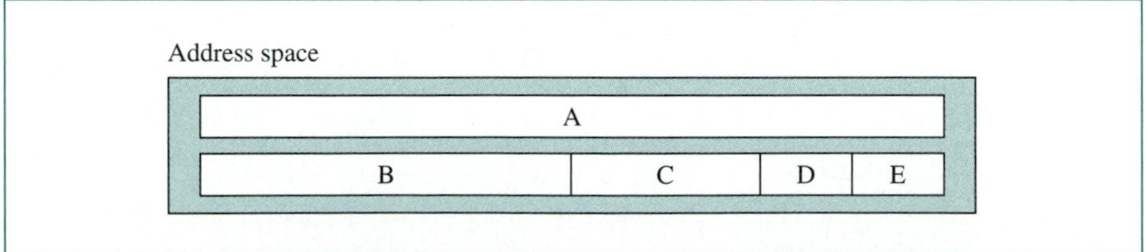

We can see from the figure that class A covers half of the address space, a serious design flaw. Class B covers 1/4 of the whole address space, another design flaw. Class C covers 1/8 of the address space, and classes D and E each cover 1/16 of the address space. Table 4.1 shows the number of addresses in each class.

Table 4.1 *Addresses per class*

Class	*Number of Addresses*	*Percentage*
A	2^{31} = 2,147,483,648	50%
B	2^{30} = 1,073,741,824	25%
C	2^{29} = 536,870,912	12.5%
D	2^{28} = 268,435,456	6.25%
E	2^{28} = 268,435,456	6.25%

In classful addressing, the address space is divided into five classes: A, B, C, D, and E.

Recognizing Classes

We can find the class of an address when the address is given in binary notation or dotted-decimal notation.

Finding the Class in Binary Notation

If the address is given in binary notation, the first few bits can immediately tell us the class of the address as shown in Figure 4.3.

Figure 4.3 *Finding the class in binary notation*

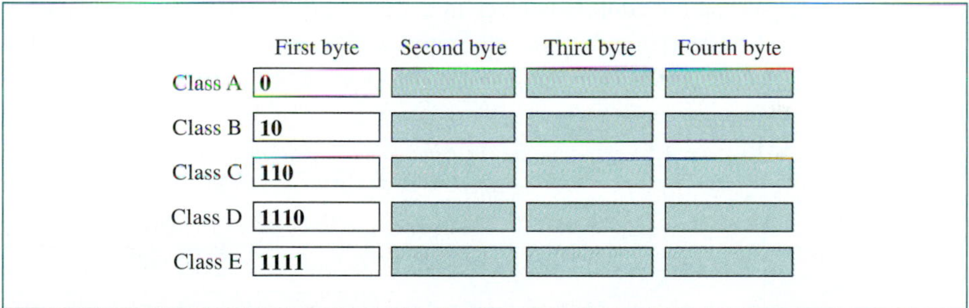

One can follow the procedure shown in Figure 4.4 to systematically check the bits and find the class. The procedure can be easily programmed in any language.

Figure 4.4 *Finding the address class*

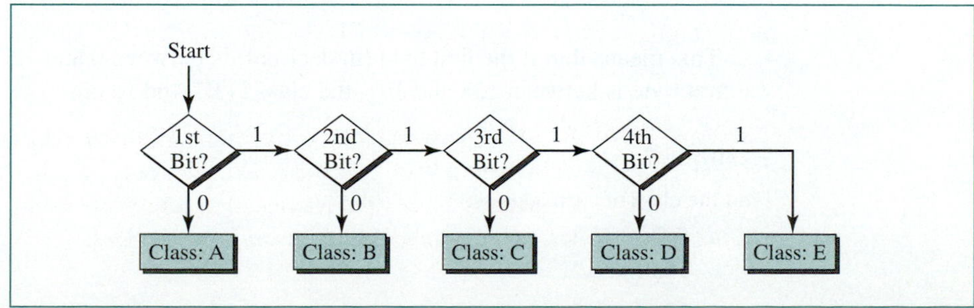

Example 5

How we can prove that we have 2,147,483,648 addresses in class A?

Solution

In class A, only 1 bit defines the class. The remaining 31 bits are available for the address. With 31 bits, we can have 2^{31} or 2,147,483,648 addresses.

Example 6

Find the class of each address:

a. **0**0000001 00001011 00001011 11101111

b. **110**00001 10000011 00011011 11111111

c. **10**100111 11011011 10001011 01101111

d. **1111**0011 10011011 11111011 00001111

Solution

See the procedure in Figure 4.4.

a. The first bit is 0. This is a class A address.

b. The first 2 bits are 1; the third bit is 0. This is a class C address.

c. The first bit is 0; the second bit is 1. This is a class B address.

d. The first 4 bits are 1s. This is a class E address.

Finding the Class in Dotted-Decimal Notation

When the address is given in dotted-decimal notation, then we need to look only at the first byte (number) to determine the class of the address. Each class has a specific range of numbers. Figure 4.5 shows the idea.

Figure 4.5 *Finding the class in decimal notation*

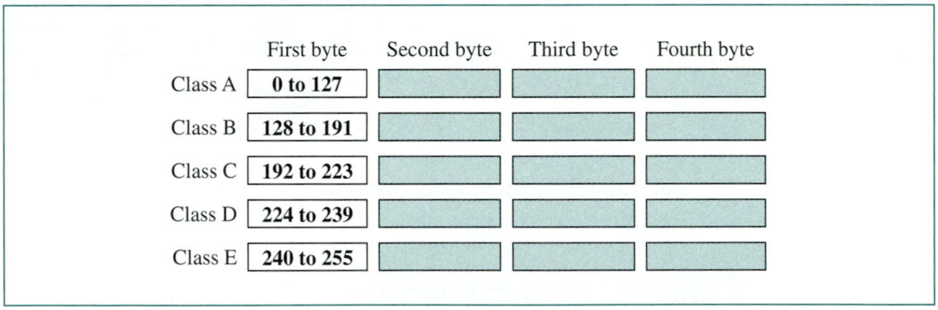

	First byte	Second byte	Third byte	Fourth byte
Class A	**0 to 127**			
Class B	**128 to 191**			
Class C	**192 to 223**			
Class D	**224 to 239**			
Class E	**240 to 255**			

This means that if the first byte (in decimal) is between 0 and 127, the class is A. If the first byte is between 128 and 191, the class is B. And so on.

Example 7

Find the class of each address:

a. **227**.12.14.87

b. **193**.14.56.22

c. **14**.23.120.8

d. **252**.5.15.111
e. **134**.11.78.56

Solution

a. The first byte is 227 (between 224 and 239); the class is D.
b. The first byte is 193 (between 192 and 223); the class is C.
c. The first byte is 14 (between 0 and 127); the class is A.
d. The first byte is 252 (between 240 and 255); the class is E.
e. The first byte is 134 (between 128 and 191); the class is B.

Example 8

In Example 4 we showed that class A has 2^{31} (2,147,483,648) addresses. How can we prove this same fact using dotted-decimal notation?

Solution

The addresses in class A range from 0.0.0.0 to 127.255.255.255. We need to show that the difference between these two numbers is 2,147,483,648. This is a good exercise because it shows us how to define the range of addresses between two addresses. We notice that we are dealing with base 256 numbers here. Each byte in the notation has a weight. The weights are as follows (see Appendix B):

$$256^3 , 256^2, 256^1, 256^0$$

Now to find the integer value of each number, we multiply each byte by its weight:

$$\text{Last address: } 127 \times 256^3 + 255 \times 256^2 + 255 \times 256^1 + 255 \times 256^0 = 2{,}147{,}483{,}647$$

$$\text{First address: } = 0$$

If we subtract the first from the last and add 1 to the result (remember we always add 1 to get the range), we get 2,147,483,648 or 2^{31}.

Netid and Hostid

In classful addressing, an IP address in classes A, B, and C is divided into netid and hostid. These parts are of varying lengths, depending on the class of the address. Figure 4.6 shows the netid and hostid bytes. Note that classes D and E are not divided into netid and hostid for reasons that we will discuss later.

Figure 4.6 *Netid and hostid*

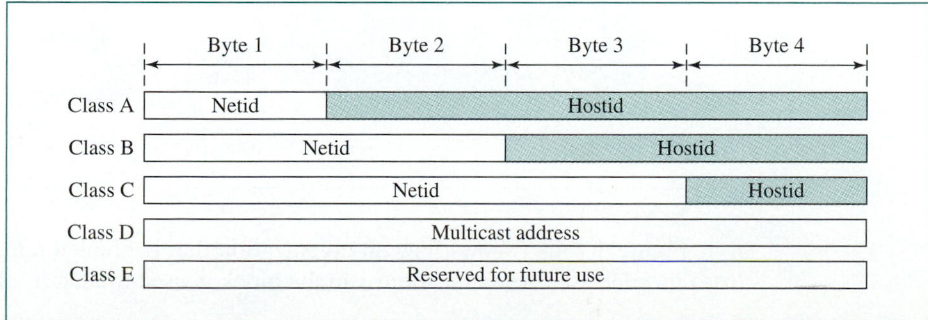

In class A, 1 byte defines the netid and 3 bytes define the hostid. In class B, 2 bytes define the netid and 2 bytes define the hostid. In class C, 3 bytes define the netid and 1 byte defines the hostid.

Classes and Blocks

One problem with classful addressing is that each class is divided into a fixed number of blocks with each block having a fixed size. Let us look at each class.

Class A

Class A is divided into 128 blocks with each block having a different netid. The first block covers addresses from **0**.0.0.0 to **0**.255.255.255 (netid **0**). The second block covers addresses from **1**.0.0.0 to **1**.255.255.255 (netid **1**). The last block covers addresses from **127**.0.0.0 to **127**.255.255.255 (netid **127**). Note that for each block of addresses the first byte (netid) is the same, but the other 3 bytes (hostid) can take any value in the given range.

The first and the last blocks in this class are reserved for special purposes as we will discuss shortly. In addition, one block (netid 10) is used for private addresses. The remaining 125 blocks can be assigned to organizations. This means that the total number of organizations that can have class A addresses is only 125. However, each block in this class contains 16,777,216 addresses, which means the organization should be a really large one to use all these addresses. Figure 4.7 shows the blocks in class A.

Figure 4.7 *Blocks in class A*

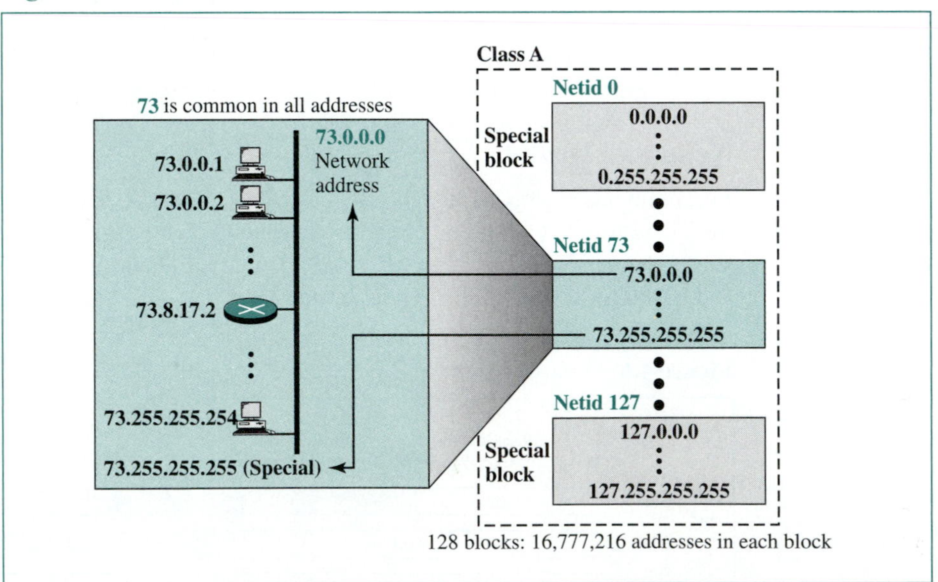

Figure 4.7 also shows how an organization that is granted a block with netid 73 uses its addresses. The first address in the block is used to identify the organization to

the rest of the Internet. This address is called the **network address;** it defines the network of the organization, not individual hosts. The organization is not allowed to use the last address; it is reserved for a special purpose as we will see shortly.

Class A addresses were designed for large organizations with a large number of hosts or routers attached to their network. However, the number of addresses in each block, 16,777,216, is probably larger than the needs of almost all organizations. Many addresses are wasted in this class.

> Millions of class A addresses are wasted.

Class B

Class B is divided into 16,384 blocks with each block having a different netid. Sixteen blocks are reserved for private addresses, leaving 16,368 blocks for assignment to organizations. The first block covers addresses from **128.0**.0.0 to **128.0**.255.255 (netid **128.0**). The last block covers addresses from **191.255**.0.0 to **191.255**.255.255 (netid **191.255**). Note that for each block of addresses the first 2 bytes (netid) are the same, but the other 2 bytes (hostid) can take any value in the given range.

There are 16,368 blocks that can be assigned. This means that the total number of organizations that can have a class B address is 16,368. However, since each block in this class contains 65,536 addresses, the organization should be large enough to use all of these addresses. Figure 4.8 shows the blocks in class B.

Figure 4.8 *Blocks in class B*

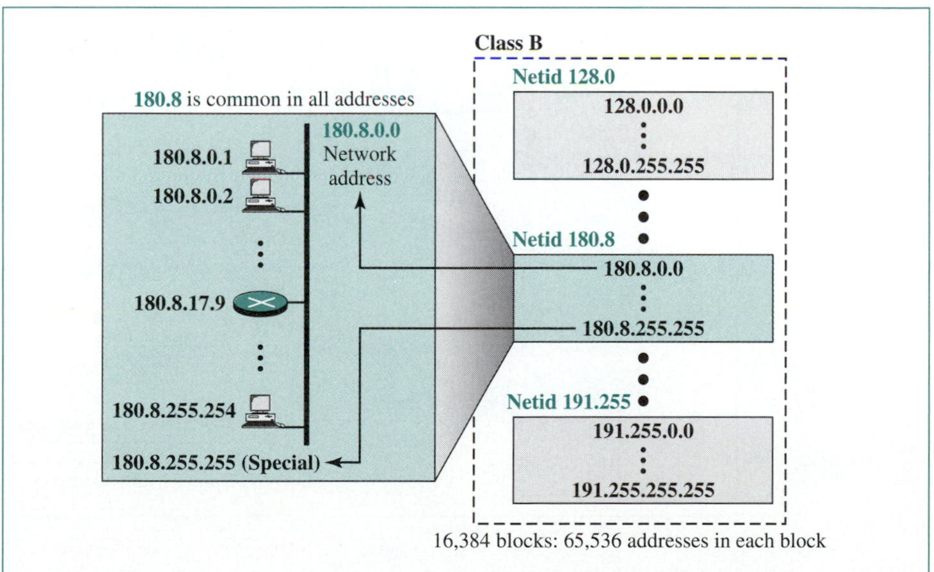

Figure 4.8 also shows how an organization that is granted a block with netid 180.8 uses its addresses. The first address is the network address; the last address is reserved for a special purpose as we will see shortly.

Class B addresses were designed for mid-size organizations that may have tens of thousands of hosts or routers attached to their networks. However, the number of addresses in each block, 65,536, is larger than the needs of most mid-size organizations. Many addresses are also wasted in this class.

Many class B addresses are wasted.

Class C

Class C is divided into 2,097,152 blocks with each block having a different netid. Two hundred fifty-six blocks are used for private addresses, leaving 2,096,896 blocks for assignment to organizations. The first block covers addresses from **192.0.0**.0 to **192.0.0**.255 (netid **192.0.0**). The last block covers addresses from **223.255.255**.0. to **223.255.255**.255 (netid **223.255.255**). Note that for each block of addresses the first 3 bytes (netid) are the same, but the remaining byte (hostid) can take any value in the given range.

There are 2,096,902 blocks that can be assigned. This means that the total number of organizations that can have a class C address is 2,096,902. However, each block in this class contains 256 addresses, which means the organization should be small enough to need less than 256 addresses. Figure 4.9 shows the blocks in class C.

Figure 4.9 *Blocks in class C*

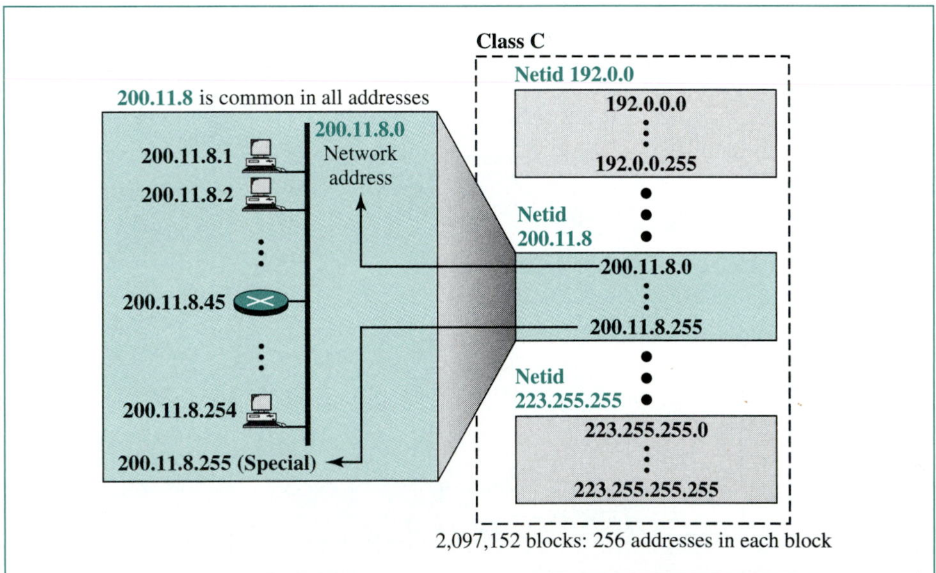

Figure 4.9 also shows how an organization that is granted a block with netid 200.11.8 uses the addresses. The first address is the network address; the last address is reserved for a special purpose as we will see shortly.

Class C addresses were designed for small organizations with a small number of hosts or routers attached to their networks. The number of addresses in each block is so limited that most organizations do not want a block in this class.

> The number of addresses in class C is smaller than the needs of most organizations.

Class D

There is just one block of class D addresses. It is designed for multicasting as we will see in a later section. Each address in this class is used to define one group of hosts on the Internet. When a group is assigned an address in this class, every host that is a member of this group will have a multicast address in addition to its normal (unicast) address.

> Class D addresses are used for multicasting; there is only one block in this class.

Class E

There is just one block of class E addresses. It was designed for use as reserved addresses. The last address in this class, 255.255.255.255 is used for a special address as we will see shortly.

> Class E addresses are reserved for special purposes; most of the block is wasted.

Network Addresses

Network addresses play a very important role in classful addressing. A network address has several properties:

1. The network address is the first address in the block.
2. The network address defines the network to the rest of the Internet. In later chapters, we learn that routers route a packet based on the network address.
3. Given the network address, we can find the class of the address, the block, and the range of the addresses in the block.

> In classful addressing, the network address (the first address in the block) is the one that is assigned to the organization. The range of addresses can automatically be inferred from the network address.

Example 9

Given the network address 17.0.0.0, find the class, the block, and the range of the addresses.

Solution

The class is A because the first byte is between 0 and 127. The block has a netid of 17. The addresses range from 17.0.0.0 to 17.255.255.255.

Example 10

Given the network address 132.21.0.0, find the class, the block, and the range of the addresses.

Solution

The class is B because the first byte is between 128 and 191. The block has a netid of 132.21. The addresses range from 132.21.0.0 to 132.21.255.255.

Example 11

Given the network address 220.34.76.0, find the class, the block, and the range of the addresses.

Solution

The class is C because the first byte is between 192 and 223. The block has a netid of 220.34.76. The addresses range from 220.34.76.0 to 220.34.76.255.

Sufficient Information

The reader may have noticed that in classful addressing, the network address gives sufficient information about the network. Given the network address, we can find the number of addresses in the block. The reason is that the number of addresses in each block is predetermined. All blocks in class A have the same range, all blocks in class B have the same range, and all blocks in class C have the same range.

Mask

In the previous section, we said that if the network address is given, we can find the block and the range of addresses in the block. What about the reverse? If an address is given, can we find the network address (the beginning address in the block)? This is important because to route a packet to the correct network, a router needs to extract a network address from the destination address (a host address) in the packet header.

One way we can find the network address is to first find the class of the address and the netid. We then set the hostid to zero to find the network address. For example, if the address 134.45.78.2 is given, we can immediately say that the address belongs to class B. The netid is 134.45 (2 bytes) and the network address is 134.45.0.0.

The above method is feasible if we have not subnetted the network; that is, if we have not divided the network into subnetworks. A general procedure that can be used involves a mask to find the network address from a given address.

Concept

A mask is a 32-bit binary number that gives the first address in the block (the network address) when bitwise ANDed with an address in the block. Figure 4.10 shows the concept of masking.

AND Operation

Masking uses the bit-wise AND operation defined in computer science. The operation is applied bit by bit to the address and the mask. For our purpose, it is enough to know

Figure 4.10 *Masking concept*

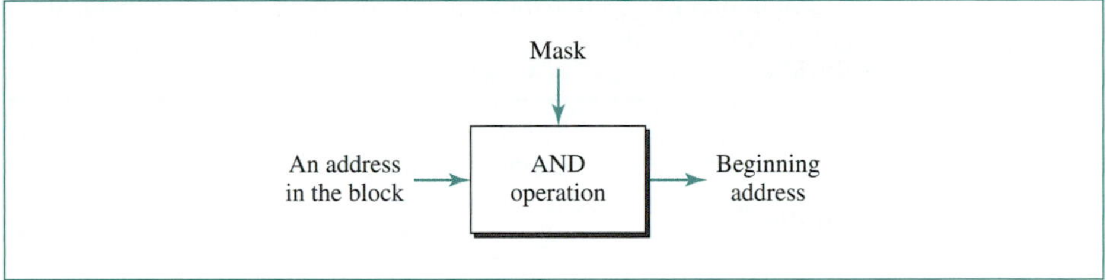

that the AND operation does the following:

1. If the bit in the mask is 1, the corresponding bit in the address is retained in the output (no change).
2. If the bit in the mask is 0, a 0 bit in the output is the result.

In other words, the bits in the address corresponding to the 1s in the mask are preserved (remain 0 or 1, as they were) and the bits corresponding to the 0s in the mask change to 0. Figure 4.11 shows the two cases.

Figure 4.11 *AND operation*

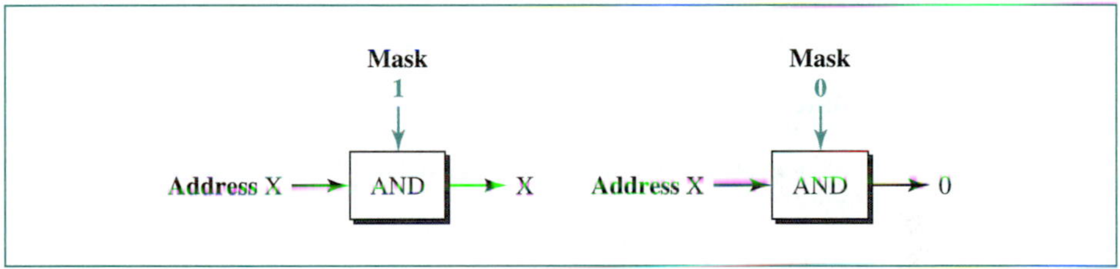

Default Masks

In the AND operation for classful addressing, there are three masks, one for each class. Table 4.2 shows the mask for each class. For class A, the mask is eight 1s and twenty-four 0s. For class B, the mask is sixteen 1s and sixteen 0s. For class C, the mask is twenty four 1s and eight 0s. The 1s preserve the netid; the 0s set the hostid to 0. Remember that the network address in any class is the netid with the hostid all 0s. Table 4.2 shows the default mask for each class.

Table 4.2 *Default masks*

Class	*Mask in binary*	*Mask in dotted-decimal*
A	**11111111** 00000000 00000000 00000000	**255**.0.0.0
B	**11111111 11111111** 00000000 00000000	**255.255**.0.0
C	**11111111 111111111 11111111** 00000000	**255.255.255**.0

Note that the number of 1s in each class matches the number of bits in the netid and the number of 0s matches the number of bits in the hostid. In other words, when a mask is ANDed with an address, the netid is retained and the hostid is set to 0s.

> The network address is the beginning address of each block. It can be found by applying the default mask to any of the addresses in the block (including itself). It retains the netid of the block and sets the hostid to zero.

Applying the Masks

Applying the mask to an unsubnetted network is simple. Two rules can help find the network address without applying the AND operation to each bit.

1. If the mask byte is 255, retain the corresponding byte in the address.
2. If the mask byte is 0, set the corresponding byte in the network address to 0.

Example 12

Given the address 23.56.7.91 and the default class A mask, find the beginning address (network address).

Solution

The default mask is 255.0.0.0, which means that only the first byte is preserved and the other 3 bytes are set to 0s. The network address is 23.0.0.0.

Example 13

Given the address 132.6.17.85 and the default class B mask, find the beginning address (network address).

Solution

The default mask is 255.255.0.0, which means that the first 2 bytes are preserved and the other 2 bytes are set to 0s. The network address is 132.6.0.0.

Example 14

Given the address 201.180.56.5 and the class C default mask, find the beginning address (network address).

Solution

The default mask is 255.255.255.0, which means that the first 3 bytes are preserved and the last byte is set to 0. The network address is 201.180.56.0.

> Note that we must not apply the default mask of one class to an address belonging to another class.

Address Depletion

Due to the classful addressing scheme and due to the fast growth of the Internet, the available addresses are almost depleted. Despite this, the number of devices on the Internet is much less than the 2^{32} address space. We have run out of addresses because many organizations have been assigned more addresses than they need (class A and B blocks), and nobody wants a class C block. In Chapter 5, we discuss some remedies to this problem.

4.3 OTHER ISSUES

In this section, we discuss some other issues that are related to addressing in general and classful addressing in particular.

Multihomed Devices

An Internet address defines the node's connection to its network. It follows, therefore, that any device connected to more than one network must have more than one Internet address. In fact, a device has a different address for each network connected to it. A computer that is connected to different networks is called a **multihomed** computer and will have more than one address, each possibly belonging to a different class. A router must be connected to more than one network, otherwise it cannot route. Therefore, a router definitely has more than one IP address, one for each interface. In Figure 4.12 we have one multihomed computer and one router. The computer is connected to two networks and its two IP addresses reflect this. Likewise, the router is connected to three networks and therefore has three IP addresses.

Figure 4.12 *Multihomed devices*

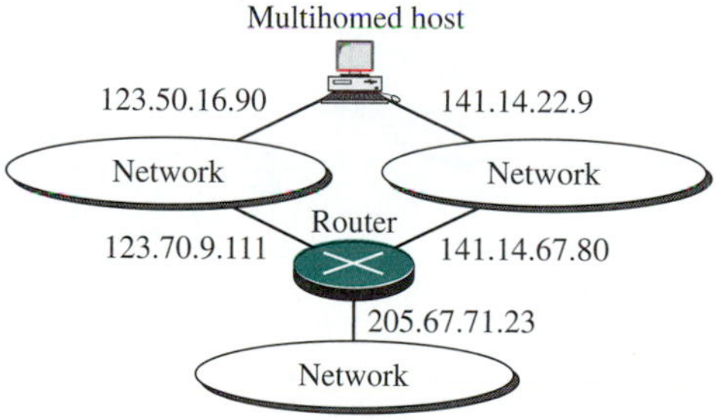

Location, Not Names

An Internet address defines the network location of a device, not its identity. In other words, because an Internet address is made of two parts (netid and hostid), it can only define the connection of a device to a specific network. One of the ramifications of this is that the movement of a computer from one network to another means that its IP address must be changed.

Special Addresses

Some parts of the address space are used for special addresses (see Table 4.3).

Table 4.3 *Special addresses*

Special Address	*Netid*	*Hostid*	*Source or Destination*
Network address	Specific	All 0s	None
Direct broadcast address	Specific	All 1s	Destination
Limited broadcast address	All 1s	All 1s	Destination
This host on this network	All 0s	All 0s	Source
Specific host on this network	All 0s	Specific	Destination
Loopback address	127	Any	Destination

Network Address

We have already covered the topic of network addresses. The first address in a block (in classes A, B, and C) defines the network address. Figure 4.13 shows three examples of network address, one for each class.

Figure 4.13 *Network address*

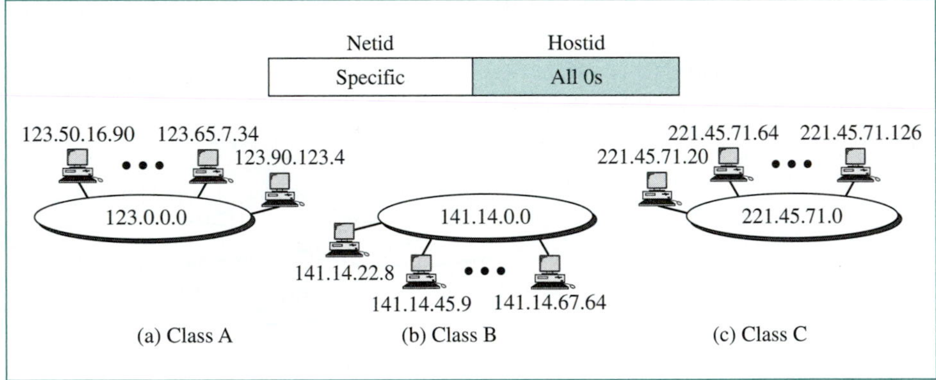

Direct Broadcast Address

In classes A, B, and C, if the hostid is all 1s, the address is called a **direct broadcast address.** It is used by a router to send a packet to all hosts in a specific network. All hosts will accept a packet having this type of destination address. Note that this address can be used only as a destination address in an IP packet. Note also that this special address also reduces the number of available hostids for each netid in classes A, B, and C. In Figure 4.14, router R sends a datagram using a destination IP address with a hostid of all 1s. All devices on this network receive and process the datagram.

Figure 4.14 *Example of direct broadcast address*

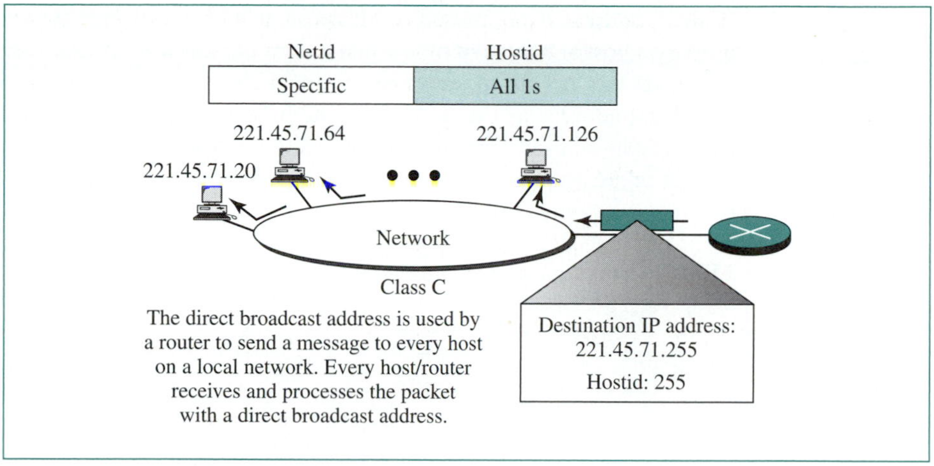

Netid | Hostid
Specific | All 1s

221.45.71.64
221.45.71.126
221.45.71.20
Network
Class C

The direct broadcast address is used by a router to send a message to every host on a local network. Every host/router receives and processes the packet with a direct broadcast address.

Destination IP address:
221.45.71.255
Hostid: 255

Limited Broadcast Address

In classes A, B, and C, an address with all 1s for the netid and hostid (32 bits) defines a broadcast address in the current network. A host that wants to send a message to every other host can use this address as a destination address in an IP packet. However, a router will block a packet having this type of address to confine the broadcasting to the local network. Note that this address belongs to class E. In Figure 4.15, a host sends a datagram using a destination IP address consisting of all 1s. All devices on this network receive and process this datagram.

Figure 4.15 *Example of limited broadcast address*

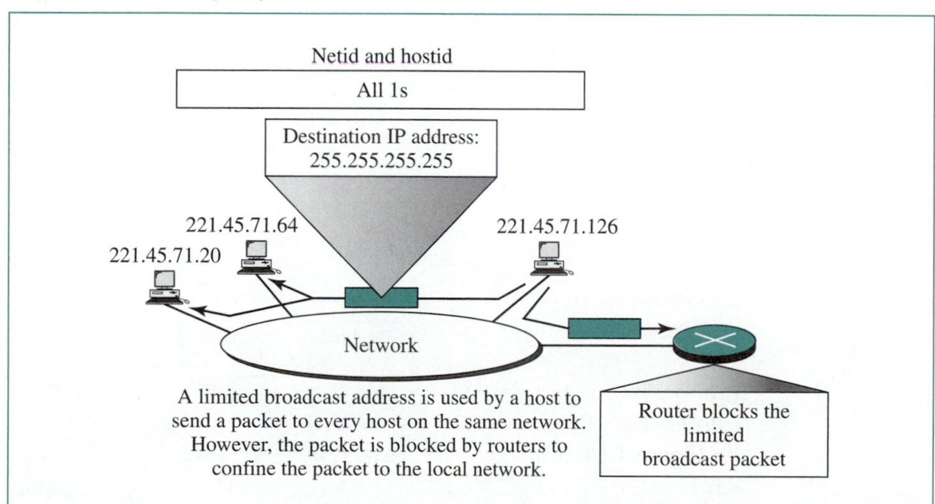

This Host on This Network

If an IP address is composed of all zeros, it means *this host on this network*. This is used by a host at bootstrap time when it does not know its IP address. The host sends an IP packet to a bootstrap server using this address as the source address and a limited broadcast address as the destination address to find its own address. Note that this address can be used only as a source address. Note also that this address is always a class A address regardless of the network. It reduces the number of networks in class A by one (see Figure 4.16).

Figure 4.16 *Examples of "this" host on "this" network address*

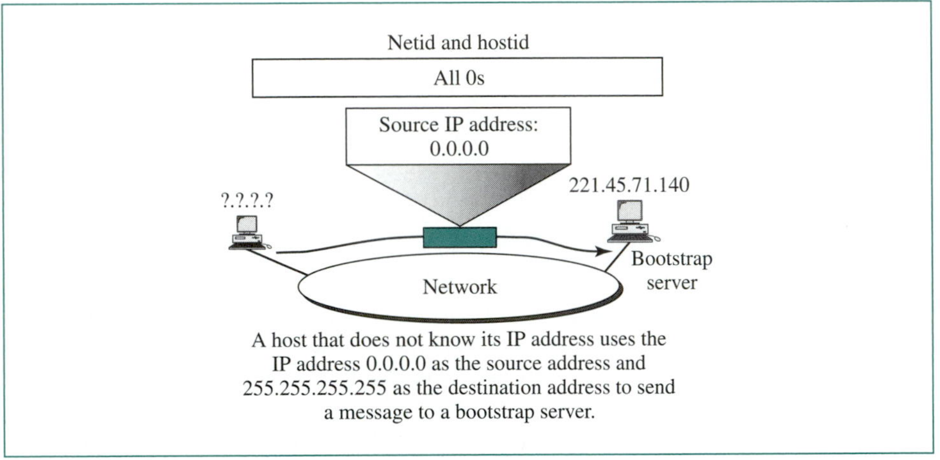

Specific Host on This Network

An IP address with a netid of all zeros means a specific host on this network. It is used by a host to send a message to another host on the same network. Because the packet is blocked by the router, it is a way of confining the packet to the local network. Note that it can be used only for a destination address. Note also it is actually a class A address regardless of the network (see Figure 4.17).

Figure 4.17 *Example of specific host on "this" network*

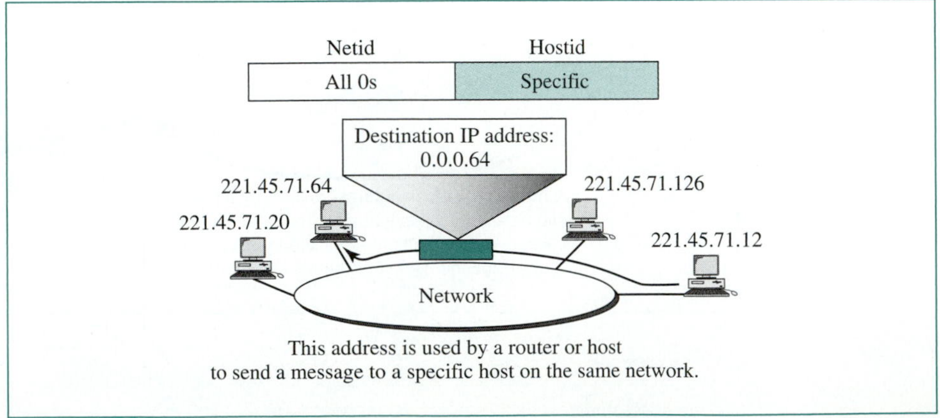

Loopback Address

The IP address with the first byte equal to 127 is used for the **loopback address,** which is an address used to test the software on a machine. When this address is used, a packet never leaves the machine; it simply returns to the protocol software. It can be used to test the IP software. For example, an application such as "ping" can send a packet with a loopback address as the destination address to see if the IP software is capable of receiving and processing a packet. As another example, the loopback address can be used by a **client process** (a running application program) to send a message to a server process on the same machine. Note that this can be used only as a destination address in an IP packet. Note also that this is actually a class A address. It reduces the number of networks in class A by 1 (see Figure 4.18).

Figure 4.18 *Example of loopback address*

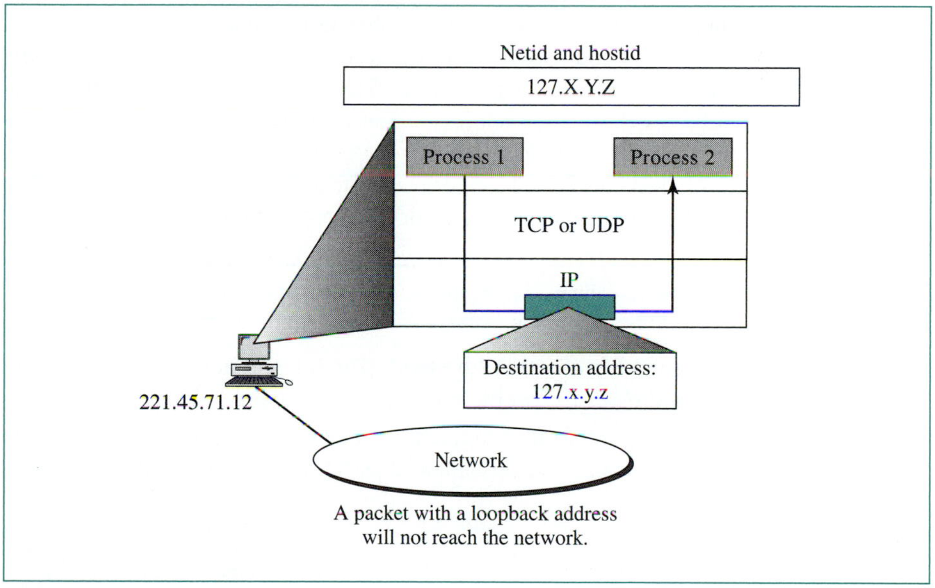

Private Addresses

A number of blocks in each class are assigned for private use. They are not recognized globally. These blocks are depicted in Table 4.4. These addresses are used either in isolation or in connection with network address translation techniques. We discuss private networks in Chapter 30.

Table 4.4 *Addresses for private networks*

Class	*Netids*	*Blocks*
A	10.0.0	1
B	172.16 to 172.31	16
C	192.168.0 to 192.168.255	256

Unicast, Multicast, and Broadcast Addresses

Communication on the Internet can be achieved using unicast, multicast, or broadcast addresses.

Unicast Addresses

Unicast communication is *one-to-one*. When a packet is sent from an individual source to an individual destination, a unicast communication takes place. All systems on the Internet have at least one unique unicast address. Unicast addresses belong to classes A, B, or C.

Multicast Addresses

Multicast communication is *one-to-many*. When a packet is sent from an individual source to a group of destinations, a multicast communication takes place. A multicast address is a class D address. The entire address defines a groupid. A system on the Internet can have one or more class D multicast addresses (in addition to its unicast address or addresses). If a system (usually a host) has seven multicast addresses, it means that it belongs to seven different groups. Note that a class D address can be used only as a destination address, not as a source address.

Multicasting on the Internet can be at the local level or at the global level. At the local level, hosts on a LAN can form a group and be assigned a multicast address. At the global level, hosts on different networks can form a group and be assigned a multicast address.

Multicast delivery will be discussed in depth in Chapter 14.

Assigned Multicast Addresses The Internet authorities have designated some multicast addresses to specific groups. We mention two here.

- **Category.** Some multicast addresses are assigned for some special use. These multicast addresses start with a 224.0.0 prefix. Table 4.5 shows some of these addresses.

Table 4.5 *Category addresses*

Address	*Group*
224.0.0.0	Reserved
224.0.0.1	All SYSTEMS on this SUBNET
224.0.0.2	All ROUTERS on this SUBNET
224.0.0.4	DVMRP ROUTERS
224.0.0.5	OSPFIGP All ROUTERS
224.0.0.6	OSPFIGP Designated ROUTERS
224.0.0.7	ST Routers
224.0.0.8	ST Hosts
224.0.0.9	RIP2 Routers
224.0.0.10	IGRP Routers
224.0.0.11	Mobile-Agents

- **Conferencing.** Some multicast addresses are for conferencing and teleconferencing. These multicast addresses start with the 224.0.1 prefix. Table 4.6 shows some of these addresses.

Table 4.6 *Addresses for conferencing*

Address	*Group*
224.0.1.7	AUDIONEWS
224.0.1.10	IETF-1-LOW-AUDIO
224.0.1.11	IETF-1-AUDIO
224.0.1.12	IETF-1-VIDEO
224.0.1.13	IETF-2-LOW-AUDIO
224.0.1.14	IETF-2-AUDIO
224.0.1.15	IETF-2-VIDEO
224.0.1.16	MUSIC-SERVICE
224.0.1.17	SEANET-TELEMETRY
224.0.1.18	SEANET-IMAGE

Broadcast Addresses

Broadcast communication is *one-to-all*. The Internet allows broadcasting only at the local level. We have already discussed two broadcast addresses used at the local level: the limited broadcast address (all 1s) and the direct broadcast address (netid: specific, hostid: all 1s).

No broadcasting is allowed at the global level. This means that a system (host or router) cannot send a message to all hosts and routers in the Internet. You can imagine the traffic that would result without this restriction.

4.4 A SAMPLE INTERNET WITH CLASSFUL ADDRESSES

Figure 4.19 shows a part of an internet with five networks.

1. A Token Ring LAN with network address 220.3.6.0 (class C).
2. An Ethernet LAN with network address 134.18.0.0 (class B).
3. An Ethernet LAN with network address 124.0.0.0 (class A).
4. A point-to-point WAN (broken line). This network (a T-1 line, for example) just connects two routers; there are no hosts. In this case, to save addresses, no network address is assigned to this type of WAN.
5. A switched WAN (such as Frame Relay or ATM) that can be connected to many routers. We have shown three. One router connects the WAN to the Token Ring network. One connects the WAN to one of the Ethernet networks, and one router connects the WAN to the rest of the Internet.

Figure 4.19 *Sample internet*

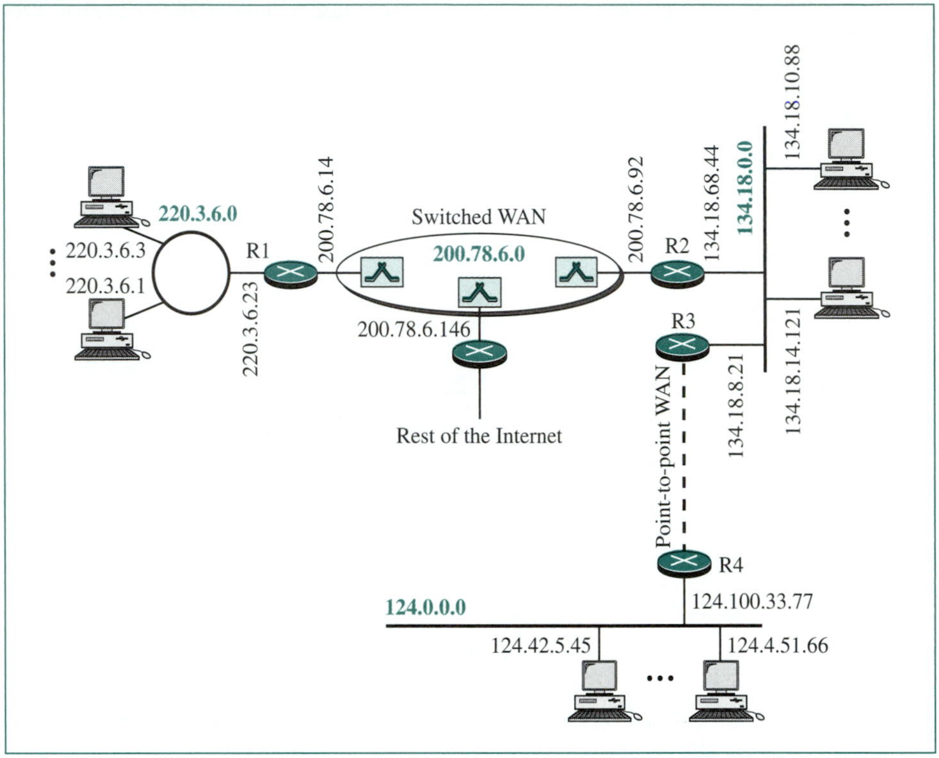

4.5 KEY TERMS

- address space
- AND operation
- binary notation
- block of addresses
- broadcast address
- class A address
- class B address
- class C address
- class D address
- class E address
- classful addressing
- classless addressing
- client process
- default mask
- direct broadcast address
- dotted-decimal notation
- flat address
- hexadecimal notation
- hostid
- internet
- Internet address
- IP address
- IP address class
- limited broadcast address

loopback address
mask
masking
multicast address
multihomed device
netid
network address
octet
specific host on this network
this host on this network
unicast address

4.6 SUMMARY

- At the network layer, a global identification system that uniquely identifies every host and router is necessary for delivery of a packet from network to network.
- The Internet address (or IP address) is 32 bits (for IPv4) that uniquely and universally defines a host or router on the Internet.
- The portion of the IP address that identifies the network is called the netid.
- The portion of the IP address that identifies the host or router on the network is called the hostid.
- An IP address defines a device's connection to a network.
- There are five classes of IP addresses. Classes A, B, and C differ in the number of hosts allowed per network. Class D is for multicasting and class E is for experimentation.
- The class of a network is easily determined by examination of the first byte.
- A multihomed device is connected to multiple networks and has an IP address for each network to which it is connected.
- For classes A, B, and C, a direct broadcast address (hostid all 1s) is used by a router to send a packet to all hosts on a specific network.
- A limited broadcast address (all 1s) is used by a host to send a packet to all hosts on its network.
- A source IP address of all 0s is used by a host at bootstrap if it does not know its IP address.
- A destination IP address with a netid of all 0s is used by a host to send a packet to another host on the same network.
- A loopback address with the first byte equal to 127 is used by a host to test its internal software.
- Unicast communication is one source sending a packet to one destination.
- Multicast communication is one source sending a packet to multiple destinations.
- Hosts with the same multicast address can either be on the same network or on different networks.
- Multicast addresses are often used for information retrieval and conferencing purposes.
- Broadcast communication is one source sending a packet to all hosts on its network.

4.7 PRACTICE SET

Multiple-Choice Questions

1. Identify the class of the following IP address: 4.5.6.7.
   a. class A
   b. class B
   c. class C
   d. class D
2. Identify the class of the following IP address: 229.1.2.3.
   a. class A
   b. class B
   c. class C
   d. class D
3. Identify the class of the following IP address: 191.1.2.3.
   a. class A
   b. class B
   c. class C
   d. class D
4. Identify the following IP address: 169.5.0.0.
   a. host IP address
   b. direct broadcast address
   c. limited broadcast address
   d. network address
5. Identify the following IP address: 169.5.1.1.
   a. host IP address
   b. direct broadcast address
   c. limited broadcast address
   d. network address
6. Identify the following IP address: 169.5.255.255.
   a. host IP address
   b. direct broadcast address
   c. limited broadcast address
   d. network address
7. Which of the following is true of the IP address 241.1.2.3?
   a. The netid is 241.
   b. The class is E.
   c. The hostid is 1.2.3.
   d. The netid is 11110.

8. A device has two IP addresses. This device could be _______.
   a. a computer
   b. a router
   c. a gateway
   d. any of the above
9. A device has two IP addresses. One address is 192.123.46.219. The other address could be _______.
   a. 192.123.46.220
   b. 192.123.46.0
   c. 192.123.47.219
   d. any of the above
10. Which of the following is true of the IP address 192.0.0.10?
    a. The netid is 192.
    b. The hostid is 0.10.
    c. The network address is 192.0.0.0.
    d. The hostid is 0.0.10.
11. Which of the following is a source IP address?
    a. this host on this network
    b. limited broadcast address
    c. loopback address
    d. specific host on this network
12. Using the direct broadcast address, a _______ sends a packet to _______ on the network.
    a. host; all other hosts
    b. router; all other hosts
    c. host; a specific host
    d. host; itself
13. Using the limited broadcast address, a _______ sends a packet to _______ on the network.
    a. host; all other hosts
    b. router; all other hosts
    c. host; a specific host
    d. host; itself
14. The loopback address is used to send a packet from the _______ to _______.
    a. host; all other hosts
    b. router; all other hosts
    c. host; a specific host
    d. host; itself

15. What destination address can be used to send a packet from a host with IP address 188.1.1.1 to all hosts on the network?
    a. 188.0.0.0
    b. 0.0.0.0
    c. 255.255.255.255
    d. b and c
16. A host can get its IP address from its server by using _______ as the source address and _______ as the destination address.
    a. 127.127.127.127; 0.0.0.0
    b. 255.255.255.255; 0.0.0.0
    c. 127.0.0.0; 255.255.255.255
    d. 0.0.0.0; 255.255.255.255
17. A host with an IP address of 142.5.0.1 needs to test internal software. What is the destination address in the packet?
    a. 127.0.0.0
    b. 127.1.1.1
    c. 127.127.127.127
    d. any of the above
18. A packet sent from a node at 198.123.46.20 to a node at 198.123.46.21 requires a _______ destination address.
    a. unicast
    b. multicast
    c. broadcast
    d. a or b
19. A packet sent from a node with IP address 198.123.46.20 to all nodes on network 198.123.46.0 requires a _______ address.
    a. unicast
    b. multicast
    c. broadcast
    d. a or b
20. A packet sent from a node with IP address 198.123.46.20 to all routers on network 198.123.46.0 requires a _______ address.
    a. unicast
    b. multicast
    c. broadcast
    d. a or b

Exercises

21. What is the address space in each of the following systems?
    a. a system with 8-bit addresses
    b. a system with 16-bit addresses
    c. a system with 64-bit addresses
22. An address space has a total of 1,024 addresses. How many bits are needed to represent an address?
23. An address space uses three symbols: 0, 1, and 2 represent addresses. If each address is made of 10 symbols, how many addresses are available in this system?
24. Change the following IP addresses from dotted-decimal notation to binary notation:
    a. 114.34.2.8
    b. 129.14.6.8
    c. 208.34.54.12
    d. 238.34.2.1
    e. 241.34.2.8
25. Change the following IP addresses from dotted-decimal notation to hexadecimal notation:
    a. 114.34.2.8
    b. 129.14.6.8
    c. 208.34.54.12
    d. 238.34.2.1
    e. 241.34.2.8
26. Change the following IP addresses from hexadecimal notation to binary notation:
    a. 0x1347FEAB
    b. 0xAB234102
    c. 0x0123A2BE
    d. 0x00001111
27. How many digits are needed to define the netid in hexadecimal notation in each of the following classes?
    a. Class A
    b. Class B
    c. Class C
28. Change the following IP addresses from binary notation to dotted-decimal notation:
    a. 01111111 11110000 01100111 01111101
    b. 10101111 11000000 11111000 00011101
    c. 11011111 10110000 00011111 01011101
    d. 11101111 11110111 11000111 00011101
    e. 11110111 11110011 10000111 11011101

29. Find the class of the following IP addresses:
    a. 208.34.54.12
    b. 238.34.2.1
    c. 114.34.2.8
    d. 129.14.6.8
    e. 241.34.2.8
30. Find the class of the following IP addresses:
    a. 11110111 11110011 10000111 11011101
    b. 10101111 11000000 11110000 00011101
    c. 11011111 10110000 00011111 01011101
    d. 11101111 11110111 11000111 00011101
    e. 01111111 11110000 01100111 01111101
31. Find the netid and the hostid of the following IP addresses:
    a. 114.34.2.8
    b. 19.34.21.5
    c. 23.67.12.1
    d. 127.23.4.0
32. Find the netid and the hostid of the following IP addresses:
    a. 129.14.6.8
    b. 132.56.8.6
    c. 171.34.14.8
    d. 190.12.67.9
33. Find the netid and the hostid of the following IP addresses:
    a. 192.8.56.2
    b. 220.34.8.9
    c. 208.34.54.12
    d. 205.23.67.8
34. Which of the following addresses does not belong to the same network (no subnetting)? Explain why.

    123.4.6.2 123.4.78.9 132.14.56.12 123.4.0.0
35. Which of the following addresses does not belong to the same network (no subnetting)? Exlain why.

    130.4.8.0 130.5.34.12 130.4.78.5 130.4.76.11
36. A host with IP address 128.23.67.3 sends a message to a host with IP address 193.45.23.7. Does the message travel through any router?
37. A host with IP address 128.23.67.3 sends a message to a host with IP address 14.45.23.7. Does the message travel through any router?
38. A host with IP address 128.23.67.3 sends a message to a host with IP address 128.45.23.7. Does the message travel through any router?

39. A host with IP address 128.23.67.3 sends a message to a host with IP address 128.23.23.7. Does the message travel through any router? Assume no subnetting (subnetting is discussed in Chapter 5).
40. A host with IP address 195.23.67.3 sends a message to a host with IP address 195.23.41.7. Does the message travel through any router? Assume no subnetting (subnetting is discussed in Chapter 5).
41. A host with IP address 195.23.67.3 sends a message to a host with IP address 195.23.67.7. Does the message travel through any router? Assume no subnetting (subnetting is discussed in Chapter 5).
42. A host with IP address 9.11.67.3 sends a message to a host with IP address 11.34.2.7. Does the message travel through any router? Assume no subnetting (subnetting is discussed in Chapter 5).
43. A host with IP address 9.11.67.3 sends a message to a host with IP address 9.34.2.7. Does the message travel through any router? Assume no subnetting (subnetting is discussed in Chapter 5).
44. Draw a diagram of a network with address 8.0.0.0 that is connected through a router to a network with IP address 131.45.0.0. Choose IP addresses for each interface of the router. Show also some hosts on each network with their IP addresses. What is the class of each network?
45. What is the class of the IP address 255.255.255.255 used in limited broadcasting?
46. What is the class of the IP address 0.0.0.0 used at bootstrap time?
47. What is the class of the IP address 0.23.56.12 used in a class A network for sending a message to a specific host located on "this" network?
48. What is the class of the IP address 0.0.52.16 used in a class B network for sending a message to a specific host located on "this" network?
49. What is the class of the IP address 0.0.0.14 used in a class C network for sending a message to a specific host located on "this" network?
50. A router has an IP address of 108.5.18.22. It sends a direct broadcast packet to all hosts in this network. What are the source and destination IP addresses used in this packet?
51. A router has an IP address of 140.15.8.20. It sends a direct broadcast packet to all hosts in this network. What are the source and destination IP addresses used in this packet?
52. A router has an IP address of 200.4.8.20. It sends a direct broadcast packet to all hosts in this network. What are the source and destination IP addresses used in this packet?
53. A host with IP address 108.67.18.70 sends a limited broadcast packet to all hosts in the same network. What are the source and destination IP addresses used in this packet?
54. A host with IP address 180.6.8.17 sends a limited broadcast packet to all hosts in the same network. What are the source and destination IP addresses used in this packet?

55. A host with IP address 202.7.8.27 sends a limited broadcast packet to all hosts in the same network. What are the source and destination IP addresses used in this packet?
56. A host with IP address 124.67.89.34 needs loopback testing. What are the source and destination addresses?
57. A host with IP address 185.42.56.88 wants to use loopback testing. What are the source and destination addresses?
58. A host with IP address 218.34.13.89 wants to use loopback testing. What are the source and destination addresses?
59. A host with IP address 123.27.19.24 sends a message to a host with IP address 123.67.89.56 using the "Specific Host on This Network" special address. What are the source and destination addresses?
60. A host with IP address 187.12.16.38 sends a message to a host with IP address 187.12.18.99 using the "Specific Host on This Network" special address. What are the source and destination addresses?
61. A host with IP address 215.14.14.9 sends a message to a host with IP address 215.14.14.22 using the "Specific Host on This Network" special address. What are the source and destination addresses?
62. A host in class A that does not know its IP address wants to send a message to a bootstrap server to find its address. What are the source and destination addresses?
63. A host in class B that does not know its IP address wants to send a message to a bootstrap server to find its address. What are the source and destination addresses?
64. A host in class C that does not know its IP address wants to send a message to a bootstrap server to find its address. What are the source and destination addresses?

Programming Exercises

65. Write a function in C (or any language you are familiar with) to change an IP address in dotted-decimal notation to binary notation.
66. Write a function in C (or any language you are familiar with) to change an IP address in binary notation to dotted-decimal notation.
67. Write a function in C (or any language you are familiar with) to change an IP address in binary notation to hexadecimal notation.
68. Write a function in C (or any language you are familiar with) that accepts an address and returns the class of the address.
69. Write a function in C (or any language you are familiar with) that accepts an address and returns the default mask for that address.
70. Write a function in C (or any language you are familiar with) that accepts an address and returns the first address (network address) in the block.
71. Write a function in C (or any language you are familiar with) that accepts an address and returns the last address in the block.

CHAPTER 5

Subnetting/Supernetting and Classless Addressing

In the previous chapter we discussed the problems associated with classful addressing. Specifically, the network addresses available for assignment to organizations are close to depletion. This is coupled with the ever-increasing demand for addresses from organizations that want connection to the Internet. In this chapter we discuss two important issues related to IP addressing: subnetting and supernetting.

5.1 SUBNETTING

In **subnetting,** a network is divided into several smaller subnetworks with each subnetwork (or subnet) having its own subnetwork address. As we learned in Chapter 4, an IP address is 32 bits long. A portion of the address indicates the network (netid), and a portion indicates the host (hostid) on the network. This means that there is a sense of hierarchy in IP addressing. To reach a host on the Internet, we must first reach the network using the first portion of the address (netid). Then we must reach the host itself using the second portion (hostid). In other words, IP addresses are designed with two levels of hierarchy.

> IP addresses are designed with two levels of hierarchy.

However, in many cases, these two levels of hierarchy are not enough. For example, imagine an organization with the network address 141.14.0.0 (a class B block). The organization has two-level hierarchical addressing, but, as shown in Figure 5.1, it cannot have more than one physical network. Note that the default mask (255.255.0.0) means that all addresses have 16 common bits. The remaining bits define the different addresses on the network. Note also that the network address is the first address in the block; the hostid part is all 0s in the network address.

With this scheme, the organization is limited to two levels of hierarchy. The hosts cannot be organized into groups; all of the hosts are at the same level. The organization has one network with many hosts.

Figure 5.1 *A network with two levels of hierarchy (not subnetted)*

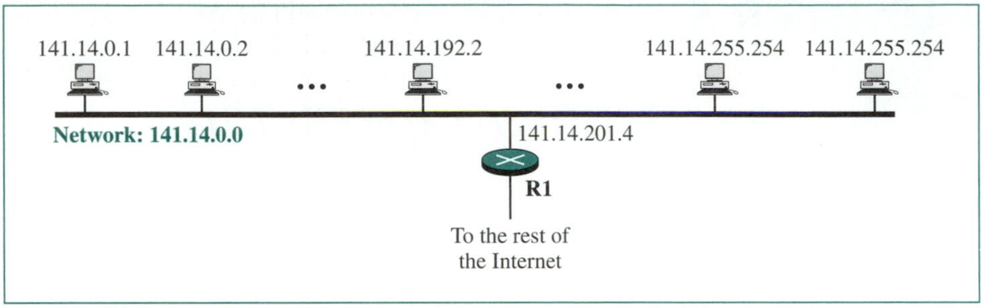

141.14.0.1
141.14.0.2
141.14.192.2
141.14.255.254
141.14.255.254
Network: 141.14.0.0
141.14.201.4
R1
To the rest of the Internet

One solution to this problem is subnetting, the further division of a network into smaller networks called *subnetworks* (or *subnets*). For example, Figure 5.2 shows the network in Figure 5.1 divided into four subnetworks.

Figure 5.2 *A network with three levels of hierarchy (subnetted)*

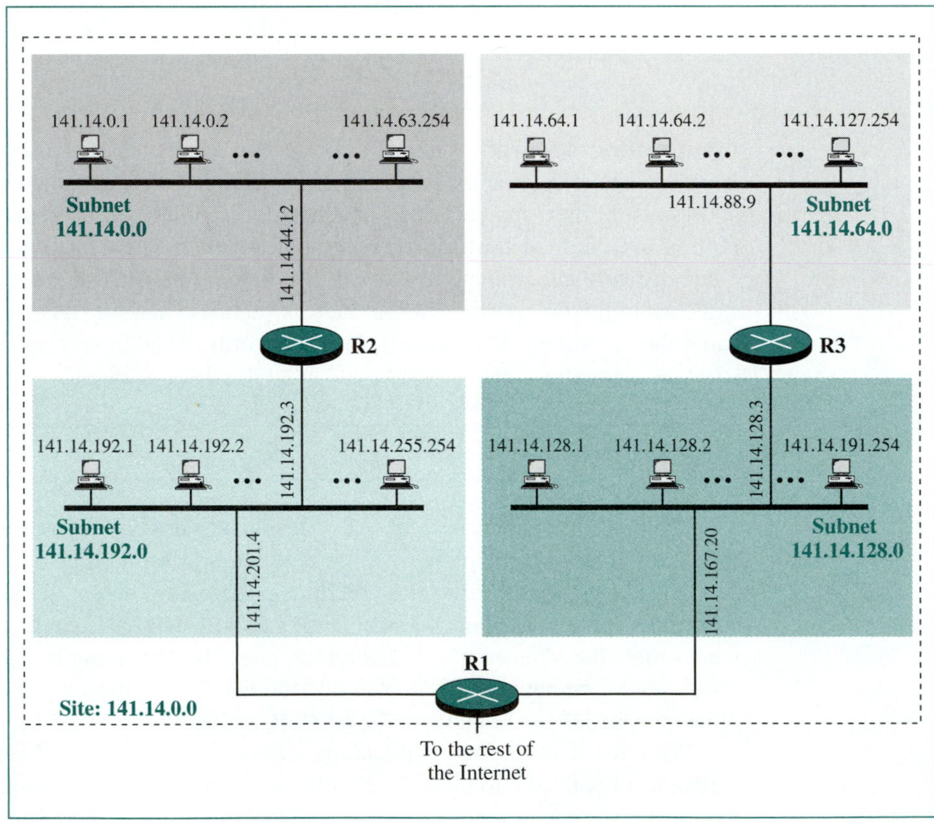

In this example, the rest of the Internet is not aware that the network is divided into physical subnetworks: The subnetworks still appear as a single network to the rest of the Internet. A packet destined for host 141.14.192.2 still reaches router R1. However, when the datagram arrives at router R1, the interpretation of the IP address changes. Router R1 knows that network 141.14 is physically divided into subnetworks. It knows that the packet must be delivered to subnetwork (subnet) 141.14.192.0.

Three Levels of Hierarchy

Adding subnetworks creates an intermediate level of hierarchy in the IP addressing system. Now we have three levels: site, subnet, and host. The site is the first level. The second level is the **subnet.** The host is the third level; it defines the connection of the host to the subnetwork. See Figure 5.3.

Figure 5.3 *Addresses in a network with and without subnetting*

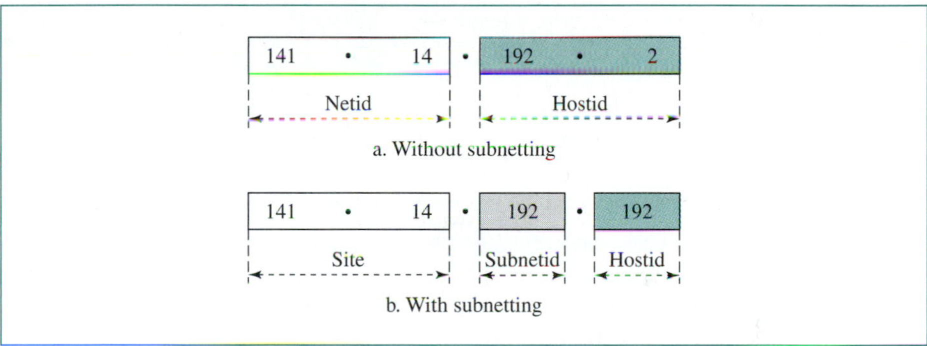

The routing of an IP datagram now involves three steps: delivery to the site, delivery to the subnetwork, and delivery to the host.

This is analogous to the 10-digit telephone number in the United States. As Figure 5.4 shows, a telephone number is divided into three levels: area code, exchange number, and connection number.

Figure 5.4 *Hierarchy concept in a telephone number*

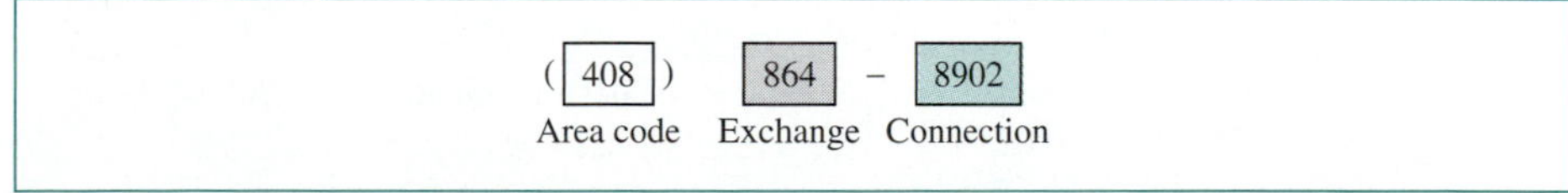

Subnet Mask

We discussed the network mask in Chapter 4. The network mask is used when a network is not subnetted. The network mask is used to find the first address in the block or the network address. However, when a mask is subnetted, the situation is different. We must have a subnet mask. The subnet has more 1s. Figure 5.5 shows the situations in two previous networks (see Figure 5.1 and Figure 5.2). The network mask creates the network address; the subnet mask creates the subnetwork address.

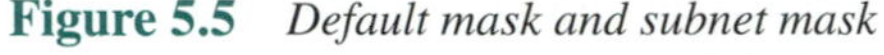

Figure 5.5 *Default mask and subnet mask*

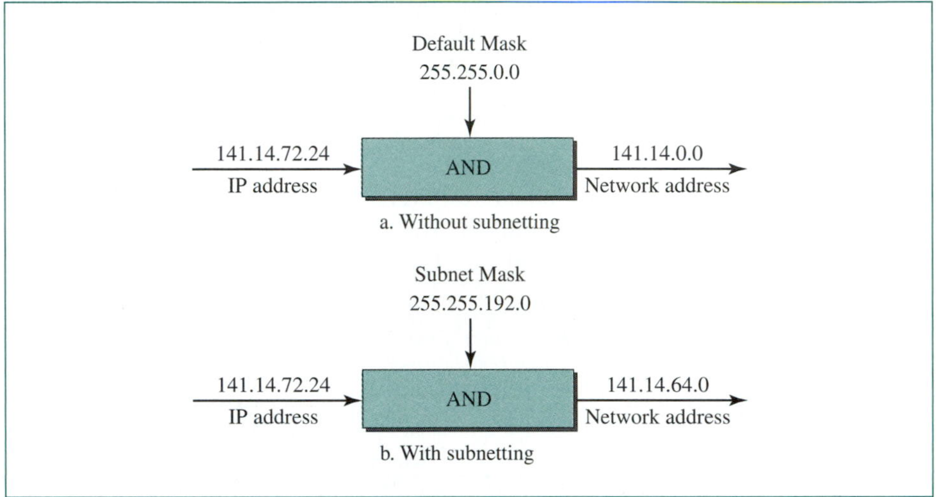

Contiguous versus Noncontiguous Subnet Mask

In the early days of subnetting, a noncontiguous subnet mask might have been used. By noncontiguous we mean a series of bits that is not a string of 1s followed by a string of 0s, but a mixture of 0s and 1s. Today, however, only contiguous masks (a run of 1s followed by a run of 0s) are used.

Finding the Subnet Address

Given an IP address, we can find the subnet address the same way we found the network address in the previous chapter. We apply the mask to the address. We can do this in two ways: straight or short-cut.

Straight Method In the straight method, we use binary notation for both the address and the mask and then apply the AND operation to find the subnet address.

Example 1

What is the subnetwork address if the destination address is 200.45.34.56 and the subnet mask is 255.255.240.0?

Solution

We apply the AND operation on the address and the subnet mask.

Address	➡	11001000 00101101 00100010 00111000
Subnet Mask	➡	11111111 11111111 11110000 00000000
Subnetwork Address	➡	11001000 00101101 00100000 00000000

The subnetwork address is 200.45.32.0.

Short-Cut Method If the subnet mask is contiguous, we can use a short cut as we did previously to find the network address using the default mask. However, we add one more rule to those learned in Chapter 4. The three rules we use are:

1. If the byte in the mask is 255, copy the byte in the address.
2. If the byte in the mask is 0, replace the byte in the address with 0.
3. If the byte in the mask is neither 255 nor 0, we write the mask and the address in binary and apply the AND operation.

Example 2

What is the subnetwork address if the destination address is 19.30.80.5 and the mask is 255.255.192.0?

Solution

Figure 5.6 shows the solution. The first, second, and fourth bytes are easy; for the third byte we use the bit-wise AND operation on 84 and 192.

Figure 5.6 *Example 2*

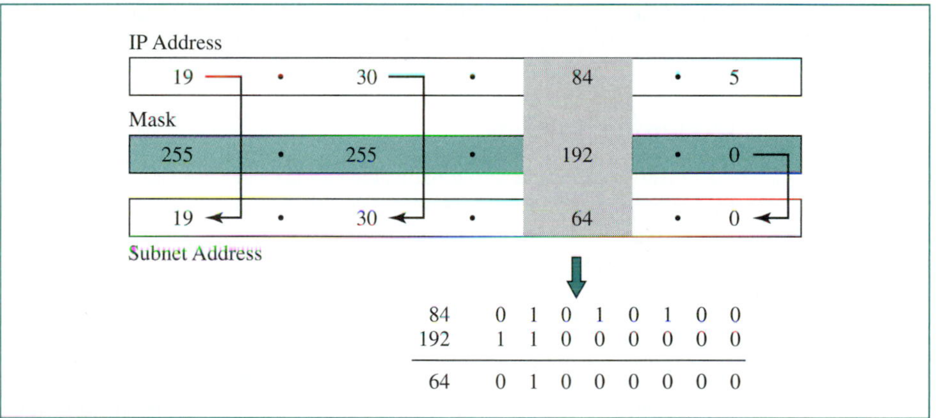

Default Mask and Subnet Mask

The number of 1s in a default mask is predetermined (8, 16, or 24). In a subnet mask the number of 1s is more than the number of 1s in the corresponding default mask. In other words, for a subnet mask, we change some of the leftmost 0s in the default mask to 1s to make a subnet mask. Figure 5.7 shows the difference between a class B default mask and a subnet mask for the same block.

Figure 5.7 *Comparison of a default mask and a subnet mask*

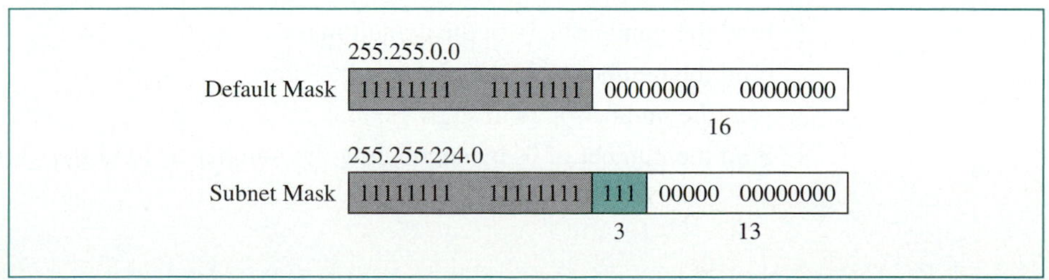

Number of Subnetworks

The number of subnetworks can be found by counting the extra 1s that are added to the default mask to make the subnet mask. For example, in Figure 5.7 the number of extra 1s is 3; therefore, the number of subnets is 2^3 or 8.

Number of Addresses per Subnet

The number of addresses per subnetwork can be found by counting the number of 0s in the subnet mask. For example, in Figure 5.7 the number of 0s is 13; therefore, the number of possible addresses in each subnet is $2^{13} = 8192$.

Special Addresses in Subnetting

With subnetting, two addresses in each subnet are added to the list of special addresses we discussed in Chapter 4. The first address in each subnet (with hostid all 0s) is the subnetwork address. The last address in each subnet (with hostid all 1s) is reserved for limited broadcast inside the subnet. Some other addresses were originally reserved as special addresses, but with the advent of classless addressing, as we will see shortly, this idea is obsolete.

Designing Subnets

To better understand subnetting, let us show how a network manager designs subnets for his company. This requires several steps:

Deciding the Number of Subnets

The first step in design is to determine the number of subnets needed for the organizaion. The decision depends on several factors: the physical location of the site (number of buildings or floors), the number of departments, the number of hosts needed for each subnet, and so on. For proper operation of masking, it is strongly recommended that the number of subnetworks be a power of 2 (0, 2, 4, 8, 16, 32, etc.). Note that a choice of 0 means no subnetting.

> The number of subnets must be a power of 2.

Finding the Subnet Mask

The second step is to find a contiguous subnet mask. The following rules can help us to find the subnet mask easily:

1. Find the number of 1s in the default mask.
2. Find the number of 1s that defines the subnets.
3. Add the number of 1s in steps 1 and 2.
4. Find the number of 0s by subtracting the number of 1s in step 3 from 32.

Finding the Range of Address in Each Subnet

After determining the subnet mask, the network administrator can find the range of addresses for each subnet. Two methods can be used to find the first and the last address in each subnet.

In the first method, we start with the first subnet. The first address in the first subnet is the first address in the block. We then add the number of addresses in each subnet to get the last address (we can also use the OR and NOT operation to do this, but we leave it as an exercise). Then we add one to this address to find the first address in the next subnet. We repeat the process for this subnet. And so on.

In the second method, we start with the last subnet. The last address in the last subnet is the last address in the block. We then apply the mask to obtain the first address in this subnet. We then subtract one from this address to obtain the last address of the subnet before the last. We repeat the procedure for this subnet. And so on.

Example 3

A company is granted the site address 201.70.64.0 (class C). The company needs six subnets. Design the subnets.

Solution

1. The number of 1s in the default mask is 24 (class C).
2. The company needs six subnets. This number 6 is not a power of 2. The next number that is a power of 2 is 8 (2^3). We need 3 more 1s in the subnet mask.
3. The total number of 1s in the subnet mask is 27 (24 + 3).
4. The total number of 0s is 5 (32 − 27).
5. The mask is

11111111 11111111 11111111 11100000

or

255.255.255.224

6. The number of subnets is 8.
7. The number of addresses in each subnet is 2^5 (5 is the number of 0s) or 32.
8. We now find the range of addresses using the first method. We start with the first subnet:
   a. The first address in this subnet is 201.70.64.0 (first address in the block).
   b. The last address in this subnet is found by adding 31 to this address (the number of addresses in each subnet is 32, but we add only 31). The last address is 201.70.64.31.
9. We now find the range of addresses in the second subnet:
   a. The first address in this subnet is 201.70.64.32 (one after the last address in the first subnet).
   b. The last address in this subnet is found by adding 31 to the first address. It is 201.70.64.63.
10. The range of addresses in the remaining subnets can be found in a similar manner. Figure 5.8 shows the procedure, which can easily be programmed.

Figure 5.8 *Example 3*

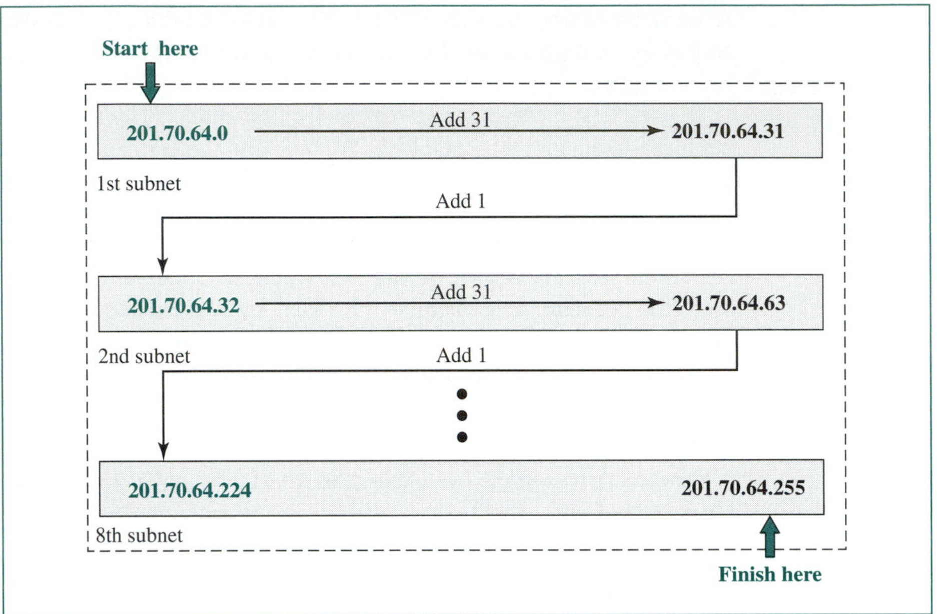

Example 4

A company is granted the site address 181.56.0.0 (class B). The company needs 1000 subnets. Design the subnets.

Solution

1. The number of 1s in the default mask is 16 (class B).
2. The company needs 1000 subnets. This number is not a power of 2. The next number that is a power of 2 is 1024 (2^{10}). We need 10 more 1s in the subnet mask.
3. The total number of 1s in the subnet mask is 26 (16 + 10).
4. The total number of 0s is 6 (32 − 26).
5. The mask is

11111111 11111111 11111111 11000000

or

255.255.255.192.

6. The number of subnets is 1024.
7. The number of addresses in each subnet is 2^6 (6 is the number of 0s) or 64.
8. We now find the range of addresses using the second method (starting from the 1024th subnet):
   a. The last address in this subnet is 181.56.255.255 (last address in the block).
   b. The first address in this subnet is found by applying the subnet mask to the last address; therefore, 181.56.255.192 is the first address.

9. We now find the range of addresses in the 1023th subnet:
   a. The last address in this subnet is 181.56.255.191 (one before the first address in the last subnet).
   b. The first address in this subnet is found by applying the subnet mask to the last address; therefore, 181.56.255.128 is the first address.
10. We now find the range of addresses in the 1022th subnet:
    a. The last address in this subnet is 181.56.255.127 (one before the first address in the last subnet).
    b. The first address in this subnet is found by applying the subnet mask to the last address; therefore, 181.56.255.64 is the first address.
11. We continue until all of the subnets are defined. However, this problem can easily be programmed using any of the modern computer languages. Figure 5.9 shows the subnets and ranges.

Figure 5.9 *Example 4*

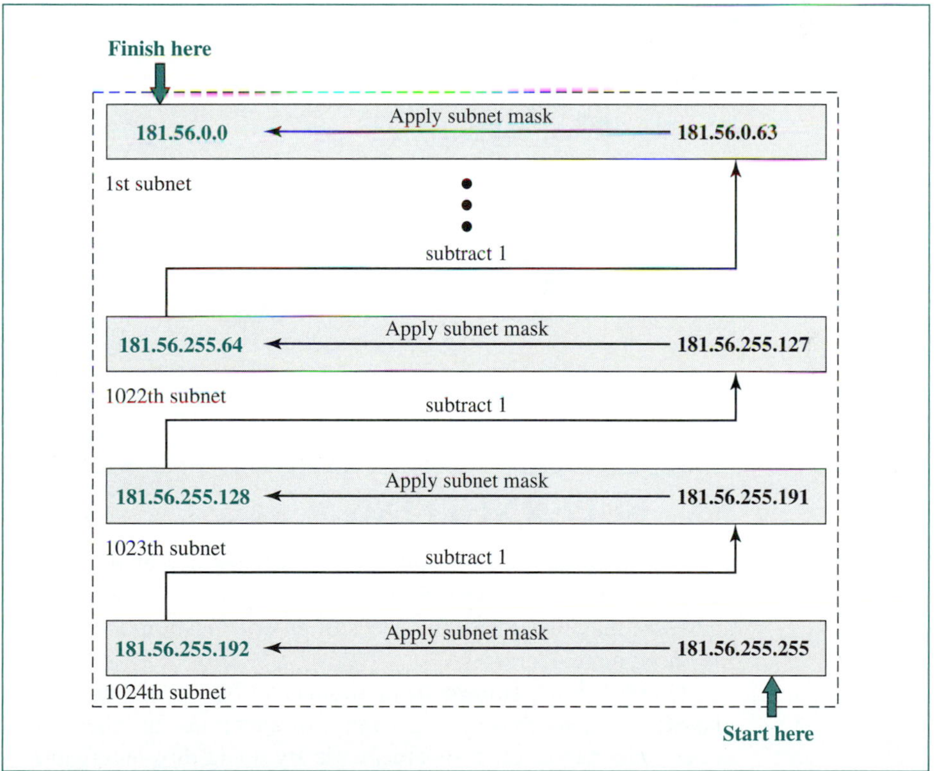

Variable-Length Subnet Mask

The Internet allows a site to use variable-length subnetting. For an example of when this may be desirable, consider a site that is granted a class C address and needs to have five subnets with the following number of hosts: 60, 60, 60, 30, 30. The site cannot use a subnet mask with only 2 bits in the subnet section because this allows only four subnetworks each with 64 addresses in each subnet. Nor can the site use a subnet mask with 3 bits in the subnet section because this allows eight subnetworks each with 32 addresses.

One solution to this site's problem is variable-length subnetting. In this configuration, the router uses two different masks, one applied after the other. It first uses the mask with 26 1s (11111111 11111111 11111111 11000000 or 255.255.255.192) to divide the network into four subnets. Then it applies the mask with 27 1s (11111111 11111111 11111111 11100000 or 255.255.255.224) to one of the subnets to divide it into two smaller subnets (see Figure 5.10).

Figure 5.10 *Variable-length subnetting*

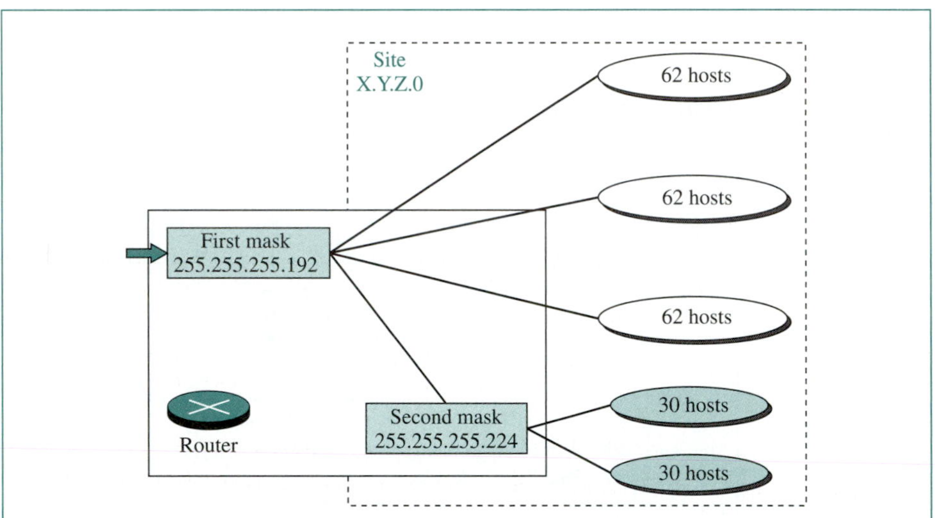

5.2 SUPERNETTING

Although classes A and B addresses are almost depleted, class C addresses are still available. However, the size of a class C block with a maximum number of 256 addresses may not satisfy the needs of an organization. Even a mid-size organization may need more addresses.

One solution is **supernetting.** In supernetting, an organization can combine several class C blocks to create a larger range of addresses. In other words, several networks are combined to create a supernetwork. By doing this, an organization can apply for a set of class C blocks instead of just one. For example, an organization that needs 1000 addresses can be granted four class C blocks. The organization can then use these addresses in one supernetwork as shown in Figure 5.11.

Assigning Addresses

When we assign a set of class C blocks to an organization, we have two choices. We can choose the blocks randomly or based on a set of rules. If we choose the blocks

Figure 5.11 *A supernetwork*

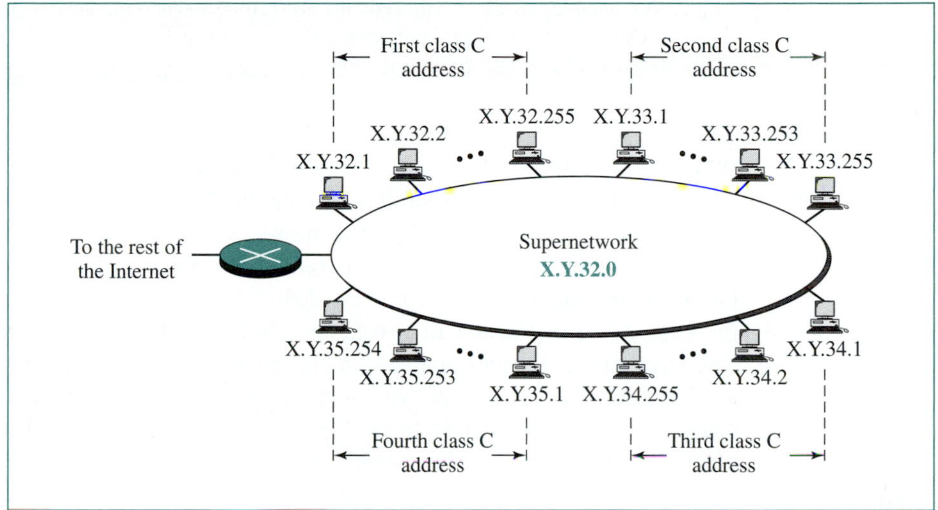

randomly, the routers outside of the organization treat each block separately; they think each block belongs to a different site. In this way, each router will have *N* entries in its routing table where *N* is the number of blocks. This strategy may increase the size of the routing table tremendously. Imagine an organization is given 100 class C blocks. Each router must have 100 entries in the routing table although all of these addresses belong to one organization, not 100.

The other choice is to make a superblock out of the blocks so that each router has only one entry in the routing table. To do so, we need to follow a set of rules when we assign the blocks:

1. The number of blocks must be a power of 2 (1, 2, 4, 8, 16, . . .).
2. The blocks must be contiguous in the address space (no gaps between the blocks).
3. The third byte of the first address in the superblock must be evenly divisible by the number of blocks. In other words, if the number of blocks is *N*, the third byte must be divisible by *N*.

Example 5

A company needs 600 addresses. Which of the following set of class C blocks can be used to form a supernet for this company?

a. **198.47.32.0** 198.47.33.0 198.47.34.0
b. **198.47.32.0** 198.47.42.0 198.47.52.0 198.47.62.0
c. **198.47.31.0** 198.47.32.0 198.47.33.0 198.47.52.0
d. **198.47.32.0** 198.47.33.0 198.47.34.0 198.47.35.0

Solution

a. Not acceptable; there are only three blocks. We need at least four blocks to make the number of blocks a power of 2.
b. Not acceptable; the blocks are not contiguous.

c. Not acceptable; 31 in the first block is not evenly divisible by 4.

d. Acceptable; all three requirements are fulfilled. The company is given more addresses than it needs, but we do not have any other choice.

Supernet Mask

When an organization is granted one block of addresses (class A, B, or C), the first address in the block and the mask define the block (the range of addresses). We always know this range of addresses since the mask is always known (default mask).

When an organization divides its block into subnets, the first address in the subblock and the subnet mask completely define the subblock (the range of addresses). In this case, however, the first address alone is not enough; we must have the subnet mask.

Similarly, when an organization combines several blocks into a superblock, we need to know the first address in the block and the supernet mask. Here also, the first address alone cannot define the range; we need a supernet mask to find how many blocks are combined to make a superblock.

> In subnetting, we need the first address of the subnet and the subnet mask to define the range of addresses.
>
> In supernetting, we need the first address of the supernet and the supernet mask to define the range of addresses.

A supernet mask is the reverse of a subnet mask. A subnet mask for class C has more 1s than the default mask for this class. A supernet mask for class C has less 1s than the default mask for this class.

Figure 5.12 shows the difference between a subnet mask and a supernet mask. A subnet mask that divides a block into eight subblocks has three more 1s ($2^3 = 8$) than the default mask; a supernet mask that combines eight blocks into one superblock has three less 1s than the default mask.

Figure 5.12 *Comparison of subnet, default, and supernet masks*

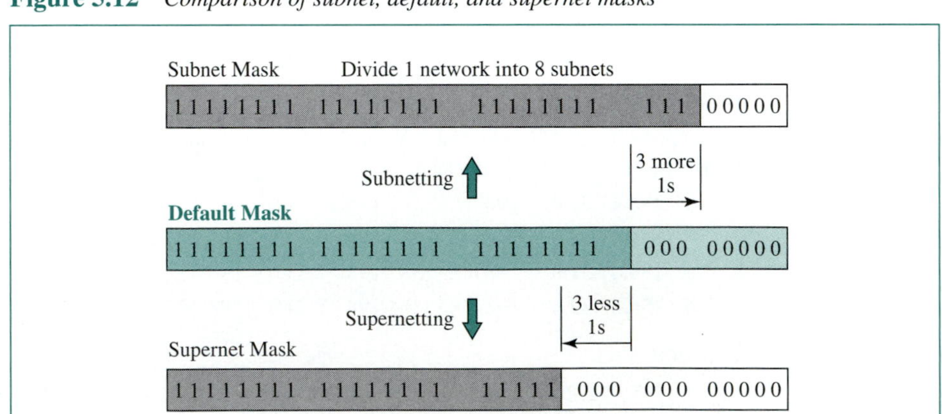

Example 6

We need to make a supernetwork out of 16 class C blocks. What is the supernet mask?

Solution

We need 16 blocks. For 16 blocks we need to change four 1s to 0s in the default mask. So the mask is

11111111 11111111 1111**0000** 00000000

or

255.255.240.0

Using the Supernet Mask to Find the First Address

The supernet mask can be used by a router to find the first address in the superblock to identify the site (the organization). A subnet mask performs the same function. When an address is given, a subnet mask finds the first address in the subnet; when an address is given, a supernet mask finds the first address in the supernet.

Example 7

A supernet has a first address of 205.16.32.0 and a supernet mask of 255.255.248.0. A router receives three packets with the following destination addresses:

a. 205.16.37.44
b. 205.16.42.56
c. 205.17.33.76

Which packet belongs the supernet?

Solution

We apply the supernet mask to see if we can find the beginning address.

a. 205.16.37.44 AND 255.255.248.0 ➡ 205.16.32.0 (first address)
b. 205.16.42.56 AND 255.255.248.0 ➡ 205.16.40.0 (not the first address)
c. 205.17.33.76 AND 255.255.248.0 ➡ 205.17.32.0 (not the first address)

This means the only address belonging to the organization is the first one. We prove this in the next section when we talk about the second usage of the supernet mask.

Using the Supernet Mask to Find the Range of Addresses

We said that the first address in the superblock coupled with the supernet mask determine the superblock (range of addresses). Comparing the supernet mask and the default mask gives us the number of blocks. We know that the default mask has 24 1s. Subtracting the number of 1s in the supernet mask from 24 gives us the number of blocks.

Example 8

A supernet has a first address of 205.16.32.0 and a supernet mask of 255.255.248.0. How many blocks are in this supernet and what is the range of addresses?

Solution

The supernet has 21 1s. The default mask has 24 1s. Since the difference is 3, there are 2^3 or 8 blocks in this supernet. The blocks are 205.16.32.0 to 205.16.39.0. The first address is 205.16.32.0. The last address is 205.16.39.255. The total number of addresses is 8×256 or 2048.

5.3 CLASSLESS ADDRESSING

The idea of classful addressing has created many problems. Until the mid-1990s, a range of addresses meant a block of addresses in class A, B, or C. The minimum number of addresses granted to an organization was 256 (class C); the maximum was 16,777,216 (class A). In between these limits an organization could have a class B block or several class C blocks. However, the choices were limited. In addition, what about a small business that needed only 16 addresses? Or a household that needed only two addresses?

During the 1990s, Internet Service Providers (ISPs) came into prominence. An ISP is an organization that provides Internet access for individuals, small businesses, and mid-size organizations that do not want to create an Internet site and become involved in providing Internet services (such as email services) for their employees. An ISP can provide these services. An ISP can be granted several class B or class C blocks and then subdivide the range of addresses (in groups of 2, 4, 8, or 16 addresses), giving a range to a household or a small business. The customers are connected via a dial-up modem, DSL, or cable modem to the ISP. However, each customer needs an IP address (we will see other solutions such as private addresses, network address translation in Chapter 30).

To facilitate this evolution, in 1996, the Internet authorities announced a new architecture called **classless addressing** that would eventually render classful addressing obsolete.

Variable-Length Blocks

The whole idea of classless addressing is to have variable-length blocks that belong to no class. We can have a block of 2 addresses, 4 addresses, 128 addresses, and so on. There are some restrictions that we will discuss shortly, but in general a block can range from very small to very large.

In this architecture, the whole address space (2^{32} addresses) is divided into blocks of different sizes. An organization will be granted a block suitable for its purposes. Figure 5.13 shows the architecture of classless addressing. Compare this figure with Figure 4.2 in Chapter 4.

Figure 5.13 *Variable-length blocks*

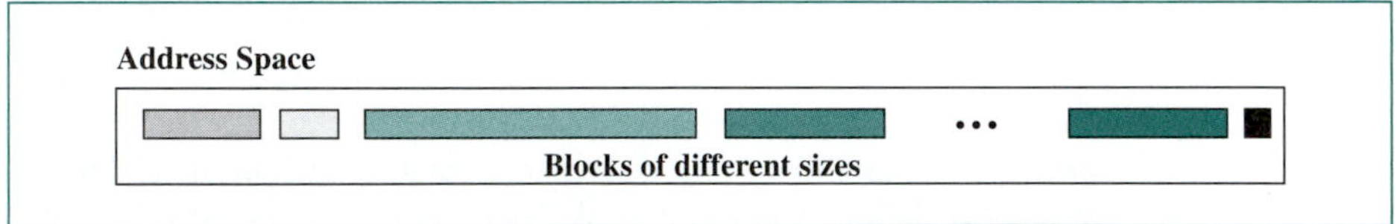

Number of Addresses in a Block

There is only one condition on the number of addresses in a block; it must be a power of 2 (2, 4, 8, . . .). A household may be given a block of 2 addresses. A small business may be given 16 addresses. A large organization may be given 1024 addresses.

Beginning Address

The beginning address must be evenly divisible by the number of addresses. For example, if a block contains 4 addresses, the beginning address must be divisible by 4. If the block has less than 256 addresses, we need to check only the rightmost byte. If it has less than 65,536 addresses, we need to check only the two rightmost bytes, and so on.

Example 9

Which of the following can be the beginning address of a block that contains 16 addresses?

a. 205.16.37.32
b. 190.16.42.44
c. 17.17.33.80
d. 123.45.24.52

Solution

Only two are eligible (a and c). The address 205.16.37.32 is eligible because 32 is divisible by 16. The address 17.17.33.80 is eligible because 80 is divisible by 16.

Example 10

Which of the following can be the beginning address of a block that contains 1024 addresses?

a. 205.16.37.32
b. 190.16.42.0
c. 17.17.32.0
d. 123.45.24.52

Solution

Only one is eligible (c). To be divisible by 1024, the rightmost byte of an address should be 0 and the second rightmost byte must be divisible by 4 (prove this to yourself). Only the address 17.17.32.0 meets this condition.

Mask

If you remember, when an organization was given a block in classful addressing the organization was given the beginning address of the block and a mask (default mask). In subnetting, when an organization was assigned a subblock, it was given the first address and the subnet mask. In supernetting, when an organization was given several class C addresses, it was given the first address and a supernet mask.

The same concept is carried over to classless addressing. When an organization is given a block, it is given the first address and the mask. These two pieces of information can define the whole block.

Slash Notation

Writing the 4-byte mask is sometimes cumbersome. We know the mask is made of some 1s at the left followed by some 0s at the right. So instead of 255.255.255.224, we can just say that the mask has 27 1s. We can attach this number to the end of a classless address. This is called **slash notation,** or **CIDR** (classless interdomain routing) notation. The CIDR conveys two ideas: the address is classless and routing is done using interdomain routing. In Chapter 6, we discuss routing and the CIDR concept. A generic address in slash notation is shown in Figure 5.14.

Note that a mask and a slash followed by a number both define the same thing: the number of common bits in every address in the block.

Figure 5.14 *Slash notation*

A.B.C.D/*n*

> Slash notation is also called CIDR notation.

The *n* after the slash defines the number of bits that are the same in every address in the block. So if *n* is 20, it means the 20 leftmost bits are identical in each address with 12 bits not the same. We can easily find the number of addresses in the block and the last address from this information.

Prefix and Prefix Length

Two terms that are often used in classless addressing are prefix and prefix length. The prefix is another name for the common part of the address range (similar to the netid). The prefix length is the length of the prefix (*n* in the slash notation).

Suffix and Suffix Length

Two other terms occasionally used in classless addressing are suffix and suffix length. The suffix is the varying part (similar to the hostid). The suffix length is the length of the suffix ($32 - n$) in slash notation.

Example 11

A small organization is given a block with the beginning address and the prefix length 205.16.37.24/29 (in slash notation). What is the range of the block?

Solution

The beginning address is 205.16.37.24. To find the last address we keep the first 29 bits and change the last 3 bits to 1s.

Beginning Address:	**11001111 00010000 00100101 00011**000
Ending Address:	**11001111 00010000 00100101 00011**111

There are only 8 addresses in this block.

Example 12

We can find the range of addresses in Example 11 by another method. We can argue that the length of the suffix is $32 - 29$ or 3. So there are $2^3 = 8$ addresses in this block. If the first address is 205.16.37.24, the last address is 205.16.37.31 ($24 + 7 = 31$).

Prefix Length and the Mask

There is a one-to-one relationship between a mask and a prefix length as shown in Table 5.1. Note that the entries in color are actually the default masks for classes A, B, and C.

Table 5.1 *Prefix lengths*

/n	Mask	/n	Mask	/n	Mask	/n	Mask
/1	128.0.0.0	/9	255.128.0.0	/17	255.255.128.0	/25	255.255.255.128
/2	192.0.0.0	/10	255.192.0.0	/18	255.255.192.0	/26	255.255.255.192
/3	224.0.0.0	/11	255.224.0.0	/19	255.255.224.0	/27	255.255.255.224
/4	240.0.0.0	/12	255.240.0.0	/20	255.255.240.0	/28	255.255.255.240
/5	248.0.0.0	/13	255.248.0.0	/21	255.255.248.0	/29	255.255.255.248
/6	252.0.0.0	/14	255.252.0.0	/22	255.255.252.0	/30	255.255.255.252
/7	254.0.0.0	/15	255.254.0.0	/23	255.255.254.0	/31	255.255.255.254
/8	**255.0.0.0**	**/16**	**255.255.0.0**	**/24**	**255.255.255.0**	/32	255.255.255.255

A block in classes A, B, and C can easily be represented in slash notation as A.B.C.D/*n* where *n* is either 8 (class A), 16 (class B), or 24 (class C).

Finding the Network Address

Can we find the network address (the first address in the block) if one of the addresses in the block and the prefix length is given? The answer is definitely yes. A prefix length is a mask. When we have the mask, we can AND the mask and the address to find the first address. However, because the addresses in classless addressing are guaranteed to be contiguous and the prefix determines the number of fixed bits, we can find the network address. Just keep the first *n* bits and change the rest of the bits to 0s.

Example 13

What is the network address if one of the addresses is 167.199.170.82/27?

Solution

The prefix length is 27, which means that we must keep the first 27 bits as is and change the remaining bits (5) to 0s. The 5 bits affect only the last byte. The last byte is 01010010. Changing the last 5 bits to 0s, we get 01000000 or 64. The network address is 167.199.170.64/27.

Subnetting

We can of course use subnetting with classless addressing. When an organization is granted a block of addresses, it can create subnets to meet its needs. The network administrator can design a subnet mask just as we discussed in classful addressing. The procedure is even simpler here. The prefix length (*n*) increases to define the subnet prefix length. For example, if the site prefix length (one given the organization) is 17, the subnet prefix length can be 20 to create eight subnets ($2^3 = 8$).

Example 14

An organization is granted the block 130.34.12.64/26. The organization needs to have four subnets. What are the subnet addresses and the range of addresses for each subnet?

Solution

The suffix length is 6. This means the total number of addresses in the block is 64 (2^6). If we create four subnets, each subnet will have 16 addresses.

1. Let us first find the subnet prefix (subnet mask). We need four subnets, which means we need to add two more 1s to the site prefix. The subnet prefix is then /28.
2. The range for the first subnet is 130.34.12.64/28 to 130.34.12.79/28.
3. The range of the second subnet is 130.34.12.80/28 to 130.34.12.95/28.
4. The range of the third subnet is 130.34.12.96/28 to 130.34.12.111/28.
5. The range of the fourth subnet is 130.34.12.112/28 to 130.34.12.127/28.

Note that we include the prefix for every address we refer to. For the main site the prefix is 26, for the subnets the prefix is 28. Figure 5.15 shows an example of a site using this block with subnetting (we have shown only the subnet addresses for simplicity).

Figure 5.15 *Example 14*

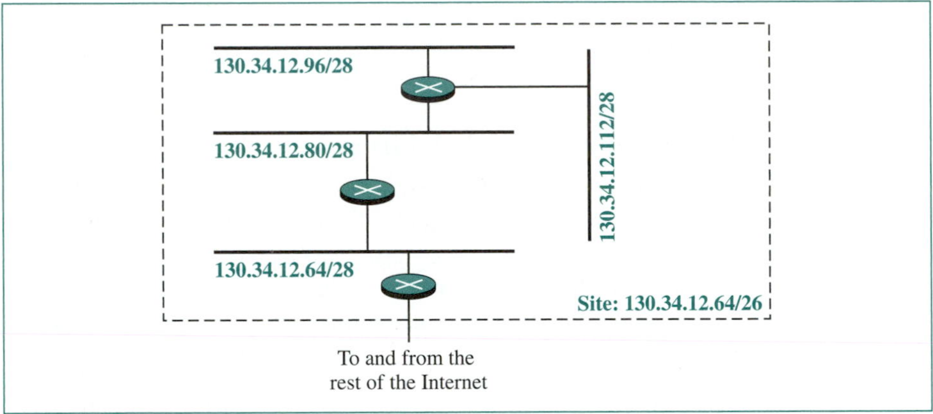

Example 15

An ISP is granted a block of addresses starting with 190.100.0.0/16. The ISP needs to distribute these addresses to three groups of customers as follows:

a. The first group has 64 customers; each needs 256 addresses.
b. The second group has 128 customers; each needs 128 addresses.
c. The third group has 128 customers; each needs 64 addresses.

Design the subblocks and give the slash notation for each subblock. Find out how many addresses are still available after these allocations.

Solution

1. Group 1

   For this group, each customer needs 256 addresses. This means the suffix length is 8 ($2^8 = 256$). The prefix length is then $32 - 8 = 24$. The addresses are:

   1st Customer 190.100.0.0/24 → 190.100.0.255/24
   2nd Customer 190.100.1.0/24 → 190.100.1.255/24
   ⋮
   64th Customer 190.100.63.0/24 → 190.100.63.255/24

   Total = $64 \times 256 = 16{,}384$

2. Group 2

   For this group, each customer needs 128 addresses. This means the suffix length is 7 ($2^7 = 128$). The prefix length is then $32 - 7 = 25$. The addresses are:

   1st Customer 190.100.64.0/25 ➡ 190.100.64.127/25
   2nd Customer 190.100.64.128/25 ➡ 190.100.64.255/25
   ⋮
   128th Customer 190.100.127.128/25 ➡ 190.100.127.255/25

   Total = 128×128 = 16,384

3. Group 3

   For this group, each customer needs 64 addresses. This means the suffix length is 6 ($2^6 = 64$). The prefix length is then $32 - 6 = 26$. The addresses are:

   1st Customer 190.100.128.0/26 ➡ 190.100.128.63/26
   2nd Customer 190.100.128.64/26 ➡ 190.100.128.127/26
   ⋮
   128th Customer 190.100.159.192/26 ➡ 190.100.159.255/26

   Total = 128×64 = 8,192

Number of granted addresses: 65,536
Number of allocated addresses: 40,960
Number of available addresses: 24,576

Supernetting

There is no need for supernetting in classless addressing. (The whole idea of classless addressing was to apply the concept of supernetting in class C to other classes.) In classless addressing, an organization is granted the right size block which means there is no need for supernetting. If an organization is granted a block and later finds it needs a larger block, a new block can be granted and the original block can be recycled.

Migration

One may ask when the idea of classless addressing will be totally implemented. The hope is that every organization will use classless addressing. Those organizations that have already been granted a block in class A, B, or C can use slash notation (/8, /16, /24) or recycle their block and request a block of the appropriate size.

Classless Interdomain Routing (CIDR)

Classless addressing has solved several critical problems associated with classful addressing, but it has created a new one. Routers need to route according to this new architecture. We will see the difficulties and the solution when we discuss routing in Chapter 6.

5.4 KEY TERMS

classless addressing
classless interdomain routing (CIDR)
contiguous mask
default mask
hostid
mask
masking
netid
noncontiguous mask
prefix
slash notation
subnet mask
subnetting
subnetwork
suffix
supernet mask
supernetting
variable-length subnetting

5.5 SUMMARY

- Subnetting divides one large network into several smaller ones.
- Subnetting adds an intermediate level of hierarchy in IP addressing.
- Classes A, B, and C addresses can be subnetted.
- The subnetid defines the physical subnetwork.
- Masking is a process that extracts the network address from an IP address.
- Subnet masking is a process that extracts the subnetwork address from an IP address.
- A network or subnet address is obtained from applying the bit-wise AND operation on the IP address and the mask.
- The concept of special addresses in IP addressing carries over to subnetting.
- A contiguous mask (a string of 1s followed by a string of 0s) is highly recommended.
- In variable length subnetting, more than one subnet mask is applied by the router.
- Supernetting combines several networks into one large one.
- In classless addressing, there are variable-length blocks that belong to no class. The entire address space is divided into blocks based on organization needs.
- The first address and the mask in classless addressing can define the whole block.
- A mask can be expressed in slash notation which is a slash followed by the number of 1s in the mask.

5.6 PRACTICE SET

Multiple-Choice Questions

1. What is the result of ANDing 255 and 15?
   a. 255
   b. 15
   c. 0
   d. undefined
2. What is the result of ANDing 0 and 15?
   a. 255
   b. 15
   c. 0
   d. undefined
3. What is the result of ANDing 254 and 15?
   a. 254
   b. 15
   c. 0
   d. 14
4. What is the result of ANDing 192 and 65?
   a. 192
   b. 65
   c. 0
   d. 64
5. A contiguous subnet mask in class A can have _______ 1s with the remaining bits 0s.
   a. 9
   b. 4
   c. 33
   d. 3
6. A contiguous subnet mask in class B can have _______ 1s with the remaining bits 0s.
   a. 9
   b. 14
   c. 17
   d. 3
7. A contiguous subnet mask in class C can have _______ 1s with the remaining bits 0s.
   a. 10
   b. 25
   c. 12
   d. 7

8. A subnet mask in class A has 14 1s. How many subnets does it define?
   a. 32
   b. 8
   c. 64
   d. 128
9. A subnet mask in class B has 19 1s. How many subnets does it define?
   a. 8
   b. 32
   c. 64
   d. 128
10. A subnet mask in class C has 25 1s. How many subnets does it define?
    a. 2
    b. 8
    c. 16
    d. 0
11. Which one is not a contiguous mask?
    a. 255.255.255.254
    b. 255.255.224.0
    c. 255.148.0.0
    d. 255.248.0.0
12. Which one cannot be a subnet mask for a class A block?
    a. 255.255.255.192
    b. 255.248.0.0
    c. 248.0.0.0
    d. 255.255.128.0
13. Which one cannot be a subnet mask for a class B block?
    a. 255.255.255.192
    b. 255.248.0.0
    c. 255.255.224.0
    d. 255.255.255.129
14. Which one can be a subnet mask for a class C block?
    a. 255.255.255.192
    b. 255.255.224.0
    c. 255.0.0.0
    d. 128.0.0.0
15. Given the IP address 201.14.78.65 and the subnet mask 255.255.255.224, what is the subnet address?
    a. 201.14.78.32
    b. 201.14.78.65
    c. 201.14.78.64
    d. 201.14.78.12

16. Given the IP address 180.25.21.172 and the subnet mask 255.255.192.0, what is the subnet address?
    a. 180.25.21.0
    b. 180.25.0.0
    c. 180.25.8.0
    d. 180.0.0.0
17. Given the IP address 18.250.31.14 and the subnet mask 255.240.0.0, what is the subnet address?
    a. 18.0.0.14
    b. 18.31.0.14
    c. 18.240.0.0
    d. 18.9.0.14
18. The subnet mask for a class C network is 255.255.255.192. How many subnetworks are available?
    a. 2
    b. 4
    c. 8
    d. 192
19. The subnet mask for a class B network is 255.255.224.0. How many subnetworks are available?
    a. 2
    b. 4
    c. 8
    d. 16
20. The subnet mask for a class C network is 255.255.255.248. How many subnetworks are available?
    a. 4
    b. 8
    c. 16
    d. 32
21. What is the supernet mask for a supernet composed of 16 class C addresses?
    a. 255.255.240.16
    b. 255.255.16.0
    c. 255.255.248.0
    d. 255.255.240.0
22. An organization is given 16 class C addresses beginning with X.Y.80.0. What is the supernet mask?
    a. 255.255.64.0
    b. 255.255.240.0
    c. 255.255.255.192
    d. 255.255.192.0

23. A supernet mask has normally __________ 24 1s.
    a. more than
    b. less than
    c. exactly
    d. none of the above
24. A supernet mask is 255.255.248.0. How many class C networks were combined to make this supernet?
    a. 2
    b. 4
    c. 6
    d. 8
25. A supernet mask has 19 1s. How many class C networks were combined to make this supernet?
    a. 2
    b. 16
    c. 32
    d. 64
26. An organization is granted a block of classless addresses with the starting address 199.34.76.64/28. How many addresses are granted?
    a. 8
    b. 16
    c. 32
    d. 64
27. An organization is granted a block of classless addresses with the starting address 199.34.76.128/29. How many addresses are granted?
    a. 8
    b. 16
    c. 32
    d. 64
28. An organization is granted a block of classless addresses with the starting address 199.34.32.0/27. How many addresses are granted?
    a. 8
    b. 16
    c. 32
    d. 64

Exercises

29. In a class A subnet, we know the IP address of one of the hosts and the mask as given below:

    IP Address: 25.34.12.56
    Mask: 255.255.0.0

What is the first address (network address) and the last address (broadcast address) in this subnet?

30. In a class B subnet, we know the IP address of one of the hosts and the mask as given below:

IP Address: 125.134.112.66
Mask: 255.255.224.0

What is the first address (network address) and the last address (broadcast address) in this subnet?

31. In a class C subnet, we know the IP address of one of the hosts and the mask as given below:

IP Address: 182.44.82.16
Mask: 255.255.255.192

What is the first address (network address) and the last address (broadcast address) in this subnet?

32. Find the masks that create the following number of subnets in class A. Assume a contiguous mask.
    a. 2
    b. 6
    c. 30
    d. 62
    e. 122
    f. 250
33. Find the masks that create the following number of subnets in class B. Assume a contiguous mask.
    a. 2
    b. 5
    c. 30
    d. 62
    e. 120
    f. 250
34. Find the masks that create the following number of subnets in class C. Assume a contiguous mask.
    a. 2
    b. 6
    c. 30
    d. 62
    e. 122
    f. 250

35. What is the maximum number of subnets in class A using the following masks?
    a. 255.255.192.0
    b. 255.192.0.0
    c. 255.255.224.0
    d. 255.255.255.0
36. What is the maximum number of subnets in class B using the following masks?
    a. 255.255.192.0
    b. 255.255.0.0
    c. 255.255.224.0
    d. 255.255. 255.0
37. What is the maximum number of subnets in class C using the following masks?
    a. 255.255.255.192
    b. 255.255.255.224
    c. 255.255.255.240
    d. 255.255. 255.0
38. For each of the following subnet masks used in class A, find the number of 1s that define the subnet.
    a. 255.255.192.0
    b. 255.192.0.0
    c. 255.255.224.0
    d. 255.255. 255.0
39. For each of the following subnet masks used in class B, find the number of 1s that define the subnet.
    a. 255.255.192.0
    b. 255.255.0.0
    c. 255.255.224.0
    d. 255.255.255.0
40. For each of the following subnet masks used in class C, find the number of 1s that define the subnet.
    a. 255.255.255.192
    b. 255.255.255.224
    c. 255.255.255.240
    d. 255.255.255.0
41. An organization is granted the block 16.0.0.0 in class A. The administrator wants to create 500 subnets.
    a. Find the subnet mask.
    b. Find the number of addresses in each subnet.
    c. Find the first and the last address in the first subnet.
    d. Find the first and the last address in the last subnet.

42. An organization is granted the block 130.56.0.0 in class B. The administrator wants to create 1024 subnets.
    a. Find the subnet mask.
    b. Find the number of addresses in each subnet.
    c. Find the first and the last address in the first subnet.
    d. Find the first and the last address in the last subnet (subnet 1024).
43. An organization is granted the block 211.17.180.0 in class C. The administrator wants to create 32 subnets.
    a. Find the subnet mask.
    b. Find the number of addresses in each subnet.
    c. Find the first and the last address in the first subnet.
    d. Find the first and the last address in the last subnet (subnet 32).
44. Write the following masks in the */n* format:
    a. 255.255.255.0
    b. 255.0.0.0
    c. 255.255.224.0
    d. 255.255.240.0
45. Find the range of addresses in the following blocks:
    a. 123.56.77.32/29
    b. 200.17.21.128/27
    c. 17.34.16.0/23
    d. 180.34.64.64/30
46. An ISP is granted a block of addresses starting with 150.80.0.0/16. The ISP wants to distribute these blocks to customers as follows:
    a. The first group has 200 medium-size businesses, each needs 128 addresses.
    b. The second group has 400 small businesses, each needs 16 addresses.
    c. The third group has 2048 households, each needs 4 addresses.

    Design the subblocks and give the slash notation for each subblock. Find out how many addresses are still available after these allocations.
47. One way to find the result of ANDing two bytes is to first write each as a sum of numbers written as powers of two (128, 64, 32, 16, 8, 4, 2, and 1) and then find and add the common ones. For example to find the result of (240 AND 84), which is 80, we can write

    240: 128 + **64** + 32 + **16**
    84: **64** + **16** + 4

    The common numbers are 64 and 16; the result is their sum, or 80.
    Find the result of the following AND operations:
    a. 192 AND 122
    b. 224 AND 191
    c. 254 AND 224
    d. 128 AND 78

48. One common operation on a mask is the complement or NOT operation. The NOT operation changes every 1 to 0 and every 0 to 1. In dotted-decimal notation the NOT operation subtracts every byte from 255. For example, NOT (255.255.224.0) is 0.0.31.255. Use the NOT operation on the following masks:
    a. 255.255.128.0
    b. 255.255.255.0
    c. 255.255.0.0
    d. 255.192.0.0
49. To find the number of addresses in a subnet, supernet, or block, we can find the complement of the mask (NOT operation) and then add 1 to the result. Find the number of addresses using the following masks.
    a. 255.255.128.0
    b. 255.255.255.0
    c. 255.255.0.0
    d. 255.192.0.0
50. Another common operation on addresses is the OR operation. In binary notation x OR 1 = 1 and x OR 0 = x. In dotted-decimal notation X OR 255 = 255 and X OR 0 = X. However, if the corresponding byte in the mask is not 255 or 0, we must use the binary operation to find the result. Find the result of the OR operation on the following:
    a. 14 OR 255
    b. 14 OR 0
    c. 14 OR 192
    d. 192 OR 128
51. Find a procedure to find the result of the OR operation similar to what we did in Exercise 47 for the AND operation.
52. When masking is contiguous, the combination of the OR and NOT operations can find the last address in a block if the first address and the mask are given:

    Last address = (First address) OR (NOT mask).

    Find the last address in each of the following blocks or subblocks using the above formula:
    a. 123.56.77.32/29
    b. 200.17.21.128/27
    c. 17.34.16.0/23
    d. 180.34.64.64/30

Programming Exercises

53. Given an address and a prefix length, write a function that returns the first address in the block.
54. Given an address and a prefix length write a function that returns the last address in the block.
55. Given an address and a prefix length write a function that returns the number of addresses in the block.
56. Given an address number (N) write a function that determines if the address can be used as the beginning address of a block with N addresses.

CHAPTER 6

Delivery and Routing of IP Packets

This chapter describes the delivery and routing of IP packets to their final destinations. By **delivery,** we mean the physical forwarding of the packets. Concepts such as connectionless and connection-oriented services, and direct and indirect delivery are discussed. By **routing,** we mean finding the route (next hop) for a datagram. We discuss routing methods, types of routing, the routing table, and the routing module.

6.1 CONNECTION-ORIENTED VERSUS CONNECTIONLESS SERVICES

Delivery of a packet in the network layer is accomplished using either a connection-oriented or a connectionless network service.

In a connection-oriented situation, the network layer protocol first makes a connection with the network layer protocol at the remote site before sending a packet. When the connection is established, a sequence of packets from the same source to the same destination can be sent one after another. In this case, there is a relationship between packets. They are sent on the same path in sequential order. A packet is logically connected to the packet traveling before it and to the packet traveling after it. When all packets of a message have been delivered, the connection is terminated.

In a connection-oriented protocol, the decision about the route of a sequence of packets with the same source and destination addresses can be made only once, when the connection is established. Routers do not recalculate the route for each individual packet.

In a connectionless situation, the network layer protocol treats each packet independently, with each packet having no relationship to any other packet. The packets in a message may or may not travel the same path to their destination.

The IP protocol is a connectionless protocol. It is designed this way because IP, as an internetwork protocol, may have to deliver the packets through several heterogeneous networks. If IP were to be connection-oriented, all of the networks in the internet should also be connection-oriented, which is not the case.

6.2 DIRECT VERSUS INDIRECT DELIVERY

The delivery of a packet to its final destination is accomplished using two different methods of delivery: direct and indirect.

Direct Delivery

In a **direct delivery,** the final destination of the packet is a host connected to the same physical network as the deliverer. Direct delivery occurs when the source and destination of the packet are located on the same physical network or if the delivery is between the last router and the destination host (see Figure 6.1).

Figure 6.1 *Direct delivery*

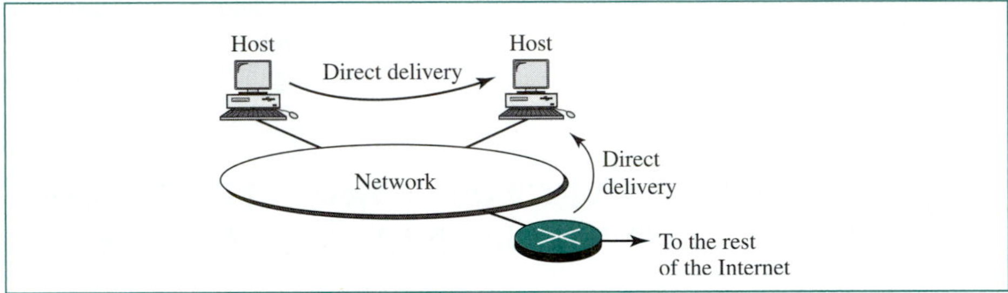

The sender can easily determine if the delivery is direct. It can extract the network address of the destination packet (setting the hostid part to all 0s) and compare this address with the addresses of the networks to which it is connected. If a match is found, the delivery is direct.

In direct delivery, the sender uses the destination IP address to find the destination physical address. The IP software then delivers the destination IP address with the destination physical address to the data link layer for actual delivery. This process is called *mapping the IP address to the physical address*. Although this mapping can be done by finding a match in a table, we will see in Chapter 8 that a protocol called address resolution protocol (ARP) dynamically maps an IP address to the corresponding physical address.

Indirect Delivery

If the destination host is not on the same network as the deliverer, the packet is delivered indirectly. In an **indirect delivery,** the packet goes from router to router until it reaches the one connected to the same physical network as its final destination (see Figure 6.2).

Note that a delivery always involves one direct delivery but zero or more indirect deliveries. Note also that the last delivery is always a direct delivery.

Figure 6.2 *Indirect delivery*

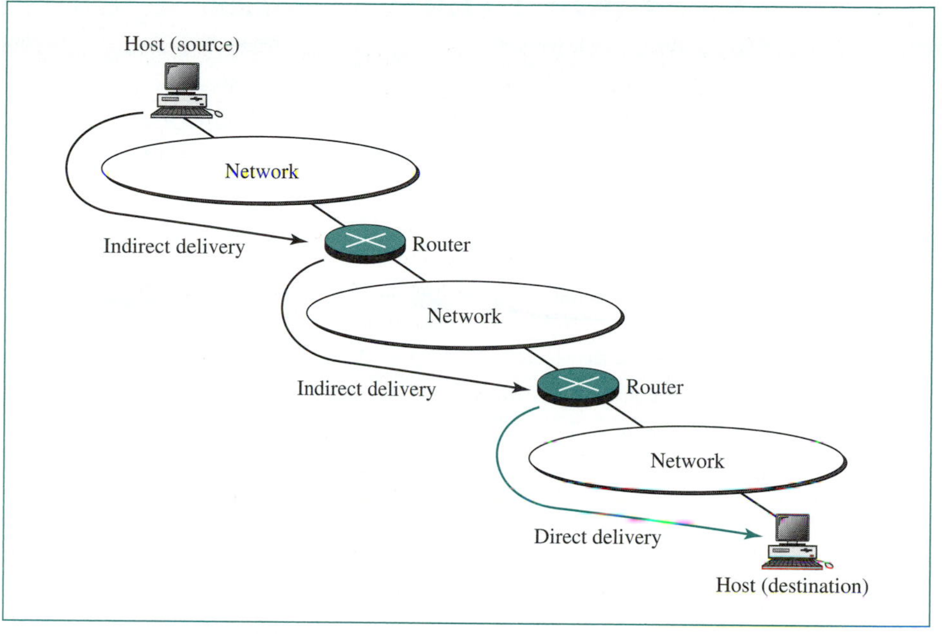

In an indirect delivery, the sender uses the destination IP address and a routing table to find the IP address of the next router to which the packet should be delivered. The sender then uses the ARP protocol to find the physical address of the next router. Note that in direct delivery, the address mapping is between the IP address of the final destination and the physical address of the final destination. In an indirect delivery, the address mapping is between the IP address of the next router and the physical address of the next router.

6.3 ROUTING METHODS

Routing requires a host or a router to have a routing table. When a host has a packet to send or when a router has received a packet to be forwarded, it looks at this table to find the route to the final destination. However, this simple solution is impossible today in an internetwork such as the Internet because the number of entries in the routing table make table lookups inefficient.

Several techniques can make the size of the routing table manageable and handle issues such as security. We will discuss these methods here.

Next-Hop Routing

One technique to reduce the contents of a routing table is called **next-hop routing.** In this technique, the routing table holds only the address of the next hop instead of holding information about the complete route. The entries of a routing table must be consistent with each other. Figure 6.3 shows how routing tables can be simplified using this technique.

Figure 6.3 *Next-hop routing*

Routing table for host A

Destination	Route
Host B	R1, R2, Host B

Routing table for R1

Destination	Route
Host B	R2, Host B

Routing table for R2

Destination	Route
Host B	Host B

a. Routing tables based on route

Host A

R1

R2

Host B

Network

Network

Network

Routing table for host A

Destination	Next Hop
Host B	R1

Routing table for R1

Destination	Next Hop
Host B	R2

Routing table for R2

Destination	Next Hop
Host B	—

b. Routing tables based on next hop

Network-Specific Routing

A second technique to reduce the routing table and simplify the searching process is called **network-specific routing.** Here, instead of having an entry for every host connected to the same physical network, we have only one entry to define the address of the network itself. In other words, we treat all hosts connected to the same network as one single entity. For example, if 1000 hosts are attached to the same network, only one entry exists in the routing table instead of 1000. Figure 6.4 shows the concept.

Figure 6.4 *Network-specific routing*

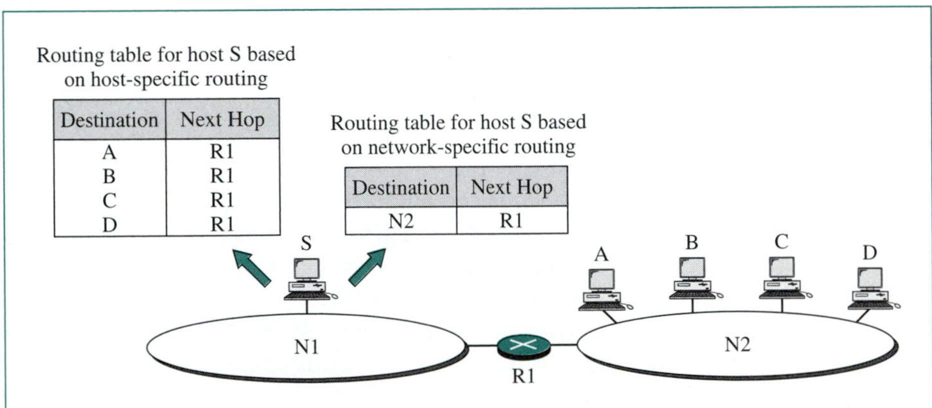

Routing table for host S based on host-specific routing

Destination	Next Hop
A	R1
B	R1
C	R1
D	R1

Routing table for host S based on network-specific routing

Destination	Next Hop
N2	R1

Host-Specific Routing

In **host-specific routing,** the destination host address is given in the routing table. The idea of host-specific routing is the inverse of network-specific routing. Here efficiency is sacrificed for other advantages: Although it is not efficient to put the host address in the routing table, there are occasions in which the administrator wants to have more control over routing. For example, in Figure 6.5 if the administrator wants all packets arriving for host B delivered to router R3 instead of R1, one single entry in the routing table of host A can explicitly define the route.

Figure 6.5 *Host-specific routing*

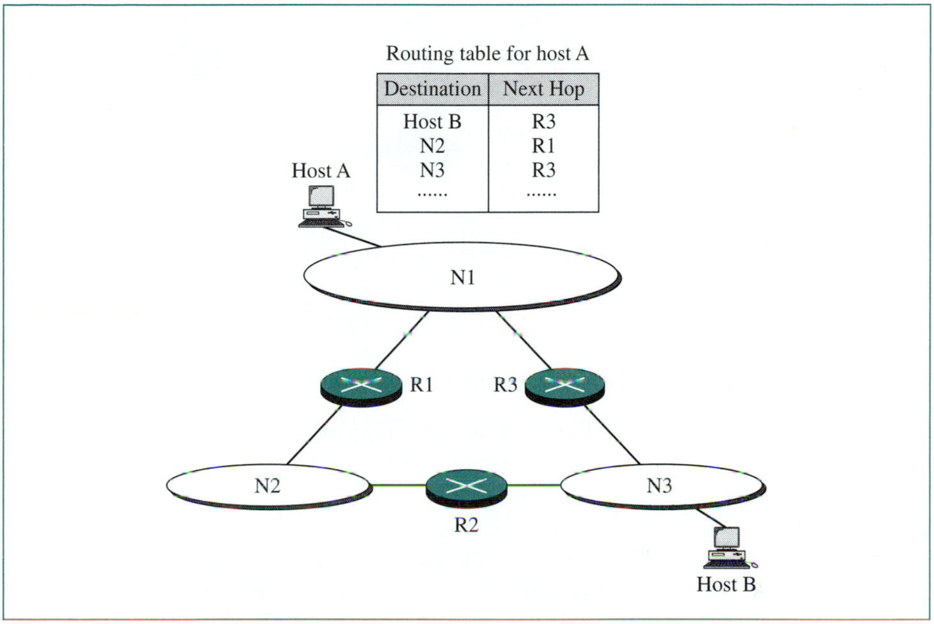

Routing table for host A

Destination	Next Hop
Host B	R3
N2	R1
N3	R3
......	......

Host-specific routing is used for specific purposes such as checking the route or providing security measures.

Default Routing

Another technique to simplify routing is **default routing.** In Figure 6.6 host A is connected to a network with two routers. Router R1 is used to route the packets to hosts connected to network N2. However, for the rest of the Internet, router R2 is used. So instead of listing all networks in the entire Internet, host A can just have one entry called the *default* (network address 0.0.0.0).

6.4 STATIC VERSUS DYNAMIC ROUTING

A host or a router keeps a routing table, with an entry for each destination, to route IP packets. The routing table can be either static or dynamic.

Figure 6.6 *Default routing*

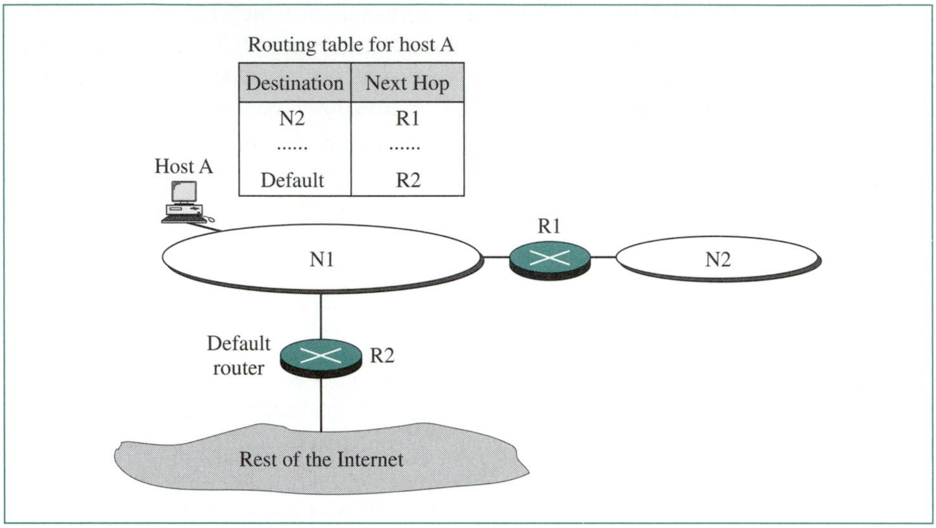

Routing table for host A

Destination	Next Hop
N2	R1
......	......
Default	R2

Static Routing Table

A **static routing table** contains information entered manually. The administrator enters the route for each destination into the table. When a table is created, it cannot update automatically when there is a change in the Internet. The table must be manually altered by the administrator.

A static routing table can be used in a small internet that does not change very often, or in an experimental internet for troubleshooting. It is not good strategy to use a static routing table in a big internet such as the Internet.

Dynamic Routing Table

A **dynamic routing table** is updated periodically using one of the dynamic routing protocols such as RIP, OSPF, or BGP (see Chapter 13). Whenever there is a change in the Internet, such as a shutdown of a router or breaking of a link, the dynamic routing protocols update all of the tables in the routers (and eventually in the host).

The routers in a big internet such as the Internet need to be updated dynamically for efficient delivery of the IP packets. We will discuss in detail the three dynamic routing protocols in Chapter 13.

6.5 ROUTING TABLE AND ROUTING MODULE

In this section, we discuss a simplified routing module. The module, presented in pseudocode, basically shows how the router can extract the outgoing interface for the packet and the next-hop address if the delivery is indirect. The next-hop address is needed, as we will see in Chapter 7, to find the physical address of the next router to which the packet should be delivered.

When looking for the route, the router must first check for direct delivery, then host-specific delivery, then network-specific delivery, and finally default delivery. This hierarchical strategy can be implemented in the routing module or in the routing table. To make our routing module as simple as possible, we have used a routing table that is organized according to the above hierarchical scheme.

The module receives an IP packet from the IP processing module (see Chapter 8). The routing module consults the routing table to find the best route for the packet. After the route is found, the packet is sent along with the next-hop address to the fragmentation module (see Chapter 8), which makes a decision on fragmentation. See Figure 6.7.

Figure 6.7 *Routing module and routing table*

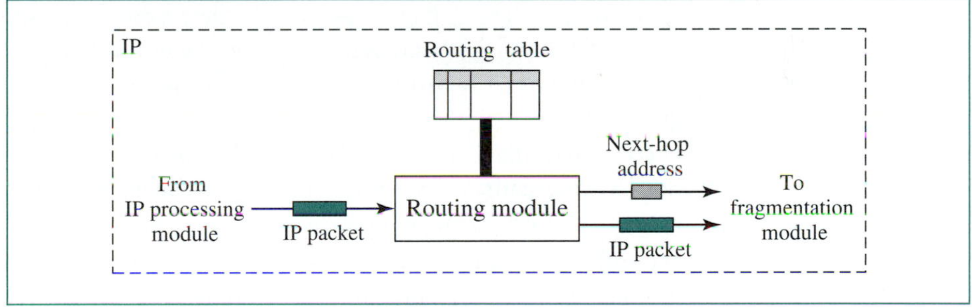

Routing Table

As mentioned previously, our routing table is organized in a hierarchical scheme with direct-delivery entries first, host-specific delivery entries next, network-specific entries third, and the default delivery entry last.

The routing table usually has these seven fields: mask, destination address, next-hop address, flags, reference count, use, and interface (see Figure 6.8).

Figure 6.8 *Fields in a routing table*

Mask	Destination address	Next-hop address	Flags	Reference count	Use	Interface
255.0.0.0	124.0.0.0	145.6.7.23	UG	4	20	m2
....	....		....	....	....	....
....	....	....	....	....	....	....

- **Mask.** This field defines the mask applied to the destination IP address of the packet to find the network or subnetwork address of the destination. In host-specific routing, the mask is 255.255.255.255. In default routing, the mask is 0.0.0.0. In an unsubnetted network, the mask is the default mask (255.0.0.0, 255.255.0.0, or 255.255.255.0 for class A, B, or C, respectively).

- **Destination address.** This field defines either the destination host address (host-specific address) or the destination network address (network-specific) address. A host-specific destination address gives the full destination address, netid and hostid. A network-specific address gives only the address of the network to which the destination entity is connected. The netid is specific, but the hostid is all 0s.
- **Next-hop address.** This field defines the address of the next-hop router to which the packet is delivered.
- **Flags.** This field defines up to five flags. Flags are on/off switches that signify either presence or absence. The five flags are U (up), G (gateway), H (host-specific), D (added by redirection), and M (modified by redirection).
    a. **U (Up).** The U flag indicates the router is up and running. If this flag is not present, it means that the router is down. The packet cannot be forwarded and is discarded.
    b. **G (Gateway).** The G flag means that the destination is in another network. The packet should be delivered to the next-hop router for delivery (indirect delivery). When this flag is missing, it means the destination is in this network (direct delivery).
    c. **H (Host-specific).** The H flag indicates that the entry in the destination field is a host-specific address. When it is missing, it means that the address is only the network address of the destination.
    d. **D (Added by redirection).** The D flag indicates that routing information for this destination has been added to the host routing table by a redirection message from ICMP. We will discuss redirection and the ICMP protocol in Chapter 9.
    e. **M (Modified by redirection).** The M flag indicates that the routing information for this destination has been modified by a redirection message from ICMP. We will discuss redirection and the ICMP protocol in Chapter 9.
- **Reference count.** This field gives the number of users that are using this route at any moment. For example, if five people at the same time are connecting to the same host from this router, the value of this column is 5.
- **Use.** This field shows the number of packets transmitted through this router for the corresponding destination.
- **Interface.** This field shows the name of the interface.

Routing Module

The routing module receives an IP packet from the IP processing module (see Chapter 8). In our example, the routing module goes from entry to entry trying to find a match. When it finds a match, it quits. Because the routing table is hierarchically organized, it is guaranteed that the module first looks for a direct-delivery match. If no match is found, the module looks for a host-specific delivery, and so on.

Routing Module

1. For each entry in the routing table
    1. Apply the mask to packet destination address
    2. If (the result matches the value in the destination field)
        1. If (the G flag is present)
            1. Use the next-hop entry in the table as next-hop address
        2. If (the G flag is missing)
            1. Use packet destination address (direct delivery)
        3. Send packet to fragmentation module with next-hop address
        4. Stop
2. If no match is found, send an ICMP error message
3. Stop

Some Examples

In this section we give some examples of routing. Figure 6.9 is used for Examples 1, 2, and 3. These three examples also use the routing table shown in Table 6.1.

Figure 6.9 *Configuration for routing examples*

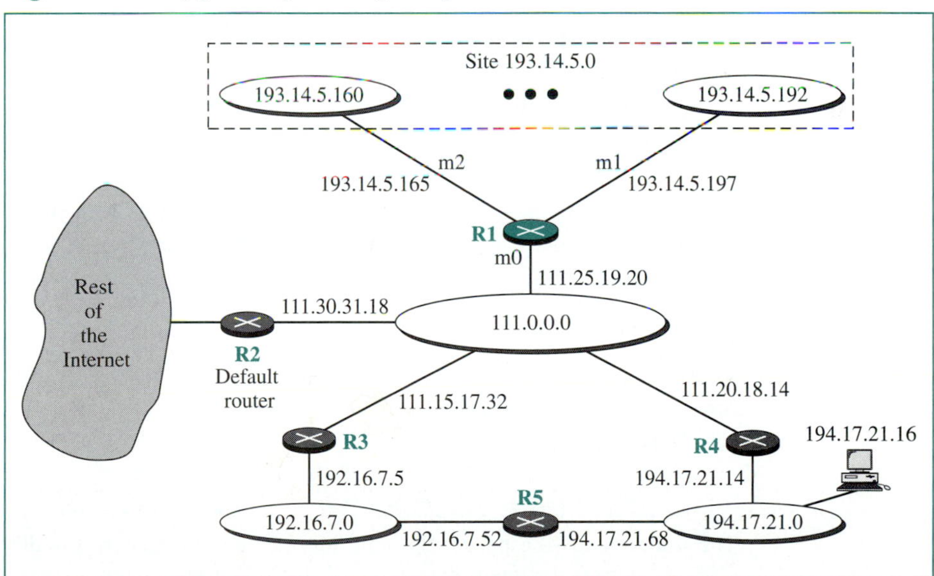

Table 6.1 *Routing table for router R1 in Figure 6.9*

Mask	*Destination*	*Next Hop*	*F.*	*R.C.*	*U.*	*I.*
255.0.0.0	111.0.0.0	-	U	0	0	m0
255.255.255.224	193.14.5.160	-	U	0	0	m2
255.255.255.224	193.14.5.192	-	U	0	0	m1
....	....	....	....	....	...	...
....	....	....	....	....	...	...
....	....	....	....	....	...	...
255.255.255.255	194.17.21.16	111.20.18.14	UGH	0	0	m0
255.255.255.0	192.16.7.0	111.15.17.32	UG	0	0	m0
255.255.255.0	194.17.21.0	111.20.18.14	UG	0	0	m0
0.0.0.0	0.0.0.0	111.30.31.18	UG	0	0	m0

Example 1

Router R1 receives 500 packets for destination 192.16.7.14; the algorithm applies the masks row by row to the destination address until a match (with the value in the second column) is found:

1. Direct delivery
   a. 192.16.7.14 & 255.0.0.0 ➡ 192.0.0.0 no match
   b. 192.16.7.14 & 255.255.255.224 ➡ 192.16.7.0 no match
   c. 192.16.7.14 & 255.255.255.224 ➡ 192.16.7.0 no match
2. Host-specific
   a. 192.16.7.14 & 255.255.255.255 ➡ 192.16.7.14 no match
3. Network-specific
   a. 192.16.7.14 & 255.255.255.0 ➡ 192.16.7.0 **match**

The router sends the packet through interface m0 along with the next-hop IP address (111.15.17.32) to the fragmentation module for further processing. It increments the use field by 500 and the reference count field by 1.

Example 2

Router R1 receives 100 packets for destination 193.14.5.176; the algorithm applies the masks row by row to the destination address until a match is found:

1. Direct delivery
   a. 193.14.5.176 & 255.0.0.0 ➡ 193.0.0.0 no match
   b. 193.14.5.176 & 255.255.255.224 ➡ 193.14.5.160 **match**

The router sends the packet through interface m2 along with the destination IP address (193.14.5.176) to the fragmentation module for further processing. It increments the use field by 100 and the reference count field by 1.

Example 3

Router R1 receives 20 packets for destination 200.34.12.34; the algorithm applies the masks row by row to the destination address until a match is found:

1. Direct delivery
   a. 200.34.12.34 & 255.0.0.0 ➡ 200.0.0.0 no match
   b. 200.34.12.34 & 255.255.255.224 ➡ 200.34.12.32 no match
   c. 200.34.12.34 & 255.255.255.224 ➡ 200.34.12.32 no match
2. Host-specific
   a. 200.34.12.34 & 255.255.255.255 ➡ 200.34.12.34 no match
3. Network-specific
   a. 200.34.12.34 & 255.255.255.0 ➡ 200.34.12.0 no match
   b. 200.34.12.34 & 255.255.255.0 ➡ 200.34.12.0 no match
4. Default
   a. 200.34.12.34 & 0.0.0.0 ➡ 0.0.0.0. **match**

The router sends the packet through interface m0 along with the next-hop IP address (111.30.31.18) to the fragmentation module for further processing. It increments the use field by 20 and the reference count field by 1.

Example 4

Make the routing table for router R1 in Figure 6.10.

Figure 6.10 *Topology for Example 4*

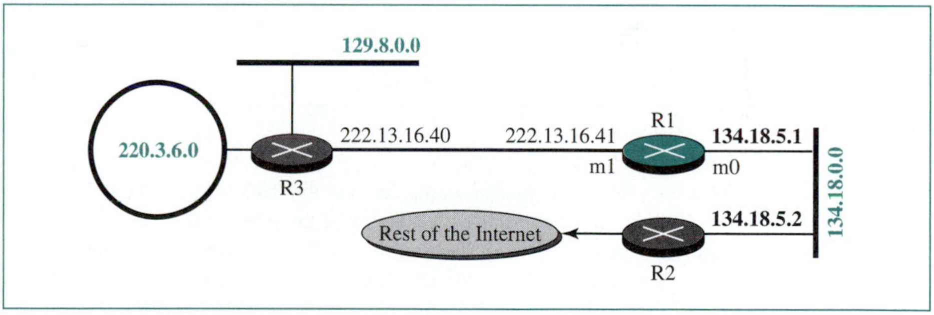

Solution

We know that there are three explicit destination networks, two class B and one class C with no subnetting (default masks). There is also one access to the rest of the Internet (default route). This means that our routing table has four rows. The routing table is shown in Table 6.2. The interface to the network 134.18.0.0 is m0 and there is no next-hop address. Access to the rest of the Internet is through interface m0 and the next-hop address is 134.18.5.2. Access to network 129.8.0.0 is through interface m1 and the next-hop address is 222.13.16.40. Access to network 220.3.6.0 is through interface m1 and the next-hop address is 222.13.16.40.

Table 6.2 *Routing table for Example 4*

Mask	*Destination*	*Next Hop*	*F.*	*R.C.*	*U.*	*I.*
255.255.0.0	134.18.0.0	---	U	0	0	m0
255.255.0.0	129.8.0.0	222.13.16.40	UG	0	0	m1
255.255.255.0	220.3.6.0	222.13.16.40	UG	0	0	m1
0.0.0.0	0.0.0.0	134.18.5.2	UG	0	0	m0

Example 5

Make the routing table for router R1 in Figure 6.11.

Figure 6.11 *Topology for Example 5*

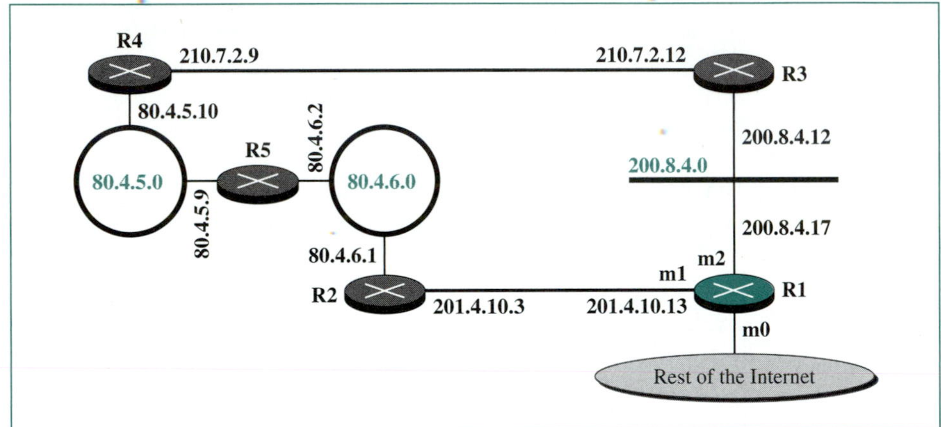

Solution

We know that there are five networks here, but two of them are point-to-point with no hosts and need not be in the routing table. The other three networks must be in the table. There is also an entry for the default. Examination of the figure shows that some information is missing. For example, we do not know the IP address of the default router. Also, there are two paths to networks 80.4.5.0 (and 80.4.6.0); one is through router R2 and one is through router R3. We do not know which route is optimal; this subject is covered in Chapter 13. For the moment, we enter both paths in the routing table (see Table 6.3).

Table 6.3 *Routing table for Example 5*

Mask	*Destination*	*Next Hop*	*F.*	*R.C.*	*U.*	*I.*
255.255.255.0	200.8.4.0	----	U	0	0	m2
255.255.255.0	80.4.5.0	201.4.10.3 or 200.8.4.12	UG	0	0	m1 or m2
255.255.255.0	80.4.6.0	201.4.10.3 or 200.4.8.12	UG	0	0	m1 or m2
0.0.0.0	0.0.0.0	???????????	UG	0	0	m0

Example 6

The routing table for router R1 is given in Table 6.4. Draw its topology.

Table 6.4 *Routing table for Example 6*

Mask	*Destination*	*Next Hop*	*F.*	*R.C.*	*U.*	*I.*
255.255.0.0	110.70.0.0	-	U	0	0	m0
255.255.0.0	180.14.0.0	-	U	0	0	m2
255.255.0.0	190.17.0.0	-	U	0	0	m1
255.255.0.0	130.4.0.0	190.17.6.5	UG	0	0	m1
255.255.0.0	140.6.0.0	180.14.2.5	UG	0	0	m2
0.0.0.0	0.0.0.0	110.70.4.6	UG	0	0	m0

Solution

We know some facts but don't have all of them for a definite topology. We know that there are three networks directly connected to router R1. We know that there are two networks indirectly connected to R1. There must be at least three other routers involved (see next-hop column). We know to which networks these routers are connected by looking at their IP addresses. So we can put them at their appropriate places. We know that one router is connected to the rest of the Internet (it is the default router). But there is some missing information. We do not know if network 130.4.0.0 is directly connected to router R2 or through a point-to-point network (WAN) and another router. We do not know if network 140.6.0.0 is connected to router R3 directly or through a point-to-point network (WAN) and another router. Point-to-point networks normally do not have an entry in the routing table because no hosts are connected to them. Figure 6.12 shows our guessed topology.

Figure 6.12 *Guessed topology for Example 6*

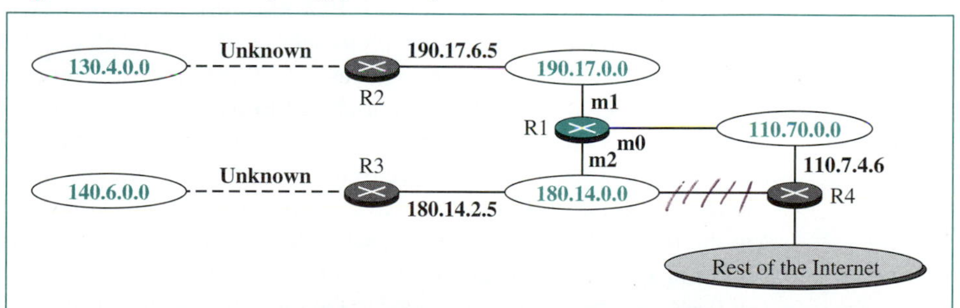

6.6 CLASSLESS ADDRESSING: CIDR

So far, the discussion on routing tables concentrated on classful addressing. Now we need to consider classless addressing and Classless InterDomain Routing (CIDR). The shift to classless addressing requires changes to the routing table organization and routing algorithms.

Routing Table Size

When we use classful addressing, there is only one entry in the routing table for each site outside the organization. The entry defines the site even if that site is subnetted. When a packet arrives at the router, the router checks the corresponding entry and forwards the packet accordingly.

When we use classless addressing, the number of entries in the router's table can either decrease or increase. It can decrease if the block of addresses assigned to an organization is larger than the block in classful addressing. For example, instead of having four entries for an organization that creates a supernet from four class C blocks, we can have one entry in classless routing.

It is more likely, however, that the number of routing table entries will increase. This is because the intent of classless addressing is to divide up the blocks of class A and class B addresses. For example, instead of assigning over 16 million addresses to just one organization, the addresses can be portioned out to many many organizations. The problem is that whereas there was just one routing table entry for the class A address, now there are many entries in classless addressing. For example, if a class B block (over 64,000 addresses) is divided up between 60 organizations, there are 60 routing table entries where before there was just one.

Hierarchical Routing

To solve the problem of gigantic routing tables, we create a sense of hierarchy in the Internet architecture and routing tables. In Chapter 1, we mentioned that the Internet today has a sense of hierarchy. We said that the Internet is divided into international and national ISPs. National ISPs are divided into regional ISPs, and regional ISPs are divided into local ISPs. If the routing table has a sense of hierarchy like the Internet architecture, the routing table can decrease in size.

Let us take the case of a local ISP. A local ISP can be assigned a single, but large block of addresses with a certain prefix length. The local ISP can divide this block into smaller blocks of different sizes, and assign these to individual users and organizations, both large and small. If the block assigned to the local ISP is A.B.C.D/*N*, the ISP can create blocks of E.F.G.H/*M*, where *M* may vary for each customer and is greater than *N*.

How does this reduce the size of the routing table? The rest of the Internet does not have to be aware of this division. All customers of the local ISP are defined as A.B.C.D/*N* to the rest of the Internet. Every packet destined for one of the addresses in this large block is routed to the local ISP. There is only one entry in every router in the world for all of these customers. They all belong to the same group. Of course, inside the local ISP, the router must recognize the subblocks and route the packet to the destined customer. If one of the customers is a large organization, it also can create another level of hierarchy by subnetting and dividing its subblock into smaller subblocks (or subsubblocks). In classless routing, the levels of hierarchy are unlimited so long as we follow the rules of classless addressing.

Geographical Routing

To decrease the size of the routing table even further, we need to extend hierarchical routing to include geographical routing. We must divide the entire address space into a few large blocks. We assign a block to North America, a block to Europe, a block to Asia, a block to Africa, and so on. The routers of ISPs outside of Europe will have only one entry for packets to Europe in their routing tables. The routers of ISPs outside of North America will have only one entry for packets to North America in their routing tables. And so on. Part of this idea has already been implemented for class C addressing. But, for real efficiency, all of classes A and B need to be recycled and reassigned.

Routing Table Search Algorithms

The algorithms that search the routing table must also be changed to make classless routing more efficient. This includes the algorithms that update routing algorithms. We will discuss this updating issue in Chapter 13.

Searching in Classful Addressing

In classful addressing, the routing table is organized as a list. However, to make searching easier, the routing table can be divided into three buckets (areas), one for each class. When the packet arrives, the router applies the default mask (which is inherent in the address itself) to find the corresponding bucket (A, B, or C). The bucket then searches the corresponding bucket instead of the whole table.

> In classful addressing, each address has self-contained information that facilitates routing table searching.

Searching in Classless Addressing

In classless addressing, we can also use buckets; specifically, 32 buckets, one for each prefix length. However, the problem is that there is no self-contained information in the destination address to help the router decide which bucket to search. The simplest, but not the most efficient, method is called the **longest match.** The router first tries to use the longest prefix (/32). If the destination address is found in this bucket, the search is complete (this bucket is for host-specific routing). If the address is not found, the bucket for the next prefix (/31) is searched. And so on. It is obvious that this type of search takes a long time; on average, 16 buckets must be searched.

The solution is to change the data structure used for searching. Instead of using a list, use other data structures (such as a tree or a binary tree). One of the candidates is a trie (a special kind of tree). However, this discussion is beyond the scope of this book.

> In classless addressing, there is no self-contained information in the destination address to facilitate routing table searching.

6.7 KEY TERMS

classful addressing
classless addressing
Classless InterDomain Routing (CIDR)
connectionless service
connection-oriented service
default mask
default routing
delivery
destination address
direct delivery
dynamic routing
dynamic routing table
gateway flag
geographical routing
hierarchical routing
host-specific flag
host-specific routing
indirect delivery
IP
IP address
mask
modified by redirection flag
network-specific routing
next-hop address
next-hop routing
physical address
reference count
routing
routing table
search algorithm
static routing
static routing table
up flag

6.8 SUMMARY

- The IP protocol is a connectionless protocol. Every packet is independent and has no relationship to any other packet.
- The delivery of a packet is called direct if the deliverer (host or router) and the destination are on the same network.
- The delivery of a packet is called indirect if the deliverer (host or router) and the destination are on different networks.
- Every host or router has a routing table to route IP packets.
- In next-hop routing, instead of a complete list of the stops the packet must make, only the address of the next hop is listed in the routing table.
- In network-specific routing, all hosts on a network share one entry in the routing table.
- In host-specific routing, the full IP address of a host is given in the routing table.

- In default routing, a router is assigned to receive all packets with no match in the routing table.
- A static routing table's entries are updated manually by an administrator.
- A dynamic routing table's entries are updated automatically by a routing protocol.
- The routing table can consist of seven fields: a mask, a destination address, a next-hop address, flags, a reference count, a use, and an interface.
- The routing module applies the mask, row by row, to the received destination address until a match is found.
- Classless addressing requires hierarchical and geographical routing to prevent immense routing tables.
- Search algorithms for classful addressing are not efficient for classless addressing.

6.9 PRACTICE SET

Multiple-Choice Questions

1. In _______ delivery, both the deliverer of the IP packet and the destination are on the same network.
   a. a connectionless
   b. a connection-oriented
   c. a direct
   d. an indirect
2. In _______ delivery, the deliverer of the IP packet and the destination are on different networks.
   a. a connectionless
   b. a connection-oriented
   c. a direct
   d. an indirect
3. In _______ delivery, packets of a message are logically connected to one another.
   a. a connectionless
   b. a connection-oriented
   c. a direct
   d. an indirect
4. In _______ delivery, a packet is not connected to any other packet.
   a. a connectionless
   b. a connection-oriented
   c. a direct
   d. an indirect

5. When a direct delivery is made, both the deliverer and receiver have the same _______.
   a. routing table
   b. IP address
   c. hostid
   d. netid
6. When an indirect delivery is made, the deliverer and receiver have _______.
   a. the same IP address
   b. different netids
   c. the same netid
   d. none of the above
7. In _______ routing, the full IP address of a destination is given in the routing table.
   a. next-hop
   b. network-specific
   c. host-specific
   d. default
8. In _______ routing, the mask and destination addresses are both 0.0.0.0 in the routing table.
   a. next-hop
   b. network-specific
   c. host-specific
   d. default
9. In _______ routing, the destination address is a network address in the routing table.
   a. next-hop
   b. network-specific
   c. host-specific
   d. default
10. In _______ routing, the routing table holds the address of just the next hop instead of complete route information.
    a. next-hop
    b. network-specific
    c. host-specific
    d. default
11. For a direct delivery, the _______ flag is missing.
    a. up
    b. gateway
    c. host-specific
    d. added by redirection

12. The _______ flag indicates the availability of a router.
    a. up
    b. gateway
    c. host-specific
    d. added by redirection
13. The _______ flag indicates that already existing information in the routing table has been modified by a redirection message.
    a. gateway
    b. host-specific
    c. modified by redirection
    d. added by redirection
14. The _______ flag indicates that the entry in the destination column is a host-specific address.
    a. gateway
    b. host-specific
    c. modified by redirection
    d. added by redirection
15. The _______ flag indicates that a redirection message has added a new entry to the routing table.
    a. gateway
    b. host-specific
    c. modified by redirection
    d. added by redirection
16. The _______ column in the routing table indicates the number of packets transmitted through the router for the corresponding destination.
    a. destination
    b. reference count
    c. use
    d. interface

Exercises

17. A host with IP address 137.23.56.23 sends a packet to a host with IP address 137.23.67.9. Is the delivery direct or indirect? Assume no subnetting.
18. A host with IP address 137.23.56.23 sends a packet to a host with IP address 142.3.6.9. Is the delivery direct or indirect? Assume no subnetting.
19. A router with IP address 109.34.56.8 sends a packet to a host with IP address 202.34.8.9. Is the delivery direct or indirect? Assume no subnetting.
20. A host with IP address 131.23.56.23 sends a packet to a host with IP address 131.23.67.9. Is the delivery direct or indirect if there is no subnetting? Can the delivery be indirect if there is subnetting?

21. Using Table 6.1, determine the next-hop address if router R1 receives a packet destined for 111.45.32.16.
22. Using Table 6.1, determine the next-hop address if router R1 receives a packet destined for 192.16.7.31.
23. Using Table 6.1, determine the next-hop address if router R1 receives a packet destined for 194.17.21.45.
24. Using Table 6.1, determine the next-hop address if router R1 receives a packet destined for 220.7.14.7.
25. Using Table 6.1, determine the next-hop address if router R1 receives a packet destined for 193.14.5.165.
26. Using Table 6.1, determine the next-hop address if router R1 receives a packet destined for 193.14.5.196.
27. Using Table 6.1, determine the next-hop address if router R1 receives a packet destined for 115.7.3.4.
28. Using Table 6.1, determine the next-hop address if router R1 receives a packet destined for 191.61.22.7.
29. Using Table 6.1, determine the next-hop address if router R1 receives a packet destined for 189.73.43.23.
30. Show the routing table for router R2 in Figure 6.9.
31. Show the routing table for router R3 in Figure 6.9.
32. Show the routing table for router R4 in Figure 6.9.
33. Show the routing table for router R5 in Figure 6.9.
34. Show the routing table for router R2 in Figure 6.10.
35. Show the routing table for router R3 in Figure 6.10.
36. Show the routing table for router R2 in Figure 6.11.
37. Show the routing table for router R3 in Figure 6.11.
38. Show the routing table for router R4 in Figure 6.11.
39. Show the routing table for router R5 in Figure 6.11.
40. Find the topology of the network if Table 6.5 is the routing table for router R1.

Table 6.5 *Routing table for Exercise 40*

Mask	*Destination*	*Next Hop*	*F.*	*R.C.*	*U.*	*I.*
255.255.192.0	145.23.129.7	----	U	0	0	m0
255.255.255.224	202.14.17.193	----	U	0	0	m1
0.0.0.0	0.0.0.0	130.56.12.4	U	0	0	m2

41. Change the routing table in Table 6.1 so that it reflects classless routing (CIDR).
42. Change the routing table in Table 6.2 so that it reflects classless routing (CIDR).
43. Change the routing table in Table 6.3 so that it reflects classless routing (CIDR).
44. Change the routing table in Table 6.4 so that it reflects classless routing (CIDR).

45. A classful routing table has four buckets in the table and a single entry for default routing. The first bucket is for host-specific routing with 10 entries. The second bucket is for class A blocks with 50 entries. The third bucket is for class B blocks with 400 entries. The fourth bucket is for class C blocks with 2000 entries. Find the average number of table lookups for each of the following cases:
    a. A packet with host-specific route has arrived.
    b. A packet with a class A address has arrived.
    c. A packet with a class B address has arrived.
    d. A packet with a class C address has arrived.
    e. A packet has arrived that must be default routed.
46. A classless routing table has 32 buckets in the table and a single entry for default routing. The average number of entries in each bucket is 100. How many table lookups are needed on average for each of the following packets:
    a. A packet with prefix /32.
    b. A packet with prefix /24.
    c. A packet with prefix /12.
    d. A packet with a prefix /8.

Programming Exercises

47. Create a header file to include all constants that you think are needed to implement the routing module and routing table in C. Use the **#define** directives.
48. Complete the following **struct** declaration for the routing table entry.

```
struct  Routing_Table_Entry
{
..........................................  Mask;
............................................................
............................................................
} ;
```

49. Write a declaration for the routing table.
50. Write a function in C to simulate the routing module.

CHAPTER 7

ARP and RARP

An internet is made of a combination of physical networks connected together by internetworking devices such as routers and gateways. A packet starting from a source host may pass through several different physical networks before finally reaching the destination host.

The hosts and routers are recognized at the network level by their logical addresses. A **logical address** is an internetwork address. Its jurisdiction is universal. A logical address is unique universally. It is called a *logical* address because it is usually implemented in software. Every protocol that deals with interconnecting networks requires logical addresses. The logical addresses in the TCP/IP protocol suite are called **IP addresses** and are 32 bits long.

However, packets pass through physical networks to reach these hosts and routers. At the physical level, the hosts and routers are recognized by their physical addresses. A physical address is a local address. Its jurisdiction is a local network. It should be unique locally, but not necessarily universally. It is called a *physical* address because it is usually (but not always) implemented in hardware. Examples of physical addresses are 48-bit MAC addresses in Ethernet and Token Ring protocols, which are imprinted on the NIC installed in the host or router.

The physical address and the logical address are two different identifiers. We need both of them because a physical network, such as Ethernet can have two different protocols at the network layer such as IP and IPX (Novell) at the same time. Likewise, a packet at a network layer such as IP may pass through different physical networks such as Ethernet and LocalTalk.

This means that delivery of a packet to a host or a router requires two levels of addressing: logical and physical. We need to be able to map a logical address to its corresponding physical address and vice versa. These can be done using either static or dynamic mapping.

Static mapping means creating a table that associates a logical address with a physical address. This table is stored in each machine on the network. Each machine that knows, for example, the IP address of another machine but not its physical address can look it up in the table. This has some limitations because physical addresses may change in the following ways:

1. A machine could change its NIC resulting in a new physical address.
2. In some LANs, such as LocalTalk, the physical address changes every time the computer is turned on.
3. A mobile computer can move from one physical network to another, resulting in a change in its physical address.

To implement these changes, a static mapping table must be updated periodically. This overhead could affect the network performance.

In **dynamic mapping** each time a machine knows one of the two addresses (logical or physical), it can use a protocol to find the other one.

Two protocols have been designed to perform dynamic mapping: **address resolution protocol (ARP)** and **reverse address resolution protocol (RARP).** The first maps a logical address to a physical address; the second maps a physical address to a logical address. Figure 7.1 shows the idea.

Figure 7.1 *ARP and RARP*

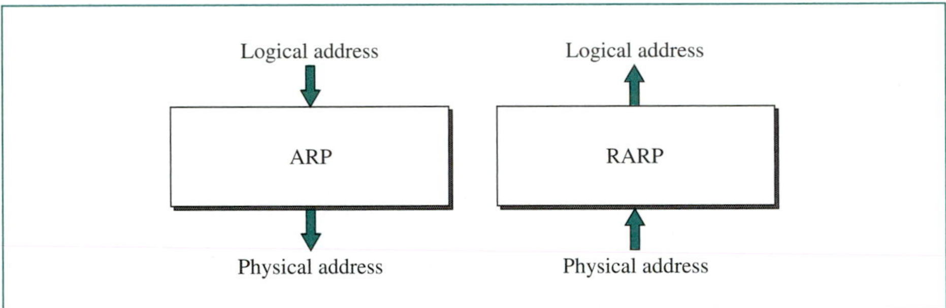

ARP and RARP use unicast and broadcast physical addresses. We discussed unicast and broadcast physical addresses in Chapter 3. We mentioned that, for example, Ethernet uses the all 1s address ($FFFFFFFFFFFF_{16}$) as the broadcast address.

Figure 7.2 shows the position of ARP and RARP protocols in the TCP/IP protocol suite.

Figure 7.2 *Position of ARP and RARP in TCP/IP protocol suite*

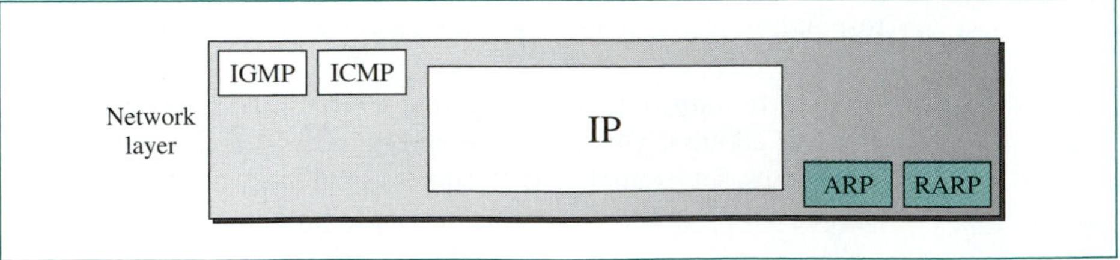

7.1 ARP

Anytime a host or a router has an IP datagram to send to another host or router, it has the logical (IP) address of the receiver. But the IP datagram must be encapsulated in a frame to be able to pass through the physical network. This means that the sender needs the physical address of the receiver. A mapping corresponds a logical address to a physical address.

As we said before, this can be done either statically or dynamically. The association between logical and physical addresses can be statically stored in a table. The sender can look in the table and find the physical address corresponding to a logical address. But as we discussed before, this is not a good solution. Every time a physical address is changed, the table must be updated. Updating tables on all machines at frequent intervals is a very demanding task.

The mapping, however, can be done dynamically, which means that the sender asks the receiver to announce its physical address when needed. ARP is designed for this purpose.

ARP associates an IP address with its physical address. On a typical physical network, such as a LAN, each device on a link is identified by a physical or station address that is usually imprinted on the NIC.

Anytime a host, or a router, needs to find the physical address of another host or router on its network, it sends an ARP query packet. The packet includes the physical and IP addresses of the sender and the IP address of the receiver. Because the sender does not know the physical address of the receiver, the query is broadcast over the network (see Figure 7.3).

Figure 7.3 *ARP operation*

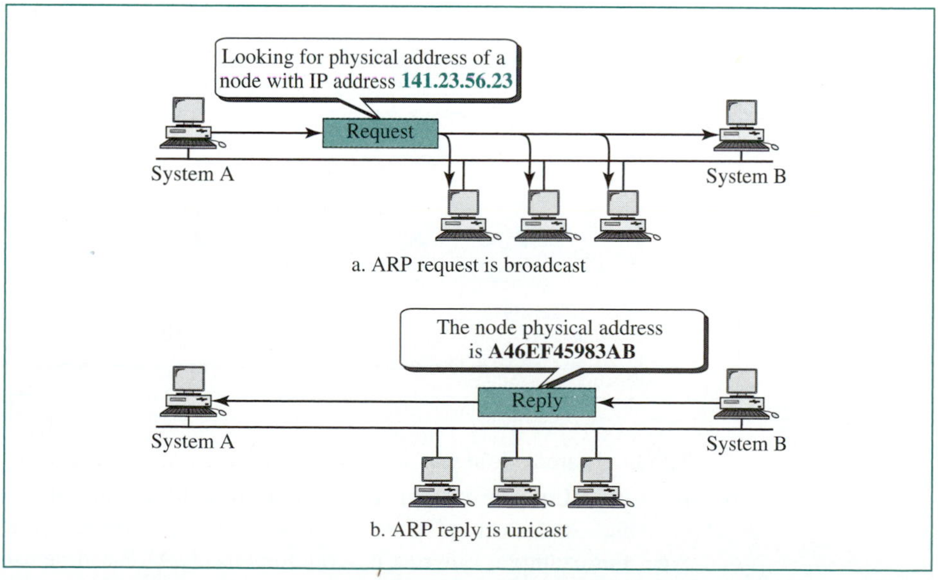

Every host or router on the network receives and processes the ARP query packet, but only the intended recipient recognizes its IP address and sends back an ARP response packet. The response packet contains the recipient's IP and physical addresses. The packet is unicast directly to the inquirer using the physical address received in the query packet.

In Figure 7.3a, the system on the left (A) has a packet that needs to be delivered to another system (B) with IP address 141.23.56.23. System A needs to pass the packet to its data link layer for the actual delivery, but it does not know the physical address of the recipient. It uses the services of ARP by asking the ARP protocol to send a broadcast ARP request packet to ask for the physical address of a system with an IP address of 141.23.56.23.

This packet is received by every system on the physical network, but only system B will answer it, as shown in Figure 7.3b. System B sends an ARP reply packet that includes its physical address. Now system A can send all the packets it has for this destination using the physical address it received.

Packet Format

Figure 7.4 shows the format of an ARP packet.

Figure 7.4 *ARP packet*

<table>
<tr><td colspan="2">Hardware Type</td><td>Protocol Type</td></tr>
<tr><td>Hardware length</td><td>Protocol length</td><td>Operation
Request 1, Reply 2</td></tr>
<tr><td colspan="3">Sender hardware address
(For example, 6 bytes for Ethernet)</td></tr>
<tr><td colspan="3">Sender protocol address
(For example, 4 bytes for IP)</td></tr>
<tr><td colspan="3">Target hardware address
(For example, 6 bytes for Ethernet)
(It is not filled in a request)</td></tr>
<tr><td colspan="3">Target protocol address
(For example, 4 bytes for IP)</td></tr>
</table>

The fields are as follows:

- **HTYPE (Hardware type).** This is a 16-bit field defining the type of the network on which ARP is running. Each LAN has been assigned an integer based on its type. For example, Ethernet is given the type 1. ARP can be used on any physical network.

- **PTYPE (Protocol type).** This is a 16-bit field defining the protocol. For example, the value of this field for the IPv4 protocol is 0800_{16}. ARP can be used with any higher-level protocol.
- **HLEN (Hardware length).** This is an 8-bit field defining the length of the physical address in bytes. For example, for Ethernet the value is 6.
- **PLEN (Protocol length).** This is an 8-bit field defining the length of the logical address in bytes. For example, for the IPv4 protocol the value is 4.
- **OPER (Operation).** This is a 16-bit field defining the type of packet. Two packet types are defined: ARP request (1), ARP reply (2).
- **SHA (Sender hardware address).** This is a variable-length field defining the physical address of the sender. For example, for Ethernet this field is 6 bytes long.
- **SPA (Sender protocol address).** This is a variable-length field defining the logical (for example, IP) address of the sender. For the IP protocol, this field is 4 bytes long.
- **THA (Target hardware address).** This is a variable-length field defining the physical address of the target. For example, for Ethernet this field is 6 bytes long. For an ARP request message, this field is all 0s because the sender does not know the physical address of the target.
- **TPA (Target protocol address).** This is a variable-length field defining the logical (for example, IP) address of the target. For the IPv4 protocol, this field is 4 bytes long.

Encapsulation

An ARP packet is encapsulated directly into a data link frame. For example, in Figure 7.5 an ARP packet is encapsulated in an Ethernet frame. Note that the type field indicates that the data carried by the frame is an ARP packet.

Figure 7.5 *Encapsulation of ARP packet*

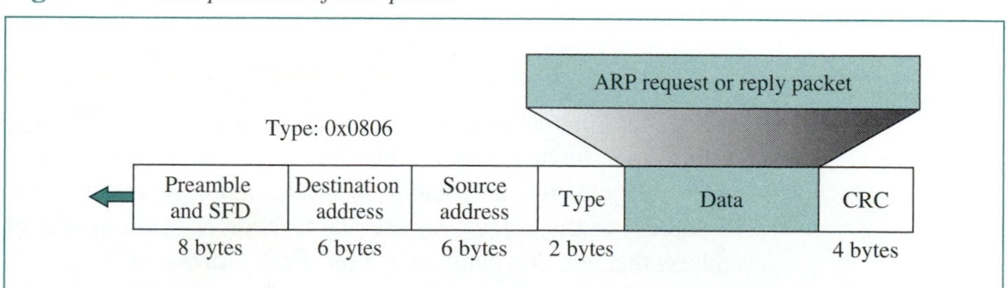

Operation

Let us see how ARP functions on a typical internet. First we describe the steps involved. Then we discuss the four cases in which a host or router needs to use ARP.

Steps Involved

These are the steps involved in an ARP process:

1. The sender knows the IP address of the target. We will see how the sender obtains this shortly.
2. IP asks ARP to create an ARP request message, filling in the sender physical address, the sender IP address, and the target IP address. The target physical address field is filled with 0s.
3. The message is passed to the data link layer where it is encapsulated in a frame using the physical address of the sender as the source address and the physical broadcast address as the destination address.
4. Every host or router receives the frame. Because the frame contains a broadcast destination address, all stations remove the message and pass it to ARP. All machines except the one targeted drop the packet. The target machine recognizes the IP address.
5. The target machine replies with an ARP reply message that contains its physical address. The message is unicast.
6. The sender receives the reply message. It now knows the physical address of the target machine.
7. The IP datagram, which carries data for the target machine, is now encapsulated in a frame and is unicast to the destination.

Four Different Cases

The following are four different cases in which the services of ARP can be used (see Figure 7.6).

1. The sender is a host and wants to send a packet to another host on the same network. In this case, the logical address that must be mapped to a physical address is the destination IP address in the datagram header.
2. The sender is a host and wants to send a packet to another host on another network. In this case, the host looks at its routing table and finds the IP address of the next hop (router) for this destination. If it does not have a routing table, it looks for the IP address of the default router. The IP address of the router becomes the logical address that must be mapped to a physical address.
3. The sender is a router that has received a datagram destined for a host on another network. It checks its routing table and finds the IP address of the next router. The IP address of the next router becomes the logical address that must be mapped to a physical address.

Figure 7.6 *Four cases using ARP*

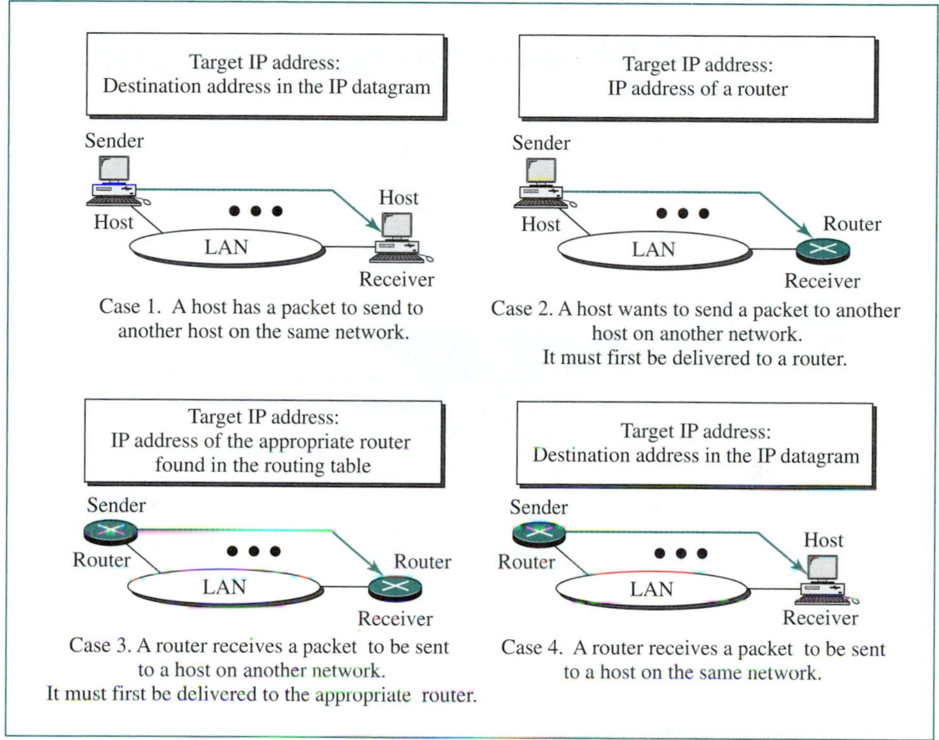
Target IP address:
Destination address in the IP datagram
Sender
Host
Host
LAN
Receiver
Case 1. A host has a packet to send to another host on the same network.
Target IP address:
IP address of a router
Sender
Host
Router
LAN
Receiver
Case 2. A host wants to send a packet to another host on another network.
It must first be delivered to a router.
Target IP address:
IP address of the appropriate router found in the routing table
Sender
Router
Router
LAN
Receiver
Case 3. A router receives a packet to be sent to a host on another network.
It must first be delivered to the appropriate router.
Target IP address:
Destination address in the IP datagram
Sender
Router
Host
LAN
Receiver
Case 4. A router receives a packet to be sent to a host on the same network.

4. The sender is a router that has received a datagram destined for a host in the same network. The destination IP address of the datagram becomes the logical address that must be mapped to a physical address.

> An ARP request is broadcast; an ARP reply is unicast.

Example 1

A host with IP address 130.23.43.20 and physical address 0xB23455102210 has a packet to send to another host with IP address 130.23.43.25 and physical address 0xA46EF45983AB. The two hosts are on the same Ethernet network. Show the ARP request and reply packets encapsulated in Ethernet frames.

Solution

Figure 7.7 shows the ARP request and reply packets. Note that the ARP data field in this case is 28 bytes, and that the individual addresses do not fit in the 4-byte boundary. That is why we do not show the regular 4-byte boundaries for these addresses. Also note that the IP addresses are shown in hexadecimal. For information on binary or hexadecimal notation see Appendix B.

Figure 7.7 *Example 1*

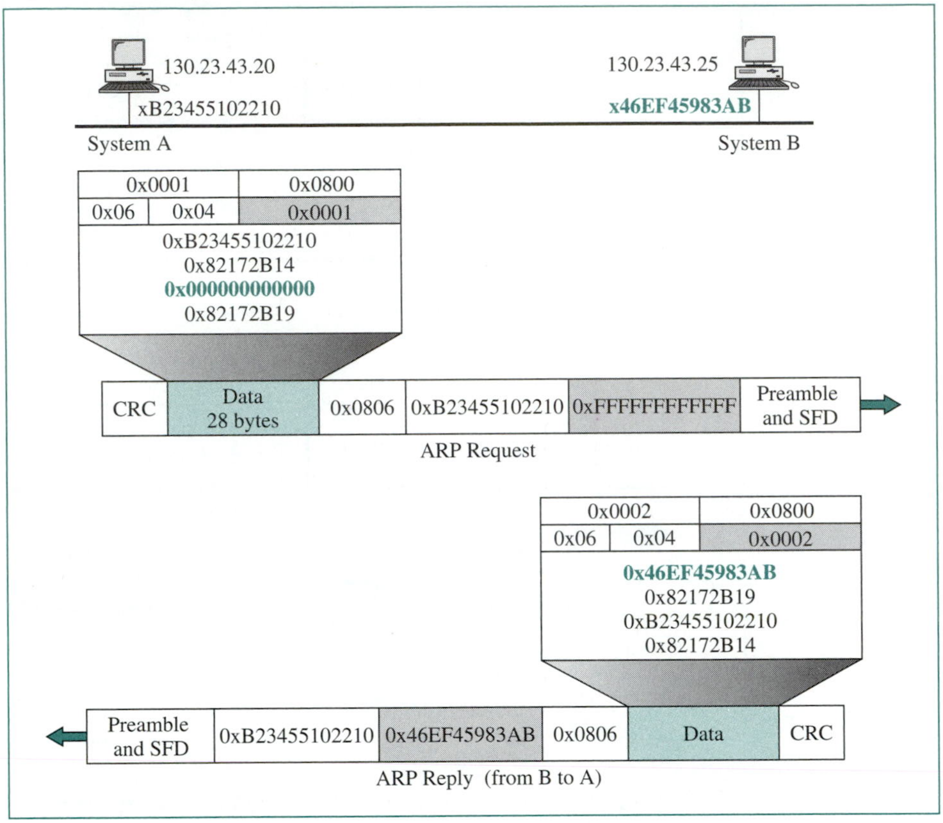

ARP Over ATM

ARP is also used when an IP packet wants to pass over an ATM network. We will talk about this aspect of ARP when we discuss IP over ATM in Chapter 26.

Proxy ARP

A technique called *proxy* (promiscuous) ARP is used to create a subnetting effect. A **proxy ARP** is an ARP that acts on behalf of a set of hosts. Whenever a router running a proxy ARP receives an ARP request looking for the IP address of one of these hosts, the router sends an ARP reply announcing its own hardware (physical) address. After the router receives the actual IP packet, it sends the packet to the appropriate host or router.

Let us give an example. In Figure 7.8 the ARP installed on the right-hand host will answer only to an ARP request with a target IP address of 141.23.56.23. We call this behavior *honest*. The other hosts or routers on the network rely on its honesty.

However, the administrator may need to create a subnet without changing the whole system to recognize subnetted addresses. One solution is to add a router running a proxy ARP. In this case, the router acts on behalf of all of the hosts installed on the subnet. When it receives an ARP request with a target IP address that matches the

Figure 7.8 *Proxy ARP*

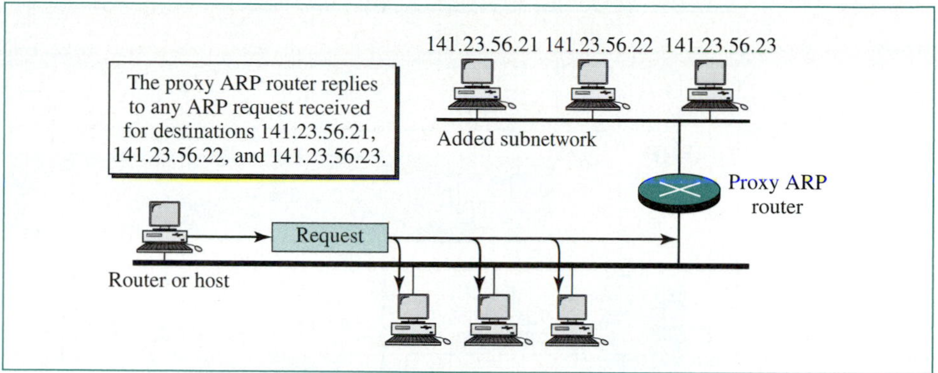

address of one its protégés (141.23.56.21, 141.23.56.22, and 141.23.56.23), it sends an ARP reply and announces its hardware address as the target hardware address. When the router receives the IP packet, it sends the packet to the appropriate host.

7.2 ARP PACKAGE

In this section, we give an example of a simplified ARP software package. The purpose is to show the components of a hypothetical ARP package and the relationship between the components.

We can say that this ARP package involves five components: a cache table, queues, an output module, an input module, and a cache-control module. Figure 7.9 shows these five components and their interactions. The package receives an IP datagram that needs to be encapsulated in a frame that needs the destination physical (hardware) address. If the ARP package finds this address, it delivers the IP packet and the physical address to the data link layer for transmission.

Cache Table

A sender usually has more than one IP datagram to send to the same destination. It is inefficient to use the ARP protocol for each datagram destined for the same host or router. The solution is the cache table. When a host or router receives the corresponding physical address for an IP datagram, the address can be saved in the cache table. This address can be used for the datagrams destined for the same receiver within the next few minutes. However, as space in the cache table is very limited, mappings in the cache are not retained for an unlimited time.

The cache table is implemented as an array of entries. In our package, each entry contains the following fields:

- **State.** This column shows the state of the entry. It can have one of three values: *FREE, PENDING,* or *RESOLVED*. The FREE state means that the time-to-live for this entry has expired. The space can be used for a new entry. The PENDING state means a request for this entry has been sent, but the reply has not yet been

Figure 7.9 *ARP components*

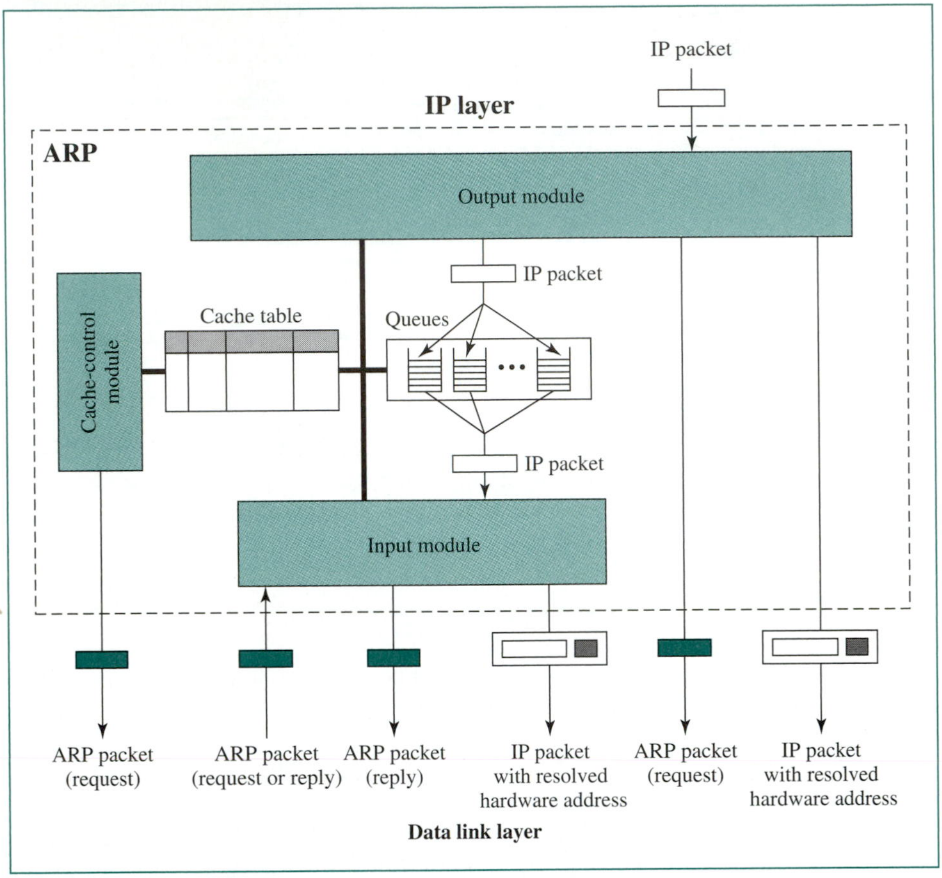

received. The RESOLVED state means that the entry is complete. The entry now has the physical (hardware) address of the destination. The packets waiting to be sent to this destination can use information in this entry.

- **Hardware type.** This field is the same as the corresponding field in the ARP packet.
- **Protocol type.** This field is the same as the corresponding field in the ARP packet.
- **Hardware length.** This field is the same as the corresponding field in the ARP packet.
- **Protocol length.** This field is the same as the corresponding field in the ARP packet.
- **Interface number.** A router (or a multihomed host) can be connected to different networks, each with a different interface number. Each network can have different hardware and protocol types.
- **Queue number.** ARP uses numbered queues to enqueue the packets waiting for address resolution. Packets for the same destination are usually enqueued in the same queue.
- **Attempts.** This column shows the number of times an ARP request is sent out for this entry.
- **Time-out.** This column shows the lifetime of an entry in seconds.

- **Hardware address.** This column shows the destination hardware address. It remains empty until resolved by an ARP reply.
- **Protocol address.** This column shows the destination IP address.

Queues

Our ARP package maintains a set of queues, one for each destination, to hold the IP packets while ARP tries to resolve the hardware address. The output module sends unresolved packets into the corresponding queue. The input module removes a packet from a queue and sends it, with the resolved physical address, to the data link layer for transmission.

Output Module

The **output module** waits for an IP packet from the IP software. The output module checks the cache table to find an entry corresponding to the destination IP address of this packet. The destination IP address of the IP packet must match the protocol address of the entry.

If the entry is found and the state of the entry is RESOLVED, the packet along with the destination hardware address is passed to the data link layer for transmission.

If the entry is found and the state of the entry is PENDING, the packet waits until the destination hardware address is found. Because the state is PENDING, there is a queue already created for this destination. The module sends the packet to this queue.

If no entry is found, the module creates a queue and enqueues the packet. A new entry with the state of PENDING is created for this destination and the value of the ATTEMPTS field is set to 1. An ARP request packet is then broadcast.

Output Module

1. Sleep until an IP packet is received from IP software.
2. Check cache table for an entry corresponding to the destination of this IP packet.
3. If (found)
    1. If (the state is RESOLVED)
        1. Extract the value of the hardware address from the entry.
        2. Send the packet and the hardware address to data link layer.
        3. Return.
    2. If (the state is PENDING)
        1. Enqueue the packet to the corresponding queue.
        2. Return.
4. If (not found)
    1. Create a cache entry with state set to PENDING and ATTEMPTS set to 1.
    2. Create a queue.
    3. Enqueue the packet.
    4. Send an ARP request.
5. Return.

Input Module

The **input module** waits until an ARP packet (request or reply) arrives. The input module checks the cache table to find an entry corresponding to this ARP packet. The target protocol address should match the protocol address of the entry.

If the entry is found and the state of the entry is PENDING, the module updates the entry by copying the target hardware address in the packet to the hardware address field of the entry and changing the state to RESOLVED. The module also sets the value of the TIME-OUT for this entry. It then dequeues the packets from the corresponding queue, one by one, and delivers them along with the hardware address to the data link layer for transmission.

If the entry is found and the state is RESOLVED, the module still updates the entry. This is because the target hardware address could have been changed. The value of the TIME-OUT field is also reset.

If the entry is not found, the module creates a new entry and adds it to the table. The protocol requires that any information received is added to the table for future use. The state is set to RESOLVED and TIME-OUT is set.

Now the module checks to see if the arrived ARP packet is a request. If it is, the module immediately creates an ARP reply message and sends it to the sender. The ARP reply packet is created by changing the value of the operation field from request to reply and filling in the target hardware address.

Input Module

1. Sleep until an ARP packet (request or reply) arrives.
2. Check the cache table to find an entry corresponding to this ARP packet.
3. If (found)
    1. Update the entry.
    2. If (the state is PENDING)
        1. While the queue is not empty
            1. Dequeue one packet.
            2. Send the packet and the hardware address to data link.
4. If (not found)
    1. Create an entry.
    2. Add the entry to the table.
5. If (the packet is a request)
    1. Send an ARP reply.
6. Return.

Cache-Control Module

The **cache-control module** is responsible for maintaining the cache table. It periodically (for example, every 5 s) checks the cache table, entry by entry.

If the state of the entry is FREE, it continues to the next entry. If the state is PENDING, the module increments the value of the attempts field by 1. It then checks the value of the attempts field. If this value is greater than the maximum number of attempts allowed, the state is changed to FREE and the corresponding queue is destroyed. However, if the number of attempts is less than the maximum, the module creates and sends another ARP request.

If the state of the entry is RESOLVED, the module decrements the value of the time-out field by the amount of time elapsed since the last check. If this value is less than or equal to zero, the state is changed to FREE and the queue is destroyed.

Cache-Control Module

1. Sleep until the periodic timer matures.
2. For every entry in the cache table
    1. If (the state is FREE)
        1. Continue.
    2. If (the state is PENDING)
        1. Increment the value of attempts by 1.
        2. If (attempts greater than maximum)
            1. Change the state to FREE.
            2. Destroy the corresponding queue.
        3. Else
            1. Send an ARP request.
        4. Continue.
    3. If (the state is RESOLVED)
        1. Decrement the value of time-out by the value of elapsed time.
        2. If (time-out less than or equal to zero)
            1. Change the state to FREE.
            2. Destroy the corresponding queue.
3. Return.

More Examples

In this section we show some examples of the ARP operation and the changes in the cache table. Table 7.1 shows some of the cache table fields at the start of our examples.

Table 7.1 *Original cache table used for examples*

State	*Queue*	*Attempt*	*Time-out*	*Protocol Addr.*	*Hardware Addr.*
R	5		900	180.3.6.1	ACAE32457342
P	2	2		129.34.4.8	
P	14	5		201.11.56.7	
R	8		450	114.5.7.89	457342ACAE32
P	12	1		220.55.5.7	
F					
R	9		60	19.1.7.82	4573E3242ACA
P	18	3		188.11.8.71	

Example 2

The ARP output module receives an IP datagram (from the IP layer) with the destination address 114.5.7.89. It checks the cache table and finds that an entry exists for this destination with the RESOLVED state (R in the table). It extracts the hardware address, which is 457342ACAE32, and sends the packet and the address to the data link layer for transmission. The cache table remains the same.

Example 3

Twenty seconds later, the ARP output module receives an IP datagram (from the IP layer) with the destination address 116.1.7.22. It checks the cache table and does not find this destination in the table. The module adds an entry to the table with the state PENDING and the Attempt value 1. It creates a new queue for this destination and enqueues the packet. It then sends an ARP request to the data link layer for this destination. The new cache table is shown in Table 7.2.

Table 7.2 *Updated cache table for example 3*

State	*Queue*	*Attempt*	*Time-out*	*Protocol Addr.*	*Hardware Addr.*
R	5		900	180.3.6.1	ACAE32457342
P	2	2		129.34.4.8	
P	14	5		201.11.56.7	
R	8		450	114.5.7.89	457342ACAE32
P	12	1		220.55.5.7	
P	23	1		116.1.7.22	
R	9		60	19.1.7.82	4573E3242ACA
P	18	3		188.11.8.71	

Example 4

Fifteen seconds later, the ARP input module receives an ARP packet with target protocol (IP) address 188.11.8.71. The module checks the table and finds this address. It changes the state of the entry to RESOLVED and sets the time-out value to 900. The module then adds the target hardware address (E34573242ACA) to the entry. Now it accesses queue 18 and sends all the packets in this queue, one by one, to the data link layer. The new cache table is shown in Table 7.3.

Table 7.3 *Updated cache table for example 4*

State	*Queue*	*Attempt*	*Time-out*	*Protocol Addr.*	*Hardware Addr.*
R	5		900	180.3.6.1	ACAE32457342
P	2	2		129.34.4.8	
P	14	5		201.11.56.7	
R	8		450	114.5.7.89	457342ACAE32
P	12	1		220.55.5.7	
P	23	1		116.1.7.22	
R	9		60	19.1.7.82	4573E3242ACA
R	18		900	188.11.8.71	E34573242ACA

Example 5

Twenty-five seconds later, the cache-control module updates every entry. The time-out values for the first three resolved entries are decremented by 60. The time-out value for the last resolved entry is decremented by 25. The state of the next-to-the last entry is changed to FREE because the time-out is zero. For each of the three entries, the value of the attempts field is incremented by one. After incrementing, the attempts value for one entry (the one with IP protocol address 201.11.56.7) is more than the maximum; the state is changed to FREE, the queue is deleted, and an ICMP message is sent to the original destination (see Chapter 9). See Table 7.4.

Table 7.4 *Updated cache table for example 5*

State	*Queue*	*Attempt*	*Time-out*	*Protocol Addr.*	*Hardware Addr.*
R	5		840	180.3.6.1	ACAE32457342
P	2	3		129.34.4.8	
F					
R	8		390	114.5.7.89	457342ACAE32
P	12	2		220.55.5.7	
P	23	2		116.1.7.22	
F					
R	18		875	188.11.8.71	E34573242ACA

7.3 RARP

RARP finds the logical address for a machine that only knows its physical address.

Each host or router is assigned one or more logical (IP) addresses, which are unique and independent of the physical (hardware) address of the machine. To create an IP datagram, a host or a router needs to know its own IP address or addresses. The IP address of a machine is usually read from its configuration file stored on a disk file.

However, a diskless machine is usually booted from ROM, which has minimum booting information. The ROM is installed by the manufacturer. It cannot include the IP address because the IP addresses on a network are assigned by the network administrator.

The machine can get its physical address (by reading its NIC, for example), which is unique locally. It can then use the physical address to get the logical address using the RARP protocol. A RARP request is created and broadcast on the local network. Another machine on the local network that knows all the IP addresses will respond with a RARP reply. The requesting machine must be running a RARP client program; the responding machine must be running a RARP server program (see Figure 7.10).

> The RARP request packets are broadcast; the RARP reply packets are unicast.

In Figure 7.10a, the diskless host on the left is booted. To get its IP address, it broadcasts a RARP request to all systems on the network.

This packet is received by every host (or router) on the physical network, but only the RARP server on the right will answer it as shown in Figure 7.10b. The server sends a RARP reply packet that includes the IP address of the requestor.

Figure 7.10 *RARP operation*

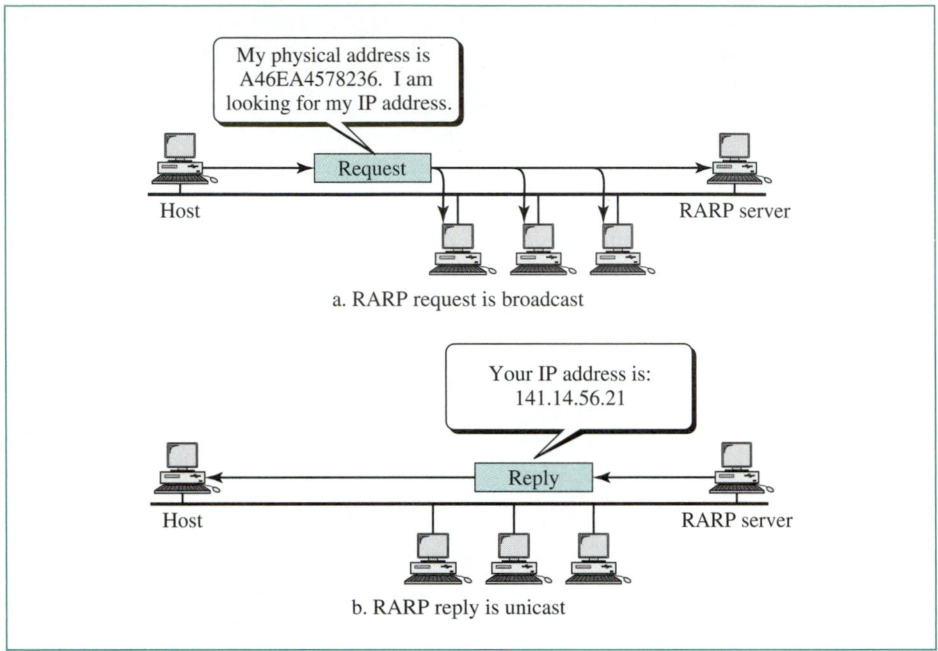

Packet Format

The format of the RARP packet is exactly the same as the ARP packet except that the operation field is either three (RARP request) or four (RARP reply). See Figure 7.11.

Figure 7.11 *RARP packet*

Hardware type		Protocol type
Hardware length	Protocol length	Operation Request 3, Reply 4
Sender hardware address (For example, 6 bytes for Ethernet)		
Sender protocol address (For example, 4 bytes for IP) (It is not filled for request)		
Target hardware address (For example, 6 bytes for Ethernet) (It is not filled for request)		
Target protocol address (For example, 4 bytes for IP) (It is not filled for request)		

Encapsulation

A RARP packet is encapsulated directly into a data link frame. For example, Figure 7.12 shows a RARP packet encapsulated in an Ethernet frame. Note that the type field shows that the data carried by the frame is a RARP packet.

Figure 7.12 *Encapsulation of RARP packet*

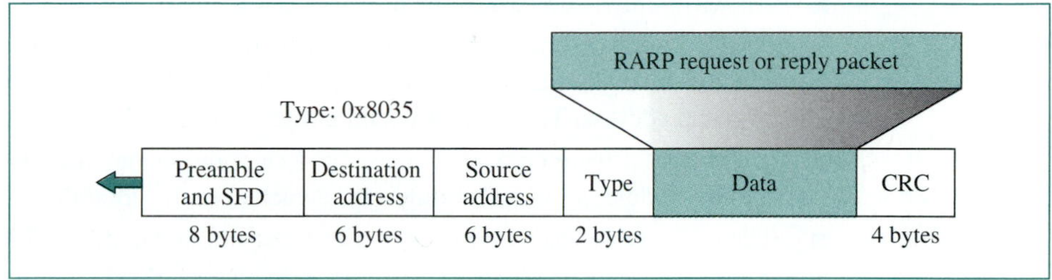

Alternative Solutions to RARP

When a diskless computer is booted, it needs more information in addition to its IP address. It needs to know its subnet mask, the IP address of a router, and the IP address of a name server. RARP cannot provide this extra information. New protocols have been developed to provide this information. In Chapter 17 we discuss two protocols, BOOTP and DHCP, that can be used instead of RARP.

7.4 KEY TERMS

address resolution protocol (ARP)

cache table

dynamic mapping

encapsulation

IP address

logical address

physical address

proxy (promiscuous) ARP

queue

reverse address resolution protocol (RARP)

static mapping

7.5 SUMMARY

- Delivery of a packet to a host or router requires two levels of addresses: logical and physical.
- A logical address identifies a host or router at the network level. TCP/IP calls this logical address an IP address.
- A physical address identifies a host or router at the physical level.

- Mapping of a logical address to a physical address can be static or dynamic.
- Static mapping involves a list of logical and physical address correspondences; maintenance of the list requires high overhead.
- The address resolution protocol (ARP) is a dynamic mapping method that finds a physical address given a logical address.
- An ARP request is broadcast to all devices on the network.
- An ARP reply is unicast to the host requesting the mapping.
- In proxy ARP (promiscuous ARP) a router represents a set of hosts. When an ARP request seeks the physical address of any host in this set, the router sends its own physical address. This creates a subnetting effect.
- The ARP software package consists of five components: a cache table, queues, an output module, an input module, and a cache-control module.
- The cache table has an array of entries used and updated by ARP messages.
- A queue contains packets going to the same destination.
- The output module takes a packet from the IP layer and sends it either to the data link layer or to a queue.
- The input module uses an ARP packet to update the cache table. The input module can also send an ARP reply.
- The cache-control module maintains the cache table by updating entry fields.
- Reverse address resolution protocol (RARP) is a form of dynamic mapping in which a given physical address is associated with a logical address.

7.6 PRACTICE SET

Multiple-Choice Questions

1. In _______ a protocol associates a logical address with a physical address.
   a. static mapping
   b. dynamic mapping
   c. physical mapping
   d. a and b
2. In _______ a table associating a logical address with a physical address is maintained on all devices on a network.
   a. static mapping
   b. dynamic mapping
   c. physical mapping
   d. a and b

3. _______ is a dynamic mapping protocol in which a logical address is found for a given physical address.
   a. ARP
   b. RARP
   c. ICMP
   d. none of the above
4. _______ is a dynamic mapping protocol in which a physical address is found for a given logical address.
   a. ARP
   b. RARP
   c. ICMP
   d. none of the above
5. A router reads the _______ address on a packet to determine the next hop.
   a. logical
   b. physical
   c. source
   d. ARP
6. The target hardware address on an Ethernet is _______ in an ARP request.
   a. 0x000000000000
   b. 0.0.0.0
   c. variable
   d. class dependent
7. An ARP reply is _______ to _______.
   a. broadcast; all hosts
   b. multicast; one host
   c. unicast; all hosts
   d. unicast; one host
8. An ARP request is _______ to _______.
   a. broadcast; all hosts
   b. multicast; one host
   c. unicast; all hosts
   d. unicast; one host
9. What does a router running proxy ARP and representing 10 hosts return in the target hardware address field in an ARP reply?
   a. any of 10 different hardware addresses
   b. any of 11 different hardware addresses
   c. just the router hardware address
   d. just the router IP address

10. The ARP component that sends an ARP reply to the data link layer is the _______.
    a. cache controller
    b. input module
    c. output module
    d. a and b
11. The ARP component that sends an IP packet to a queue is the _______.
    a. cache controller
    b. input module
    c. output module
    d. a and b
12. ARP packets are sent to the data link layer by the _______.
    a. cache-control module
    b. input module
    c. output module
    d. all of the above
13. An ARP packet from the data link layer goes to the _______.
    a. cache-control module
    b. input module
    c. output module
    d. a and c
14. An IP packet goes directly from the _______ to the data link layer if the state of the entry is RESOLVED.
    a. cache-control module
    b. input module
    c. output module
    d. a and c

Exercises

15. Is the size of the ARP packet fixed? Explain.
16. Is the size of the RARP packet fixed? Explain.
17. What is the size of an ARP packet when the protocol is IP and the hardware is Ethernet?
18. What is the size of a RARP packet when the protocol is IP and the hardware is Ethernet?
19. What is the size of an Ethernet frame carrying an ARP packet?
20. What is the size of an Ethernet frame carrying a RARP packet?
21. What is the broadcast address for Ethernet?

22. A router with IP address 125.45.23.12 and Ethernet physical address 2345AB4F67CD has received a packet for a host destination with IP address 125.11.78.10 and Ethernet physical address AABBA24F67CD. Show the entries in the ARP request packet sent by the router. Assume no subnetting.
23. Show the entries in the ARP packet sent in response to Exercise 22.
24. Encapsulate the result of Exercise 22 in a data link frame. Fill in all the fields.
25. Encapsulate the result of Exercise 23 in a data link frame. Fill in all the fields.
26. A router with IP address 195.5.2.12 and Ethernet physical address AA25AB1F67CD has received a packet for a destination with IP address 185.11.78.10. When the router checks its routing table, it finds out the packet should be delivered to a router with IP address 195.5.2.6 and Ethernet physical address AD345D4F67CD. Show the entries in the ARP request packet sent by the router. Assume no subnetting.
27. Show the entries in the ARP packet sent in response to Exercise 26.
28. Encapsulate the result of Exercise 26 in a data link frame. Fill in all the fields.
29. Encapsulate the result of Exercise 27 in a data link frame. Fill in all the fields.
30. A diskless host with an Ethernet physical address 9845234F67CD has been booted. Show the entries in the RARP packet sent by this host.
31. Show the entries in the RARP packet sent in response to Exercise 30. Assume that the IP address of the requesting host is 200.67.89.33. Choose appropriate physical and logical addresses for the server. Assume the server is on the same network as the requesting host.
32. Encapsulate the result of Exercise 30 in a data link frame. Fill in all the fields.
33. Encapsulate the result of Exercise 31 in a data link frame. Fill in all the fields.

Programming Exercises

34. Create a header file to include all constants that you think are needed to implement the ARP module in C. Use the **#define** directives.
35. Complete the following struct declaration. It is a declaration for the ARP packet.

```
struct ARP
{
unsigned short   HardwareType ;
.............................................................
.............................................................
} ;
```

36. Write the declaration for the cache table entry.
37. Write the declaration for the cache table.
38. Write a function in C to simulate the cache-control module.
39. Write a function in C to simulate the input module.
40. Write a function in C to simulate the output module.

CHAPTER 8

Internet Protocol (IP)

The Internet Protocol (IP) is the transmission mechanism used by the TCP/IP protocols. Figure 8.1 shows the position of IP in the suite.

Figure 8.1 *Position of IP in TCP/IP protocol suite*

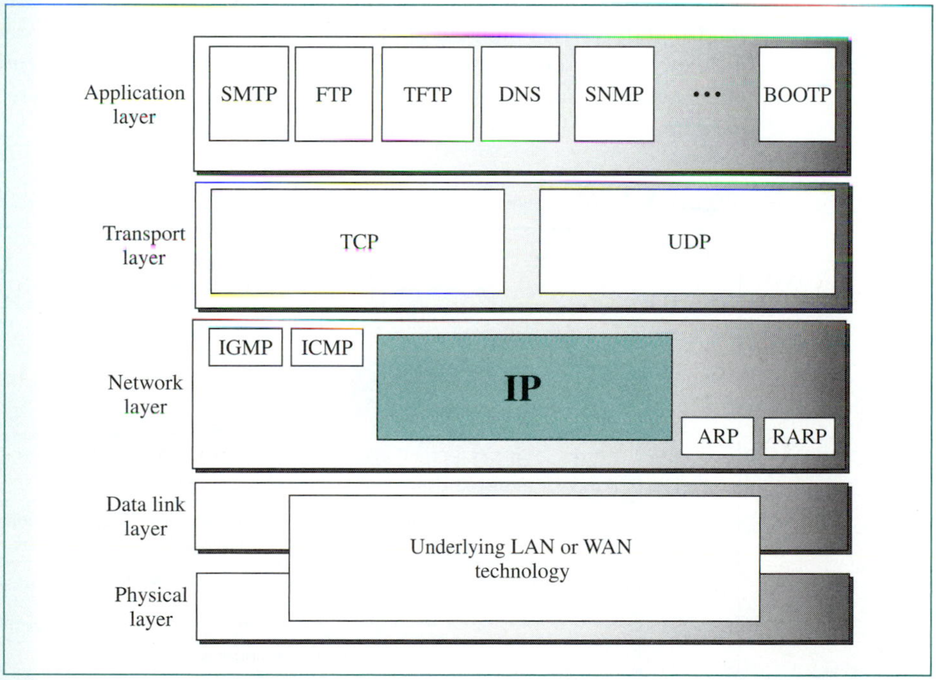

IP is an unreliable and connectionless datagram protocol—a best-effort delivery service. The term *best-effort* means that IP provides no error checking or tracking. IP assumes the unreliability of the underlying layers and does its best to get a transmission through to its destination, but with no guarantees.

If reliability is important, IP must be paired with a reliable protocol such as TCP. An example of a more commonly understood best-effort delivery service is the post office. The post office does its best to deliver the mail but does not always succeed. If an unregistered letter is lost, it is up to the sender or would-be recipient to discover the loss and rectify the problem. The post office itself does not keep track of every letter and cannot notify a sender of loss or damage.

IP is also a connectionless protocol packaged for a packet switching network that uses the datagram approach (see Chapter 6). This means that each datagram is handled independently, and each datagram can follow a different route to the destination. This implies that datagrams sent by the same source to the same destination could arrive out of order. Also, some could be lost or corrupted during transition. Again, IP relies on a higher level protocol to take care of all these problems.

8.1 DATAGRAM

Packets in the IP layer are called **datagrams.** Figure 8.2 shows the IP datagram format. A datagram is a variable-length packet consisting of two parts: header and data. The header is 20 to 60 bytes in length and contains information essential to routing and delivery. It is customary in TCP/IP to show the header in 4-byte sections. A brief description of each field is in order.

Figure 8.2 *IP datagram*

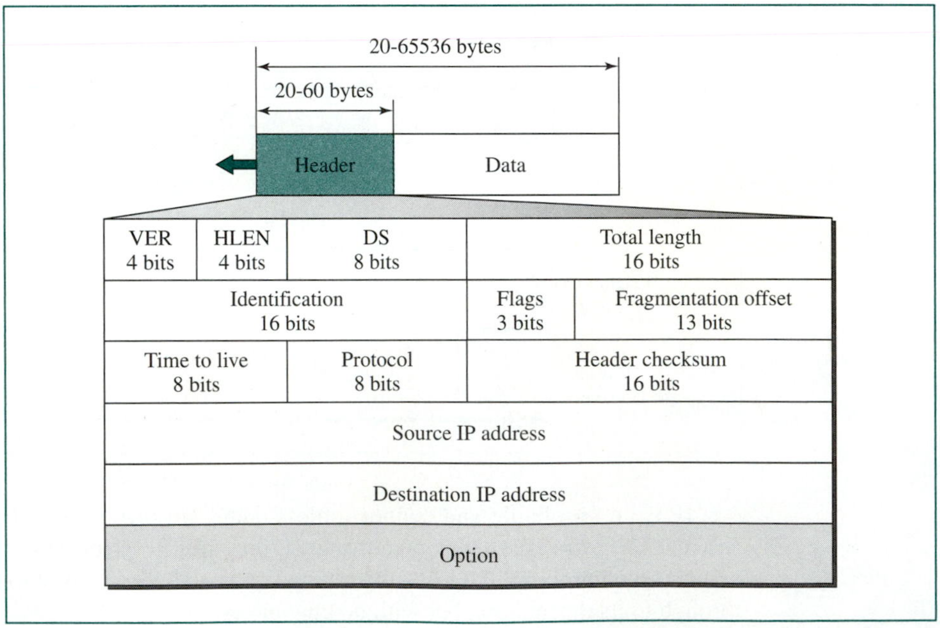

- **Version (VER).** This 4-bit field defines the version of the IP protocol. Currently the version is 4. However, version 6 (or IPng) may replace version 4 in a few years. This field tells the IP software running in the processing machine that the datagram has the format of version 4. All fields must be interpreted as specified in the fourth version of the protocol. If the machine is using some other version of IP, the datagram is discarded rather than interpreted incorrectly.
- **Header length (HLEN).** This 4-bit field defines the total length of the datagram header in 4-byte words. This field is needed because the length of the header is variable (between 20 and 60 bytes). When there are no options, the header length is 20 bytes, and the value of this field is 5 ($5 \times 4 = 20$). When the option field is at its maximum size, the value of this field is 15 ($15 \times 4 = 60$).
- **Differentiated Services (formerly Service Type).** IETF has recently changed the interpretation and name of this 8-bit field. This field, previously called Service Type, is now called Differentiated Services. We show both interpretations in Figure 8.3.

Figure 8.3 *Service Type or Differentiated Services*

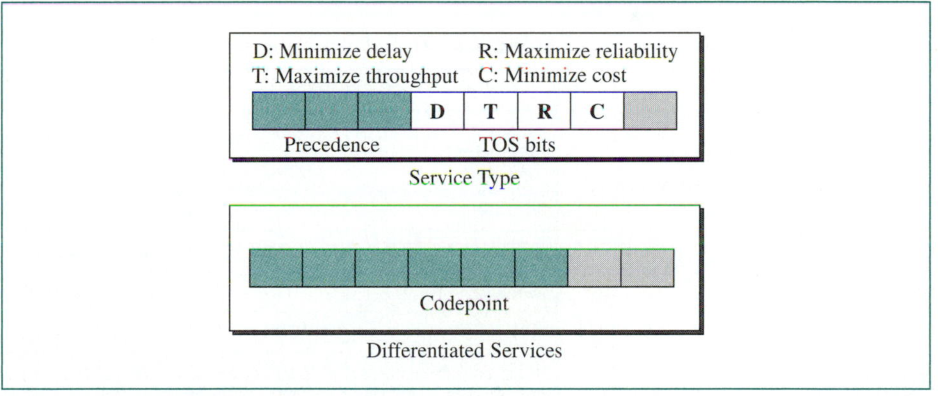

1. **Service Type**

   In this interpretation, the first 3 bits are called precedence bits. The next 4 bits are called TOS bits and the last bit is not used.

   a. **Precedence** is a 3-bit subfield ranging from 0 (000 in binary) to 7 (111 in binary). The precedence defines the priority of the datagram in issues such as congestion. If a router is congested and needs to discard some datagrams, those datagrams with lowest precedence are discarded first. Some datagrams in the Internet are more important than others. For example, a datagram used for network management is much more urgent and important than a datagram containing optional information for a group. At present, the precedence subfield, however, is not used. It is expected to be functional in future versions.

> The precedence subfield is not used in version 4.

b. **TOS bits** is a 4-bit subfield with each bit having a special meaning. Although a bit can be either 0 or 1, one and only one of the bits can have the value of 1 in each datagram. The bit patterns and their interpretations are given in Table 8.1. With only one bit set at a time, we can have five different types of services.

Table 8.1 *Types of service*

TOS Bits	*Description*
0000	Normal (default)
0001	Minimize cost
0010	Maximize reliability
0100	Maximize throughput
1000	Minimize delay

Application programs can request a specific type of service. The defaults for some applications are shown in Table 8.2.

Table 8.2 *Default types of service*

Protocol	*TOS Bits*	*Description*
ICMP	0000	Normal
BOOTP	0000	Normal
NNTP	0001	Minimize cost
IGP	0010	Maximize reliability
SNMP	0010	Maximize reliability
TELNET	1000	Minimize delay
FTP (data)	0100	Maximize throughput
FTP (control)	1000	Minimize delay
TFTP	1000	Minimize delay
SMTP (command)	1000	Minimize delay
SMTP (data)	0100	Maximize throughput
DNS (UDP query)	1000	Minimize delay
DNS (TCP query)	0000	Normal
DNS (zone)	0100	Maximize throughput

It is clear from the above table that interactive activities, activities requiring immediate attention, and activities requiring immediate response need minimum delay. Those activities that send bulk data require maximum throughput. Management activities need maximum reliability. Background activities need minimum cost.

2. **Differentiated Services**
   In this interpretation, the first 6 bits make up the **codepoint** subfield and the last two bits are not used. The codepoint subfield can be used in two different ways.
   a. When the 3 right-most bits are 0s, the 3 left-most bits are interpreted the same as the precedence bits in the Service Type interpretation. In other words, it is compatible with the old interpretation.
   b. When the 3 right-most bits are not all 0s, the 6 bits define 64 services based on the priority assignment by the Internet or local authorities according to Table 8.3. The first category contains 32 service types; the second and the third each contain 16. The first category (numbers 0, 2, 4, . . . , 62) is assigned by the Internet authorities (IETF). The second category (3, 7, 11, 15, . . . , 63) can be used by local authorities (organizations). The third category (1, 5, 9, . . . , 61) is temporary and can be used for experimental purposes. Note that the numbers are not contiguous. If they were, the first category would range from 0 to 31, the second 32 to 47, and the third 48 to 63. This would be incompatible with the TOS interpretation because XXX000 (which includes 0, 8, 16, 24, 32, 40, 48, and 56) would fall into all three categories. Instead, in this assignment method all these services belong to category 1. Note that these assignments have not yet been finalized.

Table 8.3 *Values for codepoints*

Category	*Codepoint*	*Assigning Authority*
1	XXXXX0	Internet
2	XXXX11	Local
3	XXXX01	Temporary or experimental

- **Total length.** This is a 16-bit field that defines the total length (header plus data) of the IP datagram in bytes. To find the length of the data coming from the upper layer, subtract the header length from the total length. The header length can be found by multiplying the value in the HLEN field by four.

  $$\text{length of data} = \text{total length} - \text{header length}$$

  Since the field length is 16 bits, the total length of the IP datagram is limited to 65,535 ($2^{16} - 1$) bytes, of which 20 to 60 bytes are the header and the rest is data from the upper layer.

  > The total length field defines the total length of the datagram including the header.

  Though a size of 65,535 bytes might seem large, the size of the IP datagram may increase in the near future as the underlying technologies allow even more throughput (more bandwidth).

  When we discuss fragmentation in the next section, we will see that some physical networks are not able to encapsulate a datagram of 65,535 bytes in their frames. The datagram must be fragmented to be able to pass through those networks.

One may ask why we need this field anyway. When a machine (router or host) receives a frame, it drops the header and the trailer leaving the datagram. Why include an extra field that is not needed? The answer is that in many cases we really do not need the value in this field. However, there are occasions in which the datagram is not the only thing encapsulated in a frame; it may be that padding has been added. For example, the Ethernet protocol has a minimum and maximum restriction on the size of data that can be encapsulated in a frame (46 to 1500 bytes). If the size of an IP datagram is less than 46 bytes, some padding will be added to meet this requirement. In this case, when a machine decapsulates the datagram, it needs to check the total length field to determine how much is really data and how much is padding (see Figure 8.4).

Figure 8.4 *Encapsulation of a small datagram in an Ethernet frame*

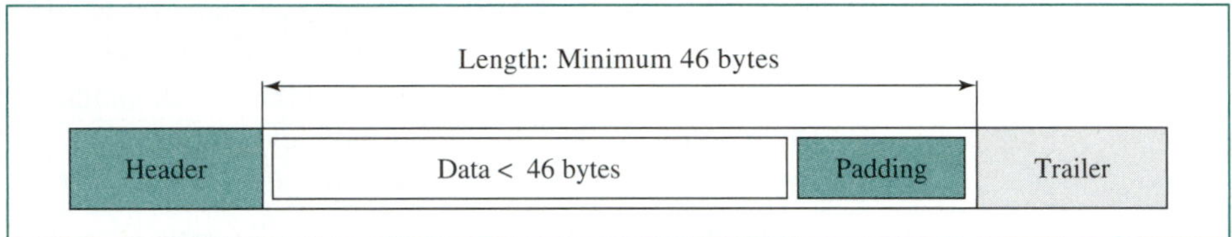

- **Identification.** This field is used in fragmentation (discussed in the next section).
- **Flags.** This field is used in fragmentation (discussed in the next section).
- **Fragmentation offset.** This field is used in fragmentation (discussed in the next section).
- **Time to live.** A datagram has a limited lifetime in its travel through an internet. This field was originally designed to hold a timestamp, which was decremented by each visited router. The datagram was discarded when the value became zero. However, for this scheme, all the machines must have synchronized clocks and must know how long it takes for a datagram to go from one machine to another. Today, this field is mostly used to control the maximum number of hops (routers) visited by the datagram. When a source host sends the datagram, it stores a number in this field. This value is approximately two times the maximum number of routes between any two hosts. Each router that processes the datagram decrements this number by one. If this value, after being decremented, is zero, the router discards the datagram.

  This field is needed because routing tables in the Internet can become corrupted. A datagram may travel between two or more routers for a long time without ever getting delivered to the destination host. Resources may become tied up. This field limits the lifetime for a datagram and prevents old datagrams from popping out of the network and perhaps confusing higher-level protocols (especially TCP).

  Another use of this field is to intentionally limit the journey of the packet. For example, if the source wants to confine the packet to the local network, it can store 1 in this field. When the packet arrives at the first router, this value is decremented to 0, and the datagram is discarded.

- **Protocol.** This 8-bit field defines the higher-level protocol that uses the services of the IP layer. An IP datagram can encapsulate data from several higher level protocols such as TCP, UDP, ICMP, and IGMP. This field specifies the final destination protocol to which the IP datagram should be delivered. In other words, since the IP protocol multiplexes and demultiplexes data from different higher-level protocols, the value of this field helps in the demultiplexing process when the datagram arrives at its final destination (see Figure 8.5).

Figure 8.5 *Multiplexing*

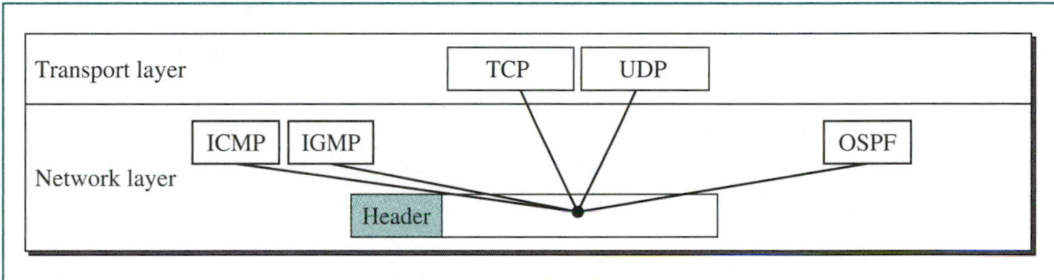

The value of this field for different higher-level protocols is shown in Table 8.4.

Table 8.4 *Protocols*

Value	*Protocol*
1	ICMP
2	IGMP
6	TCP
17	UDP
89	OSPF

- **Checksum.** The checksum concept and its calculation are discussed later in this chapter.
- **Source address.** This 32-bit field defines the IP address of the source. This field must remain unchanged during the time the IP datagram travels from the source host to the destination host.
- **Destination address.** This 32-bit field defines the IP address of the destination. This field must remain unchanged during the time the IP datagram travels from the source host to the destination host.

Example 1

An IP packet has arrived with the first 8 bits as shown:

← 01000010

The receiver discards the packet. Why?

Solution

There is an error in this packet. The 4 left-most bits (0100) show the version, which is correct. The next 4 bits (0010) show the header length, which means $(2 \times 4 = 8)$, which is wrong. The minimum number of bytes in the header must be 20. The packet has been corrupted in transmission.

Example 2

In an IP packet, the value of HLEN is 1000 in binary. How many bytes of options are being carried by this packet?

Solution

The HLEN value is 8, which means the total number of bytes in the header is 8×4 or 32 bytes. The first 20 bytes are the main header, the next 12 bytes are the options.

Example 3

In an IP packet, the value of HLEN is 5_{16} and the value of the total length field is 0028_{16}. How many bytes of data are being carried by this packet?

Solution

The HLEN value is 5, which means the total number of bytes in the header is 5×4 or 20 bytes (no options). The total length is 40 bytes, which means the packet is carrying 20 bytes of data $(40 - 20)$.

Example 4

An IP packet has arrived with the first few hexadecimal digits as shown below:

← 45000028000100000102..................

How many hops can this packet travel before being dropped? The data belong to what upper layer protocol?

Solution

To find the time-to-live field, we should skip 8 bytes (16 hexadecimal digits). The time-to-live field is the ninth byte, which is 01. This means the packet can travel only one hop. The protocol field is the next byte (02), which means that the upper layer protocol is IGMP (see Table 8.4).

8.2 FRAGMENTATION

A datagram can travel through different networks. Each router decapsulates the IP datagram from the frame it receives, processes it, and then encapsulates it in another frame. The format and size of the received frame depend on the protocol used by the physical network through which the frame has just traveled. The format and size of the sent frame depend on the protocol used by the physical network through which the frame is going to travel. For example, if a router connects an Ethernet network to a Token Ring network, it receives a frame in the Ethernet format and sends a frame in the Token Ring format.

Maximum Transfer Unit (MTU)

Each data link layer protocol has its own frame format. One of the fields defined in the format is the maximum size of the data field. In other words, when a datagram is encapsulated in a frame, the total size of the datagram must be less than this maximum size, which is defined by the restriction imposed by the hardware and software used in the network (see Figure 8.6).

Figure 8.6 *MTU*

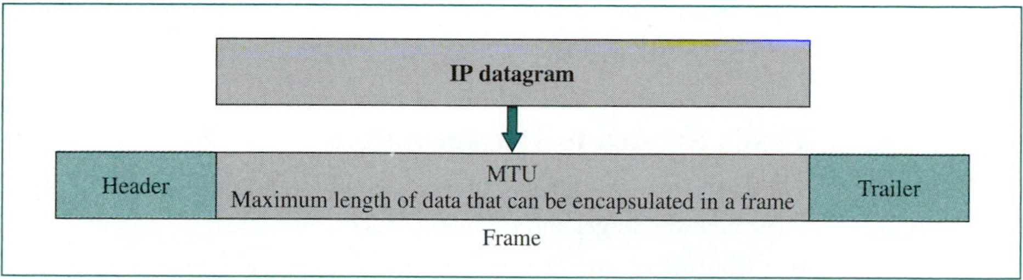

The value of the MTU differs from one physical network protocol to another. Table 8.5 shows the values for different protocols.

Table 8.5 *MTUs for different networks*

Protocol	*MTU*
Hyperchannel	65,535
Token Ring (16 Mbps)	17,914
Token Ring (4 Mbps)	4,464
FDDI	4,352
Ethernet	1,500
X.25	576
PPP	296

In order to make the IP protocol independent of the physical network, the packagers decided to make the maximum length of the IP datagram equal to the largest maximum transfer unit (MTU) defined so far (65,535 bytes). This makes transmission more efficient if we use a protocol with an MTU of this size. However, for other physical networks, we must divide the datagram to make it possible to pass through these networks. This is called **fragmentation.**

When a datagram is fragmented, each fragment has its own header with most of the fields repeated, but some changed. A fragmented datagram may itself be fragmented if it encounters a network with an even smaller MTU. In other words, a datagram can be fragmented several times before it reaches the final destination.

A datagram can be fragmented by the source host or any router in the path. The reassembly of the datagram, however, is done only by the destination host because each fragment becomes an independent datagram. Whereas the fragmented datagram can travel through different routes, and we can never control or guarantee which route a fragmented datagram may take, all of the fragments belonging to the same datagram should finally arrive at the destination host. So it is logical to do the reassembly at the final destination.

When a datagram is fragmented, required parts of the header must be copied by all fragments. The option field may or may not be copied as we will see in the next section. The host or router that fragments a datagram must change the values of three fields: flags, fragmentation offset, and total length. The rest of the fields must be copied. Of course, the value of the checksum must be recalculated regardless of fragmentation.

Fields Related to Fragmentation

The fields that are related to fragmentation and reassembly of an IP datagram are the identification, flags, and fragmentation offset fields.

- **Identification.** This 16-bit field identifies a datagram originating from the source host. The combination of the identification and source IP address must uniquely define a datagram as it leaves the source host. To guarantee uniqueness, the IP protocol uses a counter to label the datagrams. The counter is initialized to a positive number. When the IP protocol sends a datagram, it copies the current value of the counter to the identification field and increments the counter by one. As long as the counter is kept in the main memory, uniqueness is guaranteed. When a datagram is fragmented, the value in the identification field is copied into all fragments. In other words, all fragments have the same identification number, which is also the same as the original datagram. The identification number helps the destination in reassembling the datagram. It knows that all fragments having the same identification value should be assembled into one datagram.
- **Flags.** This is a three-bit field. The first bit is reserved. The second bit is called the *do not fragment* bit. If its value is 1, the machine must not fragment the datagram. If it cannot pass the datagram through any available physical network, it discards the datagram and sends an ICMP error message to the source host (see Chapter 9). If its value is 0, the datagram can be fragmented if necessary. The third bit is called the *more fragment* bit. If its value is 1, it means the datagram is not the last fragment; there are more fragments after this one. If its value is 0, it means this is the last or only fragment (see Figure 8.7).

Figure 8.7 *Flags field*

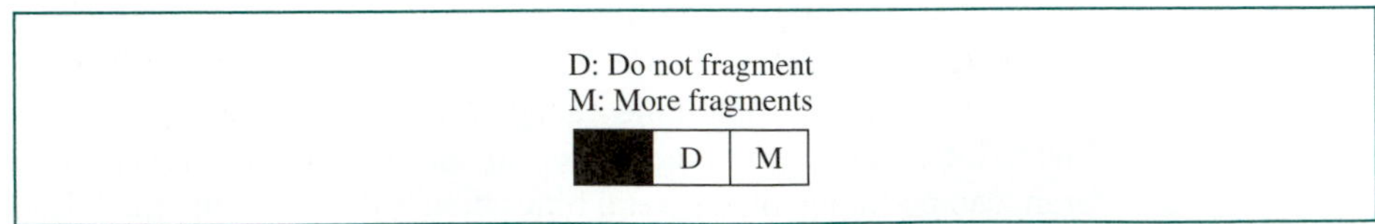

- **Fragmentation offset.** This 13-bit field shows the relative position of this fragment with respect to the whole datagram. It is the offset of the data in the original datagram measured in units of 8 bytes. Figure 8.8 shows a datagram with a data size of 4000 bytes fragmented into three fragments. The bytes in the original datagram are numbered 0 to 3999. The first fragment carries bytes 0 to 1399. The offset for this datagram is 0/8 = 0. The second fragment carries bytes 1400 to 2799; the offset value for this fragment is 1400/8 = 175. Finally, the third fragment carries bytes 2800 to 3999. The offset value for this fragment is 2800/8 = 350.

Remember that the value of the offset is measured in units of 8 bytes. This is done because the length of the offset field is only 13 bits long and cannot represent a sequence of bytes greater than 8191. This forces hosts or routers that fragment datagrams to choose the size of each fragment so that the first byte number is divisible by 8.

Figure 8.8 *Fragmentation example*

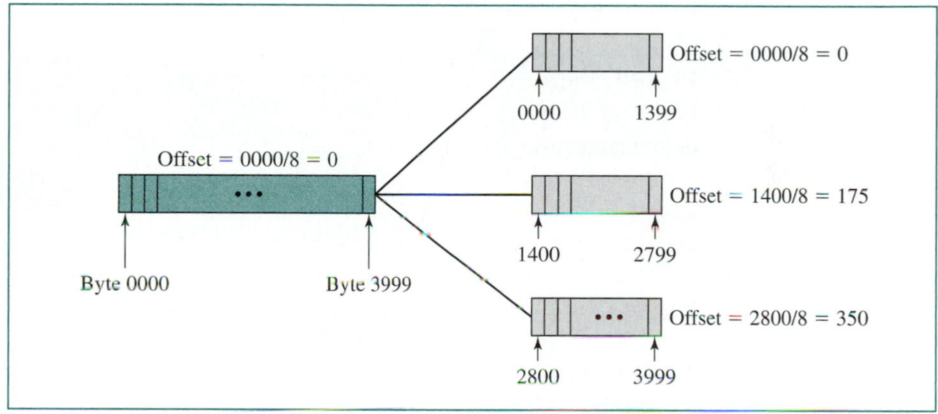

Figure 8.9 shows an expanded view of the fragments in the previous figure. Notice the value of the identification field is the same in all fragments. Notice the value of the flags field with the *more* bit set for all fragments except the last. Also, the value of the offset field for each fragment is shown.

The figure also shows what happens if a fragment itself is fragmented. In this case the value of the offset field is always relative to the original datagram. For example, in the figure, the second fragment is itself fragmented later to two fragments of 800 bytes and 600 bytes, but the offset shows the relative position of the fragments to the original data.

It is obvious that even if each fragment follows a different path and arrives out of order, the final destination host can reassemble the original datagram from the fragments received (if none of them is lost) using the following strategy:

a. The first fragment has an offset field value of zero.

b. Divide the length of the first fragment by 8. The second fragment has an offset value equal to that result.

c. Divide the total length of the first and second fragment by 8. The third fragment has an offset value equal to that result.

d. Continue the process. The last fragment has a *more* bit value of 0.

Figure 8.9 *Detailed fragmentation example*

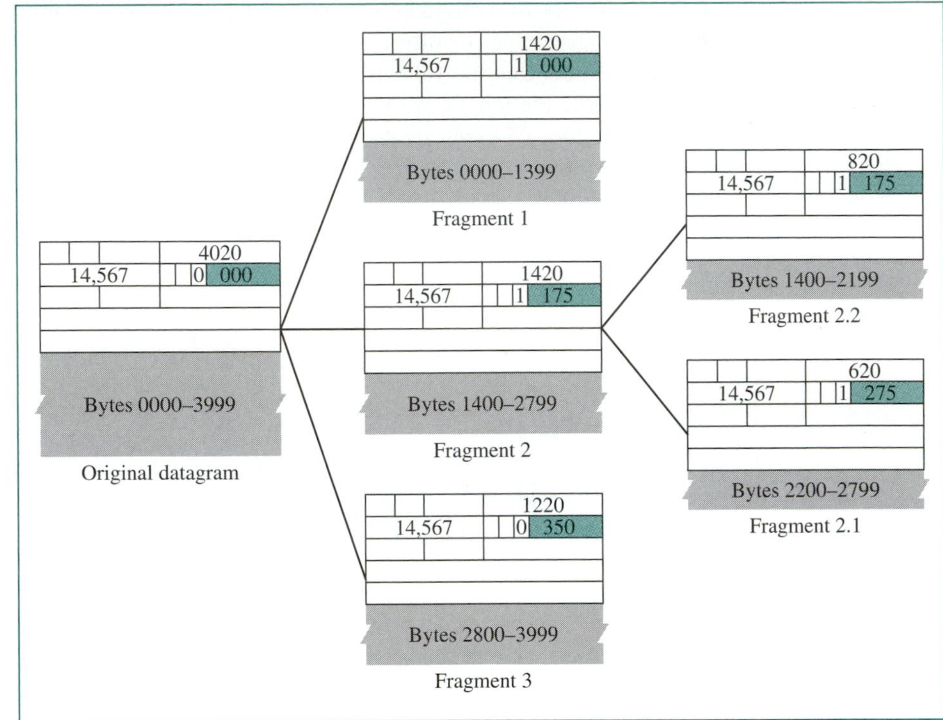

Example 5

A packet has arrived with an *M* bit value of 0. Is this the first fragment, the last fragment, or a middle fragment? Do we know if the packet was fragmented?

Solution

If the *M* bit is 0, it means that there are no more fragments; the fragment is the last one. However, we cannot say if the original packet was fragmented or not. A nonfragmented packet is considered the last fragment.

Example 6

A packet has arrived with an *M* bit value of 1. Is this the first fragment, the last fragment, or a middle fragment? Do we know if the packet was fragmented?

Solution

If the *M* bit is 1, it means that there is at least one more fragment. This fragment can be the first one or a middle one, but not the last one. We don't know if it is the first one or a middle one; we need more information (the value of the fragmentation offset). However, we can definitely say the original packet has been fragmented because the *M* bit value is 1.

Example 7

A packet has arrived with an *M* bit value of 1 and a fragmentation offset value of zero. Is this the first fragment, the last fragment, or a middle fragment?

Solution

Because the *M* bit is 1, it is either the first fragment or a middle one. Because the offset value is 0, it is the first fragment.

Example 8

A packet has arrived in which the offset value is 100. What is the number of the first byte? Do we know the number of the last byte?

Solution

To find the number of the first byte, we multiply the offset value by 8. This means that the first byte number is 800. We cannot determine the number of the last byte unless we know the length of the data.

Example 9

A packet has arrived in which the offset value is 100, the value of HLEN is 5 and the value of the total length field is 100. What is the number of the first byte and the last byte?

Solution

The first byte number is $100 \times 8 = 800$. The total length is 100 bytes and the header length is 20 bytes (5×4), which means that there are 80 bytes in this datagram. If the first byte number is 800, the last byte number must 879.

8.3 OPTIONS

The header of the IP datagram is made of two parts: a fixed part and a variable part. The fixed part is 20 bytes long and was discussed in the previous section. The variable part comprises the options that can be a maximum of 40 bytes.

Options, as the name implies, are not required for every datagram. They are used for network testing and debugging. Although options are not a required part of the IP header, option processing is required of the IP software. This means that all standards must be able to handle options if they are present in the header.

Format

Figure 8.10 shows the format of an option. It is composed of a 1-byte code field, a 1-byte length field, and a variable-sized data field.

Code

The **code field** is 8 bits long and contains three subfields: copy, class, and number.

- **Copy.** This 1-bit subfield controls the presence of the option in fragmentation. When its value is 0, it means that the option must be copied only to the first fragment. If its value is 1, it means the option must be copied to all fragments.
- **Class.** This 2-bit subfield defines the general purpose of the option. When its value is 00, it means that the option is used for datagram control. When its value is 10, it means that the option is used for debugging and management. The other two possible values (01 and 11) have not yet been defined.

Figure 8.10 *Option format*

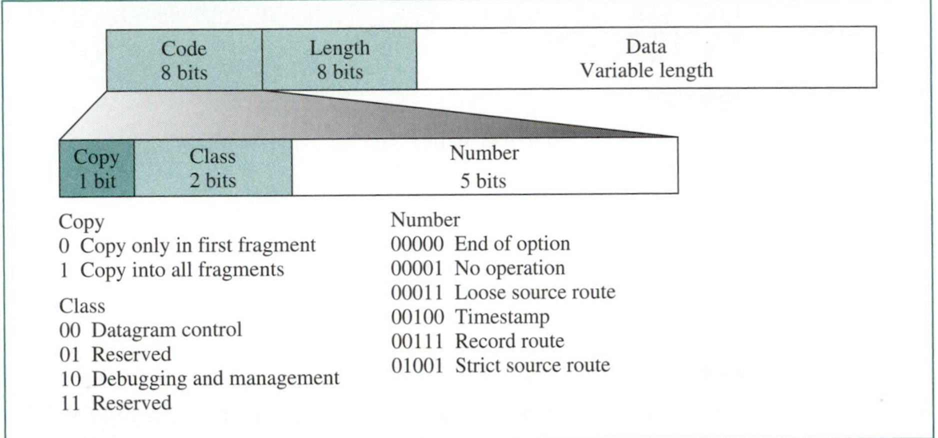

- **Number.** This 5-bit subfield defines the type of the option. Although 5 bits can define up to 32 different types, currently only 6 types are in use. These will be discussed in a later section.

Length

The **length field** defines the total length of the option including the code field and the length field itself. This field is not present in all of the option types.

Data

The **data field** contains the data that specific options require. Like the length field, this field is also not present in all option types.

Option Types

As mentioned previously, only six options are currently being used. Two of these are 1-byte options, and they do not require the length or the data fields. Four of them are multiple-byte options; they require the length and the data fields (see Figure 8.11).

Figure 8.11 *Categories of options*

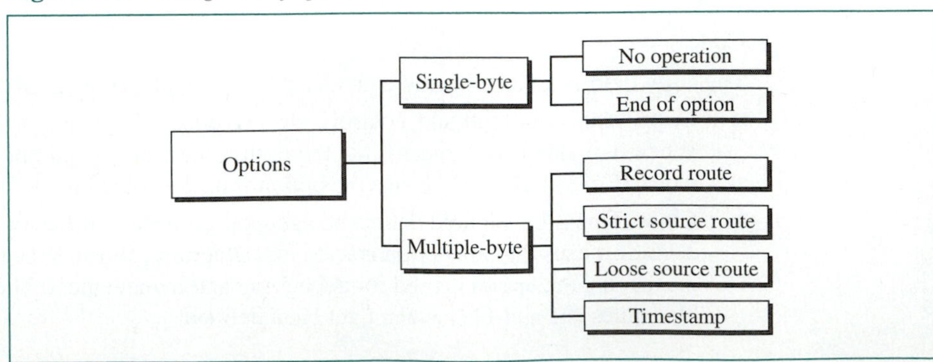

No Operation

A **no operation** option is a 1-byte option used as a filler between options. For example, it can be used to align the next option on a 16-bit or 32-bit boundary (see Figure 8.12).

Figure 8.12 *No operation option*

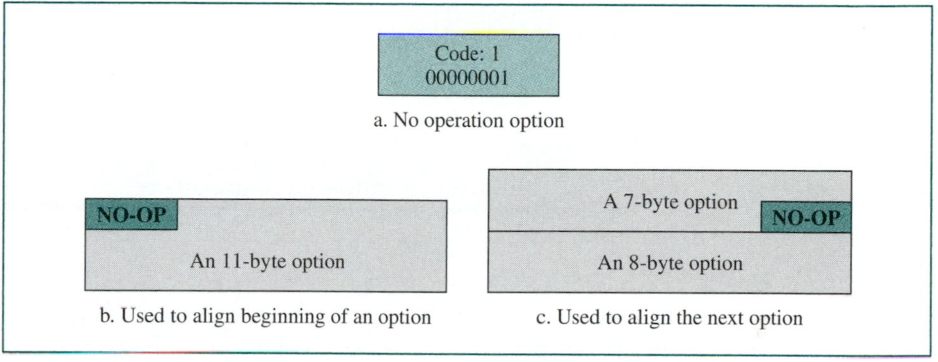

End of Option

An **end of option** option is also a 1-byte option used for padding at the end of the option field. It, however, can only be used as the last option. Only one *end of option* option can be used. After this option, the receiver looks for the payload data. This means that if more than 1 byte is needed to align the option field, some no operation options must be used followed by an end of option option (see Figure 8.13).

Figure 8.13 *End of option option*

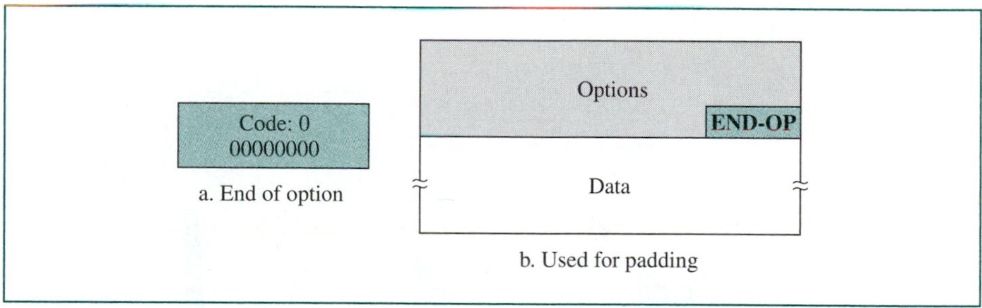

Record Route

A **record route** option is used to record the internet routers that handle the datagram. It can list up to nine router IP addresses since the maximum size of the header is 60 bytes, which must include 20 bytes for the base header. This implies that only 40 bytes are left over for the option part. The source creates placeholder fields in the option to be filled by the visited routers. Figure 8.14 shows the format of the record route option.

Both the code and length fields have been described above. The **pointer field** is an offset integer field containing the byte number of the first empty entry. In other words, it points to the first available entry.

Figure 8.14 *Record route option*

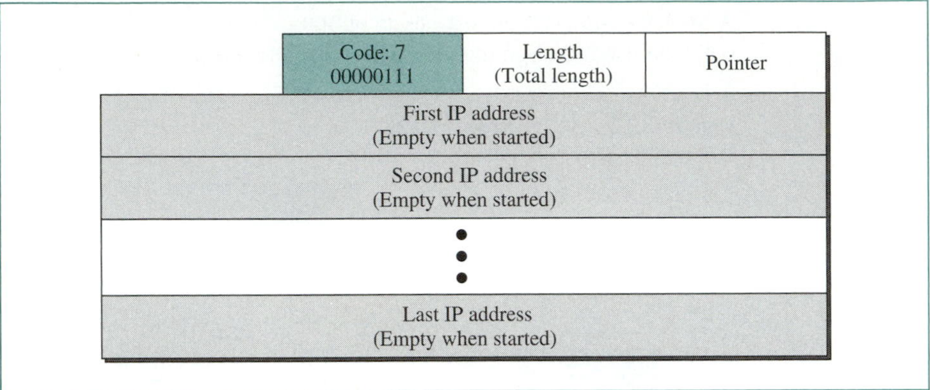

The source creates empty fields for the IP addresses in the data field of the option. When the datagram leaves the source, all of the fields are empty. The pointer field has a value of 4, pointing to the first empty field.

When the datagram is traveling, each router that processes the datagram compares the value of the pointer with the value of the length. If the value of the pointer is greater than the value of the length, the option is full and no changes are made. However, if the value of the pointer is not greater than the value of the length, the router inserts its outgoing IP address in the next empty field (remember that a router has more than one IP address). In this case, the router adds the IP address of its interface from which the datagram is leaving. The router then increments the value of the pointer by 4. Figure 8.15 shows the entries as the datagram travels left to right from router to router.

Figure 8.15 *Record route concept*

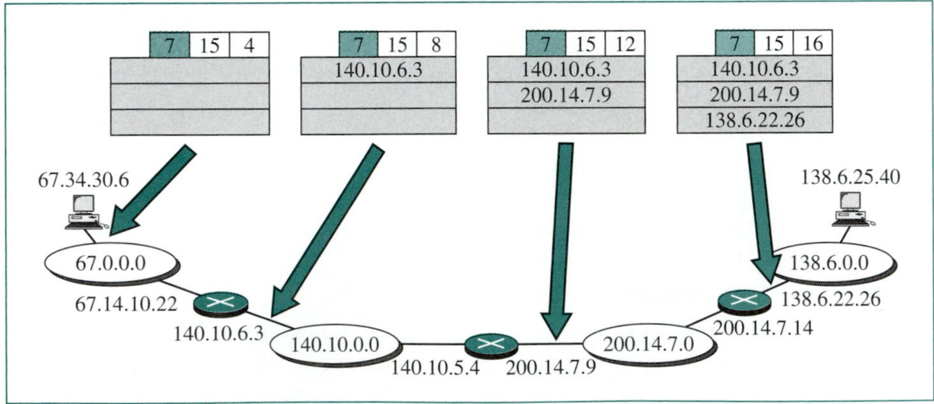

Strict Source Route

A **strict source route** option is used by the source to predetermine a route for the datagram as it travels through the Internet. Dictation of a route by the source can be useful for several purposes. The sender can choose a route with a specific type of service, such as minimum delay or maximum throughput. Alternatively, it may choose a route that is safer or more reliable for the sender's purpose. For example, a sender can choose a route so that its datagram does not travel through a competitor's network.

If a datagram specifies a strict source route, all of the routers defined in the option must be visited by the datagram. A router must not be visited if its IP address is not listed in the datagram. If the datagram visits a router that is not on the list, the datagram is discarded and an error message is issued. If the datagram arrives at the destination and some of the entries were not visited, it will also be discarded and an error message issued.

Nonprivileged users of the Internet, however, are not usually aware of the physical topology of the Internet. Consequently, strict source routing is not the choice of most users. Figure 8.16 shows the format of the strict source route option.

Figure 8.16 *Strict source route option*

Code: 137 10001001	Length (Total length)	Pointer
First IP address (Filled when started)		
Second IP address (Filled when started)		
• • •		
Last IP address (Filled when started)		

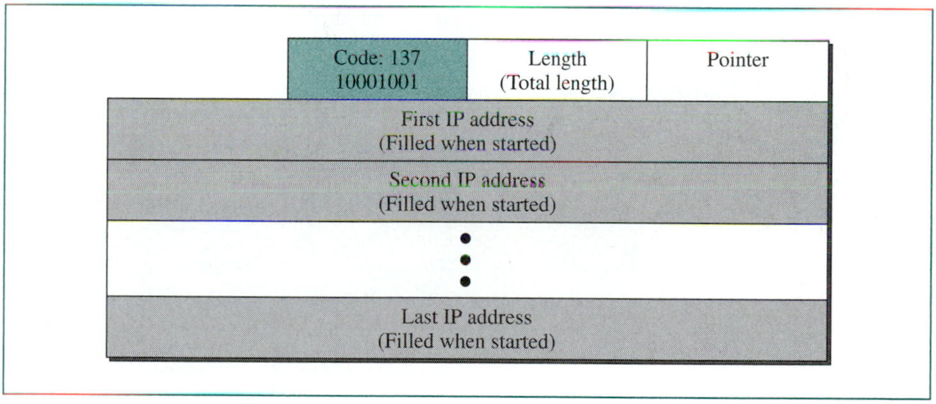

The format is similar to the record route option with the exception that all of the IP addresses are entered by the sender.

When the datagram is traveling, each router that processes the datagram compares the value of the pointer with the value of the length. If the value of the pointer is greater than the value of the length, the datagram has visited all of the predefined routers. The datagram cannot travel anymore; it is discarded and an error message is created. If the value of the pointer is not greater than the value of the length, the router compares the IP address pointed by the pointer with its incoming IP address: If they are equal, it processes the datagram, overwrites the current IP address with its outgoing IP address, increments the pointer value by 4, and forwards the datagram. If they are not equal, it discards the datagram and issues an error message. Figure 8.17 shows the actions taken by each router as a datagram travels from source to destination.

Figure 8.17 *Strict source route concept*

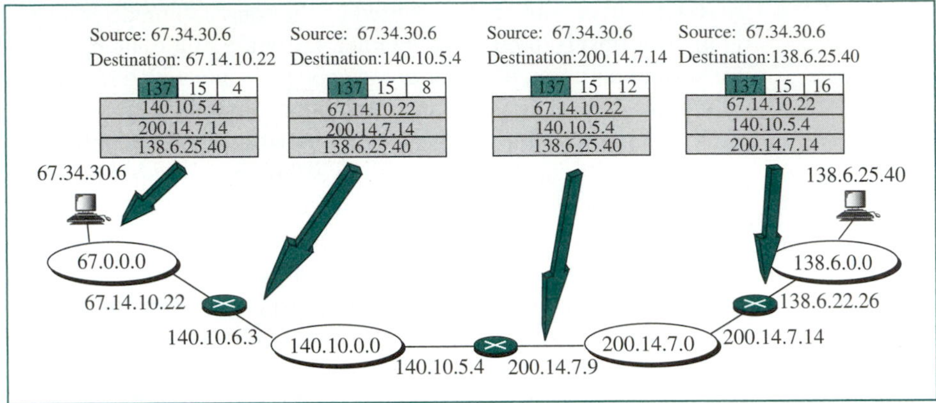

Loose Source Route

A **loose source route** option is similar to the strict source route, but it is more relaxed. Each router in the list must be visited, but the datagram can visit other routers as well. Figure 8.18 shows the format of the loose source route option.

Figure 8.18 *Loose source route option*

Code: 131 10000011	Length (Total length)	Pointer

First IP address
(Filled when started)

Second IP address
(Filled when started)

•
•
•

Last IP address
(Filled when started)

Timestamp

A **timestamp** option is used to record the time of datagram processing by a router. The time is expressed in milliseconds from midnight, Universal Time. Knowing the time a datagram is processed can help users and managers track the behavior of the routers in the Internet. We can estimate the time it takes for a datagram to go from one router to another. We say *estimate* because, although all routers may use Universal Time, their local clocks may not be synchronized.

However, nonprivileged users of the Internet are not usually aware of the physical topology of the Internet. Consequently, a timestamp option is not a choice for most users. Figure 8.19 shows the format of the timestamp option.

Figure 8.19 *Timestamp option*

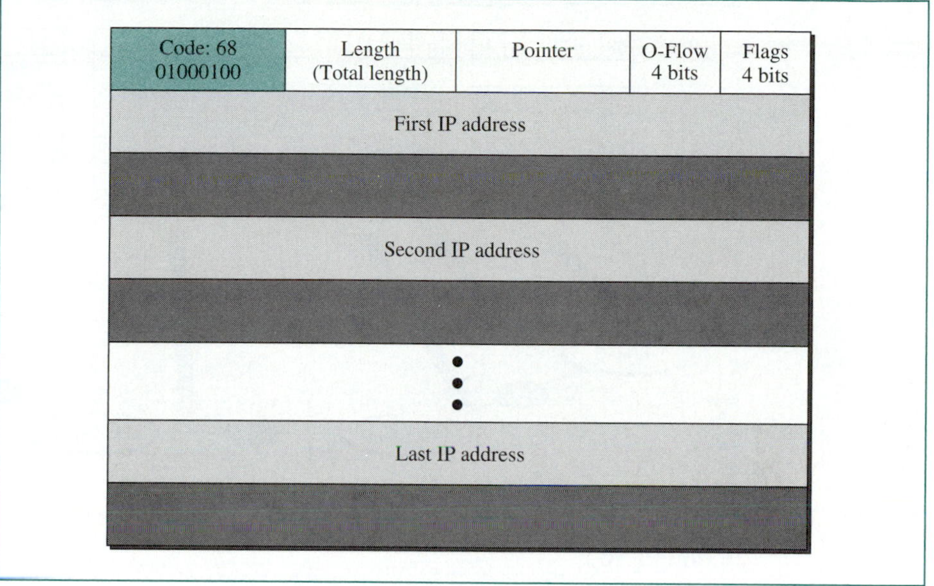

In this figure, the definition of the code and length fields are the same as before. The overflow field records the number of routers that could not add their timestamp because no more fields were available. The flags field specifies the visited router responsibilities. If the flag value is 0, each router adds only the timestamp in the provided field. If the flag value is 1, each router must add its outgoing IP address and the timestamp. If the value is 3, the IP addresses are given, and each router must check the given IP address with its own incoming IP address. If there is a match, the router overwrites the IP address with its outgoing IP address and adds the timestamp (see Figure 8.20).

Figure 8.20 *Use of flag in timestamp*

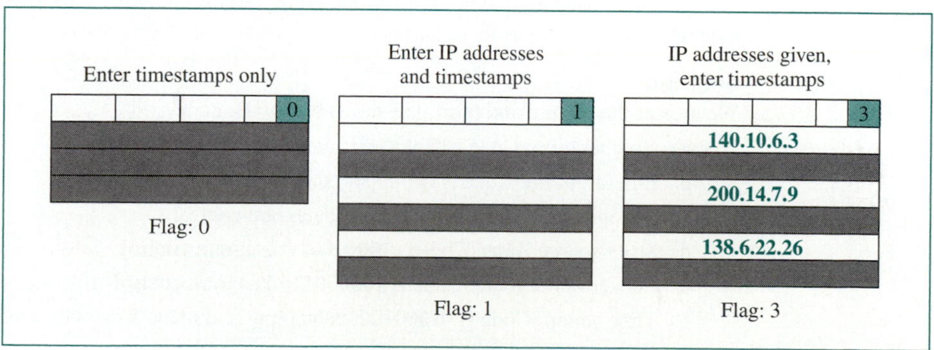

Figure 8.21 shows the actions taken by each router when a datagram travels from source to destination. The figure assumes the flag value of 1.

Figure 8.21 *Timestamp concept*

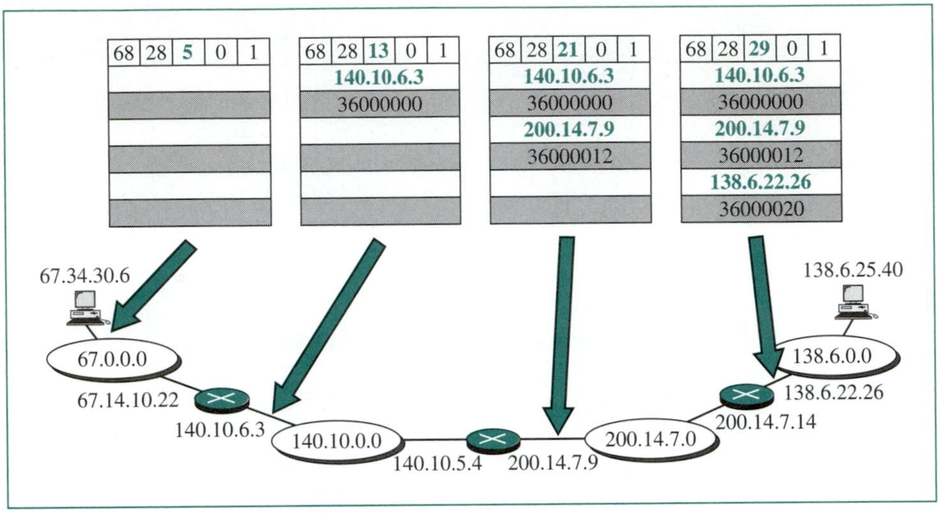

Example 10

Which of the six options must be copied to each fragment?

Solution

We look at the first (left-most) bit of the code for each option.

a. No operation: Code is **0**0000001; no copy.
b. End of option: Code is **0**0000000; no copy.
c. Record route: Code is **0**0000111; no copy.
d. Strict source route: Code is **1**0001001; it is copied to each fragment.
e. Loose source route: Code is **1**0000011; it is copied to each fragment.
f. Timestamp: Code is **0**1000100; no copy.

Example 11

Which of the six options are used for datagram control and which are used for debugging and management?

Solution

We look at the second and third (left-most) bits of the code.

a. No operation: Code is 0**00**00001; datagram control.
b. End of option: Code is 0**00**00000; datagram control.
c. Record route: Code is 0**00**00111; datagram control.
d. Strict source route: Code is 1**00**01001; datagram control.
e. Loose source route: Code is 1**00**00011; datagram control.
f. Time stamp: Code is 0**10**00100; debugging and management control.

8.4 CHECKSUM

The error detection method used by most TCP/IP protocols is called the **checksum.** The checksum protects against the corruption that may occur during the transmission of a packet. It is redundant information added to the packet.

The checksum is calculated at the sender and the value obtained is sent with the packet. The receiver repeats the same calculation on the whole packet including the checksum. If the result is satisfactory (see below), the packet is accepted; otherwise, it is rejected.

Checksum Calculation at the Sender

In the sender, the packet is divided into n-bit sections (n is usually 16). These sections are added together using one's complement arithmetic (see Appendix C) such that the sum is also n bits long. The sum is then complemented (all 0s changed to 1s and all 1s to 0s) to produce the checksum.

To create the checksum the sender does the following:

- The packet is divided into k sections, each of n bits.
- All sections are added together using one's complement arithmetic.
- The final result is complemented to make the checksum.

Checksum Calculation at the Receiver

The receiver divides the received packet into k sections and adds all sections. It then complements the result. If the final result is 0, the packet is accepted; otherwise, it is rejected.

Figure 8.22 shows graphically what happens at the sender and the receiver.

We said when the receiver adds all of the sections and complements the result, it should get zero if there is no error in the data during transmission or processing. This is true because of the rules in one's complement arithmetic.

Assume that we get a number called T when we add all the sections in the sender. When we complement the number in one's complement arithmetic, we get the negative of the number. This means that if the sum of all sections is T, the checksum is $-T$.

When the receiver receives the packet, it adds all the sections. It adds T and $-T$ which, in one's complement, is -0 (minus zero). When the result is complemented, -0 becomes 0. Thus if the final result is 0, the packet is accepted; otherwise, it is rejected (see Figure 8.23).

Checksum in the IP Packet

The implementation of the checksum in the IP packet follows the same principle discussed above. First, the value of the checksum field is set to 0. Then, the entire header

Figure 8.22 *Checksum concept*

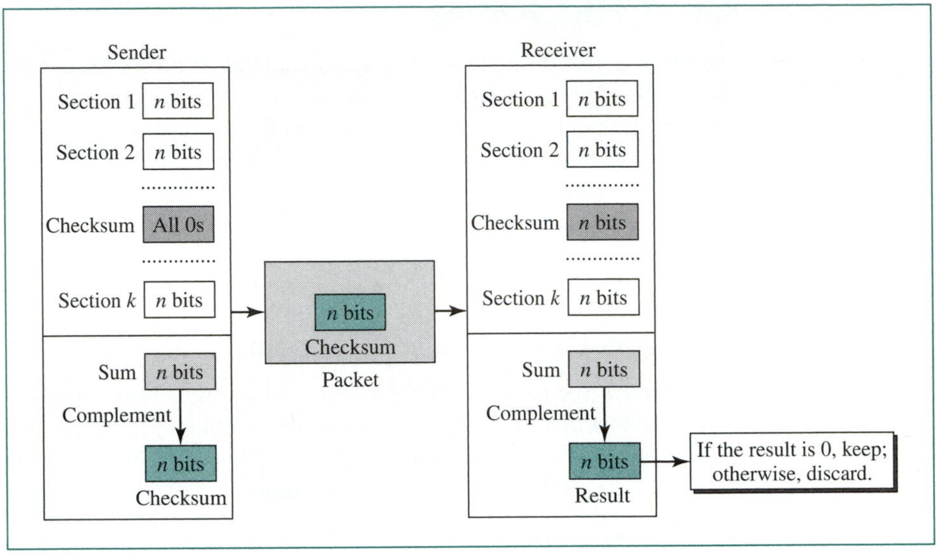

Figure 8.23 *Checksum in one's complement arithmetic*

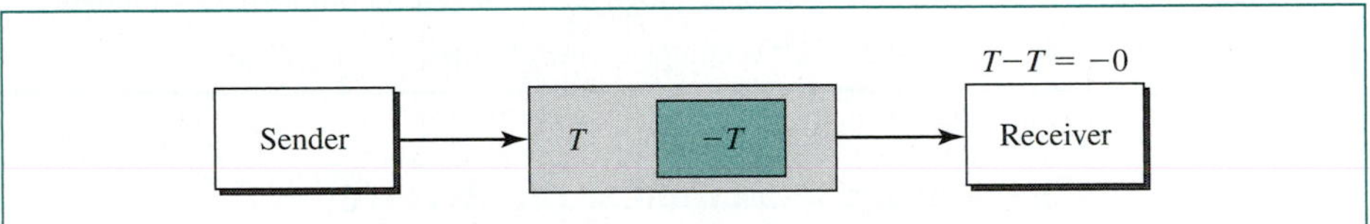

is divided into 16-bit sections and added together. The result (sum) is complemented and inserted into the checksum field.

The checksum in the IP packet covers only the header, not the data. There are two good reasons for this. First, all higher-level protocols that encapsulate data in the IP datagram have a checksum field that covers the whole packet. Therefore, the checksum for the IP datagram does not have to check the encapsulated data. Second, the header of the IP packet changes with each visited router, but the data does not. So the checksum includes only the part that has changed. If the data is included, each router must recalculate the checksum for the whole packet, which means increased processing time for each router.

Example 12

Figure 8.24 shows an example of a checksum calculation for an IP header without options. The header is divided into 16-bit sections. All the sections are added and the sum is complemented. The result is inserted in the checksum field.

Figure 8.24 *Example of checksum calculation in binary*

4	5	0	28	
1			0	0
4		17	0	
10.12.14.5				
12.6.7.9				

4, 5, and 0	→	01000101 00000000
28	→	00000000 00011100
1	→	00000000 00000001
0 and 0	→	00000000 00000000
4 and 17	→	00000100 00010001
0	→	00000000 00000000
10.12	→	00001010 00001100
14.5	→	00001110 00000101
12.6	→	00001100 00000110
7.9	→	00000111 00001001
Sum	→	**01110100 01001110**
Checksum	→	**10001011 10110001**

Example 13

Let us do the same example in hexadecimal. Each row has four hexadecimal digits. We calculate the sum first. Note that if an addition results in more than one hexadecimal digit, the right-most digit becomes the current-column digit and the rest are carried to other columns. From the sum, we make the checksum by complementing the sum. However, note that we subtract each digit from 15 in hexadecimal arithmetic (just as we subtract from 1 in binary arithmetic). This means the complement of E (14) is 1 and the complement of 4 is B (11). Figure 8.25 shows the calculation. Note that the result (8BB1) is exactly the same as in Example 11.

Figure 8.25 *Example of checksum calculation in hexadecimal*

4	5	0	28	
1			0	0
4		17	0	
10.12.14.5				
12.6.7.9				

4, 5, and 0	→	4	5	0	0
28	→	0	0	1	C
1	→	0	0	0	1
0 and 0	→	0	0	0	0
4 and 17	→	0	4	1	1
0	→	0	0	0	0
10.12	→	0	A	0	C
14.5	→	0	E	0	5
12.6	→	0	C	0	6
7.9	→	0	7	0	9
Sum	→	**7**	**4**	**4**	**E**
Checksum	→	**8**	**B**	**B**	**1**

Check Appendix C for a detailed description of checksum calculation and the handling of carries.

8.5 IP PACKAGE

In this section, we present a simplified example of a hypothetical IP package. Our purpose is to show the relationships between the different concepts discussed in this chapter. Figure 8.26 shows these eight components and their interactions.

Figure 8.26 *IP components*

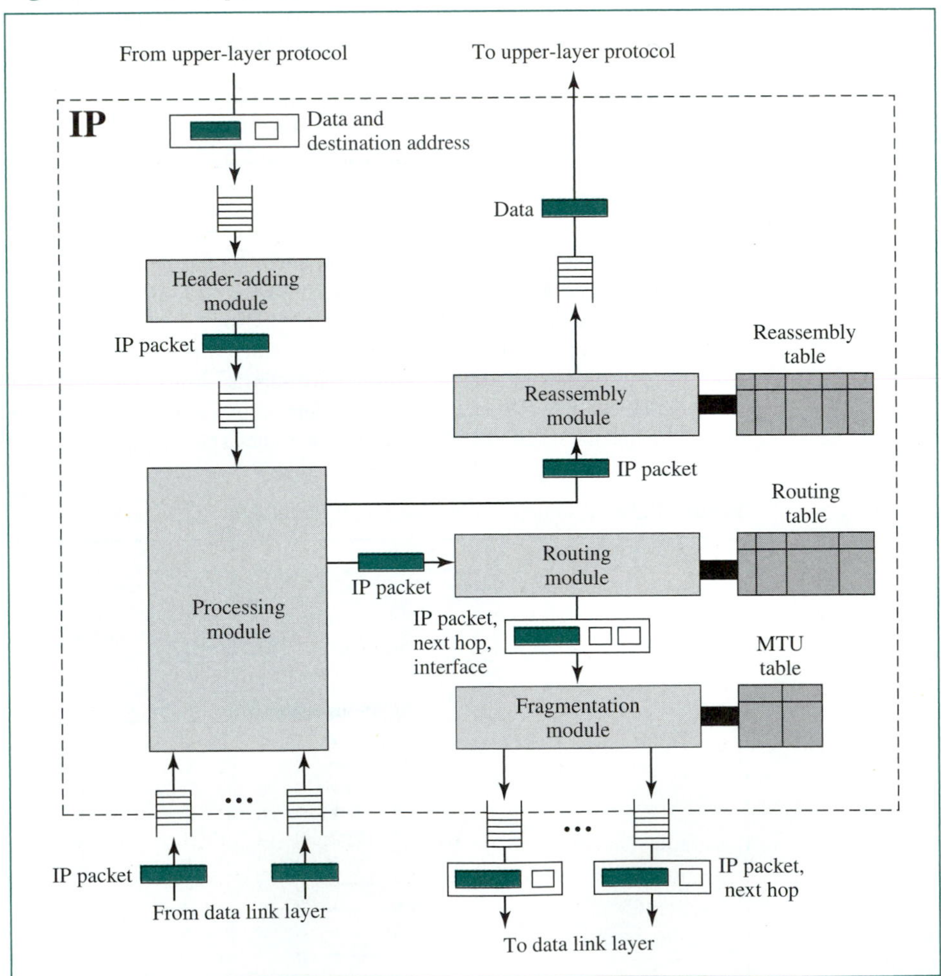

Although IP supports several options, we have omitted option processing in our package to make it easier to understand at this level. In addition, we have sacrificed efficiency for the sake of simplicity.

We can say that the IP package involves eight components: a header-adding module, a processing module, a routing module, a fragmentation module, a reassembly module, a routing table, an MTU table, and a reassembly table. In addition, the package includes input and output queues.

The package receives a packet, either from the data link layer or from a higher-level protocol. If the packet comes from an upper-layer protocol, it is delivered to the data link layer for transmission (unless it has a loopback address of 127.X.Y.Z). If the packet comes from the data link layer, it is either delivered to the data link layer for forwarding (in a router) or it is delivered to a higher-layer protocol if the destination IP address of the packet is the same as the station address.

Header-Adding Module

The **header-adding module** receives data from an upper-layer protocol along with the destination IP address. It encapsulates the data in an IP datagram by adding the IP header.

Header-Adding Module
Receive: data, destination address
1. Encapsulate the data in an IP datagram.
2. Calculate the checksum and insert it in the checksum field.
3. Send the data to the corresponding input queue.
4. Return.

Processing Module

The **processing module** is the heart of the IP package. In our package, the processing module receives a datagram from an interface or from the header-adding module. It treats both cases the same. A datagram must be processed and routed regardless of where it comes from.

The processing module first checks to see if the datagram is a loopback packet (with the destination address of 127.X.Y.Z) or a packet that has reached its final destination. In either case, the packet is sent to the reassembly module.

If the node is a router, it decrements the time-to-live (TTL) field by one. If this value is less than or equal to zero, the datagram is discarded and an ICMP message (see Chapter 9) is sent to the original sender. If the value of TTL is greater than zero after decrement, the processing module sends the datagram to the routing module (see Chapter 8).

Processing Module
1. Remove one datagram from one of the input queues.
2. If (destination address is 127.X.Y.Z or matches one of the local addresses)
1. Send the datagram to the reassembly module.
2. Return.
3. If (machine is a router)
1. Decrement TTL.
4. If (TTL less than or equal to zero)
1. Discard the datagram.
2. Send an ICMP error message.
3. Return.
5. Send the datagram to the routing module.
6. Return.

Queues

Our package uses two types of queues: input queues and output queues. The **input queues** store the datagrams coming from the data link layer or the upper-layer protocols. The **output queues** store the datagrams going to the data link layer or the upper-layer protocols. The processing module dequeues (removes) the datagrams from the input queues. The fragmentation and reassembly modules enqueue (add) the datagrams into the output queues.

Routing Table

We discussed the routing table in Chapter 6. The routing table is used by the routing module to determine the next-hop address of the packet.

Routing Module

We discussed the routing module in Chapter 6. The routing module receives an IP packet from the processing module. If the packet is to be forwarded, it is passed to this module. The module finds the IP address of the next station along with the interface number to which the packet should be sent. It then sends the packet with this information to the fragmentation module.

MTU Table

The MTU table is used by the fragmentation module to find the maximum transfer unit of a particular interface. Figure 8.27 shows the format of an MTU table.

Figure 8.27 *MTU table*

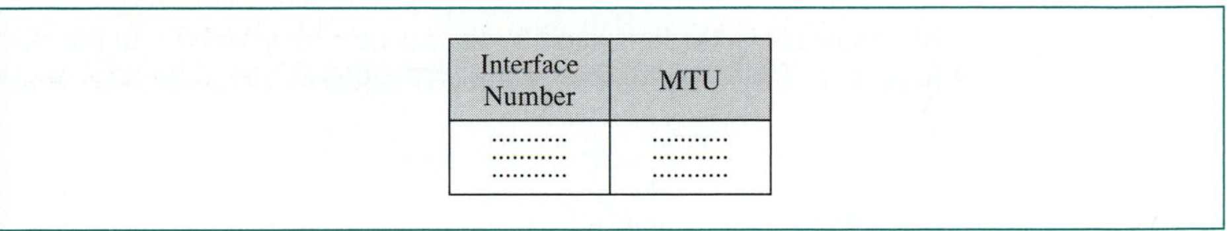

Interface Number	MTU
....	....
....	....
....	....

Fragmentation Module

In our package, the **fragmentation module** receives an IP datagram from the routing module. The routing module gives the IP datagram, the IP address of the next station (either the final destination in a direct delivery or the next router in an indirect delivery), and the interface number through which the datagram is sent out.

The fragmentation module consults the MTU table to find the MTU for the specific interface number. If the length of the datagram is larger than the MTU, the fragmentation module fragments the datagram, adds a header to each fragment, and sends them to the ARP package (see Chapter 7) for address resolution and delivery.

Fragmentation Module

Receive: an IP packet from routing module

1. Extract the size of the datagram.
2. If (size > MTU of the corresponding network)
    1. If [D (*do not fragment*) bit is set]
        1. Discard the datagram.
        2. Send an ICMP error message (see Chapter 9).
        3. Return.
    2. Else
        1. Calculate the maximum size.
        2. Divide the datagram into fragments.
        3. Add header to each fragment.
        4. Add required options to each fragment.
        5. Send the datagrams.
        6. Return.
3. Else
    1. Send the datagram.
4. Return.

Reassembly Table

The **reassembly table** is used by the reassembly module. In our package, the reassembly table has five fields: state, source IP address, datagram ID, time-out, and fragments (see Figure 8.28).

Figure 8.28 *Reassembly table*

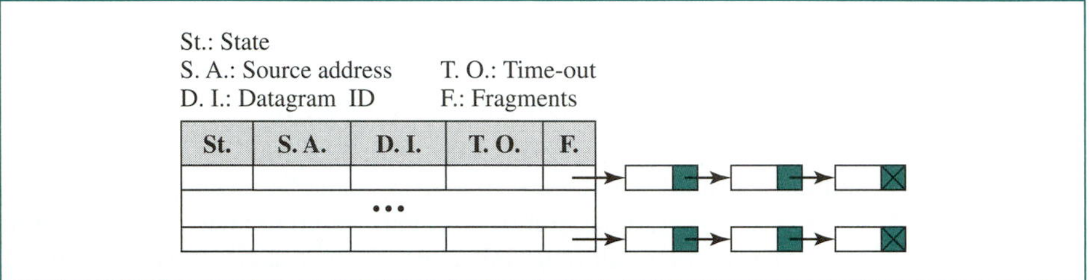

The value of the state field can be either FREE or IN-USE. The IP address field defines the source IP address of the datagram. The datagram ID is a number that uniquely defines a datagram and all of the fragments belonging to that datagram. The time-out is a predetermined amount of time in which all fragments must arrive. Finally, the fragments field is a pointer to a linked list of fragments.

Reassembly Module

The **reassembly module** receives, from the processing module, those datagram fragments that have arrived at their final destinations. In our package, the reassembly module treats an unfragmented datagram as a fragment belonging to a datagram with only one fragment.

Because the IP protocol is a connectionless protocol, there is no guarantee that the fragments arrive in order. Besides, the fragments from one datagram can be intermixed with fragments from another datagram. To keep track of these situations, the module uses a reassembly table with associated linked lists, as we described earlier.

The job of the reassembly module is to find the datagram to which a fragment belongs, to order the fragments belonging to the same datagram, and reassemble all fragments of a datagram when all have arrived. If the established time-out has expired and any fragment is missing, the module discards the fragments.

Reassembly Module

Receive: an IP datagram from the processing module
1. If (offset value is zero and the *M* bit is 0)
    1. Send the datagram to the appropriate queue.
    2. Return.
2. Search the reassembly table for the corresponding entry.
3. If (not found)
    1. Create a new entry.

Reassembly Module (continued)

4. Insert the fragment at the appropriate place in the linked list.
    1. If (all fragments have arrived)
        1. Reassemble the fragments.
        2. Deliver the datagram to the corresponding upper layer protocol.
        3. Return.
    2. Else
        1. Check the time-out.
        2. If (time-out expired)
            1. Discard all fragments.
            2. Send an ICMP error message (see Chapter 9).
5. Return.

8.6 KEY TERMS

best-effort delivery
checksum
code field
datagram
destination address
end of option option
fragmentation
fragmentation offset
header
header length
Internet Protocol (IP)
loose source route option
maximum transfer unit (MTU)
no operation option
option
pointer field
precedence
receiver
record route option
router
sender
service type
source address
strict source route option
time to live
timestamp
type of service (TOS)
version

8.7 SUMMARY

- IP is an unreliable connectionless protocol responsible for source-to-destination delivery.
- Packets in the IP layer are called datagrams.
- A datagram consists of a header (20 to 60 bytes) and data.
- The IP header contains the following information: version number, header length, differentiated services, datagram length, identification number, fragmentation flags, fragmentation offset, time to live, user of the protocol, checksum, source address, and destination address.
- The maximum length of a datagram is 65,535 bytes.
- The MTU is the maximum number of bytes that a data link protocol can encapsulate. MTUs vary from protocol to protocol.
- Fragmentation is the division of a datagram into smaller units to accommodate the MTU of a data link protocol.
- The fields in the IP header that relate to fragmentation are the identification number, the fragmentation flags, and the fragmentation offset.
- The IP datagram header consists of a fixed, 20-byte section and a variable options section with a maximum of 40 bytes.
- The options section of the IP header is used for network testing and debugging.
- The options header contains the following information: a code field that identifies the option, option length, and the specific data.
- The six IP options each have a specific function. They are as follows: filler between options for alignment purposes, padding, recording the route the datagram takes, selection of a mandatory route by the sender, selection of certain routers that must be visited, and recording of processing times at routers.
- The error detection method used by IP is the checksum.
- The checksum uses one's complement arithmetic to add equal-size sections of the IP header. The complemented result is stored in the checksum field. The receiver also uses one's complement arithmetic to check the header.
- An IP package can consist of the following: a header-adding module, a processing module, a routing module, a fragmentation module, a reassembly module, a routing table, an MTU table, and a reassembly table.

8.8 PRACTICE SET

Multiple-Choice Questions

1. What is the maximum size of the data portion of the IP datagram?
   a. 65,535 bytes
   b. 65,516 bytes
   c. 65,475 bytes
   d. 65,460 bytes

2. A best-effort delivery service such as IP does not include _______.
   a. error checking
   b. error correction
   c. datagram acknowledgment
   d. all of the above
3. An HLEN value of decimal 10 means _______.
   a. there are 10 bytes of options
   b. there are 40 bytes of options
   c. there are 10 bytes in the header
   d. there are 40 bytes in the header
4. What is the value of the total length field if the header is 28 bytes and the data field is 400 bytes?
   a. 428
   b. 407
   c. 107
   d. 427
5. What is the length of the data field given an HLEN value of 12 and total length value of 40,000?
   a. 39,988
   b. 40,012
   c. 40,048
   d. 39,952
6. A datagram is fragmented into three smaller datagrams. Which of the following is true?
   a. The *do not fragment* bit is set to 1 for all three datagrams.
   b. The *more fragment* bit is set to 0 for all three datagrams.
   c. The identification field is the same for all three datagrams.
   d. The offset field is the same for all three datagrams.
7. Which field or bit value unambiguously identifies the datagram as a fragment?
   a. Identification = 1000
   b. *Do not fragment* bit = 0
   c. *More Fragment* bit = 0
   d. Fragment offset = 1000
8. If the fragment offset has a value of 100, it means that _______.
   a. the datagram has not been fragmented
   b. the datagram is 100 bytes in size
   c. the first byte of the datagram is byte 100
   d. the first byte of the datagram is byte 800

9. What is needed to determine the number of the last byte of a fragment?
   a. identification number
   b. offset number
   c. total length
   d. b and c
10. The IP header size _______.
   a. is 20 to 60 bytes long
   b. is 20 bytes long
   c. is 60 bytes long
   d. depends on the MTU
11. What is the maximum number of IP addresses recorded if the value of the length field in the record route option is 27?
   a. 27
   b. 24
   c. 12
   d. 6
12. Which IP option is used if exactly four specific routers are to handle the datagram?
   a. record route
   b. strict source route
   c. loose source route
   d. timestamp
13. Which IP option always lists all routers visited?
   a. record route
   b. strict source route
   c. loose source route
   d. a and b
14. In the loose source route option, the number of routers visited may be _______ the number of routers listed.
   a. greater than
   b. less than
   c. equal to
   d. a and c
15. In the record route option, the number of routers visited may be _______ the number of routers listed.
   a. greater than
   b. less than
   c. equal to
   d. a and c

16. What is the maximum number of routers that can be recorded if the timestamp option has a flag value of 1?
    a. 10
    b. 9
    c. 4
    d. unlimited
17. The checksum in the IP packet covers _______.
    a. just the header
    b. just the data
    c. the header and the data
    d. just the source and destination addresses
18. If the value of the checksum field in an IP packet is decimal 255, what is the checksum as calculated at the receiver if the packet arrives intact (without error)?
    a. 00000000 11111111
    b. 00000000 00000000
    c. 11111111 00000000
    d. 11111111 11111111
19. The _______ module takes fragments of a message and puts them back in order.
    a. processing
    b. routing
    c. fragmentation
    d. reassembly
20. The _______ module sends out an IP packet, the next-hop address, and interface information.
    a. processing
    b. routing
    c. fragmentation
    d. reassembly
21. The _______ module discards datagrams with a TTL value of zero.
    a. processing
    b. routing
    c. fragmentation
    d. reassembly
22. The output of the _______ module is an IP packet destined for an upper-layer protocol.
    a. processing
    b. routing
    c. fragmentation
    d. reassembly

23. The _______ module consults the MTU table to determine the packet size necessary for transmission.
    a. processing
    b. routing
    c. fragmentation
    d. reassembly
24. Which module can send an ICMP error message?
    a. processing
    b. reassembly
    c. fragmentation
    d. all of the above

Exercises

25. Which fields of the IP header change from router to router?
26. Calculate the HLEN value if the total length is 1200 bytes, 1176 of which is data from the upper layer.
27. Table 8.5 lists the MTUs for many different protocols. The MTUs range from 296 to 65,535. What would be the advantages of having a large MTU? What would be the advantages of having a small MTU?
28. Given a fragmented datagram with an offset of 120, how can you determine the first and last byte number?
29. An IP datagram must go through router 128.46.10.5. There are no other restrictions on the routers to be visited. Draw the IP options with their values.
30. What is the maximum number of routers that can be recorded if the timestamp option has a flag value of 1? Why?
31. Can the value of the header length in an IP packet be less than 5? When is it exactly 5?
32. The value of the HLEN in an IP datagram is 7. How many option bytes are present?
33. The size of the option field of an IP datagram is 20 bytes. What is the value of HLEN? What is the value in binary?
34. The value of the total length field in an IP datagram is 36 and the value of the header length field is 5. How many bytes of data is the packet carrying?
35. A datagram is carrying 1024 bytes of data. If there is no option information, what is the value of the header length field? What is the value of the total length field?
36. A host is sending 100 datagrams to another host. If the identification number of the first datagram is 1024, what is the identification number of the last?
37. An IP datagram arrives whose fragmentation offset is 0 and the *M* bit (more fragment bit) is 0. Is this a fragment?
38. An IP fragment has arrived whose offset value is 100. How many bytes of data were originally sent by the source before the data in this fragment?

39. An IP datagram has arrived with the following information in the header (in hexadecimal):

    45 00 00 54 00 03 00 00 20 06 00 00 7C 4E 03 02 B4 0E 0F 02

    a. Are there any options?
    b. Is the packet fragmented?
    c. What is the size of the data?
    d. Is a checksum used?
    e. How many more routers can the packet travel to?
    f. What is the identification number of the packet?
    g. What is the type of service?

40. In a datagram, the *M* bit is zero, the value of HLEN is 5, the value of total length is 200, and the offset value is 200. What is the number of the first byte and number of the last byte in this datagram? Is this the last fragment, the first fragment, or a middle fragment?

Programming Exercises

41. Create a header file to include all constants that you think are needed to implement the IP modules in C. Use the **#define** directives.

42. Complete the following **struct** declaration for the IP header:

```
struct  IP_Header
{
.....     Ver;
....................
....................
} ;
```

43. Complete the following struct declaration for the IP datagram.

```
struct  IP_Datagram
{
        struct  IP_Header   ipHeader ;
        ..................           ipData ;
} ;
```

44. Write the declaration for an MTU table.
45. Write the declaration for a reassembly table.
46. Write a function in C to calculate the checksum for an IP header.
47. Write a function in C to simulate the header-adding module.
48. Write a function in C to simulate the processing module.
49. Write a function in C to simulate the fragmentation module.
50. Write a function in C to simulate the reassembly module.

CHAPTER 9

Internet Control Message Protocol (ICMP)

As discussed in Chapter 8, the IP provides unreliable and connectionless datagram delivery. It was designed this way to make efficient use of network resources. The IP protocol is a best-effort delivery service that delivers a datagram from its original source to its final destination. However, it has two deficiencies: lack of error control and lack of assistance mechanisms.

The IP protocol has no error-reporting or error-correcting mechanism. What happens if something goes wrong? What happens if a router must discard a datagram because it cannot find a router to the final destination, or because the time-to-live field has a zero value? What happens if the final destination host must discard all fragments of a datagram because it has not received all fragments within a predetermined time limit? These are examples of situations where an error has occurred and the IP protocol has no built-in mechanism to notify the original host.

The IP protocol also lacks a mechanism for host and management queries. A host sometimes needs to determine if a router or another host is alive. And sometimes a network manager needs information from another host or router.

The Internet Control Message Protocol (ICMP) has been designed to compensate for the above two deficiencies. It is a companion to the IP protocol. Figure 9.1 shows the position of ICMP in relation to IP and other protocols in the network layer.

Figure 9.1 *Position of ICMP in the network layer*

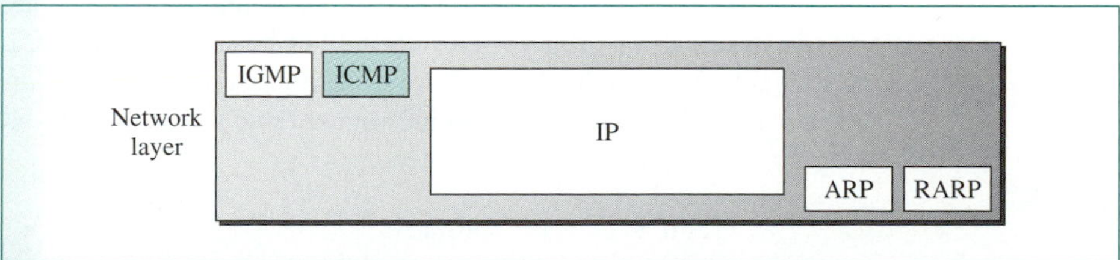

ICMP itself is a network layer protocol. However, its messages are not passed directly to the data link layer as would be expected. Instead, the messages are first encapsulated inside IP datagrams before going to the lower layer (see Figure 9.2).

Figure 9.2 *ICMP encapsulation*

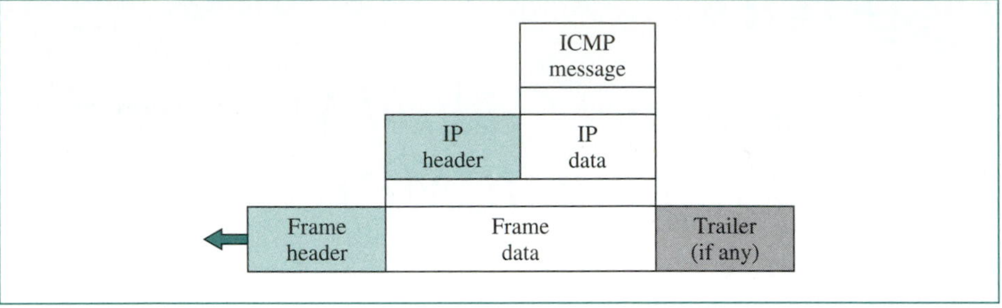

The value of the protocol field in the IP datagram is 1 to indicate that the IP data is an ICMP message.

9.1 TYPES OF MESSAGES

ICMP messages are divided into two broad categories: error-reporting messages and query messages as shown in Figure 9.3.

Figure 9.3 *ICMP messages*

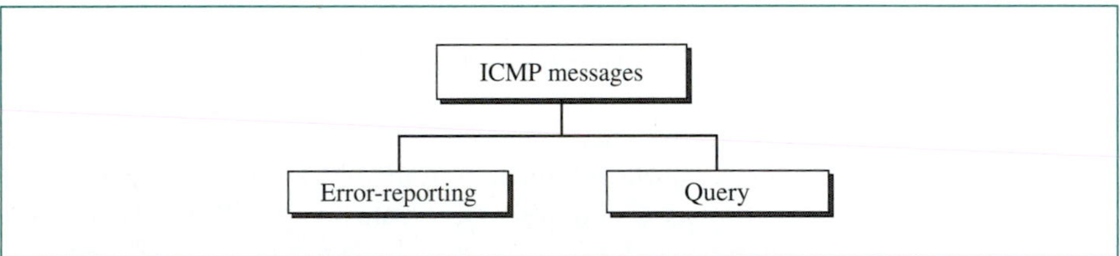

The error-reporting messages report problems that a router or a host (destination) may encounter when it processes an IP packet.

The query messages, which occur in pairs, help a host or a network manager get specific information from a router or another host. For example, nodes can discover their neighbors. Also, hosts can discover and learn about routers on their network and routers can help a node redirect its messages. Table 9.1 lists the ICMP messages in each category.

Table 9.1 *ICMP messages*

Category	*Type*	*Message*
Error-reporting messages	3	Destination unreachable
	4	Source quench
	11	Time exceeded
	12	Parameter problem
	5	Redirection

Table 9.1 *ICMP messages (continued)*

Category	*Type*	*Message*
Query messages	8 or 0	Echo request or reply
	13 or 14	Timestamp request or reply
	17 or 18	Address mask request or reply
	10 or 9	Router solicitation or advertisement

9.2 MESSAGE FORMAT

An ICMP message has an 8-byte header and a variable-size data section. Although the general format of the header is different for each message type, the first 4 bytes are common to all. As Figure 9.4 shows, the first field, ICMP type, defines the type of the message. The code field specifies the reason for the particular message type. The last common field is the checksum field (to be discussed later in the chapter). The rest of the header is specific for each message type.

The data section in error messages carries information for finding the original packet that had the error. In query messages, the data section carries extra information based on the type of the query.

Figure 9.4 *General format of ICMP messages*

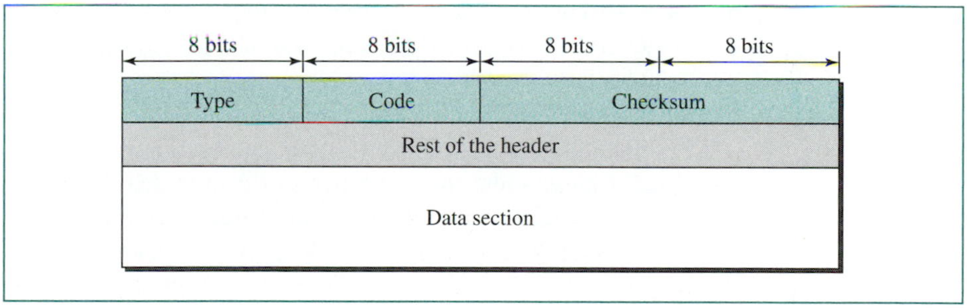

9.3 ERROR REPORTING

One of the main responsibilities of ICMP is to report errors. Although technology has produced increasingly reliable transmission media, errors still exist and must be handled. IP, as discussed in Chapter 8, is an unreliable protocol. This means that error checking and error control are not a concern of IP. ICMP was designed, in part, to compensate for this shortcoming. However, ICMP does not correct errors, it simply reports them. Error correction is left to the higher-level protocols. Error messages are always sent to the original source because the only information available in the datagram about the route is the source and destination IP addresses. ICMP uses the source IP address to send the error message to the source (originator) of the datagram.

ICMP always reports error messages to the original source.

Five types of errors are handled: destination unreachable, source quench, time exceeded, parameter problems, and redirection (see Figure 9.5).

Figure 9.5 *Error-reporting messages*

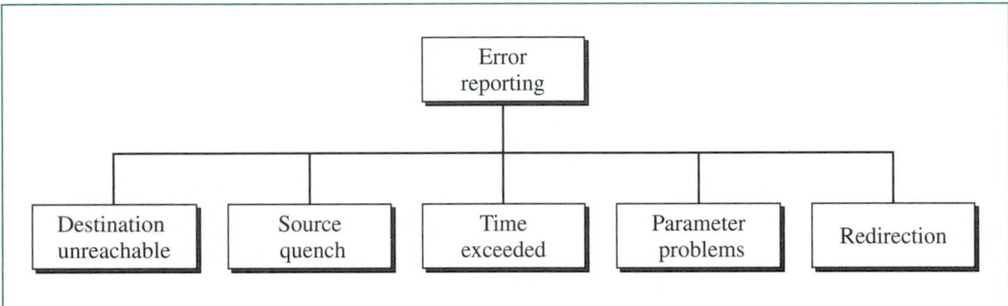

The following are important points about ICMP error messages:

- No ICMP error message will be generated in response to a datagram carrying an ICMP error message.
- No ICMP error message will be generated for a fragmented datagram that is not the first fragment.
- No ICMP error message will be generated for a datagram having a multicast address.
- No ICMP error message will be generated for a datagram having a special address such as 127.0.0.0 or 0.0.0.0.

Note that all error messages contain a data section that includes the IP header of the original datagram plus the first 8 bytes of data in that datagram. The original datagram header is added to give the original source, which receives the error message, information about the datagram itself. The 8 bytes of data are included because, as we will see in Chapters 11 and 12 on UDP and TCP protocols, the first 8 bytes provide information about the port numbers (UDP and TCP) and sequence number (TCP). This information is needed so the source can inform the protocols (TCP or UDP) about the error. ICMP forms an error packet, which is then encapsulated in an IP datagram (see Figure 9.6).

Destination Unreachable

When a router cannot route a datagram or a host cannot deliver a datagram, the datagram is discarded and the router or the host sends a destination unreachable message back to the source host that initiated the datagram. Figure 9.7 shows the format of the

Figure 9.6 *Contents of data field for the error messages*

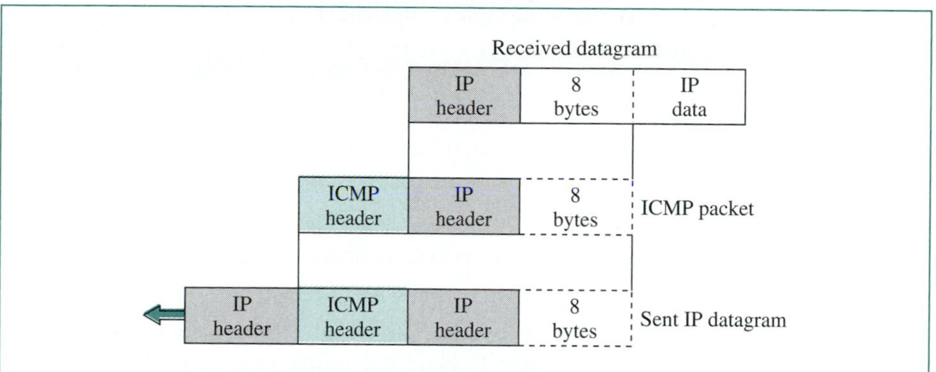

Figure 9.7 *Destination-unreachable format*

Type: 3	Code: 0 to 15	Checksum
Unused (All 0s)		
Part of the received IP datagram including IP header plus the first 8 bytes of datagram data		

destination-unreachable message. The code field for this type specifies the reason for discarding the datagram:

- **Code 0.** The network is unreachable, possibly due to hardware failure. This type of message can only be generated by a router.
- **Code 1.** The host is unreachable. This can also be due to hardware failure. This type of message can only be generated by a router.
- **Code 2.** The protocol is unreachable. An IP datagram can carry data belonging to higher-level protocols such as UDP, TCP, and OSPF. If the destination host receives a datagram that must be delivered, for example, to the TCP protocol, but the TCP protocol is not running at the moment, a code 2 message is sent. This type of message is generated only by the destination host.
- **Code 3.** The port is unreachable. The application program (process) that the datagram is destined for is not running at the moment.
- **Code 4.** Fragmentation is required, but the DF (do not fragment) field of the datagram has been set. In other words, the sender of the datagram has specified that the datagram not be fragmented, but routing is impossible without fragmentation.
- **Code 5.** Source routing cannot be accomplished. In other words, one or more routers defined in the source routing option cannot be visited.

- **Code 6.** The destination network is unknown. This is different from code 0. In code 0, the router knows that the destination network exists, but it is unreachable at the moment. For code 6, the router has no information about the destination network.
- **Code 7.** The destination host is unknown. This is different from code 1. In code 1, the router knows that the destination host exists, but it is unreachable at the moment. For code 7, the router is unaware of the existence of the destination host.
- **Code 8.** The source host is isolated.
- **Code 9.** Communication with the destination network is administratively prohibited.
- **Code 10.** Communication with the destination host is administratively prohibited.
- **Code 11.** The network is unreachable for the specified type of service. This is different from code 0. Here the router can route the datagram if the source had requested an available type of service.
- **Code 12.** The host is unreachable for the specified type of service. This is different from code 1. Here the router can route the datagram if the source had requested an available type of service.
- **Code 13.** The host is unreachable because the administrator has put a filter on it.
- **Code 14.** The host is unreachable because the host precedence is violated. The message is sent by a router to indicate that the requested precedence is not permitted for the destination.
- **Code 15.** The host is unreachable because its precedence was cut off. This message is generated when the network operators have imposed a minimum level of precedence for the operation of the network, but the datagram was sent with a precedence below this level.

Note that destination-unreachable messages can be created either by a router or the destination host. Code 2 and code 3 messages can only be created by the destination host; the messages of the remaining codes can only be created by routers.

> Destination-unreachable messages with codes 2 or 3 can be created only by the destination host.
>
> Other destination-unreachable messages can be created only by routers.

Note that even if a router does not report a destination-unreachable message, it does not necessarily mean that the datagram has been delivered. For example, if a datagram is traveling through an Ethernet network, there is no way that a router knows that the datagram has been delivered to the destination host or the next router because Ethernet does not provide any acknowledgment mechanism.

> A router cannot detect all problems that prevent the delivery of a packet.

Source Quench

The IP protocol is a connectionless protocol. There is no communication between the source host, which produces the datagram, the routers, which forward it, and the destination host, which processes it. One of the ramifications of this absence of communication is the lack of *flow control*. IP does not have a flow-control mechanism embedded in the protocol. The lack of flow control can create a major problem in the operation of IP: congestion. The source host never knows if the routers or the destination host have been overwhelmed with datagrams. The source host never knows if it is producing datagrams faster than can be forwarded by routers or processed by the destination host.

> There is no flow-control mechanism in the IP protocol.

The lack of flow control can create congestion in routers or the destination host. A router or a host has a limited-size queue (buffer) for incoming datagrams waiting to be forwarded (in the case of a router) or to be processed (in the case of a host). If the datagrams are received much faster than they can be forwarded or processed, the queue may overflow. In this case, the router or the host has no choice but to discard some of the datagrams.

The source-quench message in ICMP has been designed to add a kind of flow control to the IP. When a router or host discards a datagram due to congestion, it sends a source-quench message to the sender of the datagram. This message has two purposes. First, it informs the source that the datagram has been discarded. Second, it warns the source that there is congestion somewhere in the path and that the source should slow down (quench) the sending process. The source-quench format is shown in Figure 9.8.

Figure 9.8 *Source-quench format*

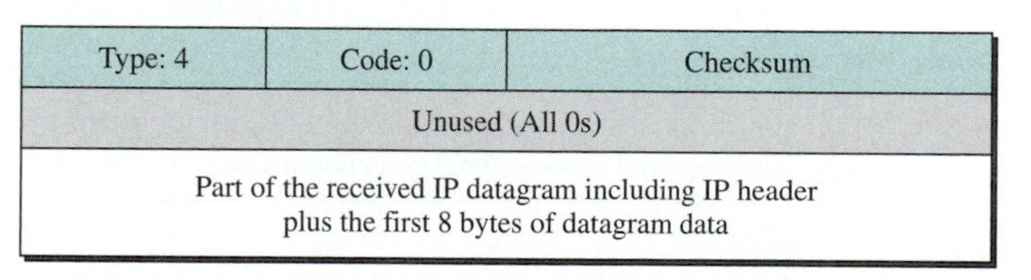

> A source-quench message informs the source that a datagram has been discarded due to congestion in a router or the destination host.
>
> The source must slow down the sending of datagrams until the congestion is relieved.

There are some points that deserve more explanation. First, the router or destination host that has experienced the congestion sends one source-quench message for each discarded datagram to the source host. Second, there is no mechanism to tell the source that the congestion has been relieved and the source can resume sending datagrams at its previous rate. The source continues to lower the rate until no more source-quench messages are received. Third, the congestion can be created either by a one-to-one or many-to-one communication. In a one-to-one communication, a single high-speed host could create datagrams faster than a router or the destination host can handle. In this case, source-quench messages can be helpful. They tell the source to slow down. In a many-to-one communication, many sources create datagrams that must be handled by a router or the destination host. In this case, each source can be sending datagrams at different speeds, some of them at a low rate, others at a high rate. In this case, the source-quench message may not be very useful. The router or the destination host has no clue which source is responsible for the congestion. It may drop a datagram from a very slow source instead of dropping the datagram from the source that has actually created the congestion.

> One source-quench message should be sent for each datagram that is discarded due to congestion.

Time Exceeded

The time-exceeded message is generated in two cases:

- As we saw in Chapter 6, routers use routing tables to find the next hop (next router) that must receive the packet. If there are errors in one or more routing tables, a packet can travel in a loop or a cycle, going from one router to the next or visiting a series of routers endlessly. As we saw in Chapter 8, each datagram contains a field called *time to live* that controls this situation. When a datagram visits a router, the value of this field is decremented by 1. When the time-to-live value is 0, after decrementing, the router discards the datagram. However, when the datagram is discarded, a time-exceeded message must be sent by the router to the original source.

  > Whenever a router receives a datagram with a time-to-live value of zero, it discards the datagram and sends a time-exceeded message to the original source.

- Second, a time-exceeded message is also generated when all fragments that make up a message do not arrive at the destination host within a certain time limit. When the first fragment arrives, the destination host starts a timer. If all the fragments have not arrived when the time expires, the destination discards all the fragments and sends a time-exceeded message to the original sender.

  > When the final destination does not receive all of the fragments in a set time, it discards the received fragments and sends a time-exceeded message to the original source.

Figure 9.9 shows the format of the time-exceeded message. Code 0 is used when the datagram is discarded by the router due to a time-to-live field value of zero. Code 1 is used when arrived fragments of a datagram are discarded because some fragments have not arrived within the time limit.

> In a time-exceeded message, code 0 is used only by routers to show that the value of the time-to-live field is zero. Code 1 is used only by the destination host to show that not all of the fragments have arrived within a set time.

Figure 9.9 *Time-exceeded message format*

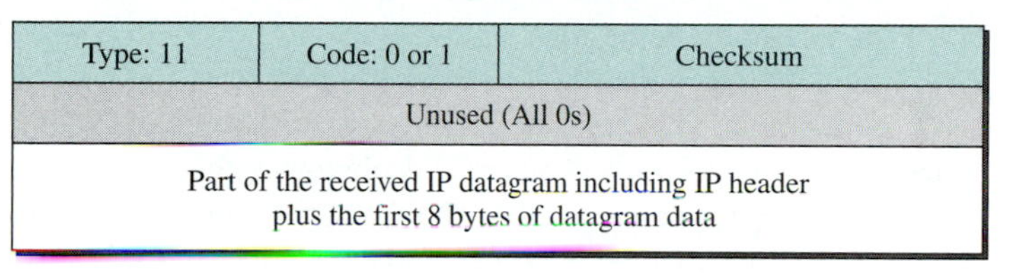

Parameter Problem

Any ambiguity in the header part of a datagram can create serious problems as the datagram travels through the Internet. If a router or the destination host discovers an ambiguous or missing value in any field of the datagram, it discards the datagram and sends a parameter-problem message back to the source.

> A parameter-problem message can be created by a router or the destination host.

Figure 9.10 shows the format of the parameter-problem message. The code field in this case specifies the reason for discarding the datagram and shows exactly what has failed:

- **Code 0.** There is an error or ambiguity in one of the header fields. In this case, the value in the pointer field points to the byte with the problem. For example, if the value is zero, then the first byte is not a valid field.
- **Code 1.** The required part of an option is missing. In this case, the pointer is not used.

Figure 9.10 *Parameter-problem message format*

Type: 12	Code: 0 or 1	Checksum
Pointer	Unused (All 0s)	
Part of the received IP datagram including IP header plus the first 8 bytes of datagram data		

Redirection

When a router needs to send a packet destined for another network, it must know the IP address of the next appropriate router. The same is true if the sender is a host. Both routers and hosts then must have a routing table to find the address of the router or the next router. Routers take part in the routing update process as we will see in Chapter 13 and are supposed to be updated constantly. Routing is dynamic.

However, for efficiency, hosts do not take part in the routing update process because there are many more hosts in an internet than routers. Updating the routing tables of hosts dynamically produces unacceptable traffic. The hosts usually use static routing. When a host comes up, its routing table has a limited number of entries. It usually knows only the IP address of one router, the default router. For this reason, the host may send a datagram, which is destined for another network, to the wrong router. In this case, the router that receives the datagram will forward the datagram to the correct router. However, to update the routing table of the host, it sends a redirection message to the host. This concept of redirection is shown in Figure 9.11. Host A wants to send a datagram to host B. Router R2 is obviously the most efficient routing choice, but host A did not choose router R2. The datagram goes to R1 instead. R1, after consulting its table, finds that the packet should have gone to R2. It sends the packet to R2 and, at the same time, sends a redirection message to host A. Host A's routing table can now be updated.

Figure 9.11 *Redirection concept*

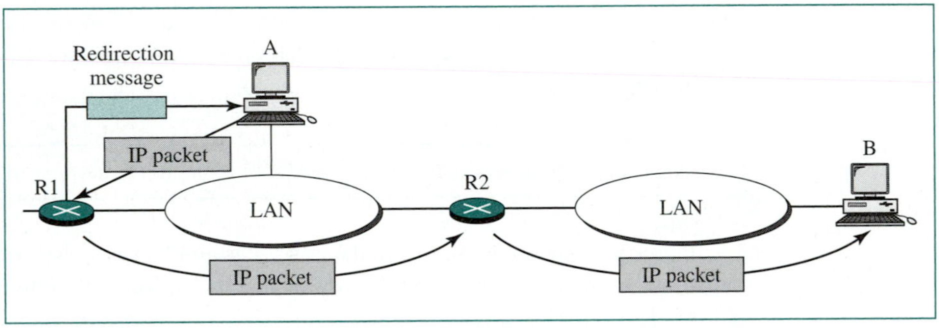

> A host usually starts with a small routing table that is gradually augmented and updated. One of the tools to accomplish this is the redirection message.

The format of the redirection message is shown in Figure 9.12. Note that the IP address of the appropriate target is given in the second row.

Although the redirection message is considered an error-reporting message, it is different from other error messages. The router does not discard the datagram in this case; it is sent to the appropriate router. The code field for the redirection message narrows down the redirection:

- **Code 0.** Redirection for a network-specific route.
- **Code 1.** Redirection for a host-specific route.
- **Code 2.** Redirection for a network-specific route based on a specified type of service.
- **Code 3.** Redirection for the host-specific route based on a specified type of service.

Figure 9.12 *Redirection message format*

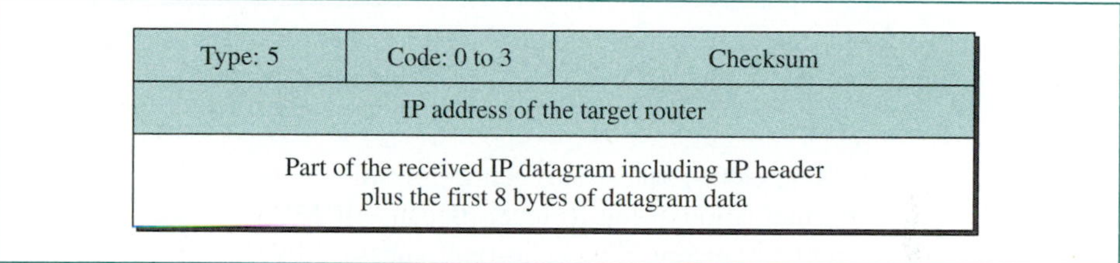

A redirection message is sent from a router to a host on the same local network.

9.4 QUERY

In addition to error reporting, ICMP can also diagnose some network problems. This is accomplished through the query messages, a group of four different pairs of messages, as shown in Figure 9.13. In this type of ICMP message, a node sends a message that is answered in a specific format by the destination node. Note that originally two other types of messages (information request and information reply) were defined, but they are now obsolete. They were designed to allow a host to get its Internet address at start-up; this function is now performed by RARP (see Chapter 7) and BOOTP (see Chapter 17).

Figure 9.13 *Query messages*

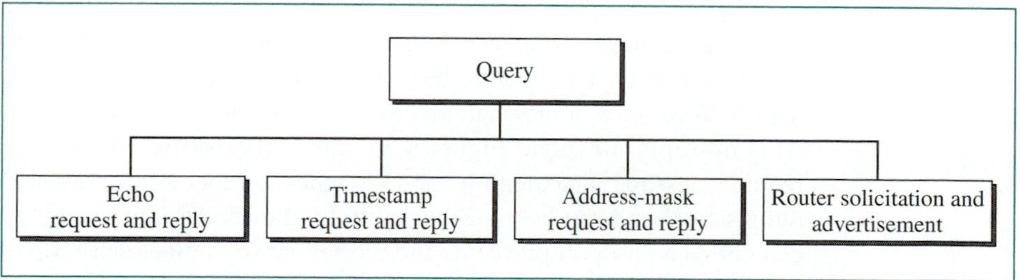

Echo Request and Reply

The echo-request and echo-reply messages are designed for diagnostic purposes. Network managers and users utilize this pair of messages to identify network problems. The combination of echo-request and echo-reply messages determines whether two systems (hosts or routers) can communicate with each other.

A host or router can send an echo-request message to another host or router. The host or router that receives an echo-request message creates an echo-reply message and returns it to the original sender.

> An echo-request message can be sent by a host or router. An echo-reply message is sent by the host or router which receives an echo-request message.

The echo-request and echo-reply messages can be used to determine if there is communication at the IP level. Because ICMP messages are encapsulated in IP datagrams, the receipt of an echo-reply message by the machine that sent the echo request is proof that the IP protocols in the sender and receiver are communicating with each other using the IP datagram. Also, it is proof that the intermediate routers are receiving, processing, and forwarding IP datagrams.

> Echo-request and echo-reply messages can be used by network managers to check the operation of the IP protocol.

The echo-request and echo-reply messages can also be used by a host to see if another host is reachable. At the user level, this is done by invoking the packet Internet groper (ping) command. Today, most systems provide a version of the ping command that can create a series (instead of just one) of echo-request and echo-reply messages, providing statistical information.

> Echo-request and echo-reply messages can test the reachability of a host. This is usually done by invoking the ping command.

Echo request, together with echo reply, can validate whether or not a node is functioning properly. The node to be tested is sent an echo-request message. The optional data field contains a message that must be repeated exactly by the responding node in its echo-reply message. Figure 9.14 shows the format of the echo-reply and echo-request message. The identifier and sequence number fields are not formally defined by the protocol and can be used arbitrarily by the sender. For example, the identifier field can define a group of problems and the sequence number can keep track of the particular echo-request messages sent. The identifier is often the same as the process ID (see Chapter 15 for the definition of process ID) of the process that originated the request.

Figure 9.14 *Echo-request and echo-reply messages*

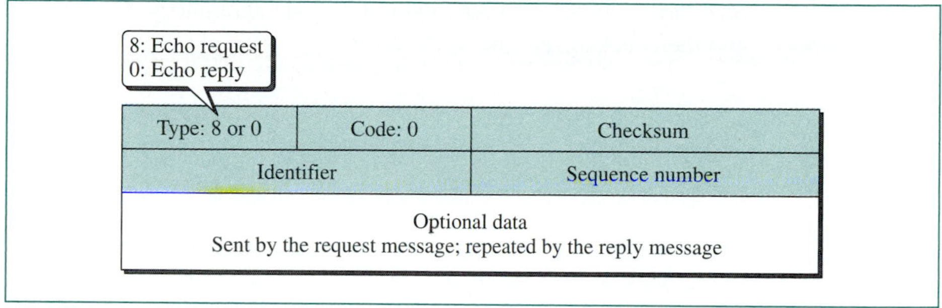

Timestamp Request and Reply

Two machines (hosts or routers) can use the timestamp-request and timestamp-reply messages to determine the round-trip time needed for an IP datagram to travel between them. It can also be used to synchronize the clocks in two machines. The format of these two messages is shown in Figure 9.15.

Figure 9.15 *Timestamp-request and timestamp-reply message format*

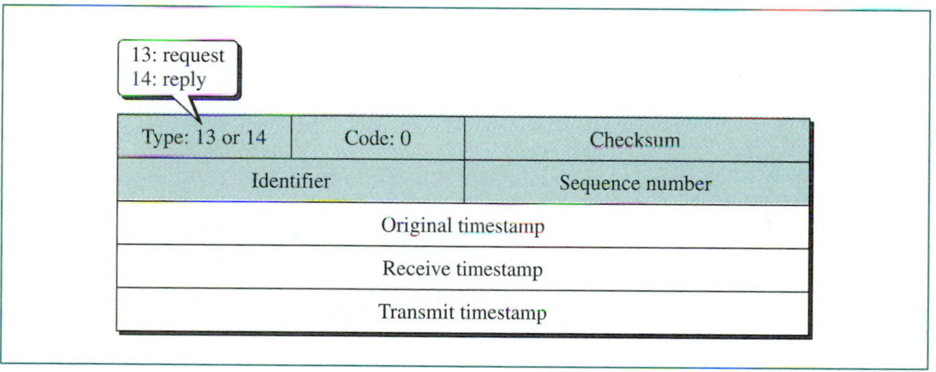

The three timestamp fields are each 32 bits long. Each field can hold a number representing time measured in milliseconds from midnight in Universal Time (formerly called Greenwich Mean Time). (Note that 32 bits can represent a number between 0 and 4,294,967,295, but a timestamp in this case cannot exceed $86{,}400{,}000 = 24 \times 60 \times 60 \times 1000$.)

The source creates a timestamp-request message. The source fills the *original timestamp* field with the Universal Time shown by its clock at departure time. The other two timestamp fields are filled with zeros.

The destination creates the timestamp-reply message. The destination copies the original timestamp value from the request message into the same field in its reply message. It then fills the *receive timestamp* field with the Universal Time shown by its clock at the time the request was received. Finally, it fills the *transmit timestamp* field with the Universal Time shown by its clock at the time the reply message departs.

The timestamp-request and timestamp-reply messages can be used to compute the one-way or round-trip time required for a datagram to go from a source to a destination and then back again. The formulas are

Sending time = value of receive timestamp – value of original timestamp
Receiving time = time the packet returned – value of transmit timestamp
Round-trip time = sending time + receiving time

Note that the sending and receiving time calculations are accurate only if the two clocks in the source and destination machines are synchronized. However, the round-trip calculation is correct even if the two clocks are not synchronized because each clock contributes twice to the round-trip calculation, thus canceling any difference in synchronization.

> Timestamp-request and timestamp-reply messages can be used to calculate the round-trip time between a source and a destination machine even if their clocks are not synchronized.

For example, given the following information:

Value of original timestamp: 46
Value of receive timestamp: 59
Value of transmit timestamp: 60
Time the packet arrived: 67

We can calculate the round-trip time to be 20 milliseconds:

Sending time = 59 – 46 = 13 milliseconds
Receiving time = 67 – 60 = 7 milliseconds
Round-trip time = 13 + 7 = 20 milliseconds

Given the actual one-way time, the timestamp-request and timestamp-reply messages can also be used to synchronize the clocks in two machines using the following formula:

Time difference = receive timestamp – (original timestamp field + one-way time duration)

The one-way time duration can be obtained either by dividing the round-trip time duration by two (if we are sure that the sending time is the same as the receiving time) or by other means. For example, we can tell that the two clocks in the previous example are 3 milliseconds out of synchronization because

Time difference = 59 – (46 + 10) = 3

> The timestamp-request and timestamp-reply messages can be used to synchronize two clocks in two machines if the exact one-way time duration is known.

Address-Mask Request and Reply

The IP address of a host contains a network address, subnet address, and host identifier. A host may know its full IP address, but it may not know which part of the address defines the network and subnetwork address and which part corresponds to the host identifier. For example, a host may know its 32-bit IP address as

10011111 00011111 11100010 10101011

But it may not know that the left 20 bits are network and subnetwork addresses and the remaining 12 bits are its host identifier. In this case, the host needs the following mask:

11111111 11111111 11110000 00000000

The 1s in the mask, as we saw in Chapter 5, identify the position of the bits used for the netid and subnetid. The 0s identify the position of the bits for the hostid.

For example, applying the above mask to the above IP address, we get

Netid and subnetid ➡ 10011111 00011111 1110
Hostid ➡ 0010 10101011

To obtain its mask, a host sends an address-mask-request message to a router on the LAN. If the host knows the address of the router, it sends the request directly to the router. If it does not know, it broadcasts the message. The router receiving the address-mask-request message responds with an address-mask-reply message, providing the necessary mask for the host. This can be applied to its full IP address to get its subnet address.

The format of the address-mask request and address-mask reply is shown in Figure 9.16. The address-mask field is filled with zeros in the request message. When the router sends the address-mask reply back to the host, this field contains the actual mask (1s for the netid and subnetid and 0s for the hostid).

Figure 9.16 *Mask-request and mask-reply message format*

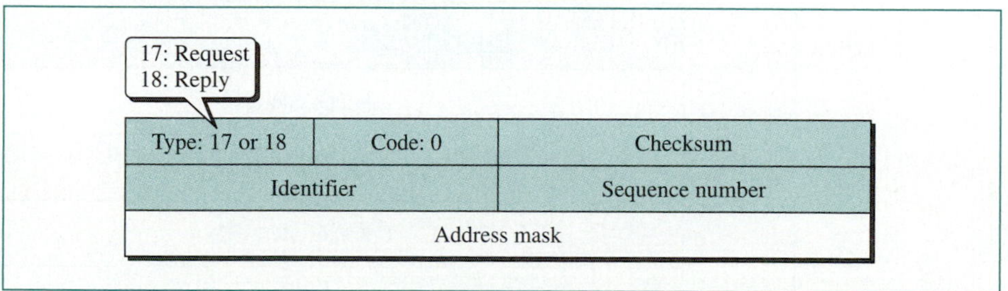

Masking is needed for diskless stations at start-up time. When a diskless station comes up for the first time, it may ask for its full IP address using the RARP protocol (see Chapter 7); after receiving its IP address, it may use the address-mask request and reply to find out which part of the address defines the subnet.

Another way to get subnet mask information is through the use of the BOOTP protocol, as we will see in Chapter 17.

Router Solicitation and Advertisement

As we discussed in the redirection message section, a host that wants to send data to a host on another network needs to know the address of routers connected to its own network. Also, the host must know if the routers are alive and functioning. The router-solicitation and router-advertisement messages can help in this situation. A host can broadcast (or multicast) a router-solicitation message. The router or routers that receive the solicitation message broadcast their routing information using the router-advertisement message. A router can also periodically send router-advertisement messages even if no host has solicited. Note that when a router sends out an advertisement, it announces not only its own presence but also the presence of all routers on the network of which it is aware. Figure 9.17 shows the format of the router-solicitation message.

Figure 9.17 *Router-solicitation message format*

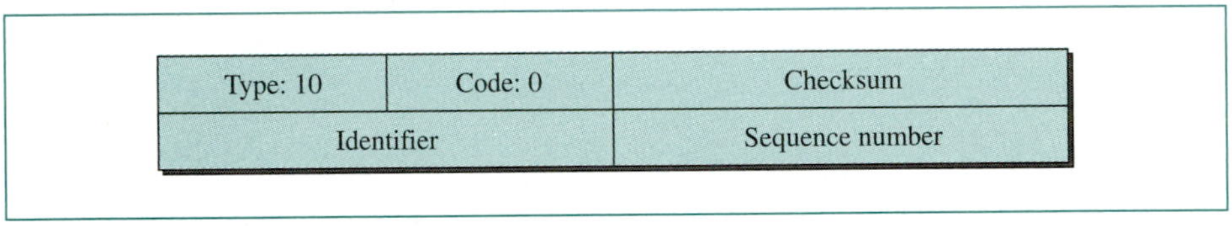

Type: 10	Code: 0	Checksum
Identifier		Sequence number

Figure 9.18 shows the format of the router-advertisement message. The lifetime field shows the number of seconds that the entries are considered to be valid. Each router entry in the advertisement contains at least two fields: the router address and the address preference level. The address preference level defines the ranking of the router.

Figure 9.18 *Router-advertisement message format*

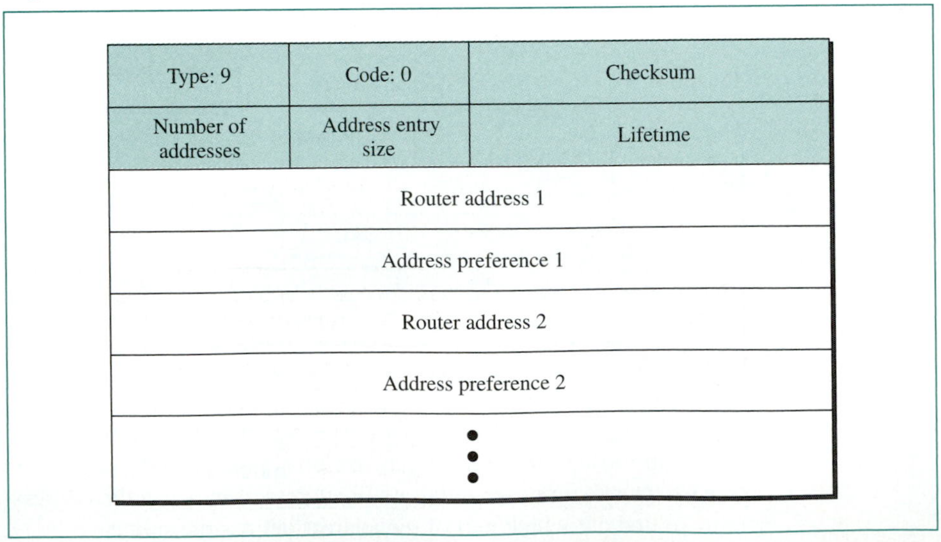

Type: 9	Code: 0	Checksum
Number of addresses	Address entry size	Lifetime
Router address 1		
Address preference 1		
Router address 2		
Address preference 2		
⋮		

The preference level is used to select a router as the default router. If the address preference level is zero, that router is considered the default router. If the address preference level is 80000000_{16}, the router should never be selected as the default router.

9.5 CHECKSUM

In Chapter 7, we learned the concept and idea of the checksum. In ICMP the checksum is calculated over the entire message (header and data).

Checksum Calculation

The sender follows these steps using one's complement arithmetic:

1. The checksum field is set to zero.
2. The sum of all the 16-bit words (header and data) is calculated.
3. The sum is complemented to get the checksum.
4. The checksum is stored in the checksum field.

Checksum Testing

The receiver follows these steps using one's complement arithmetic:

1. The sum of all words (header and data) is calculated.
2. The sum is complemented.
3. If the result obtained in step 2 is 16 0s, the message is accepted; otherwise, it is rejected.

Example

Figure 9.19 shows an example of checksum calculation for a simple echo-request message (see the section on echo request and reply). The message is divided into 16-bit (2-byte) words. The words are added together and the sum is complemented. Now the sender can put this value in the checksum field.

Figure 9.19 *Example of checksum calculation*

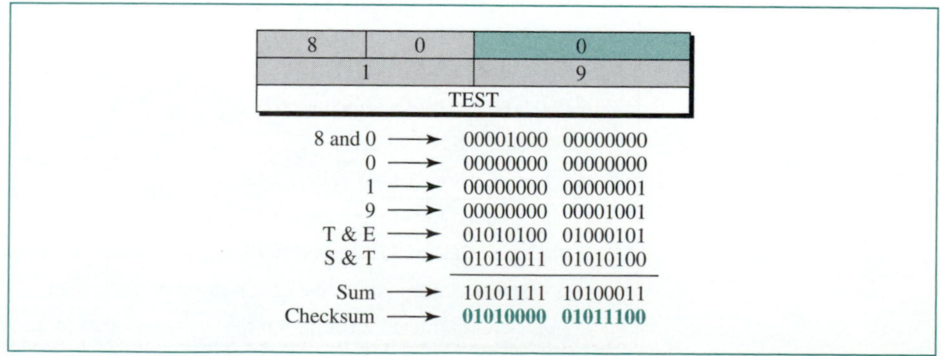

9.6 ICMP PACKAGE

To give an idea of how ICMP can handle the sending and receiving of ICMP messages, we present our version of an ICMP package made of two modules: an input module and an output module. Figure 9.20 shows these two modules.

Figure 9.20 *ICMP package*

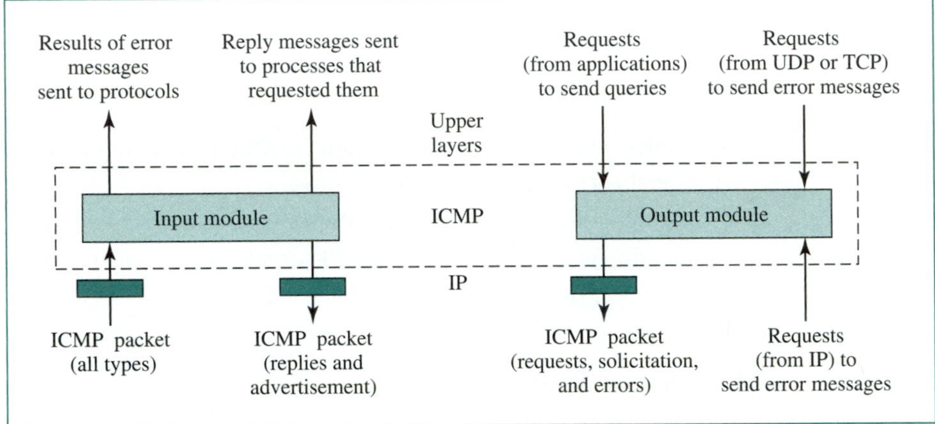

Input Module

The input module handles all received ICMP messages. It is invoked when an ICMP packet is delivered to it from the IP layer. If the received packet is a request or solicitation, the module creates a reply or an advertisement and sends it out.

If the received packet is a redirection message, the module uses the information to update the routing table. If the received packet is an error message, the module informs the protocol about the situation that caused the error. The pseudocode is shown below:

Input Module

Receive: an ICMP packet from the IP layer
1. If (the type is any of the three request types)
    1. Create a reply.
    2. Send the reply.
2. If (the type is a router solicitation)
    1. If (station is a router)
        1. Create a router advertisement.
        2. Send the advertisement.
3. If (the type is one of the three reply messages or router advertisement)
    1. Extract information in the data section of the packet.
    2. Deliver extracted information to the process that requested it.

Input Module (continued)
4. If (the type defines a redirection)
1. Modify the routing table.
5. If (the type defines an error message other than a redirection)
1. Inform the appropriate source protocol about the situation.
6. Return.

Output Module

The output module is responsible for creating request, solicitation, or error messages requested by a higher level or the IP protocol. The module receives a demand from IP, UDP, or TCP to send one of the ICMP error messages. If the demand is from IP, the output module must first check that the request is allowed. Remember, an ICMP message cannot be created for four situations: an IP packet carrying an ICMP error message, a fragmented IP packet, a multicast IP packet, or an IP packet having IP address 0.0.0.0 or 127.X.Y. Z.

The output module may also receive a demand from an application program to send one of the ICMP request or solicitation messages. The pseudocode is shown below:

Output Module
Receive: a demand
1. If (the demand defines an error message)
1. If (the demand is from IP)
1. If (the demand is forbidden)
1. Return.
2. If (the type defines a redirection message)
1. If (the station is not a router)
1. Return.
3. Create the error message using the type, the code, and the IP packet.
2. If (the demand defines a request or solicitation)
1. Create a request or solicitation message.
3. Send the message.
4. Return.

9.7 KEY TERMS

address-mask message
checksum
destination-unreachable message
echo-request and reply message
error-reporting message
Internet Control Message Protocol (ICMP)
parameter-problem message
query message
redirection
round-trip time
router-solicitation and router-advertisement message
source-quench message
time-exceeded message
timestamp message

9.8 SUMMARY

- The Internet Control Message Protocol (ICMP) sends five types of error reporting messages and four pairs of query messages to support the unreliable and connectionless Internet Protocol (IP).
- ICMP messages are encapsulated in IP datagrams.
- The destination-unreachable error message is sent to the source host when a datagram is undeliverable.
- The source-quench error message is sent in an effort to alleviate congestion.
- The time-exceeded message notifies a source host that (1) the time-to-live field has reached zero, or (2) fragments of a message have not arrived in a set amount of time.
- The parameter-problem message notifies a host that there is a problem in the header field of a datagram.
- The redirection message is sent to make the routing table of a host more efficient.
- The echo-request and echo-reply messages test the connectivity between two systems.
- The timestamp-request and timestamp-reply messages can determine the round-trip time between two systems or the difference in time between two systems.
- The address-mask-request and address-mask-reply messages are used to obtain the subnet mask.
- The router-solicitation and router-advertisement messages allow hosts to update their routing tables.
- The checksum for ICMP is calculated using both the header and the data fields of the ICMP message.
- Packet InterNet Groper (ping) is an application program that uses the services of ICMP to test the reachability of a host.
- A simple ICMP design can consist of an input module that handles incoming ICMP packets and an output module that handles demands for ICMP services.

9.9 PRACTICE SET

Multiple-Choice Questions

1. If a host needs to synchronize its clock with another host, it sends a _______ message.
   a. timestamp-request
   b. source-quench
   c. router-advertisement
   d. time-exceeded
2. Which of the following types of ICMP messages needs to be encapsulated into an IP datagram?
   a. time exceeded
   b. multicasting
   c. echo reply
   d. all of the above
3. The purpose of echo request and echo reply is to _______.
   a. report errors
   b. check node-to-node communication
   c. check packet lifetime
   d. find IP addresses
4. In error reporting the encapsulated ICMP packet goes to _______.
   a. the sender
   b. the receiver
   c. a router
   d. any of the above
5. Which field is always present in an ICMP packet?
   a. type
   b. code
   c. checksum
   d. all of the above
6. What field uniquely identifies the kind of ICMP message (for example, echo reply versus echo request)?
   a. type
   b. code
   c. option ID
   d. none of the above

7. When the hop-count field reaches zero and the destination has not been reached, a _______ error message is sent.
   a. destination-unreachable
   b. time-exceeded
   c. parameter-problem
   d. redirection
8. When all fragments of a message have not been received within the designated amount of time, a _______ error message is sent.
   a. source-quench
   b. time-exceeded
   c. parameter-problem
   d. timestamp-request
9. Errors in the header or option fields of an IP datagram require a _______ error message.
   a. parameter-problem
   b. source-quench
   c. router-solicitation
   d. redirection
10. A _______ can learn about network _______ by sending out a router-solicitation packet.
    a. router, routers
    b. router, hosts
    c. host, hosts
    d. host, routers
11. ICMP functions include:
    a. error correction
    b. detection of all unreachable datagrams
    c. reporting of some types of errors
    d. all of the above
12. Who can send ICMP error-reporting messages?
    a. routers
    b. destination hosts
    c. source hosts
    d. a and b
13. One method to alert a source host of congestion is the _______ message.
    a. redirection
    b. echo-request
    c. source-quench
    d. destination-unreachable

14. A time-exceeded message is generated if _______.
    a. the round-trip time between hosts is close to zero
    b. the time-to-live field has a zero value
    c. fragments of a message do not arrive within a set time
    d. b and c
15. To determine whether or not a node is reachable, _______ message can be sent.
    a. an echo-reply
    b. an echo-request
    c. a redirection
    d. a source-quench
16. In calculating the time difference between two clocks, a negative value indicates _______.
    a. an invalid calculation
    b. the source clock lags behind the destination clock
    c. the destination clock lags behind the source clock
    d. the one-way time has been miscalculated
17. An IP datagram (datagram A) cannot reach its destination. An ICMP error message is sent to the source. The data field of the IP datagram (datagram B) that encapsulates the ICMP packet contains _______.
    a. only the ICMP header
    b. the ICMP header plus 8 bytes of datagram A
    c. only datagram A
    d. the ICMP header, datagram A's header, and 8 bytes of datagram A's data field
18. ICMP packets are the output of _______.
    a. only the input module
    b. only the output module
    c. both the input and the output module
    d. neither the input nor the output module
19. ICMP packets are the input to _______.
    a. only the input module
    b. only the output module
    c. both the input and the output module
    d. neither the input nor the output module

Exercises

20. Host A sends a timestamp-request message to host B and never receives a reply. Discuss three possible causes and the corresponding course of action.
21. The IP address of a workstation is 198.123.46.219. If its subnet mask is 255.255.255.192, what is its identifier? What class does the network belong to?

22. Why is there a restriction on the generation of an ICMP message in response to a failed ICMP error message?
23. Host A sends a datagram to host B. Host B never receives the datagram and host A never receives notification of failure. Give two different explanations of what might have happened.
24. What is the purpose of including the IP header and the first 8 bytes of datagram data in the error reporting ICMP messages?
25. What is the maximum value of the pointer field in a parameter-problem message?
26. Give an example of a situation in which a host would never receive a redirection message.
27. Make a table showing which ICMP messages are sent by routers, which are sent by the nondestination hosts, and which are sent by the destination hosts.
28. Can the calculated sending time, receiving time, or round-trip time have a negative value? Why or why not? Give examples.
29. Why isn't the one-way time for a packet simply the round-trip time divided by two?
30. What is the minimum size of an ICMP packet? What is the maximum size of an ICMP packet?
31. What is the minimum size of an IP packet that carries an ICMP packet? What is the maximum size?
32. What is the minimum size of an Ethernet frame that carries an IP packet which in turn carries an ICMP packet? What is the maximum size?
33. How can we determine if an IP packet is carrying an ICMP packet?
34. Calculate the checksum for the following ICMP packet:

    Type: Echo Request Identifier: 123 Sequence Number: 25 Message: Hello
35. A router receives an IP packet with source IP address 130.45.3.3 and destination IP address 201.23.4.6. The router cannot find the destination IP address in its routing table. Fill in the fields (as much as you can) for the ICMP message sent.
36. TCP receives a segment with destination port address 234. TCP checks and cannot find an open port for this destination. Fill in the fields for the ICMP message sent.
37. An ICMP message has arrived with the header (in hexadecimal):

    03 0310 20 00 00 00 00

    What is the type of the message? What is the code? What is the purpose of the message?
38. An ICMP message has arrived with the header (in hexadecimal):

    05 00 11 12 11 0B 03 02

    What is the type of the message? What is the code? What is the purpose of the message? What is the value of the last 4 bytes? What do the last bytes signify?
39. A computer sends a timestamp request. If its clock shows 5:20:30 A.M. (Universal Time), show the entries for the message.
40. Repeat Exercise 39 for the time of 3:40:30 P.M. (Universal Time).

41. A computer receives a timestamp request from another computer at 2:34:20 P.M. The value of the original timestamp is 52,453,000. If the sender clock is 5 ms slow, what is the one-way time?

42. A computer sends a timestamp request to another computer. It receives the corresponding timestamp reply at 3:46:07 A.M. The values of the original timestamp, receive timestamp, and transmit timestamp are 13,560,000, 13,562,000, and 13,564,300, respectively. What is the sending trip time? What is the receiving trip time? What is the round-trip time? What is the difference between the sender clock and the receiver clock?

43. If two computers are 5000 miles apart, what is the minimum time for a message to go from one to the other?

Programming Exercises

44. Write a program in C to calculate the time elapsed from midnight in milliseconds when the time is given as X:Y:Z A.M. or P.M. format.

45. The ICMP software package usually uses the **#define** constant to declare the different types of messages. Complete the following declarations to show all the different types covered in this chapter:

```
#define ECHO_RP  0  /* Echo Reply               */
#define DEST_UR  3  /* Destination Unreachable  */
.........................................
```

46. The ICMP software package usually uses the **#define** constant to declare the different codes of different message types. Complete the following declarations to show all different codes covered in this chapter:

```
#define DU_NUR  0  /* Destination Unreachable, Network Unreachable */
#define DU_HUR  1  /* Destination Unreachable, Host Unreachable    */
................................
```

47. The ICMP software package usually uses a **struct** to declare the format of a packet header. However, the last 4 bytes of the header are specific for different types of messages. One solution is to use a **union** inside a **struct.** Complete the following declaration for different types of headers:

```
struct Icmp_Header
{
        char    type :
        char    code;
        short   checksum;
        union
        {
                ..............
                ..............
                ..............
        }....... ;
} ;
```

48. The ICMP software package usually uses a **struct** to declare the format of the entire ICMP packet including the data section. Using your answer in exercise 47, complete the following declaration:

```
struct  Icmp_Packet
{
        ...........          header ;
        ...........          data ;
} ;
```

49. Define a **struct** called **stateInformation** that contains all the local information that ICMP input module needs to access or modify.
50. Define a **struct** called **icmpPseudoHeader** that can hold entries for the pseudoheader needed to calculate the checksum for ICMP.
51. Using the declaration in the previous exercises, write a function called **icmpChSum** to calculate the checksum field for an ICMP packet. The function takes two arguments: a pointer to an ICMP packet struct and a pointer to a pseudoheader struct.
52. Using the declarations in the previous exercises and the outline given in the text, write a C function called **icmpInput** to simulate the input module. The function accepts a pointer to an ICMP packet. It uses the stateInformation struct. It sends an ICMP reply if any, or sends the information in the data section to the higher level protocols.
53. Using the declarations in the previous exercises and the outline given in the text, write a C function called **icmpOutput** to simulate the output module. The function accepts three arguments. The first argument is a pointer to an IP packet. For error messages, this pointer points to the original IP packet with a problem. For query messages, this pointer points to NULL. The second and the third arguments are characters defining the type and the code of the message to be created. Use the stateInformation struct defined previously to access the information needed to fill in the fields.
54. Write a test program that tests all of the functions written in the previous exercises. The program can print information or the values of fields instead of sending them.

CHAPTER 10

Internet Group Management Protocol (IGMP)

The IP protocol can be involved in two types of communication: unicasting and multicasting. Unicasting is the communication between one sender and one receiver. It is a one-to-one communication. However, some processes sometimes need to send the same message to a large number of receivers simultaneously. This is called *multicasting,* which is a one-to-many communication. Multicasting has many applications. For example, multiple stockbrokers can simultaneously be informed of changes in a stock price, or travel agents can be informed of a trip cancellation. Some other applications include distance learning and video-on-demand.

The **Internet Group Management Protocol (IGMP)** is one of the necessary, but not sufficient (as we will see), protocols that is involved in multicasting. IGMP is a companion to the IP protocol. Figure 10.1 shows the position of the IGMP protocol in relation to other protocols in the network layer.

Figure 10.1 *Position of IGMP in the network layer*

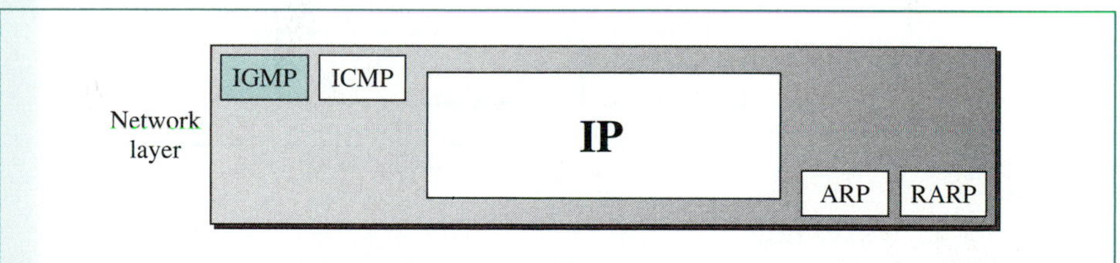

10.1 GROUP MANAGEMENT

For multicasting in the Internet we need routers that are able to route multicast packets. The routing tables of these routers must be updated using one of the multicasting routing protocols that we will discuss in Chapter 14.

IGMP is not a multicasting routing protocol; it is a protocol that manages group membership. In any network, there are one or more multicast routers that distribute multicast packets to hosts or other routers. The IGMP protocol gives the multicast routers information about the membership status of hosts (routers) connected to the network.

A multicast router may receive thousands of multicast packets every day for different groups. If a router has no knowledge about the membership status of the hosts, it must broadcast all of these packets. This creates a lot of traffic and consumes bandwidth. A better solution is to keep a list of groups in the network for which there is at least one loyal member. IGMP helps the multicast router create and update this list.

> IGMP is a group management protocol. It helps a multicast router create and update a list of loyal members related to each router interface.

10.2 IGMP MESSAGES

IGMP has gone through two versions. We discuss IGMPv2, the current version. IGMPv2 has three types of messages: the query, the membership report, and the leave report. There are two types of query messages, general and special (see Figure 10.2).

Figure 10.2 *IGMP message types*

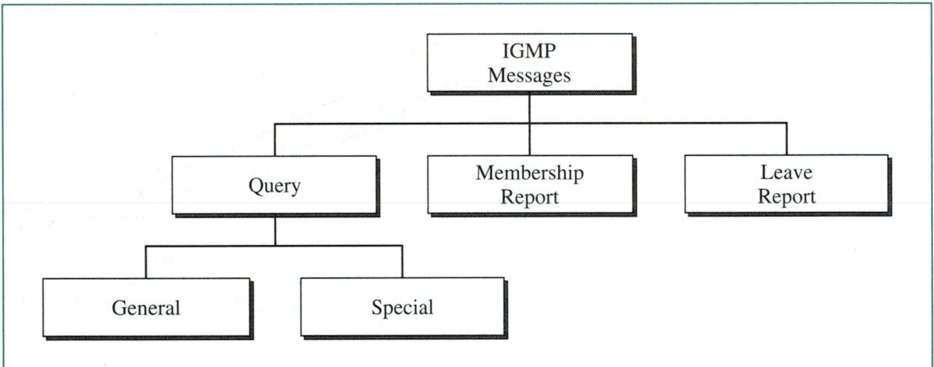

Message Format

Figure 10.3 shows the format of an IGMP (version 2) message.

Figure 10.3 *IGMP message format*

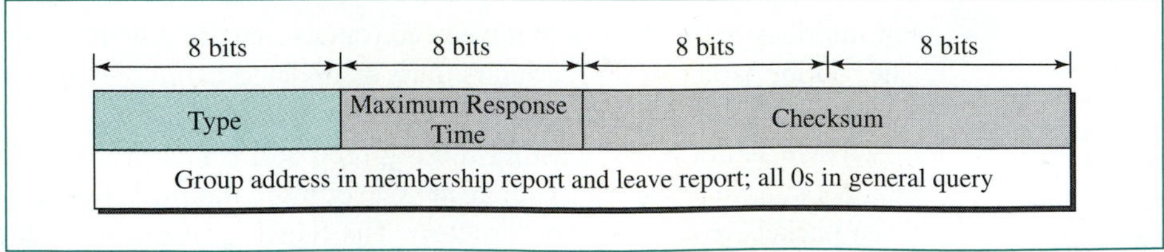

- **Type.** This 8-bit field defines the type of message as shown in Table 10.1. The value of the type is shown in both hexadecimal and binary notation.

Table 10.1 *IGMP type field*

Type	*Value*
General or Special Query	0x11 or 00010001
Membership Report	0x16 or 00010110
Leave Report	0x17 or 00010111

- **Maximum Response Time.** This 8-bit field defines the amount of time in which a query must be answered. The value is in tenths of a second; for example, if the value is 100, it means 10 s. The value is nonzero in the query message, it is set to zero in the other two message types. We will see its use shortly.
- **Checksum.** This is a 16-bit field carrying the checksum. The checksum is calculated over the 8-byte message.
- **Group address.** The value of this field is 0 for a general query message. The value defines the groupid (multicast address of the group) in the special query, the membership report, and the leave report messages.

10.3 IGMP OPERATION

IGMP operates locally. A multicast router connected to a network has a list of multicast addresses of the groups with at least one loyal member in that network (see Figure 10.4).

Figure 10.4 *IGMP operation*

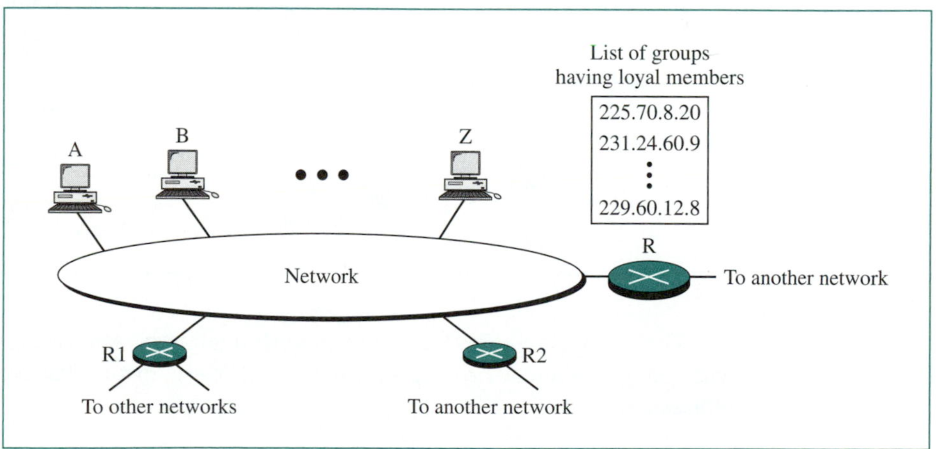

For each group, there is one router that has the duty of distributing the multicast packets destined for that group. This means that if there are three multicast routers connected to a network, their lists of groupids are mutually exclusive. For example, in the figure only router R distributes packets with the multicast address of 225.70.8.20.

A host or multicast router can have membership in a group. When a host has membership, it means that one of its processes (an application program) receives multicast packets from some group. When a router has membership, it means that a network connected to one of its other interfaces receives these multicast packets. We say that the host or the router has an *interest* in the group. In both cases, the host and the router keep a list of groupids and relay their interest to the distributing router.

For example, in Figure 10.4, router R is the distributing router. There are two other multicast routers (R1 and R2) that, depending on the group list maintained by router R, could be the recipients of router R in this network. R1 and R2 may be distributors for some of these groups in other networks, but not on this network.

Joining a Group

A host or a router can join a group. A host maintains a list of processes that have membership in a group. When a process wants to join a new group, it sends its request to the host. The host adds the name of the process and the name of the requested group to its list. If this is the first entry for this particular group, the host sends a membership report message. If this is not the first entry, there is no need to send the membership report since the host is already a member of the group; it already receives multicast packets for this group.

A router also maintains a list of groupids that shows membership for the networks connected to each interface. When there is new interest in a group for any of these interfaces, the router sends out a membership report. In other words, a router here acts like a host, but its group list is much broader because it is the accumulation of all loyal members that are connected to its interfaces. Note that the membership report is sent out of all interfaces except the one from which the new interest comes.

Figure 10.5 shows a membership report sent by a host or a router.

Figure 10.5 *Membership report*

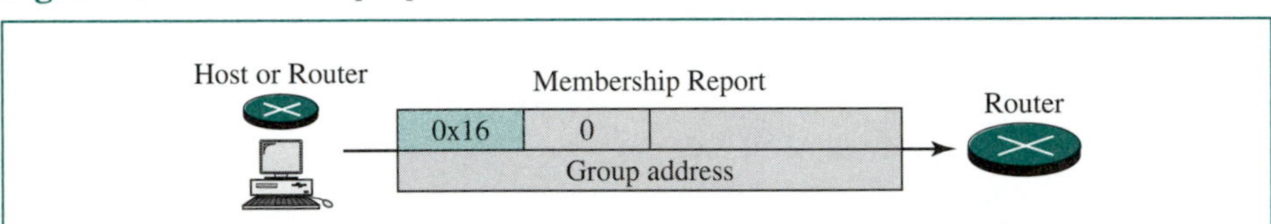

The protocol requires that the membership report be sent twice, one after the other within a few moments. In this way, if the first one is lost or damaged, the second one replaces it.

> In IGMP, a membership report is sent twice, one after the other.

Leaving a Group

When a host sees that no process is interested in a specific group, it sends a leave report. Similarly, when a router sees that none of the networks connected to its interfaces is interested in a specific group, it sends a leave report about that group.

However, when a multicast router receives a leave report, it cannot immediately purge that group from its list because the report comes from just one host or a router; there may be other hosts or routers that are still interested in that group. To make sure, the router sends a special query message and inserts the groupid (multicast address) related to the group. The router allows a specified response time for any host or router to respond. If, during this time, no interest (membership report) is received, the router assumes that there are no loyal members in the network and it purges the group from its list. Figure 10.6 shows the mechanism for leaving a group.

Figure 10.6 *Leave report*

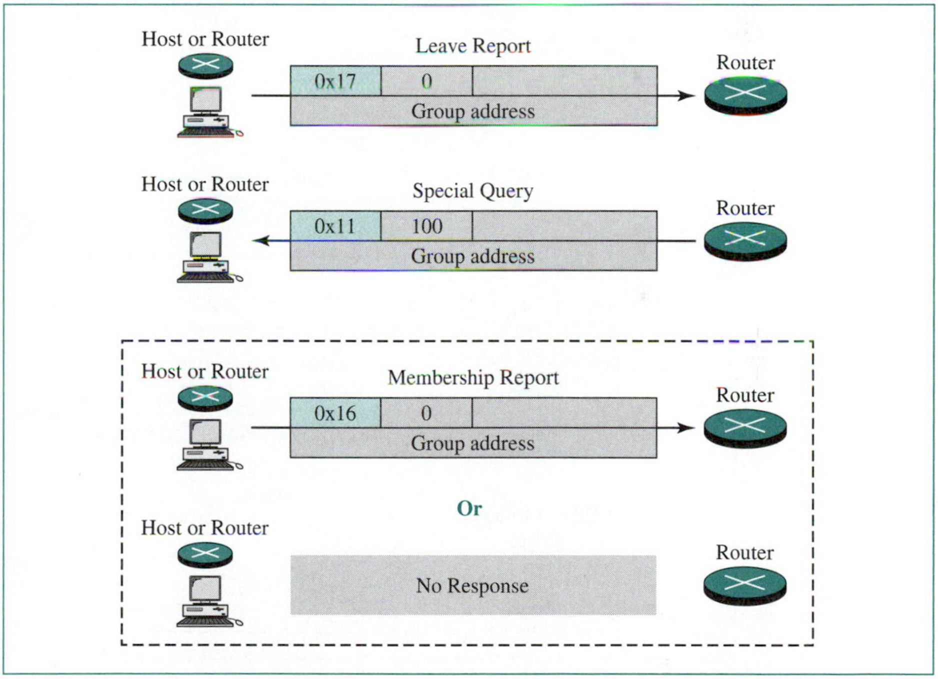

Monitoring Membership

A host or router can join a group by sending a membership report message. They can leave a group by sending a leave report message. However, sending these two types of reports is not enough. Consider the situation in which there is only one host interested in a group, but the host is shut down or removed from the system. The multicast router will never receive a leave report. How is this handled? The multicast router is responsible for monitoring all of the hosts or routers in a LAN to see if they want to continue their membership in a group.

The router periodically (by default, every 125 s) sends a general query message. In this message, the group address field is set to 0.0.0.0. This means the query for membership continuation is for all groups in which a host is involved, not just one.

> The general query message does not define a particular group.

The router expects an answer for each group in its group list; even new groups may respond. The query message has a maximum response time of 10 s (the value of the field is actually 100, but this is in tenths of a second). When a host or router receives the general query message, it responds with a membership report if it is interested in a group. However, if there is a common interest (two hosts, for example, are interested in the same group), only one response is sent for that group to prevent unnecessary traffic. This is called a delayed response and will be discussed in the next section. Note that the query message must be sent by only one router (normally called the query router), also to prevent unnecessary traffic. We discuss this issue shortly. Figure 10.7 shows the query mechanism.

Figure 10.7 *General query message*

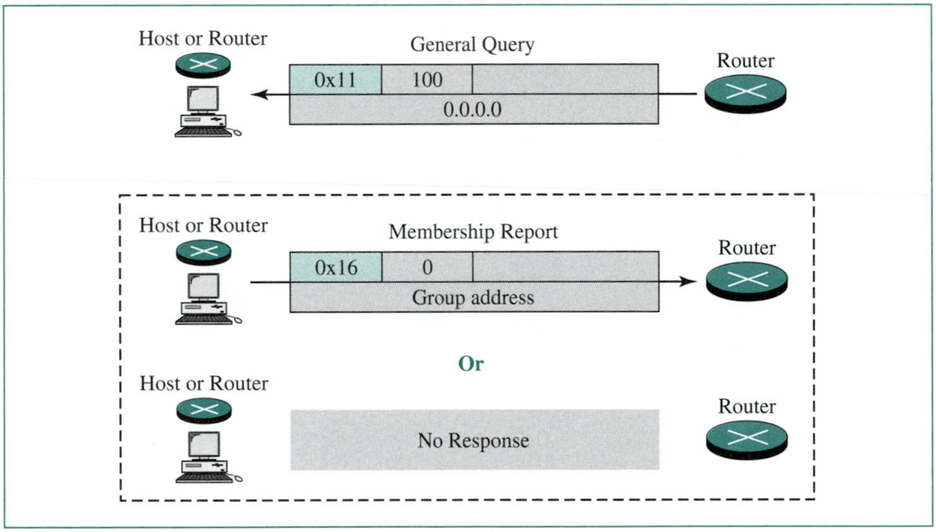

Delayed Response

To prevent unnecessary traffic, IGMP uses a delayed response strategy. When a host or router receives a query message, it does not respond immediately; it delays the response. Each host or router uses a random number to create a timer, which expires between 1 and 10 seconds. The expiration time can be in steps of 1 second or less. A timer is set for each group in the list. For example, the timer for the first group may expire in 2 seconds, but the timer for the third group may expire in 5 seconds. Each host or router waits until its timer has expired before sending a membership report message. During this waiting time, if the timer of another host or router, for the same group, expires earlier, that host or router sends a membership report. Because, as we will see shortly, the report is broadcast, the waiting host or router receives the report and knows that there is no need to send a duplicate report for this group; thus, the waiting station cancels its corresponding timer.

Example 1

Imagine there are three hosts in a network as shown in Figure 10.8.

Figure 10.8 *Example 1*

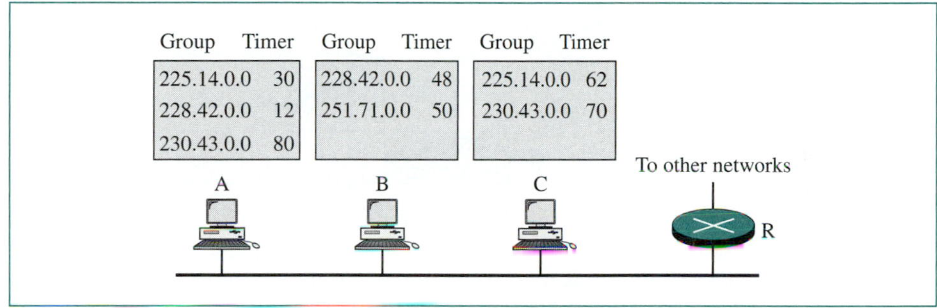

A query message was received at time 0; the random delay time (in tenths of seconds) for each group is shown next to the group address. Show the sequence of report messages.

Solution

The events occur in this sequence:

a. **Time 12:** The timer for 228.42.0.0 in host A expires and a membership report is sent, which is received by the router and every host including host B which cancels its timer for 228.42.0.0.

b. **Time 30:** The timer for 225.14.0.0 in host A expires and a membership report is sent, which is received by the router and every host including host C which cancels its timer for 225.14.0.0.

c. **Time 50:** The timer for 251.70.0.0 in host C expires and a membership report is sent, which is received by the router and every host.

d. **Time 70:** The timer for 230.43.0.0 in host A expires and a membership report is sent, which is received by the router and every host including host A which cancels its timer for 230.43.0.0.

Note that if each host had sent a report for every group in its list, there would have been seven reports; with this strategy only four reports are sent.

Query Router

Query messages may create a lot of responses. To prevent unnecessary traffic, IGMP designates one router as the query router for each network. Only this designated router sends the query message and the other routers are passive (they receive responses and update their lists).

10.4 ENCAPSULATION

The IGMP message is encapsulated in an IP datagram, which itself is encapsulated in a frame. See Figure 10.9.

Figure 10.9 *Encapsulation of IGMP packet*

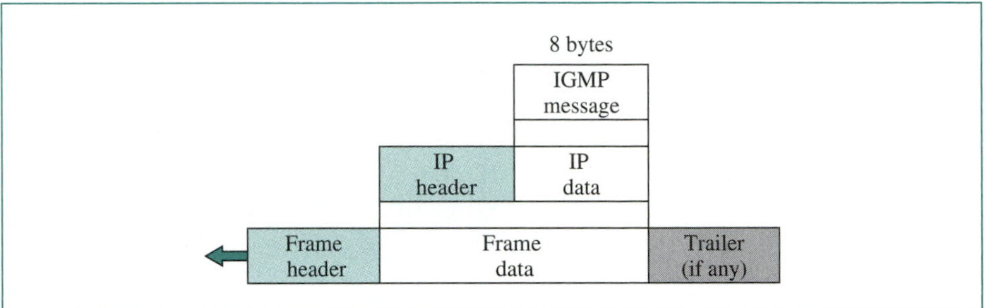

There are several issues related to this encapsulation that we need to discuss here. We first discuss the issue at the IP level and then at the data link layer.

IP Layer

At the IP layer, three fields are of concern to us: the protocol field, the TTL field, and the destination IP address.

Protocol Field

The value of the protocol field is 2 for the IGMP protocol. Every IP packet carrying this value in its protocol field has data delivered to the IGMP protocol.

> The IP packet that carries an IGMP packet has a value of 2 in its protocol field.

TTL Field

When the message is encapsulated in the IP datagram, the value of TTL must be one. This is required because the domain of IGMP is the LAN. No IGMP message should travel beyond the LAN. A TTL value of 1 guarantees that the message does not leave the LAN since this value is decremented to zero by the next router and, consequently, the packet is discarded.

> The IP packet that carries an IGMP packet has a value of 1 in its TTL field.

Destination IP Addresses

Table 10.2 shows the destination IP address for each type of message.

Table 10.2 *Destination IP addresses*

Type	*IP Destination Address*
Query	224.0.0.1 All systems on this subnet
Membership Report	The multicast address of the group
Leave Report	224.0.0.2 All routers on this subnet

A query message is multicast using the multicast address 224.0.0.1 (all systems on this subnet; see Table 4.5 in Chapter 4). All hosts and all routers will receive the message.

A membership report is multicast using a destination address equal to the multicast address being reported (groupid). Every station (host or router) that receives the packet can immediately determine (from the header) the group for which a report has been sent. As discussed previously, the timers for the corresponding unsent reports can then be cancelled. Stations do not need to open the packet to find the groupid. This address is duplicated in a packet; it's part of the message itself and also a field in the IP header. The duplication prevents errors.

A leave report message is multicast using the multicast address 224.0.0.2 (all routers on this subnet) so that routers receive this type of message. Hosts receive this message too, but disregard it.

Data Link Layer

At the network layer, the IGMP message is encapsulated in an IP packet and is treated as an IP packet. However, because the IP packet has a multicast IP address, the ARP protocol cannot find the corresponding MAC (physical) address to forward the packet at the data link layer. What happens next depends on whether or not the underlying data link layer supports physical multicast addresses.

Physical Multicast Support

Most LANs support physical multicast addressing. Ethernet is one of them. An Ethernet physical address (MAC address) is six octets (48 bits) long. If the first 25 bits in an Ethernet address are 0000000100000000010111100, this identifies a physical multicast address for the TCP/IP protocol. The remaining 23 bits can be used to define a group. To convert an IP multicast address into an Ethernet address, the multicast router extracts the least significant 23 bits of a class D IP address and inserts them into a multicast Ethernet physical address (see Figure 10.10).

However, the group identifier of a class D IP address is 28 bits long, which implies that 5 bits are not used. This means that 32 (2^5) multicast addresses at the IP level are mapped to a single multicast address. In other words, the mapping is many-to-one instead of one-to-one. If the 5 left-most bits of the group identifier of a class D address are not all zeros, a host may receive packets that do not really belong to the group in

Figure 10.10 *Mapping class D to Ethernet physical address*

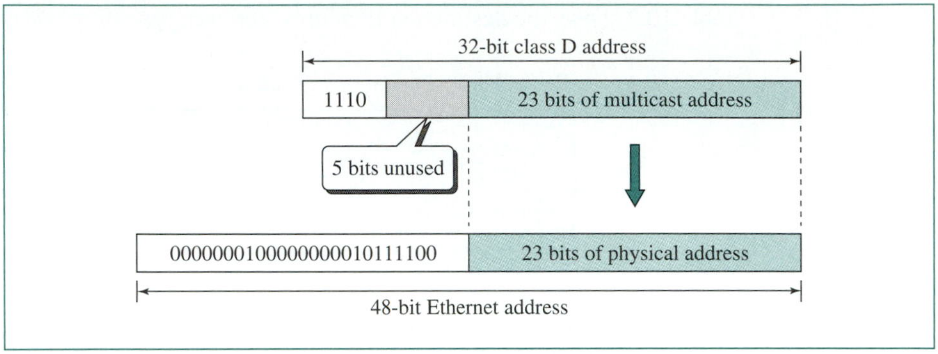

32-bit class D address

1110	(5 bits unused)	23 bits of multicast address

000000010000000001011110 0	23 bits of physical address

48-bit Ethernet address

which it is involved. For this reason, the host must check the IP address and discard any packets that do not belong to it.

Other LANs support the same concept but have different methods of mapping.

No Physical Multicast Support

Most WANs do not support physical multicast addressing. To send a multicast packet through these networks, a process called *tunneling* is used. In **tunneling,** the multicast packet is encapsulated in a unicast packet and sent through the network, where it emerges from the other side as a multicast packet (see Figure 10.11).

Figure 10.11 *Tunneling*

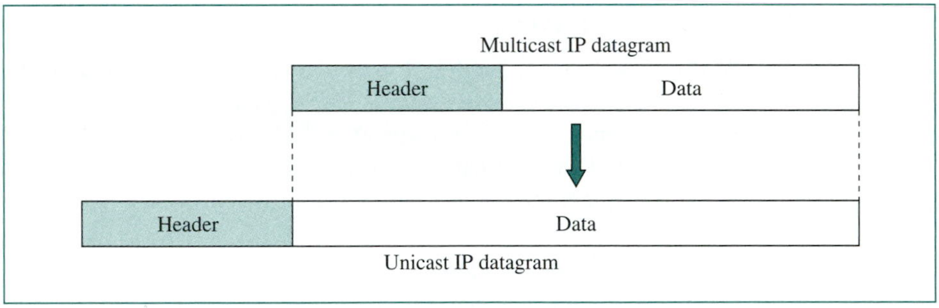

Multicast IP datagram: Header | Data

Unicast IP datagram: Header | Data

10.5 IGMP PACKAGE

We can show how IGMP can handle the sending and receiving of IGMP packets through our simplified version of an IGMP package.

The package shows only the modules used in an IGMP host. The IGMP router is left as an exercise. In our design an IGMP package involves a group table, a set of timers, and four software modules: a group-joining module, a group-leaving module, an input module, and an output module. Figure 10.12 shows these six components and their interactions.

Figure 10.12 *IGMP design*

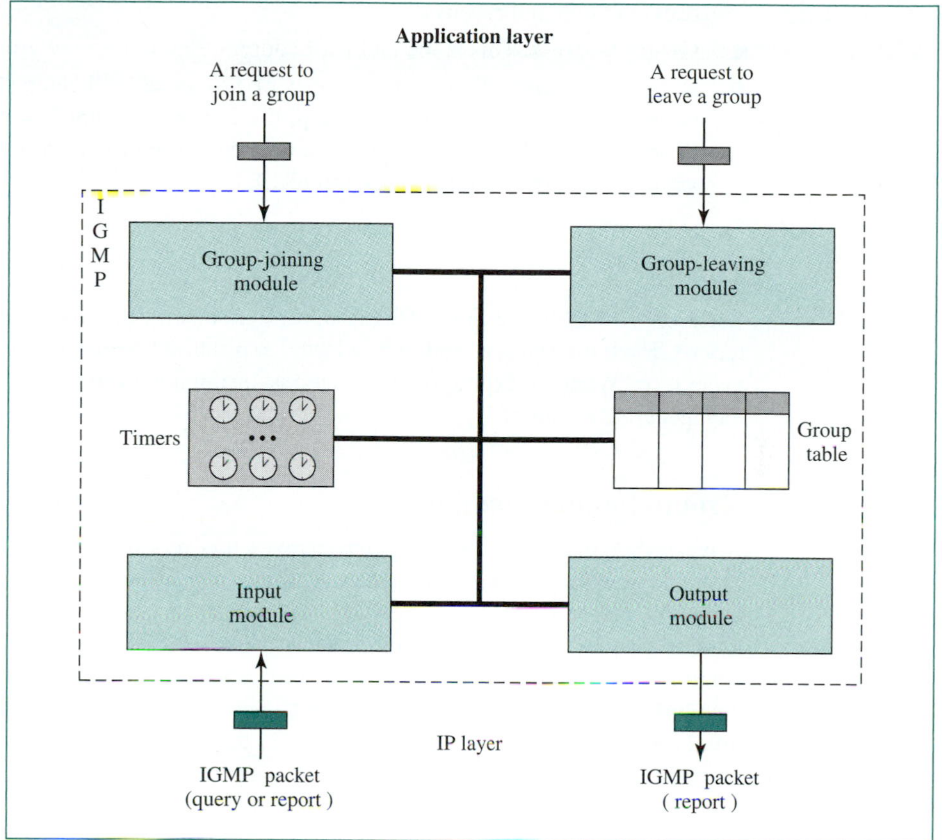

Group Table

The group table gives information about a multicast address that has at least one process as a member. The table has four fields: state, interface number, group address, and reference count (see Figure 10.13).

Figure 10.13 *Group table*

State	Interface No.	Group Address	Reference Count
....	....	....	....
....	....	....	....
....	....	....	....

- **State.** This field defines the state of the entry. It can have one of the following values: FREE, DELAYING, or IDLE. If the state is FREE, there are no processes left in the group. If the state is DELAYING, a report must be sent for this entry when the timer matures. If the state is IDLE, there is no timer running for this entry.

- **Interface number.** This field defines the interface through which the multicast packet is sent and received.
- **Group address.** This is the multicast address that defines the group.
- **Reference count.** This is the number of processes still interested in the group. Every time a process joins the group, the reference count is incremented. Every time a process leaves the group, the reference count is decremented. When this value is zero, the state is changed to FREE.

Timers

Each entry in the table in the DELAYING state has a timer to govern the sending of reports. Each timer has a randomly selected expiration time to prevent a burst of report generation. When an expiration time matures, a signal goes to the output module which then generates a report.

Group-Joining Module

A process that wants to join a group invokes this module. The module searches the group table to find an entry with the same multicast address. If found, the module increments the reference count to show that one more process has joined this group. If the multicast address is not found, the module creates a new entry and sets the reference count to one. In this case the module communicates to both the output module and the data link layer. It tells the output module to send a membership report. It tells the data link layer to update its configuration table so that this type of multicast packet can be received.

Group-Joining Module

Receive: a request from a process to join a group
1. Look for the corresponding entry in the table.
2. If (found)
    1. Increment the reference count.
3. If (not found)
    1. Create an entry with reference count set to one.
    2. Add the entry to the table.
    3. Request a membership report from the output module.
    4. Inform the data link layer to update its configuration table.
4. Return.

Group-Leaving Module

A process that wants to leave a group invokes this module. The module searches the group table to find an entry with the same multicast address. If found, the module decrements the reference count. If the count is zero, the state is changed to FREE and a leave report is sent.

Group-Leaving Module

Receive: a request from a process to leave a group
1. Look for the corresponding entry in the table.
2. If (found)
    1. Decrement the reference count.
    2. If (reference count is zero)
        1. If (any timer for this entry)
            1. Cancel the timer.
        2. Change the state to FREE.
        3. Request a leave report from the output module.
3. Return.

Input Module

The input module is invoked by an IGMP message. If the message is a query, the module starts a timer for each entry in the group table with an IDLE state and changes the state to DELAYING. To do this, the module generates a random number between zero and the maximum delay time and creates a timer with the maturation time equal to this random number. The random number generation is required so that reports will be sent by the output module at different times to prevent congestion.

If the message received is a membership report, the module checks for a corresponding entry in its table. If it is found and the state is DELAYING, it means another host on the network has sent a membership report for this group and there is no need for this host to send another report. The module cancels the timer and changes the state to IDLE. Remember that hosts do not receive leave reports.

Input Module

Receive: an IGMP message
1. Check the message type.
2. If (query)
    1. Start a timer for each entry in the table with the state IDLE.
    2. Change each IDLE state to DELAYING state.
    3. Return.
3. If (membership report)
    1. Look for the corresponding entry in the table.
    2. If (found and state is DELAYING)
        1. Cancel the timer for this entry.
        2. Change the state to IDLE.
4. Return.

Output Module

The output module is invoked by a matured timer or a request from a joining group or a leaving group. It then looks for the corresponding entry and, if the state is DELAYING, the module creates a report and sends it. It then resets the state to IDLE.

Output Module
Receive: a signal from a timer or a request from joining or leaving module
1. If the message comes from a timer.
1. If (found and state is DELAYING)
1. Create a membership report.
2. Reset the state to IDLE.
2. If the message comes from the group-joining module.
1. Create a membership report.
3. If the message comes from the group-living module.
1. Create a leave report.
4. Send the message.
5. Return.

10.6 KEY TERMS

delayed response strategy

encapsulation

general query message

group membership

groupid

Internet Group Management Protocol (IGMP)

leave report

membership report

multicast address

multicast router

multicasting

query message

query router

special query message

tunneling

10.7 SUMMARY

- Multicasting is the sending of the same message to more than one receiver simultaneously.
- The Internet Group Management Protocol (IGMP) helps multicast routers create and update a list of loyal members related to a router interface.
- The three IGMP message types are the query message, the membership report, and the leave report.

- IGMP operates locally.
- A host or router can have membership in a group.
- A host maintains a list of processes that have membership in a group.
- A router maintains a list of groupids that shows group membership for each interface.
- A router or host sends a membership report to join a group.
- A router or host sends a leave report to leave a group.
- A router sends a general query message to monitor group membership.
- A delayed response strategy prevents unnecessary traffic on a LAN.
- The IGMP message is encapsulated in an IP datagram.
- Most LANs, including Ethernet, support physical multicast addressing.
- WANs that do not support physical multicast addressing can use a process called tunneling to send multicast packets.
- An IGMP package can consist of a host group table, a set of timers, and four software modules: an input module, an output module, a group-joining module, and a group-leaving module.
- The group table holds information about each multicast group of which the host is a member.
- The timers control the sending of the reports from the host to the multicast routers.
- The group-joining module adds and updates entries in the group table.
- The group-leaving module deletes and updates entries in the group table.
- The input module handles incoming IGMP messages.
- The output module creates IGMP reports.

10.8 PRACTICE SET

Multiple-Choice Questions

1. The _______ is an IGMP message.
   a. query message
   b. membership report
   c. leave report
   d. all of the above
2. An IGMP query is sent from a _______ to a _______.
   a. host; host
   b. host; router
   c. router; router
   d. router; host or router

3. The _______ is used by a router in response to a received leave report.
   a. general query message
   b. special query message
   c. membership report
   d. leave report
4. The least significant 23 bits in a 48-bit Ethernet address unambiguously _______.
   a. identify a multicast router
   b. identify a host
   c. identify a multicast group
   d. none of the above
5. The _______ field of the IGMP message is all zeros in a query message.
   a. version
   b. type
   c. checksum
   d. group address
6. The _______ field of the IGMP message is 17 for a query message.
   a. maximum response time
   b. type
   c. checksum
   d. a and b
7. A multicast message is sent from _______ to _______.
   a. one source; one destination
   b. one source; multiple destinations
   c. multiple sources; one destination
   d. multiple sources; multiple destinations
8. In networks that do not support physical multicast addressing, multicasting can be accomplished through _______.
   a. mapping
   b. queries
   c. tunneling
   d. none of the above
9. If four hosts on a network belong to the same group, a total of _______ sent in response to a general query message.
   a. one membership report is
   b. two membership reports are
   c. three membership reports are
   d. four membership reports are

10. A query message with an IP destination address of _______ goes to all systems on the subnet.
    a. 224.0.0.0
    b. 224.0.0.1
    c. 224.0.0.2
    d. 224.0.0.3
11. A leave message with an IP destination address of _______ goes to all routers on the subnet.
    a. 224.0.0.0
    b. 224.0.0.1
    c. 224.0.0.2
    d. 224.0.0.3
12. A process called _______ sends a multicast packet through WANs that do not support physical multicast addressing.
    a. tunneling
    b. delayed response
    c. jamming
    d. multicasting
13. A group table entry is in the _______ state if there is no corresponding timer running.
    a. FREE
    b. DELAYING
    c. IDLE
    d. none of the above
14. A group table entry in the _______ state sends a request when its timer expires.
    a. FREE
    b. DELAYING
    c. IDLE
    d. none of the above
15. The _______ module receives an IGMP report or query.
    a. input
    b. output
    c. group-joining
    d. group-leaving
16. The _______ module sends out an IGMP report.
    a. input
    b. output
    c. group-joining
    d. group-leaving

17. The _______ module can create a new entry in the group table and start a timer.
    a. input
    b. output
    c. group-joining
    d. group-leaving
18. The _______ module can decrement the reference count in the group table.
    a. input
    b. output
    c. group-joining
    d. group-leaving

Exercises

19. Why is there no need for the IGMP message to travel outside its own network?
20. A multicast router list contains four groups (W, X, Y, and Z). There are three hosts on the LAN. Host A has three loyal members belonging to group W and one loyal member belonging to group X. Host B has two loyal members belonging to group W and one loyal member belonging to group Y. Host C has no processes belonging to any group. Show the IGMP messages involved in monitoring.
21. A multicast address for a group is 231.24.60.9. What is its 48-bit Ethernet address for a LAN using TCP/IP?
22. If a router has 20 entries in its group table, should it send 20 different queries periodically or just one?
23. If a host wants to continue membership in five groups, should it send five different membership report messages or just one?
24. A router with IP address 202.45.33.21 and physical Ethernet address 234A4512ECD2 sends an IGMP general query message. Show all of the entries in the message.
25. Encapsulate the message of exercise 24 in an IP packet. Fill in all the fields.
26. Encapsulate the message of exercise 25 in an Ethernet frame. Fill in all the fields.
27. A host with IP address 124.15.13.1 and physical Ethernet address 4A224512E1E2 sends an IGMP membership report message about groupid 228.45.23.11. Show all of the entries in the message.
28. Encapsulate the message of exercise 26 in an IP packet. Fill in all the fields.
29. Encapsulate the message of exercise 27 in an Ethernet frame. Fill in all the fields.
30. A router on an Ethernet network has received a multicast IP packet with groupid 226.17.18.4. When the host checks its multicast group table, it finds this address. Show how the router sends this packet to the recipients by encapsulating the IP packet in an Ethernet frame. Show all of the entries of the Ethernet frame. The outgoing IP address of the router is 185.23.5.6 and its outgoing physical address is 4A224512E1E2. Does the router need the services of ARP?
31. What if the router in exercise 30 cannot find the groupid in its table?

32. Redo exercise 30 with the physical network that does not support physical multicast addressing.
33. A host with IP address 114.45.7.9 receives an IGMP query. When it checks its group table, it finds no entries. What action should the host take? Should it send any messages? If so, show the packet fields.
34. A host with IP address 222.5.7.19 receives an IGMP query. When it checks its routing table, it finds two entries in its table: 227.4.3.7 and 229.45.6.23. What action should the host take? Should it send any messages? If so, what type and how many? Show the fields.
35. A host with IP address 186.4.77.9 receives a request from a process to join a group with groupid 230.44.101.34. When the host checks its group table, it does not find an entry for this groupid. What action should the host take? Should it send any messages? If so, show the packet field.
36. Redo exercise 35 with the host finding an entry in its table.
37. A router with IP address 184.4.7.9 receives a report from a host that wants to join a group with groupid 232.54.10.34. When the router checks its group table, it does not find an entry for this groupid. What action should the router take? Should it send any messages? If so, show the packet fields.
38. Redo exercise 37 with the router finding an entry in its table.
39. A router sends a query and receives only three reports about groupids 225.4.6.7, 225.32.56.8, and 226.34.12.9. When it checks its routing table, it finds five entries: 225.4.6.7, 225.11.6.8, 226.34.12.9, 226.23.22.67, and 229.12.4.89. What action should be taken?
40. The contents of an IGMP message in hexadecimal notation are:

    11 00 EE FF 00 00 00 00

    Answer the following questions:

    a. What is the type?
    b. What is the checksum?
    c. What is the groupid?
41. The contents of an IGMP message in hexadecimal notation are:

    16 00 F9 C0 E1 2A 13 14

    Answer the following questions:

    a. What is the type?
    b. What is the checksum?
    c. What is the groupid?
42. Is there an error in the following hexadecimal representation of an IGMP message?

    11 00 A0 11 E1 2A 13 14
43. Is there an error in the following hexadecimal representation of an IGMP message?

    17 00 A0 11 00 00 00 00
44. How many multicast addresses can be supported for the IP protocol in Ethernet?
45. How many multicast addresses can be supported by the IP protocol?

46. What is the size of address space lost when we transform a multicast IP address to an Ethernet multicast address?
47. Change the following IP multicast addresses to Ethernet multicast addresses. How many of them specify the same Ethernet address?
    a. 224.18.72.8
    b. 235.18.72.8
    c. 237.18.6.88
    d. 224.88.12.8
48. Modify the IGMP package in the text to be also applicable to a router.
49. Do some research on IGMPv1. What is the size of the type field? Is there any field in the first version that is not in the second? Are version 1 and 2 compatible? If a router supporting version 2 receives a message in version 1, what can the router do? If a router supporting version 1 receives a message in version 2, what can the router do?

Programming Exercises

50. Write a C function to determine if a given IP address (in the form x.y.z.t) is a multicast address.
51. Write a C function to determine if a given IP address (in the form of a long integer) is a multicast address.
52. Write a C function to determine if a given Ethernet address (in hexadecimal format) is an Ethernet multicast address.
53. Write a C function that changes a given IP multicast address (in long integer) to an Ethernet multicast address (in hexadecimal).
54. Write a C function that changes a given Ethernet multicast address (in hexadecimal) to an IP multicast address (in long integer).

CHAPTER 11

User Datagram Protocol (UDP)

The TCP/IP protocol suite specifies two protocols for the transport layer: UDP and TCP. We first focus on UDP, the simpler of the two, before discussing TCP in Chapter 12.

Figure 11.1 shows the relationship of UDP to the other protocols and layers of the TCP/IP protocol suite: UDP lies between the application layer and the IP layer and, like TCP, serves as the intermediary between the application programs and the network operations.

Figure 11.1 *Position of UDP in the TCP/IP protocol suite*

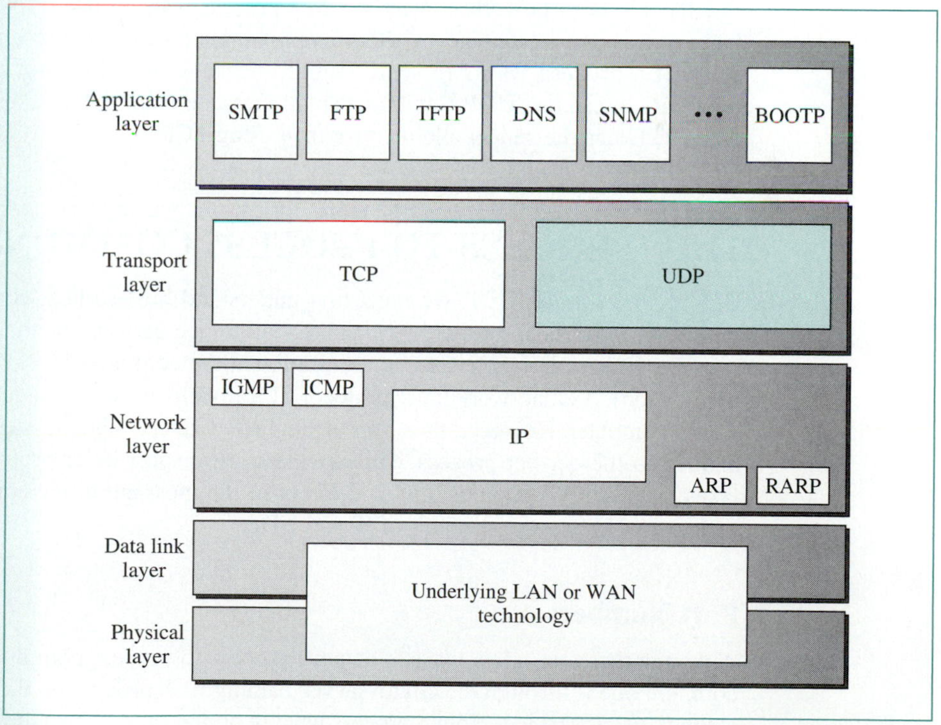

A transport layer protocol usually has several responsibilities. One is to create a process-to-process (a **process** is a running application program) communication; UDP uses port numbers to accomplish this. Another responsibility is to provide control mechanisms at the transport level. UDP does this task at a very minimal level. There is no flow control mechanism and there is no acknowledgment for received packets. UDP, however, does provide error control to some extent. If UDP detects an error in the received packet, it silently drops it.

The transport layer also provides a connection mechanism for the processes. The processes must be able to send streams of data to the transport layer. It is the responsibility of the transport layer at the sending station to make the connection with the receiver, chop the stream into transportable units, number them, and send them one by one. It is the responsibility of the transport layer at the receiving end to wait until all the different units belonging to the same process have arrived, check and pass those that are error free, and deliver them to the receiving process as a stream. After the entire stream has been sent, the transport layer closes the connection. UDP does not do any of the above. It can only receive a data unit from the processes and deliver it, unreliably, to the receiver. The data unit must be small enough to fit in a UDP packet.

UDP is called a *connectionless, unreliable* transport protocol. It does not add anything to the services of IP except for providing process-to-process communication instead of host-to-host communication. Also, it performs very limited error checking.

If UDP is so powerless, why would a process want to use it? With the disadvantages come some advantages. UDP is a very simple protocol using a minimum of overhead. If a process wants to send a small message and does not care much about reliability, it can use UDP. Sending a small message using UDP takes much less interaction between the sender and receiver than using TCP.

11.1 PROCESS-TO-PROCESS COMMUNICATION

Before we examine UDP, we must first understand host-to-host communication and process-to-process communication and the difference between them.

The IP is responsible for communication at the computer level (host-to-host communication). As a network layer protocol, IP can deliver the message only to the destination computer. However, this is an incomplete delivery. The message still needs to be handed to the correct process. This is where a transport layer protocol such as UDP takes over. UDP is responsible for delivery of the message to the appropriate process. Figure 11.2 shows the domains of IP and UDP.

Port Numbers

Although there are a few ways to achieve process-to-process communication, the most common one is through the **client-server** paradigm. A process on the local host, called a *client,* needs services from a process usually on the remote host, called a *server.*

Both processes (client and server) have the same name. For example, to get the day and time from a remote machine, we need a Daytime client process running on the local host and a Daytime server process running on a remote machine.

Figure 11.2 *UDP versus IP*

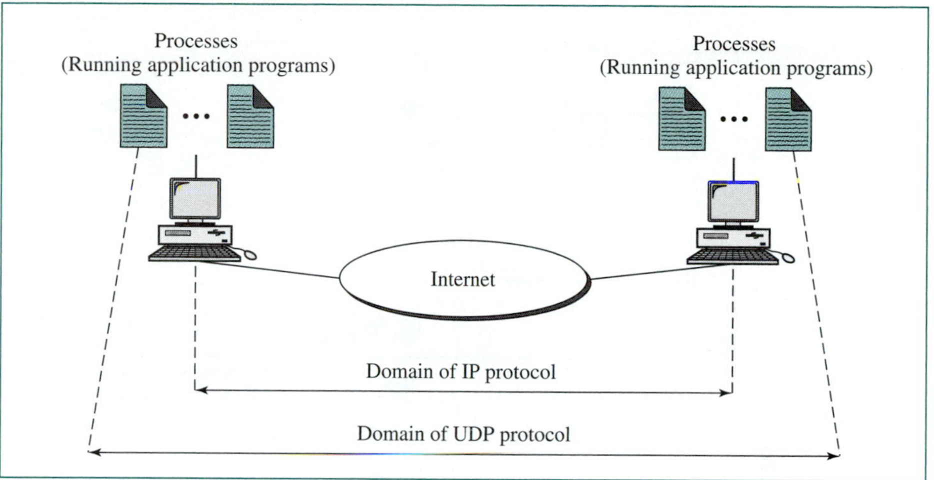

However, operating systems today support both multiuser and multiprogramming environments. A remote computer can run several server programs at the same time, just as several local computers can run one or more client programs at the same time. For communication, we must define the

- Local host
- Local process
- Remote host
- Remote process

The local host and the remote host are defined using IP addresses. To define the processes, we need second identifiers called **port numbers.** In the TCP/IP protocol suite, the port numbers are integers between 0 and 65,535.

The client program defines itself with a port number, chosen randomly by the UDP software running on the client host. This is the **ephemeral port number.**

The server process must also define itself with a port number. This port number, however, cannot be chosen randomly. If the computer at the server site runs a server process and assigns a random number as the port number, the process at the client site that wants to access that server and use its services will not know the port number. Of course, one solution would be to send a special packet and request the port number of a specific server, but this requires more overhead. TCP/IP has decided to use universal port numbers for servers; these are called **well-known port numbers.** There are some exceptions to this rule; for example, there are clients that are assigned well-known port numbers. We will talk about this later when we explore the client-server paradigm in Chapter 15. Every client process knows the well-known port number of the corresponding server process. For example, while the Daytime client process, discussed above, can use an ephemeral (temporary) port number 52,000 to identify itself, the Daytime server process must use the well-known (permanent) port number 13. Figure 11.3 shows this concept.

It should be clear by now that the IP addresses and port numbers play different roles in selecting the final destination of data. The destination IP address defines the

Figure 11.3 *Port numbers*

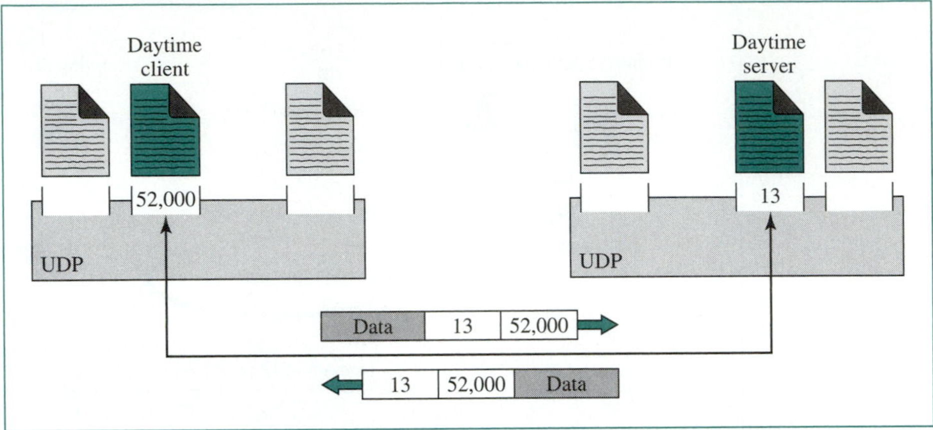

host among the different hosts in the world. After the host has been selected, the port number defines one of the processes on this particular host (see Figure 11.4).

Figure 11.4 *IP addresses versus port numbers*

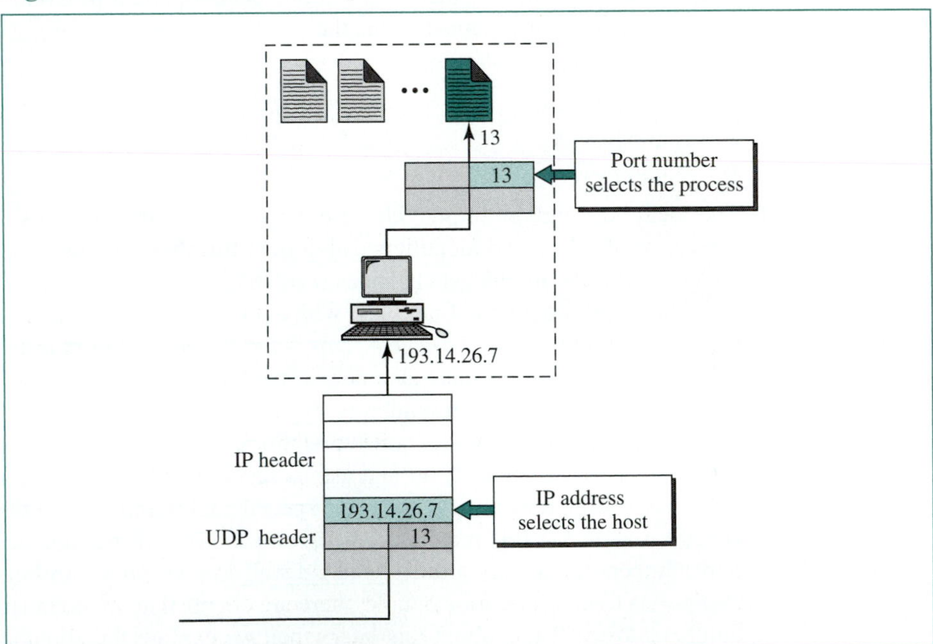

IANA Ranges

The IANA has divided the port numbers into three ranges: well-known, registered, and dynamic (or private) as shown in Figure 11.5.

Figure 11.5 *IANA ranges*

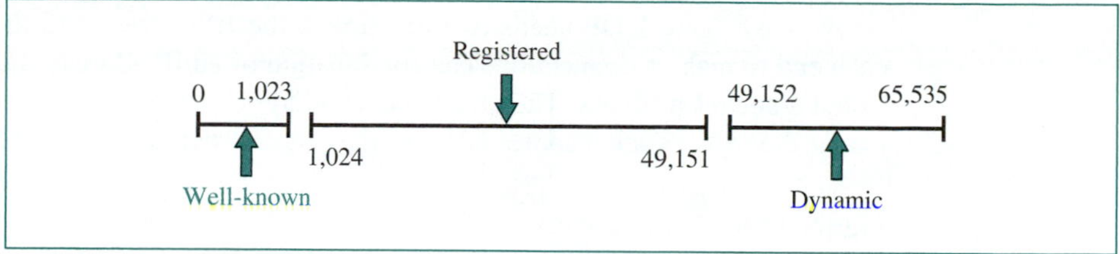

- **Well-known ports.** The ports ranging from 0 to 1,023 are assigned and controlled by IANA. These are the well-known ports.
- **Registered ports.** The ports ranging from 1,024 to 49,151 are not assigned or controlled by IANA. They can only be registered with IANA to prevent duplication.
- **Dynamic ports.** The ports ranging from 49,152 to 65,535 are neither controlled nor registered. They can be used by any process. These are the ephemeral ports.

Ranges Used by Other Systems

Note that other operating systems may use ranges other than IANA's for the well-known and ephemeral ports. For example, BSD Unix has three ranges: reserved, ephemeral, and nonprivileged.

Well-Known Ports for UDP

Table 11.1 shows some well-known port numbers used by UDP. Some port numbers can be used by both UDP and TCP. We will discuss them when we talk about TCP in Chapter 12.

Table 11.1 *Well-known ports used with UDP*

Port	*Protocol*	*Description*
7	Echo	Echoes a received datagram back to the sender
9	Discard	Discards any datagram that is received
11	Users	Active users
13	Daytime	Returns the date and the time
17	Quote	Returns a quote of the day
19	Chargen	Returns a string of characters
53	Nameserver	Domain Name Service
67	Bootps	Server port to download bootstrap information
68	Bootpc	Client port to download bootstrap information
69	TFTP	Trivial File Transfer Protocol
111	RPC	Remote Procedure Call
123	NTP	Network Time Protocol
161	SNMP	Simple Network Management Protocol
162	SNMP	Simple Network Management Protocol (trap)

Socket Addresses

As we have seen, UDP needs two identifiers, the IP address and the port number, at each end to make a connection. The combination of an IP address and a port number is called a **socket address.** The client socket address defines the client process uniquely just as the server socket address defines the server process uniquely (see Figure 11.6).

Figure 11.6 *Socket address*

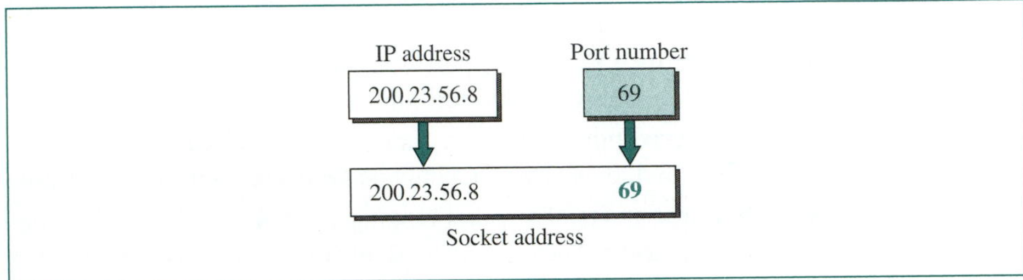

To use the services of UDP, we need a pair of socket addresses: the client socket address and the server socket address. These four pieces of information are part of the IP header and the UDP header. The IP header contains the IP addresses; the UDP header contains the port numbers.

11.2 USER DATAGRAM

UDP packets, called **user datagrams,** have a fixed-size header of 8 bytes. Figure 11.7 shows the format of a user datagram.

Figure 11.7 *User datagram format*

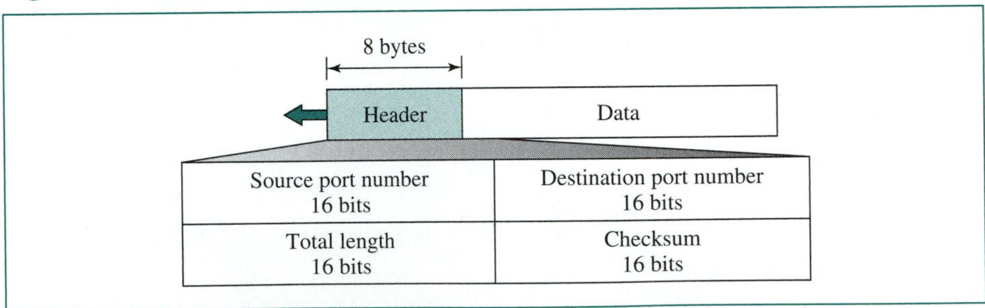

The fields are as follows:

- **Source port number.** This is the port number used by the process running on the source host. It is 16 bits long, which means that the port number can range from 0 to 65,535. If the source host is the client (a client sending a request), the port number, in most cases, is an ephemeral port number requested by the process and chosen by the UDP software running on the source host. If the source host is the server (a server sending a response), the port number, in most cases, is a well-known port number.

- **Destination port number.** This is the port number used by the process running on the destination host. It is also 16 bits long. If the destination host is the server (a client sending a request), the port number, in most cases, is a well-known port number. If the destination host is the client (a server sending a response), the port number, in most cases, is an ephemeral port number. In this case, the server copies the ephemeral port number it has received in the request packet.

- **Length.** This is a 16-bit field that defines the total length of the user datagram, header plus data. The 16 bits can define a total length of 0 to 65,535 bytes. However, the minimum length is 8 bytes, which indicates a user datagram with only header and no data. Therefore, the length of the data can be between 0 and 65,507 (65,535 – 20 – 8) bytes (20 bytes for IP header and 8 bytes for UDP header).

  The length field in a UDP user datagram is actually not necessary. A user datagram is encapsulated in an IP datagram. There is a field in the IP datagram that defines the total length. There is another field in the IP datagram that defines the length of the header. So if we subtract the value of the second field from the first, we can deduce the length of the UDP datagram that is encapsulated in an IP datagram.

  > UDP length = IP length – IP header's length

  However, the designers of the UDP protocol felt that it was more efficient for the destination UDP to calculate the length of the data from the information provided in the UDP user datagram rather than asking the IP software to supply this information. We should remember that when the IP software delivers the UDP user datagram to the UDP layer, it has already dropped the IP header.

- **Checksum.** This field is used to detect errors over the entire user datagram (header plus data). The checksum is discussed in the next section.

11.3 CHECKSUM

We have already talked about the concept of the checksum and the way it is calculated in Chapter 7. We have also shown how to calculate the checksum for the IP and ICMP packet. We now show how this is done for UDP.

UDP checksum calculation is different from the one for IP and ICMP. Here the checksum includes three sections: a pseudoheader, the UDP header, and the data coming from the application layer.

The **pseudoheader** is the part of the header of the IP packet in which the user datagram is to be encapsulated with some fields filled with 0s (see Figure 11.8).

If the checksum does not include the pseudoheader, a user datagram may arrive safe and sound. However, if the IP header is corrupted, it may be delivered to the wrong host.

Figure 11.8 *Pseudoheader added to the UDP datagram*

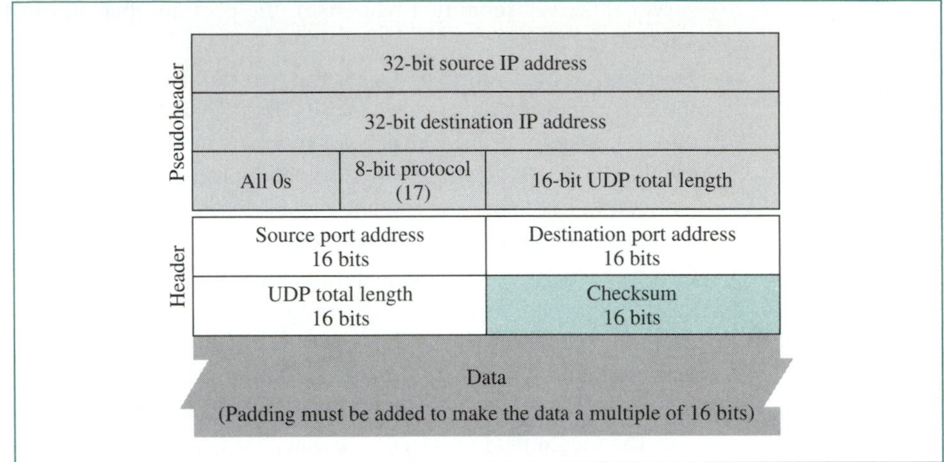

The protocol field is added to ensure that the packet belongs to UDP, and not to TCP. We will see later that if a process can use either UDP or TCP, the destination port number can be the same. The value of the protocol field for UDP is 17. If this value is changed during transmission, the checksum calculation at the receiver will detect it and UDP drops the packet. It is not delivered to the wrong protocol.

Note the similarities between the pseudoheader fields and the last 12 bytes of the IP header.

Checksum Calculation at Sender

The sender follows these eight steps to calculate the checksum:

1. Add the pseudoheader to the UDP user datagram.
2. Fill the checksum field with zeros.
3. Divide the total bits into 16-bit (2-byte) words.
4. If the total number of bytes is not even, add 1 byte of padding (all 0s). The padding is only for the purpose of calculating the checksum and will be discarded afterwards.
5. Add all 16-bit sections using one's complement arithmetic.
6. Complement the result (change all 0s to 1s and all 1s to 0s), which is a 16-bit number, and insert it in the checksum field.
7. Drop the pseudoheader and any added padding.
8. Deliver the UDP user datagram to the IP software for encapsulation.

Note that the order of the rows in the pseudoheader does not make any difference in checksum calculation. Also, adding 0s does not change the result. For this reason, the software that calculates the checksum can easily add the whole IP header (20 bytes) to the UDP datagram, set the first bytes to zero, set the TTL field to zero, replace the IP checksum with UDP length, and calculate the checksum. The result would be the same.

Checksum Calculation at Receiver

The receiver follows these six steps to calculate the checksum:

1. Add the pseudoheader to the UDP user datagram.
2. Add padding if needed.
3. Divide the total bits into 16-bit sections.
4. Add all 16-bit sections using one's complement arithmetic.
5. Complement the result.
6. If the result is all 0s, drop the pseudoheader and any added padding and accept the user datagram. If the result is anything else, discard the user datagram.

An Example

Figure 11.9 shows the checksum calculation for a very small user datagram with only 7 bytes of data. Because the number of bytes of data is odd, padding is added for checksum calculation. This pseudoheader as well as the padding will be dropped when the user datagram is delivered to the IP.

Figure 11.9 *Checksum calculation of a simple UDP user datagram*

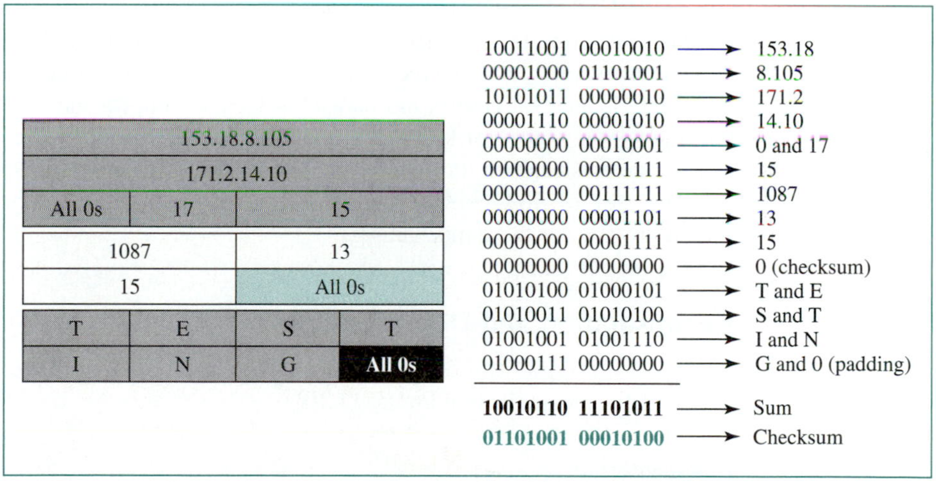

153.18.8.105			
171.2.14.10			
All 0s	17	15	
1087		13	
15		All 0s	
T	E	S	T
I	N	G	All 0s

Binary		Value
10011001 00010010	→	153.18
00001000 01101001	→	8.105
10101011 00000010	→	171.2
00001110 00001010	→	14.10
00000000 00010001	→	0 and 17
00000000 00001111	→	15
00000100 00111111	→	1087
00000000 00001101	→	13
00000000 00001111	→	15
00000000 00000000	→	0 (checksum)
01010100 01000101	→	T and E
01010011 01010100	→	S and T
01001001 01001110	→	I and N
01000111 00000000	→	G and 0 (padding)
10010110 11101011	→	Sum
01101001 00010100	→	Checksum

Optional Use of the Checksum

The calculation of the checksum and its inclusion in a user datagram is optional. If the checksum is not calculated, the field is filled with 0s. One might ask, when the UDP software on the destination computer receives a user datagram with a checksum value of zero, how it can determine if the checksum was not used or if it was used and the result happened to be all 0s? The answer is very simple. If the source does calculate the checksum and the result happens to be all 0s, it must be complemented. So what is sent is not all 0s, but all 1s, which is considered negative zero in one's complement arithmetic.

11.4 UDP OPERATION

UDP uses concepts common to the transport layer. These concepts will be discussed here briefly, and then expanded in the next chapter on the TCP protocol.

Connectionless Services

As mentioned previously, UDP provides a connectionless service. This means that each user datagram sent by UDP is an independent datagram. There is no relationship between the different user datagrams even if they are coming from the same source process and going to the same destination program. The user datagrams are not numbered. Also, there is no connection establishment and no connection termination as is the case for TCP. This means that each user datagram can travel on a different path.

One of the ramifications of being connectionless is that the process that uses UDP cannot send a stream of data to UDP and expect UDP to chop them into different related user datagrams. Instead each request must be small enough to fit into one user datagram. Only those processes sending short messages should use UDP.

Flow and Error Control

UDP is a very simple, unreliable transport protocol. There is no flow control, and hence no window mechanism. The receiver may overflow with incoming messages.

There is no error control mechanism in UDP except for the checksum. This means that the sender does not know if a message has been lost or duplicated. When the receiver detects an error through the checksum, the user datagram is silently discarded.

The lack of flow control and error control means that the process using UDP should provide for these mechanisms.

Encapsulation and Decapsulation

To send a message from one process to another, the UDP protocol encapsulates and decapsulates messages (see Figure 11.10).

Encapsulation

When a process has a message to send through UDP, it passes the message to UDP along with a pair of socket addresses and the length of data. UDP receives the data and adds the UDP header. UDP then passes the user datagram to the IP with the socket addresses. IP adds its own header, using the value 17 in the protocol field, indicating that the data has come from the UDP protocol. The IP datagram is then passed to the data link layer. The data link layer receives the IP datagram, adds its own header (and possibly a trailer), and passes it to the physical layer. The physical layer encodes the bits into electrical or optical signals and sends it to the remote machine.

Figure 11.10 *Encapsulation and decapsulation*

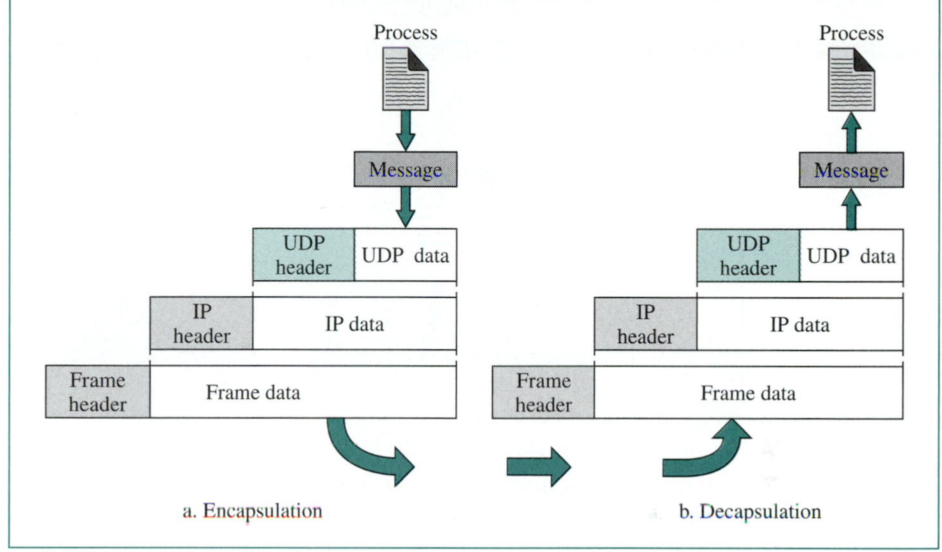

Decapsulation

When the message arrives at the destination host, the physical layer decodes the signals into bits and passes it to the data link layer. The data link layer uses the header (and the trailer) to check the data. If there is no error, the header and trailer are dropped and the datagram is passed to the IP. The IP software does its own checking. If there is no error, the header is dropped and the user datagram is passed to the UDP with the sender and receiver IP addresses. UDP uses the checksum to check the entire user datagram. If there is no error, the header is dropped and the application data along with the sender socket address is passed to the process. The sender socket address is passed to the process in case it needs to respond to the message received.

Queuing

We have talked about ports without discussing the actual implementation of them. In UDP, queues are associated with ports (see Figure 11.11).

At the client site, when a process starts, it requests a port number from the operating system. Some implementations create both an incoming and an outgoing queue associated with each process. Other implementations create only an incoming queue associated with each process.

Note that even if a process wants to communicate with multiple processes, it obtains only one port number and eventually one outgoing and one incoming queue. The queues opened by the client are, in most cases, identified by ephemeral port numbers. The queues function as long as the process is running. When the process terminates, the queues are destroyed.

Figure 11.11 *Queues in UDP*

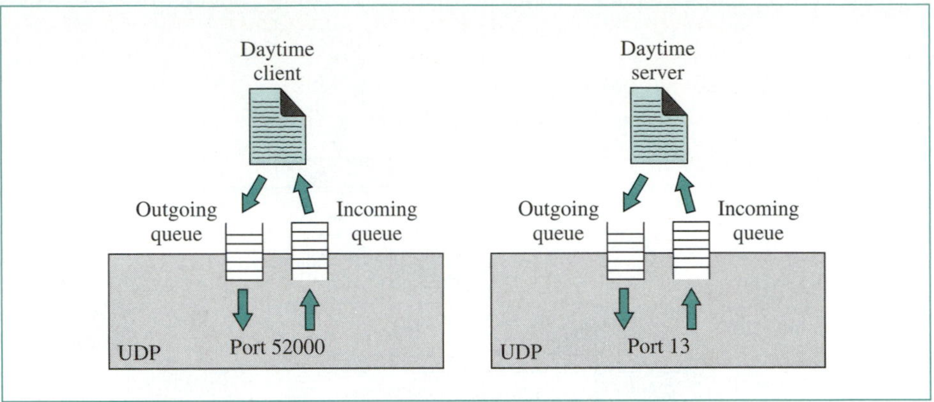

The client process can send messages to the outgoing queue by using the source port number specified in the request. UDP removes the messages one by one, and, after adding the UDP header, delivers them to IP. An outgoing queue can overflow. If this happens, the operating system can ask the client process to wait before sending any more messages.

When a message arrives for a client, UDP checks to see if an incoming queue has been created for the port number specified in the destination port number field of the user datagram. If there is such a queue, UDP sends the received user datagram to the end of the queue. If there is no such queue, UDP discards the user datagram and asks the ICMP protocol to send a *port unreachable* message to the server. All of the incoming messages for one particular client program, whether coming from the same or a different server, are sent to the same queue. An incoming queue can overflow. If this happens, UDP drops the user datagram and asks for a port unreachable message to be sent to the server.

At the server site, the mechanism of creating queues is different. We will see in future chapters that there are different types of servers. However, in its simplest form, a server asks for incoming and outgoing queues using its well-known port when it starts running. The queues remain open as long as the server is running.

When a message arrives for a server, UDP checks to see if an incoming queue has been created for the port number specified in the destination port number field of the user datagram. If there is such a queue, UDP sends the received user datagram to the end of the queue. If there is no such queue, UDP discards the user datagram and asks the ICMP protocol to send a port unreachable message to the client. All of the incoming messages for one particular server, whether coming from the same or a different client, are sent to the same queue. An incoming queue can overflow. If this happens, UDP drops the user datagram and asks for a port unreachable message to be sent to the client.

When a server wants to respond to a client, it sends messages to the outgoing queue using the source port number specified in the request. UDP removes the messages one by one, and, after adding the UDP header, delivers them to IP. An outgoing queue can overflow. If this happens, the operating system asks the server to wait before sending any more messages.

Multiplexing and Demultiplexing

In a host running a TCP/IP protocol suite, there is only one UDP but possibly several processes that may want to use the services of UDP. To handle this situation, UDP multiplexes and demultiplexes (see Figure 11.12).

Figure 11.12 *Multiplexing and demultiplexing*

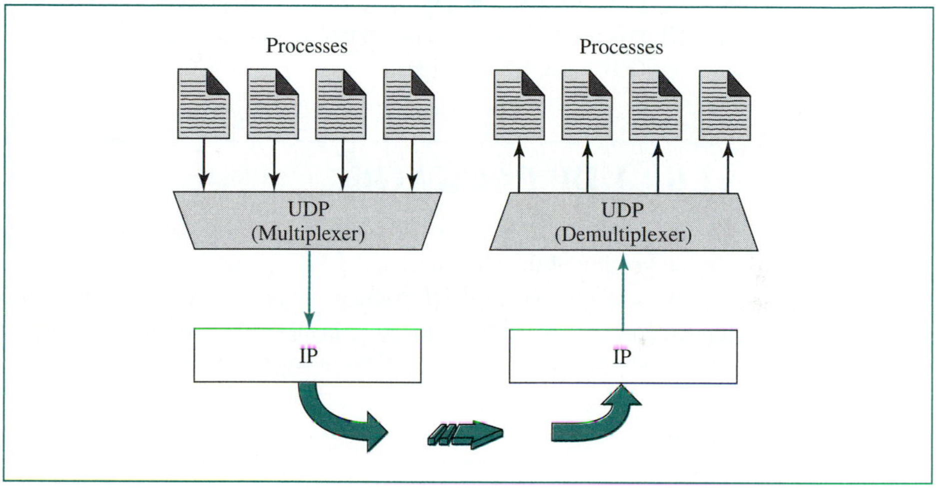

Multiplexing

At the sender site, there may be several processes that need to send user datagrams. However, there is only one UDP. This is a many-to-one relationship and requires multiplexing. UDP accepts messages from different processes, differentiated by their assigned port numbers. After adding the header, UDP passes the user datagram to the IP.

Demultiplexing

At the receiver site, there is only one UDP. However, we may have many processes that can receive user datagrams. This is a one-to-many relationship and requires demultiplexing. UDP receives user datagrams from IP. After error checking and dropping of the header, UDP delivers each message to the appropriate process based on the port numbers.

11.5 USE OF UDP

The following lists some uses of the UDP protocol:

- UDP is suitable for a process that requires simple request-response communication with little concern for flow and error control. It is not usually used for a process that needs to send bulk data, such as FTP (see Chapter 20).

- UDP is suitable for a process with internal flow and error-control mechanisms. For example, the Trivial File Transfer Protocol (TFTP) (see Chapter 21) process includes flow and error control. It can easily use UDP.
- UDP is a suitable transport protocol for multicasting and broadcasting. Multicasting and broadcasting capabilities are embedded in the UDP software but not in the TCP software.
- UDP is used for management processes such as SNMP (see Chapter 23).
- UDP is used for some route updating protocols such as Routing Information Protocol (RIP) (see Chapter 13).

11.6 UDP PACKAGE

To show how UDP handles the sending and receiving of UDP packets, we present a simple version of the UDP package.

We can say that the UDP package involves five components: a control-block table, input queues, a control-block module, an input module, and an output module. Figure 11.13 shows these five components and their interactions.

Figure 11.13 *UDP design*

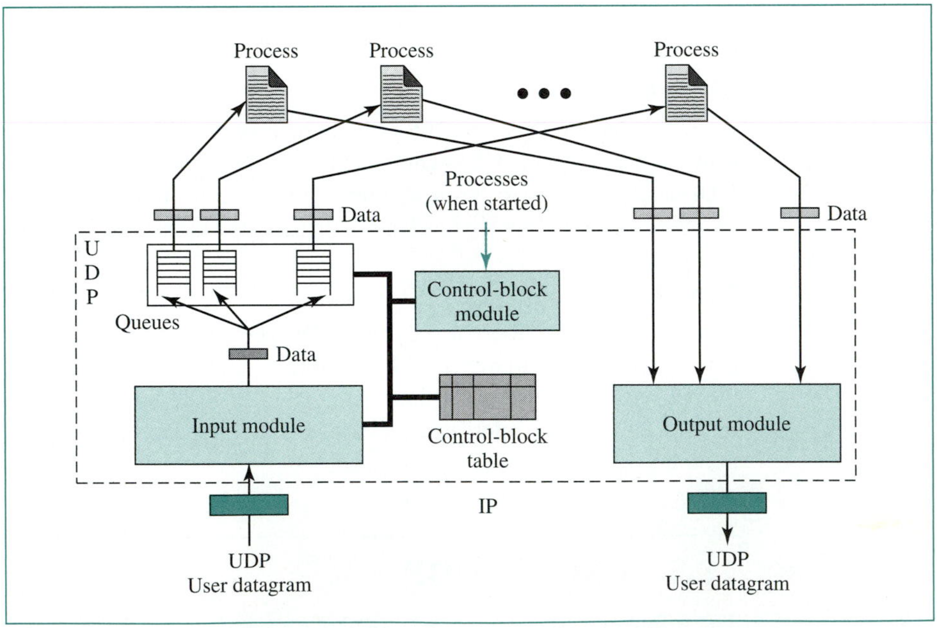

Control-Block Table

In our package, UDP has a control-block table to keep track of the open ports. Each entry in this table has a minimum of four fields: the state, which can be FREE or IN-USE, the process ID, the port number, and the corresponding queue number.

Input Queues

Our UDP package uses a set of input queues, one for each process. In this design, we do not use output queues.

Control-Block Module

The control-block module is responsible for the management of the control-block table. When a process starts, it asks for a port number from the operating system. The operating system assigns well-known port numbers to servers and ephemeral port numbers to clients. The process passes the process ID and the port number to the control-block module to create an entry in the table for the process. The module does not create the queues. The field for queue number has a value of zero. Note that we have not included a strategy to deal with a table that is full; this is left as an exercise.

Control-Block Module
Receive: a process ID and a port number
1. Search the control block table for a FREE entry.
1. If (not found)
1. Delete an entry using a predefined strategy.
2. Create a new entry with the state IN-USE.
3. Enter the process ID and the port number.
2. Return.

Input Module

The input module receives a user datagram from the IP. It searches the control-block table to find an entry having the same port number as this user datagram. If the entry is found, the module uses the information in the entry to enqueue the data. If the entry is not found, it generates an ICMP message.

Input Module
Receive: a user datagram from IP
1. Look for the corresponding entry in the control-block table.
1. If (found)
1. Check the queue field to see if a queue is allocated.
1. If (no)
1. Allocate a queue.
2. Enqueue the data in the corresponding queue.
2. If (not found)
1. Ask the ICMP module to send an "unreachable port" message.
2. Discard the user datagram.
2. Return.

Output Module

The output module is responsible for creating and sending user datagrams.

Output Module
Receive: data and information from a process
1. Create a UDP user datagram.
2. Send the user datagram.
3. Return.

Examples

In this section we show some examples of how our package responds to input and output. The control-block table at the start of our examples is shown in Table 11.2.

Table 11.2 *The control-block table at the beginning of examples*

State	*Process ID*	*Port Number*	*Queue Number*
IN-USE	2,345	52,010	34
IN-USE	3,422	52,011	
FREE			
IN-USE	4,652	52,012	38
FREE			

Example 1

The first activity is the arrival of a user datagram with destination port number 52,012. The input module searches for this port number and finds it. Queue number 38 has been assigned to this port, which means that the port has been previously used. The input module sends the data to queue 38. The control-block table does not change.

Example 2

After a few seconds, a process starts. It asks the operating system for a port number and is granted port number 52,014. Now the process sends its ID (4,978) and the port number to the control-block module to create an entry in the table. The module takes the first FREE entry and inserts the information received. The module does not allocate a queue at this moment because no user datagrams have arrived for this destination (see Table 11.3).

Table 11.3 *Control-block table after example 2*

State	*Process ID*	*Port Number*	*Queue Number*
IN-USE	2,345	52,010	34
IN-USE	3,422	52,011	
IN-USE	**4,978**	**52,014**	
IN-USE	4,652	52,012	38
FREE			

Example 3

A user datagram now arrives for port 52,011. The input module checks the table and finds that no queue has been allocated for this destination since this is the first time a user datagram has arrived for this destination. The module creates a queue and gives it a number (43). See Table 11.4.

Table 11.4 *Control-block after example 3*

State	*Process ID*	*Port Number*	*Queue Number*
IN-USE	2,345	52,010	34
IN-USE	3,422	52,011	**43**
IN-USE	4,978	52,014	
IN-USE	4,652	52,012	38
FREE			

Example 4

After a few seconds, a user datagram arrives for port 52,222. The input module checks the table and cannot find the entry for this destination. The user datagram is dropped and a request is made to ICMP to send an "unreachable port" message to the source.

Example 5

After a few seconds, a process needs to send a user datagram. It delivers the data to the output module which adds the UDP header and sends it.

11.7 KEY TERMS

application program
checksum
client
connectionless service
connectionless, unreliable transport protocol
decapsulation
dynamic port
encapsulation
ephemeral port
error control
flow control
IANA
multiplexing
port number
process
process-to-process communication
pseudoheader
queue
registered port
server
socket address
transport layer
user datagram
User Datagram Protocol (UDP)
well-known port

11.8 SUMMARY

- UDP is a transport protocol that creates a process-to-process communication.
- UDP is a (mostly) unreliable and connectionless protocol that requires little overhead and offers fast delivery.
- In the client-server paradigm, an application program on the local host, called the client, needs services from an application program on the remote host, called a server.
- Each application program has a unique port number that distinguishes it from other programs running at the same time on the same machine.
- The client program is assigned a random port number called the ephemeral port number.
- The server program is assigned a universal port number called a well-known port number.
- The IANA has specified ranges for the different types of port numbers.
- The combination of the IP address and the port number, called the socket address, uniquely defines a process and a host.
- UDP requires a pair of socket addresses: the client socket address and the server socket address.
- The UDP packet is called a user datagram.
- UDP's only attempt at error control is the checksum.
- Inclusion of a pseudoheader in checksum calculations allows source and destination IP address errors to be detected.
- UDP has no flow-control mechanism.
- A user datagram is encapsulated in the data field of an IP datagram.
- Incoming and outgoing queues hold messages going to and from UDP.
- UDP uses multiplexing to handle outgoing user datagrams from multiple processes on one host.
- UDP uses demultiplexing to handle incoming user datagrams that go to different processes on the same host.
- A UDP package can involve five components: a control-block table, a control-block module, input queues, an input module, and an output module.
- The input queues hold incoming user datagrams.
- The control-block module is responsible for maintenance of entries in the control-block table.
- The input module creates input queues.
- The output module sends out user datagrams.

11.9 PRACTICE SET

Multiple-Choice Questions

1. UDP is an acronym for _______.
   a. User Delivery Protocol
   b. User Datagram Procedure
   c. User Datagram Protocol
   d. Unreliable Datagram Protocol
2. In the sending computer, UDP receives a data unit from the _______ layer.
   a. application
   b. transport
   c. IP
   d. data link
3. In the sending computer, UDP sends a data unit to the _______ layer.
   a. application
   b. transport
   c. IP
   d. data link
4. UDP and TCP are both _______ layer protocols.
   a. physical
   b. data link
   c. network
   d. transport
5. Which of the following functions does UDP perform?
   a. process-to-process communication
   b. host-to-host communication
   c. end-to-end reliable data delivery
   d. all of the above
6. When the IP layer of a receiving host receives a datagram, _______.
   a. delivery is complete
   b. a transport layer protocol takes over
   c. a header is added
   d. b and c
7. UDP needs the _______ address to deliver the user datagram to the correct application program.
   a. port
   b. application
   c. internet
   d. physical

8. Which is a legal port address?
   a. 0
   b. 513
   c. 65,535
   d. all of the above
9. The definition of reliable delivery includes _______.
   a. error-free delivery
   b. receipt of the complete message
   c. in-order delivery
   d. all of the above
10. Which of the following does UDP guarantee?
   a. nonduplication of data
   b. in-order delivery
   c. error-free delivery
   d. a and b
11. Which of the following does UDP guarantee?
   a. sequence numbers on each user datagram
   b. acknowledgments to the sender
   c. flow control
   d. none of the above
12. Because there is no _______, UDP is considered a connectionless transport protocol.
   a. acknowledgment
   b. virtual circuit
   c. reliability
   d. data flow control
13. The source port address on the UDP user datagram header defines _______.
   a. the sending computer
   b. the receiving computer
   c. the application program of the sending computer
   d. the application program of the receiving computer
14. Which of the following is not part of the UDP user datagram header?
   a. length of header
   b. source port address
   c. checksum
   d. destination port address

15. The _______ defines the client program.
    a. ephemeral port number
    b. IP address
    c. well-known port number
    d. physical address
16. The _______ defines the server program.
    a. ephemeral port number
    b. IP address
    c. well-known port number
    d. physical address
17. If the outgoing queue of a UDP client overflows, _______.
    a. the user datagrams are discarded and a port unreachable message is sent
    b. the operating system asks the server to wait before any more messages are sent
    c. new queues are initiated
    d. the operating system asks the client process to wait before any more messages are sent
18. If the incoming queue of a UDP client overflows, _______.
    a. the user datagram is discarded and a port unreachable message is sent
    b. the operating system asks the server to wait before any more messages are sent
    c. new queues are initiated
    d. the operating system asks the client to wait before any more messages are sent
19. If the incoming queue of a UDP server overflows, _______.
    a. the user datagram is discarded and a port unreachable message is sent
    b. the operating system asks the server to wait before any more messages are sent
    c. new queues are initiated
    d. the operating system asks the client to wait before any more messages are sent
20. Which component in our UDP package allocates the queues?
    a. control-block module
    b. control-block table
    c. input module
    d. output module
21. Which component in our UDP package communicates with the ICMP software package?
    a. control-block module
    b. control-block table
    c. input module
    d. output module

22. Which component in our UDP package sends user datagrams to the IP layer?
    a. control-block module
    b. control-block table
    c. input module
    d. output module
23. Which column in the control-block table contains information from the UDP header?
    a. state
    b. process ID
    c. port number
    d. queue number

Exercises

24. In cases where reliability is not of primary importance, UDP would make a good transport protocol. Give examples of specific cases.
25. Are both UDP and IP unreliable to the same degree? Why or why not?
26. Do port addresses need to be unique? Why or why not? Why are port addresses shorter than IP addresses?
27. What is the dictionary definition of the word *ephemeral?* How does it apply to the concept of the ephemeral port number?
28. Show the entries for the header of a UDP user datagram that carries a message from a TFTP client to a TFTP server. Fill the checksum field with 0s. Choose an appropriate ephemeral port number and the correct well-known port number. The length of data is 40 bytes. Show the UDP packet using the format in Figure 11.7.
29. Show the entries for the header of a UDP user datagram that carries a message from an FTP server to an FTP client. Fill the checksum field with 0s. Choose an appropriate ephemeral port number and the correct well-known port number. The length of data is 20 bytes. Show the UDP packet using the format in Figure 11.7.
30. Calculate the checksum for the following binary numbers. Give the result in binary. Use the 16-bit format.

    11000111 11100001
    10000111 10001001
    11100101 10100011
    11111111 11100111

31. Calculate the checksum for the following decimal numbers. Give the result in decimal. Use the 16-bit format.

    23 145 78 23 114

32. Calculate the checksum for the following hexadecimal numbers. Give the result in hexadecimal. Use the16-bit format.

    3478 A233 1234 8976

33. An SNMP client residing on a host with IP address 122.45.12.7 sends a message to an SNMP server residing on a host with IP address 200.112.45.90. What is the pair of sockets used in this communication?
34. A TFTP server residing on a host with IP address 130.45.12.7 sends a message to a TFTP client residing on a host with IP address 14.90.90.33. What is the pair of sockets used in this communication?
35. What is the minimum size of a UDP datagram?
36. What is the maximum size of a UDP datagram?
37. What is the minimum size of the process data that can be encapsulated in a UDP datagram?
38. What is the maximum size of the process data that can be encapsulated in a UDP datagram?
39. A client has a packet of 68,000 bytes. Show how this packet can be transferred using only one UDP user datagram.
40. A client uses UDP to send data to a server. The data is 16 bytes. Calculate the efficiency of this transmission at the UDP level (ratio of useful bytes to total bytes).
41. Redo the previous exercise calculating the efficiency of transmission at the IP level. Assume no options for the IP header.
42. Redo the previous exercise calculating the efficiency of transmission at the data link layer. Assume no options for the IP header and use Ethernet at the data link layer.
43. The following is a dump of a UDP header in hexadecimal format.

    06 32 00 0D 00 1C E2 17

    a. What is the source port number?
    b. What is the destination port number?
    c. What is the total length of the user datagram?
    d. What is the length of the data?
    e. Is the packet directed from a client to a server or vice versa?
    f. What is the client process?

Programming Exercises

44. Create a header file to include all constants that you think are needed to implement the UDP modules in C. Use the **#define** directives.
45. Complete the following struct declaration for the UDP header.

```
struct  UDP_Header
{
unsigned short     SPortAddr  ;
...........................................................
...........................................................
} ;
```

46. Complete the following struct declaration for the UDP user datagram.

```
struct UDP_Packet
{
        struct  UDP_Header  udpHeader ;
        ..........................................  udpData ;
} ;
```

47. Write the declaration for the control-block entry.
48. Write the declaration for the control-block table.
49. Write a function that accepts a pointer to a UDP packet and a pointer to the corresponding IP header. The function should calculate and return the value of the checksum for UDP using the pseudoheader.
50. Write a function in C to simulate the control-block module.
51. Write a function in C to simulate the input module.
52. Write a function in C to simulate the output module.

CHAPTER 12

Transmission Control Protocol (TCP)

The TCP/IP protocol suite specifies two protocols for the transport layer: UDP and TCP. We studied UDP in Chapter 11; we will study TCP in this chapter.

Figure 12.1 shows the relationship of TCP to the other protocols in the TCP/IP protocol suite. TCP lies between the application layer and the network layer and serves as the intermediary between the application programs and the network operations.

Figure 12.1 *TCP/IP protocol suite*

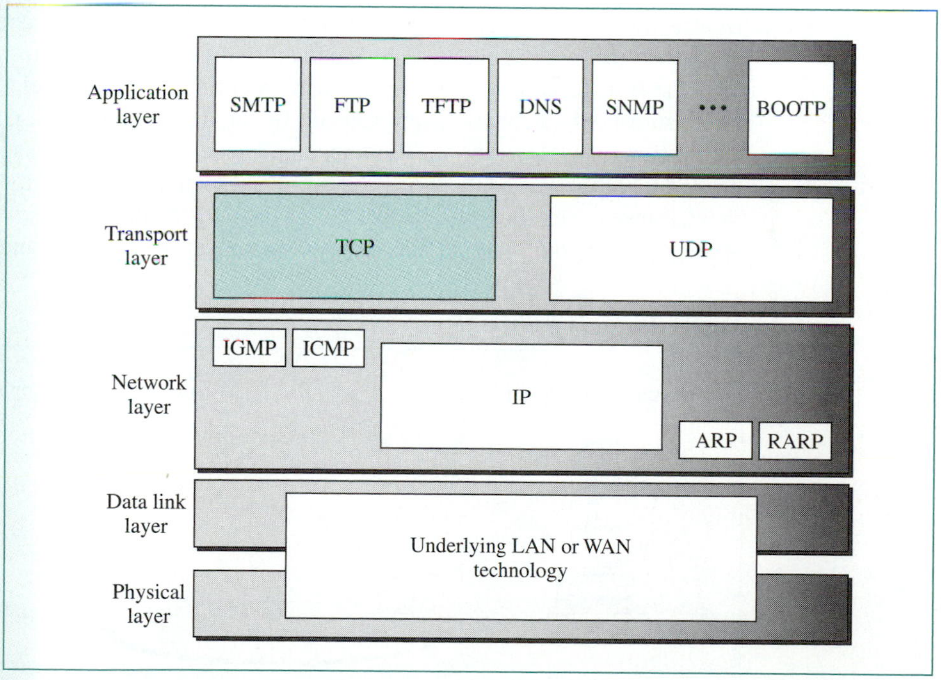

A transport layer protocol usually has several responsibilities. One is to create a process-to-process (program-to-program) communication; TCP uses port numbers to accomplish this. Another responsibility of a transport layer protocol is to create a flow- and error-control mechanism at the transport level. TCP uses a sliding window protocol to achieve flow control. It uses the acknowledgment packet, time-out, and retransmission to achieve error control.

The transport layer is also responsible for providing a connection mechanism for the application program. The application program sends streams of data to the transport layer. It is the responsibility of the transport layer at the sending station to make a connection with the receiver, chop the stream into transportable units, number them, and send them one by one. It is the responsibility of the transport layer at the receiving end to wait until all the different units belonging to the same application program have arrived, check and pass those that are error free, and deliver them to the receiving application program as a stream. After the entire stream has been sent, the transport layer closes the connection. TCP performs all these tasks.

TCP is called a *connection-oriented, reliable* transport protocol. It adds connection-oriented and reliability features to the services of IP.

12.1 PROCESS-TO-PROCESS COMMUNICATION

Before we examine TCP, we must first understand host-to-host communication and process-to-process communication and the difference between them.

The IP is responsible for communication at the computer level (host-to-host communication). As a network layer protocol, IP can deliver the message only to the destination computer. However, this is an incomplete delivery. The message still needs to be handed to the correct application program. This is where a transport layer protocol such as TCP takes over. TCP is responsible for delivery of the message to the appropriate application program. Figure 12.2 shows the scope of duties for IP and TCP.

Figure 12.2 *TCP versus IP*

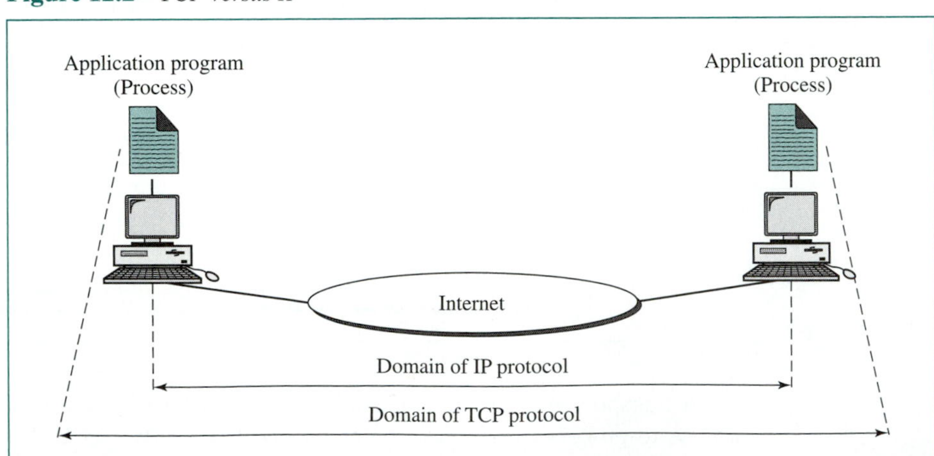

Port Addresses

As we said in the previous chapter, process-to-process communication is achieved through the client/server paradigm.

A remote computer may be running several server programs at the same time. A local computer may also be running one or more client programs at the same time. For communication, we must define the

- Local host
- Local client program
- Remote host
- Remote server program

The local host and the remote host are defined using IP addresses. To define the client and server programs, we need second identifiers called *port numbers*. In the TCP/IP protocol suite, the port numbers are integers between 0 and 65,535.

As mentioned in the UDP chapter, a client program running on the local computer defines itself with a port number, chosen randomly by the TCP software running on the local host. This is called the *ephemeral port number.*

The server program, running on the remote computer, must also define itself with a port number. As also mentioned in the UDP chapter, the server uses *well-known port numbers*. For example, in Figure 12.3 the TELNET client program uses an ephemeral (temporary) port number of 64,295 to identify itself, whereas the TELNET server program always uses the well-known (permanent) port number 23.

Figure 12.3 *Port numbers*

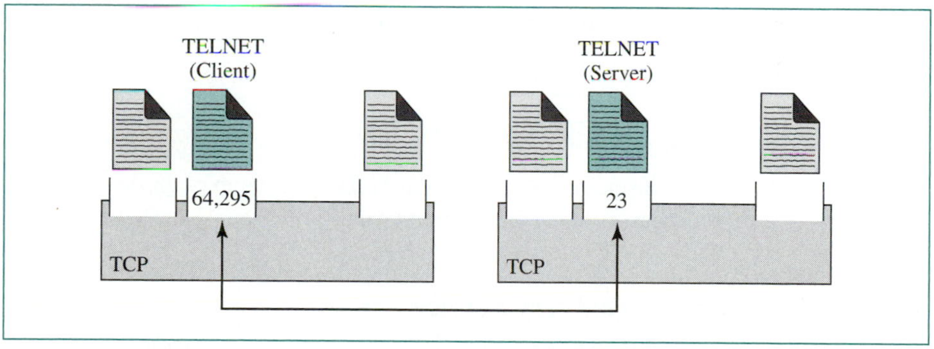

Table 12.1 lists some well-known port numbers used by TCP.

Table 12.1 *Well-known ports used by TCP*

Port	*Protocol*	*Description*
7	Echo	Echoes a received datagram back to the sender
9	Discard	Discards any datagram that is received
11	Users	Active users
13	Daytime	Returns the date and the time
17	Quote	Returns a quote of the day

Table 12.1 *Well-known ports used by TCP (continued)*

Port	*Protocol*	*Description*
19	Chargen	Returns a string of characters
20	FTP, Data	File Transfer Protocol (data connection)
21	FTP, Control	File Transfer Protocol (control connection)
23	TELNET	Terminal Network
25	SMTP	Simple Mail Transfer Protocol
53	DNS	Domain Name Server
67	BOOTP	Bootstrap Protocol
79	Finger	Finger
80	HTTP	Hypertext Transfer Protocol
111	RPC	Remote Procedure Call

Socket Addresses

Similar to UDP, TCP also needs two identifiers, the IP address and port number, for each end to make a connection. The combination of an IP address and a port number is called a **socket address.** To use the services of TCP (or UDP), we need **a pair of socket addresses:** client socket address and server socket address. The *client* socket address defines the client application program uniquely. The *server* socket address defines the server application program uniquely. These four pieces of information are part of the IP header and the TCP header. The IP header contains the IP addresses; the TCP header contains the port numbers.

12.2 TCP SERVICES

Before discussing the operation of TCP, let us explain the services offered by TCP to the processes at the application layer.

Stream Delivery Service

TCP, unlike UDP, is a stream-oriented protocol. In UDP, a process (an application program) sends a chunk of bytes to the UDP for delivery. UDP adds its own header to this chunk of data, which is now called a datagram, and delivers it to the IP for transmission. The process may deliver several chunks of data to the UDP, but UDP treats each chunk independently without seeing any connection between them.

TCP, on the other hand, allows the sending process to deliver data as a stream of bytes and the receiving process to obtain data as a stream of bytes. TCP creates an environment in which the two processes seem to be connected by an imaginary "tube" that carries their data across the Internet. This imaginary environment is depicted in

Figure 12.4. The sending process produces the stream of bytes and the receiving process consumes it.

Figure 12.4 *Stream delivery*

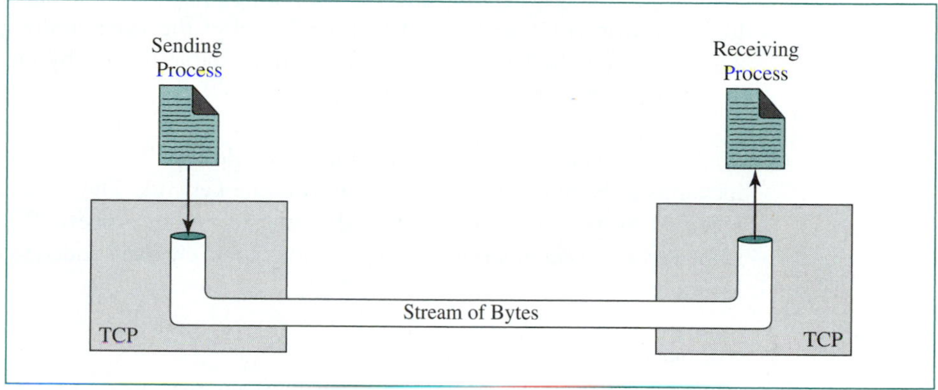

Sending and Receiving Buffers

Because the sending and the receiving processes may not produce and consume data at the same speed, TCP needs buffers for storage. There are two buffers, the sending buffer and the receiving buffer, for each direction. (We will see later that these buffers are also used in flow- and error-control mechanisms used by TCP.) One way to implement a buffer is to use a circular array of 1-byte locations as shown in Figure 12.5. For simplicity, we have shown two buffers of 20 bytes each; normally the buffers are hundreds or thousands of bytes, depending on the implementation. We also show the buffers as the same size, which is not always the case.

Figure 12.5 *Sending and receiving buffers*

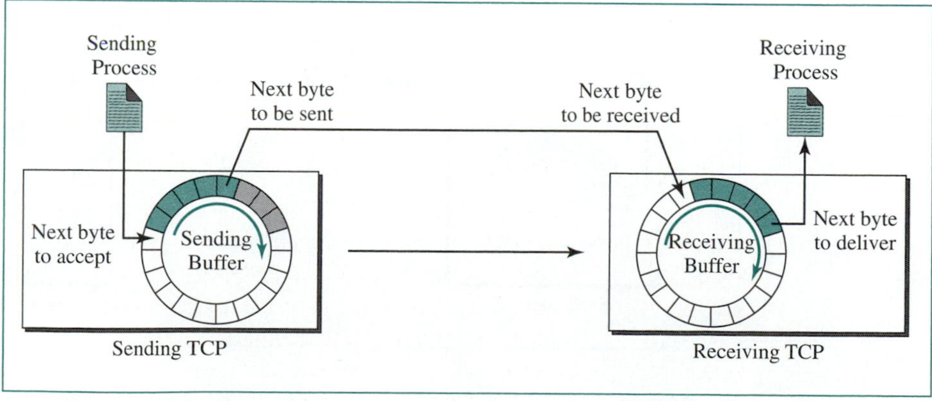

The figure shows the movement of the data in one direction. At the sending site, the buffer has three types of locations. The white section contains empty locations that can be filled by the sending process (producer). The gray area holds bytes that have been sent but not yet acknowledged. TCP keeps these bytes in the buffer until it receives an acknowledgment. The colored area are bytes to be sent by the sending TCP. However, as we will see later in this chapter, TCP may be able to send only part of this colored section. This could be due to the slowness of the receiving process or perhaps to congestion in the network. Also note that after the bytes in the gray locations are acknowledged, the location is recycled and available for use by the sending process. This is why we show a circular buffer.

The operation of the buffer at the receiver site is simpler. The circular buffer is divided into two areas (shown as white and colored). The white area contains empty locations to be filled by bytes received from the network. The colored sections contain received bytes that can be consumed by the receiving process. When a byte is consumed by the receiving process, the location is recycled and added to the pool of empty locations.

Segments

Although buffering handles the disparity between the speed of the producing and consuming processes, we need one more step before we can send data. The IP layer, as a service provider for TCP, needs to send data in packets, not as a stream of bytes. At the transport layer, TCP groups a number of bytes together into a packet called a *segment*. TCP adds a header to each segment (for control purposes) and delivers the segment to the IP layer for transmission. The segments are encapsulated in an IP datagram and transmitted. This entire operation is transparent to the receiving process. Later we will see that segments may be received out of order, lost, or corrupted and resent. All of these are handled by TCP with the receiving process unaware of any activities. Figure 12.6 shows how segments are created from the bytes in the buffers.

Figure 12.6 *TCP segments*

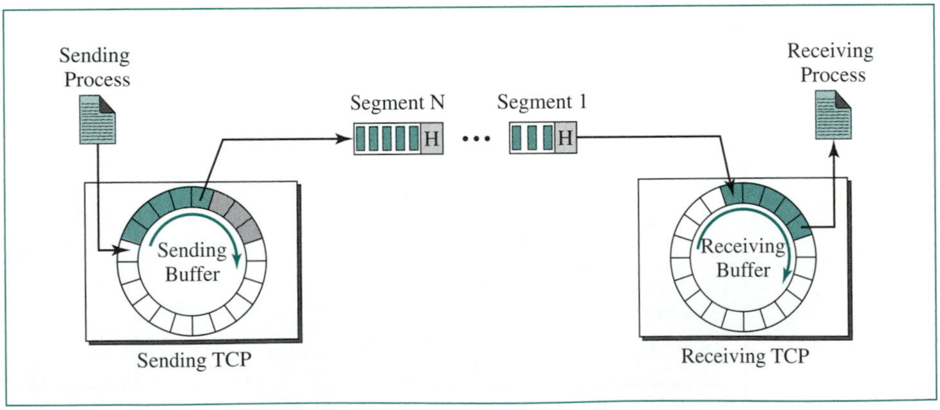

Note that the segments are not necessarily the same size. In the figure, for simplicity, we show one segment carrying 3 bytes and the other carrying 5 bytes. In reality segments carry hundreds if not thousands of bytes.

Full-Duplex Service

TCP offers **full-duplex service,** where data can flow in both directions at the same time. Each TCP then has a sending and receiving buffer and segments are sent in both direction.

Connection-Oriented Service

TCP, unlike UDP is a connection-oriented protocol. When a process at site A wants to send and receive data from another process at site B, the following occurs:

1. A's TCP informs B's TCP and gets approval from B's TCP.
2. A's TCP and B's TCP exchange data in both directions.
3. After both processes have no data left to send and the buffers are empty, the two TCPs destroy their buffers.

Note that this is a virtual connection, not a physical connection. The TCP segment is encapsulated in an IP datagram and can be sent out of order, or lost, or corrupted, and then resent. Each may use a different path to reach the destination. There is no physical connection. However, because TCP creates a stream-oriented environment in which it accepts the responsibility of delivering the bytes in order to the other site, the situation is similar to creating a bridge that spans multiple islands and passing all of the bytes from one island to another in one single connection.

Reliable Service

TCP is a reliable transport protocol. It uses an acknowledgment mechanism to check the safe and sound arrival of data. We will discuss this feature further in the section on error control.

12.3 NUMBERING BYTES

Although the TCP software keeps track of the segment being transmitted or received, there is no field for a segment number value. Instead, there are two fields called the *sequence number* and the *acknowledgment number.* These two fields refer to the byte number not the segment number.

Byte Numbers

TCP numbers all data bytes that are transmitted in a connection. Numbering is independent in each direction. When TCP receives bytes of data from the process and stores them in the sending buffer, it numbers them. The numbering does not necessarily start from 0; it starts randomly. TCP generates a random number between 0 and $2^{32} - 1$ for the number of the first byte. For example, if the random number happens to be 1,057 and the total data to be sent is 6,000 bytes, the bytes are numbered from 1,057 to 7,056. We will see that byte numbering is used for flow and error control.

> The bytes of data being transferred in each connection are numbered by TCP. The numbering starts with a randomly generated number.

Sequence Number

After the bytes have been numbered, TCP assigns a sequence number to each segment that is being sent. The sequence number for each segment is the number of the first byte carried in that segment.

Example 1

Imagine a TCP connection is transferring a file of 6000 bytes. The first byte is numbered 10010. What are the sequence numbers for each segment if data is sent in five segments with the first four segments carrying 1,000 bytes and the last segment carrying 2,000 bytes.

Solution

The following shows the sequence number for each segment:

Segment 1 ➡ Sequence Number: 10,010 (range: 10,010 to 11,009)
Segment 2 ➡ Sequence Number: 11,010 (range: 11,010 to 12,009)
Segment 3 ➡ Sequence Number: 12,010 (range: 12,010 to 13,009)
Segment 4 ➡ Sequence Number: 13,010 (range: 13,010 to 14,009)
Segment 5 ➡ Sequence Number: 14,010 (range: 14,010 to 16,009)

> The value of the sequence number field in a segment defines the number of the first data byte contained in that segment.

Acknowledgment Number

As we discussed before, communication in TCP is full duplex; when a connection is established, both parties can send and receive data at the same time. Each party numbers the bytes, usually with a different starting byte number. The sequence number in each direction shows the number of the first byte carried by the segment. Each party also uses an acknowledgment number to confirm the bytes it has received. However, the acknowledgment number defines the number of the next byte that the party expects to receive. In addition, the acknowledgment number is cumulative, which means that the party takes the number of the last byte that it has received, safe and sound, adds 1 to it, and announces this sum as the acknowledgment number. The term *cumulative* here means that if a party uses 5,643 as an acknowledgment number, it has received all bytes from the beginning up to 5,642. Note that this does not mean that the party has received 5,642 bytes because the first byte number does not have to start from 0.

> The value of the acknowledgment field in a segment defines the number of the next byte a party expects to receives. The acknowledgment number is cumulative.

12.4 FLOW CONTROL

Flow control defines the amount of data a source can send before receiving an acknowledgment from the destination. In an extreme case, a transport layer protocol could send 1 byte of data and wait for an acknowledgment before sending the next byte. But this is an extremely slow process. If the data is traveling a long distance, the source is idle while it waits for an acknowledgment.

At the other extreme, a transport layer protocol can send all of the data it has without worrying about acknowledgment. This speeds up the process, but it may overwhelm the receiver. Besides, if some part of the data is lost, duplicated, received out of order, or corrupted, the source will not know until all has been checked by the destination.

TCP has a solution that stands somewhere in between. It defines a window that is imposed on the buffer of data delivered from the application program and is ready to be sent. TCP sends as much data as is defined by the sliding window protocol.

Sliding Window Protocol

To accomplish flow control, TCP uses a sliding window protocol. With this method, both hosts use a window for each connection. The window spans a portion of the buffer containing bytes that a host can send before worrying about an acknowledgment from the other host. The window is called a **sliding window** because it can slide over the buffer as data and acknowledgments are sent and received.

> A sliding window is used to make transmission more efficient as well as to control the flow of data so that the destination does not become overwhelmed with data. TCP's sliding windows are byte oriented.

Figure 12.7 shows the sender buffer defined previously. However, instead of showing a circular buffer, we have shown a flat buffer for simplicity. Note that if we connect the two ends of the buffer, we get the circular buffer shown in Figure 12.5.

Figure 12.7 *Sender buffer*

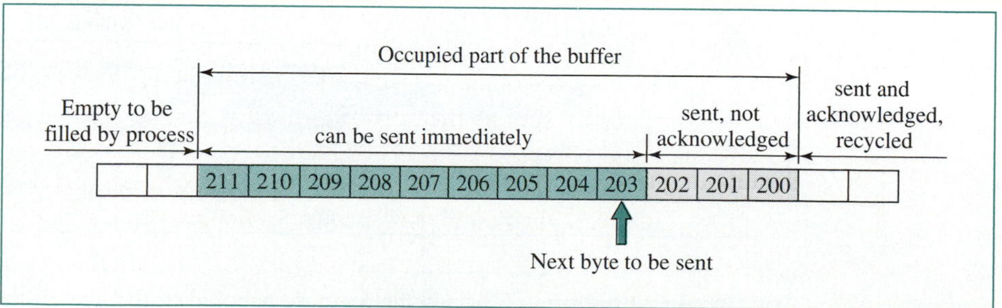

In Figure 12.7 the bytes before 200 have been sent and acknowledged. The sender can reuse these locations. Bytes 200 to 202 have been sent, but not acknowledged. The sender has to keep these bytes in the buffer in case they are lost or damaged. Bytes 203 to 211 are in the buffer (produced by the process) but have not yet been sent.

Let's examine the situation in which there is no sliding window protocol. In this case, the sender can go ahead and send all the bytes (up to 211) in its buffer, without regard to the condition of the receiver. The receiver's buffer, with its limited-size, could completely fill up because the receiving process is not consuming data fast enough. The excess bytes discarded by the receiver will require retransmission. The sender must adjust itself to the number of locations available at the receiver site.

Receiver Window

Figure 12.8 shows the receiver buffer. Note that the next byte to be consumed by the process is byte 194. The receiver expects to receive byte 200 from the sender (which has been sent but not received). How many more bytes can the receiver store? If the total size of the receiving buffer is N and M locations are already occupied, then only $N - M$ more bytes can be received. This value is called the **receiver window.** For example, if $N = 13$ and $M = 6$, this means that the value of the receiver window is 7.

Figure 12.8 *Receiver window*

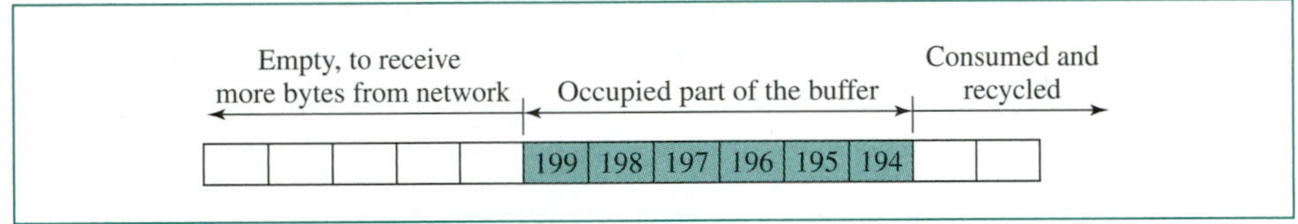

Sender Window

We have flow control if the sender creates a window (the **sender window**) with a size less than or equal to the size of the receiver window. This window includes the bytes sent and not acknowledged and those that can be sent. Figure 12.9 shows the sender buffer with the sender window.

Figure 12.9 *Sender buffer and sender window*

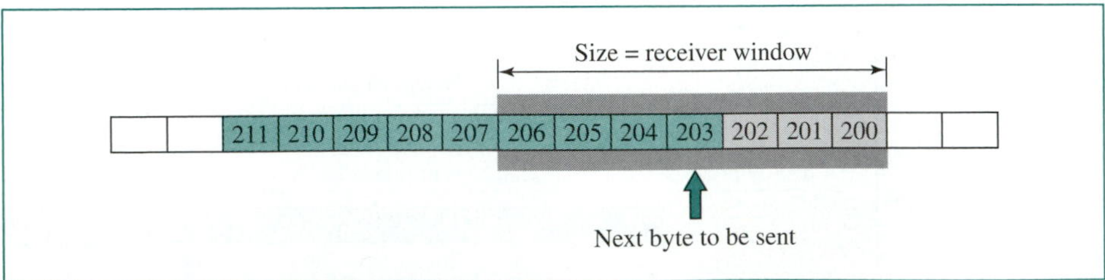

Note that the size of the sender window is equal to the size of the receiver window (7 in our example). However, this does not mean that the sender can send 7 more bytes; it can send only 4 more bytes because it has already sent 3 bytes. Note also that although bytes 207 to 211 are in the sending buffer, they also cannot be sent until more news arrives from the receiver.

Sliding the Sender Window

Let's see how messages from the receiver change the position of the sender window. In our example, suppose the sender sends 2 more bytes and an acknowledgement is received from the receiver (expecting byte 204) with no change in the size of the receiver window (still 7). The sender can now slide its window and the locations occupied by bytes 200–202 can be recycled. Figure 12.10 shows the position of the sender buffer and the sender window before and after this event. In the second part of the figure the sender can now send bytes 205 to 209 (5 more bytes).

Figure 12.10 *Sliding the sender window*

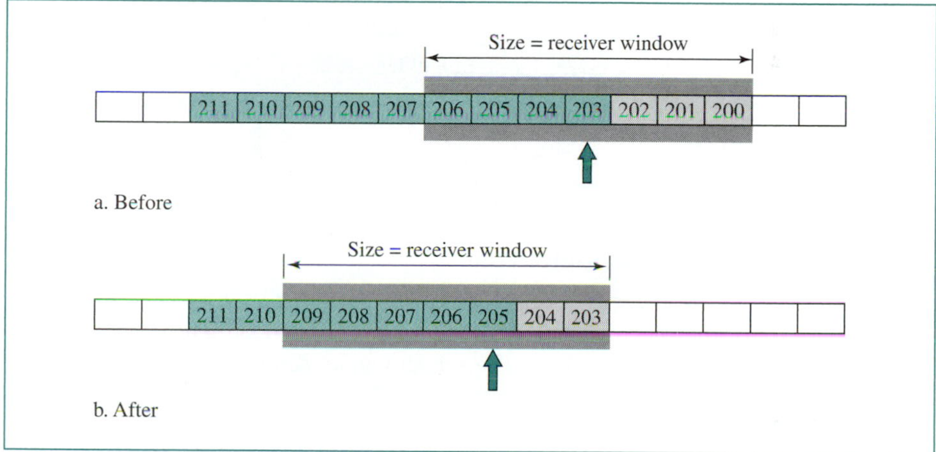

Expanding the Sender Window

If the receiving process consumes data faster than it receives, the size of the receiver window expands (the buffer has more free locations). This situation can be relayed to the sender, resulting in the increase (expansion) of the window size. In Figure 12.11, the receiver has acknowledged the receipt of 2 more bytes (expecting byte 205) and at the same time has increased the value of the receiver window to 10. In the meantime, the sending process has created 4 more bytes and the sending TCP has sent 5 bytes.

Figure 12.11 *Expanding the sender window*

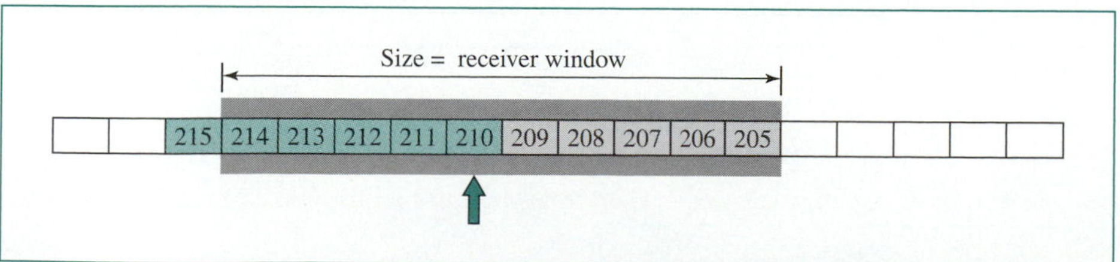

Shrinking the Sender Window

If the receiving process consumes data slower than it receives, the size of the receiver window decreases (shrinks). In this case the receiver has to inform the sender to shrink its sender window size. In Figure 12.12, the receiver has received the 5 bytes (205 to 209); however, the receiving process has consumed only 1 byte, which means the number of free locations is reduced to 6 (10 – 5 + 1). It acknowledges bytes 205 to 209 (expecting 210), but also informs the sender to shrink its window size and not to send more than 6 more bytes. If the sender has already sent 2 more bytes when it receives the news and has received 3 more bytes from the sending process, we get the window and buffer as shown in Figure 12.12.

Figure 12.12 *Shrinking the sender window*

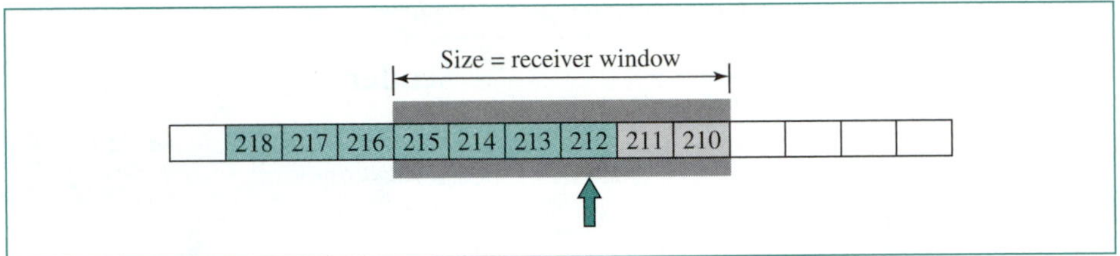

Closing the Sender Window

What happens if the receiver buffer is totally full? In this case, the receiver window value is zero. When this is relayed to the sender, the sender closes its window (left and right walls overlap). The sender cannot send any bytes until the receiver announces a nonzero receiver window value. We discuss this issue again when we talk about TCP timers.

> In TCP, the sender window size is totally controlled by the receiver window value (the number of empty locations in the receiver buffer). However, the actual window size can be smaller if there is congestion in the network.

> Some Points about TCP's Sliding Windows:
>
> - The source does not have to send a full window's worth of data.
> - The size of the window can be increased or decreased by the destination.
> - The destination can send an acknowledgment at any time.

12.5 SILLY WINDOW SYNDROME

A serious problem can arise in the sliding window operation when either the sending application program creates data slowly or the receiving application program consumes data slowly, or both. Either of these situations results in the sending of data in very small segments, which reduces the efficiency of the operation. For example, if TCP sends segments containing only 1 byte of data, it means that we are sending a 41-byte datagram (20 bytes of TCP header and 20 bytes of IP header) that transfers only 1 byte of user data. Here the overhead is 41/1, which indicates that we are using the capacity of the network very inefficiently. This problem is called the *silly window syndrome*. For each site, we first describe how the problem is created and then give the proposed solution.

Syndrome Created by the Sender

The sending TCP may create a silly window syndrome if it is serving an application program that creates data slowly, for example, 1 byte at a time. The application program writes 1 byte at a time into the buffer of the sending TCP. If the sending TCP does not have any specific instructions, it may create segments containing 1 byte of data. The result is a lot of 41-byte segments that are traveling through an internet.

The solution is to prevent the sending TCP from sending the data byte by byte. The sending TCP must be forced to wait as it collects data to send in a larger block. How long should the sending TCP wait? If it waits too long, it may delay the process. If it does not wait long enough, it may end up sending small segments. Nagle found an elegant solution.

Nagle's Algorithm

Nagle's algorithm is very simple, but it solves the problem. This algorithm is for the sending TCP:

1. The sending TCP sends the first piece of data it receives from the sending application program even if it is only 1 byte.
2. After sending the first segment, the sending TCP accumulates data in the output buffer and waits until either the receiving TCP sends an acknowledgment or until enough data has accumulated to fill a maximum-size segment. At this time, the sending TCP can send the segment.
3. Step 2 is repeated for the rest of the transmission. Segment 3 must be sent if an acknowledgment is received for segment 2 or enough data is accumulated to fill a maximum-size segment.

The elegance of Nagle's algorithm is in its simplicity and in the fact that it takes into account the speed of the application program that creates the data and the speed of the network that transports the data. If the application program is faster than the network, the segments are larger (maximum-size segments). If the application program is slower than the network, the segments are smaller (less than the maximum segment size).

Syndrome Created by the Receiver

The receiving TCP may create a silly window syndrome if it is serving an application program that consumes data slowly, for example, 1 byte at a time. Suppose that the sending application program creates data in blocks of 1K, but the receiving application program consumes data 1 byte at a time. Also suppose that the input buffer of the receiving TCP is 4K. The sender sends the first 4 kbytes of data. The receiver stores it in its buffer. Now its buffer is full. It advertises a window size of zero, which means the sender should stop sending data. The receiving application reads the first byte of data from the input buffer of the receiving TCP. Now there is 1 byte of space in the incoming buffer. The receiving TCP announces a window size of 1 byte, which means that the sending TCP, which is eagerly waiting to send data, takes this advertisement as good news and sends a segment carrying only 1 byte of data. The procedure will continue. One byte of data is consumed and a segment carrying 1 byte of data is sent. Again we have an efficiency problem and a silly window syndrome.

Two solutions have been proposed to prevent the silly window syndrome created by an application program that consumes data slower than they arrive.

Clark's Solution

Clark's solution is to send an acknowledgment as soon as the data arrives, but to announce a window size of zero until either there is enough space to accommodate a segment of maximum size or until half of the buffer is empty.

Delayed Acknowledgment

The second solution is to delay sending the acknowledgment. This means that when a segment arrives, it is not acknowledged immediately. The receiver waits until there is a decent amount of space in its incoming buffer before acknowledging the arrived segments. The delayed acknowledgment prevents the sending TCP from sliding its window. After it has sent the data in the window, it stops. This kills the syndrome.

Delayed acknowledgment also has another advantage: It reduces traffic. The receiver does not have to acknowledge each segment. However, there also is a disadvantage in that the delayed acknowledgment may force the sender to retransmit the unacknowledged segments.

The protocol balances the advantages and disadvantages. It now defines that the acknowledgment should not be delayed by more than 500 ms.

12.6 ERROR CONTROL

TCP is a reliable transport layer protocol. This means that an application program that delivers a stream of data to TCP relies on TCP to deliver the entire stream to the application program on the other end in order, without error, and without any part lost or duplicated.

TCP provides reliability using error control. Error control includes mechanisms for detecting corrupted segments, lost segments, out-of-order segments, and duplicated segments. Error control also includes a mechanism for correcting errors after they are detected.

Error Detection and Correction

Error detection in TCP is achieved through the use of three simple tools: checksum, acknowledgment, and time-out. Each segment includes the checksum field, which is used to check for a corrupted segment. If the segment is corrupted, it is discarded by the destination TCP. TCP uses the acknowledgment method to confirm the receipt of those segments that have reached the destination TCP uncorrupted. No negative acknowledgment is used in TCP. If a segment is not acknowledged before the time-out, it is considered to be either corrupted or lost.

The error-correction mechanism used by TCP is also very simple. The source TCP starts one time-out counter for each segment sent. Each counter is checked periodically. When a counter matures, the corresponding segment is considered to be either corrupted or lost, and the segment will be retransmitted.

Corrupted Segment

Figure 12.13 shows a corrupted segment arriving at the destination. In this example the source sends segments 1 through 3, each 200 bytes. The sequence number begins at

Figure 12.13 *Corrupted segment*

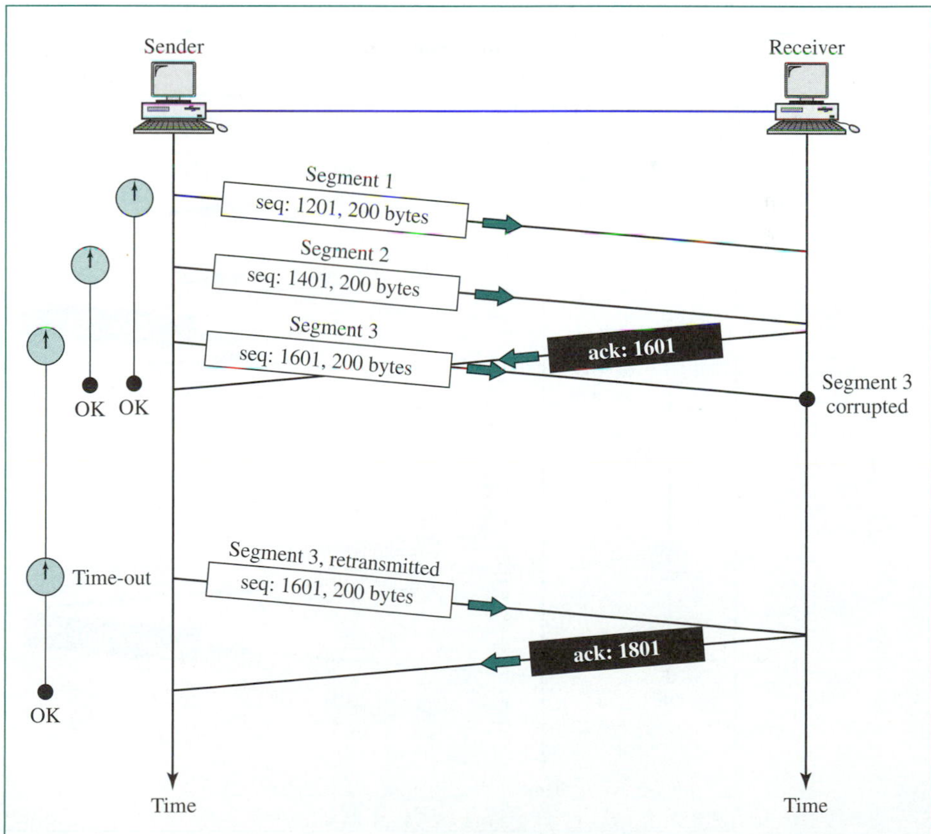

1,201 on segment 1. The receiving TCP receives segments 1 and 2 and, using the checksum, finds them error free. It acknowledges the receipt of segments 1 and 2 using acknowledgment number 1,601, which means that it has received bytes 1,201 to 1,600 safe and sound, and is expecting to receive byte 1,601. However, it finds that segment 3 is corrupted and discards segment 3. Note that although it has received bytes 1,601 to 1,800 in segment 3, the destination does not consider this as a "receipt" because this segment was corrupted. After the timer for segment 3 has matured, the source TCP will resend segment 3. After receiving segment 3, the destination sends an acknowledgment for byte 1,801, which indicates that it has received bytes 1,201 to 1,800 safe and sound.

Lost Segment

Figure 12.14 shows a lost segment. The situation is exactly the same as the corrupted segment. In other words, from the point of the source and destination, a lost segment and a corrupted segment are the same. A corrupted segment is discarded by the final destination; a lost segment is discarded by some intermediate node and never reaches the destination.

Figure 12.14 *Lost segment*

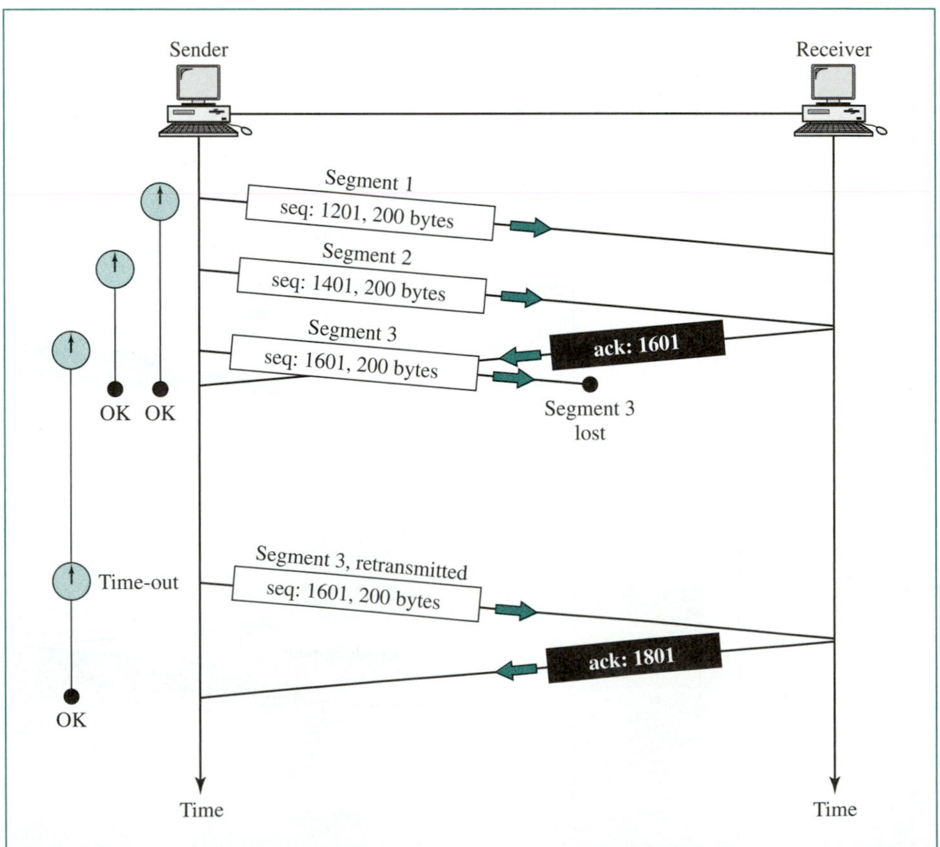

Duplicate Segment

A duplicate segment can be created, for example, by a source TCP when the acknowledgment does not arrive before the time-out. Handling the duplicated segment is a simple process for the destination TCP. The destination TCP expects a continuous stream of bytes. When a packet arrives that contains the same sequence number as another received segment, the destination TCP simply discards the packet.

Out-of-Order Segment

TCP uses the services of IP, an unreliable, connectionless network layer protocol. The TCP segment is encapsulated in an IP datagram. Each datagram is an independent entity. The routers are free to send each datagram through any route they find suitable. One datagram may follow a route with a short delay; another may follow another route with a longer delay. If datagrams arrive out of order, the TCP segments that are encapsulated in the datagrams will be out of order as well. The handling of out-of-order segments by the destination TCP is very simple: It does not acknowledge an out-of-order segment until it receives all of the segments that precede it. Of course, if the acknowledgment is delayed, the timer of the out-of-order segment may mature at the source TCP and the segment may be resent. The duplicates then will be discarded by the destination TCP.

Lost Acknowledgment

Figure 12.15 shows a lost acknowledgment sent by the destination. In the TCP acknowledgment mechanism, a lost acknowledgment may not even be noticed by the source TCP. TCP uses an accumulative acknowledgment system. Each acknowledgment is a

Figure 12.15 *Lost acknowledgment*

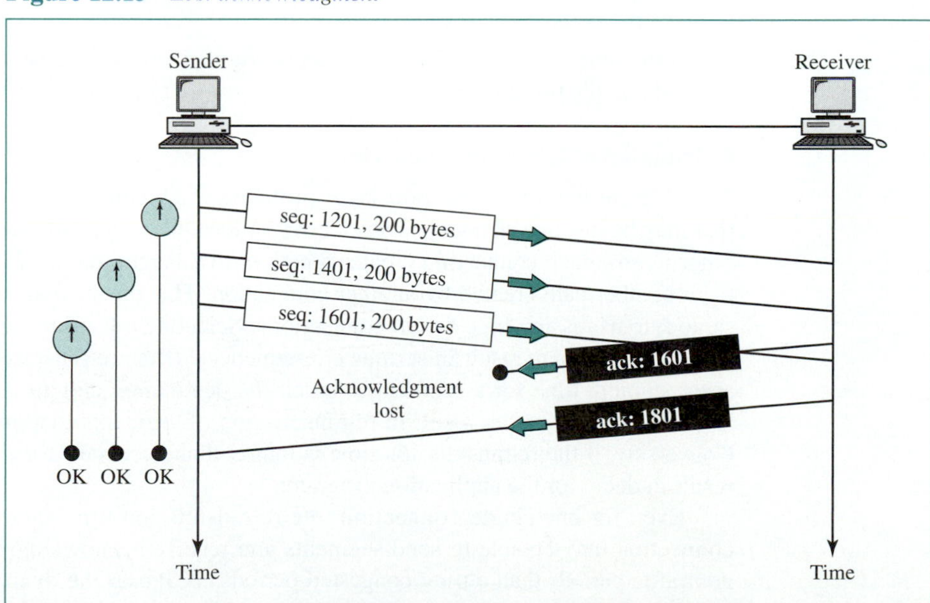

confirmation that everything up to the byte specified by the acknowledgment number has been received. For example, if the destination sends an ACK segment with an acknowledgment number for byte 1,801, it is confirming that bytes 1,201 to 1,800 have been received. If the destination had previously sent an acknowledgment for byte 1,601, meaning it has received bytes 1,201 to 1,600, loss of the acknowledgment is irrelevant.

12.7 TCP TIMERS

To perform its operation smoothly, TCP uses the four timers shown in Figure 12.16.

Figure 12.16 *TCP timers*

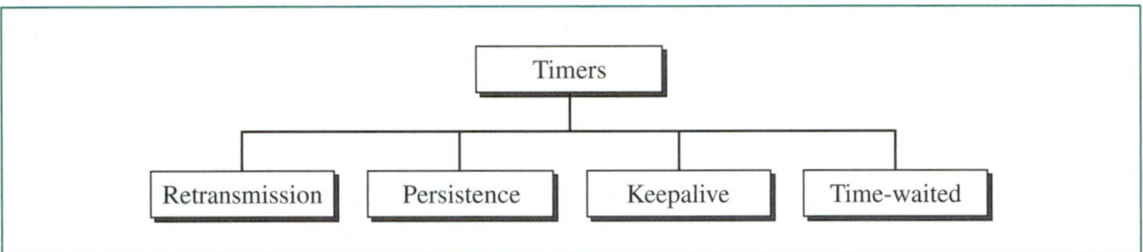

Retransmission Timer

To control a lost or discarded segment, TCP employs a retransmission timer that handles the retransmission time, the waiting time for an acknowledgment of a segment. When TCP sends a segment, it creates a retransmission timer for that particular segment. Two situations may occur:

1. If an acknowledgment is received for this particular segment before the timer goes off, the timer is destroyed.
2. If the timer goes off before the acknowledgment arrives, the segment is retransmitted and the timer is reset.

Calculation of Retransmission Time

The TCP protocol is a transport layer protocol. Each connection connects two TCPs that may be just one physical network apart or located on opposite sides of the globe. In other words, each connection creates a path with a length that may be totally different from another path created by another connection. This means that TCP cannot use the same retransmission time for all connections. Selecting a fixed retransmission time for all connections can result in serious consequences. If the retransmission time does not allow enough time for a segment to reach the destination and an acknowledgment to reach the source, it can result in retransmission of segments that are still on the way. Conversely, if the retransmission time is longer than necessary for a short path, it may result in delay for the application programs.

Even for one single connection, the retransmission time should not be fixed. A connection may be able to send segments and receive acknowledgments faster during nontraffic periods than during congested periods. TCP uses the dynamic retransmission time, a transmission time that is different for each connection and which may be changed during the same connection.

Retransmission time can be made dynamic by basing it on the round-trip time (RTT). Several formulas are used for this purpose. The most common is to consider the retransmission time to be twice the RTT:

$$\text{Retransmission time} = 2 \times \text{RTT}$$

Calculation of RTT

The question now is how do we calculate the RTT itself? RTT, too, is calculated dynamically. There are two methods. In the first method, TCP uses the timestamp option as described previously. In the second method, TCP sends a segment, starts a timer, and waits for an acknowledgment. It measures the time between the sending of the segment and the receiving of the acknowledgment. Each segment has a round-trip time. The value of the RTT used in the calculation of the retransmission time of the next segment is the updated value of the RTT according to the following formula:

$$\text{RTT} = \alpha \times \text{previous RTT} + (1 - \alpha)\ \text{current RTT}$$

The value of α is usually 90 percent. This means that the new RTT is 90 percent of the value of the previous RTT plus 10 percent of the value of the current RTT. For example, if the previous RTT is 250 microseconds and it takes a segment at this moment to be acknowledged in 70 μs, the value of the new RTT and the retransmission time would be

$$\text{RTT} = 90\% \times 250 + 10\% \times 70 = 232\ \mu\text{s}$$

$$\text{Retransmission time} = 2 \times 232 = 464\ \mu\text{s}$$

Karn's Algorithm

Suppose that a segment is not acknowledged during the retransmission period and it is therefore retransmitted. When the sending TCP receives an acknowledgment for this segment, it does not know if the acknowledgment is for the original segment or for the retransmitted one. The value of the new RTT therefore must be calculated based on the departure of the segment. However, if the original segment was lost and the acknowledgment is for the retransmitted one, the value of the current RTT must be calculated from the time the segment was retransmitted. This is a dilemma that was solved by Karn. Karn's solution is very simple. Do not consider the RTT of a retransmitted segment in the calculation of the new RTT. Do not update the value of RTT until you send a segment and receive an acknowledgment without the need for retransmission.

Persistence Timer

To deal with the zero window-size advertisement, TCP needs another timer. Suppose the receiving TCP announces a window size of zero. The sending TCP then stops transmitting segments until the receiving TCP sends an acknowledgment announcing a nonzero window size. This acknowledgment can be lost. Remember that acknowledgments are not acknowledged in TCP. If this acknowledgment is lost, the receiving TCP thinks that it has done its job and waits for the sending TCP to send more segments. The sending TCP has not received an acknowledgment and waits for the other TCP to send an acknowledgment advertising the size of the window. Both TCPs can continue to wait for each other forever.

To correct this deadlock, TCP uses a persistence timer for each connection. When the sending TCP receives an acknowledgment with a window size of zero, it starts a persistence timer. When the persistence timer goes off, the sending TCP sends a special segment called a *probe*. This segment contains only 1 byte of data. It has a sequence number, but its sequence number is never acknowledged; it is even ignored in calculating the sequence number for the rest of the data. The probe alerts the receiving TCP that the acknowledgment was lost and should be resent.

The value of the persistence timer is set to the value of the retransmission time. However, if a response is not received from the receiver, another probe segment is sent and the value of the persistence timer is doubled and reset. The sender continues sending the probe segments and doubling and resetting the value of the persistence timer until the value reaches a threshold (usually 60 s). After that the sender sends one probe segment every 60 s until the window is reopened.

Keepalive Timer

A keepalive timer is used in some implementations to prevent a long idle connection between two TCPs. Suppose that a client opens a TCP connection to a server, transfers some data, and becomes silent. Perhaps the client has crashed. In this case, the connection remains open forever.

To remedy this situation, most implementations equip a server with a keepalive timer. Each time the server hears from a client, it resets this timer. The time-out is usually two hours. If the server does not hear from the client after two hours, it sends a probe segment. If there is no response after 10 probes, each of which is 75 s apart, it assumes that the client is down and terminates the connection.

Time-Waited Timer

The time-waited timer is used during connection termination. When TCP closes a connection, it does not consider the connection really closed. The connection is held in limbo for a time-waited period (see Sections 12.12 and 12.13 and Figure 12.30). This allows duplicate FIN segments, if any, to arrive at the destination to be discarded. The value for this timer is usually two times the expected lifetime of a segment.

12.8 CONGESTION CONTROL

As we have said, an internet is a combination of networks and connecting devices (e.g., routers). A packet started at a sender may pass through several routers before reaching its final destination. A router has a buffer that stores the incoming packets, processes them, and forwards them. If a router receives packets faster than it can process them, congestion might occur, and some packets could be dropped. When a packet does not reach the destination, no acknowledgment is sent for it. The sender has no choice but to retransmit the lost packet. This may create more congestion and more dropping of packets, which means more retransmission and more congestion. A point then may be reached in which the whole system collapses and no more data can be sent. TCP therefore needs to find some way to avoid this situation.

> TCP assumes that the cause of a lost segment is due to congestion in the network.

Previously, we talked about flow control and tried to discuss solutions when the receiver is overwhelmed with data. We said that the sender window size is determined by the available buffer space in the receiver. In other words, we assumed that it is only the receiver that can dictate to the sender the size of the sender's window. We totally ignored another entity here, the network. If the network cannot deliver the data as fast as it is created by the sender, it should tell the sender to slow down. In other words, in addition to the receiver, the network should be a second entity that determines the size of the sender's window.

> If the cause of the lost segment is congestion, retransmission of the segment not only does not remove the cause, it aggravates it.

Congestion Window

Today, the sender's window size is not only determined by the receiver but also by congestion in the network.

The sender has two pieces of information: the receiver-advertised window size and the congestion window size. The actual size of the window is the minimum of these two.

> Actual window size = minimum (receiver window size, congestion window size)

Congestion Avoidance

To avoid congestion, the sender TCP uses two strategies. We call one **slow start and additive increase** and the second **multiplicative decrease.**

Slow Start and Additive Increase

This is a combination of two strategies: slow start and additive increase.

Slow Start At the beginning of a connection, TCP sets the congestion window size to the maximum segment size. For each segment that is acknowledged, TCP increases the size of the congestion window by one maximum segment size until it reaches a threshold of half the allowable window size. This is called *slow start,* which is totally misleading because the process is not slow at all. The size of the congestion window increases exponentially. The sender sends one segment, receives one acknowledgment, increases the size to two segments, sends two segments, receives acknowledgments for two segments, increases the size to four segments, sends four segments, receives acknowledgment for four segments, increases the size to eight segments, and so on. In other words, after receiving the third acknowledgment, the size of the window has been increased to eight segments. The rate is exponential ($2^3 = 8$).

Additive Increase To avoid congestion before it happens, one must slow down this exponential growth. After the size reaches the threshold, the size is increased one segment for each acknowledgment even if an acknowledgment is for several segments. The additive increase strategy continues as long as the acknowledgments arrive before their corresponding time-outs or the congestion window size reaches the receiver window value.

Multiplicative Decrease

If congestion occurs, the congestion window size must be decreased. The only way the sender can guess that congestion has occurred is through a lost segment. If the sender does not receive an acknowledgment for a segment before its retransmission timer has matured, it assumes that there is congestion. Because networks today are to some extent noise free, it is more probable that a segment is lost than that it is corrupted. The strategy says if a time-out occurs, the threshold must be set to half of the last congestion window size, and the congestion window size should start from one again. In other words, the sender returns to the slow start phase. Note that the size of threshold is reduced to half each time a time-out occurs. This means that the size of the threshold is reduced exponentially (multiplicative decrease). Figure 12.17 shows the idea.

Figure 12.17 *Multiplicative decrease*

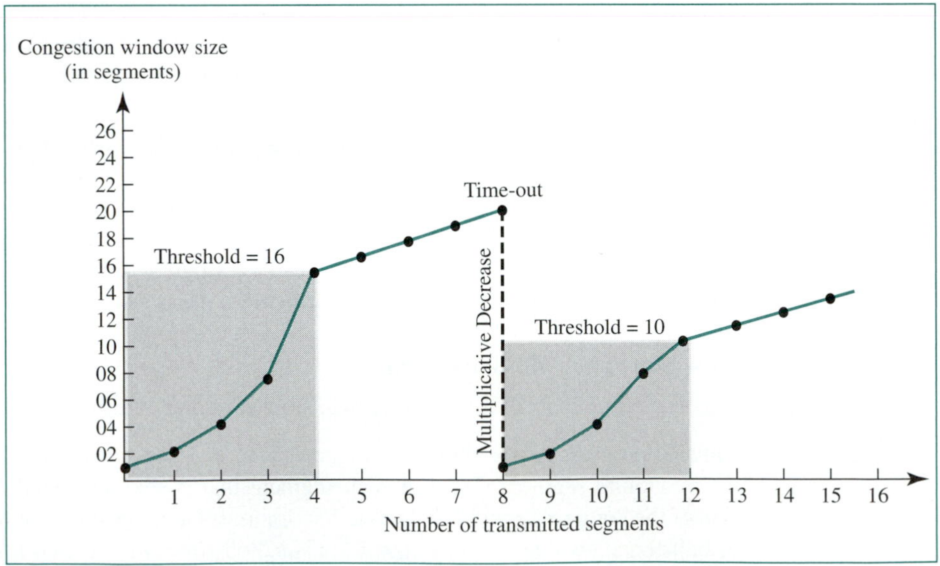

In Figure 12.17, we assume that the maximum window size is 32 segments. The threshold is set to 16 segments (half of the maximum window size). In the *slow start* procedure the window size starts from 1 and grows exponentially until it reaches the threshold with the condition that there is no timeout. After reaching the threshold, the *additive increase* procedure allows the window size to increase linearly until a timeout occurs or the maximum window size is reached. In the figure, the timeout occurs when segment 8 is sent. At this moment, the *multiplicative decrease* procedure takes over and reduces the threshold to half of the previous window size. The previous window size was 20 when the timeout happened so the new threshold is now 10.

The cycle (slow start, additive increase, multiplicative decrease) continues with the window size set at 1 again. Figure 12.18 shows the same idea. We use segments instead of characters in the window to decrease the figure size.

Figure 12.18 *Congestion avoidance strategies*

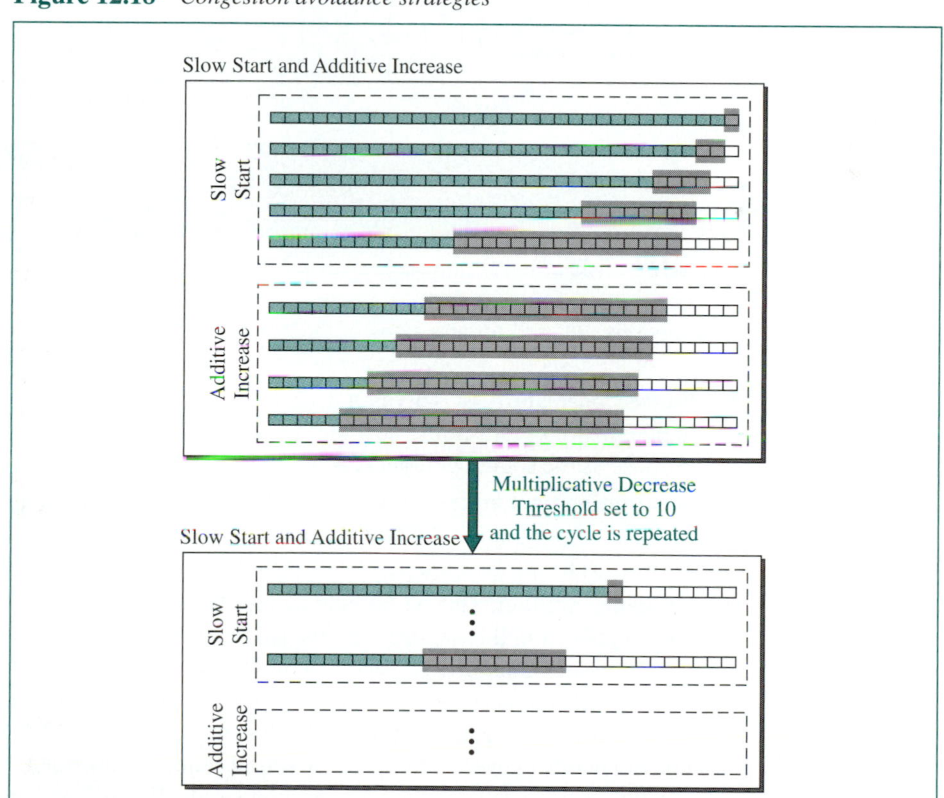

12.9 SEGMENT

The unit of data transfer between two devices using TCP is a **segment.** The format of a segment is shown in Figure 12.19.

The segment consists of a 20- to 60-byte header, followed by data from the application program. The header is 20 bytes if there are no options and up to 60 bytes if it contains

Figure 12.19 *TCP segment format*

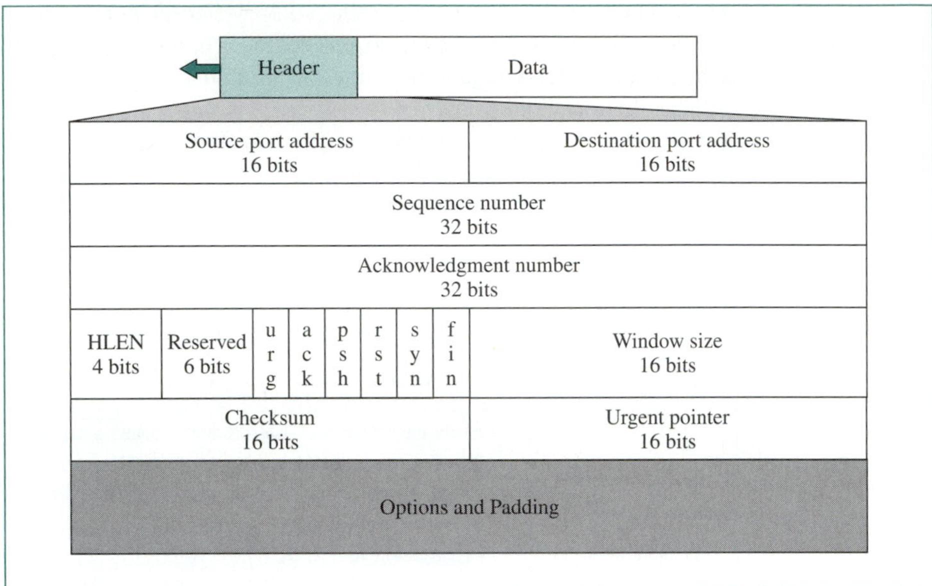

some options. We will discuss some of the header fields in this section. The meaning and purpose of these should become clearer as we proceed through the chapter.

- **Source port address.** This is a 16-bit field that defines the port number of the application program in the host that is sending the segment. This serves the same purpose as the source port address in the UDP header discussed in Chapter 11.
- **Destination port address.** This is a 16-bit field that defines the port number of the application program in the host that is receiving the segment. This serves the same purpose as the destination port address in the UDP header discussed in Chapter 11.
- **Sequence number.** This 32-bit field defines the number assigned to the first byte of data contained in this segment. As we said before, TCP is a stream transport protocol. To ensure connectivity, each byte to be transmitted is numbered. The sequence number tells the destination which byte in this sequence comprises the first byte in the segment. During connection establishment (see Section 12.12) each party uses a random number generator to create an **initial sequence number** (ISN), which is usually different in each direction. For example, if the ISN is 2,367 and the first segment is carrying 1,000 bytes, the sequence number is 2,369 (2,367 and 2,368 are used for connection establishment); the second segment, carrying 500 bytes, will have the sequence number 3,369; and so on. The destination can determine the number of the last byte by knowing the size of the data block. We discussed sequence numbers in the section on flow control and sliding window protocol.
- **Acknowledgment number.** This 32-bit field defines the byte number that the receiver of the segment is expecting to receive from the other party. If the receiver of the segment has successfully received byte number x from the other party, it defines $x + 1$ as the acknowledgment number. As mentioned previously, acknowledgment and data can be piggybacked together.

- **Header length.** This 4-bit field indicates the number of 4-byte words in the TCP header. The length of the header can be between 20 and 60 bytes. Therefore, the value of this field can be between 5 ($5 \times 4 = 20$) and 15 ($15 \times 4 = 60$).
- **Reserved.** This is a 6-bit field reserved for future use.
- **Control.** This field defines 6 different control bits or flags as shown in Figure 12.20. One or more of these bits can be set at a time.

Figure 12.20 *Control field*

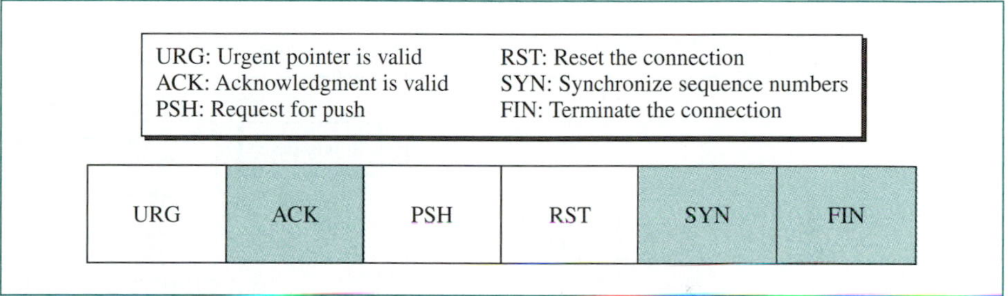

These bits enable flow control, connection establishment and termination, and the mode of data transfer in TCP. A brief description of each bit is shown in Table 12.2. We will discuss them further when we study the detailed operation of TCP later in the chapter.

Table 12.2 *Description of flags in the control field*

Flag	*Description*
URG	The value of the urgent pointer field is valid
ACK	The value of the acknowledgment field is valid
PSH	Push the data
RST	The connection must be reset
SYN	Synchronize sequence numbers during connection
FIN	Terminate the connection

- **Window size.** This field defines the size of the window, in bytes, that the other party must maintain. Note that the length of this field is 16 bits, which means that the maximum size of the window is 65,535 bytes.
- **Checksum.** This 16-bit field contains the checksum. See Section 12.11 on Checksum.
- **Urgent pointer.** This 16-bit field, which is valid only if the urgent flag is set, is used when the segment contains urgent data. It defines the number that must be added to the sequence number to obtain the number of the last urgent byte in the data section of the segment. This will be discussed later in this chapter.
- **Options.** There can be up to 40 bytes of optional information in the TCP header. We will discuss the different options currently used in the TCP header in the next section.

12.10 OPTIONS

The TCP header can have up to 40 bytes of optional information. Options convey additional information to the destination or to align other options. We can define two categories of options: 1-byte options and multiple-byte options. The first category contains two types of options: end of option and no operation. The second category contains three types of options: maximum segment size, window scale factor, and timestamp (see Figure 12.21).

Figure 12.21 *Options*

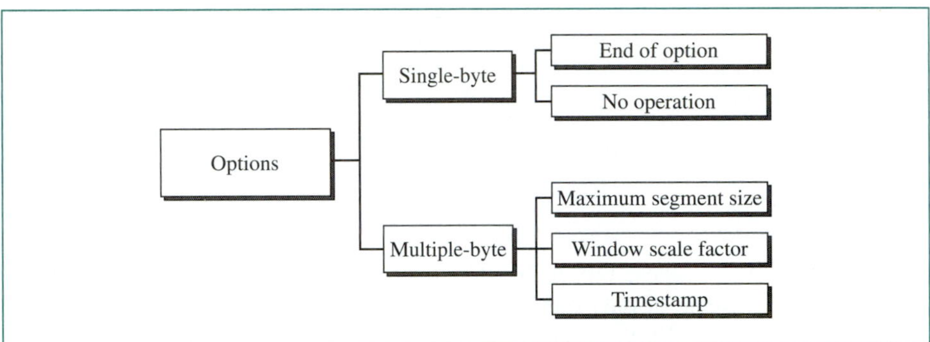

- **End of option.** This is a 1-byte option used for padding at the end of the option field. It, however, can only be used as the last option. Only one end of option can be used. After this option, the receiver looks for the payload data. This means that if more than 1 byte is needed to align the option field, some no-operation options must be used followed by an end of option (see Figure 12.22). End of option imparts three pieces of information to the destination:
  1. No more options in the header.
  2. The remainder of the 32-bit word is garbage.
  3. Data from the application program starts at the beginning of the next 32-bit word.

Figure 12.22 *End of option*

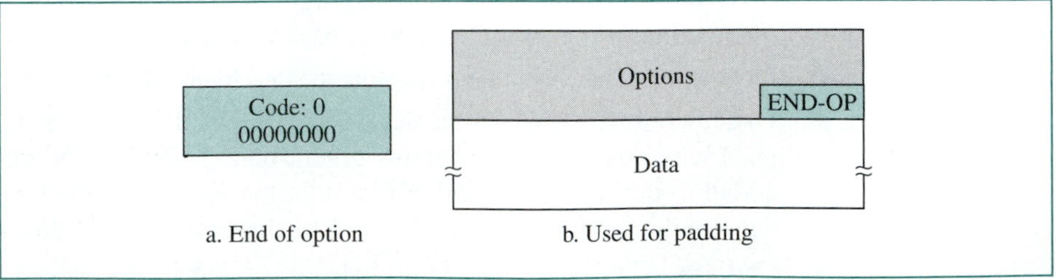

- **No operation.** This is a 1-byte option used as a filler between options. For example, it can be used to align the next option on a 32-bit boundary (see Figure 12.23).

Figure 12.23 *No operation option*

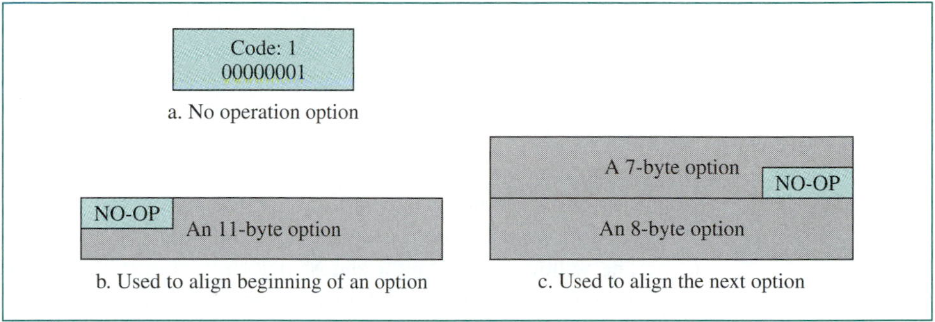

- **Maximum segment size (MSS).** This option defines the size of the biggest chunk of data that can be received by the destination of the TCP segment. In spite of its name, it defines the maximum size of the data, not the maximum size of the segment. Since the field is 16 bits long, the value can be 0 to 65,535 bytes. The default is 536.

  The maximum data size is determined during the connection establishment phase. The size is determined by the destination of the segment, not the source. So party 1 defines the MSS sent by party 2. Party 2 defines what should be the MSS sent by party 1. If neither party defines the size, the default is chosen.

  This option is used only in the segments that make the connections. It cannot be used in segments during data transfer. Figure 12.24 shows the format of this option.

Figure 12.24 *Maximum segment size option*

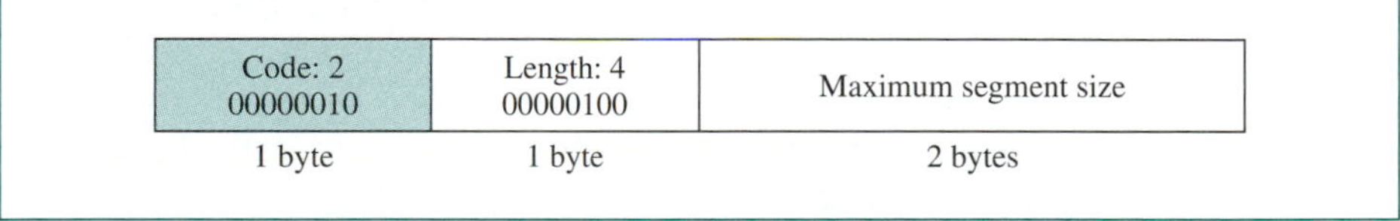

- **Window scale factor.** The window size field in the header defines the size of the sliding window. This field is 16 bits long, which means that the window can range from 0 to 65,535 bytes. Although this seems like a very large window size, it still may not be sufficient, especially if the data is traveling on a high-throughput low-delay transmission media. Consider, for example, a fiber-optic channel (OC-24), having a throughput of 1,244.160 Mbps, connecting two computers 6,000 miles apart. When one station sends data to another, it takes at least 64 ms to receive an acknowledgment. During this period, 10 Mbytes can be sent. However, the size of the window allows the station to send only 65,535 bytes.

To increase the window size, the window scale factor is used. The new window size is found by first raising 2 to the number specified in the window scale factor. Then this result is multiplied by the value of the window size in the header.

$$\text{new window size} = \text{window size defined in the header} \times 2^{\text{window scale factor}}$$

For example, if the value of the window scale factor is 3, then the actual window size is eight times the value of the window size. Although the scale factor could be as large as 255, the largest value allowed by TCP/IP is 16, which means that the maximum window size can be $2^{16} \times 2^{16} = 2^{32}$, which is the same as the maximum value for the sequence number. Note that the size of the window cannot be greater than the maximum value for the sequence number.

The window scale factor can be determined only during the connection setup phase. During data transfer, the size of the window (specified in the header) may be changed, but it must be multiplied by the same scale factor. The format of the window scale factor option is shown in Figure 12.25.

Figure 12.25 *Window scale factor option*

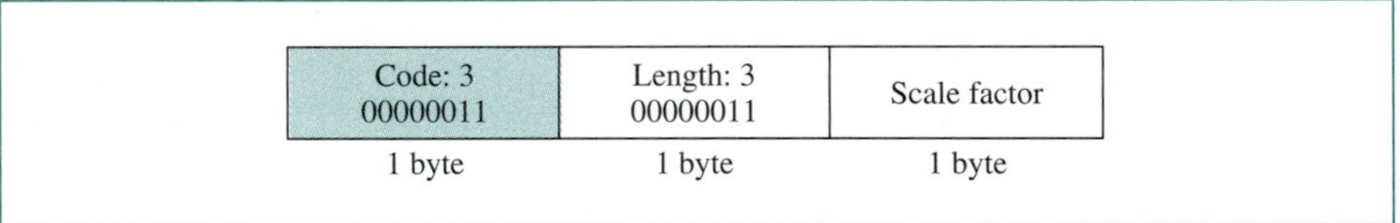

The scale factor is sometimes called the *shift count* because multiplying a number by a power of 2 is the same as a left shift in a bitwise operation.

- **Timestamp.** This is a 10-byte option with the format shown in Figure 12.26. The timestamp field is filled by the source when the segment leaves. The destination receives the segment and stores the timestamp value. When the destination sends an acknowledgment for the bytes in that segment, it enters the previously stored value in the echo reply field. The source, when it receives the acknowledgment, checks the current time versus this value. The difference is the round-trip time. The round-trip time can be used by TCP to dynamically define the retransmission time, as we have already discussed.

Figure 12.26 *Timestamp option*

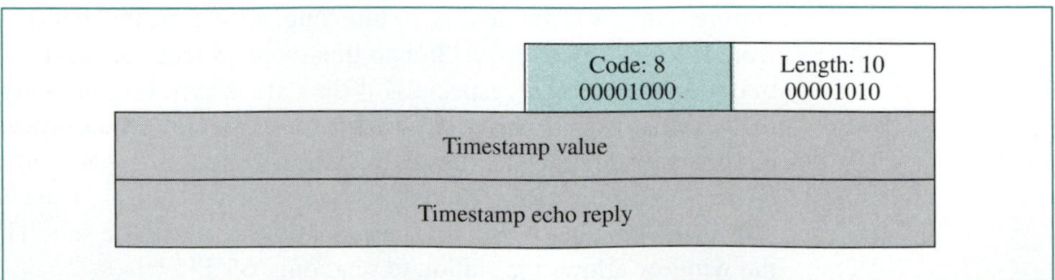

12.11 CHECKSUM

The calculation of the checksum for TCP follows the same procedure as the one described for UDP in Chapter 11. However, the inclusion of the checksum in the UDP datagram is optional, whereas the inclusion of the checksum for TCP is mandatory.

The same pseudoheader, serving the same purpose, is added to the segment. For the TCP pseudoheader, the value for the protocol field is six. See Figure 12.27.

Figure 12.27 *Pseudoheader added to the TCP datagram*

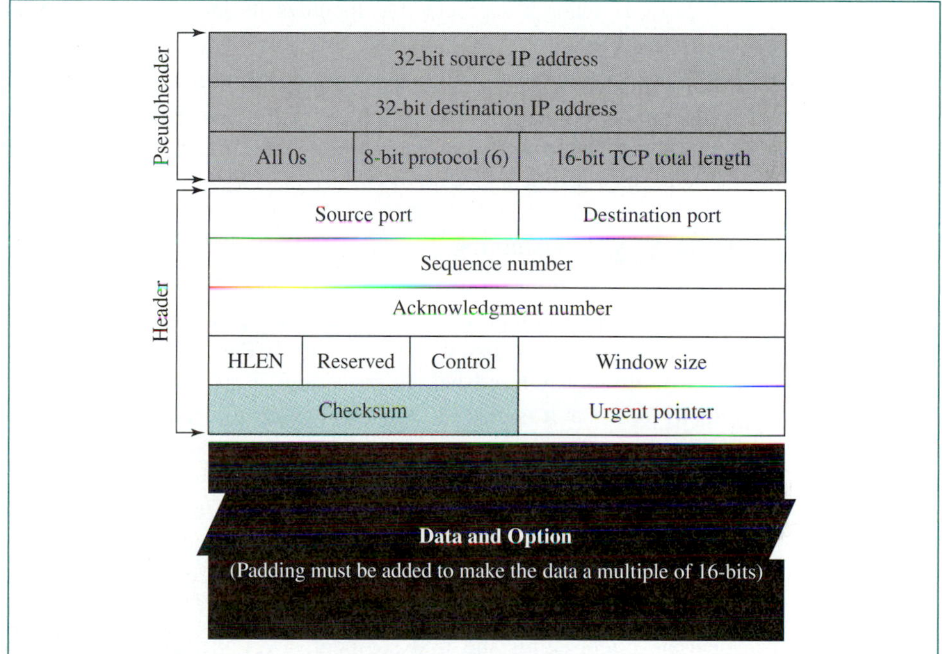

12.12 CONNECTION

TCP is a connection-oriented protocol. A connection-oriented protocol establishes a virtual path between the source and destination. All of the segments belonging to a message are then sent over this virtual path. Using a single virtual pathway for the entire message facilitates the acknowledgment process as well as retransmission of damaged or lost frames.

In TCP, connection-oriented transmission requires two procedures: connection establishment and connection termination.

Connection Establishment

TCP transmits data in full-duplex mode. When two TCPs in two machines are connected they are able to send segments to each other simultaneously. This implies that each party must initialize communication and get approval from the other party before any data transfer. Four actions are taken before the two parties, called here host A and host B, can send data:

1. Host A sends a segment to announce its wish for connection and includes its initialization information about traffic from A to B.
2. Host B sends a segment to acknowledge (confirm) the request of A.
3. Host B sends a segment that includes its initialization information about traffic from B to A.
4. Host A sends a segment to acknowledge (confirm) the request of B.

This connection establishment implies four steps. However, since steps 2 and 3 can occur at the same time, they can be combined into one step. That is, host B can confirm the request of host A and send its own request at the same time.

Three-Way Handshaking

The connection establishment described above is called *three-way handshaking*. In this procedure, an application program, called the client, wants to make a connection with another application program, called the server, using TCP as the transport layer protocol.

The three-way handshaking procedure starts with the server. The server program tells its TCP that it is ready to accept a connection. This is called a request for a *passive open*. Although the server TCP is ready to accept any connection from any machine in the world it cannot make the connection itself.

The client program makes a request for an *active open*. A client that wishes to connect to a server tells its TCP that it needs to be connected to a particular server. The TCP can now start the three-way handshaking process as shown in Figure 12.28.

The steps of the process are as follows:

1. The client sends the first segment, a SYN segment. The segment includes the source and destination port numbers. The destination port number clearly defines the server to which the client wants to be connected. The segment also contains the client initialization sequence number (ISN) used for numbering the bytes of data sent from the client to the server. If the client wants to define the MSS that it can receive from the server, it can add the corresponding option here. Also, if the client needs a large window, it defines the window scale factor here using the appropriate option. This segment defines the wish of the client to make a connection with certain parameters. Note that this segment does not contain any acknowledgment number. It does not define the window size either; a window size definition makes sense only when a segment includes an acknowledgment.
2. The server sends the second segment, a SYN and ACK segment. This segment has a dual purpose. First, it acknowledges the receipt of the first segment using the ACK flag and acknowledgment number field. The acknowledgment number is the client initialization sequence number plus one. The server must also define the client window size. Second, the segment is used as the initialization segment for the

Figure 12.28 *Three-way handshaking*

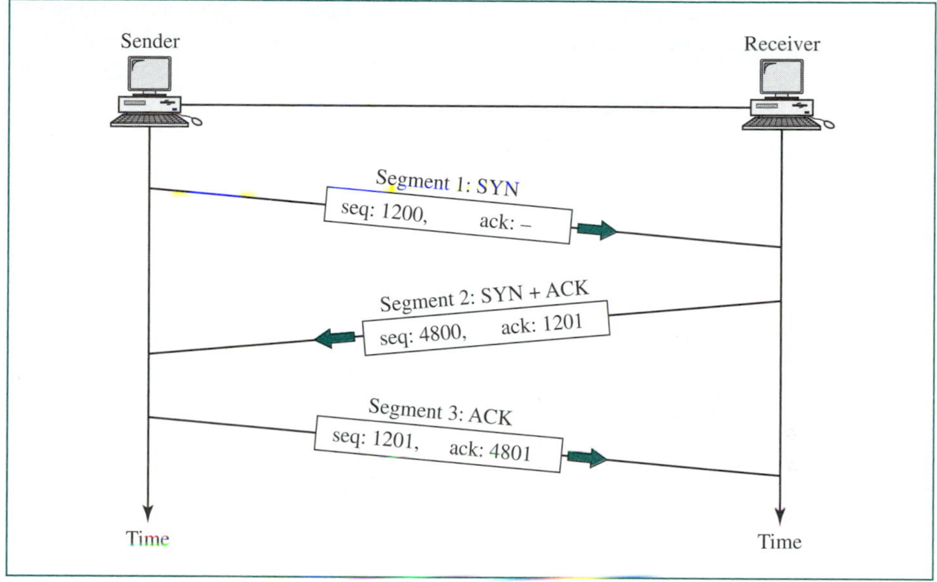

server. It contains the initialization sequence number used to number the bytes sent from the server to the client. It also contains the window scale factor option (if needed) to be used by the server and the MSS defined by the server. As we said before, this is two segments combined into one.

3. The client sends the third segment. This is just an ACK segment. It acknowledges the receipt of the second segment using the ACK flag and acknowledgment number field. The acknowledgment number is the server initialization sequence number plus one. The client must also define the server window size. Note that data can be sent with the third packet.

A rare situation may occur when both processes issue an active open. In this case, both TCPs transmit a SYN + ACK segment to each other and one single connection is established between them.

Connection Termination

Any of the two parties involved in exchanging data (client or server) can close the connection. When connection in one direction is terminated, the other party can continue sending data in the other direction. Therefore, four actions are needed to close the connections in both directions:

1. Host A sends a segment announcing its wish for connection termination.
2. Host B sends a segment acknowledging (confirming) the request of A. After this, the connection is closed in one direction, but not in the other. Host B can continue sending data to A.
3. When host B has finished sending its own data, it sends a segment to indicate that it wants to close the connection.
4. Host A acknowledges (confirms) the request of B.

This implies four steps. We cannot combine steps 2 and 3 here as we did in connection establishment. Steps 2 and 3 may or may not happen at the same time. The connection may be closed in one direction, but left open in the other direction.

Four-Way Handshaking

The connection termination described above is called *four-way handshaking*. In this procedure, an application program, usually the client, wants to terminate a connection.

The procedure starts with the client. The client program tells its TCP that it has finished sending data and wishes to terminate the connection. This is a request for an active close.

After receiving the request for an active close, the client TCP closes communication in the client-server direction. However, communication in the other direction is still open.

When the server program has finished sending data in the server-client direction, it can request from its TCP to close the connection in the server-client direction. This is usually a passive close. Four-way handshaking is shown in Figure 12.29.

Figure 12.29 *Four-way handshaking*

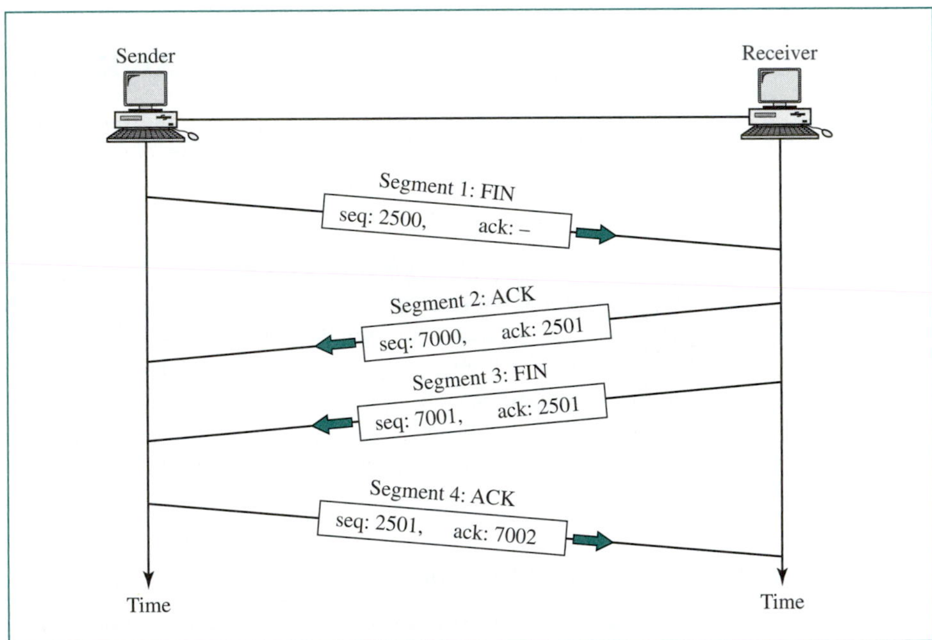

The four steps are

1. The client TCP sends the first segment, a FIN segment.
2. The server TCP sends the second segment, an ACK segment, to confirm the receipt of the FIN segment from the client. In this segment it uses the acknowledgment number, which is one plus the sequence number received in the FIN segment.
3. The server TCP can continue sending data in the server-client direction. When it does not have any more data to send, it sends the third segment. This segment is a FIN segment.

4. The client TCP sends the fourth segment, an ACK segment, to confirm the receipt of the FIN segment from the TCP server. This segment contains the acknowledgment number, which is one plus the sequence number received in the FIN segment from the server.

Connection Resetting

TCP may request the resetting of a connection. *Resetting* here means that the current connection is destroyed. This happens in one of three cases:

1. The TCP on one side has requested a connection to a nonexistent port. The TCP on the other side may send a segment with its RST bit set to annul the request.
2. One TCP may want to abort the connection due to an abnormal situation. It can send an RST segment to close the connection.
3. The TCP on one side may discover that the TCP on the other side is idle for a long time. It may send an RST segment to destroy the connection.

12.13 STATE TRANSITION DIAGRAM

To keep track of all the different events happening during connection establishment, connection termination, and data transfer, the TCP software is implemented as a finite state machine. A **finite state machine** is a machine that goes through a limited number of states. At any moment, the machine is in one of the states. It remains in that state until an event happens. The event can take the machine to a new state, or the event can also make the machine perform some actions. In other words, the event is an input applied to a state. It can change the state and can also create an output. Table 12.3 shows the states for TCP.

Table 12.3 *States for TCP*

State	*Description*
CLOSED	There is no connection
LISTEN	The server is waiting for calls from the client
SYN-SENT	A connection request is sent; waiting for acknowledgment
SYN-RCVD	A connection request is received
ESTABLISHED	Connection is established
FIN-WAIT-1	The application has requested the closing of the connection
FIN-WAIT-2	The other side has accepted the closing of the connection
CLOSING	Both sides have decided to close simultaneously
TIME-WAIT	Waiting for retransmitted segments to die
CLOSE-WAIT	The server is waiting for the application to close
LAST-ACK	The server is waiting for the last acknowledgment

To illustrate the concept we use a state transition diagram. The states are shown using ovals. The transition from one state to another is shown using the directed lines. Each line has two strings separated by a slash. The first string is the input, what TCP receives. The second is the output, what TCP sends. Figure 12.30 shows the state transition diagram for both client and server. The dotted lines of the figure represent the server, the solid lines represent the client, and the thin lines are for unusual situations.

Figure 12.30 *State transition diagram*

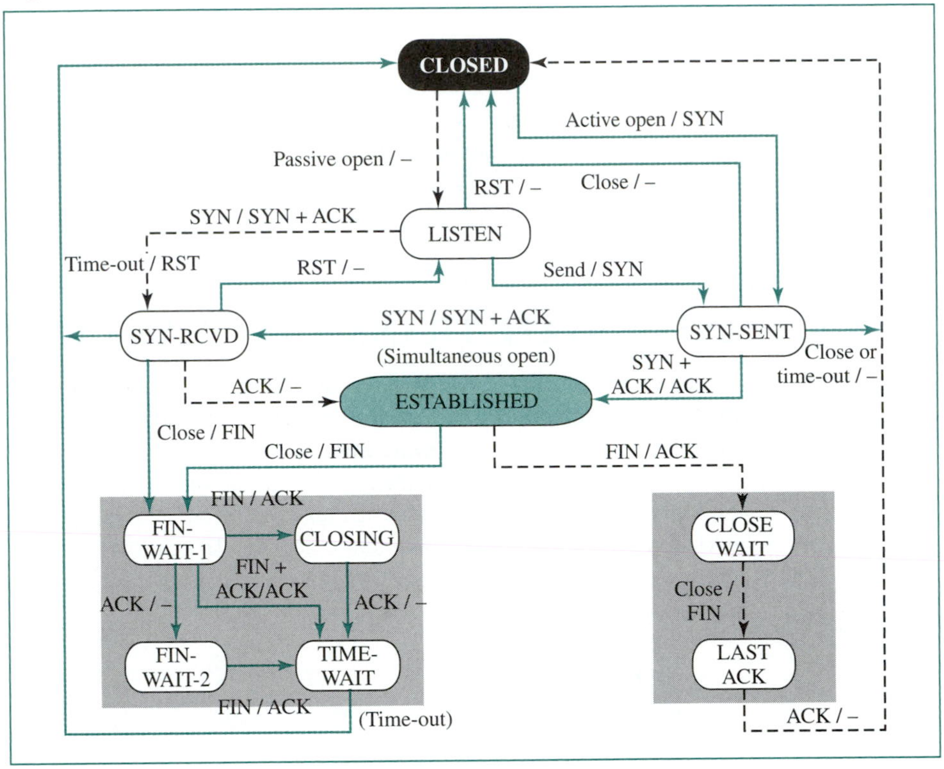

Client Diagram

The client can be in one of the following states: CLOSED, SYN-SENT, ESTABLISHED, FIN-WAIT-1, FIN-WAIT-2, and TIME-WAIT.

- The client TCP starts in the CLOSED state.
- While in this state, the client TCP can receive an active open request from the client application program. It sends a SYN segment to the server TCP and goes to the SYN-SENT state.
- While in this state, the client TCP can receive a SYN + ACK segment from the other TCP. It sends an ACK segment to the other TCP and goes to the ESTABLISHED state. This is the data transfer state. The client remains in this state as long as it is sending and receiving data.

- While in this state, the client TCP can receive a close request from the client application program. It sends a FIN segment to the other TCP and goes to the FIN-WAIT-1 state.
- While in this state, the client TCP waits to receive an ACK from the server TCP. When the ACK is received, it goes to the FIN-WAIT-2 state. It does not send anything. Now the connection is closed in one direction.
- The client remains in this state waiting for the server to close the connection from the other end. If the client receives a FIN segment from the other end, it sends an ACK segment and goes to the TIME-WAIT state.
- When the client is in this state, it starts a timer and waits until this timer goes off. The value of this timer is set to double the lifetime estimate of a segment of maximum size. The client remains in the state before totally closing to let all duplicate packets, if any, arrive at their destination to be discarded. After the time-out, the client goes to the CLOSED state, where it began.

Server Diagram

Although the server can be in any one of the 11 states, in normal operation it is in one of the following states: CLOSED, LISTEN, SYN-RCVD, ESTABLISHED, CLOSE-WAIT, and LAST-ACK.

- The server TCP starts in the CLOSED state.
- While in this state, the server TCP can receive a passive open request from the server application program. It goes to the LISTEN state.
- While in this state, the server TCP can receive a SYN segment from the client TCP. It sends an SYN + ACK segment to the client TCP and then goes to the SYN-RCVD state.
- While in this state, the server TCP can receive an ACK segment from the client TCP. It goes to the ESTABLISHED state. This is the data transfer state. The server remains in this state as long as it is receiving and sending data.
- While in this state, the server TCP can receive a FIN segment from the client, which means that the client wishes to close the connection. It can send an ACK segment to the client and goes to the CLOSE-WAIT state.
- While in this state, the server waits until it receives a close request from the server program. It then sends a FIN segment to the client and goes to the LAST-ACK state.
- While in this state, the server waits for the last ACK segment. It then goes to the CLOSED state.

Example 3

Let us show how a client process goes through the different states as it establishes a connection with a server and exchanges data. The process issues an *active open* command to TCP; TCP sends a SYN segment to the server (first segment in the connection phase in Figure 12.28). The TCP at the client site now stays in the SYN-SENT state until it receives a SYN + ACK segment from the TCP at the server site. After receiving this segment (second segment in the connection phase in Figure 12.28), the TCP at the client site sends an ACK segment (third segment in the connection phase in Figure 12.28) and goes to the ESTABLISHED state. The connection phase is completed and the client and server exchange data. See Figure 12.31.

Figure 12.31 *Client states*

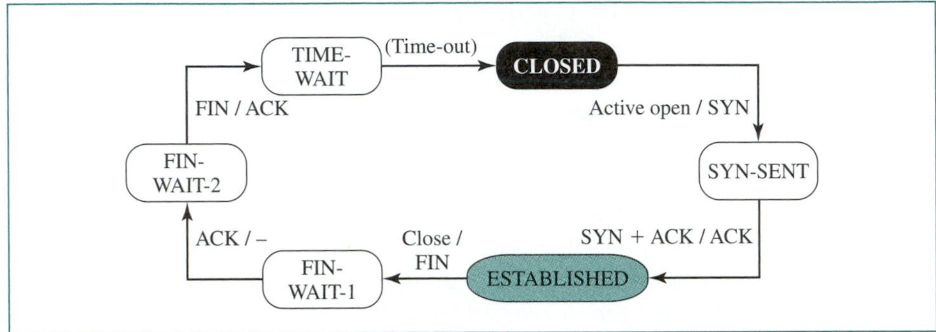

In our example, the client process closes the connection after it has sent all of its data to the server. The client process issues a *close* command to TCP. TCP sends a FIN segment to the TCP at the server site (first segment in the disconnection phase in Figure 12.29) and goes to the FIN-WAIT-1 state. It remains in this state until it receives an ACK from the TCP at the server site. After it receives the ACK segment (second segment in the disconnection phase in Figure 12.29), it goes to the FIN-WAIT-2 state and waits for the TCP server to send a FIN segment (third segment in the disconnection phase in Figure 12.29). After receiving the FIN segment (it is now sure that the server has also closed the connection), it sends an ACK segment to acknowledge the closing from the server site and goes to the TIME-WAIT state. It sets a timer and remains in this state (typically 30 to 60 s) to be sure that the last ACK sent is not lost. (There is retransmission if the ACK is lost.) It then goes to the CLOSED state. Figure 12.31 shows the transitions from state to state.

Example 4

Let us show how a server process goes through the different states as it establishes a connection with the client and exchanges data. The server process issues a *passive open.* This means that the server does not create a connection; it waits for a client to do so. After issuing the passive open, the TCP at the server site remains in the LISTEN state (perhaps for a long time) waiting for a client to show interest. After it receives a SYN segment from a client (first segment in the connection phase in Figure 12.28), it sends a SYN + ACK segment (second segment in the connection phase in Figure 12.28) and goes to the SYN-RCVD state until it receives an ACK segment from the client (third segment of the connection phase in Figure 12.28). It then goes to the ESTABLISHED state and exchanges data with the client.

Again in our example, we assume that the client terminates the connection. The server remains in the ESTABLISHED state until it receives a FIN segment (first segment in the disconnection phase in Figure 12.29) from the client. It then sends an ACK segment (second segment in the disconnection phase in Figure 12.29) and goes to the CLOSE WAIT state. It remains in this state until the server process issues a *close* command (indicating that the server does not have anything left to send to the client). The TCP then sends a FIN segment to the client and goes to the LAST-ACK state. It remains in this state until it receives an ACK segment from the client (fourth segment in the disconnection phase in Figure 12.29). See Figure 12.32.

Figure 12.32 *Server states*

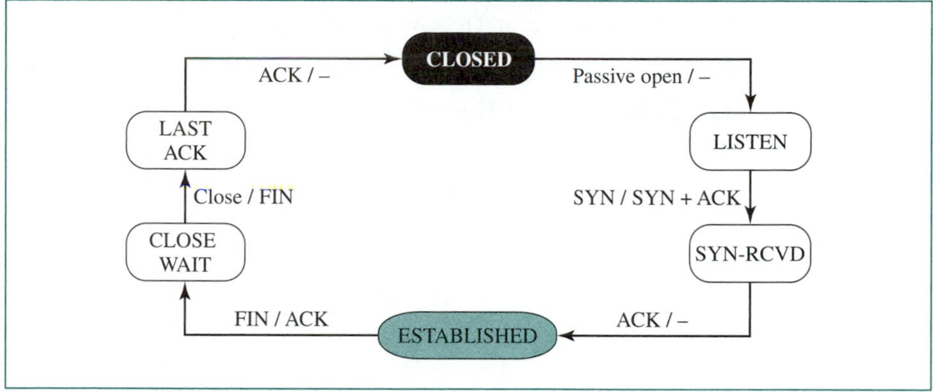

12.14 TCP OPERATION

The transport layer concepts are common to both TCP and UDP. We have discussed these concepts in the UDP chapter; we repeat them here as a review.

Encapsulation and Decapsulation

To send a message from one application program to another, the TCP protocol encapsulates and decapsulates messages (see Figure 12.33).

Figure 12.33 *Encapsulation and decapsulation*

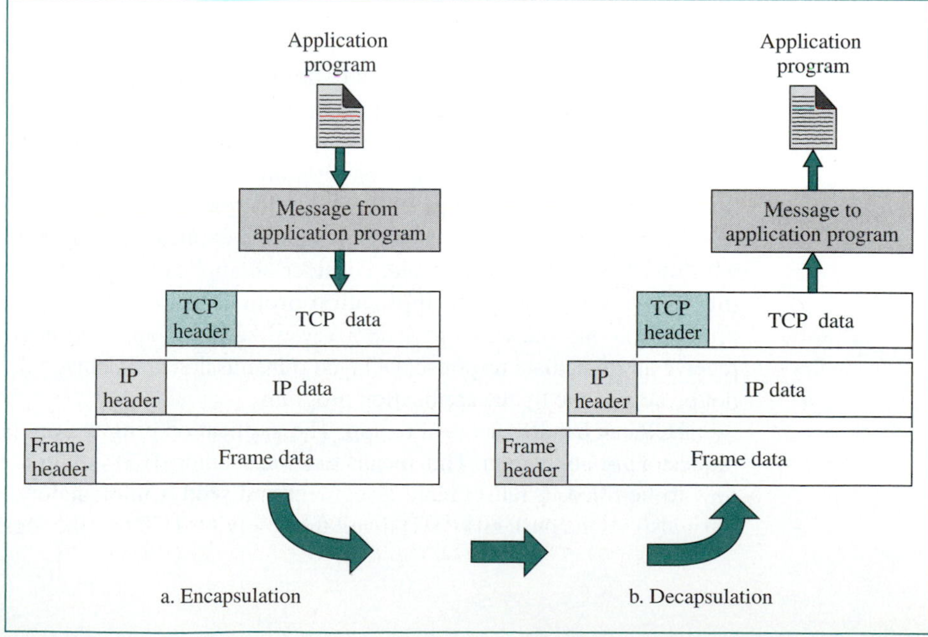

Buffering

TCP creates sending and receiving buffers for each connection as we discussed before.

Multiplexing and Demultiplexing

In the TCP/IP protocol suite, there is only one TCP but there are possibly several application programs that may want to use its services. To handle this situation, TCP does multiplexing and demultiplexing (see Figure 12.34).

Figure 12.34 *Multiplexing and demultiplexing*

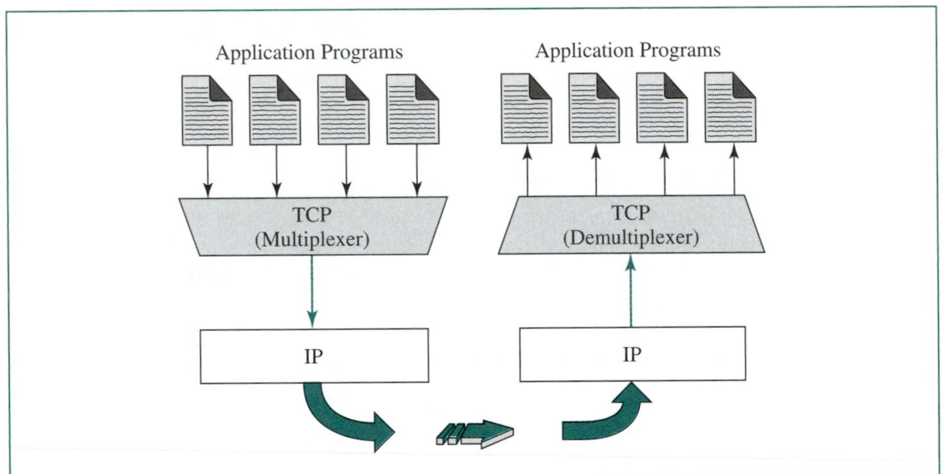

Pushing Data

We saw that the sending TCP uses a buffer to store the stream of data coming from the sending application program. The sending TCP can choose the size of the segments. The receiving TCP also buffers the data when they arrive and delivers them to the application program when the application program is ready or when the receiving TCP feels that it is convenient. This type of flexibility increases the efficiency of TCP.

However, there are occasions in which the application program is not comfortable with this flexibility. For example, consider an application program that communicates interactively with another application program on the other end. The application program on one site wants to send a keystroke to the application at the other site and receive an immediate response. Delayed transmission and delayed delivery of data may not be acceptable by the application program.

TCP can handle such a situation. The application program on the sending site can request a *push* operation. This means that the sending TCP should not wait for the window to be filled. It must create a segment and send it immediately. The sending TCP must also set the push bit (PSH) to tell the receiving TCP that the segment includes data that must be delivered to the receiving application program as soon as possible and not to wait for more data to come.

Although the push operation can be requested by the application program, today most implementations ignore such requests. TCP can choose whether or not to use this operation.

Urgent Data

TCP is a stream-oriented protocol. This means that the data is presented from the application program to TCP as a stream of characters. Each byte of data has a position in the stream. However, there are occasions in which an application program needs to send *urgent* bytes. This means that the sending application program wants a piece of data to be read out of order by the receiving application program. Suppose that the sending application program is sending data to be processed by the receiving application program. When the result of processing comes back, the sending application program finds that everything is wrong. It wants to abort the process, but it has already sent a huge amount of data. If it issues an abort command (Control + C), these two characters will be stored at the end of the receiving TCP buffer. It will be delivered to the receiving application program after all the data has been processed.

The solution is to send a segment with the URG bit set. The sending application program tells the sending TCP that the piece of data is urgent. The sending TCP creates a segment and inserts the urgent data at the beginning of the segment. The rest of the segment can contain normal data from the buffer. The urgent pointer field in the header defines the end of the urgent data and the start of normal data.

When the receiving TCP receives a segment with the URG bit set, it extracts the urgent data from the segment, using the value of the urgent pointer, and delivers it, out of order, to the receiving application program.

12.15 TCP PACKAGE

TCP is a very complex protocol. It is a stream-service, connection-oriented protocol with an involved state transition diagram. It uses flow and error control. It is so complex that the actual code is tens of thousands of lines.

In this section, we present a simplified, bare-bones TCP package. Our purpose is to show how we can simulate the heart of TCP, as represented by the state transition diagram.

The package involves tables called transmission control blocks, a set of timers, and three software modules: a main module, an input processing module, and an output processing module. Figure 12.35 shows these five components and their interactions.

Transmission Control Blocks (TCBs)

TCP is a connection-oriented transfer protocol. A connection may be open for a long period of time. To control the connection, TCP uses a structure to hold information

Figure 12.35 *TCP package*

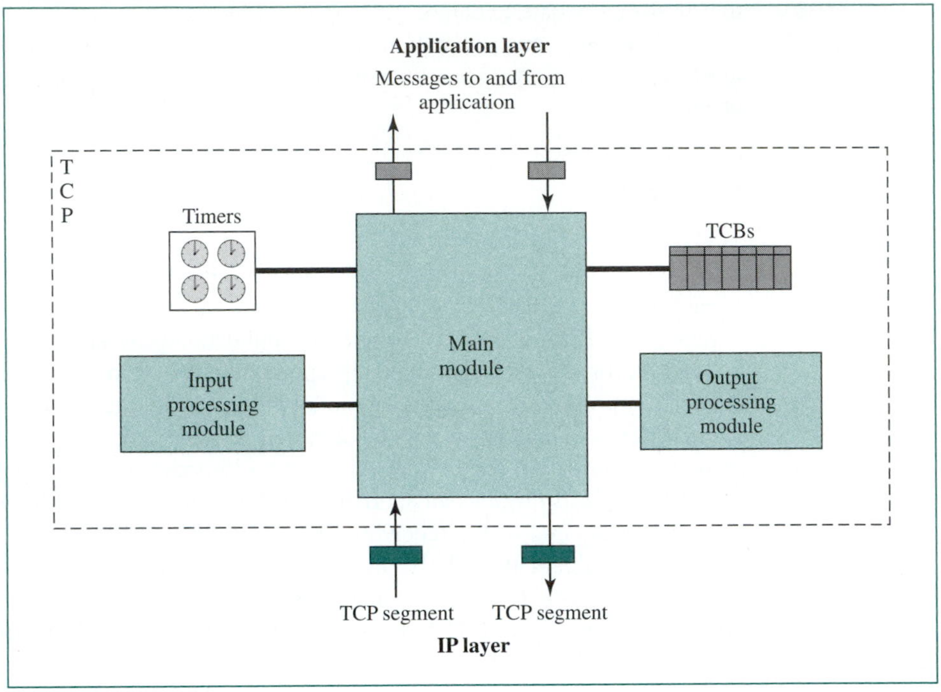

about each connection. This is called a *transmission control block* (TCB). Because at any time there can be several connections, TCP keeps an array of TCBs in the form of a table. The table is usually referred to as the TCB (see Figure 12.36).

Figure 12.36 *TCBs*

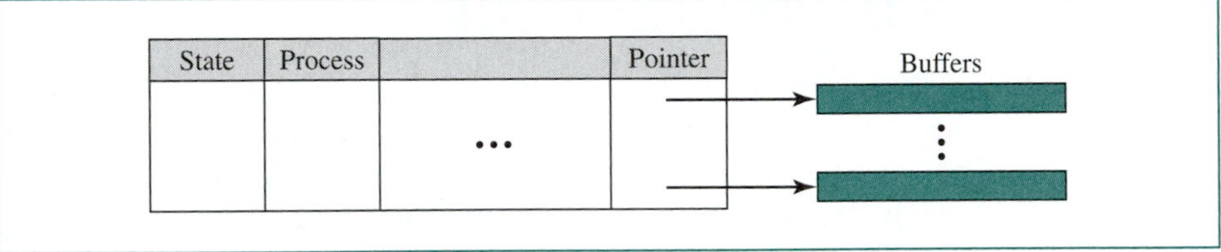

Many fields can be included in each TCB. We mention only the most common ones here.

- **State.** This field defines the state of the connection according to the state transition diagram.
- **Process.** This field defines the process using this connection at this machine as a client or a server.
- **Local IP address.** This field defines the IP address of the local machine used by this connection.

- **Local port number.** This field defines the local port number used by this connection.
- **Remote IP address.** This field defines the IP address of the remote machine used by this connection.
- **Remote port number.** This field defines the remote port number used by this connection.
- **Interface.** This field defines the local interface.
- **Local window.** This field, which can comprise several subfields, holds information about the window at the local TCP.
- **Remote window.** This field, which can comprise several subfields, holds information about the window at the remote TCP.
- **Sending sequence number.** This field holds the sending sequence number.
- **Receiving sequence number.** This field holds the receiving sequence number.
- **Sending ACK number.** This field holds the value of the ACK number sent.
- **Round-trip time.** Several fields may be used to hold information about the RTT.
- **Time-out values.** Several fields can be used to hold the different time-out values such as the retransmission time-out, persistence time-out, keepalive time-out, and so on.
- **Buffer size.** This field defines the size of the buffer at the local TCP.
- **Buffer pointer.** This field is a pointer to the buffer where the receiving data is kept until it is read by the application.

Timers

We have previously discussed the several timers TCP needs to keep track of its operations.

Main Module

The main module is invoked by an arriving TCP segment, a time-out event, or a message from an application program. This is a very complicated module because the action to be taken depends on the current state of the TCP. Several approaches have been used to implement the state transition diagram including using a process for each state, using a table (two-dimensional array), and so on. To keep our discussion simple, we use cases to handle the state. We have 11 states; we use 11 different cases. Each state is implemented as defined in the state transition diagram. The ESTABLISHED state needs further explanation. When TCP is in this state and data or an acknowledgment segment arrives, another module, the input processing module, is called to handle the situation. Also, when TCP is in this state and a "send data" message is issued by an application program, another module, the output processing module, is called to handle the situation.

Main Module

Receive: a TCP segment, a message from an application, or a time-out event
1. Search the TCB table.
2. If (corresponding TCB is not found)
    1. Create a TCB with the state CLOSED.
3. Find the state of the entry in the TCB table.
4. Case (state)
    CLOSED:
        1. If ("passive open" message from application received)
            1. Change the state to LISTEN.
        2. If ("active open" message from application received)
            1. Send a SYN segment.
            2. Change the state to SYN-SENT.
        3. If (any segment received)
            1. Send an RST segment.
        4. If (any other message received)
            1. Issue an error message.
        5. Return.
    LISTEN:
        1. If ("send data" message from application received)
            1. Send a SYN segment.
            2. Change the state to SYN-SENT.
        2. If (SYN segment received)
            1. Send a SYN + ACK segment.
            2. Change the state to SYN + RCVD.
        3. If (any other segment or message received)
            1. Issue an error message.
        4. Return.
    SYN-SENT:
        1. If (time-out)
            1. Change the state to CLOSED.
        2. If (SYN segment received)
            1. Send a SYN + ACK segment.
            2. Change the state to SYN-RCVD.
        3. If (SYN + ACK segment received)
            1. Send an ACK segment.
            2. Change the state to ESTABLISHED.
        4. If (any other segment or message received)
            1. Issue an error message.
        5. Return.

Main Module (continued)

SYN-RCVD:

1. If (ACK segment received)
    1. Change the state to ESTABLISHED.
2. If (time-out)
    1. Send an RST segment.
    2. Change the state to CLOSED.
3. If ("close" message from application received)
    1. Send a FIN segment.
    2. Change the state to FIN-WAIT-1.
4. If (RST segment received)
    1. Change the state to LISTEN.
5. If (any other segment or message received)
    1. Issue an error message.
6. Return.

ESTABLISHED:

1. If (FIN segment received)
    1. Send an ACK segment.
    2. Change the state to CLOSE-WAIT.
2. If ("close" message from application received)
    1. Send a FIN segment.
    2. Change the state to FIN-WAIT-1.
3. If (RST or SYN segment received)
    1. Issue an error message.
4. If (data or ACK segment is received)
    1. Call the input module.
5. If ("send" message from application received)
    1. Call the output module.
6. Return.

FIN-WAIT-1:

1. If (FIN segment received)
    1. Send an ACK segment.
    2. Change the state to CLOSING.
2. If (FIN + ACK segment received)
    1. Send an ACK segment.
    2. Change the state to TIME-WAIT.
3. If (ACK segment received)
    1. Change the state to FIN-WAIT-2.

Main Module (continued)

4. If (any other segment or message received)
    1. Issue an error message.
5. Return.

FIN-WAIT-2:

1. If (FIN segment received)
    1. Send an ACK segment.
    2. Change the state to TIME-WAIT.
2. Return.

CLOSING:

1. If (ACK segment received)
    1. Change the state to TIME-WAIT.
2. If (any other segment or message received)
    1. Issue an error message.
3. Return.

TIME-WAIT:

1. If (time-out)
    1. Change the state to CLOSED.
2. If (any other segment or message received)
    1. Issue an error message.
3. Return.

CLOSE-WAIT:

1. If ("close" message from application received)
    1. Send a FIN segment.
    2. Change the state to LAST-ACK.
2. If (any other segment or message received)
    1. Issue an error message.
3. Return.

LAST-ACK:

1. If (ACK segment received)
    1. Change the state to CLOSED.
2. If (any other segment or message received)
    1. Issue an error message.
3. Return.

Input Processing Module

In our design, the input processing module handles all the details needed to process data or acknowledgment received when TCP is in the ESTABLISHED state. This module sends an ACK if needed, takes care of the window size announcement, does error checking, and so on. The details of this module are not needed for an introductory textbook.

Output Processing Module

In our design, the output processing module handles all the details needed to send out data received from application program when TCP is in the ESTABLISHED state. This module handles retransmission time-outs, persistent time-outs, and so on. One of the ways to implement this module is to use a small transition diagram to handle different output conditions. Again, the details of this module are not needed for an introductory textbook.

12.16 KEY TERMS

additive increase

application program

buffer

checksum

Clark's solution

congestion control

connection establishment

connection resetting

connection termination

connection-oriented, reliable transport protocol

corrupted segment

decapsulation

duplicate segment

encapsulation

end-of-option option

ephemeral port

error control

error correction

error detection

finite state machine

flow control

four-way handshaking

full-duplex mode

header

Karn's algorithm

keepalive timer

local client program

local host

maximum segment size option

multiplexing

multiplicative decrease

Nagle's algorithm

no-operation option

option

out-of-order segment

persistence timer

piggybacking

port address

port number

process-to-process communication

program-to-program communication

pushing data

queue

remote host

remote server program

retransmission timer

round-trip time (RTT)
segment
sequence number
silly window syndrome
sliding window protocol
slow start
socket address
state transition diagram
stream transport layer
TCP timer
three-way handshaking
timestamp option
time-waited timer
Transmission Control Protocol (TCP)
transport layer
urgent data
urgent pointer
well-known port number
window scale factor
window size

12.17 SUMMARY

- Transmission Control Protocol (TCP) is a connection-oriented, reliable, stream transport layer protocol in the TCP/IP protocol suite.
- TCP is responsible for process-to-process communication.
- A process can be identified by a port number.
- The socket address, a combination of an IP address and a port number, uniquely identifies a running application program.
- The unit of data transfer between two devices using TCP software is called a segment, it has 20 to 60 bytes of header, followed by data from the application program.
- The source and destination ports define the port numbers of the application programs that are using TCP.
- The sequence number identifies the first byte of data in the segment.
- The acknowledgment number announces the successful receipt of data.
- The header length field indicates the number of 32-bit words in the header.
- The control field bits define the use of a segment or serve as a validity check for other fields.
- The window size field defines the size of the sliding window used in flow control.
- The checksum field is used for error detection.
- The urgent pointer defines the boundary between urgent data and normal data.
- The end-of-option option is used for alignment and indicates there are no more options in the header.
- The no-operation option is used for filler and alignment purposes.
- The maximum segment size is used in connection setup to define the largest allowable data segment.

- The window scale factor is a multiplier that increases the window size.
- The timestamp option shows how much time it takes for data to travel from sender to receiver.
- TCP uses a sliding window mechanism for flow control.
- Error detection is handled by the checksum, acknowledgment, and time-out.
- Corrupted and lost segments are retransmitted and duplicate segments are discarded.
- TCP uses four timers (retransmission, persistence, keepalive, and time-waited) in its operation.
- Connection establishment requires three-way handshaking; connection termination requires four-way handshaking.
- TCP software is implemented as a finite state machine.
- The TCP window size is determined by the receiver-advertised window size or the congestion window size, whichever is smaller.
- The slow start and additive increase strategy as well as the multiplicative decrease strategy are used for congestion control.
- When the push bit in the TCP header is set, a segment is sent immediately, without waiting for the window to fill with data.
- When the urgent bit in the TCP header is set, data from the segment is delivered out of order to the receiving application program.
- Transmission control blocks (TCBs) hold information about each TCP connection.
- A TCP package can contain TCBs, timers, a main module, an input processing module, and an output processing module.

12.18 PRACTICE SET

Multiple-Choice Questions

1. TCP lies between the _______ and the _______ layers of the TCP/IP protocol suite.
   a. application; UDP
   b. application; transport
   c. application; network
   d. network; data link
2. IP is responsible for _______ communication while TCP is responsible for _______ communication.
   a. host-to-host; process-to-process
   b. process-to-process; host-to-host
   c. process-to-process; network-to-network
   d. network-to-network; process-to-process

3. A host can be identified by _______ while a program running on the host can be identified by _______.
   a. an IP address; a port number
   b. a port number; an IP address
   c. an IP address; a host address
   d. an IP address; a well-known port
4. The _______ address uniquely identifies a running application program.
   a. IP address
   b. host
   c. NIC
   d. socket
5. If a segment carries data along with an acknowledgment, this is called _______.
   a. backpacking
   b. piggybacking
   c. piggypacking
   d. mother's helper
6. The _______ field is used to order packets of a message.
   a. urgent pointer
   b. checksum
   c. sequence number
   d. acknowledgment number
7. The _______ field is used for error detection.
   a. urgent pointer
   b. checksum
   c. sequence number
   d. acknowledgment number
8. Multiply the header length field by _______ to find the total number of bytes in the TCP header.
   a. 2
   b. 4
   c. 6
   d. 8
9. Urgent data requires the urgent pointer field as well as the URG bit in the _______ field.
   a. control
   b. offset
   c. sequence number
   d. reserved

10. Which of the following is not a valid acknowledgment number?
    a. 0
    b. 1
    c. $2^{32} - 1$
    d. 2^{32}
11. Which field indicates the length of the TCP header?
    a. window
    b. acknowledgment
    c. header length
    d. control
12. The options field of the TCP header ranges from 0 to _______ bytes.
    a. 10
    b. 20
    c. 40
    d. 2^{32}
13. What is the maximum number of no-operation options in one 32-bit word?
    a. one
    b. two
    c. three
    d. four
14. What is the maximum number of the end-of-option options in the entire TCP header?
    a. 30
    b. 10
    c. 9
    d. 1
15. Which option defines the maximum number of bytes in a TCP segment?
    a. maximum segment size
    b. window scale factor
    c. timestamp
    d. no operation
16. In Figure 12.7 if bytes 200 and 201 are acknowledged, bytes _______ to _______ can be sent.
    a. 203; 211
    b. 203; 205
    c. 203; 204
    d. 202; 203

17. In _______, data are sent or processed at a very inefficient rate, such as 1 byte at a time.
    a. Nagle's syndrome
    b. silly window syndrome
    c. sliding window syndrome
    d. delayed acknowledgment
18. To prevent silly window syndrome created by a receiver that processes data at a very slow rate, _______ can be used.
    a. Clark's solution
    b. Nagle's algorithm
    c. delayed acknowledgment
    d. a or c
19. To prevent silly window syndrome created by a sender that sends data at a very slow rate, _______ can be used.
    a. Clark's solution
    b. Nagle's algorithm
    c. delayed acknowledgment
    d. a or c
20. TCP uses _______ for error detection.
    a. checksum
    b. acknowledgment
    c. time-out
    d. all of the above
21. An ACK number of 1,000 always means that _______.
    a. 999 bytes have been successfully received
    b. 1,000 bytes have been successfully received
    c. 1,001 bytes have been successfully received
    d. none of the above
22. The _______ timer prevents a long idle connection between two TCPs.
    a. retransmission
    b. persistence
    c. keepalive
    d. time-waited
23. The _______ timer is needed to handle the zero window-size advertisement.
    a. retransmission
    b. persistence
    c. keepalive
    d. time-waited

24. Karn's algorithm is used in calculations by the _______ timer.
    a. retransmission
    b. persistence
    c. keepalive
    d. time-waited
25. The _______ timer is used in the termination phase.
    a. retransmission
    b. persistence
    c. keepalive
    d. time-waited
26. The _______ timer keeps track of the time between the sending of a segment and the receipt of an acknowledgment.
    a. retransmission
    b. persistence
    c. keepalive
    d. time-waited
27. A server issues _______ open while a client issues _______ open.
    a. an active; a passive
    b. a passive; an active
    c. an ephemeral; a well-known
    d. a well-known; an ephemeral
28. Connection establishment involves a _______ handshake; connection termination involves a _______ handshake.
    a. one-way; two-way
    b. two-way; three-way
    c. three-way; three-way
    d. three-way; four-way
29. In the _______ state, the server is waiting for the application to close.
    a. CLOSED
    b. ESTABLISHED
    c. CLOSE-WAIT
    d. LAST-ACK
30. In the _______ state, the server is in the data transfer state and can receive and send data.
    a. ESTABLISHED
    b. LISTEN
    c. TRANSFER
    d. OPEN

31. After the server TCP receives a passive open request from the server application program, it goes to the _______ state.
    a. CLOSED
    b. LISTEN
    c. SYN-RCVD
    d. ESTABLISHED
32. After the client TCP receives an active open request from the client application program, it goes to the _______ state.
    a. CLOSED
    b. FIN-WAIT-1
    c. SYN-SENT
    d. ESTABLISHED
33. In the _______ state, the client TCP has closed its connection to the server.
    a. CLOSED
    b. FIN-WAIT-1
    c. FIN-WAIT-2
    d. ESTABLISHED
34. In the _______ state, the client TCP waits for an ACK segment.
    a. CLOSED
    b. FIN-WAIT-1
    c. FIN-WAIT-2
    d. ESTABLISHED
35. A special segment called a probe is sent by a sending TCP when the _______ timer goes off.
    a. transmission
    b. persistence
    c. keepalive
    d. time-waited

Exercises

36. TCP sends a segment at 5:30:20. It receives the acknowledgment at 5:30:25. What is the new value for RTT if the previous RTT was 4 seconds?
37. TCP sends a segment at 4:30:20. It does not receive an acknowledgment. At 4:30:25, it retransmits the previous segment. It receives an acknowledgment at 4:30:27. What is the new value for RTT according to Karn's algorithm if the previous RTT was 4 seconds?
38. What is the maximum size of the TCP header?
39. What is the minimum size of the TCP header?
40. If the value of HLEN is 0111, how many bytes of option are included in the segment?

41. What can you say about the TCP segment in which the value of the control field is one of the following:
    a. 000000
    b. 000001
    c. 010001
    d. 000100
    e. 000010
    f. 010010
42. The control field in a TCP segment is 6 bits. We can have 64 different combinations of bits. How many of these combinations do you think are valid?
43. TCP opens a connection using an initial sequence number (ISN) of 14,534. The other party opens the connection with an ISN of 21,732. Show the three TCP segments during the connection establishment.
44. Following the previous exercise, show the contents of the segments during the data transmission if the initiator sends a segment containing the message "Hello Dear Customer" and the other party answers with a segment containing "Hi There Seller."
45. Following the previous two exercises, show the contents of the segments during the connection termination.
46. TCP is sending data at 1 megabyte per second (8 Mbps). If the sequence number starts with 7,000, how long does it take before the sequence number goes back to zero?
47. A TCP connection is using a window size of 10,000 bytes and the previous acknowledgment number was 22,001. It receives a segment with acknowledge number 24,001. Draw a diagram to show the situation of the window before and after.
48. Redo exercise 47 if the receiver has changed the window size to 11,000.
49. Redo exercise 47 if the receiver has changed the window size to 90,000.
50. In exercise 47, how low can the receiver decrease the window size?
51. A TCP connection is in the ESTABLISHED state. The following events occur one after another:
    a. A FIN segment is received.
    b. The application sends a "close" message.

    What is the state of the connection after each event? What is the action after each event?
52. A TCP connection is in the ESTABLISHED state. The following events occur one after another:
    a. The application sends a "close" message.
    b. An ACK segment is received.

    What is the state of the connection after each event? What is the action after each event?

53. A TCP connection is in the SYN-RCVD state. The following events occur one after another:

    a. The application sends a "close" message.

    b. A FIN segment is received.

    What is the state of the connection after each event? What is the action after each event?

54. A TCP connection is in the SYN-SENT state. The following events occur one after another:

    a. A SYN+ACK segment is received.

    b. A "close" message is received.

    What is the state of the connection after each event? What is the action after each event?

55. A TCP connection is in the FIN-WAIT-1 state. The following events occur one after another:

    a. An ACK segment is received.

    b. A FIN segment is received.

    c. Time-out occurs.

    What is the state of the connection after each event? What is the action after each event?

56. Show the entries for the header of a TCP segment that carries a message from a FTP client to a FTP server. Fill the checksum field with 0s. Choose an appropriate ephemeral port number and the correct well-known port number. The length of data is 40 bytes.

57. A client uses TCP to send data to a server. The data is 16 bytes. Calculate the efficiency of this transmission at the TCP level (ratio of useful bytes to total bytes).

58. Redo the previous exercise calculating the efficiency of transmission at the IP level. Assume no options for the IP header.

59. Redo the previous exercise calculating the efficiency of transmission at the data link layer. Assume no options for the IP header and use Ethernet at the data link layer.

60. The following is a dump of a TCP header in hexadecimal format.

    05320017 00000001 00000000 500207FF 00000000

    a. What is the source port number?

    b. What is the destination port number?

    c. What the sequence number?

    d. What is the acknowledgment number?

    e. What is the length of the header?

    f. What is the type of the segment?

    g. What is the window size?

Programming Exercises

61. Create a header file to include all constants that you think are needed to implement the TCP modules in C. Use the **#define** directives.
62. Complete the following struct declaration for the TCP header.

```
struct   TCP_Header
{
unsigned short     SPortAddr  ;
...............................................................
...............................................................
} ;
```

63. Complete the following struct declaration for the TCP segment.

```
struct   TCP_Segment
{
            struct    TCP_Header    tcpHeader ;
            ............................................     tcpData ;
} ;
```

64. Write the declaration for the TCBs.
65. Write a function in C to simulate the main module.

CHAPTER 13

Routing Protocols (RIP, OSPF, and BGP)

An internet is a combination of networks connected by routers. When a datagram goes from a source to a destination, it will probably pass through many routers until it reaches the router attached to the destination network.

A router receives a packet from a network and passes it to another network. A router is usually attached to several networks. When it receives a packet, to which network should it pass the packet? The decision is based on optimization: Which of the available pathways is the optimum pathway?

A **metric** is a cost assigned for passing through a network. The total metric of a particular route is equal to the sum of the metrics of networks that comprise the route. A router chooses the route with the shortest (smallest) metric.

The metric assigned to each network depends on the type of protocol. Some simple protocols, like the Routing Information Protocol (RIP), treat each network as equals. The cost of passing through each network is the same; it is one hop count. So if a packet passes through 10 networks to reach the destination, the total cost is 10 hop counts.

Other protocols, such as Open Shortest Path First (OSPF), allow the administrator to assign a cost for passing through a network based on the type of service required. A route through a network can have different costs (metrics). For example, if maximum throughput is the desired type of service, a satellite link has a lower metric than a fiber-optic line. On the other hand, if minimum delay is the desired type of service, a fiber-optic line has a lower metric than a satellite line. OSPF allows each router to have several routing tables based on the required type of service.

Other protocols define the metric totally differently. In the border gateway protocol (BGP), the criterion is the policy, which can be set by the administrator. The policy defines what paths should be chosen.

Whatever the metric, a router should have a routing table to consult when a packet is ready to be forwarded. The routing table specifies the optimum path for the packet. However, the table can be either static or dynamic. A *static table* is one that is not changed frequently. A *dynamic table,* on the other hand, is one that is updated automatically when there is a change somewhere in the internet. Today, an internet needs dynamic routing tables. The tables need to be updated as soon as there is a change in the internet. For instance, they need to be updated when a route is down, and they need to be updated whenever a better route has been created.

Routing protocols have been created in response to the demand for dynamic routing tables. A routing protocol is a combination of rules and procedures that lets routers in the internet inform each other of changes. It allows routers to share whatever they know about the internet or their neighborhood. The sharing of information allows a router in San Francisco to know about the failure of a network in Texas. The routing protocols also include procedures for combining information received from other routers.

In this chapter we discuss unicast routing protocols. Multicast routing protocols will be discussed in the next chapter.

13.1 INTERIOR AND EXTERIOR ROUTING

Today, an internet can be so large that one routing protocol cannot handle the task of updating routing tables of all routers. For this reason, an internet is divided into autonomous systems. An **Autonomous System** (AS) is a group of networks and routers under the authority of a single administration. Routing inside an autonomous system is referred to as *interior routing*. Routing between autonomous systems is referred to as *exterior routing*. Each autonomous system can choose an interior routing protocol to handle routing inside the autonomous system. However, only one exterior routing protocol is usually chosen to handle routing between autonomous systems.

Several interior and exterior routing protocols are in use. In this chapter, we cover only the most popular ones. We discuss two interior routing protocols, RIP and OSPF, and one exterior routing protocol, BGP (see Figure 13.1).

Figure 13.1 *Popular routing protocols*

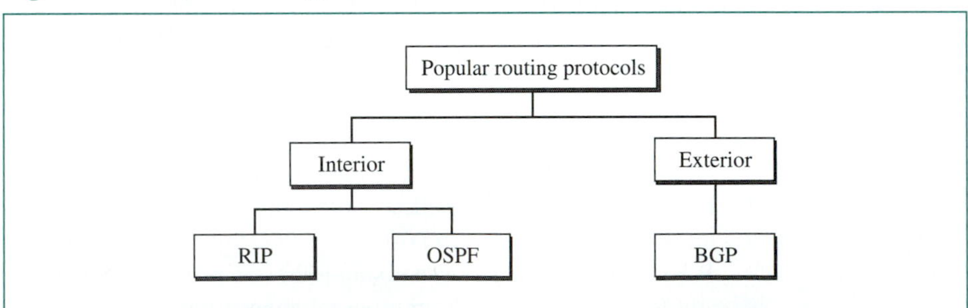

RIP and OSPF can be used to update routing tables inside an autonomous system. BGP can be used to update routing tables for routers that join the autonomous systems together.

In Figure 13.2, routers R1, R2, R3, and R4 use an interior and an exterior routing protocol. The other routers use only interior routing protocols. The solid thin lines show the communication between routers that use interior routing protocols. The broken thick lines show the communication between the routers that use an exterior routing protocol.

Figure 13.2 *Autonomous systems*

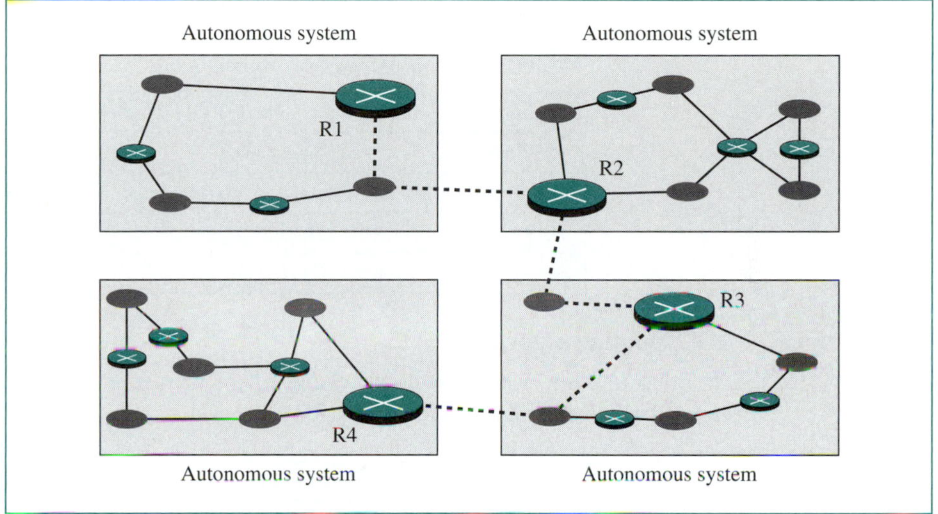

13.2 RIP

The routing information protocol is an interior routing protocol used inside an autonomous system. It is a very simple protocol based on *distance vector routing,* which uses the Bellman-Ford algorithm for calculating the routing tables. In this section, we first study the principle of distance vector routing, as it is applied to RIP, and then discuss the RIP protocol itself.

Distance Vector Routing

In **distance vector routing,** each router periodically shares its knowledge about the entire internet with its neighbors. The three keys to understanding how this algorithm works are as follows:

1. **Sharing knowledge about the entire autonomous system.** Each router shares its knowledge about the entire autonomous system with its neighbors. At the outset, a router's knowledge may be sparse. How much it knows, however, is unimportant; it sends whatever it has.
2. **Sharing only with neighbors.** Each router sends its knowledge only to neighbors. It sends whatever knowledge it has through all of its interfaces.
3. **Sharing at regular intervals.** Each router sends its knowledge to its neighbors at fixed intervals, for example, every 30 s.

Routing Table

Every router keeps a routing table that has one entry for each destination network of which the router is aware. The entry consists of the destination network address, the shortest distance to reach the destination in hop count, and the next hop (next router) to which the packet should be delivered to reach its final destination. The hop count is the number of networks a packet encounters to reach its final destination.

The table may contain other information such as the subnet mask (or prefix), or the time this entry was last updated. Table 13.1 shows an example of a routing table.

Table 13.1 *A distance vector routing table*

Destination	*Hop Count*	*Next Hop*	*Other Information*
163.5.0.0	7	172.6.23.4	
197.5.13.0	5	176.3.6.17	
189.45.0.0	4	200.5.1.6	
115.0.0.0	6	131.4.7.19	

RIP Updating Algorithm

The routing table is updated upon receipt of a RIP response message. The following shows the updating algorithm used by RIP.

RIP Updating Algorithm

Receive: a response RIP message

1. Add one hop to the hop count for each advertised destination.
2. Repeat the following steps for each advertised destination:
    1. If (destination not in the routing table)
        1. Add the advertised information to the table.
    2. Else
        1. If (next-hop field is the same)
            1. Replace entry in the table with the advertised one.
        2. Else
            1. If (advertised hop count smaller than one in the table)
                1. Replace entry in the routing table.
3. Return.

In Figure 13.3 a router receives a RIP message from router C. The message lists destination networks and their corresponding hop counts. The first step according to the updating algorithm is to increase the hop count by one. Next, this updated RIP packet and the old routing table are compared. The result is a routing table with an up-to-date hop count for each destination. For Net1 there is no new information, so the Net1 entry remains the same.

Figure 13.3 *Example of updating a routing table*

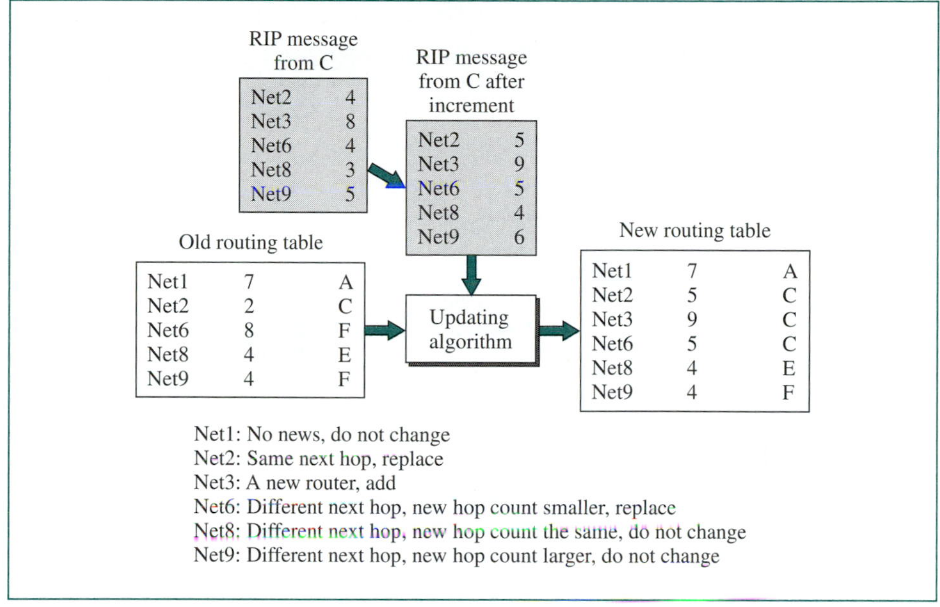

For Net2, information in the table and in the message identify the same next hop (router C). Although the value of the hop count in the table (2) is less than the one in the message (5), the algorithm selects the one received in the message because the original value has come from router C. This value is now invalid because router C is advertising a new value.

Net3 is added as a new destination. For Net6, the RIP packet contains a lower hop count and this shows up on the new routing table. Both Net8 and Net9 retain their original values since the corresponding hop counts in the message are not an improvement.

Initializing the Routing Table

When a router is added to a network, it initializes a routing table for itself using its configuration file. The table contains only the directly attached networks and the hop counts, which are initialized to 1. The next-hop field, which identifies the next router, is empty. Figure 13.4 shows the initial routing tables in a small autonomous system.

Updating the Routing Table

Each routing table is updated upon receipt of RIP messages using the RIP updating algorithm shown above. Figure 13.5 shows our previous autonomous system with final routing tables.

Figure 13.4 *Initial routing tables in a small autonomous system*

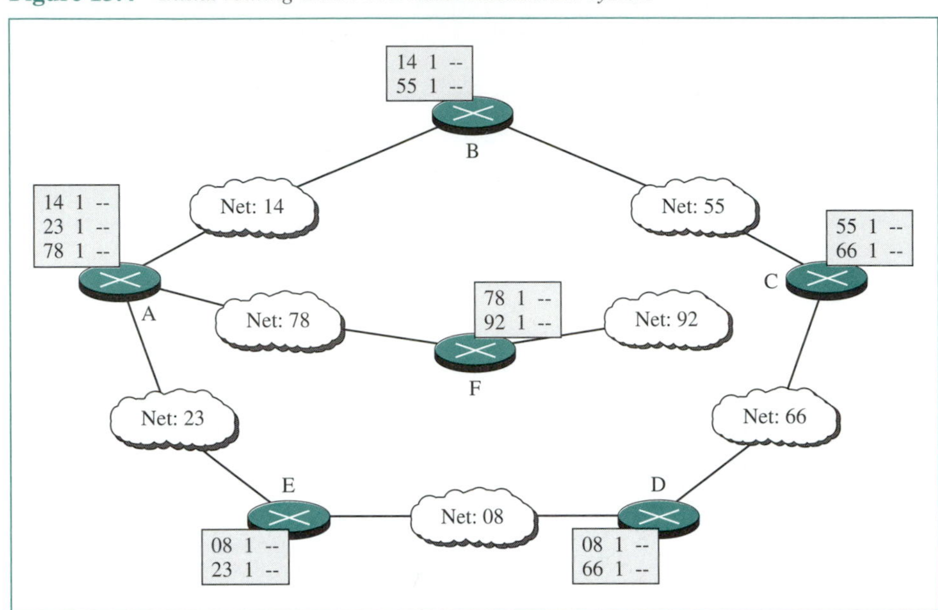

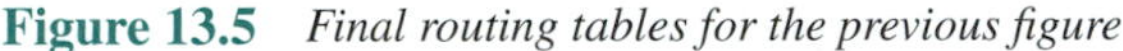

Figure 13.5 *Final routing tables for the previous figure*

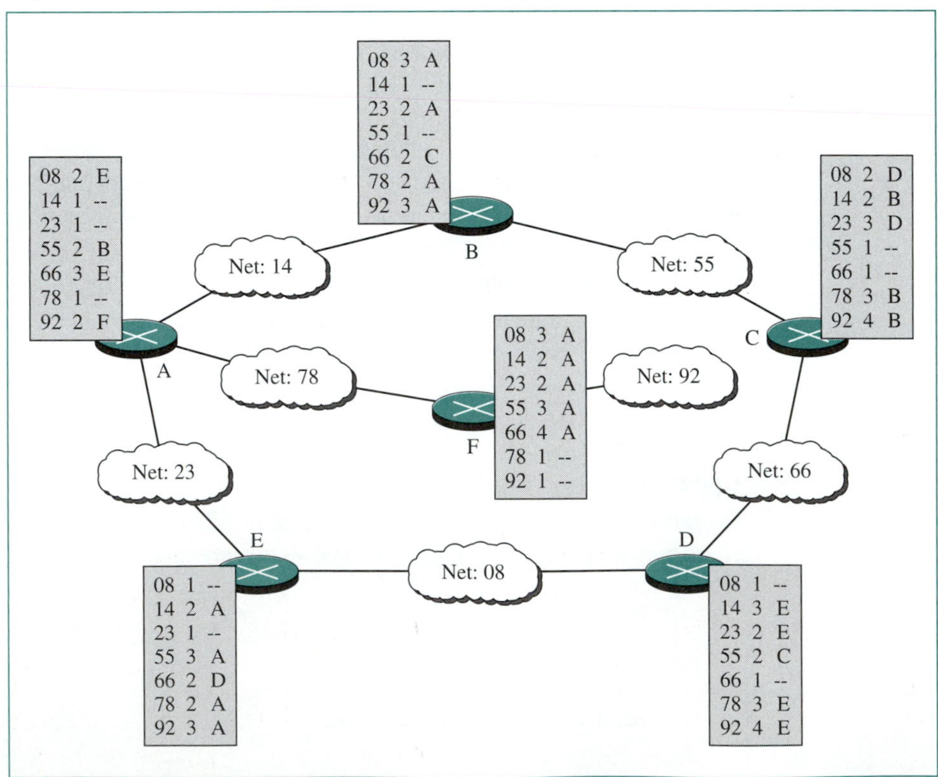

RIP Message Format

The format of the RIP message is shown in Figure 13.6.

Figure 13.6 *RIP message format*

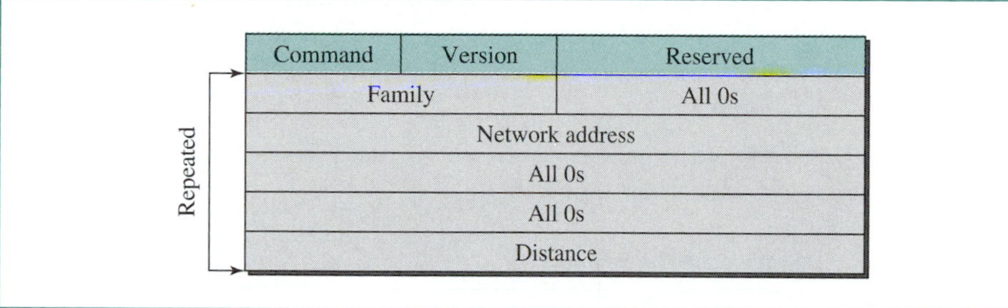

- **Command.** This 8-bit field specifies the type of message: request (1) or response (2).
- **Version.** This 8-bit field defines the version. In this book we use version 1, but at the end of this section, we give some new features of version 2.
- **Family.** This 16-bit field defines the family of the protocol used. For TCP/IP the value is 2.
- **Address.** The address field defines the address of the destination network. RIP has allocated 14 bytes for this field to be applicable to any protocol. However, IP currently uses only 4 bytes. The rest of the address is filled with 0s.
- **Distance.** This 32-bit field defines the hop count from the advertising router to the destination network.

Note that part of the message is repeated for each destination network. We refer to this as an *entry*.

Requests and Responses

RIP uses two types of messages: request and response.

Request

A request message is sent by a router that has just come up or by a router that has some time-out entries. A request can ask about specific entries or all entries (see Figure 13.7).

Figure 13.7 *Request messages*

Com: 1	Version	Reserved
Family		All 0s
Network address		
All 0s		
All 0s		
All 0s		

Repeated

a. Request for some

Com: 1	Version	Reserved
Family		All 0s
All 0s		
All 0s		
All 0s		
All 0s		

b. Request for all

Response

A response can be either solicited or unsolicited. A *solicited response* is sent only in answer to a request. It contains information about the destination specified in the corresponding request. An *unsolicited response,* on the other hand, is sent periodically, every 30 s, and contains information about the entire routing table. This periodic response is sometimes called update packet. Figure 13.6 shows the response message format.

Example 1

What is the periodic response sent by router R1 in Figure 13.8? Assume R1 knows about the whole autonomous system.

Figure 13.8 *Example 1*

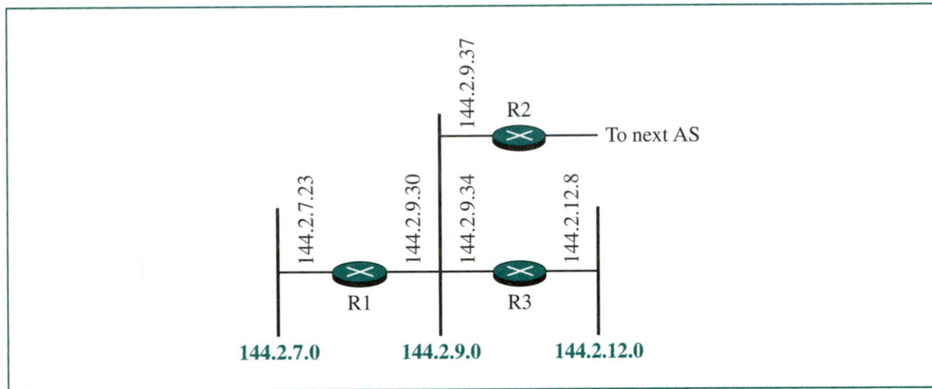

Solution

R1 can advertise three networks 144.2.7.0, 144.2.9.0, and 144.2.12.0. The periodic response (update packet) is shown in Figure 13.9.

Figure 13.9 *Solution to Example 1*

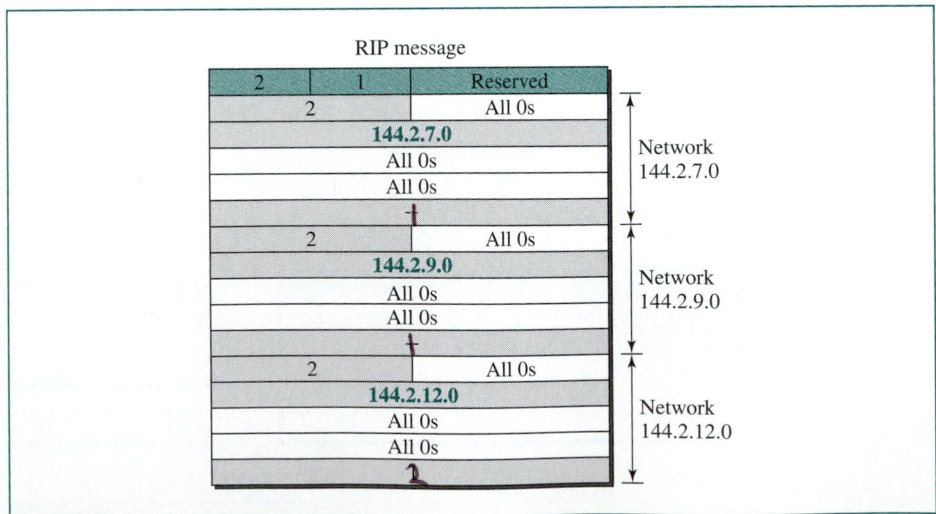

Timers in RIP

RIP uses three timers to support its operation (see Figure 13.10). The periodic timer controls the sending of messages, the expiration timer governs the validity of a route, and the garbage collection timer advertises the failure of a route.

Figure 13.10 *RIP timers*

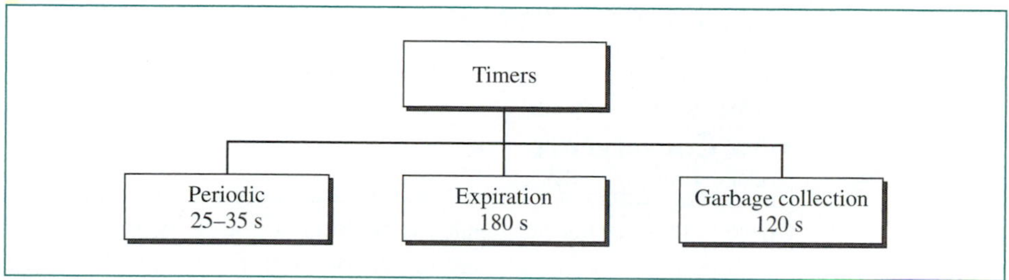

Periodic Timer

The **periodic timer** controls the advertising of regular update messages. Although the protocol specifies that this timer must be set to 30 s, the working model uses a random number between 25 and 35 s. This is to prevent any possible synchronization and therefore overload on an internet if routers update simultaneously.

Each router has one periodic timer that is set randomly to a number between 25 and 35. It counts down; when zero is reached, the update message is sent, and the timer is randomly set once again.

If RIP uses an additional timing method to send out updates (see triggered update, to follow), the periodic timer is not affected. The periodic update messages go out on their own schedule without regard to other update messages from other timing systems.

Expiration Timer

The **expiration timer** governs the validity of a route. When a router receives update information for a route, the expiration timer is set to 180 s for that particular route. Every time a new update for the route is received, the timer is reset. In normal situations this occurs every 30 s. However, if there is a problem on an internet and no update is received within the allotted 180 s, the route is considered expired and the hop count of the route is set to 16, which means the destination is unreachable. Every route has its own expiration timer.

Garbage Collection Timer

When the information about a route becomes invalid, the router does not immediately purge that route from its table. Instead, it continues to advertise the route with a metric value of 16. At the same time, a timer called the **garbage collection timer** is set to 120 s for that route. When the count reaches zero, the route is purged from the table. This timer allows neighbors to become aware of the invalidity of a route prior to purging.

Example 2

A routing table has 20 entries. It does not receive information about five routes for 200 s. How many timers are running at this time?

Solution

The timers are listed below:

Periodic timer: 1

Expiration timer: 20 – 5 = 15

Garbage collection timer: 5

Slow Convergence

One of the problems with RIP is slow convergence, which means that a change somewhere in the internet propagates very slowly through the rest of the internet. For example, suppose there is a change in network 1 in Figure 13.11. Router R1 updates itself immediately. However, since each router sends its periodic update every 30 s, this means an average of 15 s (range of 0 to 30 s) before a change reaches R2. It also takes another average 15 s before R3 receives the change, and so on. When the information finally reaches router Rn, $15 \times n$ s have passed. If n is 20, then this is 300 s. In this 300 s an ATM network can send more than one billion bits. If this change affects these bits, one billion bits are lost.

Figure 13.11 *Slow convergence*

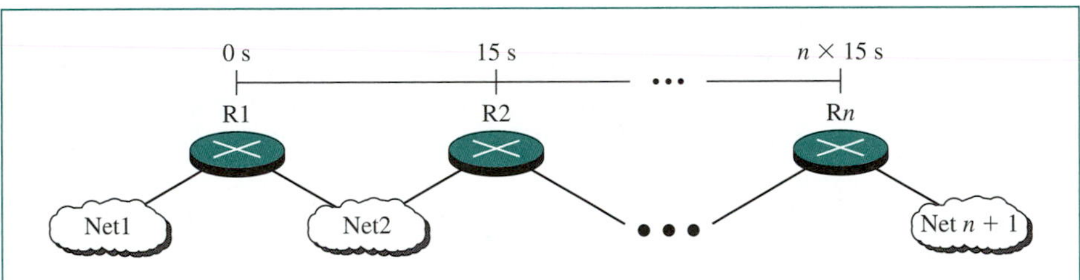

One method to deal with RIP shortcomings is to limit the hop count to 15. This prevents data packets from wandering around forever, clogging the internet. An autonomous system using RIP is limited to a diameter of 15; the number 16, therefore, is considered infinity and designates an unreachable network (see Figure 13.12).

Figure 13.12 *Hop count*

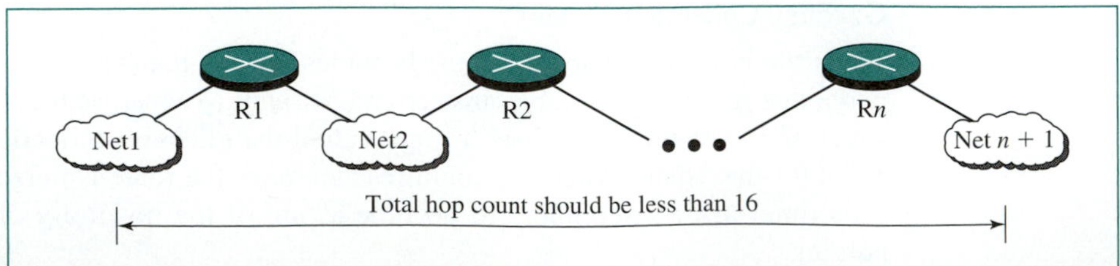

Instability

A much more important problem with RIP is instability, which means that an internet running RIP can become unstable. When this happens a packet could go from one router to another in a loop. Limiting the number of hops to 15 will improve stability but will not eliminate all of the problems.

To understand the problem, assume that the connection to Net1 in Figure 13.13 is nonfunctioning. Router A shows a cost of 1 for this network in its routing table. Router B, which can access Net1 only through router A, shows a cost of 2. When access to Net1 fails, router A immediately responds and changes the Net1 cost column to 16 (infinity). However, it may have to wait up to 30 s before it can send its update with this new information. In the meantime, it could happen that router B sends its own update message to A. Router A now has two entries for Net1: from its own table the cost is 16 and from router B the cost is 2. A is fooled into thinking that there is a backdoor access to Net1 through B. Router A then changes the cost column for Net1 to 3 (2 + 1) and this update gets sent to B. Router B's 2 cost values for Net1 are now 3 (from A) and 2 (from itself). Router B knows that Net1 is accessible only through router A so it disregards its

Figure 13.13 *Instability*

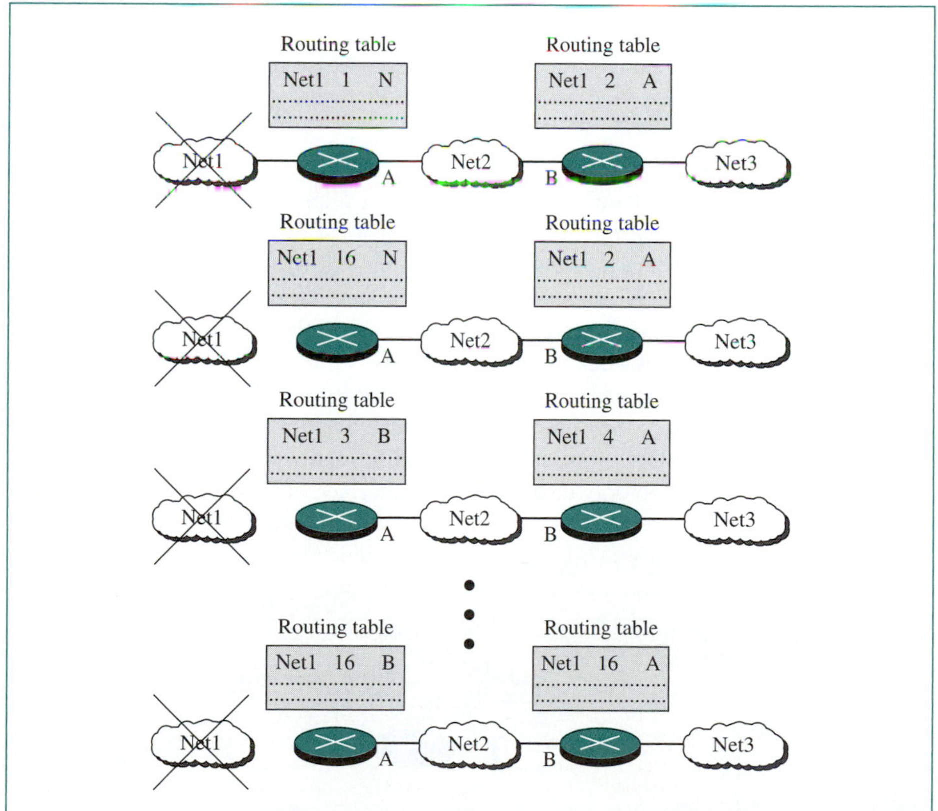

own lower cost and changes its cost to 4 (3 + 1). This back-and-forth updating continues until both routers reach a cost of 16. At this point, the routers realize there is no access to the network Net1.

Some Remedies for Instability

Some remedies have been proposed to improve the stability. However, none of them are 100 percent effective.

Triggered Update

If there are no changes on the network, updates are sent at the usual 30-s intervals. If there is a change, however, the router springs into action immediately by sending out its new table, a process called **triggered update.**

Triggered update can improve stability. Each router that receives an update with a change sends out new information at once, in considerably less time than the 15-s average. For example, in Figure 13.13, when router A realizes that Net1 is unavailable, it changes the cost to 16 in its routing table and then immediately sends this to B. Router B then changes its table, and now both tables show a cost of 16 for Net1. The sending of update messages with incremental changes in cost has been avoided as have any looping problems.

Although triggered update can vastly improve routing, it cannot solve all routing problems. For example, router failure cannot be handled by this method.

Split Horizons

Split horizons, a second method for improving stability, utilizes selectivity in the sending of routing messages; a router must distinguish between different interfaces. If a router has received route updating information from an interface, then this same updated information must not be sent back through this interface. If an interface has passed information to help update a router, this updated information must not be sent back; it is already known and thus is not needed. Figure 13.14 illustrates this concept. In this figure, router B has received information about Net1 and Net2 through its left interface; this information is updated and passed on through the right interface but not to the left. Similarly, information received by router B about Net3 is updated and passed on only through the left interface of B.

Figure 13.14 *Split horizon*

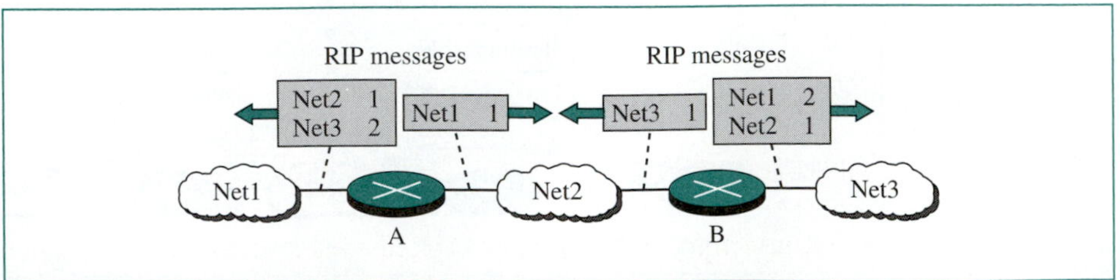

Split horizons can definitely improve stability. Assume that Net1 is inaccessible to router A in Figure 13.13. Router B receives its information about Net1 from A; it does not send information about Net1 to router A. Router A, therefore, has but one entry for the Net1 cost (16), and is not fooled into thinking that there is some back-door access to Net1. Router A sends its routing table to B and both will then end up with a cost of 16 for Net1.

Poison Reverse

Poison reverse is a variation of split horizons. In this method, information received by the router is used to update the routing table and then passed out to all interfaces. However, a table entry that has come through one interface is set to a metric of 16 as it goes out through the same interface.

Figure 13.15 illustrates this concept: Router B has received information about Net1 and Net2 through its left interface, so it sends information out about these networks with a metric of 16. Likewise, information about Net3 comes from the right interface, and the cost of Net3 in the update message going right is 16. Stability is improved using poison reverse. Assume that Net1 is inaccessible to router A in Figure 13.13. Router B receives its information about Net1 from A. In each update, B sends its routing table to A with a cost of 16 for Net1. This has no effect on A if Net1 is accessible because router A will not select B's entry for Net1. However, if Net1 does go down, both cost values are 16 and instability is thereby avoided.

Figure 13.15 *Poison reverse*

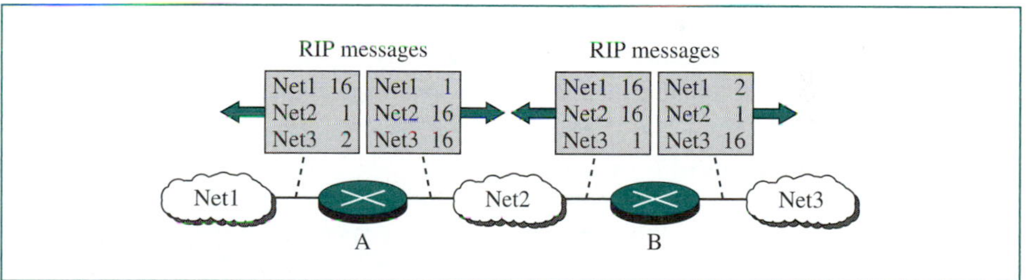

RIP Version 2

RIP version 2 was designed to overcome some of the shortcomings of version 1. The designers of version 2 have not augmented the length of the message for each entry. They have only replaced those fields in version 1 that were filled with 0s for the TCP/IP protocol with some new fields.

Message Format

Figure 13.16 shows the format of a RIP version 2 message. The new fields of this message are as follows:

- **Route Tag.** This field carries information such as the autonomous system number. It can be used to enable RIP to receive information from an exterior routing protocol.
- **Subnet mask.** This is a 4-byte field that carries the subnet mask (or prefix). This means that RIP2 supports classless addressing and CIDR.

Figure 13.16 *RIP version 2 format*

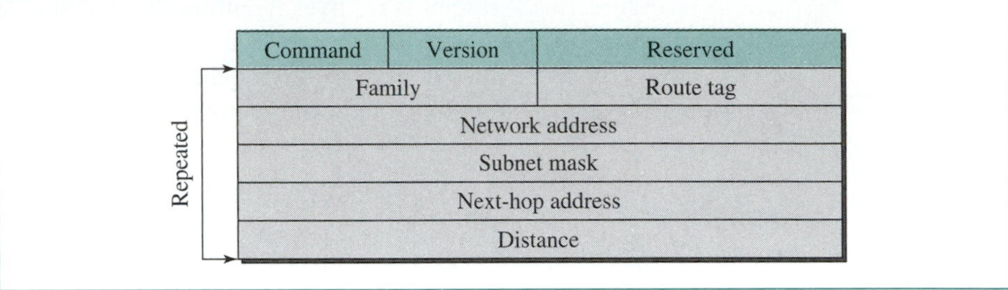

- **Next-hop address.** This field shows the address of the next hop. This is particularly useful if two autonomous systems share a network (a backbone) for example. Then the message can define the router, in the same autonomous system or other autonomous systems, to which the packet should go next.

> RIP version 2 supports CIDR.

Authentication

Authentication is added to protect the message against unauthorized advertisement. No new fields are added to the packet; instead, the first entry of the message is set aside for authentication information. To indicate that the entry is authentication information and not routing information, the value of $FFFF_{16}$ is entered in the family field (see Figure 13.17). The second field, the authentication type, defines the method used for authentication, and the third field contains the actual authentication data.

Figure 13.17 *Authentication*

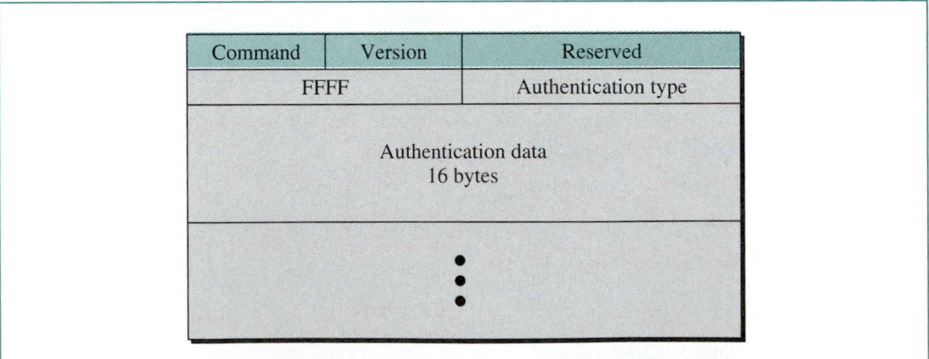

Multicasting

Version 1 of RIP uses broadcasting to send RIP messages to every neighbor. In this way, all the routers on the network receive the packets, as well as the hosts. RIP version 2, on the other hand, uses the multicast address 224.0.0.9 to multicast RIP messages only to RIP routers in the network.

Encapsulation

RIP messages are encapsulated in UDP user datagrams. A RIP message does not include a field that indicates the length of the message. This can be determined from the UDP packet. The well-known port assigned to RIP in UDP is port 520.

> RIP uses the services of UDP on well-known port 520.

13.3 OSPF

The open shortest path first (OSPF) protocol is another interior routing protocol that is gaining in popularity. Its domain is also an autonomous system. Special routers called *autonomous system boundary routers* are responsible for dissipating information about other autonomous systems into the current system. To handle routing efficiently and in a timely manner, OSPF divides an autonomous system into areas.

Areas

An **area** is a collection of networks, hosts, and routers all contained within an autonomous system. An autonomous system, in turn, can be divided into many different areas. All networks inside an area must be connected.

Routers inside an area flood the area with routing information. At the border of an area, special routers called *area border routers* summarize the information about the area and send it to other areas. Among the areas inside an autonomous system is a special area called the *backbone;* all of the areas inside an autonomous system must be connected to the backbone. In other words, the backbone serves as a primary area and the other areas as the secondary areas. This does not mean that the routers within areas cannot be connected with each other, however.

The routers inside the backbone are called the *backbone routers*. Note that a backbone router can also be an area border router.

If, due to some problem, the connectivity between a backbone and an area is broken, a *virtual link* between routers must be created by the administration to allow continuity of the functions of the backbone as the primary area.

Each area has an area identification. The area identification of the backbone is zero. Figure 13.18 shows an autonomous system and its areas.

Metric

The OSPF protocol allows the administrator to assign a cost, called the *metric,* to each route. The metric can be based on a type of service (minimum delay, maximum throughput, and so on). As a matter of fact, a router can have multiple routing tables, each based on a different type of service.

Figure 13.18 *Areas in an autonomous system*

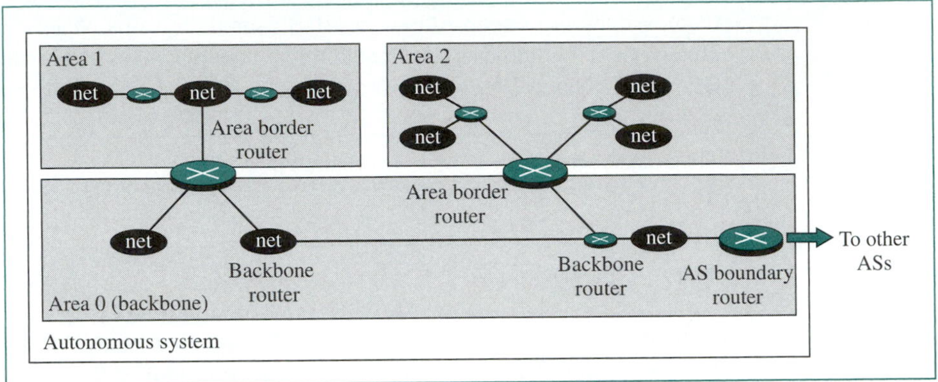

Link State Routing

OSPF uses link state routing to update the routing tables in an area. Before discussing the details of the OSPF protocol, let us discuss **link state routing,** a process by which each router shares its knowledge about its neighborhood with every router in the area. The three keys to understanding how this method works are as follows:

1. **Sharing knowledge about the neighborhood.** Each router sends the *state of its neighborhood* to every other router in the area.
2. **Sharing with every other router.** Each router sends the state of its neighborhood to *every other router in the area.* It does so by **flooding,** a process whereby a router sends its information to all of its neighbors (through all of its output ports). Each neighbor sends the packet to all of its neighbors, and so on. Every router that receives the packet sends copies to each of its neighbors. Eventually, every router (without exception) has received a copy of the same information.
3. **Sharing when there is a change.** Each router shares the state of its neighborhood only when there is a change. This rule contrasts with distance vector routing, where information is sent out at regular intervals regardless of change. This characteristic results in lower internet traffic than that required by distance vector routing.

The idea behind link state routing is that each router should have the exact topology of the internet at every moment. In other words, every router should have the whole "picture" of the internet. From this topology, a router can calculate the shortest path between itself and each network. The topology here means a graph consisting of nodes and edges. To represent an internet by a graph, however, we need more definitions.

Types of Links

In OSPF terminology, a connection is called a *link.* Four types of links have been defined: point-to-point, transient, stub, and virtual (see Figure 13.19).

Point-to-Point Link A point-to-point link connects two routers without any other host or router in between. In other words, the purpose of the link (network) is just to connect the two routers. An example of this type of link is two routers connected by a

Figure 13.19 *Types of links*

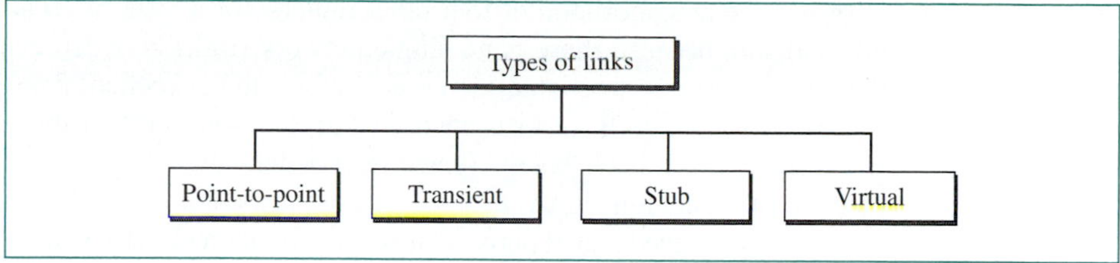

telephone line or a T-line. There is no need to assign a network address to this type of link. Graphically, the routers are represented by nodes, and the link is represented by a bidirectional edge connecting the nodes. The metrics, which are usually the same, are shown at the two ends, one for each direction. In other words, each router has only one neighbor at the other side of the link (see Figure 13.20).

Figure 13.20 *Point-to-point link*

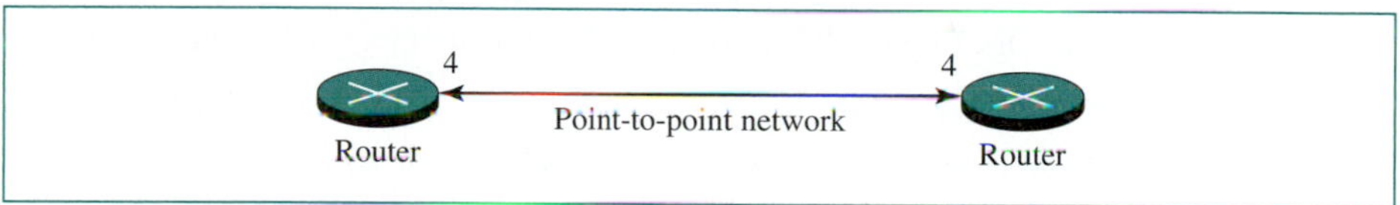

Transient Link A transient link is a network with several routers attached to it. The data can enter through any of the routers and leave through any router. All LANs and some WANs with two or more routers are of this type. In this case, each router has many neighbors. For example, consider the Ethernet in Figure 13.21a. Router A has routers B, C, D, and E as neighbors. Router B has routers A, C, D, and E as neighbors. If we want to show the neighborhood relationship in this situation, we have the graph shown in Figure 13.21b.

Figure 13.21 *Transient link*

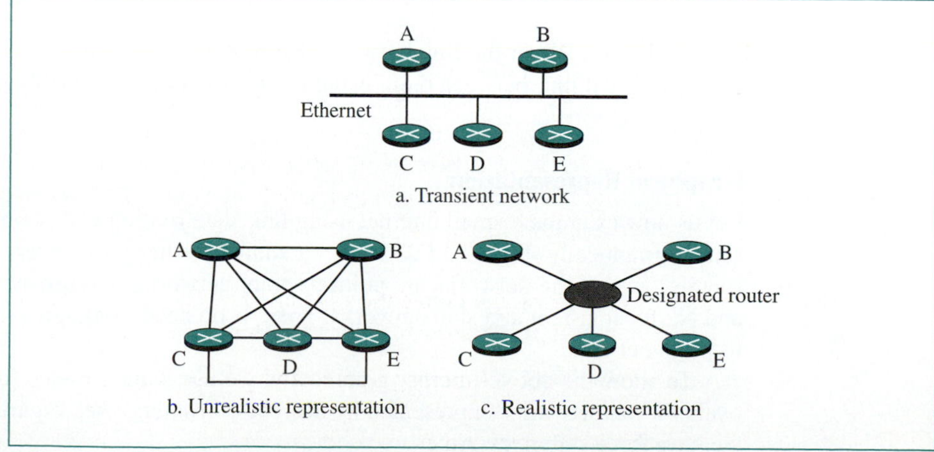

This is neither efficient nor realistic. It is not efficient because each router needs to advertise the neighborhood of four other routers, for a total of 20 advertisements. It is not realistic, because there is no single network (link) between each pair of routers; there is only one network that serves as a crossroad between all five routers.

To show that each router is connected to every other router through one single network, the network itself is represented by a node. However, because a network is not a machine, it cannot function as a router. One of the routers in the network takes this responsibility. It is assigned a dual purpose; it is a true router and a designated router. We can use the topology shown in Figure 13.21c to show the connections of a transient network.

Now each router has only one neighbor, the designated router (network). On the other hand, the designated router (the network) has five neighbors. We see that the number of neighbor announcements is reduced from 20 to 10. Still, the link is represented as a bidirectional edge between the nodes. However, while there is a metric from each node to the designated router, there is no metric from the designated router to any other node. The reason is that the designated router represents the network. We can only assign a cost to a packet that is passing through the network. We cannot charge for this twice. When a packet enters a network, we assign a cost; when a packet leaves the network to go to the router, there is no charge.

Stub Link A stub link is a network that is connected to only one router. The data packets enter the network through this single router and leave the network through this same router. This is a special case of the transient network. We can show this situation using the router as a node and using the designated router for the network. However, the link is only one-directional, from the router to the network (see Figure 13.22).

Figure 13.22 *Stub link*

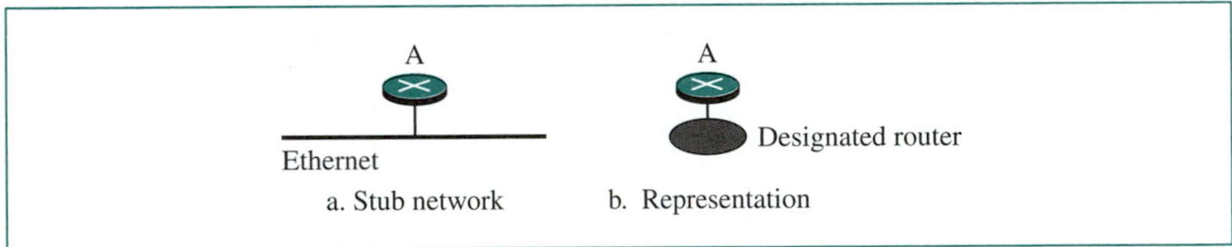

Virtual Link When the link between two routers is broken, the administration may create a virtual link between them using a longer path that probably goes through several routers.

Graphical Representation

Let us now examine a small internet using link state routing and see how we can represent it graphically. Figure 13.23 shows a small internet with seven networks and six routers. Two of the networks are point-to-point networks. We use symbols such as N1 and N2 for transient and stub networks. There is no need to assign a number to a point-to-point network.

To show the above internet graphically, we use square nodes for the routers and ovals for the networks (represented by designated routers); see Figure 13.24. Note that we have three stub networks.

Figure 13.23 *Example of an internet*

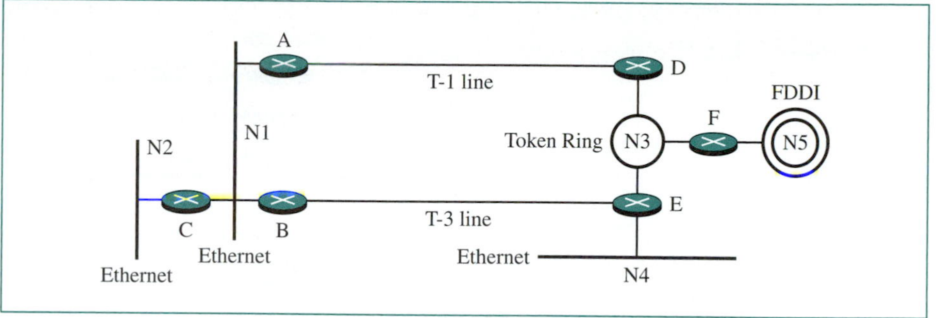

Figure 13.24 *Graphical representation of an internet*

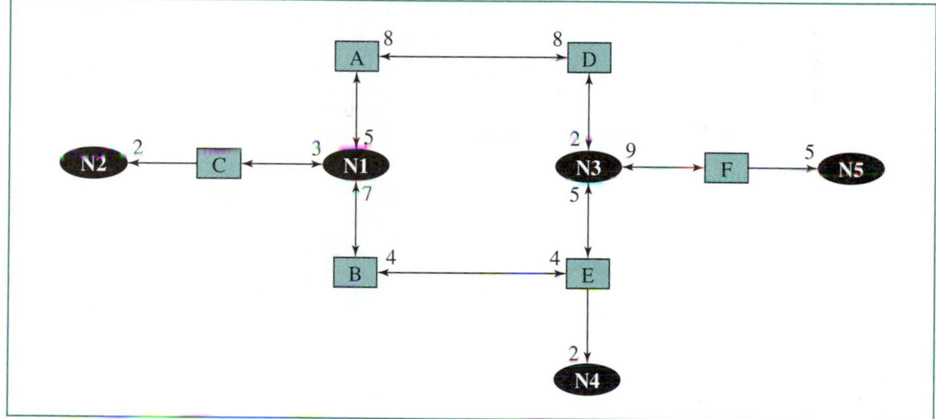

Link State Advertisements

To share information about their neighbors, each entity distributes Link State Advertisements (LSAs). An LSA announces the states of entity links. Depending on the type of entity, we can define five different LSAs (see Figure 13.25).

Figure 13.25 *Types of LSAs*

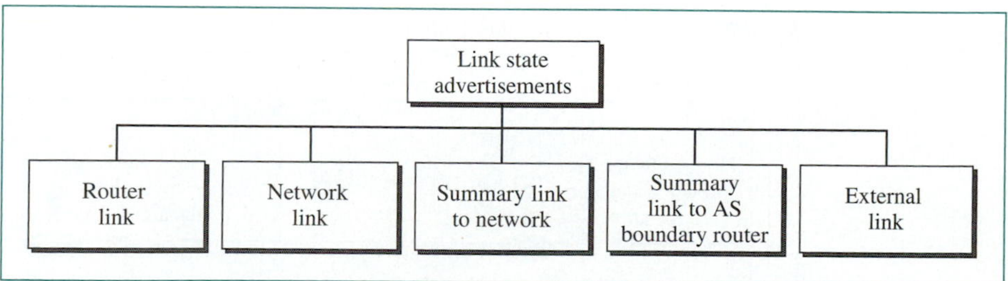

Router Link A router link defines the links of a true router. A true router uses this advertisement to announce information about all of its links and what is at the other side of the link (neighbors). See Figure 13.26 for a depiction of a router link.

Figure 13.26 *Router link*

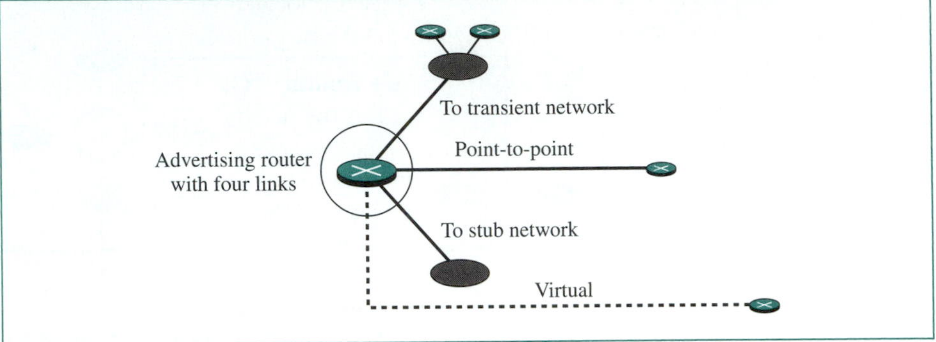

Network Link A network link defines the links of a network. A designated router, on behalf of the transient network, distributes this type of LSA packet. The packet announces the existence of all of the routers connected to the network (see Figure 13.27).

Figure 13.27 *Network link*

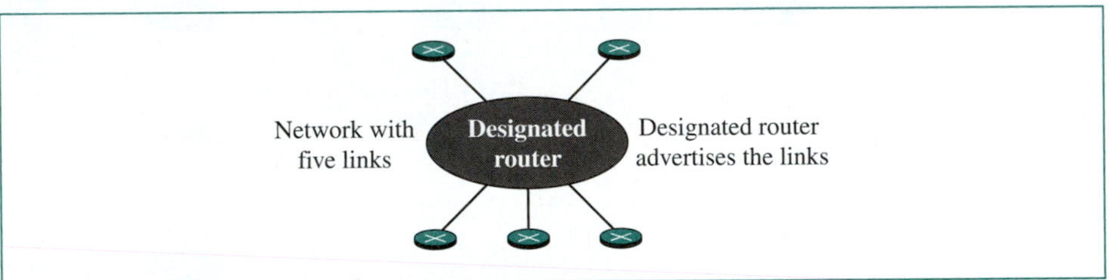

Summary Link to Network Router link and network link advertisements flood the area with information about the router links and network links inside an area. But a router must also know about the networks outside its area, and the area border routers can provide this information. An area border router is active in more than one area. It receives router link and network link advertisements, and, as we will see, creates a routing table for each area. For example, in Figure 13.28, router R1 is an area border router.

Figure 13.28 *Summary link to network*

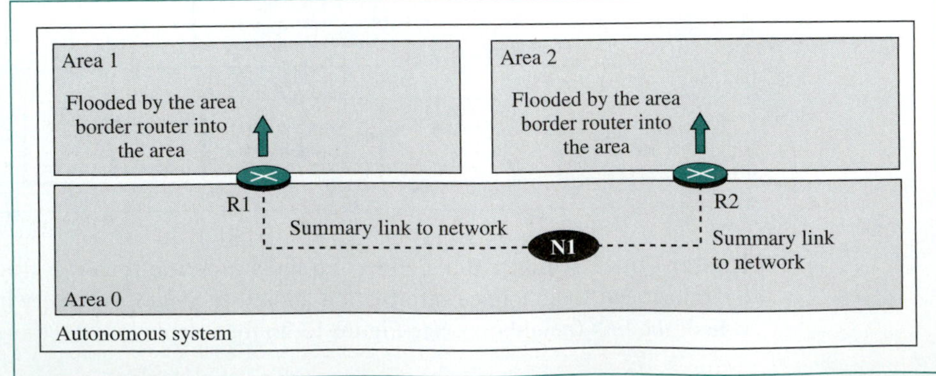

It has two routing tables, one for area 1 and one for area 0. R1 floods area 1 with information about how to reach a network located in area 0. In the same way, router R2 floods area 2 with information about how to reach the same network in area 0.

Summary Link to AS Boundary Router The previous advertisement lets every router know the cost to reach all of the networks inside the autonomous system. But what about a network outside the autonomous system? If a router inside an area wants to send a packet outside the autonomous system, it should first know the route to an autonomous boundary router; the summary link to AS boundary router provides this information. The area border routers flood their areas with this information (see Figure 13.29).

Figure 13.29 *Summary link to AS boundary router*

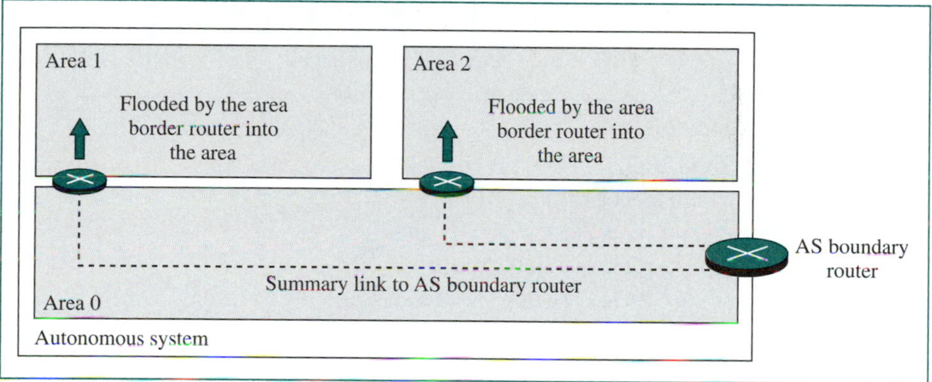

External Link Although the previous advertisement lets each router know the route to an AS boundary router, this information is not enough. A router inside an autonomous system wants to know which networks are available outside the autonomous system; the external link advertisement provides this information. The AS boundary router floods the autonomous system with the cost of each network outside the autonomous system using a routing table created by an exterior routing protocol. Each advertisement announces one single network. If there is more than one network, separate announcements are made. Figure 13.30 depicts an external link.

Figure 13.30 *External link*

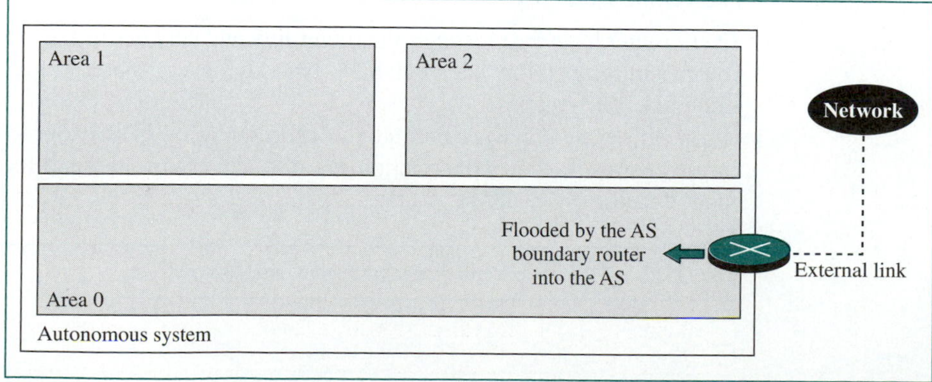

Example 3

In Figure 13.31, which router(s) sends out router link LSAs?

Figure 13.31 *Example 3 and Example 4*

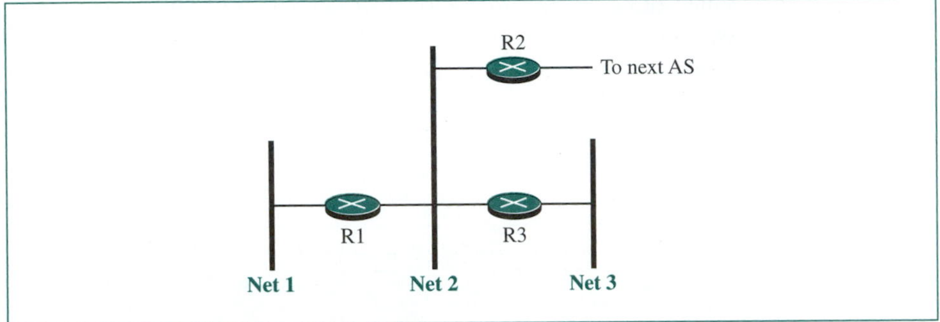

Solution

All routers advertise router link LSAs.

a. R1 has two links, Net1 and Net2.

b. R2 has one link, Net1 in this AS.

c. R3 has two links, Net2 and Net3.

Example 4

In Figure 13.31, which router(s) sends out the network link LSAs?

Solution

All three network must advertise network links:

a. Advertisement for Net1 is done by R1 because it is the only router and therefore the designated router.

b. Advertisement for Net2 can be done by either R1, R2, or R3, depending on which one is chosen as the designated router.

c. Advertisement for Net3 is done by R3 because it is the only router and therefore the designated router.

Link State Database

Every router in an area receives the router link and network link LSAs from every other router and forms a link state database. Note that every router in the same area has the same link state database.

A link state database is a tabular representation of the topology of the internet inside an area. It shows the relationship between each router and its neighbors including the metrics.

> In OSPF, all routers have the same link state database.

Dijkstra Algorithm

To calculate its routing table, each router applies the Dijkstra algorithm to its link state database. The **Dijkstra algorithm** calculates the shortest path between two points on a network using a graph made up of nodes and edge. The algorithm divides the nodes into two sets: tentative and permanent. It chooses nodes, makes them tentative, examines them, and if they pass the criteria, makes them permanent. We can informally define the algorithm using the following steps:

Dijkstra Algorithm
1. Start with the local node (router): the root of the tree.
2. Assign a cost of 0 to this node and make it the first permanent node.
3. Examine each neighbor node of the node that was the last permanent node.
4. Assign a cumulative cost to each node and make it tentative.
5. Among the list of tentative nodes
1. Find the node with the smallest cumulative cost and make it permanent.
2. If a node can be reached from more than one direction
1. Select the direction with the shortest cumulative cost.
6. Repeat steps 3 to 5 until every node becomes permanent.

Figure 13.32 shows the steps of the Dijkstra algorithm applied to node A of our sample internet in Figure 13.24. The number next to each node represents the cumulative cost from the root node. Note that in step h, network N3 is reached through two directions with cumulative costs of 14 and 10. The direction with the cumulative cost of 10 is kept and the other one is deleted.

Routing Table

Each router uses the shortest path tree method to construct its routing table. The routing table shows the cost of reaching each network in the area. To find the cost of reaching networks outside of the area, the routers use the summary link to network, the summary link to boundary router, and the external link advertisements. Table 13.2 shows the routing table for router A.

Table 13.2 *Link state routing table for router A*

Network	*Cost*	*Next Router*	*Other Information*
N1	5		
N2	7	C	
N3	10	D	
N4	11	B	
N5	15	D	

Figure 13.32 *Shortest path calculation*

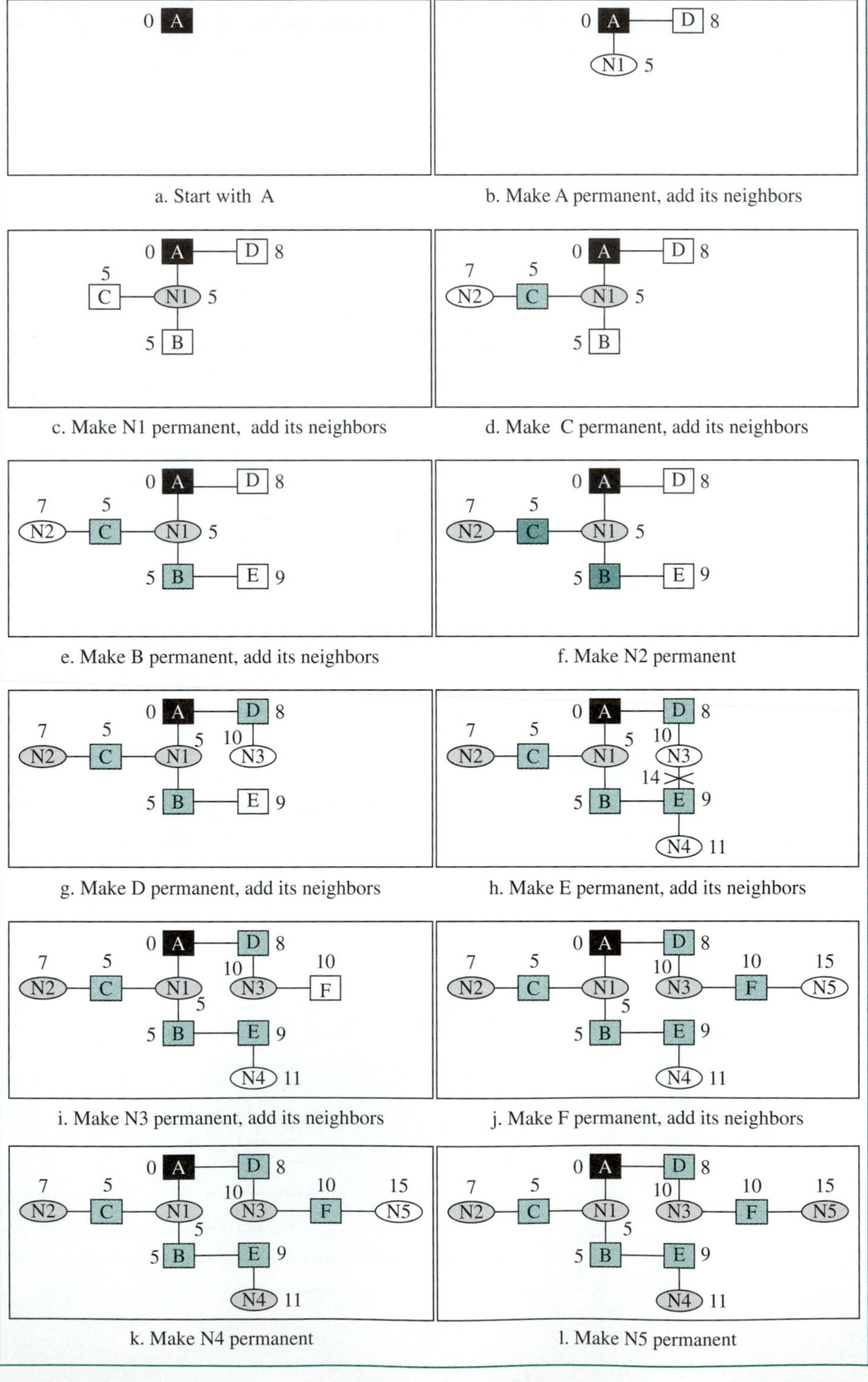

Types of Packets

OSPF uses five different types of packets: the hello packet, database description packet, link state request packet, link state update packet, and link state acknowledgment packet (see Figure 13.33).

Figure 13.33 *Types of OSPF packets*

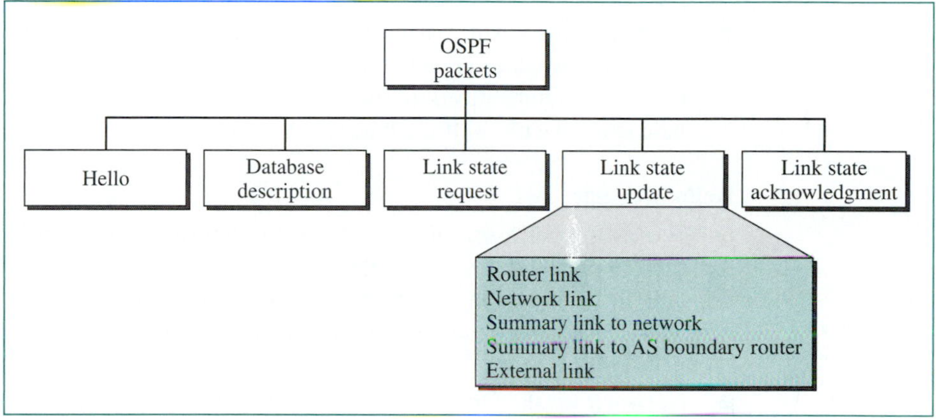

Packet Format

All OSPF packets share the same common header (see Figure 13.34). Before studying the different types of packets, let us talk about this common header.

- **Version.** This 8-bit field defines the version of the OSPF protocol. It is currently version 2.
- **Type.** This 8-bit field defines the type of the packet. As we said before, we have five types, with values 1 to 5 defining the types.
- **Message length.** This 16-bit field defines the length of the total message including the header.
- **Source router IP address.** This 32-bit field defines the IP address of the router that sends the packet.

Figure 13.34 *OSPF packet header*

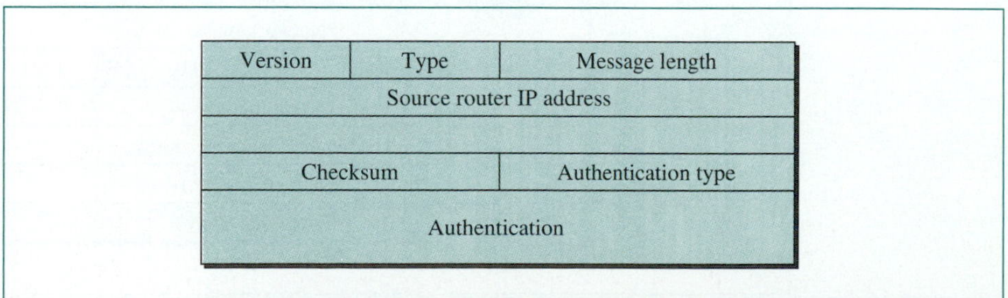

- **Area identification.** This 32-bit field defines the area within which the routing takes place.
- **Checksum.** This field is used for error detection on the entire packet excluding the authentication type and authentication data field.
- **Authentication type.** This 16-bit field defines the authentication method used in this area. At this time, two types of authentication are defined: 0 for none and 1 for password.
- **Authentication.** This 64-bit field is the actual value of the authentication data. In the future, when more authentication types are defined, this field will contain the result of the authentication calculation. For now, if the authentication type is 0, this field is filled with 0s. If the type is 1, this field carries an eight-character password.

Hello Message

OSPF uses the hello message to create neighborhood relationships and to test the reachability of neighbors. This is the first step in link state routing. Before a router can flood all of the other routers with information about its neighbors, it must first greet its neighbors. It must know if they are alive, and it must know if they are reachable (see Figure 13.35).

- **Network mask.** This 32-bit field defines the network mask of the network over which the hello message is sent.
- **Hello interval.** This 16-bit field defines the number of seconds between hello messages.
- **E flag.** This is a 1-bit flag. When it is set, it means that the area is a stub area.
- **T flag.** This is a 1-bit flag. When it is set, it means that the router supports multiple metrics.
- **Priority.** This field defines the priority of the router. The priority is used for the selection of the designated router. After all neighbors declare their priorities, the router with the highest priority is chosen as the designated router. The one with the second highest priority is chosen as the backup designated router. If the value

Figure 13.35 *Hello packet*

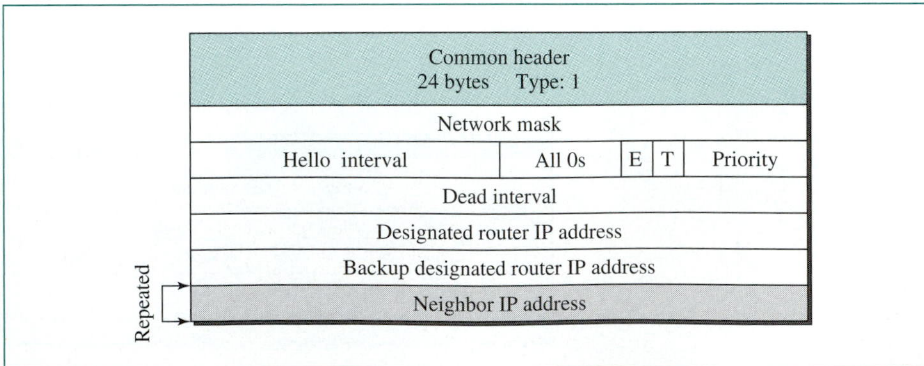

of this field is 0, it means that the router never wants to be a designated or backup designated router.

- **Dead interval.** This 32-bit field defines the number of seconds before a router assumes that a neighbor is dead.
- **Designated router IP address.** This 32-bit field is the IP address of the designated router for the network over which the message is sent.
- **Backup designated router IP address.** This 32-bit field is the IP address of the backup designated router for the network over which the message is sent.
- **Neighbor IP address.** This is a repeated 32-bit field that defines the routers that have agreed to be the neighbors of the sending router. In other words, it is a current list of all the neighbors from which the sending router has received the hello message.

Database Description Message

When a router is connected to the system for the first time or after a failure, it needs the complete link state database immediately. It cannot wait for all link state update packets to come from every other router before making its own database and calculating its routing table. Therefore, after a router is connected to the system, it sends hello packets to greet its neighbors. If this is the first time that the neighbors hear from the router, they send a database description packet. The database description packet does not contain complete database information; it only gives an outline, the title of each line in the database. The newly connected router examines the outline and finds out which lines of information it does not have. It then sends one or more link state request packets to get full information about that particular link. When two routers want to exchange database description packets, one of them takes the role of master and the other the role of slave. Because the message can be very long, the contents of the database can be divided into several messages. The format of the database description packet is shown in Figure 13.36. The fields are as follows:

- **E flag.** This 1-bit flag is set to 1 if the advertising router is an autonomous boundary router (*E* stands for external).
- **B flag.** This 1-bit flag is set to 1 if the advertising router is an area border router.

Figure 13.36 *Database description packet*

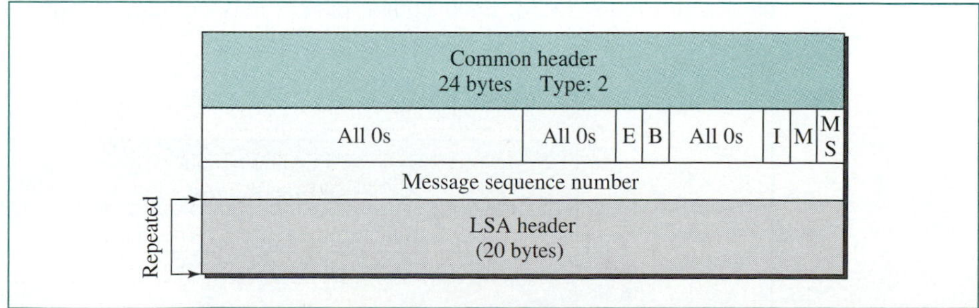

- **I flag.** This 1-bit field, the *initialization* flag, is set to 1 if the message is the first message.
- **M flag.** This 1-bit field, the *more* flag, is set to 1 if this is not the last message.
- **M/S flag.** This 1-bit field, the *master/slave* bit, indicates the origin of the packet: master (M/S = 1) or slave (M/S = 0).
- **Message sequence number.** This 32-bit field contains the sequence number of the message. It is used to match a request with the response.
- **LSA header.** This 20-byte field is used in each LSA. The format of this header is discussed in the link state update message section. This header gives the outline of each link, without details. It is repeated for each link in the link state database.

Link State Request Packet

The format of the link state request packet is shown in Figure 13.37. This is a packet that is sent by a router that needs information about a specific route or routes. It is answered with a link state update packet. It can be used by a newly connected router to request more information about some routes after receiving the database description packet. The three fields here are part of the LSA header which we will see shortly. Each set of the three fields is a request for one single LSA. The set is repeated if more than one advertisement is desired.

Figure 13.37 *Link state request packet*

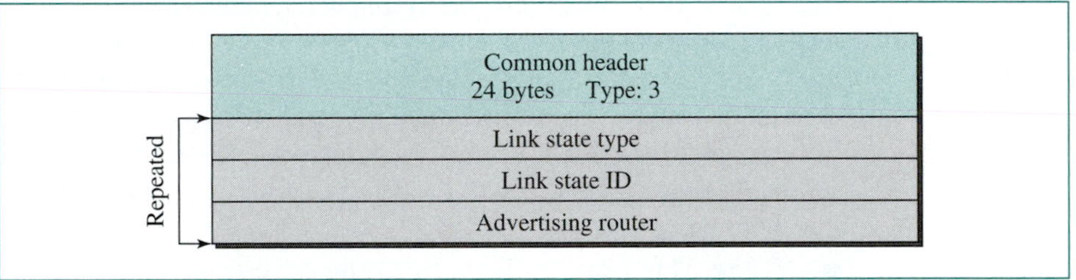

Link State Update Packet

The link state update packet is the heart of the OSPF operation. It is used by a router to advertise the states of its links. The general format of the link state update packet is shown in Figure 13.38. Each update packet may contain several different LSAs. For

Figure 13.38 *Link state update packet*

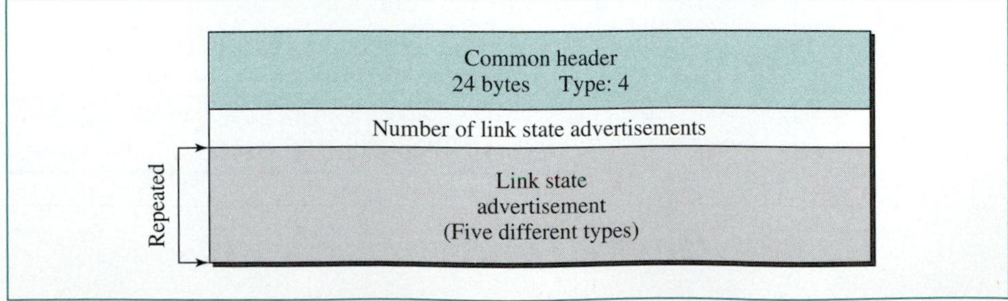

example, a link state update packet can contain 14 LSAs, four of which are router link advertisements, three of which are network link advertisements, two of which are summary link to network advertisements, two of which are summary link to AS boundary router advertisements, and three of which are external link advertisements. The fields are as follows:

- **Number of advertisements.** This 32-bit field defines the number of advertisements. One packet can advertise the states of several links.
- **Link state advertisements.** There are five different LSAs, as we discussed before, all having the same header format, but different bodies. We first discuss the general header common to all of them. The format of the LSA header is shown in Figure 13.39.

Figure 13.39 *LSA header*

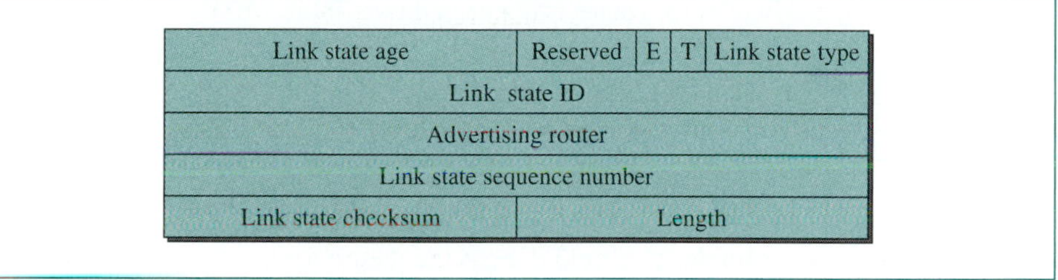

- **Link state age.** This field indicates the number of seconds elapsed since this message was first generated. Recall that this type of message goes from router to router (flooding). When a router creates the message, the value of this field is 0. When each successive router forwards this message, it estimates the transit time and adds it to the cumulative value of this field.
- **E flag.** If this 1-bit flag is set to 1, it means that the area is a stub area. A stub area is an area that is connected to the backbone area by only one path.
- **T flag.** If this 1-bit flag is set to 1, it means that the router can handle multiple types of service.
- **Link state type.** This field defines the LSA type. As we discussed before, there are five different advertisement types: router link (1), network link (2), summary link to network (3), summary link to AS boundary router (4), and external link (5).
- **Link state ID.** The value of this field depends on the type of link. For type 1 (router link), it is the IP address of the router. For type 2 (network link), it is the IP address of the designated router. For type 3 (summary link to network), it is the address of the network. For type 4 (summary link to AS boundary router), it is the IP address of the AS boundary router. For type 5 (external link), it is the address of the external network.
- **Advertising router.** This is the IP address of the router advertising this message.
- **Link state sequence number.** This is a sequence number assigned to each link state update message.

- **Link state checksum.** This is not the usual checksum field. It uses a special checksum calculation called *Fletcher's checksum,* which is based on the whole packet except for the age field.
- **Length.** This defines the length of the whole packet in bytes.

Router Link LSA The router link LSA advertises all of the links of a router (true router). The format of the router link packet is shown in Figure 13.40. The fields of the router link LSA are as follows:

- **Link ID.** The value of this field depends on the type of link. Table 13.3 shows the different link identifications based on link type.
- **Link data.** This field gives additional information about the link. Again, the value depends on the type of the link (see Table 13.3).
- **Link type.** Four different types of links are defined based on the type of network to which the router is connected (see Table 13.3).
- **Number of types of service (TOS).** This field defines the number of types of services announced for each link.
- **Metric for TOS 0.** This field defines the metric for the default type of service (TOS 0).
- **TOS.** This field defines the type of service.
- **Metric.** This field defines the metric for the corresponding TOS.

Figure 13.40 *Router link LSA*

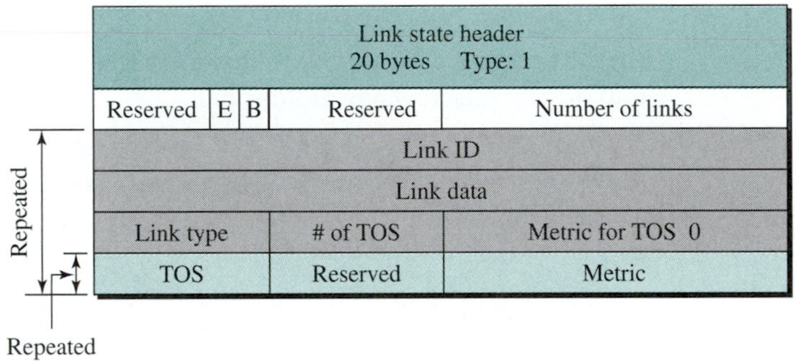

Table 13.3 *Link types, link identification, and link data*

Link Type	*Link Identification*	*Link Data*
Type 1: Point-to-point connection to another router	Address of neighbor router	Interface number
Type 2: Connection to any-to-any network	Address of designated router	Router address
Type 3: Connection to stub network	Network address	Network mask
Type 4: Virtual link	Address of neighbor router	Router address

Example 5

Give the router link LSA sent by router 10.24.7.9 in Figure 13.41.

Figure 13.41 *Example 5*

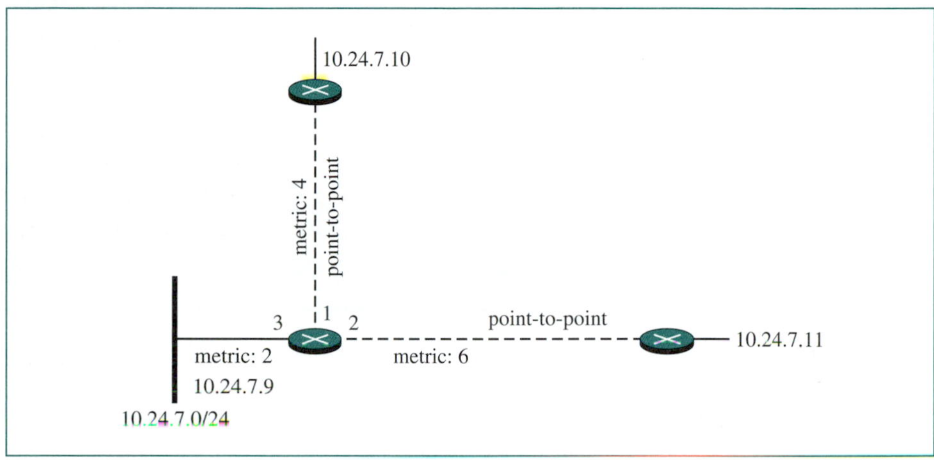

Solution

This router has three links: two of type 1 (point-to-point) and one of type 3 (stub network). Figure 13.42 shows the router link LSA.

Figure 13.42 *Solution to Example 5*

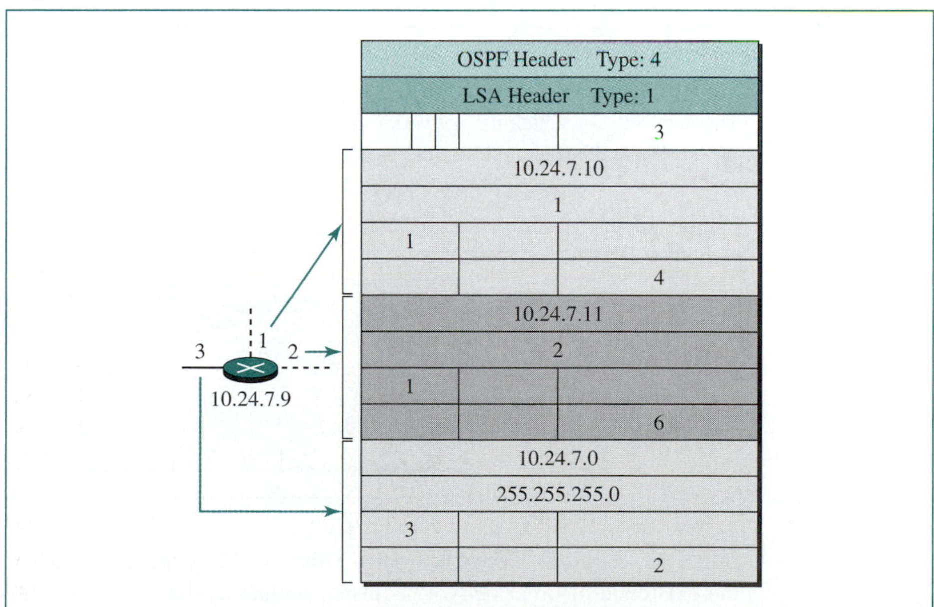

Network Link LSA The network link advertisement announces the links connected to a network. The format of the network link advertisement is shown in Figure 13.43. The fields of the network link LSA are as follows:

- **Network mask.** This field defines the network mask.
- **Attached router.** This repeated field defines the IP addresses of all attached routers.

Figure 13.43 *Network link advertisement format*

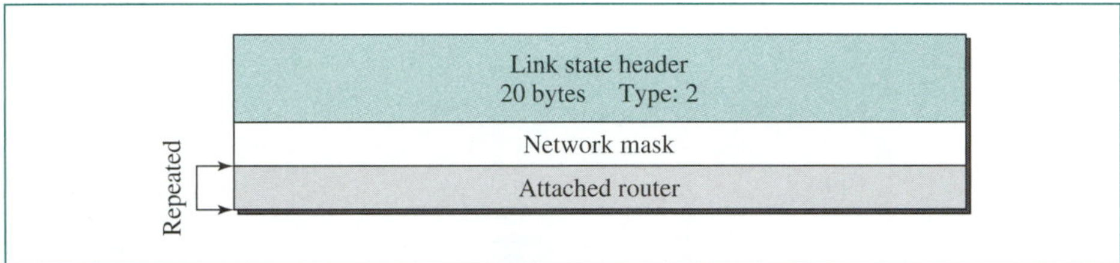

Example 6

Give the network link LSA in Figure 13.44.

Figure 13.44 *Example 6*

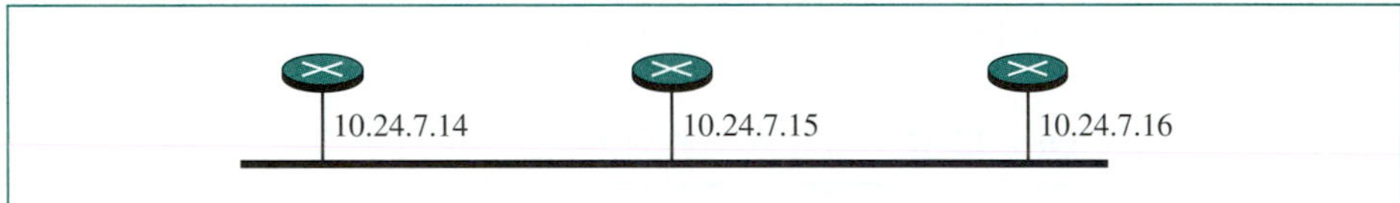

Solution

The network, for which the network link advertises, has three routers attached. The LSA shows the mask and the router addresses. Figure 13.45 shows the network link LSA.

Figure 13.45 *Solution to Example 6*

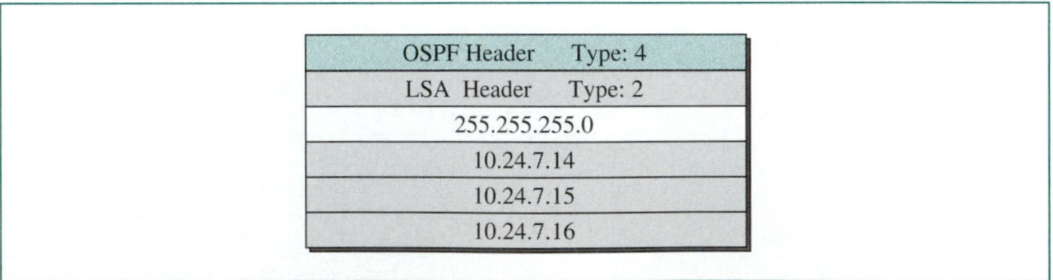

Summary Link to Network LSA This is used by the area border router to announce the existence of other networks outside the area. The summary link to network advertisement is very simple. It consists of the network mask and the metric for each type of service. Note that each advertisement announces only one single network. If there is more than one network, a separate advertisement must be issued for each. The reader may ask why only the mask of the network is advertised. What about the network address itself? The IP address of the advertising router is announced in the header of the link state advertisement. From this information and the mask, one can deduce the network address. The format of this advertisement is shown in Figure 13.46. The fields of the summary link to network LSA are as follows:

Figure 13.46 *Summary link to network LSA*

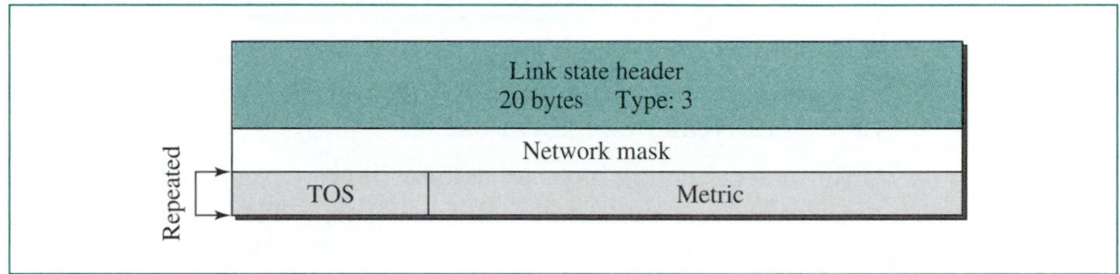

- **Network mask.** This field defines the network mask.
- **TOS.** This field defines the type of service.
- **Metric.** This field defines the metric for the type of service defined in the TOS field.

Summary Link to AS Boundary Router LSA This packet is used to announce the route to an AS boundary router. Its format is the same as the previous summary link. The packet just defines the network to which the AS boundary router is attached. If a message can reach the network, it can be picked up by the AS boundary router. The format of the packet is shown in Figure 13.47. The fields are the same as the fields in the summary link to network advertisement message.

Figure 13.47 *Summary link to AS boundary router LSA*

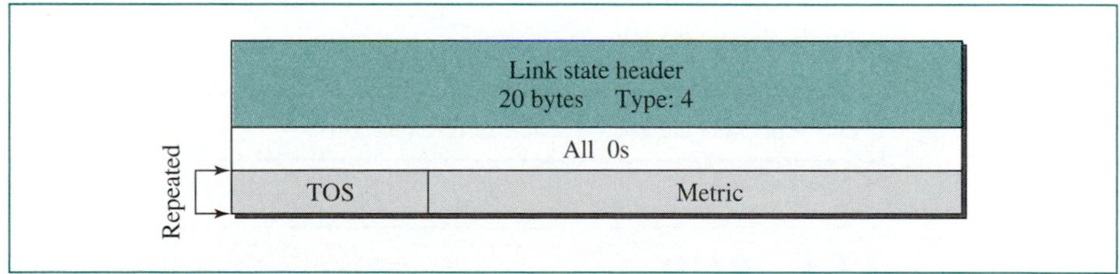

External Link LSA This is used to announce all the networks outside the AS. The format of the LSA is similar to the summary link to AS boundary router LSA, with the addition of two fields. The AS boundary router may define a forwarding router that can provide a better route to the destination. The packet also can include an external route tag, used by other protocols, but not by OSPF. The format of the packet is shown in Figure 13.48.

Figure 13.48 *External link LSA*

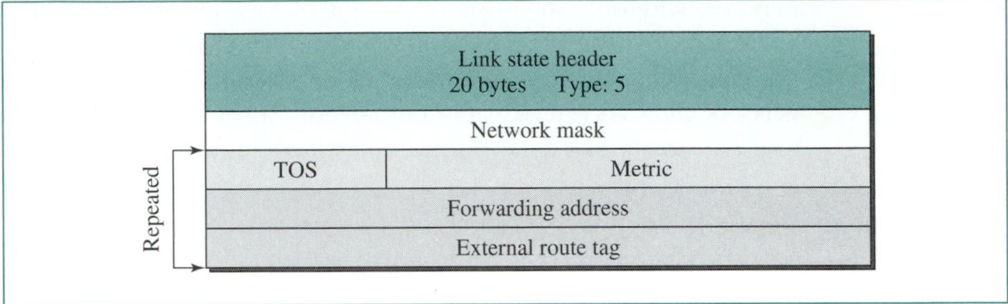

Link State Acknowledgment Packet

OSPF makes routing more reliable by forcing every router to acknowledge the receipt of every link state update packet. The format of the link state acknowledgment packet is shown in Figure 13.49. It has the common OSPF header and the generic link state update header. These two sections are sufficient to acknowledge a packet.

Figure 13.49 *Link state acknowledgment packet*

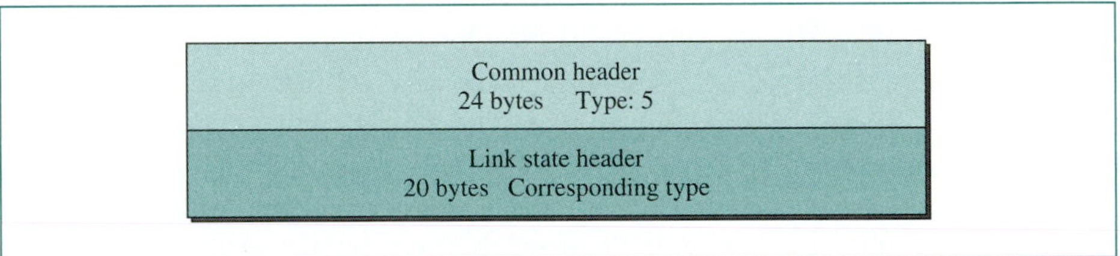

Encapsulation

OSPF packets are encapsulated in IP datagrams. They contain the acknowledgment mechanism for flow and error control. They do not need a transport layer protocol to provide these services.

> OSPF packets are encapsulated in IP datagrams.

13.4 BGP

Border Gateway Protocol (BGP) is an inter-autonomous system routing protocol. It first appeared in 1989 and has gone through four versions. BGP is based on a routing method called *path vector routing*. However, before describing the principle behind path vector routing, let us see why the two previously discussed methods—namely, distance vector routing and link state routing—are not good candidates for inter-autonomous system routing.

Distance vector is not a good candidate because there are occasions in which the route with the smallest hop count is not the preferred route. For example, we may not want a packet to pass through an autonomous system that is not secure even though it is the shortest route. Also, distance vector routing is unstable due to the fact that the routers announce only the number of hop counts to the destination without actually defining the path that leads to that destination. A router that receives a distance vector advertisement packet may be fooled if the shortest path is actually calculated through the receiving router itself.

Link state routing is also not a good candidate for inter-autonomous system routing because an internet is usually too big for this routing method. To use link state routing for the whole internet would require each router to have a huge link state database. It would also take a long time for each router to calculate its routing table using the Dijkstra algorithm.

Path Vector Routing

Path vector routing is different from both distance vector routing and link state routing. Each entry in the routing table contains the destination network, the next router, and the path to reach the destination. The path is usually defined as an ordered list of autonomous systems that a packet should travel through to reach the destination. Table 13.4 shows an example of a path vector routing table.

Table 13.4 *Path vector routing table*

Network	*Next Router*	*Path*
N01	R01	AS14, AS23, AS67
N02	R05	AS22, AS67, AS05, AS89
N03	R06	AS67, AS89, AS09, AS34
N04	R12	AS62, AS02, AS09

Path Vector Messages

The autonomous boundary routers that participate in path vector routing advertise the reachability of the networks in their own autonomous systems to neighbor autonomous boundary routers. The concept of neighborhood here is the same as the one described in the RIP or OSPF protocol. Two autonomous boundary routers connected to the same network are neighbors.

We should mention here that an autonomous boundary router receives its information from an interior routing algorithm such as RIP or OSPF.

Each router that receives a path vector message verifies that the advertised path is in agreement with its policy (a set of rules imposed by the administrator controlling the routes). If it is, the router updates its routing table and modifies the message before sending it to the next neighbor. The modification consists of adding its AS number to the path and replacing the next router entry with its own identification.

For example, Figure 13.50 shows an internet with four autonomous systems. The router R1 sends a path vector message advertising the reachability of N1. Router R2 receives the message, updates its routing table, and after adding its autonomous system to the path and inserting itself as the next router, sends the message to router R3. Router R3

Figure 13.50 *Path vector packets*

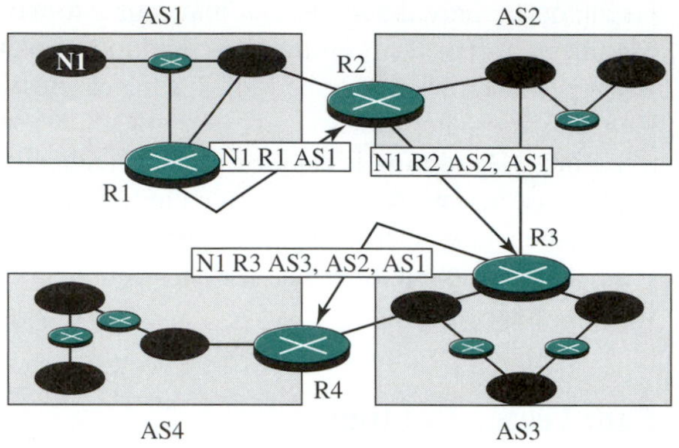

receives the message, updates its routing table, and sends the message, after changes, to router R4.

Loop Prevention

The instability of distance vector routing and the creation of loops can be avoided in path vector routing. When a router receives a message, it checks to see if its autonomous system is in the path list to the destination. If it is, looping is involved and the message is ignored.

Policy Routing

Policy routing can be easily implemented through path vector routing. When a router receives a message, it can check the path. If one of the autonomous systems listed in the path is against its policy, it can ignore that path and that destination. It does not update its routing table with this path, and it does not send this message to its neighbors. This means that the routing tables in path vector routing are not based on the smallest hop count or the minimum metric; they are based on the policy imposed on the router by the administrator.

Path Attributes

In our previous example, we discussed a path for a destination network. The path was presented as a list of autonomous systems, but is, in fact, a list of attributes. Each attribute gives some information about the path. The list of attributes helps the receiving router make a better decision when applying its policy.

Attributes are divided into two broad categories: well-known and optional. A *well-known attribute* is one that every BGP router should recognize. An *optional attribute* is one that need not be recognized by every router.

Well-known attributes are themselves divided into two categories: mandatory and discretionary. A *well-known mandatory attribute* is one that must appear in the description of a route. A *well-known discretionary attribute* is one that must be recognized by each router, but is not required to be included in every update message. One well-known mandatory attribute is ORIGIN. This defines the source of the routing information (RIP, OSPF, and so on). Another well-known mandatory attribute is AS_PATH. This defines the list of autonomous systems through which the destination can be reached. Still another well-known mandatory attribute is NEXT-HOP, which defines the next router to which the data packet should be sent.

The optional attributes can also be subdivided into two categories: transitive and nontransitive. An *optional transitive attribute* is one that must be passed to the next router by the router that has not implemented this attribute. An *optional nontransitive attribute* is one that should be discarded if the receiving router has not implemented it.

Types of Packets

BGP uses four different types of messages: open, update, keepalive, and notification (see Figure 13.51).

Figure 13.51 *Types of BGP messages*

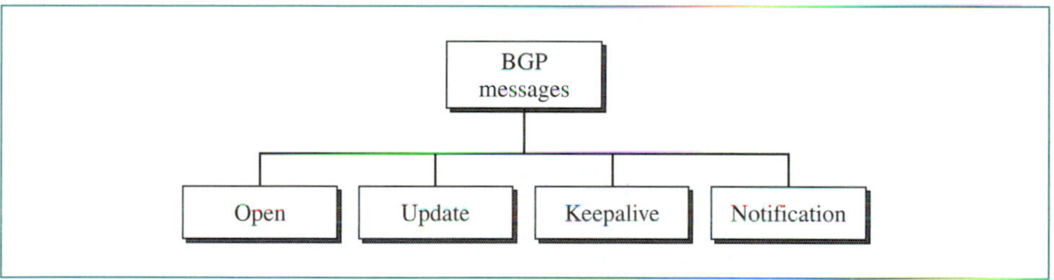

Packet Format

All BGP packets share the same common header. Before studying the different types of packets, let us talk about this common header (see Figure 13.52). The fields of this

Figure 13.52 *BGP packet header*

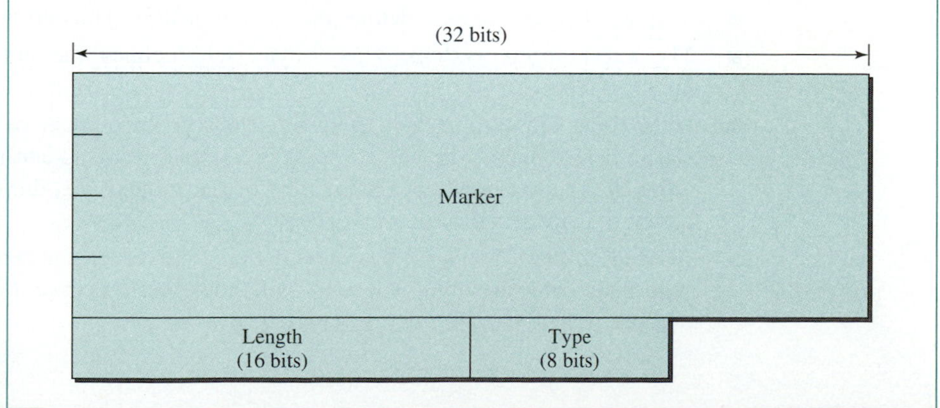

header are as follows:

- **Marker.** The 16-byte marker field is reserved for authentication.
- **Length.** This 2-byte field defines the length of the total message including the header.
- **Type.** This 1-byte field defines the type of the packet. As we said before, we have four types, and the values of 1 to 4 define those types.

Open Message

To create a neighborhood relationship, a router running BGP opens a TCP connection with a neighbor and sends an open message. If the neighbor accepts the neighborhood relationship, it responds with a keepalive message, which means that a relationship has been established between the two routers. See Figure 13.53 for a depiction of the open message format.

Figure 13.53 *Open message*

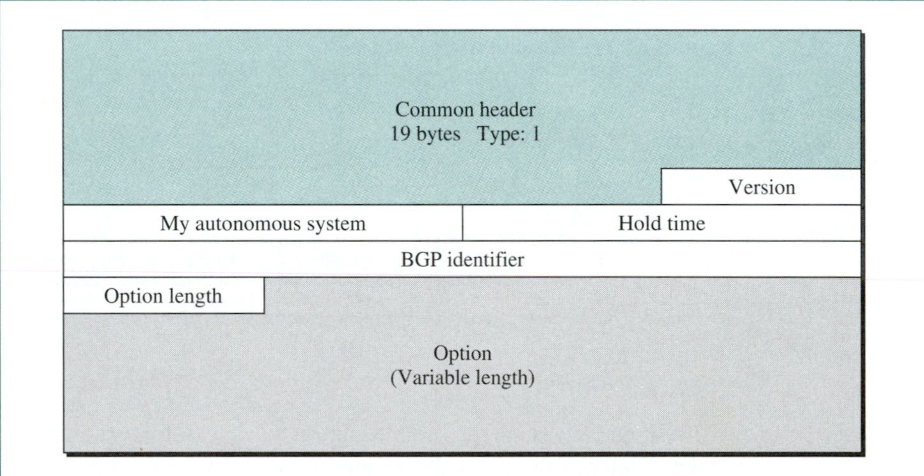

The fields of the open message are as follows:

- **Version.** This 1-byte field defines the version of BGP. The current version is 4.
- **My autonomous system.** This 2-byte field defines the autonomous system number.
- **Hold time.** This 2-byte field defines the maximum number of seconds that can elapse before one of the parties receives a keepalive or update message from the other. If a router does not receive one of these messages during the hold time period, it considers the other party dead.
- **BGP identifier.** This is a 4-byte field defining the router that sends the open message. The router usually uses one of its IP addresses (because it is unique) for this purpose.

- **Option parameter length.** The open message may also contain some option parameters. If so, this 1-byte field defines the length of the total option parameters. If there are no option parameters, the value of this field is zero.
- **Option parameters.** If the value of the option parameter length is not zero, it means that there are some option parameters. Each option parameter itself has two subfields: the length of the parameter and the parameter value. The only option parameter defined so far is authentication.

Update Message

The update message is the heart of the BGP protocol. It is used by a router to withdraw destinations that have been advertised previously, announce a route to a new destination, or both. Note that BGP can withdraw several destinations that were advertised before, but it can only advertise one new destination in a single update message. The format of the update message is shown in Figure 13.54.

Figure 13.54 *Update message*

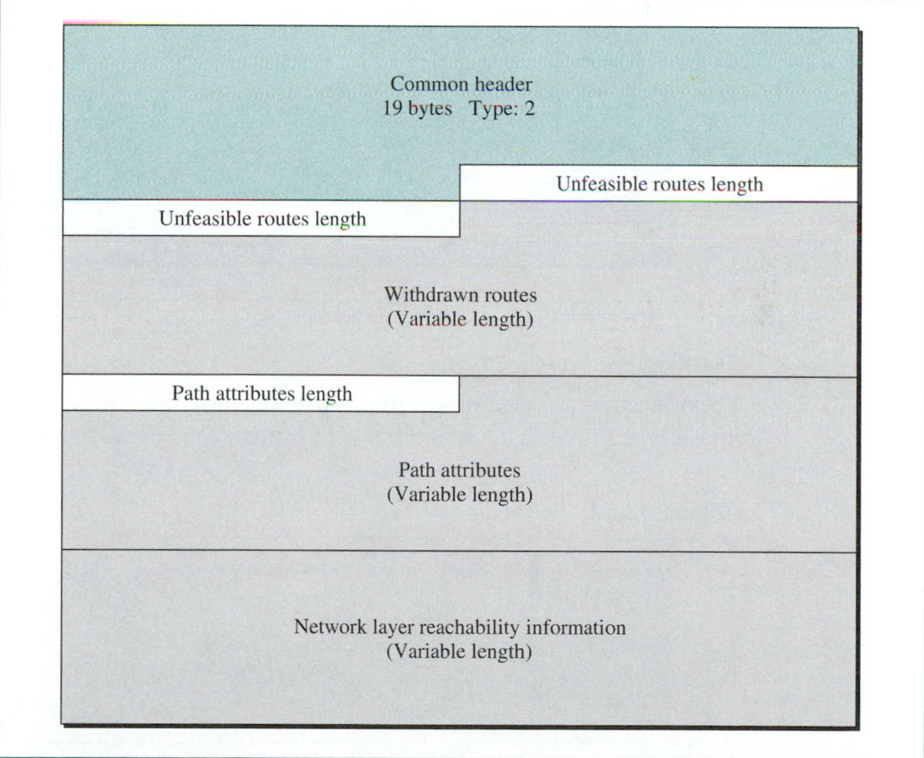

The update message fields are listed below:

- **Unfeasible routes length.** This 2-byte field defines the length of the next field.
- **Withdrawn routes.** This field lists all the routes that should be deleted from the previously advertised list.
- **Path attributes length.** This 2-byte field defines the length of the next field.

- **Path attributes.** This field defines the attributes of the path (route) to the network whose reachability is being announced in this message.
- **Network layer reachability information (NLRI).** This field defines the network that is actually advertised by this message. It has a length field and an IP address prefix. The length defines the number of bits in the prefix. The prefix defines the common part of the network address. For example, if the network is 153.18.7.0/24. The length of the prefix is 24 and the prefix is 153.18.7. This means that BGP4 supports classless addressing and CIDR.

> BGP supports classless addressing and CIDR.

Keepalive Message

The routers (called *peers* in BGP parlance), running the BGP protocols, exchange keep-alive messages regularly (before their hold time expires) to tell each other that they are alive. The keepalive message consists of only the common header shown in Figure 13.55.

Figure 13.55 *Keepalive message*

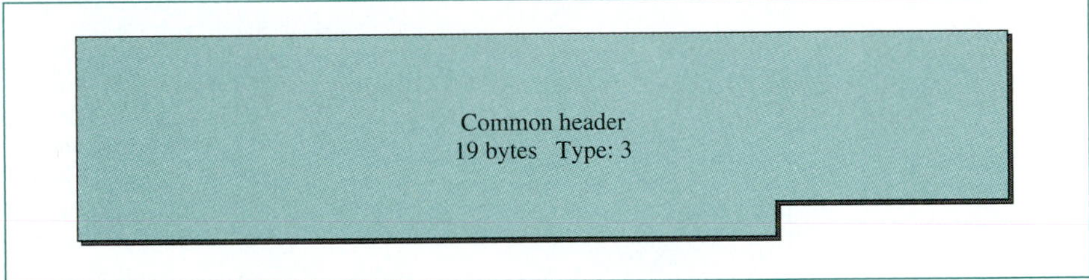

Notification Message

A notification message is sent by a router whenever an error condition is detected or a router wants to close the connection. The format of the message is shown in Figure 13.56.

Figure 13.56 *Notification message*

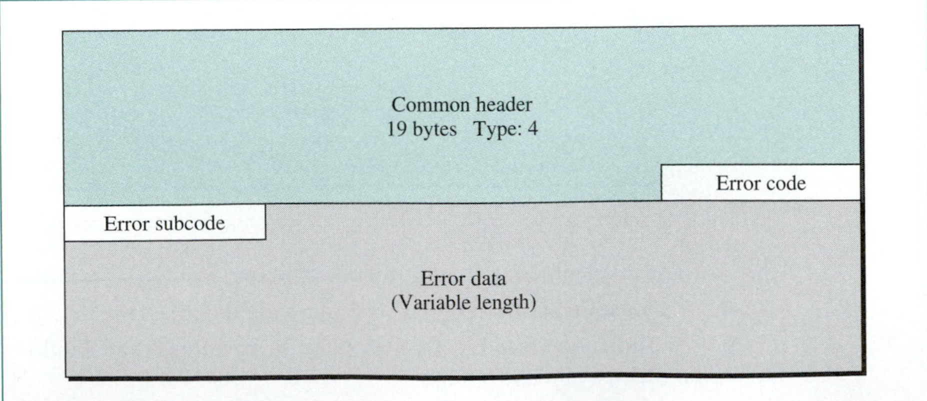

The fields comprising the notification message follow:

- **Error code.** This 1-byte field defines the category of the error. See Table 13.5.
- **Error subcode.** This 1-byte field further defines the type of error in each category.
- **Error data.** This field can be used to give more diagnostic information about the error.

Table 13.5 *Error codes*

Error Code	*Error Code Description*	*Error Subcode Description*
1	Message header error	Three different subcodes are defined for this type of error: synchronization problem (1), bad message length (2), and bad message type (3).
2	Open message error	Six different subcodes are defined for this type of error: unsupported version number (1), bad peer AS (2), bad BGP identifier (3), unsupported optional parameter (4), authentication failure (5), and unacceptable hold time (6).
3	Update message error	Eleven different subcodes are defined for this type of error: malformed attribute list (1), unrecognized well-known attribute (2), missing well-known attribute (3), attribute flag error (4), attribute length error (5), invalid origin attribute (6), AS\ routing loop (7), invalid next hop attribute (8), optional attribute error (9), invalid network field (10), malformed AS_PATH (11).
4	Hold timer expired	No subcode defined.
5	Finite state machine error	This defines the procedural error. No subcode defined.
6	Cease	No subcode defined.

Encapsulation

BGP messages are encapsulated in TCP segments using the well-known port 179. This means that there is no need for error control and flow control. When a TCP connection is opened, the exchange of update, keepalive, and notification messages is continued until a notification message of type cease is sent.

BGP uses the services of TCP on port 179.

13.5 KEY TERMS

area

area border router

area identification

authentication

autonomous system (AS)

autonomous system boundary router

backbone router

Bellman-Ford algorithm

border gateway protocol (BGP)

database description message

dead interval field

Dijkstra algorithm

distance vector multicast routing protocol (DVMRP)

distance vector routing

encapsulation

expiration timer

exterior routing

external link

external link LSA

flooding

garbage collection timer

hello interval

hello message

hop count

inter-autonomous routing protocol

interior routing

keepalive message

link state acknowledgment packet

link state advertisement (LSA)

link state database

link state request packet

link state routing

link state update packet

MBONE

metric

multicasting

network link LSA

network mask

next-hop address

notification message

open message

open shortest path first (OSPF)

optional attribute

packet

path vector routing

periodic timer

point-to-point transmission

poison reverse

policy routing

RIPv2

router

router link LSA

routing information protocol (RIP)

routing table

slow convergence

solicited response

split horizon

static routing table

stub link

subnet mask

summary link to AS boundary router LSA

summary link to network LSA

transient link

triggered update process

unsolicited response

update message

virtual link

well-known attribute

13.6 SUMMARY

- A metric is the cost assigned for passage of a packet through a network.
- A router consults its routing table to determine the best path for a packet.
- An autonomous system (AS) is a group of networks and routers under the authority of a single administration.
- RIP and OSPF are popular interior routing protocols used to update routing tables in an AS.
- RIP is based on distance vector routing, in which each router shares, at regular intervals, its knowledge about the entire AS with its neighbors.
- A RIP routing table entry consists of a destination network address, the hop count to that destination, and the IP address of the next router.
- RIP uses three timers: the periodic timer controls the advertising of the update message, the expiration timer governs the validity of a route, and the garbage collection timer advertises the failure of a route.
- Two shortcomings associated with the RIP protocol are slow convergence and instability.
- Procedures to remedy RIP instability include triggered update, split horizons, and poison reverse.
- The RIP version 2 packet format contains fields carrying AS information and authentication information.
- OSPF divides an AS into areas, defined as collections of networks, hosts, and routers.
- OSPF is based on link state routing, in which each router sends the state of its neighborhood to every other router in the area. A packet is sent only if there is a change in the neighborhood.
- OSPF defines four types of links (networks): point-to-point, transient, stub, and virtual.
- Five types of link state advertisements (LSAs) disperse information in OSPF: router link, network link, summary link to network, summary link to AS boundary router, and external link.
- A router compiles all the information from the LSAs it receives into a link state database. This database is common to all routers in an area.
- OSPF routing tables are calculated using Dijkstra's algorithm.

- There are five types of OSPF packets: hello, database description, link state request, link state update, and link state acknowledgment.
- An LSA is a multifield entry in a link state update packet.
- BGP is an inter-autonomous system routing protocol used to update routing tables.
- BGP is based on a routing method called path vector routing. In this method, the ASs through which a packet must pass are explicitly listed.
- Path vector routing does not have the instability nor looping problems of distance vector routing.
- There are four types of BGP messages: open, update, keepalive, and notification.

13.7 PRACTICE SET

Multiple-Choice Questions

1. RIP is based on _______.
   a. link state routing
   b. distance vector routing
   c. Dijkstra's algorithm
   d. path vector routing
2. In distance vector routing each router receives information directly from _______.
   a. every router on the network
   b. every router less than two units away
   c. a table stored by the network hosts
   d. its neighbors only
3. In distance vector routing a router sends out information _______.
   a. at regularly scheduled intervals
   b. only when there is a change in its table
   c. only when a new host is added
   d. only when a new network is added
4. A routing table contains _______.
   a. the destination network ID
   b. the hop count to reach the network
   c. the router ID of the next hop
   d. all of the above
5. Router B receives an update from router A that indicates Net1 is two hops away. The next update from A says Net1 is five hops away. What value is entered in B's routing table for Net1? Assume the basic RIP is being used.
   a. 2
   b. 3
   c. 6
   d. 7

6. If the routing table contains four new entries, how many update messages must the router send to its one neighbor router?
   a. 1
   b. 2
   c. 3
   d. 4
7. The hop count field of a router's first table always has a value of _______.
   a. 0
   b. 1
   c. infinity
   d. some positive integer
8. Which field in the RIP message contains the message type?
   a. command
   b. version
   c. network address
   d. distance
9. Which field in the RIP message corresponds to the cost field of the routing table?
   a. command
   b. version
   c. network address
   d. distance
10. Which field in the RIP message corresponds to the network ID field of the routing table?
   a. command
   b. version
   c. network address
   d. distance
11. Which timer schedules the sending out of regular update messages?
   a. periodic
   b. expiration
   c. garbage collection
   d. b and c
12. Which timer can set the distance field to 16?
   a. periodic
   b. expiration
   c. garbage collection
   d. b and c

13. A periodic update message goes out at time = 37 s. A triggered update follows at time = 57 s. Assuming a period of 30 s, when does the next regular periodic update message go out?
    a. at time = 67 s
    b. at time = 87 s
    c. at time = 58 s
    d. at some random time after 57 s
14. Which of the following attempts to alleviate the slow convergence problem?
    a. hop count limit
    b. triggered update
    c. looping
    d. a and b
15. Which of the following features the immediate sending of an update when a change occurs?
    a. hop count limit
    b. triggered update
    c. split horizons
    d. poison reverse
16. Which of the following sets an outgoing distance field to 16 for networks which previously sent incoming information through the same interface?
    a. hop count limit
    b. triggered update
    c. split horizons
    d. poison reverse
17. Which of the following does not allow the sending of information about the same network through the same interface?
    a. hop count limit
    b. triggered update
    c. split horizons
    d. poison reverse
18. Dijkstra's algorithm is used to _______.
    a. create LSAs
    b. flood an internet with information
    c. calculate the routing tables
    d. create a link state database
19. An area is _______.
    a. part of an AS
    b. composed of at least two ASs
    c. another term for an internet
    d. a collection of stub areas

20. In an autonomous system with n areas, how many areas are connected to the backbone?
    a. 1
    b. $n - 1$
    c. n
    d. $n + 1$
21. An area border router can be connected to _______.
    a. only another router
    b. another router or another network
    c. only another network
    d. only another area border router
22. Which of the following usually has the least number of connections to other areas?
    a. an area
    b. an autonomous system
    c. a transient link
    d. a stub link
23. Which type of network using the OSPF protocol always consists of just two connected routers?
    a. point-to-point
    b. transient
    c. stub
    d. virtual
24. Which type of network using the OSPF protocol is the result of a break in a link between two routers?
    a. point-to-point
    b. transient
    c. stub
    d. virtual
25. Which type of network using the OSPF protocol can have five routers attached to it?
    a. point-to-point
    b. transient
    c. stub
    d. all of the above
26. A WAN using the OSPF protocol that connects two routers is an example of a _______ type of OSPF network.
    a. point-to-point
    b. transient
    c. stub
    d. virtual

27. An Ethernet LAN using the OSPF protocol with five attached routers can be called a _______ network.
    a. point-to-point
    b. transient
    c. stub
    d. virtual
28. Which layer produces the OSPF message?
    a. data link
    b. network
    c. transport
    d. application
29. Which OSPF packet floods the Internet with information to update the database?
    a. link state request message
    b. link state update message
    c. link state acknowledgment message
    d. database description message
30. Which type of OSPF message must be sent prior to the others?
    a. hello message
    b. link state acknowledgment message
    c. link state request message
    d. database description message
31. Which IP address is needed in the hello message?
    a. designated router
    b. backup designated router
    c. neighbor router
    d. all of the above
32. Which of the following is an exterior routing protocol?
    a. RIP
    b. OSPF
    c. BGP
    d. a and b
33. Which of the following is an interior routing protocol?
    a. RIP
    b. OSPF
    c. BGP
    d. a and b

34. The Dijkstra algorithm is related to _______.
    a. distance vector routing
    b. link state routing
    c. path vector routing
    d. a and b
35. OSPF is based on _______.
    a. distance vector routing
    b. link state routing
    c. path vector routing
    d. a and b
36. BGP is based on _______.
    a. distance vector routing
    b. link state routing
    c. path vector routing
    d. a and b
37. Which timer is reset when a new update message for a route is received?
    a. garbage collection timer
    b. expiration timer
    c. periodic timer
    d. convergence timer
38. Which timer controls the advertising of regular update messages?
    a. garbage collection timer
    b. expiration timer
    c. periodic timer
    d. convergence timer
39. Which timer is involved in purging an invalid route from a table?
    a. garbage collection timer
    b. expiration timer
    c. periodic timer
    d. convergence timer
40. Which type of BGP message creates a relationship between two routers?
    a. open
    b. update
    c. keepalive
    d. notification
41. Which type of BGP message announces a route to a new destination?
    a. open
    b. update
    c. keepalive
    d. notification

42. Which type of BGP message is sent by a system to notify another router of the sender's existence?
    a. open
    b. update
    c. keepalive
    d. notification
43. Which type of BGP message is sent by a router to close a connection?
    a. open
    b. update
    c. keepalive
    d. notification

Exercises

44. What is the purpose of RIP?
45. What are the functions of a RIP message?
46. Why is the expiration timer value six times that of the periodic timer value?
47. How does the hop count limit alleviate RIP's problems?
48. List RIP shortcomings and their corresponding fixes.
49. Compare split horizons and poison reverse. When would one be used in preference to the other?
50. What is the basis of classification for the four types of links defined by OSPF?
51. What is the purpose of the authentication type and authentication data fields?
52. Contrast and compare distance vector routing with link state routing.
53. Draw a flowchart of the steps involved when a router receives a distance vector message from a neighbor.
54. Why do OSPF messages propagate faster than RIP messages?
55. What is the size of a RIP message that advertises only one network? What is the size of a RIP message that advertises *N* packets? Devise a formula that shows the relationship between the number of networks advertised and the size of a RIP message.
56. A router running RIP has a routing table with 20 entries. How many periodic timers are needed to handle this table?
57. A router running RIP has a routing table with 20 entries. How many expiration timers are needed to handle this table?
58. A router running RIP has a routing table with 20 entries. How many garbage collection timers are needed to handle this table if five routes are invalid?
59. A router has the following RIP routing table:

Net1	4	B
Net2	2	C
Net3	1	F
Net4	5	G

What would be the contents of the table if the router receives the following RIP message from router C:

Net1	2
Net2	1
Net3	3
Net4	7

60. How many bytes are empty in a RIP message that advertises *N* networks?
61. A router has the following RIP routing table:

Net1	4	B
Net2	2	C
Net3	1	F
Net4	5	G

Show the response message sent by this router.

62. Using Figure 13.24, show the link state update/router link advertisement for router A.
63. Using Figure 13.24, show the link state update/router link advertisement for router D.
64. Using Figure 13.24, show the link state update/router link advertisement for router E.
65. Show the link state update/network link advertisement for network N2 in Figure 13.24.
66. Show the link state update/network link advertisement for network N4 in Figure 13.24.
67. Show the link state update/network link advertisement for network N5 in Figure 13.24.
68. In Figure 13.24 assume that the designated router for network N1 is router A. Show the link state update/network link advertisement for this network.
69. In Figure 13.24 assume that the designated router for network N3 is router D. Show the link state update/network link advertisement for this network.
70. Assign IP addresses to networks and routers in Figure 13.24.
71. Using the result of exercise 70, show the OSPF hello message sent by router C.
72. Using the result of exercise 70, show the OSPF database description message sent by router C.
73. Using the result of exercise 70, show the OSPF link state request message sent by router C.
74. Show the autonomous system with the following specifications:
    a. There are eight networks (N1 to N8)
    b. There are eight routers (R1 to R8)
    c. N1, N2, N3, N4, and N5 are Ethernet networks
    d. N6 is a Token Ring
    e. N7 and N8 are point-to-point networks
    f. R1 connects N1 and N2
    g. R2 connects N1 and N7
    h. R3 connects N2 and N8
    i. R4 connects N7 and N6
    j. R5 connects N6 and N3

k. R6 connects N6 and N4
l. R7 connects N6 and N5
m. R8 connects N8 and N5

75. Draw the graphical representation of the autonomous system of exercise 74 as seen by OSPF.
76. Which of the networks in exercise 74 is a transient network? Which is a stub network?
77. Show the BGP open message for router R1 in Figure 13.50.
78. Show the BGP update message for router R1 in Figure 13.50.
79. Show the BGP keepalive message for router R1 in Figure 13.50.
80. Show the BGP notification message for router R1 in Figure 13.50.

Programming Exercises

81. Write declarations for all RIP messages in C.
82. Write declarations for all OSPF messages in C.
83. Write declarations for all BGP messages in C.
84. Write C code to implement the routing algorithm for RIP.
85. Modify the code in exercise 84 to include triggered update.
86. Modify the code in exercise 84 to include split horizon.
87. Modify the code in exercise 84 to include poison reverse.
88. Write C code to implement Dijkstra's algorithm.

CHAPTER 14

Multicasting and Multicast Routing Protocols

In this chapter, we discuss multicasting and multicast routing protocols. We first define the term multicasting and compare it to unicasting and broadcasting. We also briefly discuss the applications of multicasting. We then move on to multicast routing and the general ideas and goals related to it. Finally, we discuss five common multicast routing protocols used in the Internet today.

14.1 INTRODUCTION

Let us first introduce multicasting and its applications in this section.

Unicast, Multicast, and Broadcast

A message can be unicast, multicast, or broadcast. Let us clarify these terms as they relate to the Internet.

Unicasting

In unicast communication, there is one source and one destination. The relation between the source and the destination is one-to-one. In this type of communication, both the source and destination addresses, in the IP datagram, are the unicast addresses assigned to the host (or host interface to be more exact). In Figure 14.1, a unicast packet starts from the source S1 and passes through routers to reach the destination D1. We have shown the networks as a link between the routers to simplify the figure.

Note that in unicast routing, when a router receives a packet, it forwards the packet through only one of its interfaces (the one belonging to the optimum path) as defined in the routing table. The router may discard the packet if it cannot find the destination address in its routing table.

Multicasting

In multicast routing, there is one source and a group of destinations. The relationship is one-to-many. In this type of communication, the source address is a unicast address, but

Figure 14.1 *Unicasting*

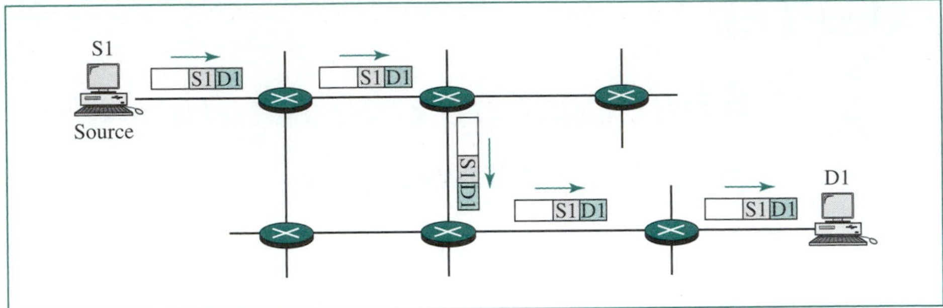

In unicast routing, the router forwards the received packet through only one of its interfaces.

the destination address is a group address (class D). The group address defines the members of the group. Figure 14.2 shows the idea behind multicasting. A multicast packet starts from the source S1 and goes to all destinations that belong to group G1.

Figure 14.2 *Multicasting*

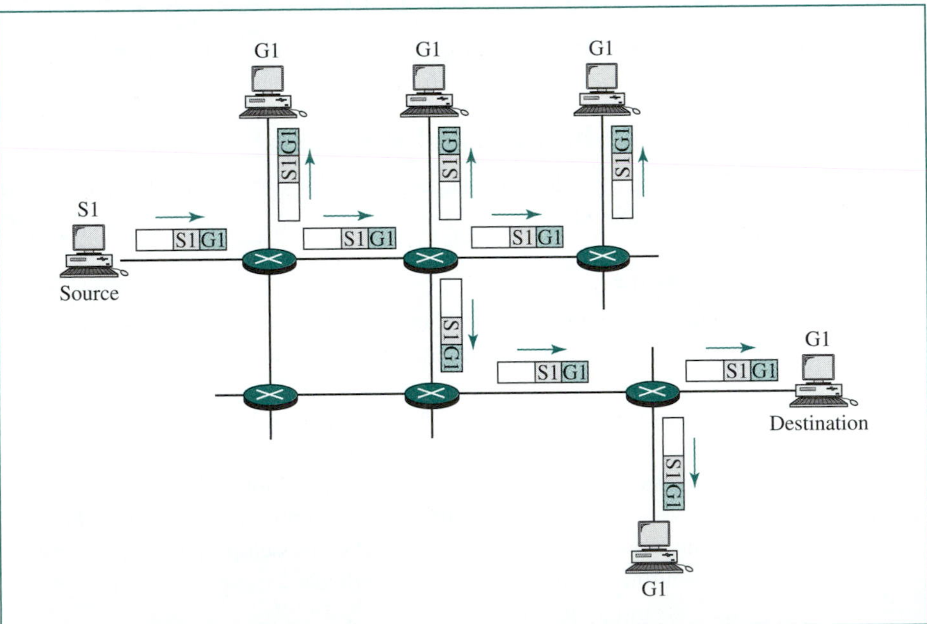

In multicast routing, when a router receives a packet, it may forward it through several of its interfaces. The router may discard the packet if it is not in the multicast path.

In multicast routing, the router may forward the received packet through several of its interfaces.

Broadcasting

In broadcast routing, the communication is one-to-all. There is only one source, but all of the other hosts are the destination. The Internet does not explicitly support broadcasting because of the huge amount of traffic it would create and because of the bandwidth it would need. Imagine the traffic generated in the Internet if 1,000 people wanted to send a message to everyone else connected to the Internet. However, as we will see shortly, broadcasting is used implicitly as a prelude to multicasting.

Multicasting Versus Multiple Unicasting

Before we finish this section we need to distinguish between multicasting and multiple unicasting. Figure 14.3 illustrates both concepts.

Figure 14.3 *Multicasting versus multiple unicasting*

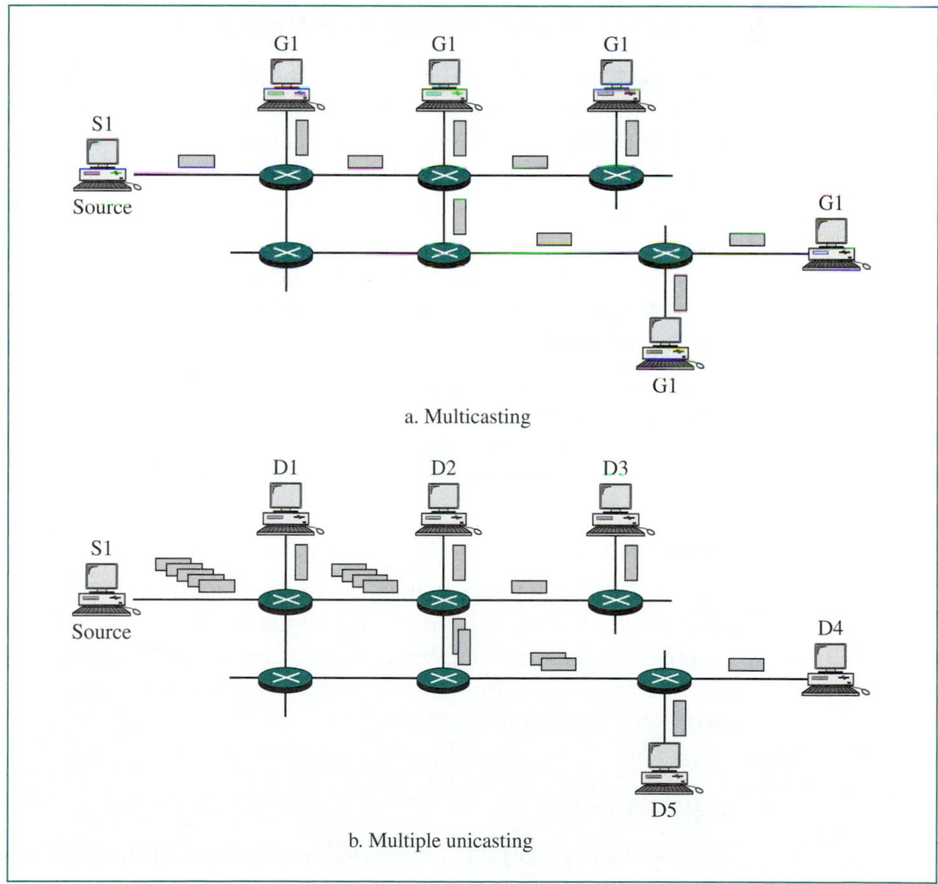

Multicasting

Multicasting starts with one single packet from the source that is duplicated by the routers. The destination address in each packet is the same for all duplicates. Note that only one single copy of the packet travels between any two routers.

Multiple Unicasting

In multiple unicasting, several packets start from the source. If there are five destinations, for example, the source sends five packets, each with a different unicast destination address. Note that there may be multiple copies traveling between two routers. For example, when a person sends an email message to a group of people, this is multiple unicasting. The email software creates replicas of the message, each with a different destination address and sends them one by one. This is not multicasting; it is multiple unicasting.

Emulation of Multicasting with Unicasting

You might wonder why we have a separate mechanism for multicasting, when it can be emulated with unicasting. There are several reasons for this; two are obvious:

1. Multicasting is more efficient than multiple unicasting. In Figure 14.3, we can see how multicasting requires less bandwidth than multiple unicasting. In multiple unicasting, some of the links must handle several copies.
2. In multiple unicasting, the packets are created by the source with a delay relative to each other. If there are 1,000 destinations, the delay between the first and the last packet may be unacceptable. In multicasting, there is little delay because of multiple packet creation.

> Emulation of multicasting through multiple unicasting is not efficient and may create long delays, particularly with a large group.

Flooding

Flooding is related to both multicasting and broadcasting. In flooding, a router forwards a packet out of all of its interfaces except the one from which the packet came. Flooding provides broadcasting, but it also creates loops. A router will receive the same packet over and over from different interfaces. Several copies of the same packet are circulated, creating traffic jams.

Applications

Multicasting has many applications today such as access to distributed databases, information dissemination, teleconferencing, and distance learning.

Access to Distributed Databases

Most of the large databases today are distributed. That is, the information is stored in more than one location, usually at the time of production. The user who needs to access the database does not know the location of the information. A user's request is multicast to all the database locations, and the location that has the information responds.

Information Dissemination

Businesses often need to send information to their customers. If the nature of the information is the same for each customer, it can be multicast. In this way a business can send one message that can reach many customers. For example, a software update can be sent to all purchasers of a particular software package.

Dissemination of News

In a similar manner the news can be easily disseminated through multicasting. One single message can be sent to those interested in a particular topic. For example, the statistics of the championship high school basketball tournament needs to be sent to the sports editors of many newspapers.

Teleconferencing

Teleconferencing involves multicasting. The individuals attending a teleconference all need to receive the same information at the same time. Temporary or permanent groups can be formed for this purpose. For example, an engineering group that holds meetings every Monday morning could have a permanent group while the group that plans the holiday party could form a temporary group.

Distance Learning

One growing area in the use of multicasting is distance learning. Lessons taught by one single professor can be received by a specific group of students. This is especially convenient for those students who find it difficult to attend classes on campus.

14.2 MULTICAST ROUTING

Now that we know what multicasting is and how it is used we need to know how a multicast packet can move efficiently from a source to a destination. The objectives of multicasting are as follows:

- Every member of the group should receive one, and only one, copy of the multicast packet. Receipt of multiple copies is not allowed.
- Nonmembers must not receive a copy.
- There must be no loops in routing; that is, a packet must not visit a router more than once.
- The path traveled from the source to each destination must be optimal (the shortest path).

Tree Versus Graph

Two common data structures used in computer science are the graph and the tree. Both are defined as a collection of nodes and edges (lines). A graph has no hierarchical structure, but a tree does. Each node on a tree has one single parent, and zero or more children. The root of the tree, the ancestor of all nodes, has no parents. A leaf of a tree has no child. A node of a graph, on the other hand, can have several predecessors and several successors. In unicasting, the Internet, or part of it, is represented by a graph; in multicasting, the Internet, or part of it, is represented by a tree. A knowledge of trees and graphs enhances the understanding of the concepts of this chapter.

Spanning Tree

For efficient multicasting, we need a tree with the source as the root and group members as leaves. Such a tree is called a **spanning tree**—a tree that connects all of the nodes.

Shortest Path Spanning Tree

For efficient multicasting, we need a spanning tree in which each path from the root to a leaf is the shortest (according to some metric) possible. This optimum tree is called a **shortest path spanning tree.**

14.3 MULTICAST TREES

Two types of trees are used for multicasting by multicasting protocols: source-based trees and group-shared trees.

Source-Based Tree

In the source-based tree method, a single tree is made for each combination of source and group. In other words, the formation of the tree is based on both the source and on the group. If there are N different groups and M different sources in the system, there can be a maximum of $N \times M$ different trees, one for each source-group combination. For example, if at this moment, a source needs to send a multicast packet to a group with a Class D address of 228.9.28.40, a corresponding tree is made for this purpose. If two minutes later, the same source wants to send a multicast packet to group 230.6.4.2 (a different group), the tree changes. In the source-based approach, the combination of source and group determines the tree.

> In a source-based tree approach, the combination of source and group determines the tree.

Although the idea of the source-based tree is simple, the implementation is not. How can we create a tree for each source/group combination? In addition, how can we be sure that each tree is optimal (the most efficient)? To have a tree for each combination, each router must have information about each particular tree. In other words, when a router receives a multicast packet, it must know the interface or interfaces through which the packet must be sent.

Two approaches have been used to create optimal source-based multicast trees. The first approach, used in DVMRP, is an extension of unicast distance vector routing (such as RIP). The second approach, used in MOSPF, is an extension of unicast link state routing (such as OSPF). Another protocol, PIM-DM uses either RIP or OSPF, depending on need. All these approaches are discussed later in the chapter.

Group-Shared Tree

In the group-shared tree method, each group in the system shares the same tree. If there are *N* groups in the whole system, there is a maximum of *N* trees, one for each group. For example, if at this moment, a source needs to send a multicast packet to a group with a Class D address of 226.7.18.10, a corresponding tree is made for this purpose. If, a few seconds later, another source needs to send another packet to the same group, the corresponding tree would be the same. But if the previous source, or any other source, needs to send a packet to group 229.5.80.10, a new tree is made. In other words, the tree changes when the group changes; the tree remains the same for the group regardless of the source. In the group-shared tree method the group determines the tree, not the source.

> In the group-shared tree approach, the group determines the tree.

This method also has two approaches to find the multicast tree: the Steiner tree and rendezvous-point tree.

Steiner Tree

In this approach, the optimal tree is the one in which the sum of the costs of the links is minimum. Note that this is different from Dijkstra's algorithm in which optimization is based on each single source. In the Steiner tree, we want to optimize the cost no matter what the source. There are good arguments for using the Steiner tree, but because of the complexity of the algorithm and the need for recalculating the tree each time there is a change in the topology or membership, no Internet protocol uses this approach. For this reason, there is no further discussion of this approach.

Rendezvous-Point Tree

In this approach, one tree is made for each group. For each group, one router is selected as the rendezvous point or core or center for the group. This router becomes the root of the tree to be formed. The CBT and PIM-SP protocols (discussed later) use this type of tree.

14.4 MULTICAST ROUTING PROTOCOLS

DVMRP, MOSPF, CBT, PIM-DM, and PIM-SM are multicast routing protocols that have been used or proposed for use in the Internet (see Figure 14.4).

Figure 14.4 *Multicast routing protocols*

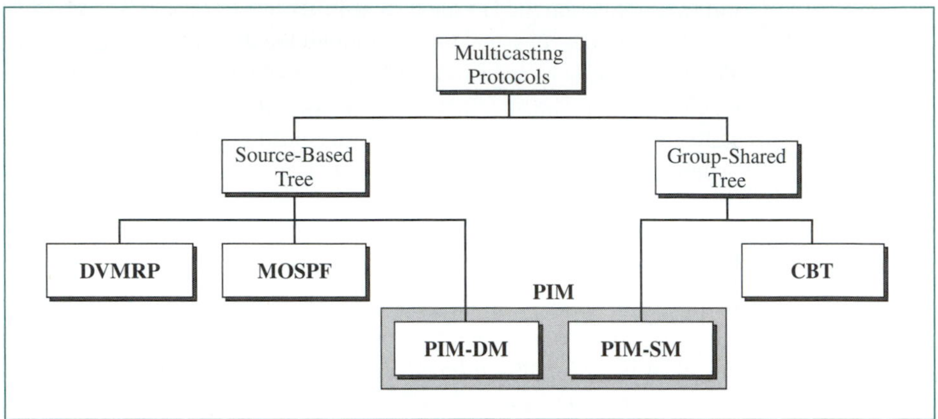

14.5 DVMRP

The Distance Vector Multicast Routing Protocol (DVMRP), a source-based routing protocol, is an extension of the Distance Vector Routing Protocol (DVRP) used in unicast routing.

Formation of Shortest Path Tree

DVMRP follows the same strategy followed by DVRP. Recall that in DVRP, no router knows the complete route for a particular destination; there is no pre-defined route. Each router knows from which interface to send out a unicast packet based on the destination address. The route is made gradually; each router contributes to the formation of the route when it receives the packet.

In DVMRP, the optimal tree is not pre-defined either. No router knows what should be the optimal tree. The tree is made gradually. When a router receives a packet, it forwards the packet through some of the interfaces and contributes to the formation of the tree; the rest of the tree is made by other downstream routers. This protocol must achieve the following:

1. It must prevent the formation of loops.
2. It must prevent duplications; no network receives more than one copy. In addition, the path traveled by a copy is the shortest path from the source to the destination.
3. It must provide for dynamic membership.

Reverse Path Forwarding (RPF)

The original idea in DVMRP was to use reverse path forwarding (RPF). RPF is a modified flooding strategy. In flooding, a router forwards each packet out of all interfaces except the one from which the packet arrived. Flooding definitely creates loops. To prevent loops, only one copy is forwarded; the other copies are dropped.

In RPF, a router forwards the copy that has traveled the shortest path from the source to the router. To find if the packet has traveled the shortest path, RPF uses the unicast routing table of DVRP. Although the unicast routing table is based on the destination address, not the source address, DVMRP interprets the destination address as the source address. Recall that a DVRP table gives the router departure information: specifically, the shortest path to the destination. In DVRMP, the router simply switches the roles of the destination and the source. The router uses the source address of the packet (which is a unicast address) to find the corresponding departing interface in the routing table (as if it wants to send a packet to that address). If the departing interface found in the table is the same as the interface from which the packet is arriving, the packet has traveled the shortest path. In other words, since the path from the router to the source is the shortest, the path from the source to the router is also the shortest because the metrics in distance vector routing (hop counts) are symmetric. Figure 14.5 shows the concept of RPF.

Figure 14.5 *Reverse path forwarding*

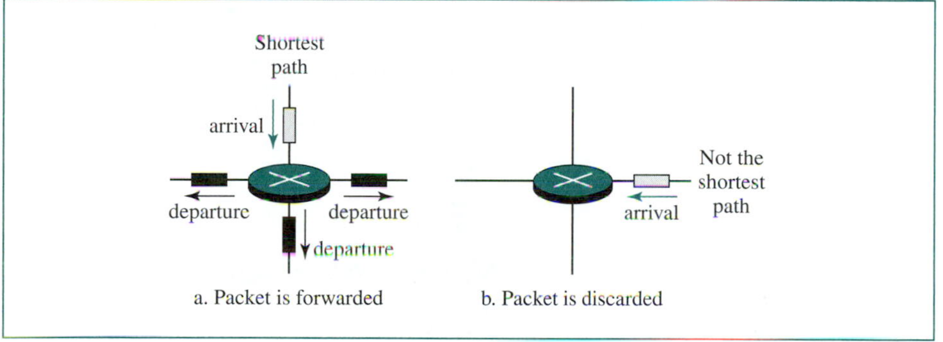

Example 1

A multicast router receives a packet with source address 195.34.23.7 and destination address 227.45.9.5 from interface 2. Should the router discard or forward the packet based on the following unicast table?

Destination	*Interface*
121.0.0.0	1
185.67.0.0	2
195.34.0.0	3

Solution

The packet must be discarded because, after interpreting the source address and applying the default mask, the router will send the packet to network 195.34.0.0 through interface 3, not interface 2. The arriving interface does not match the imaginary departure interface; the packet has not traveled the shortest path and must be dropped. The packet would be forwarded if it had arrived from interface 3.

In reverse path forwarding (RPF), the router forwards only the packets that have traveled the shortest path from the source to the router; all other copies are discarded.

RPF prevents the formation of loops.

Reverse Path Broadcasting (RPB)

RPF guarantees that each network receives a copy of the multicast packet without formation of loops. However, RPF does not guarantee that each network receives only one copy; a network may receive two or more copies. The reason is that forwarding is not based on the destination address (a group address); forwarding is based on the source address. To visualize the problem, let us look at Figure 14.6.

Figure 14.6 *Reverse path broadcasting*

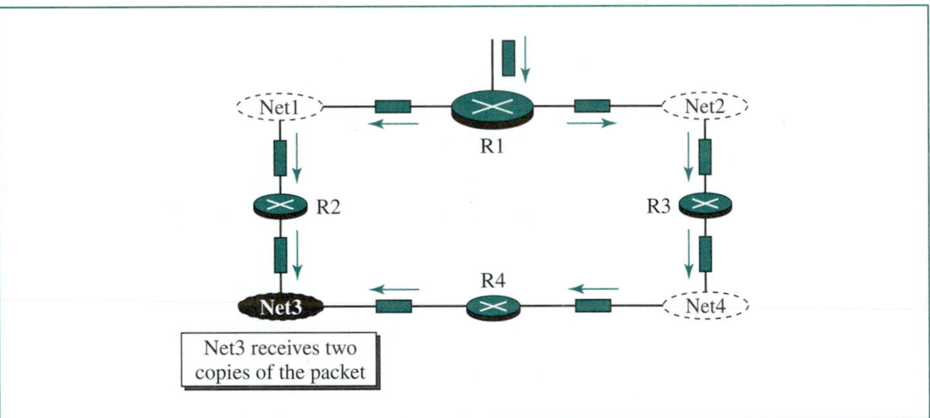

Net3 in this figure receives two copies of the packet even though each router just sends out one copy from each interface. There is duplication because a tree has not been made; instead of a tree we have a graph. Net3 has two parents: routers R2 and R4.

To eliminate duplication, we must define only one parent router for each network. We must have this restriction: A network can receive a multicast packet from a particular source only through a designated parent router.

Now the policy is clear. For each source, the router sends the packet only out of those interfaces for which it is the designated parent. This policy is called reverse path broadcasting (RPB), RPB guarantees that the packet reaches every network and that every network receives only one copy. Figure 14.7 shows the difference between RPF and RPB.

The reader may ask how the parent is determined. The designated parent router can be selected using one of several different strategies; the most common is to select the router with the shortest path to the source as the designated parent router. Because routers periodically send updating DVRP packets to each other, they can easily determine which router in the neighborhood has the shortest path to the source (when interpreting

Figure 14.7 *RPF versus RPB*

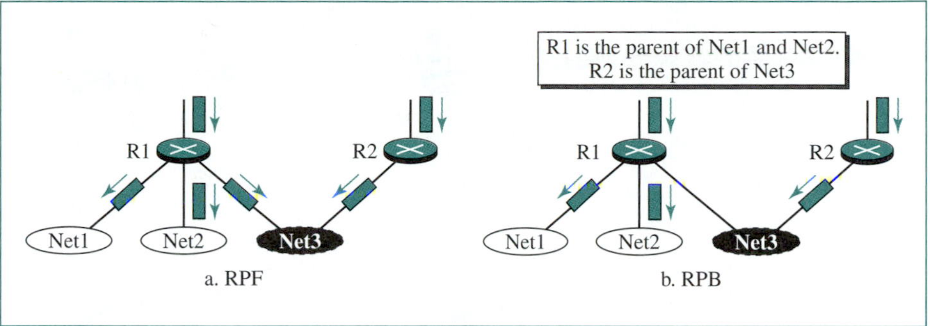

the source as the destination). If more than one router qualifies, the router with the smallest IP address is selected.

We hope that the reader is convinced that RPB creates a shortest path spanning tree that reaches each destination. We summarize the important points. First of all we need a tree to prevent duplicates. Second, the tree is the shortest path tree because the first router only forwards the packet that has traveled the shortest path; the second does the same, as does the third, and so on to the last. The tree is a shortest path broadcast tree, not a multicast tree; every network receives a copy of the packet.

> RPB creates a shortest path broadcast tree from the source to each destination. It guarantees that each destination receives one and only one copy of the packet.

Reverse Path Multicasting (RPM)

As you may have noticed, RPB does not multicast the packet, it broadcasts it. This is not efficient. To be more efficient, the multicast packet must reach only those networks that have active members for that particular group. However, the designers of DVMRP decided that the first packet is broadcast to every network. The decision regarding the remainder of the packets is the result of two procedures, pruning and grafting. This is sometimes called *reverse path multicasting* (RPM). Figure 14.8 shows the idea of pruning and grafting.

Pruning The designated parent router of each network is responsible for holding the membership information. This is done through the IGMP protocol described in Chapter 10. The process starts when a router connected to a network finds that there is no interest in a multicast packet. The router sends a prune message to the upstream router so that it can prune the corresponding interface. That is, the upstream router can stop sending multicast messages for this group through that interface. Now if this router receives prune messages from all downstream routers, it, in turn, sends a prune message to its upstream router.

Grafting What if a leaf router has sent a prune message but suddenly realizes, through IGMP, that one of its networks is again interested in receiving the multicast packet? It can send a *graft* message. The graft message forces the upstream router to resume sending the multicast messages.

Figure 14.8 *RPF, RPB, and RPM*

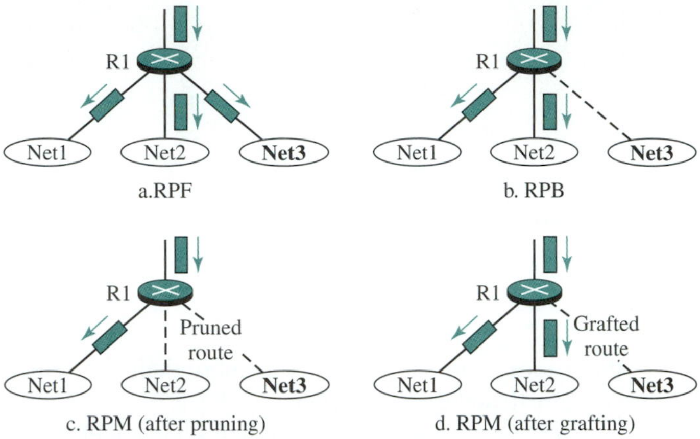

Default Lifetime All the DVMRP prune messages have a field defining the pruning lifetime. If no value is entered, the default is 2 hours. Pruning takes place only for the lifetime of the packet; after that, traffic will automatically be restored. In other words, if a router sends a prune message to the upstream router and indicates a lifetime of 1 hour, it means that the router does not want to receive multicast messages from that particular group for 1 hour. After the hour is up, the messages must resume if there is no second prune message. This implies that each router has a pruning timer for each active group.

RPM adds pruning and grafting to RPB to create a multicast shortest path tree that supports dynamic membership changes.

14.6 MOSPF

The Multicast Open Shortest Path First (MOSPF) is an extension of the OSPF protocol that uses multicast link state routing to create source-based trees. MOSPF uses an approach different from DVMRP. First, the tree is a least-cost tree (using a metric) instead of a shortest path tree. Second, the tree is made all at once instead of gradually (the tree is said to be pre-made, pre-pruned, and ready to be used).

Least-Cost Trees

This approach uses the fact that in unicast link state routing there is a common link state database and, based on this database, each router knows the topology of the entire network. In addition, each router can use Dijikstra's algorithm to create a least-cost tree that has the router as the root and the rest of the routers as nodes of the tree. However, the least-cost trees generated by Dijkstra's algorithm are different for each router, unlike the database and the topology, which are the same for each router.

The tree we need in multicasting routing is slightly different from the one used in least-cost unicast routing. We need one tree for each source/group pair and the root must be the source. The solution is not difficult, because the database is the same; we can ask each router to use Dijikstra's algorithm to create a tree with the source as the root. In this case, each router creates exactly the same tree, with the router itself as a node in the tree. Figure 14.9 shows the difference between trees.

Figure 14.9 *Unicast tree and multicast tree*

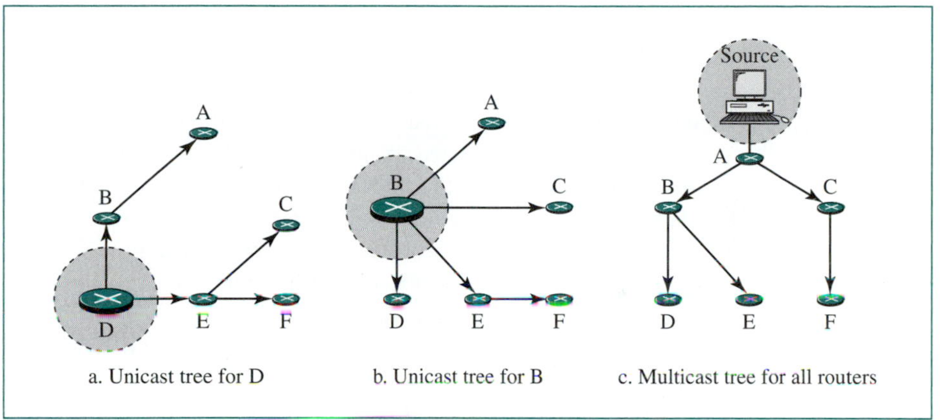

Although a tree made this way looks like a perfect solution, there are still some problems.

a. The tree based on Dijkstra's algorithm uses unicast addresses (which are unique for each host); the tree we need requires group addresses which are not unique (more than one host can belong to a group and a host may belong to several groups).

b. The membership may change frequently. A host may belong to a group at one moment but not in the next and vice versa.

c. Dijkstra's algorithm is very complex. Using the algorithm for each multicast packet is very expensive time-wise.

To solve the first problem, we can add a new link state update packet to associate the unicast address of a host with the group address or addresses the host is sponsoring. It is called a group-membership LSA. In this way, we can include in the tree only the hosts (using their unicast addresses) that belong to a particular group. In other words, we make a tree that contains all the hosts belonging to a group, but we use the unicast address of the host in the calculation.

The new link state packets can also solve the second problem if they are sent whenever there is a change in the membership.

To solve the third problem, we can make the router calculate the least-cost trees on demand (when it receives the first multicast packet). In addition, the tree can be saved in the cache memory for future use by the same source/group pair. MOSPF is a **data-driven** protocol; the first time a MOSPF router sees a datagram with a given source and group address, the router calculates the Dijkstra shortest path tree calculation.

14.7 CBT

The Core-Based Tree (CBT) protocol is a group-shared protocol that uses a core as the root of the tree. The autonomous system is divided into regions and a core (center router) is chosen for each region.

Formation of the Tree

After the rendezvous point is selected, every router is informed of the unicast address of the selected router. Each router then sends a unicast join message (similar to a grafting message) to show that it wants to join the group. This message passes through all routers that are located between the sender and the rendezvous router. Each intermediate router extracts the necessary information from the message, such as the unicast address of the sender and the interface through which the packet has arrived, and forwards the message to the next router in the past. When the rendezvous router has received all join messages from every member of the group, the tree is formed. Now every router knows its upstream router (the router that leads to the root) and the downstream router (the router that leads to the leaf).

If a router wants to leave the group, it sends a leave message to its upstream router. The upstream router, removes the link to that router from the tree and forwards the message to the upstream router, and so on. Figure 14.10 shows the a shared-group tree with rendezvous router.

Figure 14.10 *Shared-group tree with rendezvous router*

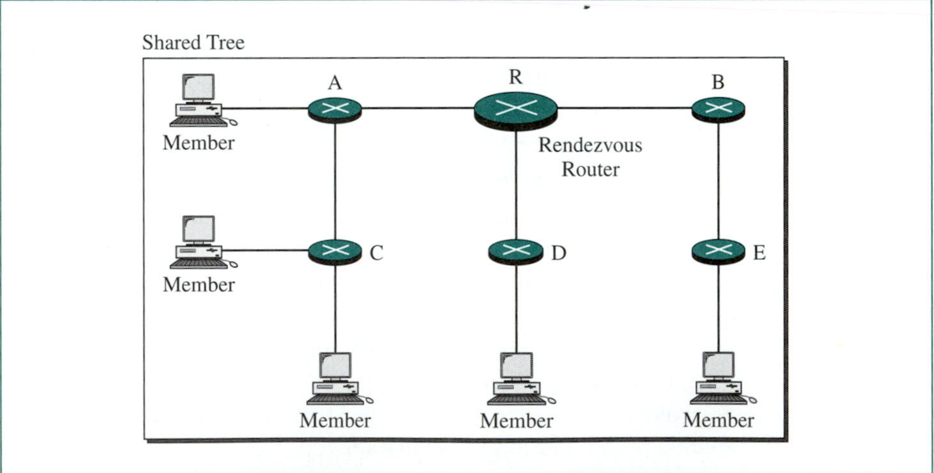

The reader may have noticed two differences between DVMRP and MOSPF, on one hand, and CBT, on the other. First, the tree for the first two is made from the root; the tree for CBT is formed from the leaves. Second, in DVMRP, the tree is first made (broadcasting) and then pruned; in CBT, there is no tree at the beginning; the joining (grafting) gradually makes the tree.

Sending Multicast Packets

After formation of the tree, any source (belonging to the group or not) can send a multicast packet to all members of the group. It simply sends the packet to the rendezvous router, using the unicast address of the rendezvous router; the rendezvous router distributes the packet to all members of the group. Figure 14.11 shows how a host can send a multicast packet to all members of the group. Note that the source host can be any of the hosts inside the shared tree or any host outside the shared tree. In the figure we show one located outside the shared tree.

Figure 14.11 *Sending a multicast packet to the rendezvous router*

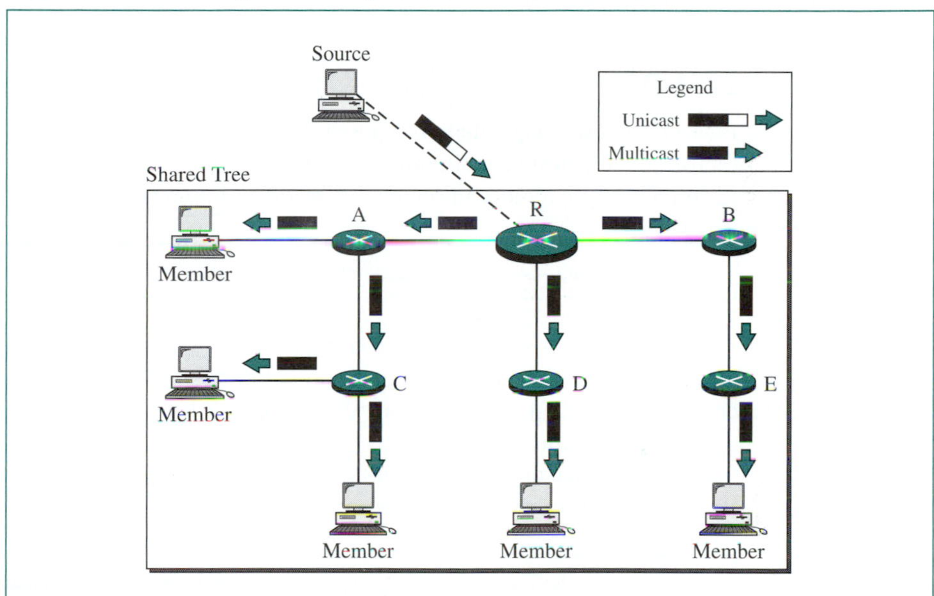

Selecting the Rendezvous Router

This approach is simple except for one point. How do we select a rendezvous router to optimize the process and multicasting as well? Several methods have been implemented. However, this topic is beyond the scope of this book and we leave it to more advanced books.

In summary, the Core-Based Tree (CBT) is a shared-group tree, center-based protocol using one tree per group. One of the routers in the tree is called the core. A packet is sent from the source to members of the group following this procedure:

1. The source, which may or may not be part of the tree, encapsulates the multicast packet inside a unicast packet with the unicast destination address of the core and sends it to the core. This part of delivery is done using a unicast address; the only recipient is the core router.
2. The core decapsulates the unicast packet and forwards it to all "interested" interfaces (we define interested interfaces later).
3. Each router that receives the multicast packet, in turn, forwards it to all interested interfaces.

> In CBT, the source sends the multicast packet (encapsulated in a unicast packet) to the core router. The core router decapsulates the packet and forwards it to all interested hosts.

14.8 PIM

Protocol Independent Multicast (PIM) is the name given to two independent multicast routing protocols: Protocol Independent Multicast, Dense Mode (PIM-DM) and Protocol Independent Multicast, Sparse Mode (PIM-SM). Both protocols are unicast-protocol dependent, but the similarity ends here. We discuss each separately.

PIM-DM

PIM-DM is used when there is a possibility that each router is involved in multicasting (dense mode). In this environment, the use of a protocol that broadcasts the packet is justified because almost all routers are involved in the process.

> PIM-DM is used in a dense multicast environment, such as a LAN environment.

PIM-DM is a source-based routing protocol that uses RPF and pruning/grafting strategies for multicasting. Its operation is like DVMRP; however, unlike DVMRP, it does not depend on a specific unicasting protocol. It assumes that the autonomous system is using a unicast protocol and each router has a table that can find the outgoing interface that has an optimal path to a destination. This unicast protocol can be a distance vector protocol (RIP) or link state protocol (OSPF).

> PIM-DM uses RPF and pruning/grafting strategies to handle multicasting. However, it is independent from the underlying unicast protocol.

PIM-SM

PIM-SM is used when there is slight possibility that each router is involved in multicasting (sparse mode). In this environment, the use of a protocol that broadcasts the packet is not justified, but a protocol such as CBT that uses a group-shared tree is more appropriate.

> PIM-SM is used in a sparse multicast environment such as a WAN.

PIM-SM is a group-shared routing protocol that has a rendezvous point (RP) as the source of the tree. Its operation is like CBT; however, it is simpler because it does not require acknowledgment from a join message. In addition, it creates a backup set of RPs for each region to cover RP failures.

One of the characteristics of PIM-SM is that it can switch from a group-shared tree strategy to a source-based tree strategy when necessary. This can happen if there is a dense area of activity far from the RP. That area can be more efficiently handled with a source-based tree strategy instead of a group-shared tree strategy.

PIM-SM is similar to CBT but uses a simpler procedure.

14.9 MBONE

Multimedia and real-time communication have increased the need for multicasting in the Internet. However, only a small fraction of Internet routers are multicast routers. In other words, a multicast router may not find another multicast router in the neighborhood to forward the multicast packet. Although, this problem may be solved in the next few years by adding more and more multicast routers, there is another solution for this problem. The solution is tunneling. The multicast routers are seen as a group of routers on the top of unicast routers. The multicast routers may not be connected directly, but they are connected logically. Figure 14.12 shows the idea. In this figure, only the routers enclosed in the shaded circles are capable of multicasting. Without tunneling, these routers are isolated islands. To enable multicasting, we make a multicast backbone (MBONE) out of these isolated routers using the concept of tunneling.

Figure 14.12 *Logical tunneling*

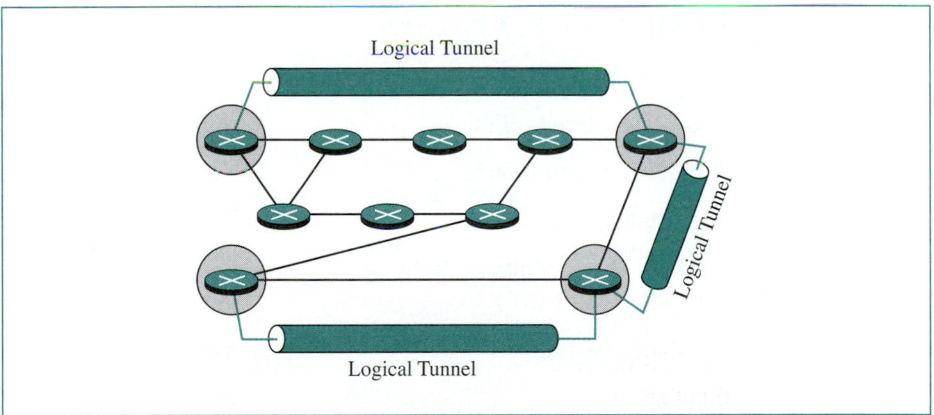

A logical tunnel is established by encapsulating the multicast packet inside a unicast packet. The multicast packet becomes the payload (data) of the unicast packet. The intermediate (nonmulticast) routers route the packet as unicast routers and deliver the packet from one island to another. It's as if the unicast routers do not exist and the two multicast routers are neighbors. Figure 14.13 shows the concept.

So far the only protocol that supports MBONE and tunneling is DVMRP.

Figure 14.13 *MBONE*

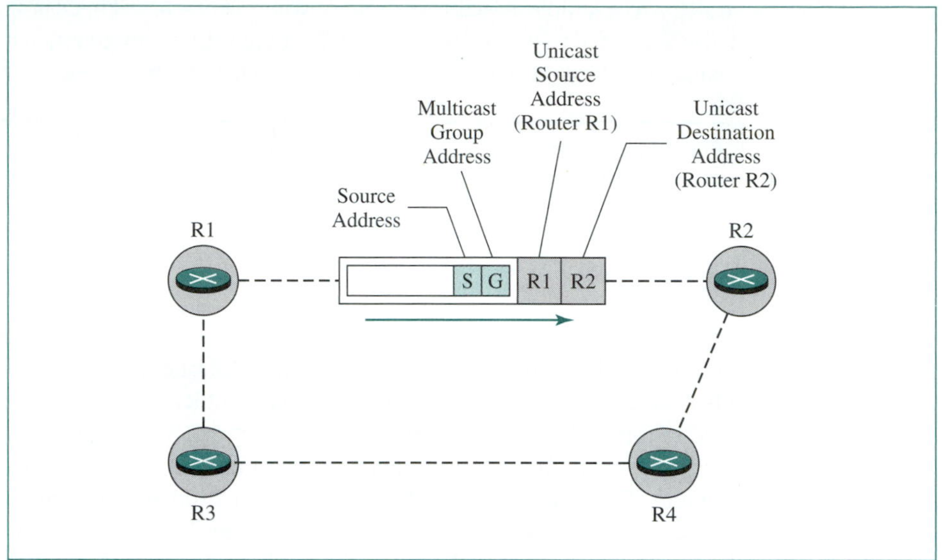

DVMRP supports MBONE.

14.10 KEY TERMS

broadcasting

Core-Based Tree (CBT)

designated parent router

distance learning

Distance Vector Multicast Routing Protocol (DVMRP)

distributed database

flooding

grafting

graph

group-shared tree

least-cost tree

logical tunnel

multicast backbone (MBONE)

Multicast Open Shortest Path First (MOSPF)

multicast router

multicast routing

multicasting

multiple unicasting

Protocol Independent Multicast (PIM)

Protocol Independent Multicast, Dense Mode (PIM-DM)

Protocol Independent Multicast, Sparse Mode (PIM-SM).

pruning

rendezvous router
rendezvous-point tree
reverse path broadcasting (RPB)
reverse path forwarding (RPF)
reverse path multicasting (RPM)
shortest path
source-based tree
spanning tree
Steiner tree
teleconferencing
tree
tunneling
unicasting

14.11 SUMMARY

- In multicasting there is one source and a group of destinations.
- In multiple unicasting multiple copies of a message, each with a different unicast destination address, are sent from a source.
- Multicasting applications include distributed databases, information dissemination, teleconferencing, and distance learning.
- For efficient multicasting we use a shortest path spanning tree to represent the communication path.
- In a source-based tree approach to multicast routing, the source/group combination determines the tree.
- In a group-shared tree approach to multicast routing, the group determines the tree.
- DVRMP is a multicast routing protocol that uses the distance routing protocol to create a source-based tree.
- In reverse path forwarding (RPF), the router forwards only the packets that have traveled the shortest path from the source to the router.
- Reverse path broadcasting (RPB) creates a shortest path broadcast tree from the source to each destination. It guarantees that each destination receives one and only one copy of the packet.
- Reverse path multicasting (RPM) adds pruning and grafting to RPB to create a multicast shortest path tree that supports dynamic membership changes.
- MOSPF is a multicast protocol that uses multicast link state routing to create a source-based least-cost tree.
- The Core-Based Tree (CBT) protocol is a multicast routing protocol that uses a core as the root of the tree.
- PIM-DM is a source-based routing protocol that uses RPF and pruning/grafting strategies to handle multicasting.
- PIM-SM is a group-shared routing protocol that is similar to CBT and uses a rendezvous point as the source of the tree.
- For multicasting between two noncontiguous multicast routers, we make a multicast backbone (MBONE) to enable tunneling.

14.12 PRACTICE SET

Multiple-Choice Questions

1. A one-to-all communication between a source and all hosts on a network is classified as a _______ communication.
   a. unicast
   b. multicast
   c. broadcast
   d. a and b
2. A one-to-many communication between a source and a specific group of hosts is classified as a _______ communication.
   a. unicast
   b. multicast
   c. broadcast
   d. a and b
3. A one-to-one communication between a source and one destination is classified as a _______ communication.
   a. unicast
   b. multicast
   c. broadcast
   d. a and b
4. We can use _______ to emulate multicasting, but it is inefficient and could result in unacceptable delays.
   a. unicasting
   b. multiple unicasting
   c. broadcasting
   d. multiple broadcasting
5. A router has four interfaces: A, B, C, and D. It receives a packet from interface A. To flood the network with this packet, the router sends the packet through interface(s) _______.
   a. A
   b. B, C, and D
   c. A, B, C, and D
   d. A, B, C, or D
6. ________ is a multicasting application.
   a. Teleconferencing
   b. Distance learning
   c. Information dissemination
   d. All of the above

7. A _______ is a data structure with nodes and edges and a hierarchical structure.
   a. tree
   b. graph
   c. leaf
   d. root
8. In unicasting, the Internet, or part of it, can be represented by a _______.
   a. tree
   b. graph
   c. leaf
   d. root
9. In multicasting, the Internet, or part of it, can be represented by a _______.
   a. tree
   b. graph
   c. leaf
   d. root
10. A system uses source-based trees for multicasting. If there are 100 sources and 5 groups, there is a maximum of _______ different trees.
    a. 5
    b. 20
    c. 100
    d. 500
11. In a _______ tree approach to multicasting, the combination of source and group determines the tree.
    a. spanning-source
    b. shortest-group
    c. source-based
    d. group-shared
12. In a _______ tree approach to multicasting, the group determines the tree.
    a. spanning-source
    b. shortest-group
    c. source-based
    d. group-shared
13. A system uses group-shared trees for multicasting. If there are 100 sources and 5 groups, there is a maximum of _______ different trees.
    a. 5
    b. 20
    c. 100
    d. 500

14. _______ is a multicast routing protocol using source-based trees.
    a. DVRMP
    b. MOSPF
    c. CBT
    d. a and b
15. _______ is a multicast routing protocol using group-shared trees.
    a. DVRMP
    b. MOSPF
    c. CBT
    d. a and b
16. In _______ a network can receive a multicast packet from a particular source only through a designated parent router.
    a. RPF
    b. RPB
    c. RPM
    d. all of the above
17. Pruning and grafting are strategies used in _______.
    a. RPF
    b. RPB
    c. RPM
    d. all of the above
18. A _______ message tells an upstream router to stop sending multicast messages for a specific group through a specific router.
    a. weed
    b. graft
    c. prune
    d. plum
19. A _______ message tells an upstream router to start sending multicast messages for a specific group through a specific router.
    a. weed
    b. graft
    c. prune
    d. plum
20. _______ uses multicast link state routing concepts to create source-based trees.
    a. DVMRP
    b. MOSPF
    c. CBT
    d. BVD

21. In the _______ protocol, a multicast packet is encapsulated inside a unicast packet with the core router as the destination.
    a. DVMRP
    b. MOSPF
    c. CBT
    d. BVD
22. _______ is used in a dense multicast environment while _______ is used in a sparse multicast environment.
    a. PIM-DM; PIM-SM
    b. PIM-SM; PIM-DM
    c. PIM; PIM-DM
    d. PIM; PIM-SM
23. When a multicast router is not directly connected to another multicast router, a _______ can be formed to connect the two.
    a. physical tunnel
    b. logical tunnel
    c. logical core
    d. spanning tree

Exercises

24. A router using DVMRP receives a packet with source address 10.14.17.2 from interface 2. If the router forwards the packet, what are the contents of the entry related to this address in the unicast routing table?
25. Router A sends a unicast RIP update packet to router B that says 134.23.0.0/16 is 7 hops away. Network B sends an update packet to router A that says 13.23.0.0/16 is 4 hops away. If these two routers are connected to the same network, which one is the designated parent router?
26. Does RPF actually create a spanning tree? Explain.
27. Does RPB actually create a spanning tree? Explain. What are the leaves of the tree?
28. Does RPM actually create a spanning tree? Explain. What are the leaves of the tree?

Projects

29. Do some research on the Internet on DVMRP. What is the format of the prune message? What is the format of the graft message?
30. Do some research on the Internet on MOSPF. What is the format of the group-membership LSA packet that associates a network with a group?
31. CBT uses nine types of packets. Use the Internet to find the purpose and format of each packet.
32. Use the Internet to find how CBT messages are encapsulated.
33. Use the Internet to find information regarding the scalability of each multicast routing protocol we discussed. Make a table and compare them.
34. Use the Internet to find information about the inter-autonomous multicast protocols.

CHAPTER 15

Application Layer and Client-Server Model

Because the TCP/IP protocol suite was designed before the OSI model, the layers in TCP/IP do not correspond exactly to the OSI layers. The application layer in TCP/IP is equivalent to the combined session, presentation, and application layers of the OSI model. This means that all of the functionalities associated with those three layers are handled in one single layer, the application layer (see Figure 15.1).

Figure 15.1 *Comparison between OSI and TCP/IP*

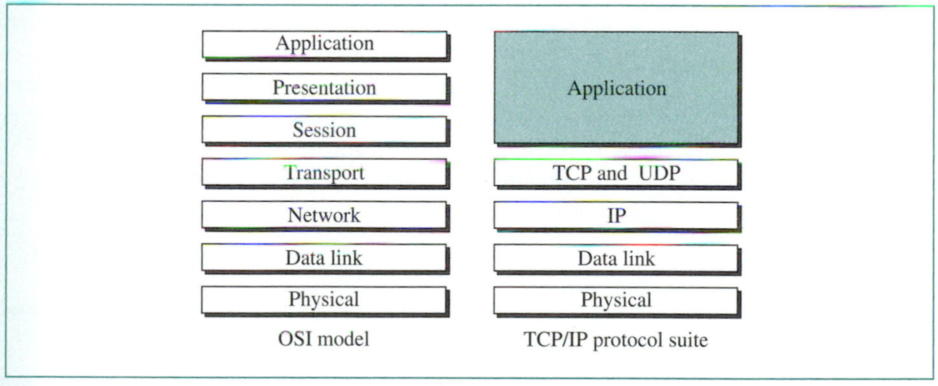

In other words, every application program must include all tasks assigned to the session, presentation, and application layers of the OSI model. This has some advantages and some disadvantages. One advantage is that each application program is independent. It requires only those functions needed for the job for which the application is designed. This saves needless calls to services that just pass parameters. One disadvantage is that the same tasks appear in different application programs, making them more complex. In addition, this kills the whole idea of modularity and layered architecture of the OSI model.

15.1 CLIENT-SERVER MODEL

The purpose of a network, or an internetwork, is to provide services to users. A user at a local site wants to receive a service from a computer at a remote site. There is only one way for a computer to do the job; it must run a program. A computer runs a program to request a service from another program and also to provide a service to another computer. This means that two computers, connected by an internet, must each run a program, one to provide a service and one to request a service.

It should be clear now that if we want to use the services available on an internet, application programs, running at two end computers and communicating with each other, are needed. In other words, in an internet, the application programs are the entities that communicate with each other, not the computers or users.

At first glance, it looks simple to enable communication between two application programs, one running at the local site, the other running at the remote site. But many questions arise when we want to implement the approach. Some of the questions that we may ask are:

1. Should both application programs be able to request services and provide services or should the application programs just do one or the other? One solution is to have an application program, called the *client,* running on the local machine, request a service from another application program, called the *server,* running on the remote machine. In other words, the tasks of requesting a service and providing a service are separate from each other. An application program is either a requester (a client), or a provider (a server). If a machine needs to request a service and provide a service, two application programs must be installed. In other words, application programs come in pairs, client and server, both having the same name. Figure 15.2 illustrates this.

Figure 15.2 *Client-server model*

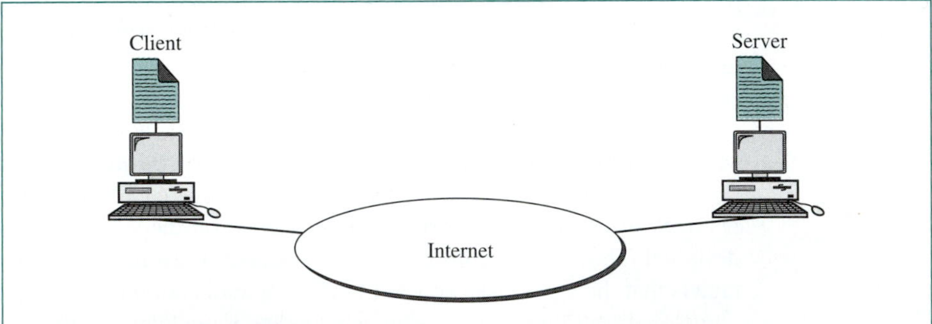

2. Should an application program provide services only to one specific application program installed somewhere in an internet or should it provide services for any application program that requests this service? The most common solution is a server providing a service for any client, not a particular client. In other words, the

client-server relationship is many-to-one. Many clients can use the services of one server (see Figure 15.3).

Figure 15.3 *Client-server relationship*

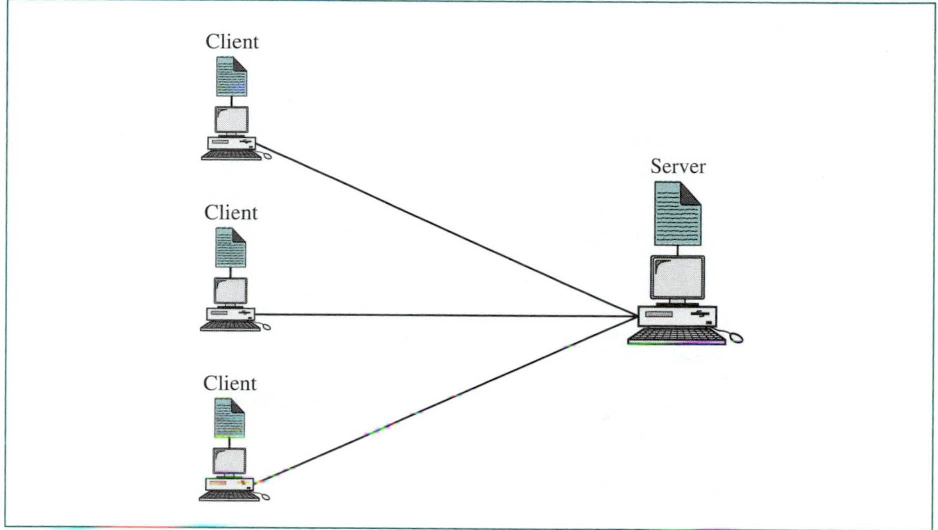

3. When should an application program be running? All of the time or just when there is a need for the service? Generally, a client program, which requests a service, should run only when it is needed. The server program, which provides a service, should run all of the time because it does not know when its service will be needed.
4. Should there be only one universal application program that can provide any type of service a user wants? Or should there be one application program for each type of service? In TCP/IP, services needed frequently and by many users have specific client-server application programs. For example, we have separate client-server application programs that allow users to access files, send email, and so on. For services that are more customized, we should have one generic application program that allows users to access the services available on a remote computer. For example, we should have a client-server application program that allows the user to log onto a remote computer and then use the services provided by that computer. However, we will see that there is a security problem with this type of client-server pair.

Client

A **client** is a program running on the local machine requesting service from a server. A client program is **finite,** which means it is started by the user (or another application program) and terminates when the service is complete. A client opens the communication channel using the IP address of the remote host and the well-known port address of the specific server program running on that machine. This is called an *active open*. After a channel of communication is opened, the client sends its request and receives a response. Although the request-response part may be repeated several times, the whole process is finite and eventually comes to an end. At that moment, the client closes the communication channel with an *active close*.

Server

A **server** is a program running on the remote machine providing service to the clients. When it starts, it opens the door for incoming requests from clients, but it never initiates a service until it is requested to do so. This is called a *passive open*.

A server program is an **infinite** program. When it starts it runs infinitely unless a problem arises. It waits for incoming requests from clients. When a request arrives, it responds to the request, either iteratively or concurrently as we will see shortly.

15.2 CONCURRENCY

Both clients and servers can run in concurrent mode.

Concurrency in Clients

Clients can be run on a machine either iteratively or concurrently. Running clients iteratively means running them one by one; one client must start, run, and terminate before the machine can start another client. Most computers today, however, allow concurrent clients, that is, two or more clients can run at the same time.

Concurrency in Servers

An iterative server can process only one request at a time; it receives a request, processes it, and sends the response to the requestor before it handles another request. A concurrent server, on the other hand, can process many requests at the same time and thus can share its time between many requests.

The servers use either UDP, a connectionless transport layer protocol, or TCP, a connection-oriented transport layer protocol. Server operation, therefore, depends on two factors: the transport layer protocol and the service method. Theoretically we can have four types of servers: connectionless iterative, connectionless concurrent, connection-oriented iterative, and connection-oriented concurrent (see Figure 15.4). However, only the first and the last are commonly used. We discuss only these two here.

Connectionless Iterative Server

The servers that use UDP are normally iterative, which, as we have said, means that the server processes one request at a time. A server gets the request received in a datagram from UDP, processes the request, and gives the response to UDP to send to the client. The server pays no attention to the other datagrams. These datagrams are stored in a queue, waiting for service. They could all be from one client or from many clients. In either case they are processed one by one in order of arrival.

Figure 15.4 *Server types*

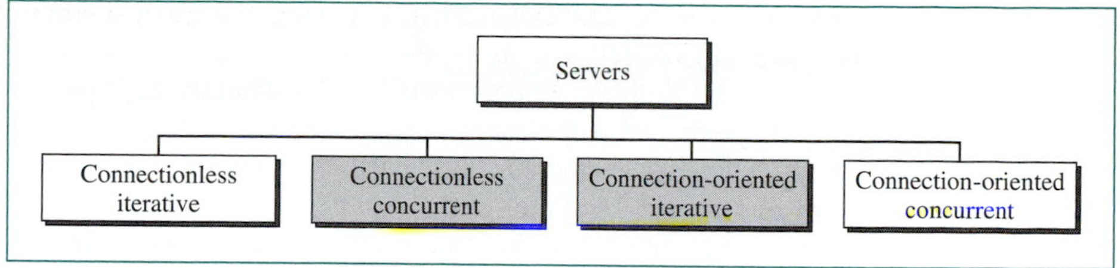

The server uses one single port for this purpose, the well-known port. All the datagrams arriving at this port wait in line to be served, as is shown in Figure 15.5.

Figure 15.5 *Connectionless iterative server*

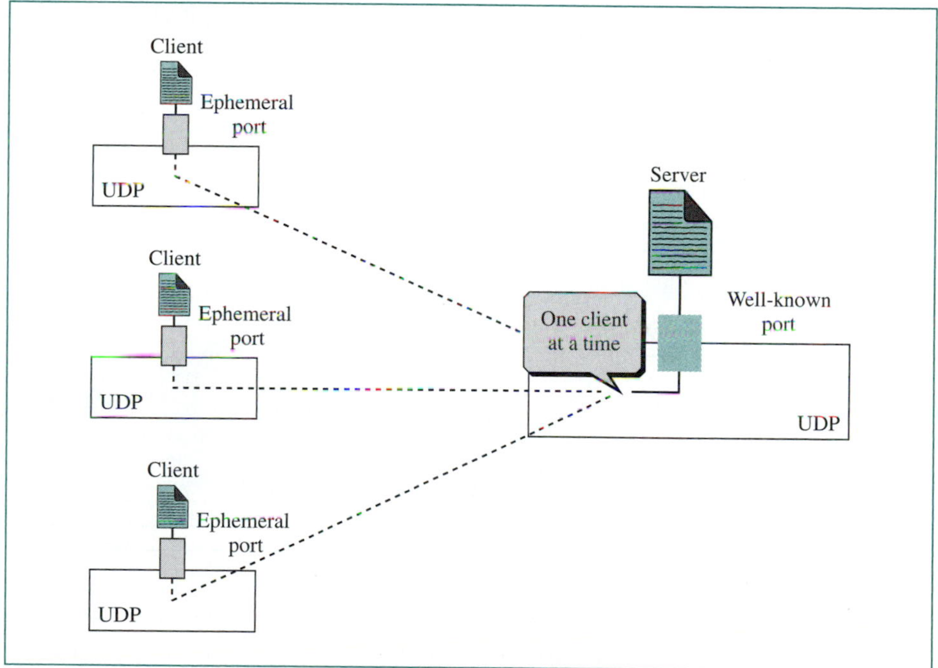

Connection-Oriented Concurrent Server

The servers that use TCP are normally concurrent. This means that the server can serve many clients at the same time. Communication is connection-oriented, which means that a request is a stream of bytes that can arrive in several segments and the response can occupy several segments. A connection is established between the server and each client, and the connection remains open until the entire stream is processed and the connection is terminated.

This type of server cannot use only one well-known port because each connection needs a port and many connections may be open at the same time. Many ports are needed, but a server can use only one well-known port. The solution is to have one well-known port and many ephemeral ports. The server makes a passive open at the well-known port. A client can make its initial approach to this port to make the connection. After the connection is made, the server assigns a temporary port to this connection to free the well-known port. Data transfer can now take place between these two temporary ports, one at the client site and the other at the server site. The well-known port is now free for another client to make the connection. The idea is to push demultiplexing to TCP instead of the server.

The server must also have one buffer for each connection. The segments come from the client, are stored in the appropriate buffer, and will be served concurrently by the server.

To provide this service, most implementations use the concept of parent and child servers. A server running infinitely and accepting connections from the clients is called a *parent server.* The parent server uses the well-known port. After it makes a connection, the parent server creates a *child server* and a temporary (ephemeral) port and lets the child server handle the service. It thereby frees itself so that it can wait for another connection. See Figure 15.6 for this configuration.

Figure 15.6 *Connection-oriented concurrent server*

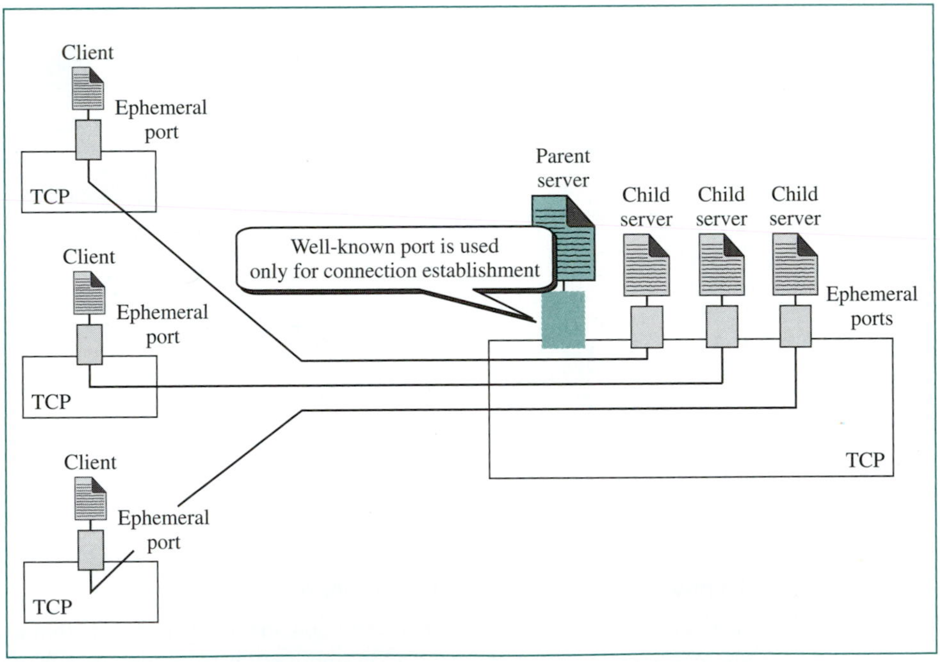

15.3 PROCESSES

Understanding the concept of a **process** is necessary to comprehend the client-server model. In this section, we discuss this concept and its relationship to the client-server model, particularly concurrent processing.

Concept

Most operating systems, including UNIX, distinguish a program from a process. Whereas a program and a process are related to each other, they are not the same thing. In UNIX, a program is code. The code defines all the variables and actions to be performed on those variables. A process, on the other hand, is an instance of a program. When the operating system executes a program, an instance of the program, a process, is created. The operating system can create several processes from one program, which means several instances of the same program are running at the same time (concurrently). Memory is allocated for each process separately.

To handle processes, an operating system usually associates a structure with a process. The structure holds information needed to control a process. Among other things, a structure holds a pointer pointing to the line of the program being executed at this moment for this specific process, the processid, the userid, the program name, and a pointer to the memory where allocation for variables is made and data belonging to this process is stored.

Figure 15.7 shows the concept. Here the operating system is running two instances of the program, and therefore, there are two structures, one for each process.

Figure 15.7 *Program and processes*

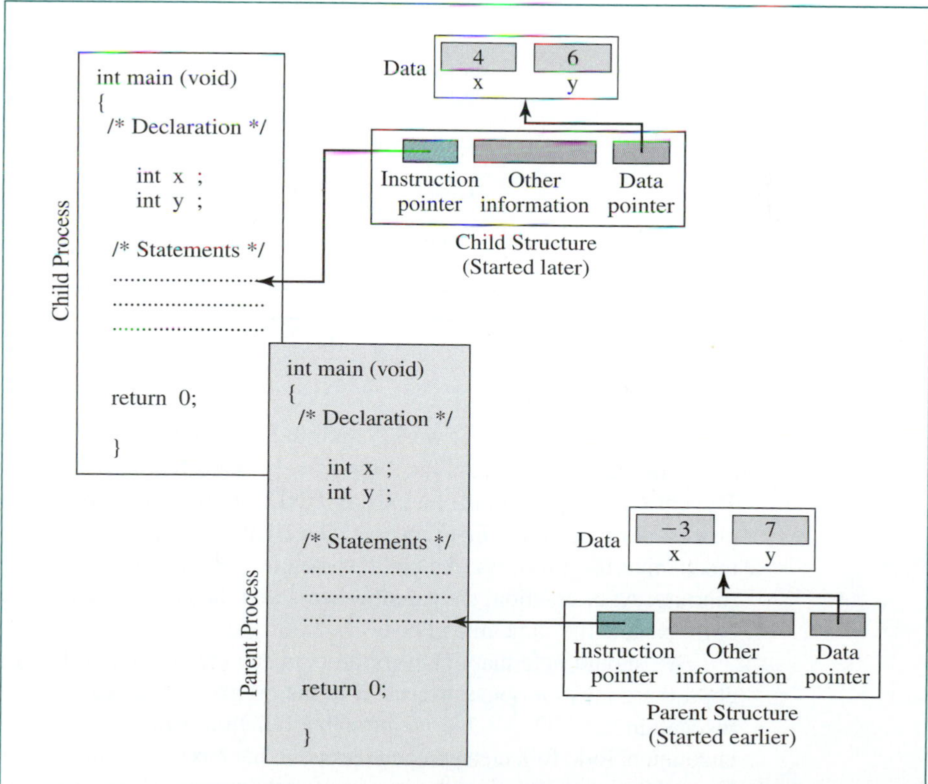

Process Identification

Each process in UNIX is uniquely defined by an integer called the *process identification* number or *processid*. There is a UNIX function that can return the process identification number of a process. Figure 15.8 shows the prototype declaration. The **pid_t** is a data type that is often cast to long integer.

Figure 15.8 *Prototype for the getpid function*

```
pid_t    getpid (void) ;
```

For example, the program in Figure 15.9, when run, is a process; it prints its own processid. However, the printed processid is different each time the program is run. Each time, the operating system assigns a different processid to the process.

Figure 15.9 *A program that prints its own processid*

```
#include <stdio.h>
#include <sys/types.h>
#include <unistd.h>

int main (void)
{
  printf ("My process id  is %ld", (long) getpid());

  return  0;
}
```

Process Creation

Just as creation in the real world is normally done by replication, process creation in an operating system occurs the same way. In real life, a pair of parents creates a child. The child is a replica of the parents. In UNIX, a process can be created only by a parent process (except for the first process). The created process is called a *child process*. This means that for a process (the child) to be created, another process (the parent) must be running. After creation, the parent process and the child process run concurrently; they both execute the same line of codes.

We should note that not every process can create a child. For a process to create a child there must be some invocation in the program code that triggers the process. This invocation in UNIX is achieved through a function named *fork*. When the parent process encounters fork, fork creates a child process that has exactly the same image as its parent. From this time forward, both parent and child execute all remaining lines of code. However, the lines of code prior to fork are executed only by the parent. Figure 15.10 shows the prototype of the fork function.

Figure 15.10 *Prototype for the fork function*

```
pid_t    fork (void) ;
```

Figure 15.11 shows an example of a program with the function fork. The parent process runs the program. When it encounters fork, a child process is born and, after that, both run the remaining code. The message "Hello World" is printed once and only by the parent. The message "Bye World" is printed twice; once by the parent and once by the child.

Figure 15.11 *A program with one parent and one child*

```
#include <stdio.h>
#include <sys/types.h>
#include <unistd.h>

int main (void)
{
  printf ("Hello World\n") ;

  fork () ;

  printf ("Bye World\n") ;

  return 0;
}
```

Hello World

Printed by parent

Bye World
Bye World

Printed by parent and child

An interesting point in process creation is that a child process can also create a child (a grandchild). Figure 15.12 shows how fork is called twice in a program. The

Figure 15.12 *A program with two fork functions*

```
#include <stdio.h>
#include <sys/types.h>
#include <unistd.h>

int main (void)
{

  printf ("Parent\n") ;
  fork () ;
  printf ("Parent and first child\n") ;
  fork () ;
  printf ("Parent, first child, second child, and grandchild");

  return 0;
}
```

first fork is called by the parent process and creates a child; the second fork, however, is called by two processes: the parent and the child. When fork is called by the parent process, it creates a new child (second child). When fork is called by the first child, it creates another child (a grandchild). After the first fork, only two processes are running (the parent and the first child); after the second fork, four processes are running: the parent, the first child, the second child, and the grandchild (the child of the first child).

Figure 15.13 shows the result of the previous program. The first line is printed only once, the second line twice, and the third line four times.

Figure 15.13 *The output of the program in Figure 15.12*

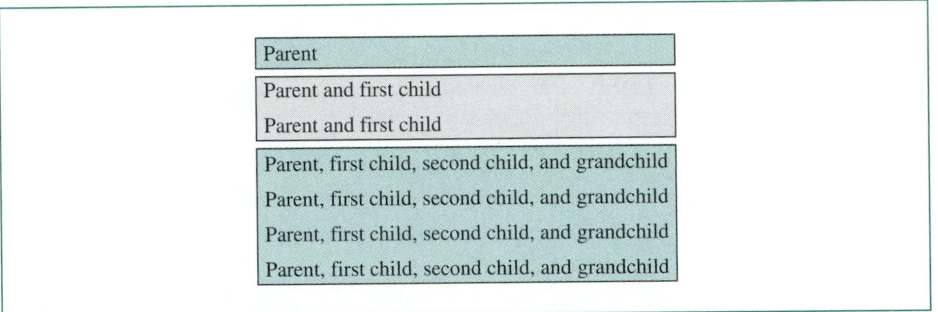

```
Parent
Parent and first child
Parent and first child
Parent, first child, second child, and grandchild
Parent, first child, second child, and grandchild
Parent, first child, second child, and grandchild
Parent, first child, second child, and grandchild
```

A very interesting point about fork is that when it is called, it returns two values. The returned value available to the parent process is the processid of the created child. The returned value available to the child process is simply 0. These dual returned values allow the programmer to write a program to separate the parent process from the child process. The program in Figure 15.14 prints the processids of the parent and child. The program separates these two processes by testing the return value of the fork function.

Figure 15.14 *A program that prints the processids of the parent and the child*

```
#include <stdio.h>
#include <sys/types.h>
#include <unistd.h>

int main (void)
{
  pid_t  pid ;
  pid  = fork () ;
  if (pid > 0 )
     printf ("Parent process id  is %ld", (long) getpid());
  if (pid == 0 )
     printf ("Child process id  is %ld", (long) getpid());
  return  0;
}
```

The separation of the parent and the child is the key to the design of concurrent servers. A parent server can run infinitely and wait for a client to make a connection. As soon as a client requests the connection, the parent can create a child server to serve the client while it continues to look for other clients. For every client, a new child server is created and assigned to serve that client. Figure 15.15 shows the idea. We will give more details in Chapter 16 when we discuss the socket interface.

Figure 15.15 *Example of a server program with parent and child processes*

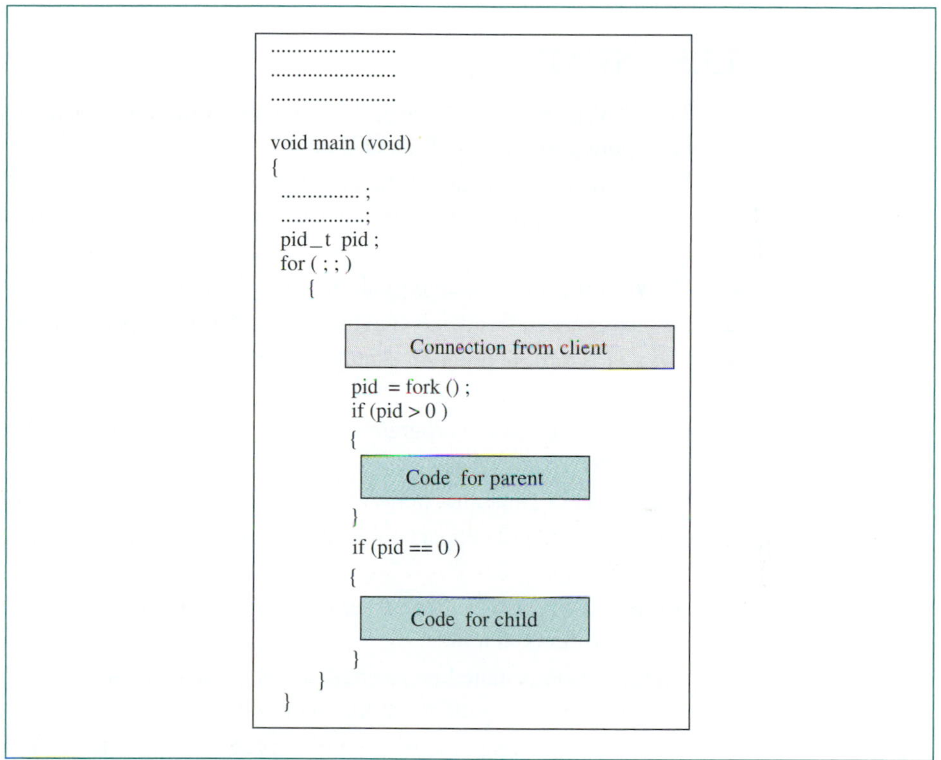

15.4 KEY TERMS

- active close
- active open
- application layer
- child process
- child server
- client
- client-server model
- code
- concurrent client
- concurrent server
- connectionless iterative server
- connection-oriented concurrent server
- finite program
- fork

infinite program
iterative client
iterative server
OSI model
parent server
passive open
process
process identification (processid)
program
server

15.5 SUMMARY

- The TCP/IP application layer corresponds to the combined session, presentation, and application layers of the OSI model.
- In the client-server model the client runs a program to request a service and the server runs a program to provide the service. These two programs communicate with each other.
- One server program can provide services for many client programs.
- Services needed frequently and by many users have specific client-server programs.
- A client is a finite program running on the local machine requesting service from a server.
- A server is an infinite program running on the remote machine providing service to the clients.
- Clients can be run either iteratively (one at a time) or concurrently (many at a time).
- Servers can handle clients either iteratively (one at a time) or concurrently (many at a time).
- A connectionless iterative server uses UDP as its transport layer protocol and can serve one client at a time.
- A connection-oriented concurrent server uses TCP as its transport layer protocol and can serve many clients at the same time.
- When the operating system executes a program, an instance of the program, called a process, is created.
- Each program in UNIX is uniquely identified by an integer called the process identification number (processid).
- The fork function enables the creation of a child process from a parent process.
- The fork function returns two values that enable the separation of the parent from the child.

15.6 PRACTICE SET

Multiple-Choice Questions

1. _______ can request a service.
   a. A socket interface
   b. A port
   c. A client
   d. A server
2. _______ can provide a service.
   a. An iterative server
   b. A concurrent server
   c. A client
   d. a and b
3. The client program is _______ because it terminates after it has been served.
   a. active
   b. passive
   c. finite
   d. infinite
4. The server program is _______ because it is always available, waiting for a client request.
   a. active
   b. passive
   c. finite
   d. infinite
5. A connection-oriented concurrent server uses _______ ports.
   a. ephemeral
   b. well-known
   c. active
   d. a and b
6. A connectionless iterative server uses _______ ports.
   a. ephemeral
   b. well-known
   c. active
   d. a and b
7. The TCP/IP application layer corresponds to the OSI model's _______ layer.
   a. physical, data link, and network
   b. transport and network
   c. session and transport
   d. session, presentation, and application

8. Machine A requests service X from machine B. Machine B requests service Y from machine A. What is the total number of application programs required?
   a. 1
   b. 2
   c. 3
   d. 4
9. A client issues _______ when it needs service from a server.
   a. an active open
   b. a passive open
   c. an active request
   d. a finite open
10. A server program, once it issues _______, waits for clients to request its service.
    a. an active open
    b. a passive open
    c. an active request
    d. a finite open
11. _______ processes requests one at a time.
    a. An iterative client
    b. An iterative server
    c. A concurrent client
    d. A concurrent server
12. _______ processes many requests simultaneously.
    a. An iterative client
    b. An iterative server
    c. A concurrent client
    d. A concurrent server
13. In a connection-oriented concurrent server, the _______ is used for connection only.
    a. infinite port
    b. ephemeral port
    c. well-known port
    d. b and c
14. A _______ is an instance of a _______.
    a. process; program
    b. program; process
    c. process; service
    d. structure; process

15. Four processes from one program are created: one parent, two child, and one grandchild. How many processids are there?
    a. 1
    b. 2
    c. 3
    d. 4
16. When program A is run, its processid is 12,345. When it is run again, its processid is _______.
    a. 12,344
    b. 12,345
    c. 12,346
    d. some number assigned by the operating system
17. The _______ function creates a child process.
    a. child
    b. get_child
    c. getpid
    d. fork
18. In the program in Figure 15.12, the parent process prints _______ statements.
    a. 1
    b. 2
    c. 3
    d. 4
19. In the program in Figure 15.12, the first child process prints _______ statements.
    a. 1
    b. 2
    c. 3
    d. 4
20. In the program in Figure 15.12, the second child process prints _______ statements.
    a. 1
    b. 2
    c. 3
    d. 4
21. In the program in Figure 15.12, the grandchild process prints _______ statements.
    a. 1
    b. 2
    c. 3
    d. 4

Exercises

22. Can a child process have more than one parent process?
23. Can a parent process have more than one child process?
24. Show how a parent can print the processid of its child.
25. Show how a child can print the processid of its parent. Use the *getppid()* function which is similar to *getpid,* but it prints the processid of the parent.
26. What is the output of the following program segment?

```
fork ();
printf ("Hello\n") ;
printf ("Hello\n") ;
fork ();
printf ("Bye\n") ;
return 0 ;
```

27. What is the output of the following program segment?

```
for (i =1 ; i<= 4 ; i++)
{
  pid = fork () ;
  if (pid > 0)
     printf ("%d\n", pid) ;
}
```

28. What is the output of the following program segment?

```
for (i =1 ; i<= 4 ; i++)
{
  pid = fork () ;
  if (pid == 0)
     continue ;
  else
     printf ("%d\n", pid) ;
}
```

29. What is the output of the following program segment?

```
pid  = fork ();
if (pid == 0)
     {
     printf ("Hello\n") ;
     fork ();
     printf ("Bye\n") ;
     }
else
     {
     printf ("Hi\n") ;
     fork ();
     printf ("Dear\n") ;
     fork ();
     printf ("Friend\n");
     }
```

Programming Exercises

30. Write a program that creates a child and prints the processid of the child first and the parent next.
31. Write a program that creates a child and a grandchild. The program should print the processid of the parent, the child, and the grandchild in this order.
32. Write a program that creates a child and a grandchild. The program should print the processid of the grandchild, the child, and the parent in this order.
33. Write a program that creates two children and four grandchildren (two for each child). The program should then print the processid of the parent, the two children, and the four grandchildren in this order.
34. Write the client program for the program in Figure 15.9.
35. Rewrite the program of Figure 15.9 as an iterative server.

CHAPTER 16

Socket Interface

In a client-server model, two application programs, one running on the local system (a client for example) and the other running on the remote system (a server for example), need to communicate with one another. To standardize network programming, application programming interfaces (APIs) have been developed. An API is a set of declarations, definitions, and procedures followed by programmers to write client-server programs. Among the more common APIs are the Socket Interface, the Transport Layer Interface (TLI), the Stream Interface, the Thread Interface, and the Remote Procedure Call (RPC). The Socket Interface, which is very common today, is the implementation we will discuss in this chapter.

The Socket Interface was developed as part of UNIX BSD. It is based on UNIX and defines a set of system calls (procedures) that are an extension of system calls used in UNIX to access files. This chapter shows the fundamentals of Socket Interface programming though it by no means teaches Socket Interface programming; there are whole books devoted to this subject. Instead, we introduce the concept and idea, and, maybe, provide motivation for those readers who want to learn more.

In this chapter, we first introduce some data types and functions used in network programming. Then we define sockets and introduce socket interface calls. Finally we give two pairs of examples of client-server programs.

16.1 SOME DEFINITIONS

In this section, we introduce some data types and structures that are needed for writing client-server programs.

Data Types Defined

Figure 16.1 lists six data types used extensively in client-server programs. These are int8_t, int16_t, int32_t, uint8_t, uint16_t, and uint32_t data types.

Figure 16.1 *Data types*

int8_t	Signed 8-bit integer
int16_t	Signed 16-bit integer
int32_t	Signed 32-bit integer
uint8_t	Unsigned 8-bit integer
uint16_t	Unsigned 16-bit integer
uint32_t	Unsigned 32-bit integer

Internet Address Structure

An IPv4 address is defined as a structure (struct in C) called *in_addr,* which contains only one field called *s_addr* of type in_addr_t. The structure holds an IP address as a 32-bit binary number. Figure 16.2 shows the structure and the corresponding declaration.

Figure 16.2 *Internet address structure*

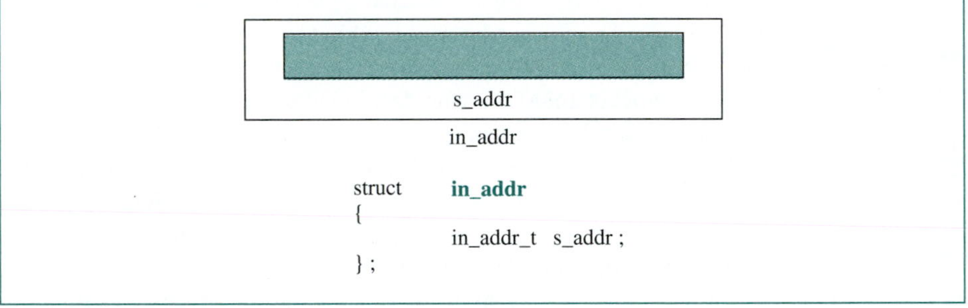

Internet Socket Address Structure

The application programs that use the TCP/IP protocol suite need a structure called a **socket address,** which mainly holds an IP address, a port number, and the protocol family. The structure is called *sockaddress* and has five fields; the first and the last field are normally not used, however. Figure 16.3 shows the structure and its declaration.

16.2 SOCKETS

The communication structure that we need in socket programming is a **socket.** A socket acts as an end point. Two processes need a socket at each end to communicate with each other.

Figure 16.3 *Socket address structure*

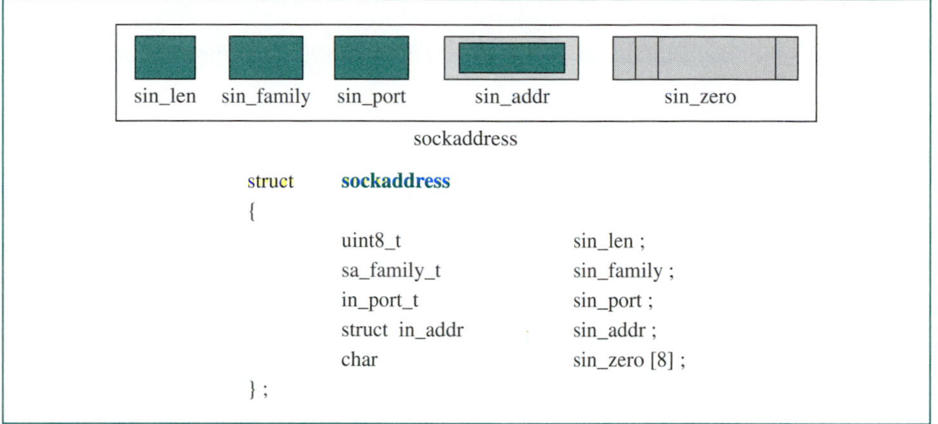

A socket is defined in the operating system as a structure. Figure 16.4 shows a simplified version of a socket structure with five fields. These fields are listed below.

- **Family.** This field defines the protocol group: IPv4, IPv6, UNIX domain protocols, and so on.
- **Type.** This field defines the type of socket: stream socket, datagram socket, or raw socket. These are discussed in the next section.
- **Protocol.** This field is usually set to zero for TCP and UDP.
- **Local socket address.** This field defines the local socket address, a structure of type sockaddress, as defined previously.
- **Remote socket address.** This field defines the remote socket address, a structure of type sockaddress, as defined previously.

Figure 16.4 *Socket structure*

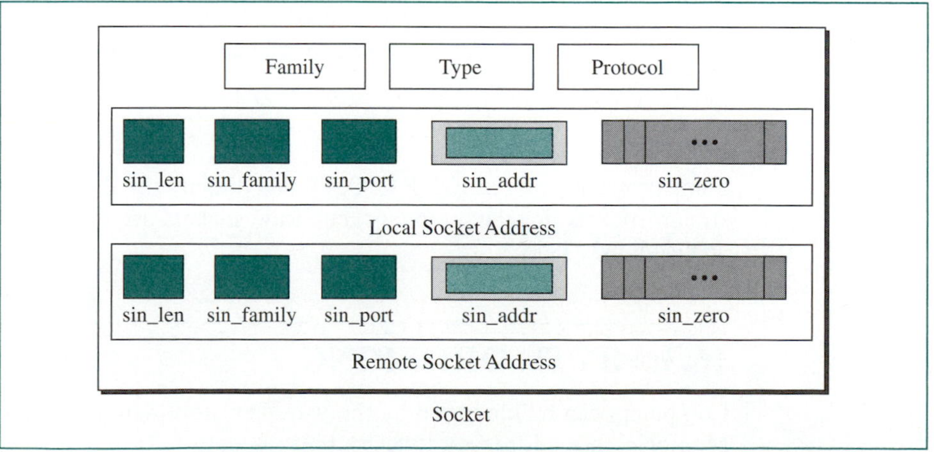

Socket Types

The socket interface defines three types of sockets: the stream socket, the datagram socket, and the raw socket. All three types can be used in a TCP/IP environment (see Figure 16.5).

Figure 16.5 *Socket types*

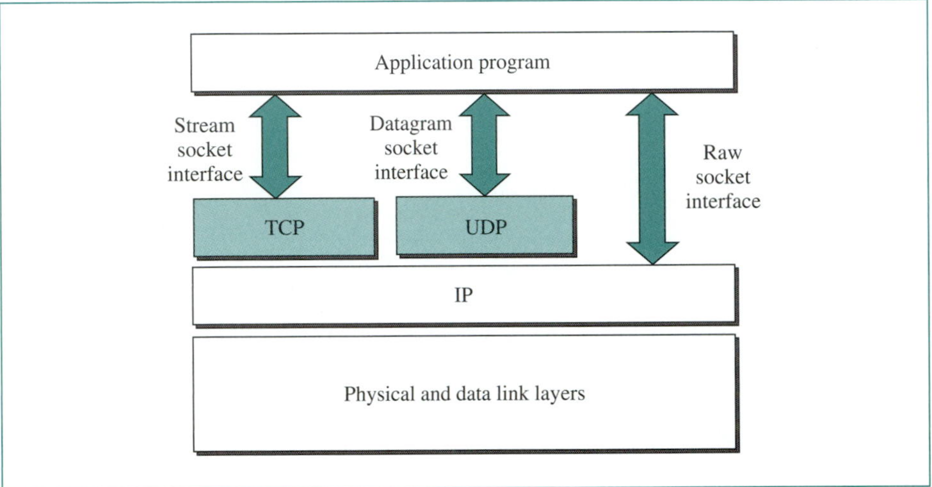

Stream Socket

A stream socket is designed to be used with a connection-oriented protocol such as TCP. TCP uses a pair of stream sockets to connect one application program to another across the Internet.

Datagram Socket

A datagram socket is designed to be used with a connectionless protocol such as UDP. UDP uses a pair of datagram sockets to send a message from one application program to another across the Internet.

Raw Socket

Some protocols such as ICMP or OSPF that directly use the services of IP use neither stream sockets nor datagram sockets. Raw sockets are designed for these types of applications.

16.3 BYTE ORDERING

Computers can be classified by the way they store data in their internal memories. Memories are addressed byte by byte. A data unit can span more than 1 byte, however. For example, in most computers, a short integer is 2 bytes (16 bits) and a long integer is 4 bytes (32 bits). How a 2-byte short integer or a 4-byte long integer is stored in bytes of memory defines the category of computer: big endian or little endian.

Big-Endian Byte Order

A computer that uses the **big-endian** system stores the most significant byte (the big end) of data in the starting address of the data unit. For example, an IP address such as 10.23.14.6, when expressed as a 32-bit binary number (long integer), can be stored in a big-endian computer as shown in Figure 16.6.

Figure 16.6 *Big-endian byte order*

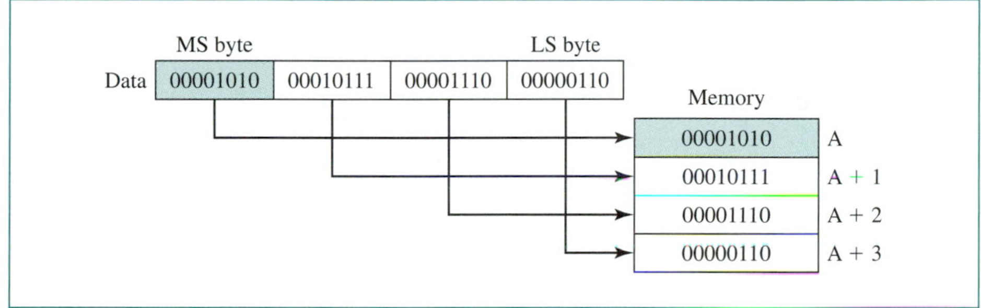

IBM mainframe computers as well as computers based on Motorola microprocessors are based on the big-endian system.

Little-Endian Byte Order

If a computer uses the **little-endian** system, it stores the least significant byte (the little end) of data in the starting address of the data unit. For example, an IP address such as 10.23.14.6, when expressed as a 32-bit binary number (long integer), can be stored in a little-endian computer as shown in Figure 16.7.

Figure 16.7 *Little-endian byte order*

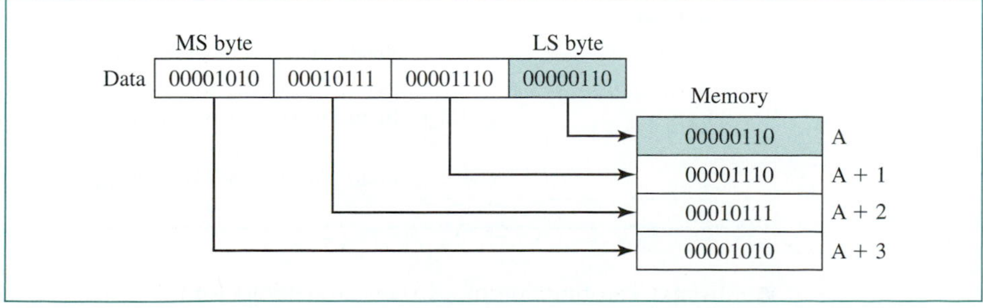

DEC VAX computers and computers using Intel microprocessors are based on the little-endian system.

Network Byte Order

Networking protocols can also choose their own byte order. The TCP/IP protocol suite has chosen the big-endian byte order.

> The byte order for the TCP/IP protocol suite is big endian.

Byte-Order Transformation

To create portability in application programs, TCP/IP software provides a set of functions that transforms integers from a host byte order (big endian or little endian) to network byte order (big endian). Four functions are designed for this purpose: htons, htonl, ntohs, and ntohl (see Figure 16.8).

Figure 16.8 *Byte-order transformation functions*

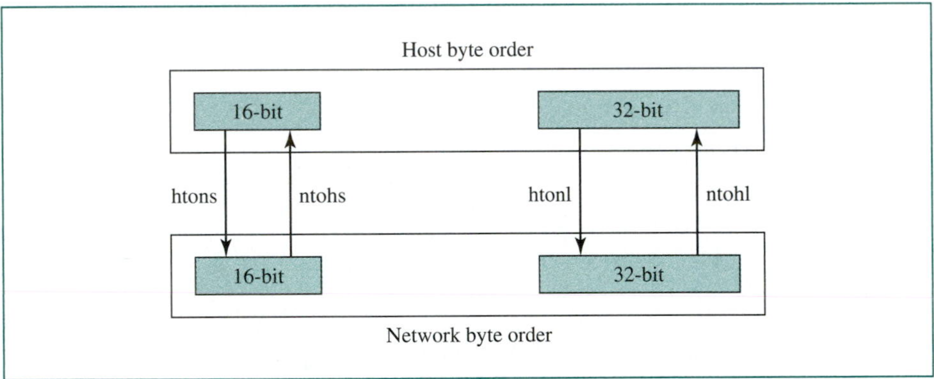

The prototypes are shown in Figure 16.9.

Figure 16.9 *Declarations for byte-order transformation*

```
uint16_t  htons ( uint16_t  host_short ) ;

uint16_t  ntohs ( uint16_t  network_short ) ;

uint32_t  htonl ( uint32_t  host_long ) ;

uint32_t  ntohl ( uint32_t  network_long ) ;
```

- **htons.** The function htons (host to network short) converts a 16-bit integer from host byte order to network byte order.
- **htonl.** The function htonl (host to network long) converts a 32-bit integer from host byte order to network byte order.

- **ntohs.** The function ntohs (network to host short) converts a 16-bit integer from network byte order to host byte order.
- **ntohl.** The function ntohl (network to host long) converts a 32-bit integer from network byte order to host byte order.

16.4 ADDRESS TRANSFORMATION

Network software provides functions to transform an IP address from ASCII dotted decimal format to 32-bit binary format and vice versa. Two of these functions are discussed here: inet_aton and inet_ntoa (see Figure 16.10).

Figure 16.10 *Address transformation*

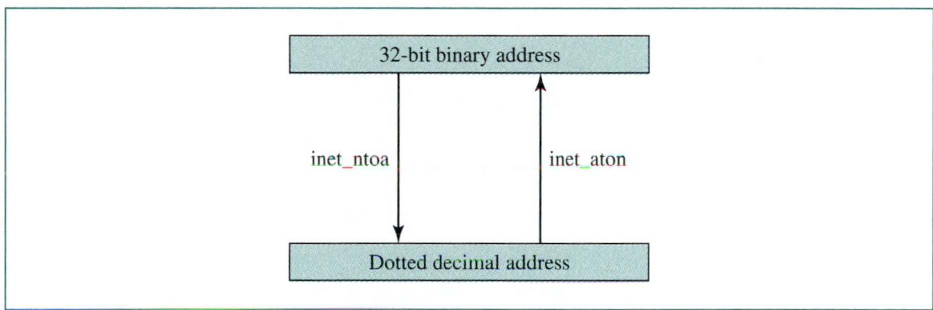

The prototypes of transformation functions are shown in Figure 16.11.

Figure 16.11 *Declarations for transformation functions*

```
int      inet_aton ( const char *strptr , struct in_addr *addrptr ) ;
char    *inet_ntoa (struct in_addr inaddr ) ;
```

- **inet_aton.** This function transforms an ASCII string that contains up to four segments separated by dots to a 32-bit binary address in network byte order.
- **inet_ntoa.** This function transforms a 32-bit binary address in network byte order to an ASCII string with four segments separated by dots.

16.5 BYTE MANIPULATION FUNCTIONS

In network programming, we often need to initialize a field, copy the contents of one field to another, or compare the contents of two fields. We cannot use string functions such as *strcpy* or *strcmp* because these functions assume that a field is terminated with a null character, which is not true in network programming. As a matter of fact, we may need to copy a sequence of bytes from one field to another that may contain a zero byte. The string functions interpret this zero as a terminator and stop at that point.

Several functions have been defined in the <string.h> header file for these byte manipulations. We introduce the three most common: *memset, memcpy,* and *memcmp*. Their prototypes are shown in Figure 16.12.

Figure 16.12 *Declaration for byte-manipulation functions*

```
void    *memset ( void *dest , int chr , size_t len ) ;

void    *memcpy ( void *dest , const void  *src , size_t len ) ;

int      memcmp ( const void *first , const void  *second , size_t len ) ;
```

- **Memset.** This function sets a specified number of bytes to a value. The first argument is a pointer to the destination, the field to be set. The second argument is the value, and the third argument is the number of bytes. One can use the sizeof operator to fill the entire field. For example, the following stores zeros in a field called *x*:

  memset (&x , 0 , sizeof(x)) ;

- **Memcpy.** This function copies the value of one field to another. The first argument is a pointer to the destination. The second argument is a pointer to the source. The third argument is the number of bytes to be copied. For example, the following copies the value of the *y* field to the *x* field:

  memcpy (&x , &y , sizeof(x)) ;

- **Memcmp.** This function compares two fields. The first argument is a pointer to the first field. The second argument is a pointer to the second field. The third argument is the number of bytes to be compared. This function returns zero if the two fields are the same. It returns a number less than zero if the first field is smaller than the second. It returns a number greater than zero if the first field is greater than the second. For example, the following compares the first 10 bytes of fields *x* and *y*:

  memcmp (&x , &y , 10) ;

16.6 INFORMATION ABOUT REMOTE HOST

A process often needs information about a remote host. Several functions have been designed to provide this information. We discuss one such function, called *gethostbyname*. This function is actually a call to the DNS. The function accepts the domain name of the host and returns structured information called *hostent* that is actually the contents of a resource record. The prototype of the function is given in Figure 16.13.

Figure 16.13 *Declaration for gethostbyname*

```
struct hostent *gethostbyname ( const char *hostname ) ;
```

The hostname is the domain name of the host in the form xxx.yyy.zzz. The function returns a pointer to the hostent structure.

The struct hostent provides several pieces of information. The first field is a pointer to the name of the host. The second field is a pointer to an array of pointers with each pointer pointing to an alias by which the host can be called. The third field is the type of address (AF_INET in the Internet). The next field is the length of the address (4 bytes for IPv4). The last field is a pointer to an array of pointers with each pointer pointing to one of the host addresses (the host can be a multihomed host). See Figure 16.14.

Figure 16.14 *The hostent structure*

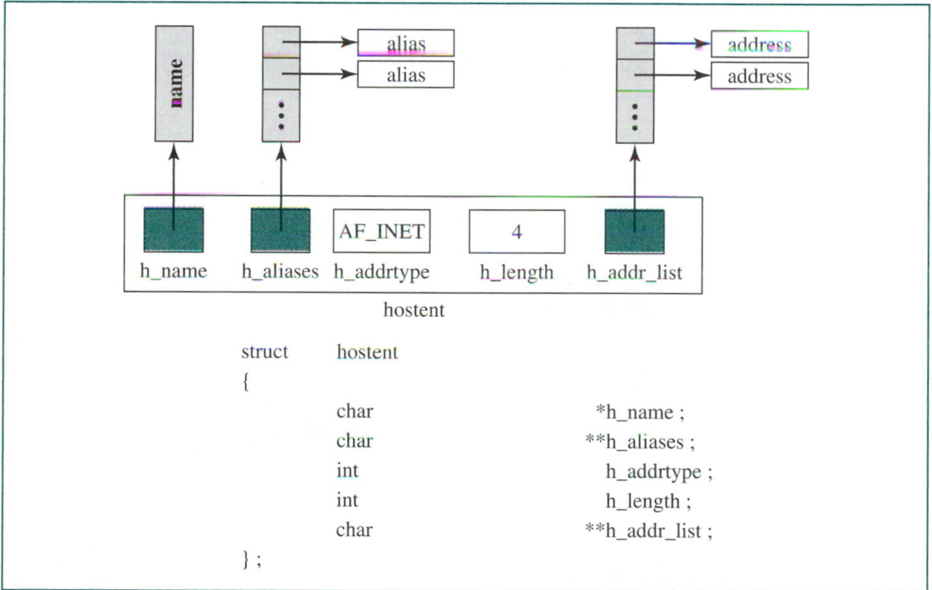


```
struct    hostent
{
          char          *h_name ;
          char          **h_aliases ;
          int           h_addrtype ;
          int           h_length ;
          char          **h_addr_list ;
} ;
```

16.7 SOCKET SYSTEM CALLS

Several functions have been defined that can be called by an application program to communicate with another application program. We introduce some of these in this section for later use in our client-server programs.

Socket

The socket function is used by a process to create a socket. The prototype for this function is given in Figure 16.15. The family, type, and protocol fields were defined in Figure 16.4. For TCP/IP, the value of family is the constant AF_INET. The value of

Figure 16.15 *Declaration for socket function*

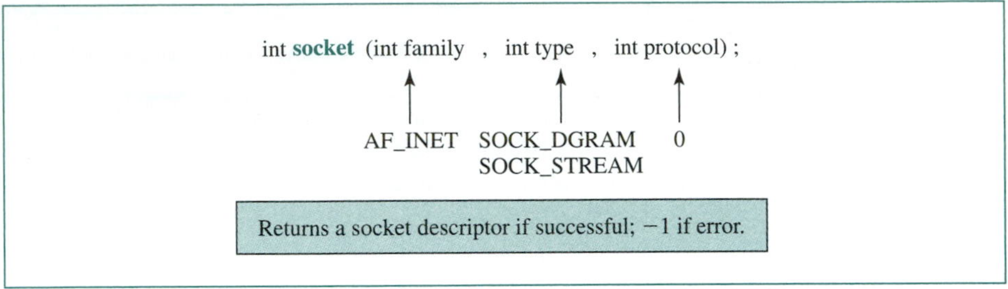

type as used in this chapter is either the constant SOCK_STREAM (used by stream sockets) or SOCK_DGRAM (used by datagram sockets).

Although this function creates a socket, it sets values for only the first three fields (family, type, and protocol) of the socket structure. The other fields are set by the other functions or by the operating system, as we will discuss later.

The function returns an integer called the *socket descriptor,* which uniquely defines the created socket if the creation is successful. It returns –1 if there is an error. The socket descriptor is used by other functions to refer to the socket.

Bind

The bind function binds a socket to a local socket address by adding the local socket address to an already created socket. The prototype is given in Figure 16.16.

Figure 16.16 *Declaration for bind function*

```
int bind (int sockfd , const struct sockaddress *localaddr , socklen_t localaddrlen) ;
```

Returns 0 if successful; −1 if error.

Sockfd is the socket descriptor returned by the socket function; *localaddr* is a pointer to the socket address of the local machine; and *localaddrlen* is the length of the local socket address.

To use this function, the client first needs to call the socket function in order to use the returned value as the socket descriptor. The function sets values for the local socket address. Note that this function is not usually called by the client. In a client, the information about the local socket address is usually provided by the operating system. This function returns an integer, 0 for success and –1 for any error.

Connect

The connect function is used by a process (usually a client) to establish an active connection to a remote process (normally a server). The prototype is given in Figure 16.17.

Figure 16.17 *Declaration for connect function*

```
int connect (int sockfd , const struct sockaddress *serveraddr , socklen_t serveraddrlen) ;
```

Returns 0 if successful; −1 if error.

Sockfd is the socket descriptor returned by the socket function; *serveraddr* is a pointer to the remote socket address; and *serveraddrlen* is the length of that address.

To use this function, the client first needs to call the socket function in order to use the returned value as the socket descriptor. This function sets values for the remote socket address. The local socket address is either provided by the bind function or set by the operating system. The function returns an integer, 0 for success and –1 for any error.

Listen

The listen function is called only by the TCP server. It creates a passive socket from an unconnected socket. Before calling the listen function, the socket must already be created and the local socket address fields set. This function informs the operating system that the server is ready to accept connection through this socket. Figure 16.18 shows the prototype.

Figure 16.18 *Declaration for listen function*

```
int listen (int sockfd , int backlog) ;
```

Returns 0 if successful; −1 if error.

Sockfd is the socket descriptor returned by the socket function; *backlog* is the number of requests that can be queued for this connection. This function returns an integer, 0 for success and −1 for any error.

Accept

The accept function is called by a TCP server to remove the first connection request from the corresponding queue. If there are no requests (the queue is empty), the accept function is put to sleep. The prototype is given in Figure 16.19.

Figure 16.19 *Declaration for accept function*

```
int accept (int sockfd , struct sockaddress *clientaddr , socklen_t *clientaddrlen) ;
```

Returns a socket descriptor if successful; −1 if error.

Sockfd is the socket descriptor; *clientaddr* is the pointer to the address of the client that has requested the connection; and *clientaddrlen* is a pointer to the client address length. Note that the socket address is not passed to the function but is returned from it. The length, however, is passed to the function as a value; it is also returned as a result.

This function actually creates a new socket (child socket) that can be used by a child server to connect to the client. All of the information needed for a new socket is provided by the operating system. The return value is the new socket descriptor.

Sendto

The sendto function is used by a process using UDP to send a message to another process usually running on a remote machine. The prototype is given in Figure 16.20.

Figure 16.20 *Declaration for sendto function*

```
ssize_t sendto (int sockfd , const void *buf , size_t buflen , int flags ,
        const struct sockaddress *toaddr , socklen_t toaddrlen) ;
```

Returns number of bytes sent if successful; −1 if error.

Sockfd is the socket descriptor, *buf* is a pointer to the buffer holding the message to be sent, *buflen* defines the length of the buffer, and the *flags* field specifies out-of-band data or lookahead messages. Normally it is set to zero. *Toaddr* is a pointer to the socket address of the receiver, and *toaddrlen* is the length of the socket address. The function returns the number of characters sent if there is no error and –1 otherwise.

Recvfrom

The recvfrom function extracts the next message that arrives at a socket. It also extracts the sender's socket address. In this way, the process that uses this function can record the socket address and use it to send a reply back to the sender. It is used mostly by a UDP process. The prototype is given in Figure 16.21.

Figure 16.21 *Declaration for recvfrom function*

```
ssize_t recvfrom (int sockfd , void *buf , size_t buflen , int flags,
        struct sockaddress *fromaddr , socklen_t *fromaddrlen) ;
```

Returns number of bytes received if successful; −1 if error.

Sockfd is the socket descriptor, *buf* is a pointer to the buffer where the message will be stored, *buflen* defines the length of the buffer, and the *flags* field specifies out-of-band data or lookahead messages. Normally it is set to zero. *Fromaddr* is a pointer to the socket address of the sender, and *fromaddrlen* is a pointer to the length of the socket address. The function returns the number of characters received if there is no error and −1 otherwise. Note that the socket address is not passed to the function, it is returned from it. It can be used by the process to respond to the remote process. The length, however, is passed as a value and is also returned as a result.

Read

The read function is used by a process to receive data from another process running on a remote machine. This function assumes that there is already an open connection between two machines; therefore, it can only be used by TCP processes. The prototype is given in Figure 16.22.

Figure 16.22 *Declaration for read function*

```
ssize_t read (int sockfd , void *buf , size_t buflen ) ;
```

Returns number of bytes read if successful; 0 for end of file; −1 if error.

Sockfd is the socket descriptor, *buf* is a pointer to the buffer where data will be stored, and *buflen* is the length of the buffer. This function returns the number of bytes received (read) if successful, 0 if an end-of-file condition is detected, and −1 if there is an error.

Write

The write function is used by a process to send data to another process running on a remote machine. This function assumes that there is already an open connection between two machines. Therefore, it can only be used by TCP processes. The prototype is given in Figure 16.23.

Figure 16.23 *Declaration for write function*

```
ssize_t write (int sockfd , const void *buf , size_t buflen ) ;
```

Returns number of bytes written if successful; −1 if error.

Sockfd is the socket descriptor, *buf* is a pointer to the buffer where data to be sent is stored, and *buflen* is the length the buffer. This function returns the number of bytes sent (written) if successful and −1 if there is an error.

Close

The close function is used by a process to close a socket and terminate a TCP connection. The prototype is given in Figure 16.24.

Figure 16.24 *Declaration for close function*

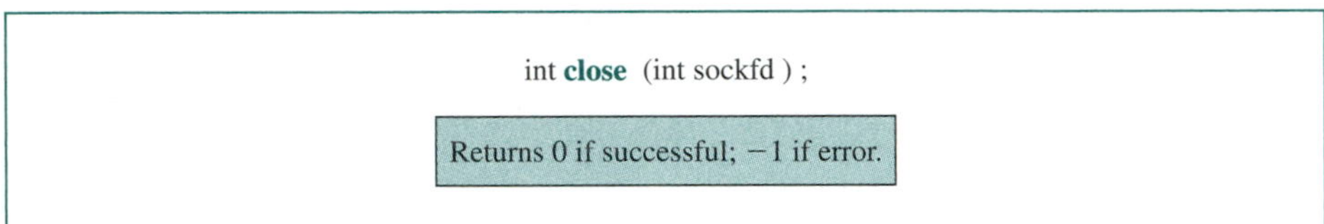

```
int close (int sockfd ) ;
```

Returns 0 if successful; −1 if error.

The socket descriptor is not valid after calling this function. The socket returns an integer, 0 for success and −1 for error.

16.8 CONNECTIONLESS ITERATIVE SERVER

In this section, we discuss connectionless, iterative client-server communication using UDP and datagram sockets. As we discussed in Chapter 14, a server that uses UDP is usually connectionless iterative. This means that the server serves one request at a time. A server gets the request received in a datagram from UDP, processes the request, and gives the response to UDP to send to the client. The server pays no attention to the other datagrams. These datagrams, which could all be from one client or from many clients, are stored in a queue, waiting for service. They are processed one by one in order of arrival.

The server uses one single port for this purpose, the well-known port. All the datagrams arriving at this port wait in line to be served. Figure 16.25 shows the flowchart of events in connectionless iterative communication.

Server

The server performs the following functions:

1. **Opening a socket.** The server issues the socket call to ask the operating system to create a socket. The socket call in the socket interface is like the open call in the file interface. The socket call creates a new socket structure, and the open call creates a new file structure. The application program makes this call and passes three pieces of information: family, type, and protocol. The operating system creates a socket and enters the received information. However, the information for the socket is not complete. The operating system returns an integer to define the socket uniquely. This integer is called the *socket descriptor* and is used to refer to the socket in the following calls.

Figure 16.25 *Socket interface for connectionless iterative server*

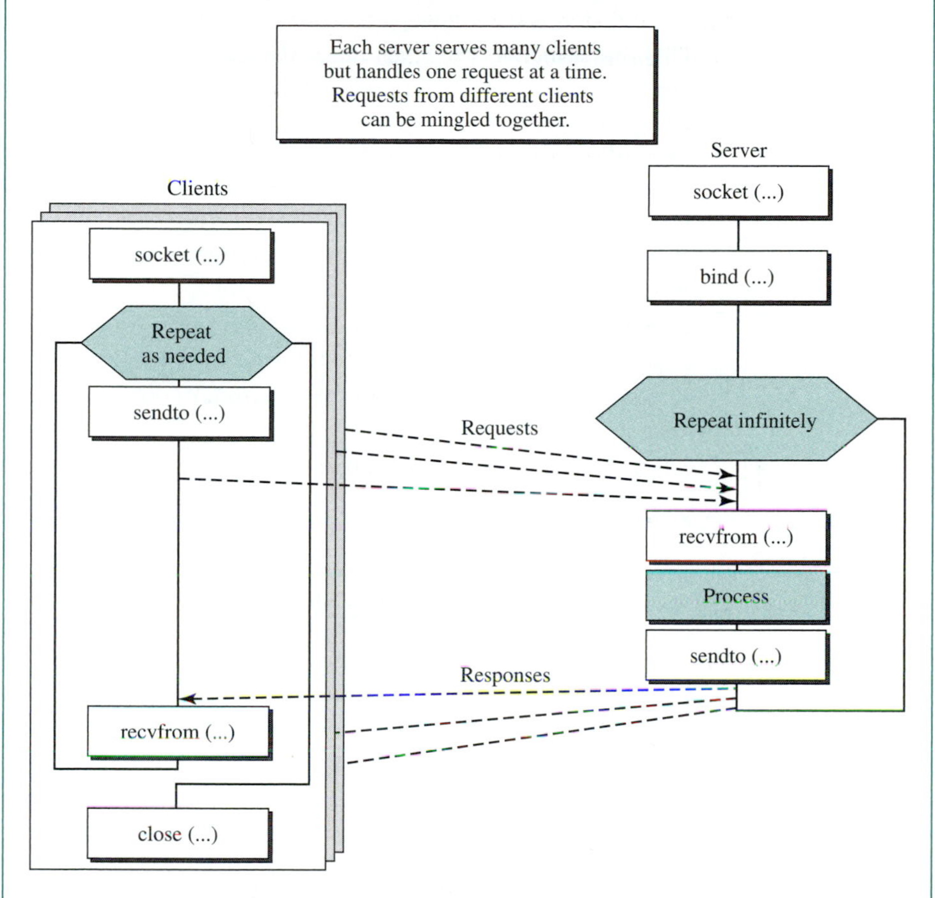

2. **Binding.** The server issues the bind call to ask the operating system to enter information in the socket structure created in the previous step. This information consists of the local socket address.
3. **Repeating the steps.** The server repeats the following steps infinitely:
   a. **Receiving.** The server issues the recvfrom call to read, from the incoming queue, a datagram sent by a client.
   b. **Sending.** After processing the datagram, the server issues the sendto call to send the datagram that contains the result to the outgoing queue. Because the communication is connectionless, the sendto call provides the remote socket address (client IP address and the client ephemeral port address) for each datagram to be sent to the client. These two pieces of information are obtained by the recvfrom system call.

Client

The client performs the following functions:

1. **Opening a socket.** The client issues the socket call to ask the operating system to create a socket. The client does not have to do binding because the local socket address can be provided by the operating system. The operating system enters the local IP address and the ephemeral port number in the local socket address field of the created socket. In some implementations, the client also issues the bind call so that stray data from another program do not enter that port.
2. **Repeating the steps.** The client repeats the following steps as long as it has requests to make:
   a. **Sending.** After receiving the socket descriptor from the operating system, the client issues the sendto calls to send its request to the server.
   b. **Receiving.** The client issues the recvfrom to obtain the response of its request from the operating system.
3. **Closing.** When the client has no more requests, it issues a close call to destroy the socket.

16.9 UDP CLIENT-SERVER PROGRAMS

This section contains one simple server program and one simple client program. The server is a generic server. We have included one PROCESS call that is used to define the server function. For the sake of simplicity, we have not included any error-checking or error-handling statements.

Server Program

The server program is shown in Program 16.1.

Program 16.1

UDP Iterative Server Program

```
#include <sys/types.h>
#include <sys/socket.h>
#include <netdb.h>
#include <netinet/in.h>
#include <stdio.h>
#include <string.h>

#define MAXBUF   256

void main (void)
{
```

Program 16.1 ***(Continued)***

UDP Iterative Server Program

```
12  char buf [ MAXBUF] ;
13  int passiveSocket ;
14  socklen_t clientAddrLen ;
15  struct sockaddress    serverAddr ;
16  struct sockaddress    clientAddr ;
17  passiveSocket =  socket (AF_INET, SOCK_DGRAM, 0) ;
18  memset (&serverAddr ,  0 , sizeof (serverAddr) ) ;
19  serverAddr.sin_family = AF_INET ;
20  serverAddr.sin_port = htons (a-well-known-port)  ;
21  serverAddr.sin_addr.s_addr = htonl (INADDR_ANY) ;
22  bind (passiveSocket, &serverAddr, sizeof (serverAddr) );
23  clientAddrLen = sizeof (serverAddr) ;
24  memset (buf , 0, MAXBUF) ;
25  for ( ; ; )
26  {
27    while (recvfrom (passiveSocket, buf, MAXBUF, 0,
28          &clientAddr, &clientAddrLen) > 0 )
29    {
30      PROCESS (............) ;
31
32      sendto (passiveSocket,  buf  , MAXBUF , 0 ,
33        &clientAddr ,  clientAddrLen) ;
34      memset (buf , 0  , MAXBUF) ;
35    }
36  }
37 }
```

- Lines 1–6 are the header files.
- Line 8 defines the buffer size.
- Line 17 creates a socket.
- Line 18 initializes a server socket address.
- Lines 19–21 set the values for the server socket address. Note that we use htons and htonl to create network byte-order integers.
- Line 22 binds the created socket to the local socket address (server socket address).
- Line 24 initializes the buffer.
- Line 25 starts an infinite loop.
- Line 27 receives the client messages.

- Line 30 uses a procedure to process the data.
- Line 32 sends the results back to the client.
- Line 34 reinitializes the buffer for the next iteration.

Client Program

The client program is shown in Program 16.2.

Program 16.2

UDP Iterative Client Program

```
#include <sys/types.h>
#include <sys/socket.h>
#include <netdb.h>
#include <netinet/in.h>
#include <stdio.h>
#include <string.h>

#define MAXBUF   256

void main (void)
{
   char buf [ MAXBUF] ;
   int activeSocket ;
   socklen_t remoteAddrLen ;
   struct sockaddress     remoteAddr ;
   struct sockaddress     localAddr ;
   struct hostent   *hptr ;
   activeSocket =  socket (AF_INET, SOCK_DGRAM, 0) ;
   memset (&remoteAddr , 0  , sizeof (remoteAddr) ) ;
   remoteAddr.sin_family = AF_INET ;
   remoteAddr.sin_port = htons (a-well-known-port)  ;
   hptr = gethostbyname (" a-domain-name") ;
   memcpy  ((char*) &remoteAddr.sin_addr.s_addr,
         hptr ->h_addr_list[0], hptr  ->h_length ) ;

   memset (buf , 0, MAXBUF) ;
   remoteAddrLen = sizeof (remoteAddr) ;
   while (gets (buf) )
   {
   sendto (activeSocket,  buf  , sizeof (buf) , 0 ,
         &remoteAddr ,  sizeof (remoteAddr) ) ;
```

Program 16.2 *(Continued)*

UDP Iterative Client Program

```
32      memset (buf, 0, sizeof (buf) ) ;
33      recvfrom (activeSocket, buf , MAXBUF, 0 ,
34          &remoteAddr , &remoteAddrLen ) ;
35      printf ("%s\n", buf) ;
36      memset (buf , 0 , sizeof (buf) ) ;
37      }
38   close (activeSocket ) ;
39   }
```

- Lines 1–6 are the header files.
- Line 8 defines the buffer size.
- Line 18 creates a socket.
- Line 19 initializes a remote socket address.
- Lines 20–24 set the values for the remote socket address.
- Line 26 initializes the buffer.
- Line 30 sends the buffer contents to the server.
- Line 33 receives the responses from the server.
- Line 35 prints the received message.
- Line 36 reinitializes the buffer for the next iteration.
- Line 38 closes the connection.

16.10 CONNECTION-ORIENTED CONCURRENT SERVER

In this section, we discuss connection-oriented, concurrent client-server communication using TCP and stream sockets. As mentioned in Chapter 14, the servers that use TCP are normally concurrent. This means that the server serves many clients at the same time. Communication is connection-oriented, which means that a request is a stream of bytes that could arrive in several segments, and the response could occupy several segments. A connection is established between the server and each client; the connection remains open until the entire stream is processed, and the connection is terminated.

For this type of server, many connections may be open at the same time. Many ports are needed, but the server can use only one well-known port. The solution is to use one well-known port and many ephemeral ports. The server issues a passive open at the well-known port. A client makes its initial approach to this port to make the connection. After the connection is made, the server assigns an ephemeral port to this connection to free the well-known port. Data transfer can now take place between these two ephemeral ports, one at the client site and the other at the server site. The well-known port is now free for another client connection.

The server must have one buffer for each connection. The segments from the clients are stored in the appropriate buffers and handled concurrently by the server.

To provide this service, most implementations use the concept of parent and child servers. A server running infinitely and accepting connections from clients is called a *parent server.* The parent server uses the well-known port. After the connection is made, the parent server creates a *child server* and an ephemeral port and lets the child server handle the client. It frees itself so that it can wait for another connection. In this section, we show how a server can serve several clients concurrently using the services of TCP. Figure 16.26 shows the flowchart of events for a server and a client.

Server

The server performs the following functions:

1. **Opening a socket.** The server issues the socket call to ask the operating system to create a socket.
2. **Binding.** The server issues the bind call to ask the operating system to enter information in the socket structure created in the previous step. This information consists of the local socket address.
3. **Listening.** The server issues the listen call to convert a socket into a passive socket, usually called the listening socket. A listening socket does not connect itself to a socket at the other end; it just waits for a connection from the other end. The server passes the socket descriptor and the maximum number of requests for connection.
4. **Repeating the steps.** The server repeats the following steps infinitely:
   a. **Accepting.** The accept call creates a new socket, called the *accepting socket,* for actual communication and connects the next client in line. After this call, the client is connected to the new socket and the previous socket is freed.
   b. **Forking.** The server now uses the fork call (see Chapter 14) to create a process just like itself. This is called the *child process;* and the creator is called the *parent process*. After this operation, the client is connected to both the parent and the child. Both parent and child have a listening and accepting socket.
   c. **Closing the accepting socket.** The parent issues the close call to close its accepting socket, but its listening socket remains open for the next client.
   d. **Closing the listening socket.** The child issues the close call to close its listening socket, but its accepting socket remains open.
   e. **Repeating.** The child repeats the following steps as long as it has requests from the client:

      Reading. The child issues the read call to read as much data as it can process in one shot from the incoming buffer assigned to the client.

      Processing. The child processes the data read from the buffer.

      Writing. The child issues the write call to write the result of processing to the outgoing buffer assigned to the client.

   f. **Closing the communicating socket.** After the client has been served, the child issues the close call to close the communicating socket.

Figure 16.26 *Socket interface for connection-oriented concurrent server*

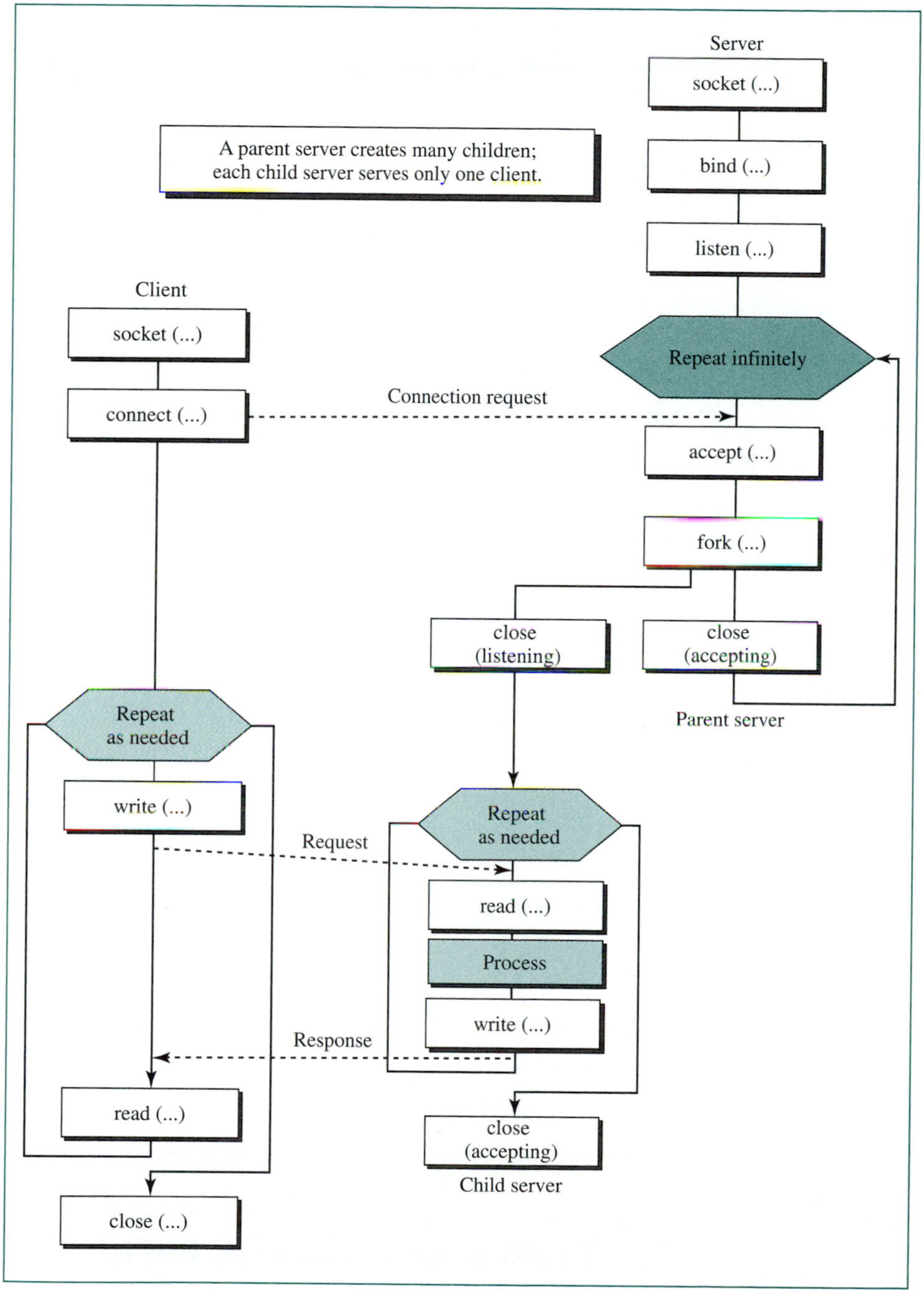

Client

The client performs the following functions:

1. **Opening a socket.** The client issues the socket call to ask the operating system to create a socket.
2. **Connecting.** The client issues the connect call to ask the operating system to enter the socket address of the server into the created socket structure. This call also requests a connection with the TCP on the other side.
3. **Repeating the steps.** The client repeats the following steps as long as it has requests to make.
   a. **Writing.** The client issues the write call to write data into the outgoing TCP buffer.
   b. **Reading.** The client issues the read call to get data from the incoming buffer.
4. **Closing.** After the client has finished, it issues a close call to request TCP to close the connection. It also sends an application-defined "quit" packet to notify the server.

Figure 16.27 shows the relationships between the client, the parent server, and the child server.

Figure 16.27 *Relationship between the client and the server*

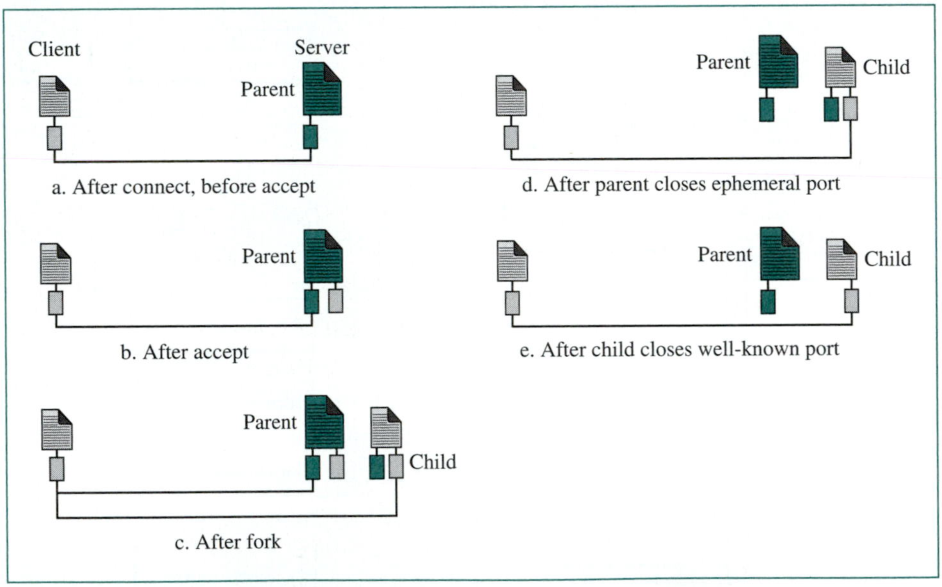

16.11 TCP CLIENT-SERVER PROGRAMS

This section contains one simple server program and one simple client program. The server is a generic server. We have included one PROCESS call that is used to define the server function. For the sake of simplicity, we have not included any error-checking or error-handling statements.

Server Program

Program 16.3 shows the server program.

Program 16.3

TCP Concurrent Server Program

```
#include <sys/types.h>
#include <sys/socket.h>
#include <netdb.h>
#include <netinet/in.h>
#include <stdio.h>
#include <string.h>

#define MAXBUF   256

void main (void)
{
  char buf [ MAXBUF] ;
  int listenSocket ;
  int acceptSocket ;
  socklen_t clientAddrLen ;
  struct sockaddress     serverAddr ;
  struct sockaddress     clientAddr ;
  listenSocket =  socket (AF_INET, SOCK_STREAM, 0) ;
  memset (&serverAddr , 0 , sizeof (serverAddr)) ;
  serverAddr.sin_family = AF_INET ;
  serverAddr.sin_port = htons (a-well-known-port)  ;
  serverAddr.sin_addr.s_addr = htonl(INADDR_ANY) ;
  bind (listenSocket, &serverAddr, sizeof (serverAddr) ) ;
  listen (listenSocket ,  1 ) ;
  clientAddrLen = sizeof (clientAddr) ;
  for ( ; ;  )
  {
    acceptSocket = accept (listenSocket &clientAddr,
                                   &clientAddrLen ) ;
    pid  =  fork () ;
    if (pid > 0)    /* parent */
    {
      close ( acceptSocket)  ;
      continue ;
    }
```

Program 16.3 ***(Continued)***

TCP Concurrent Server Program

```
36        else    /* child */
37      {
38        close (listenSocket) ;
39        memset (buf , 0, MAXBUF) ;
40        while (read (acceptSocket , buf, MAXBUF)> 0 )
41        {
42          PROCESS (............) ;
43        memset (buf, 0, MAXBUF);
44        write  (acceptSocket,  buf  , MAXBUF ) ;
45        memset (buf , 0  , MAXBUF) ;
46        } /* while */
47      close (acceptSocket) ;
48      } /* else */
49    } /* for */
50  }
```

- Lines 1–6 are the header files.
- Line 8 defines the buffer size.
- Line 18 creates a passive socket.
- Line 23 binds the passive socket to the server socket address.
- Line 24 creates a listening socket from the passive socket.
- Line 28 creates an accepting socket.
- Line 30 creates the child process using fork.
- Line 33 closes the parent accepting socket.
- Line 38 closes the child listening socket.
- Line 40 makes the child read from the accepting socket in a loop.
- Line 42 processes the data read.
- Line 44 makes the child write the result to the accepting socket.
- Line 47 closes the accepting socket.

Client Program

The client program is shown Program 16.4.

Program 16.4

TCP Concurrent Client Program

```
#include <sys/types.h>
#include <sys/socket.h>
#include <netdb.h>
#include <netinet/in.h>
#include <stdio.h>
#include <string.h>

#define MAXBUF   256

void main (void)
{
    char buf [ MAXBUF] ;
    int activeSocket ;
    struct sockaddress     remoteAddr ;
    struct sockaddress     localAddr ;
    struct hostent   *hptr ;
    activeSocket =  socket (AF_INET, SOCK_STREAM, 0) ;
    memset (&remoteAddr , 0  , sizeof (remoteAddr)) ;
    remoteAddr.sin_family = AF_INET ;
    remoteAddr.sin_port = htons (a-well-known-port)  ;
    hptr = gethostbyname (" a-domain-name") ;
    memcpy   ((char*) &remoteAddr.sin_addr.s_addr ,
        hptr ->h_addr_list[0], hptr  ->h_length ) ;
    connect (activeSocket, remoteAddr, sizeof struct sockaddress) ;
    memset (buf , 0, MAXBUF) ;
    while (gets (buf) )
    {
        write  (activeSocket,  buf  , MAXBUF) ;
       memset (buf, 0, MAXBUF);
       read (activeSocket ,  buf , MAXBUF) ;
       printf ("%s\n", buf) ;
       memset (buf , 0 , MAXBUF) ;
    }
close (activeSocket) ;
}
```

- Lines 1–6 are the header files.
- Line 8 defines the buffer size.
- Line 17 creates an active socket.
- Line 21 gets information about the remote host (server) and stores it in a variable pointing to a hostent structure.
- Lines 22–23 copy the socket address in hostent to the remote socket address structure.
- Line 24 connects the client to the server.
- Line 26 uses a loop to get data from the user and stores it in a buffer.
- Line 28 writes the buffer contents to the active socket.
- Line 30 reads what is received from the server from the active socket.
- Line 31 prints the contents of the received buffer.
- Line 34 closes the active socket.

16.12 KEY TERMS

address transformation

application program

application programming interfaces (APIs)

big-endian byte order

child server

client

connectionless iterative server

connection-oriented concurrent server

datagram socket

little-endian byte order

parent server

raw socket

server

socket

socket address

Socket Interface

stream socket

16.13 SUMMARY

- If two application programs, one running on a local system and the other running on the remote system, need to communicate with each other, network programming is required.
- The socket interface is a set of declarations, definitions, and procedures for writing client-server programs.
- The communication structure needed for socket programming is called a socket.
- A stream socket is used with a connection-oriented protocol such as TCP.
- A datagram socket is used with a connectionless protocol such as UDP.

- A raw socket is used by protocols such as ICMP or OSPF that directly use the services of IP.
- In big-endian byte order, the most significant byte is stored in the lowest memory address of the data unit.
- In little-endian byte order, the least significant byte is stored in the lowest memory address of the data unit.
- TCP/IP uses the big-endian byte order.
- Three functions to manipulate bytes in network programming are memset, memcpy, and memcmp.
- A function to provide information about the remote host is gethostbyname.
- The socket system call creates a socket.
- The bind system call adds the local socket address to an already created socket.
- The connect system call establishes an active connection to a remote process.
- The listen system call converts a socket into a passive socket.
- The accept system call creates a new socket for actual communication and connects the next client in line.
- A connectionless process issues the sendto system call to send data to a remote process.
- A connectionless process issues the recvfrom system call to receive, from the incoming queue, the datagrams sent by a remote process.
- A connection-oriented process issues the read system call to receive datagrams from a remote process.
- A connection-oriented process issues the write system call to send datagrams to a remote process.
- The close system call closes a socket and terminates a TCP connection.
- A connectionless, iterative server uses the services of UDP and can serve only one client at a time.
- A connection-oriented, concurrent server uses the services of TCP and can serve many clients simultaneously.
- A server running infinitely and accepting connections from clients is called a parent server.
- A parent server creates a child server that actually handles the client.

16.14 PRACTICE SET

Multiple-Choice Questions

1. An API is a set of _______.
   a. declarations
   b. definitions
   c. procedures
   d. all of the above

2. The structure to define an IPv4 address is called _______ and contains a field called _______.
   a. uint8_t; s_addr
   b. s_addr; in_addr
   c. in_addr; s_addr
   d. in_addr; uint8_t
3. The _______ field in the socket structure is usually set to 0 for a process using the services of TCP or UDP.
   a. family
   b. type
   c. protocol
   d. local socket address
4. The _______ field in the socket structure defines the protocol group.
   a. family
   b. type
   c. protocol
   d. local socket address
5. The _______ field in the socket structure is a structure of type sockaddress.
   a. family
   b. local socket address
   c. remote socket address
   d. b and c
6. The _______ socket is used with a connection-oriented protocol.
   a. stream
   b. datagram
   c. raw
   d. remote
7. The _______ socket is used with a connectionless protocol.
   a. stream
   b. datagram
   c. raw
   d. remote
8. The _______ socket is used with a protocol that directly uses the services of IP.
   a. stream
   b. datagram
   c. raw
   d. remote

9. On an IBM mainframe computer, the starting address in memory for the IP address 7.8.9.10 contains _______.
   a. 00000111
   b. 00001000
   c. 00001001
   d. 00001010
10. On a PC with an Intel processor, the starting address in memory for the IP address 7.8.9.10 contains _______.
    a. 00000111
    b. 00001000
    c. 00001001
    d. 00001010
11. To convert a dotted decimal address to a 32-bit binary address, use the _______ function.
    a. htons
    b. htonl
    c. inet_ntoa
    d. inet_aton
12. To convert a 16-bit integer to network byte order, use the _______ function.
    a. htons
    b. ntohs
    c. htonl
    d. ntohl
13. To convert a 32-bit integer from network byte order to host byte order, use the _______ function.
    a. htons
    b. ntohs
    c. htonl
    d. ntohl
14. In network programming, the _______ function copies the value of one field to another.
    a. memset
    b. memcpy
    c. memcmp
    d. memstr
15. In network programming, the _______ function sets a specified number of bytes.
    a. memset
    b. memcpy
    c. memcmp
    d. memstr

16. If the memcmp function returns a value of 1, it means _______.
    a. the first field is the same as the second field
    b. the first field is greater than the second field
    c. the first field is less than the second field
    d. the first field has a value of 1
17. The _______ function provides information about the remote host.
    a. hostent
    b. hostname
    c. gethostbyname
    d. getnameofhost
18. A connectionless process issues the _______ system call to receive, from the incoming queue, the datagrams sent by a remote process.
    a. listen
    b. receive
    c. bind
    d. recvfrom
19. A connection-oriented process issues the _______ system call to send datagrams to a remote process.
    a. sendto
    b. bind
    c. accept
    d. write
20. A connectionless process issues the _______ system call to send data to a remote process.
    a. sendto
    b. bind
    c. listen
    d. remote
21. The _______ system call adds the local socket address to an already created socket.
    a. address
    b. create
    c. bind
    d. socket
22. The _______ system call creates a socket.
    a. create
    b. socket
    c. open
    d. bind

23. The _______ system call closes a socket and terminates a TCP connection.
    a. recvfrom
    b. close
    c. shut
    d. bind
24. The _______ system call creates a new socket for actual communication and connects the next client in line.
    a. accept
    b. connect
    c. bind
    d. create
25. The _______ system call converts a socket into a passive socket.
    a. convert
    b. listen
    c. socket
    d. bind
26. The _______ system call establishes an active connection to a remote process.
    a. accept
    b. bind
    c. socket
    d. connect
27. A connection-oriented process issues the _______ system call to receive datagrams from a remote process.
    a. read
    b. recvfrom
    c. listen
    d. sendto
28. The client program is _______ because it terminates after it has been served.
    a. active
    b. passive
    c. finite
    d. infinite
29. The server program is _______ because it is always available, waiting for a client request.
    a. active
    b. passive
    c. finite
    d. infinite

30. A connection-oriented concurrent server uses _______ ports.
    a. ephemeral
    b. well-known
    c. active
    d. a and b
31. A connectionless iterative concurrent server uses _______ ports.
    a. ephemeral
    b. well-known
    c. active
    d. a and b
32. A _______ server serves multiple clients, handling one request at a time.
    a. connection-oriented iterative
    b. connection-oriented concurrent
    c. connectionless iterative
    d. connectionless concurrent
33. A _______ server serves multiple clients simultaneously.
    a. connection-oriented iterative
    b. connection-oriented concurrent
    c. connectionless iterative
    d. connectionless concurrent
34. A _______ server uses the sendto and recvfrom system.
    a. connection-oriented iterative
    b. connection-oriented concurrent
    c. connectionless iterative
    d. connectionless concurrent
35. A _______ server uses the read and write system calls.
    a. connection-oriented iterative
    b. connection-oriented concurrent
    c. connectionless iterative
    d. connectionless concurrent

Exercises

36. Explain the difference between the bind function and the connect function.
37. Explain the difference between the bind function and the listen function.
38. Explain the difference between the socket function and the accept function.
39. Write the necessary lines of code to connect a socket to the remote TELNET server at site xxx.yyy.edu.
40. Write the necessary lines of code to connect a socket to the remote FTP server at site yy.zz.edu.

41. Write the necessary lines of code to bind a socket to the local server.
42. Write the necessary lines of code to create a listening socket with a queue size of 100.
43. Write the necessary lines of code to create a child socket.
44. Describe the differences between the sendto and the write functions.
45. Describe the differences between the recvfrom and the read functions.
46. Describe the relationship between the connect function and the TCP state transition diagram. (See Chapter 12.) What is the state of TCP after the connect function?
47. Describe the relationship between the bind function and the TCP state transition diagram. (See Chapter 12.) What is the state of TCP after the bind function?
48. Describe the relationship between the listen function and the TCP state transition diagram. (See Chapter 12.) What is the state of TCP after the listen function?
49. Describe the relationship between the accept function and the TCP state transition diagram. (See Chapter 12.) What is the state of TCP after the accept function?

Programming Exercises

50. Write a UDP client program that sends a string of characters to a server. The client does not use a loop.
51. Write a UDP server program that receives a string of characters from a client. The server receives the string from the client program in exercise 50.
52. Write a TCP client program that does the same job as the client program in exercise 50.
53. Write a TCP server program that does the same job as the server program in exercise 51.
54. Write a UDP client program that asks for the time from a UDP server.
55. Write a UDP server program that responds to the client in exercise 54.
56. Write a TCP client program that asks for the time from a TCP server.
57. Write a TCP server program that responds to the client in exercise 56.
58. Write a UDP client program that behaves like a simple TFTP client.
59. Write a UDP server program that behaves like a simple TFTP server.
60. Write a TCP client program that behaves like a simple FTP client.
61. Write a TCP server program that behaves like a simple FTP server.
62. Write a TCP client program that behaves like a simple TELNET client.
63. Write a TCP server program that behaves like a simple TELNET server.

CHAPTER 17

BOOTP and DHCP

Each computer that is attached to a TCP/IP internet must know the following information:

- Its IP address
- Its subnet mask
- The IP address of a router
- The IP address of a name server

This information is usually stored in a configuration file and accessed by the computer during the bootstrap process. But what about a diskless workstation or a computer with a disk that is booted for the first time?

In the case of a diskless computer, the operating system and the networking software can be stored in read-only memory (ROM). However, the above information is not known to the manufacturer and thus cannot be stored in ROM. The information is dependent on the individual configuration of the machine and defines the network to which the machine is connected.

17.1 BOOTP

BOOTP (Bootstrap Protocol) is a client/server protocol designed to provide the four previously mentioned pieces of information for a diskless computer or a computer that is booted for the first time. We have already studied one protocol, RARP, that provides the IP address for a diskless computer. Why do we need yet another protocol? The answer is that RARP provides only the IP address and not the other information. If we use BOOTP, we do not need RARP. For this reason RARP is not implemented in most systems, and it is totally removed from TCP/IP version 6.

Packet Format

Figure 17.1 shows the format of a BOOTP packet.

Figure 17.1 *BOOTP packet format*

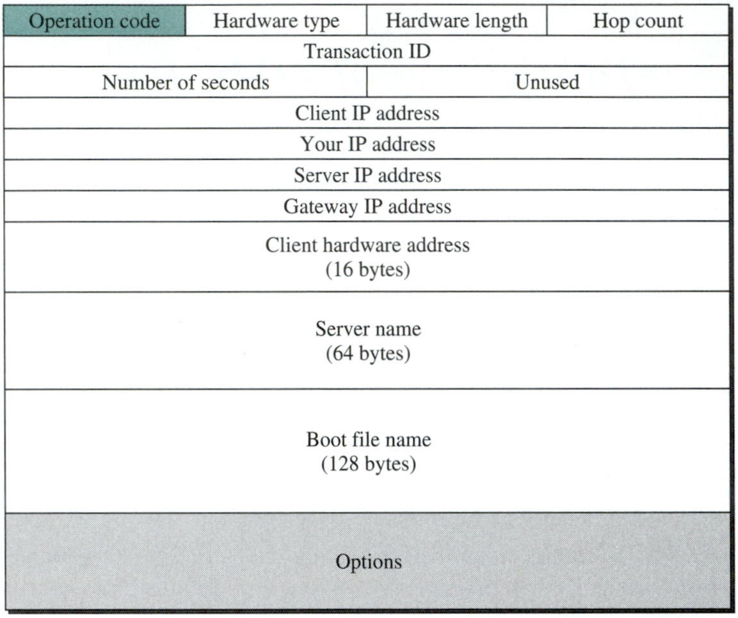

Operation code	Hardware type	Hardware length	Hop count
Transaction ID			
Number of seconds		Unused	
Client IP address			
Your IP address			
Server IP address			
Gateway IP address			
Client hardware address (16 bytes)			
Server name (64 bytes)			
Boot file name (128 bytes)			
Options			

- **Operation code.** This 8-bit field defines the type of BOOTP packet: request (1) or reply (2).
- **Hardware type.** This is an 8-bit field defining the type of physical network. Each type of local area network has been assigned an integer. For example, for Ethernet the value is 1.
- **Hardware length.** This is an 8-bit field defining the length of the physical address in bytes. For example, for Ethernet the value is 6.
- **Hop count.** This is an 8-bit field defining the maximum number of hops the packet can travel.
- **Transaction ID.** This is a 4-byte field carrying an integer. The transaction identification is set by the client and is used to match a reply with the request. The server returns the same value in its reply.
- **Number of seconds.** This is a 16-bit field that indicates the number of seconds elapsed since the time the client started to boot.
- **Client IP address.** This is a 4-byte field that contains the client IP address. If the client does not have this information, this field has a value of 0.
- **Your IP address.** This is a 4-byte field that contains the client IP address. It is filled by the server (in the reply message) at the request of the client.
- **Server IP address.** This is a 4-byte field containing the server IP address. It is filled by the server in a reply message.

- **Gateway IP address.** This is a 4-byte field containing the IP address of a router. It is filled by the server in a reply message.
- **Client hardware address.** This is the physical address of the client. Although the server can retrieve this address from the frame sent by the client, it is more efficient if the address is supplied explicitly by the client in the request message.
- **Server name.** This is an optional 64-byte field filled by the server in a reply packet. It contains a null-terminated string consisting of the domain name of the server.
- **Boot filename.** This is an optional 128-byte field that can be filled by the server in a reply packet. It contains a null-terminated string consisting of the full pathname of the boot file. The client can use this path to retrieve other booting information.
- **Options.** This is a 64-byte field with a dual purpose. It can carry either additional information (such as the network mask or default router address) or some specific vendor information. The field is used only in a reply message. The server uses a number, called a *magic cookie,* in the format of an IP address with the value of 99.130.83.99. When the client finishes reading the message, it looks for this magic cookie. If present, the next 60 bytes are options. An option is composed of three fields: a 1-byte tag, a 1-byte length, and a variable-length value. The length field defines the length of the value field, not the whole option. See Figure 17.2.

Figure 17.2 *Option format*

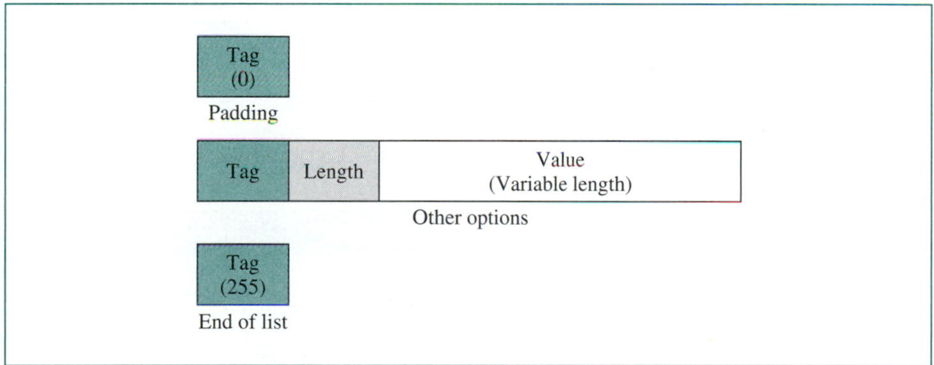

The list of options is shown in Table 17.1.

Table 17.1 *Options for BOOTP*

Description	*Tag*	*Length*	*Value*
Padding	0		
Subnet mask	1	4	Subnet mask
Time offset	2	4	Time of the day
Default routers	3	Variable	IP addresses
Time servers	4	Variable	IP addresses
DNS servers	6	Variable	IP addresses

Table 17.1 *Options for BOOTP (Continued)*

Description	*Tag*	*Length*	*Value*
Print servers	9	Variable	IP addresses
Host name	12	Variable	DNS name
Boot file size	13	2	Integer
Vendor specific	128–254	Variable	Specific information
End of list	255		

The length of the fields that contain IP addresses are multiples of 4 bytes. The padding option, which is only 1-byte long, is used only for alignment. The end-of-list option, which is also only 1-byte long, indicates the end of the option field. Vendors can use option tags 128 to 254 to supply extra information in a reply message.

Operation

Figure 17.3 shows the steps involved in using the BOOTP protocol.

Figure 17.3 *BOOTP operation*

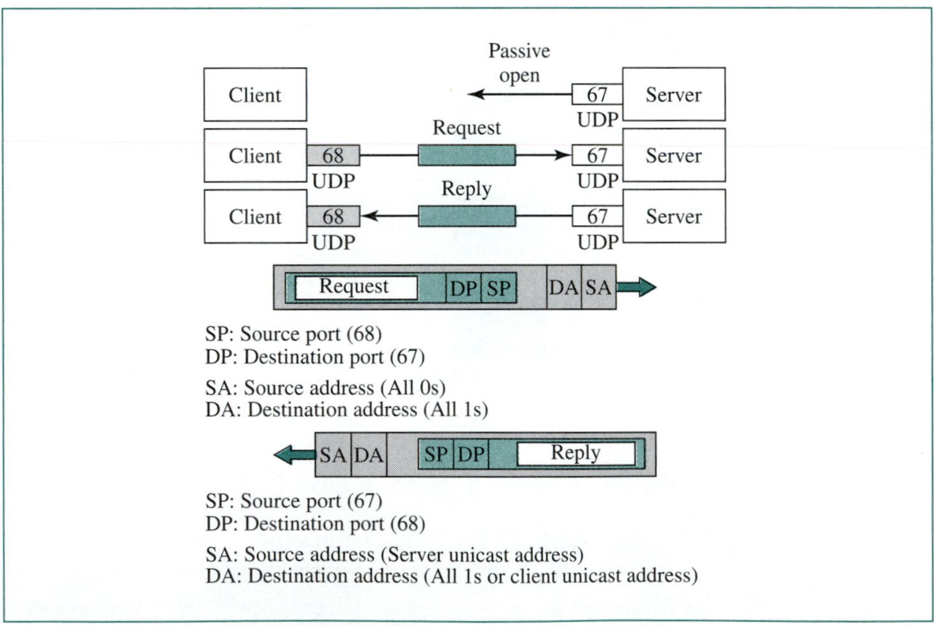

1. The BOOTP server uses UDP port number 67 and waits for a client.
2. The client sends a BOOTP request message to the server. The message is encapsulated in a UDP user datagram, using the UDP port number 68. The UDP user datagram, in turn, is encapsulated in an IP datagram. The reader may ask how the client can send an IP datagram when it knows neither its own IP address (the source

address) nor the server's IP address (the destination address). The client uses all 0s as the source address and all 1s as the destination address (see special addresses in Chapter 4).

3. The server replies to the client with either a broadcast or a unicast message using UDP destination port 68. The unicast reply message is preferred because it does not involve other hosts on the network. Note that if the server uses the unicast message to reply, it cannot use the services of ARP. The ARP protocol requires that the other party (the client) know its own IP address, which is not true in this case. This means that, the server must manually add the client's IP address to the ARP table, which is not allowed in some systems. In this systems, the server has to broadcast the reply.

UDP Ports

An unusual aspect of BOOTP is the client's use of the well-known port 68 instead of an ephemeral port. This is because the reply from the server can be broadcast and therefore the response will be received by all hosts. However, what if two clients, one using BOOTP, the other DAYTIME, select the same ephemeral ports? The broadcast message will be sent to both clients, and because the port numbers are the same, two clients will receive the same messages. One client is expecting a BOOTP reply, the other a DAYTIME reply. However, if the BOOTP client uses the well-known port 68, the BOOTP reply will not be received by a DAYTIME process.

The reader may ask what happens if two hosts use BOOTP at the same time. Both use the well-known port 68. If the server broadcasts the reply, both hosts receive the message. In this case, the Transaction ID field can help. It is very improbable that the two hosts used the same transaction identifier in their request. In this way, the host can recognize its reply from another host's reply.

Using TFTP

The server does not send all of the information that a client may need for booting. In the reply message, the server defines the pathname of a file in which the client can find complete booting information. The client can then use a TFTP message, which is encapsulated in a UDP user datagram, to obtain the rest of the needed information.

Relay Agent

It may happen that the administrator has decided not to include a BOOTP server for each LAN. Instead, a remote BOOTP server may serve several LANs.

In this case, if a client needs to be booted, it cannot reach the remote server using the broadcast address because an address of all 1s has only local jurisdiction. The problem is solved, however, with the use of a *relay agent*. A relay agent is a router that can help send local requests to remote servers.

The relay agent that receives the client request adds its IP address in the field provided for this purpose, and sends it to the remote server. The remote server sends the reply to the relay agent, which is then forwarded to the client.

Error Control

What if a request is lost, or damaged? What if the response is damaged? There is a need for error control when using BOOTP. BOOTP uses UDP, which does not provide error control. Therefore, BOOTP must provide error control. Error control is accomplished through two strategies:

1. BOOTP requires that the UDP uses checksum. Remember that the use of checksum in UDP is optional.
2. The BOOTP client uses timers and a retransmission policy if it does not receive the BOOTP reply to a request. However, to prevent a traffic jam when several hosts need to retransmit a request (for example, after a power failure), BOOTP forces the client to use a random number to set its timers.

17.2 DYNAMIC HOST CONFIGURATION PROTOCOL (DHCP)

BOOTP is not a dynamic configuration protocol. When a client requests its IP address, the BOOTP server consults a table that matches the physical address of the client with its IP address. This implies that the binding between the physical address and the IP address of the client should already exist. The binding is predetermined.

However, what if a host moves from one physical network to another? What if a host wants a temporary IP address? BOOTP cannot handle these problems because the binding between the physical and IP addresses is static and fixed in a table until changed by the administrator. BOOTP is a static configuration protocol.

The **Dynamic Host Configuration Protocol** (DHCP) has been devised to provide dynamic configuration. DHCP is an extension to BOOTP. It enhances BOOTP and is backward compatible with BOOTP. This means a host running the BOOTP client can request a static configuration from a DHCP server.

DHCP is also needed when a host moves from network to network or is connected and disconnected from a network (like a subscriber to a service provider). DHCP provides temporary IP addresses for a limited period of time.

A DHCP server has two databases. The first database statically binds physical addresses with IP addresses. This is the same type of database a BOOTP server has. DHCP has a second database with a pool of available IP addresses. This second database makes DHCP dynamic. When a DHCP client requests a temporary IP address, the DHCP server goes to the pool of available (unused) IP addresses and assigns an IP address for a negotiable period of time.

When a DHCP client sends a request to a DHCP server, the server first checks its static database. If an entry with the requested physical address exists in the static database, the permanent IP address of the client is returned. On the other hand, if the entry does not exist in the static database, the server selects an IP address from the available pool and assigns the address to the client and adds the entry to the dynamic database.

Leasing

The addresses assigned from the pool are temporary addresses. The DHCP server issues a lease for a specific period of time. When the lease expires, the client must either stop using the IP address or renew the lease. The server has the choice to agree or disagree with renewal. If the server disagrees, the client stops using the address.

Packet Format

To make DHCP backward compatible with BOOTP, the designers of DHCP have decided to use almost the same packet format. They have only added a 1-bit flag to the packet. However, to allow different interactions with the server, extra options have been added to the option field. Figure 17.4 shows the format of a DHCP message.

Figure 17.4 *DHCP packet*

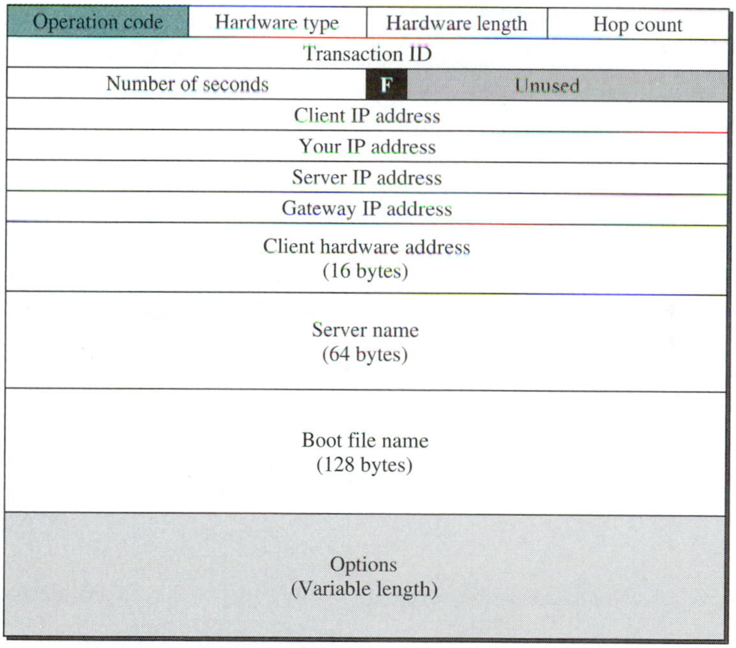

<table>
<tr><td>Operation code</td><td>Hardware type</td><td>Hardware length</td><td>Hop count</td></tr>
<tr><td colspan="4">Transaction ID</td></tr>
<tr><td colspan="2">Number of seconds</td><td>F</td><td>Unused</td></tr>
<tr><td colspan="4">Client IP address</td></tr>
<tr><td colspan="4">Your IP address</td></tr>
<tr><td colspan="4">Server IP address</td></tr>
<tr><td colspan="4">Gateway IP address</td></tr>
<tr><td colspan="4">Client hardware address
(16 bytes)</td></tr>
<tr><td colspan="4">Server name
(64 bytes)</td></tr>
<tr><td colspan="4">Boot file name
(128 bytes)</td></tr>
<tr><td colspan="4">Options
(Variable length)</td></tr>
</table>

The fields are as follows:

- **Flag.** A 1-bit flag has been added to the packet (the first bit of the unused field) to let the client specify a forced broadcast reply (instead of unicast) from the server. If the reply is unicast to the client, the destination IP address of the IP packet is the address assigned to the client. Since the client does not know its IP address, it may discard the packet. However if the IP datagram is broadcast, every host receives and processes the broadcast message.

- **Options.** Several options have been added to the list of options. One option, with the value 53 for the tag subfield, is used to define the type of interaction between the client and the server (see Table 17.2). Other options define parameters such as lease time and so on. The options field in DHCP can be up to 312 bytes.

Table 17.2 *Options for DHCP*

Value	*Value*
1 DHCPDISCOVER	5 DHCPACK
2 DHCPOFFER	6 DHCPNACK
3 DHCPREQUEST	7 DHCPRELEASE
4 DHCPDECLINE	

We will see the use of these options in the next section.

Transition States

The DHCP client transitions from one state to another depending on the messages it receives or sends. See Figure 17.5.

Figure 17.5 *DHCP transition diagram*

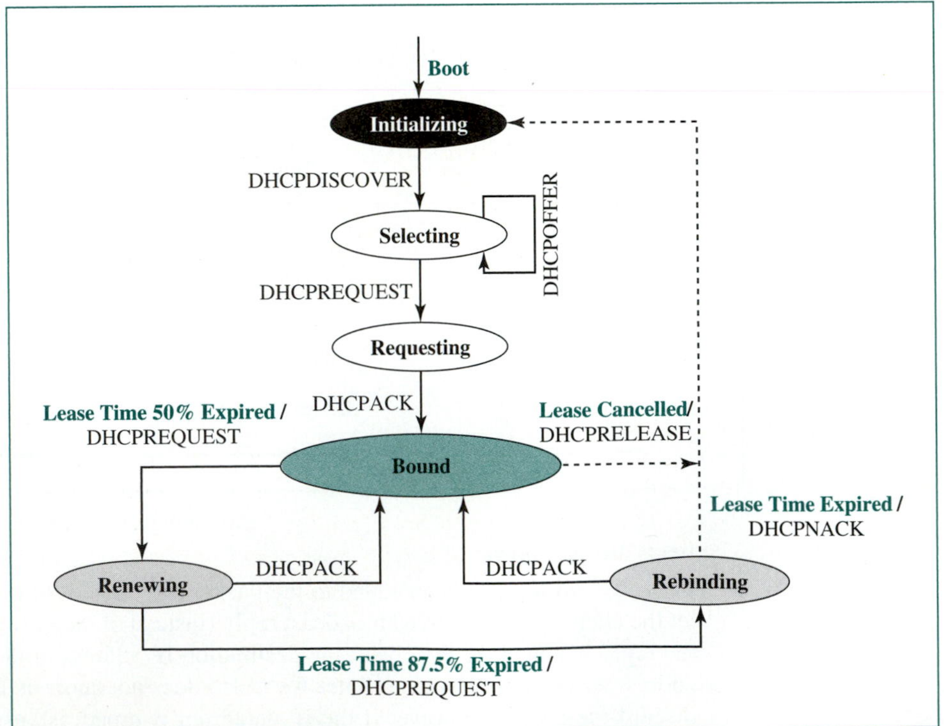

Initializing State

When the DHCP client first starts, it is in the initializing state. The client broadcasts a DHCPDISCOVER message (a request message with the DHCPDISCOVER option) using port 67.

Selecting State

After sending the DHCPDISCOVER message, the client goes to the selecting state. Those servers that can provide this type of service respond with a DHCPOFFER message. In these messages, the servers offer an IP address. They can also offer the lease duration. The default is 1 h. The server that sends a DHCPOFFER locks the offered IP address so that it is not available to any other clients. The client chooses one of the offers and sends a DHCPREQUEST message to the selected server. It then goes to the selecting state. If the client receives no DHCPOFFER message, it tries four more times, each with a span of 2 s. If there is no reply to any of these DHCPDISCOVERs, the client sleeps for 5 min before trying again.

Requesting State

The client remains in the selecting state until it receives a DHCPACK message from the server which creates the binding between the client physical address and its IP address.

Bound State

In this state, the client can use the IP address until the lease expires. When 50 percent of the lease period is reached, the client sends another DHCPREQUEST to ask for renewal. It then goes to the renewing state. When in the bound state, the client can also cancel the lease and go to the initializing state.

Renewing State

The client remains in the renewing state until one of the two events happens. It can receive a DHCPACK, which renews the lease agreement. In this case, the client resets its timer and goes back to the bound state. Or, if a DHCPACK is not received, and 87.5% of the lease time expires, the client goes to the rebinding state.

Rebinding State

The client remains in the rebinding state, until one of the three events happens. If the client receives a DHCPNACK or the lease expires, it goes back to the initializing state and tries to get another IP address. If the client receives a DHCPACK it goes to the bound state and resets the timer.

Exchanging Messages

Figure 17.6 shows the exchange of messages related to the transition diagrams.

Figure 17.6 *Exchanging messages*

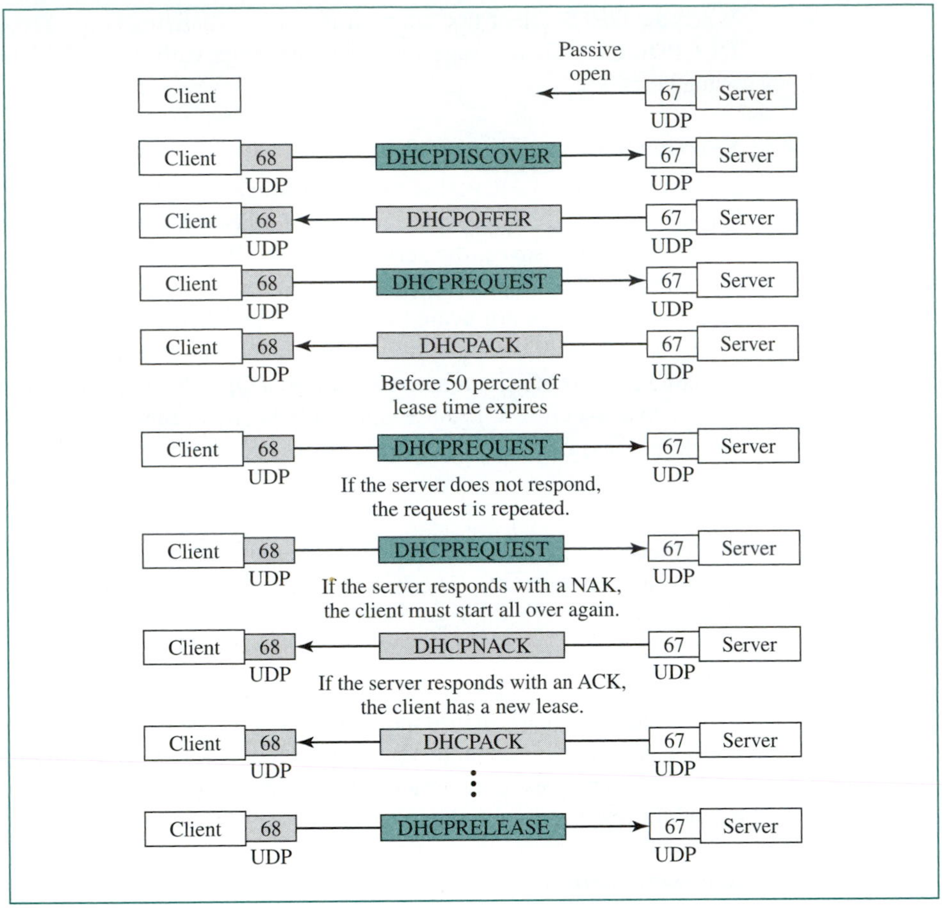

17.3 KEY TERMS

bootstrap process

Bootstrap Protocol (BOOTP)

broadcast message

configuration file

dynamic configuration protocol

Dynamic Host Configuration Protocol (DHCP)

gateway

hardware address

IP address

magic cookie

name server

RARP

read-only memory (ROM)

relay agent

router
static configuration protocol
subnet mask
TFTP
UDP
unicast message
user datagram
well-known port

17.4 SUMMARY

- Every computer attached to a TCP/IP internet must know its IP address, the IP address of a router, the IP address of a name server, and its subnet mask (if it is part of a subnet).
- BOOTP and Dynamic Host Configuration Protocol (DHCP) are client-server applications that deliver vital network information to either diskless computers or computers at first boot.
- One BOOTP packet format is used for both the client request and the server reply.
- The BOOTP server waits passively for a client request.
- A server reply can be either broadcast or unicast.
- A BOOTP request is encapsulated in a UDP user datagram.
- BOOTP, a static configuration protocol, uses a table that maps IP addresses to physical addresses.
- A relay agent is a router that helps send local BOOTP requests to remote servers.
- DHCP is a dynamic configuration protocol with two databases: one is similar to BOOTP and the other is a pool of IP addresses available for temporary assignment.
- The DHCP server issues a lease for an IP address to a client for a specific period of time.
- The DHCP packet format is similar to that of BOOTP. DHCP added a flag field and extra options.
- DHCP is backward compatible with BOOTP.

17.5 PRACTICE SET

Multiple-Choice Questions

1. The server can supply the _______ during the BOOTP process.
   a. client IP address
   b. your IP address
   c. gateway IP address
   d. all of the above

2. The _______ field in a BOOTP packet identifies a specific client request with a specific server response.
   a. operation code
   b. hardware type
   c. transaction ID
   d. hop count
3. The _______ field in a BOOTP packet identifies the type of network.
   a. operation code
   b. hardware type
   c. transaction ID
   d. hop count
4. The _______ field in a BOOTP packet identifies the packet as either a request or a reply.
   a. operation code
   b. hardware type
   c. transaction ID
   d. hop count
5. A relay agent is a router on a LAN that can help send _______ requests to _______ servers.
   a. all; local
   b. remote; local
   c. local; remote
   d. none of the above
6. The DHCP client may not send a _______.
   a. DHCPDISCOVER
   b. DHCPOFFER
   c. DHCPREQUEST
   d. DHCPRELEASE
7. The DHCP server may not send a _______.
   a. DHCPOFFER
   b. DHCPACK
   c. DHCPNACK
   d. DHCPRELEASE
8. The _______ message offers the client an IP address.
   a. DHCPOFFER
   b. DHCPREQUEST
   c. DHCPNACK
   d. DHCPRELEASE

9. When a client receives a _______ message, it must relinquish its IP address.
   a. DHCPOFFER
   b. DHCPDISCOVER
   c. DHCPNACK
   d. DHCPREQUEST
10. The _______ field in the reply packet is the full pathname of the boot file.
   a. server name
   b. transaction ID
   c. magic cookie
   d. boot filename
11. A computer booted for the first time has its _______ stored on ROM.
   a. IP address
   b. subnet mask
   c. IP address of a name server
   d. none of the above
12. _______ can supply a diskless computer with its IP address.
   a. RARP
   b. ARP
   c. BOOTP
   d. a and c
13. _______ can supply a diskless computer with the IP address of a router.
   a. RARP
   b. ARP
   c. BOOTP
   d. a and c
14. Which fields are most likely to contain the same information?
   a. client IP address and your IP address
   b. client IP address and server IP address
   c. client IP address and gateway IP address
   d. your IP address and server IP address
15. The BOOTP client uses _______ port number _______.
   a. ephemeral; 67
   b. ephemeral; 68
   c. well-known; 67
   d. well-known; 68
16. The BOOTP server reply uses _______ as the destination address.
   a. all 0s
   b. all 1s
   c. client IP address
   d. b or c

Exercises

17. What is the minimum length of a BOOTP packet? What is the maximum length?
18. A BOOTP packet is encapsulated in a UDP packet, which is encapsulated in an IP packet, which is encapsulated in a frame. A RARP packet, on the other hand, is encapsulated only in a frame. Find the efficiency of a BOOTP packet versus a RARP packet.
19. Show an example of a BOOTP packet with a padding option.
20. Show an example of a BOOTP packet with an end-of-list option.
21. What is the maximum number of seconds that can be stored in the Number of Seconds field of a BOOTP packet?
22. Show the contents of all fields for a BOOTP request packet sent from a client with physical address 00112115EA21.
23. Show the contents of all fields for a BOOTP reply sent in response to the request in exercise 22.
24. Encapsulate the packet in exercise 22 in a UDP user datagram. Fill all the fields.
25. Encapsulate the packet in exercise 23 in a UDP user datagram. Fill all the fields.
26. Encapsulate the packet in exercise 24 in an IP datagram. Fill all the fields.
27. Encapsulate the packet in exercise 25 in an IP datagram. Fill all the fields.
28. Why does a newly added host need to know its subnetmask?
29. Why does a newly added host need to know the IP address of a router?
30. Why does a newly added host need to know the IP address of a name server?
31. Why do you think BOOTP needs to use TFTP to get additional information? Why can't all information be retrieved using BOOTP?
32. Show the format and contents of a DHCPDISCOVER message.
33. Show the format and contents of a DHCPOFFER message.
34. Show the format and contents of a DHCPREQUEST message.
35. Show the format and contents of a DHCPDECLINE message.
36. Show the format and contents of a DHCPACK message.
37. Show the format and contents of a DHCPNACK message.
38. Show the format and contents of a DHCPRELEASE message.
39. A diskless client on a Class C Ethernet network uses BOOTP. The BOOTP server is on a Class B Ethernet network. Draw a figure of the networks with appropriate IP addresses for the client, server, and relay agent. Fill out a BOOTP request and reply packet.
40. Design an algorithm for a BOOTP client.
41. Design an algorithm for a BOOTP server.
42. Design an algorithm for a DHCP client.
43. Design an algorithm for a DHCP server.

Programming Exercises

44. Create a header file to include all constants that you think are needed to implement a BOOTP algorithm in C. Use the #define directives.
45. Create a header file to include all constants that you think are needed to implement a DHCP algorithm in C. Use the #define directives.
46. Complete the following struct declaration for the BOOTP packet.

```
struct   BOOTP
{
unsigned short     Operation_Code  ;
................................................................
................................................................
} ;
```

47. Write a C program for the algorithm you developed in exercise 40.
48. Write a C program for the algorithm you developed in exercise 41.
49. Write a C program for the algorithm you developed in exercise 42.
50. Write a C program for the algorithm you developed in exercise 43.

CHAPTER 18

Domain Name System (DNS)

To identify an entity, TCP/IP protocols use the IP address, which uniquely identifies the connection of a host to the Internet. However, people prefer to use names instead of addresses. Therefore, we need a system that can map a name to an address or an address to a name.

When the Internet was small, mapping was done using a *host file*. The host file had only two columns comprising name and address. Every host could store the host file on its disk and update it periodically from a master host file. When a program or a user wanted to map a name to an address, the host consulted the host file and found the mapping.

Today, however, it is impossible to have one single host file to relate every address with a name or vice versa. The host file would be too large to store in every host. In addition, it would be impossible to update all the host files in the world every time there is a change.

One solution would be to store the entire host file in a single computer and allow access to this centralized information to every computer that needs mapping. But we know that this would create a huge amount of traffic on the Internet.

Another solution, the one used today, is to divide this huge amount of information into smaller parts and store each part on a different computer. In this method, the host that needs mapping can contact the closest computer holding the needed information. This method is used by the Domain Name System (DNS). In this chapter, we first discuss the concepts and ideas behind the DNS. We then describe the DNS protocol itself.

18.1 NAME SPACE

To be unambiguous, the names assigned to machines should be carefully selected from a name space with complete control over the binding between the names and IP addresses. In other words, the names should be unique because the addresses are unique. A name space that maps each address to a unique name can be organized in two ways: flat and hierarchical.

Flat Name Space

In a **flat name space,** a name is assigned to an address. A name in this space is a sequence of characters without structure. The names may or may not have a common section; if they do, it has no meaning. The main disadvantage of a flat name space is that it cannot be used in a large system such as the Internet because it must be centrally controlled to avoid ambiguity and duplication.

Hierarchical Name Space

In a **hierarchical name space,** each name is made of several parts. The first part can define the nature of the organization, the second part can define the name of an organization, the third part can define departments in the organization, and so on. In this case, the authority to assign and control the name spaces can be decentralized. A central authority can assign the part of the name that defines the nature of the organization and the name of the organization. The responsibility of the rest of the name can be given to the organization itself. The organization can add suffixes (or prefixes) to the name to define its host or resources. The management of the organization need not worry that the prefix chosen for a host is taken by another organization because, even if part of an address is the same, the whole address is different. For example, assume two colleges and a company call one of their computers *challenger.* The first college is given a name by the central authority such as *fhda.edu,* the second college is given the name *berkeley.edu,* and the company is given the name *smart.com.* When each of these organizations add the name *challenger* to the name they have already been given, the end result is three distinguishable names: *challenger.fhda.edu, challenger.berkeley.edu,* and *challenger.smart.com.* The names are unique without the need to be assigned by a central authority. The central authority controls only part of the name, not the whole.

18.2 DOMAIN NAME SPACE

To have a hierarchical name space, a **domain name space** was designed. In this design the names are defined in an inverted-tree structure with the root at the top. The tree can have only 128 levels: level 0 (root) to level 127. Whereas the root glues the whole tree together, each level of the tree defines a hierarchical level (see Figure 18.1).

Label

Each node in the tree has a **label,** which is a string with a maximum of 63 characters. The root label is a null string (empty string). DNS requires that children of a node (nodes that branch from the same node) have different labels, which guarantees the uniqueness of the domain names.

Domain Name

Each node in the tree has a domain name. A full **domain name** is a sequence of labels separated by dots (.). The domain names are always read from the node up to the root.

Figure 18.1 *Domain name space*

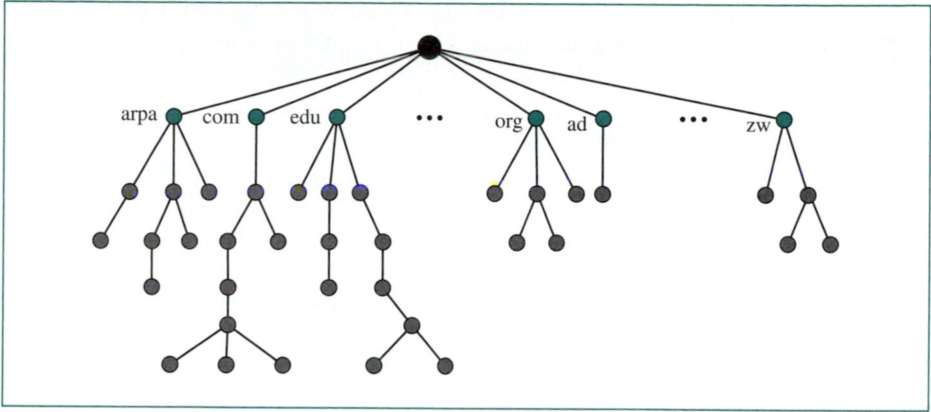

The last label is the label of the root (null). This means that a full domain name always ends in a null label, which means the last character is a dot because the null string is nothing. Figure 18.2 shows some domain names.

Figure 18.2 *Domain names and labels*

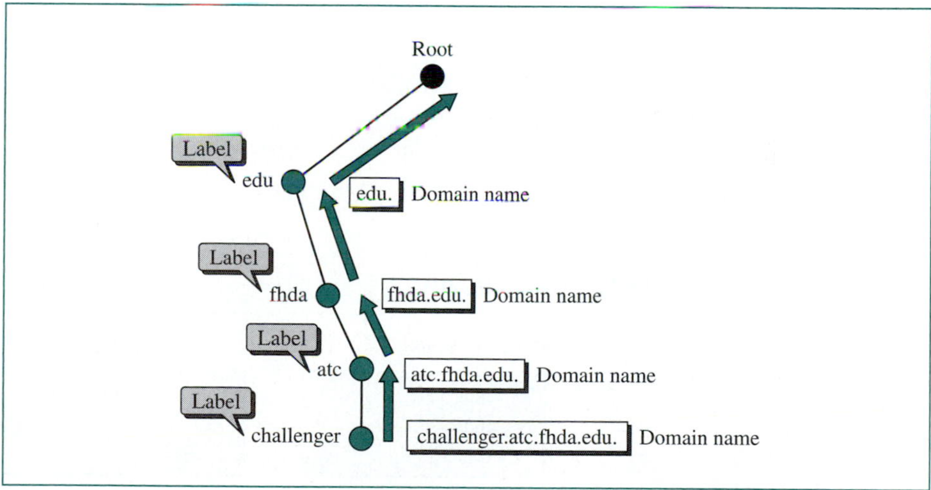

Fully Qualified Domain Name (FQDN)

If a label is terminated by a null string, it is called a fully qualified domain name (FQDN). An FQDN is a domain name that contains the full name of a host. It contains all labels, from the most specific to the most general, that uniquely defines the name of the host. For example, the domain name

challenger.atc.fhda.edu.

is the FQDN of a computer named *challenger* and installed at the Advanced Technology Center (ATC) at De Anza College. A DNS server can only match an FQDN to an address. Note that the name must end with a null label, but because null here means nothing, the label ends with a dot (.).

Partially Qualified Domain Name (PQDN)

If a label is not terminated by a null string, it is called a partially qualified domain name (PQDN). A PQDN starts from a node, but it does not reach the root. It is used when the name to be resolved belongs to the same site as the client. Here the resolver can supply the missing part, called the *suffix,* to create an FQDN. For example, if a user at the *fhda.edu.* site wants to get the IP address of the challenger computer, he or she can define the partial name

challenger

The DNS client adds the suffix *atc.fhda.edu.* before passing the address to the DNS server.

The DNS client normally holds a list of suffixes. The following can be the list of suffixes at De Anza College. The null suffix defines nothing. This suffix is added when the user defines an FQDN.

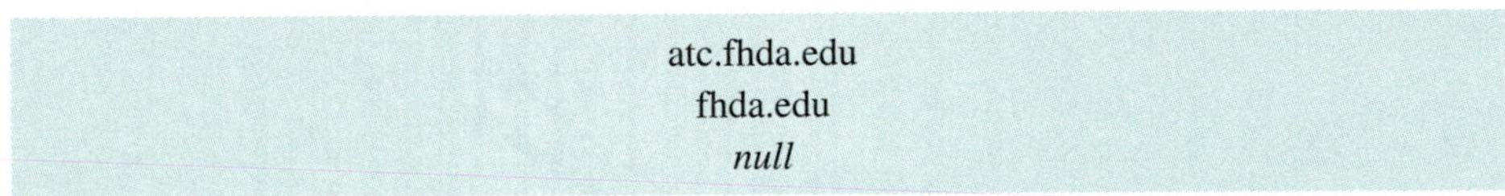

atc.fhda.edu
fhda.edu
null

Figure 18.3 shows some FQDNs and PQDNs.

Figure 18.3 *FQDN and PQDN*

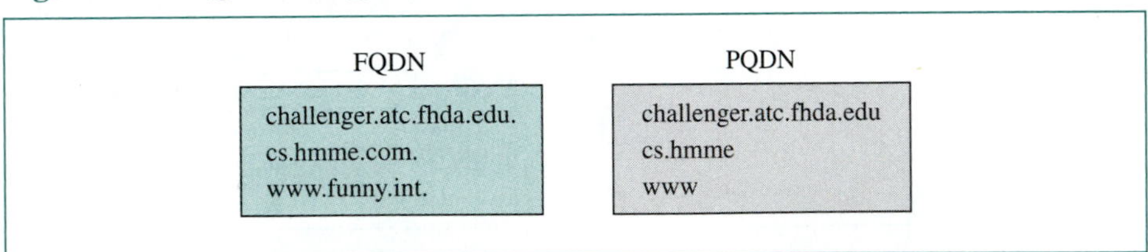

Domain

A **domain** is a subtree of the domain name space. The name of the domain is the domain name of the node at the top of the subtree. Figure 18.4 shows some domains. Note that a domain may itself be divided into domains (or *subdomains* as they are sometimes called).

Figure 18.4 *Domains*

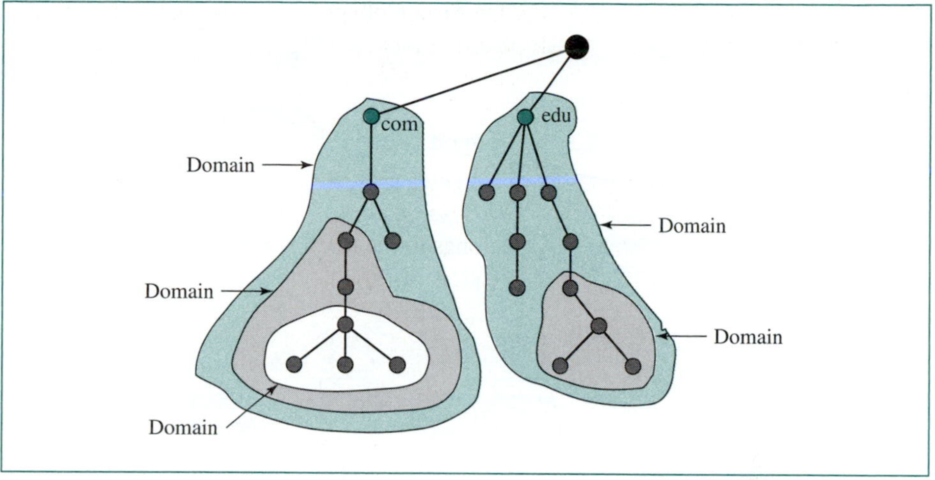

18.3 DISTRIBUTION OF NAME SPACE

The information contained in the domain name space should be stored. However, it is very inefficient and also not reliable to have just one computer store such a huge amount of information. It is inefficient because responding to requests from all over the world places a heavy load on the system. It is not reliable because any failure makes the data inaccessible.

Hierarchy of Name Servers

The solution to these problems is to distribute the information among many computers called *DNS servers*. One way to do this is to divide the whole space into many domains based on the first level. In other words, we let the root stand alone and create as many domains (subtrees) as there are first-level nodes. Because a domain created this way could be very large, DNS allows domains to be divided further into smaller domains (subdomains). Each server can be responsible (authoritative) for either a large or small domain. In other words, we have a hierarchy of servers in the same way that we have a hierarchy of names (see Figure 18.5).

Zone

What a server is responsible for or has authority over is called a *zone*. If a server accepts responsibility for a domain and does not divide the domain into smaller domains, the "domain" and the "zone" refer to the same thing. The server makes a database called a *zone file* and keeps all the information for every node under that domain. However, if a server divides its domain into subdomains and delegates part of its authority to other servers, "domain" and "zone" refer to different things. The information about the nodes in the subdomains is stored in the servers at the lower levels, with

Figure 18.5 *Hierarchy of name servers*

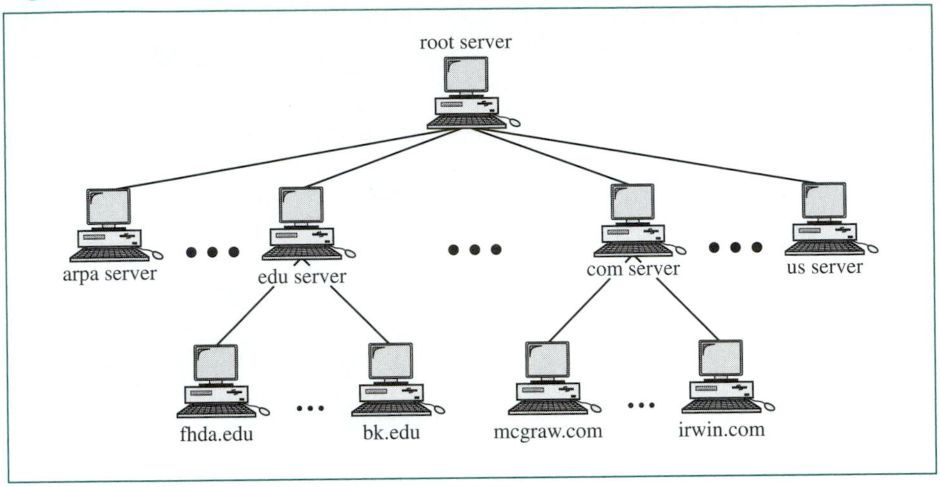

the original server keeping some sort of reference to these lower-level servers. Of course the original server does not free itself from responsibility totally: It still has a zone, but the detailed information is kept by the lower-level servers (see Figure 18.6).

Figure 18.6 *Zones and domains*

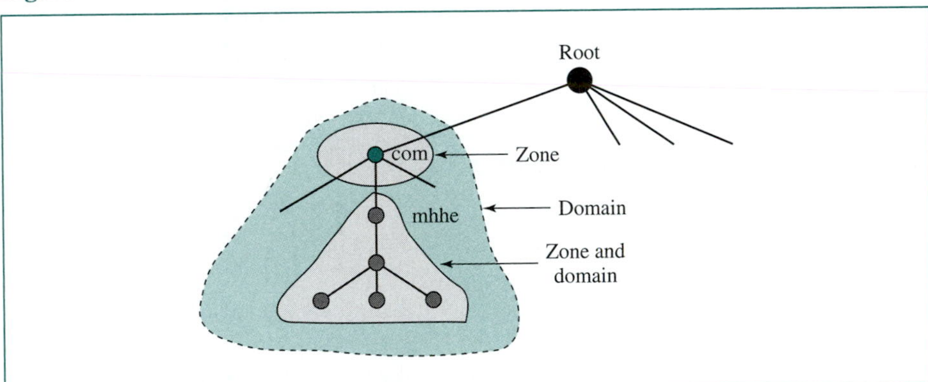

A server can also divide part of its domain and delegate responsibility but still keep part of the domain for itself. In this case, its zone is made of detailed information for the part of the domain that is not delegated and references to those parts that are delegated.

Root Server

A **root server** is a server whose zone consists of the whole tree. A root server usually does not store any information about domains but delegates its authority to other servers, keeping references to those servers. Currently there are more than 13 root servers, each covering the whole domain name space. The servers are distributed all around the world.

Primary and Secondary Servers

DNS defines two types of servers: primary and secondary. A **primary server** is a server that stores a file about the zone for which it is an authority. It it responsible for creating, maintaining, and updating the zone file. It stores the zone file on a local disk.

A **secondary server** is a server that transfers the complete information about a zone from another server (primary or secondary) and stores the file on its local disk. The secondary server neither creates nor updates the zone files. If updating is required, it must be done by the primary server, which sends the updated version to the secondary.

The primary and secondary servers are both authoritative for the zones they serve. The idea is not to put the secondary server at a lower level of authority but to create redundancy for the data so that if one server fails, the other can continue serving clients. Note also that a server can be a primary server for a specific zone and a secondary server for another zone. Therefore, when we refer to a server as a primary or secondary server, we should be careful to which zone we refer.

> A primary server loads all information from the disk file; the secondary server loads all information from the the primary server. When the primary downloads information from the secondary, it is called **zone transfer.**

18.4 DNS IN THE INTERNET

DNS is a protocol that can be used in different platforms. In the Internet, the domain name space (tree) is divided into three different sections: generic domains, country domains, and inverse domain (see Figure 18.7).

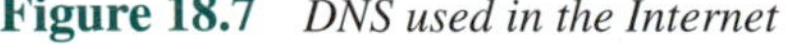

Figure 18.7 *DNS used in the Internet*

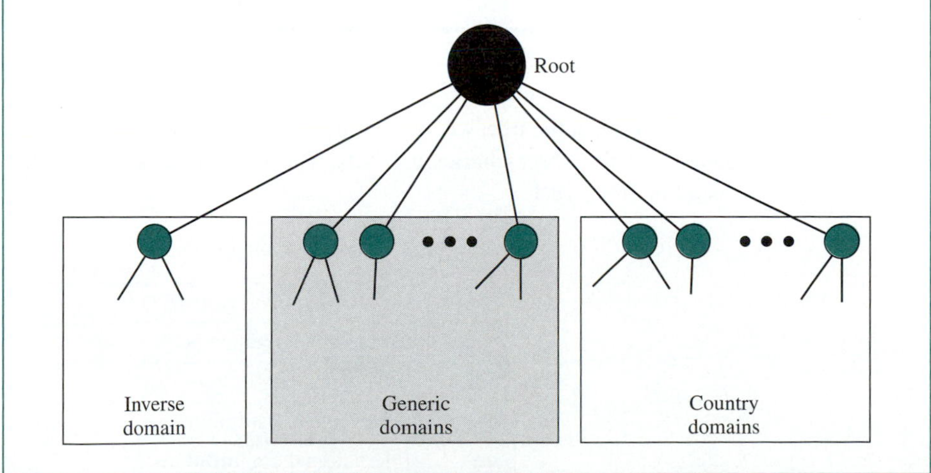

Generic Domains

The **generic domains** define registered hosts according to their generic behavior. Each node in the tree defines a domain, which is an index to the domain name space database (see Figure 18.8).

Figure 18.8 *Generic domains*

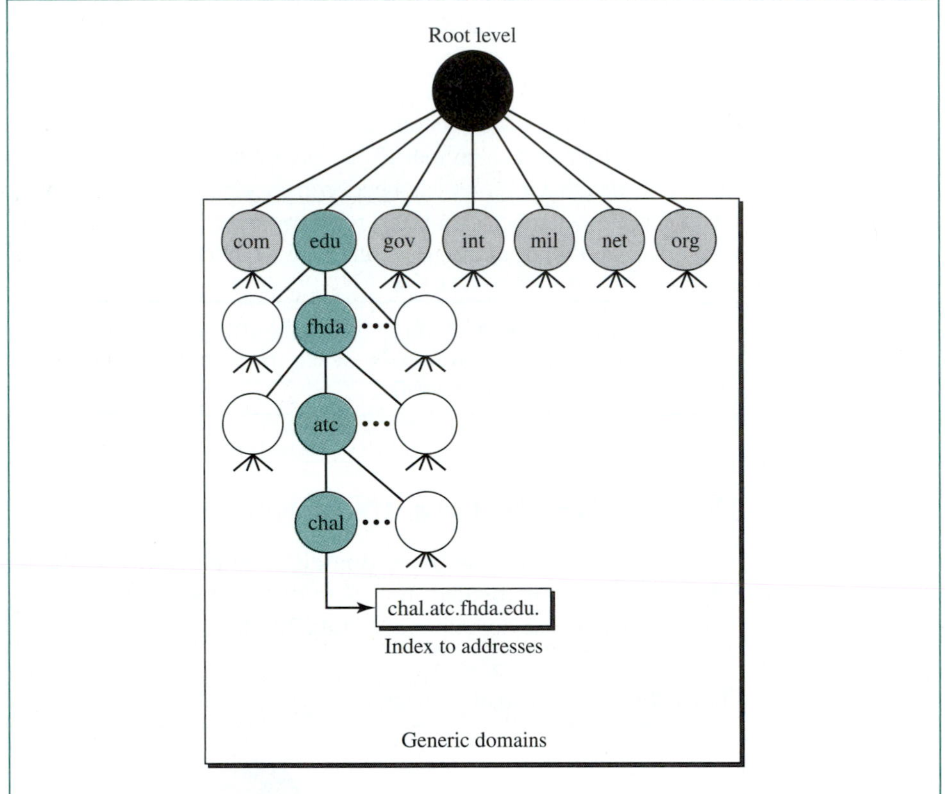

Looking at the tree, we see that the first level in the generic domains section allows seven possible three-character labels. These labels describe the organization types as listed in Table 18.1.

Table 18.1 *Generic domain labels*

Label	*Description*
com	Commercial organizations
edu	Educational institutions
gov	Government institutions
int	International organizations

Table 18.1 *Generic domain labels (continued)*

Label	*Description*
mil	Military groups
net	Network support centers
org	Nonprofit organizations

Recently a few more first-level labels have been approved; these are shown in Table 18.2.

Table 18.2 *New generic domain labels*

Label	*Description*
aero	Airlines and aerospace companies
biz	Businesses or firms (similar to "com")
coop	Cooperative business organizations
info	Information service providers
museum	Museums and other non-profit organizations
name	Personal names (individuals)
pro	Professional individual organizations

Country Domains

The **country domains** section follows the same format as the generic domains but uses two-character country abbreviations (e.g., us for United States) in place of the three-character organizational abbreviations at the first level. Second-level labels can be organizational, or they can be more specific, national designations. The United States, for example, uses state abbreviations as a subdivision of us (e.g., ca.us.).

Figure 18.9 shows the country domains section. The address *anza.cup.ca.us* can be translated to De Anza College in Cupertino in California in the United States.

Inverse Domain

The **inverse domain** is used to map an address to a name. This may happen, for example, when a server has received a request from a client to do a task. Whereas the server has a file that contains a list of authorized clients, the server lists only the IP address of the client (extracted from the received IP packet). To determine if the client is on the authorized list, it can ask its resolver to send a query to the DNS server and ask for a mapping of address to name.

This type of query is called an inverse or pointer (PTR) query. To handle a pointer query, the inverse domain is added to the domain name space with the first-level node called *arpa* (for historical reasons). The second level is also one single node named *in-addr* (for inverse address). The rest of the domain defines IP addresses.

Figure 18.9 *Country domains*

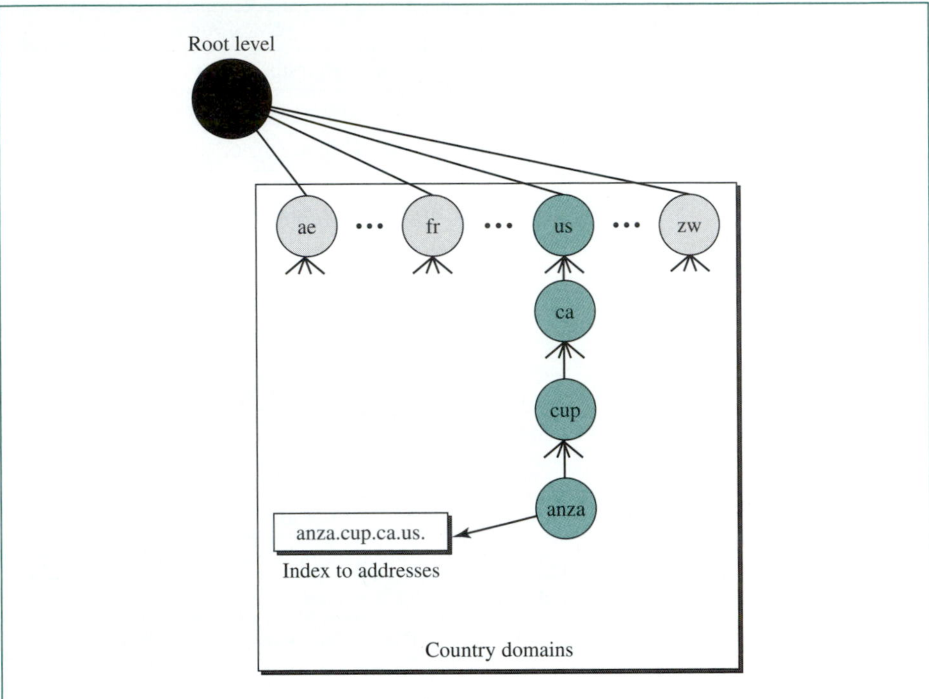

The servers that handle the inverse domain are also hierarchical. This means the netid part of the address should be at a higher level than the subnetid part, and the subnetid part higher than the hostid part. In this way, a server serving the whole site is at a higher level than the servers serving each subnet. This configuration makes the domain look inverted when compared to a generic or country domain. To follow the convention of reading the domain labels from the bottom to the top, an IP address such as 132.34.45.121 (a class B address with netid 132.34) is read as 121.45.34.132.in-addr.arpa. See Figure 18.10 for an illustration of the inverse domain configuration.

18.5 RESOLUTION

Mapping a name to an address or an address to a name is called *name-address resolution.*

Resolver

DNS is designed as a client-server application. A host that needs to map an address to a name or a name to an address calls a DNS client called a *resolver.* The resolver accesses the closest DNS server with a mapping request. If the server has the information, it satisfies the resolver; otherwise, it either refers the resolver to other servers or asks other servers to provide the information.

Figure 18.10 *Inverse domain*

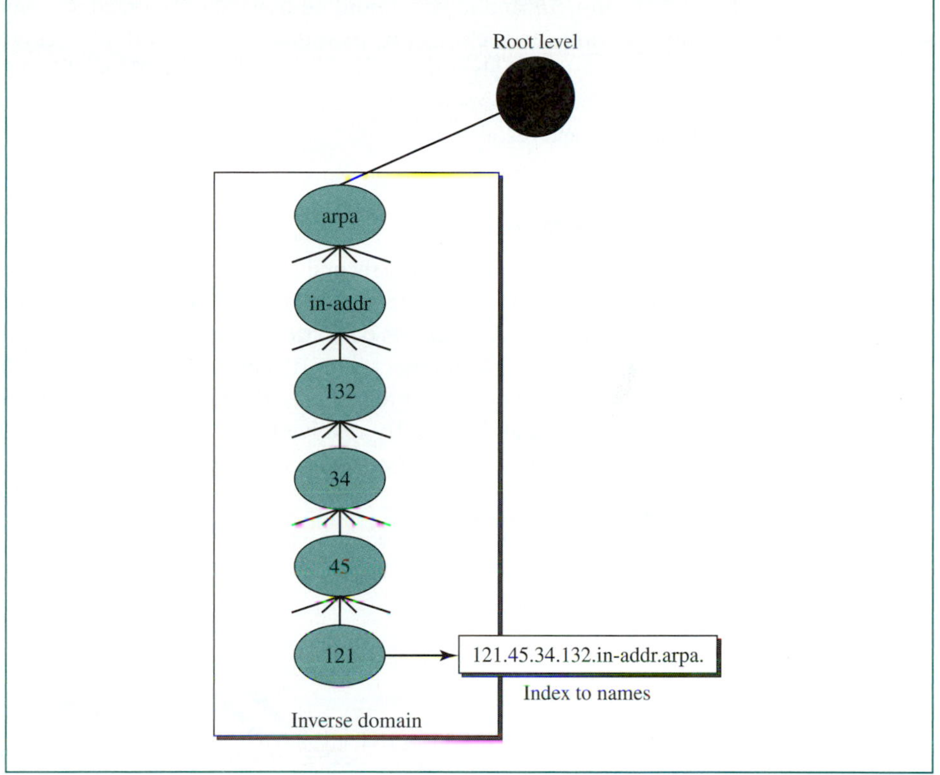

After the resolver receives the mapping, it interprets the response to see if it is a real resolution or an error, and finally delivers the result to the process that requested it.

Mapping Names to Addresses

Most of the time, the resolver gives a domain name to the server and asks for the corresponding address. In this case, the server checks the generic domains or the country domains to find the mapping.

If the domain name is from the generic domains section, the resolver receives a domain name such as "*chal.atc.fhda.edu.*". The query is sent by the resolver to the local DNS server for resolution. If the local server cannot resolve the query, it either refers the resolver to other servers or asks other servers directly.

If the domain name is from the country domains section, the resolver receives a domain name such as "*ch.fhda.cu.ca.us.*". The procedure is the same.

Mapping Addresses to Names

A client can send an IP address to a server to be mapped to a domain name. As mentioned before, this is called a PTR query. To answer queries of this kind, DNS uses the inverse domain. However, in the request, the IP address should be reversed and two labels, *in-addr* and *arpa,* should be appended to create a domain acceptable by the inverse domain section. For example, if the resolver receives the IP address 132.34.45.121, the resolver first inverts the address and then adds the two labels before sending. The domain name sent is "*121.45.34.132.in-addr.arpa.*", which is received by the local DNS and resolved.

Recursive Resolution

The client (resolver) can ask for a recursive answer from a name server. This means that the resolver expects the server to supply the final answer. If the server is the authority for the domain name, it checks its database and responds. If the server is not the authority, it sends the request to another server (the parent usually) and waits for the response. If the parent is the authority, it responds; otherwise, it sends the query to yet another server. When the query is finally resolved, the response travels back until it finally reaches the requesting client. This is shown in Figure 18.11.

Figure 18.11 *Recursive resolution*

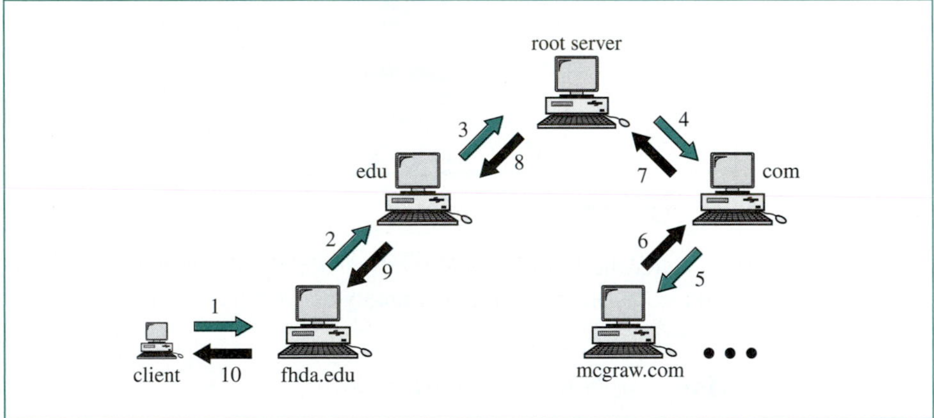

Iterative Resolution

If the client does not ask for a recursive answer, the mapping can be done iteratively. If the server is an authority for the name, it sends the answer. If it is not, it returns (to the client) the IP address of the server that it thinks can resolve the query. The client is responsible for repeating the query to this second server. If the newly addressed server can resolve the problem, it answers the query with the IP address; otherwise, it returns the IP address of a new server to the client. Now the client must repeat the query to the third server. This process is called *iterative* because the client repeats the same query to multiple servers. In Figure 18.12 the client queries four servers before it gets an answer from the mcgraw.com server.

Figure 18.12 *Iterative resolution*

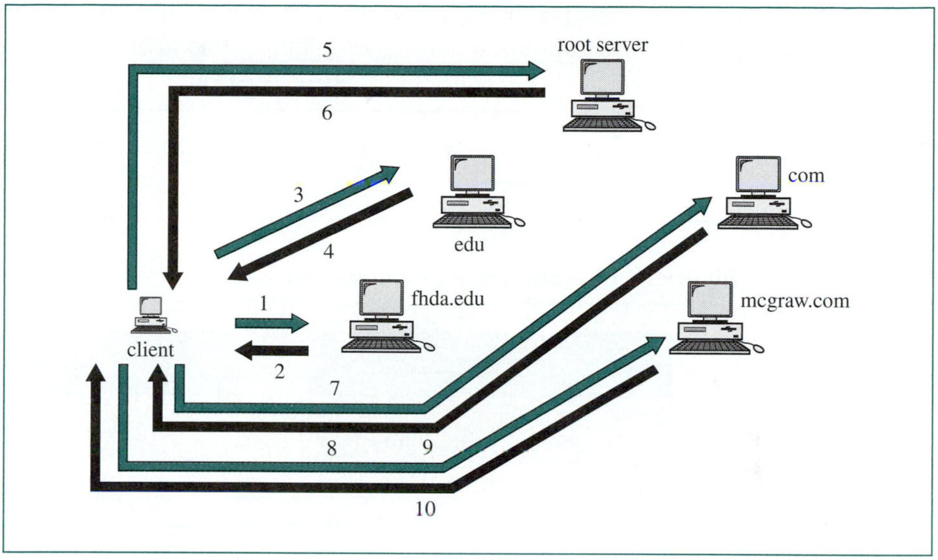

Caching

Each time a server receives a query for a name that is not in its domain, it needs to search its database for a server IP address. Reduction of this search time would increase efficiency. DNS handles this with a mechanism called *caching*. When a server asks for a mapping from another server and receives the response, it stores this information in its cache memory before sending it to the client. If the same or another client asks for the same mapping, it can check its cache memory and resolve the problem. However, to inform the client that the response is coming from the cache memory and not from an authoritative source, the server marks the response as *unauthoritative.*

Caching speeds up resolution, but it can also be problematic. If a server caches a mapping for a long time, it may send an outdated mapping to the client. To counter this, two techniques are used. First, the authoritative server always adds a piece of information to the mapping called *time-to-live* (TTL). It defines the time in seconds that the receiving server can cache the information. After that time, the mapping is invalid and any query must be sent again to the authoritative server. Second, DNS requires that each server keep a TTL counter for each mapping it caches. The cache memory must be searched periodically and those mappings with an expired TTL must be purged.

18.6 DNS MESSAGES

DNS has two types of messages: query and response (see Figure 18.13). Both types have the same format. The query message consists of a header and the question records; the response message consists of a header, question records, answer records, authoritative records, and additional records (see Figure 18.14).

Figure 18.13 *DNS messages*

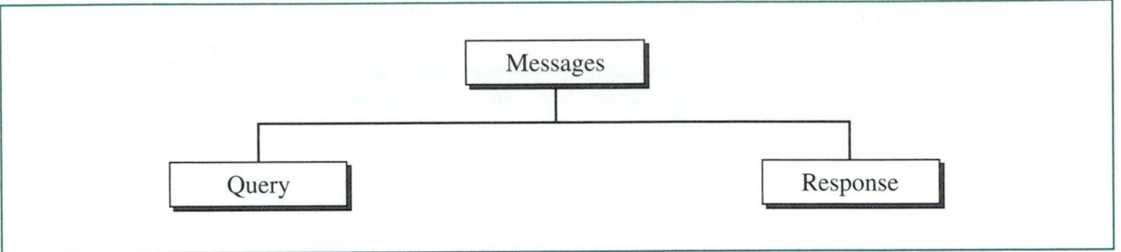

Figure 18.14 *Query and response messages*

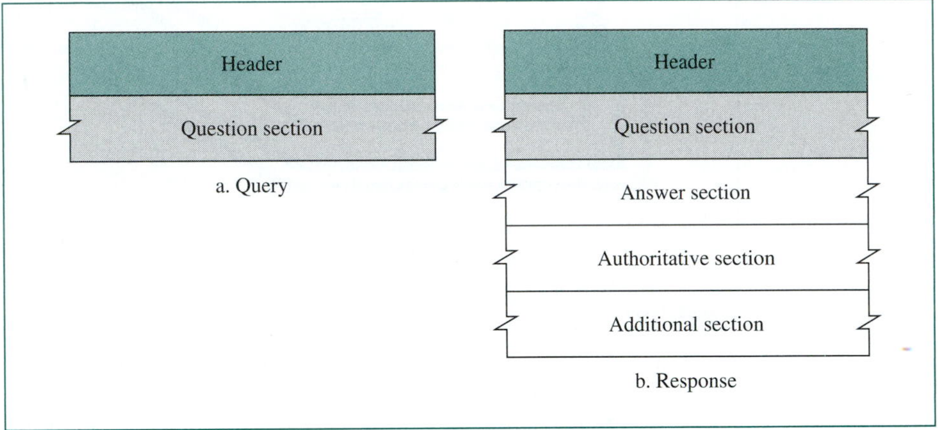

Header

Both query and response messages have the same header format with some fields set to zero for the query messages. The header is 12 bytes and its format is shown in Figure 18.15.

Figure 18.15 *Header format*

Identification	Flags
Number of question records	Number of answer records (All 0s in query message)
Number of authoritative records (All 0s in query message)	Number of additional records (All 0s in query message)

The header fields are as follows:

- **Identification.** This is a 16-bit field used by the client to match the response with the query. The client uses a different identification number each time it sends a query. The server duplicates this number in the corresponding response.
- **Flags.** This is a 16-bit field consisting of the subfields shown in Figure 18.16.

Figure 18.16 *Flags field*

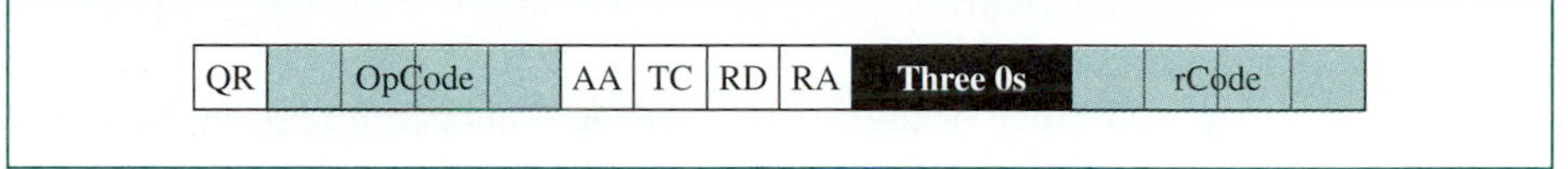

A brief description of each flag subfield follows.

a. **QR (query/response).** This is a 1-bit subfield that defines the type of message. If it is 0, the message is a query. If it is 1, the message is a response.

b. **OpCode.** This is a 4-bit subfield that defines the type of query or response (0 if standard, 1 if inverse, and 2 if a server status request).

c. **AA (authoritative answer).** This is a 1-bit subfield. When it is set (value of 1) it means that the name server is an authoritative server. It is used only in a response message.

d. **TC (truncated).** This is a 1-bit subfield. When it is set (value of 1), it means that the response was more than 512 bytes and truncated to 512. It is used when DNS uses the services of UDP (see Section 16.11 on Encapsulation).

e. **RD (recursion desired).** This is a 1-bit subfield. When it is set (value of 1) it means the client desires a recursive answer. It is set in the query message and repeated in the response message.

f. **RA (recursion available).** This is a 1-bit subfield. When it is set in the response, it means that a recursive response is available. It is set only in the response message.

g. **Reserved.** This is a 3-bit subfield set to 000.

h. **rCode.** This is a 4-bit field that shows the status of the error in the response. Of course, only an authoritative server can make such a judgment. Table 18.3 shows the possible values for this field.

Table 18.3 *Values of rCode*

Value	*Meaning*
0	No error
1	Format error
2	Problem at name server
3	Domain reference problem
4	Query type not supported
5	Administratively prohibited
6–15	Reserved

- **Number of question records.** This is a 16-bit field containing the number of queries in the question section of the message.
- **Number of answer records.** This is a 16-bit field containing the number of answer records in the answer section of the response message. Its value is zero in the query message.

- **Number of authoritative records.** This is a 16-bit field containing the number of authoritative records in the authoritative section of a response message. Its value is zero in the query message.
- **Number of additional records.** This is a 16-bit field containing the number of additional records in the additional section of a response message. Its value is zero in the query message.

Question Section

This is a section consisting of one or more question records. It is present on both query and response messages. We will discuss the question records in a following section.

Answer Section

This is a section consisting of one or more resource records. It is present only on response messages. This section includes the answer from the server to the client (resolver). We will discuss resource records in a following section.

Authoritative Section

This is a section consisting of one or more resource records. It is present only on response messages. This section gives information (domain name) about one or more authoritative servers for the query.

Additional Information Section

This is a section consisting of one or more resource records. It is present only on response messages. This section provides additional information that may help the resolver. For example, a server may give the domain name of an authoritative server to the resolver in the authoritative section, and include the IP address of the same authoritative server in the additional information section.

18.7 TYPES OF RECORDS

As we saw in the previous section, two types of records are used in DNS. The question records are used in the question section of the query and response messages. The resource records are used in the answer, authoritative, and additional information sections of the response message.

Question Record

A question record is used by the client to get information from a server. This contains the domain name. Figure 18.17 shows the format of a question record. The list below describes question record fields.

Figure 18.17 *Question record format*

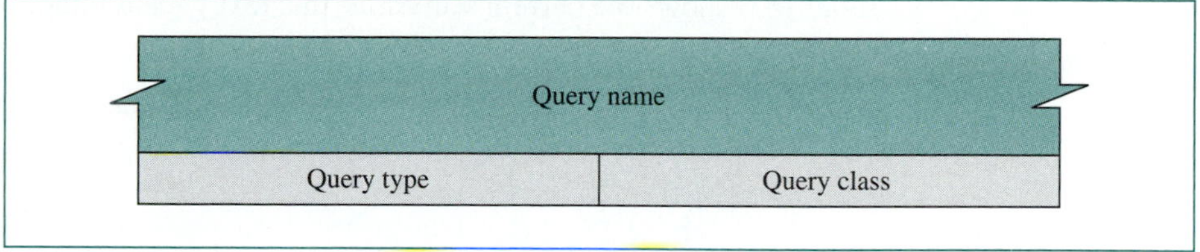

- **Query name.** This is a variable-length field containing a domain name (see Figure 18.18).

Figure 18.18 *Query name format*

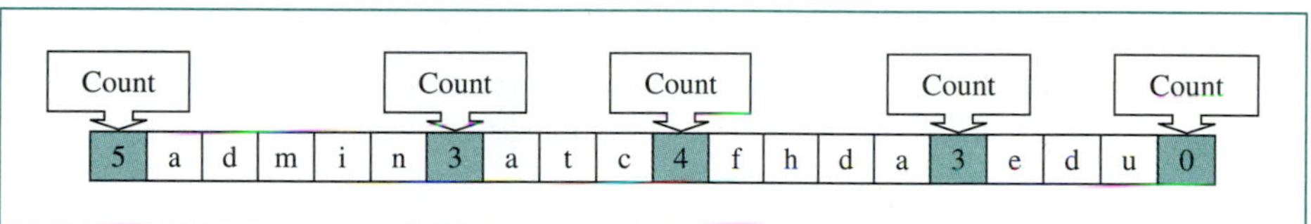

- **Query type.** This is a 16-bit field defining the type of query. Table 18.4 shows some of the types commonly used. The last two can be used only in a query.

Table 18.4 *Types*

Type	*Mnemonic*	*Description*
1	A	Address. A 32-bit IPv4 address. It is used to convert a domain name to an IPv4 address.
2	NS	Name server. It identifies the authoritative servers for a zone.
5	CNAME	Canonical name. It defines an alias for the official name of a host.
6	SOA	Start of authority. It marks the beginning of a zone. It is usually the first record in a zone file.
11	WKS	Well-known services. It defines the network services that a host provides.
12	PTR	Pointer. It is used to convert an IP address to a domain name.
13	HINFO	Host information. It gives the description of the hardware and the operating system used by a host.
15	MX	Mail exchange. It redirects mail to a mail server.
28	AAAA	Address. An IPv6 address (see Chapter 31).
252	AXFR	A request for the transfer of the entire zone.
255	ANY	A request for all records.

- **Query class.** This is a 16-bit field defining the specific protocol using DNS. Table 18.5 shows the current values. In this text we are interested only in class 1 (the Internet).

Table 18.5 *Classes*

Class	*Mnemonic*	*Description*
1	IN	Internet
2	CSNET	CSNET network (obsolete)
3	CS	The COAS network
4	HS	The Hesiod server developed by MIT

Resource Record

Each domain name (each node on the tree) is associated with a record called the *resource record.* The server database consists of resource records. Resource records are also what is returned by the server to the client. Figure 18.19 shows the format of a resource record.

Figure 18.19 *Resource record format*

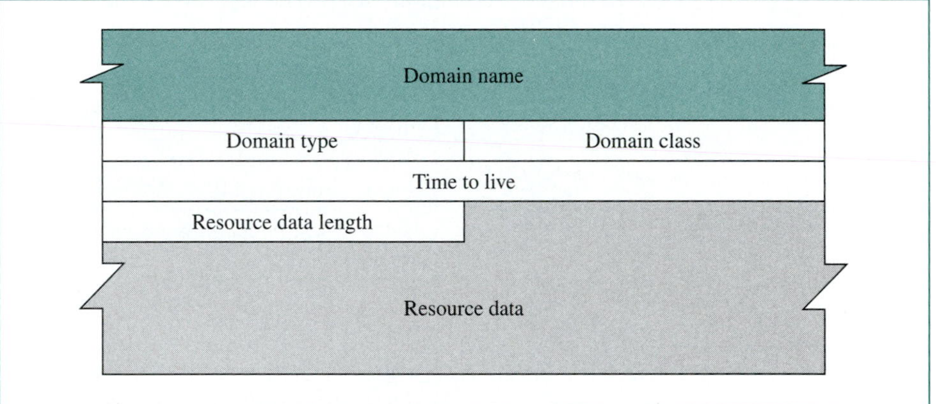

- **Domain name.** This is a variable-length field containing the domain name. It is the duplication of the domain name in the question record. Since DNS requires the use of compression everywhere a name is repeated, this field is a pointer offset to the corresponding domain name field in the question record. See Section 18.8 on Compression.
- **Domain type.** This field is the same as the query type field in the question section except the last two types are not allowed. Refer to Table 18.4 for more information.
- **Domain class.** This field is the same as the query class field in the question section (see Table 18.5).

- **Time to live.** This is a 32-bit field that defines the number of seconds the answer is valid. The receiver can cache the answer for this period of time. A zero value means that the resource record is used only in a single transaction and should not be cached.
- **Resource data length.** This is a 16-bit field defining the length of the resource data.
- **Resource data.** This is a variable-length field containing the answer to the query (in the answer section) or the domain name of the authoritative server (in the authoritative section) or additional information (in the additional information section). The format and contents of this field depend on the value of the type field. It can be one of the following:
  a. **A number.** This is written in octets. For example, an IPv4 address is a 4-octet integer and an IPv6 address is a 16-octet integer.
  b. **A domain name.** Domain names are expressed as a sequence of labels. Each label is preceded by a 1-byte length field that defines the number of characters in the label. Since every domain name ends with the null label, the last byte of every domain name is the length field with the value of 0. To distinguish between a length field and an offset pointer (as we will discuss later), the two high-order bits of a length field should always be zero (00). This will not create a problem because the length of a label cannot be more than 63, which is a maximum of 6 bits (111111).
  c. **An offset pointer.** Domain names can be replaced with an offset pointer. An offset pointer is a 2-byte field with the 2 high-order bits set to 1 (11).
  d. **A character string.** A character string is represented by a 1-byte length field followed by the number of characters defined in the length field. The length field is not restricted like the domain name length field. The character string can be as long as 256 characters (including the length field).

18.8 COMPRESSION

DNS requires that a domain name be replaced by an offset pointer when it is repeated. For example, in a resource record the domain name is usually a repetition of the domain name in the question record. To avoid duplication, DNS defines a 2-byte offset pointer that points to a previous occurrence of the domain or part of it. The format of the field is shown in Figure 18.20.

Figure 18.20 *Format of an offset pointer*

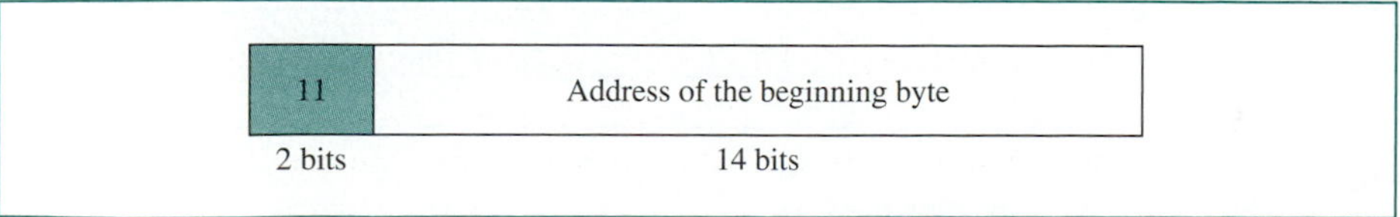

The first 2 high-order bits are two 1s to distinguish an offset pointer from a length field. The other 14 bits represent a number that points to the corresponding byte number in the message. The bytes in a message are counted from the beginning of the message with the first byte counted as byte 0. For example, if an offset pointer refers to byte 12 (the thirteenth byte) of the message, the value should be 1100000000001100. Here the 2 leftmost bits define the field as an offset pointer and the other bits define the decimal number 12. We will show the use of the offset pointers in the following examples.

18.9 EXAMPLES

In this section we show some examples of DNS queries and responses.

Example 1

A resolver sends a query message to a local server to find the IP address for the host "*chal.fhda.edu.*". We discuss the query and response messages separately.

Query Message Figure 18.21 shows the query message sent by the resolver. The first 2 bytes show the identifier (1333). It is used as a sequence number and relates a response to a query. Because a resolver may send many queries even to the same server, the identifier helps to sort responses that arrive out of order. The next bytes contain the flags with the value of 0x0100 in hexadecimal. In binary it is 0000000100000000, but it is more meaningful to divide it into the fields as shown below:

QR	OpCode	AA	TC	RD	RA	Reserved	rCode
0	0000	0	0	1	0	000	0000

Figure 18.21 *Example of a query message*

0x1333		0x0100	
1		0	
0		0	
4	'c'	'h'	'a'
'l'	4	'f'	'h'
'd'	'a'	3	'e'
'd'	'u'	0	Continued on next line
1	1		

The QR bit defines the message as a query. The OpCode is 0000, which means standard query. The recursion desired (RD) bit is set. (Refer back to Figure 18.16 for the flags field descriptions.) The message contains only one question record. The domain name is ***4chal4fhda3edu0***. The next 2 bytes define the query type as an IP address; the last 2 bytes define the class as Internet.

Response Message Figure 18.22 shows the response of the server. The response is similar to the query except that the flags are different and the number of answer records is one. The flags value is 0x8180 in hexadecimal. In binary it is 1000000110000000, but again we divide it into fields as shown below:

QR	OpCode	AA	TC	RD	RA	Reserved	rCode
1	0000	0	0	1	1	000	0000

Figure 18.22 *Example of a response message*

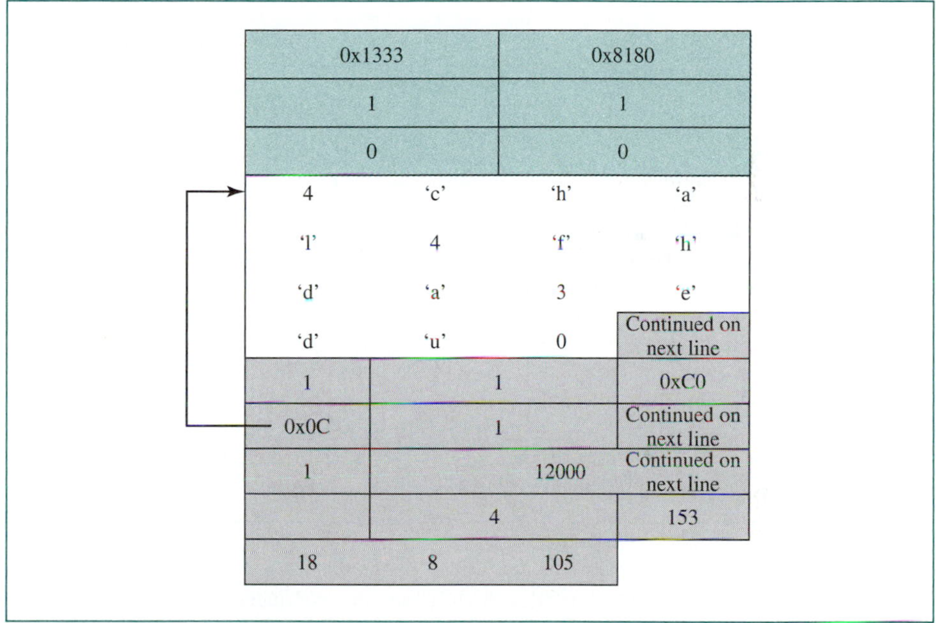

The QR bit defines the message as a response. The OpCode is 0000, which means standard query. The recursion available (RA) and RD bits are set. The message contains one question record and one answer record. The question record is repeated from the query message. The answer record has a pointer 0xC00C (split in two lines), which refers to the question record instead of repeating the domain name. The next field defines the domain type (address). The field after that defines the class (Internet). The field with the value 12,000 is the TTL (12,000 s). The next field is the length of the resource data, which is an IP address (153.18.8.105).

Example 2

An FTP server has received a packet from an FTP client with IP address 153.2.7.9. The FTP server wants to verify that the FTP client is an authorized client. The FTP server can consult a file containing the list of authorized clients. However, the file consists only of domain names. The FTP server has only the IP address of the requesting client, which was the source IP address in the IP datagram received. The FTP server asks the resolver (DNS client) to send an inverse query to a DNS server to ask for the name of the FTP client. We discuss the query and response messages separately.

Query Message Figure 18.23 shows the query message sent from the resolver to the server. The first 2 bytes show the identifier (0x1200). The flags value is 0x0900 in hexadecimal. In binary it is 0000100100000000, and we divide it into fields as shown below:

QR	OpCode	AA	TC	RD	RA	Reserved	rCode
0	0001	0	0	1	0	000	0000

Figure 18.23 *Example of inverse query message*

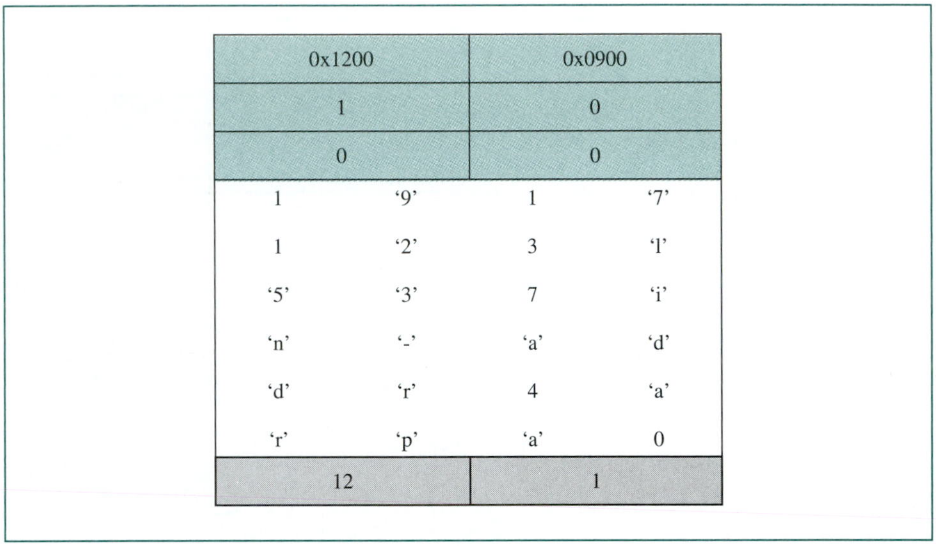

0x1200		0x0900	
1		0	
0		0	
1	'9'	1	'7'
1	'2'	3	'1'
'5'	'3'	7	'i'
'n'	'-'	'a'	'd'
'd'	'r'	4	'a'
'r'	'p'	'a'	0
12		1	

The OpCode is 0001, which means inverse query. The message contains only one question record. The domain name is ***19171231537in-addr4arpa***. The next 2 bytes define the query type as PTR, and the last 2 bytes define the class as Internet.

Response Message Figure 18.24 shows the response. The flags value is 0x8D80 in hexadecimal. In binary it is 1000110110000000, and we divide it into fields as shown below:

QR	OpCode	AA	TC	RD	RA	Reserved	rCode
1	0001	1	0	1	1	000	0000

The message contains one question record and one answer record. The question record is repeated from the query message. The answer record has a pointer 0xC00C, which refers to the question record instead of repeating the domain name. The next field defines the domain type (PTR). The field after that defines the class (Internet), and the field after that defines the TTL (24,000 s). The next field is the length of the resource data (10). The last field is the domain name ***4mhhe3com0***, which means "mhhe.com.".

Figure 18.24 *Example of inverse response message*

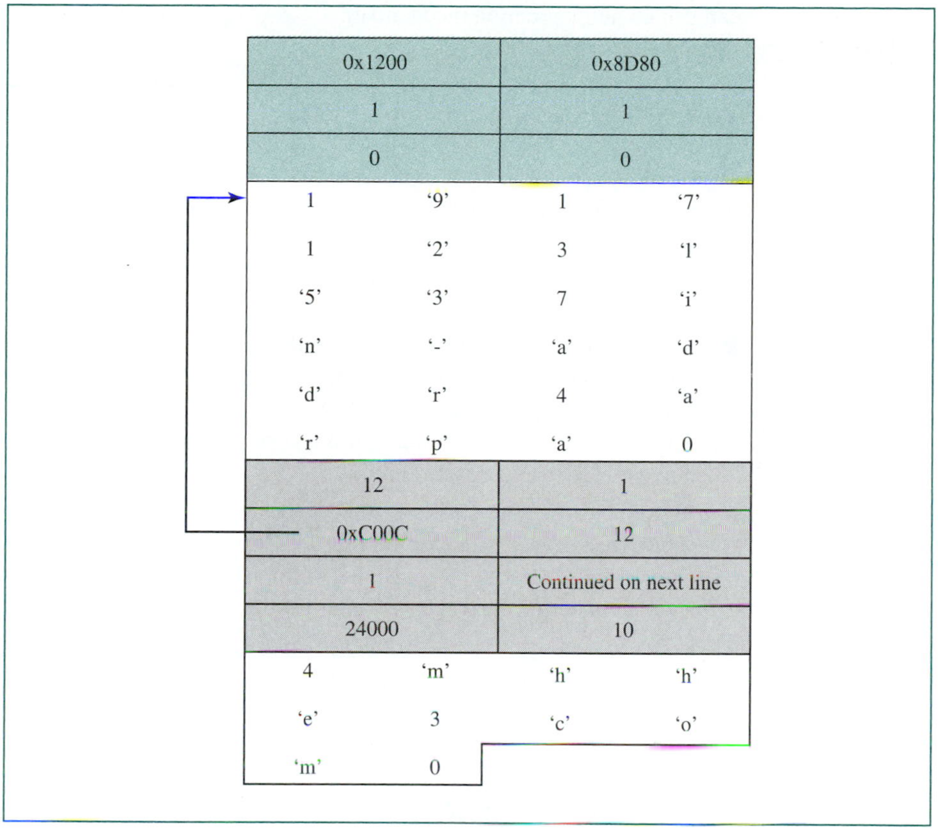

0x1200		0x8D80	
1		1	
0		0	
1	'9'	1	'7'
1	'2'	3	'I'
'5'	'3'	7	'i'
'n'	'-'	'a'	'd'
'd'	'r'	4	'a'
'r'	'p'	'a'	0
12		1	
0xC00C		12	
1		Continued on next line	
24000		10	
4	'm'	'h'	'h'
'e'	3	'c'	'o'
'm'	0		

18.10 DDNS

When the DNS was designed, no one predicted that there would be so many changes made to addresses. In DNS, when there is a change, such as adding a new host, removing a host, or changing an IP address, the change must be made to the DNS master file. These types of changes involve a lot of manual updating. The size of today's Internet does not allow this kind of manual operation.

The DNS master file must be updated dynamically. The Dynamic Domain Name System (DDNS) therefore has been devised to respond to this need. In DDNS, when a binding between a name and an address is determined, the information is sent, usually by DHCP (see Chapter 17) to a primary DNS server. The primary server updates the zone. The secondary servers are notified either actively or passively. In active notification, the primary server sends a message to the secondary servers about the change in the zone, whereas in passive notification, the secondary servers periodically check for any changes. In either case, after being notified about the change, the secondary requests information about the entire zone (zone transfer).

To provide security and prevent unauthorized changes in the DNS records, DDNS can use an authentication mechanism.

18.11 ENCAPSULATION

DNS can use either UDP or TCP. In both cases the well-known port used by the server is port 53. UDP is used when the size of the response message is less than 512 bytes because most UDP packages have a 512-byte packet size limit. If the size of the response message is more than 512 bytes, a TCP connection should be used. In that case, one of two scenarios can occur:

- If the resolver has prior knowledge that the size of the response message is more than 512 bytes, it should use the TCP connection. For example, if a secondary name server (acting as a client) needs a zone transfer from a primary server, it should use the TCP connection because the size of the information being transferred usually exceeds 512 bytes.
- If the resolver does not know the size of the response message, it can use the UDP port. However, if the size of the response message is more than 512 bytes, the server truncates the message and turns on the TC bit. The resolver now opens a TCP connection and repeats the request to get a full response from the server.

DNS can use the services of UDP or TCP using the well-known port 53.

18.12 KEY TERMS

caching

compression

country domain

DNS server

domain

domain name

domain name space

Domain Name System (DNS)

Dynamic Domain Name System (DDNS)

flat name space

fully qualified domain name (FQDN)

generic domain

hierarchical name space

host file

inverse domain

iterative resolution

name space

name-address resolution

partially qualified domain name (PQDN)

primary server

query message

question record

recursive resolution

resolver

- resource record
- response message
- root label
- root server
- secondary server
- subdomain
- suffix
- zone

18.13 SUMMARY

- Domain Name System (DNS) is a client-server application that identifies each host on the Internet with a unique user-friendly name.
- DNS organizes the name space in a hierarchical structure to decentralize the responsibilities involved in naming.
- DNS can be pictured as an inverted hierarchical tree structure with one root node at the top and a maximum of 128 levels.
- Each node in the tree has a domain name.
- A domain is defined as any subtree of the domain name space.
- The name space information is distributed among DNS servers. Each server has jurisdiction over its zone.
- A root server's zone is the entire DNS tree.
- A primary server creates, maintains, and updates information about its zone.
- A secondary server gets its information from a primary server.
- The domain name space is divided into three sections: generic domains, country domains, and inverse domain.
- There are seven generic domains, each specifying an organization type.
- Each country domain specifies a country.
- The inverse domain finds a domain name for a given IP address. This is called address-to-name resolution.
- Name servers, computers that run the DNS server program, are organized in a hierarchy.
- The DNS client, called a resolver, maps a name to an address or an address to a name.
- In recursive resolution, the client sends its request to a server that eventually returns a response.
- In iterative resolution, the client may send its request to multiple servers before getting an answer.
- Caching is a method whereby an answer to a query is stored in memory (for a limited time) for easy access to future requests.
- A fully qualified domain name (FQDN) is a domain name consisting of labels beginning with the host and going back through each level to the root node.
- A partially qualified domain name (PQDN) is a domain name that does not include all the levels between the host and the root node.

- There are two types of DNS messages: queries and responses.
- There are two types of DNS records: question records and resource records.
- DNS uses an offset pointer for duplicated domain name information in its messages.
- Dynamic DNS (DDNS) automatically updates the DNS master file.
- DNS uses the services of UDP for messages of less than 512 bytes; otherwise, TCP is used.

18.14 PRACTICE SET

Multiple-Choice Questions

1. In the domain name chal.atc.fhda.edu, _______ is the least specific label.
   a. chal
   b. atc
   c. fhda
   d. edu
2. In the domain name chal.atc.fhda.edu, _______ is the most specific label.
   a. chal
   b. atc
   c. fhda
   d. edu
3. Which of the following domain names would most likely use a country domain to resolve its IP address?
   a. chal.atac.fhda.edu
   b. gsfc.nasa.gov
   c. kenz.acct.sony.jp
   d. mac.eng.sony.com
4. A DNS response is classified as _______ if the information comes from a cache memory.
   a. authoritative
   b. unauthoritative
   c. iterative
   d. recursive
5. In _______ resolution the client is in direct contact with at most one server.
   a. a recursive
   b. an iterative
   c. a cache
   d. all of the above

6. In _______ resolution the client could directly contact more than one server.
   a. a recursive
   b. an iterative
   c. a cache
   d. all of the above
7. What is the maximum length of the query name subfield?
   a. 4 bytes
   b. 63 bytes
   c. 32 bytes
   d. none of the above
8. In address-to-name resolution the _______ domain is used.
   a. inverse
   b. reverse
   c. generic
   d. country
9. How is the lifetime of a name-to-address resolution in cache memory controlled?
   a. by the time-to-live field set by the server
   b. by the time-to-live counter set by the server
   c. by the time-to-live field set by the authoritative server
   d. b and c
10. In the string 219.46.123.107.in-addr.arpa what is the network address of the host we are looking for?
    a. 219.46.123.0
    b. 107.123.0.0
    c. 107.123.46.0
    d. 107.0.0.0
11. A host with the domain name "pit.arc.nasa.gov." is on the _______ level of the DNS hierarchical tree. (The root is level one.)
    a. third
    b. fourth
    c. fifth
    d. not enough information
12. A host with the domain name "trinity.blue.vers.inc" is on the _______ level of the DNS hierarchical tree. (The root is level one.)
    a. third
    b. fourth
    c. fifth
    d. not enough information

13. A DNS _______ server gets its data from another DNS server.
    a. primary
    b. secondary
    c. root
    d. all of the above
14. A DNS _______ server creates, maintains, and updates the zone file.
    a. primary
    b. secondary
    c. root
    d. all of the above
15. A DNS _______ server's zone is the entire DNS tree.
    a. primary
    b. secondary
    c. root
    d. all of the above
16. A resolver is the _______.
    a. DNS client
    b. DNS server
    c. host machine
    d. root server
17. A pointer query involves the _______ domain.
    a. inverse
    b. reverse
    c. root
    d. recursive
18. To find the IP address of a host when the domain name is known, the _______ can be used.
    a. inverse domain
    b. generic domains
    c. country domains
    d. b or c
19. Which field has a zero value in the DNS query message?
    a. number of answer records
    b. number of authoritative records
    c. number of additional records
    d. all of the above
20. Question records are found in the _______ record section.
    a. question
    b. answer
    c. authoritative
    d. additional information

Exercises

21. Compare and contrast the DNS structure with the UNIX directory structure.
22. What is the equivalent of dots in the DNS structure in the UNIX directory structure?
23. A DNS domain name starts with a node and goes up to the root of the tree. Do the pathnames in UNIX do the same?
24. Can we say that the FQDNs in DNS are the same as absolute pathnames in UNIX and PQDNs are the same as relative pathnames in UNIX?
25. Determine which of the following is an FQDN and which is a PQDN:
    a. xxx
    b. xxx.yyy.
    c. xxx.yyy.net
    d. zzz.yyy.xxx.edu.
26. Determine which of the following is an FQDN and which one is a PQDN:
    a. mil.
    b. edu.
    c. xxx.yyy.net
    d. zzz.yyy.xxx.edu
27. Find the value of the flags field (in hexadecimal) for a query message requesting an address and demanding a recursive answer.
28. Find the value of the flags field (in hexadecimal) for an unauthoritative message carrying an inverse response. The resolver had asked for a recursive response, but the recursive answer was not available.
29. Analyze the flag 0x8F80.
30. Analyze the flag 0x0503. Is it valid?
31. Is the size of a question record fixed?
32. Is the size of a resource record fixed?
33. What is the size of a question record containing the domain name fhda.edu?
34. What is the size of a question record containing an IP address?
35. What is the size of a resource record containing the domain name fhda.edu?
36. What is the size of a resource record containing an IP address?
37. What is the size of a query message requesting the IP address for challenger.atc.fhda.edu?
38. What is the size of a query message requesting the domain name for 185.34.23.12?
39. What is the size of the response message responding to the query message in exercise 37?
40. What is the size of the response message responding to the query message in exercise 38?
41. Redo Example 1 using a response message with one answer record and one authoritative record which defines “fhda.edu.” as the authoritative server.

42. Redo exercise 41, but add one additional record that defines the address of the authoritative server as 153.18.9.0.
43. A DNS client is looking for the IP address of xxx.yyy.com. Show the query message with values for each field.
44. Show the response message of a DNS server to exercise 43. Assume the IP address is 201.34.23.12.
45. A DNS client is looking for the IP addresses corresponding to xxx.yyy.com and aaa.bbb.edu. Show the query message.
46. Show the response message of a DNS server to the query in exercise 45 if the addresses are 14.23.45.12 and 131.34.67.89.
47. Show the response message of exercise 46 if the DNS server can resolve the first enquiry but not the second.
48. A DNS client is looking for the name of the computer with IP address 132.1.17.8. Show the query message.
49. Show the response message sent by the server to the query in exercise 48.
50. Encapsulate the query message of exercise 43 in a UDP user datagram.
51. Encapsulate the response message of exercise 44 in a UDP user datagram.

CHAPTER 19

TELNET and Rlogin

The main task of the Internet and its TCP/IP protocol suite is to provide services for users. For example, users want to be able to run different application programs at a remote site and create results that can be transferred to their local site. One way to satisfy these demands is to create different client-server application programs for each desired service. Programs such as file transfer programs (FTP and TFTP), email (SMTP), and so on are already available. However, it would be impossible to write a specific client-server program for each demand.

The better solution is a general-purpose client-server program that lets a user access any application program on a remote computer; in other words, allow the user to log on to a remote computer. After logging on, a user can use the services available on the remote computer and transfer the results back to the local computer.

In this chapter, we discuss two client-server application programs: TELNET and Rlogin. TELNET is an abbreviation for *TErminaL NETwork*. It is the standard TCP/IP protocol for virtual terminal service as proposed by ISO. TELNET enables the establishment of a connection to a remote system in such a way that the local terminal appears to be a terminal at the remote system. Rlogin is a remote login protocol provided by BSD UNIX.

> TELNET and Rlogin are general-purpose client-server application programs.

19.1 CONCEPT

TELNET is related to several concepts that we briefly describe here.

Time-sharing Environment

TELNET was designed at a time when most operating systems, such as UNIX, were operating in a time-sharing environment. In a time-sharing environment, a large computer supports multiple users. The interaction between a user and the computer occurs through a terminal, which is usually a combination of keyboard, monitor, and mouse. Even a microcomputer can simulate a terminal with a terminal emulator.

In a time-sharing environment, all of the processing must be done by the central computer. When a user types a character on the keyboard, the character is usually sent to the computer and echoed to the monitor. Time-sharing creates an environment in which each user has the illusion of a dedicated computer. The user can run a program, access the system resources, switch from one program to another, and so on.

Login

In a time-sharing environment, users are part of the system with some right to access resources. Each authorized user has an identification and probably a password. The user identification defines the user as part of the system. To access the system, the user logs into the system with a user id or login name. The system also facilitates password checking to prevent an unauthorized user from accessing the resources.

Local Login

When a user logs into a local time-sharing system, it is called *local login.* As a user types at a terminal or at a workstation running a terminal emulator, the keystrokes are accepted by the terminal driver. The terminal driver passes the characters to the operating system. The operating system, in turn, interprets the combination of characters and invokes the desired application program or utility (see Figure 19.1).

Figure 19.1 *Local login*

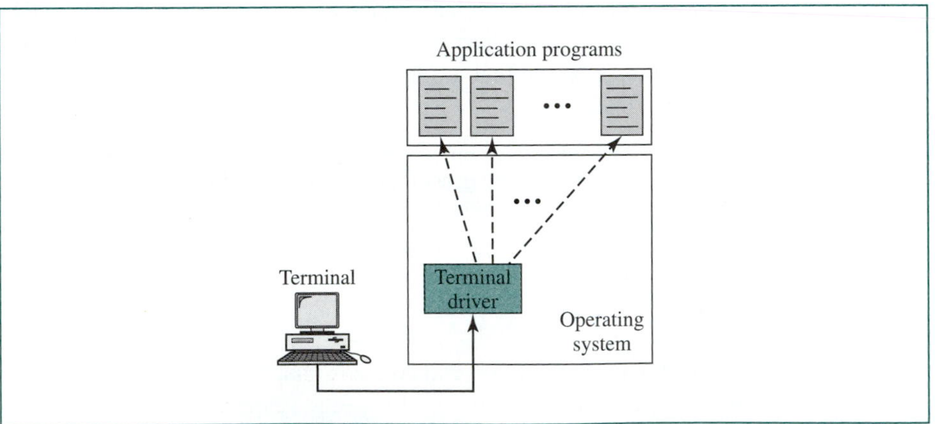

The mechanism, however, is not as simple as it seems because the operating system may assign special meanings to special characters. For example, in UNIX some combinations of characters have special meanings, such as the combination of the control character with the character "z," which means suspend; the combination of the control character with the character "c," which means abort; and so on. Whereas these special situations do not create any problem in local login because the terminal emulator and the terminal driver know the exact meaning of each character or combination of characters, they may create problems in remote login. Which process should interpret special characters? The client or the server? We will clarify this situation later in the chapter.

Remote Login

When a user wants to access an application program or utility located on a remote machine, he or she performs remote login. Here the TELNET client and server programs come into use. The user sends the keystrokes to the terminal driver where the local operating system accepts the characters but does not interpret them. The characters are sent to the TELNET client, which transforms the characters to a universal character set called *Network Virtual Terminal characters* and delivers them to the local TCP/IP stack (see Figure 19.2).

Figure 19.2 *Remote login*

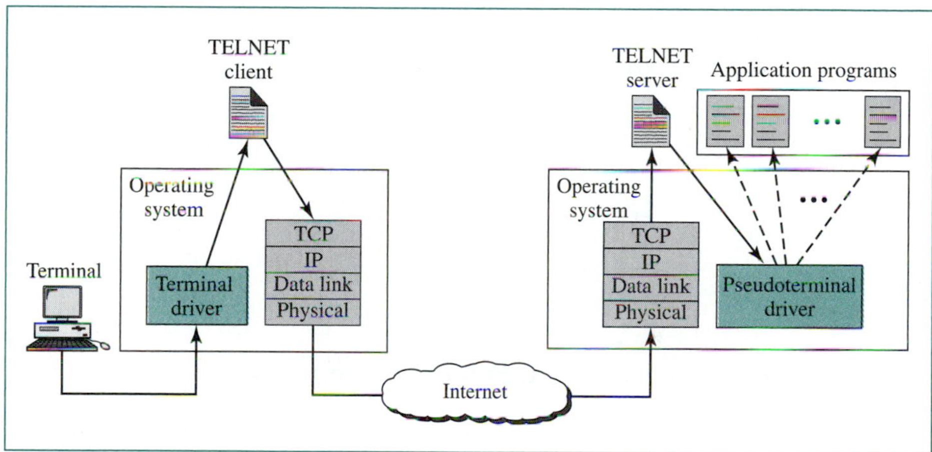

The commands or text, in NVT form, travel through the Internet and arrive at the TCP/IP stack at the remote machine. Here the characters are delivered to the operating system and passed to the TELNET server, which changes the characters to the corresponding characters understandable by the remote computer. However, the characters cannot be passed directly to the operating system because the remote operating system is not designed to receive characters from a TELNET server: It is designed to receive characters from a terminal driver. The solution is to add a piece of software called a *pseudoterminal driver* which pretends that the characters are coming from a terminal. The operating system then passes the characters to the appropriate application program.

19.2 NETWORK VIRTUAL TERMINAL (NVT)

The mechanism to access a remote computer is complex. This is because every computer and its operating system accepts a special combination of characters as tokens. For example, the end-of-file token in a computer running the DOS operating system is Ctrl+z, while the UNIX operating system recognizes Ctrl+d.

We are dealing with heterogeneous systems. If we want to access any remote computer in the world, we must first know what type of computer we will be connected to, and we must also install the specific terminal emulator used by that computer. TELNET solves this problem by defining a universal interface called the Network Virtual Terminal (NVT) character set. Via this interface, the client TELNET translates characters (data or commands) that come from the local terminal into NVT form and delivers them to the network. The server TELNET, on the other hand, translates data and commands from NVT form into the form acceptable by the remote computer. For an illustration of this concept, see Figure 19.3.

Figure 19.3 *Concept of NVT*

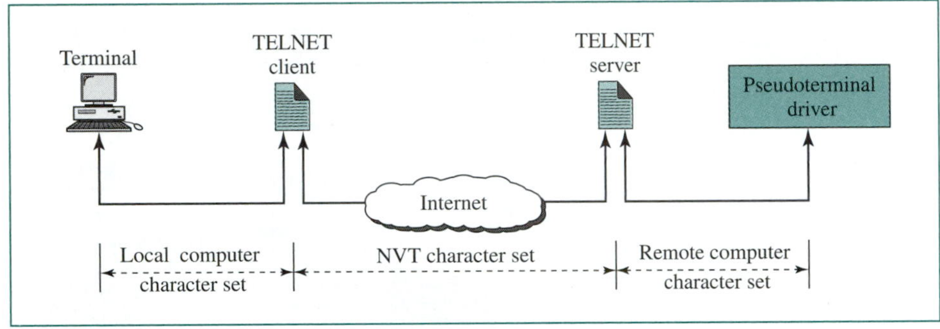

19.3 NVT CHARACTER SET

NVT uses two sets of characters, one for data and one for control. Both are 8-bit bytes.

Data Characters

For data, NVT normally uses what is called NVT ASCII. This is an 8-bit character set in which the seven lowest order bits are the same as US ASCII and the highest order bit is 0 (see Figure 19.4). Although it is possible to send an 8-bit ASCII (with the highest order bit set to be 0 or 1), this must first be agreed upon between the client and the server using option negotiation.

Figure 19.4 *Format of data characters*

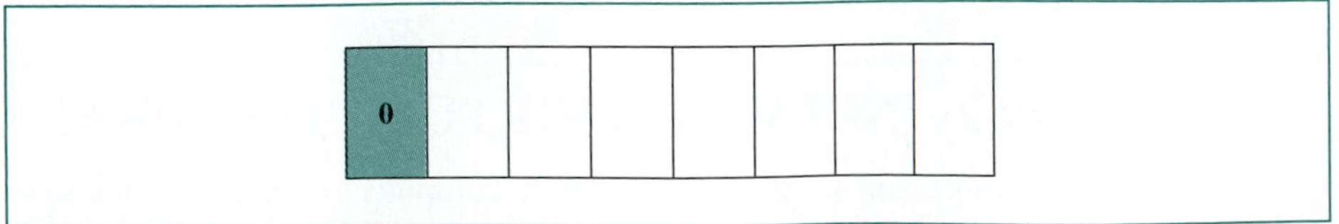

Remote Control Characters

To send control characters between computers (from client to server or vice versa), NVT uses an 8-bit character set in which the highest order bit is set (see Figure 19.5).

Figure 19.5 *Format of control characters*

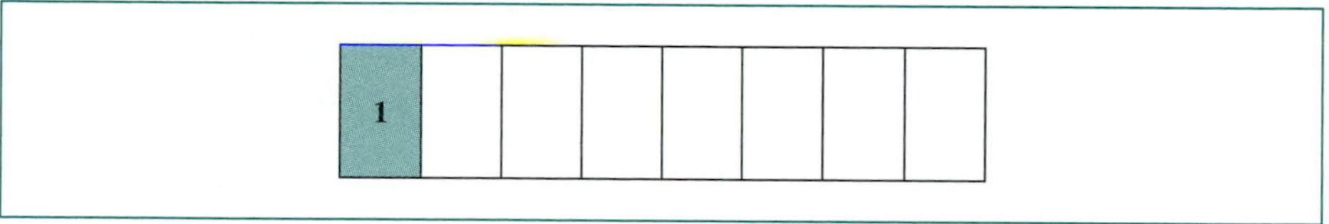

Table 19.1 lists some of the remote control characters and their meanings. We will describe these control characters later in groups based on their functionalities.

Table 19.1 *Some NVT remote control characters*

Character	*Decimal*	*Binary*	*Meaning*
EOF	236	11101100	End of file
EOR	239	11101111	End of record
SE	240	11110000	Suboption end
NOP	241	11110001	No operation
DM	242	11110010	Data mark
BRK	243	11110011	Break
IP	244	11110100	Interrupt process
AO	245	11110101	Abort output
AYT	246	11110110	Are you there?
EC	247	11110111	Erase character
EL	248	11111000	Erase line
GA	249	11111001	Go ahead
SB	250	11111010	Suboption begin
WILL	251	11111011	Agreement to enable option
WONT	252	11111100	Refusal to enable option
DO	253	11111101	Approval to option request
DONT	254	11111110	Denial of option request
IAC	255	11111111	Interpret (the next character) as control

19.4 EMBEDDING

TELNET uses only one TCP connection. The server uses the well-known port 23 and the client uses an ephemeral port. The same connection is used for sending both data and control characters. TELNET accomplishes this by embedding the control characters in a data stream. However, to distinguish data from control characters, each sequence of control characters is preceded by a special control character called *interpret as control* (IAC). For example, imagine a user wants to send a sequence of data characters to the remote server to display a file (*file1*):

cat file1

However, the name of the file has been mistyped (*filea* instead of *file1*). The user uses the backspace key to correct this situation.

cat filea<backspace>1

However, in a default implementation of TELNET, the user cannot edit locally; the editing should be done at the remote server. The backspace character is translated into two remote characters (IAC EC), which is embedded in the data and sent to the remote server. What is sent to the server is shown in Figure 19.6.

Figure 19.6 *An example of embedding*

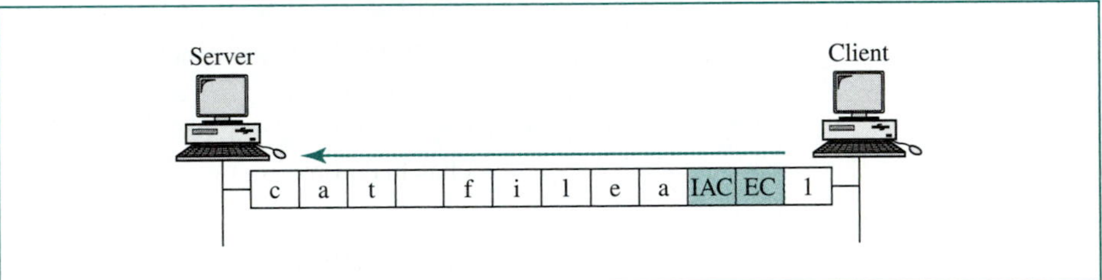

19.5 OPTIONS

TELNET lets the client and server negotiate options before or during the use of the service. Options are extra features available to a user with a more sophisticated terminal. Users with simpler terminals can use minimum features. Some of the remote control characters discussed previously are used to define options. Table 19.2 shows some common options.

Table 19.2 *Options*

Code	*Option*	*Meaning*
0	Binary	Use 8-bit binary transmission
1	Echo	Echo the data received on one side to the other
3	Suppress go ahead	Suppress go-ahead signals after data
5	Status	Request the status of TELNET
6	Timing mark	Define the timing marks
24	Terminal type	Set the terminal type
32	Terminal speed	Set the terminal speed
34	Line mode	Change to line mode

The option descriptions are as follows:

- **Binary.** This option allows the receiver to interpret every 8-bit character received, except IAC, as binary data. When IAC is received, the next character or characters are interpreted as commands. However, if two consecutive IAC characters are received, the first is discarded and the second is interpreted as data.
- **Echo.** This option allows the server to echo data received from the client. This means that every character sent by the client to the sender will be echoed back to the screen of the client terminal. In this case, the user terminal usually does not echo display characters when they are typed but waits until it receives them from the server.
- **Suppress go-ahead.** This option suppresses the go-ahead (GA) character. We will discuss the GA character in Section 19.11 on TELNET modes.
- **Status.** This option allows the user or the process running on the client machine to get the status of the options being enabled at the server site.
- **Timing mark.** This option allows one party to issue a timing mark that indicates all previously received data has been processed.
- **Terminal type.** This option allows the client to send its terminal type.
- **Terminal speed.** This option allows the client to send its terminal speed.
- **Line mode.** This option allows the client to switch to the line mode. We will discuss the line mode later.

19.6 OPTION NEGOTIATION

To use any of the options mentioned in the previous section first requires negotiation between the client and the server. Four control characters are used for this purpose; these are shown in Table 19.3.

Table 19.3 *NVT character set for option negotiation*

Character	*Decimal*	*Binary*	*Meaning*
WILL	251	11111011	1. Offering to enable 2. Accepting a request to enable
WONT	252	11111100	1. Rejecting a request to enable 2. Offering to disable 3. Accepting a request to disable
DO	253	11111101	1. Approving an offer to enable 2. Requesting to enable
DONT	254	11111110	1. Disapproving an offer to enable 2. Approving an offer to disable 3. Requesting to disable

Enabling an Option

Some options can only be enabled by the server, some only by the client, and some by both. An option is enabled either through an *offer* or a *request.*

Offer to Enable

A party can offer to enable an option if it has the right to do so. The offering can be approved or disapproved by the other party. The offering party sends the *WILL* command, which means "Will I enable the option?" The other party sends either the *DO* command, which means "Please Do," or the *DONT* command, which means "Please Don't." See Figure 19.7.

Figure 19.7 *Offer to enable an option*

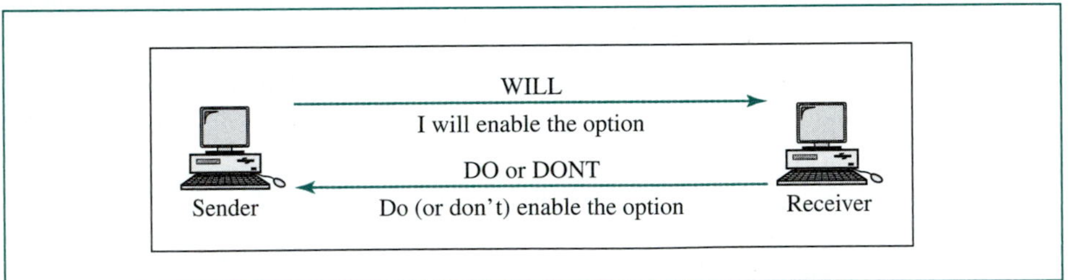

Request to Enable

A party can request from the other party the enabling of an option. The request can be accepted or refused by the other party. The requesting party sends the *DO* command, which means "Please do enable the option." The other party sends either the *WILL* command, which means "I will," or the *WONT* command, which means "I won't." See Figure 19.8.

Figure 19.8 *Request to enable an option*

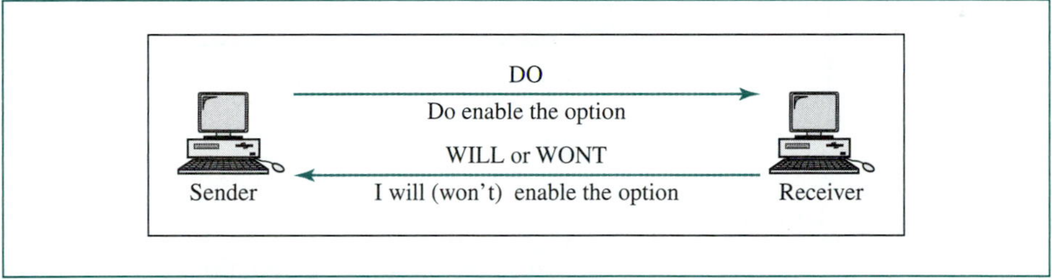

Disabling an Option

An option that has been enabled can be disabled by one of the parties. An option is disabled either through an *offer* or a *request*.

Offer to Disable

A party can offer to disable an option. The other party must approve the offering; it cannot be disapproved. The offering party sends the *WONT* command, which means "I won't use this option any more." The answer must be the *DONT* command, which means "Don't use it anymore." Figure 19.9 shows an offer to disable an option.

Figure 19.9 *Offer to disable an option*

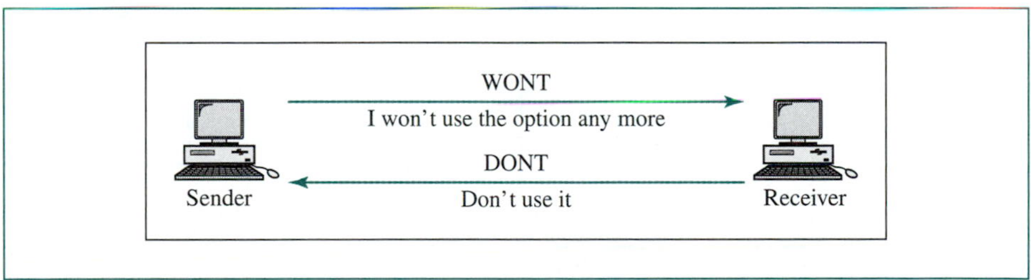

Request to Disable

A party can request from another party the disabling of an option. The other party must accept the request; it cannot be rejected. The requesting party sends the *DONT* command, which means "Please don't use this option anymore." The answer must be the *WONT* command, which means "I won't use it anymore." Figure 19.10 shows a request to disable an option.

Figure 19.10 *Request to disable an option*

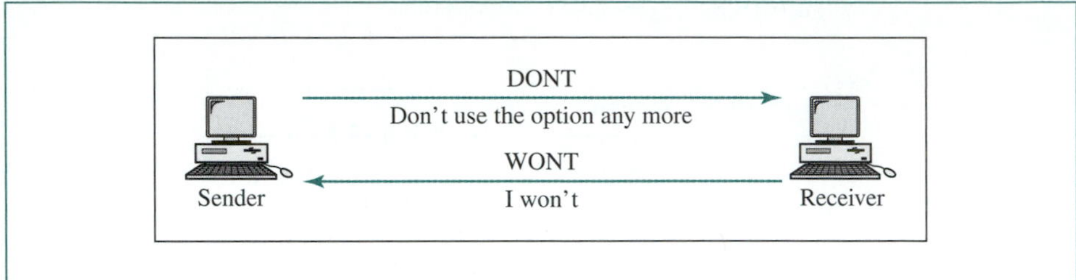

Example

Figure 19.11 shows an example of option negotiation. In this example, the client wants the server to echo each character sent to the server. In other words, when a character is typed at the user keyboard terminal, it should go to the server and be sent back to the screen of the user before being processed. The echo option should be enabled by the server because it is the server that sends the characters back to the user terminal. Therefore, the client should *request* from the server the enabling of the option using DO. The request consists of three characters: IAC, DO, and ECHO. The server accepts the request and enables the option. It informs the client by sending the three-character approval: IAC, WILL, and ECHO.

Figure 19.11 *Echo option example*

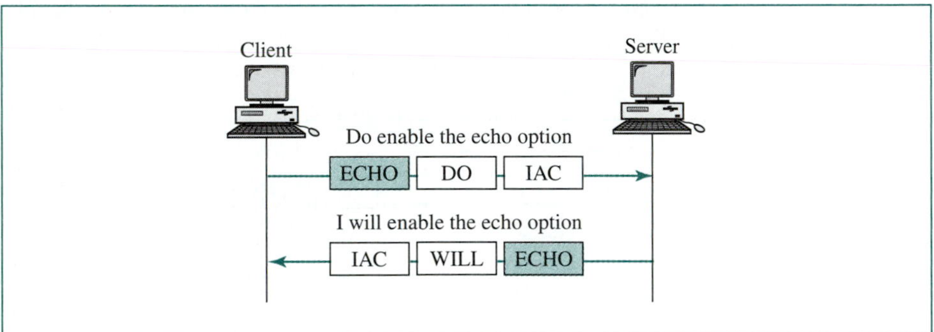

Symmetry

One interesting feature of TELNET is its symmetric option negotiation in which the client and server are given equal opportunity. This means that, at the beginning of connection, it is assumed that both sides are using a simple TELNET implementation with no options enabled. If one party wants an option enabled, it can offer or request. The other party has the right to approve the offer or reject the request if the party is not capable of using the option or does not want to use the option. This allows for the expansion of TELNET. A client or server can install a more sophisticated version of TELNET with more options. When it is connected to a party, it can offer or request these new options. If the other party also supports these options, the options can be enabled; otherwise, they are rejected.

19.7 SUBOPTION NEGOTIATION

Some options require additional information. For example, to define the type or speed of a terminal, the negotiation includes a string or a number to define the type or speed. In either case, the two suboption characters indicated in Table 19.4 are needed for suboption negotiation.

Table 19.4 *NVT character set for suboption negotiation*

Character	*Decimal*	*Binary*	*Meaning*
SE	240	11110000	Suboption end
SB	250	11111010	Suboption begin

For example, the type of the terminal is set by the client, as is shown in Figure 19.12.

Figure 19.12 *Example of suboption negotiation*

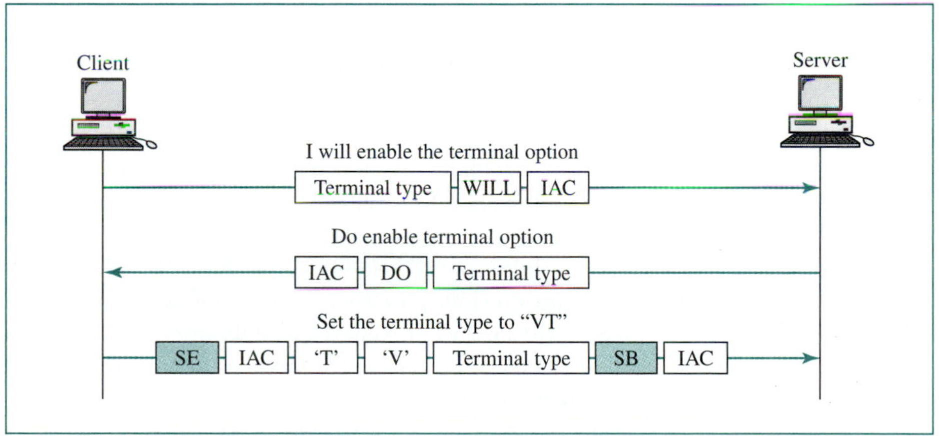

19.8 CONTROLLING THE SERVER

Some of the control characters can be used to control the remote server. When an application program is running on the local computer, special characters are used to interrupt (abort) the program (for example, Ctrl+c), or erase the last character typed (for example, delete key or backspace key), and so on. However, when a program is running on a remote computer, these control characters should be sent to the remote machine.

The user still types the same sequences, but they are changed to special characters and sent to the server. Table 19.5 shows some of the characters that can be sent to the server to control the application program that is running there.

Table 19.5 *Characters used to control the application program running on remote server*

Character	*Decimal*	*Binary*	*Meaning*
IP	244	11110100	Interrupt process
AO	245	11110101	Abort output
AYT	246	11110110	Are you there?
EC	247	11110111	Erase the last character
EL	248	11111000	Erase line

Let's look at these characters in more detail:

- **IP (interrupt process).** When a program is being run locally, the user can interrupt (abort) the program if, for example, the program has gone into an infinite loop. The user can depress the Ctrl+c combination, the operating system calls a function, and the function aborts the program. However, if the program is running on a remote machine, the appropriate function should be called by the operating system of the remote machine. TELNET defines the IP (interrupt process) control character that is read and interpreted as the appropriate command for invoking the interrupting function in the remote machine.
- **AO (abort output).** This is the same as IP, but it allows the process to continue without creating output. This is useful if the process has another effect in addition to creating output. The user wants this effect but not the output. For example, most commands in UNIX generate output and have an exit status. The user may want exit status for future use but is not interested in the output data.
- **AYT (are you there?).** This control character is used to determine if the remote machine is still up and running, especially after a long silence from the server. When this character is received, the server usually sends an audible or visual signal to confirm that it is running.
- **EC (erase character).** When a user sends data from the keyboard to the local machine, the delete or backspace character can erase the last character typed. To do the same in a remote machine, TELNET defines the EC control character.
- **EL (erase line).** This is used to erase the current line in the remote host.

For example, Figure 19.13 shows how to interrupt a runaway application program at the server site. The user types Ctrl+c, but the TELNET client sends the combination of IAC and IP to the server.

Figure 19.13 *Example of interrupting an application program*

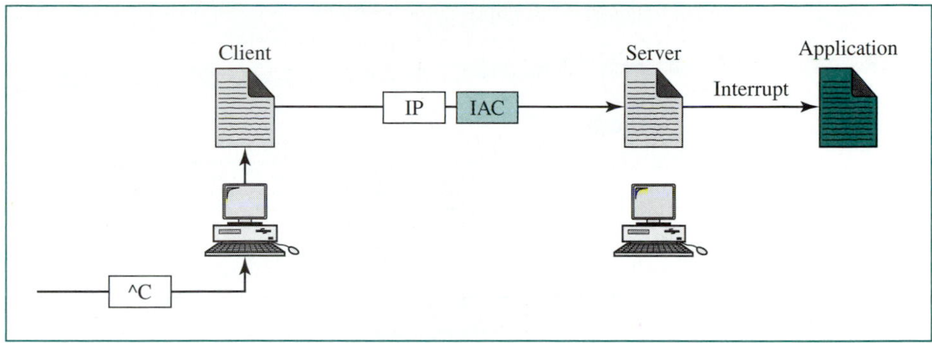

19.9 OUT-OF-BAND SIGNALING

To make control characters effective in special situations, TELNET uses out-of-band signaling. In out-of-band signaling, the control characters are preceded by IAC and are sent to the remote process out of order.

Imagine a situation in which an application program running at the server site has gone into an infinite loop and does not accept any more input data. The user wants to interrupt the application program, but the program does not read data from the buffer. The TCP at the server site has found that the buffer is full and has sent a segment specifying that the client window size should be zero. In other words, the TCP at the server site is announcing that no more regular traffic is accepted. To remedy such a situation, an urgent TCP segment should be sent from the client to the server. The urgent segment overrides the regular flow-control mechanism. Although TCP is not accepting normal segments, it must accept an urgent segment.

When a TELNET process (client or server) wants to send an out-of-band sequence of characters to the other process (client or server), it embeds the sequence in the data stream and inserts a special character called DM (data mark). However, to force the other party to handle the sequence out of order, it creates a TCP segment with the urgent bit set and the urgent pointer pointing to the DM character. When the receiving TCP receives the segment, it reads the data and discards any data preceding the control characters (IAC and IP, for example). When it reaches the DM character, the remaining data are handled normally. In other words, the DM character is used as a *synchronization* character that switches the receiving TCP from the urgent mode to the normal mode and *resynchronizes* the two ends (see Figure 19.14).

In this way, the control character (IP) is delivered out of band to the operating system, which uses the appropriate function to interrupt the running application program.

Figure 19.14 *Out-of-band signaling*

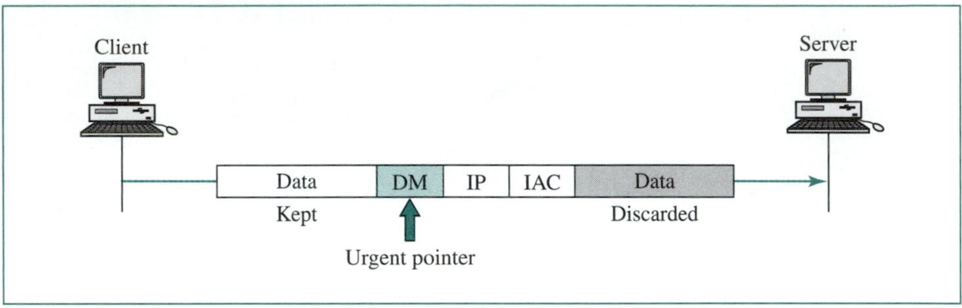

19.10 ESCAPE CHARACTER

A character typed by the user is normally sent to the server. However, sometimes the user wants characters interpreted by the client instead of the server. In this case, the user can use an *escape* character, normally Ctrl+] (shown as ^]). This is a signal to the client that the command is not for the remote server, it is for the client. Figure 19.15 compares the interruption of an application program at the remote site with the interruption of the client process at the local site using the escape character.

Figure 19.15 *Two different interruptions*

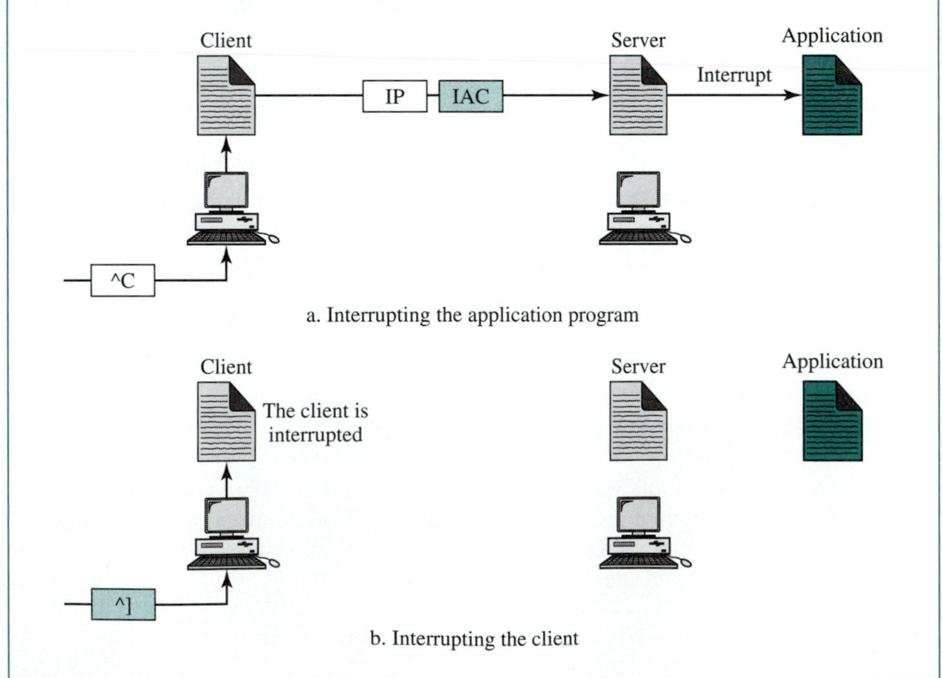

19.11 MODE OF OPERATION

Most TELNET implementations operate in one of three modes: default mode, character mode, or line mode.

Default Mode

The default mode is used if no other modes are invoked through option negotiation. In this mode, the echoing is done by the client. The user types a character and the client echoes the character on the screen (or printer) but does not send it until a whole line is completed. After sending the whole line to the server, the client waits for the GA (go ahead) command from the server before accepting a new line from the user. The operation is half-duplex. Half-duplex operation is not efficient when the TCP connection itself is full-duplex, and so this mode is becoming obsolete.

Character Mode

In the character mode, each character typed is sent by the client to the server. The server normally echoes the character back to be displayed on the client screen. In this mode the echoing of the character can be delayed if the transmission time is long (such as in a satellite connection). It also creates overhead (traffic) for the network because three TCP segments must be sent for each character of data:

1. The user enters a character that is sent to the server.
2. The server acknowledges the received character and echos the character back (in one segment).
3. The client acknowledges the receipt of the echoed character.

Line Mode

A new mode has been proposed to compensate for the deficiencies of the default mode and the character mode. In this mode, called the line mode, line editing (echoing, character erasing, line erasing, and so on) is done by the client. The client then sends the whole line to the server.

Although the line mode looks like the default mode, it is not. The default mode operates in the half-duplex mode; the line mode is full-duplex with the client sending one line after another, without the need for an intervening GA (go ahead) character from the server.

19.12 EXAMPLES

In this section, we show two examples of TELNET interaction between the client and the server.

Example 1

In this example, we use the default mode to show the concept and its deficiencies even though it is almost obsolete today. The client and the server negotiate the terminal type and terminal speed and then the server checks the login and password of the user (see Figure 19.16).

Figure 19.16 *Example 1*

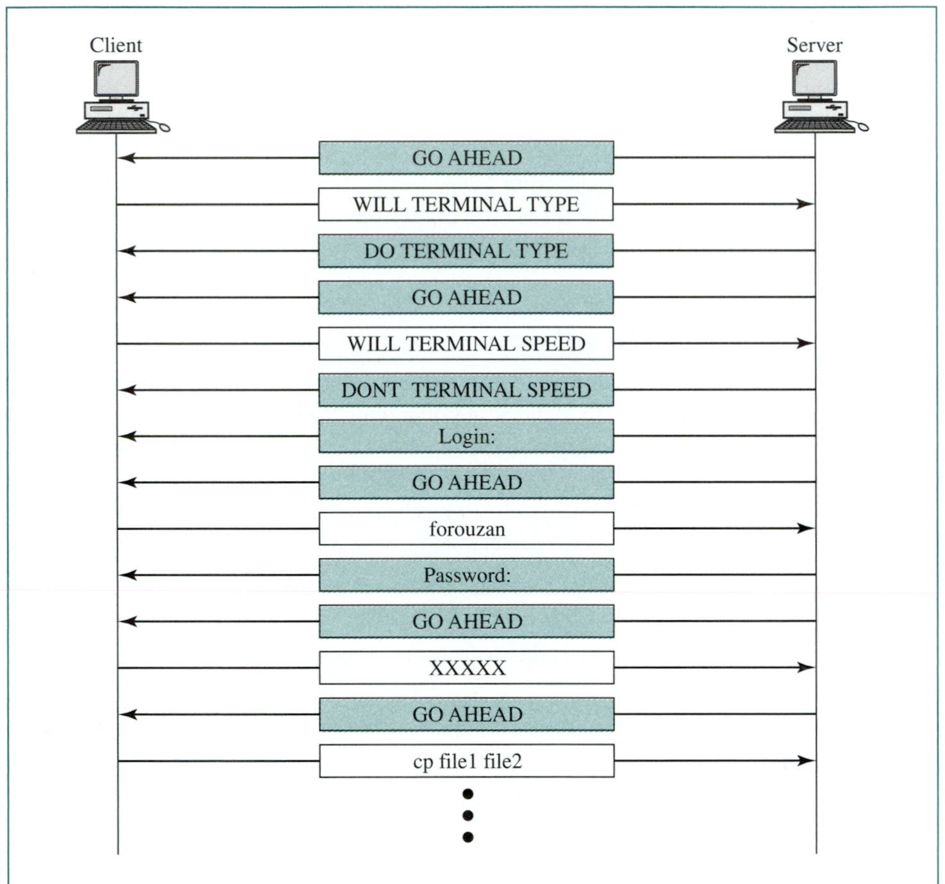

Example 2

In this example, we show how the client switches to the character mode. This requires that the client request the server to enable the SUPPRESS GO AHEAD and ECHO options (see Figure 19.17).

Figure 19.17 *Example 2*

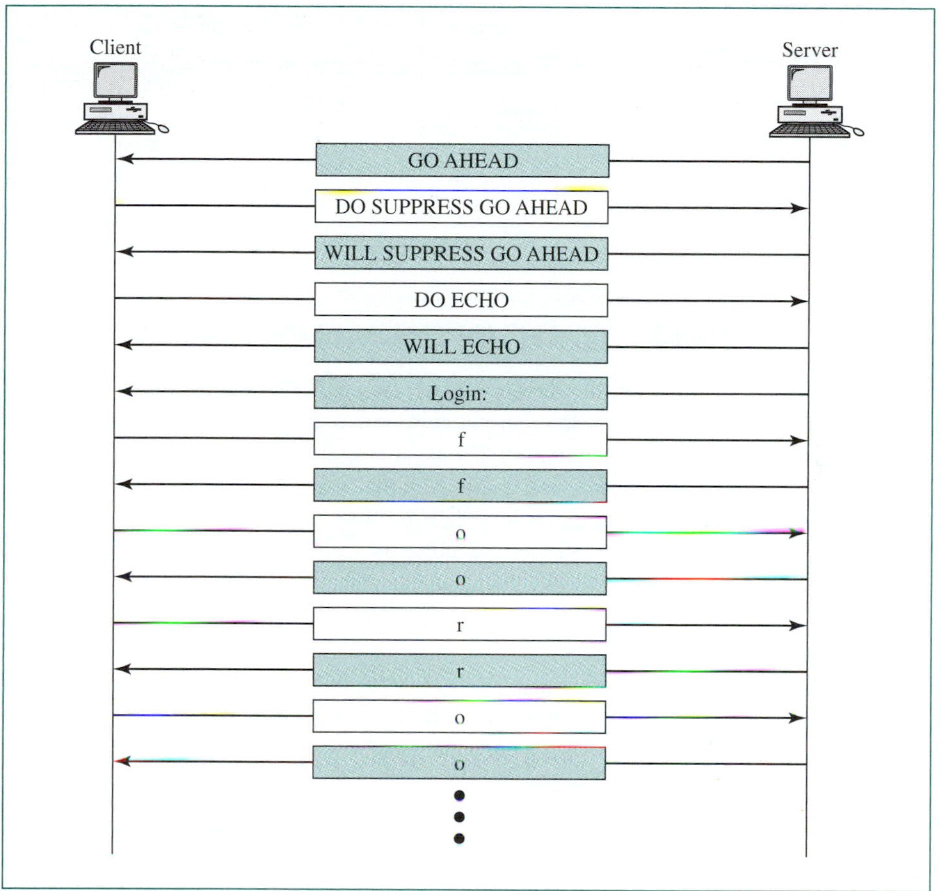

19.13 USER INTERFACE

The normal user does not use TELNET commands as defined above. Normally, the operating system (UNIX, for example) defines an interface with user-friendly commands. An example of such a set of commands can be found in Table 19.6. Note that the interface is responsible for translating the user-friendly commands to the previously defined commands in the protocol.

Table 19.6 *Example of interface commands*

Command	*Meaning*
open	Connect to a remote computer
close	Close the connection
display	Show the operating parameters

Table 19.6 *Example of interface commands (continued)*

Command	*Meaning*
mode	Change to line mode or character mode
set	Set the operating parameters
status	Display the status information
send	Send special characters
quit	Exit TELNET

19.14 RLOGIN (REMOTE LOGIN)

Another remote login client-server application in common use is Rlogin (remote login). This is not an Internet standard but was designed by BSD UNIX to provide access to remote computers. We discuss it here briefly to compare it with TELNET.

Rlogin was originally designed to be used on the UNIX operating system as a simple remote login facility. It, therefore, does not provide option negotiation. The server accepts the terminal type of the user.

TCP Port

Rlogin uses only one TCP connection. The server uses the well-known port 513 and the client uses an ephemeral port. The one TCP connection is used both for data and commands. We will see how data and commands are distinguished by the client and the server.

> The Rlogin process uses the TCP port 513.

Connection

The client starts the connection. After the usual TCP connection is established on port 513, the client sends four null-terminated strings.

1. The first string is actually empty. It is just a null character (\0).
2. The second string defines the login name of the user on the client host and terminates with a null character (\0), for example, *forouzan\0.*
3. The third string defines the login name of the user on the server host and terminates with a null character (\0), for example, *baf3652\0.*
4. The fourth string defines the name of the user's terminal followed by a slash, followed by the terminal speed, and terminated with a null character (\0), for example, *vt100/9600\0.*

The server responds with only one null character (\0). Figure 19.18 shows the interaction between the client and the server. Although everything is sent character by character and each character is echoed, we have shown only strings to conserve space.

Figure 19.18 *Connection establishment*

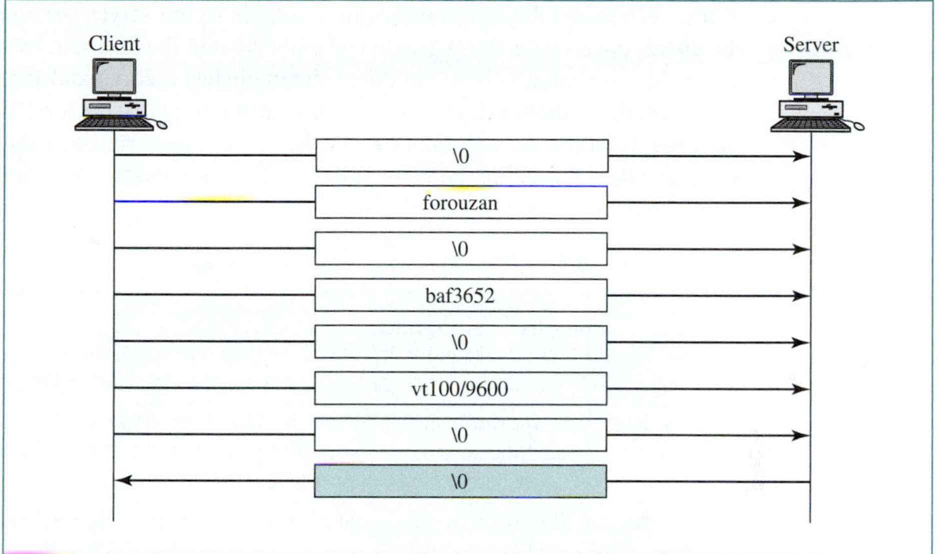

Flow Control

The output sent by the server to the client is shown on the client screen. Two special characters (Stop and Start) control the displaying of the output on the screen. The Stop and Start keys (normally Ctrl+s and Ctrl+q) can be handled either by the client or by the server.

Local Flow Control

In local flow control, the Start and Stop keys are handled by the client. The client does not send these two characters to the server. If the user types the Stop key (Ctrl+s), the client stops showing on the screen the output received from the server. It buffers them. When the user types the Start key (Ctrl+q), the buffered data are then displayed. This is the default setting. We will see that the server can change this situation.

Remote Flow Control

In remote flow control, the Start and Stop keys are handled by the server. The Stop and Start keys are passed to the server as data. When the server receives the Stop key, it stops sending data to the client. When it receives the Start key, it sends the buffered data to the client. In remote flow control, by the time the Stop key reaches the server, it may have already sent a lot of characters to the client screen.

Commands

As mentioned previously, Rlogin uses only one TCP connection. This means that data and commands are sent over the same connection. Somehow commands must be distinguished from data. In Rlogin, the commands from the server and the client are handled differently.

Commands from Server to Client

Table 19.7 shows the four commands available to the server for communication with the client. Each command is 1 byte and embedded in the data sent from the server to the client. The question is how the client distinguishes a command from data. When the server sends a command, it enters the urgent mode (see Chapter 12). The last byte of the urgent data is the command byte. When the client receives the TCP segment, it stores the data preceding the command byte and first handles the command before handling the data.

Table 19.7 *Rlogin commands from server to client*

Code	*Description*
02_{16}	The client should discard all the data received from the server. This command is sent when the client has sent an interrupt key to the server.
10_{16}	Flow control should be remote. The client should not handle the Start and Stop keys (Ctrl+s and Ctrl+q). They will be sent as data to the server. The server will handle them.
20_{16}	The client should switch to local flow control and interpret the Stop and Start keys locally.
80_{16}	The server requests the client to send its current window size.

Commands from Client to Server

The client can send commands to the server. To distinguish a command from data, the commands should start with two special characters, two FF_{16}. The next 2 bytes define the type of command. Note that if the client sends a stream of data starting with two FF_{16} characters, the server may be confused. However, it is very unlikely that these two characters are part of the data stream.

So far only one command has been defined. It is the *ss* (screen size) command, used to announce the screen window size. The client sends two characters of all 1s (FF_{16}) followed by ss, followed by 2 bytes showing the number of characters per row, followed by 2 bytes showing the number of characters per column, followed by 2 bytes showing the number of pixels (picture elements) in the X (horizontal) direction, followed by 2 bytes showing the number of pixels in the Y (vertical) direction (see Figure 19.19). Although everything is sent character by character and each character is echoed, we have shown strings to conserve space.

Mode

Rlogin works only in the character mode. The data are sent from the client to the server one character at a time. Each character is then echoed to the user terminal.

Escape Characters

During data transfer, every character typed by the user is interpreted as data and is sent to the server (unless there are two FF_{16} characters). However, sometimes the user wants

Figure 19.19 *Sending ss command from the client to the server*

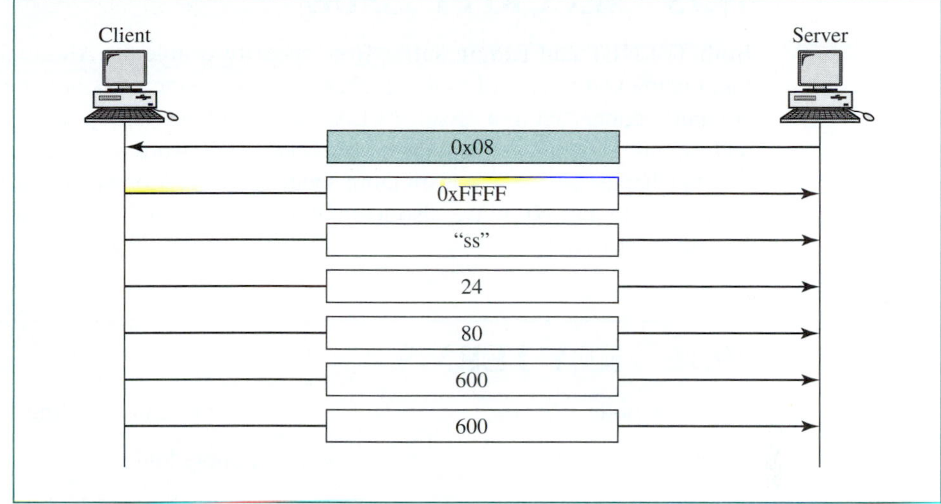

the characters to be interpreted by the client instead of the server. In this case, the user can type an escape character, usually a tilde (~). Table 19.8 shows the list of characters that can be used after the escape character to accomplish a local task.

Table 19.8 *Rlogin commands used after the escape character*

Character	*Description*
Terminator (period or Ctrl+d)	This terminates the client process.
Job suspender (Ctrl+z)	This suspends the client. The user can run other programs and later return to Rlogin. The client program can be resumed using UNIX commands such as fg (foreground).
Input suspender (Ctrl+y)	This suspends only the client input. The user can run another program. Everything the user types is interpreted as the input for that program, not for Rlogin. However, everything sent from the server will show on the screen.

Interruption

Sometimes the user needs to interrupt (abort) the Rlogin process. It is possible to send the interrupt key (usually Ctrl+c) to the server to end the sending of data. However, when the interrupt character reaches the server, a full window of data may have already been sent to the client. The better solution would be to let the client handle the interrupt key. When the user types the interrupt key (Ctrl+c), the client discards everything in the buffer and terminates the TCP connection.

19.15 SECURITY ISSUE

Both TELNET and Rlogin suffer from security problems. Although both require a login name and password (when exchanging text), often this is not enough. A microcomputer connected to a broadcast LAN can easily eavesdrop using snooper software and capture a login name and the corresponding password (even if it is encrypted).

In Chapter 29, we will learn more about authentication and security and how it can be applied to TELNET. We also learn about Secure Shell (SSH), which can be used instead of TELNET.

19.16 KEY TERMS

character mode
client
control character
default mode
flow control
line mode
local login
network virtual terminal (NVT)
option negotiation
out-of-band signaling
remote login
remote login (Rlogin)
remote server
server
suboption negotiation
terminal network (TELNET)
time-sharing
well-known port

19.17 SUMMARY

- TELNET is a client-server application that allows a user to log on to a remote machine, giving the user access to the remote system.
- When a user accesses a remote system via the TELNET process, this is comparable to a time-sharing environment.
- A terminal driver correctly interprets the keystrokes on the local terminal or terminal emulator. This may not occur between a terminal and a remote terminal driver.
- TELNET uses the Network Virtual Terminal (NVT) system to encode characters on the local system. On the server machine, NVT decodes the characters to a form acceptable to the remote machine.
- NVT uses a set of characters for data and a set of characters for remote control.
- In TELNET, control characters are embedded in the data stream and preceded by the interpret as control (IAC) control character.
- Options are features that enhance the TELNET process.
- TELNET allows negotiation to set transfer conditions between the client and server before and during the use of the service.

- Some options can only be enabled by the server, some only by the client, and some by both.
- An option is enabled or disabled through an offer or a request.
- An option that needs additional information requires the use of suboption characters.
- Control characters can be used to handle the remote server.
- In out-of-band signaling, commands are sent out of order.
- A TELNET implementation operates in the default, character, or line mode.
- In the default mode, the client sends one line at a time to the server and waits for the go ahead (GA) character before a new line from the user can be accepted.
- In the character mode, the client sends one character at a time to the server.
- In the line mode, the client sends one line at a time to the server, one after the other, without the need for an intervening GA character.
- TELNET is usually not accessed directly by the user. User-friendly software acts as an interface between TELNET and the user.
- Rlogin is a BSD UNIX product that provides a simple remote login service. Options negotiation is not involved.
- Rlogin uses the TCP port 513.
- Rlogin allows either local or remote flow control.
- Rlogin allows the server to send commands to the client and vice versa.
- Rlogin supports local tasking and local program interruption.
- Security is an issue with both TELNET and Rlogin, although the former does allow an authentication option.

19.18 PRACTICE SET

Multiple-Choice Questions

1. In a time-sharing environment _______.
   a. each user can access only his own computer
   b. one computer supports multiple users
   c. each user has a dedicated computer
   d. all of the above
2. In _______, the local operating system always correctly interprets the keystrokes accepted by the local terminal driver.
   a. dedicated login
   b. remote login
   c. local login
   d. b or c

3. Remote login can involve _______.
   a. NVT
   b. TELNET
   c. TCP/IP
   d. all of the above
4. When commands travel from _______, they are in NVT form.
   a. the terminal to the terminal driver
   b. the terminal driver to the TELNET client
   c. the TELNET client to the local TCP/IP stack
   d. none of the above
5. The _______ at the remote site sends received characters to the operating system.
   a. terminal driver
   b. pseudoterminal driver
   c. TELNET client
   d. TELNET server
6. The _______ translates local characters into NVT form.
   a. terminal driver
   b. pseudoterminal driver
   c. TELNET client
   d. TELNET server
7. The _______ translates NVT characters into a form acceptable by the remote operating system.
   a. terminal driver
   b. pseudoterminal driver
   c. TELNET client
   d. TELNET server
8. If the sender wants to disable an option, it sends a _______ command.
   a. WILL
   b. DO
   c. WONT
   d. DONT
9. If the sender wants to enable an option, it sends a _______ command.
   a. WILL
   b. DO
   c. WONT
   d. DONT
10. If the sender wants an option disabled by the receiver, it sends a _______ command.
    a. WILL
    b. DO
    c. WONT
    d. DONT

11. If the sender wants an option enabled by the receiver, it sends a _______ command.
    a. WILL
    b. DO
    c. WONT
    d. DONT
12. A TELNET control character _______.
    a. has its high-order bit set to 0
    b. has its high-order bit set to 1
    c. has its low-order bit set to 1
    d. has its low-ordered bit set to 0
13. The _______ character precedes characters used for control.
    a. IP
    b. IAC
    c. SB
    d. GA
14. The _______ option allows the specification of terminal type.
    a. binary
    b. echo
    c. status
    d. terminal type
15. The _______ option suppresses the GA character.
    a. echo
    b. get alternate
    c. suppress go ahead
    d. terminal speed
16. The _______ option allows the server to echo data received from the client.
    a. binary
    b. echo
    c. repeat
    d. b or c
17. The _______ option conveys to the client the options enabled at the server site.
    a. echo
    b. status
    c. options
    d. terminal mode
18. What is needed to set the terminal speed?
    a. IAC
    b. terminal speed option
    c. SB
    d. all of the above

19. The _______ control character aborts a process running at the remote site.
    a. IP
    b. AO
    c. AYT
    d. EC
20. What is needed in option negotiation?
    a. an option
    b. an IAC control character
    c. an option control character (WILL, WONT, DO, or DONT)
    d. all of the above
21. The _______ control character determines whether or not the remote machine is up and running.
    a. IP
    b. AO
    c. AYT
    d. EC
22. The _______ control character allows a remote process to continue without creating output.
    a. IP
    b. AO
    c. AYT
    d. EC
23. To interrupt an application running at the remote site, type _______.
    a. Ctrl+c
    b. Ctrl+] followed by Ctrl+c
    c. Ctrl+]
    d. Ctrl+z
24. To interrupt the TELNET client, type _______.
    a. Ctrl+c
    b. Ctrl+]
    c. Ctrl+z
    d. none of the above
25. In the TELNET _______ mode, three TCP segments are needed for each typed character.
    a. default
    b. character
    c. line
    d. b and c

26. In the TELNET _______ mode, the GA character is sent after every line of characters is received.
    a. default
    b. character
    c. line
    d. b and c
27. In the TELNET _______ mode, no GA character is sent.
    a. default
    b. character
    c. line
    d. b and c
28. In Rlogin, a command from the server to the client is accomplished through _______.
    a. the urgent mode
    b. the use of FF_{16}
    c. Ctrl+z
    d. Ctrl+c
29. In Rlogin, a command from the client to the server begins with _______.
    a. the tilde
    b. the use of FF_{16}
    c. Ctrl+z
    d. Ctrl+c
30. In Rlogin, a _______ can be used to let typed characters be interpreted by the client instead of the server.
    a. tilde
    b. FF_{16}
    c. Ctrl+z
    d. Ctrl+c
31. Which of the following is not common to both local and remote login?
    a. terminal driver
    b. local operating system
    c. application programs
    d. pseudoterminal

Exercises

32. Show the sequence of bits sent from a client TELNET for the binary transmission of 11110011 00111100 11111111.
33. If TELNET is using the character mode, how many characters are sent back and forth between the client and server to copy a file named file1 to another file named file2 in UNIX (*cp file1 file2*)?

34. What is the minimum number of bits sent at the TCP level to accomplish the task in exercise 32?
35. What is the minimum number of bits sent at the data link layer level (using Ethernet) to accomplish the task in exercise 32?
36. What is the ratio of the useful bits to the total bits in exercise 35?
37. Show the sequence of characters exchanged between the TELNET client and the server to switch from the default mode to the character mode.
38. Show the sequence of characters exchanged between the TELNET client and the server to switch from the character mode to the default mode.
39. Show the sequence of characters exchanged between the TELNET client and the server to switch from the default mode to line mode.
40. Show the sequence of characters exchanged between the TELNET client and the server to switch from the character mode to the line mode.
41. Show the sequence of characters exchanged between the TELNET client and the server to switch from the line mode to the character mode.
42. Show the sequence of characters exchanged between the TELNET client and the server to switch from the line mode to the default mode.
43. Interpret the following sequence of characters (in hexadecimal) received by a TELNET client or server:
    a. FF FB 01
    b. FF FE 01
    c. FF F4
    d. FF F9
44. Encode the interaction in Example 1 using NVT remote control characters.
45. Encode the interaction in Example 1 using hexadecimal digits.
46. Encode the interaction in Example 2 using NVT remote control characters.
47. Encode the interaction in Example 2 using hexadecimal digits.
48. Compare the modes of operations between TELNET and Rlogin.
49. Compare the escape characters in TELNET and Rlogin.
50. What is the equivalent of the IAC character in Rlogin?
51. How is the functionality of control characters in Table 19.7 accomplished in TELNET?
52. Make a table comparing the features of TELNET and Rlogin (data characters, remote control characters, escape control characters, option negotiation, etc.).
53. Do some research and find the extended options proposed for TELNET.

CHAPTER 20

File Transfer Protocol (FTP)

File Transfer Protocol (FTP) is the standard mechanism provided by TCP/IP for copying a file from one host to another. Transferring files from one computer to another is one of the most common tasks expected from a networking or internetworking environment.

Although transferring files from one system to another seems simple and straightforward, some problems must be dealt with first. For example, two systems may use different file name conventions. Two systems may have different ways to represent text and data. Two systems may have different directory structures. All of these problems have been solved by FTP in a very simple and elegant approach.

FTP differs from other client-server applications in that it establishes two connections between the hosts. One connection is used for data transfer, the other for control information (commands and responses). Separation of commands and data transfer makes FTP more efficient. The control connection uses very simple rules of communication. We need to transfer only a line of command or a line of response at a time. The data connection, on the other hand, needs more complex rules due to the variety of data types transferred.

FTP uses two well-known TCP ports: Port 21 is used for the control connection, and port 20 is used for the data connection.

> FTP uses the services of TCP. It needs two TCP connections.
> The well-known port 21 is used for the control connection and the well-known port 20 for the data connection.

Figure 20.1 shows the basic model of FTP. The client has three components: user interface, client control process, and the client data transfer process. The server has two components: the server control process and the server data transfer process. The control connection is made between the control processes. The data connection is made between the data transfer processes.

The control connection remains connected during the entire interactive FTP session. The data connection is opened and then closed for each file transferred. It opens each time commands that involve transferring files are used, and it closes when the file is transferred. In other words, when a user starts an FTP session, the control connection opens. While the control connection is open, the data connection can be opened and closed multiple times if several files are transferred.

Figure 20.1 *FTP*

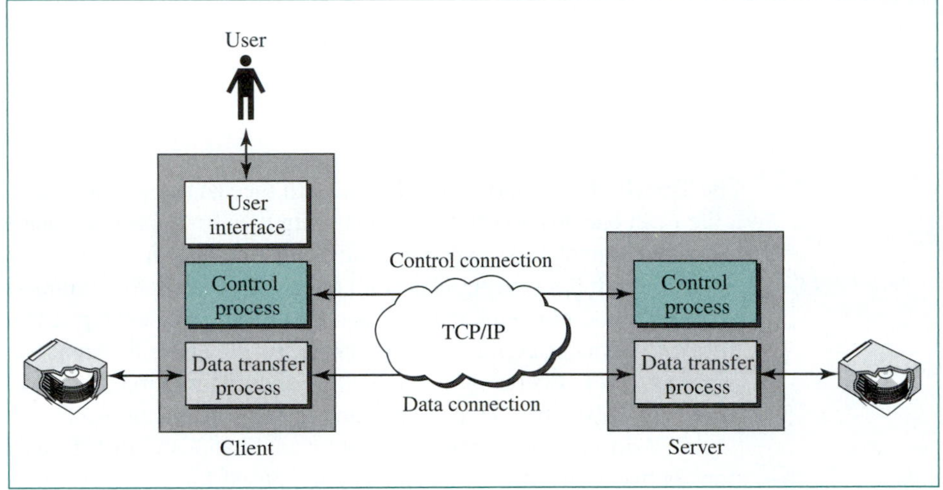

20.1 CONNECTIONS

The two FTP connections, control and data, use different strategies and different port numbers.

Control Connection

The control connection is created in the same way as other application programs described so far. There are two steps:

1. The server issues a passive open on the well-known port 21 and waits for a client.
2. The client uses an ephemeral port and issues an active open.

The connection remains open during the entire process. The service type, used by the IP protocol, is *minimize delay* because this is an interactive connection between a user (human) and a server. The user types commands and expects to receive responses without significant delay. Figure 20.2 shows the initial connection between the server and the client. Of course, after the initial connection, the server process creates a child process and assigns the duty of serving the client to the child process using an ephemeral port.

Figure 20.2 *Opening the control connection*

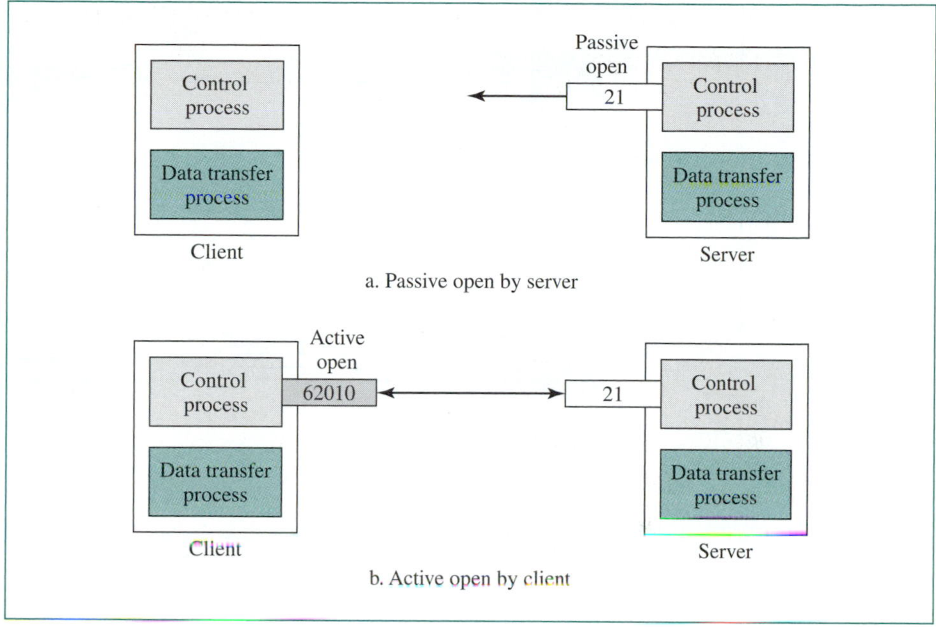

Data Connection

The data connection uses the well-known port 20 at the server site. However, the creation of a data connection is different from what we have seen so far. The following shows how FTP creates a data connection:

1. The client, not the server, issues a passive open using an ephemeral port. This must be done by the client because it is the client that issues the commands for transferring files.
2. The client sends this port number to the server using the PORT command (we will discuss this command shortly).
3. The server receives the port number and issues an active open using the well-known port 20 and the received ephemeral port number.

The steps for creating the initial data connection are shown in Figure 20.3. Of course, after the initial connection, the server process creates a child process and assigns the duty of serving the client to the child process using an ephemeral port.

Later we will see that these steps are changed if the PASV command is used.

20.2 COMMUNICATION

The FTP client and server, which run on different computers, must communicate with each other. These two computers may use different operating systems, different character sets, different file structures, and different file formats. FTP must make this heterogeneity compatible.

Figure 20.3 *Creating the data connection*

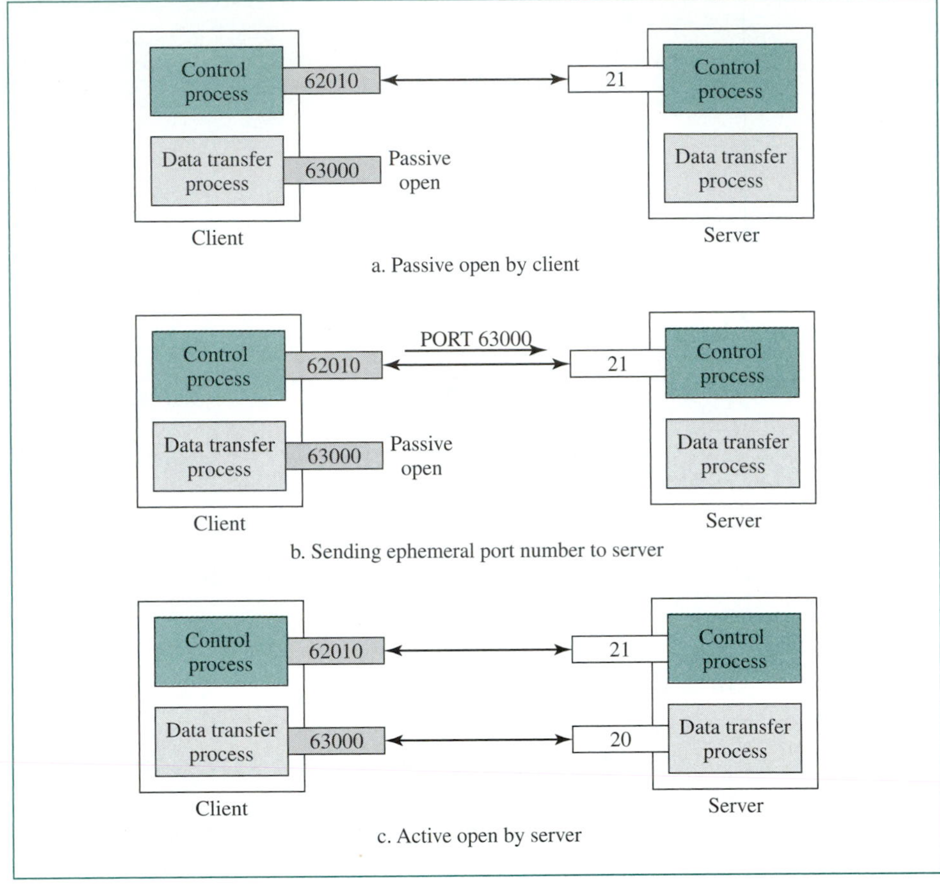

FTP has two different approaches, one for the control connection and one for the data connection. We will study each approach separately.

Communication over Control Connection

FTP uses the same approach as TELNET or SMTP to communicate across the control connection. It uses the NVT ASCII character set (see Figure 20.4). Communication is achieved through commands and responses. This simple method is adequate for the control connection because we send one command (response) at a time. Each command or response is only one short line so we need not worry about file format or file structure. Each line is terminated with a two-character (carriage return and line feed) end-of-line token.

Communication over Data Connection

The purpose and implementation of the data connection are different from that of the control connection. We want to transfer files through the data connection. The client

Figure 20.4 *Using the control connection*

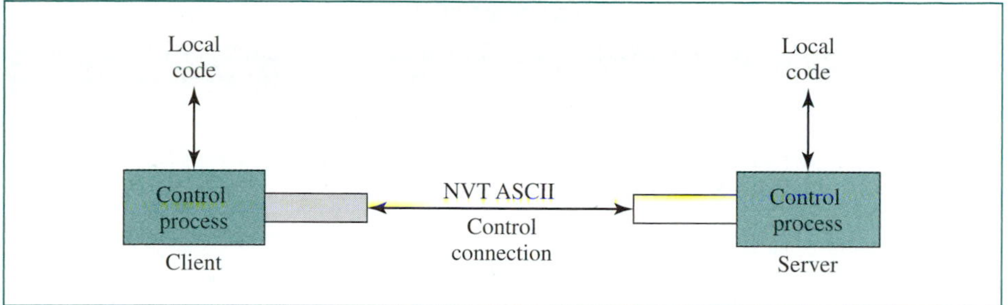

must define the type of file to be transferred, the structure of the data, and the transmission mode. Before sending the file through the data connection, we prepare for transmission through the control connection. The heterogeneity problem is resolved by defining three attributes of communication: file type, data structure, and transmission mode (see Figure 20.5).

Figure 20.5 *Using the data connection*

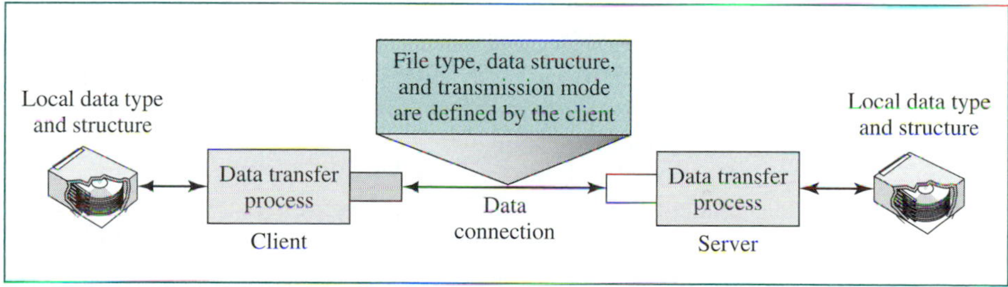

File Type

FTP can transfer one of the following file types across the data connection:

- **ASCII file.** This is the default format for transferring text files. Each character is encoded using NVT ASCII. The sender transforms the file from its own representation into NVT ASCII characters and the receiver transforms the NVT ASCII characters to its own representation.
- **EBCDIC file.** If one or both ends of the connection use EBCDIC encoding, the file can be transferred using EBCDIC encoding.
- **Image file.** This is the default format for transferring binary files. The file is sent as continuous streams of bits without any interpretation or encoding. This is mostly used to transfer binary files such as compiled programs.

If the file is encoded in ASCII or EBCDIC, another attribute must be added to define the printability of the file.

a. **Nonprint.** This is the default format for transferring a text file. The file contains no vertical specifications for printing. This means that the file cannot be printed without further processing because there are no characters to be interpreted for vertical movement of the print head. This format is used for files that will be stored and processed later.

b. **TELNET.** In this format the file contains NVT ASCII vertical characters such as CR (carriage return), LF (line feed), NL (new line), and VT (vertical tab). The file is printable after transfer.

Data Structure

FTP can transfer a file across the data connection using one of the following interpretations about the structure of the data:

- **File structure (default).** The file has no structure. It is a continuous stream of bytes.
- **Record structure.** The file is divided into records (or structs in C). This can be used only with text files.
- **Page structure.** The file is divided into pages, with each page having a page number and a page header. The pages can be stored or accessed randomly or sequentially.

Transmission Mode

FTP can transfer a file across the data connection using one of the following three transmission modes:

- **Stream mode.** This is the default mode. Data are delivered from FTP to TCP as a continuous stream of bytes. TCP is responsible for chopping data into segments of appropriate size. If the data is simply a stream of bytes (file structure), no end-of-file is needed. End-of-file in this case is the closing of the data connection by the sender. If the data is divided into records (record structure), each record will have a 1-byte end-of-record (EOR) character and the end of the file will have a 1-byte end-of-file (EOF) character.
- **Block mode.** Data can be delivered from FTP to TCP in blocks. In this case, each block is preceded by a 3-byte header. The first byte is called the *block descriptor;* the next two bytes define the size of the block in bytes.
- **Compressed mode.** If the file is big, the data can be compressed. The compression method used is normally run-length encoding. In this method, consecutive appearances of a data unit are replaced by one occurrence and the number of repetitions. In a text file, this is usually spaces (blanks). In a binary file, null characters are usually compressed.

20.3 COMMAND PROCESSING

FTP uses the control connection to establish a communication between the client control process and the server control process. During this communication, the commands are sent from the client to the server and the responses are sent back from the server to the client (see Figure 20.6).

Figure 20.6 *Command processing*

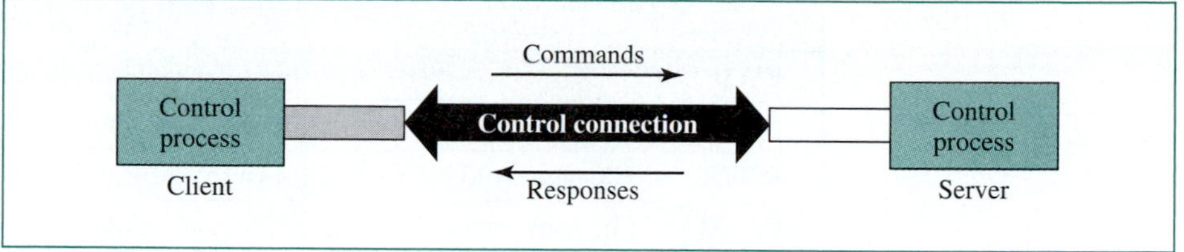

Commands

Commands, which are sent from the FTP client control process, are in the form of ASCII uppercase, which may or may not be followed by an argument. We can roughly divide the commands into six groups: access commands, file management commands, data formatting commands, port defining commands, file transferring commands, and miscellaneous commands.

- **Access commands.** These commands let the user access the remote system. Table 20.1 lists common commands in this group.

Table 20.1 *Access commands*

Command	*Argument(s)*	*Description*
USER	User id	User information
PASS	User password	Password
ACCT	Account to be charged	Account information
REIN		Reinitialize
QUIT		Log out of the system
ABOR		Abort the previous command

- **File management commands.** These commands let the user access the file system on the remote computer. They allow the user to navigate through the directory structure, create new directories, delete files, and so on. Table 20.2 gives common commands in this group.

Table 20.2 *File management commands*

Command	*Argument(s)*	*Description*
CWD	Directory name	Change to another directory
CDUP		Change to the parent directory
DELE	File name	Delete a file
LIST	Directory name	List subdirectories or files
NLIST	Directory name	List the names of subdirectories or files without other attributes
MKD	Directory name	Create a new directory

Table 20.2 *File management commands (continued)*

Command	*Argument(s)*	*Description*
PWD		Display name of current directory
RMD	Directory name	Delete a directory
RNFR	File name (old file name)	Identify a file to be renamed
RNTO	File name (new file name)	Rename the file
SMNT	File system name	Mount a file system

- **Data formatting commands.** These commands let the user define the data structure, file type, and transmission mode. The defined format is then used by the file transfer commands. Table 20.3 shows common commands in this group.

Table 20.3 *Data formatting commands*

Command	*Argument(s)*	*Description*
TYPE	A (ASCII), E (EBCDIC), I (Image), N (Nonprint), or T (TELNET)	Define the file type and if necessary the print format
STRU	F (File), R (Record), or P (Page)	Define the organization of the data
MODE	S (Stream), B (Block), or C (Compressed)	Define the transmission mode

- **Port defining commands.** These commands define the port number for the data connection on the client site. There are two methods to do this. In the first method, using the PORT command, the client can choose an ephemeral port number and send it to the server using a passive open. The server uses that port number and creates an active open. In the second method, using the PASV command, the client just asks the server to first choose a port number. The server does a passive open on that port and sends the port number in the response (see response numbered 227 in Table 20.7). The client issues an active open using that port number. Table 20.4 shows the port defining commands.

Table 20.4 *Port defining commands*

Command	*Argument(s)*	*Description*
PORT	6-digit identifier	Client chooses a port
PASV		Server chooses a port

- **File transfer commands.** These commands actually let the user transfer files. Table 20.5 lists common commands in this group.

Table 20.5 *File transfer commands*

Command	*Argument(s)*	*Description*
RETR	File name(s)	Retrieve files; file(s) are transferred from server to the client
STOR	File name(s)	Store files; file(s) are transferred from the client to the server
APPE	File name(s)	Similar to STOR except if the file exists, data must be appended to it
STOU	File name(s)	Same as STOR except that the file name will be unique in the directory; however, the existing file should not be overwritten
ALLO	File name(s)	Allocate storage space for the files at the server
REST	File name(s)	Position the file marker at a specified data point
STAT	File name(s)	Return the status of files

- **Miscellaneous commands.** These commands deliver information to the FTP user at the client site. Table 20.6 shows common commands in this group.

Table 20.6 *Miscellaneous commands*

Command	*Argument(s)*	*Description*
HELP		Ask information about the server
NOOP		Check if server is alive
SITE	Commands	Specify the site-specific commands
SYST		Ask about operating system used by the server

Responses

Every FTP command generates at least one response. A response has two parts: a three-digit number followed by text. The numeric part defines the code; the text part defines needed parameters or extra explanations. We represent the three digits as *xyz*. The meaning of each digit is described below.

First Digit

The first digit defines the status of the command. One of five digits can be used in this position:

- **1yz (positive preliminary reply).** The action has started. The server will send another reply before accepting another command.
- **2yz (positive completion reply).** The action has been completed. The server will accept another command.
- **3yz (positive intermediate reply).** The command has been accepted, but further information is needed.

- **4yz (transient negative completion reply).** The action did not take place, but the error is temporary. The same command can be sent later.
- **5yz (permanent negative completion reply).** The command was not accepted and should not be retried again.

Second Digit

The second digit also defines the status of the command. One of six digits can be used in this position:

- **x0z (syntax).**
- **x1z (information).**
- **x2z (connections).**
- **x3z (authentication and accounting).**
- **x4z (unspecified).**
- **x5z (file system).**

Third Digit

The third digit provides additional information. Table 20.7 shows a brief list of possible responses.

Table 20.7 *Responses*

Code	*Description*
	Positive Preliminary Reply
120	Service will be ready shortly
125	Data connection open; data transfer will start shortly
150	File status is OK; data connection will be open shortly
	Positive Completion Reply
200	Command OK
211	System status or help reply
212	Directory status
213	File status
214	Help message
215	Naming the system type (operating system)
220	Service ready
221	Service closing
225	Data connection open
226	Closing data connection
227	Entering passive mode; server sends its IP address and port number
230	User login OK
250	Request file action OK

Table 20.7 *Responses (continued)*

Code	*Description*
	Positive Intermediate Reply
331	User name OK; password is needed
332	Need account for logging
350	The file action is pending; more information needed
	Transient Negative Completion Reply
425	Cannot open data connection
426	Connection closed; transfer aborted
450	File action not taken; file not available
451	Action aborted; local error
452	Action aborted; insufficient storage
	Permanent Negative Completion Reply
500	Syntax error; unrecognized command
501	Syntax error in parameters or arguments
502	Command not implemented
503	Bad sequence of commands
504	Command parameter not implemented
530	User not logged in
532	Need account for storing file
550	Action is not done; file unavailable
552	Requested action aborted; exceeded storage allocation
553	Requested action not taken; file name not allowed

20.4 FILE TRANSFER

File transfer occurs over the data connection under the control of the commands sent over the control connection. However, we should remember that file transfer in FTP means one of three things (see Figure 20.7).

- A file is to be copied from the server to the client. This is called *retrieving a file*. It is done under the supervision of the RETR command.
- A file is to be copied from the client to the server. This is called *storing a file*. It is done under the supervision of the STOR command.
- A list of directory or file names is to be sent from the server to the client. This is done under the supervision of the LIST command. Note that FTP treats a list of directory or file names as a file. It is sent over the data connection.

Figure 20.7 *File transfer*

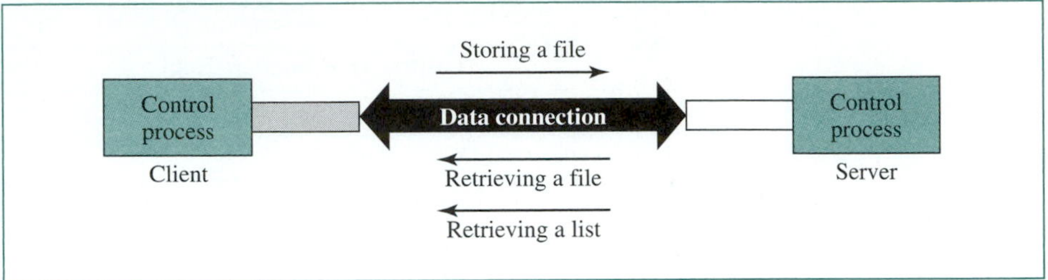

Example 1

Figure 20.8 shows an example of using FTP for retrieving a list of items in a directory.

Figure 20.8 *Example 1*

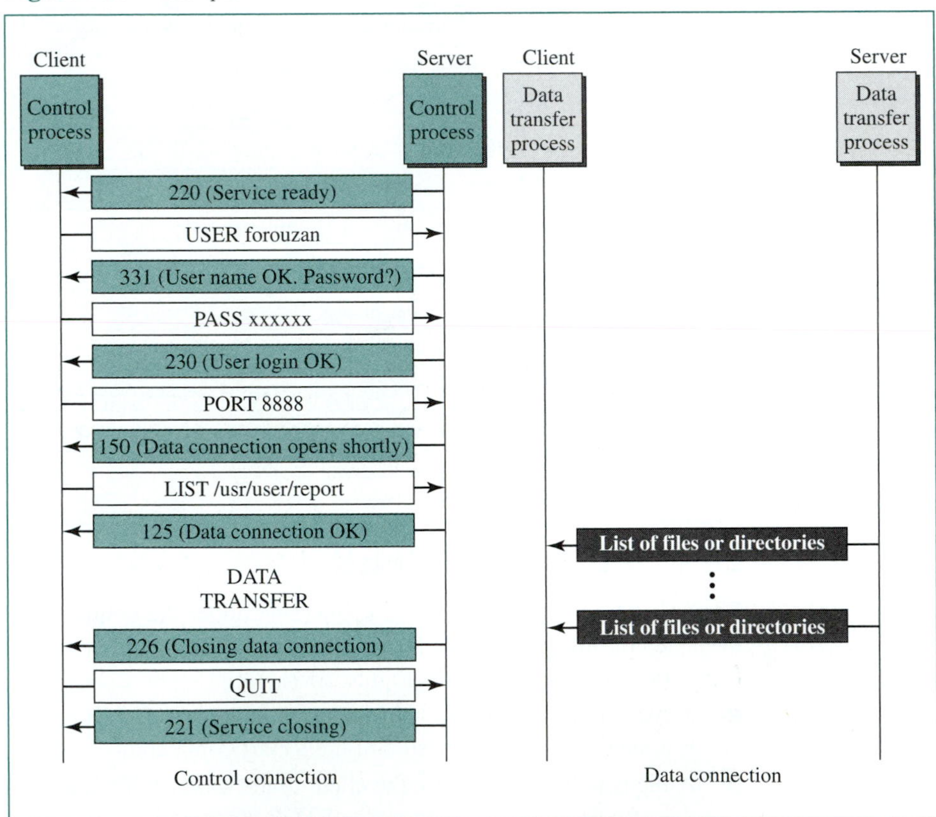

1. After the control connection to port 21 is created, the FTP server sends the 220 (service ready) response on the control connection.
2. The client sends the USER command.
3. The server responds with 331 (user name is OK, password is required).
4. The client sends the PASS command.

5. The server responds with 230 (user login is OK)
6. The client issues a passive open on an ephemeral port for the data connection and sends the PORT command (over the control connection) to give this port number to the server.
7. The server does not open the connection at this time, but it prepares itself for issuing an active open on the data connection between port 20 (server side) and the ephemeral port received from the client. It sends response 150 (data connection will open shortly).
8. The client sends the LIST message.
9. Now the server responds with 125 and opens the data connection.
10. The server then sends the list of the files or directories (as a file) on the data connection. When the whole list (file) is sent, the server responds with 226 (closing data connection) over the control connection.
11. The client now has two choices. It can use the QUIT command to request the closing of the control or it can send another command to start another activity (and eventually open another data connection). In our example, the client sends a QUIT command.
12. After receiving the QUIT command, the server responds with 221 (service closing) and then closes the control connection.

Example 2

Figure 20.9 shows an example of how an image (binary) file is stored.

1. After the control connection to port 21 is created, the FTP server sends the 220 (service ready) response on the control connection.
2. The client sends the USER command.
3. The server responds with 331 (user name is OK, a password is required).
4. The client sends the PASS command.
5. The server responds with 230 (user login is OK).
6. The client issues a passive open on an ephemeral port for data connection and sends the PORT command (over the control connection) to give this port number to the server.
7. The server does not open the connection at this time, but prepares itself for issuing an active open on the data connection between port 20 (server side) and the ephemeral port received from the client. It sends the response 150 (data connection will open shortly).
8. The client sends the TYPE command.
9. The server responds with the response 200 (command OK).
10. The client sends the STRU command.
11. The server responds with 200 (command OK).
12. The client sends the STOR command.
13. The server opens the data connection and sends the message 250.
14. The client sends the file on the data connection. After the entire file is sent the data connection is closed. Closing the data connection means end-of-file.
15. The server sends the response 226 on the control connection.
16. The client sends the QUIT command or uses other commands to open another data connection for transferring another file. In our example, the QUIT command is sent.
17. The server responds with 221 (service closing) and it closes the control connection.

Figure 20.9 *Example 2*

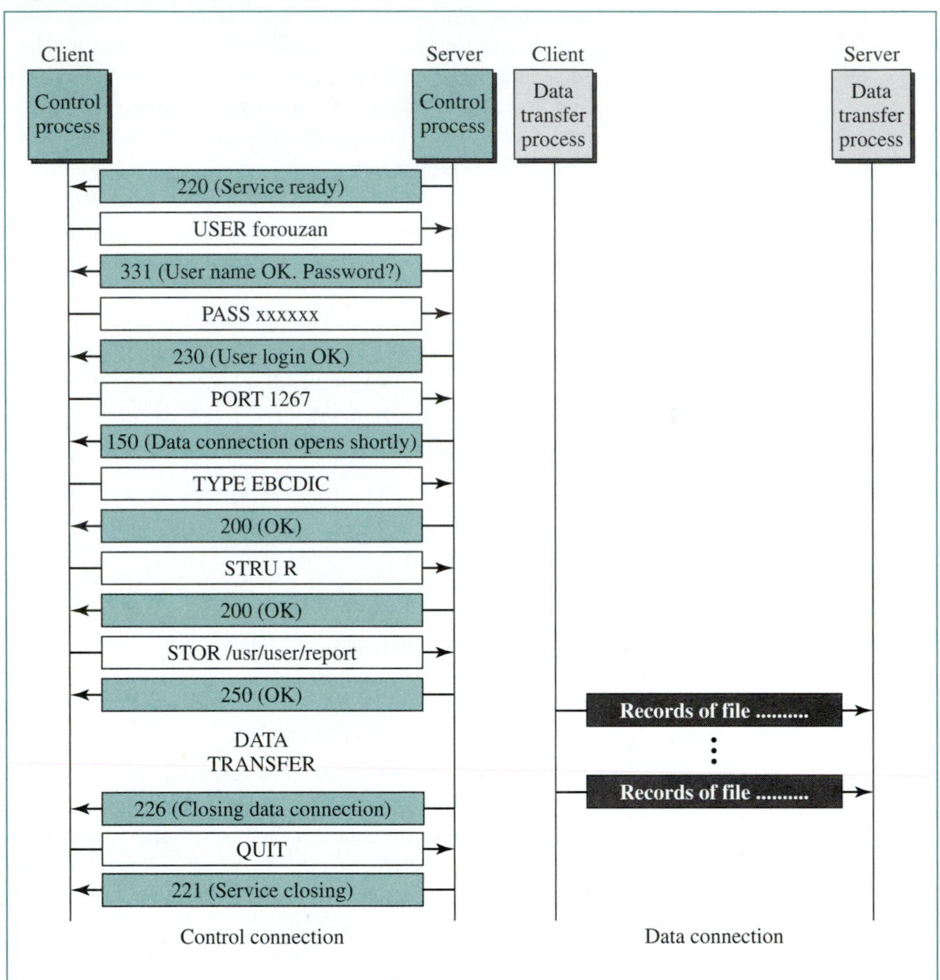

20.5 USER INTERFACE

Most operating systems provide a user-friendly interface to access the services of FTP. The interface prompts the user for the appropriate input. After the user types a line, the FTP interface reads the line and changes it to the corresponding FTP command. Table 20.8 shows the interface commands provided in UNIX FTP. Some of the commands can be abbreviated as long as there is no ambiguity.

Table 20.8 *List of FTP commands in UNIX*

Commands
!, $, account, append, ascii, bell, binary, bye, case, cd, cdup, close, cr, delete, debug, dir, discount, form, get, glob, hash, help, lcd, ls, macdef, mdelete, mdir, mget, mkdir, mls, mode, mput, nmap, ntrans, open, prompt, proxy, sendport, put, pwd, quit, quote, recv, remotehelp, rename, reset, rmdir, runique, send, status, struct, sunique, tenex, trace, type, user, verbose,?

Example 3

We show some of the user interface commands that accomplish the same task as in Example 1. The user input is shown in boldface. As shown below, some of the commands are provided automatically by the interface. For example, the user does not have to type any command corresponding to the USER, PASS, or PORT commands. The interface does this. The user receives a prompt and provides only the arguments.

```
% ftp challenger.atc.fhda.edu
Connected to challenger.atc.fhda.edu
220 Server ready
Name: forouzan
Password: xxxxxxx
ftp > ls /usr/user/report
200 OK
150 Opening ASCII mode
...........
...........
226 transfer complete
ftp > close
221 Goodbye
ftp > quit
```

20.6 ANONYMOUS FTP

To use FTP, a user needs an account (user name) and a password on the remote server. Some sites have a set of files available for public access. To access these files, a user does not need to have an account or password. Instead, the user can use *anonymous* as the user name and *guest* as the password.

User access to the system is very limited. Some sites allow anonymous users only a subset of commands. For example, most sites allow the user to copy some files, but do not allow navigation through the directories.

Example 4

We show an example of using anonymous FTP. We assume that some public data are available at internic.net.

```
% ftp internic.net
Connected to internic.net
220 Server ready
Name: anonymous
331 Guest login OK, send "guest" as password
Password: guest
ftp > pwd
257 '/' is current directory
ftp > ls
200 OK
150 Opening ASCII mode
bin
...
ftp > close
221 Goodbye
ftp > quit
```

20.7 KEY TERMS

anonymous FTP

ASCII file

block mode

compressed mode

control connection

data connection

EBCDIC file

ephemeral port

file structure

File Transfer Protocol (FTP)

flow control

image file

record structure

stream mode

user interface

well-known port

20.8 SUMMARY

- File Transfer Protocol (FTP) is a TCP/IP client-server application for copying files from one host to another.
- FTP requires two connections for data transfer: a control connection and a data connection.
- FTP employs NVT ASCII for communication between dissimilar systems.

- Prior to the actual transfer of files, the file type, data structure, and transmission mode are defined by the client through the control connection.
- There are six classes of commands sent by the client to establish communication with the server. They are:
  a. access commands
  b. file management commands
  c. data formatting commands
  d. port defining commands
  e. file transferring commands
  f. miscellaneous commands
- Responses are sent from the server to the client during connection establishment.
- There are three types of file transfer:
  a. a file is copied from the server to the client
  b. a file is copied from the client to the server
  c. a list of directories or filenames is sent from the server to the client
- Most operating systems provide a user-friendly interface between FTP and the user.
- Anonymous FTP provides a method for the general public to access files on remote sites.

20.9 PRACTICE SET

Multiple-Choice Questions

1. Which of the following is true?
   a. FTP allows systems with different directory structures to transfer files.
   b. FTP allows a system using ASCII and a system using EBCDIC to transfer files.
   c. FTP allows a PC and a SUN workstation to transfer files.
   d. all of the above
2. During an FTP session the control connection is opened _______.
   a. exactly once
   b. exactly twice
   c. as many times as necessary
   d. all of the above
3. During an FTP session the data connection is opened _______.
   a. exactly once
   b. exactly twice
   c. as many times as necessary
   d. all of the above

4. What attributes must be defined by the client prior to transmission?
   a. data type
   b. file structure
   c. transmission mode
   d. all of the above
5. A file can be organized into records, pages, or a stream of bytes. These are types of an attribute called _______.
   a. file types
   b. data structures
   c. transmission modes
   d. all of the above
6. There are three types of _______: stream, block, and compressed.
   a. file types
   b. data structures
   c. transmission modes
   d. all of the above
7. ASCII, EBCDIC, and image define an attribute called _______.
   a. file type
   b. data structure
   c. transmission mode
   d. all of the above
8. Which category of commands is used to store and retrieve files?
   a. file transfer commands
   b. access commands
   c. file management commands
   d. data formatting commands
9. Which category of commands defines the port number for the data connection on the client site?
   a. file transfer commands
   b. access commands
   c. file management commands
   d. port defining commands
10. Which category of commands sets the attributes (file type, data structure, and transmission modes) of a file to be transferred?
   a. file transfer commands
   b. access commands
   c. file management commands
   d. data formatting commands

11. Which category of commands lets a user switch directories and create or delete directories?
    a. file transfer commands
    b. access commands
    c. file management commands
    d. data formatting commands
12. When you _______, it is copied from the server to the client.
    a. retrieve a file
    b. store a file
    c. retrieve a list
    d. a and c
13. When you _______, it is copied from the client to the server.
    a. retrieve a file
    b. store a file
    c. retrieve a list
    d. a and c
14. In anonymous FTP, the user can usually _______.
    a. retrieve files
    b. navigate through directories
    c. store files
    d. all of the above

Exercises

15. What do you think would happen if the control connection is accidentally severed during an FTP transfer?
16. Explain why the client issues an active open for the control connection and a passive open for the data connection.
17. Why should there be limitations on anonymous FTP? What could an unscrupulous user do?
18. Explain why FTP does not have a message format.
19. Show a TCP segment carrying one of the FTP commands.
20. Show a TCP segment carrying one of the FTP responses.
21. Show a TCP segment carrying FTP data.
22. Explain what will happen if the file in Example 2 already exists.
23. Redo Example 1 using the PASV command instead of the PORT command.
24. Redo Example 2 using the STOU command instead of the STOR command to store a file with a unique name. What happens if a file already exists with the same name?
25. Redo Example 2 using the RETR command instead of the STOR command to retrieve a file.

26. Give an example of the use of the HELP command. Follow the format of Example 1.
27. Give an example of the use of the NOOP command. Follow the format of Example 1.
28. Give an example of the use of the SYST command. Follow the format of Example 1.
29. A user wants to make a directory called *Jan* under the directory */usr/usrs/letters*. The host is called "*mcGraw.com.*". Show all of the commands and responses using Examples 1 and 2 as a guide.
30. A user wants to move to the parent of its current directory. The host is called "*mcGraw.com.*". Show all of the commands and responses using Examples 1 and 2 as a guide.
31. A user wants to move a file named *file1* from */usr/usrs/report* directory to */usr/usrs/letters* directory. The host is called "*mcGraw.com.*". Show all the commands and responses using Examples 1 and 2 as a guide.
32. A user wants to retrieve an EBCDIC file named *file1* from */usr/usrs/report* directory. The host is called "*mcGraw.com.*". The file is so large that the user wants to compress it before transferring. Show all the commands and responses using Examples 1 and 2 as a guide.
33. Show how the user interface commands in UNIX are translated to FTP commands (see Table 20.8).

CHAPTER 21

Trivial File Transfer Protocol (TFTP)

There are occasions when we need to simply copy a file without the need for all of the functionalities of the FTP protocol. For example, when a diskless workstation or a router is booted, we need to download the bootstrap and configuration files. Here we do not need all of the sophistication provided in FTP. We just need a protocol that quickly copies the files.

Trivial File Transfer Protocol (TFTP) is designed for these types of file transfer. It is so simple that the software package can fit into the read-only memory of a diskless workstation. It can be used at bootstrap time. TFTP can read or write a file for the client. *Reading* means copying a file from the server site to the client site. *Writing* means copying a file from the client site to the server site.

> TFTP uses the services of UDP on the well-known port 69.

21.1 MESSAGES

There are five types of TFTP messages, RRQ, WRQ, DATA, ACK, and ERROR, as shown in Figure 21.1.

Figure 21.1 *Message categories*

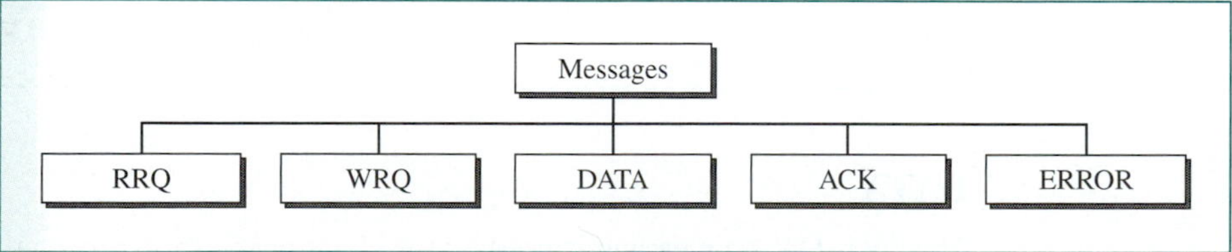

RRQ

The read request (RRQ) message is used by the client to establish a connection for reading data from the server. Its format is shown in Figure 21.2.

Figure 21.2 *RRQ format*

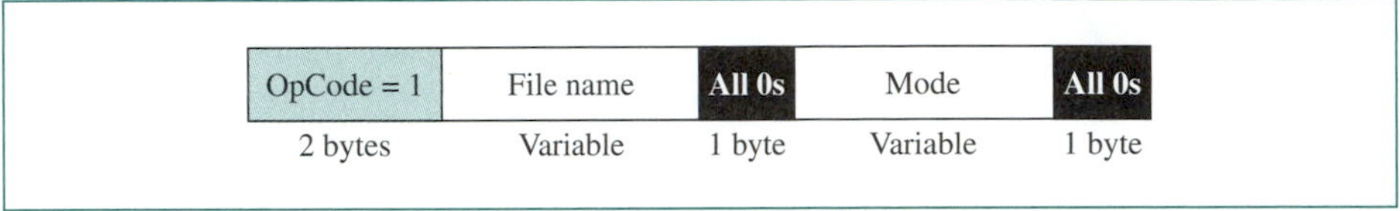

The RRQ message fields are as follows:

- **OpCode.** The first field is a 2-byte operation code. The value is 1 for the RRQ message.
- **File name.** The next field is a variable-size string (encoded in ASCII) that defines the name of the file. Since the file name varies in length, termination is signaled by a 1-byte field of 0s.
- **Mode.** The next field is another variable-size string defining the transfer mode. The mode field is terminated by another 1-byte field of 0s. The mode can be one of two strings: "netascii" (for an ASCII file) or "octet" (for a binary file). Originally there was another file mode, "mail," which is now obsolete. The file name and mode fields can be in upper- or lowercase, or a combination of both.

WRQ

The write request (WRQ) message is used by the client to establish a connection for writing data to the server. The format is the same as RRQ except that the OpCode is 2 (see Figure 21.3).

Figure 21.3 *WRQ format*

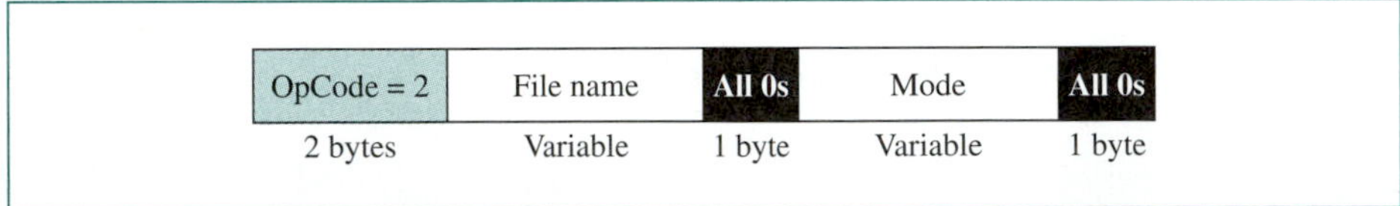

DATA

The data (DATA) message is used by the client or the server to send blocks of data. Its format is shown in Figure 21.4. The DATA message fields are as follows:

- **OpCode.** The first field is a 2-byte operation code. The value is 3 for the DATA message.
- **Block number.** This is a 2-byte field containing the block number. The sender of the data (client or server) uses this field for sequencing. All blocks are numbered

Figure 21.4 *DATA format*

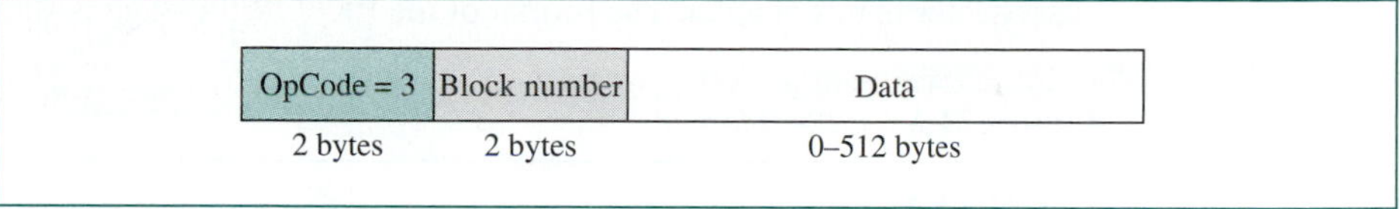

sequentially starting with 1. The block number is necessary for acknowledgment as we will see shortly.

- **Data.** This block must be exactly 512 bytes in all DATA messages except the last block which must be between 0 and 511 bytes. A non-512 byte block is used as a signal that the sender has sent all the data. In other words, it is used as an end-of-file indicator. If the data in the file happens to be an exact multiple of 512 bytes, the sender must send one extra block of zero bytes to show the end of transmission. Data can be transferred in either NVT ASCII (netascii) or binary octet (octet).

ACK

The acknowledge (ACK) message is used by the client or server to acknowledge the receipt of a data block. The message is only 4 bytes long. Its format is shown in Figure 21.5.

Figure 21.5 *ACK format*

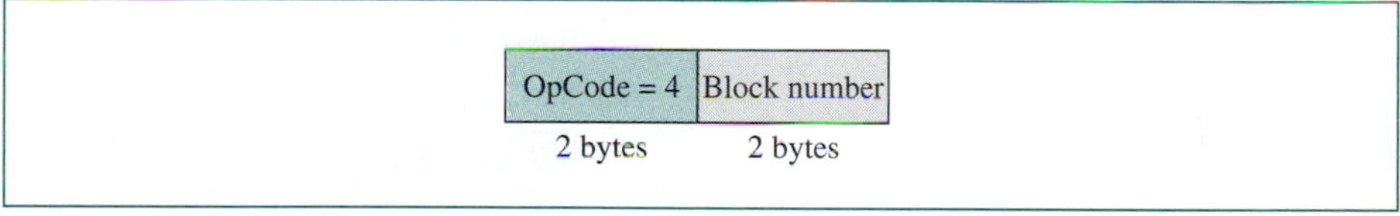

The ACK message fields are as follows:

- **OpCode.** The first field is a 2-byte operation code. The value is 4 for the ACK message.
- **Block number.** The next field is a 2-byte field containing the number of the block received.

The ACK message can also be a response to a WRQ. It is sent by the server to indicate that it is ready to receive data from the client. In this case the value of the block number field is 0. An example of an ACK message is in a later section.

ERROR

The ERROR message is used by the client or the server when a connection cannot be established or when there is a problem during data transmission. It can be sent as a negative response to RRQ or WRQ. It can also be used if the next block cannot be transferred during the actual data transfer phase. The error message is not used to declare a damaged or duplicated message. These problems are resolved by error-control mechanisms discussed later in this chapter. The format of the ERROR message is shown in Figure 21.6.

Figure 21.6 *ERROR format*

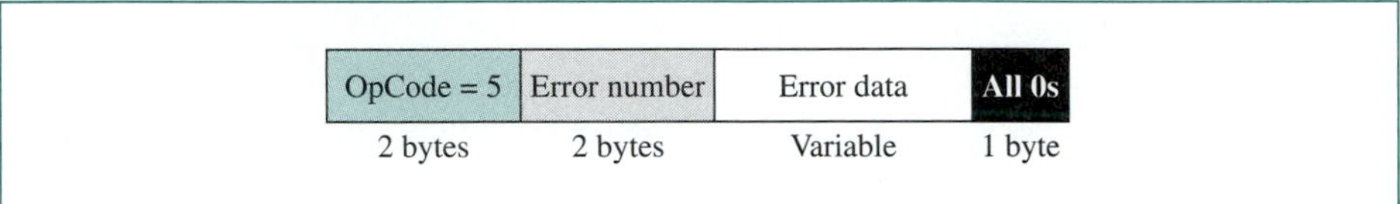

The ERROR message fields are as follows:

- **OpCode.** The first field is a 2-byte operation code. The value is 5 for the ERROR message.
- **Error number.** This 2-byte field defines the type of error. Table 21.1 shows the error numbers and their corresponding meanings.

Table 21.1 *Error numbers and their meanings*

Number	*Meaning*
0	Not defined
1	File not found
2	Access violation
3	Disk full or quota on disk exceeded
4	Illegal operation
5	Unknown port number
6	File already exists
7	No such user

- **Error data.** This variable-byte field contains the textual error data and is terminated by a 1-byte field of 0s.

21.2 CONNECTION

TFTP uses UDP services. Because there is no provision for connection establishment and termination in UDP, UDP transfers each block of data encapsulated in an independent user datagram. In TFTP, however, we do not want to transfer only one block of data; we do not want to transfer the file as independent blocks either. We need connections for the blocks of data being transferred as they all belong to the same file. TFTP uses RRQ, WRQ, ACK, and ERROR messages to establish connection. It uses the DATA message with a block of data of fewer than 512 bytes (0–511) to terminate connection.

Connection Establishment

Connection establishment for reading files is different from connection establishment for writing files (see Figure 21.7).

Figure 21.7 *Connection establishment*

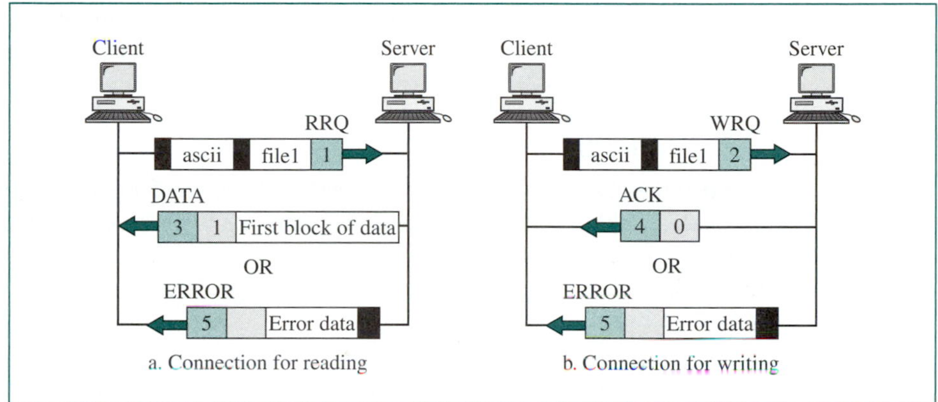

- **Reading.** To establish a connection for reading, the TFTP client sends the RRQ message. The name of the file and the transmission mode is defined in this message. If the server can transfer the file, it responds positively with a DATA message containing the first block of data. If there is a problem, such as difficulty in opening the file or permission restriction, the server responds negatively by sending an ERROR message.
- **Writing.** To establish a connection for writing, the TFTP client uses the WRQ message. The name of the file and the transmission mode is defined in this message. If the server can accept a copy of the file, it responds positively with an ACK message using a value of 0 for the block number. If there is any problem, the server responds negatively by sending an ERROR message.

Connection Termination

After the entire file is transferred, the connection must be terminated. As mentioned previously, TFTP does not have a special message for termination. Termination is accomplished by sending the last block of data, which is less than 512 bytes.

21.3 DATA TRANSFER

The data transfer phase occurs between connection establishment and termination. TFTP uses the services of UDP, which is unreliable.

The file is divided into blocks of data, in which each block except the last one is exactly 512 bytes. The last block must be between 0 and 511 bytes. TFTP can transfer data in ASCII or binary format.

UDP does not have any mechanism for flow and error control. TFTP has to create a flow- and error-control mechanism to transfer a file made of continuous blocks of data.

Flow Control

TFTP sends a block of data using the DATA message and waits for an ACK message. If the sender receives an acknowledgment before the time-out, it sends the next block. Thus, flow control is achieved by numbering the data blocks and waiting for an ACK before the next data block is sent.

Retrieve a File

When the client wants to retrieve (read) a file, it sends the RRQ message. The server responds with a DATA message sending the first block of data (if there is no problem) with a block number of 1.

Store a File

When the client wants to store (write) a file, it sends the WRQ message. The server responds with an ACK message (if there is no problem) using 0 for the block number. After receiving this acknowledgment, the client sends the first data block with a block number of 1.

Error Control

The TFTP error-control mechanism is different from those of other protocols. It is *symmetric,* which means that the sender and the receiver both use time-outs. The sender uses a time-out for data messages; the receiver uses a time-out for acknowledgment messages. If a data message is lost, the sender retransmits it after time-out expiration. If an acknowledgment is lost, the receiver retransmits it after time-out expiration. This guarantees a smooth operation.

Error control is needed in four situations: damaged message, lost message, lost acknowledgment, or duplicated message.

Damaged Message

There is no negative acknowledgment. If a block of data is damaged, it is detected by the receiver and the block is discarded. The sender waits for the acknowledgment and does not receive it within the time-out period. The block is then sent again. Note that there is no checksum field in the DATA message of TFTP. The only way the receiver can detect data corruption is through the checksum field of the UDP user datagram.

Lost Message

If a block is lost, it never reaches the receiver and no acknowledgment is sent. The sender resends the block after the time-out.

Lost Acknowledgment

If an acknowledgment is lost, we can have two situations. If the timer of the receiver matures before the timer of the sender, the receiver retransmits the acknowledgment; otherwise, the sender retransmits the data.

Duplicate Message

Duplication of blocks can be detected by the receiver through block number. If a block is duplicated, it is simply discarded by the receiver.

Sorcerer's Apprentice Bug

Although the flow- and error-control mechanism is symmetric in TFTP, it can lead to a problem known as the *sorcerer's apprentice bug,* named for the cartoon character who inadvertently conjures up a mop that continuously replicates itself. This will happen if the ACK message for a packet is not lost but delayed. In this situation, every succeeding block is sent twice and every succeeding acknowledgment is received twice.

Figure 21.8 shows the problem. The acknowledgment for the fifth block is delayed. After the time-out expiration, the sender retransmits the fifth block, which will be acknowledged by the receiver again. The sender receives two acknowledgments for the fifth block, which triggers it to send the sixth block twice. The receiver receives the sixth block twice and again sends two acknowledgments, which result in sending the seventh block twice. And so on.

Figure 21.8 *Sorcerer's apprentice bug*

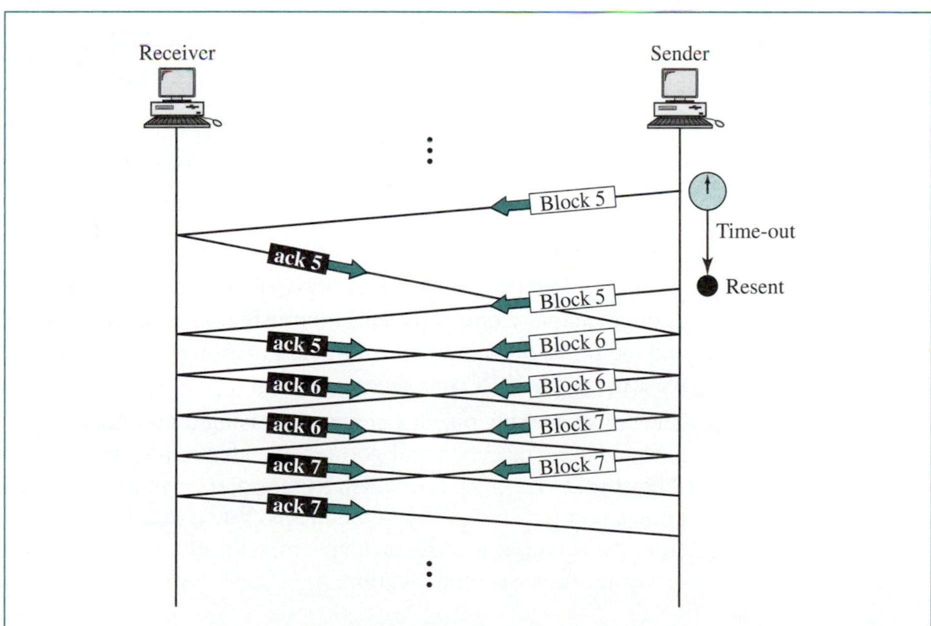

21.4 UDP PORTS

When a process uses the services of UDP, the server process issues the passive open on the well-known port and waits for the client process to issue the active open on an ephemeral port. After the connection is established, the client and server communicate using these two ports.

TFTP follows a different set of steps because the communication between a client TFTP and a server TFTP can be quite lengthy (seconds or even minutes). If a TFTP server uses the well-known port 69 to communicate with a single client, no other clients can use these services during that time. The solution to this problem, as shown in Figure 21.9, is to use the well-known port for the initial connection and an ephemeral port for the remaining communication.

Figure 21.9 *UDP port numbers used by TFTP*

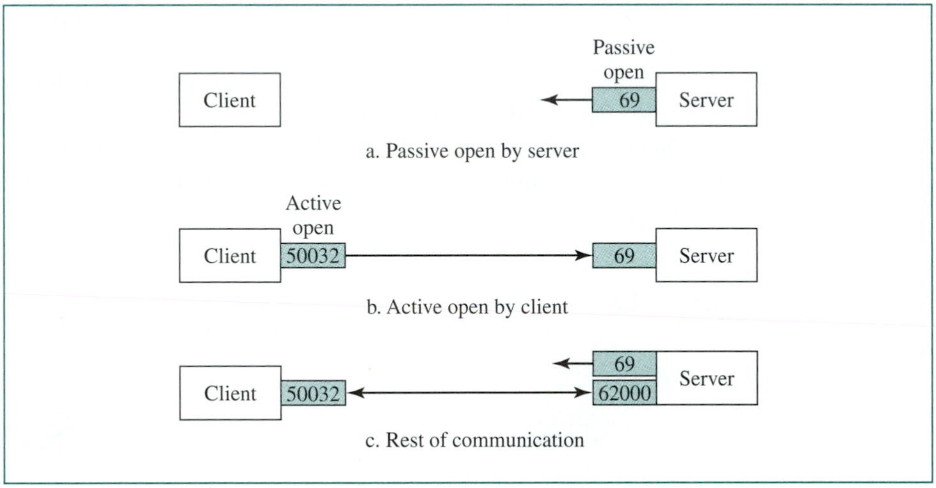

The steps are as follows:

1. The server passively opens the connection using the well-known port 69.
2. A client actively opens a connection using an ephemeral port for the source port and the well-known port 69 for the destination port. This is done through the RRQ message or the WRQ message.
3. The server actively opens a connection using a new ephemeral port for the source port and uses the ephemeral port received from the client as the destination port. It sends the DATA or ACK or ERROR message using these ports. This frees the well-known port (69) for use by other clients. When the client receives the first message from the server, it uses its own ephemeral port and the ephemeral port sent by the server for future communication.

21.5 TFTP EXAMPLE

Figure 21.10 shows an example of a TFTP transmission. The client wants to retrieve a copy of the contents of a 2,000-byte file called *file1*. The client sends an RRQ message. The server sends the first block, carrying the first 512 bytes, which is received intact and acknowledged. These two messages are the connection establishment. The second block, carrying the second 512 bytes, is lost. After the time-out, the server retransmits the block, which is received. The third block, carrying the third 512 bytes, is received intact, but the acknowledgment is lost. After the time-out, the receiver retransmits the acknowledgment. The last block, carrying the remaining 464 bytes, is received damaged, so the client simply discards it. After the time-out, the server retransmits the block. This message is considered the connection termination because the block carries fewer than 512 bytes.

Figure 21.10 *TFTP example*

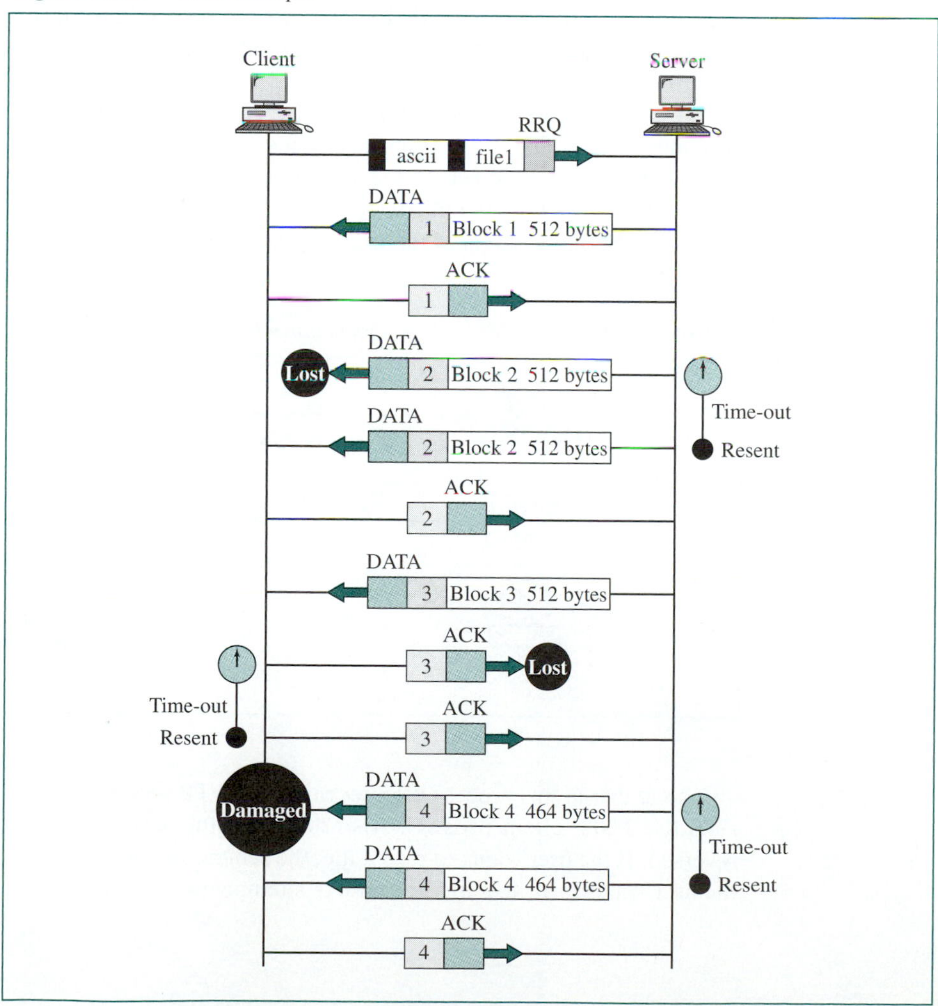

21.6 TFTP OPTIONS

An extension to the TFTP protocol that allows the appending of options to the RRQ and WRQ messages has been proposed. The options are mainly used to negotiate the size of the block and possibly the initial sequence number. Without the options the size of a block is 512 bytes except for the last block. The negotiation can define a size of block to be any number of bytes so long as the message can be encapsulated in a UDP user datagram.

A new type of message, option acknowledgment (OACK), to let the other party accept or reject the options, has also been proposed.

21.7 SECURITY

One important point about TFTP is that there is no provision for security: There is no user identification or password. Today, however, precautions must be taken to prevent hackers from accessing files. One security measure is to limit the access of TFTP to noncritical files.

Another way to add security is to use an application program, such as TELNET in conjunction with TFTP. The user must first access TELNET. TELNET checks whether the user has the right to access the system and the corresponding file. It then calls the TFTP client and passes the file name to the client. The client then makes the TFTP connection to the TFTP server at the user site (see Figure 21.11).

Figure 21.11 *Using TELNET in conjunction with TFTP to provide security*

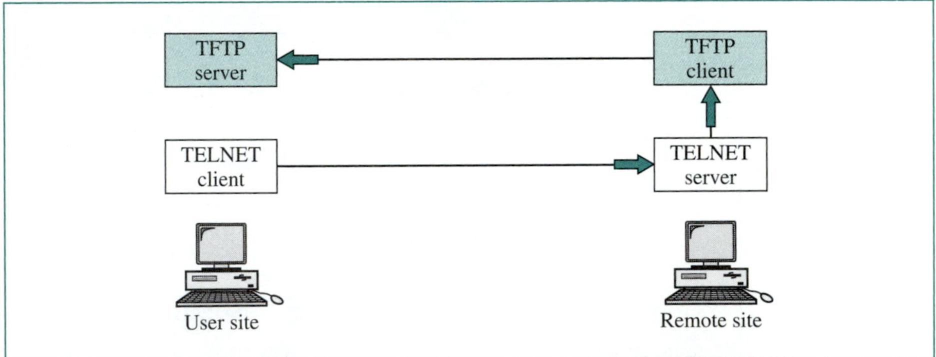

Note that in this process the user runs the TFTP server process and the remote site runs the TFTP client process. Also note that the action performed by the user is reversed: If the user wants to read a file, the remote site now uses the write operation; if the user wants to write a file, the remote site now uses the read operation.

21.8 APPLICATIONS

TFTP is very useful for basic file transfer where security is not a big issue. It can be used to initialize devices such as bridges or routers. Its main application is in conjunction with the BOOTP or DHCP protocols. TFTP requires only a small amount of memory and uses only the services of UDP and IP. It can easily be configured in ROM (or PROM). When the station is powered on, TFTP will be connected to a server and can download the configuration files from there. Figure 21.12 shows the idea. The powered-on station uses the BOOTP (or DHCP) client to get the name of the configuration file from the BOOTP server. The station then passes the name of the file to the TFTP client to get the contents of the configuration file from the TFTP server.

Figure 21.12 *Use of TFTP with BOOTP*

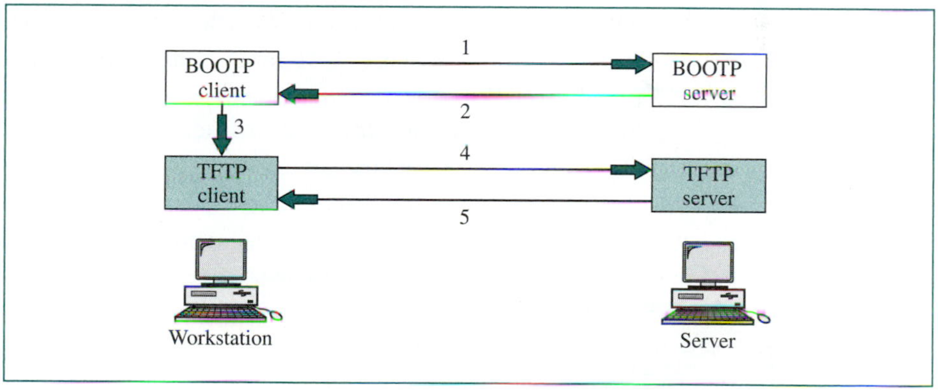

21.9 KEY TERMS

BOOTP

client

connection establishment

connection termination

damaged message

DHCP

duplicate message

ephemeral port

error control

flow control

lost acknowledgment

lost message

reading

server

sorcerer's apprentice bug

stop-and-wait protocol

Trivial File Transfer Protocol (TFTP)

UDP

well-known port

writing

21.10 SUMMARY

- Trivial File Transfer Protocol (TFTP) is a simple File Transfer Protocol without the complexities and sophistication of FTP.
- A client uses the services of TFTP to retrieve a copy of a file or send a copy of a file to a server.
- There are five types of TFTP messages:
  a. RRQ is a client message that establishes a connection for reading data from the server.
  b. WRQ is a client message that establishes a connection for writing data to the server.
  c. DATA is a client or server message that sends blocks of data.
  d. ACK acknowledges the receipt of a data block.
  e. ERROR is a message to convey a connection or transmission problem.
- TFTP is an application that uses UDP for its transport mechanism.
- TFTP uses RRQ, WRQ, ACK, and ERROR to establish connection. A DATA message with a block of data less than 512 bytes terminates connection.
- Each DATA message, except the last, carries 512 bytes of data from the file.
- TFTP uses a stop-and-wait protocol for flow control.
- Error control is needed in four situations: damaged message, lost message, lost acknowledgment, or duplicated message.
- TFTP employs symmetric transmission whereby both sender and receiver use time-outs for error handling.
- The sorcerer's apprentice bug is the duplication of both acknowledgments and data messages caused by TFTP's flow- and error-control mechanism.
- An extension to the TFTP protocol to allow options regarding the data block size has been proposed.
- TFTP has no provision for security. A second application program such as TELNET can be used in conjunction with TFTP to provide security.
- TFTP can be used in conjunction with BOOTP or DHCP to initialize devices by downloading configuration files.

21.11 PRACTICE SET

Multiple-Choice Questions

1. What type of message is sent in response to an RRQ that fails to establish a connection?
   a. WRQ
   b. DATA
   c. ACK
   d. ERROR

2. What type of message is sent to establish a connection to retrieve a file?
   a. RRQ
   b. WRQ
   c. DATA
   d. ACK
3. Which type of message is always a set number of bytes?
   a. RRQ
   b. WRQ
   c. DATA
   d. ACK
4. A DATA block is sent in response to a _______ message.
   a. RRQ
   b. WRQ
   c. ACK
   d. a or c
5. TFTP uses the _______ message for flow control.
   a. RRQ
   b. WRQ
   c. ACK
   d. ERROR
6. TFTP uses the _______ message for connection termination.
   a. DATA
   b. ACK
   c. ERROR
   d. a and b
7. An unauthorized user tries to send a file to a server using TFTP. What should be the response of the server?
   a. ACK
   b. ERROR
   c. DATA
   d. WRQ
8. The block number on a DATA message is 22. This always means _______.
   a. there were 21 previous blocks
   b. there were 20 previous blocks
   c. this is the last block
   d. none of the above
9. Which TFTP message contains a block number field?
   a. ERROR
   b. DATA
   c. ACK
   d. b and c

10. The ERROR message can follow a _______ message.
    a. RRQ
    b. WRQ
    c. DATA
    d. all of the above
11. Connection termination is signaled by a DATA message with _______ bytes.
    a. any positive number of
    b. 512
    c. 0 to 511
    d. all of the above
12. The flow-control mechanism in TFTP _______.
    a. is called stop-and-wait
    b. is called sliding window
    c. is nonexistent
    d. depends on the TFTP purpose (read or write)
13. If a message is _______, it is resent.
    a. damaged
    b. lost
    c. duplicated
    d. a and b
14. If a duplicate DATA message is received, _______.
    a. the sender sends an error message
    b. the connection is terminated
    c. the sender discards the duplicate
    d. the receiver discards the duplicate
15. One symptom of the sorcerer's apprentice bug is that _______.
    a. time-outs malfunction
    b. ACKS are duplicated
    c. DATA messages are duplicated
    d. b and c
16. When TFTP services are used in conjunction with TELNET for security reasons, the user site acts as the _______ and _______.
    a. TFTP server; TELNET client
    b. TFTP client; TELNET server
    c. TFTP server; TELNET server
    d. TFTP client; TELNET client

Exercises

17. Why do we need an RRQ or WRQ message in TFTP but not in FTP?
18. Show the encapsulation of an RRQ message in a UDP user datagram. Assume the file name is "Report" and the mode is ASCII. What is the size of the UDP datagram?
19. Show the encapsulation of a WRQ message in a UDP user datagram. Assume the file name is "Report" and the mode is ASCII. What is the size of the UDP datagram?
20. Show the encapsulation of a TFTP data message, carrying block number 7, in a UDP user datagram. What is the total size of the user datagram?
21. Host A uses TFTP to read 2,150 bytes of data from host B. Show all the TFTP commands including commands needed for connection establishment and termination. Assume no error.
22. Show all the user datagrams exchanged between the two hosts in exercise 21.
23. Redo exercise 21 but assume the second block is in error.
24. Show all the user datagrams exchanged between the two hosts in exercise 23.
25. Do some research and find the format of the proposed OACK message.
26. Do some research and find the types of options proposed to be appended to the RRQ and WRQ messages.

CHAPTER 22

Simple Mail Transfer Protocol (SMTP)

One of the most popular network services is electronic mail (email). The TCP/IP protocol that supports electronic mail on the Internet is called Simple Mail Transfer Protocol (SMTP). It is a system for sending messages to other computer users based on email addresses. SMTP provides for mail exchange between users on the same or different computers. SMTP supports:

- Sending a single message to one or more recipients.
- Sending messages that include text, voice, video, or graphics.
- Sending messages to users on networks outside the Internet.

Figure 22.1 shows the basic idea. The SMTP server uses the TCP well-known port 25.

Figure 22.1 *SMTP concept*

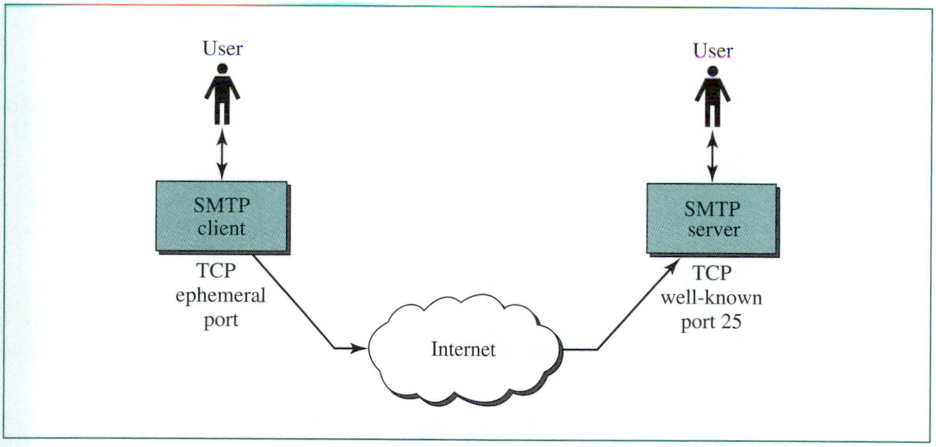

Starting with this simple figure, we will examine the components of the SMTP system, gradually adding complexity. Let us begin by breaking down both the SMTP client and server into two components: user agent (UA) and mail transfer agent (MTA).

The UA prepares the message, creates the envelope, and puts the message in the envelope. The MTA transfers the mail across the Internet. Figure 22.2 shows the previous figure with the addition of these two components.

Figure 22.2 *UAs and MTAs*

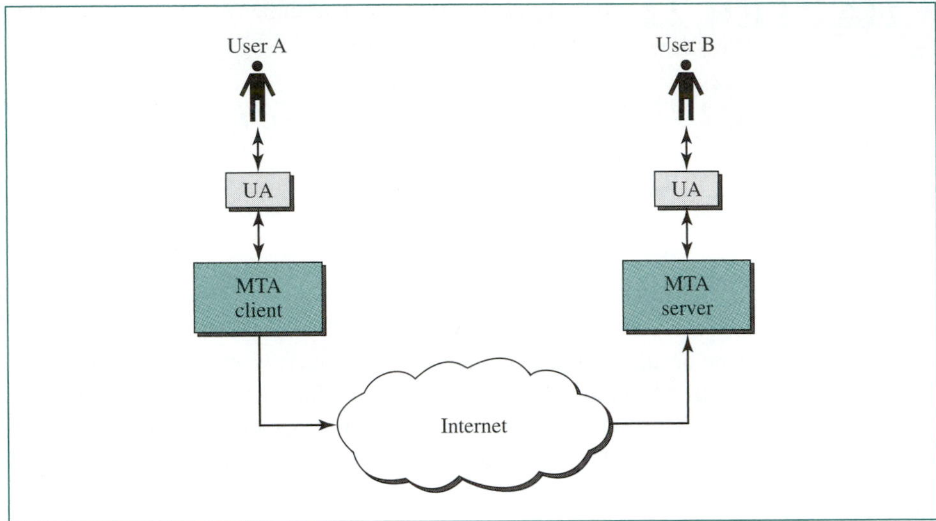

SMTP protocol allows a more complex system than the one shown. Relaying could be involved. Instead of just one MTA at the sender site and one at the receiving site, other MTAs, acting either as client or server, can relay the mail (see Figure 22.3).

Figure 22.3 *Relay MTAs*

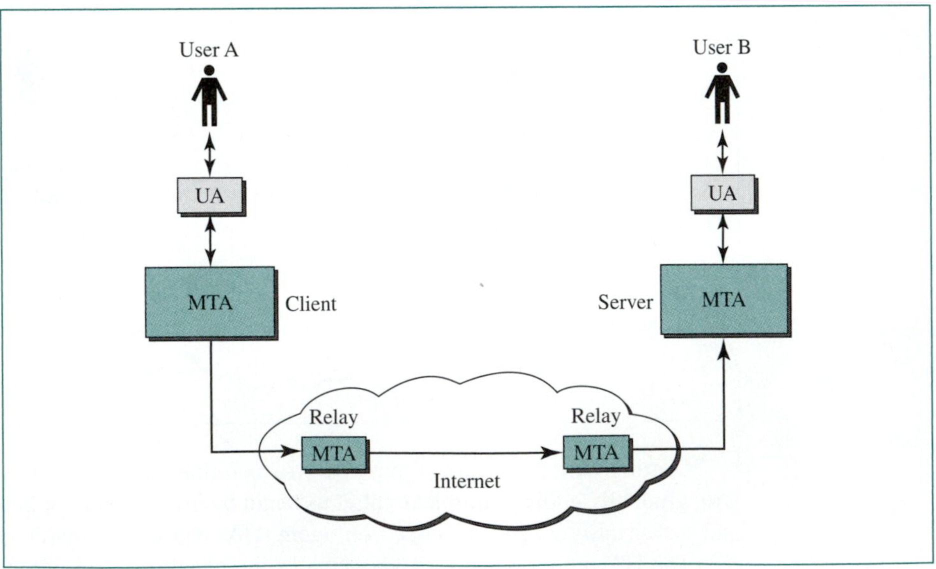

The relaying system allows sites that do not use the TCP/IP protocol suite to send email to users on other sites that may or may not use the TCP/IP protocol suite. This is accomplished through the use of a **mail gateway,** which is a relay MTA that can receive mail prepared by a protocol other than SMTP and transform it to SMTP format before sending it. It can also receive mail in SMTP format and change it to another format before sending it (see Figure 22.4).

Figure 22.4 *Mail gateway*

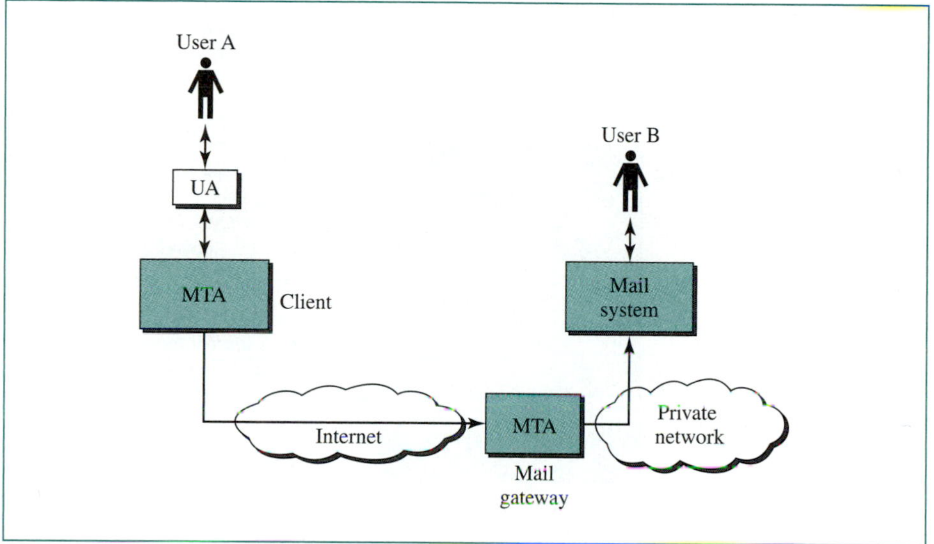

22.1 USER AGENT (UA)

A user agent is defined in SMTP, but the implementation details are not. The UA is normally a program used to send and receive mail. Popular user agent programs are MH, Berkeley Mail, Elm, Zmail, and Mush.

Some user agents have an extra user interface that allows window-type interactions with the system. Eudora is an example of this type of interface.

Sending Mail

To send mail, the user, through the UA, creates mail that looks very similar to postal mail. It has an *envelope* and a *message* (see Figure 22.5).

Envelope

The envelope usually contains the sender address, the receiver address, and other information.

Message

The message contains the *headers* and the *body*. The headers of the message define the sender, the receiver, the subject of the message, and some other information. The body of the message contains the actual information to be read by the recipient.

Figure 22.5 *Format of an email*

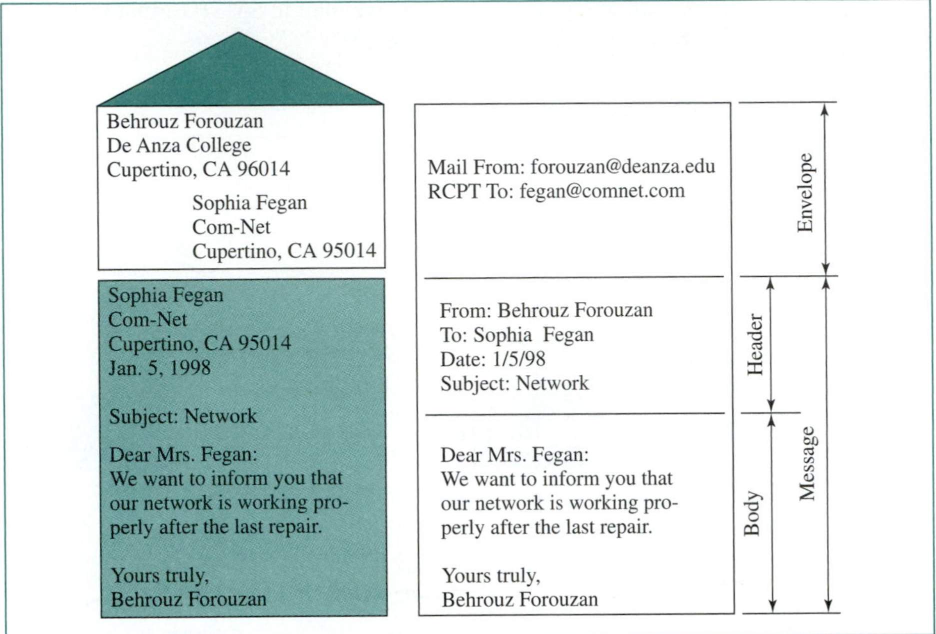

Receiving Mail

The user agent periodically checks the mailboxes. If a user has mail, the UA informs the user first by giving a notice. If the user is ready to read the mail, a list is displayed in which each line contains a summary of the information about a particular message in the mailbox. The summary usually includes the sender mail address, the subject, and the time the mail was sent or received. The user can select any of the messages and display its contents on the screen.

22.2 ADDRESSES

To deliver mail, a mail handling system must use an addressing system with unique addresses. The addressing system used by SMTP consists of two parts: a *local part* and a *domain name,* separated by an @ sign (see Figure 22.6).

Figure 22.6 *Email address*

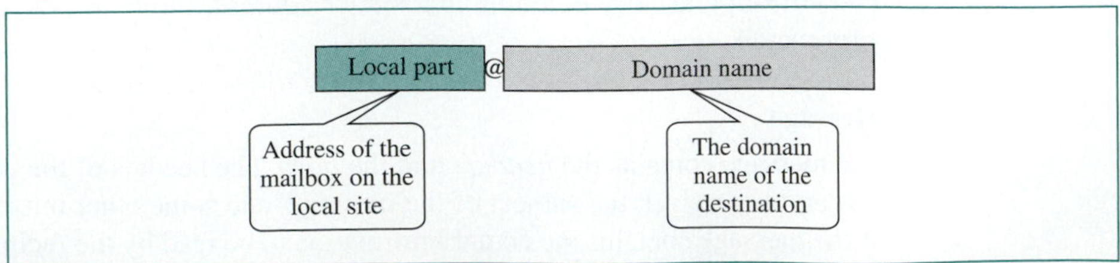

Local Part

The local part defines the name of a special file, called the user mailbox, where all of the mail received for a user is stored for retrieval by the user agent.

Domain Name

The second part of the address is the domain name. An organization usually selects one or more hosts to receive and send email; they are sometimes called *mail exchangers*. The domain name assigned to each mail exchanger either comes from the DNS database or it is a logical name (for example, the name of the organization).

The email addresses become more complex when we use mail gateways. In this case, the email address must define both the address of the gateway and the address of the actual recipient. The domain name must define the name of the mail gateway in the DNS database and the local part must define the local physical network, the computer attached to that network, and the user mailbox. Because some mailing systems do not use the mailing address format defined by the SMTP, this can create problems and confusion.

22.3 DELAYED DELIVERY

SMTP is different from other application programs that we have seen so far because it allows delayed delivery. This means that the message does not necessarily have to be delivered immediately but can be delayed at the sender site, the receiver site, or the intermediate servers.

Sender-Site Delay

The sending of a message can be delayed at the sender site. SMTP stipulates that the sender site must accommodate a *spooling* system in which messages are stored before being sent. After the user agent creates a message, it is delivered to the spool, which is a storage structure. The mail transfer system periodically (every 10 to 30 minutes) checks the mail stored in the spool to see if the mail can be sent. This depends on whether the IP address of the server has been obtained through DNS, if the receiver is ready, and so on. If the message cannot be sent, it remains in the spool to be checked in the next cycle. If a message cannot be delivered in the time-out period (usually three to five days), the mail returns to the sender (see Figure 22.7).

Receiver-Site Delay

After the message has been received, it does not have to be read by the recipient immediately. The mail can be stored in the mailbox of the receiver (see Figure 22.8).

Figure 22.7 *Sender-site delay*

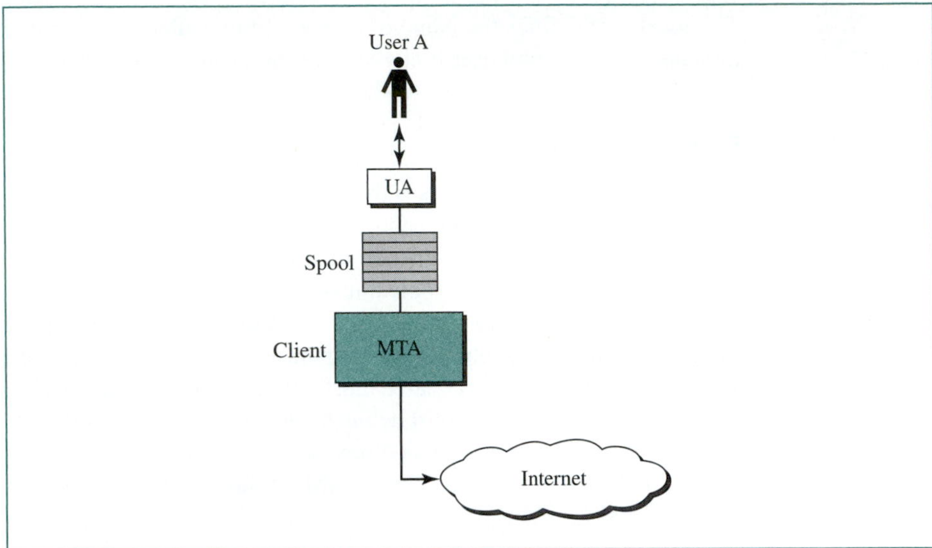

Figure 22.8 *Receiver-site delay*

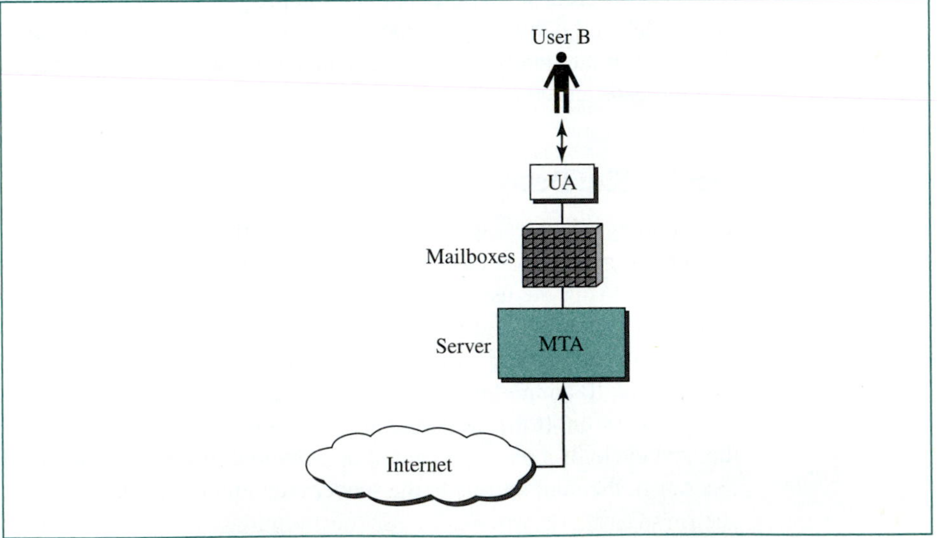

Intermediate Delay

As previously mentioned, SMTP allows intermediate MTAs to serve as clients and servers. They too can receive mail, keep mail messages in their own mailboxes and spools, and send them when appropriate.

22.4 ALIASES

SMTP allows one name, an *alias,* to represent several different email addresses; this is called *one-to-many alias expansion*. Also a single user can be defined by several different email addresses, called *many-to-one alias expansion*. To handle these, the system must include an alias expansion facility at both the sender and receiver site (see Figure 22.9).

Figure 22.9 *Alias expansion*

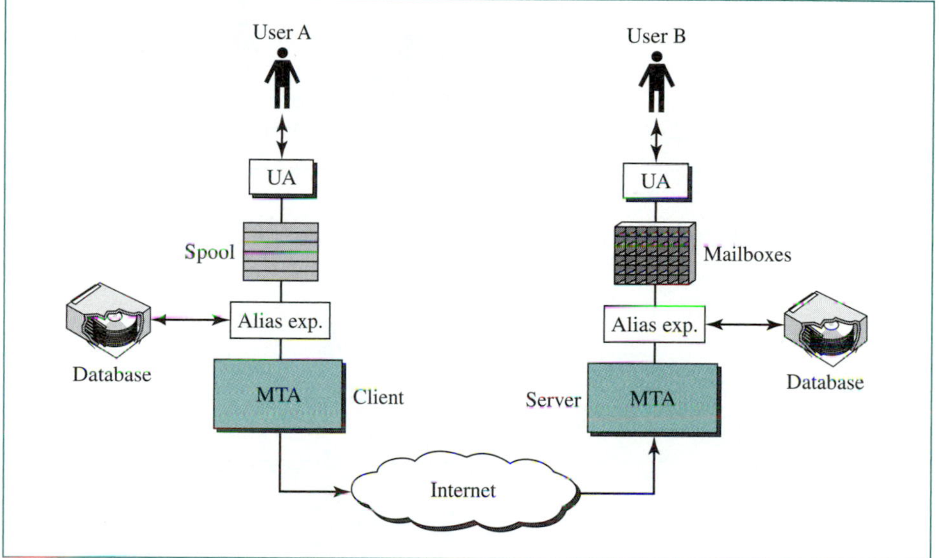

One-to-Many Expansion

In situations where the same message is to be sent to different recipients, the user can create an alias that is mapped to the list of the recipients. Every time a message is sent, the system checks the recipient's name against the alias expansion database; if there is an expansion for the defined name, separate messages, one for each entry in the expansion, must be prepared and handed to the mail delivery system. If there is no expansion for the recipient name, the name itself is the receiving address and a single message is delivered to the mail transfer entity (see Figure 22.10).

Many-to-One Expansion

A user can have several email addresses, but the user agent recognizes only one mailbox name. Usually the local parts of the address will differ. When a system receives mail, it checks the many-to-one expansion database. If a mailbox name corresponding to the local part of the received address is found, the mail is sent to that mailbox; otherwise, the mail is discarded (see Figure 22.11).

Figure 22.10 *One-to-many expansion*

Figure 22.11 *Many-to-one expansion*

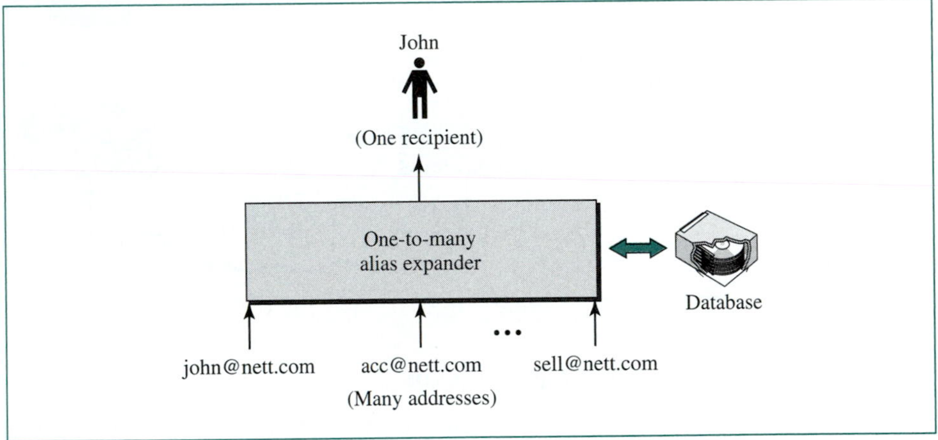

22.5 MAIL TRANSFER AGENT (MTA)

The actual mail transfer is done through mail transfer agents (MTAs). To send mail, a system must have the client MTA, and to receive mail, a system must have a server MTA. Although SMTP does not define a specific MTA, **Sendmail** is a commonly used UNIX system MTA.

SMTP simply defines how commands and responses must be sent back and forth. Each network is free to choose a software package for implementation. We will discuss the mechanism of mail transfer by the SMTP in the remainder of the chapter. However, first we present the whole picture of a bidirectional email system as defined by SMTP. Figure 22.12 illustrates the process of sending and receiving email as described above.

For a computer to be able to send and receive mail using SMTP, it must have most of the entities (the user interface is not necessary) defined in the figure. The user interface is a component that creates a user-friendly environment. A popular example of a user interface is Eudora.

Figure 22.12 *The entire email system*

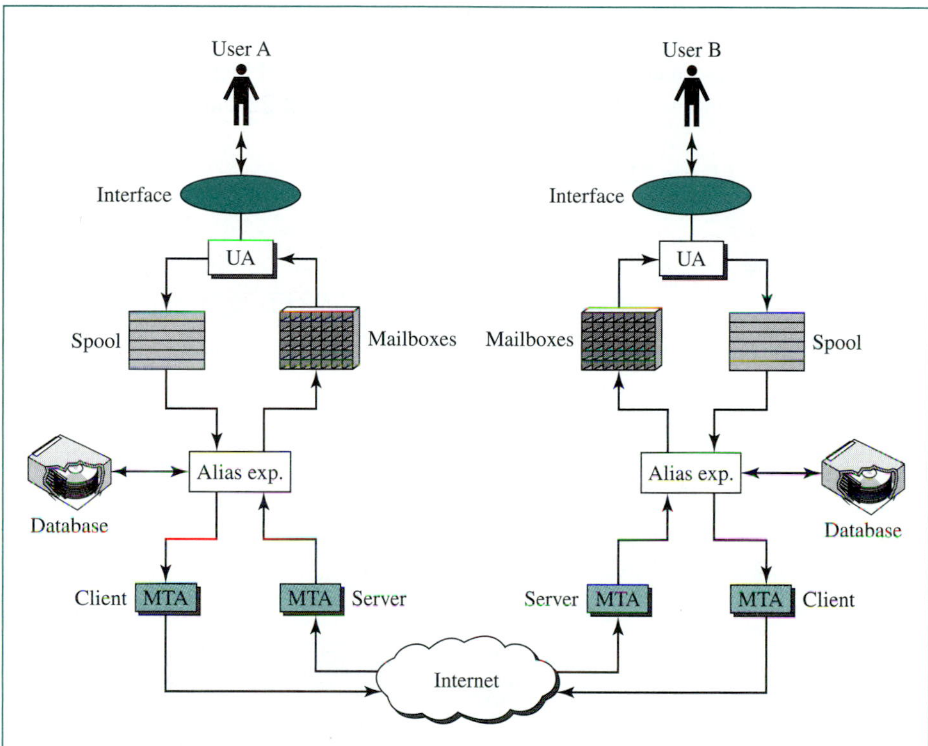

22.6 COMMANDS AND RESPONSES

SMTP uses commands and responses to transfer messages between an MTA client and an MTA server (see Figure 22.13).

Figure 22.13 *Commands and responses*

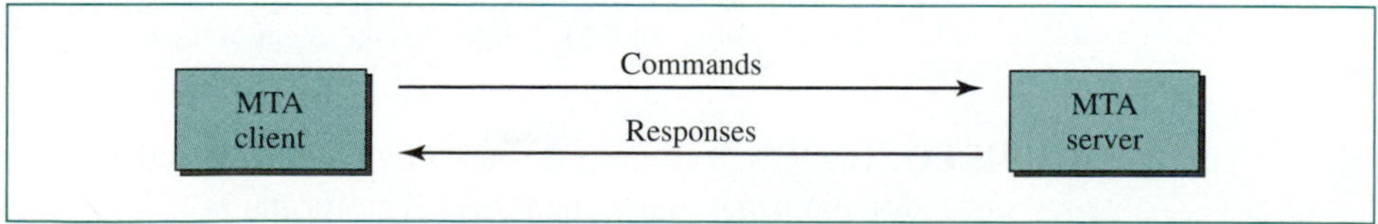

Each command or reply is terminated by a two-character (carriage return and line feed) end-of-line token.

Commands

Commands are sent from the client to the server. The format of a command is shown in Figure 22.14. It consists of a keyword followed by zero or more arguments. SMTP defines 14 commands. The first five are mandatory; every implementation must support these five commands. The next three are often used and highly recommended. The last six are seldom used. The commands are listed in Table 22.1 and described in more detail below.

Figure 22.14 *Command format*

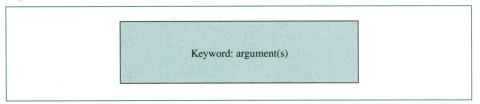

Keyword: argument(s)

Table 22.1 *Commands*

Keyword	*Argument(s)*
HELO	Sender's host name
MAIL FROM	Sender of the message
RCPT TO	Intended recipient of the message
DATA	Body of the mail
QUIT	
RSET	
VRFY	Name of recipient to be verified
NOOP	
TURN	
EXPN	Mailing list to be expanded
HELP	Command name
SEND FROM	Intended recipient of the message
SMOL FROM	Intended recipient of the message
SMAL FROM	Intended recipient of the message

- **HELO.** The HELO command is used by the client to identify itself. The argument is the domain name of the client host. The format is

HELO: challenger.atc.fhda.edu

- **MAIL FROM.** The MAIL command is used by the client to identify the sender of the message. The argument is the email address of the sender (local part plus the domain name). The format is

MAIL FROM: forouzan@challenger.atc.fhda.edu

- **RCPT TO.** The RCPT (Recipient) command is used by the client to identify the intended recipient of the message. The argument is the email address of the recipient. If there are multiple recipients, the command is repeated. The format is

RCPT TO: betsy@mcgraw-hill.com

- **DATA.** The DATA command is used to send the actual message. All lines that follow the DATA command are treated as the mail message. The message is terminated by a line containing just a period. The format is

DATA
This is the message
to be sent to the McGraw-Hill
Company.
.

- **QUIT.** The QUIT command terminates the message. The format is

QUIT

- **RSET.** The RSET (reset) command aborts the current mail transaction. The stored information about the sender and recipient is deleted. The connection will be reset.

RSET

- **VRFY.** The VRFY (verify) command is used to verify the address of the recipient, which is sent as the argument. The sender can ask the receiver to confirm that a name identifies a valid recipient. Its format is

VRFY: betsy@mcgraw-hill.com

- **NOOP.** The NOOP (no operation) command is used by the client to check the status of the recipient. It requires an answer from the recipient. Its format is

NOOP

- **TURN.** The TURN command lets the sender and the recipient switch positions, whereby the sender becomes the recipient and vice versa. However, most SMTP implementations today do not support this feature. The format is

TURN

- **EXPN.** The EXPN (expand) command asks the receiving host to expand the mailing list sent as the arguments and to return the mailbox addresses of the recipients that comprise the list. The format is

EXPN: x y z

- **HELP.** The HELP command asks the recipient to send information about the command sent as the argument. The format is

HELP: mail

- **SEND FROM.** The SEND command specifies that the mail is to be delivered to the terminal of the recipient, and not the mailbox. If the recipient is not logged in, the mail is bounced back. The argument is the address of the sender. The format is

SEND FROM: forouzan@fhda.atc.edu

- **SMOL FROM.** The SMOL (send to the mailbox or terminal) command specifies that the mail is to be delivered to the terminal or the mailbox of the recipient. This means that if the recipient is logged in, the mail is delivered only to the terminal. If the recipient is not logged in, the mail is delivered to the mailbox. The argument is the address of the sender. The format is

SMOL FROM: forouzan@fhda.atc.edu

- **SMAL FROM.** The SMAL (send to the mailbox and terminal) command specifies that the mail is to be delivered to the terminal and the mailbox of the recipient. This means that if the recipient is logged in, the mail is delivered to the terminal and the mailbox. If the recipient is not logged in, the mail is delivered only to the mailbox. The argument is the address of the sender. The format is

SMAL FROM: forouzan@fhda.atc.edu

Responses

Responses are sent from the server to the client. A response is a three-digit code that may be followed by additional textual information. The meanings of the first digit are as follows:

- **2yz (positive completion reply).** If the first digit is 2 (digit 1 is not in use today), it means that the requested command has been successfully completed and a new command can be started.
- **3yz (positive intermediate reply).** If the first digit is 3, it means that the requested command has been accepted, but the recipient needs some more information before completion can occur.
- **4yz (transient negative completion reply).** If the first digit is 4, it means the requested command has been rejected, but the error condition is temporary. The command can be sent again.
- **5yz (permanent negative completion reply).** If the first digit is 5, it means the requested command has been rejected. The command cannot be sent again.

The second and the third digits provide further details about the responses. Table 22.2 lists some of the responses.

Table 22.2 *Responses*

Code	*Description*
	Positive Completion Reply
211	System status or help reply
214	Help message
220	Service ready
221	Service closing transmission channel
250	Request command completed
251	User not local; the message will be forwarded
	Positive Intermediate Reply
354	Start mail input
	Transient Negative Completion Reply
421	Service not available
450	Mailbox not available
451	Command aborted: local error
452	Command aborted; insufficient storage

Table 22.2 *Responses (continued)*

Code	*Description*
Permanent Negative Completion Reply	
500	Syntax error; unrecognized command
501	Syntax error in parameters or arguments
502	Command not implemented
503	Bad sequence of commands
504	Command temporarily not implemented
550	Command is not executed; mailbox unavailable
551	User not local
552	Requested action aborted; exceeded storage location
553	Requested action not taken; mailbox name not allowed
554	Transaction failed

22.7 MAIL TRANSFER PHASES

The process of transferring a mail message occurs in three phases: connection establishment, mail transfer, and connection termination.

Connection Establishment

After a client has made a TCP connection to the well-known port 25, the SMTP server starts the connection phase. This phase involves the following three steps, which are illustrated in Figure 22.15.

Figure 22.15 *Connection establishment*

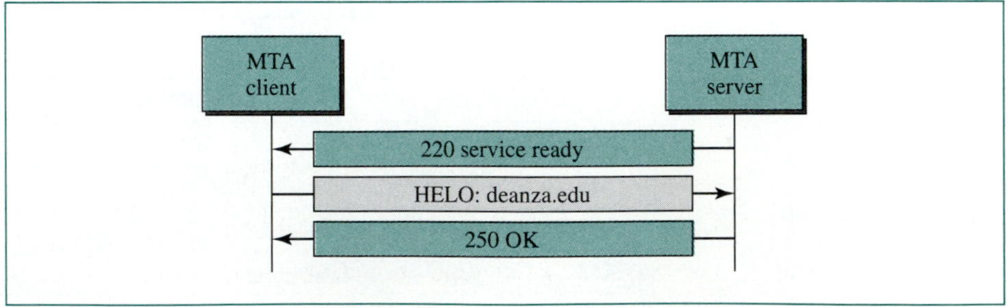

1. The server sends code 220 (service ready) to tell the client that it is ready to receive mail. If the server is not ready, it sends code 421 (service not available).
2. The client sends the HELO message to identify itself using its domain name address. This step is necessary to inform the server of the domain name of the

client. Remember that during TCP connection establishment, the sender and receiver know each other through their IP addresses.

3. The server responds with code 250 (request command completed) or some other code depending on the situation.

Message Transfer

After connection has been established between the SMTP client and server, a single message between a sender and one or more recipients can be exchanged. This phase involves eight steps. Steps 3 and 4 are repeated if there is more than one recipient (see Figure 22.16).

Figure 22.16 *Message transfer*

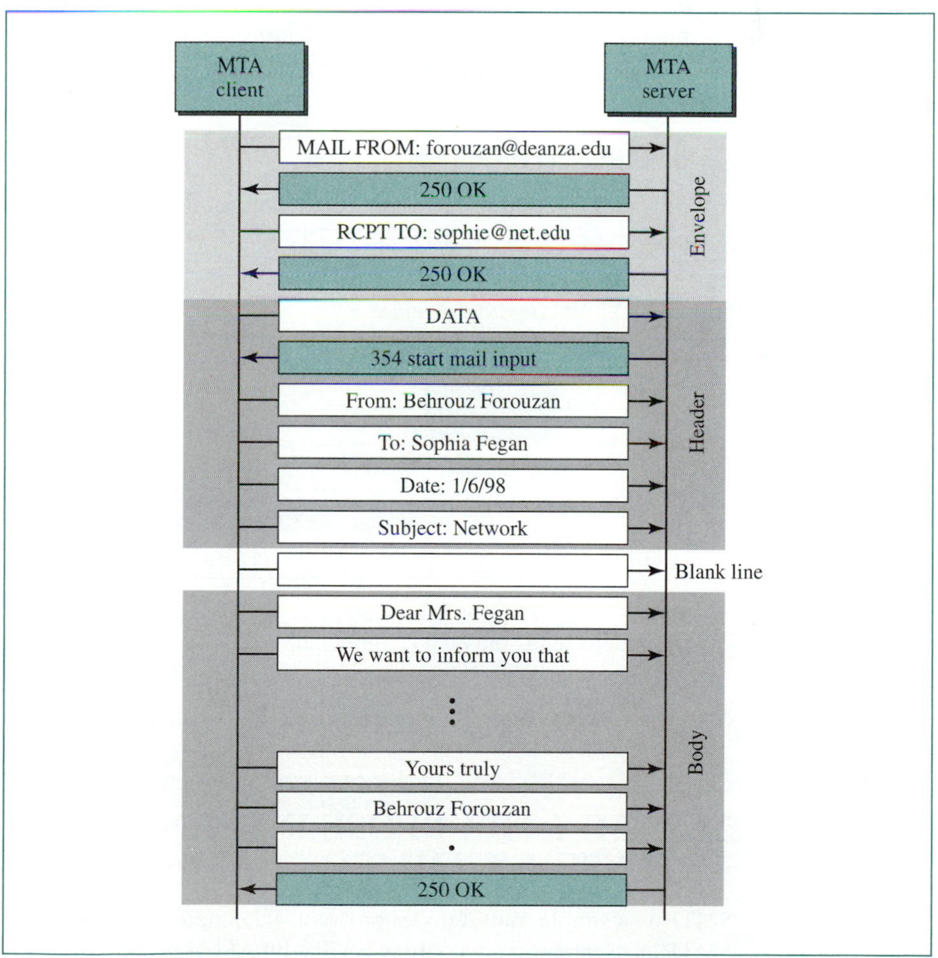

1. The client sends the MAIL message to introduce the sender of the message. It includes the mail address of the sender (mailbox and the domain name). This step is needed to give the server the return mail address for returning errors and reporting messages.
2. The server responds with code 250 or some other appropriate code.
3. The client sends the RCPT (recipient) message, which includes the mail address of the recipient.
4. The server responds with code 250 or some other appropriate code.
5. The client sends the DATA message to initialize the message transfer.
6. The server responds with code 354 (start mail input) or some other appropriate message.
7. The client sends the contents of the message in consecutive lines. Each line is terminated by a two-character end-of-line token (carriage return and line feed). The message is terminated by a line containing just a period.
8. The server responds with code 250 (OK) or some other appropriate code.

Connection Termination

After the message is transferred successfully, the client terminates the connection. This phase involves two steps (see Figure 22.17).

Figure 22.17 *Connection termination*

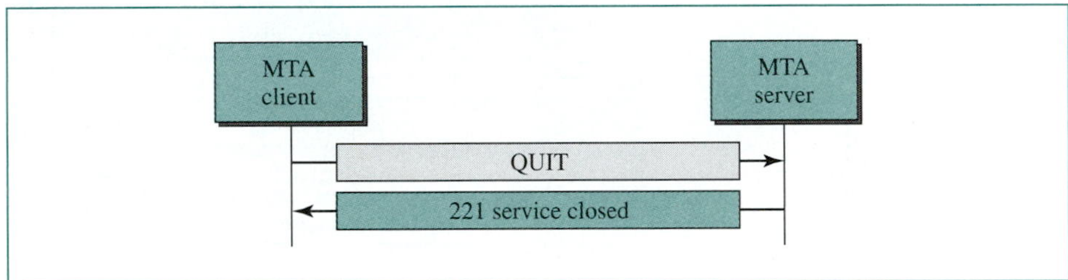

1. The client sends the QUIT command.
2. The server responds with code 221 or some other appropriate code.

After the connection termination phase, the TCP connection must be closed.

22.8 MULTIPURPOSE INTERNET MAIL EXTENSIONS (MIME)

SMTP is a simple mail transfer protocol. Its simplicity, however, comes with a price. SMTP can send messages only in NVT 7-bit ASCII format. In other words, it has some limitations. For example, it cannot be used for languages that are not supported by 7-bit ASCII characters (such as French, German, Hebrew, Russian, Chinese, and Japanese). Also, it cannot be used to send binary files or to send video or audio data.

Multipurpose Internet Mail Extensions (MIME) is a supplementary protocol that allows non-ASCII data to be sent through SMTP. MIME is not a mail protocol and cannot replace SMTP; it is only an extension to SMTP.

MIME transforms non-ASCII data at the sender site to NVT ASCII data and delivers it to the client SMTP to be sent through the Internet. The server SMTP at the receiving side receives the NVT ASCII data and delivers it to MIME to be transformed back to the original data.

We can think of MIME as a set of software functions that transforms non-ASCII data to ASCII data and vice versa (see Figure 22.18).

Figure 22.18 *MIME*

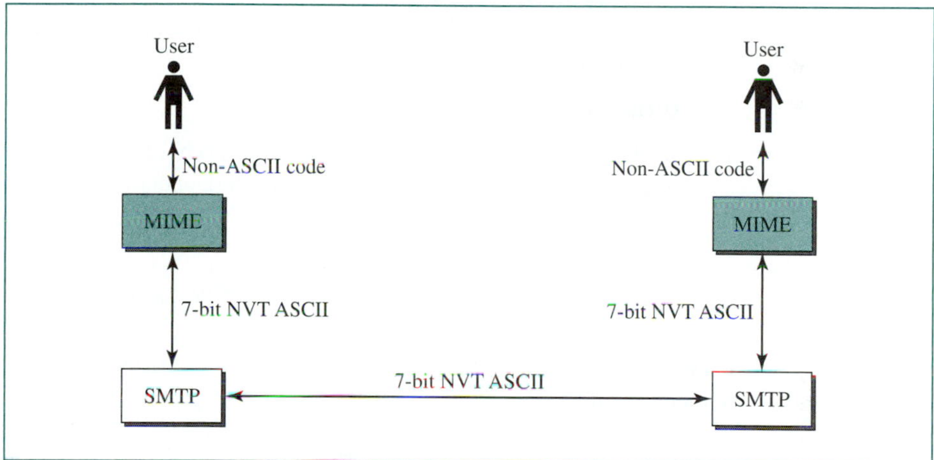

MIME defines five headers that can be added to the original SMTP header section to define the transformation parameters:

1. MIME-Version
2. Content-Type
3. Content-Transfer-Encoding
4. Content-Id
5. Content-Description

Figure 22.19 shows the original header and the extended header. We will describe each header in detail.

MIME-Version

This header defines the version of MIME used. The current version is 1.1.

MIME-Version: 1.1

Figure 22.19 *MIME header*

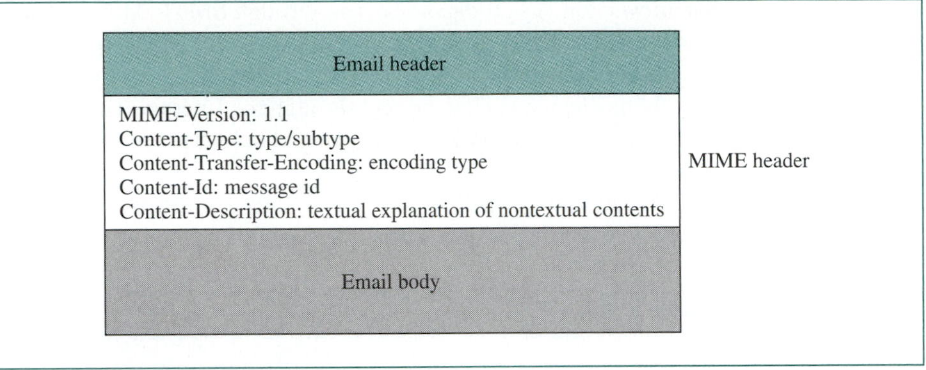

Content-Type

This header defines the type of data used in the body of the message. The content type and the content subtype are separated by a slash. Depending on the subtype, the header may contain other parameters.

Content-Type: <type / subtype; parameters>

MIME allows seven different types of data. These are listed in Table 22.3 and described in more detail below.

Table 22.3 *Data types and subtypes in MIME*

Type	*Subtype*	*Description*
Text	Plain	Unformatted text
Multipart	Mixed	Body contains ordered parts of different data types
	Parallel	Same as above, but no order
	Digest	Similar to Mixed, but the default is message/RFC822
	Alternative	Parts are different versions of the same message
Message	RFC822	Body is an encapsulated message
	Partial	Body is a fragment of a bigger message
	External-Body	Body is a reference to another message
Image	JPEG	Image is in JPEG format
	GIF	Image is in GIF format
Video	MPEG	Video is in MPEG format
Audio	Basic	Single channel encoding of voice at 8 KHz
Application	PostScript	Adobe PostScript
	Octet-stream	General binary data (eight-bit bytes)

- **Text.** The original message is in 7-bit ASCII format and no transformation by MIME is needed. There is only one subtype currently used, *plain*.
- **Multipart.** The body contains multiple, independent parts. The multipart header needs to define the boundary between each part. The boundary is used as a parameter. It is a string token that is repeated before each part on a separate line by itself and preceded by two hyphens. The body will be terminated using the boundary token preceded and terminated by two hyphens.

  Four subtypes are defined for this type: *mixed, parallel, digest,* and *alternative*. In the mixed subtype, the parts must be presented to the recipient in the exact order as in the message. Each part has a different type and is defined at the boundary. The parallel subtype is similar to the mixed subtype, except that the order of the parts is unimportant. The digest subtype is also similar to the mixed subtype except that the default type/subtype is message/RFC822 as defined below. In the alternative subtype, the same message is repeated using different formats. The following is an example of a multipart message using a mixed subtype:

```
Content-Type: multipart/mixed; boundary=xxxx

     --xxxx
     Content-Type: text/plain;
     ..............................................
     --xxxx
     Content-Type: image/gif;
     ..............................................
     --xxxx--
```

- **Message.** In the message type, the body is itself a whole mail message, a part of a mail message, or a pointer to a message. Three subtypes are currently used: *RFC822, partial,* or *external-body.* The subtype RFC822 is used if the body is encapsulating another message (including header and the body). The subtype partial is used if the original message has been fragmented into different mail messages and this mail message is one of the fragments. The fragments must be reassembled at the destination by MIME. Three parameters must be added: *id, number,* and the *total*. The id identifies the message and is present in all the fragments. The number defines the sequence order of the fragment. The total defines the number of fragments that comprise the original message. The following is an example of a message with three fragments:

```
Content-Type: message/partial;
id="forouzan@challenger.atc.fhda.edu";
number=1;
total=3;

........................
........................
```

The subtype external-body indicates that the body does not contain the actual message but is only a reference (pointer) to the original message. The parameters following the subtype define how to access the original message. The following is an example:

```
Content-Type: message/external-body;
name="report.txt";
site="fhda.edu";
access-type="ftp";

........................
........................
```

- **Image.** The original message is a stationary image, indicating that there is no animation. The two currently used subtypes are Joint Photographic Experts Group (*JPEG*), which uses image compression, and Graphics Interchange Format (*GIF*).
- **Video.** The original message is a time-varying image (animation). The only subtype is Motion Picture Experts Group (*MPEG*). If the animated image contains sounds, it must be sent separately using the audio content type.
- **Audio.** The original message is a sound. The only subtype is basic, which uses 8 kHz standard audio data.
- **Application.** The original message is a type of data not previously defined. There are only two subtypes used currently: *octet-stream* and *PostScript.* Octet-stream is used when the data must be interpreted as a sequence of 8-bit bytes (binary file). PostScript is used when the data is in Adobe PostScript format.

Content-Transfer-Encoding

This header defines the method to encode the messages into 0s and 1s for transport:

Content-Transfer-Encoding: <type>

The five types of encoding are listed in Table 22.4.

Table 22.4 *Content-transfer-encoding*

Type	*Description*
7bit	NVT ASCII characters and short lines
8bit	Non-ASCII characters and short lines
binary	Non-ASCII characters with unlimited-length lines
Base64	6-bit blocks of data are encoded into 8-bit ASCII characters
Quoted-printable	Non-ASCII characters are encoded as an equal sign followed by an ASCII code

- **7bit.** This is 7-bit NVT ASCII encoding. Although no special transformation is needed, the length of the line should not exceed 1,000 characters.
- **8bit.** This is 8-bit encoding. Non-ASCII characters can be sent, but the length of the line still should not exceed 1,000 characters. MIME does not do any encoding here; the underlying SMTP protocol must be able to transfer 8-bit non-ASCII characters. It is, therefore, not recommended. Base64 and quoted-printable types are preferable.
- **Binary.** This is 8-bit encoding. Non-ASCII characters can be sent, and the length of the line can exceed 1,000 characters. MIME does not do any encoding here; the underlying SMTP protocol must be able to transfer binary data. It is, therefore, not recommended. Base64 and quoted-printable types are preferable.
- **Base64.** This is a solution for sending data made of bytes when the highest bit is not necessarily zero. Base64 transforms this type of data to printable characters, which can then be sent as ASCII characters or any type of character set supported by the underlying mail transfer mechanism.

  Base64 divides the binary data (made of streams of bits) into 24-bit blocks. Each block is then divided into four sections, each made of 6 bits (see Figure 22.20).

Figure 22.20 *Base64*

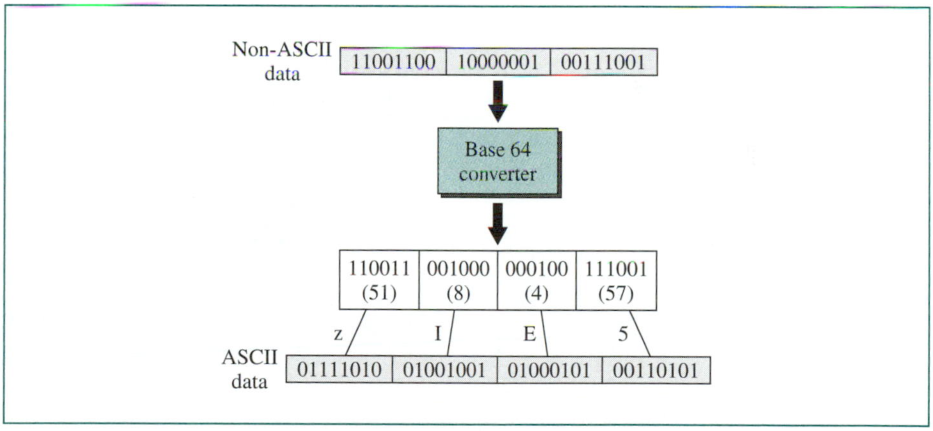

Each 6-bit section is interpreted as one character according to Table 22.5.

- **Quoted-printable.** Base64 is a redundant encoding scheme; that is, 24 bits becomes four characters, and eventually sent as 32 bits. We have an overhead of 25 percent. If the data consist of mostly ASCII characters with a small non-ASCII portion, we can use quoted-printable encoding. If a character is ASCII, it is sent as is. If a character is not ASCII, it is sent as three characters. The first character is the equal sign (=). The next two characters are the hexadecimal representation of the byte. Figure 22.21 shows an example.

Table 22.5 *Base64 encoding table*

Value	*Code*	*Value*	*Code*	*Value*	*Code*	*Value*	*Code*	*Value*	*Code*	*Value*	*Code*
0	**A**	11	**L**	22	**W**	33	**h**	44	**s**	55	**3**
1	**B**	12	**M**	23	**X**	34	**i**	45	**t**	56	**4**
2	**C**	13	**N**	24	**Y**	35	**j**	46	**u**	57	**5**
3	**D**	14	**O**	25	**Z**	36	**k**	47	**v**	58	**6**
4	**E**	15	**P**	26	**a**	37	**l**	48	**w**	59	**7**
5	**F**	16	**Q**	27	**b**	38	**m**	49	**x**	60	**8**
6	**G**	17	**R**	28	**c**	39	**n**	50	**y**	61	**9**
7	**H**	18	**S**	29	**d**	40	**o**	51	**z**	62	+
8	**I**	19	**T**	30	**e**	41	**p**	52	**0**	63	/
9	**J**	20	**U**	31	**f**	42	**q**	53	**1**		
10	**K**	21	**V**	32	**g**	43	**r**	54	**2**		

Figure 22.21 *Quoted-printable*

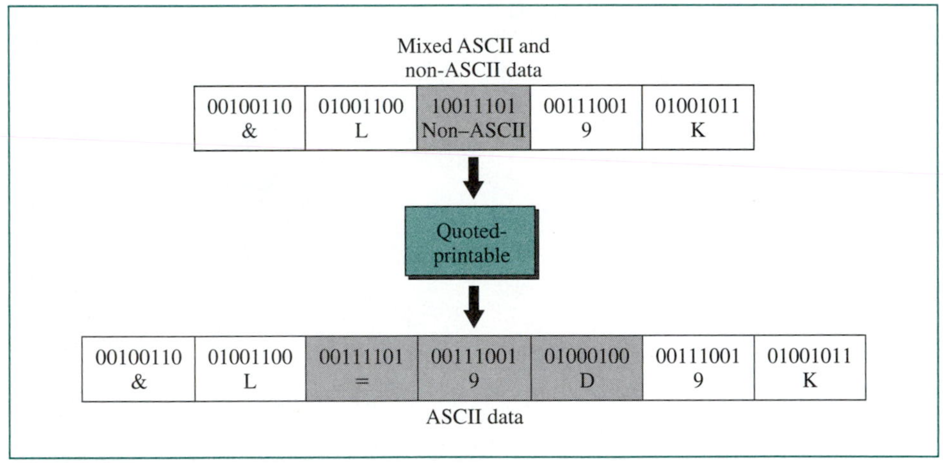

Content-Id

This header uniquely identifies the whole message in a multiple message environment.

Content-Id: id=<content-id>

Content-Description

This header defines whether the body is image, audio, or video.

Content-Description: <description>

22.9 MAIL DELIVERY

The delivery of email from the sender to the receiver consists of three stages (see Figure 22.22).

Figure 22.22 *Email delivery*

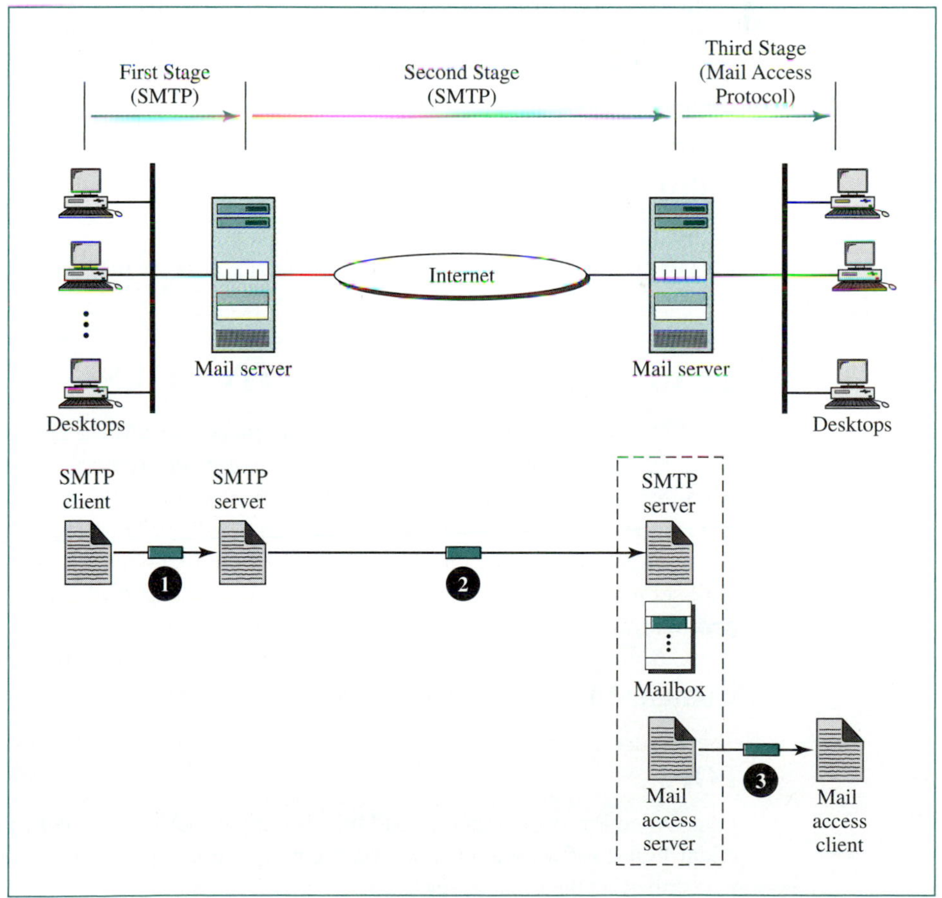

First Stage

In the first stage, the email goes from the user agent to the local server. The mail does not go directly to the remote server because it (the remote server) may not be available at all times. Therefore, the mail is stored in the local server until it can be sent. The user agent uses SMTP client software and the local server uses SMTP server software.

Second Stage

In the second stage, the email is relayed by the local server, which now acts as the SMTP client, to the remote server, which is the SMTP server in this stage. The email is delivered to the remote server not to the remote user agent. The reason is that SMTP messages must be received by a server that is always running since mail can arrive at any time. However, people often turn off their computers at the end of the day, and those with laptops or mobile computers do not normally have them on all the time. So usually an organization (or an ISP) assigns a computer to be the email server and run the SMTP server program. The email is received by this mail server and stored in the mailbox of the user for later retrieval.

Third Stage

In the third stage, the remote user agent uses a mail access protocol such as POP3 or IMAP4 (both discussed in the next section) to access the mailbox and obtain the mail.

22.10 MAIL ACCESS PROTOCOLS

The first and the second stages of mail delivery use SMTP. However, SMTP is not involved in the third stage because SMTP is a *push* protocol; it pushes the message from the sender to the receiver even if the receiver does not want it. The operation of SMTP starts with the sender not the receiver. On the other hand, the third stage needs a *pull* protocol; the operation must start with the recipient. The mail must stay in the mail server mailbox until the recipient retrieves it. The third stage uses a **mail access protocol.**

Currently two mail access protocols are available: Post Office Protocol, version 3 (POP3) and Internet Mail Access Protocol, version 4 (IMAP4).

POP3

Post Office Protocol, version 3 (POP3) is simple, but it is limited in functionality. The client POP3 software is installed on the recipient computer; the server POP3 software is installed on the mail server.

Mail access starts with the client when the user needs to download its email from the mailbox on the mail server. The client (user agent) opens a connection with the server on TCP port 110. It then sends its user name and password to access the mailbox. The user can then list and retrieve the mail messages, one by one. Figure 22.23 shows an example of downloading using POP3.

Figure 22.23 *POP3*

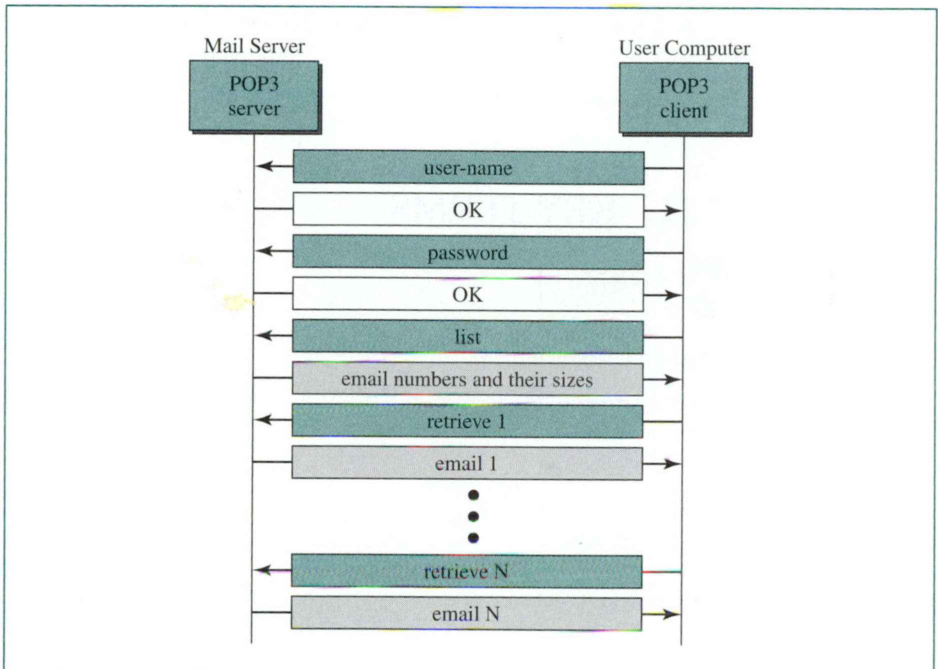

POP3 has two modes: the delete mode and the keep mode. In the delete mode, the mail is deleted from the mailbox after each retrieval. In the keep mode, the mail remains in the mailbox after retrieval. The delete mode is normally used when the user is working at her permanent computer and can save and organize the received mail after reading or replying. The keep mode is normally used when the user accesses her mail away from her primary computer (e.g., a laptop). The mail is read but kept in the system for later retrieval and organizing.

IMAP4

Another mail access protocol is Internet Mail Access Protocol, version 4 (IMAP4). IMAP4 is similar to POP3, but it has more features; IMAP4 is more powerful and more complex.

POP3 is deficient in several ways. It does not allow the user to organize her mail on the server; the user cannot have different folders on the server. (Of course, the user can create folders on her own computer.) In addition, POP3 does not allow the user to partially check the contents of the mail before downloading.

IMAP4 provides the following extra functions:

- A user can check the email header prior to downloading.
- A user can search the contents of the email for a specific string of characters prior to downloading.
- A user can partially download email. This is especially useful if bandwidth is limited and the email contains multimedia with high bandwidth requirements.
- A user can create, delete, or rename mailboxes on the mail server.
- A user can create a hierarchy of mailboxes in a folder for email storage.

22.11 KEY TERMS

alias

body

connection establishment

connection termination

domain name

envelope

header

Internet Mail Access Protocol, version 4 (IMAP4)

local address

mail access protocol

mail exchanger

mail gateway

mail transfer agent (MTA)

many-to-one alias expansion

message

message transfer

Multipurpose Internet Mail Extensions (MIME)

one-to-many alias expansion

Post Office Protocol, version 3 (POP3)

relay MTA

Simple Mail Transfer Protocol (SMTP)

spooling system

user agent (UA)

22.12 SUMMARY

- The TCP/IP protocol that supports email on the Internet is called Simple Mail Transfer Protocol (SMTP).
- Both SMTP client and server require a user agent (UA) and a mail transfer agent (MTA).
- The UA prepares the message, creates the envelope, and puts the message in the envelope.
- The mail address consists of two parts: a local address (user mailbox) and a domain name. The form is localname@domainname.

- A mail gateway translates mail formats.
- Delivery of SMTP messages can be delayed at the sender site, the receiver site, or at intermediate servers.
- An alias allows one user to have multiple email addresses or many users to share the same email address.
- The MTA transfers the mail across the Internet.
- Sendmail is a commonly used UNIX system MTA.
- SMTP uses commands and responses to transfer messages between an MTA client and an MTA server.
- The steps in transferring a mail message are:
  a. connection establishment
  b. mail transfer
  c. connection termination
- Multipurpose Internet Mail Extension (MIME) is an extension of SMTP that allows the transfer of multimedia messages.
- Post Office Protocol, version 3 (POP3) and Internet Mail Access Protocol, version 4 (IMAP4) are protocols used by a mail server in conjunction with SMTP to receive and hold mail for hosts.

22.13 PRACTICE SET

Multiple-Choice Questions

1. The purpose of the UA is _______.
   a. message preparation
   b. envelope creation
   c. transferal of messages across the Internet
   d. a and b
2. The purpose of the MTA is _______.
   a. message preparation
   b. envelope creation
   c. transferal of messages across the Internet
   d. a and b
3. When a message is sent using SMTP _______ UAs are involved.
   a. only one
   b. only two
   c. only three
   d. at least two

4. Email cannot be sent _______.
   a. if the sending site does not use TCP/IP
   b. if the receiving site does not use TCP/IP
   c. through private networks
   d. none of the above
5. Which part of the mail created by the UA contains the sender and receiver addresses?
   a. envelope
   b. message
   c. header
   d. body
6. Which part of the mail created by the UA contains the sender and receiver names?
   a. envelope
   b. address
   c. header
   d. body
7. Hosts in a LAN that send and receive email are called _______.
   a. mail spools
   b. mail gateways
   c. mail files
   d. mail exchangers
8. A _______ can transform non-SMTP mail to SMTP format and vice versa.
   a. mail spools
   b. mail gateways
   c. mail files
   d. mail exchangers
9. In the mail address mackenzie@pit.arc.nasa.gov, what is the domain name?
   a. mackenzie
   b. pit.arc.nasa.gov
   c. mackenzie@pit.arc.nasa.gov
   d. a and b
10. Delayed delivery means that delivery of email is delayed at _______.
    a. the sender site
    b. the receiver site
    c. the intermediate server
    d. any of the above

11. The _______ is a storage structure that can hold outgoing mail.
    a. MTA
    b. alias expander
    c. spool
    d. mail exchanger
12. A very common MTA in use is _______.
    a. Sendmail
    b. Eudora
    c. MIME
    d. all of the above
13. This command identifies the recipient of the mail.
    a. HELO
    b. MAIL FROM
    c. RCPT TO
    d. RSET
14. This command identifies the sender of the mail.
    a. HELO
    b. MAIL FROM
    c. RCPT TO
    d. VRFY
15. This command identifies the client host.
    a. HELO
    b. MAIL FROM
    c. RCPT TO
    d. RSET
16. The _______ command specifies that mail is not delivered if the recipient is not logged on.
    a. EXPN
    b. SEND FROM
    c. SMOL FROM
    d. SMAL FROM
17. The _______ command specifies that mail is delivered only to the terminal if the recipient is logged on.
    a. EXPN
    b. SEND FROM
    c. SMOL FROM
    d. SMAL FROM

18. In the _______ command, mail is delivered to the terminal and mailbox if the recipient is logged on.
    a. EXPN
    b. SEND TO
    c. SMOL FROM
    d. SMAL FROM
19. A _______ reply is sent in response to a successfully completed command.
    a. positive completion
    b. positive intermediate
    c. transient negative completion
    d. permanent negative completion
20. A _______ reply is sent in response to a rejected command that cannot be resent.
    a. positive completion
    b. positive intermediate
    c. transient negative completion
    d. permanent negative completion
21. MIME allows _______ data to be sent through SMTP.
    a. audio
    b. non-ASCII data
    c. image
    d. all of the above
22. The _______ field in the MIME header is useful for mail with multiple messages.
    a. content-type
    b. content-transfer-encoding
    c. content-Id
    d. content-description
23. The _______ field in the MIME header uses text to describe the data in the body of the message.
    a. content-type
    b. content-transfer-encoding
    c. content-Id
    d. content-description
24. The _______ field in the MIME header describes the method used to encode the data.
    a. content-type
    b. content-transfer-encoding
    c. content-Id
    d. content-description

25. The _______ field in the MIME header has type and subtype subfields.
    a. content-type
    b. content-transfer-encoding
    c. content-Id
    d. content-description
26. A JPEG image is sent as email. What is the content-type?
    a. multipart/mixed
    b. multipart/image
    c. image/JPEG
    d. image/basic
27. An email contains a textual birthday greeting, a picture of a cake, and a song. The text must precede the image. What is the content-type?
    a. multipart/mixed
    b. multipart/parallel
    c. multipart/digest
    d. multipart/alternative
28. An email contains a textual birthday greeting, a picture of a cake, and a song. The order is not important. What is the content-type?
    a. multipart/mixed
    b. multipart/parallel
    c. multipart/digest
    d. multipart/alternative
29. A message is fragmented into three mail messages. What is the content-type?
    a. multipart/mixed
    b. message/RFC822
    c. message/partial
    d. multipart/partial
30. A client machine powers off at the end of the day. It probably needs _______ to receive email.
    a. only SMTP
    b. only POP
    c. both SMTP and POP
    d. none of the above
31. A client machine usually needs _______ to send email.
    a. only SMTP
    b. only POP
    c. both SMTP and POP
    d. none of the above

Exercises

32. Give an example of a situation in which a one-to-many alias expander would be useful. Do the same for a many-to-one alias expander.
33. Are the HELO and MAIL FROM commands both necessary? Why or why not?
34. In Figure 22.16 what is the difference between MAIL FROM in the envelope and the FROM in the header?
35. Why is a connection establishment for mail transfer needed if TCP has already established a connection?
36. Show the connection establishment phase from aaa@xxx.com to bbb@yyy.com.
37. Show the message transfer phase from aaa@xxx.com to bbb@yyy.com. The message is "Good morning my friend."
38. Show the connection termination phase from aaa@xxx.com to bbb@yyy.com.
39. User aaa@xxx.com sends a message to user bbb@yyy.com, which is forwarded to user ccc@zzz.com. Show all SMTP commands and responses.
40. User aaa@xxx.com sends a message to user bbb@yyy.com. The latter replies. Show all SMTP commands and responses.
41. In SMTP, if we send a one-line message between two users, how many lines of commands and responses are exchanged?
42. A sender is sending unformatted text. Show the MIME header.
43. A sender is sending a JPEG message. Show the MIME header.
44. A non-ASCII message of 1,000 bytes is encoded using base64. How many bytes are in the encoded message? How many bytes are redundant? What is the ratio of redundant bytes to the total message?
45. A message of 1,000 bytes is encoded using quoted-printable. The message consists of 90 percent ASCII and 10 percent non-ASCII characters. How many bytes are in the encoded message? How many bytes are redundant? What is the ratio of redundant bytes to the total message?
46. Compare the results of exercises 44 and 45. How much is the efficiency improved if the message is a combination of ASCII and non-ASCII characters?
47. Encode the following message in base64:

    01010111 00001111 11110000 10101111 01110001 01010100

48. Encode the following message in quoted-printable:

    01010111 00001111 11110000 10101111 01110001 01010100

49. Encode the following message in base64:

    01010111 00001111 11110000 10101111 01110001

50. Encode the following message in quoted-printable:

    01010111 00001111 11110000 10101111 01110001

CHAPTER 23

Simple Network Management Protocol (SNMP)

The Simple Network Management Protocol (SNMP) is a framework for managing devices in an internet using the TCP/IP protocol suite. It provides a set of fundamental operations for monitoring and maintaining an internet.

23.1 CONCEPT

SNMP uses the concept of manager and agent. That is, a manager, usually a host, controls and monitors a set of agents, usually routers (see Figure 23.1).

Figure 23.1 *SNMP concept*

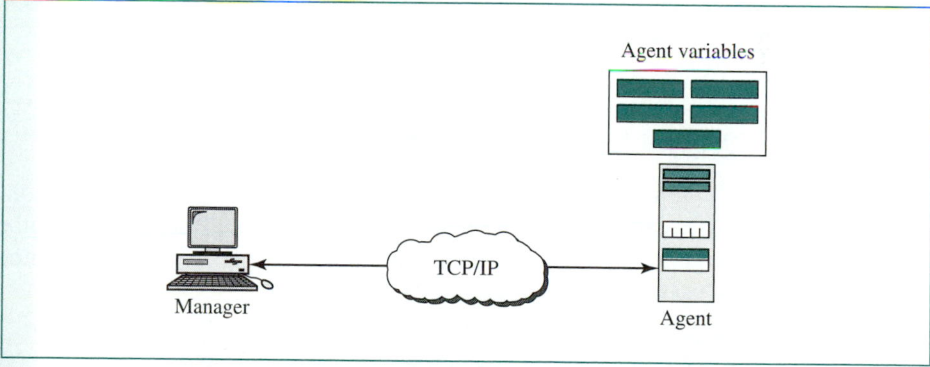

SNMP is an application-level protocol in which a few manager stations control a set of agents. The protocol is designed at the application level so that it can monitor devices made by different manufacturers and installed on different physical networks. In other words, SNMP frees management tasks from both the physical characteristics of the managed devices and the underlying networking technology. It can be used in a heterogeneous internet made of different LANs and WANs connected by routers made by different manufacturers.

Managers and Agents

A management station, called a *manager,* is a host that runs the SNMP client program. A managed station, called an *agent,* is a router (or a host) that runs the SNMP server program. Management is achieved through simple interaction between a manager and an agent.

The agent keeps performance information in a database. The manager has access to the values in the database. For example, a router can store in appropriate variables the number of packets received and forwarded. The manager can fetch and compare the values of these two variables to see if the router is congested or not.

The manager can also make the router perform certain actions. For example, a router periodically checks the value of a reboot counter to see when it should reboot itself. It reboots itself, for example, if the value of the counter is 0. The manager can use this feature to reboot the agent remotely at any time. It simply sends a packet to force a 0 value in the counter.

Agents can also contribute to the management process. The server program running on the agent can check the environment and, if it notices something unusual, it can send a warning message (called a *trap*) to the manager.

In other words, management with SNMP is based on three basic ideas:

1. A manager checks an agent by requesting information that reflects the behavior of the agent.
2. A manager forces an agent to perform a task by resetting values in the agent database.
3. An agent contributes to the management process by warning the manager of an unusual situation.

23.2 MANAGEMENT COMPONENTS

To do management tasks, SNMP uses other two protocols: Structure of Management Information (SMI) and Management Information Base (MIB). In other words, management on the Internet is done through the cooperation of three protocols: SNMP, SMI, and MIB as shown in Figure 23.2.

Figure 23.2 *Components of network management on the Internet*

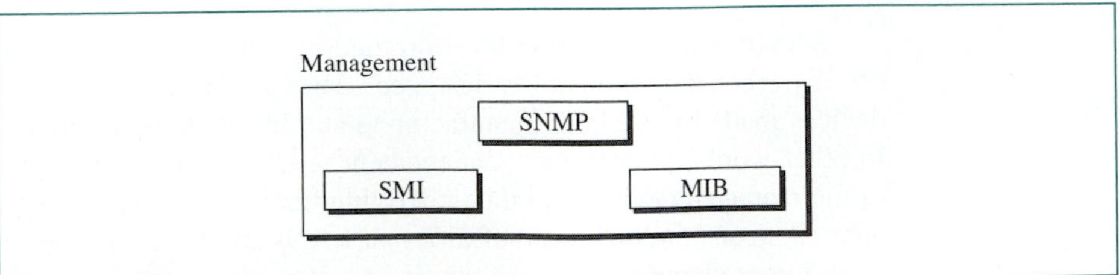

Let us elaborate on the interactions between these protocols.

Role of SNMP

SNMP has some very specific roles in network management. It defines the format of the packet to be sent from a manager to an agent and vice versa. It also interprets the result and creates statistics (often with the help of other management software). The packets exchanged contain the object (variable) names and their status (values). SNMP is responsible for reading and changing these values.

> SNMP defines the format of packets exchanged between a manager and an agent. It reads and changes the status (values) of objects (variables) in SNMP packets.

Role of SMI

To use SNMP, we need rules. We need rules for naming objects. This is particularly important because the objects in SNMP form a hierarchical structure (an object may have a parent object and some children objects). Part of a name can be inherited from the parent. We also need rules to define the type of the objects. What types of objects are handled by SNMP? Can SNMP handle simple types or structured types? How many simple types are available? What are the sizes of these types? What is the range of these types? In addition, how are each of these types encoded?

We need these universal rules because we do not know the architecture of the computers that send, receive, or store these values. The sender may be a powerful computer in which an integer is stored as 8-byte data; the receiver may be a small computer that stores an integer as 4-byte data.

SMI is a protocol that defines these rules. However, we must understand that SMI only defines the rules; it does not define how many objects are managed in an entity or which object uses which type. SMI is a collection of general rules to name objects and to list their types. The association of an object with the type is not done by SMI.

> SMI defines the general rules for naming objects, defining object types (including range and length), and showing how to encode objects and values.
>
> SMI defines neither the number of objects an entity should manage, nor names the objects to be managed nor defines the association between the objects and their values.

Role of MIB

We hope it is clear that we need another protocol. For each entity to be managed, this protocol must define the number of objects, name them according to the rules defined by SMI, and associate a type to each named object. This protocol is MIB. MIB creates a set of objects defined for each entity similar to a database (mostly meta data in a database, name and types without values).

> MIB creates a collection of named objects, their types, and their relationships to each other in an entity to be managed.

An Analogy

Before discussing each of these protocols in more detail, let us give an analogy. The three network management components are similar to what we need when we write a program in a computer language to solve a problem.

Before we write a program, the syntax of the language (such as C or C++) must be predefined. The language also defines the structure of variables (simple, structured, pointer, and so on) and how the variables must be named. For example, a variable name must be 1 to *N* characters in length and start with a letter followed by alphanumeric characters. The language also defines the type of data to be used (integer, float, char, etc.). In programming the rules are defined by the language. In network management the rules are defined by SMI.

Most computer languages require that variables be declared in each specific program. The declaration names each variable and defines the predefined type. For example, if a program has two variables (an integer named *counter* and an array named *grades* of type char), they must be declared at the beginning of the program:

```
int counter ;
char grades [40] ;
```

Note that the declarations name the variables (counter and grades) and define the type of each variable. Because the types are predefined in the language, the program knows the range and size of each variable.

MIB does this task in network management. MIB names each object and defines the type of the objects. Because the type is defined by SMI, SNMP knows the range and size.

After declaration in programming, the program needs to write statements to store values in the variables and change them if needed. SNMP does this task in network management. SNMP stores, changes, and interprets the values of objects already declared by MIB according to the rules defined by SMI.

> We can compare the task of network management to the task of writing a program.
> - Both tasks need rules. In network management this is handled by SMI.
> - Both tasks need variable declarations. In network management this is handled by MIB.
> - Both tasks have actions performed by statements. In network management this is handled by SNMP.

23.3 SMI

The Structure of Management Information, version 2 (SMIv2) is a component for network management. Its functions are:

1. To name objects.
2. To define the type of data that can be stored in an object.
3. To show how to encode data for transmission over the network.

SMI is a guideline for SNMP. It emphasizes three attributes to handle an object: name, data type, and encoding method (see Figure 23.3).

Figure 23.3 *Object attributes*

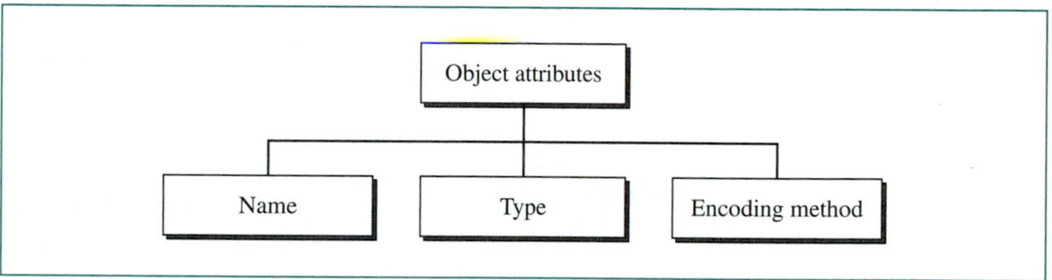

Name

SMI requires that each managed object (such as a router, a variable in a router, a value, etc.) have a unique name. To name objects globally, SMI uses an **object identifier,** which is a hierarchical identifier based on a tree structure (see Figure 23.4).

Figure 23.4 *Object identifier*

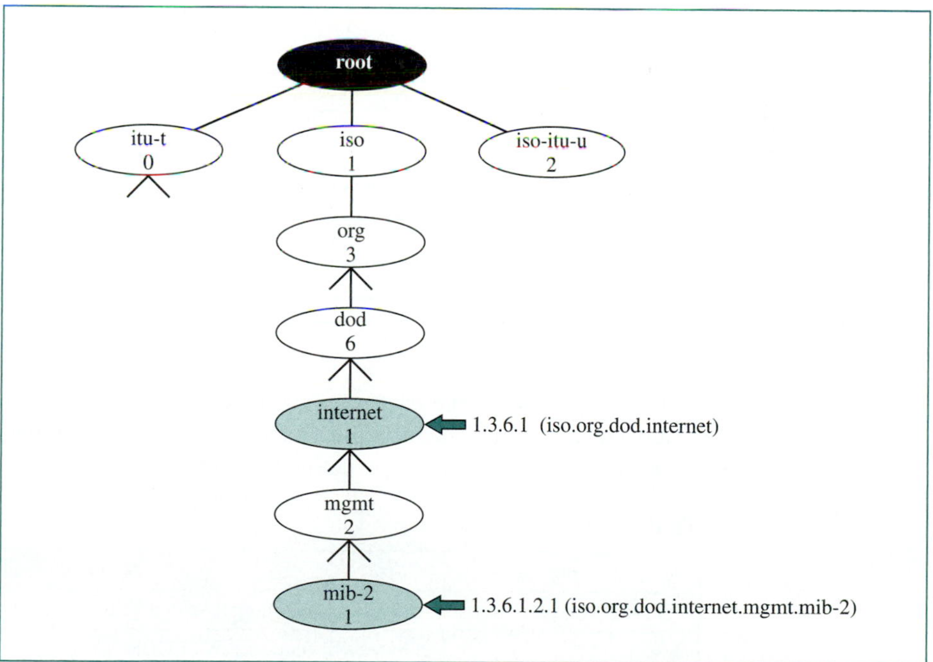

The tree structure starts with an unnamed root. Each object can be defined using a sequence of integers separated by dots. The tree structure can also define an object using a sequence of textual names separated by dots. The integer-dot representation is used in SNMP. The name-dot notation is used by people. For example, the following shows the same object in two different notations:

iso.org.dod.internet.mgmt.mib-2 ⟷ 1.3.6.1.2.1

The objects that are used in SNMP are located under the *mib-2* object, so their identifiers always start with 1.3.6.1.2.1.

> All objects managed by SNMP are given an object identifier. The object identifier always starts with 1.3.6.1.2.1.

Type

The second attribute of an object is the type of data stored in it. To define the data type, SMI uses fundamental ASN.1 definitions and adds some new definitions. In other words, SMI is both a subset and a superset of ASN.1.

SMI uses two broad categories of data type: *simple* and *structured.* We first define the simple types and then show how the structured types can be constructed from the simple ones (see Figure 23.5).

Figure 23.5 *Data type*

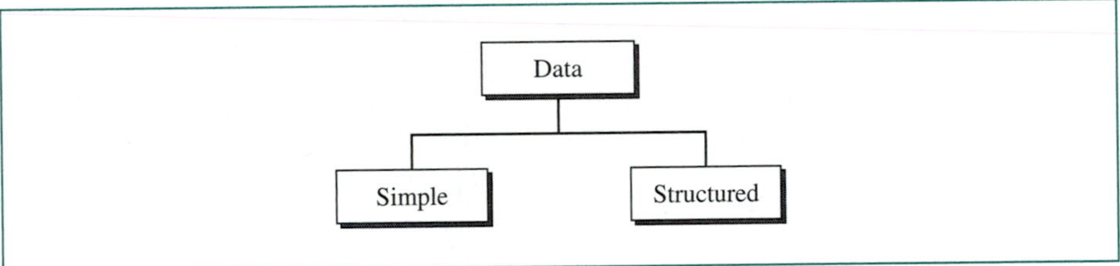

Simple Type

The simple types are atomic data types. Some of them are directly taken from ASN.1; some are added by SMI. The most important ones are given in Table 23.1. The first five are from ASN.1; the next seven are defined by SMI.

Table 23.1 *Data types*

Type	*Size*	*Description*
INTEGER	4 bytes	An integer with a value between -2^{31} and $2^{31}-1$
Integer32	4 bytes	Same as INTEGER
Unsigned32	4 bytes	Unsigned with a value between 0 and $2^{32}-1$
OCTET STRING	Variable	Byte-string up to 65,535 bytes long

Table 23.1 *Data types (continued)*

Type	*Size*	*Description*
OBJECT IDENTIFIER	Variable	An object identifier
IPAddress	4 bytes	An IP address made of four integers
Counter32	4 bytes	An integer whose value can be incremented from zero to 2^{32}; when it reaches its maximum value it wraps back to zero
Counter64	8 bytes	64-bit counter
Gauge32	4 bytes	Same as Counter32, but when it reaches its maximum value, it does not wrap; it remains there until it is reset
TimeTicks	4 bytes	A counting value that records time in 1/100ths of a second
BITS		A string of bits
Opaque	Variable	Uninterpreted string

Structured Type

By combining simple and structured data types, we can make new structured data types. SMI defines two structured data types: *sequence* and *sequence of*.

- **Sequence.** A *sequence* data type is a combination of simple data types, not necessarily of the same type. It is analogous to the concept of a *struct* or a *record* used in programming languages such as C.
- **Sequence of.** A *sequence of* data type is a combination of simple data types all of the same type or a combination of sequence data types all of the same type. It is analogous to the concept of an *array* used in programming languages such as C.

Figure 23.6 shows a conceptual view of data types.

Figure 23.6 *Conceptual data types*

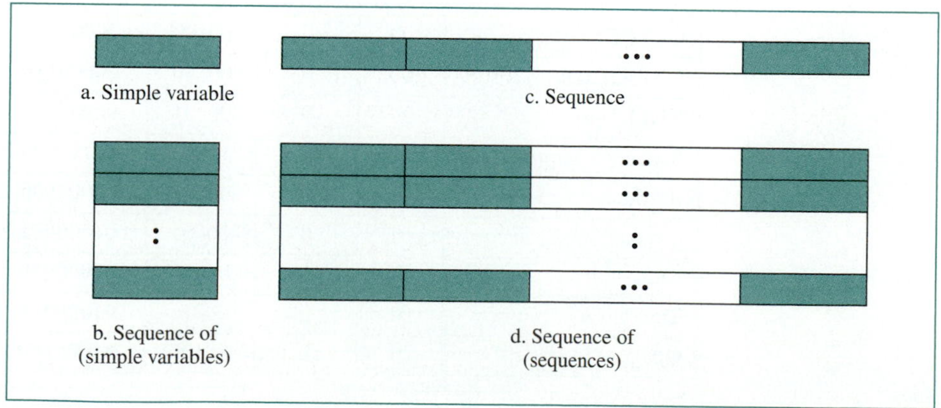

Encoding Method

SMI uses another standard, Basic Encoding Rules (BER), to encode data to be transmitted over the network. BER specifies that each piece of data be encoded in triplet format: tag, length, and value, as illustrated in Figure 23.7.

Figure 23.7 *Encoding format*

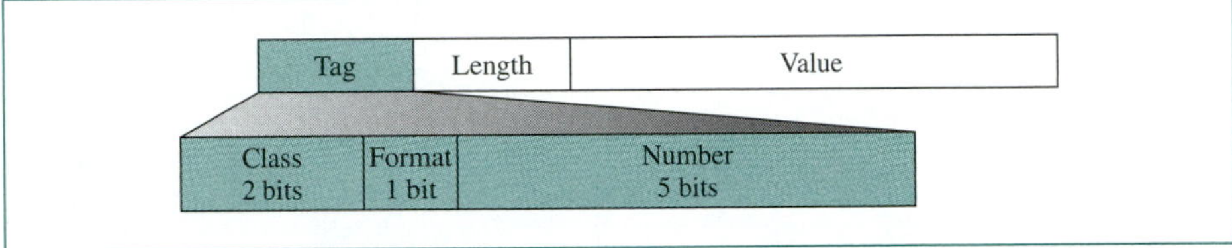

- **Tag.** The tag is a 1-byte field that defines the type of data. It is composed of three subfields: *class* (2 bits), *format* (1 bit), and *number* (5 bits). The class subfield defines the scope of the data. Four classes are defined: universal (00), application-wide (01), context-specific (10), and private (11). The universal data types are those taken from ASN.1 (INTEGER, OCTET STRING, and ObjectIdentifier). The application-wide data types are those added by SMI (IPAddress, Counter, Gauge, and TimeTicks). The five context-specific data types have meanings that may change from one protocol to another. The private data types are vendor-specific.

  The format subfield indicates whether the data is simple (0) or structured (1). The number subfield further divides simple or structured data into subgroups. For example, in the universal class, with simple format, INTEGER has a value of 2, OCTET STRING has a value of 4, and so on. Table 23.2 shows the data types we use in this chapter and their tags in binary and hexadecimal numbers.

Table 23.2 *Codes for data types*

Data Type	*Class*	*Format*	*Number*	*Tag (Binary)*	*Tag (Hex)*
INTEGER	00	0	00010	**00000010**	**02**
OCTET STRING	00	0	00100	**00000100**	**04**
OBJECT IDENTIFIER	00	0	00110	**00000110**	**06**
NULL	00	0	00101	**00000101**	**05**
Sequence, sequence of	00	1	10000	**00110000**	**30**
IPAddress	01	0	00000	**01000000**	**40**
Counter	01	0	00001	**01000001**	**41**
Gauge	01	0	00010	**01000010**	**42**
TimeTicks	01	0	00011	**01000011**	**43**
Opaque	01	0	00100	**01000100**	**44**

- **Length.** The length field is 1 or more bytes. If it is 1 byte, the most significant bit must be 0. The other 7 bits define the length of the data. If it is more than 1 byte, the most significant bit of the first byte must be 1. The other 7 bits of the first byte define the number of bytes needed to define the length. See Figure 23.8 for a depiction of the length field.

Figure 23.8 *Length format*

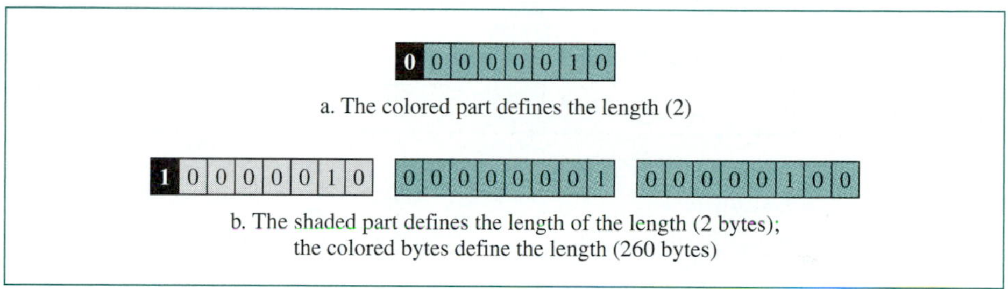

- **Value.** The value field codes the value of the data according to the rules defined in BER.

To show how these three fields—tag, length, and value—can define objects, we give some examples.

Example 1

Figure 23.9 shows how to define INTEGER 14.

Figure 23.9 *Example 1, INTEGER 14*

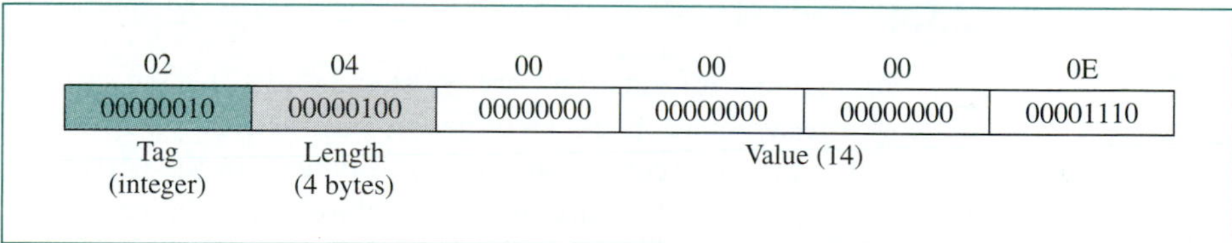

Example 2

Figure 23.10 shows how to define the OCTET STRING "HI."

Figure 23.10 *Example 2, OCTET STRING "HI"*

04	02	48	49
00000100	00000010	01001000	01001001
Tag (String)	Length (2 bytes)	Value (H)	Value (I)

Example 3

Figure 23.11 shows how to define ObjectIdentifier 1.3.6.1 (iso.org.dod.internet).

Figure 23.11 *Example 3, ObjectIdentifier 1.3.6.1*

06	04	01	03	06	01
00000110	00000100	00000001	00000011	00000110	00000001
Tag (ObjectId)	Length (4 bytes)	Value (1)	Value (3)	Value (6)	Value (1)
		1.3.6.1 (iso.org.dod.internet)			

Example 4

Figure 23.12 shows how to define IPAddress 131.21.14.8.

Figure 23.12 *Example 4, IPAddress 131.21.14.8*

40	04	83	15	0E	08
01000000	00000100	10000011	00010101	00001110	00001000
Tag (IpAddress)	Length (4 bytes)	Value (131)	Value (21)	Value (14)	Value (8)
		131.21.14.8			

23.4 MIB

The Management Information Base, version 2 (MIB2) is the second component used in network management. Each agent has its own MIB2, which is a collection of all the objects that the manager can manage. The objects in the MIB2 are categorized under ten different groups: system, interface, address translation, ip, icmp, tcp, udp, egp, transmission, and snmp. These groups are under the mib-2 object in the object identifier tree (see Figure 23.13).

Figure 23.13 *mib-2*

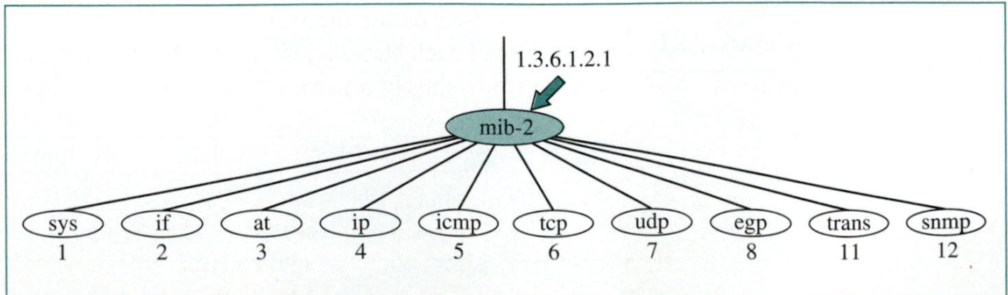

Each group has defined variables and/or tables.

Accessing MIB Variables

To show how to access different variables, we use the udp group as an example. There are four simple variables in the udp group and one sequence of (table of) records. Figure 23.14 shows the variables and the table.

Figure 23.14 *udp group*

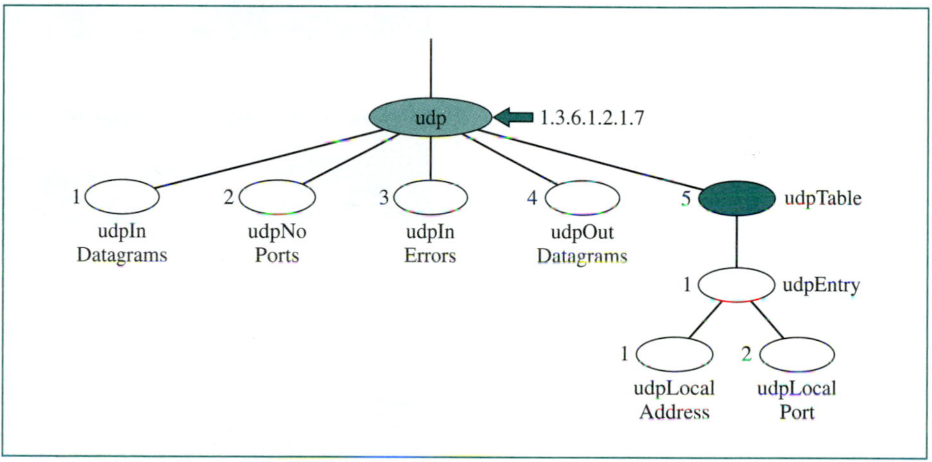

We will show how to access each entity.

Simple Variables

To access any of the simple variables, we use the id of the group (1.3.6.1.2.1.7) followed by the id of the variable. The following shows how to access each variable.

udpInDatagrams	➡	1.3.6.1.2.1.7.1
udpNoPorts	➡	1.3.6.1.2.1.7.2
udpInErrors	➡	1.3.6.1.2.1.7.3
udpOutDatagrams	➡	1.3.6.1.2.1.7.4

However, these object identifiers define the variable, not the instance (contents). To show the instance or the contents of each variable, we must add an instance suffix. The instance suffix for a simple variable is simply a zero. In other words, to show an instance of the above variables, we use the following:

udpInDatagrams.0	➡	1.3.6.1.2.1.7.1.**0**
udpNoPorts.0	➡	1.3.6.1.2.1.7.2.**0**
udpInErrors.0	➡	1.3.6.1.2.1.7.3.**0**
udpOutDatagrams.0	➡	1.3.6.1.2.1.7.4.**0**

Tables

To identify a table, we first use the table id. The udp group has only one table (with id 5) as illustrated in Figure 23.15.

Figure 23.15 *udp variables and tables*

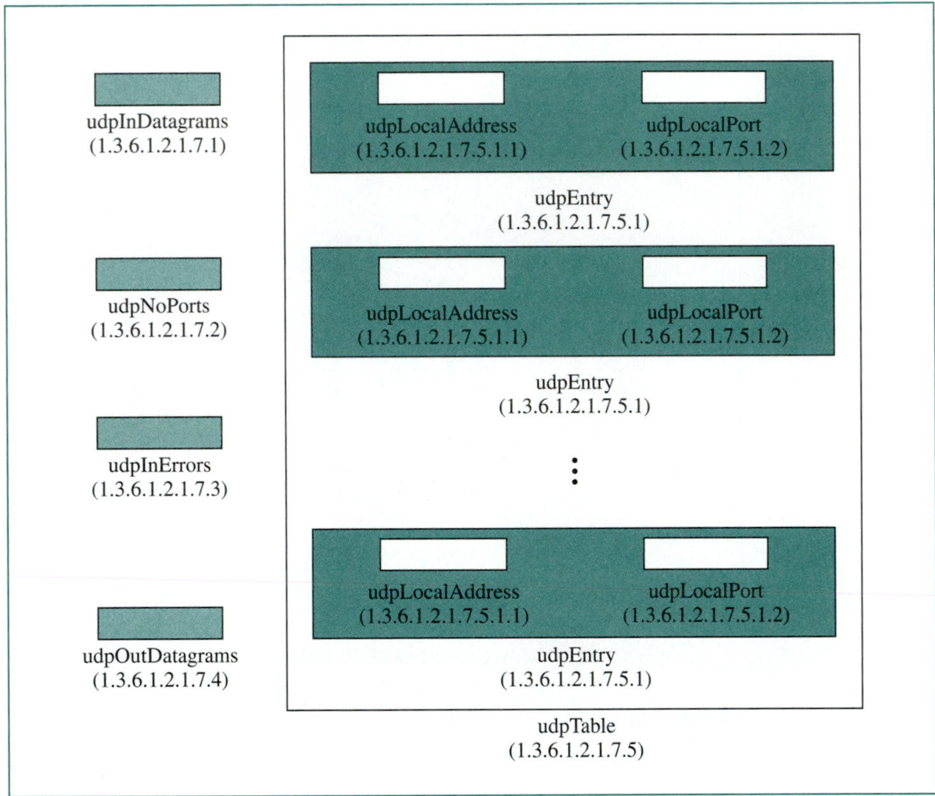

So to access the table, we should use the following:

udpTable ➡ 1.3.6.1.2.1.7.5

However, the table is not at the leaf level in the tree structure. We cannot access the table; we define the entry (sequence) in the table (with id of 1), as follows:

udpEntry ➡ 1.3.6.1.2.1.7.5.**1**

This entry is also not a leaf and we cannot access it. We need to define each entity (field) in the entry.

udpLocalAddress ➡ 1.3.6.1.2.1.7.5.**1.1**
udpLocalPort ➡ 1.3.6.1.2.1.7.5.**1.2**

These two variables are at the leaf of the tree. Although we can access their instances, we need to define *which* instance. At any moment, the table can have several values for each local address/local port pair. To access a specific instance (row) of the table, we should add the index to the above ids. In MIB, the indexes of arrays are not integers (like most programming languages). The indexes are based on the value of one or more fields in the entries. In our example, the udpTable is indexed based on both local address and local port number. For example, Figure 23.16 shows a table with four rows and values for each field. The index of each row is a combination of two values.

Figure 23.16 *Indexes for udpTable*

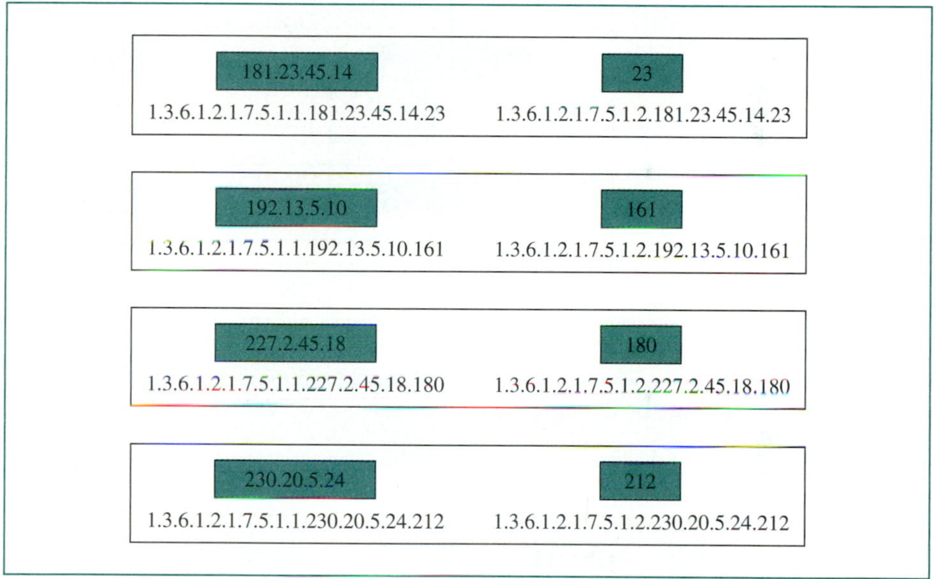

To access the instance of the local address for the first row, we use the identifier augmented with the instance index:

udpLocalAddress.181.23.45.14.23 ➡ 1.3.6.1.2.7.5.1.1.181.23.45.14.23

Note that not all tables are indexed the same way. Some tables are indexed using the value of one field, some using the value of two fields, and so on. See Appendix F for details.

Lexicographic Ordering

One interesting point about the MIB variables is that the object identifiers (including the instance identifiers) are in lexicographic order. Tables are ordered according to column-row rules, which means one should go column by column. In each column, one should go from the top to the bottom, as shown in Figure 23.17.

Figure 23.17 *Lexicographic ordering*

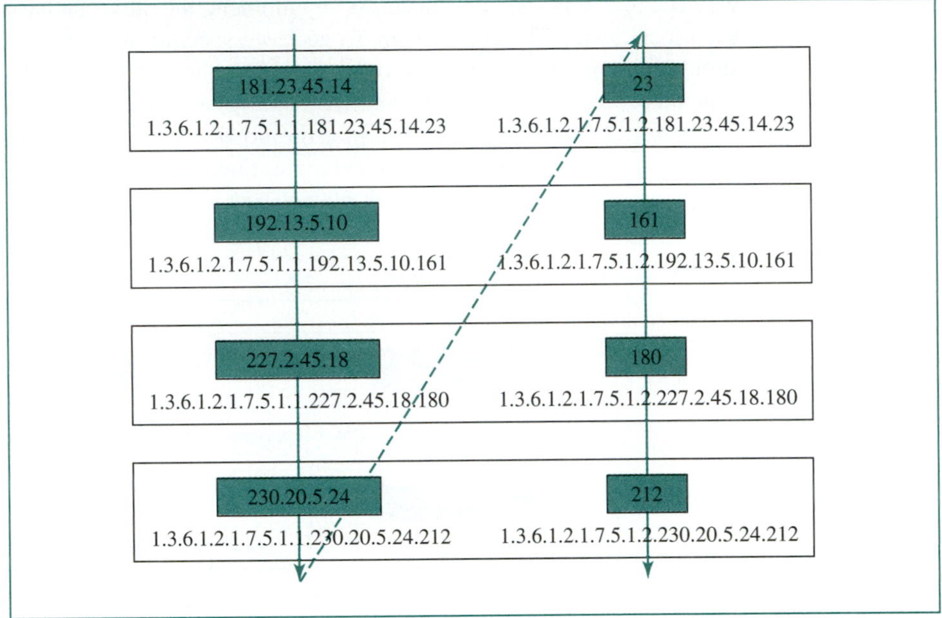

The lexicographic ordering enables a manager to access a set of variables one after another by defining the first variable, as we will see in the GetNextRequest command in the next section.

23.5 SNMP

SNMP uses both SMI and MIB in Internet network management. It is an application program that allows:

1. A manager to retrieve the value of an object defined in an agent.
2. A manager to store a value in an object defined in an agent.
3. An agent to send an alarm message about an abnormal situation to the manager.

PDUs

SNMPv3 defines eight types of packets (or PDUs): GetRequest, GetNextRequest, GetBulkRequest, SetRequest, Response, Trap, InformRequest, and Report (see Figure 23.18).

GetRequest

The GetRequest PDU is sent from the manager (client) to the agent (server) to retrieve the value of a variable or a set of variables.

Figure 23.18 *SNMP PDUs*

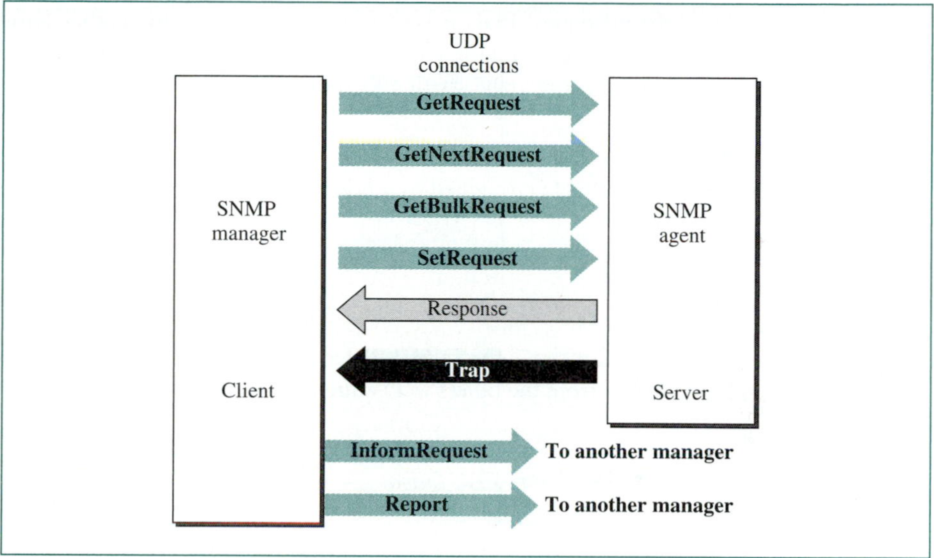

GetNextRequest

The GetNextRequest PDU is sent from the manager to the agent to retrieve the value of a variable. The retrieved value is the value of the object following the defined ObjectId in the PDU. It is mostly used to retrieve the values of the entries in a table. If the manager does not know the indexes of the entries, it cannot retrieve the values. However, it can use GetNextRequest and define the ObjectId of the table. Because the first entry has the ObjectId immediately after the ObjectId of the table, the value of the first entry is returned. The manager can use this ObjectId to get the value of the next one, and so on.

GetBulkRequest

The GetBulkRequest PDU is sent from the manager to the agent to retrieve a large amount of data. It can be used instead of multiple GetRequest and GetNextRequest PDUs.

SetRequest

The SetRequest PDU is sent from the manager to the agent to set (store) a value in a variable.

Response

The Response PDU is sent from an agent to a manager in response to GetRequest or GetNextRequest. It contains the value(s) of the variable(s) requested by the manager.

Trap

The Trap (also called SNMPv2 Trap to distinguish it from SNMPv1 Trap) PDU is sent from the agent to the manager to report an event. For example, if the agent is rebooted, it informs the manager and reports the time of rebooting.

InformRequest

The InformRequest PDU is sent from one manager to another remote manager to get the value of some variables from agents under the control of the remote manager. The remote manager responds with a Response PDU.

Report

The Report PDU is designed to report some types of errors between managers. It is not yet in use.

Format

The format for the eight SNMP PDUs is shown in Figure 23.19. The GetBulkRequest PDU differs from the others in two areas as shown in the figure.

Figure 23.19 *SNMP PDU format*

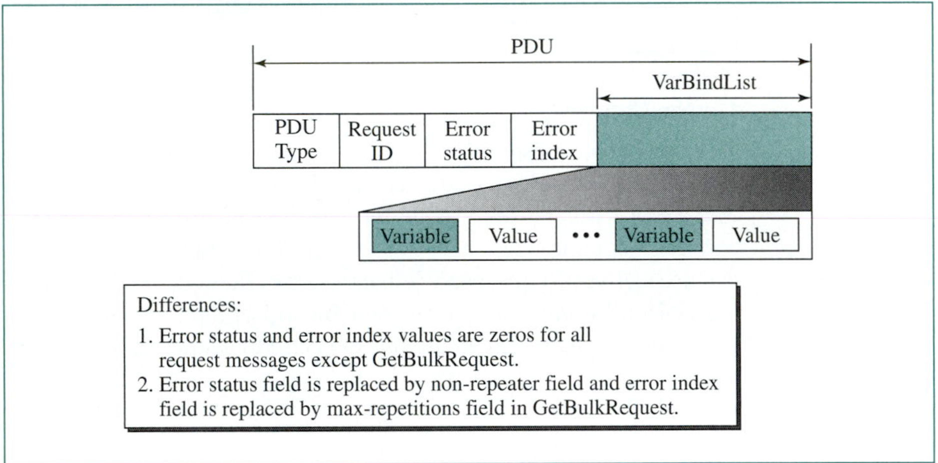

The fields are listed below:

- **PDU type.** This field defines the type of the PDU (see Table 23.4).
- **Request ID.** This field is a sequence number used by the manager in a request PDU and repeated by the agent in a response. It is used to match a request to a response.
- **Error status.** This is an integer that is used only in response PDUs to show the types of errors reported by the agent. Its value is 0 in request PDUs. Table 23.3 lists the types of errors that can occur.
- **Non-repeaters.** This field is used only in GetBulkRequest and replaces the error status field, which is empty in request PDUs.

Table 23.3 *Types of errors*

Status	*Name*	*Meaning*
0	noError	No error
1	tooBig	Response too big to fit in one message
2	noSuchName	Variable does not exist
3	badValue	The value to be stored is invalid
4	readOnly	The value cannot be modified
5	genErr	Other errors

- **Error index.** The error index is an offset that tells the manager which variable caused the error.
- **Max-repetition.** This field is also used only in GetBulkRequest and replaces the error index field, which is empty in request PDUs.
- **VarBindList.** This is a set of variables with the corresponding values the manager wants to retrieve or set. The values are null in GetRequest and GetNextRequest. In a Trap PDU, it shows the variables and values related to a specific PDU.

23.6 MESSAGES

SNMP does not send only a PDU, it embeds the PDU in a message. A message in SNMPv3 is made of four elements: version, header, security parameters, and data (which includes the encoded PDU) as shown in Figure 23.20.

Because the length of these elements is different from message to message, SNMP uses BER to encode each element. Remember that BER uses the tag and the length to define a value. The version defines the current version (3). The header contains values for message identification, message maximum size (the maximum size of the reply), message flag (one octet of data type OCTET STRING where each bit defines security type, such as privacy or authentication, or other information), and a message security model (defining the security protocol). The message security parameter is used to create a message digest (see Chapter 29). The data contains the PDU. If the data are encrypted, there is information about the encrypting engine (the manager program that did the encryption) and the encrypting context (the type of encryption) followed by the encrypted PDU. If the data are not encrypted, the data consists of just the PDU.

To define the type of PDU, SNMP uses a tag. The class is context-sensitive (10), the format is structured (1), and the numbers are 0, 1, 2, 3, 5, 6, 7, 8 (see Table 23.4). Note that SNMPv1 defined A4 for Trap, which is obsolete today.

Figure 23.20 *SNMP message*

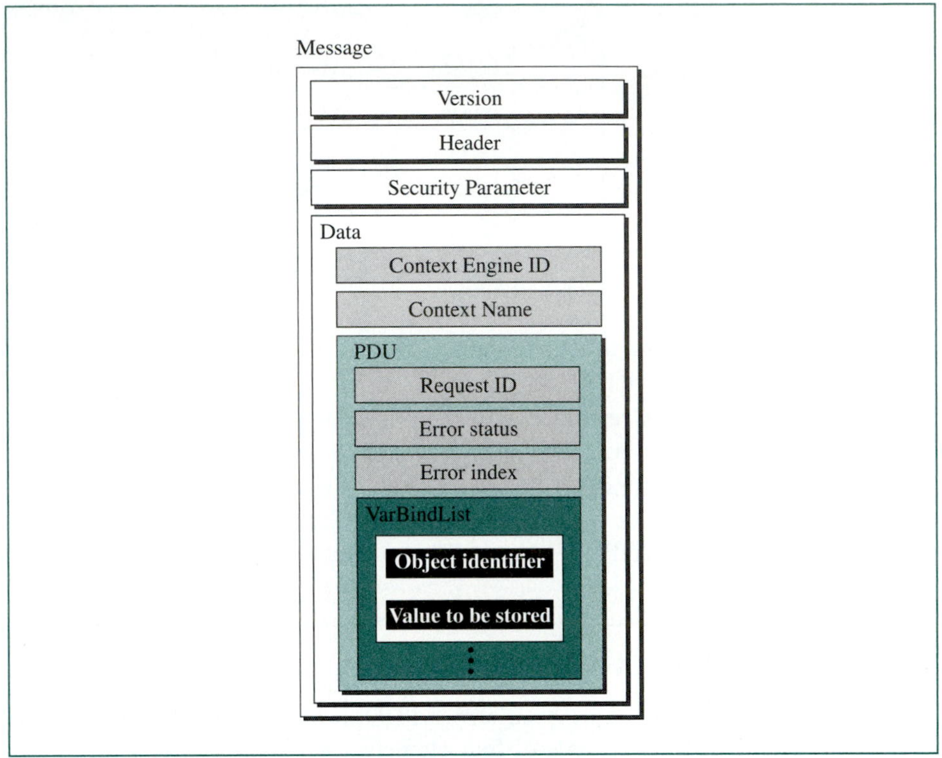

Table 23.4 *Codes for SNMP messages*

Data	*Class*	*Format*	*Number*	*Whole Tag (Binary)*	*Whole Tag (Hex)*
GetRequest	10	1	00000	**10100000**	**A0**
GetNextRequest	10	1	00001	**10100001**	**A1**
Response	10	1	00010	**10100010**	**A2**
SetRequest	10	1	00011	**10100011**	**A3**
GetBulkRequest	10	1	00101	**10100101**	**A5**
InformRequest	10	1	00110	**10100110**	**A6**
Trap (SNMPv2)	10	1	00111	**10100111**	**A7**
Report	10	1	01000	**10101000**	**A8**

Example 1

In this example, a manager station (SNMP client) uses the GetRequest message to retrieve the number of UDP datagrams that a router has received. The encoding is shown in Table 23.5.

The corresponding MIB variable related to this information is udpInDatagrams with the object identifier 1.3.6.1.2.1.7.1. The manager wants to retrieve a value (not to store a value), so the last section defines a null entity of value zero. To make the message very simple, we ignore several fields.

Table 23.5 *Example 1*

GetRequest Encoding	
30 34	Sequence of length 52
02 01 03	INTEGER of length 1, version=3
30 0C	Sequence of length 12 (header)
02 01 40	INTEGER of length 1, message ID=64
02 02 04 00	INTEGER of length 2, maximum size=1024
04 01 00	OCTET STRING of length 1, all flags zero
02 00	OCTET STRING of length 0, no security model
04 00	OCTET STRING of length 0, no security parameter
30 1F	Sequence of length 31, Data
A0 1D	GetRequest PDU (no encryption) of length 29
02 04 00 01 06 11	INTEGER of length 04, Request ID=00010611_{16}
02 01 00	INTEGER of length 01, Error Status=00_{16}
02 01 00	INTEGER of length 01, Error Index=00_{16}
30 0F	Sequence of length 15
30 0D	Sequence of length 13
06 09 01 03 06 01 02 01 07 01 00	ObjectId of length 09, udpInDatagram
05 00	Null entity of length 00

Figure 23.21 shows the actual message sent by the manager station (client) to the agent (server).

Figure 23.21 *GetRequest message*

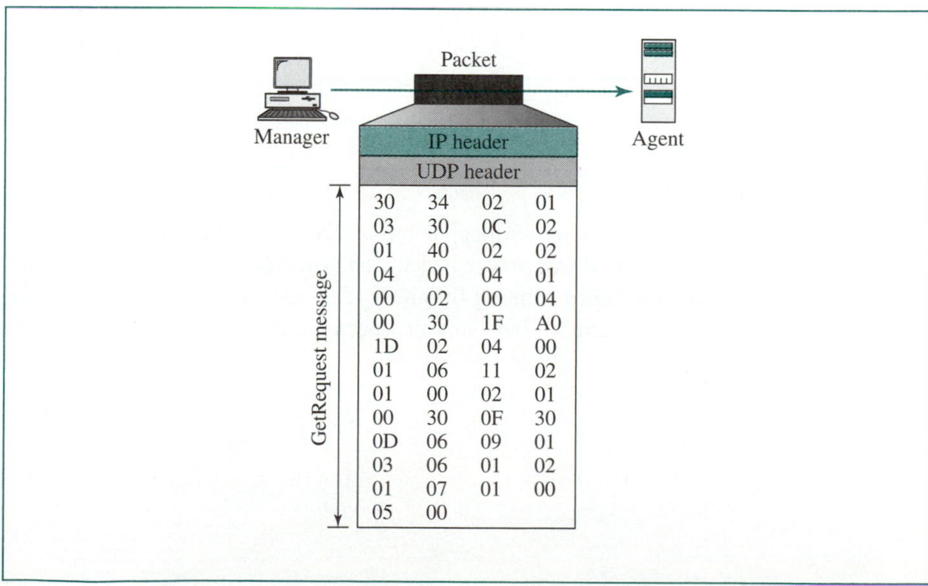

23.7 UDP PORTS

SNMP uses the services of UDP on two well-known ports, 161 and 162. The well-known port 161 is used by the server (agent), and the well-known port 162 is used by the client (manager).

The agent (server) issues a passive open on port 161. It then waits for a connection from a manager (client). A manager (client) issues an active open using an ephemeral port. The request messages are sent from the client to the server using the ephemeral port as the source port and the well-known port 161 as the destination port. The response messages are sent from the server to the client using the well-known port 161 as the source port and the ephemeral port as the destination port.

The manager (client) issues a passive open on port 162. It then waits for a connection from an agent (server). An agent (server) issues an active open, using an ephemeral port, whenever it has a Trap message to send. This connection is only one-way, from the server to the client (see Figure 23.22).

Figure 23.22 *Port numbers for SNMP*

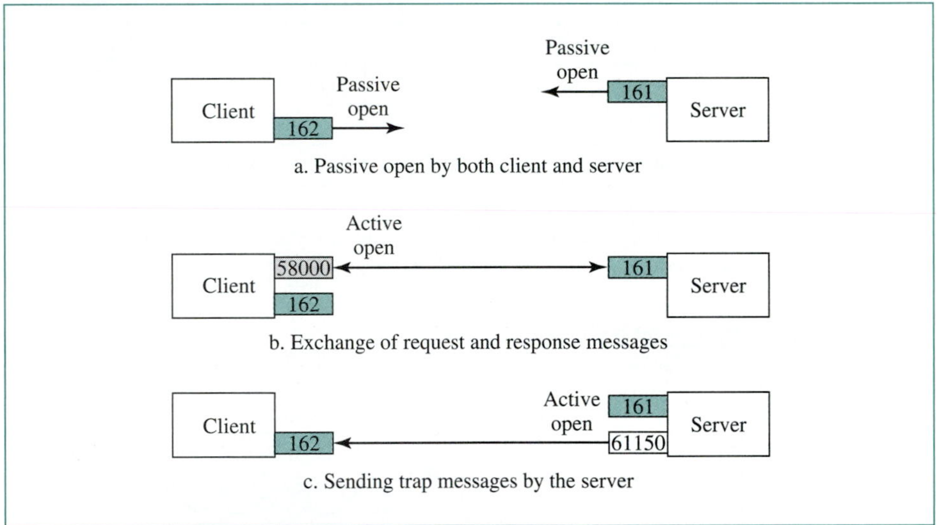

The client-server mechanism in SNMP is different from other protocols. Here both the client and the server use well-known ports. In addition, both the client and the server should be running infinitely. The reason is that request messages are initiated by a manager (client), but Trap messages are initiated by an agent (server).

23.8 SECURITY

The main difference between SNMPv3 and SNMPv2 is the enhanced security. SNMPv3 provides two types of security: general and specific. SNMPv3 provides message authentication, privacy, and manager authorization. We discuss these three aspects in Chapter 29. In addition, SNMPv3 allows a manager to remotely change the security configuration, which means that the manager does not have to be physically present at the manager station.

23.9 KEY TERMS

Abstract Syntax Notation 1 (ASN.1)

agent

Basic Encoding Rules (BER)

host

lexicographic ordering

Management Information Base (MIB)

manager

object

object identifier

router

simple data type

Simple Network Management Protocol (SNMP)

Structure of Management Information (SMI)

structured data type

trap

23.10 SUMMARY

- Simple Network Management Protocol (SNMP) is a framework for managing devices in an internet using the TCP/IP protocol suite.
- A manager, usually a host, controls and monitors a set of agents, usually routers.
- The manager is a host that runs the SNMP client program.
- The agent is a router or host that runs the SNMP server program.
- SNMP frees management tasks from both the physical characteristics of the managed devices and the underlying networking technology.
- SNMP uses the services of two other protocols: Structure of Management Information (SMI) and Management Information Base (MIB).
- SMI names objects, defines the type of data that can be stored in an object, and encodes the data.
- SMI objects are named according to a hierarchical tree structure.
- SMI data types are defined according to Abstract Syntax Notation 1 (ASN.1).
- SMI uses Basic Encoding Rules (BER) to encode data.
- MIB is a collection of groups of objects that can be managed by SNMP.

- MIB uses lexicographic ordering to manage its variables.
- SNMP functions in three ways:
  a. A manager can retrieve the value of an object defined in an agent.
  b. A manager can store a value in an object defined in an agent.
  c. An agent can send an alarm message to the manager.
- SNMP defines eight types of packets: GetRequest, GetNextRequest, SetRequest, GetBulkRequest, Trap, InformRequest, Response, and Report.
- SNMP uses the services of UDP on two well-known ports, 161 and 162.
- SNMPv3 has enhanced security features over previous versions.

23.11 PRACTICE SET

Multiple-Choice Questions

1. Which of the following is associated with SNMP?
   a. MIB
   b. SMI
   c. BER
   d. all of the above
2. _______ runs the SNMP client program; _______ runs the SNMP server program.
   a. A manager; a manager
   b. An agent; an agent
   c. A manager; an agent
   d. An agent; a manager
3. SNMP uses _______ in its management tasks.
   a. SMI
   b. MBI
   c. SMTP
   d. a and b
4. _______ names objects, defines the type of data that can be stored in an object, and encodes data for network transmission.
   a. MIB
   b. SMI
   c. SNMP
   d. ASN.1
5. Which of the following creates a collection of objects to be managed?
   a. MIB
   b. SMI
   c. SNMP
   d. ASN.1

6. INTEGER, OCTET STRING, and ObjectIdentifier are _______ definitions used by SMI.
   a. MIB
   b. SNMP
   c. ASN.1
   d. BER
7. Which of the following could be a legitimate MIB object identifier?
   a. 1.3.6.1.2.1.1
   b. 1.3.6.1.2.2.1
   c. 2.3.6.1.2.1.2
   d. 1.3.6.2.2.1.3
8. Which is a manager duty?
   a. Retrieve the value of an object defined in an agent.
   b. Store the value of an object defined in an agent.
   c. Send an alarm message to the agent.
   d. a and b
9. _______ specifies which data types are available for the MIB.
   a. BER
   b. SNMP
   c. ASN.1
   d. SMI
10. For a 1-byte length field, what is the maximum value for the data length?
    a. 127
    b. 128
    c. 255
    d. 256
11. An object id defines a _______. Add a zero suffix to define the _______.
    a. variable; table
    b. table; variable
    c. variable; variable contents
    d. variable contents; variable
12. An SNMP agent can send _______ messages.
    a. GetRequest
    b. SetRequest
    c. GetNextRequest
    d. Trap
13. An SNMP manager can send _______ messages.
    a. GetRequest
    b. SetRequest
    c. GetNextRequest
    d. all of the above

14. An SNMP agent can send _______ messages.
    a. Response
    b. GetRequest
    c. SetRequest
    d. GetNextRequest
15. The _______ field in the SNMP PDU is an offset that points to the variable in error.
    a. community
    b. enterprise
    c. error status
    d. error index
16. The _______ field in the SNMP PDU reports an error in a response message.
    a. community
    b. enterprise
    c. error status
    d. error index
17. The _______ field in the SNMP PDU consists of a sequence of variables and their corresponding values.
    a. version
    b. community
    c. VarBindList
    d. agentAddress
18. A request message from the client to the server uses the _______ as the source port and the _______ as the destination port.
    a. ephemeral port; well-known port 162
    b. ephemeral port; well-known port 161
    c. well-known port 161; ephemeral port
    d. well-known port 162; ephemeral port
19. A response message from the server to the client uses the _______ as the source port and the _______ as the destination port.
    a. ephemeral port; well-known port 162
    b. ephemeral port; well-known port 161
    c. well-known port 161; ephemeral port
    d. well-known port 162; ephemeral port
20. A Trap message from the server to the client uses the _______ as the source port and the _______ as the destination port.
    a. ephemeral port; well-known port 162
    b. ephemeral port; well-known port 161
    c. well-known port 161; ephemeral port
    d. well-known port 162; ephemeral port

Exercises

21. Show the encoding for the INTEGER 1456.
22. Show the encoding for the OCTET STRING "Hello World."
23. Show the encoding for an arbitrary OCTET STRING of length 1,000.
24. Show how the following record (sequence) is encoded.

INTEGER	OCTET STRING	IP Address
2345	"COMPUTER"	185.32.1.5

25. Show how the following record (sequence) is encoded.

Time Tick	INTEGER	Object Id
12000	14564	1.3.6.1.2.1.7

26. Show how the following array (sequence of) is encoded. Each element is an integer.

2345

1236

122

1236

27. Show how the following array of records (sequence of sequence) is encoded.

INTEGER	OCTET STRING	Counter
2345	"COMPUTER"	345
1123	"DISK"	1430
3456	"MONITOR"	2313

28. Decode the following:
    a. 02 04 01 02 14 32
    b. 30 06 02 01 11 02 01 14
    c. 30 09 04 03 41 43 42 02 02 14 14
    d. 30 0A 40 04 23 51 62 71 02 02 14 12

CHAPTER 24

Hypertext Transfer Protocol (HTTP)

The Hypertext Transfer Protocol (HTTP) is a protocol used mainly to access data on the World Wide Web (see Chapter 25). The protocol transfers data in the form of plain text, hypertext, audio, video, and so on. However, it is called the Hypertext Transfer Protocol because its efficiency allows its use in a hypertext environment where there are rapid jumps from one document to another.

HTTP functions like a combination of FTP and SMTP. It is similar to FTP because it transfers files and uses the services of TCP. However, it is much simpler than FTP because it uses only one TCP connection (well-known port 80). There is no separate control connection; only data are transferred between the client and the server.

HTTP is like SMTP because the data transferred between the client and the server looks like SMTP messages. In addition, the format of the messages is controlled by MIME-like headers (see Chapter 22). However, HTTP differs from SMTP in the way the messages are sent from the client to the server and from the server to the client. Unlike SMTP, the HTTP messages are not destined to be read by humans; they are read and interpreted by the HTTP server and HTTP client (browser). SMTP messages are stored and forwarded, but the HTTP messages are delivered immediately.

The idea of HTTP is very simple. A client sends a request, which looks like mail, to the server. The server sends the response, which looks like a mail reply to the client. The request and response messages carry data in the form of a letter with MIME-like format.

The commands from the client to the server are embedded in a letter-like request message. The contents of the requested file or other information are embedded in a letter-like response message.

> HTTP uses the services of TCP on well-known port 80.

24.1 HTTP TRANSACTION

Figure 24.1 illustrates the HTTP transaction between the client and server. Although HTTP uses the services of TCP, HTTP itself is a stateless protocol. The client initializes the transaction by sending a request message. The server replies by sending a response.

Figure 24.1 *HTTP transaction*

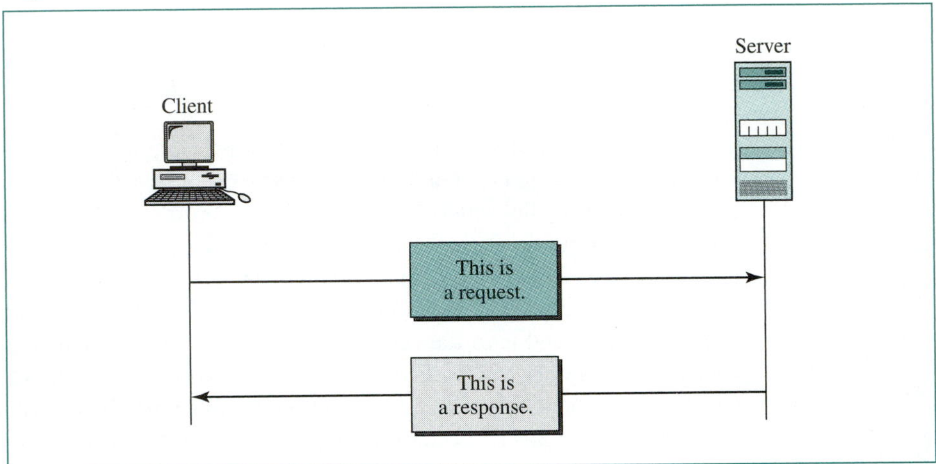

Messages

There are two general types of HTTP messages; these are shown in Figure 24.2.

Figure 24.2 *Message categories*

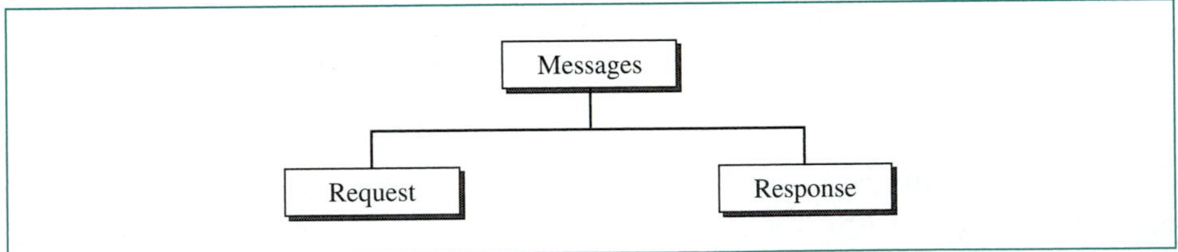

Both message types follow almost the same format.

24.2 REQUEST MESSAGES

A request message consists of a request line, a header, and sometimes a body. See Figure 24.3.

Figure 24.3 *Request message*

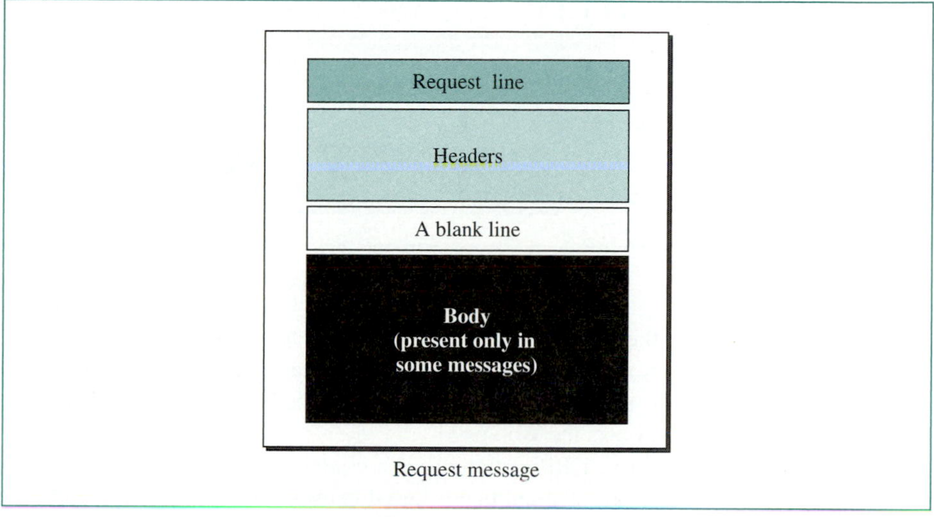

Request Line

The request line defines the request type, resource (URL), and HTTP version (see Figure 24.4). The request line consists of a request type, a space, a URL, a space, and HTTP version.

Figure 24.4 *Request line*

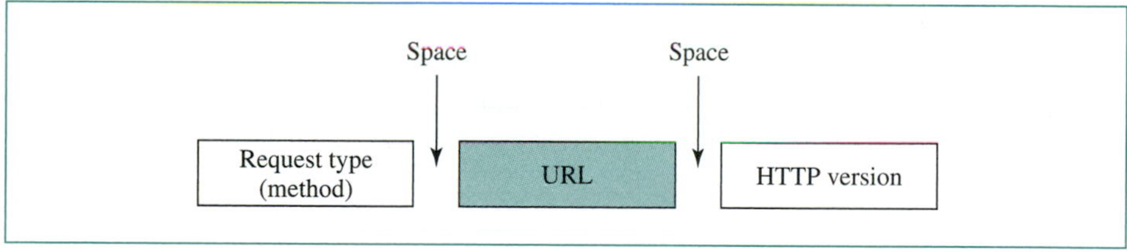

- **Request type.** In version 1.1 of HTTP, several request types are defined. The request type categorizes the request messages into several methods, which we will discuss later.
- **Uniform Resource Locator (URL).** A client that wants to access a Web page needs an address. To facilitate the access of documents distributed throughout the world, HTTP uses the concept of locators. The URL is a standard for specifying any kind of information on the Internet. The URL defines four things: method, host computer, port, and path (see Figure 24.5).

  The *method* is the protocol used to retrieve the document. Several different protocols can retrieve a document; among them are Gopher, FTP, HTTP, News, and TELNET.

Figure 24.5 *URL*

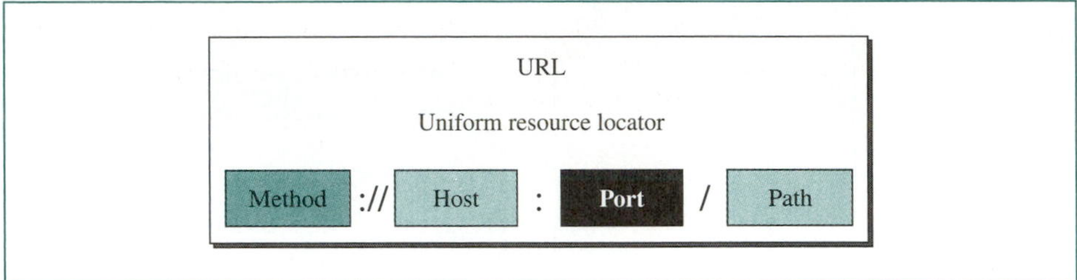

The *host* is the computer where the information is located, although the name of the computer can be an alias. Web pages are usually stored in computers, and computers are given alias names that usually begin with the characters "www". This is not mandatory, however, as the host can be any name given to the computer that hosts the Web page.

The URL optionally can contain the port number of the server. If the *port* is included, it should be inserted between the host and the path, and it should be separated from the host by a colon.

Path is the pathname of the file where the information is located. Note that the path can itself contain slashes that, in the UNIX operating system, separate the directories from the subdirectories and files.

- **Version.** Although the most current version of HTTP is 1.1, HTTP versions 1.0 and 0.9 are still in use.

Methods

The request type field in a request message defines several kinds of messages referred to as *methods*. The request method is the actual command or request that a client issues to the server. We briefly discuss the purpose of some methods here.

GET

The GET method is used when the client wants to retrieve a document from the server. The address of the document is defined in the URL; this is the main method for retrieving a document. The server usually responds with the contents of the document in the body of the response message unless there is an error.

HEAD

The HEAD method is used when the client wants some information about a document but not the document itself. It is similar to GET, but the response from the server does not contain a body.

POST

The POST method is used when the client provides some information for the server. For example, it can be used to send input to a server.

PUT

The PUT method is used by the client to provide a new or replacement document to be stored on the server. The document is included in the body of the request and will be stored in the location defined by the URL.

PATCH

PATCH is similar to PUT except that the request contains only a list of differences that should be implemented in the existing file.

COPY

The COPY method is used to copy a file to another location. The location of the source file is given in the request line (URL); the location of the destination is given in the entity header (discussed in the Header section).

MOVE

The MOVE method is used to move a file to another location. The location of the source file is given in the request line (URL); the location of the destination is given in the entity header.

DELETE

The DELETE method is used to remove a document on the server.

LINK

The LINK method is used to create a link or links from a document to another location. The location of the file is given in the request line (URL); the location of the destination is given in the entity header.

UNLINK

The UNLINK method is used to delete links created by the LINK method.

OPTION

The OPTION method is used by the client to ask the server about available options.

24.3 RESPONSE MESSAGE

A response message consists of a status line, a header, and sometimes a body. See Figure 24.6.

Status Line

The status line defines the status of the response message. It consists of the HTTP version, a space, a status code, a space, a status phrase. See Figure 24.7.

Figure 24.6 *Response message*

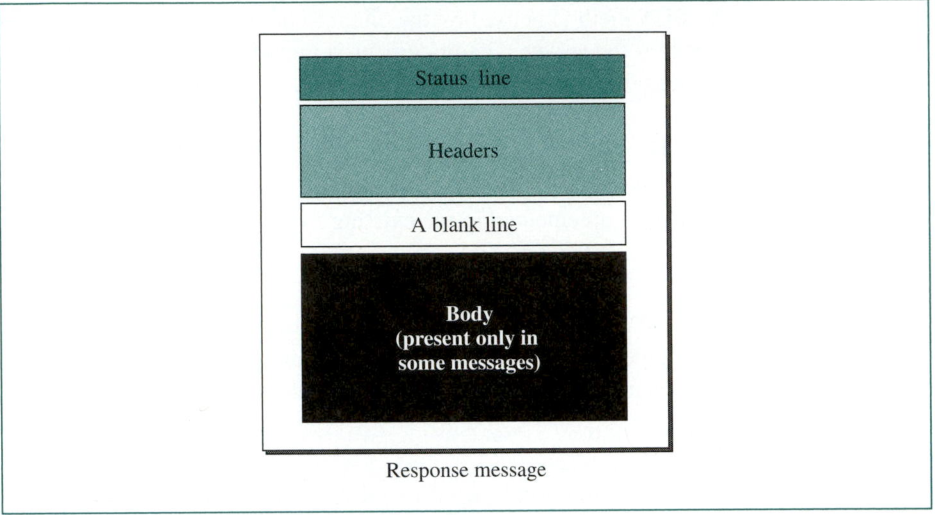

Figure 24.7 *Status line*

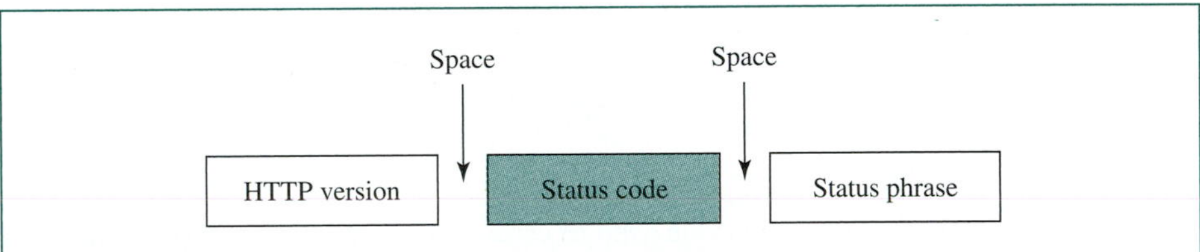

- **HTTP version.** This field is the same as the field in the request line.
- **Status code.** The status code field is similar to those in the FTP and the SMTP protocols. It consists of three digits. Whereas the codes in the 100 range are only informational, the codes in the 200 range indicate a successful request. The codes in the 300 range redirect the client to another URL, and the codes in the 400 range indicate an error at the client site. Finally, the codes in the 500 range indicate an error at the server site. We list the most common codes in Table 24.1.

Table 24.1 *Status codes*

Code	*Phrase*	*Description*
	Informational	
100	Continue	The initial part of the request has been received and the client may continue with its request
101	Switching	The server is complying with a client request to switch protocols defined in the upgrade header

Table 24.1 *Status codes (continued)*

Code	*Phrase*	*Description*
		Success
200	OK	The request is successful
201	Created	A new URL is created
202	Accepted	The request is accepted, but it is not immediately acted upon
204	No content	There is no content in the body
		Redirection
301	Multiple choices	The requested URL refers to more than one resource
302	Moved permanently	The requested URL is no longer used by the server
304	Moved temporarily	The requested URL has moved temporarily
		Client Error
400	Bad request	There is a syntax error in the request
401	Unauthorized	The request lacks proper authorization
403	Forbidden	Service is denied
404	Not found	The document is not found
405	Method not allowed	The method is not supported in this URL
406	Not acceptable	The format requested is not acceptable
		Server Error
500	Internal server error	There is an error, such as a crash, in the server site
501	Not implemented	The action requested cannot be performed
503	Service unavailable	The service is temporarily unavailable, but may be requested in the future

- **Status phrase.** This field explains the status code in text form. Table 24.1 also gives the status phrase.

24.4 HEADER

The header exchanges additional information between the client and the server. For example, the client can request that the document be sent in a special format or the server can send extra information about the document.

The header can be one or more header lines. Each header line is made of a header name, a colon, a space, and a header value (see Figure 24.8). We will show some header lines in the examples at the end of this chapter.

A header line belongs to one of four categories: general header, request header, response header, and entity header. A request message can contain only general,

Figure 24.8 *Header format*

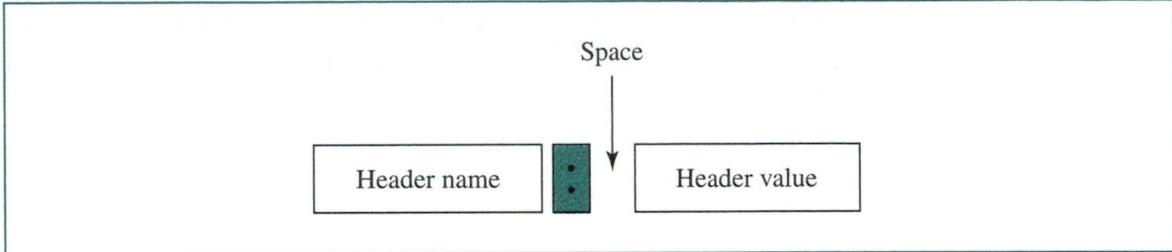

request, and entity headers. A response message, on the other hand, can contain only general, response, and entity headers. Figure 24.9 diagrams a request message and a response message.

Figure 24.9 *Headers*

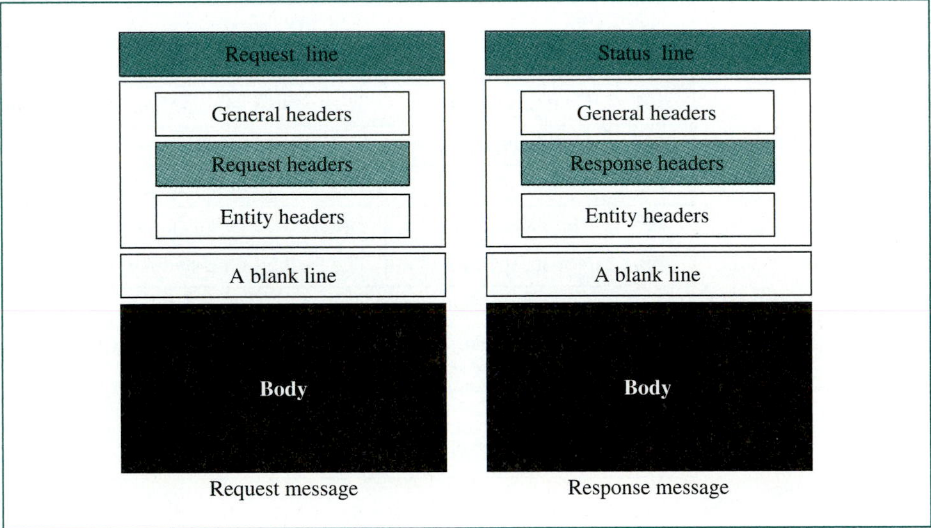

General Header

The general header gives general information about the message and can be present in both a request and a response. Table 24.2 list some general headers with their descriptions.

Table 24.2 *General headers*

Header	*Description*
Cache-control	Specifies information about caching
Connection	Shows whether the connection should be closed or not
Date	Shows the current date
MIME-version	Shows the MIME version used
Upgrade	Specifies the preferred communication protocol

Request Header

The request header can be present only in a request message. It specifies the client's configuration and the client's preferred document format. See Table 24.3 for a list of some request headers and their descriptions.

Table 24.3 *Request headers*

Header	*Description*
Accept	Shows the media format the client can accept
Accept-charset	Shows the character set the client can handle
Accept-encoding	Shows the encoding scheme the client can handle
Accept-language	Shows the language the client can accept
Authorization	Shows what permissions the client has
From	Shows the email address of the user
Host	Shows the host and port number of the client
If-modified-since	Send the document if newer than specified date
If-match	Send the document only if it matches given tag
If-non-match	Send the document only if it does not match given tag
If-range	Send only the portion of the document that is missing
If-unmodified-since	Send the document if not changed since specified date
Referrer	Specifies the URL of the linked document
User-agent	Identifies the client program

Response Header

The response header can be present only in a response message. It specifies the server's configuration and special information about the request. See Table 24.4 for a list of some response headers with their descriptions.

Table 24.4 *Response headers*

Header	*Description*
Accept-range	Shows if server accepts the range requested by client
Age	Shows the age of the document
Public	Shows the supported list of methods
Retry-after	Specifies the date after which the server is available
Server	Shows the server name and version number

Entity Header

The entity header gives information about the body of the document. Although it is mostly present in response messages, some request messages, such as POST or PUT methods, that contain a body also use this type of header. See Table 24.5 for a list of some entity headers and their descriptions.

Table 24.5 *Entity headers*

Header	*Description*
Allow	List valid methods that can be used with a URL
Content-encoding	Specifies the encoding scheme
Content-language	Specifies the language
Content-length	Shows the length of the document
Content-range	Specifies the range of the document
Content-type	Specifies the media type
Etag	Gives an entity tag
Expires	Gives the date and time when contents may change
Last-modified	Gives the date and time of the last change
Location	Specifies the location of the created or moved document

24.5 EXAMPLES

In this section, we give three simple examples of request and response messages.

Example 1

This example retrieves a document. We use the GET method to retrieve an image with the path /usr/bin/image1. The request line shows the method (GET), the URL, and the HTTP version (1.1). The header has two lines that show that the client can accept images in the GIF and JPEG format. The request does not have a body. The response message contains the status line and four lines of header. The header lines define the date, server, MIME version, and length of the document. The body of the document follows the header (see Figure 24.10).

Example 2

This example retrieves information about a document. We use the HEAD method to retrieve information about an HTML document (see Chapter 25). The request line shows the method (HEAD), URL, and HTTP version (1.1). The header is one line showing that the client can accept the document in any format (wild card). The request does not have a body. The response message contains the status line and five lines of header. The header lines define the date, server, MIME version, type of document, and length of the document (see Figure 24.11). Note that the response message does not contain a body.

Figure 24.10 *Example 1*

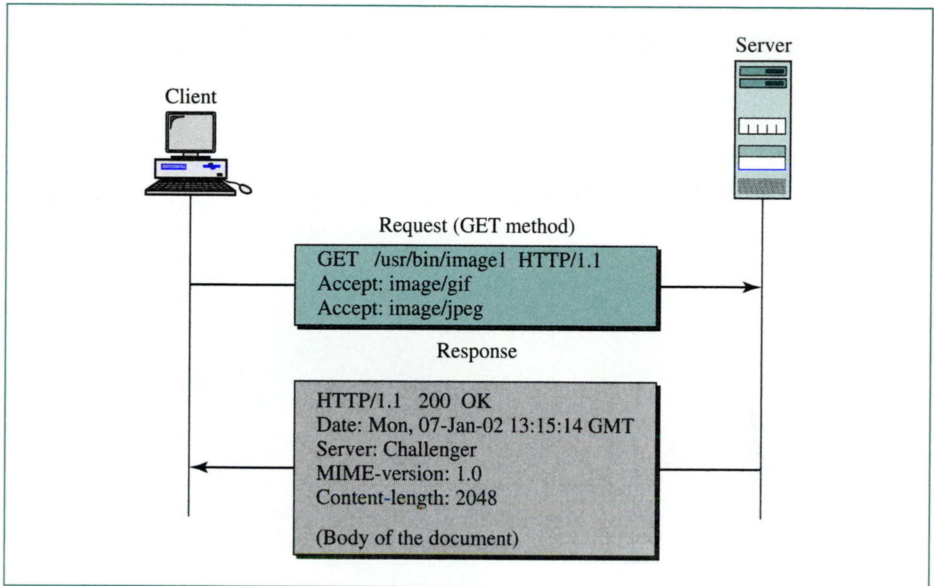

Figure 24.11 *Example 2*

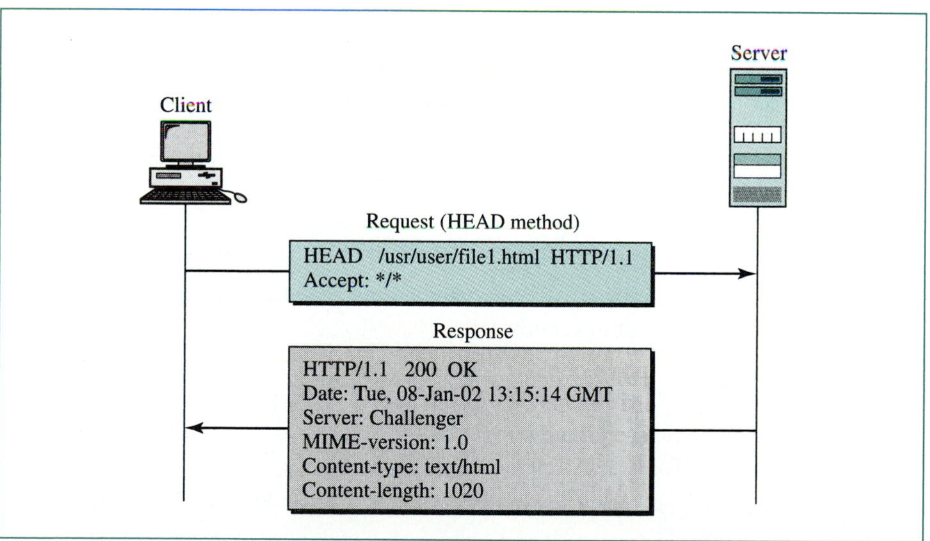

Example 3

In this example, the client wants to send input data to the server. We use the POST method. The request line shows the method (POST), URL, and HTTP version (1.1). There are four lines of headers. The request contains the input information in the body. The response message contains the status line and four lines of headers. The created document, which is a CGI document (see Chapter 25), is included as the body (see Figure 24.12).

Figure 24.12 *Example 3*

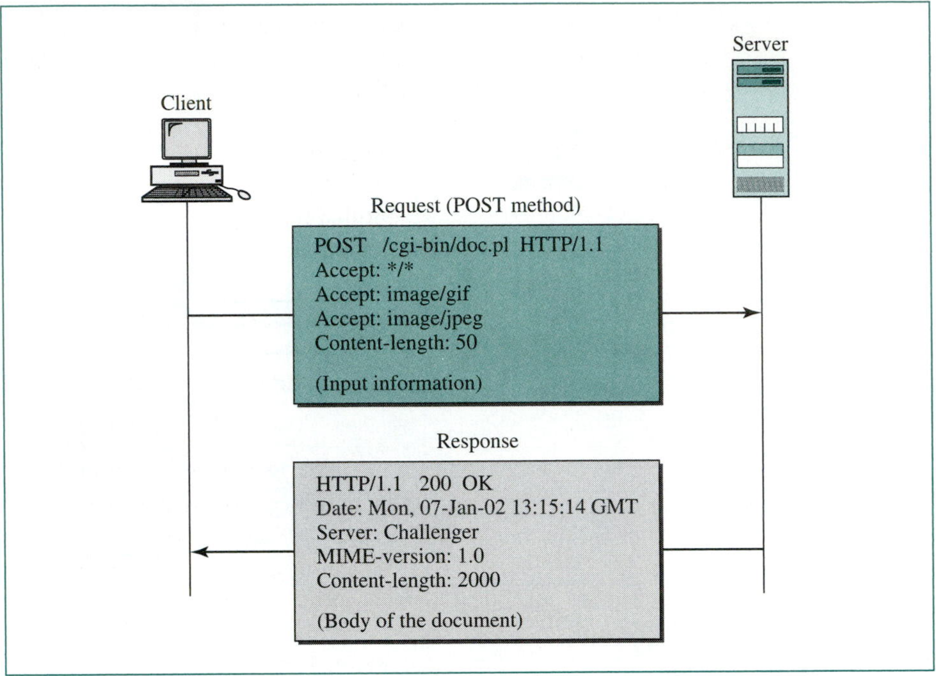

24.6 SOME OTHER FEATURES

In this section, we briefly discuss some other features of HTTP in version 1.1.

Persistent versus Nonpersistent Connection

HTTP version 1.0 specified a nonpersistent connection, while a persistent connection is the default in version 1.1.

Nonpersistent Connection

In a nonpersistent connection, one TCP connection is made for each request/response. The following lists the steps in this strategy:

1. The client opens a TCP connection and sends a request.
2. The server sends the response and closes the connection.
3. The client reads the data until it encounters an end-of-file marker; it then closes the connection.

In this strategy, for N different pictures in different files, the connection must be opened and closed N times. The nonpersistent strategy imposes high overhead on the server because the server needs N different buffers and requires a slow start procedure each time a connection is opened.

Persistent Connection

HTTP version 1.1 specifies a persistent connection by default. In a persistent connection, the server leaves the connection open for more requests after sending a response. The server can close the connection at the request of a client or if a timeout has been reached. The sender usually sends the length of the data with each response. However, there are some occasions when the sender does not know the length of the data. This is the case when a document is created dynamically or actively (see Chapter 25). In these cases, the server informs the client that the length is not known and closes the connection after sending the data so the client knows that the end of the data has been reached.

> HTTP version 1.1 specifies a persistent connection by default.

Proxy Server

HTTP supports proxy servers. A proxy server is a computer that keeps copies of responses to recent requests. In the presence of a proxy server, the HTTP client sends a request to the proxy server. The proxy server checks its cache. If the response is not stored in the cache, the proxy server sends the request to the corresponding server. Incoming responses are sent to the proxy server and stored for future requests from other clients.

The proxy server reduces the load on the original server, decreases traffic, and improves latency. However, to use the proxy server, the client must be configured to access the proxy instead of the target server.

24.7 KEY TERMS

entity header

general header

host

Hypertext Transfer Protocol (HTTP)

nonpersistent connection

path

persistent connection

port

proxy server

request header

request line

request type

response header

status code

status line

uniform resource locator (URL)

24.8 SUMMARY

- The Hypertext Transfer Protocol (HTTP) is the main protocol used to access data on the World Wide Web (WWW).
- HTTP uses a TCP connection to transfer files.
- An HTTP message is similar in form to an SMTP message.
- An HTTP message (request or response) consists of a request or status line, headers, and a body (required only for certain types of messages).
- The request line consists of a request type, a URL, and the HTTP version number.
- The uniform resource locator (URL) consists of a method, host computer, optional port number, and pathname to locate information on the WWW.
- The request type or method is the actual command or request issued by the client to the server.
- The status line consists of the HTTP version number, a status code, and a status phrase.
- The status code relays general information, information related to a successful request, redirection information, or error information.
- The header relays additional information between the client and server.
- A header consists of a header name and a header value.
- A general header gives general information about the request or response message.
- A request header specifies a client's configuration and preferred document format.
- A response header specifies a server's configuration and special information about the request.
- An entity header provides information about the body of a document.
- HTTP, version 1.1 specifies a persistent connection.
- A proxy server keeps copies of responses to recent requests.

24.9 PRACTICE SET

Multiple-Choice Questions

1. HTTP has similarities to both _______ and _______.
   a. FTP; SNMP
   b. FTP; SMTP
   c. FTP; MTV
   d. FTP; URL
2. A request message always contains _______.
   a. a header and a body
   b. a request line and a header
   c. a status line, a header, and a body
   d. a status line and a header

3. Which of the following is present in both a request line and a status line?
   a. HTTP version number
   b. URL
   c. status code
   d. status phrase
4. What does the URL need to access a document?
   a. pathname
   b. host computer
   c. retrieval method
   d. all of the above
5. Which of the following is a retrieval method?
   a. HTTP
   b. FTP
   c. TELNET
   d. all of the above
6. A user wants to replace a document with a newer version; the request line contains the _______ method.
   a. GET
   b. POST
   c. COPY
   d. PUT
7. A user wants to copy a file to another location; the request line contains the _______ method.
   a. PUT
   b. PATCH
   c. COPY
   d. POST
8. A user needs to retrieve a document from the server; the request line contains the _______ method.
   a. GET
   b. HEAD
   c. POST
   d. PUT
9. A user needs to send the server some information. The request line method is _______.
   a. OPTION
   b. PATCH
   c. MOVE
   d. POST

10. A user needs to move a file to another location. The request line method is _______.
    a. MOVE
    b. PUT
    c. GET
    d. PATCH
11. A response message always contains _______.
    a. a header and a body
    b. a request line and a header
    c. a status line, a header, and a body
    d. a status line and a header
12. Status codes that send the client to another URL are in the _______ range.
    a. 100
    b. 200
    c. 300
    d. 400
13. Status codes that indicate a successful request are in the _______ range.
    a. 100
    b. 200
    c. 300
    d. 400
14. Status codes that indicate a client error are in the _______ range.
    a. 100
    b. 200
    c. 300
    d. 400
15. The _______ header supplies information about the body of a document.
    a. general
    b. request
    c. response
    d. entity
16. The _______ header can specify the server configuration or provide information about a request.
    a. general
    b. request
    c. response
    d. entity

17. The _______ header can specify the client configuration and the client's preferred document format.
    a. general
    b. request
    c. response
    d. entity

Exercises

18. Show a request that retrieves the document /usr/users/doc/doc1. Use at least two general headers, two request headers, and one entity header.
19. Show the response to exercise 18 for a successful request.
20. Show the response to exercise 18 if the document has permanently moved to /usr/deads/doc1.
21. Show the response to exercise 18 if there is a syntax error in the request.
22. Show the response to exercise 18 if the client is unauthorized to access the document.
23. Show a request that asks for information about a document at /bin/users/file. Use at least two general headers and one request header.
24. Show the response to exercise 23 for a successful request.
25. Show the request to copy the file at location /bin/usr/bin/file1 to /bin/file1.
26. Show the response to exercise 25.
27. Show the request to delete the file at location /bin/file1.
28. Show the response to exercise 27.
29. Show a request to retrieve the file at location /bin/etc/file1. The client needs the document only if it was modified after January 23, 1999.
30. Show the response to exercise 29.
31. Show a request to retrieve the file at location /bin/etc/file1. The client should identify itself.
32. Show the response to exercise 31.
33. Show a request to store a file at location /bin/letter. The client should identify the types of documents it can accept.
34. Show the response to exercise 33. The response should show the age of the document as well as the date and time when the contents may change.

CHAPTER 25

World Wide Web (WWW)

The **World Wide Web** (WWW) is a repository of information spread all over the world and linked together. The WWW has a unique combination of flexibility, portability, and user-friendly features that distinguish it from other services provided by the Internet.

The WWW project was initiated by CERN (European Laboratory for Particle Physics) to create a system to handle distributed resources necessary for scientific research.

The WWW today is a distributed client-server service, in which a client using a browser can access a service using a server. However, the service provided is distributed over many locations called *websites* (see Figure 25.1).

Figure 25.1 *Distributed services*

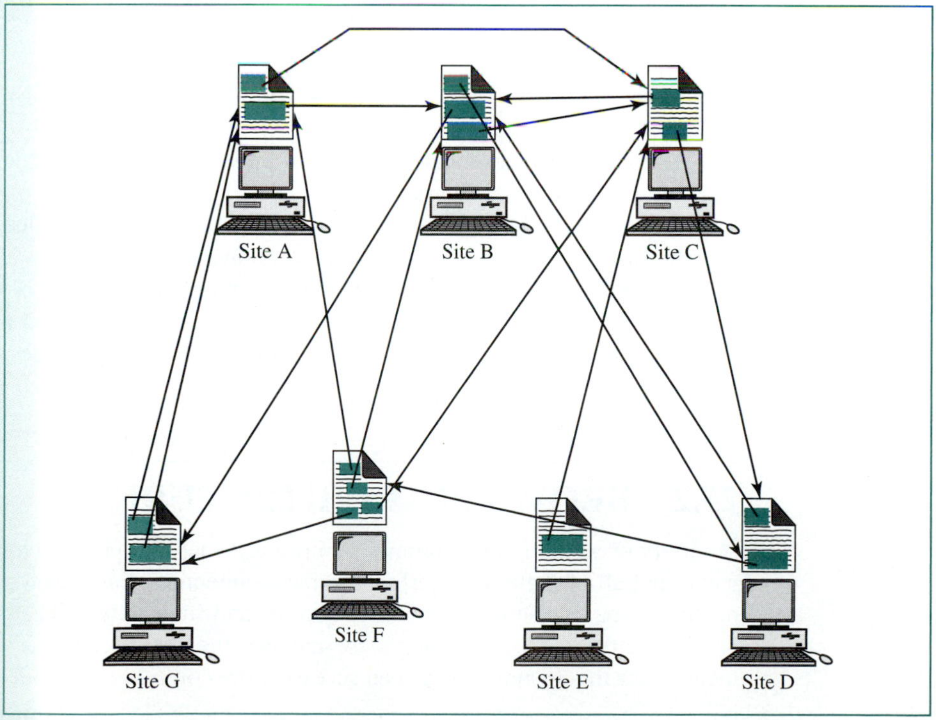

25.1 HYPERTEXT AND HYPERMEDIA

The WWW uses the concept of hypertext and hypermedia. In a hypertext environment, information is stored in a set of documents that are linked together using the concept of pointers. An item can be associated with another document using a pointer. The reader who is browsing through the document can move to other documents by choosing (clicking) the items that are linked to other documents. Figure 25.2 shows the concept of hypertext.

Figure 25.2 *Hypertext*

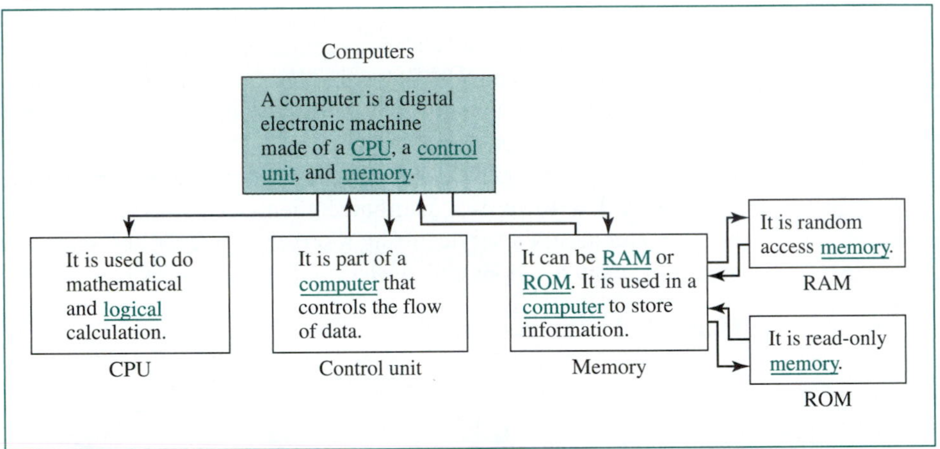

Whereas hypertext documents contain only text, hypermedia documents can contain pictures, graphics, and sound.

A unit of hypertext or hypermedia available on the Web is called a *page*. The main page for an organization or an individual is known as a *homepage*.

Information about one specific subject can be undistributed or distributed. In the first case, all of the information may consist of one or more Web pages on the same server. In the second case, the information is made of multiple pages distributed on different servers.

25.2 BROWSER ARCHITECTURE

A variety of vendors offer commercial browsers that interpret and display a Web document, and all of them use nearly the same architecture. Each browser usually consists of three parts: a controller, client programs, and interpreters. The controller receives input from the keyboard or the mouse and uses the client programs to access the document. After the document has been accessed, the controller uses one of the interpreters to display the document on the screen. The client programs can be one of the methods (protocols) described previously such as HTTP, FTP, Gopher, or TELNET. The interpreter can be HTML or Java, depending on the type of document (see Figure 25.3).

Figure 25.3 *Browser architecture*

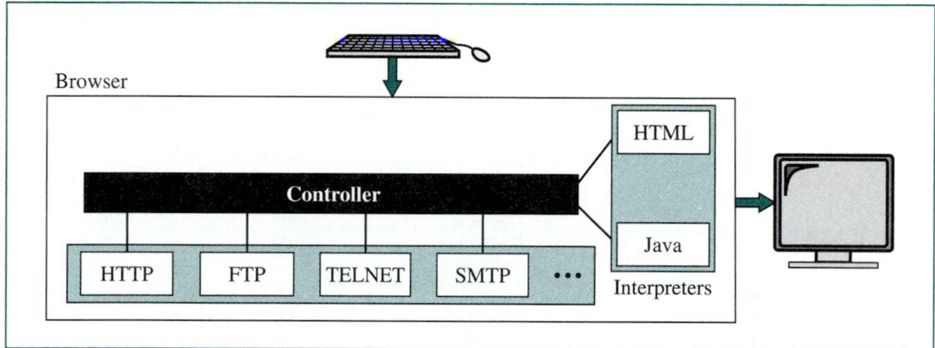

The documents in the WWW can be grouped into three broad categories: static, dynamic, and active (see Figure 25.4). The category is based on the time the contents of the document are determined.

Figure 25.4 *Categories of Web documents*

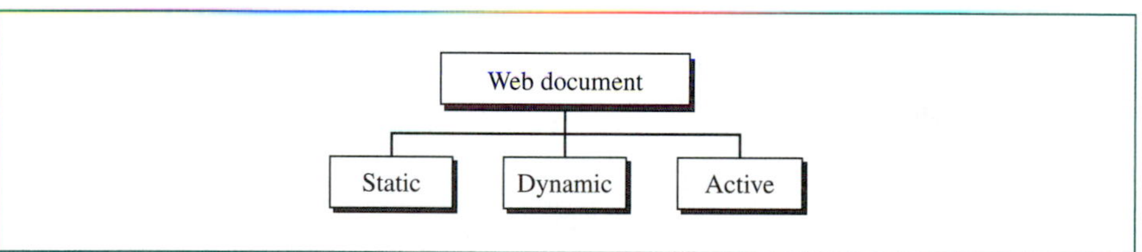

25.3 STATIC DOCUMENTS

Static documents are fixed-content documents that are created and stored in a server. The client can get only a copy of the document. In other words, the contents of the file are determined when the file is created, not when it is used. Of course, the contents in the server can be changed, but the user cannot change it. When a client accesses the document, a copy of the document is sent. The user can then use a browsing program to display the document (see Figure 25.5).

Figure 25.5 *Static document*

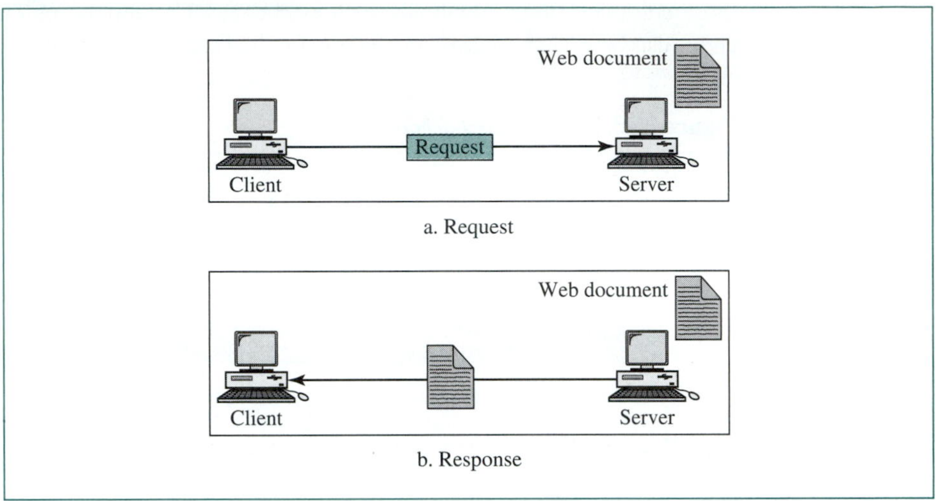

25.4 HTML

Hypertext Markup Language (HTML) is a language for creating Web pages. The term *markup language* comes from the book publishing industry. Before a book is typeset and printed, a copy editor reads the manuscript and puts a lot of marks on it. These marks tell the designer how to format the text. For example, if the copy editor wants part of a line to be printed in boldface, he or she draws a wavy line under that part. In the same way, data for a Web page is formatted for interpretation by a browser.

Let us clarify the idea with an example. To make part of a text displayed in boldface with HTML, we must include the beginning and ending boldface tags (marks) in the text as shown in Figure 25.6.

Figure 25.6 *Boldface tags*

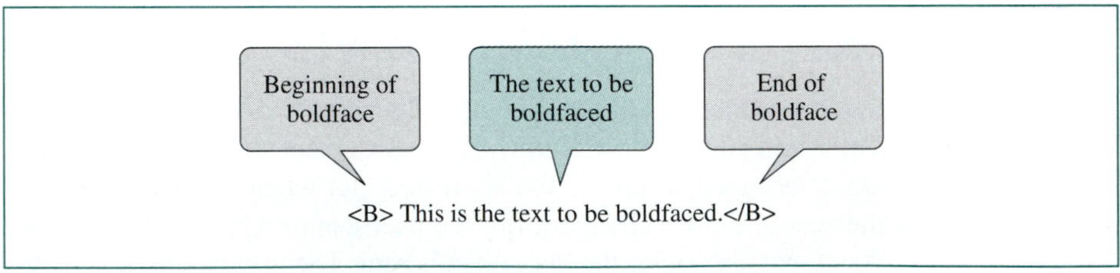

The two tags <B> and </B> are instructions for the browser. When the browser sees these two marks, it knows that the text must be boldfaced (see Figure 25.7).

A markup language such as HTML allows us to embed formatting instructions in the file itself. The instructions are stored with the text. In this way, any browser can read the instructions and format the text according to the workstation being used. One might

Figure 25.7 *Effect of boldface tags*

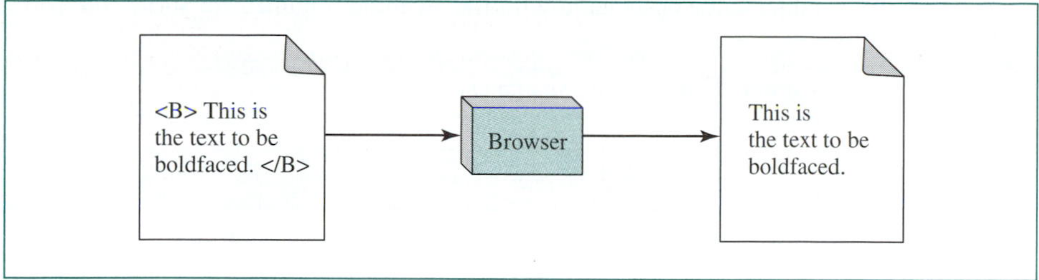

ask why we do not use the formatting capabilities of word processors to create and save formatted text. The answer is that different word processors use different techniques or procedures for formatting text. For example, imagine that a user creates formatted text on a Macintosh computer and stores it in a Web page. Another user who is on an IBM computer is not able to receive the Web page because the two computers are using different formatting procedures.

HTML lets us use only ASCII characters for both the main text and formatting instructions. In this way, every computer can receive the whole document as an ASCII document. The main text is the data, and the formatting instructions can be used by the browser to format the data.

Structure of a Web Page

A Web page is made up of two parts: the head and body.

Head

The head is the first part of a Web page. The head contains the title of the page and other parameters that the browser will use.

Body

The actual contents of a page are in the body, which includes the text and the tags. Whereas the text is the actual information contained in a page, the tags define the appearance of the document. Every HTML tag is a name followed by an optional list of attributes, all enclosed between less-than and greater-than brackets.

An attribute, if present, is followed by an equal sign and the value of the attribute. Some tags can be used alone; some must be used in pairs. Those that are used in pairs are called *starting* and *ending* tags. The starting tag can have attributes and values. The ending tag cannot have attributes or values but must have a slash before the name.

Tags

The browser makes a decision about the structure of the text based on the tags, which are marks that are embedded into the text. A tag is enclosed in two brackets (< and >) and usually comes in pairs. The beginning tag starts with the name of the tag, and the ending tag starts with a slash followed by the name of the tag.

A tag can have a list of attributes, each of which can be followed by an equal sign and a value associated with the attribute. Figure 25.8 shows the format of a tag.

Figure 25.8 *Beginning and ending tags*

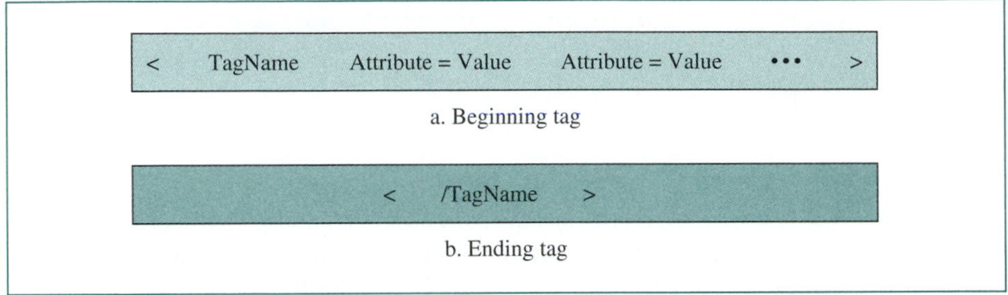

Table 25.1 shows some of the most common tags. We explain some of these tags based on their category.

Table 25.1 *Common tags*

Beginning Tag	*Ending Tag*	*Meaning*
Skeletal Tags		
<HTML>	</HTML>	Defines an HTML document
<HEAD>	</HEAD>	Defines the head of the document
<BODY>	</BODY>	Defines the body of the document
Title and Header Tags		
<TITLE>	</TITLE>	Defines the title of the document
<Hn>	</Hn>	Defines different headers (n is an integer)
Text Formatting Tags		
<B>	</B>	Boldface
<I>	</I>	Italic
<U>	</U>	Underlined
_		Subscript
[	]	Superscript
Data Flow Tags		
<CENTER>	</CENTER>	Centered
 		Line break
List Tags		
<OL>	</OL>	Ordered list
<UL>	</UL>	Unordered list
<LI>	</LI>	An item in a list
Image Tags		
<IMG>		Defines an image

Table 25.1 *Common tags (continued)*

Beginning Tag	*Ending Tag*	*Meaning*
	Hyperlink Tags	
<A>	</A>	Defines an address (hyperlink)
	Executable Contents	
<APPLET>	</APPLET>	The document is an applet

Skeletal Tags

Skeletal tags show the skeleton of the document and show how it is divided into a head and body.

- **<HTML> and </HTML>.** Every HTML document must start and finish with these two tags. They are the signals to the browser that an HTML document is embedded between these two tags.
- **<HEAD> and </HEAD>.** The head contains information about the document itself. The head must be defined using the two head tags.
- **<BODY> and </BODY>.** The body of the page contains the actual information. The body is encapsulated between the two body tags.

Title and Header Tags

The following tags are used to show titles or headers.

- **<TITLE> and </TITLE>.** The title of the page is usually embedded in the head. The title is encapsulated between the two title markers. The title may or may not be displayed or printed when the page is accessed by the browser.
- **<Hn> and </Hn>.** Headers are inserted into a page by using header tags. We can create different levels of headers, with each in a different font size. The header marker is the character H followed by a digit. For example, H1 creates the biggest header, H2 is the second level header, and so on.

Text Formatting Tags

The following tags are used to recommend the format of the text.

- **<B> and </B>.** The text between these tags should be bold.
- **<I> and </I>.** The text between these tags should be italic.
- **<U> and </U>.** The text between these tags should be underlined.
- **_{and}.** The text between these tags should be subscript.
- **^{and}.** The text between these tags should be superscript.

Data Flow Tags

The following tags are used to control the flow of data.

- **
.** This tag inserts a line break into the text.
- **<CENTER> and </CENTER>.** The text enclosed between these tags should be centered.

List Tags

The following tags are used to create a list of items.

- **<UL> and </UL>.** We often need to create a list of items. HTML has a mechanism to create several types of lists. The simplest of these is the unordered list, in which items are listed one after another with a bullet in front. To create a list, use the <UL> tag at the beginning and the </UL> tag at the end of the list. Each item listed must be preceded by the <LI> tag.
- **<OL> and </OL>.** These tags are similar to <UL> and </UL> except that the items in the list are numbered instead of bulleted.
- **<LI> and </LI>.** These tags define an item in a list. The ending tag is usually omitted.

Image Tags

The following tag is used to insert a figure in the document.

- **<IMG......>.** Nontextual information such as digitized photos or graphic images are not a physical part of an HTML document. But we can use an image tag to point to the file of the photo or image. The image tag defines the address of the image to be retrieved (a URL). It also specifies how the image can be inserted after retrieval. The following shows the format of the image tag. We can choose from among several attributes. The most common are SRC (source), which defines the source (address), and ALIGN, which defines the alignment of the image. The SRC attribute is required. Most browsers accept images in the GIF or JPEG formats.

```
<IMG  SRC="..........."  ALIGN=............ ................>
```

For example, the following tag can retrieve an image stored as image1.gif in the directory /bin/images:

```
<IMG  SRC="/bin/images/image1.gif"  ALIGN=MIDDLE >
```

Hyperlink Tags

The following tags are used to allow one document to be linked to another.

- **<A......> and </A>.** A hypertext markup language needs to link documents together. Any item (word, phrase, paragraph, or image) can refer to another document. A mechanism called an *anchor* does this job. The anchor is defined by <A.....> and </A> tags, and the anchored items use the URL to refer to another document. When the document is displayed, the anchored items are underlined, blinking, or boldfaced. The user can click on the anchored item to go to another document, which may or may not be stored on the same server as the original document.

  The following shows the format of the anchor tags. The reference phrase is embedded between the beginning and ending tags. The beginning tag can have several attributes, but the one required is the HREF (hyperlink reference), which defines the address (URL) of the linked document.

```
<A HREF= "......................" > Ref-Phrase </A>
```

For example, to link to the author of a book we might see:

```
<A HREF= "http://www.deanza.edu/somebody"> Author </A>
```

What appears in the text is the word "Author," on which the user can click to go to the author's Web page.

Executable Contents Tags

The executable contents tags show that the contents enclosed between the two tags are binary code or bytecode. They should be executed to create the output. We discuss only the tags that define a document as an applet (see the section on Java).

- **<APPLET...> and </APPLET>.** These tags define the document as an **applet,** a small program written in the Java language. Several attributes can be used with applet tags; we show only the most common ones.

```
<APPLET CODE=..... HEIGHT=..... WIDTH=......>
.........................................................
.........................................................
.........................................................
</APPLET>
```

We will see how these tags are used when we discuss Java applets.

Examples

In this section, we give some simple examples of HTML documents to show the implementation of the tags previously described.

Example 1

This simple example shows how the skeletal tags are used to define the parts of an HTML document.

First HTML Program

```
<HTML>
    <HEAD>
        <TITLE>
            First Sample Document
        </TITLE>
```

First HTML Program (continued)

```
        </HEAD>

        <BODY>
                The body of the first sample program
                ..................................................................
                ..................................................................
        </BODY>
</HTML>
```

Example 2

This example shows how tags are used to let the browser format the appearance of the text.

Second HTML Program

```
<HTML>
        <HEAD>
                <TITLE> Second Sample Document </TITLE>
        </HEAD>
        <BODY>
                <CENTER>
                <H1><B>  ATTENTION </B></H1>
                </CENTER>
                You can get a copy of this document by:
                <UL>
                <LI> Writing to the publisher
                <LI> Ordering on-line
                <LI> Ordering through a bookstore
                </UL>
        </BODY>
</HTML>
```

Example 3

This example shows how tags are used to import an image and insert it into the text.

Third HTML Program

```
<HTML>
        <HEAD>
                <TITLE> Third Sample Document </TITLE>
        </HEAD>
```

Third HTML Program (continued)

```
        <BODY>
            This is the picture of a book:
            <IMG SRC="Pictures/book1.gif"  ALIGN=MIDDLE>
        </BODY>
</HTML>
```

Example 4

This example shows how tags are used to make a hyperlink to another document.

Fourth HTML Program

```
<HTML>
        <HEAD>
                <TITLE> Fourth Sample Document </TITLE>
        </HEAD>
        <BODY>
            This is a wonderful product that can save you money and time.
            To get information about the producer, click on
            <A HREF="http://www.phony.producer">
            Producer </A>
        </BODY>
</HTML>
```

25.5 DYNAMIC DOCUMENTS

Dynamic documents do not exist in a predefined format. Instead, a dynamic document is created by a Web server whenever a browser requests the document. When a request arrives, the Web server runs an application program that creates the dynamic document. The server returns the output of the program as a response to the browser that requested the document. Because a fresh document is created for each request, the contents of a dynamic document can vary from one request to another. A very simple example of a dynamic document is getting the time and date from the server. Time and date are kinds of information that are dynamic in that they change from moment to moment. The client can request that the server run a program such as the *date* program in UNIX and send the result of the program to the client. Figure 25.9 illustrates the steps in sending and responding to a dynamic document.

A server that handles dynamic documents follows these steps:

1. The server examines the URL to find if it defines a dynamic document.
2. If the URL defines a dynamic document, the server executes the program.
3. It sends the output of the program to the client (browser).

Figure 25.9 *Dynamic document*

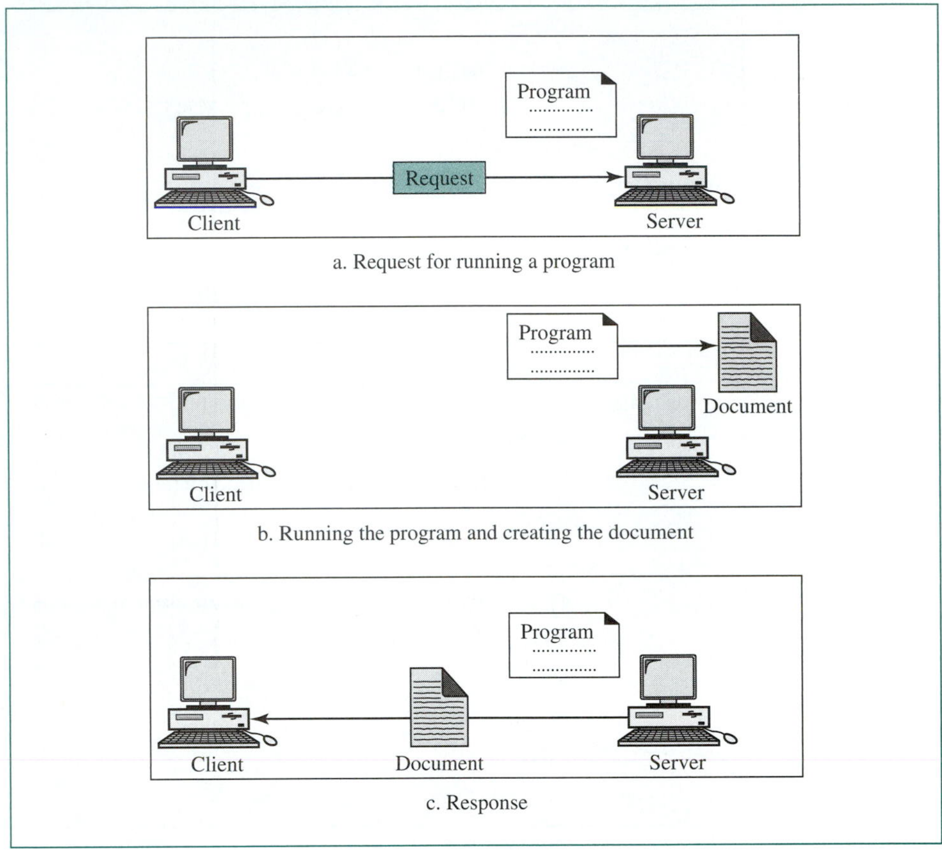

25.6 COMMON GATEWAY INTERFACE (CGI)

Common Gateway Interface (CGI) is a technology that creates and handles dynamic documents. CGI is a set of standards that defines how a dynamic document should be written, how input data should be supplied to the program, and how the output result should be used.

CGI is not a new language; instead, it allows programmers to use any of several languages such as C, C++, Bourne Shell, Korn Shell, C Shell, Tcl, or Perl. The only thing that CGI defines is a set of rules and terms that the programmer should follow.

The use of "common" in CGI indicates that the standard defines a set of rules that are common to any language or platform. The term *gateway* here means that a CGI program is a gateway that can be used to access other resources such as databases, graphic packages, and so on. The term *interface* here means that there are a set of predefined terms, variables, calls, and so on that can be used in any CGI program.

CGI Program

A CGI program in its simplest form is code written in one of the languages supporting CGI. Any programmer who can encode a sequence of thoughts in a program and knows the syntax of one of the above-mentioned languages can write a simple CGI program.

Environment Variables

To answer queries from a browser and access resources, a CGI program uses a list of environment variables. These environment variables either inherit their values from the parent process or the values are supplied by the browser (input). Table 25.2 shows the list.

Table 25.2 *Environment variable in CGI*

Beginning Tag	*Meaning*
AUTH_TYPE	Authentication method used to validate a user
CONTENT_LENGTH	The length of data passed to CGI
CONTENT_TYPE	The MIME type of the query data
DOCUMENT_ROOT	Directory of the Web document
GATEWAY_INTERFACE	Version of CGI
HTTP_ACCEPT	A list of MIME types that client can accept
HTTP_FORM	Email address of the user
HTTP_REFERER	URL of the document pointed to by the client
HTTP_USER_AGENT	Name of the client program (browser)
PATH_INFO	Extra path information given by URL
PATH_TRANSLATED	Translation of the contents of PATH_INFO
QUERY_STRING	Input information supplied by the user
REMOTE_ADDR	IP address of the client
REMOTE_HOST	Name of the client
REMOTE_IDENT	Username of the user
REMOTE_USER	Authenticated name of the user
SCRIPT_NAME	Path of the script being executed
SERVER_NAME	Server name or IP address
SERVER_PORT	Port number of the server
SERVER_PROTOCOL	Name and version of protocol used to receive request
SERVER_SOFTWARE	Name and version of the protocol used to send response

Input

In traditional programming, when a program is executed, parameters can be passed to the program. Parameter passing allows the programmer to write a generic program that can be used in different situations. For example, a generic copy program can be written to copy any file to another. A user can use the program to copy a file named *x* to another file named *y* by passing *x* and *y* as parameters.

The input from a browser to a server is sent using a *form*. If the information in a form is small (such as a word), it can be appended to the URL after a question mark. For example, the following URL is carrying form information (file1, the name of a file):

http://www.deanza/cgi-bin/prog.pl?file1

When the server receives the URL, it uses the part of the URL before the question mark to access the program to be run, and it interprets the part after the question mark ("file1") as the input sent by the client. It stores this string in an environment variable called QUERY_STRING. When the CGI program is executed, it can access this value.

If input from a browser is too long to fit in the query string, the browser can request the server to send a form. The browser can then fill the form with the input data and send it to the server. The information in the form can be used as the input to the CGI program.

Output

The whole idea of CGI is to execute a CGI program at the server site and send the output to the client (browser). The output is usually plain text or a text with HTML structures; however, the output can be a variety of other things. It can be graphics or binary data, a status code, instructions to the browser to cache the result, or instructions to the server to send an existing document instead of the actual output.

To tell the client the type of document sent, a CGI program should create headers. As a matter of fact, the output of the CGI program always consists of two parts: a header and a body. The header is separated by a blank line from the body. This means any CGI program first creates the header, then a blank line, and then the body. Although the header and the blank line are not shown on the browser screen, the header is used by the browser to interpret the body.

Several different headers are defined for the output from a CGI program. They are similar to the MIME headers discussed in Chapter 22. We briefly list some common ones here.

- **CONTENT_LENGTH.** This defines the length of the output data in bytes. It is normally defined for binary data (graphics, for example). For example, a program with the header *CONTENT_LENGTH: 2000* means that the output contains 2,000 bytes of binary data.
- **CONTENT_TYPE.** This defines the type of the output data. For example, a program with the header *CONTENT_TYPE: text/plain* contains plain text while *CONTENT-TYPE: text/html* contains HTML text.
- **EXPIRES.** This shows the date and time when the document is no longer valid.
- **LOCATION.** This shows the redirection. (We will discuss redirection later.)
- **PRAGMA.** This turns document caching on and off.
- **STATUS.** This shows the status of the request.

Redirection

The output of a CGI program can be the address of a file. This is called *redirection*. The output of the program can be an address to redirect the request to a static document. The browser can now use the address (URL) to fetch that static document.

Examples

In this section, we have given some examples of CGI programming that show the concept and idea. Programs are written in different languages to show the reader that CGI is language independent.

Example 1

Example 1 is a CGI program written in Bourne shell script. The program accesses the UNIX utility (*date*) that returns the date and the time. Note that the program output is in plain text.

First Example of CGI

```
#!/bin/sh
# The head of the program
echo Content_type: text/plain
echo
# The body of the program
now='date'
echo  $now
exit 0
```

Example 2

Example 2 is similar to Example 1 except that program output is in HTML.

Second Example of CGI

```
#!/bin/sh
#  The head of the program
echo Content_type: text/html
echo
#  The body of the program
echo <HTML>
echo <HEAD><TITLE> Date and Time </TITLE></HEAD>
echo <BODY>
now='date'
echo <CENTER><B> $now </B></CENTER>
echo </BODY>
echo </HTML>
exit 0
```

Example 3

Example 3 is similar to Example 2 except that the program is written in Perl.

Third Example of CGI

```
#!/bin/perl
# The head of the program
print "Content_type: text/html\n" ;
print "\n" ;
# The body of the program
print "<HTML>\n" ;
print "<HEAD><TITLE> Date and Time </TITLE></HEAD>\n" ;
print "<BODY>\n" ;
$now = 'date';
print "<CENTER><B> $now </B></CENTER>\n" ;
print "</BODY>\n" ;
print "</HTML>\n"
exit 0
```

Example 4

Example 4 creates information about the server and returns it to the client.

Fourth Example of CGI

```
#!/bin/perl
# The head of the program
print "Content/type: text/html\n" ;
print "\n" ;
# The body of the program
print "<HTML>\n" ;
print "<HEAD><TITLE> Server Information </TITLE></HEAD>\n" ;
print "<BODY>\n" ;
print " Server name:" , $ENV {'SERVER_NAME'}, "\n" ;
print " Port Number:" , $ENV {'SERVER_PORT'}, "\n" ;
print "</BODY>\n" ;
print "</HTML>\n" ;
exit 0
```

Example 5

Example 5 is a CGI program that requires user input. The program is written in C.

Fifth Example of CGI

```
#include <stdio.h>
#include <stdlib.h>
#include <string.h>
int main (void)
{
char *query = getenv ("QUERY_STRING");
float balance;
printf ("Content_type: text/plain\n\n");
if (query == NULL)
    {
    printf ("Sorry, you did not supply the name of the account.\n") ;
    printf ("To access the database, the account name is needed.\n") ;
    }
else
    {
    balance = Access_Balance (query) ;
    printf ("The balance is: %f\n", balance);
    }
return 0 ;
}
```

25.7 ACTIVE DOCUMENTS

For many applications, we need a program to be run at the client site. These are called **active documents.** For example, imagine we want to run a program that creates animated graphics on the screen or interacts with the user. The program definitely needs to be run at the client site where the animation or interaction takes place. When a browser requests an active document, the server sends a copy of the document in the form of bytecode. The document is then run at the client (browser) site (see Figure 25.10).

An active document in the server is stored in the form of binary code. However, it does not create overhead for the server in the same way that a dynamic document does. Although an active document is not run on the server, it is stored as a binary document that it is retrieved by a client. When a client receives the document, it can also store it in its own storage area. In this way, the client can run the document again without making another request.

An active document is transported from the server to the client in binary form. This means that it can be compressed at the server site and decompressed at the client site, saving both bandwidth and transmission time.

Figure 25.10 *Active document*

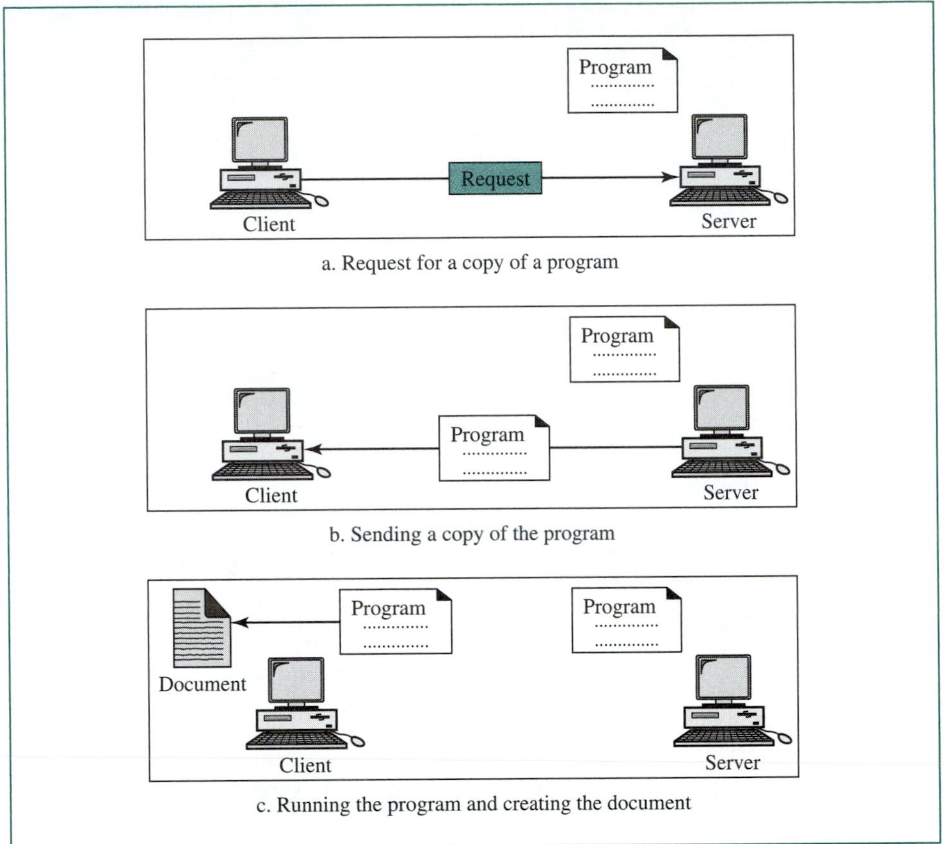

Creation, Compilation, and Execution

The following steps show how an active document is created, compiled, and executed.

1. At the server site, a programmer writes a program, in source code, and stores it in a file.
2. At the server site, the program is compiled and binary code is created, which is stored in a file. The pathname of this file is the one used by a URL to refer to the file. In this file, each program command (statement) is in binary form and each identifier (variable, constants, function names, and so on) is referred to by a binary offset address.
3. A client (browser) requests a copy of the binary code, which is probably transported in compressed form from the server to the client (browser).
4. The client (browser) uses its own software to change the binary code into executable code. The software links all the library modules and makes it ready for execution.
5. The client (browser) runs the program and creates the result that can include animation or interaction with the user.

25.8 JAVA

Java is a combination of a high-level programming language, a run-time environment, and a class library that allows a programmer to write an active document (an applet) and a browser to run it. It can also be used as a stand-alone program without using a browser.

Java is an object-oriented language which is, syntactically and semantically, very similar to C++. However, it does not have some of the complexities of C++ such as operator overloading or multiple inheritance. Java is also platform independent and does not use pointer arithmetic. In Java, like any other object-oriented language, a programmer defines a set of objects and a set of operations (methods) to operate on those objects. It is a *typed* language which means that the programmer must declare the type of any piece of data before using it. Java is also a concurrent language, which indicates the programmer can use multiple threads to create concurrency.

Classes and Objects

Java, as an object-oriented language, uses the concept of classes and objects. An object is an instance of a class that uses methods (procedures or functions) to manipulate encapsulated data.

Both data and methods can be private, protected, or public. Public data can be accessed by any procedure or program outside the class definition. Private data, on the other hand, can be accessed only by methods defined inside the class. Public methods can be invoked by any procedure or program; private methods can be invoked only by the methods defined inside the class. Protected data and methods can be accessed by methods in inherited classes (see inheritance).

Instantiation

To use an object, a process should instantiate an object, which means it should create an instance of the object. The instance encapsulates a set of data defined in the class. The process can use any of the public methods to manipulate the data encapsulated in an object.

Inheritance

One of the main ideas in object-oriented programming is the concept of inheritance. Inheritance defines a hierarchy of objects, in which one object can inherit data and methods from other objects. In Java we can define a class as the base class that contains data and methods common to many classes. Inherited classes can inherit these data and methods and can also have their own data and methods.

Packages

Java has a rich library of classes, which allows the programmer to create and use different objects in an applet. The classes are organized in packages. Six packages are common in Java today: java.lang, java.io, java.net, java.util, java.applet, and java.awt.

- **java.lang.** This package contains methods such as threads and exception handling that are part of the language itself. Standard libraries such as mathematical and string functions are also included in this package.
- **java.io.** This package contains classes that handle input/output operations.
- **java.net.** This package contains classes that handle transmission of messages over the network. It contains methods for creating IP datagrams, accessing the socket interface, and so on.
- **java.util.** This package contains classes that handle common data structures such as stacks, vectors, time, date, and hash tables.
- **java.applet.** This package contains methods for getting and displaying Web pages. It also includes a very special class called an object class. This is an abstract class, from which all other objects are derived.
- **java.awt.** This is the Abstract Window Toolkit (AWT), which is a package designed to make the Java language portable. It contains classes and methods that make an applet capable of being run on any client environment. It contains classes and methods that enable an applet to draw on the screen. The java.awt package creates the necessary interface with the local operating system. Event handling (which includes detecting a keystroke, mouse motion, etc.) is also included in this package. This package includes two subpackages called *java.awt.image,* which manages images, and *java.awt.peer,* which is used to access the window system. Note that in Java 2, the javax.swing packages are used instead of java.out.

Skeleton of an Applet

An applet is a dynamic document written in Java. It is actually the definition of a publicly inherited class, which inherits from the applet class defined in the java.applet library. The programmer can define private data and public and private methods in this definition (see Figure 25.11).

Figure 25.11 *Skeleton of an applet*

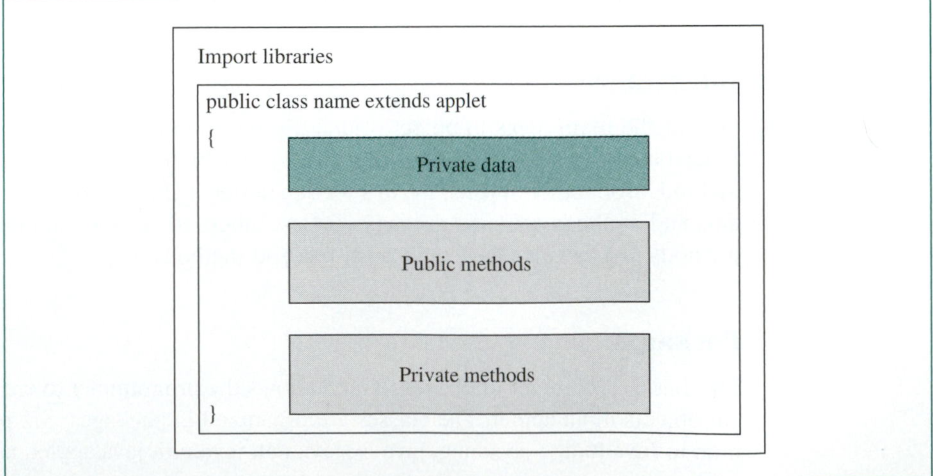

The client process (browser) creates an instance of this applet. The browser then uses the public methods defined in the applet to invoke private methods or to access data. Figure 25.12 shows this relationship.

Figure 25.12 *Instantiation of the object defined by an applet*

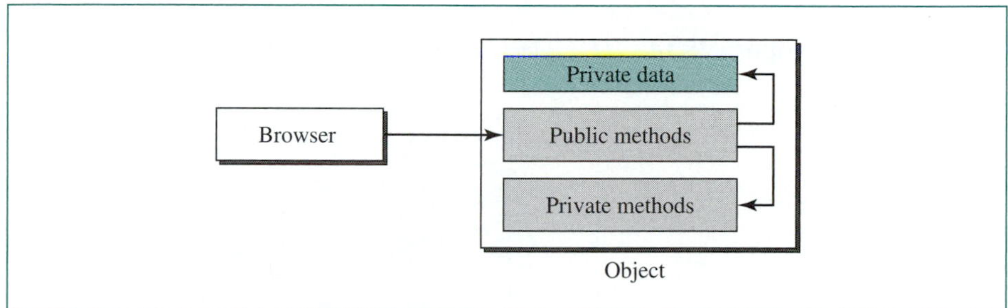

Creation and Compilation

To be used as an applet, the class definition is created using a text editor. The name of the file is the same as the name of the publicly inherited class with the "java" extension. The Java compiler creates bytecode out of this file, which has the same name with the "class" extension (see Figure 25.13).

Figure 25.13 *Creation and compilation*

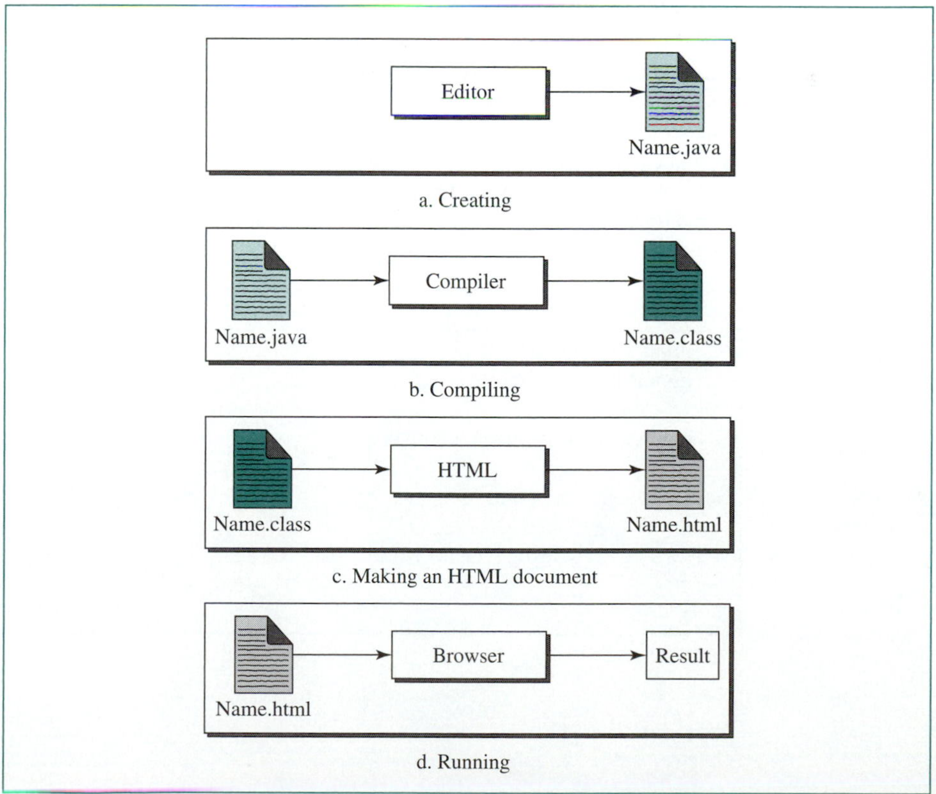

HTML Document

To use the applet, an HTML document is created and the name of the applet is inserted between the <APPLET> tags. The tag also defines the size of the window used for the applet (see Figure 25.14).

Figure 25.14 *HTML document carrying an applet*

```
<HTML>

    <APPLET  CODE = "Name.class"
    WIDTH = mmm
    HEIGHT = nnn  ....  >
    </APPLET >

</HTML>
```

Examples

In this section, we give some very simple examples of Java programs. The purpose is not to teach Java but to show how Java can be used to create active documents.

Example 1

In this example, we first import two packages java.awt and java.applet. They contain the declarations and definitions of classes and methods that we need. Our example uses only one publicly inherited class called *First*. We define only one public method, *paint*. The browser can access the instance of First through the public method paint. The paint method, however, calls another method called *drawString,* which is defined in java.awt.*. Three parameters are passed to drawString: a string that we want to display, the *x* coordinate, and the *y* coordinate. The coordinates are measured from the top left of the browser window in pixels.

First Example of Java

```
import java.applet.* ;
import java.awt.* ;

public class First extends Applet
{
    public void paint (Graphics  g)
    {
      g.drawString ("Hello World", 100, 100 ) ;
    }
}
```

Example 2

In this example, we modify the program in Example 1 to draw a line. Instead of method drawString, we use another method called *drawLine*.This method needs four parameters: the *x* and *y* coordinates of the beginning of the line and the *x* and *y* coordinates of the end of the line. We use 0 and 0 for the beginning and 80 and 90 for the end.

Second Example of Java

```
import java.applet.* ;
import java.awt.* ;

public class Second extends Applet
{
    public void paint (Graphics  g)
    {
      g.drawLine (0, 0, 80, 90 ) ;
    }
}
```

Example 3

In this example, we modify the program in Example 2 to draw a rectangle. We use a method called *drawRect*. The drawRect method needs four parameters: The first two define the *x* and *y* coordinates of the top left corner of the rectangle, and the next two parameters define the width and the height. We also use two more methods to fill in the rectangle: The first method sets the color of filling; the second fills the rectangle we have drawn.

Third Example of Java

```
import java.applet.* ;
import java.awt.* ;

public class Third extends Applet
{
    public void paint (Graphics  g)
    {
      g.drawRect (30, 30, 80, 20 ) ;
      g.setColor (Color.black) ;
      g.fillRect (30, 30, 80, 20) ;
    }
}
```

Example 4

In this example, we draw a triangle given the coordinates of its vertices. We define our own private method, called *drawTriangle*. We can use this method as many times as we want to draw different triangles in different places in the browser window.

Fourth Example of Java

```
import java.applet.* ;
import java.awt.* ;

public class Fourth extends Applet
{
        public void paint (Graphics  g)
            {
            g.drawTriangle (g, 10, 10, 10, 30, 50, 30 ) ;
            g.drawTriangle (g, 50, 30, 50, 10, 70, 10) ;
            }
            private void drawTriangle (Graphics g, int x1, int y1,
                                  int x2, int y2, int x3, int y3 )
           {
             g.drawLine (x1, y1, x2, y2 );
             g.drawLine (x2, y2, x3, y3 );
             g.drawLine (x3, y3, x1, y1 );
           }
 }
```

Example 5

In all previous examples, only one public method, paint, was defined in the inherited class. This means that the browser can access the object defined by the inherited class, using only this method. Now we want to define other public methods that can be used by the browser to access the object. We use two new public methods: the *init* method that can create a new object on the screen (a scrollbar in this case) and the *handleEvent* method that is invoked by an event such as scrolling the scrollbar.

The init method creates the scrollbar. There are four numbers involved: the initial value, the increments, and the range (from and to). When the user scrolls the bar, the value associated with the bar is captured by the handleEvent method. This method uses the *repaint* method to "repaint" the value of the bar on the screen.

Fifth Example of Java

```
import java.applet.* ;
import java.awt.* ;
public class Fifth extends Applet
{
  private Scrollbar  bar  ;
  private int barValue = 0 ;

public void init ()
  {
  bar = new Scrollbar (Scrollbar.HORIZONTAL, 0, 2, 1, 100) ;
  add (bar) ;
  }
```

Fifth Example of Java (continued)

```
public void paint (Graphics  g)
   {
    g.drawString ("Value is " + barValue, 100, 100 ) ;
   }

public boolean handleEvent (Event  e)
   {
   barValue = bar.getValue ( ) ;
   repaint () ;
   return true ;
   }
}
```

25.9 KEY TERMS

active document
applet
browser
class
Common Gateway Interface (CGI)
dynamic document
homepage
hypermedia
hypertext
Hypertext Markup Language (HTML)
Hypertext Transfer Protocol (HTTP)
inheritance
instantiation
Java
object
page
redirection
static document
tag
web
World Wide Web (WWW)

25.10 SUMMARY

- The World Wide Web (WWW) is a repository of information spread all over the world and linked together.
- Hypertext and hypermedia are documents linked to one another through the concept of pointers.
- Browsers interpret and display a Web document.

- The Hypertext Transfer Protocol (HTTP) is an advanced file-retrieving application program that can access distributed and linked documents on the WWW.
- A browser consists of a controller, client programs, and interpreters.
- A Web document can be classified as static, dynamic, or active.
- A static document is one in which the contents are fixed and stored in a server. The client can make no changes in the server document.
- Hypertext Markup Language (HTML) is a language used to create static Web pages.
- Any browser can read formatting instructions (tags) embedded in an HTML document.
- A Web page has a head and a body.
- Tags provide structure to a document, define titles and headers, format text, control the data flow, insert figures, link different documents together, and define executable code.
- A dynamic Web document is created by a server only at a browser request.
- The Common Gateway Interface (CGI) is a standard for creating and handling dynamic Web documents.
- A CGI program with its embedded CGI interface tags can be written in a language such as C, C++, shell script, or Perl.
- The server receives input from a browser through a form.
- The server sends the output of the CGI program to the browser.
- The output of a CGI program can be text, graphics, binary data, status codes, instructions, or an address of a file.
- An active document is a copy of a program retrieved by the client and run at the client site.
- Java is a combination of a high-level programming language, a run-time environment, and a class library that allows a programmer to write an active document and a browser to run it.
- Java is used to create applets (small application programs).
- Java is an object-oriented typed language with a rich library of classes.

25.11 PRACTICE SET

Multiple-Choice Questions

1. Hypertext documents are linked through _______.
   a. DNS
   b. TELNET
   c. pointers
   d. homepages

2. Which of the following is not a client program in WWW?
   a. FTP
   b. TELNET
   c. HTTP
   d. HTML
3. Which of the following is an interpreter?
   a. HTTP
   b. HTML
   c. CGI
   d. FTP
4. What are the components of a browser?
   a. retrieval method, host computer, pathname
   b. controller, client program, interpreter
   c. hypertext, hypermedia, HTML
   d. all of the above
5. Which type of Web document is run at the client site?
   a. static
   b. dynamic
   c. active
   d. all of the above
6. Which type of Web document is created at the server site only when requested by a client?
   a. static
   b. dynamic
   c. active
   d. all of the above
7. Which type of Web document is fixed-content and is created and stored at the server site?
   a. static
   b. dynamic
   c. active
   d. all of the above
8. The _______ of a Web page contains the title and parameters used by the browser.
   a. tags
   b. head
   c. body
   d. attributes

9. In <IMG SRC="Pictures/book1.gif" ALIGN=middle> ALIGN is _______.
   a. a tag
   b. the head
   c. the body
   d. an attribute
10. An ending tag is usually of the form _______.
    a. </tagname>
    b. <\tagname>
    c. <tagname>
    d. <tagname!>
11. Which category of HTML tags inserts a figure in a document?
    a. document
    b. text formatting
    c. image
    d. list
12. Which category of HTML tags allows the listing of documents?
    a. image
    b. list
    c. hyperlink
    d. executable contents
13. The _______ tags enclose binary code or bytecode.
    a. image
    b. list
    c. hyperlink
    d. executable contents
14. A program can use _______ to write a CGI program.
    a. Bourne shell script
    b. Perl
    c. C
    d. any of the above
15. An unemployed actor has posted his resume on the Web. This is probably a(n) _______ document.
    a. active
    b. static
    c. passive
    d. dynamic
16. The server receives input from a browser through _______.
    a. an attribute
    b. a tag
    c. a form
    d. any of the above

17. Output from a CGI program is _______.
    a. text
    b. graphics
    c. binary data
    d. any of the above
18. The _______ MIME header turns document caching on and off.
    a. expires
    b. location
    c. pragma
    d. status
19. Which type of Web document is transported from the server to the client in binary form?
    a. static
    b. dynamic
    c. active
    d. all of the above
20. An applet is a small application program written in _______.
    a. C
    b. C++
    c. shell script
    d. Java
21. The _______ package contains classes that handle common data structures.
    a. java.lang
    b. java.io
    c. java.net
    d. java.util
22. The _______ package contains methods for getting and displaying Web pages.
    a. java.applet
    b. java.lang
    c. java.io
    d. java.net
23. The _______ package contains classes and methods that make an applet capable of being run on any client environment.
    a. java.applet
    b. java.lang
    c. java.io
    d. java.awt

24. _______ is used to enable the use of active documents.
    a. HTML
    b. CGI
    c. Java
    d. all of the above
25. Java is _______.
    a. a programming language
    b. a run-time environment
    c. a class library
    d. all of the above
26. An applet is _______ document application program.
    a. a static
    b. an active
    c. a passive
    d. a dynamic
27. Stock quotations are posted on the Web. This is probably a(n) _______ document.
    a. active
    b. static
    c. passive
    d. dynamic
28. Updates for a satellite's coordinates can be obtained on the WWW. This is probably a(n) _______ document.
    a. active
    b. static
    c. passive
    d. dynamic

Exercises

29. Show the effect of the tags in the following line:

    This is <BR> a line of
 HTML

30. Show the effect of the tags in the following line:

    This is

 another line of

 HTML

31. Show the effect of the tags in the following lines:

    <H1> DOCUMENT </H1>
    <H2> This is an HTML document </H2>
    <H1> It shows the effect of H-tags </H1>

32. Show the effect of the tags in the following lines:

    <UL>
    <LI> Last Name, First Name, Initial </LI>
    <LI> Street Address, City </LI>
    <LI> State, Zip Code </LI>
    </UL>

33. Where will each figure be shown on the screen?

    Look at the following picture:
    then tell me what you feel:
    <IMG SRC="Pictures/Funny1.gif" ALIGN=middle>
    <IMG SRC="Pictures/Funny2.gif" ALIGN=bottom>
    <B>What is your feeling? </B>

34. Show the effect of the following HTML segment.

    The publisher of this book is <A HREF="www.mhhe">
    McGraw-Hill Publisher </A>

Programming Exercises

35. Write an HTML document to create the following screen:

    List of items offered at ***discount price:***
    1. Books
    2. Pens
    3. Pencil
    4. Notebook

36. Write an HTML document to create the following screen:

    This is the picture of a book:
    "Put the picture here. It is in a file called pic.fig"
    Look at it carefully.

37. Write an HTML document to create the following screen. Use your own URL for hyperlink connection.

    A Web document can be either **Static, Dynamic,** or **Active.**
    If you want to learn more about each type click on the boldfaced word.

38. Write the first example of CGI in Korn Shell.
39. Write the first example of CGI in C shell.
40. Write the fourth example of CGI in Bourne shell.
41. Write the fourth example of CGI in C language.
42. Write the fifth example of CGI in Perl.
43. Write a CGI program that returns the IP address of the browser.
44. Write a CGI program that returns the port number of the server.
45. Write a CGI program that echoes the query string sent by the browser.

46. Write a Java applet to draw a line from the top-left corner of the window to the bottom right of the window for a window size of 300 (horizontal) by 400 (vertical) pixels.
47. Write a Java applet to draw a line from the middle top of the window to the middle bottom of the window for a window size of 300 (horizontal) by 400 (vertical) pixels.
48. Write a Java applet to draw a line from the middle left of the window to the middle right of the window for a window size of 300 (horizontal) by 400 (vertical) pixels.
49. Write a Java applet to draw a square of size 100 pixels at the middle of the window for a window size of 300 (horizontal) by 400 (vertical) pixels.
50. Write a Java program that creates and manipulates two scrollbars, one horizontal and the other vertical. Choose the range and increments.

CHAPTER 26

IP over ATM

Throughout this book, we have defined an internet (and the Internet) as a combination of LANs, MANs, and WANs connected together by routers. This means that an IP datagram, from its source to its destination, may travel through several of these networks.

We have shown how a datagram is encapsulated in a frame to pass through a LAN. The frame uses the physical address defined by the LAN protocol and the binding between the IP address and the physical address attained through ARP. If the size of the IP packet is larger than the MTU of the LAN, the IP layer fragments the IP packet; the LAN has no responsibility here.

In this chapter we show how an IP datagram can pass through an ATM WAN. We will see that there are similarities as well as differences. The IP packet is encapsulated in cells (not just one). An ATM network has its own definition for the physical address of a device. Binding between an IP address and a physical address is attained through a protocol called ATMARP. Fragmentation occurs at two levels: at the IP layer to break the packet into a default size, and at the AAL level to divide a packet into even smaller chunks.

Let us review some features of the ATM WAN needed to understand IP over ATM.

26.1 ATM WANS

We discussed ATM WANs in Chapter 3. ATM, a cell-switched network, can be a highway for an IP datagram. Figure 26.1 shows how an ATM network can be used in the Internet.

Layers

We discussed ATM layers in Chapter 3 (see Figure 3.23). Routers connected to an ATM network use all three layers (AAL, ATM, and physical), but the switches inside the network use only the bottom two layers (ATM and physical) as shown in Figure 26.2.

Figure 26.1 *An ATM WAN in the Internet*

Figure 26.2 *ATM layers in routers and switches*

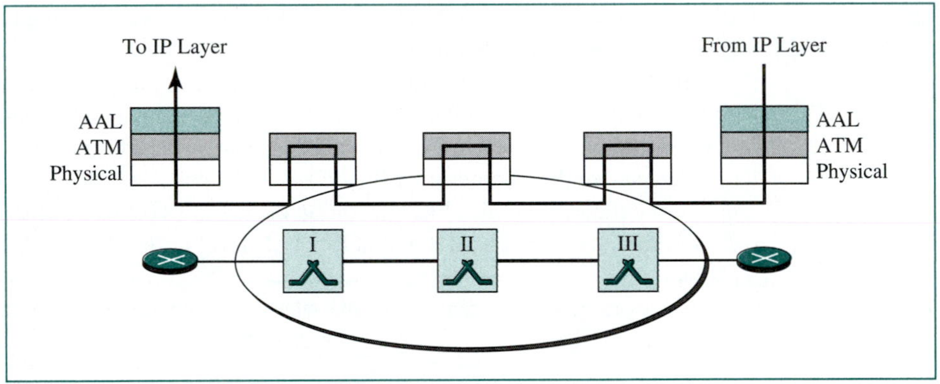

> End devices such as routers use all three layers, while switches use only the bottom two layers.

AAL5 Layer

In Chapter 3, we discussed different AALs and their applications. The only AAL used by the Internet is AAL5. It is sometimes called the *simple and efficient adaptation layer* (SEAL). AAL5 assumes that all cells belong to a single message. AAL5 therefore provides no addressing, sequencing, or other header information. Instead, only padding and a four-field trailer are added to the IP packet.

AAL5 accepts an IP packet of no more than 65,535 bytes and adds an 8-byte trailer as well as any padding required to ensure that the position of the trailer falls where the receiving equipment expects it (at the last 8 bytes of the last cell). See Figure 26.3. Once the padding and trailer are in place, AAL5 passes the message in 48-byte segments to the ATM layer.

Figure 26.3 *AAL5*

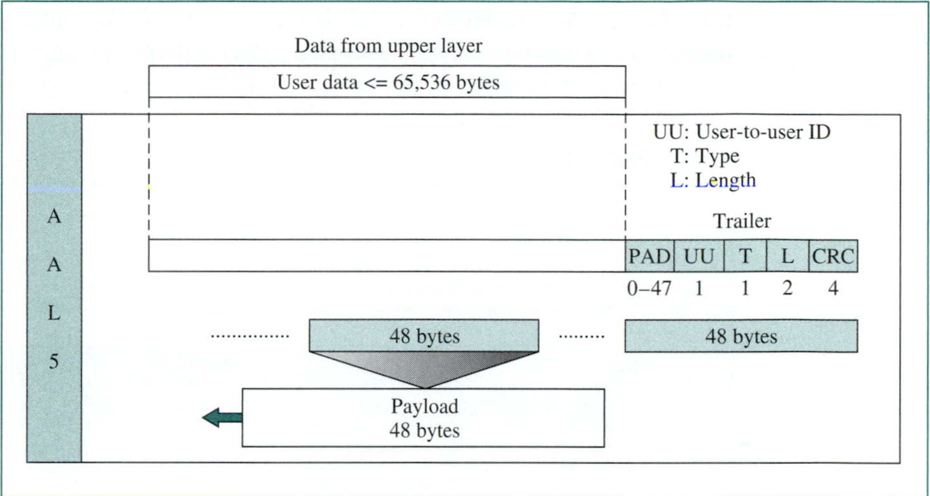

Fields added at the end of the message include the following:

- **Pad (PAD).** The total padding for a packet is between 0 and 47 bytes.
- **User-to-user ID (UU).** Use of the 1-byte UU field is left to the discretion of the user.
- **Type (T).** The 1-byte T field is reserved but not yet defined.
- **Length (L).** The 2-byte L field indicates how much of the message is data.
- **CRC.** The last 4 bytes are an error check for the entire data unit.

> The AAL layer used by the IP protocol is AAL5.

ATM Layer

The ATM layer provides routing, traffic management, switching, and multiplexing services. It processes outgoing traffic by accepting 48-byte segments from the AAL sublayer. The addition of a 5-byte header transforms the segment into a 53-byte cell (see Figure 26.4).

Figure 26.4 *ATM layer*

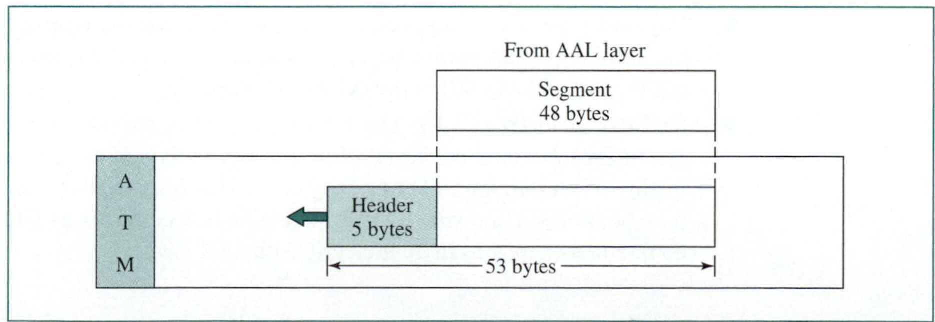

Header Format

ATM has two formats for this header, one for user-to-network interface (UNI) cells and another for network-to-network interface (NNI) cells. Figure 26.5 shows these headers in the byte-by-byte format preferred by the ITU-T (each row represents a byte).

Figure 26.5 *ATM headers*

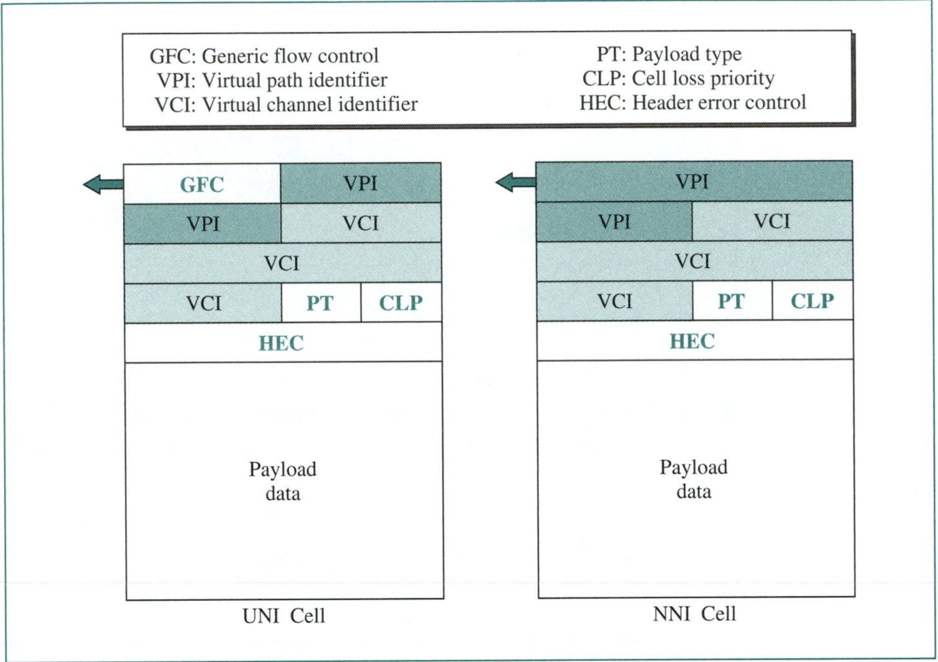

- **Generic flow control (GFC).** The 4-bit GFC field provides flow control at the UNI level. The ITU-T has determined that this level of flow control is not necessary at the NNI level. In the NNI header, therefore, these bits are added to the VPI. The longer VPI allows more virtual paths to be defined at the NNI level. The format for this additional VPI has not yet been determined. Currently, it is not used.
- **Virtual path identifier (VPI).** The VPI is an 8-bit field in a UNI cell and a 12-bit field in an NNI cell.
- **Virtual channel identifier (VCI).** The VCI is a 16-bit field in both frames.
- **Payload type (PT).** This 3-bit field is used to define the type of the payload. When the cell is carrying part of an IP packet, the value of this field is 000 if the cell is not the last cell and 001 if the cell is the last cell.
- **Cell loss priority (CLP).** The 1-bit CLP field is provided for congestion control. When links become congested, low-priority cells may be discarded to protect the quality of service for higher priority cells. This bit indicates to a switch which cells may be dropped and which must be retained. A cell with its CLP bit set to 1 must be retained as long as there are cells with a CLP of 0.

- **Header error correction (HEC).** The HEC is an error correction method computed over the first four bytes of the header. It is a CRC with the divisor $x^8 + x^2 + x + 1$ that can correct single-bit errors as well as a large class of multiple-bit errors.

Physical Layer

The physical layer defines the transmission medium, bit transmission, encoding, and electrical to optical transformation. It provides convergence with physical transport protocols, such as SONET (described in Chapter 3) and T-3, as well as the mechanisms for transforming the flow of cells into a flow of bits.

26.2 CARRYING A DATAGRAM IN CELLS

As an example, let us show how a datagram of 140 bytes is encapsulated in four cells and transmitted through an ATM network. Before encapsulation, an 8-byte trailer is added to the datagram. However, the size of the packet is now 148, which is not divisible by 48. We must add 44 bytes of padding, which makes the total length 192 bytes. The packet is then divided into four chunks of 48 bytes each as shown in Figure 26.6.

Figure 26.6 *Fragmentation*

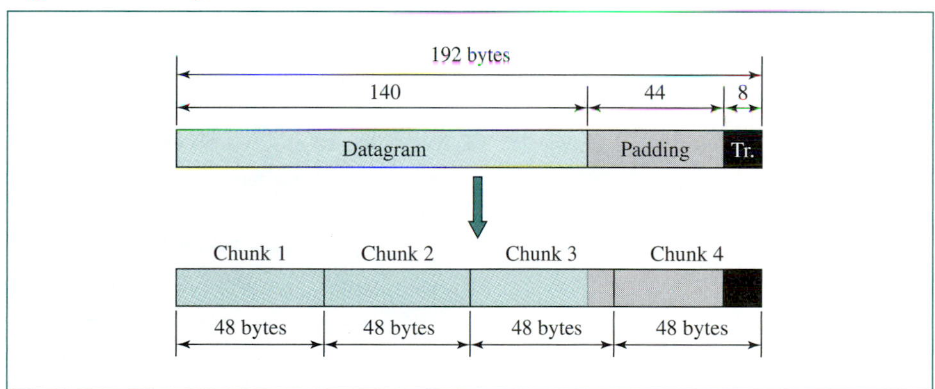

> Only the last cell carries the 8-byte trailer added to the IP datagram. Padding can be added only to the last cell or the last two cells.

At the ATM layer, each chunk of data is encapsulated into a cell as shown in Figure 26.7. Note that the last cell carries no data. Also note that the value of the PT field in the last cell is 001 to show that this is the last cell.

> The value of the PT field is 000 in all cells carrying an IP datagram fragment except for the last cell; the value is 001 in the last cell.

Figure 26.7 *ATM cells*

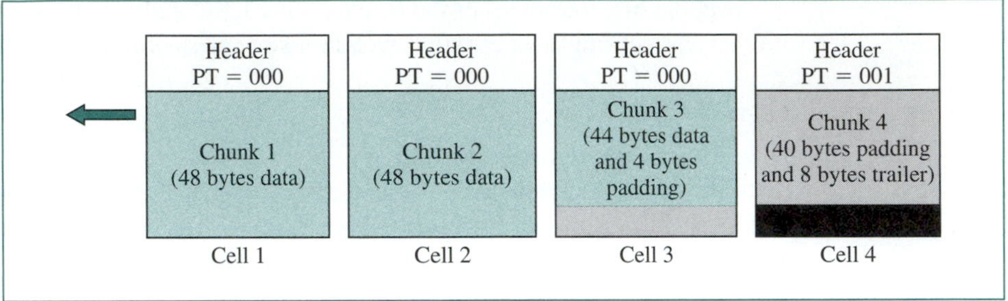

26.3 ROUTING THE CELLS

The ATM network creates a route between two routers. We call these routers entering-point and exiting-point routers. The cells start from the entering-point router and end at the exiting-point router as shown in Figure 26.8.

Figure 26.8 *Entering-point and exiting-point routers*

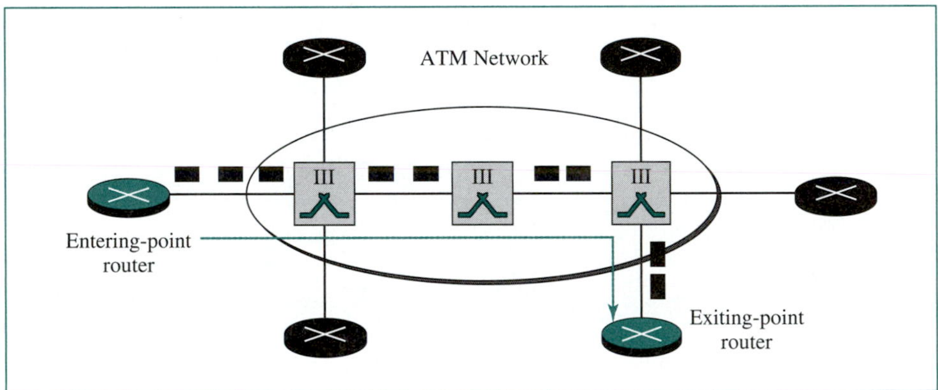

Addresses

Routing the cells from one specific entering-point router to one specific exiting-point router requires three types of addressing: IP addresses, physical addresses, and virtual circuit identifiers.

IP Addresses

Each router connected to the ATM network has an IP address. Later we will see that the addresses may or may not have the same prefix. The IP address defines the router at the IP layer. It does not have anything to do with the ATM network.

Physical Addresses

Each router (or any other device) connected to the ATM network has also a physical address. The physical address is associated with the ATM network and does not have anything to do with the Internet. The ATM Forum defines 20-byte addresses for ATM networks. Each address must be unique in a network and is defined by the network administrator. The physical addresses in an ATM network play the same role as the MAC addresses in a LAN. The physical addresses are used during connection establishment.

Virtual Circuit Identifiers

The switches inside the ATM network route the cells based on the virtual circuit identifiers (VPIs and VCIs) as we discussed in Chapter 3. The virtual circuit identifiers are used during the data transfer.

Address Binding

An ATM network needs virtual circuit identifiers to route the cells. The IP datagram contains only source and destination IP addresses. Virtual circuit identifiers must be determined from the destination IP address. These are the steps:

1. The entering-point router receives an IP datagram. It uses the destination address and its routing table to find the IP address of the next router, the exiting-point router. This is exactly the same step as when a datagram must pass through a LAN.
2. The entering-point router uses the services of a protocol called ATMARP to find the physical address of the exiting-point router. ATMARP is similar to ARP (discussed in Chapter 7). We discuss ATMARP in the next section.
3. The virtual circuit identifiers are bound to the physical addresses.

26.4 ATMARP

A protocol is needed to find (map) the IP address of the exiting-point router given the physical address of the exiting-point router. This is the same task performed by ARP on a LAN. However, there is a difference between a LAN and an ATM network. A LAN is a broadcast network (at the data link layer); ARP uses the broadcasting capability of a LAN to send (broadcast) an ARP request. An ATM network is not a broadcast network; some other solution is needed to handle the task.

Packet Format

The format of an ATMARP packet, which is similar to the ARP packet, is shown in Figure 26.9.

The fields are as follows:

- **Hardware type (HTYPE).** This 16-bit HTYPE field defines the type of the physical network. Its value is 0013_{16} for an ATM network.
- **Protocol type (PTYPE).** This 16-bit PTYPE field defines the type of the protocol. For IPv4 protocol the value is 0800_{16}.

Figure 26.9 *ARP packet*

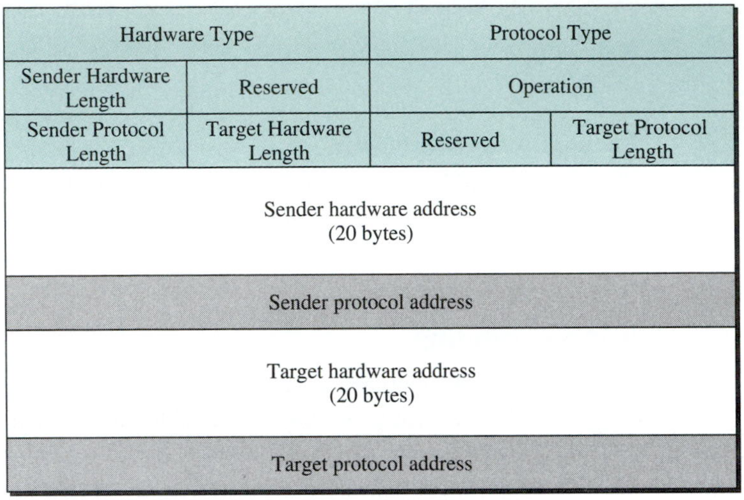

<table>
<tr><td colspan="2">Hardware Type</td><td colspan="2">Protocol Type</td></tr>
<tr><td>Sender Hardware Length</td><td>Reserved</td><td colspan="2">Operation</td></tr>
<tr><td>Sender Protocol Length</td><td>Target Hardware Length</td><td>Reserved</td><td>Target Protocol Length</td></tr>
<tr><td colspan="4">Sender hardware address
(20 bytes)</td></tr>
<tr><td colspan="4">Sender protocol address</td></tr>
<tr><td colspan="4">Target hardware address
(20 bytes)</td></tr>
<tr><td colspan="4">Target protocol address</td></tr>
</table>

- **Sender hardware length (SHLEN).** This 8-bit SHLEN field defines the length of the sender's physical address in bytes. For an ATM network the value is 20. Note that if the binding is done across an ATM network and two levels of hardware addressing are necessary, the neighboring 8-bit **reserved** field is used to define the length of the second address.
- **Operation (OPER).** This 16-bit OPER field defines the type of the packet. Five packet types are defined as shown in Table 26.1.

Table 26.1 *OPER field*

Message	*OPER value*
Request	1
Reply	2
Inverse Request	8
Inverse Reply	9
NACK	10

- **Sender protocol length (SPLEN).** This 8-bit SPLEN field defines the length of the protocol address in bytes. For IPv4 the value is four.
- **Target hardware length (TLEN).** This 8-bit TLEN field defines the length of the receiver's physical address in bytes. For an ATM network the value is 20. Note that if the binding is done across an ATM network and two levels of hardware addressing are necessary, the neighboring 8-bit **reserved** field is used to define the length of the second address.
- **Target protocol length (TPLEN).** This 8-bit TPLEN field defines the length of the protocol address in bytes. For IPv4 the value is four.

- **Sender hardware address (SHA).** This variable-length SHA field defines the physical address of the sender. For ATM networks defined by the ATM Forum, the length is 20 bytes.
- **Sender protocol address (SPA).** This variable-length SPA field defines the protocol address of the sender. For IPv4 the length is 4 bytes.
- **Target hardware address (THA).** This variable-length THA field defines the physical address of the receiver. For ATM networks defined by the ATM Forum, the length is 20 bytes. This field is left empty for request messages and filled in for reply and NACK messages.
- **Target protocol address (TPA).** This variable-length TPA field defines the protocol address of the receiver. For IPv4 the length is 4 bytes.

ATMARP Operation

There are two methods to connect two routers on an ATM network: through a permanent virtual circuit (PVC) or through a switched virtual circuit (SVC). The operation of ATMARP depends on the connection method.

PVC

A permanent virtual circuit (PVC) connection is established between two end points by the network provider. The VPIs and VCIs are defined for the permanent connections and the values are entered in a table for each switch.

If a permanent virtual circuit is established between two routers, there is no need for an ATMARP server. However, the routers must be able to bind a physical address to an IP address. The inverse request and reply messages can be used for the binding. When a PVC is established for a router, the router sends an inverse request message. The router at the other end of the connection receives the message (which contains the physical and IP address of the sender) and sends back a reply (which contains its own physical and IP address).

After the exchange, both routers add a table entry that maps the physical addresses to the PVC. Now, when a router receives an IP datagram, the table provides information so that the router can encapsulate the datagram using the virtual circuit identifier. Figure 26.10 shows the exchange of messages between two routers.

SVC

In a switched virtual circuit (SVC) connection, each time a router wants to make a connection with another router (or any computer), a new virtual circuit must be established. However, the virtual circuit can be created only if the entering-point router knows the physical address of the exiting-point router (ATM does not recognize IP addresses).

To map the IP addresses to physical addresses, each router runs a client ATMARP program, but only one computer runs an ATMARP server program. To understand the difference between ARP and ATMARP, remember that ARP operates on a LAN, which is a broadcast network. An ARP client can broadcast an ARP request message and each router on the network will receive it; only the target router will respond. ATM is a

Figure 26.10 *Binding with PVC*

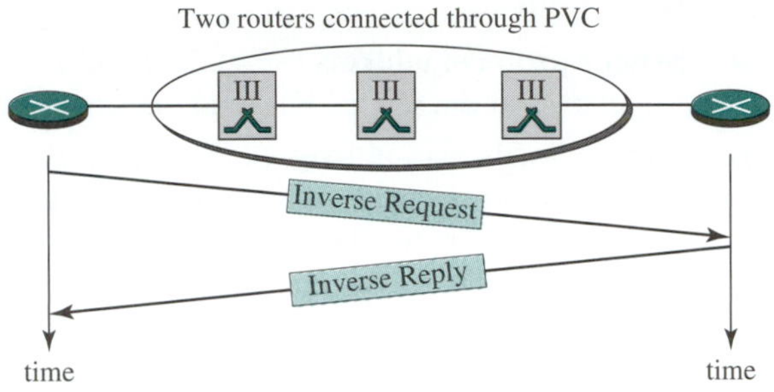

> The inverse request and inverse reply messages can bind the physical address to an IP address in a PVC situation.

nonbroadcast network; an ATMARP request cannot reach all routers connected to the network.

The process of establishing a virtual connection requires three steps: connecting to the server, receiving the physical address, and establishing the connection. Figure 26.11 shows the steps.

Connecting to the Server Normally, there is a permanent virtual circuit established between each router and the server. If there is no PVC connection between the router and the server, the server must at least know the physical address of the router to create an SVC connection just for exchanging ATMARP request and reply messages.

Receiving the Physical Address When there is a connection between the entering-point router and the server, the router sends an *ATMARP request* to the server. The server sends back an *ATMARP reply* if the physical address can be found or an *ATMARP NACK* otherwise. If the entering-point router receives a NACK, the datagram is dropped.

Establishing Virtual Circuits After the entering-point router receives the physical address of the exiting-point router, it can request an SVC between itself and the exiting-point router. The ATM network uses the two physical addresses to set up a virtual circuit which lasts until the entering-point router asks for disconnection. In this step, each switch inside the network adds an entry to their tables to enable them to route the cells carrying the IP datagram.

Building the Table

How does the ATM server build its mapping table? This is also done through the use of ATMARP and the two inverse messages (inverse request and inverse reply). When a router is connected to an ATM network for the first time and a permanent virtual connection is established between the router and the server, the server sends an inverse request message to the router. The router sends back an inverse reply message which

Figure 26.11 *Binding with ATMARP*

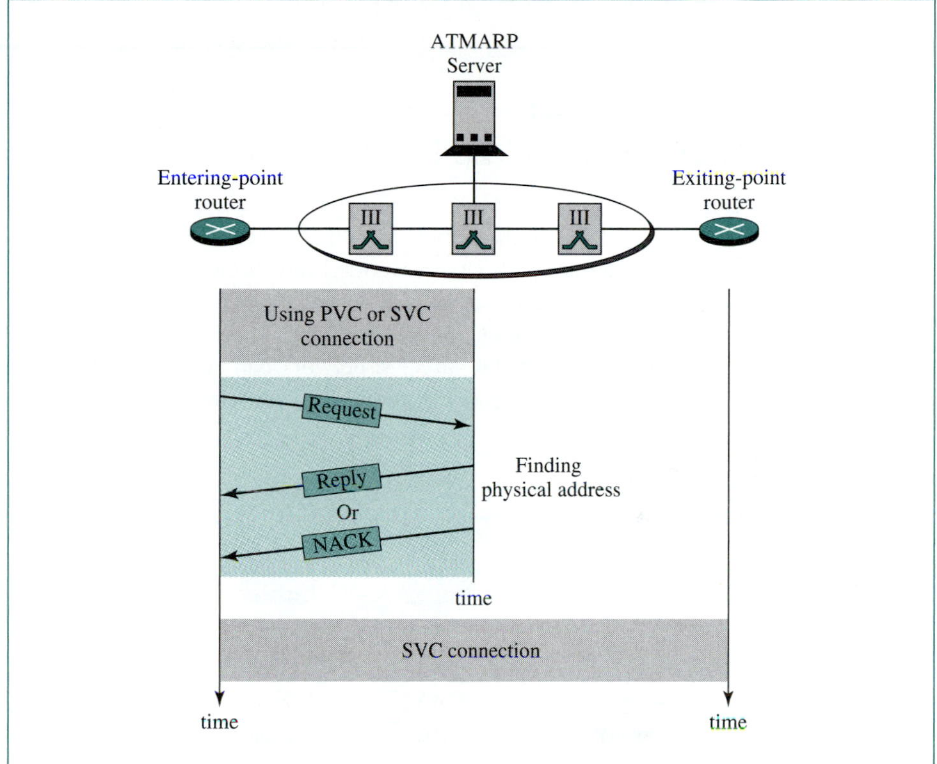

> The request and reply message can be used to bind a physical address to an IP address in an SVC situation.

includes its IP address and physical address. Using these two addresses, the server creates an entry in its routing table to be used if the router becomes an exiting-point router in the future. Figure 26.12 shows the inverse operation of ATMARP.

Figure 26.12 *Building a table*

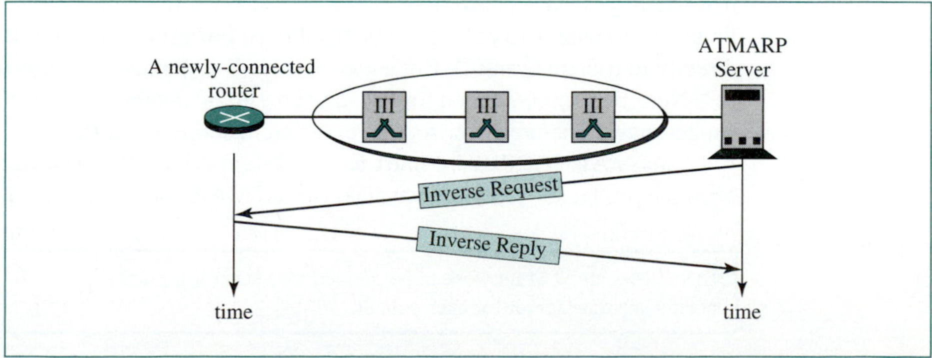

> The inverse request and inverse reply can also be used to build the server's mapping table.

26.5 LOGICAL IP SUBNET (LIS)

Before we leave the subject of IP over ATM, we need to discuss a concept called logical IP subnet (LIS). For the same reason that a large LAN can be divided into several subnets, an ATM network can be divided into logical (not physical) subnetworks. This facilitates the operation of ATMARP and other protocols (such as IGMP) that need to simulate broadcasting on an ATM network.

Routers connected to an ATM network can belong to one or more logical subnets. as shown in Figure 26.13. In the figure, routers B, C, and D belong to one logical

Figure 26.13 *LIS*

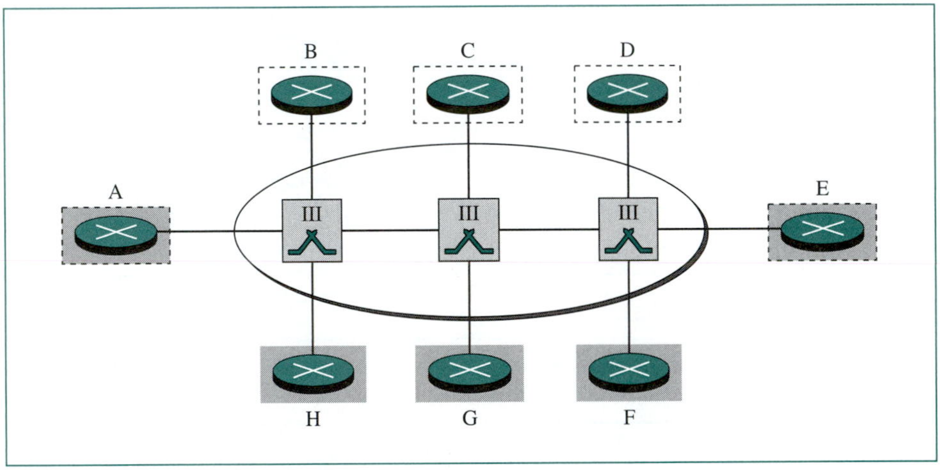

subnet (shown by broken-line boxes); routers F, G, and H belong to another logical subnet (shown by shaded boxes). Routers A and E belong to both logical subnets. A router can communicate and send IP packets directly to a router in the same subnet; however, if it needs to send a packet to a router that belongs to another subnet, the packet must first go to a router that belongs to both subnets. For example, router B can send a packet directly to routers C and D. But a packet from B to F must first pass through A or E.

Note that routers belonging to the same logical subnet share the same prefix and subnet mask. The prefix for routers in different subnets is different.

To use ATMARP, there must be a different ATMARP server in each subnet. For example, in the above figure, we need two ATMARP servers, one for each subnet.

> LIS allows an ATM network to be divided into several logical subnets. To use ATMARP, we need a separate server for each subnet.

26.6 KEY TERMS

AAL5 layer

application adaptation layer (AAL)

asynchronous transfer mode (ATM)

ATMARP

cell

entering-point router

exiting-point router

inverse reply message

inverse request message

logical IP subnet (LIS)

network-to-network interface (NNI)

permanent virtual circuit (PVC)

reply message

request message

switched virtual circuit (SVC)

user-to-network interface (UNI)

virtual channel identifier (VCI)

virtual circuit identifier (VCI)

virtual path identifier (VPI)

26.7 SUMMARY

- The AAL layer used by the IP protocol is AAL5.
- The ATM layer accepts 48-byte segments from the AAL and transforms them into 53-byte cells through the addition of a 5-byte header.
- An ATM network creates a route between an entering-point router and an exiting-point router.
- ATM can use a permanent virtual circuit (PVC) or a switched virtual circuit (SVC).
- If there is a PVC between an entering-point router and an exiting-point router, inverse request and inverse reply messages are exchanged to bind IP addresses to physical addresses. Then physical addresses can be bound to the PVC.
- ATMARP is a protocol used on ATM networks that binds a physical address to an IP address.
- To establish a SVC between an entering-point router and an exiting-point router, the services of an ATMARP server are needed to find the physical address of the exiting-point router.
- The ATMARP server's mapping table is built through the use of the inverse request and the inverse reply messages.
- An ATM network can be divided into logical subnetworks to facilitate ATMARP and other protocol operations.

26.8 PRACTICE SET

Multiple-Choice Questions

1. A router connected to an ATM network uses the _______ layers.
   a. AAL and ATM
   b. AAL and physical
   c. ATM and physical
   d. AAL, ATM, and physical
2. A switch inside an ATM network uses the _______ layers.
   a. AAL and ATM
   b. AAL and physical
   c. ATM and physical
   d. AAL, ATM, and physical
3. Which ATM layer adds an 8-byte trailer to an IP packet?
   a. AAL5
   b. ATM
   c. physical
   d. network
4. Which ATM layer has a 53-byte cell as an end product?
   a. physical
   b. ATM
   c. AAL5
   d. network
5. The _______ field on a UNI cell header provides flow control.
   a. VPI
   b. VCI
   c. CLP
   d. GFC
6. A _______ field on a cell header in the ATM layer determines whether a cell can be dropped.
   a. VPI
   b. VCI
   c. CLP
   d. GFC
7. The VPI of a UNI is _______ bits in length.
   a. 8
   b. 12
   c. 16
   d. 24

8. The VPI of an NNI is _______ bits in length.
   a. 8
   b. 12
   c. 16
   d. 24
9. The _______ field of the ATM header provides error control.
   a. CLP
   b. HEC
   c. VPC
   d. VPI
10. A datagram of 1010 bytes needs _______ bytes of padding.
    a. 0
    b. 38
    c. 46
    d. 48
11. A datagram of 402 bytes is divided into _______ cells.
    a. 6
    b. 7
    c. 8
    d. 9
12. The maximum amount of padding that can be added is _______ bytes.
    a. 0
    b. 47
    c. 48
    d. there is no maximum amount
13. The ATM _______ address is 20 bytes in length.
    a. IP
    b. network
    c. circuit
    d. physical
14. The routing of a cell from the entering-point router to the exiting-point router requires _______.
    a. IP addresses
    b. physical addresses
    c. virtual circuit identifiers
    d. all of the above
15. The _______ field is empty in a request message.
    a. sender hardware address
    b. target hardware address
    c. sender protocol address
    d. target protocol address

16. When a _______ exists between two routers on an ATM network, ATMARP is not needed.
    a. permanent virtual circuit
    b. switched virtual circuit
    c. logical IP subnet
    d. permanent logical switch
17. What is the first step in establishing a virtual connection between an entering-point router and an exiting-point router on an ATM network?
    a. connecting to an ATMARP server
    b. connecting to the exiting-point router
    c. formation of a logical IP subnet
    d. receiving a physical address
18. If there are five subnets on an ATM network, how many ATMARP servers are needed?
    a. 1
    b. 4
    c. 5
    d. 6

Exercises

19. What is the minimum number of cells resulting from an IP datagram? What is the maximum number of cells resulting from an IP datagram?
20. Explain why padding is necessary in AAL5.
21. Using AAL5, show a situation where we need _______ of padding.
    a. zero bytes (no padding)
    b. 40 bytes
    c. 47 bytes
22. In a 53-byte cell (not the last cell), how many bytes belong to the IP packet if there is no padding? How many bytes belong to the IP packet in the last cell if there is no padding?
23. How many cells are created from an IP packet of 42 bytes? Show the contents of each cell.
24. Explain why no more than two cells can carry padding.
25. Show the contents of ATMARP inverse packets exchanged between two routers that have a PVC connection. The IP addresses are 172.14.20.16/16 and 180.25.23.14/24. Choose two arbitrary 20-byte physical addresses. Use hexadecimal values in filling the fields.
26. Show the contents of ATMARP packets (request and reply) exchanged between a router and a server. The IP address of the router is 14.56.12.8/16 and the IP address of the server is 200.23.54.8/24. Choose two arbitrary 20-byte physical addresses. Use hexadecimal values in filling the fields.

27. Add IP addresses for the routers in Figure 26.13. Note that the prefix in each LIS must be the same, but it must be different for the two LISs. Note also that the routers that belong to two LISs must have two IP addresses.
28. An ATMARP packet must also be carried in cells. How many cells are needed to carry an ATMARP packet discussed in this chapter?
29. A datagram is sent through an ATM network. What happens if the network is congested and one of the cells is discarded by one of the switches?
30. A datagram is sent through an ATM network. The last cell carries only padding and a trailer. What happens if the network is congested and the last cell is discarded by one of the switches? Can the IP datagram be recovered? Explain your answer.

CHAPTER 27

Mobile IP

Mobile communication has received a lot of attention in the last decade. The interest in mobile communication on the Internet means that the IP protocol, originally designed for stationary devices, must be enhanced to allow the use of mobile computers, computers that move from one network to another.

27.1 ADDRESSING

The main problem that must be solved in providing mobile communication using the IP protocol is addressing.

Stationary Hosts

The original IP addressing was based on the assumption that a host is stationary, attached to one specific network. A router uses the hierarchical structure of an IP address to route an IP datagram. As we learned in Chapter 4, an IP address has two parts: a prefix (net or subnet address) and a suffix (hostid). The prefix associates a host to a network. For example, an IP address 10.3.4.24/8 defines a host attached to the network 10.0.0.0/8. This implies that a host in the Internet does not have an address that it can carry with itself from one place to another. The address is valid only when the host is attached to the network. If the network changes, the address is no longer valid. Routers use this association to route a packet; they use the prefix to deliver the packet to the network to which the host is attached. This scheme works perfectly with stationary hosts.

> The IP addresses are designed to work with stationary hosts because part of the address defines the network to which the host is attached.

Mobile Hosts

When a host moves from one network to another, the IP addressing structure needs to be modified. Several solutions have been proposed.

Changing the Address

One simple solution is to let the mobile host change its address as it goes to the new network. The host can use DHCP to obtain a new address to associate it with the new network. This approach has several drawbacks. First, the configuration files would need to be changed. Second, each time the computer moves from one network to another, it must be rebooted. Third, the DNS tables need to be revised so that every other host in the Internet is aware of the change. Fourth, if the host roams from one network to another during a transmission, the data exchange will be interrupted. This is because the ports and IP addresses of the client and the server must remain constant for the duration of the connection.

Two Addresses

The approach that is more feasible is the use of two addresses. The host has its original address, called the *home address* and a temporary address, called the *care-of address*. The home address is permanent; it associates the host to its *home network,* the network that is the permanent home of the host. The care-of address is temporary. When a host moves from one network to another, the care-of address changes; it is associated with the *foreign network,* the network to which the host moves. Figure 27.1 shows the concept.

Figure 27.1 *Home address and care-of address*

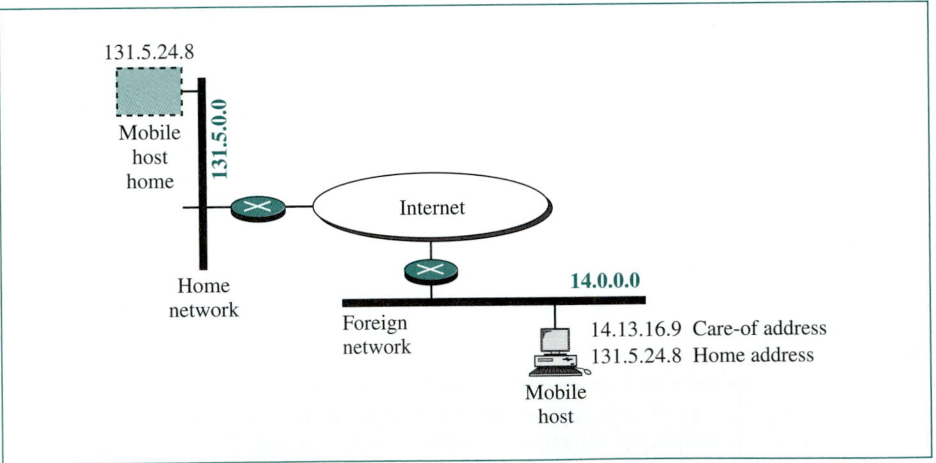

> Mobile IP has two addresses for a mobile host: one home address and one care-of address. The home address is permanent; the care-of address changes as the mobile host moves from one network to another.

When a mobile host visits a foreign network, it receives its care-of address during the agent discovery and registration phase.

27.2 AGENTS

To make the change of address transparent to the rest of the Internet requires a *home agent* and a *foreign agent*. Figure 27.2 shows the position of a home agent relative to the home network and a foreign agent relative to the foreign network.

Figure 27.2 *Home agent and foreign agent*

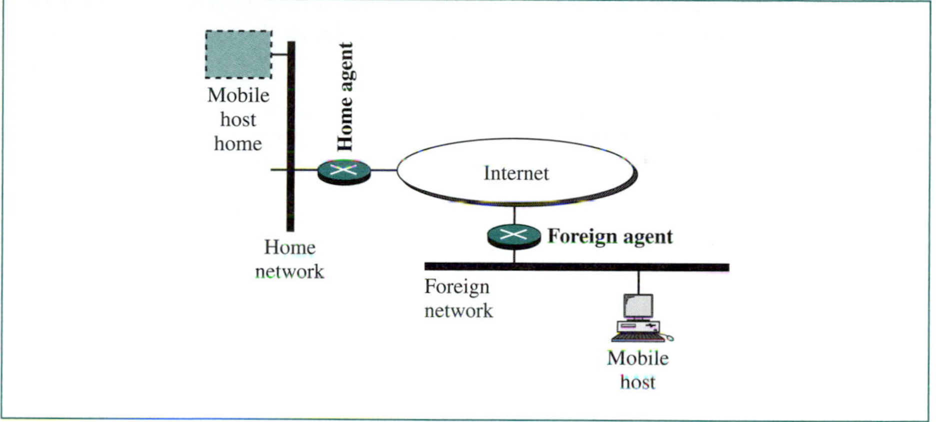

Home Agent

The home agent is usually a router attached to the home network of the mobile host. The home agent acts on behalf of the mobile host when a remote host sends a packet to the mobile host. The home agent receives the packet and sends it to the foreign agent.

Foreign Agent

The *foreign agent* is usually a router attached to the foreign network. The foreign agent receives and delivers packets sent by the home agent to the mobile host.

The mobile host can also act as a foreign agent. In other words, the mobile host and the foreign agent can be the same. However, to do this, a mobile host must be able to receive a care-of address by itself, which can be done through the use of DHCP. In addition, the mobile host needs the necessary software to allow it to communicate with the home agent and to have two addresses: its home address and its care-of address. This dual addressing must be transparent to the application programs.

When the mobile host acts as a foreign agent, the care-of address is called a *co-located care-of address*.

> When the mobile host and the foreign agent are the same, the care-of address is called a co-located care-of address.

The advantage of using a co-located care-of address is that the mobile host can move to any network without worrying about the availability of a foreign agent. The disadvantage is that the mobile host needs extra software to act as its own foreign agent.

27.3 THREE PHASES

To communicate with a remote host, a mobile host goes through three phases: agent discovery, registration, and data transfer as shown in Figure 27.3.

Figure 27.3 *Remote host and mobile host communication*

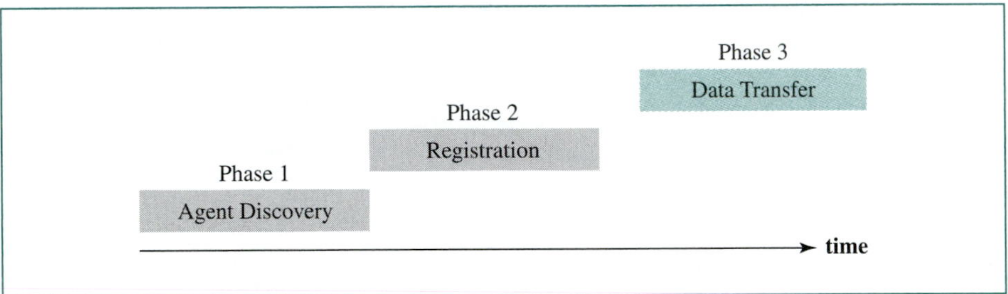

The first phase, agent discovery, involves the mobile host, the foreign agent, and the home agent. The second phase, registration, also involves the mobile host and the two agents. Finally, in the third phase, all four entities are involved. We discuss each phase separately.

27.4 AGENT DISCOVERY

The first phase in mobile communication, agent discovery, consists of two subphases. A mobile host must discover (learn the address of) a home agent before it leaves its home network. A mobile host must also discover a foreign agent after it has moved to a foreign network. This discovery consists of learning the care-of address as well as the foreign agent's address. The discovery involves two types of messages: advertisement and solicitation.

Agent Advertisement

When a router advertises its presence on a network using an ICMP router advertisement, it can append an agent advertisement to the packet if it acts as an agent. Figure 27.4 shows how an agent advertisement is piggybacked to the router advertisement packet.

Figure 27.4 *Agent advertisement*

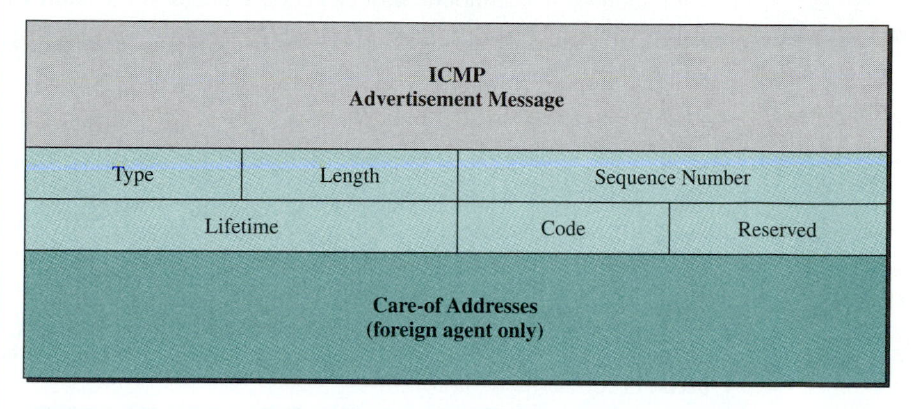

> Mobile IP does not use a new packet type for agent advertisement; it uses the router advertisement packet of ICMP, and appends an agent advertisement message.

The field descriptions are as follows:

- **Type.** The 8-bit type field is set to 16.
- **Length.** The 8-bit length field defines the total length of the extension message (not the length of the ICMP advertisement message).
- **Sequence Number.** The 16-bit sequence number field holds the message number. The recipient can use the sequence number to determine if a message is lost.
- **Lifetime.** The lifetime field defines the number of seconds that the agent will accept requests. If the value is a string of 1s, the lifetime is infinite.
- **Code.** The code field is an 8-bit flag in which each bit is set (1) or unset (0). The meanings of the bits are shown in Table 27.1.

Table 27.1 *Code bits*

Bit	*Meaning*
0	Registration required. No co-located care-of address.
1	Agent is busy and does not accept registration at this moment.
2	Agent acts as a home agent.
3	Agent acts as a foreign agent.
4	Agent uses minimal encapsulation.
5	Agent uses generic routing encapsulation (GRE).
6	Agent supports header compression
7	Unused (0)

- **Care-of Addresses.** This field contains a list of addresses available for use as care-of addresses. The mobile host can choose one of these addresses. The selection of this care-of address is announced in the registration request. Note that this field is used only by a foreign agent.

Agent Solicitation

When a mobile host has moved to a new network and has not received agent advertisements, it can initiate an agent solicitation. It can use the ICMP solicitation message to inform an agent that it needs assistance.

> Mobile IP does not use a new packet type for agent solicitation; it uses the router solicitation packet of ICMP.

27.5 REGISTRATION

The second phase in mobile communication is registration. After a mobile host has moved to a foreign network and discovered the foreign agent, it must register. There are four aspects of registration:

1. The mobile host must register itself with the foreign agent.
2. The mobile host must register itself with its home agent. This is done normally by the foreign agent on behalf of the mobile host.
3. The mobile host must renew registration if it has expired.
4. The mobile host must cancel its registration (deregistration) when it returns home.

Request and Reply

To register with the foreign agent and the home agent, the mobile host uses a registration request and a registration reply as shown in Figure 27.5.

Figure 27.5 *Registration request and reply*

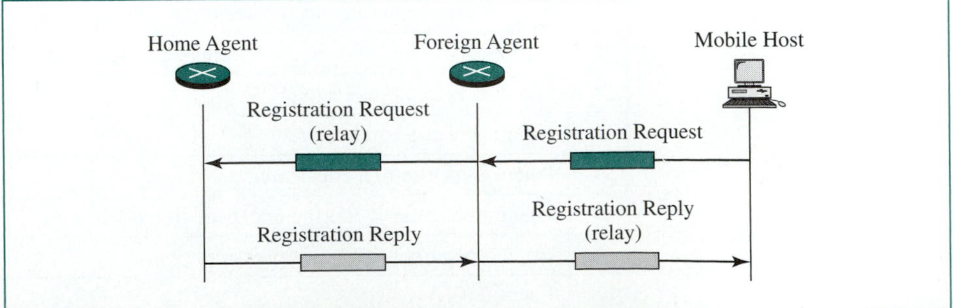

Registration Request

A registration request is sent from the mobile host to the foreign agent to register its care-of address and also to announce its home address and home agent address. The foreign agent, after receiving and registering the request, relays the message to the home agent. Note that the home agent now knows the address of the foreign agent because the IP packet that is used for relaying has the IP address of the foreign agent as the source address. Figure 27.6 shows the format of the registration request.

Figure 27.6 *Registration request format*

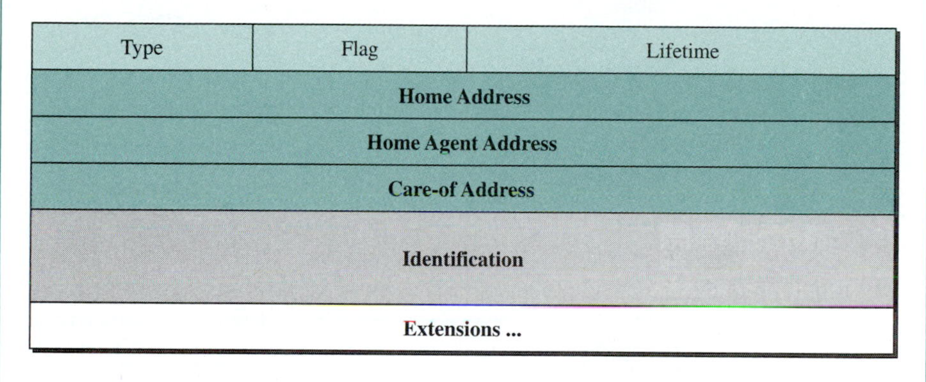

The field descriptions are as follows:

- **Type.** The 8-bit type field defines the type of the message. For a request message the value of this field is 1.
- **Flag.** The 8-bit flag field defines forwarding information. The value of each bit can be set or unset. The meaning of each bit is given in Table 27.2.

Table 27.2 *Registration request flag field bits*

Bit	*Meaning*
0	Mobile host requests that home agent retain its prior care-of address.
1	Mobile host requests that home agent tunnel any broadcast message.
2	Mobile host is using co-located care-of address.
3	Mobile host requests that home agent use minimal encapsulation.
4	Mobile host requests generic routing encapsulation (GRE).
5	Mobile host requests header compression.
6-7	Reserved bits.

- **Lifetime.** This field defines the number of seconds the registration is valid. If the field is a string of 0s, the request message is asking for deregistration. If the field is a string of 1s, the lifetime is infinite.

- **Home Address.** This field contains the permanent (first) address of the mobile host.
- **Home Agent Address.** This field contains the address of the home agent.
- **Care-of Address.** This field is the temporary (second) address of the mobile host.
- **Identification.** This field contains a 64-bit number that is inserted into the request by the mobile host and repeated in the reply message. It matches a request with a reply.
- **Extensions.** Variable length extensions are used for authentication. They allow a home agent to authenticate the mobile agent. We discuss authentication in Chapter 29.

Registration Reply

A registration reply is sent from the home agent to the foreign agent and then relayed to the mobile host. The reply confirms or denies the registration request. Figure 27.7 shows the format of the registration reply.

Figure 27.7 *Registration reply format*

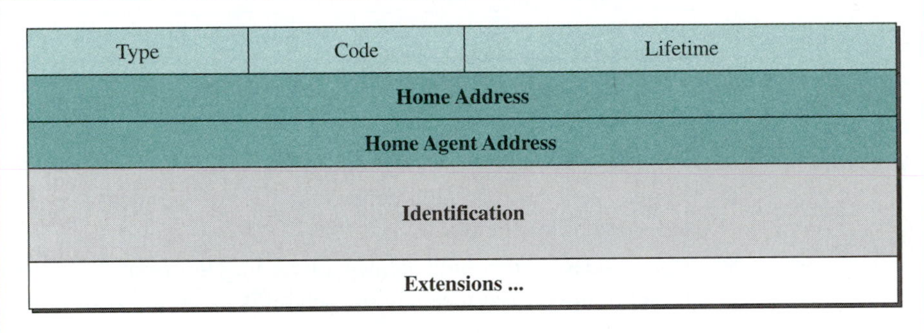

The fields are similar to those of the registration request with the following exceptions. The value of the type field is 3. The code field replaces the flag field and shows the result of the registration request (acceptance or denial). The care-of address field is not needed.

Encapsulation

Registration messages are encapsulated in a UDP user datagram. An agent uses the well-known port 434; a mobile host uses a temporary port.

> A registration request or reply is sent by UDP using the well-known port 434.

27.6 DATA TRANSFER

After agent discovery and registration, a mobile host can communicate with a remote host. Figure 27.8 shows the idea.

Figure 27.8 *Data transfer*

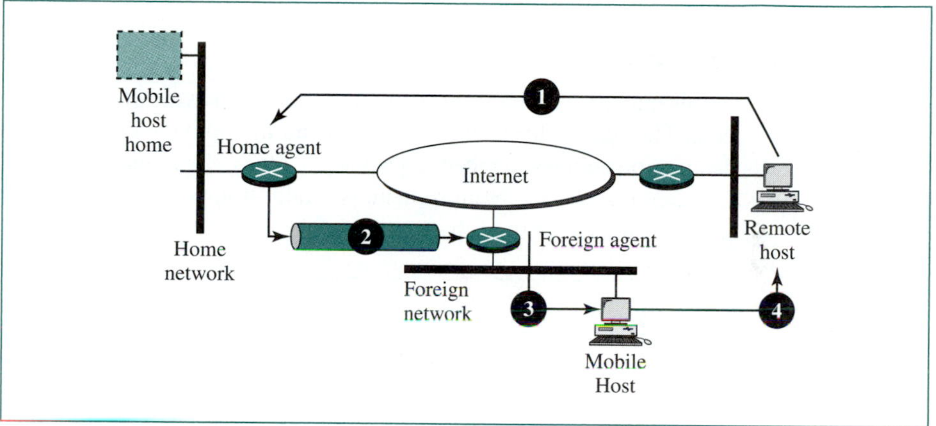

From Remote Host to Home Agent

When a remote host wants to send a packet to the mobile host, it uses its address as the source address and the home address of the mobile host as the destination address. In other words, the remote host sends a packet as though the mobile host is at its home network. The packet, however, is intercepted by the home agent, which pretends it is the mobile host. This is done using the proxy ARP technique discussed in Chapter 7. Path 1 of Figure 27.8 shows this step.

From Home Agent to Foreign Agent

After receiving the packet, the home agent sends the packet to the foreign agent using the tunneling concept discussed in Chapter 14. The home agent encapsulates the whole IP packet inside another IP packet using its address as the source and the foreign agent's address as the destination. Path 2 of Figure 27.8 shows this step.

From Foreign Agent to Mobile Host

When the foreign agent receives the packet, it removes the original packet. However, since the destination address is the home address of the mobile host, the foreign agent consults a registry table to find the care-of address of the mobile host. (Otherwise, the packet would just be sent back to the home network.) The packet is then sent to the care-of address. Path 3 of Figure 27.8 shows this step.

From Mobile Host to Remote Host

When a mobile host wants to send a packet to a remote host (for example, a response to the packet it has received), it sends as it does normally. The mobile host prepares a packet with its home address as the source, and the address of the remote host as the destination. Although the packet comes from the foreign network, it has the home address of the mobile host. Path 4 of Figure 27.8 shows this step.

Transparency

In this data transfer process, the remote host is unaware of any movement by the mobile host. The remote host sends packets using the home address of the mobile host as the destination address; it receives packets that have the home address of the mobile host as the source address. The movement is totally transparent. The rest of the Internet is not aware of the mobility of the moving host.

> The movement of the mobile host is transparent to the rest of the Internet.

27.7 INEFFICIENCY IN MOBILE IP

Communication involving mobile IP can be inefficient. The inefficiency can be severe or moderate. The severe case is called *double crossing* or *2X*. The moderate case is called *triangle routing* or *dog-leg routing*.

Double Crossing

Double crossing occurs when a remote host communicates with a mobile host that has moved to the same network (or site) as the remote host. When the mobile host sends a packet to the remote host, there is no inefficiency; the communication is local. However, when the remote host sends a packet to the mobile host, the packet crosses the Internet twice (see Figure 27.9).

Figure 27.9 *Double crossing*

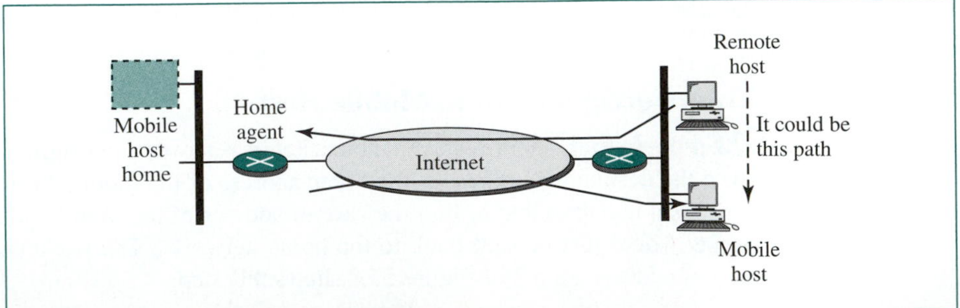

Since a computer usually communicates with other local computers (principle of locality), the inefficiency from double crossing is significant.

Triangle Routing

Triangle routing, the less severe case, occurs when the remote host communicates with a mobile host that is not attached to the same network (or site) as the mobile host. When the mobile host sends a packet to the remote host, there is no inefficiency. However, when the remote host sends a packet to the mobile host, the packet goes from the remote host to the home agent and then to the mobile host. The packet travels the two sides of a triangle, instead of just one side (see Figure 27.10).

Figure 27.10 *Triangle routing*

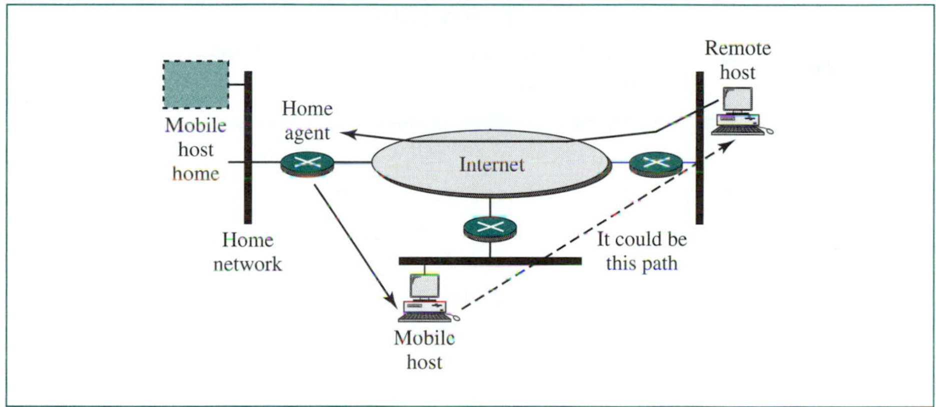

Solution

One solution to inefficiency is for the remote host to bind the care-of address to the home address of a mobile host. For example, when a home agent receives the first packet for a mobile host, it forwards the packet to the foreign agent; it could also send an *update binding packet* to the remote host so that future packets to this host could be sent to the care-of address. The remote host can keep this information in a cache.

The problem with this strategy is that the cache entry becomes outdated once the mobile host moves. In this case the home agent needs to send a *warning packet* to the remote host to inform it of the change.

27.8 KEY TERMS

agent advertisement

agent discovery

agent solicitation

care-of address

co-located care-of address

double crossing

foreign agent

foreign network

- home address
- home agent
- home network
- mobile host
- registration
- registration reply
- registration request
- stationary host
- triangle routing
- update binding packet
- warning packet

27.9 SUMMARY

- Mobile IP, designed for mobile communication, is an enhanced version of the Internetworking Protocol (IP).
- A mobile host has a home address on its home network and a care-of address on its foreign network.
- When the mobile host is on a foreign network, a home agent relays messages (for the mobile host) to a foreign agent.
- A foreign agent sends relayed messages to a mobile host.
- A mobile host on its home network learns the address of a home agent through a process called agent discovery. A mobile host on a foreign network learns the address of a foreign agent through agent discovery or agent solicitation.
- A mobile host on a foreign network must register itself with both the home and foreign agents.
- A message from a remote host goes from the remote host to the home agent, to the foreign agent, and then to the mobile host.
- Mobile communication can be inefficient due to the extra distance a message must travel. Double crossing and triangle routing are two instances of inefficient routing.

27.10 PRACTICE SET

Multiple-Choice Questions

1. The home network address of a mobile host with a home address of 17.1.2.3/8 is _______.
   a. 17.0.0.0
   b. 17.1.0.0
   c. 17.1.2.0
   d. not enough information to answer the question

2. The home network address of a mobile host with a care-of address of 17.1.2.3/8 is _______.
   a. 17.0.0.0
   b. 17.1.0.0
   c. 17.1.2.0
   d. not enough information to answer the question
3. The foreign network address of a mobile host with a care-of address of 47.1.2.3/8 is _______.
   a. 47.0.0.0
   b. 47.1.0.0
   c. 47.1.2.0
   d. not enough information to answer the question
4. The temporary address of a mobile host is called a _______ address.
   a. home
   b. not-at-home
   c. carrier
   d. care-of
5. The permanent address of a mobile host is called a _______ address.
   a. home
   b. stable
   c. everlasting
   d. forever
6. When the mobile host acts as a foreign agent, the care-of address is called a _______ address.
   a. double crossing
   b. co-located care-of
   c. double care-of
   d. co-double
7. The _______ agent is usually a router attached to the home network of the mobile host.
   a. double
   b. home
   c. foreign
   d. co-located
8. In the _______ phase, a mobile host must learn the address of its home agent.
   a. agent discovery
   b. registration
   c. data transfer
   d. none of the above

9. In the _______ phase, a mobile host must learn the address of its foreign agent.
   a. agent discovery
   b. registration
   c. data transfer
   d. none of the above
10. If a router acts as an agent, it advertises its presence in a network by appending an agent _______ message to an ICMP router advertisement.
   a. solicitation
   b. advertisement
   c. discovery
   d. registration
11. A mobile host can send an agent _______ message if it has not received any agent advertisements.
   a. solicitation
   b. discovery
   c. registration
   d. request
12. When a mobile host wants to register with its foreign agent, it sends _______ message.
   a. an agent solicitation
   b. an agent advertisement
   c. a registration request
   d. a registration reply
13. The registration reply is sent by the _______ agent to the foreign agent.
   a. home
   b. care-of
   c. discovery
   d. a and b
14. Registration messages are encapsulated in _______.
   a. an IP datagram
   b. a data link layer frame
   c. a UDP user datagram
   d. a TCP datagram
15. The home agent intercepts a message sent by the remote host to the mobile host using a method called _______.
   a. proxy ARP
   b. tunneling
   c. double crossing
   d. co-location

16. The home agent sends a packet to the foreign agent using a method called _______.
    a. proxy ARP
    b. tunneling
    c. double crossing
    d. co-location
17. The _______ uses a registry table to find the care-of address of the mobile host.
    a. home agent
    b. foreign agent
    c. remote host
    d. none of the above
18. If the mobile host is on the same network as the remote host, an inefficient situation called _______ occurs when the remote host sends a message to the mobile host.
    a. transparency
    b. double crossing
    c. triangle routing
    d. registration
19. In a situation called _______, a message from a remote host to a mobile host travels two sides of a triangle instead of just one side.
    a. transparency
    b. double crossing
    c. triangle routing
    d. registration
20. _______ can be sent from a home agent to a remote host to improve efficiency.
    a. An update binding packet
    b. A registration request
    c. A router advertisement
    d. A solicitation message

Exercises

21. Is registration required if the mobile host acts as a foreign agent? Explain your answer.
22. Redraw Figure 27.5 if the mobile host acts as a foreign agent.
23. Create a home agent advertisement message using 1456 as the sequence number and a lifetime of 3 hours. Select your own values for the bits in the code field. Calculate and insert the value for the length field.
24. Create a foreign agent advertisement message using 1672 as the sequence number and a lifetime of 4 hours. Select your own values for the bits in the code field. Use at least three care-of addresses of your choice. Calculate and insert the value for the length field.

25. Discuss how the ICMP router solicitation message can also be used for agent solicitation. Why are there no extra fields?
26. Which protocol is the carrier of the agent advertisement and solicitation messages?
27. Show the encapsulation of the advertisement message in Exercise 23 in an IP datagram. What is the value for the protocol field?
28. Explain why the registration request and reply are not directly encapsulated in an IP datagram. Why is there a need for the UDP user datagram?
29. We have the following information:

    Mobile host home address: 130.45.6.7/16
    Mobile host care-of address: 14.56.8.9/8
    Remote host address: 200.4.7.14/24
    Home agent address: 130.45.10.20/16
    Foreign agent address: 14.67.34.6/8

    Show the contents of the IP datagram header sent from the remote host to the home agent.
30. Using the information in exercise 29, show the contents of the IP datagram sent by the home agent to the foreign agent. Use tunneling.
31. Using the information in exercise 29, show the contents of the IP datagram sent by the foreign agent to the mobile host.
32. Using the information in exercise 29, show the contents of the IP datagram sent by the mobile host to the remote host.
33. What type of inefficiency do we have in exercise 29? Explain your answer.

CHAPTER 28

Real-Time Traffic over the Internet

In this chapter, we introduce real-time traffic and how it can be handled on the Internet. Most people use the terms *real-time traffic* and *multimedia traffic* interchangeably. However, not all multimedia traffic needs real-time handling. We must separate the two. Figure 28.1 shows the concept.

Figure 28.1 *Real-time multimedia traffic*

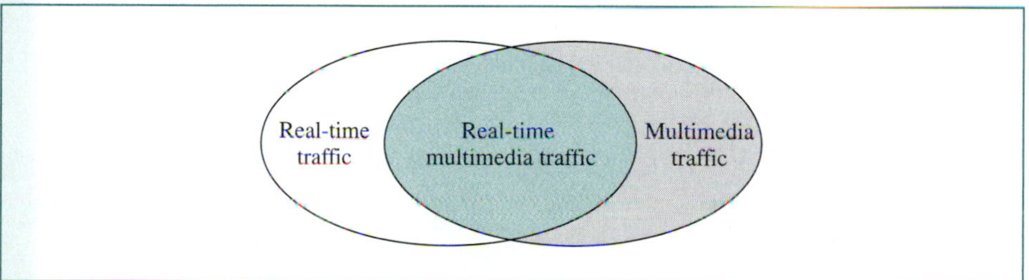

To distinguish real-time communication from other types of communication, we must define real-time traffic. Informally, ignoring short delays in transmission, real-time traffic is the almost simultaneous production and use of data. In other words, the sender produces data, sends it on the Internet, and the receiver uses it. Usually, when the receiver is using the received data, the next part is still in production.

> In real-time traffic, if we ignore propagation delay, the production, transmission, and use of data takes place at the same time.

Example 1

An example of non-real-time multimedia traffic is the downloading of a video from the Internet. The video has already been made; it's a finished product. A client HTTP is used to download the video from an HTTP server and the user views the video at a later time. The production, transmission, and use all happen at different times. Figure 28.2 shows this situation.

Figure 28.2 *Non-real-time multimedia traffic*

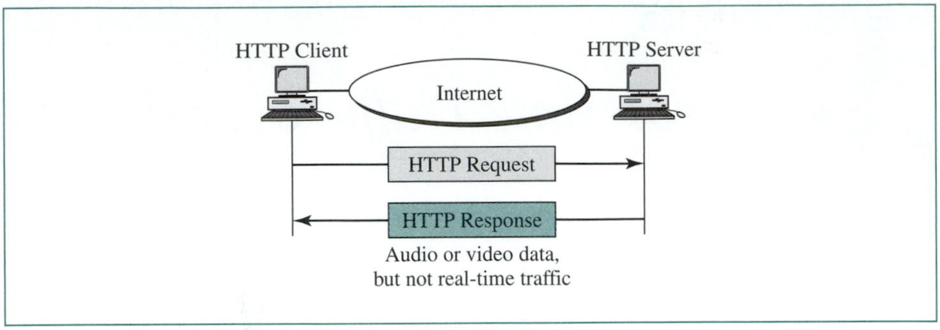

Example 2

Now let us consider an example of real-time multimedia traffic. Consider a video conference in which a camera is connected to a server that transmits video information as it is produced. Everything that happens at the server site can be displayed on the computer at the client site. This is both multimedia (video) and real-time traffic (production and use at the same time). Figure 28.3 shows the situation.

Figure 28.3 *Real-time multimedia traffic*

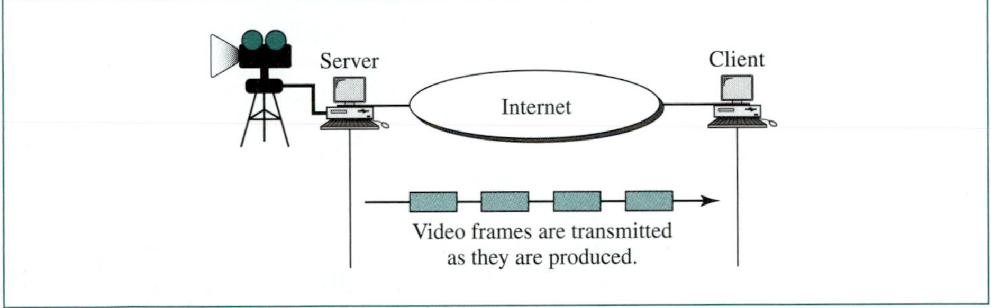

28.1 CHARACTERISTICS

Real-time traffic has characteristics common to all data types (audio, video, and text).

Time Relationship

Real-time data on a packet-switched network requires the preservation of the time relationship between packets of a session. For example, let us assume that a real-time video server creates live video images and sends them on line. The video is digitized and packetized. There are only three packets and each packet holds 10 seconds of video information. The first packet starts at 00:00:00, the second packet starts at 00:00:10, and the third packet at 00:00:20. Also imagine that it takes one second (an exaggeration for simplicity) for each packet to reach the destination (equal delay). The receiver can play back the first packet at 00:00:01, the second packet at 00:00:11, and the third packet at 00:00:21. Although there is a 1-s time difference between what the cameraman sees at the sender site and what the remote viewer sees on the computer screen, the action is happening in real time. The time relationship between the packets is preserved. The 1-s delay is not important. Figure 28.4 shows the idea.

Figure 28.4 *Time relationship*

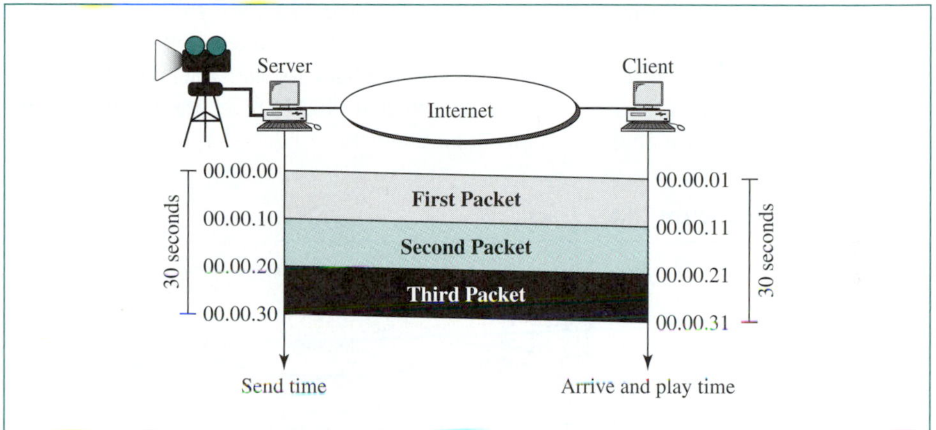

But what happens if the packets arrive with different delays? For example, the first packet arrives at 00:00:01 (1-s delay), the second arrives at 00:00:15 (5-s delay), and the third arrives at 00:00:27 (7-s delay). If the receiver starts playing the first packet at 00:00:01, it will finish at 00:00:11. However, the next packet has not yet arrived; it arrives 4 s later. There is a gap between the first and second packet and between the second and the third as the video is viewed at the remote site. This phenomenon is called *jitter*. Figure 28.5 shows the situation.

Figure 28.5 *Jitter*

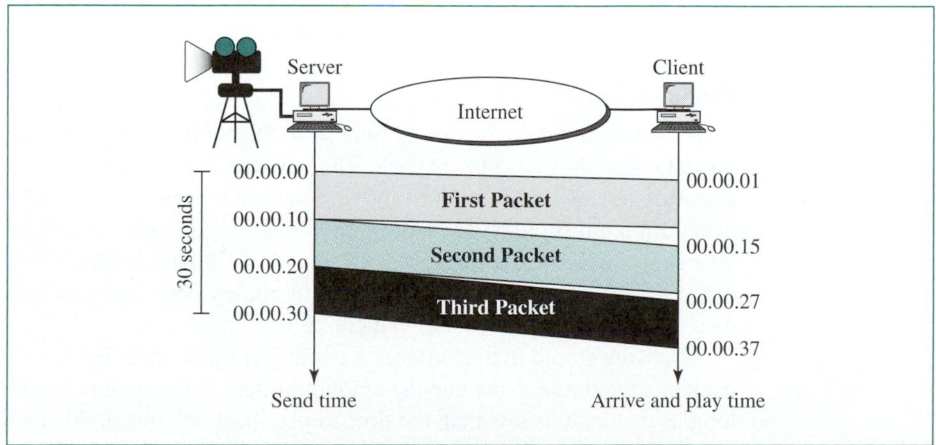

Jitter is introduced in real-time data by the delay between packets.

Timestamp

One solution to jitter is the use of a timestamp. If each packet has a timestamp that shows the time it was produced relative to the first (or previous) packet, then the receiver can add this time to the time it starts the playback. In other words, the receiver knows when each packet is to be played. Imagine the first packet in the previous example has a timestamp of 0, the second has a timestamp of 10, and the third a timestamp of 20. If the receiver starts playing back the first packet at 00:00:08, the second will be played at 00:00:18, and the third at 00:00:28. There are no gaps between the packets. Figure 28.6 shows the situation.

Figure 28.6 *Timestamp*

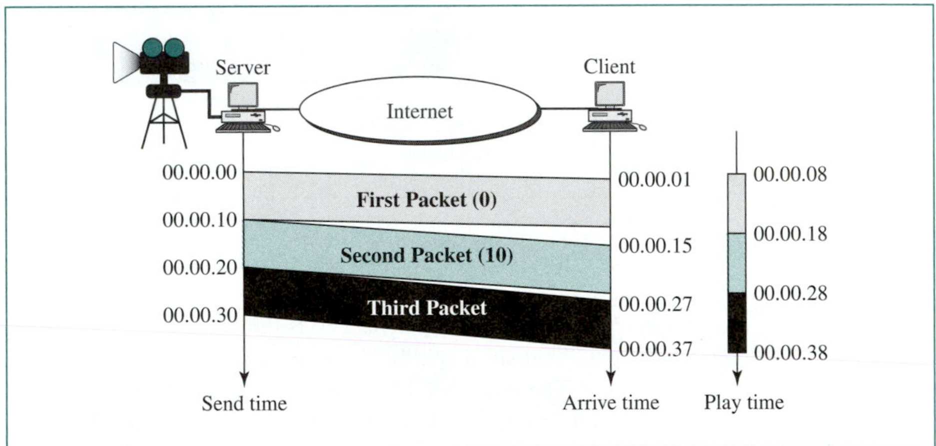

To prevent jitter, we can timestamp the packets and separate the arrival time from the playback time.

Playback Buffer

To be able to separate the arrival time from the playback time, we need a buffer to store the data until they are played back. The buffer is referred to as a *playback buffer.* When a session begins (the first bit of the first packet arrives), the receiver delays playing the data until a threshold is reached. In the previous example, the first bit of the first packet arrives at 00:00:01; the threshold is 7 s, and the playback time is 00:00:08. The threshold is measured in time units of data. The replay does not start until the time units of data are equal to the threshold value.

Data are stored in the buffer at a possibly variable rate, but it is extracted and played back at a fixed rate. Note that the amount of data in the buffer shrinks or expands, but as long as the delay is less than the time to play back the threshold amount of data, there is no jitter. Figure 28.7 shows the buffer at different times for our example.

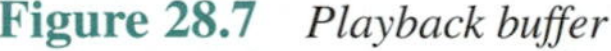

Figure 28.7 *Playback buffer*

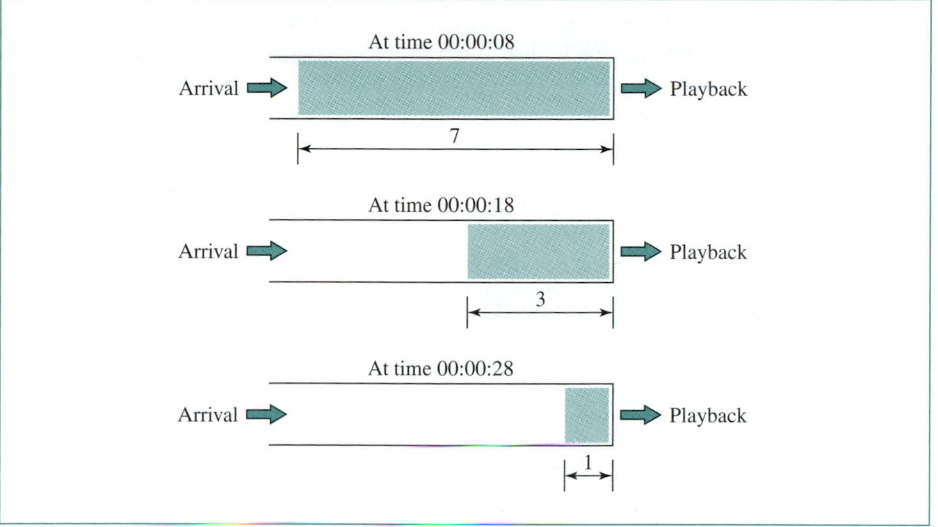

> A playback buffer is required for real-time traffic.

Ordering

In addition to time relationship information and timestamps for real-time traffic, one more feature is needed. We need a *sequence number* for each packet. The timestamp alone cannot inform the receiver if a packet is lost. For example, suppose the timestamps are 0, 10, and 20. If the second packet is lost, the receiver receives just two packets with timestamps 0 and 20. The receiver assumes that the packet with timestamp 20 is the second packet, produced 20 seconds after the first. The receiver has no way of knowing that the second packet has actually been lost. A sequence number to order the packets is needed to handle this situation.

> A sequence number on each packet is required for real-time traffic.

Multicasting

Multimedia play a primary role in audio and video conferencing. The traffic can be heavy and the data are distributed using multicasting methods. Conferencing requires two-way communication between receivers and senders.

> Real-time traffic needs the support of multicasting.

Translation

Sometimes real-time traffic needs translators. A translator is a computer that can change the format of a high-bandwidth video signal to a lower quality narrow-bandwidth signal. This is needed, for example, for a source creating a high-quality video signal at 5 Mbps, and sending to a recipient having a bandwidth less than 1 Mbps. To receive the signal, a translator is needed to decode the signal and encode it again at a lower quality that needs less bandwidth.

> Translation means changing the encoding of a payload to a lower quality to match the bandwidth of the receiving network.

Mixing

If there is more than one source that can send data at the same time (as in a video or audio conference), the traffic is made of multiple streams. To reduce the traffic to one stream, data from different sources can be mixed into one stream. A mixer mathematically adds signals coming from different sources to create one single signal.

> Mixing means combining several streams of traffic into one stream.

Support from Transport Layer Protocol

The procedures mentioned in the previous sections can be implemented in the application layer. However, they are so common in real-time applications that implementation in the Transport Layer Protocol is preferable. Let's see which of the existing transport layers is suitable for this type of traffic.

TCP is not suitable for real-time traffic. It has no provision for timestamping and it does not support multicasting. However, it does provide ordering (sequence numbers). One feature of TCP that makes it particularly unsuitable for real-time traffic is its error control mechanism. In real-time traffic, we cannot allow the retransmission of a lost or corrupted packet. If a packet is lost or corrupted in real-time traffic, it must just be ignored. Retransmission upsets the whole idea of timestamping and playback. Today there is so much redundancy in audio and video signals (even with compression) that we can simply ignore a lost packet. The listener or viewer at the remote site may not even notice it.

> TCP, with all its sophistication, is not suitable for real-time multimedia traffic because we cannot allow retransmission of packets.

UDP is more suitable for real-time multimedia traffic. UDP supports multicasting and has no retransmission strategy. However, UDP has no provision for timestamping, sequencing, or mixing.

To use UDP and at the same time provide support for the missing features, we use UDP in conjunction with a new transport protocol, Real-time Transport Protocol (RTP), for real-time traffic on the Internet.

> UDP is more suitable than TCP for real-time traffic. However, we need the services of RTP, another Transport Layer Protocol to make up the deficiencies of UDP.

28.2 RTP

Real-time Transport Protocol (RTP) is the protocol designed to handle real-time traffic on the Internet. RTP does not have a delivery mechanism (multicasting, port numbers, and so on); it must be used with UDP. RTP stands between UDP and the application program. The main contributions of RTP are timestamping, sequencing, and mixing facilities. Figure 28.8 shows the position of RTP in the protocol suite.

Figure 28.8 *RTP*

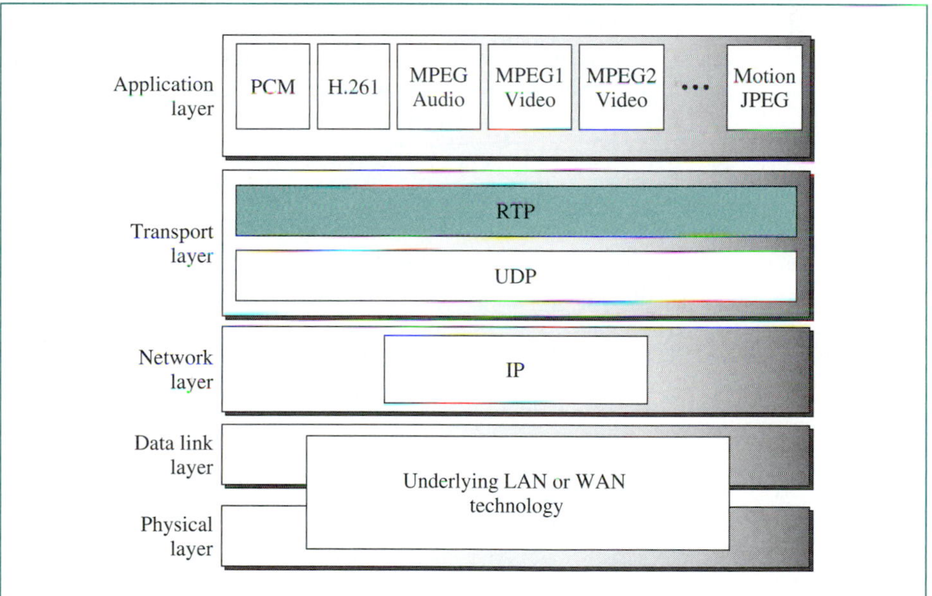

RTP Packet Format

Figure 28.9 shows the format of the RTP packet header.

The format is very simple and general enough to cover all real-time applications. An application that needs more information adds it to the beginning of its payload. A description of each field follows.

- **Ver.** This 2-bit field defines the version number. The current version is 2.
- **P.** This 1-bit field, if set to 1, indicates the presence of padding at the end of the packet. In this case, the value of the last byte in the padding defines the length of the padding. Padding is the norm if a packet is encrypted. There is no padding if the value of the P field is 0.

Figure 28.9 *RTP packet header format*

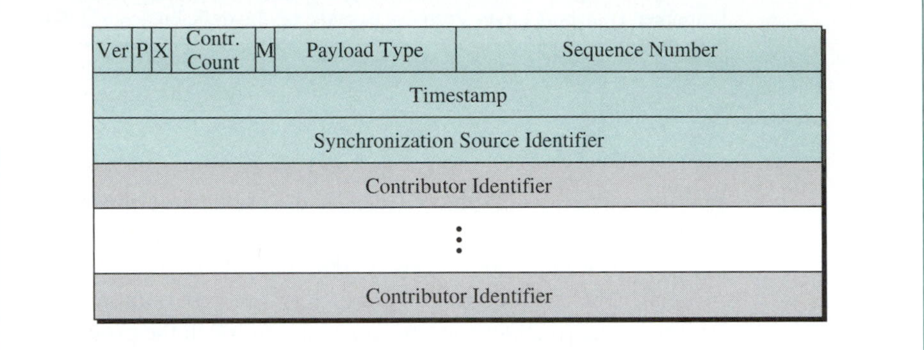

- **X.** This 1-bit field, if set to 1, indicates an extra extension header between the basic header and the data. There is no extra extension header if the value of this field is 0.
- **Contributor Count.** This 4-bit field indicates the number of contributors. Note that we can have a maximum of 15 contributors because a 4-bit field only allows a number between 0 and 15.
- **M.** This 1-bit field is a marker used by the application to indicate, for example, the end of its data.
- **Payload Type.** This 8-bit field indicates the type of the payload. Several payload types have been defined so far. We list some common applications in Table 28.1. A discussion of the types is beyond the scope of this book.

Table 28.1 *Payload types*

Type	*Application*	*Type*	*Application*	*Type*	*Application*
0	PCMμ Audio	7	LPC audio	15	G728 audio
1	1016	8	PCMA audio	26	Motion JPEG
2	G721 audio	9	G722 audio	31	H.261
3	GSM audio	10-11	L16 audio	32	MPEG1 video
5-6	DV14 audio	14	MPEG audio	33	MPEG2 video

- **Sequence Number.** This field is 16 bits in length. It is used to number the RTP packets. The sequence number of the first packet is chosen randomly; it is incremented by 1 for each subsequent packet. The sequence number is used by the receiver to detect lost or out of order packets.
- **Timestamp.** This is a 32-bit field that indicates the time relationship between packets. The timestamp for the first packet is a random number. For each succeeding packet, the value is the sum of the preceding timestamp plus the time the first byte is produced (sampled). The value of the clock tick depends on the application. For example, audio applications normally generate chunks of 160 bytes; the clock tick for this application is 160. The timestamp for this application increases 160 for each RTP packet.

- **Synchronization Source Identifier.** If there is only one source, this 32-bit field defines the source. However, if there are several sources, the mixer is the synchronization source and the other sources are contributors. The value of the source identifier is a random number chosen by the source. The protocol provides a strategy in case of conflict (two sources start with the same sequence number).
- **Contributor Identifier.** Each of these 32-bit identifiers (a maximum of 15) defines a source. When there is more than one source in a session, the mixer is the synchronization source and the remaining sources are the contributors.

UDP Port

Although RTP is itself a Transport Layer Protocol, the RTP packet is not encapsulated directly in an IP datagram. Instead, RTP is treated like an application program and is encapsulated in a UDP user datagram. However, unlike other application programs, no well-known port is assigned to RTP. The port can be selected on demand with only one restriction: The port number must be an even number. The next number (an odd number) is used by the companion of RTP, Real-time Transport Control Protocol (RTCP).

> RTP uses a temporary even-numbered UDP port.

28.3 RTCP

RTP allows only one type of message, one that carries data from the source to the destination. In many cases, there is a need for other messages in a session. These messages control the flow and quality of data and allow the recipient to send feedback to the source or sources. Real-time Transport Control Protocol (RTCP) is a protocol designed for this purpose. RTCP has five types of messages as shown in Figure 28.10. The number next to each box defines the type of the message.

Figure 28.10

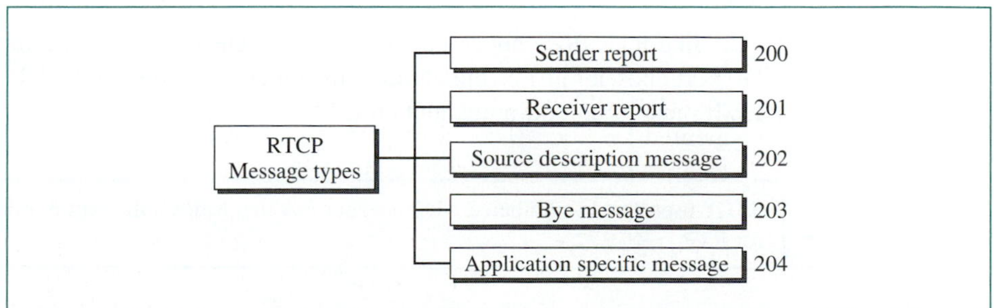

Sender Report

The sender report is sent periodically by the active senders in a conference to report transmission and reception statistics for all RTP packets sent during the interval. The sender report includes an absolute timestamp, which is the number of seconds elapsed since midnight January 1, 1970. The absolute timestamp allows the receiver to synchronize different RTP messages. It is particularly important when both audio and video are transmitted (audio and video transmissions use separate relative timestamps).

Receiver Report

The receiver report is for passive participants, those that do not send RTP packets. The report informs the sender and other receivers about the quality of service.

Source Description Message

The source periodically sends a source description message to give additional information about itself. This information can be the name, email address, telephone number, and address of the owner or controller of the source.

Bye Message

A source sends a bye message to shut down a stream. It allows the source to announce that it is leaving the conference. Although other sources can detect the absence of a source, this message is a direct announcement. It is also very useful to a mixer.

Application Specific Message

The application specific message is a packet for an application that wants to use new applications (not defined in the standard). It allows the definition of a new message type.

UDP Port

RTCP, like RTP, does not use a well-known UDP port. It uses a temporary port. The UDP port chosen must be the number immediately following the UDP port selected for RTP. It must be an odd-numbered port.

> RTCP uses an odd-numbered UDP port number that follows the port number selected for RTP.

28.4 KEY TERMS

application specific message
bye message
jitter
mixer
multicasting
multimedia traffic
playback buffer
real-time multimedia traffic
real-time traffic
Real-time Transport Control Protocol (RTCP)
Real-time Transport Protocol (RTP)
receiver report
sender report
sequence number
source description message
threshold
timestamp
translator

28.5 SUMMARY

- Real-time traffic is the production, transmission, and use of data at the same time.
- Real-time data on a packet-switched network requires the preservation of the time relationship between packets of a session.
- Gaps between consecutive packets at the receiver cause a phenomenon called jitter.
- Jitter can be controlled through the use of timestamps and a judicious choice of the playback time.
- A playback buffer holds data until they can be played back.
- A receiver delays playing back real-time data held in the playback buffer until a threshold level is reached.
- Sequence numbers on real-time data packets provide a form of error control.
- Real-time data are multicast to receivers.
- Real-time traffic sometimes requires a translator to change a high-bandwidth signal to a lower quality narrow-bandwidth signal.
- A mixer combines signals from different sources into one signal.
- Real-time multimedia traffic requires both UDP and Real-time Transport Protocol (RTP).
- RTP handles timestamping, sequencing, and mixing.
- Real-time Transport Control Protocol (RTCP) provides flow control, quality of data control, and feedback to the sources.

28.6 PRACTICE SET

Multiple-Choice Questions

1. The downloading of last year's award-winning video for later viewing is _______ traffic.
   a. real-time
   b. multimedia
   c. real-time multimedia
   d. none of the above
2. We want to view a presidential press conference as it actually takes place. This is classified as _______ traffic.
   a. real-time
   b. multimedia
   c. real-time multimedia
   d. none of the above
3. A real-time video performance lasts 10 min. If there is jitter in the system, the viewer spends _______ min watching the performance.
   a. less than 10
   b. greater than 10
   c. exactly 10
   d. exactly 11
4. A _______ stores real-time data.
   a. timestamp
   b. playback buffer
   c. sequence number
   d. threshold
5. A _______ shows when a packet was produced relative to the first or previous packet.
   a. timestamp
   b. playback buffer
   c. sequence number
   d. threshold
6. _______ are used to number the packets of a real-time transmission.
   a. Timestamps
   b. Playback buffers
   c. Sequence numbers
   d. Translators

7. In a real-time video conference, data from the server is _______ to the client sites.
   a. unicast
   b. multicast
   c. broadcast
   d. none of the above
8. A _______ adds signals from different sources to create a single signal.
   a. timestamp
   b. sequence number
   c. mixer
   d. translator
9. A _______ changes the format of a high-bandwidth video signal to a lower quality narrow-bandwidth signal.
   a. timestamp
   b. sequence number
   c. mixer
   d. translator
10. An RTP packet is encapsulated in _______.
    a. a UDP user datagram
    b. a TCP segment
    c. an IP datagram
    d. an RTCP packet
11. TCP is not suitable for real-time traffic because ______.
    a. there is no provision for timestamping
    b. there is no support for multicasting
    c. missing packets are retransmitted
    d. all of the above
12. If an RTP packet is padded and the value of the last byte is 10, this means _______.
    a. the RTP version is 10
    b. the timestamping value is 10 units
    c. the packet is the tenth of a series
    d. there are 10 bytes of padding
13. If there is an extra extension header in the RTP packet, the _______ field is set to 1.
    a. Ver
    b. P
    c. X
    d. M
14. If an RTP packet carries MPEG audio data, the _______ field is set to 14.
    a. contributor identifier
    b. M
    c. contributor count
    d. payload type

15. When there is more than one source, the _______ identifier defines the mixer.
    a. synchronization source
    b. contributor
    c. timestamp
    d. payload
16. There is a maximum of 15 contributor identifier fields because the contributor count field is _______ bits.
    a. 2
    b. 4
    c. 8
    d. 15
17. _______ messages carry flow control information for real-time transmissions.
    a. RTP
    b. RTCP
    c. TCP
    d. all of the above
18. _______ messages carry real-time data.
    a. RTP
    b. RTCP
    c. TCP
    d. all of the above

Exercises

19. In Figure 28.7 what is the amount of data in the playback buffer at each of the following times:
    a. 00:00:17
    b. 00:00:20
    c. 00:00:25
    d. 00:00:30
20. Show the contents of an RTP packet that has 5 bytes of padding, no extensions, four contributors, and one synchronization source (choose arbitrary identifications). The payload is MPEG1 video.
21. In exercise 20, what is the total length of the RTP header?
22. Encapsulate the message created in exercise 20 in a UDP user datagram. Choose the port number.
23. Do some research on the Internet or the library to find the format of an RTCP sender report. Pay particular attention to the packet length and the parts repeated for each source. Describe each field.
24. In exercise 23, what is the total length of the header if there are five sources?

25. Do some research on the Internet or the library to find the format of an RTCP receiver report. Pay particular attention to the packet length and the parts repeated for each source. Describe each field.
26. In exercise 25, what is the total length of the header if there are five sources?
27. Do some research on the Internet or the library to find the format of an RTCP source description. Pay particular attention to the packet length and the parts repeated for each source. Describe each field.
28. In exercise 27, what is the total length of the header if there are five sources?
29. Do some research and find the meaning of the source description items used in the RTCP source description packet. Specifically, find the meaning of CNAME, NAME, EMAIL, PHONE, LOC, TOOL, NOTE, and PRIV.
30. Do some research on the Internet or the library to find the format of an RTCP bye message. Pay particular attention to the packet length and the parts repeated for each source. Describe each field.
31. If five sources are leaving simultaneously in exercise 30, what is the total length of the packet? Is it fixed, or is it variable? Does the reason for leaving have to be given? If yes, must it be given for each source?
32. Do some research on the Internet or the library to find the format for the RTCP application-specific packet.

CHAPTER 29

Internet Security

29.1 INTRODUCTION

Security is becoming more and more crucial as the volume of data being exchanged on the Internet increases. When people use the Internet, they have certain expectations. They expect confidentiality and data integrity. They want to be able to identify the sender of a message. They want to be able to prove that a message has in fact been sent by a certain sender even if the sender denies it.

Based on the above expectations, we can say that security involves four aspects: privacy (confidentiality), message authentication, message integrity, and nonrepudiation (see Figure 29.1).

Figure 29.1 *Aspects of security*

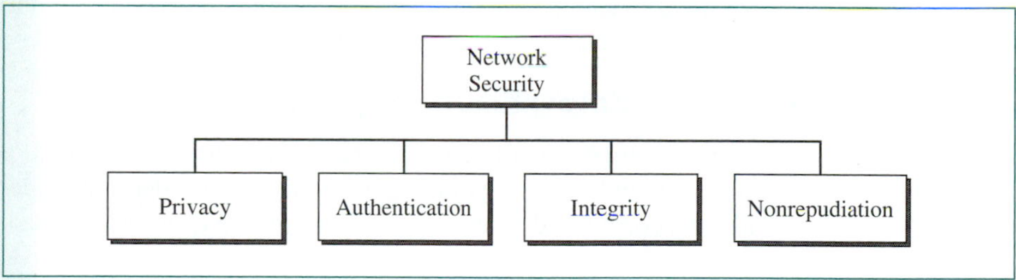

Privacy

Privacy means that the sender and the receiver expect confidentiality. The transmitted message must make sense to only the intended receiver. To all others, the message must be unintelligible.

Authentication

Authentication means that the receiver is sure of the sender's identity and that an imposter has not sent the message.

Integrity

Integrity means that the data must arrive at the receiver exactly as it was sent. There must be no changes during the transmission, either accidental or malicious. As more and more monetary exchanges occur over the Internet, integrity is crucial. For example, it would be disastrous if a request for transferring $100 changes to a request for $10,000 or $100,000. The integrity of the message must be preserved in a secure communication.

Nonrepudiation

Nonrepudiation means that a receiver must be able to prove that a received message came from a specific sender. The sender must not be able to deny sending a message that he, in fact, did send. The burden of proof falls on the receiver. For example, when a customer sends a message to transfer money from one account to another, the bank must have proof that the customer actually requested this transaction.

29.2 PRIVACY

The concept of how to achieve privacy has not changed for thousands of years: The message must be encrypted. That is, the message must be rendered unintelligible to unauthorized parties. A good privacy technique guarantees to some extent that a potential intruder (eavesdropper) cannot understand the contents of the message.

The data to be encrypted at the sender site is called plaintext. The encrypted data are called ciphertext and are decrypted at the receiver. There are two categories of encryption/decryption methods: the secret-key methods and the public-key methods.

Secret-Key Encryption/Decryption

In secret-key encryption/decryption, the same key is used by both parties. The sender uses this key and an encryption algorithm to encrypt data; the receiver uses the same key and the corresponding decryption algorithm to decrypt the data (see Figure 29.2).

Figure 29.2 *Secret-key encryption*

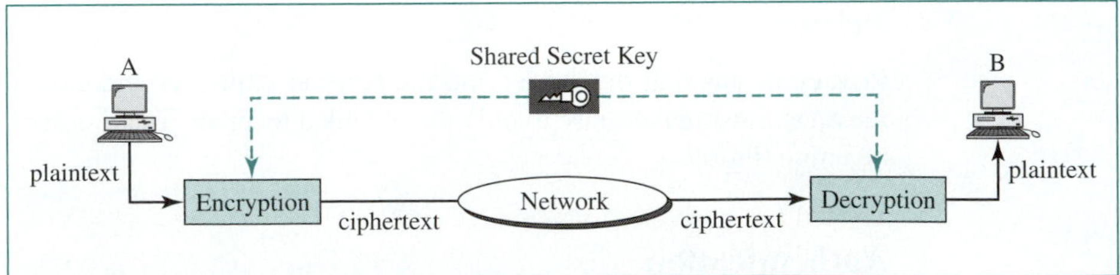

> In secret-key encryption, the same key is used by the sender (for encryption) and the receiver (for decryption). The key is shared.

In secret-key encryption/decryption, the algorithm used for decryption is the inverse of the algorithm used for encryption. This means that if the encryption algorithm uses a combination of addition and multiplication, the decryption algorithm uses a combination of division and subtraction.

Note that the secret-key encryption algorithms are often referred to as symmetric encryption algorithms because the same secret key can be used in bidirectional communication.

> Secret-key encryption is often called symmetric encryption because the same key can be used in both directions.

Advantages

Secret-key algorithms are efficient; it takes less time to encrypt a message using a secret-key algorithm than it takes to encrypt using a public-key algorithm. The reason is that the key is usually smaller. For this reason, secret-key algorithms are used to encrypt and decrypt long messages.

> Secret-key encryption is often used for long messages.

Disadvantages

Secret-key encryption/decryption has two major disadvantages.

1. Each pair of users must have a secret key. This means that if N people in the world want to use this method, there needs to be $N (N - 1)/2$ secret keys. For example, for one million people to communicate, 500 billion secret keys are needed.
2. The distribution of the keys between two parties can be difficult. We will see shortly how we can solve this problem.

> We discuss one secret-key algorithm in Appendix E.

Key Distribution Center (KDC)

One drawback of secret-key encryption is that two parties (who may never be in contact with each other) must agree on a shared secret key. One acceptable solution to this problem is for both to trust a third party, a key distribution center (KDC). The KDC is normally a server that shares a key with each user. The users use their shared key with the server to establish a one-time shared key with each other.

> KDC can solve the problem of secret-key distribution.

Public-Key Encryption

In public-key encryption, there are two keys: a private key and a public key. The private key is kept by the receiver. The public key is announced to the public.

Imagine user A as shown in Figure 29.3 wants to send a message to user B. A uses the public key to encrypt the message. When the message is received by B, the private key is used to decrypt the message.

Figure 29.3 *Public-key encryption*

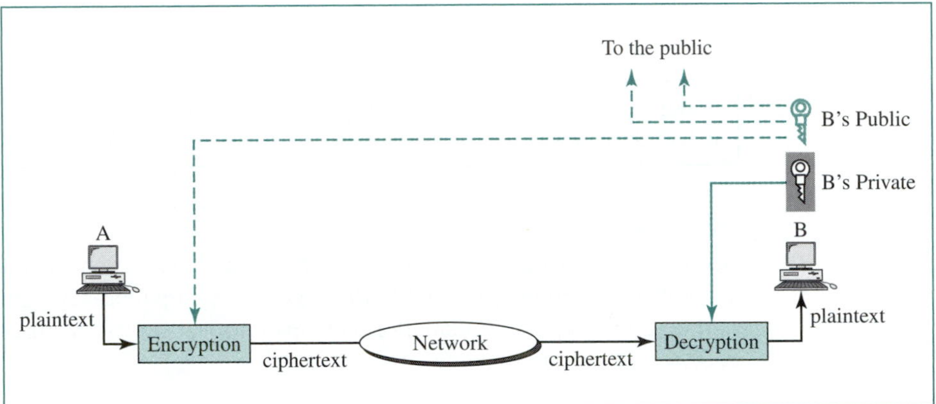

In public-key encryption/decryption, the public key that is used to encrypt the algorithm is different from the private key that is used to decrypt the algorithm. The public key is available to the public; the private key is kept by each individual.

Advantages

Public-key encryption/decryption has two advantages:

1. The whole idea behind public-key encryption is to remove the restriction of a shared secret key between two entities (persons, for example) who need to communicate with each other. This key is shared by the two parties and cannot be used when one of them wants to communicate with a third party. In public-key encryption/decryption, each entity can create a pair of keys, keep the private one, and publicly distribute the other one. Each entity is independent and the pair of keys created can be used to communicate with any other entity.
2. The number of keys needed is reduced tremendously. In this system, for one million users to communicate, only two million keys are needed, not 500 billion as was the case in secret-key encryption.

Disadvantage

Public-key encryption also has two disadvantages:

1. The big disadvantage of the public-key method is the complexity of the algorithm. If we want the method to be effective, the algorithm needs large numbers. Calculating the ciphertext from plaintext using the long keys takes a lot of time. That is

the main reason that public-key encryption is not recommended for large amounts of text.

> Public-key algorithms are more efficient for short messages.

2. The second disadvantage of the public-key method is that the association between an entity and its public key must be verified. If A sends its public key via an email to B, B must be sure that the public key really belongs to A and nobody else. We will see that this certification is really important when we use public-key encryption for authentication. However, this disadvantage can be overcome using Certification Authority (CA) as we will see shortly.

Certification Authority (CA)

One drawback of public-key encryption is that the owner of the public key must be verified. A Certification Authority (CA) is an agency such as a federal or state organization that binds a public key to an entity and issues a certificate. CA combines a public key and information about an entity, such as name, organization name, or router IP address, into one document. It then encrypts the document with its private key and sends it to everyone registered to that authority. The registered users can use their public key to decrypt the certificate and find the public key of the entity.

> A CA can certify the binding between a public key and the owner.

Using the Combination

We can combine the advantage of the secret-key method (efficiency) with the advantage of the public-key method (easy distribution of keys). The public key is used to encrypt the secret key; the secret key is used to encrypt the message. The procedure is as follows:

1. The sender chooses a secret key. This secret key is called the one-session key; it is used only once.
2. The sender uses the public key of the receiver to encrypt the secret key (as text). and sends the encrypted secret key to the receiver. Remember that we said the public-key method is good for short messages. A secret key is a short text message.
3. The receiver uses its private key to decrypt the secret key.
4. The sender uses the shared secret key to encrypt the actual message.

Figure 29.4 shows encryption using a combination of methods.

29.3 DIGITAL SIGNATURE

We said that security has four aspects: privacy, authentication, integrity, and nonrepudiation. We have already discussed privacy. The other three can be achieved using what is called **digital signature.**

Figure 29.4 *Combination*

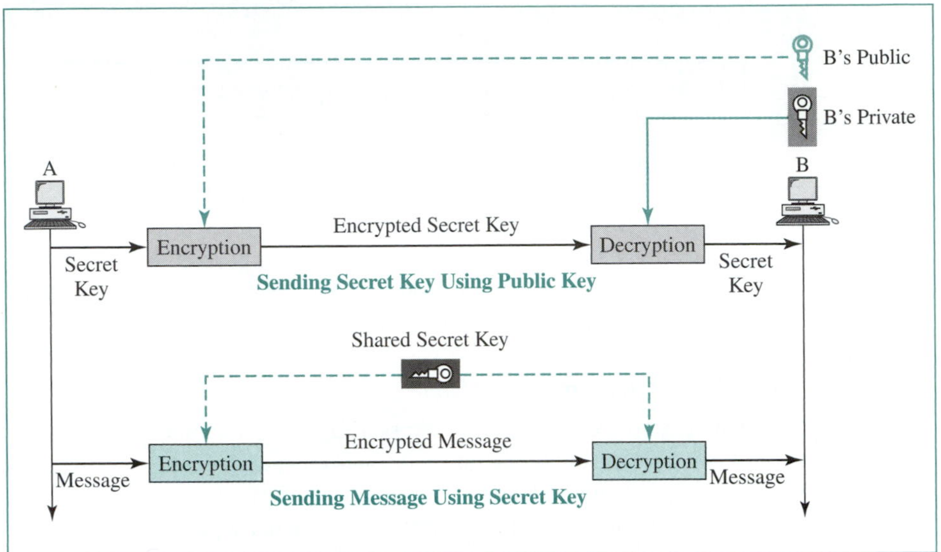

> To have the advantages of both secret-key and public-key encryption, we can encrypt the secret key using the public key and encrypt the message using the secret key.

The idea is similar to the signing of a document. When we send a document electronically, we can also sign it. We have two choices: we can sign the entire document or we can sign a digest (condensed version) of the document.

Signing the Whole Document

Public-key encryption can be used to sign a document. However, the roles of the public and private key are different here. The sender uses her private key to encrypt (sign) the message just as a person uses her signature (which is private in the sense that it is difficult to forge) to sign a paper document. The receiver, on the other hand, uses the public key of the sender to decrypt the message just as a person verifies from memory another person's signature.

In digital signature the private key is used for encryption and the public key for decryption. This is possible because the encryption and decryption algorithms used today, such as RSA, are mathematical formulas and their structures are similar. Figure 29.5 shows how this is done.

Digital signature can provide integrity, authentication, and nonrepudiation.

Integrity The integrity of a message is preserved because, if an intruder intercepts the message and partially or totally changes it, the decrypted message would be (with a high probability) unreadable.

Figure 29.5 *Signing the whole document*

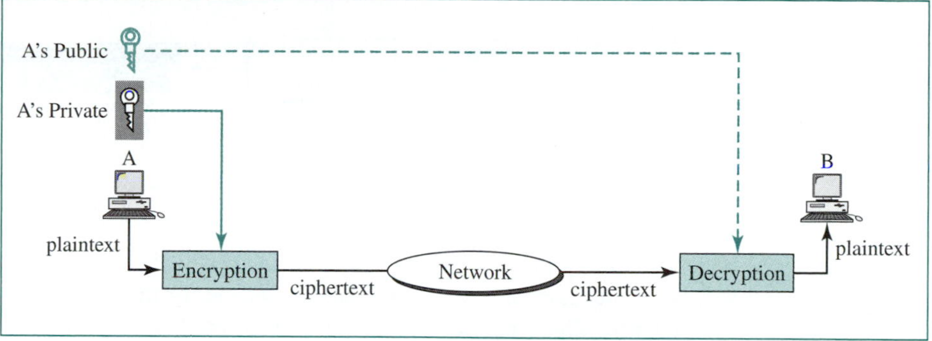

> Digital signature cannot be achieved using only secret keys

Authentication We can use the following reasoning to show how a message can be authenticated. If an intruder (user X) sends a message pretending that it is coming from someone else (user G), she must use her own private key (private X) for encryption. The message is then decrypted with the public key of user G and will therefore be non-readable. Encryption with X's private key and decryption with G's public key results in garbage.

Nonrepudiation Digital signature also provides for nonrepudiation. If the sender denies sending the message, her private key corresponding to her public key can be tested on the original plaintext. If the result of decryption matches the original message then we know the sender sent the message.

> Digital signature does not provide privacy. If there is a need for privacy, another layer of encryption/decryption must be applied.

Signing the Digest

We said before that public-key encryption is efficient if the message is short. Using a public key to sign the entire message is very inefficient if the message is very long. The solution is to let the sender sign a digest of the document instead of the whole document. The sender creates a miniature version of the document and signs it; the receiver then checks the signature on the miniature.

To create a digest of the message, we use a hash function. The hash function creates a fixed-size digest from a variable-length message as shown in Figure 29.6.

The two most common hash functions are called MD5 (Message Digest 5) and SHA-1 (Secure Hash Algorithm 1). The first one produces a 120-bit digest. The second produces a 160-bit digest.

Note that a hash function must have two properties to guarantee its success. First, hashing is one-way; the digest can only be created from the message, not vice versa.

Figure 29.6 *Signing the digest*

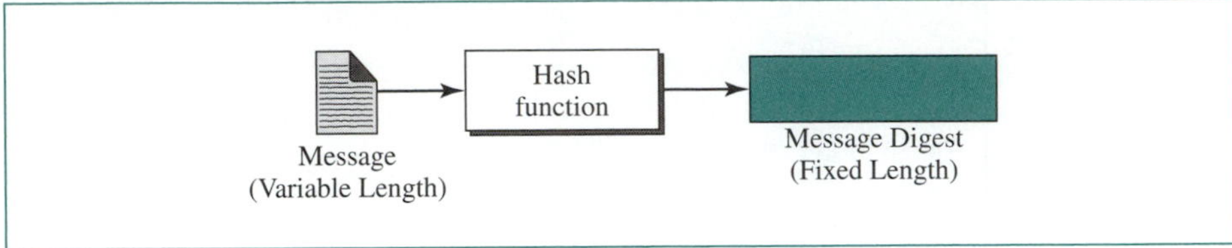

Second, hashing is a one-to-one function; there is little probability that two messages will create the same digest. We will see the reason for this condition shortly.

After the digest has been created, it is encrypted (signed) using the sender's private key. The encrypted digest is attached to the original message and sent to the receiver. Figure 29.7 shows the sender site.

Figure 29.7 *Sender site*

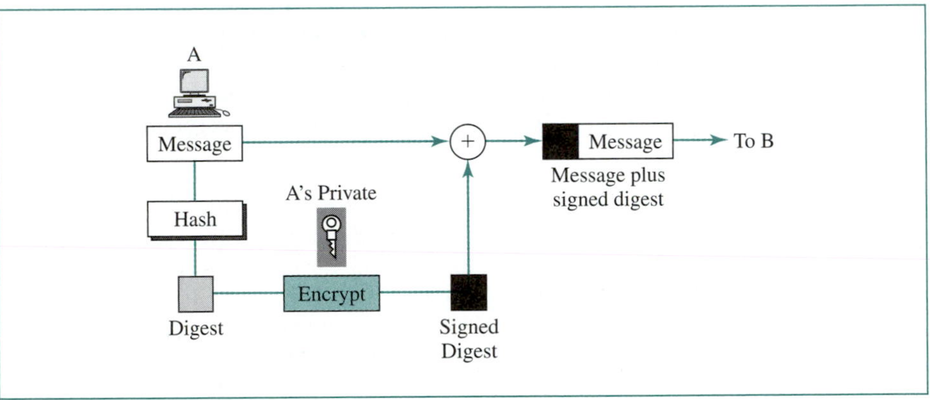

The receiver receives the original message and the encrypted digest. She separates the two. She applies the same hash function to the message to create a second digest. She also decrypts the received digest using the public key of the sender. If the two digests are the same, all three aspects of security are preserved. Figure 29.8 shows the receiver site.

According to the previous section, we know that the digest is secure in terms of integrity, authentication, and nonrepudiation, but what about the message itself? The following reasoning shows that these aspects are indeed provided for the message too:

1. The digest has not been changed (integrity) and the digest is a replica of the message. So the message has not been changed (remember no two messages can create the same digest). Integrity has been provided.
2. The digest comes from the true sender, so the message also comes from the true sender. If an intruder had initiated the message, the message would not have created the same digest (no two messages can create the same digest).
3. The sender cannot deny the message since she cannot deny the digest; the only message that can create that digest is the received message.

Figure 29.8 *Receiver site*

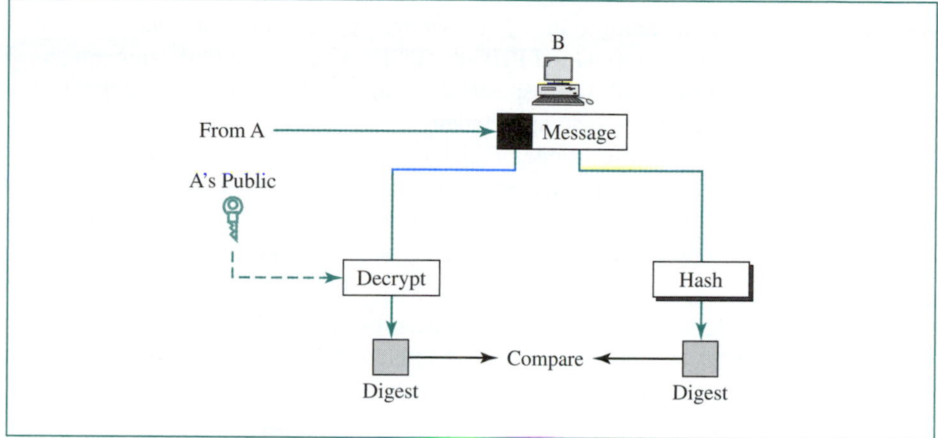

29.4 SECURITY IN THE INTERNET

All of the principles and concepts discussed can be used in the Internet to provide all aspects of security. In particular, security measures can be applied to the application layer, transport layer, and the IP layer.

At the application layer, each application is responsible for providing security. The implementation of security at this level is the simplest. It concerns two entities: the client and the server. We discuss two security methods at the application layer in this chapter.

At the transport layer, security is more complicated. We could modify the application or modify the transport layer for security. Instead, we discuss a protocol that "glues" a new layer to the transport layer to provide security on behalf of the transport layer.

At the IP layer, implementation of security features is very complicated, especially since every device must be able to handle it. IP not only provides services for user applications, but it also provides services to other protocols such as OSPF, ICMP, and IGMP. This means that implementation of security at this level is not very effective until all devices are ready to use it. We discuss security at this level later in the chapter.

29.5 APPLICATION LAYER SECURITY

The implementation of security at the application layer is more feasible and simpler particularly when the Internet communication involves only two parties, as in the case of email and TELNET. The sender and the receiver can agree to use the same protocol and to use any type of security services they desire. In this section, we discuss two protocols used at the application layer to provide security: PGP and SSH.

Pretty Good Privacy (PGP)

As an example of a good secure system, let us discuss a common security scheme called **Pretty Good Privacy** (PGP), invented by Phil Zimmermann. PGP was designed to provide all four aspects of security (privacy, integrity, authentication, and nonrepudiation) in the sending of email.

PGP uses digital signature (a combination of hashing and public-key encryption) to provide integrity, authentication, and nonrepudiation. It uses a combination of secret-key and public-key encryption to provide privacy. Specifically, it uses one hash function, one secret key, and two private-public key pairs. See Figure 29.9.

Figure 29.9 *PGP at the sender site*

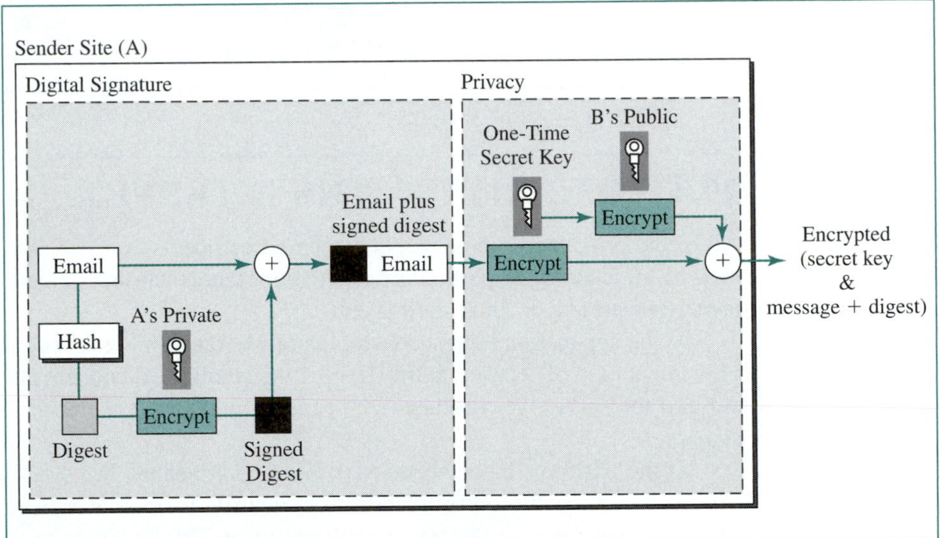

The figure shows how PGP creates secure email at the sender site. The email message is hashed to create a digest. The digest is encrypted (signed) using A's private key. The message and the digest are encrypted using the one-time secret key created by A. The secret-key is encrypted using B's public key and sent together with the encrypted combination of message and digest. Figure 29.10 shows how PGP uses hashing and a combination of three keys to extract the original message at the receiver site.

The combination of encrypted secret key and message plus digest is received. The encrypted secret key first is decrypted (using B's private key) to get the one-time secret key created by the sender. The secret key then is used to decrypt the combination of the message plus digest.

Secure Shell (SSH)

Despite its name, secure shell (SSH) is not a true shell such as the UNIX C shell or Korn shell. SSH is in fact a client-server program that provides security. We can think

Figure 29.10 *PGP at the receiver site*

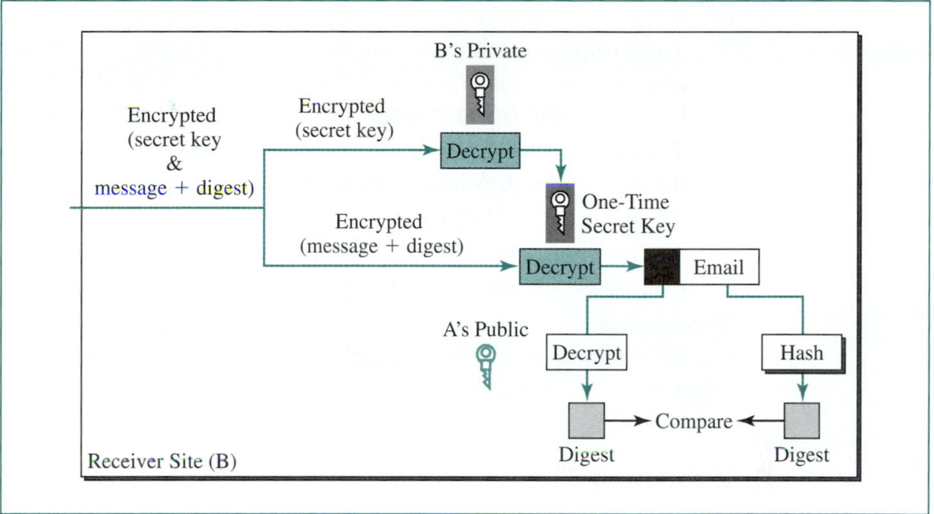

of SSH as a secure form of the *rlogin* client-server application program discussed in Chapter 19.

Authentication

When a user logs into the system, the authentication test must be passed. SSH uses public-key encryption to provide authentication.

Authorization

SSH uses sophisticated authorization methods to allow access to files.

Privacy

Data exchanged between the user (client) and the system (server) are encrypted to provide privacy.

Integrity

SSH guarantees the integrity of the message in both directions.

Tunneling

SSH uses application level tunneling to encapsulate other applications inside itself.

29.6 TRANSPORT LAYER SECURITY: TLS

Transport Layer Security (TLS) was designed to provide security at the transport layer. TLS was derived from a security protocol called Secure Sockets Layer (SSL) designed by Netscape to provide security on the WWW. TLS is a nonproprietary version of SSL designed by IETF. For transactions on the Internet, a browser needs the following:

1. The customer needs to be sure that the server belongs to the actual vendor, not an imposter. For example, a customer does not want an imposter to make charges on her credit card. In other words, the server must be authenticated.
2. The customer needs to be sure that the contents of the message are not modified during transition. A bill for $100 must not be changed to $1000. The integrity of the message must be preserved.
3. The customer needs to be sure that an imposter does not intercept sensitive information such as a credit card number. There is a need for privacy.

There are other optional security aspects that can be added to the above list. For example, the vendor may also need to authenticate the customer. TLS can provide additional features to cover these aspects of security.

Position of TLS

TLS lies between the application layer and the transport layer (TCP) as shown in Figure 29.11.

Figure 29.11 *Position of TLS*

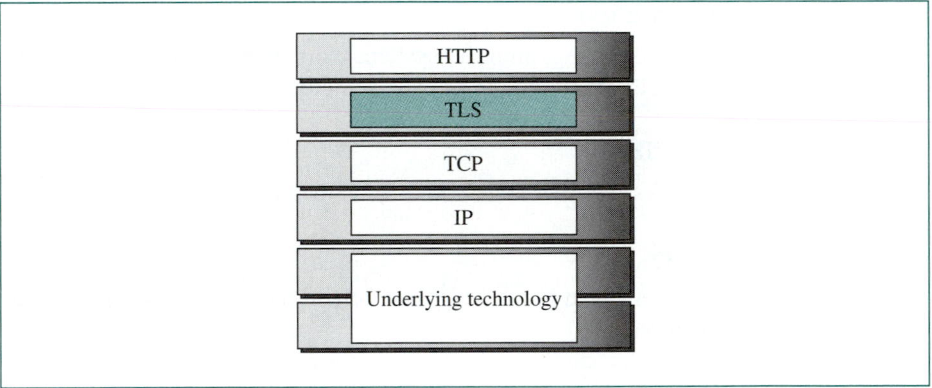

The application layer protocol, in this case HTTP, uses the services of TLS and TLS uses the services of the transport layer.

Two Protocols

TLS is actually two protocols: the handshake protocol and the data exchange (sometimes called record) protocol.

Handshake Protocol

The handshake protocol is responsible for negotiating security, authenticating the server to the browser, and optionally, defining other communication parameters. The handshake protocol defines the exchange of a series of messages between the browser and server. We discuss a simplified version as shown in Figure 29.12.

Figure 29.12 *Handshake protocol*

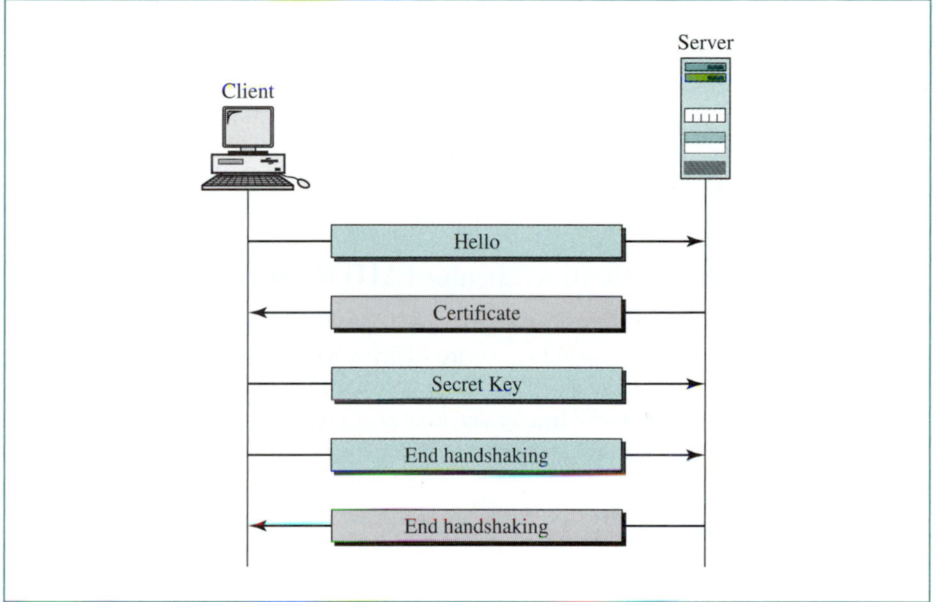

1. The browser sends a hello message that includes the TLS version and some preferences.
2. The server sends a certificate message that includes the public key of the server. The public key is certified by some CA, which means that the public key is encrypted by a CA private key.

   The browser has a list of CAs and their public keys. It uses the corresponding key to decrypt the certificate and finds the server public key. This also authenticates the server because the public key is certified by the CA.
3. The browser generates a secret key, encrypts it with the server public key and sends it to the server.
4. The browser sends a message, encrypted by the secret key, to inform the server that handshaking is terminating from the browser side.
5. The server decrypts the secret key using its private key and decrypts the message using the secret key. It then sends a message, encrypted by the secret key, to inform the browser that handshaking is terminating from the server side.

Note that handshaking uses the public key for two purposes: to authenticate the server and to encrypt the secret key, which is used in the data exchange protocol.

Data Exchange Protocol

The data exchange (record) protocol uses the secret key to encrypt the data for secrecy and to encrypt the message digest for integrity. The details and specification of algorithms is agreed upon during the handshake phase.

29.7 SECURITY AT THE IP LAYER: IPSEC

IP Security (IPSec) is a collection of protocols designed by the IETF (Internet Engineering Task Force) to provide security for a packet carried on the Internet. IPSec does not define the use of any specific encryption or authentication method. Instead, it provides a framework and a mechanism; it leaves the selection of the encryption/authentication and hashing methods to the user.

IPSec defines two protocols to be used at the IP (network layer): Authentication Header (AH) protocol and Encapsulating Security Payload protocol. We discuss both of these protocols here.

Authentication Header (AH) Protocol

The Authentication Header (AH) protocol is designed to provide integrity. The method involves a digital signature using a hashing function. The message digest created by applying the hashing function is included in a header (AH header), and inserted between the IP header and transport layer data and header. Figure 29.13 shows the position of the AH header in an IP datagram.

Figure 29.13 *Authentication*

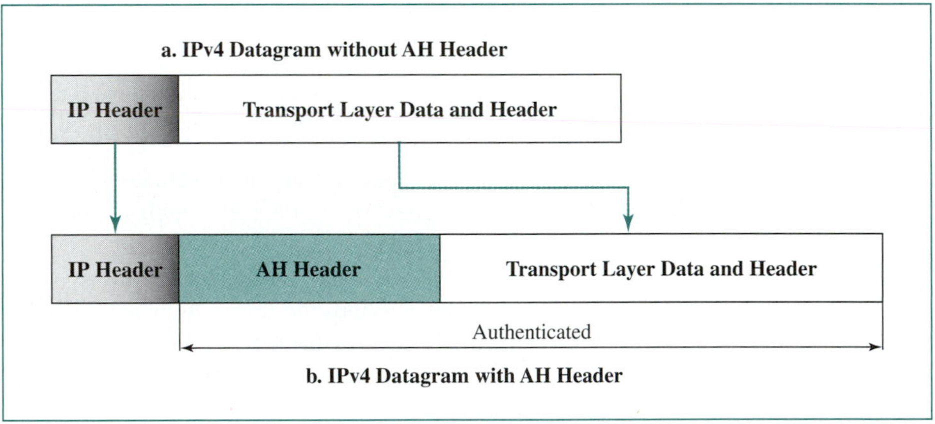

When an IP datagram carries an authentication header, the original value in the protocol field of the IP header is replaced by the value 51. A field inside the AH header (next header field) defines the original value of the protocol field (the type of payload being carried by the IP datagram).

Addition of an AH header follows the steps below:

1. An AH header is added to the payload with the authentication data field set to zero.
2. The AH header and the payload are hashed to create the authentication data.
3. The authentication data are inserted into the AH header.
4. The IP header is added after changing the value of the protocol field to 51.

Header Format

Figure 29.14 shows the format of the header. A brief description of each field follows:

Figure 29.14 *Header format*

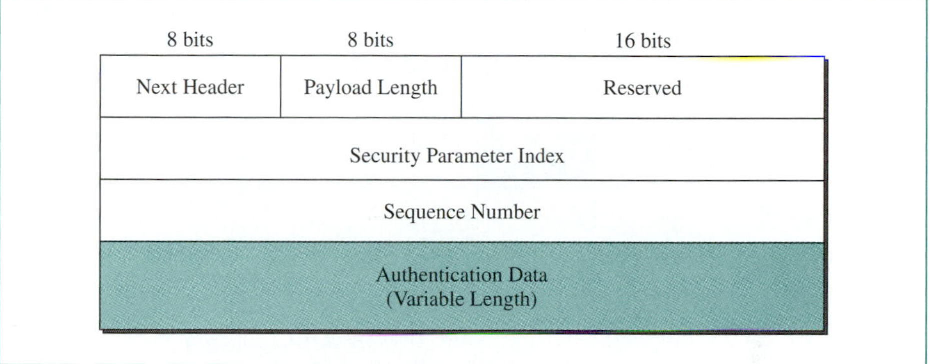

- **Next Header.** The 8-bit next header field defines the type of the payload carried by the IP datagram (TCP, UDP, ICMP, OSPF, and so on). It has the same functions as the protocol field in the IP header before encapsulation. In other words, the process copies the value of the protocol field in the IP datagram to this field. The value of the protocol field in the IP datagram is changed to 51 to show that the packet carries an AH header.
- **Payload Length.** The name of this 8-bit payload length field is misleading. It does not define the length of the payload; it defines the length of the AH header in multiples of 4 bytes.
- **Security Parameter Index.** The 32-bit security parameter index field defines the security method used in creating the authentication data.
- **Sequence Number.** A 32-bit sequence number provides ordering information for a sequence of datagrams. As we learned previously, we need sequence numbers to prevent the loss of packets during a playback.
- **Authentication Data.** Finally, the authentication data field is the result of applying a hash function to the entire IP datagram except for the fields that are changed during transit (time-to-live, for example).

Encapsulating Security Payload

The AH protocol does not provide privacy, only integrity and message authentication (digital signature). IPSec defines another protocol that provides privacy as well as a combination of integrity and message authentication. The protocol is called Encapsulating Security Payload (ESP). Figure 29.15 shows how an IP packet is encrypted and authenticated using ESP.

When an IP datagram carries an ESP header and trailer, the value in the protocol field in the IP header changes to 50. A field inside the ESP trailer (the next header field) holds the original value of the protocol field (the type of payload being carried by the IP datagram, such as TCP or UDP).

Figure 29.15 *ESP*

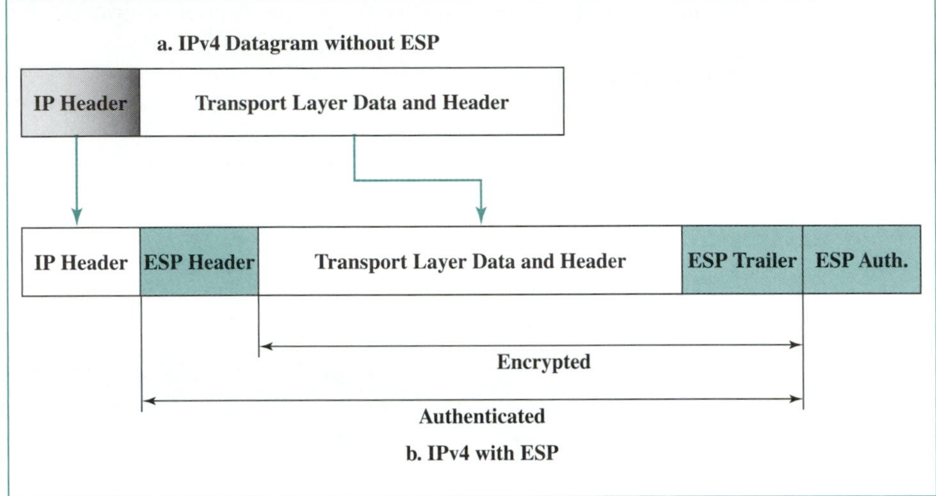

The ESP procedure follows these steps:

1. An ESP trailer is added to the payload.
2. The payload and the trailer are encrypted.
3. The ESP header is added.
4. The ESP header, payload, and the ESP trailer are used to create authentication data.
5. The authentication data are added at the end of the ESP trailer.
6. The IP header is added after changing the protocol value to 50.

Format of Header and Trailer

Figure 29.16 shows the format of an ESP header and trailer. It also shows the authentication data that is created and added after the trailer.

The fields are described as follows:

- **Security Parameter Index.** The 32-bit security parameter field is similar to that defined for the AH protocol.
- **Sequence Number.** The 32-bit sequence number field is similar to that defined for the AH protocol.
- **Padding.** This is a variable length field (0 to 255 bytes) of 0s to serve as padding. Padding may be needed to make the length of data to be encrypted a multiple of some predefined value. It may also be needed for alignment. As shown in the figure, the authentication data normally start at a 4-byte boundary and the payload and the trailer must be aligned for that reason.
- **Pad Length.** The 8-bit pad length field defines the number of padding bytes. The value is between 0 and 255. However, the padding is rarely the maximum value.
- **Next Header.** The 8-bit next header field is similar to that defined in the AH protocol. It serves the same purpose as the protocol field in the IP header before

Figure 29.16 *ESP format*

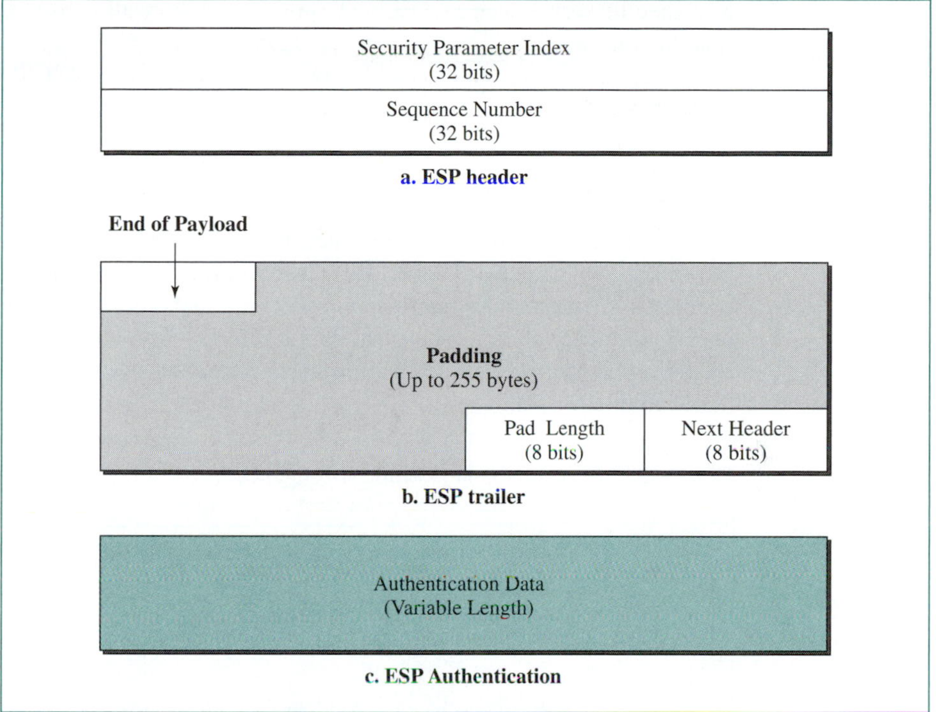

encapsulation. In other words, the value of the protocol field in the IP datagram is copied to this field. The value of the protocol field in the IP header is changed to 50 to show that the packet carries an ESP.

- **Authentication Data.** Finally, the authentication data field is the result of applying an authentication scheme to parts of the datagram as discussed previously.

29.8 FIREWALLS

A firewall is a router installed between the internal network of an organization and the the rest of the Internet. It is designed to forward some packets and filter (not forward) others. Figure 29.17 shows a firewall.

Figure 29.17 *Firewall*

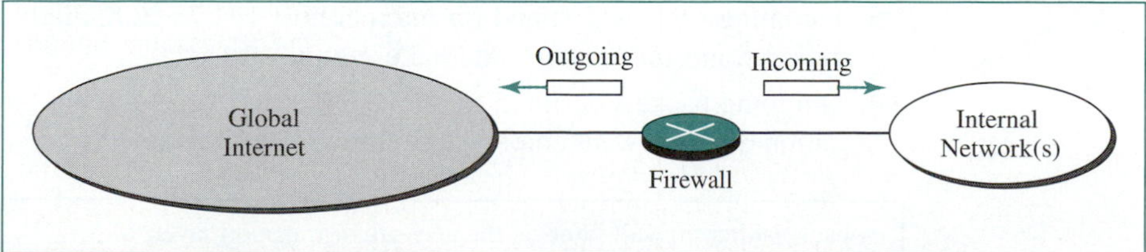

For example, a firewall may filter all incoming packets destined for a specific host or a specific server such as TELNET (port 23). A firewall is used to deny access to a specific host or a specific service in the organization.

Firewalls are normally used for two purposes: as a packet-filter firewall or as a proxy-based firewall.

Packet-Filter Firewall

A firewall can be used as a packet filter. It can forward or block packets based on the information in the network layer and transport layer headers: source and destination IP addresses, source and destination port addresses, and type of protocol (TCP or UDP). A packet-filter firewall is a router that uses a filtering table to decide which packet must be discarded (not forwarded). Figure 29.18 shows an example of a filtering table for this kind of a firewall.

Figure 29.18 *Packet-filter firewall*

Packet Filter Firewall

To and From Global Internet — 1 — 2 — Internal Network(s)

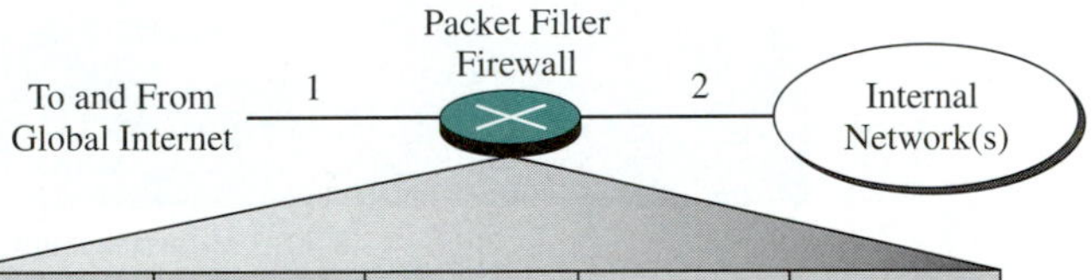

Interface	Source IP	Source Port	Destination IP	Destination Port
1	131.34.0.0	*	*	*
1	*	*	*	23
1	*	*	194.78.20.8	*
2	*	80	*	*

According to the table, the following packets are filtered:

1. Incoming packets from network 131.34.0.0. are blocked (security precaution). Note that the "*" (asterisk) means "any."
2. Incoming packets destined for any internal TELNET server (port 23) are blocked.
3. Incoming packets destined for internal host 194.78.20.8. are blocked. The organization wants this host for internal use only.
4. Outgoing packets destined for an HTTP server (port 80) are blocked. The organization does not want employees to browse the Internet.

A packet-filter firewall filters at the network or transport layer.

Proxy Firewall

The packet-filter firewall is based on the information available on the network layer and transport layer headers (IP and TCP/UDP). However, sometimes we need to filter a message based on the information available in the message itself (at the application layer). As an example, assume that an organization wants to implement the following policies regarding its Web pages: Only those Internet users who have previously established business relations with the company can have access; access to other users must be blocked. In this case, a packet-filter firewall is not feasible because the router cannot distinguish between the packets arriving at TCP port 80 (HTTP). Testing must be done at the application level (using URLs).

One solution is to install a proxy computer (sometimes called an application gateway), which stands between the customer (user client) computer and the corporation computer. When the user client process sends a message, the proxy computer runs a server process to receive the request. The server opens the packet at the application level and finds out if the request is legitimate. If it is, the server acts as a client process and sends the message to the real server in the corporation. If it is not, the message is dropped and an error message is sent to the external user. In this way, the requests of the external users are filtered based on the contents at the application layer. Figure 29.19 shows a proxy firewall implementation.

Figure 29.19 *Proxy firewall*

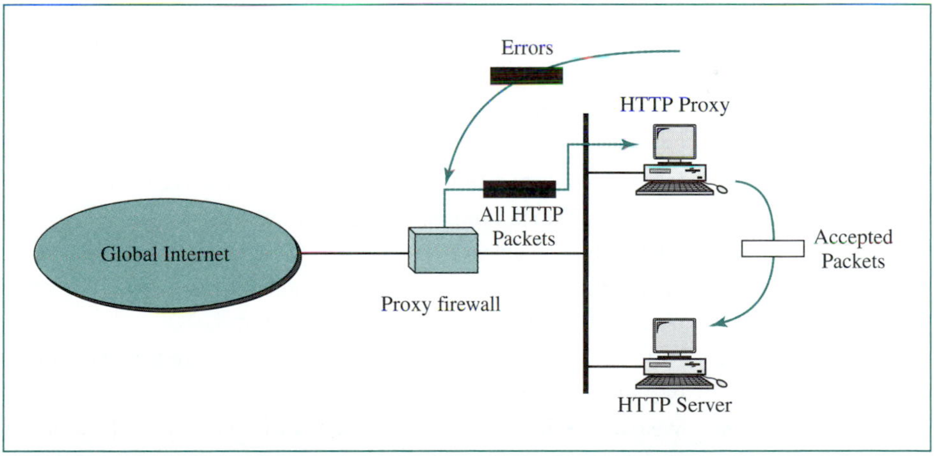

A proxy firewall filters at the application layer.

29.9 KEY TERMS

authentication

Authentication Header Protocol

Certification Authority (CA)

ciphertext

confidentiality

data exchange protocol

decryption
digest
digital signature
Encapsulating Security Payload (ESP)
encryption
firewall
handshake protocol
hash function
integrity
IP Security (IPSec)
key distribution center (KDC)
nonrepudiation
packet-filter firewall
plaintext
Pretty Good Privacy (PGP)
privacy
private key
proxy firewall
public key
public-key encryption
secret key
secret-key encryption
secure shell (SSH)
security
Transport Layer Security (TLS)

29.10 SUMMARY

- The issues involved in security are privacy, authentication, integrity, and nonrepudiation.
- Privacy is achieved through encryption of the plaintext and decryption of the ciphertext.
- In secret-key encryption, the sender and the receiver share a secret key.
- In public-key encryption, the public key is known to everyone but the private key is known only to the receiver.
- Techniques that use both secret-key encryption and public-key encryption are efficient and provide for easy key distribution.
- Authentication, integrity, and nonrepudiation are achieved through a method called digital signature.
- We can use digital signature on the entire message or on a digest of the message. A hash function creates the digest from the original document.
- Security methods can be applied in the application layer, transport layer, and IP layer.
- Pretty Good Privacy (PGP) provides security for the transmission of email.
- Secure shell (SSH) is a secure form of the rlogin client-server application program.
- Transport Layer Security (TLS) provides security at the transport layer through its handshake protocol and data exchange protocol.
- IP Security (IPSec) is a collection of protocols designed by the IETF to provide security for an Internet packet.

- The Authentication Header Protocol provides integrity and message authentication.
- The Encapsulating Security Payload Protocol provides integrity, message authentication, and privacy.
- A firewall is a router installed between the internal network of an organization and the rest of the Internet.
- A packet-filter firewall blocks or forwards packets based on information in the network and transport layers.
- A proxy firewall blocks or forwards packets based on information in the application layer.

29.11 PRACTICE SET

Multiple-Choice Questions

1. Encryption/decryption provides a network with _______.
   a. privacy
   b. authentication
   c. integrity
   d. nonrepudiation
2. Secret-key encryption involves the use of _______.
   a. one key
   b. two keys
   c. hash functions
   d. all of the above
3. Public-key encryption involves the use of _______.
   a. one key
   b. two keys
   c. hash functions
   d. all of the above
4. In secret-key encryption, the secret key is used for _______.
   a. encryption
   b. decryption
   c. hashing
   d. a and b
5. In public-key encryption, the public key is used for _______.
   a. encryption
   b. decryption
   c. hashing
   d. a and b

6. In public-key encryption, the private key is used for _______.
   a. encryption
   b. decryption
   c. hashing
   d. a and b
7. If user A wants to send an encrypted message to user B, the plaintext is encrypted with the public key of _______.
   a. user A
   b. user B
   c. the network
   d. a or b
8. When secret-key encryption is combined with private-key encryption, the _______ key is encrypted with the public key.
   a. private
   b. public
   c. secret
   d. skeleton
9. Digital signature can provide _______ for a network.
   a. authentication
   b. integrity
   c. nonrepudiation
   d. all of the above
10. In the digital signature technique, the sender of the message uses _______ to create ciphertext.
    a. her own secret key
    b. her own private key
    c. her own public key
    d. the receiver's private key
11. In the digital signature technique, the receiver of the message uses _______ to create plaintext.
    a. her own secret key
    b. her own private key
    c. her own public key
    d. the sender's public key
12. A method to provide for the secure transmission of email is called _______.
    a. RSA
    b. DES
    c. BVD
    d. PGP

13. A _______ is a trusted third party that solves the problem of secret-key distribution.
    a. CA
    b. KDC
    c. TLS
    d. firewall
14. A _______ certifies the biding between a public key and its owner.
    a. CA
    b. KDC
    c. TLS
    d. firewall
15. _______ is a protocol that provides security at the application layer level.
    a. CA
    b. PGP
    c. SSH
    d. b and c
16. _______ is a protocol that provides security at the transport layer level.
    a. CA
    b. KDC
    c. TLS
    d. SSH
17. The handshake protocol and data exchange protocol are part of _______.
    a. CA
    b. KDC
    c. TLS
    d. SSH
18. _______ is a collection of protocols that provide security at the IP layer level.
    a. TLS
    b. SSH
    c. PGP
    d. IPSec
19. _______ is an IP layer security protocol that only provides integrity and authentication.
    a. AH
    b. PGP
    c. ESP
    d. IPSec

20. _______ is an IP layer security protocol that provides privacy as well as integrity and authentication.
    a. AH
    b. PGP
    c. ESP
    d. IPSec
21. An IP datagram carries an AH header if the _______ field of the IP header has a value of 51.
    a. next header
    b. protocol
    c. security parameter index
    d. sequence number
22. A _______ can forward or block packets based on the information in the network layer and transport layer headers.
    a. proxy firewall
    b. packet-filter firewall
    c. message digest
    d. private key
23. A _______ can forward or block messages based on the information in the message itself.
    a. proxy firewall
    b. packet-filter firewall
    c. message digest
    d. private key

Exercises

24. An early secret-key encryption method called monoalphabetic substitution (or Caesar Cipher) was attributed to Julius Caesar. Each character in the plaintext is shifted forward n characters; if necessary, characters are wrapped around. For example, if n is 6, then character A is replaced by character G, character B by H, and so on. What is the encryption algorithm? What is the decryption algorithm?
25. Encrypt the message "beeswax" using the Caesar Cipher. Let $n = 6$.
26. How effective is the Caesar Cipher? Can the key be guessed by looking only at the ciphertext? Explain your answer.
27. One secret-key encryption method involves the permutation of bits. For example, an 8-bit plaintext is permuted (scrambled); bit 8 becomes bit 3, bit 1 becomes bit 2, and so on. Draw a diagram to show the mapping of each bit to its new designation. Scramble the bits as you please. What is the encryption algorithm? What is the decryption algorithm?

28. One secret-key encryption method involves the XOR operation. A bit pattern (plaintext) of a fixed-size is XORed with a block of bits of the same size to create a fixed-sized ciphertext. What is the encryption algorithm here? What is the decryption algorithm here? Remember that an XOR algorithm is a reversible algorithm.
29. Discuss why secret-key encryption/decryption cannot be used for nonrepudiation.
30. Discuss why secret-key encryption/decryption cannot be used for authentication.
31. Add a layer of secret-key encryption/decryption to Figure 29.5 to provide privacy.
32. Add a layer of public-key encryption/decryption to Figure 29.5 to provide privacy.
33. Kerberos is a method that uses KDC. Do some investigation on the Internet to find how Kerberos uses KDC.
34. Use the RSA algorithm in Appendix E and the public key (15, 3) to encrypt the number 5. Use the private the key (15, 11) to decrypt the result of the previous encryption. Draw a diagram to show the flow of information between the sender and receiver.
35. Prove that the roles of the public key and private key can be exchanged by redoing the previous exercise. Encrypt the number 5 with the private key (15, 11) and decrypt it with the public key (15, 3). Draw a diagram to show the flow of information between the sender and receiver.

CHAPTER 30

Private Networks, Virtual Private Networks, and Network Address Translation

In this chapter, we discuss three related topics that are becoming increasingly important as the Internet grows and as security in the Internet becomes more crucial. We first discuss the idea of private networks—networks that are isolated from the Internet but use the TCP/IP protocol suite. We then discuss virtual private networks—networks that use the Internet and at the same time require privacy like a private network. Finally, we discuss network address translation—a technology that allows a private network to use two sets of addresses: one private and one global.

30.1 PRIVATE NETWORKS

A private network is designed to be used inside an organization. It allows access to shared resources and, at the same time, provides privacy. Before we discuss some aspects of these networks, let us define two commonly used related terms: intranet and extranet.

Intranet

An **intranet** is a private network (LAN) that uses the TCP/IP protocol suite. However, access to the network is limited only to the users inside the organization. The network uses application programs defined for the global Internet, such as HTTP, and may have web servers, print servers, file servers, and so on.

Extranet

An **extranet** is the same as an intranet with one major difference. Some resources may be accessed by specific groups of users outside the organization under the control of the network administrator. For example, an organization may allow authorized customers access to product specifications, availability, and on-line ordering. A university or a college can allow distance learning students access to the computer lab after passwords have been checked.

Addressing

A private network that uses the TCP/IP protocol suite must use IP addresses. Three choices are available:

1. The network can apply for a set of addresses from the Internet authorities and use them without being connected to the Internet. This strategy has an advantage. If in the future the organization decides to be connected to the Internet, it can do so with relative ease. However, there is also a disadvantage: The address space is wasted.
2. The network can use any set of addresses without registering with the Internet authorities. Because the network is isolated, the addresses do not have to be unique. However, this strategy has a serious drawback: Users might mistakenly confuse the addresses as part of the global Internet.
3. To overcome the problems associated with the first and second strategies, the Internet authorities have reserved three sets of addresses, shown in Table 30.1.

Table 30.1 *Addresses for private networks*

Prefix	*Range*	*Total*
10/8	10.0.0.0 to 10.255.255.255	2^{24}
172.16/12	172.16.0.0 to 172.31.255.255	2^{20}
192.168/16	192.168.0.0 to 192.168.255.255	2^{16}

Any organization can use an address out of this set without permission from the Internet authorities. Everybody knows that these reserved addresses are for private networks. They are unique inside the organization, but they are not unique globally. No router will forward a packet that has one of these addresses as the destination address.

30.2 VIRTUAL PRIVATE NETWORKS (VPN)

Virtual private network (VPN) is a technology that is gaining popularity among large organizations that use the global Internet for both intra- and interorganization communication, but require privacy in their intraorganization communication.

Achieving Privacy

To achieve privacy, organizations can use one of three strategies: private networks, hybrid networks, and virtual private networks.

Private Networks

An organization that needs privacy when routing information inside the organization can use a private network as discussed previously. A small organization with one single site can use an isolated LAN. People inside the organization can send data to one another that totally remain inside the organization, secure from outsiders. A larger organization with several sites can create a private internet. The LANs at different sites can be connected to each other using routers and leased lines. In other words, an internet can be made out of private LANs and private WANs. Figure 30.1 shows such a situation for an organization with two sites. The LANs are connected to each other using routers and one leased line.

Figure 30.1 *Private network*

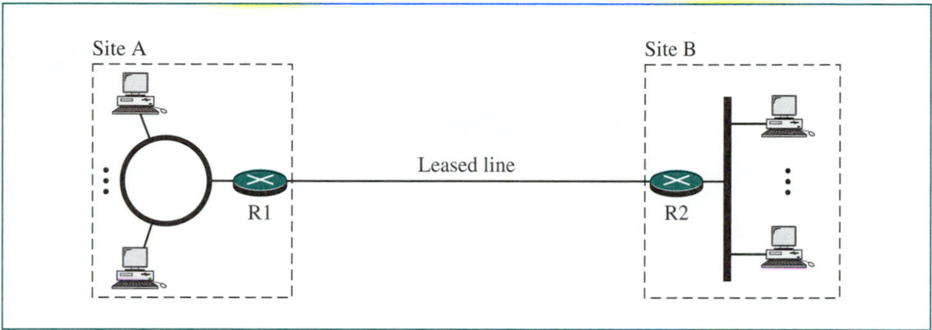

In this situation, the organization has created a private internet that is totally isolated from the global Internet. For end-to-end communication between stations at different sites, the organization can use the TCP/IP protocol suite. However, there is no need for the organization to apply for IP addresses with the Internet authorities. It can use private IP addresses. The organization can use any IP class and assign network and host addresses internally. Because the internet is private, duplication of addresses by another organization in the global Internet is not a problem.

Hybrid Networks

Today, most organizations need to have privacy in intraorganization data exchange, but, at the same time, they need to be connected to the global Internet for data exchange with other organizations. One solution is the use of a hybrid network. A hybrid network allows an organization to have its own private internet and, at the same time, access to the global Internet. Intraorganization data is routed through the private internet; interorganization data is routed through the global Internet. Figure 30.2 shows an example of this situation.

An organization with two sites uses routers R1 and R2 to connect the two sites privately through a leased line; it uses routers R3 and R4 to connect the two sites to the rest of the world. The organization uses global IP addresses for both types of communication. However, packets destined for internal recipients are routed only through routers R1 and R2. Routers R3 and R4 route the packets destined for outsiders.

Virtual Private Networks

Both private and hybrid networks have a major drawback: cost. Private wide area networks are expensive. To connect several sites, an organization needs several leased lines, which means a high monthly cost. One solution is to use the global Internet for both private and public communication. A technology called virtual private network (VPN) allows organizations to use the global Internet for both purposes.

Figure 30.2 *Hybrid network*

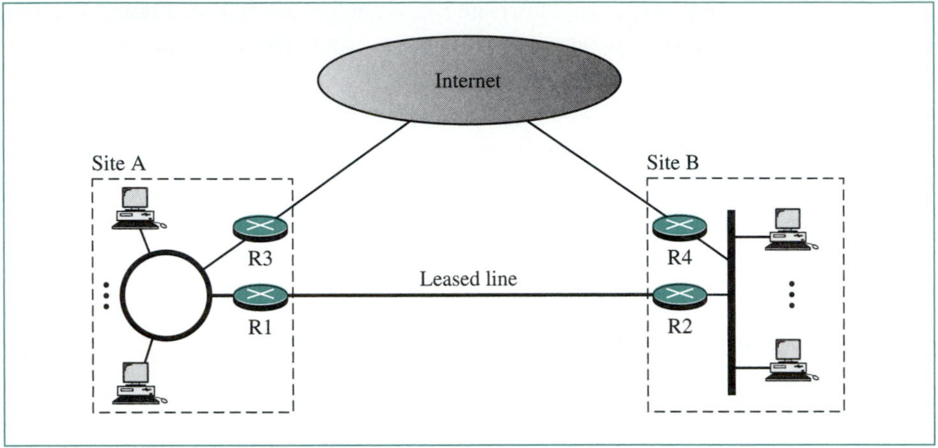

VPN creates a network that is private but virtual. It is private because it guarantees privacy inside the organization. It is virtual because it does not use real private WANs; the network is physically public but virtually private.

Figure 30.3 shows the idea of a virtual private network. Routers R1 and R2 use VPN technology to guarantee privacy for the organization.

Figure 30.3 *Virtual private network*

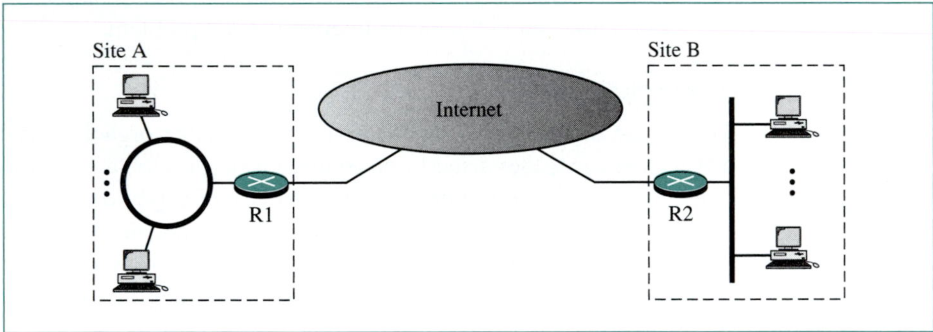

VPN Technology

VPN technology uses two simultaneous techniques to guarantee privacy for an organization: IPSec and tunneling.

IPSec

We discussed IPSec in Chapter 29. A virtual private network can use either AH or ESP for authentication and privacy.

Tunneling

To guarantee privacy for an organization, VPN specifies that each IP datagram destined for private use in the organization must be encapsulated in another datagram as shown in Figure 30.4.

Figure 30.4 *Tunneling*

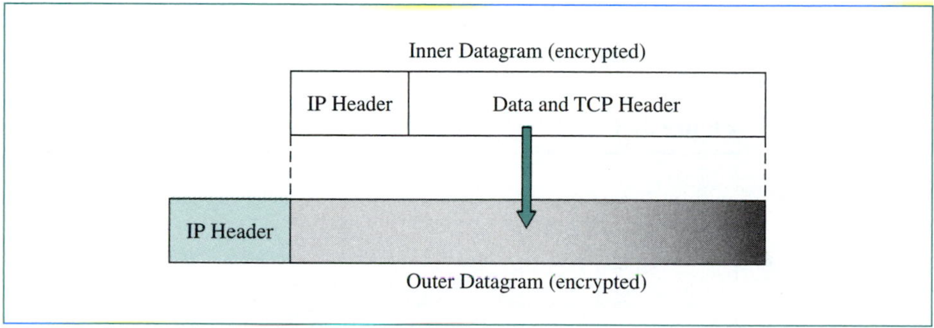

This is called tunneling because the original datagram is hidden inside the outer datagram after exiting R1 in Figure 30.5 and becomes invisible until it reaches R2. It appears that the original datagram has gone through a tunnel spanning R1 and R2.

As the figure shows, the entire IP datagram (including the header) is first encrypted and then encapsulated in another datagram with a new header. The inner datagram here carries the actual source and destination address of the packet (two stations inside the organization). The outer datagram header carries the source and destination of the two routers at the boundary of the private and public networks as shown in Figure 30.5.

Figure 30.5 *Addressing in a VPN*

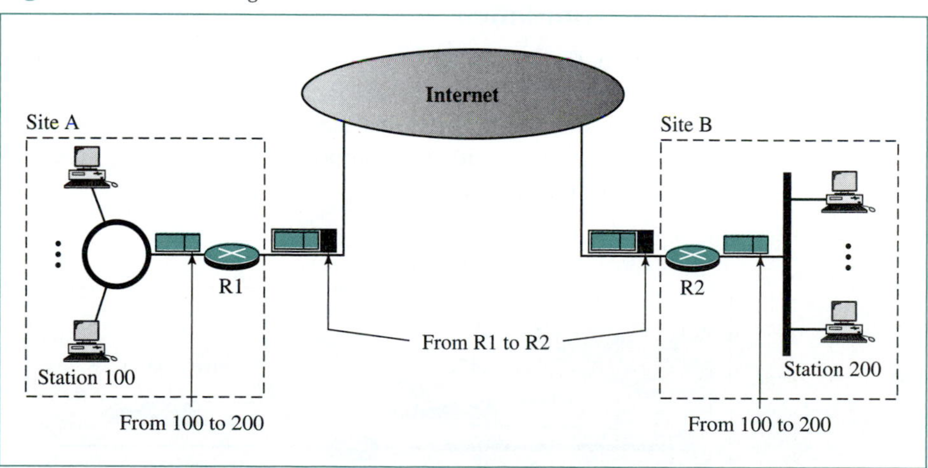

The public network (Internet) is responsible for carrying the packet from R1 to R2. Outsiders cannot decipher the contents of the packet or the source and destination addresses. Deciphering takes place at R2, which finds the destination address of the packet and delivers it.

30.3 NETWORK ADDRESS TRANSLATION (NAT)

A technology that is related to private networks and virtual private networks is **network address translation** (NAT). The technology allows a site to use a set of private addresses for internal communication and a set of (at least one) global Internet addresses for communication with another site. The site must have only one single connection to the global Internet through a router that runs the NAT software. Figure 30.6 shows a simple implementation of NAT.

Figure 30.6 *NAT*

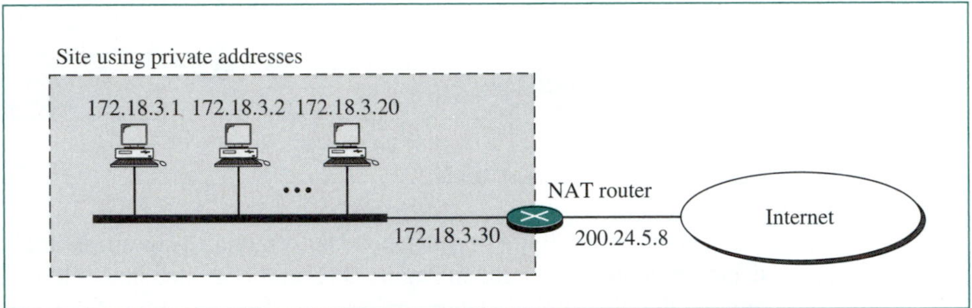

As the figure shows, the private network uses private addresses. The router that connects the network to the global address uses one private address and one global address. The private network is transparent to the rest of the Internet; the rest of the internet sees only the NAT router with the address 200.24.5.8.

Address Translation

All of the outgoing packets go through the NAT router, which replaces the *source address* in the packet with the global NAT address. All incoming packets also pass through the NAT router, which replaces the *destination address* in the packet (the NAT router global address) with the appropriate private address. Figure 30.7 shows an example of address translation.

Figure 30.7 *Address translation*

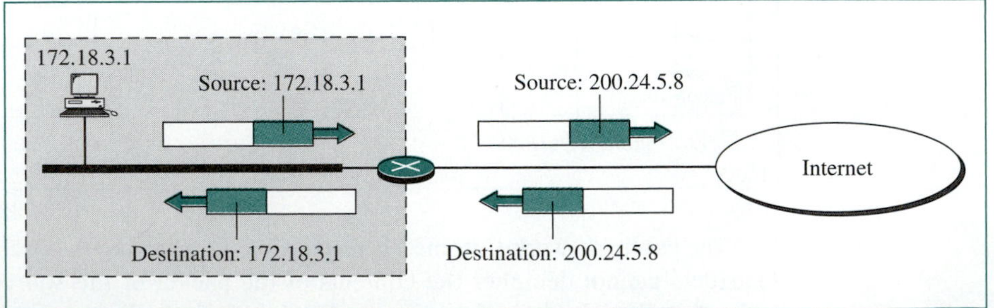

Translation Table

The reader may have noticed that translating the source addresses for an outgoing packets is straightforward. But how does the NAT router know the destination address for a packet coming from the Internet? There may be tens or hundreds of private IP addresses, each belonging to one specific host. The problem is solved if the NAT router has a translation table.

Using One IP Address

In its simplest form, a translation table has only two columns: the private address and the external address (destination address of the packet). When the router translates the source address of the outgoing packet, it also makes note of the destination address—where the packet is going. When the response comes back from the destination, the router uses the source address of the packet (as the external address) to find the private address of the packet. Figure 30.8 shows the idea. Note that the addresses that are changed (translated) are shown in color.

Figure 30.8 *Translation*

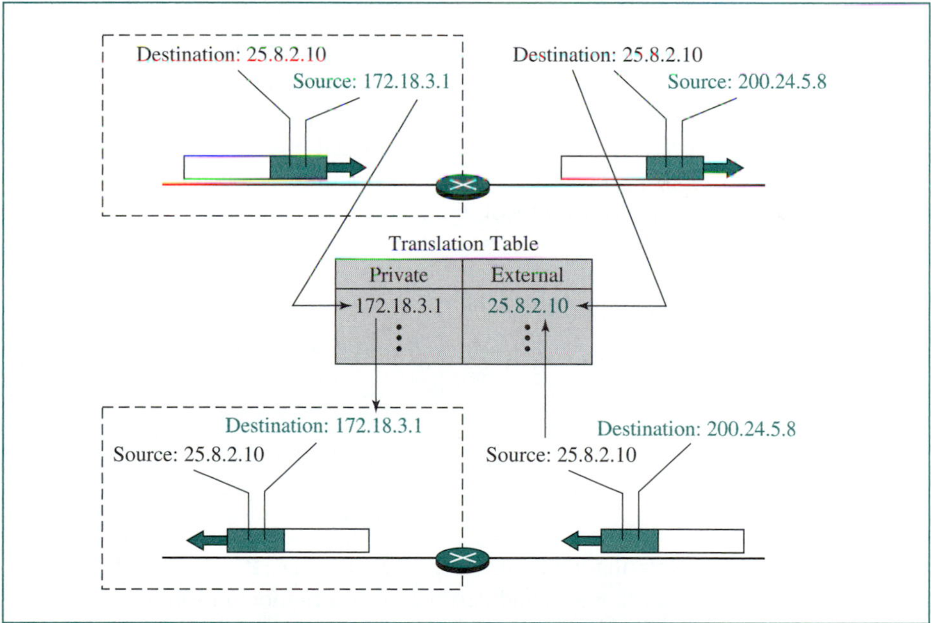

In this strategy, communication must always be initiated by the private network. The NAT mechanism described requires that the private network start the communication. As we will see, NAT is used mostly by ISPs which assign one single address to a customer. The customer, however, may be a member of a private network that has many private addresses. In this case, communication with the Internet is always initiated from the customer site, using a client program such as HTTP, TELNET, or FTP to access the corresponding server program. For example, when email that originates from a noncustomer site is received by the ISP email server it is stored in the mailbox of the customer until retrieved with a protocol such as POP.

A private network cannot run a server program for clients outside of its network if it is using NAT technology.

Using a Pool of IP Addresses

Using only one global address by the NAT router allows only one private-network host to access the same external host. To remove this restriction, the NAT router can use a pool of global addresses. For example, instead of using only one global address (200.24.5.8), the NAT router can use four addresses (200.24.5.8, 200.24.5.9, 200.24.5.10, and 200.24.5.11). In this case, four private-network hosts can communicate with the same external host at the same time because each pair of addresses defines a connection. However, there are still some drawbacks. No more than four connections can be made to the same destination. No private-network host can access two external server programs (e.g., HTTP and TELNET) at the same time. And, likewise, two private-network hosts cannot access the same external server program (e.g., HTTP or TELNET) at the same time.

Using Both IP Addresses and Port Numbers

To allow a many-to-many relationship between private-network hosts and external server programs, we need more information in the translation table. For example, suppose two hosts inside a private network with addresses 172.18.3.1 and 172.18.3.2 need to access the HTTP server on external host 25.8.3.2. If the translation table has five columns, instead of two, that include the source and destination port numbers and the transport layer protocol, the ambiguity is eliminated. Table 30.2 shows an example of such a table.

Table 30.2 *Five-column translation table*

Private Address	*Private Port*	*External Address*	*External Port*	*Transport Protocol*
172.18.3.1	1400	25.8.3.2	80	TCP
172.18.3.2	1401	25.8.3.2	80	TCP
...	...	...	...	...

Note that when the response from HTTP comes back, the combination of source address (25.8.3.2) and destination port number (1400) defines the private network host to which the response should be directed. Note also that for this translation to work, the temporary port numbers (1400 and 1401) must be unique.

NAT and ISP

An ISP that serves dial-up customers can use NAT technology to conserve addresses. For example, imagine an ISP is granted 1000 addresses, but has 100,000 customers. The ISP can divide the customers into 1000 groups, with each group covering 100 customers. Each of the customers in a group is assigned a private network address. The customers in each group form an imaginary private network. The ISP translates each of the 100 source addresses in outgoing packets to one global address; it translates the global destination address in incoming packets to the corresponding private address. There is one translation table for each group. Figure 30.9 shows this concept.

Figure 30.9 *An ISP and NAT*

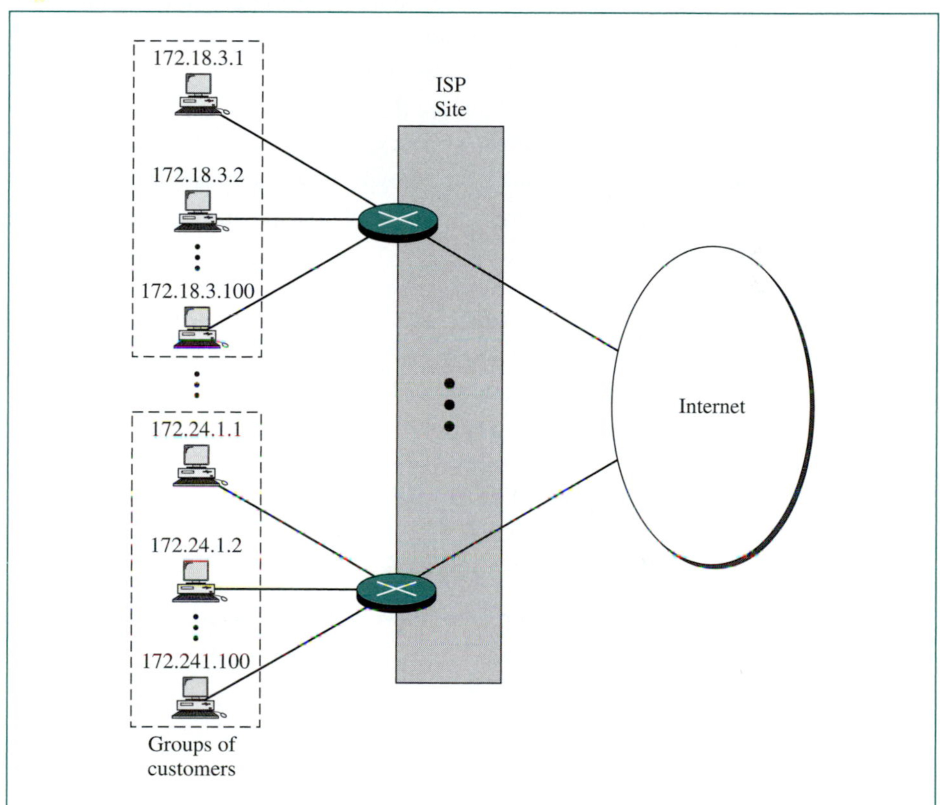

30.4 KEY TERMS

extranet

global Internet

hybrid network

intranet

network address translation (NAT)

private network

reserved addresses

translation table

tunneling

virtual private network (VPN)

30.5 SUMMARY

- A private network is used inside an organization.
- An intranet is a private network that uses the TCP/IP protocol suite.
- An extranet is an intranet that allows authorized access from outside users.
- The Internet authorities have reserved addresses for private networks.
- A virtual private network (VPN) provides privacy for LANs that must communicate through the global Internet.
- VPN technology involves the simultaneous use of encryption/authentication and tunneling to guarantee privacy.
- A common technique to encrypt and authenticate in VPNs is IP security (IPSec).
- Tunneling involves the encapsulation of an encrypted IP datagram in a second outer datagram.
- Network address translation allows a private network to use a set of private addresses for internal communication and a set of global Internet addresses for external communication.
- NAT uses translation tables to route messages.

30.6 PRACTICE SET

Multiple-Choice Questions

1. An _______ is a private network with no external access that uses the TCP/IP protocol suite.
   a. Internet
   b. internet
   c. intranet
   d. extranet
2. An _______ is a private network with limited external access that uses the TCP/IP protocol suite.
   a. Internet
   b. internet
   c. intranet
   d. extranet
3. A network has addresses that range from 192.168.4.0 to 192.168.5.0. This is probably a(n) _______ network.
   a. private
   b. hybrid
   c. public
   d. open

4. A _______ network is totally isolated from the global Internet.
   a. private
   b. hybrid
   c. virtual private
   d. any of the above
5. A _______ network can use a leased line for intraorganization communication and the Internet for interorganization communication.
   a. private
   b. hybrid
   c. virtual private
   d. any of the above
6. A VPN uses _______ to guarantee privacy.
   a. IPSec
   b. tunneling
   c. both a and b
   d. none of the above
7. In a VPN, _____ encrypted.
   a. the inner datagram is
   b. the outer datagram is
   c. both inner and outer datagram are
   d. neither inner and outer datagram are
8. Tunneling is a technique in which the IP datagram is first _______ and then _______.
   a. encapsulated in another datagram; encrypted
   b. encrypted; encapsulated in another datagram
   c. authenticated; encrypted
   d. encrypted; authenticated
9. _______ is a technology using a set of global Internet addresses and a set of private addresses.
   a. VPN
   b. ISP
   c. HTTP
   d. NAT
10. On a network that uses NAT, the _______ has a translation table.
    a. switch
    b. router
    c. server
    d. none of the above

11. On a network that uses NAT, _______ initiates the communication.
    a. an external host
    b. an internal host
    c. the router
    d. a or b
12. On a network that uses NAT, the router can use _______ global address(es).
    a. 1
    b. 2
    c. a pool of
    d. none of the above
13. An ISP using NAT has 200 customers and is granted 5 global Internet addresses. How many private addresses are needed?
    a. 5
    b. 40
    c. 200
    d. none of the above

Exercises

14. Find out how Point-to-Point Tunneling Protocol (PPTP) can be used in VPN technology.
15. Find out how Layer 2 Forwarding (L2F) can be used in VPN technology.
16. Find out how Layer 2 Tunneling Protocol (L2TP) can be used in VPN technology.
17. Find out how Multiprotocol Label Switching (MPLS) can be used in VPN technology.
18. Explain how a personal computer using a dial-up connection to the Internet can access a private network using VPN technology.
19. Find out how Security Association (SA) in IPSec is used in VPN technology.
20. Find out how Internet Key Exchange (IKE) in IPSec is used in VPN technology.
21. How can one prevent a translation table from constantly expanding? When can an entry be deleted from the table? What strategy can you propose?
22. Do some research and find out if there is a way for communication to be initiated from the external host on a network using NAT.
23. Do some research and find out how DNS can be used in NAT.

CHAPTER 31

Next Generation: IPv6 and ICMPv6

The network layer protocol in the TCP/IP protocol suite is currently IPv4 (Internetworking Protocol, version 4). IPv4 provides the host-to-host communication between systems in the Internet. Although IPv4 is well designed, data communication has evolved since the inception of IPv4 in the 1970s. IPv4 has some deficiencies that make it unsuitable for the fast-growing Internet, including the following:

- IPv4 has a two-level address structure (netid and hostid) categorized into five classes (A, B, C, D, and E). The use of address space is inefficient. For instance, when an organization is granted a class A address, 16 million addresses from the address space are assigned for the organization's exclusive use. If an organization is granted a class C address, on the other hand, only 256 addresses are assigned to this organization, which may not be a sufficient number. Also, millions of addresses are wasted in classes D and E. This method of addressing has depleted the address space of IPv4, and soon there will not be any addresses left to assign to any new system that wants to be connected to the Internet. Although the subnetting and supernetting strategies have alleviated some of the addressing problems, subnetting and supernetting make routing more complicated as we have seen in previous chapters.
- The Internet must accommodate real-time audio and video transmission. This type of transmission requires minimum delay strategies and reservation of resources not provided in the IPv4 design.
- The Internet must accommodate encryption and authentication of data for some applications. No encryption or authentication is provided by IPv4.

To overcome these deficiencies, IPv6 (Internet Protocol, version 6), also known as IPng (Internetworking Protocol, next generation) was proposed and is now a standard. In IPv6, the Internet protocol was extensively modified to accommodate the unforeseen growth of the Internet. The format and the length of the IP addresses were changed along with the packet format. Related protocols, such as ICMP, were also modified. Other protocols in the network layer, such as ARP, RARP, and IGMP, were either deleted or included in the ICMPv6 protocol. Routing protocols, such as RIP and OSPF, were also slightly modified to accommodate these changes. Communication experts predict that IPv6 and its related protocols will soon replace the current IP version. In this chapter we talk first about IPv6. Then we discuss ICMPv6. Finally we explore the strategies used for the transition from version 4 to version 6.

31.1 IPv6

The next-generation IP, or IPv6, has some advantages over IPv4 that can be summarized as follows:

- **Larger address space.** An IPv6 address is 128 bits long. Compared with the 32-bit address of IPv4, this is a huge (2^{96}) increase in the address space.
- **Better header format.** IPv6 uses a new header format in which options are separated from the base header and inserted, when needed, between the base header and the upper-layer data. This simplifies and speeds up the routing process because most of the options do not need to be checked by routers.
- **New options.** IPv6 has new options to allow for additional functionalities.
- **Allowance for extension.** IPv6 is designed to allow the extension of the protocol if required by new technologies or applications.
- **Support for resource allocation.** In IPv6, the type-of-service field has been removed, but a mechanism (called *flow label*) has been added to enable the source to request special handling of the packet. This mechanism can be used to support traffic such as real-time audio and video.
- **Support for more security.** The encryption and authentication options in IPv6 provide confidentiality and integrity of the packet.

31.2 IPv6 ADDRESSES

An IPv6 address consists of 16 bytes (octets); it is 128 bits long (see Figure 31.1).

Figure 31.1 *IPv6 address*

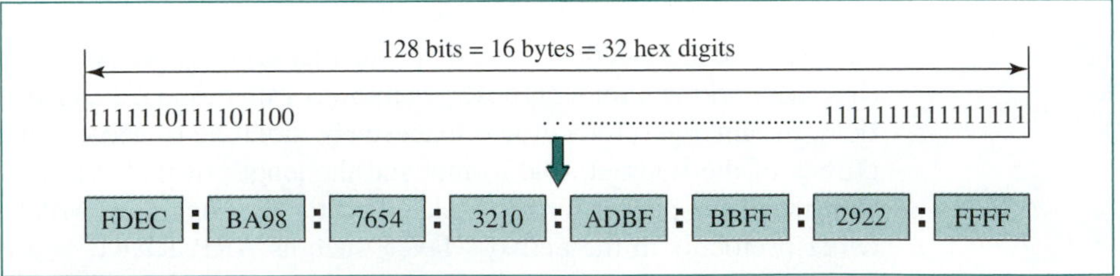

Hexadecimal Colon Notation

To make addresses more readable, IPv6 specifies hexadecimal colon notation. In this notation, 128 bits are divided into eight sections, each 2 bytes in length. Two bytes in hexadecimal notation require four hexadecimal digits. Therefore, the address consists of 32 hexadecimal digits, with every four digits separated by a colon.

Abbreviation

Although the IP address, even in hexadecimal format, is very long, many of the digits are zeros. In this case, we can abbreviate the address. The leading zeros of a section (four digits between two colons) can be omitted. Only the leading zeros can be dropped, not the trailing zeros. For an example, see Figure 31.2.

Figure 31.2 *Abbreviated address*

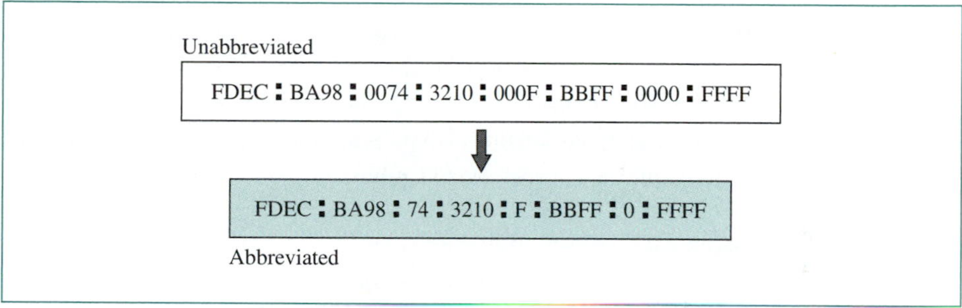

Using this form of abbreviation, 0074 can be written as 74, 000F as F, and 0000 as 0. Note that 3210 cannot be abbreviated. Further abbreviations are possible if there are consecutive sections consisting of zeros only. We can remove the zeros altogether and replace them with a double semicolon. Figure 31.3 shows the concept.

Figure 31.3 *Abbreviated address with consecutive zeros*

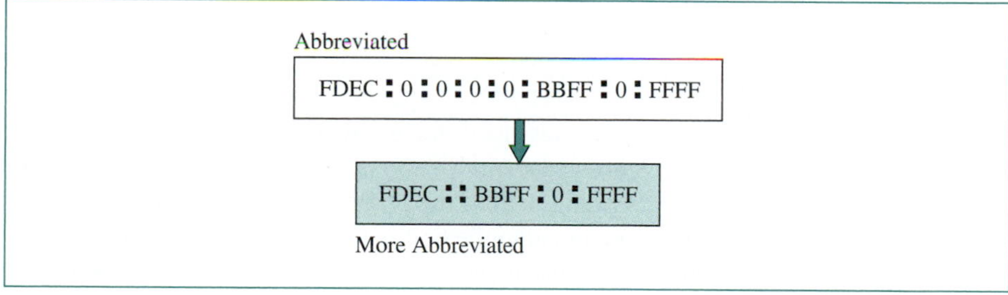

Note that this type of abbreviation is allowed only once per address. If there are two runs of zero sections, only one of them can be abbreviated. Reexpansion of the abbreviated address is very simple: Align the unabbreviated portions and insert zeros to get the original expanded address.

CIDR Notation

IPv6 allows classless addressing and CIDR notation. For example, Figure 31.4 shows how we can define a prefix of 60 bits using CIDR.

Figure 31.4 *CIDR address*

FDEC : 0 : 0 : 0 : 0 : BBFF : 0 : FFFF/60

Categories of Addresses

IPv6 defines three types of addresses: unicast, anycast, and multicast.

Unicast Addresses

A unicast address defines a single computer. The packet sent to a unicast address must be delivered to that specific computer.

Anycast Addresses

An anycast address defines a group of computers with addresses that have the same prefix. For example, all computers connected to the same physical network share the same prefix address. A packet sent to an anycast address must be delivered to exactly one of the members of the group—the closest or the most easily accessible.

Multicast Addresses

A multicast address defines a group of computers that may or may not share the same prefix and may or may not be connected to the same physical network. A packet sent to a multicast address must be delivered to each member of the set.

Address Space Assignment

The address space has many different purposes. The designers of the IP addresses divided the address space into two parts, with the first part called the *type prefix*. This variable-length prefix defines the purpose of the address. The codes are designed such that no code is identical to the first part of any other code. In this way, there is no ambiguity; when an address is given, the type prefix can easily be determined. Figure 31.5 shows the IPv6 address format.

Figure 31.5 *Address structure*

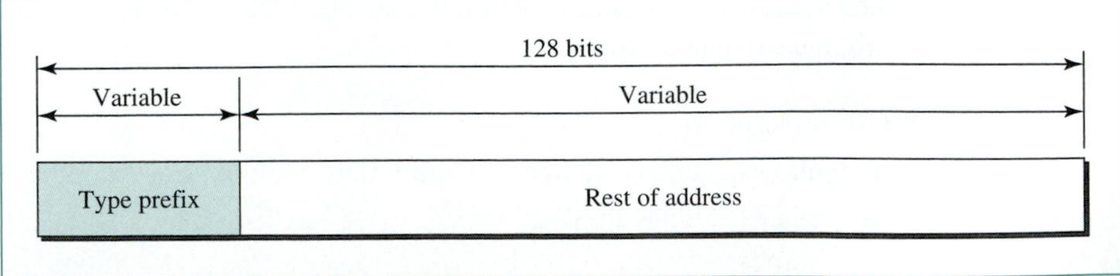

Table 31.1 shows the prefix for each type of address. The third column shows the fraction of each type of address relative to the whole address space.

Table 31.1 *Type prefixes for IPv6 addresses*

Type Prefix	*Type*	*Fraction*
0000 0000	Reserved	1/256
0000 0001	Reserved	1/256
0000 001	NSAP (Network Service Access Point)	1/128
0000 010	IPX (Novell)	1/128
0000 011	Reserved	1/128
0000 100	Reserved	1/128
0000 101	Reserved	1/128
0000 110	Reserved	1/128
0000 111	Reserved	1/128
0001	Reserved	1/16
001	Reserved	1/8
010	**Provider-based unicast addresses**	**1/8**
011	Reserved	1/8
100	Geographic unicast addresses	1/8
101	Reserved	1/8
110	Reserved	1/8
1110	Reserved	1/16
1111 0	Reserved	1/32
1111 10	Reserved	1/64
1111 110	Reserved	1/128
1111 1110 0	Reserved	1/512
1111 1110 10	Link local addresses	1/1024
1111 1110 11	Site local addresses	1/1024
1111 1111	Multicast addresses	1/256

Provider-Based Unicast Addresses

The provider-based address is generally used by a normal host as a unicast address. The address format is shown in Figure 31.6.

Fields for the provider-based addresses are as follows:

- **Type identifier.** This 3-bit field defines the address as a provider-based address.
- **Registry identifier.** This 5-bit field indicates the agency that has registered the address. Currently three registry centers have been defined. INTERNIC (code 11000) is the center for North America; RIPNIC (code 01000) is the center for European registration; and APNIC (code 10100) is for Asian and Pacific countries.

Figure 31.6 *Provider-based address*

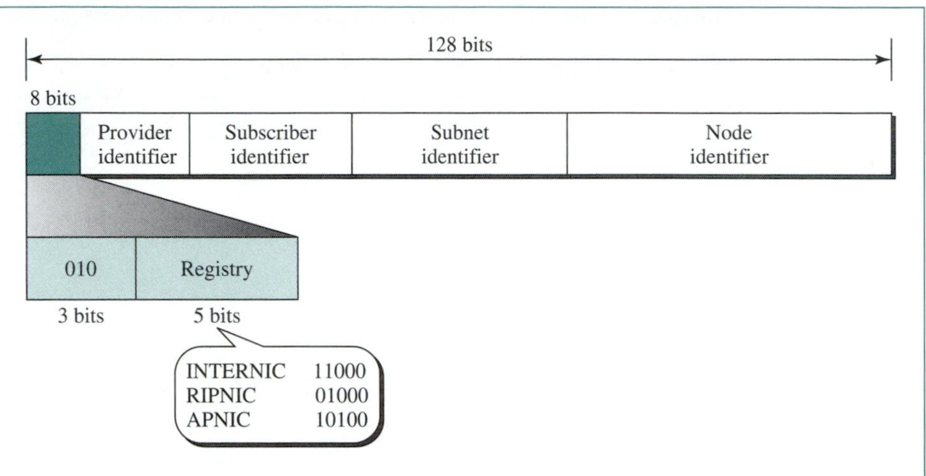

- **Provider identifier.** This variable-length field identifies the provider for Internet access. A 16-bit length is recommended for this field.
- **Subscriber identifier.** When an organization subscribes to the Internet through a provider, it is assigned a subscriber identification. A 24-bit length is recommended for this field.
- **Subnet identifier.** Each subscriber can have many different subnetworks and each network can have different identifiers. The subnet identifier defines a specific network under the territory of the subscriber. A 32-bit length is recommended for this field.
- **Node identifier.** The last field defines the identity of the node connected to a subnet. A length of 48 bits is recommended for this field to make it compatible with the 48-bit link (physical) address used by Ethernet. In the future, this link address will probably be the same as the node physical address.

We can think of a provider-based address as a hierarchical identity having several prefixes. As shown in Figure 31.7, each prefix defines a level of hierarchy. The type prefix defines the type, the registry prefix uniquely defines the registry level, the provider prefix uniquely defines a provider, the subscriber prefix uniquely defines a subscriber, and the subnet prefix uniquely defines a subnet.

Figure 31.7 *Address hierarchy*

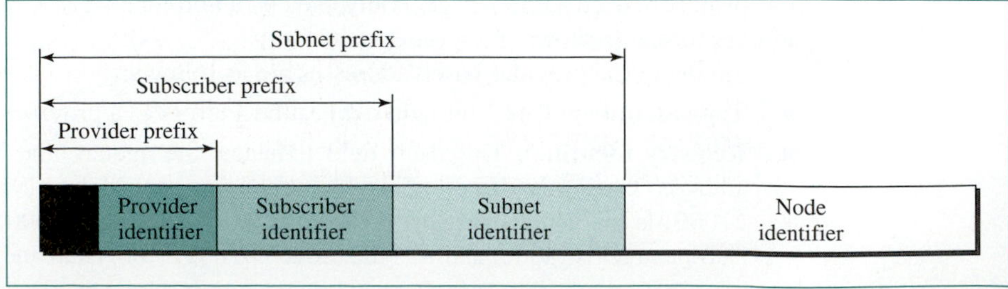

Reserved Addresses

Addresses that use the reserved prefix (00000000) will be discussed here briefly.

- **Unspecified address.** This is an address in which the nonprefix part is also zero. In other words, the entire address consists of zeros. This address is used when a host does not know its own address and sends an inquiry to find its address. However, in the inquiry it must define a source address. The unspecified address can be used for this purpose. Note that the unspecified address cannot be used as a destination address. The unspecified address format is shown in Figure 31.8.

Figure 31.8 *Unspecified address*

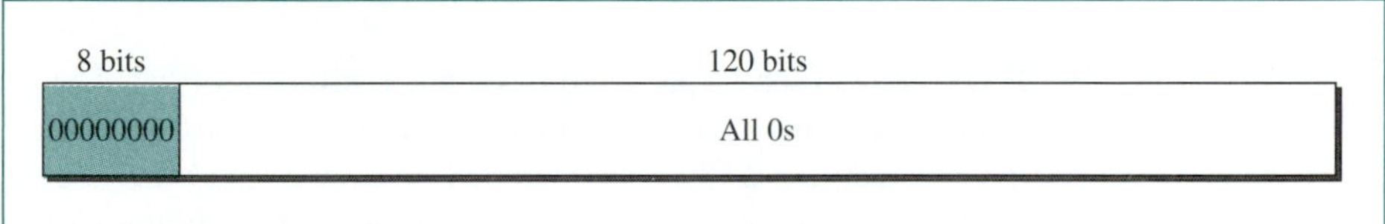

- **Loopback address.** This is an address used by a host to test itself without going into the network. In this case, a message is created in the application layer, sent to the transport layer, and passed to the network layer. However, instead of going to the physical network, it returns to the transport layer and then passes to the application layer. This is very useful for testing the functions of software packages in these layers before even connecting the computer to the network. The address as shown in Figure 31.9 consists of the prefix 0000000 followed by 119 zero bits and 1 one bit.

Figure 31.9 *Loopback address*

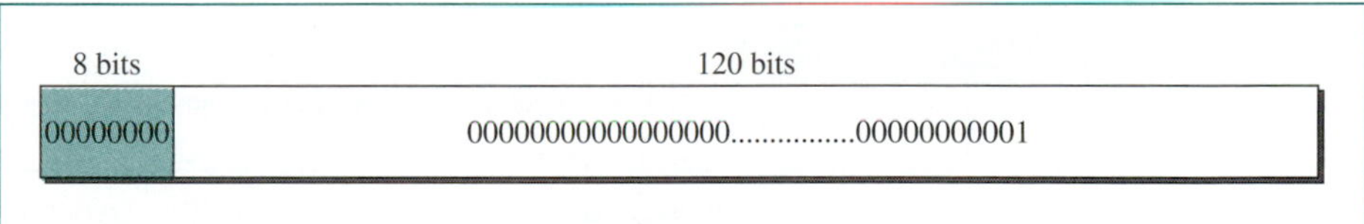

- **IPv4 addresses.** As we will see later in this chapter, during transition from IPv4 to IPv6, hosts can use their IPv4 addresses embedded in IPv6 addresses. Two formats have been designed for this purpose: compatible and mapped. A *compatible address* is an address of 96 bits of zero followed by 32 bits of IPv4 address. It is used when a computer using IPv6 wants to send a message to another computer using IPv6. However, the packet should pass through a region where the networks are still using IPv4. The sender uses the IPv4-compatible address to facilitate passing the packet through the IPv4 region (see Section 31.5 on Transition Strategies). For example, the IPv4 address 2.13.17.14 (in decimal dotted format) becomes 0::020D:110E (in hexadecimal colon format). The IPv4 address is prepended with 96 zeros to create a 128-bit IPv6 address (see Figure 31.10).

  A *mapped address* comprises 80 bits of zero, followed by 16 bits of one, followed by the 32-bit IPv4 address. It is used when a computer that has migrated to

Figure 31.10 *Compatible address*

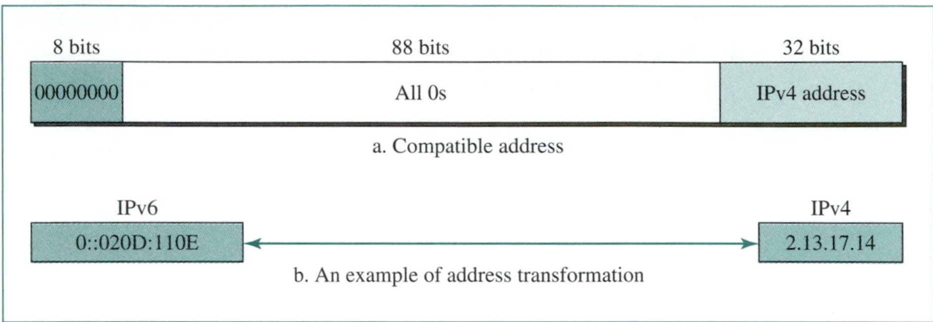

IPv6 wants to send a packet to a computer still using IPv4. The packet travels mostly through IPv6 networks but is finally delivered to a host that uses IPv4. For example, the IPv4 address 2.13.17.14 (in dotted decimal format) becomes 0::FFFF:020D:110E (in hexadecimal colon format). The IPv4 address is prepended with 16 ones and 80 zeros to create a 128-bit IPv6 address (see Section 31.5 on Transition Strategies). Figure 31.11 shows a mapped address.

Figure 31.11 *Mapped address*

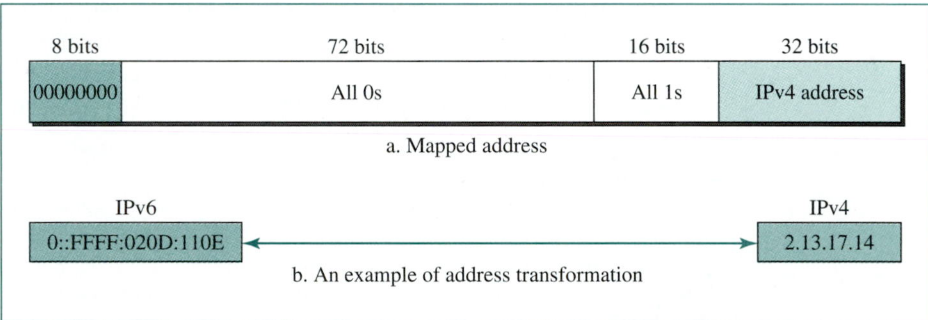

A very interesting point about mapped and compatible addresses is that they are designed in such a way that, when calculating the checksum, one can use either the embedded address or the total address because extra 0s or 1s in multiples of 16 do not have any effect in checksum calculation. This is important because if the address of the packet is changed from IPv6 to IPv4 by a router, the checksum calculation is not affected.

Local Addresses

Addresses that use the reserved prefix (11111110) are discussed here briefly.

- **Link local address.** These addresses are used if a LAN is to use the Internet protocols but is not connected to the Internet for security reasons. This type of addressing uses the prefix 1111 1110 10. The link local address is used in an isolated network and does not have a global effect. Nobody outside an isolated network can send a message to the computers attached to a network using these addresses (see Figure 31.12).

Figure 31.12 *Link local address*

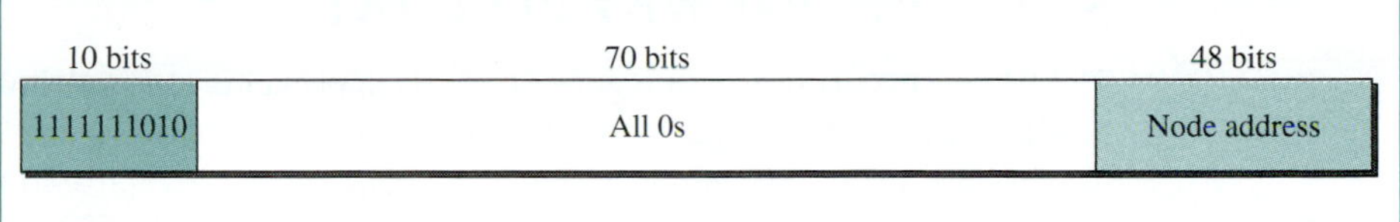

- **Site local address.** These addresses are used if a site having several networks uses the Internet protocols but is not connected to the Internet, also for security reasons. This type of addressing uses the prefix 1111 1110 11. The site local address is used in isolated networks and does not have a global effect. Nobody outside the isolated networks can send a message to any of the computers attached to a network using these addresses (see Figure 31.13).

Figure 31.13 *Site local address*

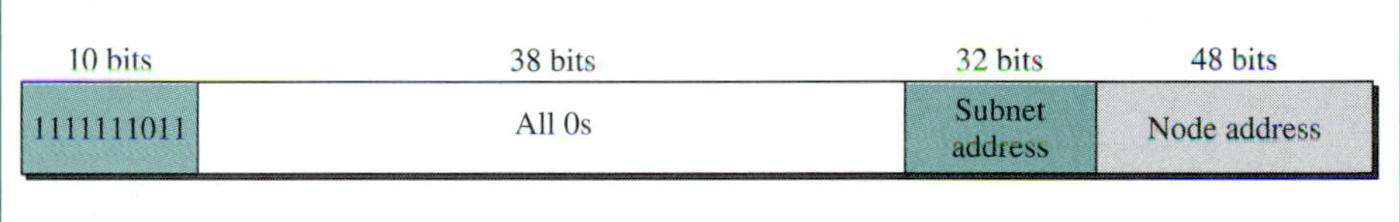

Multicast Addresses

Multicast addresses are used to define a group of hosts instead of just one. All use the prefix 11111111 in the first field. The second field is a flag that defines the group address as either permanent or transient. A permanent group address is defined by the Internet authorities and can be accessed at all times. A transient group address, on the other hand, is used only temporarily. Systems engaged in a teleconference, for example, can use a transient group address. The third field defines the scope of the group address. Many different scopes have been defined, as shown in Figure 31.14.

Figure 31.14 *Multicast address*

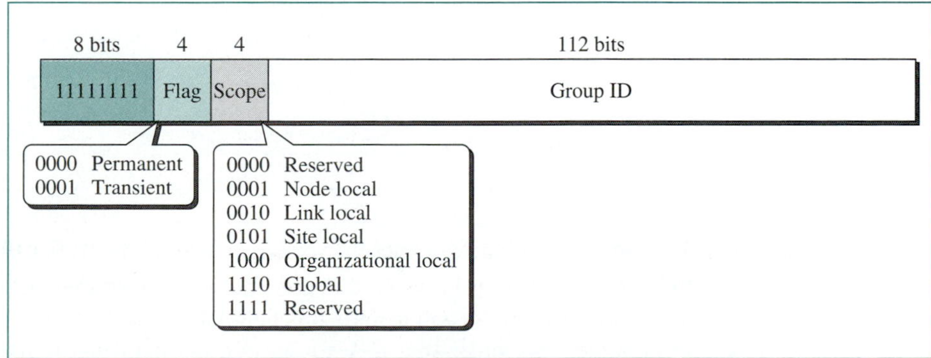

31.3 IPv6 PACKET FORMAT

The IPv6 packet is shown in Figure 31.15. Each packet is composed of a mandatory base header followed by the payload. The payload consists of two parts: optional extension headers and data from an upper layer. The base header occupies 40 bytes, whereas the extension headers and data from the upper layer contain up to 65,535 bytes of information.

Figure 31.15 *IPv6 datagram*

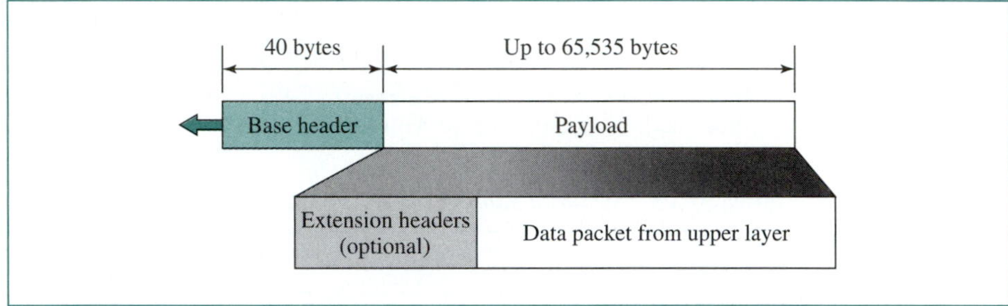

Base Header

Figure 31.16 shows the base header with its eight fields. These fields are as follows:

Figure 31.16 *Format of an IPv6 datagram*

VER
PRI
Flow label
Payload length
Next header
Hop limit
Source address
Destination address
Payload
extension headers
+
Data packet from the upper layer

- **Version.** This 4-bit field defines the version number of the IP. For IPv6, the value is 6.
- **Priority.** The 4-bit priority field defines the priority of the packet with respect to traffic congestion. We will discuss this field later.
- **Flow label.** The flow label is a 3-byte (24-bit) field that is designed to provide special handling for a particular flow of data. We will discuss this field later.

- **Payload length.** This 2-byte payload length field defines the total length of the IP datagram excluding the base header.
- **Next header.** The next header is an 8-bit field defining the header that follows the base header in the datagram. The next header is either one of the optional extension headers used by IP or the header for an upper-layer protocol such as UDP or TCP. Each extension header also contains this field. Table 31.2 shows the values of next headers. Note that this field in version 4 is called the *protocol.*

Table 31.2 *Next header codes*

Code	*Next Header*
0	Hop-by-hop option
2	ICMP
6	TCP
17	UDP
43	Source routing
44	Fragmentation
50	Encrypted security payload
51	Authentication
59	Null (No next header)
60	Destination option

- **Hop limit.** This 8-bit hop limit field serves the same purpose as the TTL field in IPv4.
- **Source address.** The source address field is a 16-byte (128-bit) Internet address that identifies the original source of the datagram.
- **Destination address.** The destination address field is a 16-byte (128-bit) Internet address that usually identifies the final destination of the datagram. However, if source routing is used, this field contains the address of the next router.

Priority

The priority field of the IPv6 packet defines the priority of each packet with respect to other packets from the same source. For example, if one of two consecutive datagrams must be discarded due to congestion, the datagram with the lower priority will be discarded. IPv6 divides traffic into two broad categories: congestion-controlled and noncongestion-controlled.

Congestion-Controlled Traffic

If a source adapts itself to traffic slowdown when there is congestion, the traffic is referred to as *congestion-controlled traffic*. For example, the TCP protocol, which uses the sliding window protocol, can easily respond to the traffic. In congestion-controlled traffic, it is understood that packets may arrive delayed or even lost or received out of order. Congestion-controlled data are assigned priorities from 0 to 7, as listed in Table 31.3. A priority of 0 is the lowest; a priority of 7 is the highest.

Table 31.3 *Priorities for congestion-controlled traffic*

Priority	*Meaning*
0	No specific traffic
1	Background data
2	Unattended data traffic
3	Reserved
4	Attended bulk data traffic
5	Reserved
6	Interactive traffic
7	Control traffic

The priority descriptions are as follows:

- **No specific traffic.** The priority 0 is assigned to a packet when the process does not define a priority.
- **Background data.** This group (priority 1) defines data that is usually delivered in the background. Delivery of the news is a good example.
- **Unattended data traffic.** If the user is not waiting (attending) for the data to be received, the packet will be given priority 2. Email belongs to this group. A user initiates an email message to another user, but the receiver does not know that an email will arrive soon. In addition, an email is usually stored before it is forwarded. A little bit of delay is of little consequence.
- **Attended bulk data traffic.** The protocol that transfers the bulk of data while the user is waiting (attending) to receive the data (possibly with delay) is given priority 4. FTP and HTTP belong to this group.
- **Interactive traffic.** Protocols such as TELNET that need interaction with the user are assigned the second highest priority (6) in this group.
- **Control traffic.** Control traffic has been given the highest priority (7) in this category. Routing protocols such as OSPF and RIP and management protocols such as SNMP use this priority.

Noncongestion-Controlled Traffic

This refers to a type of traffic that expects minimum delay. Discarding of packets is not desirable. Retransmission in most cases is impossible. In other words, the source does not adapt itself to congestion. Real-time audio and video are good examples of this type of traffic.

Priority numbers from 8 to 15 are assigned to noncongestion-controlled traffic. Although there are not yet any particular standard assignments for this type of data, the priorities are usually assigned based on how much the quality of received data can be affected by discarding some packets. Data containing less redundancy (such as low-fidelity audio or video) can be given a higher priority (15). Data containing more redundancy (such as high-fidelity audio or video) should be given lower priority (8). See Table 31.4.

Table 31.4 *Priorities for noncongestion-controlled traffic*

Priority	*Meaning*
8	Data with most redundancy
. . .	. . .
15	Data with least redundancy

Flow Label

A sequence of packets, sent from a particular source to a particular destination, that needs special handling by routers is called a *flow* of packets. The combination of the source address and the value of the *flow label* (see above) uniquely defines a flow of packets.

To a router, a flow is a sequence of packets that share the same characteristics, such as traveling the same path, using the same resources, having the same kind of security, and so on. A router that supports the handling of flow labels has a flow label table. The table has an entry for each active flow label; each entry defines the services required by the corresponding flow label. When the router receives a packet, it consults its flow label table to find the corresponding entry for the flow label value defined in the packet. It then provides the packet with the services mentioned in the entry. However, note that the flow label itself does not provide the information for the entries of the flow label table; the information is provided by other means such as the hop-by-hop options or other protocols.

In its simplest form, a flow label can be used to speed up the processing of a packet by a router. When a router receives a packet, instead of consulting the routing table and going through a routing algorithm to define the address of the next hop, it can easily look in a flow label table for the next hop.

In its more sophisticated form, a flow label can be used to support the transmission of real-time audio and video. Real-time audio or video, particularly in digital form, requires resources such as high bandwidth, large buffers, long processing time, and so on. A process can make a reservation for these resources beforehand to guarantee that real-time data will not be delayed due to a lack of resources. The use of real-time data and the reservation of these resources require other protocols such as Real-Time Protocol (RTP) and Resource Reservation Protocol (RSVP) in addition to IPv6.

To allow the effective use of flow labels, three rules have been defined:

1. The flow label is assigned to a packet by the source host. The label is a random number between 1 and $2^{24} - 1$. A source must not reuse a flow label for a new flow while the existing flow is still alive.
2. If a host does not support the flow label, it sets this field to zero. If a router does not support the flow label, it simply ignores it.
3. All packets belonging to the same flow should have the same source, same destination, same priority, and same options.

Comparison between IPv4 and IPv6 Headers

Table 31.5 compares IPv4 and IPv6 headers.

Table 31.5 *Comparison between IPv4 and IPv6 packet header*

Comparison
1. The header length field is eliminated in IPv6 because the length of the header is fixed in this version.
2. The service type field is eliminated in IPv6. The priority and flow label fields together take over the function of the service type field.
3. The total length field is eliminated in IPv6 and replaced by the payload length field.
4. The identification, flag, and offset fields are eliminated from the base header in IPv6. They are included in the fragmentation extension header.
5. The TTL field is called hop limit in IPv6.
6. The protocol field is replaced by the next header field.
7. The header checksum is eliminated because the checksum is provided by upper layer protocols; it is therefore not needed at this level.
8. The option fields in IPv4 are implemented as extension headers in IPv6.

Extension Headers

The length of the base header is fixed at 40 bytes. However, to give more functionality to the IP datagram, the base header can be followed by up to six extension headers. Many of these headers are options in IPv4. Figure 31.17 shows the extension header format.

Figure 31.17 *Extension header format*

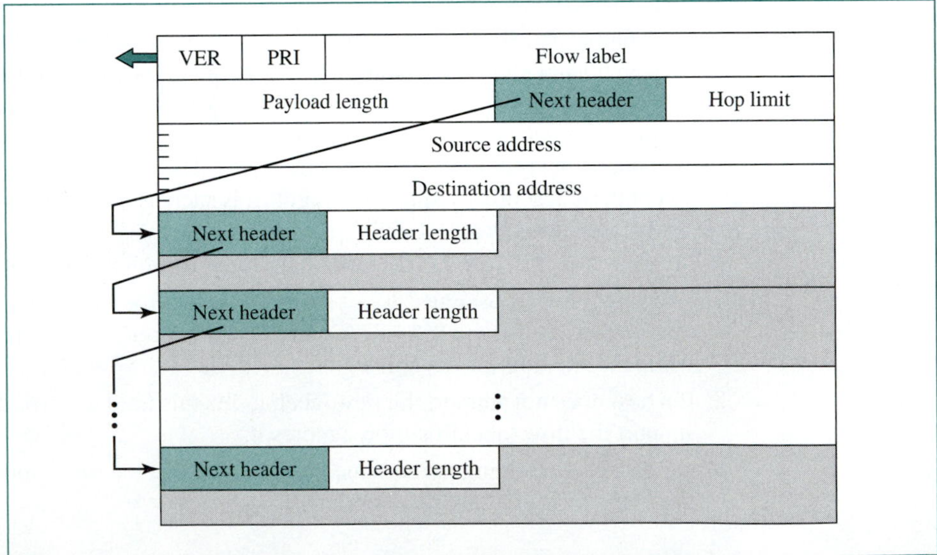

Six types of extension headers have been defined. These are hop-by-hop option, source routing, fragmentation, authentication, encrypted security payload, and destination option (see Figure 31.18).

Figure 31.18 *Extension header types*

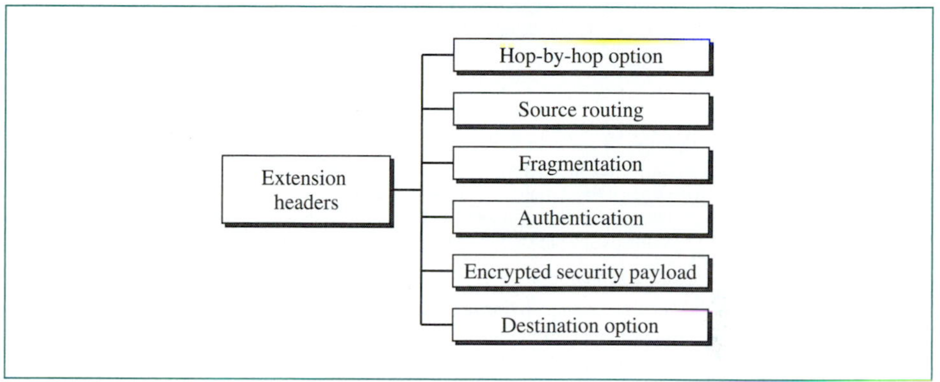

Hop-by-Hop Option

The hop-by-hop option is used when the source needs to pass information to all routers visited by the datagram. For example, perhaps routers must be informed about certain management, debugging, or control functions. Or, if the length of the datagram is more than the usual 65,535 bytes, routers must have this information. Figure 31.19 shows the format of the hop-by-hop option header. The first field defines the next header in the chain of headers. The header length defines the number of bytes in the header (including the next header field). The rest of the header contains different options.

Figure 31.19 *Hop-by-hop option header format*

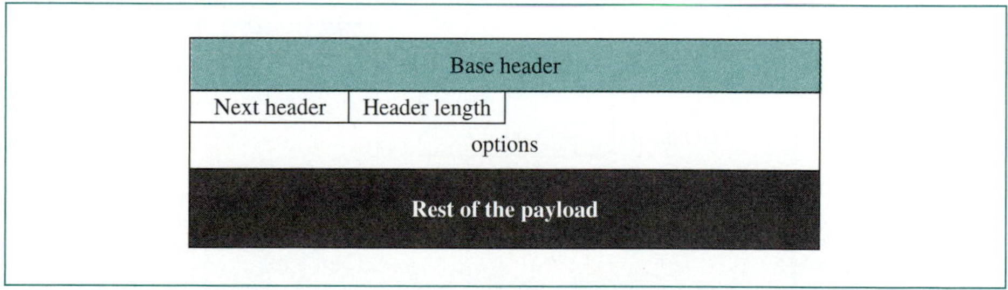

So far, only three options have been defined: Pad1, PadN, and jumbo payload. Figure 31.20 shows the general format of the option.

Figure 31.20 *The format of options in a hop-by-hop option header*

Code 8 bits	Length 8 bits	Data (Variable length)

Action	C	Type
2 bits	1 bit	5 bits

Action: To be taken if the option is not recognized

00 Skip over this option
01 Discard the datagram, no more action
10 Discard the datagram and send an error message
11 Same as 10, but only if the destination is not a multicast address

C: Change in option value

0 Does not change in transit
1 May be changed in transit

Type

00000 Pad1
00001 PadN
00010 Jumbo payload

- **Pad1.** This option is 1 byte long and is designed for alignment purposes. Some options need to start at a specific bit of the 32-bit word (see the jumbo payload description to come). If an option falls short of this requirement by exactly one byte, Pad1 is added to make up the difference. Pad1 contains neither the option length field nor the option data field. It consists solely of the option code field with all bits set to 0 (action is 00, the change bit is 0, and type is 00000). Pad1 can be inserted anywhere in the hop-by-hop option header (see Figure 31.21).

Figure 31.21 *Pad1*

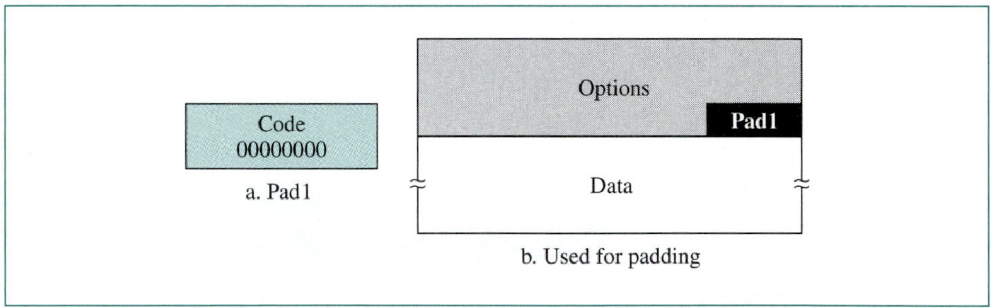

- **PadN.** PadN is similar in concept to Pad1. The difference is that PadN is used when 2 or more bytes are needed for alignment. This option consists of 1 byte of option code, 1 byte of the option length, and a variable number of zero padding bytes. The value of the option code is 1 (action is 00, the change bit is 0, and type is 00001). The option length contains the number of padding bytes. See Figure 31.22.

Figure 31.22 *PadN*

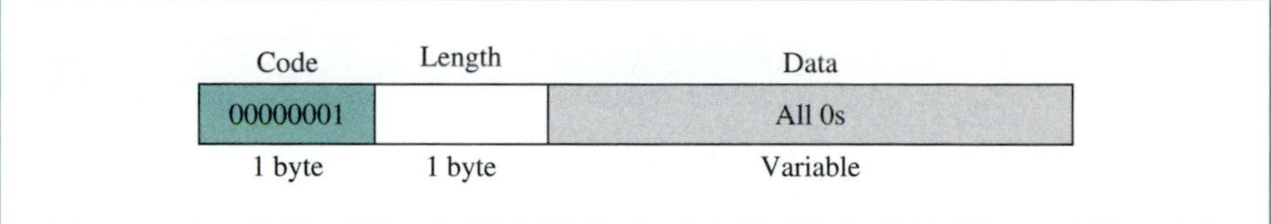

- **Jumbo payload.** Recall that the length of the payload in the IP datagram can be a maximum of 65,535 bytes. However, if for any reason a longer payload is required, we can use the jumbo payload option to define this longer length. The 1-byte option code has a value of 194 (11 for action, 0 for the change bit, and 00010 for type). The 1-byte option length defines the size in bytes of the next field and has a fixed value of 4. This means that the maximum length of the jumbo payload is $2^{32} - 1$ (4,294,967,295) bytes.

  This option has an alignment restriction. The jumbo payload option must always start at a multiple of 4 bytes plus 2 from the beginning of the extension headers. The jumbo payload option starts at the $(4n + 2)$ byte, where n is a small integer. See Figure 31.23.

Figure 31.23 *Jumbo payload*

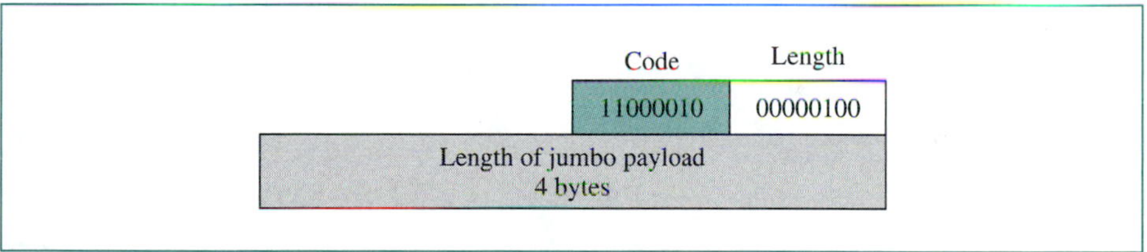

Source Routing

The source routing extension header combines the concepts of the strict source route and the loose source route options of IPv4. The source routing header contains a minimum of seven fields (see Figure 31.24). The first two fields, next header and header length, are identical to that of the hop-by-hop extension header. The type field defines loose or strict routing. The addresses left field indicates the number of hops still needed to reach the destination. The strict/loose mask field determines the rigidity of routing. If set to strict, routing must follow exactly as indicated by the source. If, instead, the mask is loose, other routers may be visited in addition to those in the header.

The destination address in source routing does not conform to our previous definition (the final destination of the datagram). Instead, it changes from router to router. For example, in Figure 31.25, Host A wants to send a datagram to Host B using a specific route: A to R1 to R2 to R3 to B. Notice the destination address in the base headers. It is not constant as you might expect. Instead, it changes at each router. The addresses in the extension headers also change from router to router.

Figure 31.24 *Source routing*

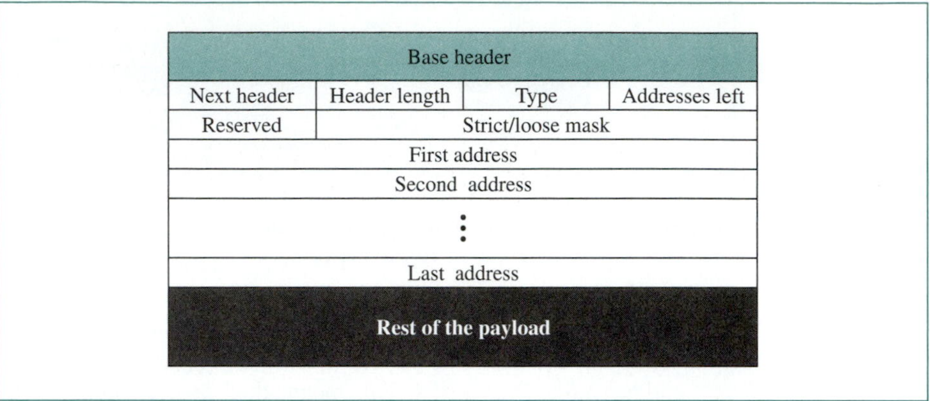

Figure 31.25 *Source routing example*

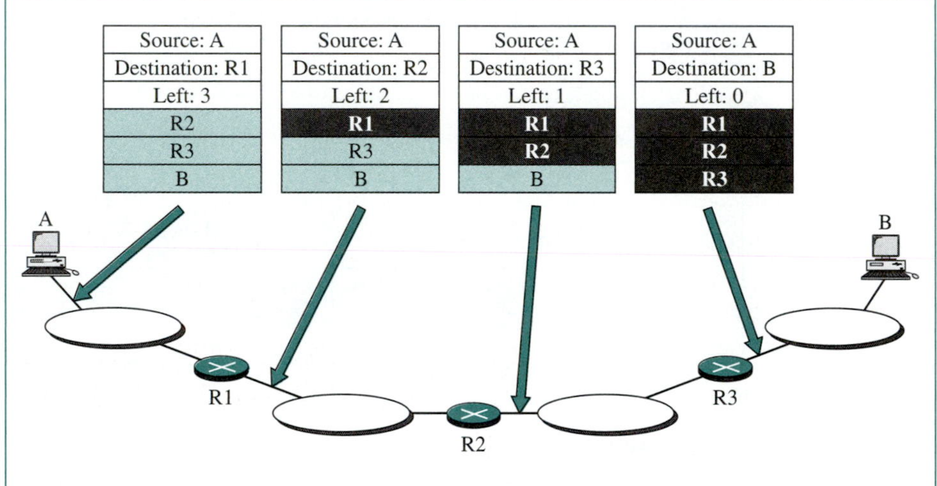

Fragmentation

The concept of fragmentation is the same as that in IPv4. However, the place where fragmentation takes place differs. In IPv4, the source or a router is required to fragment if the size of the datagram is larger than the MTU of the network over which the datagram should travel. In IPv6, only the original source can fragment. A source must use a Path MTU Discovery technique to find the smallest MTU supported by any network on the path. The source then fragments using this knowledge.

If the source does not use the Path MTU Discovery technique, it should fragment the datagram to a size of 576 bytes or smaller. This is the minimum size of MTU required for each network connected to the Internet. Figure 31.26 shows the format of the fragmentation extension header.

Figure 31.26 *Fragmentation*

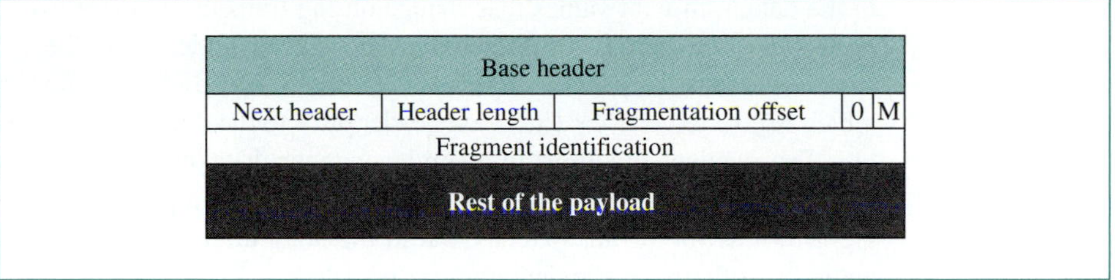

Authentication

The authentication extension header has a dual purpose: it validates the message sender and ensures the integrity of data. The former is needed so the receiver can be sure that a message is from the genuine sender and not from an imposter. The latter is needed to check that the data is not altered in transition by some hacker.

The format of the authentication extension header is shown in Figure 31.27. The security parameter index field defines the algorithm used for authentication. The authentication data field contains the actual data generated by the algorithm. We discussed authentication in Chapter 29.

Figure 31.27 *Authentication*

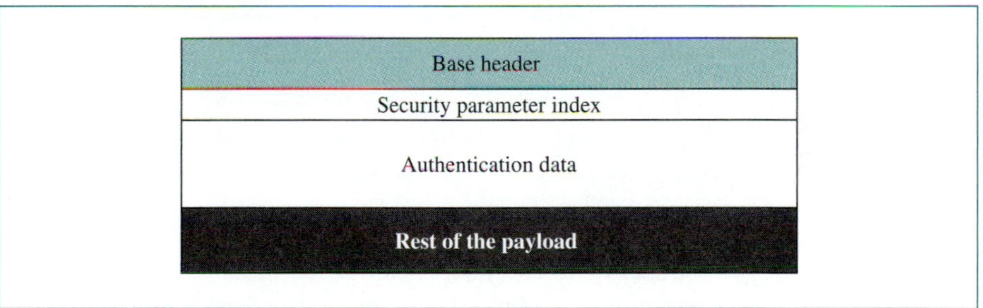

Many different algorithms can be used for authentication. Figure 31.28 outlines the method for calculating the authentication data field. The sender passes a 128-bit security

Figure 31.28 *Calculation of authentication data*

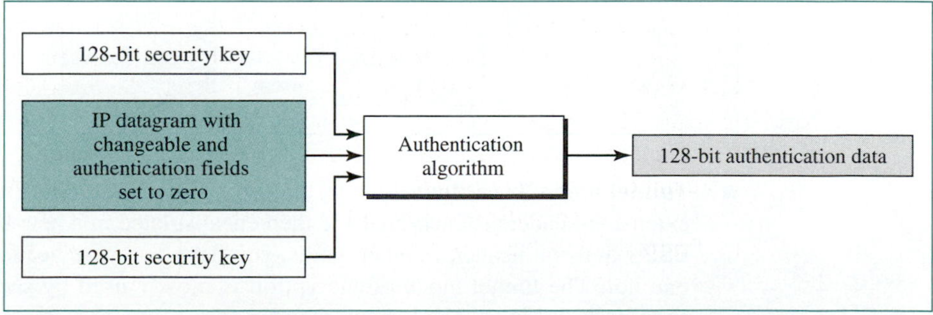

key, the entire IP datagram, and the 128-bit security key again to the algorithm. Those fields in the datagram with values that change during transmission (for example, hop count) are set to zero. The datagram passed to the algorithm includes the authentication header extension, with the authentication data field set to zero. The algorithm creates authentication data which is inserted into the extension header prior to datagram transmission.

The receiver functions in a similar manner. It takes the secret key and the received datagram (again, with changeable fields set to zero) and passes them to the authentication algorithm. If the result matches that in the authentication data field, the IP datagram is authentic; otherwise, the datagram is discarded.

Encrypted Security Payload

The encrypted security payload (ESP) is an extension that provides confidentiality and guards against eavesdropping. Figure 31.29 shows the format. The security parameter index field is a 32-bit word that defines the type of encryption/decryption used. The other field contains the data being encrypted along with any extra parameters needed by the algorithm. Encryption can be implemented in two ways: transport mode and tunnel mode.

Figure 31.29 *Encrypted security payload*

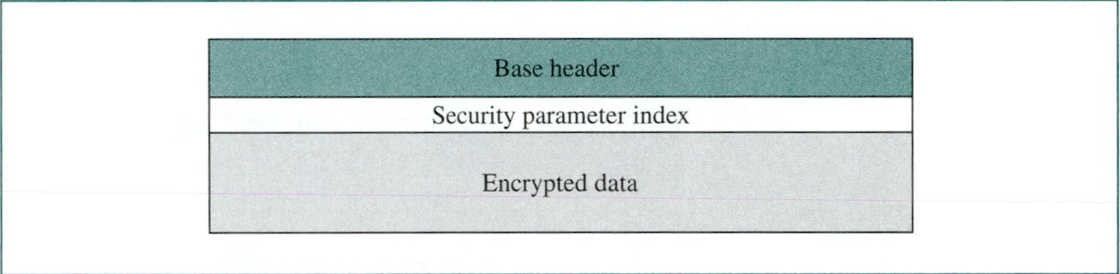

- **Transport mode.** In the transport mode, a TCP segment or a UDP user datagram is first encrypted and then encapsulated in an IPv6 packet. The transport mode of encryption is used mostly to encrypt data from host to host (see Figure 31.30).

Figure 31.30 *Transport mode encryption*

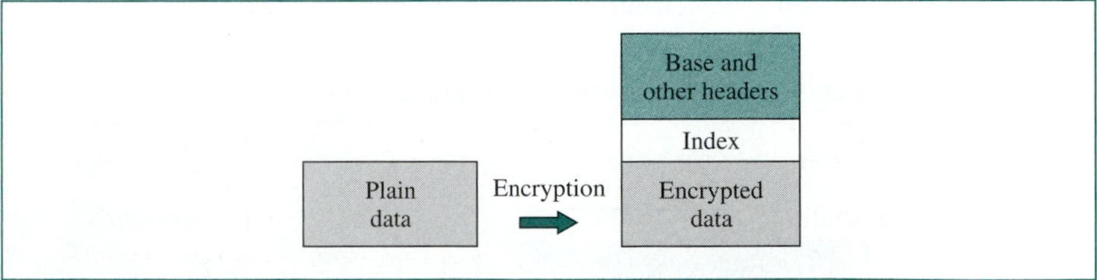

- **Tunnel mode.** In the tunnel mode, the entire IP datagram with its base header and extension headers is encrypted and then encapsulated in a new IP packet using the ESP extension header. In other words, you have two base headers: one encrypted, one not. The tunnel mode of encryption is mostly used by security gateways to encrypt data. Figure 31.31 shows the idea.

Figure 31.31 *Tunnel-mode encryption*

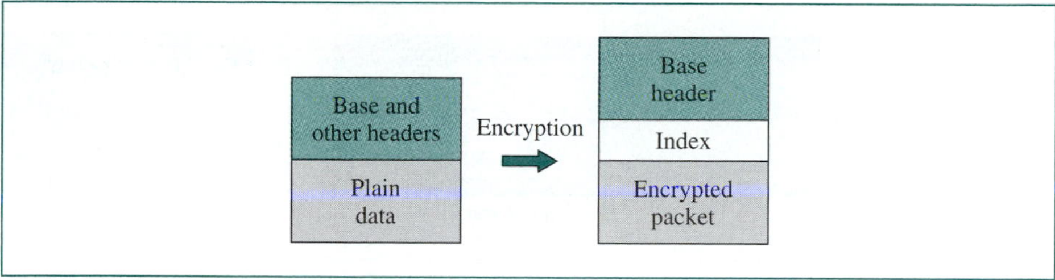

Destination Option

The destination option is used when the source needs to pass information to the destination only. Intermediate routers are not permitted access to this information. The format of the destination option is the same as the hop-by-hop option (refer back to Figure 31.19). So far, only the Pad1 and PadN options have been defined.

Comparison between IPv4 and IPv6

Table 31.6 compares the options in IPv4 with the extension headers in IPv6.

Table 31.6 *Comparison between IPv4 and IPv6 packet header*

Comparison
1. The no-operation and end-of-option options in IPv4 are replaced by Pad1 and PadN options in IPv6.
2. The record route option is not implemented in IPv6 because it was not used.
3. The timestamp option is not implemented because it was not used.
4. The source route option is called the source route extension header in IPv6.
5. The fragmentation fields in the base header section of IPv4 have moved to the fragmentation extension header in IPv6.
6. The authentication extension header is new in IPv6.
7. The encrypted security payload extension header is new in IPv6.

31.4 ICMPv6

Another protocol that has been modified in version 6 of the TCP/IP protocol suite is ICMP (ICMPv6). This new version follows the same strategy and purposes of version 4. ICMPv4 has been modified to make it more suitable for IPv6. In addition, some protocols that were independent in version 4 are now part of ICMPv6. Figure 31.32 compares the network layer of version 4 to version 6.

The ARP and IGMP protocols in version 4 are combined in ICMPv6. The RARP protocol is dropped from the suite because it is not used often. In addition, BOOTP does the job of RARP.

Figure 31.32 *Comparison of network layers in version 4 and version 6*

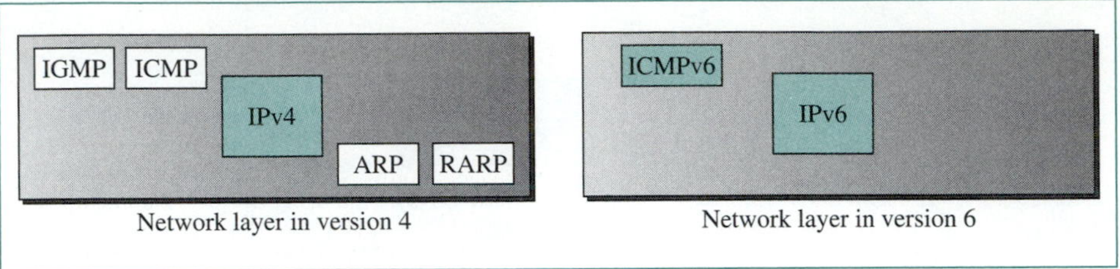

Just as in ICMPv4, we divide the ICMP messages into two categories. However, each category has more types of messages than before (see Figure 31.33). Although the general format of an ICMP message is different for each message type, the first 4 bytes are common to all, as is shown in Figure 31.34. The first field, the ICMP type, defines the broad category of the message. The code field specifies the reason for the particular message type. The last common field is the checksum field, calculated in the same manner as was described for ICMP version 4.

Figure 31.33 *Categories of ICMPv6 messages*

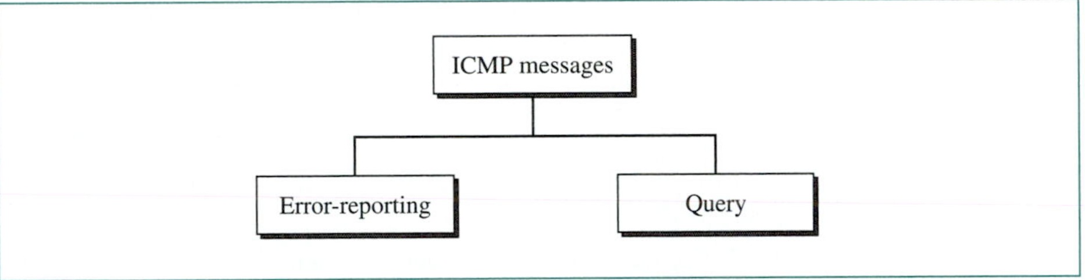

Figure 31.34 *General format of ICMP messages*

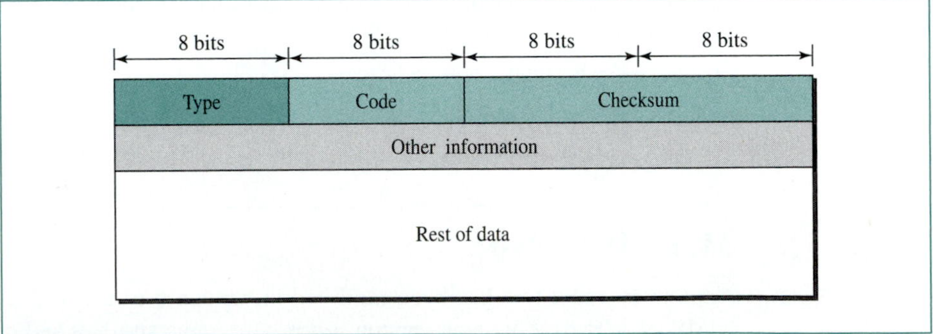

Error Reporting

As we saw in our discussion of version 4, one of the main responsibilities of ICMP is to report errors. Five types of errors are handled: destination unreachable, packet too big, time exceeded, parameter problems, and redirection (see Figure 31.35). ICMPv6 forms

Figure 31.35 *Error-reporting messages*

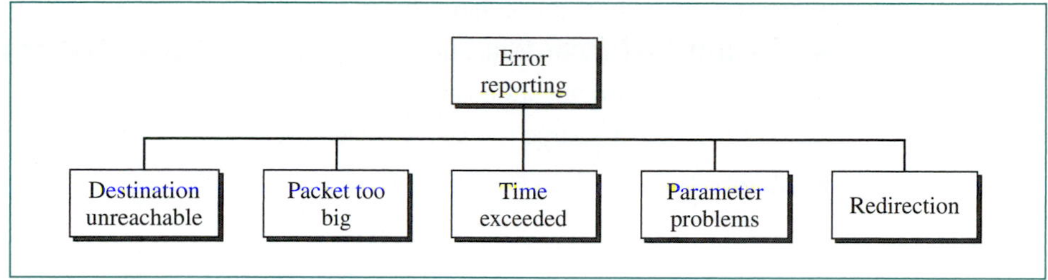

an error packet, which is then encapsulated in an IP datagram. This is delivered to the original source of the failed datagram.

Table 31.7 compares the error-reporting messages of ICMPv4 with ICMPv6. The source-quench message is eliminated in version 6 because the priority and the flow label fields allow the router to control congestion and discard the least important messages. In this version, there is no need to inform the sender to slow down. The packet-too-big message is added because fragmentation is the responsibility of the sender in IPv6. If the sender does not make the right packet size decision, the router does not have any choice except to drop the packet and send an error message to the sender.

Table 31.7 *Comparison of error-reporting messages in ICMPv4 and ICMPv6*

Type of Message	*Version 4*	*Version 6*
Destination unreachable	Yes	Yes
Source quench	Yes	No
Packet too big	No	Yes
Time exceeded	Yes	Yes
Parameter problem	Yes	Yes
Redirection	Yes	Yes

Destination Unreachable

The concept of the destination unreachable message is exactly the same as we described for ICMP version 4. Figure 31.36 shows the format of the destination-unreachable message. It is similar to the one defined for version 4, with the type value equal to 1.

Figure 31.36 *Destination-unreachable message format*

Type: 1	Code: 0 to 4	Checksum
Unused (All 0s)		
Part of the received IP datagram including IP header plus the first 8 bytes of datagram data		

The code field for this type specifies the reason for discarding the datagram and explains exactly what has failed:

- **Code 0.** No path to destination.
- **Code 1.** Communication is prohibited.
- **Code 2.** Strict source routing is impossible.
- **Code 3.** Destination address is unreachable.
- **Code 4.** Port is not available.

Packet Too Big

This is a new type of message added to version 6. If a router receives a datagram that is larger than the maximum transmission unit (MTU) size of the network through which the datagram should pass, two things happen. First, the router discards the datagram and then an ICMP error packet is sent to the source. Figure 31.37 shows the format of the packet. Note that there is only one code (0) and that the MTU field informs the sender of the maximum size packet accepted by the network.

Figure 31.37 *Packet-too-big message format*

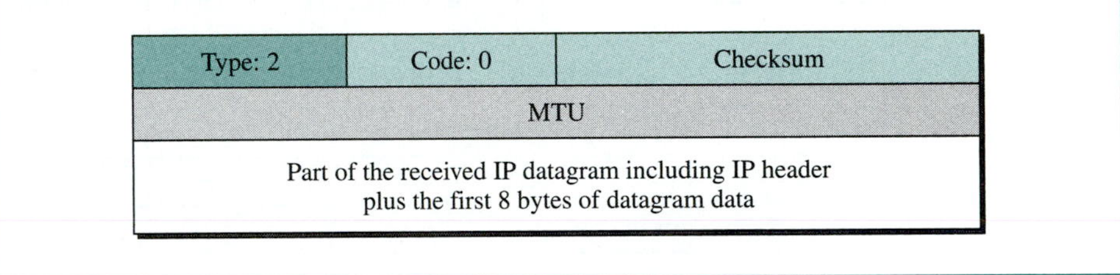

Time Exceeded

This message is similar to the one in version 4. The only difference is that the type value has changed to 3. Figure 31.38 shows the format of the time-exceeded message.

Figure 31.38 *Time-exceeded message format*

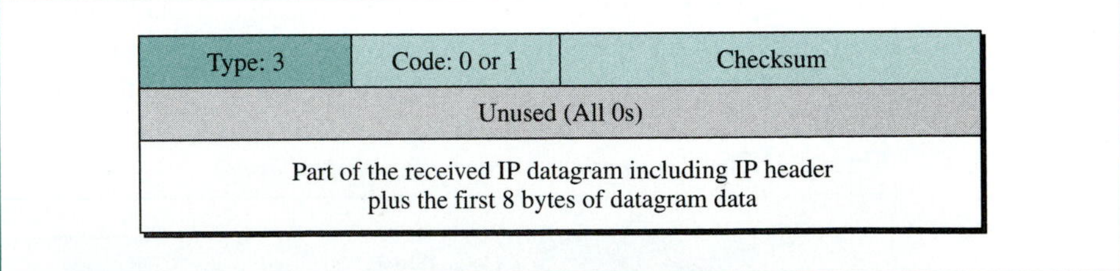

As in version 4, code 0 is used when the datagram is discarded by the router due to a hop-limit field value of zero. Code 1 is used when fragments of a datagram are discarded because other fragments have not arrived within the time limit.

Parameter Problem

This message is similar to its version 4 counterpart. However, the type value has been changed to 4 and the size of the offset pointer field has been increased to 4 bytes. There are also three different codes instead of two. The code field specifies the reason for discarding the datagram and the cause of failure:

- **Code 0.** There is error or ambiguity in one of the header fields. In this case the value in the pointer field points to the byte with the problem. For example, if the value is zero, then the first byte is not a valid field.
- **Code 1.** This defines an unrecognizable extension header.
- **Code 2.** This defines an unrecognizable option.

Figure 31.39 shows the format of the parameter problem message.

Figure 31.39 *Parameter-problem message format*

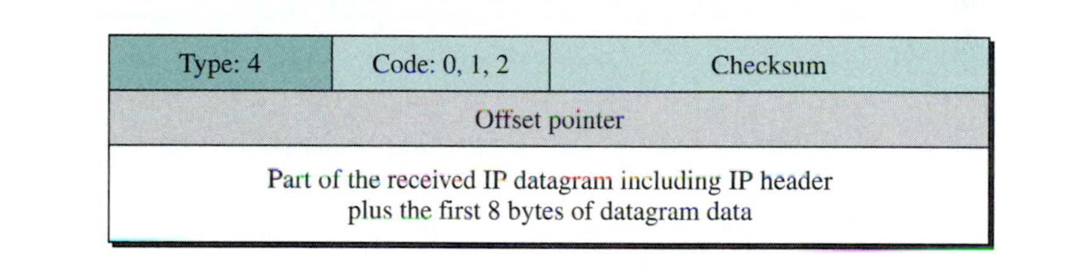

Redirection

The purpose of this message is the same as we described for version 4. However, the format of the packet is changed to accommodate the size of the IP address in version 6. Also, an option is added to let the host know the physical address of the target router (see Figure 31.40).

Figure 31.40 *Redirection message format*

Type: 137	Code: 0	Checksum
Reserved		
Target (router) IP address		
Destination IP address		
OPT. code	OPT. length	
Target (router) physical address		
Part of the received IP datagram including IP header plus the first 8 bytes of datagram data		

Query

In addition to error reporting, ICMP can also diagnose some network problems. This is accomplished through the query messages. Four different groups of messages have been defined: echo request and reply, router solicitation and advertisement, neighbor solicitation and advertisement, and group membership (see Figure 31.41).

Figure 31.41 *Query messages*

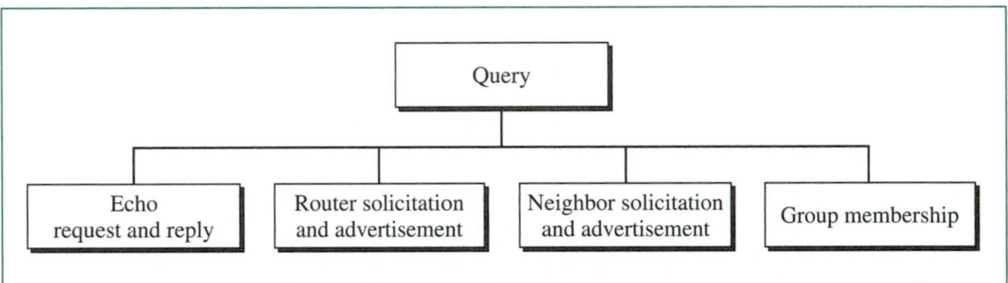

Table 31.8 shows the comparison between the query messages in versions 4 and 6. Two sets of query messages are eliminated from ICMPv6: timestamp request and reply and address mask request and reply. The timestamp request and reply messages are eliminated because they are implemented in other protocols such as TCP and because they were not used in the past. The address-mask request and reply messages are eliminated in IPv6 because the subnet section of an address allows the subscriber to use up to $2^{32} - 1$ subnets. Therefore, subnet masking, as defined in IPv4, is not needed here.

Table 31.8 *Comparison of query messages in ICMPv4 and ICMPv6*

Type of Message	*Version 4*	*Version 6*
Echo request and reply	Yes	Yes
Timestamp request and reply	Yes	No
Address mask request and reply	Yes	No
Router solicitation and advertisement	Yes	Yes
Neighbor solicitation and advertisement	ARP	Yes
Group membership	IGMP	Yes

Echo Request and Reply

The idea and format of the echo request and reply messages are the same as those in version 4. The only difference is the value for the type as shown in Figure 31.42.

Router Solicitation and Advertisement

The idea behind the router-solicitation and advertisement messages is the same as in version 4. The router-solicitation format is the same as the one in ICMPv4. However, an option is added to allow the host to announce its physical address to make it easier for the router to respond. The router-advertisement format is different from the one in

Figure 31.42 *Echo request and reply messages*

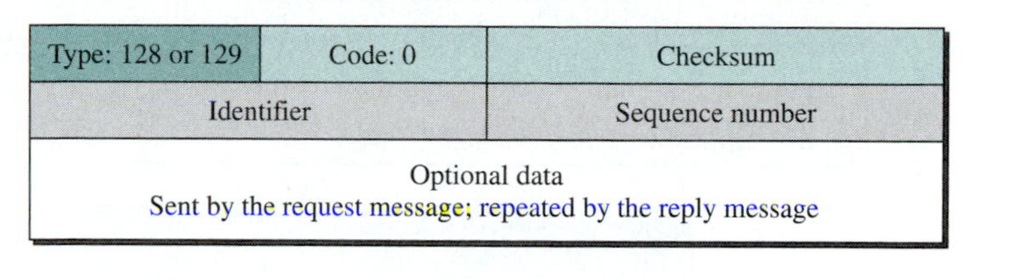

ICMPv4; here the router announces just itself and not any other router. Options can be added to the packet. One option announces the router physical address for the convenience of the host. Another option lets the router announce the MTU size. A third option allows the router to define the valid and preferred lifetime. Figure 31.43 shows the format of the router-solicitation and advertisement messages.

Figure 31.43 *Router-solicitation and advertisement message formats*

Type: 133
Code: 0
Checksum
Unused (All 0s)
Option code: 1
Option length
Host physical address

a. Router solicitation format

Type: 134
Code: 0
Checksum
Max hop
M
O
Unused(All 0s)
Router lifetime
Reachability lifetime
Reachability transmission interval
Option code: 1
Option length
Router physical address
Option code: 5
Option length
Unused (All 0s)
MTU size

b. Router advertisement format

Neighbor Solicitation and Advertisement

As previously mentioned, the network layer in version 4 contains an independent protocol called ARP. In version 6, this protocol is eliminated, and its duties are included in

ICMPv6. The idea is exactly the same, but the format of the message has changed. Figure 31.44 shows the format of neighbor solicitation and advertisement. The only option announces the sender physical address for the convenience of the receiver.

Figure 31.44 *Neighbor-solicitation and advertisement message formats*

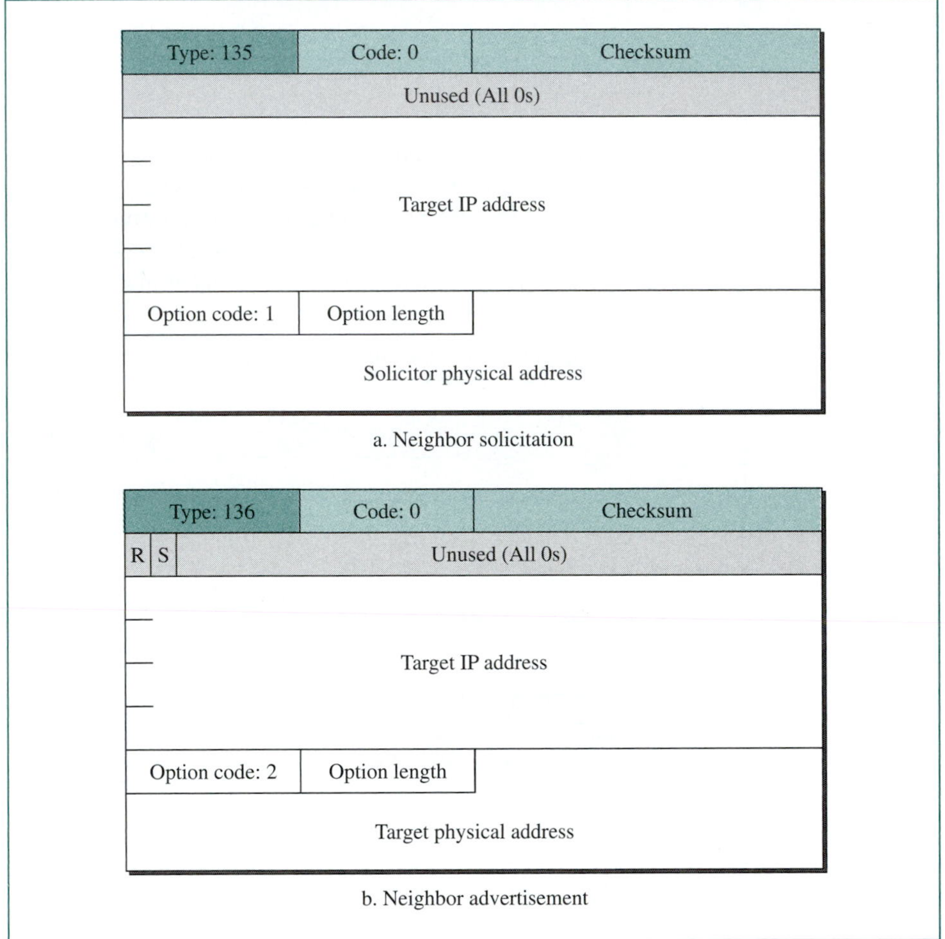

Group Membership

As previously mentioned, the network layer in version 4 contains an independent protocol called IGMP. In version 6, this protocol is eliminated, and its duties are included in ICMPv6. The purpose is exactly the same.

There are three types of group-membership messages: report, query, and termination (see Figure 31.45). The report and termination messages are sent from the host to the router. The query message is sent from the router to the host. Figure 31.46 shows the formats of group-membership messages.

Figure 31.45 *Group-membership messages*

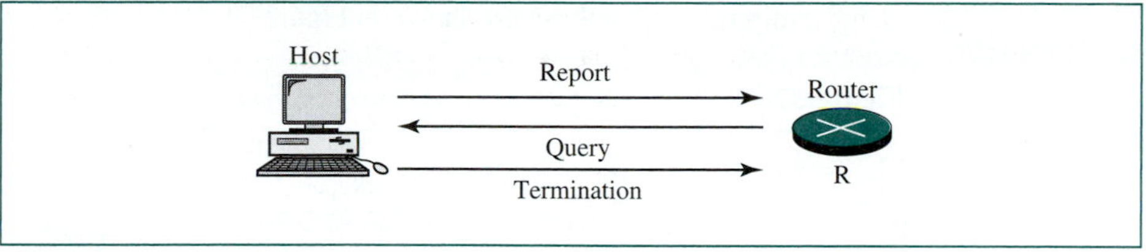

Figure 31.46 *Group-membership message formats*

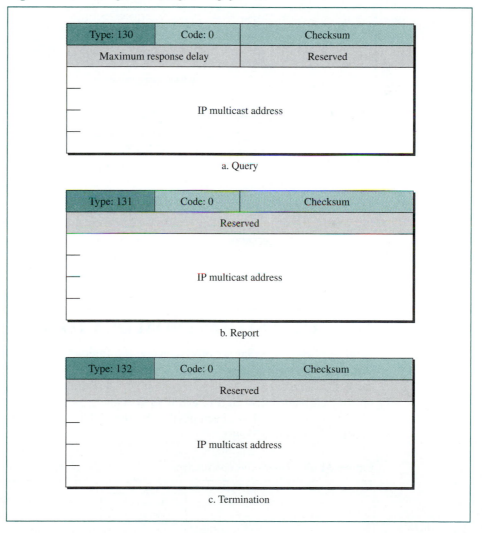

Type: 130	Code: 0	Checksum
Maximum response delay		Reserved
IP multicast address		

a. Query

Type: 131	Code: 0	Checksum
Reserved		
IP multicast address		

b. Report

Type: 132	Code: 0	Checksum
Reserved		
IP multicast address		

c. Termination

As we noted in our discussion of version 4, four different situations involve group-membership messages; these are shown in Figure 31.47.

Figure 31.47 *Four situations of group-membership operation*

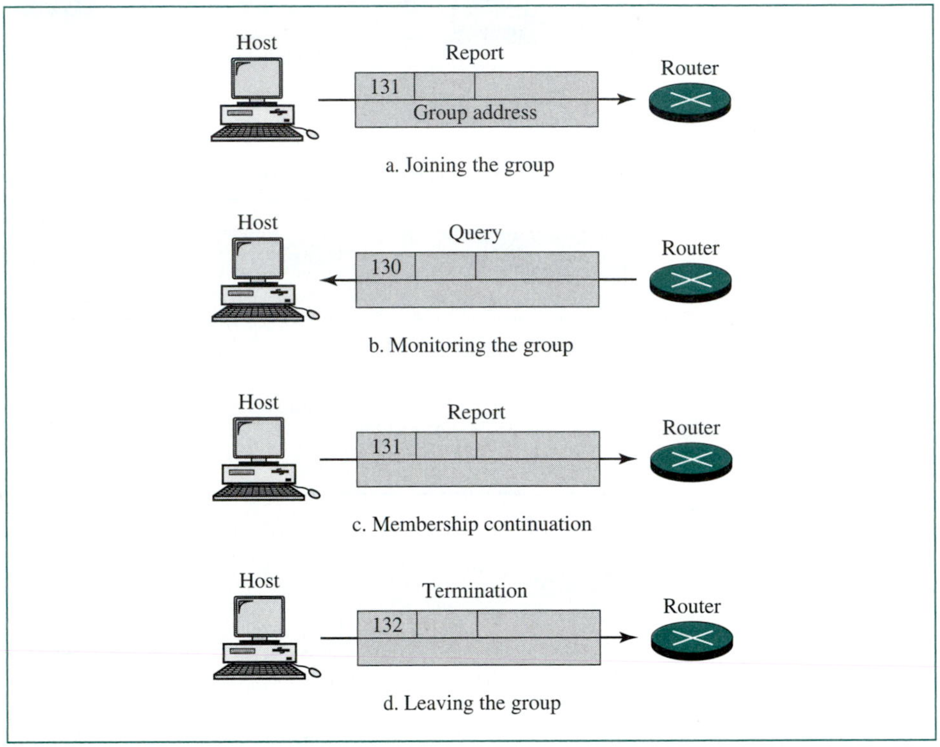

31.5 TRANSITION FROM IPv4 TO IPv6

Because of the huge number of systems on the Internet, the transition from IPv4 to IPv6 cannot happen suddenly. It takes a considerable amount of time before every system in the Internet can move from IPv4 to IPv6. The transition should be smooth to prevent any problems between IPv4 and IPv6 systems.

Three strategies have been devised by the IETF to make the transition period smoother (see Figure 31.48).

Figure 31.48 *Three transition strategies*

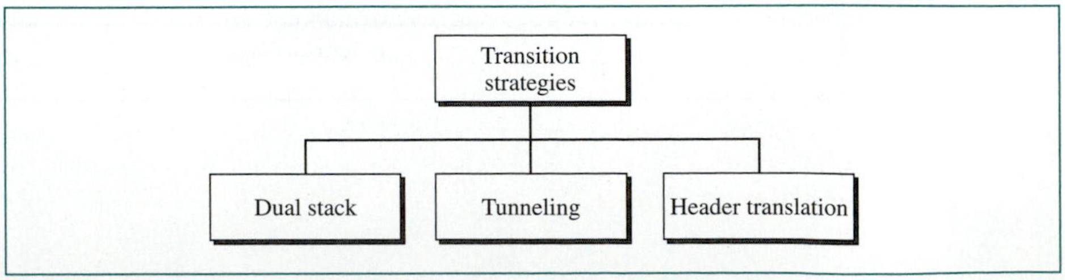

Dual Stack

It is recommended that all hosts, before migrating completely to version 6, have a dual stack of protocols. In other words, a station should run IPv4 and IPv6 simultaneously until all of the Internet uses IPv6. See Figure 31.49 for the layout of dual-stack configuration.

Figure 31.49 *Dual stack*

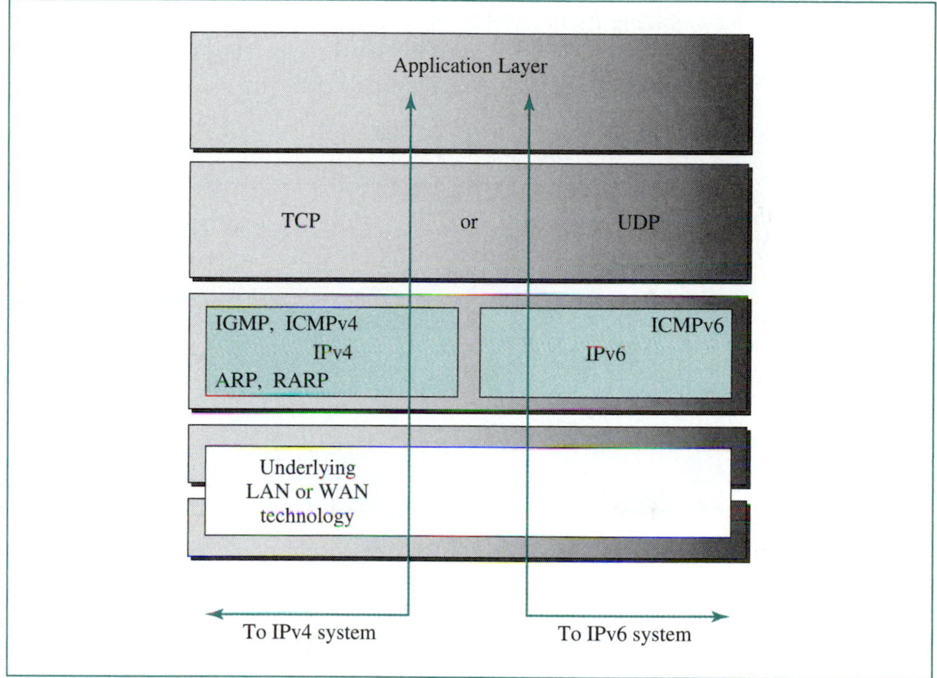

To determine which version to use when sending a packet to a destination, the source host queries the DNS. If the DNS returns an IPv4 address, the source host sends an IPv4 packet. If the DNS returns an IPv6 address, the source host sends an IPv6 packet.

Tunneling

Tunneling is a strategy used when two computers using IPv6 want to communicate with each other when the packet must pass through a region that uses IPv4. To pass through this region, the packet must have an IPv4 address. So the IPv6 packet is encapsulated in an IPv4 packet when it enters the region, and it leaves its capsule when it exits the region. It seems as if the IPv6 packet goes through a tunnel at one end and emerges at the other end. To make it clear that the IPv4 packet is carrying an IPv6 packet as data, the protocol value is set to 41. Tunneling uses the compatible addresses discussed in Section 31.2.

Automatic Tunneling

If the receiving host uses a compatible IPv6 address, tunneling occurs automatically without any reconfiguration. The sender sends the receiver an IPv6 packet using the IPv6 compatible address as the destination address. When the packet reaches the boundary of the IPv4 network, the router encapsulates it in an IPv4 packet, which should have an IPv4 address. To get this address, the router extracts the IPv4 address embedded in the IPv6 address. The packet then travels the rest of its journey as an IPv4 packet. The destination host, which is using a dual stack, now receives an IPv4 packet. Recognizing its IPv4 address, it reads the header, and finds (through the protocol field value) that the packet is carrying an IPv6 packet. It then passes the packet to the IPv6 software for processing (see Figure 31.50).

Figure 31.50 *Automatic tunneling*

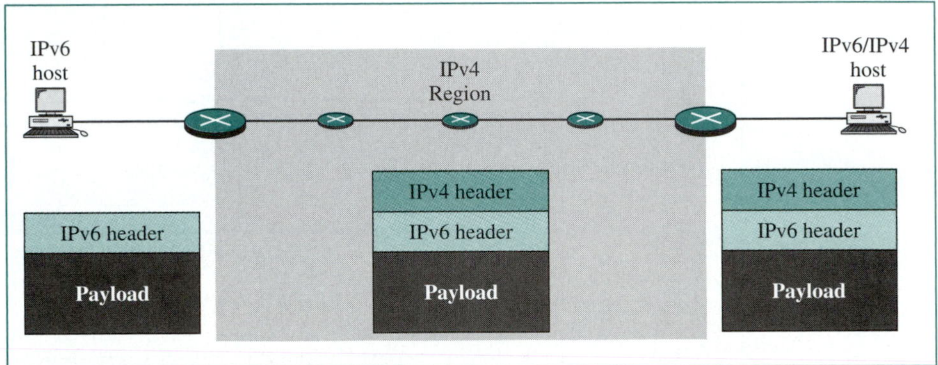

Configured Tunneling

If the receiving host does not support an IPv6-compatible address, the sender receives a noncompatible IPv6 address from the DNS. In this case, the sender sends the IPv6 packet with the receiver's noncompatible IPv6 address. However, the packet cannot pass through the IPv4 region without first being encapsulated in an IPv4 packet. The two routers at the boundary of the IPv4 region are configured to pass the packet encapsulated in an IPv4 packet. The router at one end sends the IPv4 packet with its own IPv4 address as the source and the other router's IPv4 address as the destination. The other router receives the packet, decapsulates the IPv6 packet, and sends it to the destination host. The destination host then receives the packet in IPv6 format and processes it (see Figure 31.51).

Header Translation

Header translation is necessary when the majority of the Internet has moved to IPv6 but some systems still use IPv4. The sender wants to use IPv6, but the receiver does not understand IPv6. Tunneling does not work in this situation because the packet must be in the IPv4 format to be understood by the receiver. In this case, the header format must be changed totally through header translation. The header of the IPv6 packet is converted to an IPv4 header (see Figure 31.52).

Figure 31.51 *Configured tunneling*

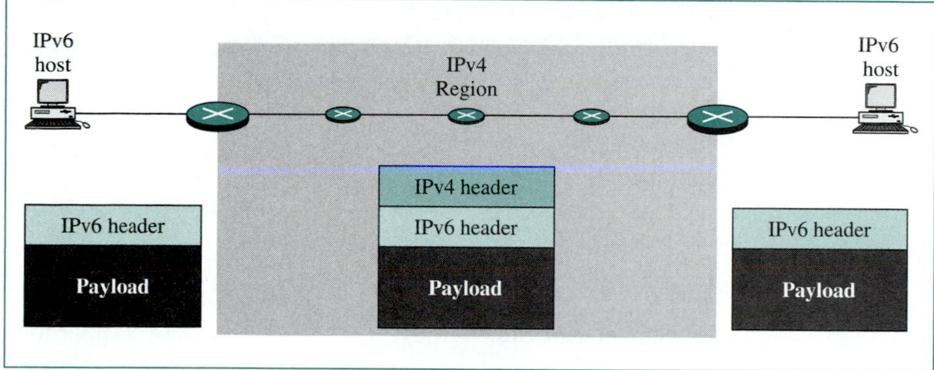

Figure 31.52 *Header translation*

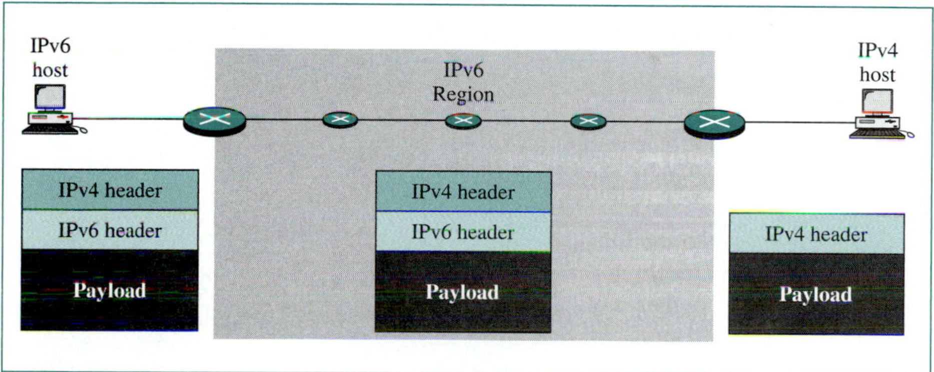

Header translation uses the mapped address to translate an IPv6 address to an IPv4 address. Table 31.9 lists some rules used in transforming an IPv6 packet header to an IPv4 packet header.

Table 31.9 *Header translation*

Header Translation Procedure
1. The IPv6 mapped address is changed to an IPv4 address by extracting the rightmost 32 bits.
2. The value of the IPv6 priority field is discarded.
3. Set the type of service field in IPv4 to zero.
4. The checksum for IPv4 is calculated and inserted in the corresponding field.
5. The IPv6 flow label is ignored.
6. Compatible extension headers are converted to options and inserted in the IPv4 header.
7. The length of IPv4 header is calculated and inserted into the corresponding field.
8. The total length of the IPv4 packet is calculated and inserted in the corresponding field.

31.6 KEY TERMS

abbreviation

address-mask request and reply message

Address Resolution Protocol (ARP)

address space

anycast address

attended bulk data traffic

authentication

automatic tunneling

background data

base header

compatible address

configured tunneling

congestion-controlled traffic

control traffic

destination address

destination option

destination-unreachable message

dual stack

echo request and reply message

encrypted security payload (ESP)

encryption

error-reporting message

extension header

flow label

fragmentation

group-membership message

header translation

hexadecimal colon notation

hop limit

hop-by-hop option

hostid

interactive traffic

Internet

Internetworking Control Message Protocol, version 6 (ICMPv6)

Internetworking Protocol, next generation (IPng)

Internetworking Protocol, version 4 (IPv4)

Internetworking Protocol, version 6 (Ipv6)

jumbo payload

link local address

loopback address

mapped address

multicast address

neighbor-solicitation and advertisement message

netid

next header

noncongestion-controlled traffic

packet priority

packet-too-big message

Pad1

PadN

parameter problem message

Path MTU Discovery technique

query message

redirection message

reserved address

resource allocation

router-solicitation and advertisement message

site local address

source address

source-quench message

source routing

subnet

supernet

time-exceeded message

timestamp request and reply message

traffic

Transmission Control Protocol/ Internetworking Protocol (TCP/IP)

transport mode

tunnel mode

tunneling

unattended data traffic

unicast address

unspecified address

31.7 SUMMARY

- IPv6, the latest version of the Internet Protocol, has a 128-bit address space, a revised header format, new options, an allowance for extension, support for resource allocation, and increased security measures.
- IPv6 uses hexadecimal colon notation with abbreviation methods available.
- There are three types of addresses: unicast, anycast, and multicast.
- The variable-type prefix field defines the address type or purpose.
- An IP datagram is composed of a base header and a payload.
- The 40-byte base header consists of the version, priority, flow label, payload length, next header, hop limit, source address, and destination address fields.
- The priority field is a measure of the importance of a datagram.
- The flow label identifies the special-handling needs of a sequence of packets.
- A payload consists of optional extension headers and data from an upper layer.
- Extension headers add functionality to the IPv6 datagram.
- The hop-by-hop option is used to pass information to all routers in the path.
- The source routing extension is used when the source wants to specify the transmission path.
- The fragmentation extension is used if the payload is a fragment of a message.
- The authentication extension validates the sender of the message and protects the data from hackers.
- The encrypted security payload extension provides confidentiality between sender and receiver.
- The destination extension passes information from the source to the destination exclusively.
- ICMPv6, like version 4, reports errors, handles group memberships, updates specific router and host tables, and checks the viability of a host.

- The five error-reporting messages deal with unreachable destinations, packets that are too big, expired timers for fragments and hop counts, header problems, and inefficient routing.
- Query messages are in the form of a response and a reply.
- The echo request and reply query messages test the connectivity between two systems.
- The router-solicitation and advertisement messages allow routers to update their routing tables.
- The group-membership messages (IGMP in version 4) can add a host to a group, terminate a group membership, monitor a group, or maintain group membership.
- Three strategies used to make the transition from version 4 to version 6 are dual stack, tunneling, and header translation.

31.8 PRACTICE SET

Multiple-Choice Questions

1. Which of the following is a necessary part of the IPv6 datagram?
   a. base header
   b. extension header
   c. data packet from the upper layer
   d. a and c
2. The _______ field in the base header restricts the lifetime of a datagram.
   a. version
   b. priority
   c. next header
   d. hop limit
3. When a datagram needs to be discarded in a congested network, the decision is based on the _______ field in the base header.
   a. version
   b. priority
   c. next header
   d. hop limit
4. The _______ field in the base header and the sender IP address combine to indicate a unique path identifier for a specific flow of data.
   a. version
   b. flow label
   c. next header
   d. hop limit

5. The source address in the base header always contains the address of the _______.
   a. last router
   b. next router
   c. original sender
   d. any of the above
6. For a maximum number of hops, set the hop limit field to decimal _______.
   a. 16
   b. 15
   c. 42
   d. 255
7. For time-sensitive data, assign the priority field a value of decimal _______.
   a. 0
   b. 7
   c. 8 to 15
   d. 16
8. Real-time packets being sent at a constant rate are classified as _______.
   a. congestion-controlled data
   b. noncongestion-controlled data
   c. low-priority data
   d. none of the above
9. _______ data can adapt itself to the network flow.
   a. Congestion-controlled
   b. Noncongestion-controlled
   c. Compressed
   d. Modulated
10. A datagram with a priority of _______ will be discarded before a datagram with a priority of 12.
    a. 11
    b. 7
    c. 0
    d. any of the above
11. A 6000-byte packet needs to be routed through an Ethernet LAN. What extension header must be used?
    a. source routing
    b. fragmentation
    c. authentication
    d. destination option

12. In the _______ extension header, the destination address changes from router to router.
    a. source routing
    b. fragmentation
    c. authentication
    d. payload
13. An IP datagram is 80,000 bytes. What extension header must be used?
    a. hop-by-hop
    b. fragmentation
    c. authentication
    d. destination option
14. The maximum size for an IPv6 datagram is _______ bytes.
    a. 65,535
    b. 65,575
    c. 2^{32}
    d. $2^{32} + 40$
15. What is the minimum length for a hop-by-hop extension header?
    a. 1 byte
    b. 3 bytes
    c. 4 bytes
    d. 8 bytes
16. To request the physical address of a host whose IP address is known, a _______ message is sent.
    a. membership-query
    b. router-solicitation
    c. neighbor-solicitation
    d. neighbor-advertisement
17. If a host needs information about routers on the network, it sends a _______ message.
    a. membership-report
    b. router-solicitation
    c. neighbor-solicitation
    d. neighbor-advertisement
18. Which of the following types of ICMP messages need to be encapsulated into an IP datagram?
    a. neighbor solicitation
    b. echo response
    c. redirection
    d. all of the above

19. The ARP function in version 4 is part of _______ in version 6.
    a. echo request and reply
    b. router solicitation and advertisement
    c. neighbor solicitation and advertisement
    d. group membership
20. The IGMP functions in version 4 are part of _______ in version 6.
    a. echo request and reply
    b. router solicitation and advertisement
    c. neighbor solicitation and advertisement
    d. group membership
21. To join a group, a host sends a _______.
    a. group-membership report
    b. group-membership query
    c. group-membership termination
    d. any of the above
22. The purpose of echo request and echo reply is to _______.
    a. report errors
    b. check node-to-node communication
    c. check group memberships
    d. find physical addresses
23. A router sends a _______ message to the host to monitor group membership.
    a. report
    b. query
    c. termination
    d. none of the above
24. In error reporting the encapsulated ICMP packet goes to _______.
    a. the source
    b. the destination
    c. a router
    d. any of the above
25. In error reporting, a destination can send a _______ message if an option is not recognized.
    a. parameter-problem
    b. packet-too-big
    c. time-exceeded
    d. destination-unreachable
26. Which field is always present in an ICMP packet?
    a. type
    b. code
    c. checksum
    d. all of the above

27. An MTU field is found on the _______ error message to inform the sender about packet size.
    a. destination-unreachable
    b. time-exceeded
    c. parameter-problem
    d. packet-too-big
28. When the hop count field reaches zero and the destination has not been reached, a _______ error message is sent.
    a. destination-unreachable
    b. time-exceeded
    c. parameter-problem
    d. packet-too-big
29. When all fragments of a message have not been received within the designated amount of time, a _______ error message is sent.
    a. destination-unreachable
    b. time-exceeded
    c. parameter-problem
    d. packet-too-big
30. Errors in the header or option fields of an IP datagram require a _______ error message.
    a. destination-unreachable
    b. time-exceeded
    c. parameter-problem
    d. packet-too-big
31. If a member of a group wishes to terminate membership, it can _______ in response to a group membership query.
    a. send a group membership report
    b. send a group membership termination
    c. send a group membership query
    d. none of the above
32. In version 6, an independent protocol called _______ is eliminated.
    a. ICMP
    b. IP
    c. IGMP
    d. all of the above
33. A _______ can learn about network _______ by sending out a router solicitation packet.
    a. router, routers
    b. router, hosts
    c. host, hosts
    d. host, routers

34. The _______ packet contains information about a router.
    a. router solicitation
    b. router information
    c. router advertisement
    d. router option
35. When a host has the _______ address of a host but needs the _______ address, it uses a neighbor solicitation packet.
    a. physical, protocol port
    b. physical, data link layer
    c. physical, IP
    d. IP, physical
36. A router can send a _______ message to a host to inform it of a more efficient path.
    a. neighbor-solicitation
    b. router-solicitation
    c. redirection
    d. neighbor-advertisement
37. Which version 4 protocols are still viable and known by their same names in version 6?
    a. IGMP
    b. ARP
    c. RARP
    d. none of the above
38. Which error-reporting message from version 4 has been eliminated in version 6?
    a. packet too big
    b. destination unreachable
    c. parameter problem
    d. source quench
39. Which error-reporting message is found in version 6 but not in version 4?
    a. packet too big
    b. destination unreachable
    c. parameter problem
    d. time exceeded

Exercises

40. Show the shortest form of the following addresses:
    a. 2340:1ABC:119A:A000:0000:0000:0000:0000
    b. 0000:00AA:0000:0000:0000:0000:119A:A231
    c. 2340:0000:0000:0000:0000:119A:A001:0000
    d. 0000:0000:0000:2340:0000:0000:0000:0000

41. Show the original (unabbreviated) form of the following addresses:
    a. 0::0
    b. 0:AA::0
    c. 0:1234::3
    d. 123::1:2
42. What is the type of each of the following addresses:
    a. FE80::12
    b. FEC0::24A2
    c. FF02::0
    d. 0::01
43. What is the type of each of the following addresses:
    a. 0::0
    b. 0::FFFF:0:0
    c. 582F:1234::2222
    d. 4821::14:22
    e. 54EF::A234:2
44. Show the provider prefix (in hexadecimal colon notation) of an address assigned to a subscriber if it is registered in the USA with the provider identification ABC1.
45. Show in hexadecimal colon notation the IPv6 address compatible to the IPv4 address 129.6.12.34.
46. Show in hexadecimal colon notation the IPv6 address mapped to the IPv4 address 129.6.12.34.
47. Show in hexadecimal colon notation the IPv6 loopback address.
48. Show in hexadecimal colon notation the link local address in which the node identifier is 0::123/48.
49. Show in hexadecimal colon notation the site local address in which the node identifier is 0::123/48.
50. Show in hexadecimal colon notation the permanent multicast address used in a link local scope.
51. What are the possible first two bytes for a multicast address?
52. A host has the address 581E:1456:2314:ABCD::1211. If the node identification is 48 bits, find the address of the subnet to which the host is attached.
53. A host has the address 581E:1456:2314:ABCD::1211. If the node identification is 48 bits, and the subnet identification is 32 bits, find the provider prefix.
54. A site with 200 subnets has the class B address of 132.45.0.0. The site recently migrated to IPv6 with the subscriber prefix 581E:1456:2314::ABCD/80. Design the subnets and define the subnet address using a subnet identifier of 32 bits.
55. An IPv6 packet consists of the base header and a TCP segment. The length of data is 320 bytes. Show the packet and enter a value for each field.
56. An IPv6 packet consists of a base header and a TCP segment. The length of data is 128,000 bytes (jumbo payload). Show the packet and enter a value for each field.

57. What types of ICMP messages contain part of the IP datagram? Why is this included?
58. Compare and contrast, field by field, the destination-unreachable message format in ICMPv4 and ICMPv6.
59. Compare and contrast, field by field, the time-exceeded message format in ICMPv4 and ICMPv6.
60. Compare and contrast, field by field, the parameter-problem message format in ICMPv4 and ICMPv6.
61. Compare and contrast, field by field, the redirection-message format in ICMPv4 and ICMPv6.
62. Compare and contrast, field by field, the echo-request and reply messages format in ICMPv4 and ICMPv6.
63. Compare and contrast, field by field, the router-solicitation and advertisement messages format in ICMPv4 and ICMPv6.
64. Compare and contrast, field by field, the neighbor-solicitation and advertisement messages format in ICMPv6 with the query and reply messages in ARP.
65. Compare and contrast, field by field, the group-membership messages in IPv6 with the corresponding messages in IGMP.
66. Why are the IPv4-compatible addresses and the IPv4-mapped addresses different?
67. What is the IPv4-compatible address for 119.254.254.254?
68. What is the IPv4-mapped address for 119.254.254.254?
69. How many more addresses are available with IPv6 than IPv4?
70. In designing the IPv4-mapped address, why didn't the designers just prepend 96 1s to the IPv4 address?

Programming Exercises

71. Write a function in C to convert an address in binary format to hexadecimal colon notation.
72. Write a function in C to convert an address in hexadecimal notation to its shortest length.
73. Write a function in C to convert an IPv4 address to the corresponding IPv6 compatible address.
74. Write a function in C to convert an IPv4 address to the corresponding IPv6 mapped address.
75. Write a function in C to find the type of an IPv6 address.

APPENDIX A

ASCII Code

The American Standard Code for Information Interchange (ASCII) is the most commonly used code for encoding printable and nonprintable (control) characters.

ASCII uses seven bits to encode each character. It can therefore represent up to 128 characters. Table A.1 lists the ASCII characters and their codes in both binary and hexadecimal form.

Table A.1 *ASCII table*

Decimal	*Hexadecimal*	*Binary*	*Character*	*Description*
0	00	0000000	NUL	Null
1	01	0000001	SOH	Start of header
2	02	0000010	STX	Start of text
3	03	0000011	ETX	End of text
4	04	0000100	EOT	End of transmission
5	05	0000101	ENQ	Enquiry
6	06	0000110	ACK	Acknowledgment
7	07	0000111	BEL	Bell
8	08	0001000	BS	Backspace
9	09	0001001	HT	Horizontal tab
10	0A	0001010	LF	Line feed
11	0B	0001011	VT	Vertical tab
12	0C	0001100	FF	Form feed
13	0D	0001101	CR	Carriage return
14	0E	0001110	SO	Shift out
15	0F	0001111	SI	Shift in
16	10	0010000	DLE	Data link escape

Table A.1 *ASCII table (continued)*

Decimal	*Hexadecimal*	*Binary*	*Character*	*Description*
17	11	0010001	DC1	Device control 1
18	12	0010010	DC2	Device control 2
19	13	0010011	DC3	Device control 3
20	14	0010100	DC4	Device control 4
21	15	0010101	NAK	Negative acknowledgment
22	16	0010110	SYN	Synchronous idle
23	17	0010111	ETB	End of transmission block
24	18	0011000	CAN	Cancel
25	19	0011001	EM	End of medium
26	1A	0011010	SUB	Substitute
27	1B	0011011	ESC	Escape
28	1C	0011100	FS	File separator
29	1D	0011101	GS	Group separator
30	1E	0011110	RS	Record separator
31	1F	0011111	US	Unit separator
32	20	0100000	SP	Space
33	21	0100001	!	Exclamation mark
34	22	0100010	“	Double quote
35	23	0100011	#	Pound sign
36	24	0100100	$	Dollar sign
37	25	0100101	%	Percent sign
38	26	0100110	&	Ampersand
39	27	0100111	’	Apostrophe
40	28	0101000	(	Open parenthesis
41	29	0101001	)	Close parenthesis
42	2A	0101010	*	Asterisk
43	2B	0101011	+	Plus sign
44	2C	0101100	,	Comma
45	2D	0101101	-	Hyphen
46	2E	0101110	.	Period
47	2F	0101111	/	Slash
48	30	0110000	0	
49	31	0110001	1	
50	32	0110010	2	

Table A.1 *ASCII table (continued)*

Decimal	*Hexadecimal*	*Binary*	*Character*	*Description*
51	33	0110011	3	
52	34	0110100	4	
53	35	0110101	5	
54	36	0110110	6	
55	37	0110111	7	
56	38	0111000	8	
57	39	0111001	9	
58	3A	0111010	:	Colon
59	3B	0111011	;	Semicolon
60	3C	0111100	<	Less than sign
61	3D	0111101	=	Equal sign
62	3E	0111110	>	Greater than sign
63	3F	0111111	?	Question mark
64	40	1000000	@	At sign
65	41	1000001	A	
66	42	1000010	B	
67	43	1000011	C	
68	44	1000100	D	
69	45	1000101	E	
70	46	1000110	F	
71	47	1000111	G	
72	48	1001000	H	
73	49	1001001	I	
74	4A	1001010	J	
75	4B	1001011	K	
76	4C	1001100	L	
77	4D	1001101	M	
78	4E	1001110	N	
79	4F	1001111	O	
80	50	1010000	P	
81	51	1010001	Q	
82	52	1010010	R	
83	53	1010011	S	
84	54	1010100	T	

Table A.1 *ASCII table (continued)*

Decimal	*Hexadecimal*	*Binary*	*Character*	*Description*
85	55	1010101	U	
86	56	1010110	V	
87	57	1010111	W	
88	58	1011000	X	
89	59	1011001	Y	
90	5A	1011010	Z	
91	5B	1011011	[	Open bracket
92	5C	1011100	\	Backslash
93	5D	1011101	]	Close bracket
94	5E	1011110	^	Caret
95	5F	1011111	_	Underscore
96	60	1100000	`	Grave accent
97	61	1100001	a	
98	62	1100010	b	
99	63	1100011	c	
100	64	1100100	d	
101	65	1100101	e	
102	66	1100110	f	
103	67	1100111	g	
104	68	1101000	h	
105	69	1101001	i	
106	6A	1101010	j	
107	6B	1101011	k	
108	6C	1101100	l	
109	6D	1101101	m	
110	6E	1101110	n	
111	6F	1101111	o	
112	70	1110000	p	
113	71	1110001	q	
114	72	1110010	r	
115	73	1110011	s	
116	74	1110100	t	
117	75	1110101	u	
118	76	1110110	v	

Table A.1 *ASCII table (continued)*

Decimal	*Hexadecimal*	*Binary*	*Character*	*Description*
119	77	1110111	w	
120	78	1111000	x	
121	79	1111001	y	
122	7A	1111010	z	
123	7B	1111011	{	Open brace
124	7C	1111100	|	Bar
125	7D	1111101	}	Close brace
126	7E	1111110	~	Tilde
127	7F	1111111	DEL	Delete

APPENDIX B

Numbering Systems and Transformation

Today's computers make use of four numbering systems: decimal, binary, octal, and hexadecimal. Each has advantages for different levels of digital processing. In Section B.1 of this appendix, we describe each of the four systems. In Section B.2, we show how a number in one system can be transformed into a number in another system.

B.1 NUMBERING SYSTEMS

All of the numbering systems examined here are positional, meaning that the position of a symbol in relation to other symbols determines its value. Within a number, each symbol is called a digit (decimal digit, binary digit, octal digit, or hexadecimal digit). For example, the decimal number 798 has three decimal digits. Digits are arranged in order of ascending value, moving from the lowest value on the right to the highest on the left. For this reason, the leftmost digit is referred to as the most significant and the rightmost as the least significant digit (see Figure B.1). For example, in the decimal number 1234, the most significant digit is the 1 and the least significant is the 4.

Figure B.1 *Digit positions and their significance*

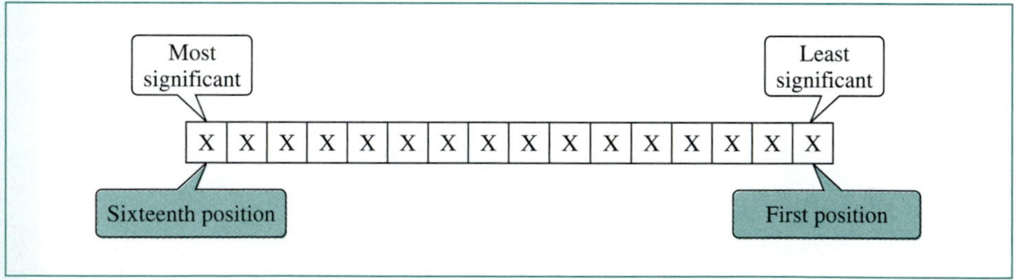

Decimal Numbers

The decimal system is the one most familiar to us in everyday life. All of our terms for indicating countable quantities are based on it, and, in fact, when we speak of other numbering systems, we tend to refer to their quantities by their decimal equivalents. Also called base 10, the name *decimal* is derived from the Latin stem *deci,* meaning ten. The decimal system uses 10 symbols to represent quantitative values: 0, 1, 2, 3, 4, 5, 6, 7, 8, and 9.

> Decimal numbers use 10 symbols: 0, 1, 2, 3, 4, 5, 6, 7, 8, and 9.

Weight and Value

In the decimal system, each weight equals 10 raised to the power of its position. The weight of the first position, therefore, is 10^0, which equals 1. So the value of a digit in the first position is equal to the value of the digit times 1. The weight of the second position is 10^1, which equals 10. The value of a digit in the second position, therefore, is equal to the value of the digit times 10. The weight of the third position is 10^2. The value of a digit in the third position is equal to the value of the digit times 100 (see Table B.1).

Table B.1 *Decimal weights*

Position	Fifth	Fourth	Third	Second	First
Weight	10^4 (10,000)	10^3 (1,000)	10^2 (100)	10^1 (10)	10^0 (1)

The value of the number as a whole is the sum of each digit times its weight. Figure B.2 shows the weightings of the decimal number 4567.

Figure B.2 *Example of a decimal number*

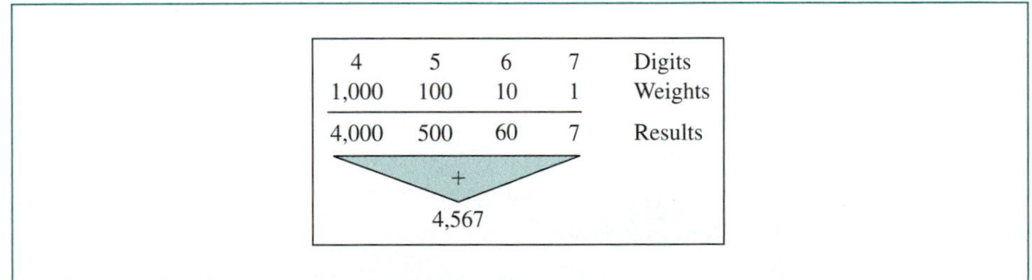

Binary Numbers

The binary number system provides the basis for all computer operations. Computers work by manipulating electrical current on and off. The binary system uses two symbols, *0* and *1,* so it corresponds naturally to a two-state device, such as a switch, with 0 to represent the off state and 1 to represent the on state. Also called base 2, the word *binary* derives from the Latin stem *bi,* meaning two.

> Binary numbers use two symbols: 0 and 1.

Weight and Value

The binary system is also a weighted system. Each digit has a weight based on its position in the number. Weight in the binary system is two raised to the power represented by a position, as shown in Table B.2. Note that the value of the weightings is shown in decimal terms next to the weight itself. The value of a specific digit is equal to its face value times the weight of its position.

Table B.2 *Binary weights*

Position	Fifth	Fourth	Third	Second	First
Weight	2^4 (16)	2^3 (8)	2^2 (4)	2^1 (2)	2^0 (1)

To calculate the value of a number, multiply each digit by the weight of its position, and then add together the results. Figure B.3 demonstrates the weighting of the binary number 1101. As you can see, 1101 is the binary equivalent of decimal 13.

Figure B.3 *Example of a binary number*

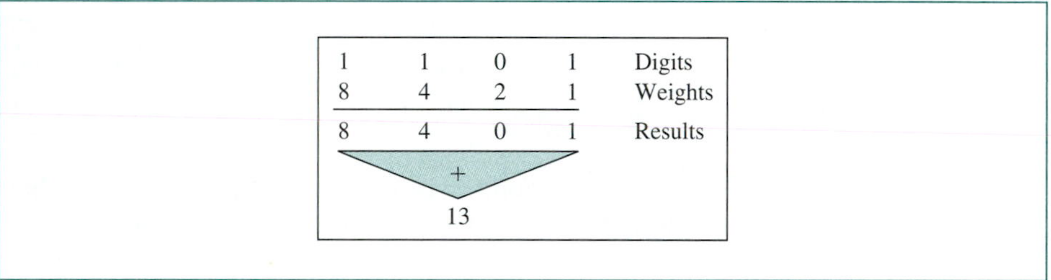

Octal Numbers

The octal number system is used by computer programmers to represent binary numbers in a compact form. Also called base 8, the term *octal* derives from the Greek stem *octa,* meaning eight. Eight is a power of two (2^3) and therefore can be used to model binary concepts. The octal system uses eight symbols to represent quantitative values: 0, 1, 2, 3, 4, 5, 6, and 7.

> Octal numbers use eight symbols: 0, 1, 2, 3, 4, 5, 6, and 7.

Weight and Value

The octal system is also a weighted system. Each digit has a weight based on its position in the number. Weight in octal is eight raised to the power represented by a position, as shown in Table B.3. Once again, the value represented by each weighting is given in decimal terms next to the weight itself. The value of a specific digit is equal to its face value times the weight of its position. For example, a 4 in the third position has the equivalent decimal value 4 × 64, or 256.

Table B.3 *Octal weights*

Position	Fifth	Fourth	Third	Second	First
Weight	8^4	8^3	8^2	8^1	8^0
	(4096)	(512)	(64)	(8)	(1)

To calculate the value of an octal number, multiply the value of each digit by the weight of its position, then add together the results. Figure B.4 shows the weighting for the octal number 3471. As you can see, 3471 is the octal equivalent of decimal 1,849.

Figure B.4 *Example of an octal number*

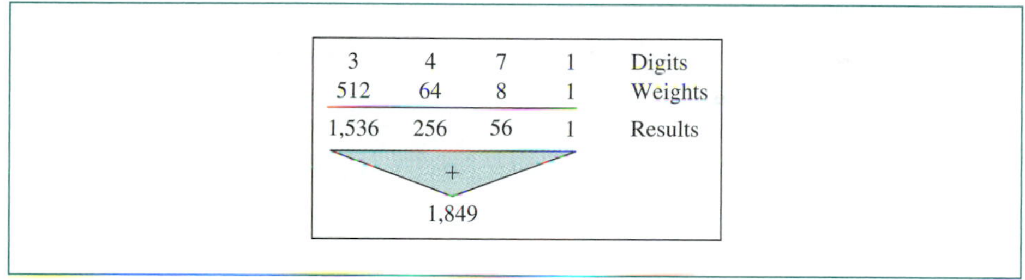

Hexadecimal Numbers

The term *hexadecimal* is derived from the Greek stem *hexadeca,* meaning 16 (*hex* means 6, and *deca* means 10). So the hexadecimal number system is base 16. Sixteen is also a power of 2 (2^4). Like octal, therefore, the hexadecimal system is used by programmers to represent binary numbers in a compact form. Hexadecimal uses 16 symbols to represent data: 0, 1, 2, 3, 4, 5, 6, 7, 8, 9, A, B, C, D, E, and F.

Hexadecimal numbers use 16 symbols: 0, 1, 2, 3, 4, 5, 6, 7, 8, 9, A, B, C, D, E, and F.

Weight and Value

Like the others, the hexadecimal system is a weighted system. Each digit has a weight based on its position in the number. The weight is used to calculate the value represented by the digit. Weight in hexadecimal is 16 raised to the power represented by a position, as shown in Table B.4. Once again, the value represented by each weighting is given in decimal terms next to the weight itself. The value of a specific digit is equal to its face value times the weight of its position. For example, a 4 in the third position has the equivalent decimal value 4 × 256, or 1024. To calculate the value of a hexadecimal number, multiply the value of each digit by the weight of its position, then add together the results. Figure B.5 shows the weighting for the hexadecimal number 3471. As you can see, 3471 is the hexadecimal equivalent of decimal 13,425.

Table B.4 *Hexadecimal weights*

Position	Fifth	Fourth	Third	Second	First
Weight	16^4 (65,536)	16^3 (4096)	16^2 (256)	16^1 (16)	16^0 (1)

Figure B.5 *Example of a hexadecimal number*

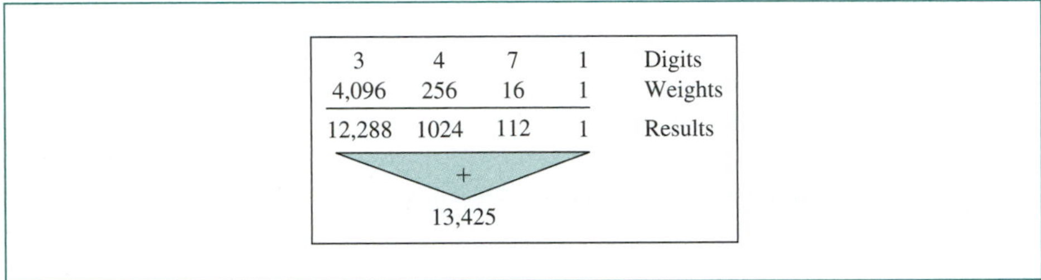

B.2 TRANSFORMATION

The different numbering systems provide different ways of thinking about a common subject: quantities of single units. A number from any given system can be transformed into its equivalent in any other system. For example, a binary number can be converted to a decimal number, and vice versa, without altering its value. Table B.5 shows how each system represents the decimal numbers 0 through 15. As you can see, decimal 13 is equivalent to binary 1101, which is equivalent to octal 15, which is equivalent to hexadecimal D.

Table B.5 *Comparison of four systems*

Decimal	*Binary*	*Octal*	*Hexadecimal*
0	0	0	0
1	1	1	1
2	10	2	2
3	11	3	3
4	100	4	4
5	101	5	5
6	110	6	6
7	111	7	7
8	1000	10	8
9	1001	11	9
10	1010	12	A
11	1011	13	B

Table B.5 *Comparison of four systems (continued)*

Decimal	*Binary*	*Octal*	*Hexadecimal*
12	1100	14	C
13	1101	15	D
14	1110	16	E
15	1111	17	F

From Other Systems to Decimal

As we saw in the discussions above, binary, octal, and hexadecimal numbers can be transformed easily to their decimal equivalents by using the weights of the digits. Figure B.6 shows the decimal value 78 represented in each of the other three systems.

Figure B.6 *Transformation from other systems to decimal*

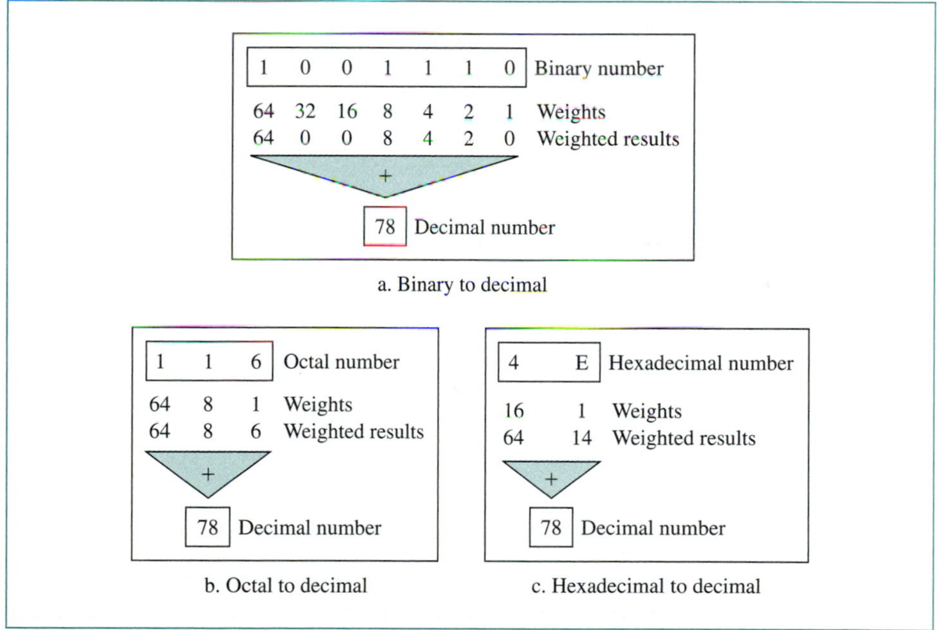

From Decimal to Other Systems

A simple division trick gives us a convenient way to convert a decimal number to its binary, octal, or hexadecimal equivalent (see Figure B.7).

To convert a number from decimal to binary, divide the number by 2 and write down the resulting remainder (1 or 0). That remainder is the least significant binary digit. Now, divide the result of that division by 2 and write down the new remainder in the second position. Repeat this process until the quotient becomes zero.

Figure B.7 *Transformation from decimal to other systems*

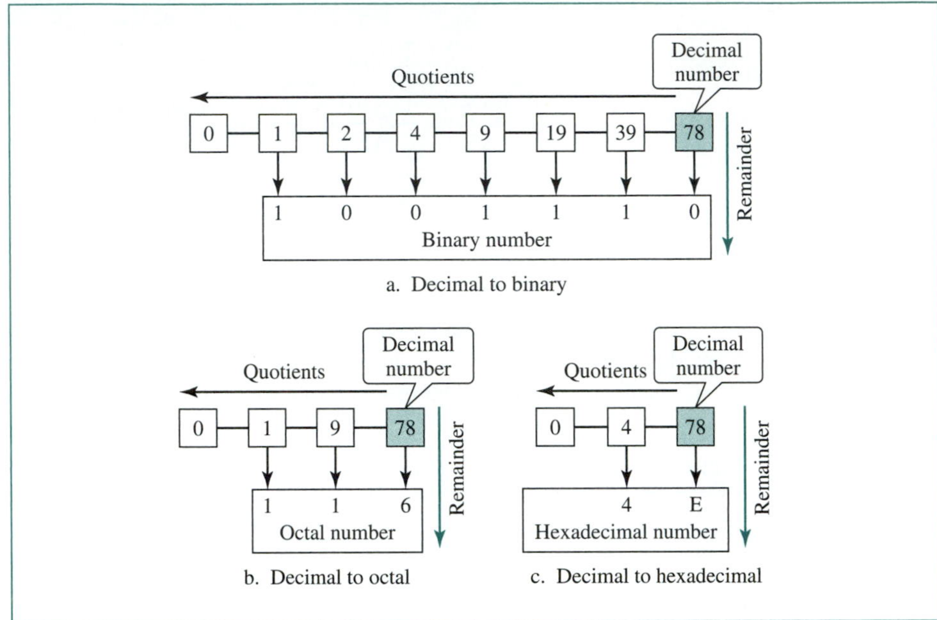

In Figure B.7, we convert the decimal number 78 to its binary equivalent. To check the validity of this method, we convert 1001110 to decimal using the weights of each position.

$$2^6 + 2^3 + 2^2 + 2^1 \rightarrow 64 + 8 + 4 + 2 \rightarrow 78$$

To convert a number from decimal to octal, the procedure is the same but the divisor is 8 instead of 2. To convert from decimal to hexadecimal, the divisor is 16.

From Binary to Octal or Hexadecimal

To change a number from binary to octal, we first group the binary digits from right to left by threes. Then we convert each tribit to its octal equivalent and write the result under the tribit. These equivalents, taken in order (not added), are the octal equivalent of the original number. In Figure B.8, we convert binary 1001110.

To change a number from binary to hexadecimal, we follow the same procedure but group the digits from right to left by fours. This time we convert each quadbit to its hexadecimal equivalent (use Table B.5). In Figure B.8, we convert binary 1001110 to hexadecimal.

Figure B.8 *Transformation from binary to octal or hexadecimal*

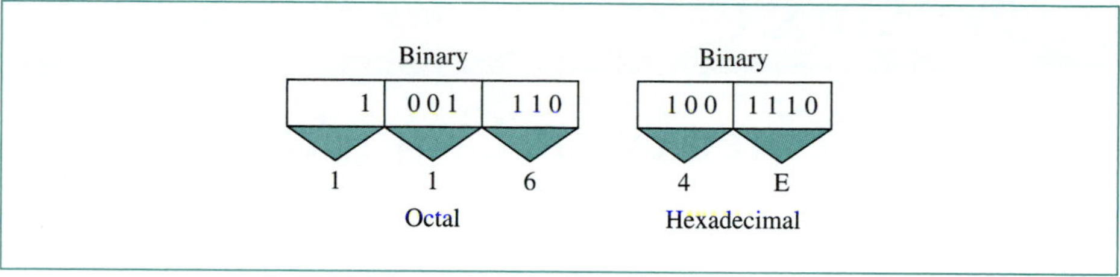

From Octal or Hexadecimal to Binary

To convert from octal to binary, we reverse the procedure above. Starting with the least significant digit, we convert each octal digit into its equivalent three binary digits. In Figure B.9, we convert octal 116 to binary.

Figure B.9 *Transformation from octal or hexadecimal to binary*

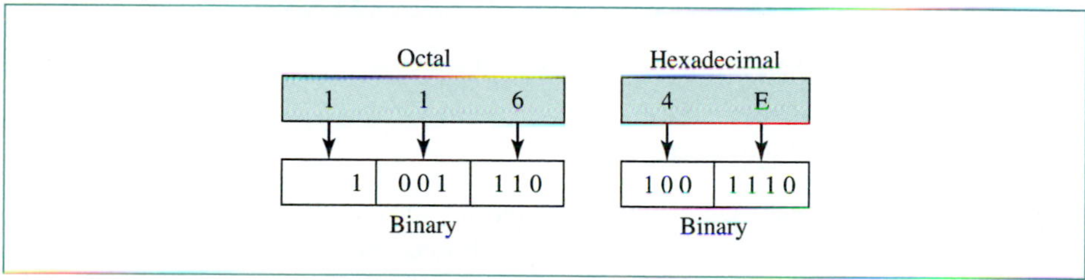

To convert a number from hexadecimal to binary, we convert each hexadecimal digit to its equivalent four binary digits, again starting with the least significant digit. In Figure B.9, we convert hexadecimal 4E to binary.

APPENDIX C

Checksum Calculation

This appendix shows how to calculate a checksum in both binary and hexadecimal notation.

C.1 BINARY NOTATION

To show a binary checksum calculation, we use Figure 11.9 in Chapter 11.

Partial Sum

First we calculate the partial sum as shown in Figure C.1. We add each column and carry to the next columns, if necessary. Note the following points:

- When we add the first (rightmost) column, we get 7. The number 7 in binary is 111. We keep the rightmost 1 and carry the rest to columns 2 and 3.
- When we add the second column, we include the carry from the first column. The result is 8, which is 1000 in binary. We keep the first bit (rightmost) and carry the rest (100) to columns 3, 4, and 5.
- We repeat the above procedure for each column.
- When we finish adding the last column, we have two 1s for which there is no column left for addition. We add these two 1s to the partial sum in the next step.

Sum

If there is no carry from the last column, the partial sum is the sum. However, if there are extra columns (in this example, there is one column with two rows), these are added to the partial sum to obtain the sum. Figure C.2 shows this calculation. Now we have the sum.

Figure C.1 *Partial sum for binary notation*

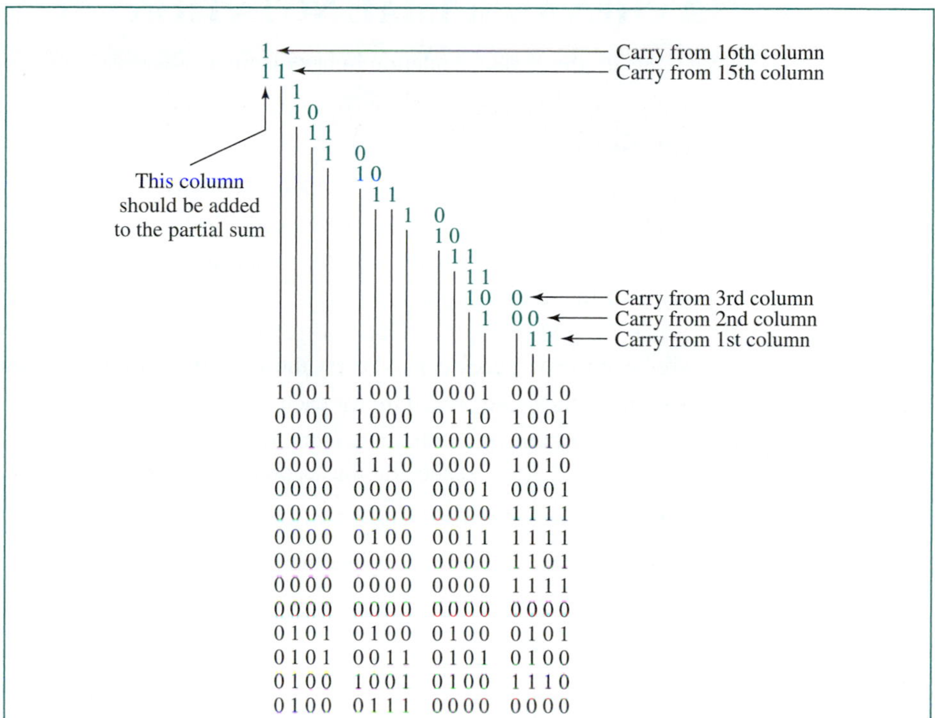

Checksum

After the sum is calculated, we complement each bit to get the checksum. Figure C.2 also shows the checksum.

Figure C.2 *Sum and checksum for binary notation*

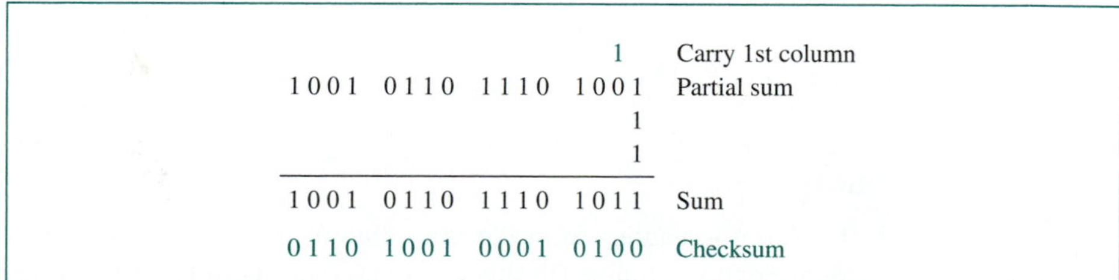

C.2 HEXADECIMAL NOTATION

Now let us do the same calculation in hexadecimal.

Partial Sum

First we calculate the partial sum as shown in Figure C.3. We add each column and carry to the next columns, if necessary. Note the following points:

- We use 10, 11, 12, 13, 14, and 15 instead of A, B, C, D, E, and F when we add hexadecimal digits.
- When we add the first column, we get 105. This number in hexadecimal is 69_{16}. We keep the first digit (9) and carry the second digit (6) to column 2.
- We repeat the same procedure for each column.
- When we add the last column, we get 41. This number in hexadecimal is 29_{16}. We keep the first digit (9) and add the second digit to the partial sum in the next step.

Figure C.3 *Partial sum for hexadecimal notation*

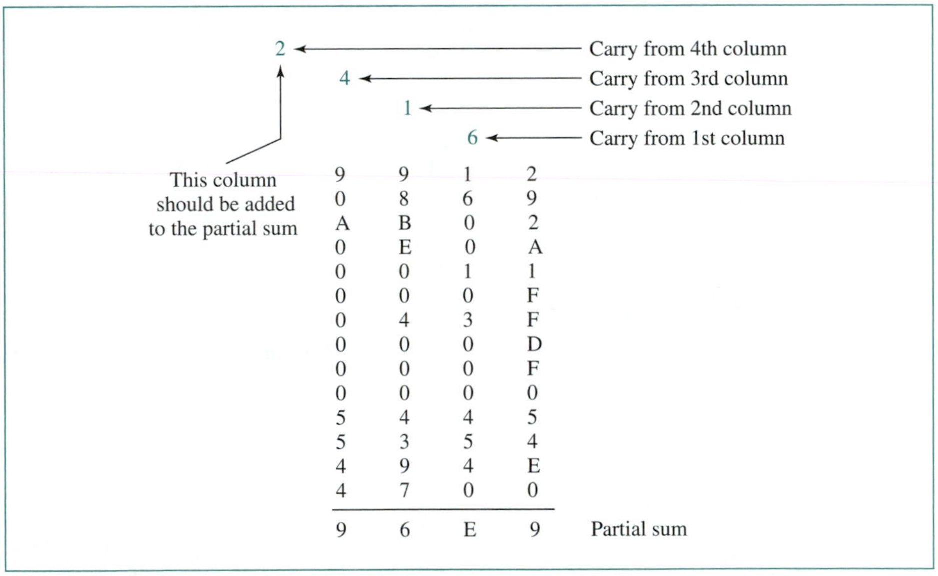

2					Carry from 4th column
	4				Carry from 3rd column
		1			Carry from 2nd column
			6		Carry from 1st column
This column should be added to the partial sum	9	9	1	2	
	0	8	6	9	
	A	B	0	2	
	0	E	0	A	
	0	0	1	1	
	0	0	0	F	
	0	4	3	F	
	0	0	0	D	
	0	0	0	F	
	0	0	0	0	
	5	4	4	5	
	5	3	5	4	
	4	9	4	E	
	4	7	0	0	
	9	6	E	9	Partial sum

Sum

If there are no carries from the last column, the partial sum is the sum. However, if there are extra columns (in this example, there is only one column), these are added to the partial sum to obtain the sum. Figure C.4 shows this calculation. Now we have the sum.

Figure C.4 *Sum and checksum for hexadecimal notation*

9	6	E	9	Partial sum
			2	Carry from last column
9	6	E	B	Sum
6	9	1	4	Checksum
0110	1001	0001	0100	Checksum (binary)

Checksum

After the sum is calculated, we complement each hexadecimal digit to get the checksum. Figure C.4 also shows the checksum. Note that when we calculate the complement, we subtract each digit from 15 to get the complement (one's complement in hexadecimal). The figure also shows how to represent the checksum in binary.

APPENDIX D

Error Detection

Networks must be able to transfer data from one device to another with complete accuracy. A system that cannot guarantee that the data received by one device are identical to the data transmitted by another device is essentially useless. Yet anytime data are transmitted from source to destination, they can become corrupted in passage. In fact, it is more likely that some part of a message will be altered in transit than that the entire contents will arrive intact. Many factors, including line noise, can alter or wipe out one or more bits of a given data unit. Reliable systems must have a mechanism for detecting and correcting such errors.

> Data can be corrupted during transmission. For reliable communication, errors must be detected and corrected.

Error detection and correction are implemented either at the data link layer or the transport layer of the OSI model.

D.1 TYPES OF ERRORS

Whenever an electromagnetic signal flows from one point to another, it is subject to unpredictable interference from heat, magnetism, and other forms of electricity. This interference can change the shape or timing of the signal. If the signal is carrying encoded binary data, such changes can alter the meaning of the data. In a single-bit error, a 0 is changed to a 1 or a 1 to a 0. In a burst error, multiple bits are changed. For example, a 0.01-second burst of impulse noise on a transmission with a data rate of 1200 bps might change all or some of 12 bits of information (see Figure D.1).

Single-Bit Error

The term *single-bit error* means that only 1 bit of a given data unit (such as a byte, character, data unit, or packet) is changed from 1 to 0 or from 0 to 1.

Figure D.1 *Types of errors*

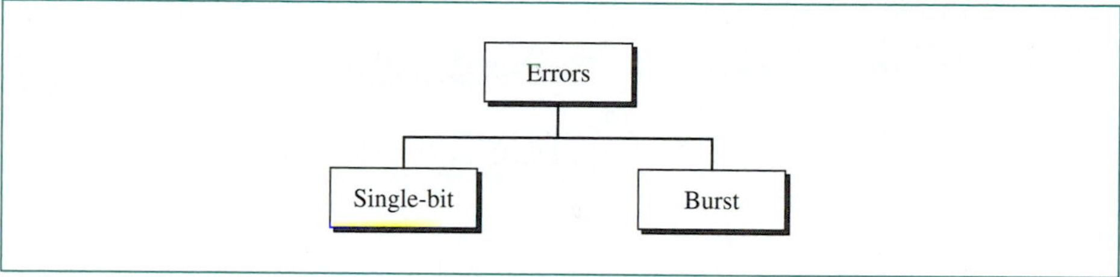

> In a single-bit error, only 1 bit in the data unit has changed.

Figure D.2 shows the effect of a single-bit error on a data unit. To understand the impact of the change, imagine that each group of 8 bits is an ASCII character with a 0 bit added to the left. In the figure, 00000010 (ASCII *STX*) was sent, meaning *start of text,* but 00001010 (ASCII *LF*) was received, meaning *line feed.* (For more information about ASCII code, see Appendix A.)

Figure D.2 *Single-bit error*

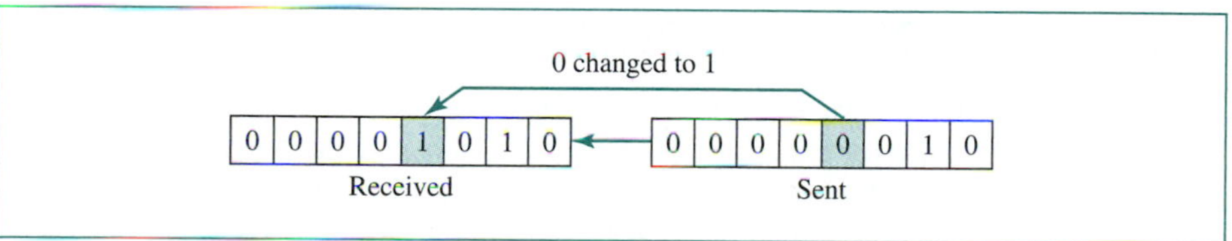

Single-bit errors are the least likely type of error in serial data transmission. To see why, imagine a sender sends data at 1 Mbps. This means that each bit lasts only 1/1,000,000 second, or 1 μs. For a single-bit error to occur, the noise must have a duration of only 1 μs, which is very rare; noise normally lasts much longer than this.

However, a single-bit error can happen if we are sending data using parallel transmission. For example, if eight wires are used to send all of the 8 bits of a byte at the same time and one of the wires is noisy, 1 bit can be corrupted in each byte. Think of parallel transmission inside a computer, between CPU and memory, for example.

Burst Error

The term *burst error* means that two or more bits in the data unit have changed from 1 to 0 or from 0 to 1.

> A burst error means that two or more bits in the data unit have changed.

Figure D.3 shows the effect of a burst error on a data unit. In this case, 0100010001000011 was sent, but 0101110101000011 was received. Note that a burst error does not necessarily mean that the errors occur in consecutive bits. The length of the burst is measured from the first corrupted bit to the last corrupted bit. Some bits in between may not have been corrupted.

Figure D.3 *Burst error of length five*

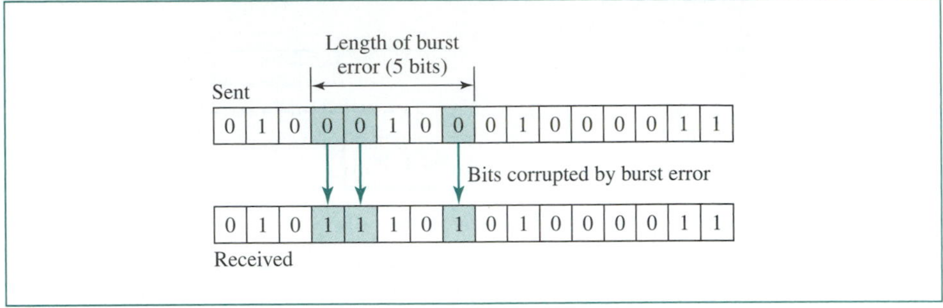

Burst error is most likely to happen in a serial transmission. The duration of noise is normally longer than the duration of a bit, which means that when noise affects data, it affects a set of bits. The number of bits affected depends on the data rate and duration of noise. For example, if we are sending data at 1 Kbps, a noise of 1/100 seconds can affect 10 bits; if we are sending data at 1 Mbps, the same noise can affect 10,000 bits.

D.2 DETECTION

Even if we know what types of errors can occur, will we recognize one when we see it? If we have a copy of the intended transmission for comparison, of course we will. But what if we don't have a copy of the original? Then we will have no way of knowing we have received an error until we have decoded the transmission and failed to make sense of it. For a machine to check for errors this way would be slow, costly, and of questionable value. We don't need a system where computers decode whatever comes in, then sit around trying to decide if the sender really meant to use the word *glbrshnif* in the middle of an array of weather statistics. What we need is a mechanism that is simple and completely objective.

Redundancy

One *error detection* mechanism that would satisfy these requirements would be to send every data unit twice. The receiving device would then be able to do a bit-for-bit comparison between the two versions of the data. Any discrepancy would indicate an error, and an appropriate correction mechanism could be set in place. This system would be completely accurate (the odds of errors being introduced onto exactly the same bits in both sets of data are infinitesimally small), but it would also be insupportably slow. Not only would the transmission time double, but the time it takes to compare every unit bit by bit must be added.

The concept of including extra information in the transmission solely for the purposes of comparison is a good one. But instead of repeating the entire data stream, a shorter group of bits may be appended to the end of each unit. This technique is called *redundancy* because the extra bits are redundant to the information; they are discarded as soon as the accuracy of the transmission has been determined.

> Error detection uses the concept of redundancy, which means adding extra bits for detecting errors at the destination.

Figure D.4 shows the process of using redundant bits to check the accuracy of a data unit. Once the data stream has been generated, it passes through a device that analyzes it and adds on an appropriately coded redundancy check. The data unit, now enlarged by several bits (in this illustration, seven), travels over the link to the receiver. The receiver puts the entire stream through a checking function. If the received bit stream passes the checking criteria, the data portion of the data unit is accepted and the redundant bits are discarded.

Figure D.4 *Redundancy*

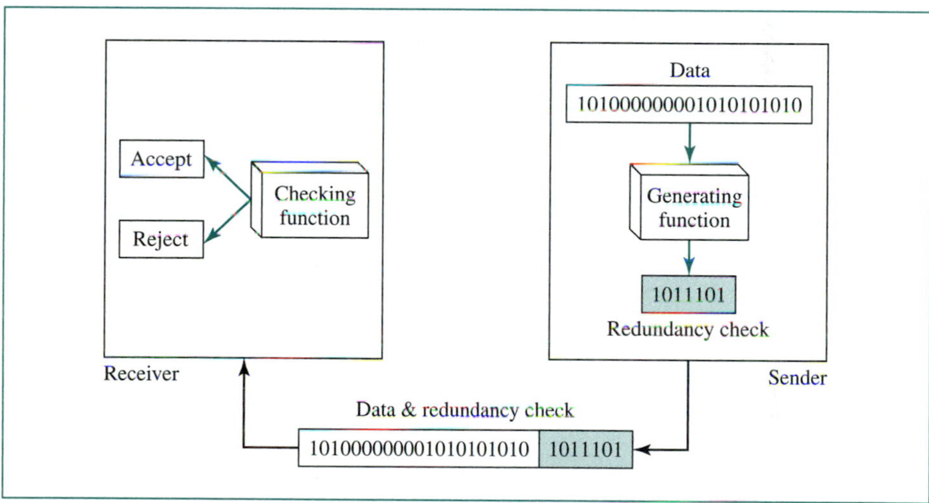

Four types of redundancy checks are used in data communications: vertical redundancy check (VRC) (also called parity check), longitudinal redundancy check (LRC), cyclical redundancy check (CRC), and checksum. The first three, VRC, LRC, and CRC, are normally implemented in the physical layer for use in the data link layer. The fourth, checksum, is used primarily by upper layers (see Figure D.5).

Figure D.5 *Detection methods*

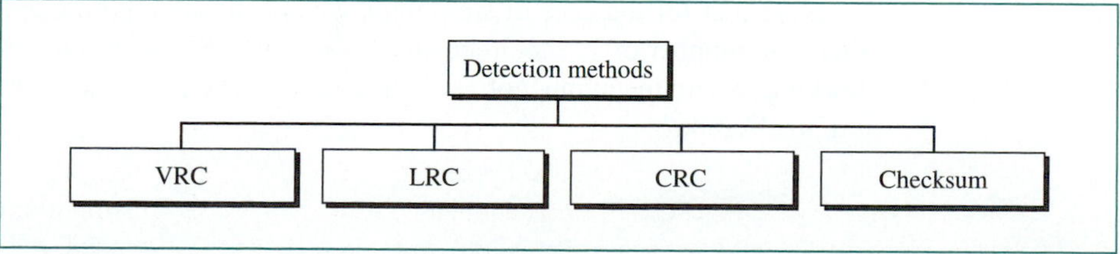

D.3 VERTICAL REDUNDANCY CHECK (VRC)

The most common and least expensive mechanism for error detection is the **vertical redundancy check (VRC),** often called a **parity check.** In this technique, a redundant bit, called a **parity bit,** is appended to every data unit so that the total number of 1s in the unit (including the parity bit) becomes even.

Suppose we want to transmit the binary data unit 1100001 [ASCII *a* (97)]; see Figure D.6. Adding together the number of 1s gives us 3, an odd number. Before transmitting, we pass the data unit through a parity generator. The parity generator counts the 1s and appends the parity bit (a 1 in this case) to the end. The total number of 1s is now four, an even number. The system now transmits the entire expanded unit across the network link. When it reaches its destination, the receiver puts all eight bits through an **even-parity** checking function. If the receiver sees 11100001, it counts four 1s, an even number, and the data unit passes. But what if the data unit has been damaged in transit? What if, instead of 11100001, the receiver sees 11100101? Then, when the parity checker counts the 1s, it gets 5, an odd number. The receiver knows that an error has been introduced into the data somewhere and therefore rejects the whole unit.

Figure D.6 *Even parity VRC concept*

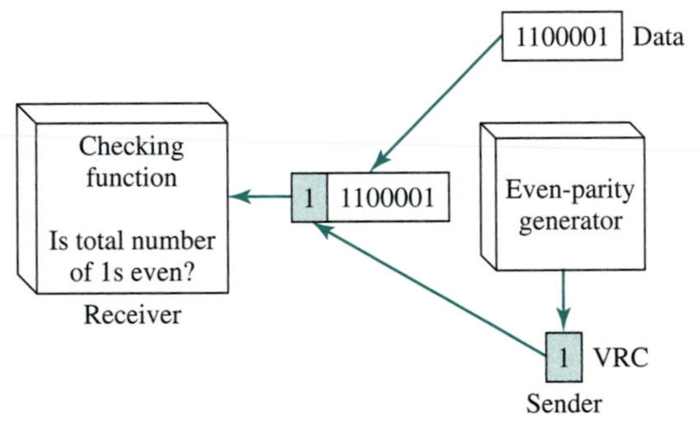

> In vertical redundancy check (VRC), a parity bit is added to every data unit so that the total number of 1s becomes even.

Note that for the sake of simplicity, we are discussing here even-parity checking, where the number of 1s should be an even number. Some systems may use **odd-parity** checking, where the number of 1s should be odd. The principle is the same; the calculation is different.

D.4 LONGITUDINAL REDUNDANCY CHECK (LRC)

In **longitudinal redundancy check (LRC),** a block of bits is organized in a table (rows and columns). For example, instead of sending a block of 32 bits, we organize them in a table made of four rows and eight columns, as shown in Figure D.7. We then calculate the parity bit for each column and create a new row of 8 bits, which are the parity bits for the whole block. Note that the first parity bit in the fifth row is calculated based on all first bits. The second parity bit is calculated based on all second bits, and so on. We then attach the 8 parity bits to the original data and send them to the receiver.

In longitudinal redundancy check (LRC), a block of bits is divided into rows and a redundant row of bits is added to the whole block.

Figure D.7 *LRC*

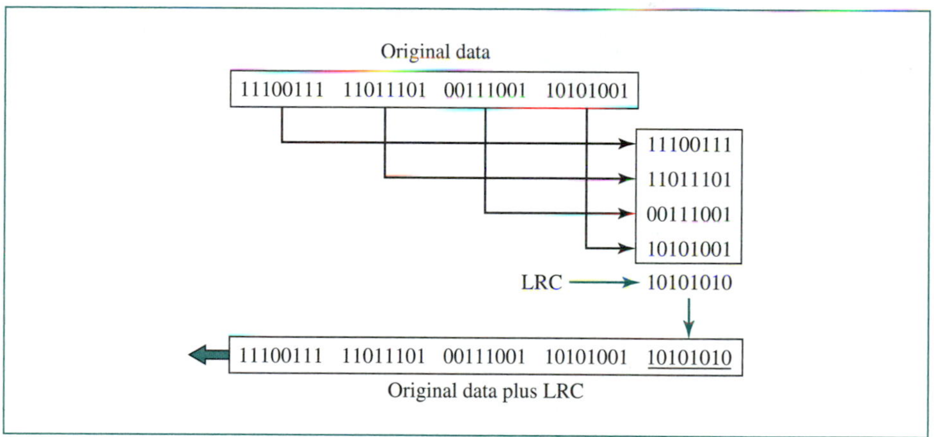

Performance

LRC increases the likelihood of detecting burst errors. As we showed in the previous example, an LRC of n bits can easily detect a burst error of n bits. A burst error of more than n bits is also detected by LRC with a very high probability. There is, however, one pattern of errors that remains elusive. If 2 bits in one data unit are damaged and 2 bits *in exactly the same positions* in another data unit are also damaged, the LRC checker will not detect an error.

D.5 CYCLIC REDUNDANCY CHECK (CRC)

The third and most powerful of the redundancy checking techniques is the **cyclic redundancy check (CRC).** Unlike VRC and LRC, which are based on addition, CRC is based on binary division. In CRC, instead of adding bits together to achieve a desired parity, a sequence of redundant bits, called the CRC or the CRC remainder, is appended to the end of a data unit so that the resulting data unit becomes exactly divisible by a second, predetermined binary number. At its destination, the incoming data unit is divided by the same number. If at this step there is no remainder, the data unit is assumed to be intact and is therefore accepted. A remainder indicates that the data unit has been damaged in transit and therefore must be rejected.

The redundancy bits used by CRC are derived by dividing the data unit by a predetermined divisor; the remainder is the CRC. To be valid, a CRC must have two qualities: it must have exactly one less bit than the divisor, and appending it to the end of the data string must make the resulting bit sequence exactly divisible by the divisor.

Both the theory and the application of CRC error detection are straightforward. The only complexity is in deriving the CRC. In order to clarify this process, we will start with an overview and add complexity as we go. Figure D.8 provides an outline of the three basic steps.

Figure D.8 *CRC generator and checker*

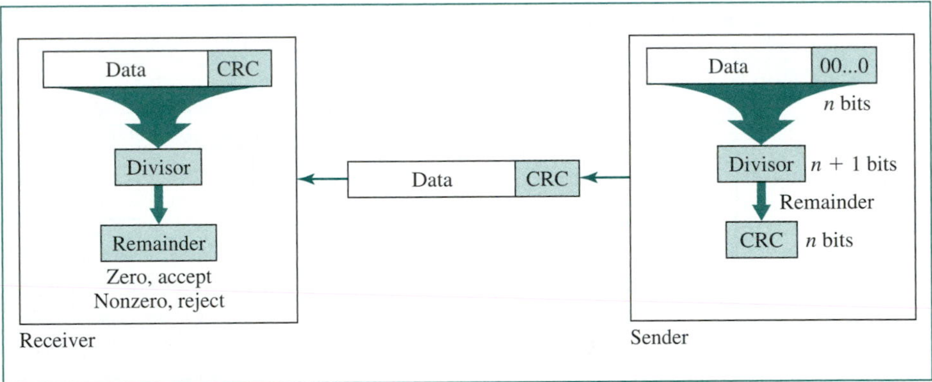

First, a string of n 0s is appended to the data unit. The number n is one less than the number of bits in the predetermined divisor, which is $n + 1$ bits.

Second, the newly elongated data unit is divided by the divisor using a process called binary division. The remainder resulting from this division is the CRC.

Third, the CRC of n bits derived in step 2 replaces the appended 0s at the end of the data unit. Note that the CRC may consist of all 0s.

The data unit arrives at the receiver data first, followed by the CRC. The receiver treats the whole string as a unit and divides it by the same divisor that was used to find the CRC remainder.

If the string arrives without error, the CRC checker yields a remainder of zero and the data unit passes. If the string has been changed in transit, the division yields a nonzero remainder and the data unit does not pass.

The CRC Generator

A CRC generator uses modulo-2 division. Figure D.9 shows this process. In the first step, the 4-bit divisor is subtracted from the first 4 bits of the dividend. Each bit of the

Figure D.9 *Binary division in a CRC generator*

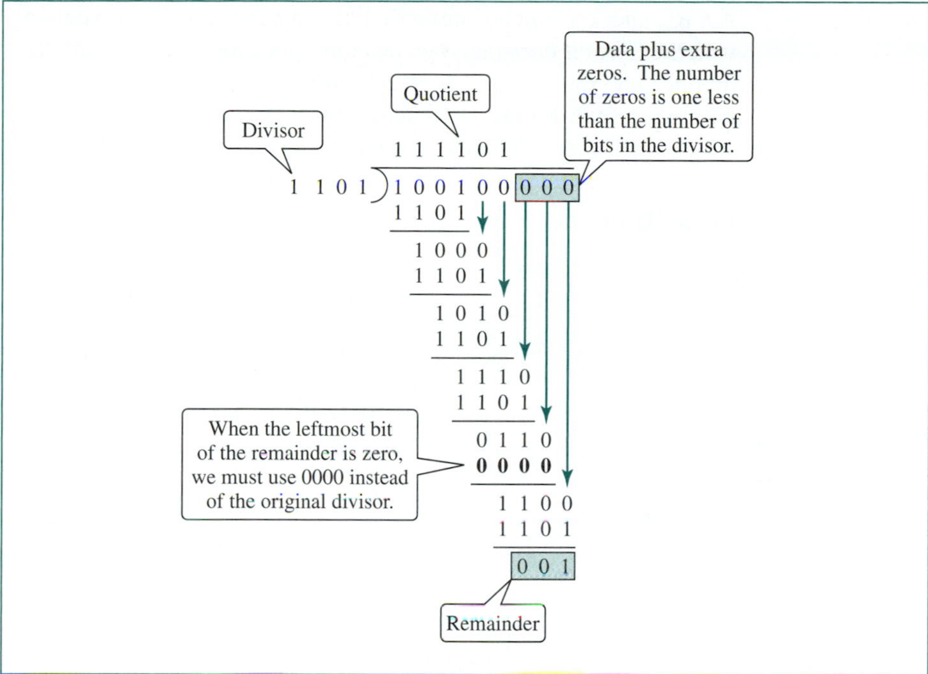

divisor is subtracted from the corresponding bit of the dividend without disturbing the next higher bit. In our example, the divisor, 1101, is subtracted from the first 4 bits of the dividend, 1001, yielding 100 (the leading 0 of the remainder is dropped off). The next unused bit from the dividend is then pulled down to make the number of bits in the remainder equal to the number of bits in the divisor. The next step, therefore, is 1000 – 1101, which yields 101, and so on.

In this process, the divisor always begins with a 1; the divisor is subtracted from a portion of the previous dividend/remainder that is equal to it in length; the divisor can only be subtracted from a dividend/remainder whose leftmost bit is 1. Anytime the leftmost bit of the dividend/remainder is 0, a string of 0s, of the same length as the divisor, replaces the divisor in that step of the process. For example, if the divisor is 4 bits long, it is replaced by four 0s. (Remember, we are dealing with bit patterns, not with quantitative values; 0000 is not the same as 0.) This restriction means that, at any step, the leftmost subtraction will be either 0 – 0 or 1 – 1, both of which equal 0. So, after subtraction, the leftmost bit of the remainder will always be a leading zero, which is dropped off, and the next unused bit of the dividend is pulled down to fill out the remainder. Note that only the first bit of the remainder is dropped—if the second bit is also 0, it is retained, and the dividend/remainder for the next step will begin with 0. This process repeats until the entire dividend has been used.

The CRC Checker

A CRC checker functions exactly like the generator. After receiving the data appended with the CRC, it does the same modulo-2 division. If the remainder is all 0s, the CRC is dropped and the data accepted; otherwise, the received stream of bits is discarded and data are resent. Figure D.10 shows the same process of division in the receiver. We assume that there is no error. The remainder is therefore all 0s and the data are accepted.

Figure D.10 *Binary division in CRC checker*

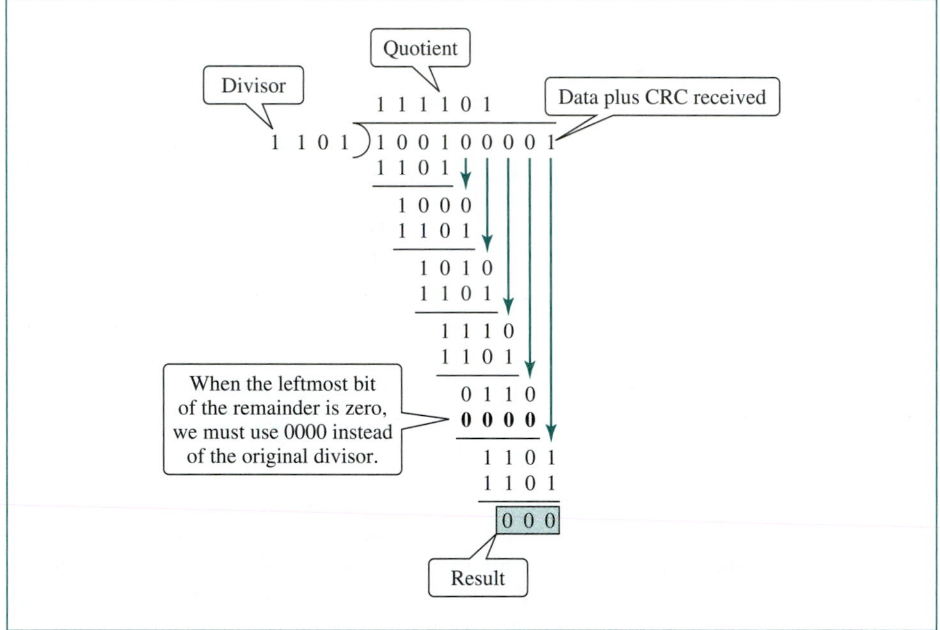

Polynomials

The CRC generator (the divisor) is most often represented not as a string of 1s and 0s, but as an algebraic polynomial (see Figure D.11). The polynomial format is useful for two reasons: It is short, and it can be used to prove the concept mathematically (which is beyond the scope of this book).

Figure D.11 *A polynomial*

$$x^7 + x^6 + x^4 + x^3 + x + 1$$

The relationship of a polynomial to its corresponding binary representation is shown in Figure D.12.

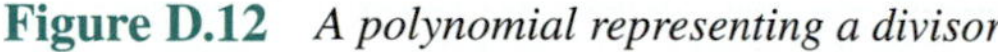

Figure D.12 *A polynomial representing a divisor*

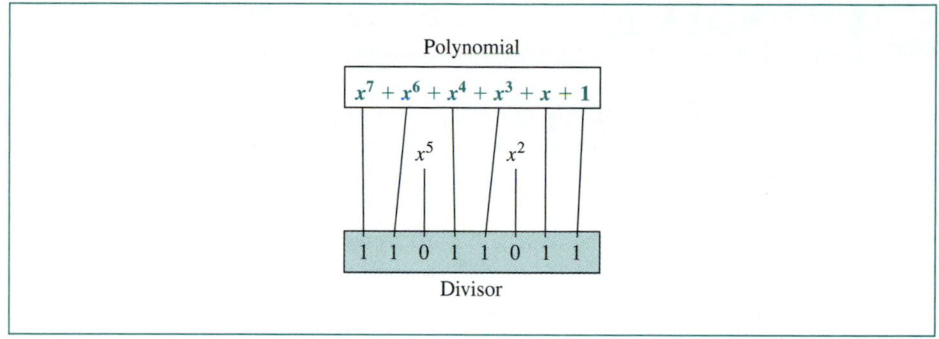

A polynomial should be selected to have at least the following properties:

- It should not be divisible by x.
- It should be divisible by $(x + 1)$.

The first condition guarantees that all burst errors of a length equal to the degree of the polynomial are detected. The second condition guarantees that all burst errors affecting an odd number of bits are detected (the proof is beyond the scope of this book).

The standard polynomials used by popular protocols for CRC generation are shown in Figure D.13. The numbers 12, 16, and 32 refer to the size of the CRC remainder. The CRC divisors are 13, 17, and 33 bits, respectively.

Figure D.13 *Standard polynomials*

CRC-12: $x^{12} + x^{11} + x^3 + x^2 + x + 1$

CRC-16: $x^{16} + x^{15} + x^2 + 1$

CRC-ITU-T: $x^{16} + x^{12} + x^5 + 1$

CRC-32: $x^{32} + x^{26} + x^{23} + x^{22} + x^{16} + x^{12} + x^{11} + x^{10} + x^8 + x^7 + x^5 + x^4 + x^2 + x + 1$

D.6 CHECKSUM

The error detection method used by the higher-layer protocols is called *checksum*. Like VRC, LRC, and CRC, checksum is based on the concept of redundancy. We discussed checksum in Chapter 8 and Appendix C.

APPENDIX E

Encryption Methods

E.1 SECRET-KEY METHODS

We discussed the principles of secret-key (symmetric) encryption in Chapter 29. Secret-key encryption methods have been in use for more than two millennia. Today, a method called data encryption standard (DES) is prevalent.

DES

Data encryption standard (DES) encrypts and decrypts at the bit-level. The data are first transformed into a string of bits. The string is broken into segments of 64 bits; if the last segment is less than 64 bits, 0s are added to make up the difference. Each section is then encrypted using a 56-bit key (the key is actually 64 bits long, with the extra 8 bits for error control). Figure E.1 shows the general layout of this method.

Figure E.1 *DES*

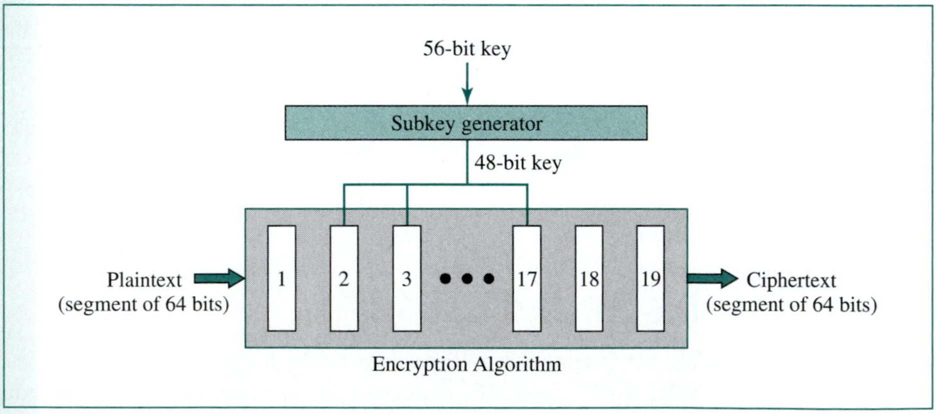

56-bit key
Subkey generator
48-bit key
Plaintext (segment of 64 bits)
1 2 3 • • • 17 18 19
Ciphertext (segment of 64 bits)
Encryption Algorithm

The whole idea is to scramble the data and the key in such a way that every bit of ciphertext is a function of every bit of the plaintext and the key.

The encryption algorithm consists of 19 stages. The first, 18th, and 19th stages are just simple scrambling operations and do not involve the key. Stages 2 to 17 use identical methods. The rightmost 32 bits of the stage become the leftmost 32 bits of the next stage. The leftmost 32 bits of the stage are scrambled with the key and become the rightmost 32 bits of the next stage.

E.2 PUBLIC KEY METHODS

We discussed the principles of public key (asymmetric) encryption in Chapter 29. Public-key encryption methods are relatively new. Several methods have been used during the last few decades, but the one in use today is based on the RSA algorithm.

RSA

The most common public key algorithm is called RSA after its inventors (Rivest, Shamir, and Adleman). The private key here is a pair of numbers (N, d); the public key is also a pair of numbers (N, e). Note that N is common to the private and public keys.

The sender uses the following algorithm to encrypt the message:

$$C = P^e \bmod N$$

In this algorithm, P is the plaintext, which is represented as a number. C is the number that represents the ciphertext. The two numbers e and N are components of the public key. P is raised to the power e and divided by N. The mod term indicates that the remainder is sent as the ciphertext.

The receiver uses the following algorithm to decrypt the message:

$$P = C^d \bmod N$$

In this algorithm, P and C are the same as before. The two numbers d and N are components of the private key. Figure E.2 shows an example.

Figure E.2 *RSA*

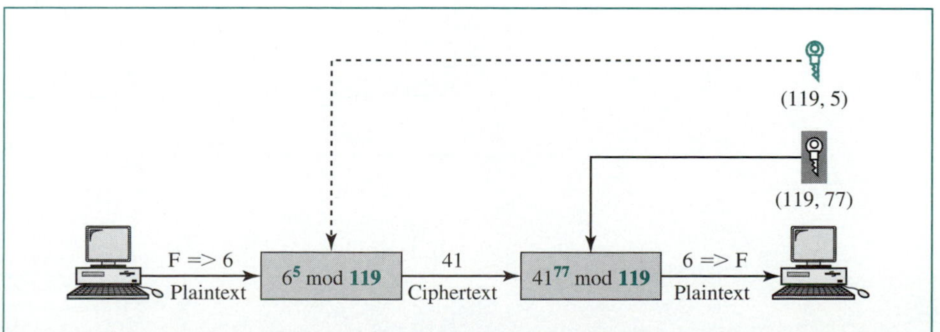

Imagine the private key is the pair (119, 77) and the public key is the pair (119, 5). The sender needs to send the character F. This character can be represented as number 6 (F is the 6th character in the alphabet). The encryption algorithm calculates $C = 6^5$ mod 119 = 41. This number is sent to the receiver as the ciphertext. The receiver uses the decryption algorithm to calculate $P = 41^{77}$ mod 119 = 6 (the original number). The number 6 is then interpreted as F.

The reader may question the effectiveness of this algorithm. If an intruder knows the decryption algorithm and $N = 119$, the only thing missing is $d = 77$. Why couldn't the intruder use trial and error to find d? The answer is yes, that in this trivial example, an intruder could easily guess the value of d. But a major concept of the RSA algorithm is to use very large numbers for d and e. In practice, the numbers are so large (on the scale of tens of digits) that the trial and error approach of breaking the code takes a long time (years, if not months) even with the fastest computers available today.

Choosing Public and Private Keys

One question that comes to mind is how to choose the three numbers N, d, and e for encryption and decryption to work. The inventors of the RSA algorithm mathematically proved that using the following procedure will guarantee that the algorithms will work. Although the proof is beyond the scope of this book, we outline the procedure:

1. Choose two large prime numbers, p and q.
2. Compute $N = p \times \text{q}$.
3. Choose e (less than N) such that e and $(p - 1)(q - 1)$ are relatively prime (having no common factor other than 1).
4. Choose d such that $(e \times d)$ mod $((p - 1)(q - 1))$ is equal to 1.

APPENDIX F

Project 802

In 1985, the Computer Society of the IEEE started Project 802, a drive to set standards to enable intercommunication between equipment from a variety of manufacturers. Project 802 does not seek to replace any part of the OSI model. Instead, it is a way of specifying functions of the physical layer, the data link layer, and to a lesser extent the network layer to support interconnectivity of major LAN protocols.

> In 1985, the Computer Society of IEEE developed Project 802. It covers the first two layers and part of the third level of the OSI model.

The relationship of Project 802 to the OSI model is shown in Figure F.1. The IEEE has subdivided the data link layer into two sublayers: logical link control (LLC) and media access control (MAC).

Figure F.1 *LAN compared with the OSI model*

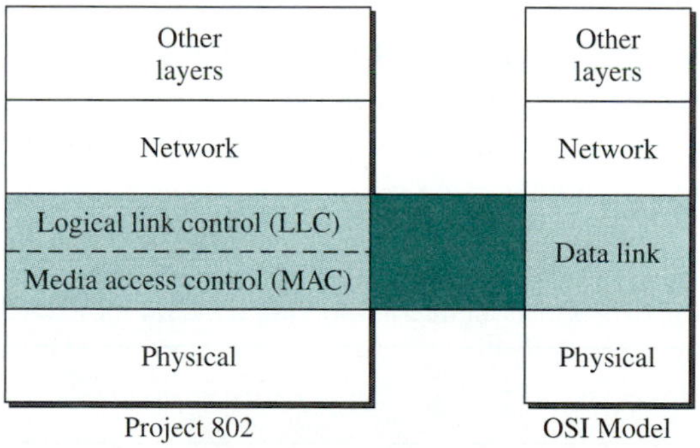

The LLC is nonarchitecture-specific; that is it is the same for all IEEE-defined LANs. The MAC sublayer, on the other hand, contains a number of distinct modules; each carries proprietary information specific to the LAN product being used.

Project 802 has split the data link layer into two different sublayers: logical link control (LLC) and media access control (MAC).

The strength of Project 802 is modularity. By subdividing the functions necessary for LAN management, the designers were able to standardize those that can be generalized and isolate those that must remain specific. Each subdivision is identified by a number: 802.1 (internetworking); 802.2 (LLC); and the MAC modules 802.3 (CSMA/CD), 802.4 (Token Bus), 802.5 (Token Ring), and others (see Figure F.2).

Figure F.2 *Project 802*

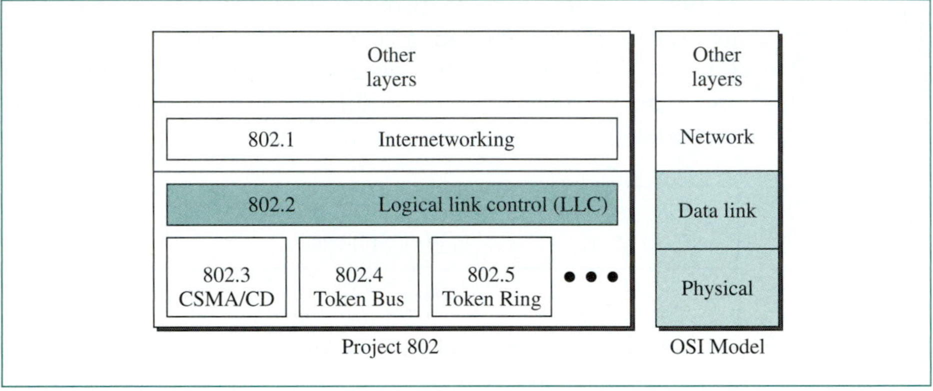

F.1 PROJECT 802.1

802.1 is the section of Project 802 devoted to internetworking issues in LANs and MANs. It seeks to resolve the incompatibilities between network architectures without requiring modifications in existing addressing, access, and error-recovery mechanisms, among others.

IEEE 802.1 is an internetworking standard for LANs.

F.2 PROJECT 802.2

802.2 is the section of Project 802 related to the physical and data link layers. It divides the data link layer into two sublayers: LLC and MAC.

LLC

In general, the IEEE Project 802 model takes the structure of an HDLC frame and divides it into two sets of functions. One set contains the end-user portions of the frame: the logical addresses, control information, and data. These functions are handled by the IEEE 802.2 LLC protocol. LLC is considered the upper layer of the IEEE 802 data link layer and is common to all LAN protocols.

> IEEE 802.2 logical link control (LLC) is the upper sublayer of the data link layer.

PDU

The data unit at the LLC level is the protocol data unit. The PDU contains four fields familiar from HDLC: a destination service access point (DSAP), a source service access point (SSAP), a control field, and an information field (see Figure F.3).

Figure F.3 *PDU format*

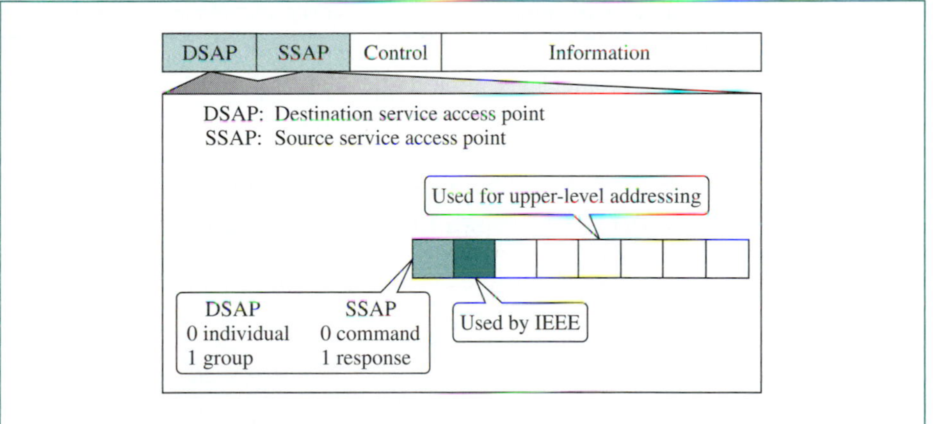

- **DSAP and SSAP.** The DSAP and SSAP are addresses used by the LLC to identify the protocol stacks on the receiving and sending machines that are generating and using the data. The first bit of the DSAP indicates whether the frame is intended for an individual or a group. The first bit of the SSAP indicates whether the communication is a command or response PDU (see Figure F.3).
- **Control.** The control field of the PDU is identical to the control field in HDLC. As in HDLC, PDU frames can be I-frames, S-frames, or U-frames and carry all of the codes and information that the corresponding HDLC frames carry (see Figure F.4).

MAC

The second set of functions, the media access control sublayer, resolves the contention for the shared media. It contains the synchronization, flag, flow, and error control specifications necessary to move information from one place to another, as well as the

Figure F.4 *Control fields in a PDU*

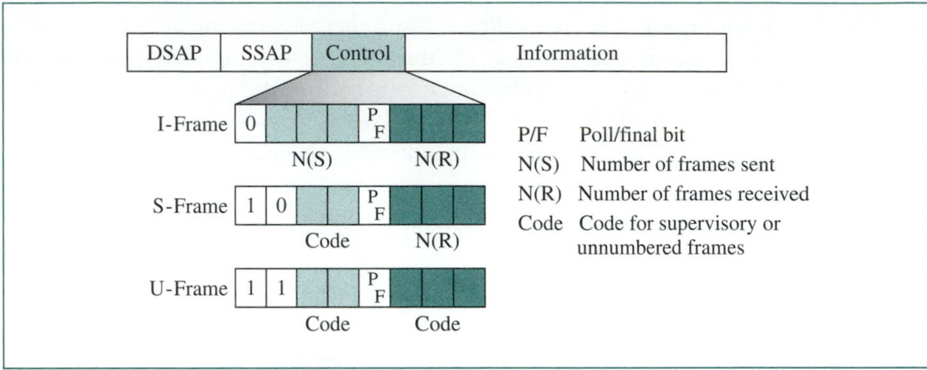

physical address of the next station to receive and route a packet. MAC protocols are specific to the LAN using them (Ethernet, Token Ring, and Token Bus, etc.).

> Media access control (MAC) is the lower sublayer of the data link layer.

In the MAC layer, Project 802 is itself divided into several projects to answer the de facto standards used by the industry. Two of them are related to the LANs we discussed in Chapter 3.

- Project 802.3 defines a LAN using a CSMA/CD access method similar to Ethernet.
- Project 802.5 defines a LAN with Token Ring access method.

APPENDIX G

Contact Addresses

The following is a list of contact addresses for various organizations mentioned in the text.

- **ATM Forum**
  Presidio of San Francisco
  P.O. Box 29920 (mail)
  572B Ruger Street (surface)
  San Francisco, CA 94129-0920
  Telephone: 415 561-6275
  Email: info@atmforum.com
  http://www.atmforum.com
- **Federal Communications Commission (FCC)**
  445 12th Street S.W.
  Washington, DC 20554
  Telephone: 1-888-225-5322
  Email: fccinfo@fcc.gov
  http://www.fcc.gov
- **Institute of Electrical and Electronics Engineers (IEEE)**
  Operations Center
  445 Hoes Lane
  Piscataway, NJ 08855-1331
  Telephone: 732 981-0060
  http://www.ieee.gov

- **International Organization for Standardization (ISO)**
  1, rue de Varembe
  Case postale 56
  CH-1211 Geneve 20
  Switzerland
  Telephone: 41 22 749 0111
  Email: central@iso.ch
  http://www.iso.org
- **International Telecommunication Union (ITU)**
  Place des Nations
  CH-1211 Geneva 20
  Switzerland
  Telephone: 41 22 730 5852
  Email: tsbmail@itu.int
  http://www.itu.int/ITU-T
- **Internet Architecture Board (IAB)**
  Email: IAB@isi.edu
  http://www.iab.org
- **Internet Corporation for Assigned Names and Numbers (ICANN)**
  4676 Admiralty Way, Suite 330
  Marina del Rey, CA 90292-6601
  Telephone: 310 823-9358
  Email: icann@icann.org
  http://www.icann.org
- **Internet Engineering Steering Group (IESG)**
  Email: iesg@ietf.org
  http://www.ietf.org/iesg.html
- **Internet Engineering Task Force (IETF)**
  Email: ietf-infor@ietf.org
  http://www.ietf.org
- **Internet Research Task Force (IRTF)**
  Email: irtf-chair@ietf.org
  http://www.irtf.org
- **Internet Society (ISOC)**
  775 Weihle Avenue, Suite 102
  Reston, VA 20190-5108
  Telephone: 703 326-9880
  Email: info@isoc.org
  http://www.isoc.org

APPENDIX H

RFCs

There are approximately 2500 RFCs. In Table H.1, we list alphabetically, by protocol, those that are directly related to the material in this text. The main RFCs for each protocol are in boldface. For a complete listing, go to http://www.faqs.org/rfcs.

Table H.1 *RFCs for each protocol*

Protocol	*RFC*
ARP and RARP	**826, 903,** 925, 1027, 1293, 1329, 1433
BGP	1092, 1105, 1163, 1265, 1266, 1267, 1364, 1392, 1403, 1565, 1654, 1655, 1665, 1745, 1997, 2238, 2439
BOOTP and DHCP	**951,** 1048, 1084, 1395, 1497, 1531, 1532, 1533, 1534, 1541, 1542, 2131, 2132
DHCP	See BOOTP and DHCP
DNS	799, 811, 819, 830, 881, 882, 883, 897, 920, 921, **1034, 1035,** 1386, 1480, 1535, 1536, 1537, 1591, 1637, 1664, 1706, 1712, 1713, 1995, 2317
FTP	114, 133, 141, 163, 171, 172, 238, 242, 250, 256, 264, 269, 281, 291, 354, 385, 412, 414, 418, 430, 438, 448, 463, 468, 478, 486, 505, 506, 542, 553, 624, 630, 640, 691, 765, 913, **959,** 1635, 2460, 2577
HTML	1866
HTTP	**2068,** 2109
ICMP	777, **792,** 1016, 1018, 1256, 1788, 1885, 2521
IGMP	988, 1054, 1112, 2236
IP	760, 781, **791,** 815, 950, 919, 922, 1025, 1063, 1141, 1190, 1191, 1624, 2113
IPv6	1365, 1550, 1678, 1680, 1682, 1683, 1686, 1688, 1726, 1752, 1826, 1883, 1884, 2133, 2147, 2492, 2553, 2590, 2675

Table H.1 *RFCs for each protocol (continued)*

Protocol	*RFC*
MIME	See SNMP, MIME, SMI
OSPF	1131, 1245, 1246, 1247, 1370, 1583, 1584, 1585, 1586, 1587, 2178, 2328, 2329, 2370
PIM	2362
PPP	1134, 1171, 1172, 1331, 1332, 1547, 1570, 1663
RARP	See ARP and RARP
RIP	1131, 1245, 1246, 1247, 1370, 1583, 1584, 1585, 1586, 1587, 1722, 1723, 2082, 2453
SMI	See SNMP, MIB, SMI
SMTP, MIME, POP	196, 221, 224, 278, 524, 539, 753, 772, 780, 806, **821,** 934, 974, 1047, 1081, 1082, 1225, 1460, 1496, 1426, 1427, 1652, 1653, 1711, 1725, 1734, 1740, 1741, 1767, 1869, **1870,** 2045, 2449, 2487, 2554, 2633, 2683
SNMP, MIB, SMI	1065, 1067, 1098, 1155, **1157, 1212, 1213,** 1229, 1231, 1243, 1284, 1351, 1352, 1354, 1389, 1398, 1414, 1441, 1442, 1443, 1444, 1445, 1446, 1447, 1448, 1449, 1450, 1451, 1452, 1461, 1472, 1474, 1537, 1623, 1643, 1650, 1657, 1665, 1666, 1696, 1697, 1724, 1742, 1743, 1748, 1749, 1905, 1906, 2001, 2037, 2320, 2593, 2581, 2582, 2579, 2677
TCP	675, 721, 761, **793,** 879, 896, 1078, 1106, 1110, 1144, 1145, 1146, 1263, 1323, 1337, 1379, 1644
TELNET	137, 340, 393, 426, 435, 452, 466, 495, 513, 529, 562, 595, 596, 599, 669, 679, 701, 702, 703, 728, 764, 782, 818, **854, 855,** 1184, 1205, 1411, 1412
TFTP	**1350,** 1782, 1783, 1784, 1785
UDP	768
WWW	1614, 1630, 1737, 1738

APPENDIX I

UDP and TCP Ports

Table I.1 lists the common well-known ports ordered by port number.

Table I.1 *Ports by port number*

Port Number	*UDP/TCP*	*Protocol*
7	TCP	ECHO
13	UDP/TCP	DAYTIME
19	UDP/TCP	CHARACTER GENERATOR
20	TCP	FTP-DATA
21	TCP	FTP-CONTROL
23	TCP	TELNET
25	TCP	SMTP
37	UDP/TCP	TIME
67	UDP	BOOTP-SERVER
68	UDP	BOOTP-CLIENT
69	UDP	TFTP
70	TCP	GOPHER
79	TCP	FINGER
80	TCP	HTTP
109	TCP	POP-2
110	TCP	POP-3
111	UDP/TCP	RPC
161	UDP	SNMP
162	UDP	SNMP-TRAP
179	TCP	BGP
520	UDP	RIP

Table I.2 lists the ports ordered alphabetically by protocol.

Table I.2 *Port numbers by protocol*

Protocol	*UDP/TCP*	*Port Number*
BGP	TCP	179
BOOTP-SERVER	UDP	67
BOOTP-CLIENT	UDP	68
CHARACTER GENERATOR	UDP/TCP	19
DAYTIME	UDP/TCP	13
ECHO	TCP	7
FINGER	TCP	79
FTP-CONTROL	TCP	21
FTP-DATA	TCP	20
GOPHER	TCP	70
HTTP	TCP	80
POP-2	TCP	109
POP-3	TCP	110
RIP	UDP	520
RPC	UDP/TCP	111
SMTP	TCP	25
SNMP	UDP	161
SNMP-TRAP	UDP	162
TELNET	TCP	23
TFTP	UDP	69
TIME	UDP/TCP	37

Glossary

1000BASE-CX A two-wire implementation of Gigabit Ethernet using shielded twisted pair cables.

1000BASE-LX A two-wire implementation of Gigabit Ethernet using optical fibers transmitting long-wave laser signals.

1000BASE-SX A two-wire implementation of Gigabit Ethernet using optical fibers transmitting short-wave laser signals.

1000BASE-T A four-wire implementation of Gigabit Ethernet using twisted-pair cables.

100BASE-FX A two-wire implementation of Fast Ethernet using fiber-optic cable.

100BASE-T4 A four-wire implementation of Fast Ethernet using twisted-pair cable.

100BASE-TX A two-wire implementation of Fast Ethernet using twisted-pair cable.

100BASE-X A two-wire implementation of Fast Ethernet.

10BASE-FL The IEEE 802.3 standard for twisted-pair Ethernet. The standard specifies a star topology with stations connected by a pair of fiber-optic cables to a hub. The data rate is defined to be 10 Mbps.

10BASE-T The IEEE 802.3 standard for twisted-pair Ethernet. The standard specifies a star topology using twisted-pair cable. The data rate is defined to be 10 Mbps.

10BASE2 The IEEE 802.3 standard for Thin Ethernet. The standard specifies a bus topology using thin coaxial cable with a maximum segment length of 185 meters. The data rate is defined to be 10 Mbps. (Also called cheapernet or cheapnet.)

10BASE5 The IEEE 802.3 standard for Thick Ethernet. The standard specifies a bus topology using thick coaxial cable with a maximum segment length of 500 meters. The data rate is defined to be 10 Mbps.

A

AAL5 An AAL layer in the ATM protocol that processes data with extensive header information from upper-layer protocols; also called the simple and efficient adaptation layer (SEAL).

abbreviation A method to shorten the IPv6 address by eliminating certain 0 digits.

abort frame A token ring frame with no information—just starting and ending delimiters.

abstract syntax notation 1 (ASN.1) A formal language using abstract syntax for defining the structure of a protocol data unit (PDU).

access control Management to determine which device has control over a link.

active close Closing a TCP connection by a client.

active document In the World Wide Web, a document executed at the local site using Java.

active open Establishment of a connection with a server by a client.

additive increase With slow start, a congestion avoidance strategy in which the window size is increased by just one segment instead of exponentially.

address mask 32 bits that extract a network address or a subnetwork address.

address-mask request and reply message An ICMP query request or reply that finds the network mask.

address resolution protocol (ARP) In TCP/IP, a protocol for obtaining the physical address of a node when the Internet address is known.

address space The total number of addresses used by a protocol.

address transformation The conversion of an IP address from ASCII dotted-decimal format to 32-bit binary format and vice versa.

ADSL See *asymmetric digital subscriber line.*

Advanced Networks and Services (ANS) The owner and operator of the Internet since 1995.

Advanced Networks and Services Network (ANSNET) The high-speed Internet backbone.

Advanced Research Project Agency (ARPA) The government agency that funded ARPANET.

Advanced Research Project Agency Network (ARPANET) The packet switching network that was funded by ARPA.

agent A router or a host that runs the SNMP server program.

agent advertisement A process in which a router informs a mobile host of its address.

agent discovery A process through which a mobile host on its home network learns the address of a home agent.

agent solicitation A process in which a mobile host on a foreign network uses ICMP to learn an agent's address.

alias In SMTP, a name that represents a group of recipients.

American National Standards Institute (ANSI) A national standards organization that defines standards in the United States.

American Standard Code for Information Interchange (ASCII) A character code developed by ANSI and used extensively for data communication.

AND operation A logical operation that is true if and only if both operands are true.

anonymous FTP A protocol in which a remote user can access another machine without an account or password.

ANS See *Advanced Networks and Services.*

ANSI See *American National Standards Institute.*

ANSNET See *Advanced Networks and Services Network.*

anycast address An address that defines a group of computers with addresses that have the same prefix.

API See *application programming interface.*

applet A computer program for creating an active Web document. It is usually written in Java.

AppleTalk A protocol suite developed by Apple Computer, Inc.

application adaptation layer (AAL) A layer in ATM protocol that breaks user data into 48-byte payloads.

application layer The seventh layer in the OSI model; provides access to network resources.

application program Application layer software that accomplishes a specific task.

application programming interface (API) A set of declarations, definitions, and procedures followed by programmers to write client-server programs.

application specific message An RTCP packet sent by an application that wants to use new applications (not defined in the standard). It allows the definition of a new message type.

area A collection of networks, hosts, and routers all contained within an autonomous system.

area border router A router inside an area that summarizes the information about the area and sends it to other areas.

area identification A 32-bit field that defines the area within which the routing takes place.

ARP See *address resolution protocol.*

ARPA See *Advanced Research Project Agency.*

ARPANET See *Advanced Research Project Agency Network.*

AS See *autonomous system.*

ASCII See *American Standard Code for Information Interchange.*

ASN.1 See *abstract syntax notation 1.*

asymmetric digital subscriber line (ADSL) A communication technology in which the downstream data rate is higher than the upstream rate.

asynchronous time division multiplexing Time division multiplexing in which link time is allocated dynamically according to whether a terminal is active or not.

asynchronous transfer mode (ATM) A wide area protocol featuring high data rates and equal-sized packets (cells); ATM is suitable for transferring text, audio, and video data.

ATM See *asynchronous transfer mode.*

ATM consortium A group of ATM software and hardware vendors.

ATM forum A group of parties interested in the promotion and rapid development of ATM.

ATM switch An ATM device providing both switching and multiplexing functions.

ATMARP A protocol that finds (maps) the IP address of an exiting-point router given the physical address of the exiting-point router.

attended bulk data traffic Traffic in which the user is waiting to receive the data.

authentication Verification of the sender of a message.

Authentication Header Protocol A protocol defined by IPSec at the network layer that provides integrity to a message through the creation of a digital signature by a hashing function.

automatic tunneling Tunneling in which the receiving host has an IPv6 compatible address; no reconfiguration is necessary.

autonomous system (AS) A group of networks and routers under the authority of a single administration.

autonomous system boundary router Routers responsible for dissipating information about other autonomous systems into the current system.

B

backbone The major transmission path in a network.

backbone router A router inside the backbone.

background data In IPv6, traffic consisting of data that is usually delivered in the background; low priority data.

bandwidth The difference between the highest and the lowest frequencies of a composite signal. It also measures the information-carrying capacity of a line or a network.

bandwidth on demand A digital service that allows subscribers higher speeds through the use of multiple lines.

base 2 A number system based on two symbols; also called the binary system.

base 8 A number system based on eight symbols; also called the octal system.

base 10 A number system based on 10 symbols; also called the decimal system.

base 16 A number system based on 16 symbols; also called the hexadecimal system.

base header In IPv6, the main header of the datagram.

Basic Encoding Rules (BER) A standard that encodes data to be transferred through a network.

Basic Service Set (BSS) The building block of a wireless LAN as defined by the IEEE 802.11 standard.

Bellman-Ford algorithm An algorithm used to calculate routing tables in the distance vector routing method.

BER See *Basic Encoding Rules.*

best-effort delivery The unreliable transmission mechanism by IP that does not guarantee message delivery.

BGP See *Border Gateway Protocol.*

big endian A format in which the most significant byte is stored or transmitted first.

binary notation Expressing a number as bits.

binary number system A method of representing information using only two symbols (0 and 1).

bit A binary digit; the smallest unit of information; 1 or 0.

bit rate The number of bits transmitted per second.

bit synchronization Agreement in time of the data rate at the sender and the receiver.

bits per second (bps) A measurement of data speed; bits transmitted per second.

block mode Delivery of the data from FTP to TCP in blocks.

body The part of an email message that contains the actual information to be read by the recipient.

BOOTP See *Bootstrap Protocol.*

bootstrap process The booting up of a computer that requires its IP address, subnet mask, default router address, and name server address.

Bootstrap Protocol (BOOTP) The protocol that provides configuration information from a table (file).

Border Gateway Protocol (BGP) An interautonomous system routing protocol based on path vector routing.

bps See *bits per second.*

bridge A network device operating at the first two layers of the OSI model with filtering and forwarding capabilities.

broadcast address An address that allows transmission of a message to all nodes of a network.

broadcast message A message sent to all nodes of a network.

broadcast/unknown server (BUS) A server connected to an ATM switch that can multicast and broadcast frames.

broadcasting Transmission of a message to all nodes in a network.

browser An application program that displays a WWW document. A browser usually uses other Internet services to access the document.

BSS See *Basic Service Set.*

buffer Memory set aside for temporary storage.

BUS See *broadcast/unknown server.*

bye message An RTCP message sent by a source to shut down a stream.

byte A group of 8 bits.

byte rate The number of bytes transmitted per second.

C

CA See *Certification Authority.*

cache table An ARP mechanism that saves ARP resolutions.

caching The storing of information in a small, fast memory used to hold data items that are being processed.

care-of address The temporary address of a mobile host on its foreign network.

carrier sense multiple access (CSMA) A contention access method in which each station listens to the line before transmitting data.

carrier sense multiple access with collision detection (CSMA/CD) An access method in which stations transmit whenever the transmission medium is available and retransmit when collision occurs.

CBT See *Core-Based Tree.*

CCITT See *Consultative Committee for International Telegraphy and Telephony.*

cell A small, fixed-size data unit; also, in cellular telephony, a geographical area served by a cell office.

cell network A network using the cell as its basic data unit.

cell relay A communication technology using a fixed-size data unit as the packet; used by ATM.

Certification Authority (CA) An agency such as a federal or state organization that binds a public key to an entity and issues a certificate.

CGI See *Common Gateway Interface.*

channel A communications pathway.

character mode A TELNET operation mode in which each character typed is sent by the client to the server.

checksum A field used for error detection. It is formed by adding bit streams using one's complement arithmetic and then complementing the result.

child process A process created by a parent running application program.

child server A server created by a parent server and using an ephemeral port; it frees the parent server for another connection on the well-known port.

CIDR See *Classless Inter-Domain Routing.*

ciphertext The encrypted data.

Clark's solution A solution to prevent the silly window syndrome; an acknowledgment is sent as soon as the data arrives, but to announce a window size of zero until either there is enough space to accommodate a segment of maximum size or until half of the buffer is empty.

class The joining of data and functions to form a type.

class A address An IPv4 address with the first octet between 0 and 127.

class B address An IPv4 address with the first octet between 128 and 191.

class C address An IPv4 address with the first octet between 192 and 223.

class D address An IPv4 multicast address.

class E address An IPv4 address reserved for special purposes.

classful addressing An IPv4 addressing mechanism in which the IP address space is divided into 5 classes: A, B, C, D, and E. Each class occupies some part of the whole address space.

classless addressing An addressing mechanism in which the IP address space is not divided into classes.

Classless InterDomain Routing (CIDR) A technique to reduce the number of routing table entries when supernetting is used.

client See *client process.*

client process A running application program on a local site that requests service from a running application program on a remote site.

client-server model The model of interaction between two application programs in which a program at one end (client) requests a service from a program at the other end (server).

CLNS See *connectionless network service.*

CLTS See *connectionless transport service.*

code An arrangement of symbols to stand for a word or an action.

code field A field in the option portion of the IP header; it contains the copy, class, and number subfields.

collision The event that occurs when two transmitters send at the same time on a channel designed for only one transmission at a time; data will be destroyed.

co-located care-of address A care-of address of a mobile host acting as a foreign agent.

common gateway interface (CGI) A standard for communication between HTTP servers and executable programs. CGI is used in creating dynamic documents.

compatible address An IPv6 address consisting of 96 bits of zero followed by 32 bits of IPv4 address.

compressed mode Delivery of compressed data from FTP to TCP.

compression The reduction of a message without significant loss of information.

concurrent client A client running the same time as another client of the same process.

concurrent server A server that can process many requests at the same time and share its time between many requests.

confidentiality Privacy.

configuration file A file containing information needed when a computer is booted; the file contains the computer's IP address, subnet mask, a default router address, and a name server address.

configured tunneling Tunneling in which the receiving host does not support an IPv6-compatible address; reconfiguration is necessary.

congestion Excessive network or internetwork traffic causing a general degradation of service.

congestion-controlled traffic Traffic in which a source adapts itself to traffic slowdown when there is congestion.

connecting device A tool that connects computers or networks.

connection control The technique used by the transport layer to deliver segments.

connection establishment The preliminary setup necessary for a logical connection prior to actual data transfer.

connection resetting Destroying a connection.

connection termination A message sent to end a connection.

connectionless iterative server A connectionless server that processes one request at a time.

connectionless protocol A protocol for data transfer without connection establishment or termination.

connectionless service A service for data transfer without connection establishment or termination.

connectionless, unreliable transport protocol A transport layer protocol without connection establishment or termination.

connection-oriented concurrent server A connection-oriented server that can serve many clients at the same time.

connection-oriented protocol A protocol for data transfer with connection establishment and termination.

connection-oriented reliable transport protocol A transport layer protocol with connection establishment and termination.

connection-oriented service A service for data transfer involving establishment and termination of a connection.

Consultative Committee for International Telegraphy and Telephony (CCITT) An international standards group now known as the ITU-T.

contiguous mask A mask composed of a run of 1s followed by a run of 0s.

control character A character that conveys information about the transmission rather than the actual data.

control connection The FTP connection used for control information (commands and responses).

control traffic Highest priority traffic such as routing and management messages.

Core-Based Tree (CBT) In multicasting, a group-shared protocol that uses a center router as the root of the tree.

corrupted segment A data segment with errors.

country domain A subdomain in the Domain Name System that uses two characters as the last suffix.

CRC See *cyclic redundancy check.*

CS See *convergence sublayer.*

CSMA See *carrier sense multiple access.*

CSMA/CD See *carrier sense multiple access with collision detection.*

CSNET A network sponsored by the National Science Foundation originally intended for universities.

D

DARPA See *Defense Advanced Research Projects Agency.*

data connection The FTP connection used for data transfer.

data encryption standard (DES) The U.S. government standard encryption method for nonmilitary and nonclassified use.

data exchange protocol A protocol that uses the secret key to encrypt the data for secrecy and to encrypt the message digest for integrity.

data link layer The second layer in the OSI model. It is responsible for node-to-node delivery.

database description message A first-time message sent by a router to its neighbors; it only gives an outline, the title of each line in the database.

datagram In packet-switching, an independent data unit.

datagram socket A structure designed to be used with a connectionless protocol such as UDP.

DDN See *Defense Data Network.*

DDNS See *dynamic domain name system.*

de facto standard A protocol that has not been approved by an organized body but adopted as a standard through widespread use.

de jure standard A protocol that has been legislated by an officially recognized body.

dead interval field A field that defines the number of seconds before a router assumes that a neighbor is dead.

decapsulation Removal of a header and trailer from a message.

decimal number system A method of representing information using 10 symbols (0, 1, . . . to 9).

decryption Recovery of the original message from the encrypted data.

default mask The mask for a network that is not subnetted.

default mode A TELNET operation mode that is used if no other modes are invoked during option negotiation.

default routing A routing method in which a router is assigned to receive all packets with no match in the routing table.

Defense Advanced Research Projects Agency (DARPA) A government organization, which, under the name of ARPA funded ARPANET and the Internet.

Defense Data Network (DDN) The military portion of the Internet.

delayed response strategy A technique used by IGMP to prevent unnecessary traffic on a LAN.

delivery The physical forwarding of packets.

DES See *data encryption standard.*

designated parent router In multicasting, the router that distributes a multicast packet from a particular source to a network.

destination address The address of the receiver of the data unit.

destination option An IPv6 extension used if the source needs to pass information to the destination only. Intermediate routers are not permitted access to this information.

destination-unreachable message An ICMP error-reporting message sent to a source when a router cannot route a datagram or a host cannot deliver a datagram.

DHCP See *Dynamic Host Configuration Protocol.*

dialog The exchange between two communicating devices.

dialog control The technique used by the session layer to control the dialog.

digest A condensed version of a document.

digital signature A method to authenticate the sender of a message.

digital subscriber line (DSL) A technology using existing telecommunication networks to accomplish high-speed delivery of data, voice, video, and multimedia.

Dijkstra's algorithm In link state routing, an algorithm that finds the shortest path to other routers.

direct broadcast address A special address used by a router to send a packet to all hosts in a specified network.

direct delivery A delivery in which the final destination of the packet is a host connected to the same physical network as the deliverer.

direct sequence spread spectrum (DSSS) A wireless transmission method in which each bit to be sent by the sender is replaced by a sequence of bits called a chip code.

directory service (DS) A service that can provide the email address of an individual.

distance learning Schooling through multicast lectures.

Distance Vector Multicast Routing Protocol (DVMRP) A protocol based on distance vector routing that handles multicast routing in conjunction with IGMP.

distance vector routing A routing method in which each router sends its neighbors a list of networks it can reach and the distance to that network.

distributed database Information stored in many locations.

DNS See *domain name system.*

DNS server A computer that holds information about the name space.

domain A subtree of the domain name space.

domain name In the DNS, a sequence of labels separated by dots.

domain name space A structure for organizing the name space in which the names are defined in an inverted-tree structure with the root at the top.

domain name system (DNS) A TCP/IP application service that converts user-friendly names to IP addresses.

dotted-decimal notation A notation devised to make the IP address easier to read; each byte is converted to its decimal equivalent and then set off from its neighbor by a decimal.

double crossing An inefficient situation that results when a remote host communicates with a mobile host that has moved to the same network (or site) as the remote host.

DS See *directory service.*

DSL See *digital subscriber line.*

DSSS See *direct sequence spread spectrum.*

dual stack Two protocols (IPv4 and IPv6) on a station.

duplex mode See *full-duplex mode.*

duplicate segment A segment identical to another.

DVMRP See *Distance Vector Multicast Routing Protocol.*

dynamic configuration protocol A protocol that features tables that are automatically updated as changes occur.

dynamic document A Web document created by running a CGI program at the server site.

dynamic domain name system (DDNS) A method to update the DNS master file dynamically.

dynamic host configuration protocol (DHCP) An extension to BOOTP that dynamically assigns configuration information.

dynamic mapping A technique in which a protocol is used for address resolution.

dynamic port An ephemeral port; a port that is neither controlled nor registered and can be used by any process.

dynamic routing Routing in which the routing table entries are updated automatically by the routing protocol.

dynamic routing table A routing table that has its entries updated automatically by the routing protocol.

E

EBCDIC See *extended binary coded decimal interchange code.*

echo-request and reply message An ICMP query message that determines whether two systems (hosts or routers) can communicate with each other.

EGP See *Exterior Gateway Protocol.*

EHF See *extremely high frequency.*

EIA See *Electronics Industries Association.*

electromagnetic interference (EMI) A noise on the data transmission line that can corrupt the data. It can be created by motors, generators, and so on.

electronic mail (email) A method of sending messages electronically based on mailbox addresses rather than a direct host-to-host exchange.

Electronics Industries Association (EIA) An organization that promotes electronics manufacturing concerns. It has developed interface standards such as EIA-232, EIA-449, and EIA-530.

email See *electronic mail.*

EMI See *electromagnetic interference.*

Encapsulating Security Payload (ESP) A protocol defined by IPSec that provides privacy as well as a combination of integrity and message authentication.

encapsulation The technique in which a data unit from one protocol is placed within the data field portion of the data unit of another protocol.

Encrypted Security Payload (ESP) An IPv6 extension that provides confidentiality and guards against eavesdropping.

encryption Converting a message into an unintelligible form that is unreadable unless decrypted.

end-of-option option A 1-byte option used for padding at the end of the option field in the IP header. It can only be used as the last option.

end-to-end message delivery Delivery of all parts of a message from the sender to the receiver.

entering-point router In an ATM network, the router from which the cell begins its transmission.

entity Anything capable of sending or receiving information.

entity header A part of the HTTP request or response message that gives information about the body of the document.

envelope The part of the email that contains the sender address, the receiver address, and other information.

ephemeral port A port number used by the client.

error control The detection and handling of errors in data transmission.

error correction The process of correcting bits that have been changed during transmission.

error detection The process of determining whether or not some bits have been changed during transmission.

error-reporting message An ICMP message sent to the source to report an error.

ESP See *Encapsulating Security Payload* or *Encrypted Security Payload.*

ESS See *Extended Service Set.*

Ethernet A local area network using CSMA/CD access method. See *IEEE Project 802.3.*

exiting-point router In an ATM network, the router from which the cell ends its transmission.

expiration timer A timer that governs the validity of a route.

extended binary coded decimal interchange code (EBCDIC) An 8-bit character code developed and used by IBM.

Extended Service Set (ESS) A wireless LAN service composed of two or more BSSs with APs as defined by the IEEE 802.11 standard.

extension header Extra headers in the IPv6 datagram that provide additional functionality.

exterior routing Routing between autonomous systems.

external link An advertisement that allows a router inside an autonomous system to know which networks are available outside the autonomous system.

external link LSA A message that announces all the networks outside the AS.

extranet A private network that uses the TCP/IP protocol suite that allows authorized access from outside users.

F

Fast Ethernet See *100BASE-T.*

FCC See *Federal Communications Commission.*

FCS See *frame check sequence.*

Federal Communications Commission (FCC) A government agency that regulates radio, television, and telecommunications.

FHSS See *frequency hopping spread spectrum.*

file transfer, access, and management (FTAM) In the OSI model, an application layer service for remote file handling.

File Transfer Protocol (FTP) In TCP/IP, an application layer protocol that transfers files between two sites.

finite program A program that is started by the user (or another application program) and terminates when the service is complete.

finite state machine A machine that goes through a limited number of states.

firewall A device (usually a router) installed between the internal network of an organization and the rest of the Internet to provide security.

flat namespace A method to map a name to an address in which there is no hierarchical structure.

flooding Saturation of a network with a message.

flow control A technique to control the rate of flow of frames (packets or messages).

flow label An IPv6 mechanism to enable the source to request special handling of a packet.

foreign agent Usually a router attached to a foreign network that receives and delivers packets sent by the home agent to the mobile host.

foreign network The network to which a mobile host moves.

fork A UNIX function that creates a child process that has exactly the same image as its parent.

forum An organization that tests, evaluates, and standardizes a specific new technology.

four-way handshake A sequence of events for connection termination consisting of four steps between the client and server.

FQDN See *fully qualified domain name.*

fractional T line A service that allows several subscribers to share one line by multiplexing their transmissions.

fragmentation The division of a packet into smaller units to accommodate a protocol's MTU.

fragmentation offset A field in the IP header used in fragmentation to show the relative position of the fragment with respect to the whole datagram.

frame A group of bits representing a block of data.

frame check sequence (FCS) The HDLC error-detection field containing either a 2- or 4-byte CRC.

frame relay A packet-switching specification defined for the first two layers of the OSI model. There is no network layer. Error checking is done on end-to-end basis instead of on each link.

Frame Relay Forum A group formed by Digital Equipment Corporation, Northern Telecom, Cisco, and StrataCom to promote the acceptance and implementation of frame relay.

frequency hopping spread spectrum (FHSS) A wireless transmission method in which the sender transmits at one carrier frequency for a short period of time, then hops to another carrier frequency for the same amount of time, hops again for the same amount of time, and so on. After N hops, the cycle is repeated.

FTAM See *file transfer, access, and management.*

FTP See *File Transfer Protocol.*

full-duplex Ethernet An Ethernet implementation in which every station is connected by two separate paths to the central hub.

full-duplex mode A transmission mode in which communication can be two way simultaneously.

fully qualified domain name (FQDN) A domain name consisting of labels beginning with the host and going back through each level to the root node.

G

garbage collection timer A timer that advertises the failure of a route.

gateway A device used to connect two separate networks that use different communication protocols.

general header A part of an HTTP request or response message that gives general information about the message.

general query message A message sent by a router to monitor group membership.

generic domain A subdomain in the domain name system that uses generic suffixes.

geographical routing A routing technique in which the entire address space is divided into blocks based on physical land masses.

Gigabit Ethernet Ethernet with a 1000 Mbps data rate.

global Internet The Internet.

grafting Resumption of multicast messages.

graph A data structure with no hierarchy.

group membership Belonging to a group.

group membership message An IPv6 message that serves the same purpose as the IGMP message.

groupid The multicast address of a group.

group-shared tree A multicast routing feature in which each group in the system shares the same tree.

H

half-duplex mode A transmission mode in which communication can be two-way but not at the same time.

handshaking A process to establish or terminate a connection.

hardware address An address used by a data link layer to identify a device.

hash function An algorithm that creates a fixed-size digest from a variable-length message.

HDSL See *high bit rate digital subscriber line.*

header Control information added to the beginning of a data packet. Also, in an email, the part of the message that defines the sender, the receiver, the subject of the message, and other information.

header length A 4-bit field in the IP header defining the total length of the datagram header in 4-byte words.

header translation Conversion of the IPv6 header to IPv4.

hello interval A field defining the number of seconds between hello messages.

hello message An OSPF message that creates neighborhood relationships and tests the reachability of neighbors.

hexadecimal colon notation In IPv6, an address notation consisting of 32 hexadecimal digits, with every four digits separated by a colon.

hexadecimal number system A method of representing information using 16 symbols (0, 1, . . . , 9, A, B, C, D, E, and F).

hierarchical name space A name space made of several parts, with each succeeding part becoming more and more specific.

hierarchical routing A routing technique in which the entire address space is divided into levels based on specific criteria.

high bit rate digital subscriber line (HDSL) A service similar to the T1-line that can operate at lengths up to 3.6 km.

home address A mobile host's permanent address on its home network.

home agent Usually a router attached to the home network of the mobile host that receives and sends packets (for the mobile host) to the foreign agent.

home network A network that is the permanent home of the mobile host.

homepage A unit of hypertext or hypermedia available on the Web that is the main page for an organization or an individual.

hop count The number of nodes along a route. It is a measurement of distance in routing algorithms.

hop limit An IPv6 field that limits the number of routers that a packet can visit.

hop-by-hop option An IPv6 option used when the source needs to pass information to all routers visited by the datagram.

host A station or node on a network.

host file A file, used when the Internet was small, that mapped host names to host addresses.

host specific flag In a routing table, a field that specifies that the entry in the destination field is a host-specific address.

host-specific routing A routing method in which the full IP address of a host is given in the routing table.

hostid The part of an IP address that identifies a host.

host-to-host protocol A protocol that can deliver a packet from one physical device to another.

HTML See *hypertext markup language.*

HTTP See *hypertext transfer protocol.*

hybrid network A network with a private internet and access to the global Internet.

hypermedia Information containing text, pictures, graphics, and sound that is linked to other documents through pointers.

hypertext Information containing text that is linked to other documents through pointers.

hypertext markup language (HTML) The computer language for specifying the contents and format of a Web document. It allows additional text to include codes that define fonts, layouts, embedded graphics, and hypertext links.

hypertext transfer protocol (HTTP) An application service for retrieving a Web document.

I

IAB See *Internet Architecture Board.*

IANA See *Internet Assigned Numbers Authority.*

ICANN See *Internet Corporation for Assigned Names and Numbers.*

ICMP See *Internet Control Message Protocol.*

ICMPv6 See *Internet Control Message Protocol, version 6.*

IEEE See *Institute of Electrical and Electronics Engineers.*

IESG See *Internet Engineering Steering Group.*

IETF See *Internet Engineering Task Force.*

IGMP See *Internet Group Management Protocol.*

IGP See *Interior Gateway Protocol.*

image file In FTP, the default format for transferring binary files. The file is sent as continuous streams of bits without any interpretation or encoding.

IMAP4 See *Internet Mail Access Protocol, version 4.*

indirect delivery A delivery in which a packet goes from one router to another router until it reaches the one connected to the same physical network as its final destination.

infinite program A program running on a server all the time.

infrared (IR) light Electromagnetic waves with frequencies just below the visible spectrum.

inheritance The extension of data and methods from one object to another.

instantiation Creation of an instance of an object.

Institute of Electrical and Electronics Engineers (IEEE) A group consisting of professional engineers which has specialized societies whose committees prepare standards in members' areas of specialty.

integrity A data quality of being noncorrupted.

interactive traffic Traffic in which interaction with the user is necessary.

interautonomous-routing protocol A protocol to handle transmissions between autonomous systems.

interface The boundary between two pieces of equipment. It also refers to mechanical, electrical, and functional characteristics of the connection.

interior routing Routing inside an autonomous system.

International Organization of Standardization (ISO) A worldwide organization that defines and develops standards on a variety of topics.

International Telecommunications Union–Telecommunication Standardization Sector (ITU–T) A standards organization formerly known as the CCITT.

internet A collection of networks connected by internetworking devices such as routers or gateways.

Internet A global internet that uses the TCP/IP protocol suite.

Internet address A 32-bit or 128-bit network-layer address used to uniquely define a host on an internet using the TCP/IP protocol.

Internet Architecture Board (IAB) The technical adviser to the ISOC; oversees the continuing development of the TCP/IP protocol suite.

Internet Assigned Numbers Authority (IANA) A group supported by the U.S. government that was responsible for the management of Internet domain names and addresses until October 1998.

Internet Control Message Protocol (ICMP) A protocol in the TCP/IP protocol suite that handles error and control messages.

Internet Control Message Protocol, version 6 (ICMPv6) A protocol in IPv6 that handles error and control messages.

Internet Corporation for Assigned Names and Numbers (ICANN) A private, nonprofit corporation managed by an international board that assumed IANA operations.

Internet draft A working Internet document (a work in progress) with no official status and a six-month lifetime.

Internet Engineering Steering Group (IESG) An organization that oversees the activity of IETF.

Internet Engineering Task Force (IETF) A group working on the design and development of the TCP/IP protocol suite and the Internet.

Internet Group Management Protocol (IGMP) A protocol in the TCP/IP protocol suite that handles multicasting.

Internet Mail Access Protocol, version 4 (IMAP4) A complex and powerful protocol to handle the transmission of electronic mail.

Internet Network Information Center (INTERNIC) An agency responsible for collecting and distributing information about TCP/IP protocols.

Internet Protocol See *Internetworking Protocol.*

Internet Research Task Force (IRTF) A forum of working groups focusing on long-term research topics related to the Internet.

Internet service provider (ISP) Usually, a company that provides Internet services.

Internet Society (ISOC) The nonprofit organization established to publicize the Internet.

Internet standard A thoroughly tested specification that is useful to and adhered to by those who work with the Internet. It is a formalized regulation that must be followed.

internetwork See *internet.*

internetworking Connecting several networks together using internetworking devices such as routers and gateways.

internetworking devices Electronic devices such as routers and gateways that connect networks together to form an internet.

Internetworking Protocol (IP) The network-layer protocol in the TCP/IP protocol suite governing connectionless transmission across packet-switching networks.

Internetworking Protocol, next generation (IPng) Another term for the sixth version of the Internetworking Protocol.

Internetworking Protocol, version 6 (IPv6) The sixth version of the Internetworking Protocol; it features major IP addressing changes.

INTERNIC See *Internet Network Information Center.*

intranet A private network that uses the TCP/IP protocol suite.

inverse domain A subdomain in the DNS that finds the domain name given the IP address.

inverse reply message In an ATM network, a message sent from a router to a server containing address (physical and IP) information to build a routing table.

inverse request message In an ATM network, a message sent from a server to a router to get address (physical and IP) information to build its routing table.

IP See *Internetworking Protocol.*

IP address See *Internet address.*

IP address class In IPv4, one of the five groups of addresses; classes A, B, and C consist of a netid, hostid, and class ID; class D holds multicast addresses; class E is reserved for future use.

IP datagram The Internetworking Protocol data unit.

IP Security (IPSec) A collection of protocols designed by the IETF (Internet Engineering Task Force) to provide security for a packet carried on the Internet.

IPng (IP next generation) See *IPv6.*

IPSec See *P Security.*

IPv4 The Internetworking Protocol, version 4. It is the current version.

IPv6 See *Internetworking Protocol, version 6.*

IR See *infrared.*

IRTF See *Internet Research Task Force.*

ISDN See *integrated services digital network.*

ISO See *International Organization of Standardization.*

ISOC See *Internet Society.*

ISP See *Internet service provider.*

iterative resolution Resolution of the IP address in which the client may send its request to multiple servers before getting an answer.

ITU–T See *International Telecommunications Union–Telecommunication Standardization Sector.*

J

Java A programming language used to create active Web documents.

jitter A phenomenon in real-time traffic caused by gaps between consecutive packets at the receiver.

jumbo payload An IPv6 header option used to define a payload longer than the maximum.

K

Karn's Algorithm An algorithm that does not include the retransmitted segments in calculation of round-trip time.

Kbps Kilobits per second.

KDC See *key distribution center.*

keepalive message A message that establishes a relationship between the two routers.

keepalive timer A timer that prevents a long idle connection between two TCPs.

key distribution center (KDC) In secret key encryption, a trusted third party that shares a key with each user.

L

LAN See *local area network.*

LAN emulation (LANE) A client-server model that allows the use of ATM technology in LANs.

LAN emulation client (LEC) Client software that receives requests for a LAN service; part of a LANE.

LAN emulation configuration server (LECS) Server software used for the initial connection in LANE.

LAN emulation server (LES) Server software that creates a virtual circuit between the source and destination; part of a LANE.

LANE See *LAN emulation.*

layered architecture A model based on ordered tiers.

LCP See *Link Control Protocol.*

least-cost tree An MOSPF feature in which the tree is based on a chosen metric instead of shortest path.

leave report An IGMP message sent by a host when no process is interested in a specific group.

LEC See *LAN emulation client.*

LECS See *LAN emulation configuration server.*

legacy LAN A LAN in which ATM technology is used as a backbone to connect traditional LANs.

LES See *LAN emulation server.*

lexicographic ordering A table arranged such that the sequence is from the top to the bottom of a column and then from the top to the bottom of the adjacent column and so on.

limited broadcast address An address consisting of all 1s used by a host to send a packet to all hosts on its network.

line configuration The relationship between communication devices and their pathway.

line mode A TELNET operation mode in which line editing (echoing, character erasing, line erasing, and so on) is done by the client.

Link Control Protocol (LCP) A PPP protocol responsible for establishing, maintaining, configuring, and terminating links.

link local address An IPv6 address that is used if a LAN is to use the Internet protocols but is not connected to the Internet for security reasons.

link state acknowledgment packet An OSPF mechanism in which every router must acknowledge the receipt of every link state update packet.

link state advertisement (LSA) In OSPF, a method that disperses information.

link state database In link state routing, a database common to all routers and made from LSP information.

link state packet (LSP) In link state routing, a small packet containing routing information sent by a router to all other routers.

link state request packet An OSPF packet containing full information about a particular link.

link state update packet A packet that provides information about a specific route or routes.

LIS See *logical IP subnet.*

little-endian byte format A format in which the least significant byte is stored or transmitted first.

local address The part of an email address that defines the name of a special file, called the user mailbox, where all of the mail received for a user is stored for retrieval by the user agent.

local area network (LAN) A network connecting devices inside a single building or inside buildings close to each other.

local client program A program run locally that requests a service from a remote server program.

local host The computer at which a user is physically using.

local ISP The same as an ISP.

local login Using a terminal directly connected to the computer.

local loop The link that connects a subscriber to the telephone central office.

logical address An address defined in the network layer.

logical IP subnet (LIS) A grouping of nodes of an ATM network in which the connection is logical, not physical.

logical tunnel The encapsulation of a multicast packet inside a unicast packet to enable multicast routing by non-multicast routers.

longitudinal redundancy check (LRC) An error-detection method dividing a data unit into rows and columns and performing parity checks on corresponding bits of each column.

loopback address An address used by a host to test its internal software.

loose source route option An IP header option listing the routers that must be visited.

LRC See *longitudinal redundancy check.*

LSA See *link state advertisement.*

LSP See *link state packet.*

M

magic cookie In BOOTP, the number in the format of an IP address with the value of 99.130.83.99; indicates that options are present.

mail access protocol A protocol used by the remote user agent to access the mailbox and obtain the mail.

mail exchanger Any computer capable of receiving email.

mail gateway A relay MTA that can receive both SMTP mail and non-SMTP mail.

mail service The handling of email.

mail transfer agent (MTA) An SMTP component that transfers the mail across the Internet.

MAN See *metropolitan area network.*

Management Information Base (MIB) The database used by SNMP that holds the information necessary for management of a network.

manager The host that runs the SNMP client program.

Manchester encoding A digital-to-digital polar encoding method in which a transition occurs at the middle of each bit interval for the purpose of synchronization.

many-to-one alias expansion In SMTP, the defining of a single user by several different email addresses.

mapped address An IPv6 address used when a computer that has migrated to IPv6 wants to send a packet to a computer still using IPv4.

mask For IPv4, a 32-bit binary number that gives the first address in the block (the network address) when ANDed with an address in the block.

masking A process that extracts the address of the physical network from an IP address.

maturity level The phases through which an RFC goes.

MAU See *multistation access unit.*

maximum segment size (MSS) option A TCP header option defining the biggest chunk of data that the destination can receive; the size is negotiated during connection establishment.

maximum transfer unit (MTU) The largest size data unit a specific network can handle.

MBONE See *multicast backbone.*

Mbps Megabits per second.

membership report An IGMP message sent by a host or router interested in joining a specific group.

message Data sent from source to destination. Or, in SMTP, the headers and the body portion of email.

metric A cost assigned for passing through a network.

metropolitan area network (MAN) A network that can span a geographical area the size of a city.

MIB See *management information base.*

Military Network (MILNET) A network for military use that was originally part of ARPANET.

MILNET See *Military Network.*

MIME See *Multipurpose Internet Mail Extension.*

mixed architecture LAN An ATM LAN that combines the features of a pure ATM LAN and a legacy ATM LAN.

mixer A device that combines real-time signals from different sources into one signal.

mobile host A host that can move from one network to another.

modified by redirection flag In a routing table, a field that indicates that the routing information for this destination has been modified by a redirection message from ICMP.

MOSPF See *Multicast Open Shortest Path First.*

MPEG See *motion picture experts group.*

MSS See *maximum segment size.*

MTA See *mail transfer agent.*

MTU See *maximum transfer unit.*

multicast address An address used for multicasting.

multicast backbone (MBONE) A set of internet routers supporting multicasting through the use of tunneling.

Multicast Open Shortest Path First (MOSPF) A multicast protocol that uses multicast link state routing to create a source-based least cost tree.

multicast router A router with a list of loyal members related to each router interface that distributes the multicast packets.

multicast routing Moving a multicast packet to its destination.

multicasting A transmission method that allows copies of a single packet to be sent to a selected group of receivers.

multihomed device A device connected to more than one network.

multimedia traffic Traffic consisting of data, video, and audio.

multiple unicasting Sending multiple copies of a message, each with a different unicast destination address, from one source.

multiplexing The process of combining signals from multiple sources for transmission across a single data link.

multiplicative decrease A congestion avoidance technique in which the threshold is set to half of the last congestion window size, and the congestion window size starts from one again.

Multipurpose Internet Mail Extension (MIME) A supplement to SMTP that allows non-ASCII data to be sent through SMTP.

multistation access unit (MAU) In token ring, a device that houses individual automatic switches.

N

Nagle's algorithm An algorithm that attempts to prevent silly window syndrome at the sender's site; both the rate of data production and the network speed are taken into account.

name server A computer that maps computer names to IP addresses.

name space All the names assigned to machines on an internet.

name-address resolution Mapping a name to an address or an address to a name.

NAP See *Network Access Point.*

NAT See *network address translation.*

National Science Foundation (NSF) A government agency responsible for Internet funding.

National Science Foundation Network (NSFNET) A backbone funded by NSF.

national service provider (NSP) A backbone network created and maintained by a specialized company.

NCP See *Network Control Protocol.*

neighbor solicitation and advertisement message An ICMPv6 message that functions like ARP.

netid The part of an IP address that identifies the network.

network A system consisting of connected nodes made to share data, hardware, and software.

Network Access Point (NAP) A complex switching station that connects backbone networks.

network address An address that identifies a network to the rest of the Internet; it is the first address in a block.

network address translation (NAT) A technology that allows a private network to use a set of private addresses for internal communication and a set of global Internet addresses for external communication.

Network Control Protocol (NCP) In PPP, a set of control protocols that allows the encapsulation of data coming from network layer protocols.

network file system (NFS) A TCP/IP application protocol that allows a user to access and manipulate remote file systems as if they were local. It uses the services of remote procedure call protocol.

Network Information Center (NIC) An agency responsible for collecting and distributing information about TCP/IP protocols.

network interface card (NIC) An electronic device, internal or external to a station, that contains circuitry to enable the station to be connected to the network.

network layer The third layer in the OSI model, responsible for the delivery of a packet to the final destination.

network link LSA An LSA packet that announces the existence of all of the routers connected to the network.

network mask A field in the OSPF hello message that defines the network mask of the network over which the hello message is sent.

network support layers The physical, data link, and network layers.

network-specific routing Routing in which all hosts on a network share one entry in the routing table.

network-to-network interface (NNI) In ATM, the interface between two networks.

Network Virtual Terminal (NVT) A TCP/IP application protocol that allows remote login.

next header In IPv6, an 8-bit field defining the header that follows the base header in the datagram.

next-hop address The address of the first router to which the packet is delivered.

next-hop routing A routing method in which only the address of the next hop is listed in the routing table instead of a complete list of the stops the packet must make.

NFS See *network file system.*

NIC See *network interface card* or *Network Information Center.*

NNI See *network-to-network interface.*

node-to-node delivery Transfer of a data unit from one node to the next.

noise Random electrical signals that can be picked by the transmission medium and result in degradation or distortion of the data.

noncongestion-controlled traffic Traffic in which the source does not adapt itself to congestion; requires minimum delay.

noncontiguous mask A mask composed of a series of bits that is not a string of 1s followed by a string of 0s, but a mixture of 0s and 1s.

nonpersistent connection A connection in which one TCP connection is made for each request/response.

nonrepudiation A security aspect in which a receiver must be able to prove that a received message came from a specific sender.

no-operation option A 1-byte option in the IP header used as a filler between options.

notification message A BGP message sent by a router whenever an error condition is detected or a router wants to close the connection.

NRM See *normal response mode.*

NSF See *National Science Foundation.*

NSFNET See *National Science Foundation Network.*

NSP See *national service provider.*

NVT See *network virtual terminal.*

O

object A variable in an SNMP packet. Or, in object oriented programming, any instantiation of a class including its members and methods.

object identifier A hierarchical method used by SMI to name variables managed by SNMP.

OC See *optical carrier.*

octal number system A method of representing information using eight symbols (0, 1, . . . , 6, and 7).

octet Eight bits.

one's complement A representation of binary numbers in which the complement of a number is found by complementing all bits.

one-to-many alias expansion The use of an alias to represent several different email addresses.

open message A BGP message sent by a router to create a neighborhood relationship.

open shortest path first (OSPF) An interior routing protocol based on link state routing.

open systems interconnection (OSI) A seven-layer model for data communication defined by ISO.

optical carrier (OC) The hierarchy of fiber-optic carriers defined in SONET. The hierarchy defines up to 10 different carriers (OC-1, OC-3, OC-12, . . . , OC-192), each with a different data rate.

option In the IP header, a selection that may or may not be used for network testing and debugging.

option negotiation In TELNET, a client and server interaction to decide which options to use.

optional attribute A BGP path attribute that need not be recognized by every router.

OSI See *open systems interconnection.*

OSPF See *open shortest path first.*

out-of-band signaling A method of signaling in which control data and user data travel on different channels.

out-of-order segment A TCP segment that arrives in the incorrect sequence.

P

packet Synonym for data unit, mostly used in the network layer.

Packet Internet Groper (PING) An application program to determine the reachability of a destination using an ICMP echo request and reply.

packet-too-big message An ICMPv6 error message sent in response to a datagram that is discarded because it is larger than the MTU.

packet-filter firewall A firewall that forwards or blocks packets based on the information in the network-layer and transport-layer headers.

pad1 An IPv6 option used for alignment when only 1 byte is needed.

padN An IPv6 option when two or more bytes are needed for alignment.

page A unit of hypertext or hypermedia available on the Web.

parallel transmission Transmission in which bits in a group are sent simultaneously, each using a separate link.

parameter-problem message An ICMP message that notifies a host that there is an ambiguous or missing value in any field of the datagram.

parent server A server running infinitely and accepting connections from the clients.

partially qualified domain name (PQDN) A domain name that does not include all the levels between the host and the root node.

passive open The state of a server as it waits for incoming requests from a client.

path The channel through which a signal travels.

Path MTU Discovery technique An IPv6 method to find the smallest MTU supported by any network on a path.

path vector routing A routing method on which BGP is based; in this method, the ASs through which a packet must pass are explicitly listed.

peer-to-peer process A process on a sending and a receiving machine that communicate at a given layer.

periodic timer A RIP timer that controls the sending of messages.

permanent virtual circuit (PVC) A virtual circuit transmission method in which the same virtual circuit is used between source and destination on a continual basis.

persistence timer A technique to handle the zero window-size advertisement.

persistent connection A connection in which the server leaves the connection open for more requests after sending a response.

PGP See *Pretty Good Privacy.*

physical address The address of a device used at the data link layer (MAC address).

physical layer The first layer of the OSI model, responsible for the mechanical and electrical specifications of the medium.

physical topology The manner in which devices are connected in a network.

piggybacking The inclusion of acknowledgment on a data frame.

PIM See *Protocol Independent Multicast.*

PIM-DM See *Protocol Independent Multicast, Dense Mode.*

PIM-SM See *Protocol Independent Multicast, Sparse Mode.*

PING See *Packet Internet Groper.*

plaintext In encryption/decryption, the original message.

playback buffer A buffer that stores the data until they are ready to be played.

pointer field In the IP header, an offset integer field containing the byte number of the first empty entry.

point-to-point link A dedicated transmission link between two devices.

Point-to-Point Protocol (PPP) A protocol for data transfer across a serial line.

poison reverse A variation of split horizons. In this method, information received by the router is used to update the routing table and then passed out to all interfaces. However, a table entry that has come through one interface is set to a metric of 16 as it goes out through the same interface.

policy routing A path vector routing feature in which the routing tables are based on rules set by the network administrator rather than a metric.

POP3 See *Post Office Protocol, version 3.*

port address In TCP/IP protocol an integer identifying a process.

port number An integer that defines a process running on a host.

Post Office Protocol, version 3 (POP3) A popular but simple SMTP mail access protocol.

PPP See *Point-to-Point Protocol.*

PQDN See *partially qualified domain name.*

preamble The 7-byte field of an IEEE 802.3 frame consisting of alternating 1s and 0s that alert and synchronize the receiver.

precedence A 3-bit subfield in the IP header that defines the priority of the datagram in issues such as congestion.

prefix For a network, another name for the common part of the address range (similar to the netid).

presentation layer The sixth layer of the OSI model responsible for translation, encryption, authentication, and data compression.

Pretty Good Privacy (PGP) A protocol that provides all four aspects of security in the sending of email.

primary server A server that stores a file about the zone for which it is an authority.

privacy A security aspect in which the message makes sense only to the intended receiver.

private key In conventional encryption, a key shared by only one pair of devices, a sender and a receiver. In public-key encryption, the private key is known only to the receiver.

private network A network that is isolated from the Internet.

process A running application program.

process identification (processid) A number that uniquely defines a UNIX process.

process-to-process communication Communication between two running application programs.

program-to-program communication Same as a process-to-process communication.

promiscuous ARP (proxy ARP) A technique that creates a subnetting effect; one device answers ARP requests for multiple hosts.

protocol Rules for communication.

Protocol Independent Multicast (PIM) A multicasting protocol family with two members, PIM-DM and PIM-SM; both protocols are unicast-protocol dependent.

Protocol Independent Multicast, Dense Mode (PIM-DM) A source-based routing protocol that uses RPF and pruning/grafting strategies to handle multicasting.

Protocol Independent Multicast, Sparse Mode (PIM-SM) A group-shared routing protocol that is similar to CBT and uses a rendezvous point as the source of the tree.

protocol suite A stack or family of protocols defined for a complex communication system.

proxy ARP See *promiscuous ARP.*

proxy firewall A firewall that filters a message based on the information available in the message itself (at the application layer).

proxy server A computer that keeps copies of responses to recent requests.

pruning Stopping the sending of multicast messages from an interface.

pseudoheader Information from the IP header used only for checksum calculation in UDP and TCP packets.

public key In public-key encryption, a key known to everyone.

public-key encryption A method of encryption based on a nonreversible encryption algorithm. The method uses two types of keys: The public key is known to the public; the private key (secret key) is known only to the receiver.

pure ATM LAN A LAN in which an ATM switch is used to connect the stations in a LAN, in the same way stations are connected to an Ethernet switch.

push data Data that must be sent with minimum delay; marked by setting the push bit in the TCP header.

pushing data A technique in which the application program on the sending site does not wait for the window to be filled. It creates a segment and sends it immediately.

PVC See *permanent virtual circuit.*

Q

query message An ICMP message that helps a host or a network manager get specific information from a router or another host. Or, an IGMP message that requests group information from a router or a host. Or, a DNS message that requests information.

query router The router on a network that sends a query message.

question record A DNS record used in the question section of the query and response messages; used by the client to get information from a server.

queue A waiting list.

R

radio frequency wave Electromagnetic energy in the 3-kHz to 300-GHz range.

RADSL See *rate adaptive asymmetrical digital subscriber line.*

RARP See *reverse address resolution protocol.*

rate adaptive asymmetrical digital subscriber line (RADSL) A DSL-based technology that features different data rates depending on the type of communication.

raw socket A structure designed for protocols that directly use the services of IP and use neither stream sockets nor datagram sockets.

reading Copying a file from the server site to the client site.

read-only memory (ROM) Permanent memory with contents that cannot be changed.

real-time multimedia traffic Traffic consisting of data, audio, and video that is simultaneously produced and used.

real-time traffic Traffic in one form that is simultaneously produced and used.

Real-time Transport Control Protocol (RTCP) A companion protocol to RTP with messages that control the flow and quality of data and allow the recipient to send feedback to the source or sources.

Real-time Transport Protocol (RTP) A protocol for real-time traffic; used in conjunction with UDP.

receiver The target point of a transmission.

receiver report An RTCP packet that informs the sender and other receivers about the quality of service.

record route option An IP header option that is used to record the routers that handle the datagram.

recursive resolution Resolution of the IP address in which the client sends its request to a server that eventually returns a response.

redirection message An ICMP message that informs the sender of a preferred route. Or, a method to redirect a CGI request to a static document.

reference count In a routing table, a field that gives the number of users that are using this route at any moment.

regional ISP A small ISP that is connected to one or more NSPs.

registered port A port number, ranging from 1,024 to 49,151, not assigned or controlled by IANA.

registration A phase of communication between a remote host and a mobile host in which the mobile host gives information about itself to the foreign agent.

registration reply A packet sent from the home agent to the foreign agent and then relayed to the mobile host to confirm or deny the registration request.

registration request A packet sent from the mobile host to the foreign agent to register its care-of address and also to announce its home address and home agent address.

relay agent For BOOTP, a router that can help send local requests to remote servers.

relay MTA An MTA that can relay email.

remote host The computer that a user wishes to access while seated physically at another computer.

remote login (rlogin) The process of logging on to a remote computer from a terminal connected to a local computer.

remote server A program run at a site physically removed from the user.

rendezvous router A router that is the core or center for each multicast group; it becomes the root of the tree.

rendezvous-point tree A group-shared tree method in which there is one tree for each group.

repeater A device that extends the distance a signal can travel by regenerating the signal.

Request for Comment (RFC) A formal Internet document concerning an Internet issue.

request header A part of the HTTP request message that specifies the client's configuration and the client's preferred document format.

request line A line in the HTTP request message consisting of a request type, a space, a URL, a space, and HTTP version.

request type In HTTP, a field defining the category of the request message.

requirement level One of five RFC levels.

reserved address IP addresses set aside by the Internet authorities for the use of private networks. Or, an IPv6 address with a reserved prefix.

resolver The DNS client that is used by a host that needs to map an address to a name or a name to an address.

resource record A DNS record used in the answer, authoritative, and additional information sections of the response message; returned by the server to the client.

response header A part of the HTTP response message that specifies the server's configuration and special information about the request.

response message A DNS message type that returns information.

retransmission timer A timer that controls the waiting time for an acknowledgment of a segment.

Reverse Address Resolution Protocol (RARP) A TCP/IP protocol that allows a host to find its Internet address given its physical address.

reverse path broadcasting (RPB) A technique in which the router forwards only the packets that have traveled the shortest path from the source to the router.

reverse path forwarding (RPF) A technique in which the router forwards only the packets that have traveled the shortest path from the source to the router.

reverse path multicasting (RPM) A technique that adds pruning and grafting to RPB to create a multicast shortest path tree that supports dynamic membership changes.

RFC See *Request for Comment.*

ring topology A topology in which the devices are connected in a ring. Each device on the ring receives the data unit from the previous device, regenerates it, and forwards it to the next device.

RIP See *routing information protocol.*

RIPv2 See *routing information protocol, version 2.*

rlogin A remote login application designed by BSD UNIX.

ROM See *read-only memory.*

root label In DNS, a null (empty) string.

root server In DNS, a server whose zone consists of the whole tree. A root server usually does not store any information about domains but delegates its authority to other servers, keeping references to those servers.

round-trip time (RTT) The time required for a datagram to go from a source to a destination and then back again.

router An internetworking device operating at the first three OSI layers. A router is attached to two or more networks and forwards packets from one network to another.

router link LSA An LSA packet that advertises all of the links of a router.

router-solicitation and advertisement message An ICMP message sent to obtain and disperse router information.

routing The process performed by a router; finding the next hop for a datagram.

Routing Information Protocol (RIP) A routing protocol based on the distance vector routing algorithm.

routing information protocol, version 2 A second RIP version in which fields in version 1 that were filled with 0s for the TCP/IP protocol have been replaced with some new fields.

routing table A table containing information a router needs to route packets. The information may include the network address, the cost, the address of the next hop, and so on.

RPB See *reverse path broadcasting.*

RPC See *remote procedure call.*

RPF See *reverse path forwarding.*

RPM See *reverse path multicasting.*

RS232 See *EIA-232.*

RSA encryption A popular public-key encryption method developed by Rivest, Shamir, and Adleman.

RTCP See *Real-time Transport Control Protocol.*

RTP See *Real-time Transport Protocol.*

RTT See *round-trip time.*

RZ See *return to zero.*

S

SDH See *synchronous digital hierarchy.*

SDSL See *symmetric digital subscriber line.*

search algorithm A rule for finding the next hop.

secondary server In DNS, a server that transfers the complete information about a zone from another server (primary or secondary) and stores the file on its local disk.

secret-key encryption A security method in which the key for encryption is the same as the key for decryption; both sender and receiver have the same key.

secure shell (SSH) A client-server program that provides security.

security The protection of a network from unauthorized access, viruses, and catastrophe.

segment The packet at the TCP layer.

segmentation The splitting of a message into multiple packets; usually performed at the transport layer.

semantics The meaning of each section of bits.

sender The originator of a message.

sender report An RTCP packet sent periodically by the active senders in a conference to report transmission and reception statistics for all RTP packets sent during the interval.

sequence number The number that denotes the location of a frame or packet in a message.

server See *server process.*

service type An 8-bit field in the IP header that contains the precedence and TOS bits; the field has been renamed and redefined by IETF.

service-point address See *port address.*

session layer The fifth layer of the OSI model, responsible for the establishment, management, and termination of logical connections between two end users.

SFD See *start frame delimiter.*

shortest path The optimal path from the source to the destination.

silly window syndrome A situation in which a small window size is advertised by the receiver and a small segment sent by the sender.

simple data type An atomic SMI data type from which other data types are constructed.

Simple Mail Transfer Protocol (SMTP) The TCP/IP protocol defining electronic mail service on the Internet.

Simple Network Management Protocol (SNMP) The TCP/IP protocol that specifies the process of management in the Internet.

Simple Network Management Protocol version 3 (SNMPv3) The third version of SNMP.

simplex mode A transmission mode in which communication is one way.

site local address An IPv6 address used if a site having several networks uses the Internet protocols but is not connected to the Internet for security reasons.

slash notation A shorthand method to indicate the number of 1s in the mask.

sliding window protocol A protocol that allows several data units to be in transition before receiving an acknowledgment.

slow convergence A RIP shortcoming apparent when a change somewhere in the internet propagates very slowly through the rest of the internet.

slow start A congestion-control method in which the congestion window size increases exponentially at first.

SMI See *Structure of Management Information.*

SMTP See *simple mail transfer protocol.*

SNMP See *simple network management protocol.*

SNMPv3 See *simple network management protocol, version 3.*

socket An end point for a process; two sockets are needed for communication.

socket address A structure holding an IP address and a port number.

socket interface An API based on UNIX that defines a set of system calls (procedures) that are an extension of system calls used in UNIX to access files.

solicited response A RIP response sent only in answer to a request.

sorcerer's apprentice bug A TFTP problem for a packet that is not lost, but delayed in which every succeeding block is sent twice and every succeeding acknowledgment is received twice.

source address The address of the sender of the message.

source description message An RTP message sent by a source that contains additional information about the source.

source quench A method, used in ICMP for flow control, in which the source is advised to slow down or stop the sending of datagrams because of congestion.

source-quench message An ICMP message sent to slow down or stop the sending of datagrams.

source routing In IPv6, routing that combines the concepts of the strict source route and the loose source route options of IPv4.

source-based tree A tree used for multicasting by multicasting protocols in which a single tree is made for each combination of source and group.

source-to-destination delivery The transmission of a message from the original sender to the intended recipient.

spanning tree A tree with the source as the root and group members as leaves; a tree that connects all of the nodes.

special-query message An IGMP query message sent by a router to ensure that no host or router is interested in continuing membership in a group.

specific host on this network A special address in which the netid is all 0s and the hostid is explicit.

spectrum The range of frequencies of a signal.

split horizon A method to improve RIP stability in which the router selectively chooses the interface from which updating information is sent.

spooling system An SMTP feature in which messages are stored before being sent.

spread spectrum A wireless transmission technique that requires a bandwidth several times the original bandwidth.

SSH See *secure shell.*

standard A basis or model to which everyone has agreed.

standards creation committee A group that produces a basis or model to which everyone has agreed.

star topology A topology in which all stations are attached to a central device (hub).

start frame delimiter (SFD) A 1-byte field in the IEEE 802.3 frame that signals the beginning of the readable (nonpreamble) bit stream.

state transition diagram A diagram to illustrate the states of a finite state machine.

static configuration protocol A protocol, such as BOOTP, in which the binding between the physical and IP addresses is static and fixed in a table until changed by the administrator.

static document On the World Wide Web, a fixed-content document that is created and stored in a server.

static mapping A technique in which a list of logical and physical address correspondences is used for address resolution.

static routing A type of routing in which the routing table remains unchanged.

static-routing table A routing table used in static routing; usually manually updated.

stationary host A host that remains attached to one network.

status code Bits in the HTTP response message that relay general information, information related to a successful request, redirection information, or error information.

status line In the HTTP response message a line that consists of the HTTP version, a space, a status code, a space, a status phrase.

Steiner tree A method to find the multicast tree in which the optimal tree is the one in which the sum of the costs of the links is minimum.

STM See *synchronous transport module.*

stop-and-wait A flow-control method in which each data unit must be acknowledged before the next one can be sent.

stop-and-wait ARQ An error-control protocol using stop-and-wait flow control.

store and forward Another name for message switching.

stream mode An FTP transmission mode in which data is delivered from FTP to TCP as a continuous stream of bytes.

stream socket A structure designed to be used with a connection-oriented protocol such as TCP.

strict source route option An IP header option used to predetermine a route for a datagram as it travels through the Internet.

Structure of Management Information (SMI) In SNMP, a component used in network management.

structured data type An SMI data type composed of a combination of simple data types.

STS See *synchronous transport signal.*

stub link A network that is connected to only one router.

subdomain A part of a DNS domain.

subnet See *subnetwork.*

subnet address The network address of a subnet.

subnet mask The mask for a subnet.

subnetting Dividing a network into smaller units.

subnetwork A part of a network.

suboption negotiation The interaction between a client and server to decide on the suboption to use.

suffix For a network, the varying part (similar to the hostid) of the address. In DNS, a string used by an organization to define its host or resources.

summary link to AS boundary router LSA An LSA packet that lets a router inside an area know the route to an autonomous boundary router.

summary link to network LSA An LSA packet that finds the cost of reaching networks outside of the area.

supernet A network formed from two or more smaller networks.

supernet mask The mask for a supernet.

supernetting The combining of several class C blocks to create a larger range of addresses.

SVC See *switched virtual circuit.*

switch A device connecting multiple communication lines together.

switched Ethernet An Ethernet in which a switch, replacing the hub, can direct a transmission to its destination.

switched virtual circuit (SVC) A virtual circuit transmission method in which a virtual circuit is created and in existence only for the duration of the exchange.

symmetric digital subscriber line (SDSL) A DSL-based technology similar to HDSL, but using only one single twisted-pair cable.

synchronization points Reference points introduced into the data by the session layer for the purpose of flow and error control.

synchronous digital hierarchy (SDH) The ITU-T equivalent of SONET.

Synchronous Optical Network (SONET) A standard developed by ANSI for fiber-optic technology that can transmit high-speed data. It can be used to deliver text, audio, and video.

synchronous transport module (STM) A signal in the SDH hierarchy.

synchronous transport signal (STS) A signal in the SONET hierarchy.

syntax The structure or format of data, meaning the order in which they are presented.

T

T-1 line A 1.544-Mbps digital transmission line.

T-2 line A 6.312-Mbps digital transmission line.

T-3 line A 44.736-Mbps digital transmission line.

T-4 line A 274.176-Mbps digital transmission line.

T-lines A hierarchy of digital lines designed to carry speech and other signals in digital forms. The hierarchy defines T-1, T-2, T-3, and T-4 lines.

tag A formatting instruction embedded in an HTML document.

TCP See *transmission control protocol.*

TCP timer The timers used by TCP to handle retransmission, zero window-size advertisements, long idle connections, and connection termination.

TCP/IP See *transmission control protocol/internetworking protocol.*

TCP/IP protocol suite A group of hierarchical protocols used in an internet.

TDM See *time-division multiplexing.*

teleconferencing Audio and visual communication between remote users.

TELNET See *Terminal Network.*

Terminal Network (TELNET) A general purpose client-server program that allows remote login.

TFTP See *trivial file transfer protocol.*

this host on this network A special address in which the netid and hostid are all 0s; used by a host at bootstrap time when it does not know its IP address.

three-way handshake A sequence of events for connection establishment or termination consisting of the request, then the acknowledgment of the request, and then confirmation of the acknowledgment.

time to live (TTL) See *packet lifetime.*

time-exceeded message An ICMP message sent to inform a source that (1) its datagram has a time-to-live value of zero, or (2) the fragments of a message have not been received within a set time limit.

time-sharing Multiple users sharing the resources of a large computer.

timestamp An IP header option used to record the time of datagram processing by a router.

timestamp option A TCP option that shows how much time it takes for data to travel from sender to receiver.

timestamp-request and reply message An ICMP message sent to determine the round-trip time or to synchronize clocks.

time-waited timer A TCP timer used in connection termination that allows late segments to arrive.

timing Referring to when data must be sent and how fast it can be sent.

TLS See *Transport Layer Security.*

token A small packet used in token-passing access method.

token bus A LAN using a bus topology and token-passing access method.

token passing An access method in which a token is circulated in the network. The station that captures the token can send data.

Token Ring A LAN using a ring topology and token-passing access method.

topology The structure of a network including physical arrangement of devices.

TOS See *type of service.*

TPDU See *transport protocol data unit.*

traffic Communication.

trailer Control information appended to a data unit.

transient link A network with several routers attached to it.

translation Changing from one code or protocol to another.

translation table A table used by a NAT router to resolve a private address with an external address.

translator A computer that can change the format of a high-bandwidth video signal to a lower quality narrow-bandwidth signal.

Transmission Control Protocol (TCP) A transport protocol in the TCP/IP protocol suite.

Transmission Control Protocol/Internetworking Protocol (TCP/IP) A five-layer protocol suite that defines the exchange of transmissions across the Internet.

transmission mode The direction(s) of the communication as governed by the physical layer.

transparency The ability to send any bit pattern as data without it being mistaken for control bits.

transport layer The fourth layer in the OSI model; responsible for reliable end-to-end delivery and error recovery.

Transport Layer Security (TLS) A security protocol at the transport level designed to provide security on the WWW.

transport mode Encryption in which a TCP segment or a UDP user datagram is first encrypted and then encapsulated in an IPv6 packet.

trap An SNMP warning message sent by an agent to a manager.

tree A hierarchical data structure in which each node on a tree has one single parent, and zero or more children.

tree topology A topology in which stations are attached to a hierarchy of hubs. Tree topology is an extension of star topology with more than one level.

triangle routing An inefficient routing that occurs when a remote host sends a packet to the mobile host; the packet goes from the remote host to the home agent and then to the mobile host.

tribit A unit of data consisting of three bits.

triggered update process A RIP feature to remedy instability in which an update is sent immediately following a change.

Trivial File Transfer Protocol (TFTP) An unreliable TCP/IP protocol for file transfer that does not require complex interaction between client and server.

TTL See *time to live.*

tunnel mode Encryption in which the entire IP datagram with its base header and extension headers is encrypted and then encapsulated in a new IP packet using the ESP extension header.

tunneling In multicasting, a process in which the multicast packet is encapsulated in a unicast packet and then sent through the network. In VPN, the encapsulation of an encrypted IP datagram in a second outer datagram. For IPv6, a strategy used when two computers using IPv6 want to communicate with each other when the packet must pass through a region that uses IPv4.

two's complement A representation of binary numbers in which the complement of a number is found by complementing all bits and adding a 1 after that.

type of service (TOS) A criteria or value that specifies the handling of the datagram.

U

UA See *user agent.*

UDP See *User Datagram Protocol.*

unattended data traffic Traffic in which the user is not waiting (attending) for the data.

UNI See *user network interface.*

unicast address An address belonging to one destination.

unicast message A message sent to just one destination.

unicasting The sending of a packet to just one destination.

Uniform Resource Locator (URL) A string of characters (address) that identifies a page on the World Wide Web.

unsigned number A representation of binary numbers without sign (plus or minus).

unsolicited response A RIP response sent periodically, every 30 seconds that contains information about the entire routing table.

unspecified address An IPv6 address consisting entirely of 0s.

up flag In a routing table, a field that indicates whether or not the router is up and running.

update binding packet A packet that binds the care-of address to the home address of a mobile host.

update message A BGP message used by a router to withdraw destinations that have been advertised previously or to announce a route to a new destination.

urgent data In TCP/IP, data that must be delivered to the application program as quickly as possible.

urgent pointer A pointer to the boundary between urgent data and normal data.

URL See *uniform resource locator.*

user agent (UA) An SMTP component that prepares the message, creates the envelope, and puts the message in the envelope.

user datagram The name of the packet in the UDP protocol.

User Datagram Protocol (UDP) A connectionless TCP/IP transport layer protocol.

user interface The interface between the user and the application.

user network interface (UNI) The interface between a user and the ATM network.

user support layers The session, presentation, and application layers.

V

variable-length subnetting The use of different masks to create subnets on a network.

VCI See *virtual channel identifier* or *virtual connection identifier.*

VDSL See *very high bit rate digital subscriber line.*

version A 4-bit IP header field that defines the version of the IP protocol.

vertical redundancy check (VRC) An error-detection method based on per-character parity check.

very high bit rate digital subscriber line (VDSL) A DSL-based technology for short distances.

videotex The process of accessing remote databases interactively.

virtual channel identifier (VCI) A field in an ATM cell header that defines a channel.

virtual circuit A logical circuit made between the sending and receiving computer. The connection is made after both computers do handshaking. After the connection, all packets follow the same route and arrive in sequence.

virtual connection identifier A VCI or VPI.

virtual link An OSPF connection between two routers that is created when the physical link is broken. The link between them uses a longer path that probably goes through several routers.

virtual path identifier (VPI) A field in an ATM cell header that identifies a path.

virtual private network (VPN) A technology that creates a network that is physically public, but virtually private.

virus Unauthorized software introduced for destructive purposes onto a computer.

VPI See *virtual path identifier.*

VPI/VCI See *virtual path identifier/virtual channel identifier.*

VPN See *virtual private network.*

VRC See *vertical redundancy check.*

W

WAN See *wide area network.*

warning packet A packet sent by the home agent to inform the remote host that a mobile host has moved.

Web Synonym for World Wide Web (WWW).

well-known attribute Path information that every BGP router must recognize.

well-known port A port number that identifies a process on the server.

wide area network (WAN) A network that uses a technology that can span a large geographical distance.

window scale factor A multiplier that increases the window size.

window size field The size of the sliding window used in flow control.

wireless transmission Communication using unguided media.

working group An IETF committee concentrating on a specific Internet topic.

World Wide Web (WWW) A multimedia Internet service that allows users to traverse the Internet by moving from one document to another via links that connect them together.

writing Copying a file from the client site to the server site.

WWW See *World Wide Web.*

X

X.25 An ITU-T standard that defines the interface between a data terminal device and a packet-switching network.

Z

zone In DNS, what a server is responsible for or has authority over.

References

Comer, Douglas E. *Internetworking with TCP/IP,* vol. 1, 4th ed. Upper Saddle River, NJ: Prentice-Hall, 2000.

———. *Internetworking with TCP/IP,* vol. 2. Upper Saddle River, NJ: Prentice-Hall, 1999.

———. *Internetworking with TCP/IP,* vol. 3. Upper Saddle River, NJ: Prentice-Hall, 1996.

Dickie, Mark. *Routing in Today's Internetworks*. New York, NY: Van Nostrand Reinhold, 1994.

Forouzan, Behrouz. *Introduction to Data Communication and Networking,* 2nd ed. Burr Ridge, IL: McGraw-Hill, 2001.

Forouzan, Behrouz. *Local Area Networks*. Burr Ridge, IL: McGraw-Hill, 2003.

Halsall, Fred. *Data Communications, Computer Networks and Open Systems,* 4th ed. Reading, MA: Addison-Wesley, 1995.

Huitema, Christian. *Routing in the Internet*. Upper Saddle River, NJ: Prentice-Hall, 1995.

Johnson, Howard W. *Fast Ethernet*. Upper Saddle River, NJ: Prentice-Hall, 1996.

Moy, John. *OSPF.* Reading, MA: Addison-Wesley, 1998.

Partridge, Craig. *Gigabit Networking*. Reading, MA: Addison-Wesley, 1994.

Perlman, Radia. *Interconnections,* 2nd ed. Reading, MA: Addison-Wesley, 2000.

Stallings, William. *High-Speed Network,* Upper Saddle River, NJ: Prentice-Hall, 1998.

Stevens, W. Richard. *TCP/IP Illustrated,* vol. 1. Reading, MA: Addison-Wesley, 1994.

———. *TCP/IP Illustrated,* vol. 3. Reading, MA: Addison-Wesley, 1996.

Tanenbaum, Andrew S. *Computer Networks,* 3rd ed. Upper Saddle River, NJ: Prentice-Hall, 1996.

Wright, Gary R., and W. Richard Stevens. *TCP/IP Illustrated,* vol. 2. Reading, MA: Addison-Wesley, 1995.

Index

Numerics

A

C

D

E

F

I

N

O

P

Q

R

S

T

U

V

W

X

Z

MBONE multicast backbone

MIB management information base

MILNET Military Network

MIME Multipurpose Internet Mail Extension

MOSPF Multicast Open Shortest Path First

MSS maximum segment size

MTA mail transfer agent

MTU maximum transfer unit

NAP Network Access Point

NAT network address translation

NCP Network Control Protocol

NFS network file system

NIC Network Information Center

NIC network interface card

NNI network-to-network interface

NSF National Science Foundation

NSFNET National Science Foundation Network

NSP national service provider

NVT network virtual terminal

OC optical carrier

OSI open systems interconnection

OSPF open shortest path first

PGP Pretty Good Privacy

PIM Protocol Independent Multicast

PIM-DM Protocol Independent Multicast, Dense Mode

PIM-SM Protocol Independent Multicast, Sparse Mode

PING Packet Internet Groper

POP3 Post Office Protocol, version 3

PPP Point-to-Point Protocol

PQDN partially qualified domain name

proxy ARP promiscuous ARP proxy

PVC permanent virtual circuit

RADSL rate adaptive asymmetrical digital subscriber line

RARP reverse address resolution protocol

RFC Request for Comment

RIP routing information protocol

RIPv2 routing information protocol, version 2

ROM read-only memory

RPB reverse path broadcasting

RPF reverse path forwarding

RPM reverse path multicasting

RTCP Real-time Transport Control Protocol

RTP Real-time Transport Protocol

RTT round-trip time

SDH synchronous digital hierarchy

SDSL symmetric digital subscriber line

SFD start frame delimiter

SMI Structure of Management Information

SMTP simple mail transfer protocol

SNMP simple network management protocol

SNMPv3 simple network management protocol, version 3